COST ACCOUNTING

PRENTICE HALL SERIES IN ACCOUNTING

Charles T. Horngren, Consulting Editor

NINTH EDITION

COST ACCOUNTING

A MANAGERIAL EMPHASIS

Charles T. Horngren

Stanford University

George Foster

Stanford University

Srikant M. Datar

Stanford University

PRENTICE HALL
Upper Saddle River, NJ 07458

Library of Congress Cataloging-in-Publication Data

Horngren, Charles T., 1926–
    Cost accounting: a managerial emphasis / Charles T. Horngren,
George Foster, Srikant M. Datar. —9th ed.
      p. cm. —(Prentice Hall series in accounting)
    Includes indexes.
    ISBN 0-13-232901-8
    1. Cost accounting.   2. Costs, Industrial.   I. Foster, George, 1948– .
    II. Datar, Srikant M.   III. Title.   IV. Series.
HF5686.C8H59 1996
658.15'4—dc20   96-15750
             CIP

Executive Editor: *P.J. Boardman*
Senior Development Editor: *David Cohen*
Associate Editor: *Diane deCastro*
Editorial Assistant: *Jane Avery*
Editor-in-Chief: *Richard Wohl*
Director of Development: *Steve Deitmer*
Executive Marketing Manager: *Deborah Hoffman Emry*
Book Production: *Progressive Publishing Alternatives*
Production Coordinator: *Renee Pelletier*
Managing Editor: *Katherine Evancie*
Senior Manufacturing Supervisor: *Paul Smolenski*
Manufacturing Manager: *Vincent Scelta*
Senior Designer: *Suzanne Behnke*
Design Director: *Patricia Wosczyk*
Interior Design: *Maureen Eide*
Cover Design: *Maureen Eide*
Illustrator (Interior): *TSI Graphics*
Composition: *TSI Graphics*
Cover Art/Photo: *Kunio Owaki, The Stock Market*

Printed in the United States of America
10 9 8 7 6 5 4 3 2 1

ISBN 0-13-232901-8

Prentice-Hall International (UK) Limited, *London*
Prentice-Hall of Australia Pty. Limited, *Sydney*
Prentice-Hall Canada Inc., *Toronto*
Prentice-Hall Hispanoamericana, S.A., *Mexico City*
Prentice-Hall of India Private Limited, *New Delhi*
Prentice-Hall of Japan, Inc., *Tokyo*
Simon & Schuster Asia Pte. Ltd., *Singapore*
Editora Prentice-Hall do Brasil, Ltda., *Rio de Janiero*

ABOUT THE AUTHORS

CHARLES T. HORNGREN is the Edmund W. Littlefield Professor Emeritus of Accounting at Stanford University. A graduate of Marquette University, he received his MBA from Harvard University and his Ph.D. from the University of Chicago. He is also the recipient of honorary doctorates from Marquette University and DePaul University.

A Certified Public Accountant, Horngren served on the Accounting Principles Board for six years, the Financial Accounting Standards Board Advisory Council for five years, and the Council of the American Institute of Certified Public Accountants for three years. In addition, he served as a trustee of the Financial Accounting Foundation, which oversees the Financial Accounting Standards Board and the Government Accounting Standards Board for six years.

A member of the American Accounting Association, Horngren has also served as its President and Director of Research. He received the Outstanding Accounting Educator Award in 1973, when the association initiated an annual series of such awards.

The California Certified Public Accountants Foundation gave Horngren its Faculty Excellence Award in 1975 and its Distinguished Professor Award in 1983. He is the first person to have received both awards. In 1985, the American Institute of Certified Public Accountants presented him with its first Outstanding Educator Award. Five years later, he was elected to the Accounting Hall of Fame.

In 1993, Horngren was named Accountant of the Year, Education, by the national professional accounting fraternity, Beta Alpha Psi.

Professor Horngren is a member of the National Association of Accountants, and served on its research planning committee for three years. He was also a member of the Board of Regents, Institute of Management Accounting, which administers the Certified Management Accountant examinations.

Charles T. Horngren, the Consulting Editor for the Prentice Hall Series in Accounting, is the coauthor of six other books published by Prentice Hall: *Principles of Financial and Management Accounting: A Sole Proprietorship Approach* and *Principles of Financial and Management Accounting: A Corporate Approach*, 1994 (with Walter T. Harrison, Jr., and Michael A. Robinson); *Introduction to Financial Accounting*, Fifth Edition, 1993 (with Gary L. Sundem and John Elliott), *Introduction to Management Accounting*, Ninth Edition, 1993 (with Gary L. Sundem), *Financial Accounting*, 1992, and *Accounting*, Second Edition, 1993 (with Walter T. Harrison, Jr.).

GEORGE FOSTER is the Paul L. and Phyllis Wattis Professor of Management at Stanford University. He graduated with a university medal from the University of Sydney and has a Ph.D. from Stanford University. He has been awarded honorary doctorates from the University of Ghent, Belgium, and from the University of Vaasa, Finland. He has received the Outstanding Educator Award from the American Accounting Association.

Foster has received the Distinguished Teaching Award at Stanford University and the Faculty Excellence Award from the California Society of Certified Public Accountants. He has been a Visiting Professor to Mexico for the American Accounting Association.

Research awards Foster has received include the Competitive Manuscript Competition Award of the American Accounting Association, the Notable Contribution to Accounting Literature Award of the American Institute of Certified Public Accountants, and the Citation for Meritorious Contribution to Accounting Literature Award of the Australian Society of Accountants.

He is the author of *Financial Statement Analysis,* published by Prentice Hall. He is co-author of *Activity-Based Management Consortium Study (APQC and CAM–I)* and *Marketing, Cost Management and Management Accounting (CAM–I).* He is also co-author of two monographs published by the American Accounting Association— *Security Analyst Multi-Year Earnings Forecasts and The Capital Market* and *Market Microstructure and Capital Market Information Content Research.* Journals publishing his articles include *Abacus, The Accounting Review, Harvard Business Review, Journal of Accounting and Economics, Journal of Accounting Research, Journal of Cost Management, Journal of Management Accounting Research,* and *Management Accounting.*

Foster works actively with many companies, including Apple Computer, ARCO, BHP, Digital Equipment Corp., Exxon, Frito-Lay Corp., Hewlett-Packard, McDonalds Corp., Octel Communications, PepsiCo, Santa Fe Corp., and Wells Fargo. He also has worked closely with Computer Aided Manufacturing-International (CAM-I) in the development of a framework for modern cost management practices. Foster has presented seminars on new developments in cost accounting in North America, Asia, Australia, and Europe.

SRIKANT M. DATAR is the Edmund W. Littlefield Professor of Accounting and Management at Stanford University. A graduate with distinction from the University of Bombay, he received gold medals upon graduation from the Indian Institute of Management, Ahmedabad, and the Institute of Cost and Works Accountants of India. A Chartered Accountant, he holds two masters degrees and a Ph.D. from Stanford University.

Cited by his students as a dedicated and innovative teacher, Datar received the George Leland Bach Award for Excellence in the Classroom at Carnegie Mellon University and the Distinguished Teaching Award at Stanford University.

Datar has published his research in various journals, including *The Accounting Review, Contemporary Accounting Research, Journal of Accounting, Auditing and Finance, Journal of Accounting and Economics, Journal of Accounting Research,* and *Management Science.* He has also served on the editorial board of several journals and presented his research to corporate executives and academic audiences in North America, South America, Asia, and Europe.

Datar has worked with many corporations, including AT&T, Boeing, British Columbia Telecommunications, The Cooperative Bank, Du Pont, Ford, General Motors, Hewlett-Packard, Mellon Bank, Solectron, TRW, and VISA, on field-based projects in management accounting. He is a member of the American Accounting Association and the Institute of Management Accountants.

BRIEF CONTENTS

PART FIVE QUALITY AND JIT

PART SIX CAPITAL BUDGETING

PART SEVEN MANAGEMENT CONTROL SYSTEMS

CONTENTS

PART TWO
TOOLS FOR PLANNING AND CONTROL

6
MASTER BUDGET AND RESPONSIBILITY ACCOUNTING   175

7
FLEXIBLE BUDGETS, VARIANCES, AND MANAGEMENT CONTROL: I   217

8

FLEXIBLE BUDGETS, VARIANCES, AND MANAGEMENT CONTROL: II   253

9

INCOME EFFECTS OF ALTERNATIVE INVENTORY-COSTING METHODS   297

PART THREE
COST INFORMATION FOR DECISIONS

10
DETERMINING HOW COSTS BEHAVE 335

11
RELEVANT REVENUES, RELEVANT COSTS, AND THE DECISION PROCESS 383

12

PRICING DECISIONS, PRODUCT PROFITABILITY DECISIONS, AND COST MANAGEMENT 429

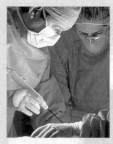

PART FOUR
COST ALLOCATION AND REVENUES

13

COST ALLOCATION: I 471

PART FIVE
QUALITY AND JIT

18
SPOILAGE, REWORKED UNITS, AND SCRAP 651

19
COST MANAGEMENT: QUALITY, TIME, AND THE THEORY OF CONSTRAINTS 681

PART SIX
CAPITAL BUDGETING

PREFACE

Studying cost accounting is one of the best business decisions a student can make. Why? Because success in any business—from the smallest corner store to the largest multinational corporation—requires the use of cost accounting principles and practices. Cost accounting provides key data to managers for planning and controlling, as well as for costing products, services, and customers. Today especially, as more and more cost accountants are being called on to become decision makers instead of data providers, our theme of "different costs for different purposes," which we stress throughout the book, is essential for a thorough and useful accounting education. By focusing on basic concepts, analyses, uses, and procedures instead of procedures alone, we recognize cost accounting as a managerial tool for business strategy and implementation, and we also prepare students for the rewards and challenges facing them in the world of professional cost accounting both today and tomorrow.

STRENGTHS OF THE EIGHTH EDITION RETAINED AND ENHANCED

Reviewers of the eighth edition praised the following features, which have been retained and strengthened in the ninth edition:

- ◆ Clarity and understandability of the text
- ◆ Coverage of important topics, including current developments in actual practice
- ◆ Extensive use of real-world examples
- ◆ Excellent quantity, quality, and range of assignment material
- ◆ Helpful Problems for Self-Study for each chapter
- ◆ Flexible organization through a modular approach

The first fourteen chapters provide the essence of a one-term (quarter or semester) course. There is ample text and assignment material in the book's twenty-six chapters for a two-term course. This book can be used immediately after the student has had an introductory course in financial accounting. Alternatively, this book can build on an introductory course in managerial accounting.

Deciding on the sequence of chapters in a textbook is a challenge. Every instructor has a favorite way of organizing his or her course. Hence, we present a modular, flexible organization that permits a course to be custom-tailored. *This organization facilitates diverse approaches to teaching and learning.*

As an example of the book's flexibility, consider our treatment of process costing. Process costing is described in Chapters 17 and 18. Instructors interested in filling out a student's perspective of costing systems can move directly from job-order costing described in Chapters 4 and 5 to Chapter 17 without interruption in the flow of material. Other instructors may want their students to delve into budgeting and more decision-oriented topics early in the course. These instructors may prefer to postpone discussion of process costing.

CHANGES IN CONTENT AND PEDAGOGY OF THE NINTH EDITION

The pace of change in organizations continues to be rapid. The ninth edition of *Cost Accounting* reflects changes occurring in the role of cost accounting in organizations and in research on cost accounting. We have shortened and streamlined individual chapters, focused on the major issues facing the management accountant, and achieved greater integration across chapters. Each chapter was scrutinized by knowledgeable critics before a final draft was reached.

1. *Newly evolving management themes.* These themes guided us in choosing the topics to be given increased emphasis.

   ◆ *Focus on customers.* Chapter 1 takes a customer-driven perspective on changes in cost accounting. The customer focus is emphasized in many other chapters. For example, Chapters 11 and 16 include sections on customer costing and profitability analysis.

   ◆ *Key success factors*, such as cost, quality, and time. Chapters 8 and 12 include discussion on cost planning and cost management. Chapter 19 discusses cost management aspects of quality and time. Chapter 21 describes cost management issues in just-in-time environments.

   ◆ *Total value-chain analysis.* The value chain is systematically emphasized throughout the book. Chapter 1 introduces the value chain. The text in many areas (such as Chapter 2 on cost drivers, Chapter 6 on budgeting, Chapter 7 on explanations for variances, and Chapter 12 on pricing decisions) emphasizes the importance of considering all areas of the value chain. We have also integrated value-chain analysis in our discussion of quality in Chapter 19 and just-in-time in Chapter 21.

   ◆ *Dual internal/external focus.* Topics such as benchmarking (Chapter 7) and customer satisfaction (Chapter 19) highlight the increased attention given to external factors in management accounting. Greater recognition is given to how cost accounting is expanding its horizons to incorporate environment-related considerations, for example in capital budgeting (Chapter 22) and performance evaluation (Chapter 26).

   ◆ *Continuous improvement.* Topics such as kaizen budgeting (Chapter 6) and productivity (Chapter 24) focus on the heightened emphasis companies now give to continuous improvement.

2. *Broad coverage of the service sector.* The service sector is now the single largest sector in the economy, and it is sometimes easier to use in teaching because there is no work in process to consider. Chapter 2 discusses cost concepts in the service sector as well as in the merchandising and manufacturing sectors. Chapter 4 illustrates job costing in the service sector. Chapter 16 on revenue analysis, Chapter 22 on capital budgeting, Chapter 25 on transfer pricing, and Chapter 26 on performance evaluation are discussed using service-sector illustrations.

3. *Expanded global content of the text.* Our coverage of international business is highly visible in our continued use of boxed features: Surveys of Company Practice and Concepts in Action. Both types of boxes, described in more detail later, draw on businesses from around the globe. In addition, company examples from many different countries are cited throughout the chapter material. Chapter 16 on revenue analysis, Chapter 25 on transfer pricing, and Chapter 26 on performance evaluation have expanded discussions within multinational contexts.

4. *Professional ethics.* The ninth edition continues our emphasis on ethics. The second-to-last problem in every chapter of the book has a component on ethics. This feature gives the instructor the flexibility to reinforce the importance of ethics in as many areas as is deemed appropriate.

5. *Cost management.* The eighth edition expanded its coverage of cost management. The ninth edition continues this expansion. Each chapter has an explicit discussion

of how the ideas described in it help the management accountant to plan, manage, and control costs.

Activity-based management is integrated into many chapters of the ninth edition. Chapter 2 discusses cost drivers and value-added costs. Chapters 4 and 5 illustrate how an activity-based costing approach can be used to refine job-costing systems. Chapter 6 illustrates activity-based budgeting. Chapter 11 applies activity-based costing to decisions regarding adding or dropping customers. Chapter 12 discusses how companies can reduce costs by reengineering product design or by reducing individual activity costs. Chapters 5, 14 and 16 present cost hierarchies. Chapter 15 examines capacity costing issues. Chapter 19 describes how activity-based costing can be used to manage quality.

6. *Performance evaluation.* Corporations have continued to innovate in their performance evaluation systems, placing greater emphasis on nonfinancial measures and combining these measures with financial measures. We describe performance evaluation considerations throughout the text, for example, when describing costing systems, variance analysis, relevant costs, overhead cost allocations, quality, productivity, and just-in-time. Chapter 26 develops a conceptual framework, based on recent research, for understanding performance evaluation issues.

Major Changes in Content and Sequence

1. The sequence of topics in Chapters 1 through 12 of the eighth edition is unchanged in the ninth edition, except that Process Costing previously introduced in Chapter 5 is instead presented comprehensively in Chapter 17. Material within these chapters is updated, reorganized, and integrated to facilitate student learning. For example, the discussion of cost hierarchies in Chapter 10 of the eighth edition is integrated with activity-based costing in Chapter 5 of the ninth edition; Chapters 4 and 5 streamline the presentation of job costing, cost-system refinements, and activity-based costing; and Chapter 10 on estimating cost functions and determining how costs behave is presented in a more graphical way.

2. The topics covered in the eighth edition Chapter 13 ("Management Control Systems") have been integrated into other chapters. Benchmarking is combined with variance analysis in Chapter 7; discretionary and engineered costs are described in an Appendix to Chapter 8 as an extension of overhead-variance analysis; value-added and nonvalue-added distinctions are discussed in the context of value engineering in Chapter 12; and management control issues are integrated with the transfer pricing discussion in Chapter 25.

3. Old Chapters 14 through 16 (on cost allocation and joint costs) are now Chapters 13 through 15.

4. Chapter 16 in the ninth edition is a new chapter that focuses on revenue management. Part One is new material on revenue tracing and revenue allocation. Part Two covers sales variances from old Chapter 22, and Part Three describes the customer profitability analysis from old Chapter 4.

5. Old Chapters 17 and 18 (on process costing and spoilage) continue as Chapters 17 and 18. However, the ninth edition introduces a new method for process costing. This method uses inventory-costing procedures that are virtually identical to inventory-costing methods, which students encountered in their introductory financial accounting classes. The only additional feature is the equivalent unit cost calculations.

6. Old Chapters 19 and 24 (on operation costing, backflush costing, inventory management, and just-in-time) have been reorganized into new Chapters 20 and 21 to achieve an expanded and integrated treatment of costing and cost management in a just-in-time environment.

7. Old Chapters 20 and 21 (on capital budgeting) are now Chapters 22 and 23. The new capital budgeting chapters include the topics of breakeven time (BET) from old Chapter 23, control of projects from old Chapter 19, and expanded discussions of post-investment audits and tax aspects.

8. Old Chapter 22 (Part Two on input variances and Part Three on productivity measurement) is now Chapter 24.

9. Old Chapter 23 (on quality and time) is now Chapter 19. The discussion of quality cost management in new Chapter 19 builds on the accounting for spoilage, rework, and scrap in new Chapter 18.

10. Old Chapters 25 and 26 (on transfer pricing and performance evaluation) continue as Chapters 25 and 26 but with an expanded multinational flavor.

Assignment Material

The ninth edition continues the widely applauded tight linkage between text and assignment material formed in previous editions. We have also significantly expanded the assignment material, provided more structure, and added greater variety. Notable changes are as follows:

◆ End-of-chapter assignment material are divided into three groups: Exercises, Problems, and a Collaborative Learning Problem. Exercises are short, structured assignments that test basic issues presented in the chapter. Problems are longer and more difficult assignments. The Collaborative Learning Problem is the last assignment in each chapter. These problems are group assignments that require students to think critically about a particular problem or specific business situation.

◆ Each of the seven parts of the book has a video case. The video case covers and integrates material from the various chapters in that part. For example, Nally & Gibson Georgetown, Inc., a limestone mining and processing company, is used to illustrate cost allocation and process costing at the end of Part Four. Instructors can use these video cases and the accompanying photo walkthroughs to summarize major segments of the course and to challenge their students' comprehension of the topics covered in those segments.

ILLUSTRATIONS OF ACTUAL BUSINESSES

Students become highly motivated to learn cost accounting if they can relate the subject matter to the real world. We have spent considerable time interacting with the business community, investigating new uses of cost accounting data and gaining insight into how changes in technology are affecting the roles of cost accounting information. Real-world illustrations are found in many parts of the text.

Concepts in Action Boxes   Found in many chapters, these boxes discuss how cost accounting concepts are applied by individual companies. Examples are drawn from many different countries, including the United States (Motorola on p. 15, Harley-Davidson on p. 41, General Motors on p. 68, Clark-Hurth on p. 149, Parker-Hannifin on p. 231), Canada (Ontario Hydro on p. 799), France (CFM International on p. 441), Germany (Porsche on p. 757), Japan (Nissan and Toyota on p. 441 and Japanese National Tax Agency on p. 916), Mexico (Crysel on p. 690), and the United Kingdom (Allied-Signal Skelmersdale on p. 700).

Surveys of Company Practice Boxes   Results from surveys in more than 15 countries are cited in the many Surveys of Company Practice boxes found throughout the book. Examples include

◆ Growing Interest in Activity-Based Costing (p. 113)—cites evidence from the United States, Canada, the United Kingdom, and New Zealand.
◆ Budgeting Practices (p. 188)—cites evidence from the United States, Australia, Holland, Japan, and the United Kingdom.

- ◆ Standard Costing (p. 225)—cites evidence from the United States, Canada, Ireland, Japan, Sweden, and the United Kingdom.
- ◆ Variable Costing (p. 312)—cites evidence from the United States, Australia, Canada, Japan, Sweden, and the United Kingdom.
- ◆ Pricing Practices (p. 445)—cites evidence from the United States, Australia, Ireland, Japan, and the United Kingdom.
- ◆ Purposes of Cost Allocation (p. 490)—cites evidence from the United States, Australia, Canada, and the United Kingdom.
- ◆ Performance Measures in Just-in-Time Systems (p. 761)—cites evidence from the United States, Canada, Ireland, Italy, and the United Kingdom.
- ◆ Capital Budgeting Methods (p. 794)—cites evidence from the United States, Australia, Canada, Ireland, Japan, Poland, Scotland, South Korea, and the United Kingdom.
- ◆ Transfer Pricing Methods (p. 912)—cites evidence from the United States, Australia, Canada, India, Japan, New Zealand, and the United Kingdom.

This extensive survey evidence enables students to see that many of the concepts they are learning are widely used across the globe.

Photos from Actual Companies   All chapters open with a photo that illustrates an important concept discussed in that chapter. These photos feature companies from many different countries, including the United States (Ben & Jerry's), Canada (Cott Corporation), and the United Kingdom (Tomkins, PLC). Each Concepts in Action box has an accompanying photo.

- ◆ Photo Walkthroughs are a new feature of the ninth edition. These appear at the end of each of the seven parts of the book and provide visual images of a manufacturing or business process described in that part. Visualizing a process helps students better understand the text descriptions. Video cases, tied to the photo essays, help students to further consolidate their thinking.

SUPPLEMENTS TO THE NINTH EDITION

A complete package of supplements is available to assist students and instructors in using this book. Supplements available to students include the following:

- ◆ *Student Guide and Review Manual* by John K. Harris and Dudley W. Curry.
- ◆ *Student Solutions Manual* by Charles T. Horngren, George Foster, and Srikant M. Datar.
- ◆ *Applications in Cost Accounting Using Excel* by David M. Buehlmann and Dennis P. Curtin.
- ◆ *Spreadsheet Templates* by Albert Fisher.

Supplements available to instructors include the following:

- ◆ *Annotated Instructor's Edition* with annotations by Linda S. Bamber.
- ◆ *Prentice Hall Course Manager.*
- ◆ *Instructor's Manual and Media Guide* by Michael C. Nibbelin.
- ◆ *Test Item File* by Marvin L. Bouillon.
- ◆ *Prentice Hall Custom Test* by ESA, Inc.
- ◆ *Solutions Manual* by Charles T. Horngren, George Foster, and Srikant M. Datar.
- ◆ *Solutions Transparencies.*
- ◆ *Solutions Manual for Applications in Cost Accounting Using Excel* by David M. Buehlmann and Dennis P. Curtin.

Supplements new to the ninth edition include the following:

◆ *PH Professor: A Classroom Presentation on PowerPoint* by William O. Stratton. Approximately 20 PowerPoint slides are available for each chapter of the text. This software allows instructors to offer an interactive presentation that uses colorful graphics, outlines of chapter material, additional examples, and graphical explanations of difficult topics. Some slides also have hidden spreadsheets that allow instructors to do what-if analyses for the situation being discussed in the slide. It is not necessary to have PowerPoint to run the presentations. However, if PowerPoint is available, you will be able to add, delete, revise, and change the order of the slides. Students may purchase a copy of *Power Notes,* which is a print out of all of the slides along with additional space for taking notes.

◆ *Power Notes* by William O. Stratton. This handy note-taking tool contains print-outs of all PowerPoint slides available for the text. Students can focus their attention on the lecture because they already possess the information on the slide. Extra space is provided next to each slide to jot down additional explanations, examples, and so on that are supplied by the instructor.

◆ *CD-ROM—Career Paths in Accounting* by Convergence Multimedia. With *Career Paths*, students can explore facts and trends in business, find out where the jobs are, and find out how to succeed in marketing themselves in the information age. Each CD-ROM contains 250 original video clips describing the nature of specific jobs, successful applicant profiles and entry requirements in today's volatile business world; interviews with key practitioners in the field; modules for preparing a winning resume, interviewing, networking, and negotiating; and interactive aptitude tests to determine skills and preferences.

◆ *ABC News/PH Video Library for Cost Accounting.* Video is a dynamic way to enhance your class presentations. However, the quality of the video material and how well it relates to your course can still make all the difference. For these reasons, Prentice Hall and ABC News worked together to bring you the best and most comprehensive video ancillaries available in the college market.

◆ In addition to the *ABC News Videos*, and ON LOCATION! Videos, company-specific plant tours from Fortune 500 service and manufacturing companies are also provided. Through these videos your students are able to experience shop floors like Chrysler and AT&T.

Through its wide variety of award-winning programs—"Nightline," "Business World," "On Business," "This Week with David Brinkley," "World News Tonight," and "The Wall Street Journal Report"—ABC offers a resource for feature and documentary-style videos related to text concepts and applications. The programs have extremely high production quality, present substantial content, and are hosted by well-versed, well-known anchors. Prentice Hall—its authors and its editors—provides videos on topics that work well with this course and text and gives instructors teaching notes on using them in the classroom.

◆ *ON LOCATION! Custom Case Videos for Cost Accounting.* Broadcast journalism and accounting education meet to create a series of custom produced case videos that have all the fast-paced and engaging qualities of TV and focus on the successful cost accounting activities of five dynamic companies. Take your students on a field trip to Dell Computers or Deer Valley Ski Resort to see the impact of cost accounting on their business strategies. Each video is approximately six to eight minutes in length and is tied directly to the issue-oriented end-of-part video case studies in *Cost Accounting*.

The ABC News/PH Video Library *ON LOCATION!* for *Cost Accounting* offers video material for almost every chapter in the text. An excellent video guide that is included in your *Instructor's Manual* carefully and completely integrates the videos into your lecture.

We are indebted to many for their ideas and assistance. Our primary thanks go to the many academics and practitioners who have advanced our knowledge of cost accounting.

The package of teaching material we present is the work of many skillful and valued team members. John K. Harris aided us immensely at all stages in the development and production of this book. He critiqued the eighth edition and gave a detailed review of the manuscript for the ninth edition. Linda S. Bamber reviewed the manuscript and gave suggestions for improvement in addition to working on the *Annotated Instructor's Edition*. Beverly Amer proved to be an invaluable resource in researching and writing the photo essays and video cases.

Professors providing detailed written reviews of the previous edition or comments on our drafts of this edition include

Tarek S. Amer, Northern Arizona University
Charles D. Bailey, University of Central Florida
Ken M. Boze, University of Alaska, Anchorage
Somnath Das, University of California, Berkeley
Peggy deProphetis, University of Pennsylvania
Amin A. Elmallah, California State University, Sacramento
David P. Franz, San Francisco State University
James M. Fremgen, Naval Postgraduate School
David O. Green, City University of New York-Baruch College
Horace W. Harrell Jr., Georgia Southern University
Cliff Harrison, Palliser Institute, Saskatchewan Institute of Applied Science and Technology
Ennis Hawkins, Sam Houston State University
Eleanor G. Henry, State University of New York, Oswego
Jiunn C. Huang, San Francisco State University
M. Zafar Iqbal, California Polytechnic State University, San Luis Obispo
Holly H. Johnston, Boston University
S. Joseph Lambert III, University of New Orleans
Peter Luckett, University of New South Wales
Frank F. S. Luh, Lehigh University
Allan MacQuarrie, University of Massachusetts-Boston
Gary J. Mann, University of Texas at El Paso
C. Michael Merz, Boise State University
Arijit Mukherji, University of Minnesota
Lee H. Nicholas, University of Northern Iowa
Manyong Park, Georgia State University
Emanuel Schwarz, San Francisco State University, Emeritus
Gim S. Seow, University of Connecticut
Robert J. Shepherd, University of California, Santa Cruz and San Jose State University
Harry Soltermann, Northern Alberta Institute of Technology
William A. Stahlin, Drexel University
Neil A. Wilner, University of North Texas
Tony B. Wong, Northern Alberta Institute of Technology
Russell Yerkes, Roosevelt University, Emeritus
Marilyn T. Zarzeski, University of Central Florida

The faculty participating in the many focus groups on the eighth edition provided highly valued feedback. Many students provided helpful input on this and the previous edition, including Michael Clements, Susan Cohen, Donald Cram, Sheryl Powers, Ratna Sarkar, and Daniel Serra. In addition, we have received helpful suggestions from many users, unfortunately too numerous to be mentioned here. The ninth edition is much improved by the feedback and interest of all these people. We are very appreciative of this support.

Our association with CAM-I has been a source of much stimulation as well as enjoyment. CAM-I has played a pivotal role in extending the frontiers of knowledge on cost management. We appreciate our extended and continued interaction with Jim Brimson, Callie Berliner, Charles Marx, R. Steven Player, Tom Pryor, Mike Roberts, and Pete Zampino.

We thank the people at Prentice Hall. Katherine Evancie (the managing editor) and David Cohen (the development editor) greatly exceeded their calls of duty in producing and developing a quality book in a timely fashion. Many others at Prentice Hall gave important assistance, including Jane Avery, P. J. Boardman, Diane deCastro, Patti Dant, Lisa DiMaulo, Deborah Hoffman Emry, Richard Wohl, Pat Wosczyk, Elaine Mast, Robert Prokop, Suzanne Behnke, Renée Pelletier, Paul Smolenski, Vincent Scelta, Joanne Jay, Richard Breten, Joe Tomasso, Veronica Schwartz, Steve Deitmer, Janet Ferruggia, and Ruta Fiorino.

Jiranee Tongudai managed the production aspects of all the manuscript preparation with superb skill and much grace. Her capacity and willingness to handle the many tasks never wavered. We are deeply appreciative of her good spirits, loyalty, and ability to stay calm in the most hectic of times. We also appreciate the help of Mathew Lonergan and Jeannette Ochoa.

Appreciation also goes to the American Institute of Certified Public Accountants, the Institute of Management Accountants, the Society of Management Accountants of Canada, the Certified General Accountants Association of Canada, the Financial Executive Institute of America, and many other publishers and companies for their generous permission to quote from their publications. Problems from the Uniform CPA examinations are designated (CPA); problems from the Certificate in Management Accounting examinations are designated (CMA); problems from the Canadian examinations administered by the Society of Management Accountants are designated (SMA); problems from the Certified General Accountants Association are designated (CGA). Many of these problems are adapted to highlight particular points.

We are grateful to the professors who contributed assignment material for this edition. Their names are indicated in parentheses at the start of their specific problems.

Comments from users are welcome.

CHARLES T. HORNGREN
GEORGE FOSTER
SRIKANT M. DATAR

TO OUR FAMILIES

Joan, Scott, Mary, Susie, Cathy (CH)

The Foster Family (GF)

Swati, Radhika, Gayatri, Sidharth (SD)

1

THE ACCOUNTANT'S ROLE
IN THE ORGANIZATION

Modern cost management emphasizes the role of research and development and product design as well as other areas of the value chain such as production and marketing. Textron uses "Integrated Product Teams" with members from all areas of the value chain at its Bell-Boeing Aircraft facility to reduce product costs and aircraft weight while increasing quality.

LEARNING OBJECTIVES

After studying this chapter, you should be able to

1. Identify five broad purposes of accounting systems
2. Describe cost accounting and its relationship to management accounting and financial accounting
3. Describe the set of business functions in a value chain
4. Understand how accounting can facilitate planning, control, and decision making
5. Describe the difference between line management and staff management
6. Distinguish among the scorekeeping, attention-directing, and problem-solving functions of the controller
7. Understand the importance of professional ethics to management accountants
8. Describe evolving management themes that are shaping developments in management accounting systems

ormer accountants currently are senior executives in many large companies, including Coca-Cola, Nike, PepsiCo, Bell Canada, Cadbury Schweppes, and Nissan Motors. Accounting provides a superb training field for executives because it cuts across all facets of the organization. The accountant's duties are intertwined with management planning, control, and decision making.

The study of modern cost accounting yields numerous insights into both the manager's *and* the accountant's role in an organization. What types of decisions do managers make? How can accounting help managers make these decisions? This book addresses these questions. In this chapter we look at where the accountant fits in the organization; this will give us a framework for studying the succeeding chapters.

THE MAJOR PURPOSES OF ACCOUNTING SYSTEMS

The accounting system is the principal—and the most credible—quantitative information system in almost every organization. This system should provide information for five broad purposes:

◆ *Purpose 1: Formulating overall strategies and long-range plans.* This includes new product development and investment in both tangible (equipment) and intangible (brands, patents, or people) assets, and frequently involves special purpose reports.

◆ *Purpose 2: Resource allocation decisions such as product and customer emphasis and pricing.* This frequently involves reports on the profitability of products or services, brand categories, customers, distribution channels, and so on.

◆ *Purpose 3: Cost planning and cost control of operations and activities.* This involves reports on revenues, costs, assets, and the liabilities of divisions, plants, and other areas of responsibility.

◆ *Purpose 4: Performance measurement and evaluation of people.* This includes comparisons of actual results with planned results. It can be based on financial or nonfinancial measures.

◆ *Purpose 5: Meeting external regulatory and legal reporting requirements.* Regulations and statutes typically prescribe the accounting methods to be followed here. Consider financial reports that are provided to shareholders who are making decisions to buy, hold, or sell shares in the company. These reports must follow generally accepted accounting principles, as heavily influenced by regulatory bodies such as the Financial Accounting Standards Board in the United States or the Accounting Standards Board in Canada.

Each of the purposes stated here may require a different presentation or reporting method. An ideal data base for presentations and reports (sometimes called a data warehouse or infobarn) is very detailed and cuts across business functions. Accountants combine or adjust ("slice or dice") these data to answer the questions from particular internal or external users.

Management Accounting, Financial Accounting, and Cost Accounting

A distinction is often made in practice between management accounting and financial accounting. **Management accounting** measures and reports financial information as well as other types of information that assist managers in fulfilling the goals of the organization. It is thus concerned with purposes 1–4. **Financial accounting** focuses on external reporting that is guided by generally accepted accounting principles. It is thus concerned with purpose 5. **Cost accounting** measures and reports financial and other information related to the organization's acquisition or consumption of resources. It provides information for both management accounting and financial accounting.

Financial accounting, as mentioned, is constrained by generally accepted accounting principles. These principles restrict the set of revenue and cost measurement rules and the types of items that are classified as assets, liabilities, or owners' equity in balance sheets. In contrast, management accounting is not restricted to those accounting principles acceptable for financial reporting. For example, for purposes 3 and 4, a consumer products company may present a particular estimated "value" of a brand name (say, the Coca-Cola brand name) in its *internal* financial reports for marketing managers, although doing so is not in accordance with generally accepted accounting principles.

Do not assume that management accounting focuses exclusively on internal parties. Managers are increasingly sharing accounting information with external parties such as suppliers and customers.

Cost Management and Accounting Systems

A central task of managers is *cost management.* We use **cost management** to describe the actions managers undertake to satisfy customers while continuously reducing and controlling costs. The Toyota Motor Company in a recent Annual Report noted that

> Cost management is . . . for the automobile industry in the 1990s what quality control was in the 1970s and 80s.

An important component of cost management is the recognition that prior management decisions often commit the organization to the subsequent incurrence of costs. Consider the costs of handling materials in a production plant. Decisions about plant layout and the extent of physical movement of materials required for production typically are made before production begins. These decisions greatly influence the level of day-to-day materials-handling costs once production begins.

MODERN COST ACCOUNTING

Managers as Customers of Accounting

Managers around the globe are becoming increasingly aware of the importance of the quality and timeliness of products and services sold to their external customers. In turn, accountants are becoming increasingly sensitive to the quality and timeliness of accounting information required by managers. For example, a management accounting group at Johnson & Johnson (the manufacturer of many consumer products, such as Band Aids) has a vision statement that includes the phrases "delight our customers" and "be the best." The success of management accounting depends on whether managers' decisions are improved by the accounting information provided to them.

The Value Chain of Business Functions

Throughout this book we organize our look at organizations by using the value chain of the business functions, which appears as Exhibit 1-1. The **value chain** is the sequence of business functions in which utility (usefulness) is added to the products or services of an organization. These functions are as follows:

OBJECTIVE 3

Describe the set of business functions in a value chain

- ◆ **Research and development (R&D)**—the generation of, and experimentation with, ideas related to new products, services, or processes.
- ◆ **Design of products, services, or processes**—the detailed planning and engineering of products, services, or processes.
- ◆ **Production**—the coordination and assembly of resources to produce a product or deliver a service.
- ◆ **Marketing**—the manner by which individuals or groups (a) learn about and value the attributes of products or services, and (b) purchase those products or services.
- ◆ **Distribution**—the mechanism by which products or services are delivered to the customer.
- ◆ **Customer service**—the support activities provided to customers.

EXHIBIT 1-1
The Value Chain of Business Functions

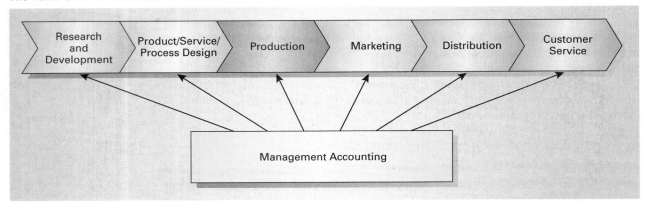

Do not interpret Exhibit 1-1 as implying that managers should proceed sequentially through the value chain. There are important gains to be realized (in terms of, say, cost, quality, and the speed with which new products are developed) from having the individual parts of the value chain work concurrently.

Senior managers of an organization (including those from individual parts of the value chain) have the responsibility of deciding on its overall strategy, how resources are to be obtained and used, and how rewards are to be given. This task covers the entire value chain.

Accounting is a major means of helping managers to administer each of the business functions presented in Exhibit 1-1 and to coordinate their activities within the framework of the organization as a whole. This book focuses on how accounting does in fact assist managers in these tasks.

ELEMENTS OF MANAGEMENT CONTROL

Is Microsoft's management control system better than Novell's? Is Nestlé's better than Cadbury's? This section provides an overview of management control systems, illustrating the role of accounting information.

Planning and Control

There are countless definitions of planning and control. Study the left side of Exhibit 1-2, which uses planning and control at *The Daily Sporting News* (DSN) as an illustration. We define **planning** (the top box) as choosing goals, predicting results under various ways of achieving those goals, and then deciding how to attain the desired goals. For example, one goal of DSN may be to increase operating income. Three main alternatives are considered to achieve this goal:

1. Change the price per newspaper.
2. Change the rate per page charged to advertisers.
3. Reduce labor costs by having fewer workers at DSN's printing facility.

Assume that the publisher, Naomi Crawford, increases advertising rates by 4% to $5,200 per page for March 19_7. She budgets advertising revenue to be $4,160,000 ($5,200 × 800 pages predicted to be sold in March 19_7). A **budget** is the quantitative expression of a plan of action and an aid to the coordination and implementation of the plan.

Control (the bottom box in Exhibit 1-2) covers both the action that implements the planning decision and the performance evaluation of the personnel and operations. With our DSN example, the action would include communicating the new advertising-rate schedule to DSN's marketing sales representatives and advertisers. The performance evaluation provides feedback on the actual results.

EXHIBIT 1-2
How Accounting Facilitates Planning and Control

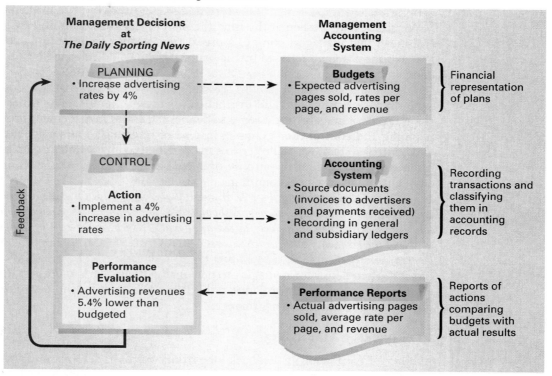

During March 19_7, DSN sells advertising, sends out invoices, and receives payments. These invoices and receipts are recorded in the accounting system. Exhibit 1-3 shows the March 19_7 advertising revenue performance report for DSN. This report indicates that 760 pages of advertising (40 pages less than the budgeted 800 pages) were sold in March 19_7. The average rate per page was $5,080 compared with the budgeted $5,200 rate, yielding actual advertising revenue in March 19_7 of $3,860,800. The actual advertising revenue in March 19_7 is $299,200 less than the budgeted $4,160,000. Understanding the reasons for any difference between actual results and budgeted results is an important part of **management by exception,** which is the practice of concentrating on areas not operating as expected (such as a cost overrun on a project) and placing less attention on areas operating as expected. The term **variance** in Exhibit 1-3 refers to the difference between the actual results and the budgeted amounts.

The performance report in Exhibit 1-3 could spur investigation. For example, did other newspapers experience a comparable decline in advertising revenue? Did the marketing department make sufficient efforts to convince advertisers that, even with the new rate of $5,200 per page, advertising in the DSN was a good buy? Why was the actual average rate per page $5,080 instead of the budgeted rate of $5,200? Did some sales representatives offer discounted rates? Did a major advertiser threaten to transfer its advertising to another newspaper unless it was given a large rate per page reduction? Answers to these questions could prompt Crawford to take

EXHIBIT 1-3
Advertising Revenue Performance Report at *The Daily Sporting News* for March 19_7

	Actual Results	Budgeted Amounts	Variance
Advertising Pages Sold	760	800	40 unfavorable
Average Rate Per Page	$5,080	$5,200	$120 unfavorable
Advertising Revenue	$3,860,800	$4,160,000	$299,200 unfavorable

subsequent actions, including, for example, pushing marketing personnel to renew efforts to promote advertising by existing and potential advertisers.

A well-conceived plan includes enough flexibility so that managers can seize opportunities unforeseen at the time the plan is formulated. In no case should control mean that managers cling to a preexisting plan when unfolding events indicate that actions not encompassed by the original plan would offer the best results to the company.

Planning and control are so strongly intertwined that managers do not spend time drawing artificially rigid distinctions between them. Unless otherwise stated, we use control in its broadest sense to denote the entire management process of both planning and control. For example, instead of referring to a management planning and control system, we will refer to a management control system. Similarly, we will often refer to the control purpose of accounting instead of the awkward planning and control purpose of accounting.

Do not underestimate the role of individuals and groups in management control systems. Both accountants and managers should always remember that management control systems are not confined exclusively to technical matters such as the type of computer systems used and the frequency with which reports are prepared. Management control is primarily a human activity that should focus on how to help individuals do their jobs better. For example, it is often better for managers to personally discuss with underperforming workers how to improve performance rather than just sending those workers a report highlighting their underperformance.

Feedback: A Major Key

Exhibit 1-2 (p. 5) shows a feedback loop from control back to planning. Feedback involves managers examining past performance and systematically exploring alternative ways to improve future performance. It can lead to a variety of responses, including the following:

USE OF FEEDBACK	EXAMPLE
◆ Changing goals.	◆ Continental Airlines increases emphasis on cash flow rather than income, after prior liquidity problems led to bankruptcy.
◆ Searching for alternative means of operating.	◆ London University Hospital compares internal processing versus third-party managing (outsourcing) of its accounts receivable operations.
◆ Changing methods for making decisions.	◆ Chrysler adopts a team-based new product development process with input from both manufacturing and marketing.
◆ Making predictions.	◆ British Columbia Telecom incorporates average inflation forecasts for wages when predicting future labor costs.
◆ Changing operations.	◆ Sony has materials delivered directly to the assembly floor instead of to a storeroom.
◆ Changing the reward system.	◆ IBM considers basing its marketing bonuses on the profitability of sales rather than on the dollar amount of sales.

COST-BENEFIT APPROACH

This book takes a general approach to accounting, which is referred to as the **cost-benefit approach.** That is, the primary criterion for choosing among alternative accounting systems is how well they help achieve organizational goals in relation to the costs of those systems.

As customers, managers buy a more elaborate management accounting system when its perceived expected benefits exceed its perceived expected costs. Although the benefits may take many forms, they can be summarized as the collective set of decisions that will better attain organizational goals.

Consider the installation of a company's first budgeting system. Previously the company had probably been using some historical recordkeeping and little formal planning. A major benefit of installing the budgeting system is that it compels managers to plan more formally. They may make a different, more profitable set of decisions than would have been done by using only a historical system. Thus the expected benefits exceed the expected costs of the new budgeting system. These costs include investments in computer hardware and software, in training people, and in ongoing operating costs of the system.

Admittedly, the measurement of these costs and benefits is seldom easy. Therefore, you may want to call this approach a conceptual rather than a practical guide. Nevertheless, the cost-benefit approach provides a starting point for analyzing virtually all accounting issues.

ORGANIZATION STRUCTURE AND THE MANAGEMENT ACCOUNTANT

Line and Staff Relationships

OBJECTIVE 5

Describe the difference between line management and staff management

Most organizations distinguish between line and staff management. **Line management** is directly responsible for attaining the objectives of the organization. For example, managers of manufacturing divisions may have objectives for a specified amount of operating income plus targets for product quality, safety, and compliance with environmental laws. **Staff management,** such as management accountants, exists to provide advice and assistance to line management. For example, a plant manager (a line function) may be responsible for investing in new equipment. A plant management accountant (a staff function) may prepare detailed operating-cost comparisons for potential pieces of equipment.

Increasingly, organizations are emphasizing the importance of teams in promoting their objectives. These teams often include both line and staff management with the result that the traditional distinctions between line and staff are less clear-cut than they were a decade ago. Line management and staff management designations are best viewed as different ends of a spectrum.

The Chief Financial Officer and the Controller

The **chief financial officer (CFO)**—also called the **finance director**—is the senior officer empowered with overseeing the financial operations of an organization. The responsibilities of the CFO vary among organizations, but they almost always encompass the following four areas:

◆ *Controllership* includes providing financial information for both reports to managers and reports to investors.

◆ *Treasury* includes short- and long-term financing, banking, and foreign exchange and derivatives management.

◆ *Tax* includes income taxes, sales taxes, and international tax planning.

◆ *Internal audit* includes reviewing and analyzing the financial records and other records to attest to the integrity of its financial reports and adherence to the organization's policies and procedures.

In some organizations, the CFO also has responsibility for information systems. In other organizations, an officer of equivalent rank to the CFO—termed *chief information officer*—has responsibility for information systems.

The **controller** is the financial executive primarily responsible for both management accounting and financial accounting. This book focuses on the management accounting function of the controller. The modern controller does not do any controlling in terms of line authority except over his or her own department. Yet the

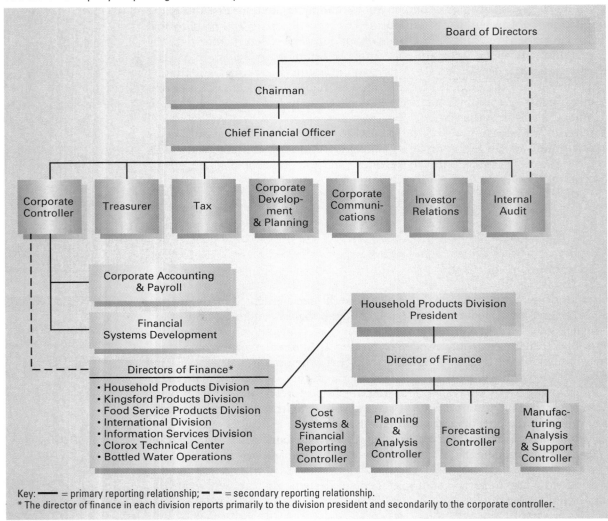

Key: ——— = primary reporting relationship; — — — = secondary reporting relationship.
* The director of finance in each division reports primarily to the division president and secondarily to the corporate controller.

modern concept of controllership maintains that the controller does control in a special sense. That is, by reporting and interpreting relevant data, the controller exerts a force or influence that impels management toward making better informed decisions.

Exhibit 1-4 presents an organization chart showing the reporting responsibilities of the CFO and the corporate controller at the Clorox Company. Clorox is a leading bleach-producing company and also has major brands in charcoal and salad dressing. The CFO is a staff management function that reports to the most senior line managers (who in turn report to the board of directors). As in most organizations, the corporate controller at Clorox reports to the CFO. Organization charts like that in Exhibit 1-4 show formal reporting relationships. In most organizations, informal relationships also exist that are essential to understand when managers attempt to implement their decisions.

O B J E C T I V E 6

Distinguish among the scorekeeping, attention-directing, and problem-solving functions of the controller

Scorekeeping, Attention-Directing, and Problem-Solving Functions

Management accountants perform three important functions—scorekeeping, attention directing, and problem solving.

◆ **Scorekeeping**—accumulating data and reporting reliable results to all levels of management. Examples are the recording of sales, purchases of materials, and payroll payments.

- **Attention directing**—making visible both opportunities and problems on which managers need to focus. Examples are highlighting rapidly growing markets where the company may be underfunding its investment and highlighting products with higher-than-expected rework rates or customer-return rates. Attention directing should focus on all opportunities to add value to an organization and not just on cost-reduction opportunities.
- **Problem solving**—comparative analysis to identify the best alternatives in relation to the organization's goals. An example is comparing the financial advantages of leasing a fleet of vehicles rather than owning those vehicles.

Accountants serving the scorekeeping function accumulate data and report the results to all levels of management. Accountants serving this function are responsible for the reliability of the reported information. In this regard, accountants are watchdogs for top management. The scorekeeping function in many organizations requires processing numerous data items (millions of items in some cases). The mechanics of the task should be well understood by those handling it and executed as flawlessly as possible.

Many organizations now have management accountants who concentrate solely on the attention-directing or problem-solving function. The titles of these individuals differ. As shown in Exhibit 1-4, Clorox has special staff positions for "cost systems and financial reporting," "planning and analysis," "forecasting," and "manufacturing analysis and support." The Yoplait Company, the French yogurt company, has staff positions for "operations analysis," "budget analysis and reporting," and "marketing and sales analysis."

Many controllers' departments actively promote their attention-directing and problem-solving abilities to their internal customers in the organization. For example, Swissair's corporate controller's group was reorganized so that each of the 13 staff members in the group was assigned responsibility for assisting an individual Swissair division (such as engineering and maintenance, flight services, and marketing for Europe). Their challenge was to demonstrate to the managers of each division the value of their assistance in areas such as financial analysis, the budgeting process, and cost management.

PROFESSIONAL ETHICS

Ethical Guidelines

Professional accounting organizations representing management accountants exist in many countries. Appendix D discusses professional organizations in the United States, Canada, Australia, Japan, and the United Kingdom. Each of these organizations provides certification programs. For example, the **Institute of Management Accountants (IMA)**—the largest association of management accountants in the United States—provides a program leading to the **Certified Management Accountant (CMA)** certificate. This certificate signals that the holder has passed the admission criteria and demonstrated the competency of technical knowledge required by the IMA.

Accountants consistently rank high in public opinion surveys on the ethics exhibited by members of different professions. Professional accounting organizations play an important role in promoting a high standard of ethics. The IMA has issued a *Standards of Ethical Conduct for Management Accountants*. Exhibit 1-5 presents the IMA's guidance on issues relating to competence, confidentiality, integrity, and objectivity.

Typical Ethical Challenges

Ethical issues can confront management accountants in many ways. The following examples are illustrative.

OBJECTIVE 7

Understand the importance of professional ethics to management accountants

EXHIBIT 1-5
Standards of Ethical Conduct for Management Accountants

Management accountants have an obligation to the organizations they serve, their profession, the public, and themselves to maintain the highest standards of ethical conduct. In recognition of this obligation, the Institute of Certified Management Accountants and the Institute of Management Accountants have adopted the following standards of ethical conduct for management accountants. Adherence to these standards is integral to achieving the objectives of management accounting. Management accountants shall not commit acts contrary to these standards, nor shall they condone the commission of such acts by others within their organizations.

COMPETENCE

Management accountants have a responsibility to

◆ Maintain an appropriate level of professional competence by ongoing development of their knowledge and skills.

◆ Perform their professional duties in accordance with relevant laws, regulations, and technical standards.

◆ Prepare complete and clear reports and recommendations after appropriate analysis of relevant and reliable information.

CONFIDENTIALITY

Management accountants have a responsibility to

◆ Refrain from disclosing confidential information acquired in the course of their work except when authorized, unless legally obligated to do so.

◆ Inform subordinates as appropriate regarding the confidentiality of information acquired in the course of their work and monitor their activities to assure the maintenance of that confidentiality.

◆ Refrain from using or appearing to use confidential information acquired in the course of their work for unethical or illegal advantage either personally or through third parties.

INTEGRITY

Management accountants have a responsibility to

◆ Avoid actual or apparent conflicts of interest and advise all appropriate parties of any potential conflict.

◆ Refrain from engaging in any activity that would prejudice their ability to carry out their duties ethically.

◆ Refuse any gift, favor, or hospitality that would influence or would appear to influence their actions.

◆ Refrain from either actively or passively subverting the attainment of the organization's legitimate and ethical objectives.

◆ Recognize and communicate professional limitations or other constraints that would preclude responsible judgment or successful performance of an activity.

◆ Communicate unfavorable as well as favorable information and professional judgments or opinions.

◆ Refrain from engaging in or supporting any activity that would discredit the profession.

OBJECTIVITY

Management accountants have a responsibility to

◆ Communicate information fairly and objectively.

◆ Disclose fully all relevant information that could reasonably be expected to influence an intended user's understanding of the reports, comments, and recommendations presented.

Source: Institute of Management Accounting, *Standards of Ethical Conduct for Management Accountants* (Montvale, N.J.).

◆ **Case A** A management accountant, knowing that reporting a loss for a software division will result in yet another "rightsizing initiative" (a euphemism for layoffs), has concerns about the commercial viability of software for which R&D costs are currently being capitalized. The division manager argues vehemently that the new product will be a "winner" but has no credible evidence to support the opinion. The last two products from this division have not been successful in the market. The management accountant has many friends in the division and wants to avoid a personal confrontation with the division manager. Should the management accountant require the R&D to be expensed immediately due to the lack of evidence as to its commercial viability?

◆ **Case B** A packaging supplier, bidding for a new contract, offers the management accountant of its customer an all-expenses-paid weekend to the Superbowl. The supplier does not mention the new contract when making the invitation. The accountant is not a personal friend of the supplier. He knows operating-cost issues are critical in approving the new contract and is concerned that the supplier will ask details about bids by competing packaging companies.

In each case the management accountant is faced with an ethical challenge. Case A involves competence, objectivity, and integrity, whereas case B involves confidentiality and integrity. Ethical issues are not always black or white. For example, the supplier in case B may have no intention of raising issues associated with the bid. However, the appearance of a conflict of interest in case B is sufficient for many companies to prohibit employees from accepting free "favors" from suppliers. Exhibit 1-6 presents the IMA's guidelines on resolution of ethical conflict.

A survey of 1,500 members of the Australian Society of Accountants found the following to be among the most frequently encountered ethical issues:

1. Proposals by clients or managers for tax evasion.
2. Conflicts of interest.
3. Proposals to manipulate financial statements.
4. Integrity in admitting mistakes made by oneself.
5. Coping with superior's instructions to carry out unethical acts.[1]

Most professional accounting organizations around the globe issue statements about professional ethics. While these statements include many of the same issues discussed by the IMA in Exhibits 1-5 and 1-6, differences do exist in their content. For example, the Chartered Institute of Management Accountants (CIMA) in the United Kingdom identifies the same four fundamental principles as the IMA did in Exhibit 1-5—competency, confidentiality, integrity, and objectivity. Yet, while the IMA code states that "except where legally prescribed, communication of such problems to authorities or individuals not employed or engaged by the organization is not considered appropriate,"[2] the CIMA code permits the accountant to hire an independent legal counsel if the issue cannot be resolved internally.

[1]P. Leung and B. J. Cooper, "Ethical Dilemmas in Accountancy Practice," *The Australian Accountant* (May 1995).
[2]R. L. Madison and J. R. Boafright, "Comparing IMA and CIMA Ethical Standards," *Management Accounting* (April 1995).

EXHIBIT 1-6
Resolution of Ethical Conflict

In applying the standards of ethical conduct, management accountants may encounter problems in identifying unethical behavior or in resolving an ethical conflict. When faced with significant ethical issues, management accountants should follow the established policies of the organization bearing on the resolution of such conflict. If these policies do not resolve the ethical conflict, management accountants should consider the following course of action:

◆ Discuss such problems with the immediate superior except when it appears that the superior is involved, in which case the problem should be presented initially to the next higher managerial level. If satisfactory resolution cannot be achieved when the problem is initially presented, submit the issues to the next higher managerial level.

   If the immediate superior is the chief executive officer, or equivalent, the acceptable reviewing authority may be a group such as the audit committee, executive committee, board of directors, board of trustees, or the owners. Contact with levels above the immediate superior should be initiated only with the superior's knowledge, assuming the superior is not involved.

◆ Clarify relevant concepts by confidential discussion with an objective advisor to obtain an understanding of a possible course of actions.

◆ If the ethical conflict still exists after exhausting all levels of internal review, the management accountant may have no other recourse on significant matters other than to resign from the organization and to submit an informative memorandum to an appropriate representative of the organization.

   Except where legally prescribed, communication of such problems to authorities or individuals not employed or engaged by the organization is not considered appropriate.

Source: Institute of Management Accountants, *Statements on Management Accounting: Objectives of Management Accounting. Statement No. 1B*, (Montvale, N.J.).

NEWLY EVOLVING MANAGEMENT THEMES AROUND THE GLOBE

OBJECTIVE 8

Describe evolving management themes that are shaping developments in management accounting systems

Management accounting exists to help managers make better decisions. Changes in the way managers operate require reevaluating the design and operation of the management accounting systems themselves. Exhibit 1-7 presents key themes in the new management approach.

1. *Customer satisfaction is priority one.* This theme is central. Customers are pivotal to the success of an organization. The number of organizations aiming to be "customer-driven" is large and increasing. The organization chart of Furon (a manufacturer of polymer) in Exhibit 1-8 shows how the customer is positioned at the apex of its organizational structure.

   We discuss this theme in Chapter 16 when we look at customer profitability analysis and Chapter 26 when we address customer feedback in performance measures.

2. *Key success factors.* Customers are demanding ever-improving levels of performance regarding several (or even all) of the following factors:

Common Ethical Dilemmas and Codes of Ethics

Ethical dilemmas occur in many areas. Kirk Hanson, a noted scholar in business ethics, lists the following as most common:

◆ When the boss asks you to do something questionable or unethical

◆ When you have knowledge of the unethical actions of others

◆ When you are tempted to cut corners to meet your performance goals

◆ When you are tempted to oversell your product to close the deal

◆ When disclosing confidential information will greatly help your career or your company

◆ When you are tempted to cover up past subperformance

One survey found 83% of U.S., 68% of Canadian, and 50% of European companies have instituted codes of ethics. Examples of issues covered in these ethics statements are

◆ Fundamental guiding principles—for example, Vulcan Materials states, "Integrity: We will work constantly to earn the respect and trust of all parties we interact with by acting fairly and honorably."

◆ Purchasing guidelines—Provident Mutual states, "Employees may not give or receive anything of more than token value ($50 or more) to or from any individual or organization with whom Provident Mutual does business."

◆ Environmental and safety guidelines—Neste OY states, "Our aim is to develop the best possible solutions in terms of the environment, occupational safety, and product user safety."

Other issues covered in codes of ethics statements include proprietary information, intellectual property, and confidentiality of employee records.

Source: K. O. Hanson, "Unavoidable Ethical Dilemmas in a Business Career" (Stanford University, 1995) and R. E. Berenbeim, *Corporate Ethics Practices* (New York: The Conference Board, 1992).

EXHIBIT 1-7
Key Themes in the New Management Approach

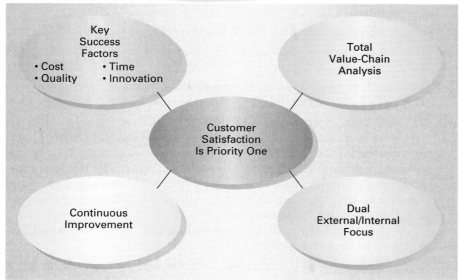

EXHIBIT 1-8
The Pivotal Position of Customers in the Organization Chart of the Furon Corporation

◆ *Cost.* Organizations are under continuous pressure to reduce the cost of the products or services they sell to their customers.

◆ *Quality.* Customers are expecting higher levels of quality and are less tolerant of low quality than in the past.

◆ *Time.* Time has many components, including the time taken to develop and bring new products to market, the speed at which an organization responds to customer requests, and the reliability with which promised delivery dates are met. Organizations are under pressure to complete activities faster and to meet promised delivery dates more reliably than in the past in order to increase customer satisfaction.

◆ *Innovation.* There is heightened recognition that a continuing flow of innovative products or services is a prerequisite for the ongoing success of most organizations.

Factors that directly affect customer satisfaction, such as cost, quality, time, and innovative products and services, are termed **key success factors.**
  We discuss this theme in Chapters 4 and 5 when we address using activity-based costing to guide cost reductions and in Chapter 19 when we examine cost of quality reports.

3. *Total value-chain analysis.* This theme has two related aspects:

◆ Treating each area of the business functions in Exhibit 1-1 (p. 4) as an essential and valued contributor

◆ Integrating and coordinating the efforts of all business functions in addition to developing the capabilities of each individual business function

Total value-chain analysis means focusing on all the business functions related to a product or service from its cradle to its grave ("womb to tomb"), irrespective of whether those functions occur in the same organization or in a set of legally independent organizations. For example, Pepsi-Cola bottlers work with their materials suppliers to reduce Pepsi's materials-handling costs. Similarly, Fujitsu works with the customers of its microchip division to better plan its production scheduling of microchips.
  We discuss this theme in Chapter 6 as we look at budgeting and Chapter 12 when we address target costing.

4. *Continuous improvement.* Continuous improvement by competitors creates a never-ending search for higher levels of performance within many organizations. Phrases such as the following capture this theme:

Quality in Accounting at Motorola

Providing a quality product or service is often defined in terms of consistently meeting or exceeding customers' expectations. Motorola, a $20 billion global company, is a winner of many awards for the quality of its products. The accounting group at Motorola views Motorola managers as its customers and is constantly seeking ways to meet or exceed their expectations. Consider the timeliness of the financial reports. Motorola managers place a premium on receiving timely reports. For many years, monthly results were not available to managers until 8 working days after month end. While an 8 working day "close period" is faster than that in most companies, managers viewed the provision of more timely reports as very important. The accounting group at Motorola decided to set itself a target of a 2 working day close.

Motorola now requires its six operating groups and its administrative group "to send monthly numbers no later than 2 working days after month end in a uniform layout that is compatible with the accounting group's software." As numbers are received, accounting performs real-time checks for "unusual transactions, numbers that don't jibe, and other potentially inaccurate entries." The consolidated financial reports are now provided to senior company executives and board members by noon of the third work day after the month end.

Motorola managers, with more timely information about business trends, can now make any adjustments at least 6 working days earlier than before. Moreover, the streamlining undertaken to speed the closing process has resulted in lower costs of monthly closing (a 30% reduction in employees) and a lower errors rate (less than 1,000 errors per 2 million transactions).

What has been the response of the accounting group to this success? They now have a goal of closing in 1½ days! Motorola has a culture of continuous improvement that is applied to all aspects of its business.

Source: B. Ettorre, "How Motorola Closes Its Books in Two Days," *Management Review* (March 1995) plus discussions with Motorola management.

♦ A journey with no end.

♦ We are running harder just to stand still.

♦ If you're not going forward, you're going backward.

Sumitomo Electric Industries, the Japanese manufacturer of electric wires and cables, has daily meetings so that all employees maintain a continuous focus on cost reduction.

We discuss this theme in Chapter 6 (kaizen budgeting), Chapter 7 (continuous improvement standard costs), and Chapter 10 (learning curves).

5. *Dual external/internal focus.* Managers operate in both an external and an internal environment. The external environment includes customers, competitors, suppliers, and government bodies. Many organizations now are restructuring the definition of manager responsibilities to give much greater emphasis to the external environment. This greater emphasis increases the likelihood that managers will anticipate external changes and take advantage of such external changes as the introduction of competitors' new products or shifts in customer preferences. The internal environment covers each part of the value chain as well as the coordination of its components.

We discuss this theme in Chapter 7 when we examine benchmarking and Chapter 25 when we look at market-based transfer pricing.

Over time, the emphasis placed on the five themes in Exhibit 1-7 may change, and new themes may be added. If management accountants are to remain useful to managers, they must keep up to date with changes in the field of management.

(Try to solve this problem before examining the solution that follows.)

PROBLEM

The Campbell Soup Company incurs the following costs:

a. Purchase of tomatoes by canning plant for Campbell's tomato soup products.

b. Materials purchased for redesigning Pepperidge Farm biscuit containers to make biscuits stay fresh longer.

c. Payment to Bates, the advertising agency for the Healthy Request line of soup products.

d. Salaries of food technologists researching feasibility of a Prego pizza sauce that has zero calories.

e. Payment to Safeway for shelf space to display Campbell's food products.

f. Cost of a toll-free telephone line used for customer inquiries about possible taste problems with Campbell's Soups.

g. Cost of gloves used by line operators on the Swanson Fiesta breakfast food production line.

h. Cost of hand-held computers used by Pepperidge Farm delivery staff serving major supermarket accounts.

REQUIRED

Classify each cost item (a–h) into a component of the value chain shown in Exhibit 1-1 (p. 4).

SOLUTION

a. Production

b. Design of products, services, or processes

c. Marketing

d. Research and development

e. Marketing

f. Customer service

g. Production

h. Distribution

SUMMARY

The following points are linked to the chapter's learning objectives.

1. Accounting systems provide information for five broad purposes: (a) formulating overall strategies and long-range plans, (b) resource allocation decisions such as product and customer emphasis, (c) cost planning and cost control, (d) performance measurement, and (e) meeting external regulatory and legal reporting obligations.

2. Cost accounting measures and reports financial and other information related to an organization's acquisition or consumption of resources. It is an important component of both management accounting and financial accounting.

3. Managers in all areas of the value chain are customers of accounting information. The business functions in the value chain are research and development; design of products, services, or processes; production; marketing; distribution; and customer service.

4. Accounting helps facilitate planning, control, and decision making through budgets and other financial benchmarks, its systematic recording of actual results, and its role in performance evaluation.

5. Management accountants and controllers are staff management in most organizations. Staff management exists to provide advice and assistance to line managers, who are directly responsible for attaining the objectives of the organization.

6. In most organizations, management accountants perform scorekeeping, attention-directing, and problem-solving functions. The first function emphasizes the importance of the integrity of information, while the other two emphasize the helper role of the accountant.

7. Management accountants have important ethical responsibilities that are related to competence, confidentiality, integrity, and objectivity.

8. Important management themes that are shaping developments in management accounting systems around the globe include (a) the primacy of customer satisfaction, (b) linking planning and control to key success factors, (c) total value-chain analysis, (d) continuous improvement, and (e) dual external/internal focus.

▼ TERMS TO LEARN

Each chapter will include this section. Like all technical subjects, accounting contains many terms with precise meanings. Pin down the definitions of new terms when you initially encounter them. The meaning of each of the following terms is explained in this chapter and also in the Glossary at the end of this book.

attention directing (p. 9)
budget (4)
Certified Management Accountant
   (CMA) (9)
chief financial officer (CFO) (7)
control (4)
controller (7)
cost accounting (2)
cost-benefit approach (6)
cost management (3)
customer service (3)
design of products, services, or
   processes (3)
distribution (3)
finance director (7)
financial accounting (2)

Institute of Management Accountants
   (IMA) (9)
key success factors (14)
line management (7)
management accounting (2)
management by exception (5)
marketing (3)
planning (4)
problem solving (9)
production (3)
research and development (R&D) (3)
scorekeeping (8)
staff management (7)
value chain (3)
variance (5)

▼ ASSIGNMENT MATERIAL

QUESTIONS

1-1 The accounting system should provide information for five broad purposes. Describe them.

1-2 Distinguish between *management accounting* and *financial accounting*.

1-3 "Management accounting should not fit the straitjacket of financial accounting." Explain and give an example.

1-4 Describe the business functions in the value chain.

1-5 Explain the meaning of *cost management*.

1-6 Feedback may be used for a variety of purposes. Identify at least five uses of feedback.

1-7 "Knowledge of technical issues such as computer technology is necessary but not sufficient to becoming a successful accountant." Do you agree? Why?

1-8 Peter Drucker, a noted business observer, made the following comment in an address to management accountants: "I am not saying that you do not need a 'cop on the beat,' you do. . . But your great challenge is to get across to your associates your ability to identify the opportunities—to identify the wealth-producing characteristics." Do you agree? Explain.

1-9 As a new controller, reply to this comment by a plant manager: "As I see it, our accountants may be needed to keep records for stockholders and Uncle Sam—but I don't want them sticking their noses in my day-to-day operations. I do the best I know how. No pencil-pushing bean-counter knows enough about my responsibilities to be of any use to me."

1-10 As used in accounting, what do IMA and CMA stand for?

1-11 Name the four areas in which standards of ethical conduct exist for management accountants in the United States. What organization sets forth these standards?

1-12 What steps should a management accountant take if established written policies provide insufficient guidance on how to handle an ethical conflict?

1-13 When explaining a motor vehicle market-share turnaround, General Motors stated: "We listened to what our customers wanted and acted on what they said. Good things happen when you pay attention to the boss." How might management accountants at General Motors apply this same perspective to their own tasks?

1-14 A leading management observer stated that the most successful companies are those who have an obsession for their customers. Is this statement pertinent to management accountants? Explain.

1-15 Changes in the way managers operate require rethinking the design and operation of management accounting systems. Describe five themes that are affecting both the way managers operate and developments in management accounting.

EXERCISES

1-16 **Financial and management accounting.** David Colhane, an able electrical engineer, was informed that he was going to be promoted to assistant plant manager. David was elated but uneasy. In particular, his knowledge of accounting was sparse. He had taken one course in financial accounting but had not been exposed to the management accounting that his superiors found helpful.

Colhane planned to enroll in a management accounting course as soon as possible. Meanwhile, he asked Susan Hansley, an assistant controller, to state two or three of the principal distinctions between financial and management accounting using some concrete examples.

As the assistant controller, prepare a written response to Colhane.

1-17 **Purposes of accounting systems.** The International Sports Management Group (ISMG) manages and promotes sporting events and sporting personalities. Its managers are currently examining the following reports and accounting statements:

a. Five-year projections for expanding into managing sports television networks for cable television.

b. Income statement to be included in a six-month interim report to be sent to investors and filed with the Securities & Exchange Commission.

c. Profitability comparison of golf tournaments directed by different managers, each of whom receives a percentage of that tournament's profits.

d. Monthly reports of office costs for each of the 14 ISMG offices worldwide.

e. Statement showing the revenues ISMG earns from different types of sporting events (for example, golf, motor racing, and tennis).

REQUIRED
Classify the reports in parts a–e into one of the five major purposes of accounting systems (on p. 2).

1-18 **Purposes of accounting systems.** Managers at Coca-Cola are examining the following reports and accounting statements:

managers at Coca-cola are examining the following reports and accounting statement

a. Report on the profitability of Minute Maid Orange Juice in different regions; regional managers receive a bonus based on region profitability.

b. Consolidated balance sheet to be reported in the Annual Report to investors. *①financial*

c. Ten-year projections of revenues, costs, and investments for entering into joint venture agreements in the new Russian republics. *③ management*

d. Monthly manufacturing cost report of the Toronto bottling plant. *③*

e. Report comparing profitability of soft drink sales in retail outlets, fast-food franchises, and sporting stadium vendors for most recent month. *②*

REQUIRED

1. Classify the reports in parts a–e into one of the five major purposes of accounting systems (p. 2).

2. How might a report developed for the financial-reporting purpose differ from a report for one of the four management accounting purposes? Illustrate by referring to two of the Coca-Cola reports in parts a–e.

1-19 Value chain and classification of costs, computer company. Apple Computer incurs the following costs:

a. Electricity costs for the plant assembling the Macintosh computer line of products. *production*

b. Transportation costs for shipping Macintosh software to a retail chain. *distribution*

c. Payment to David Kelley Designs for design of the Powerbook carrying case. *Design stage*

d. Salary of a computer scientist working on the next generation of mini-computers. *Research and Development*

e. Cost of Apple employees' visit to a major customer to illustrate Apple's ability to interconnect with other computers. *On going customer service*

f. Purchase of competitors' products for testing against potential future Apple products. *Research and development*

g. Payment to a television station for running Apple advertisements. *marketing*

h. Cost of cables purchased from an outside supplier to be used with the Macintosh printer. *production*

REQUIRED

Classify each of the cost items in parts a–h into a component of the value chain shown in Exhibit 1-1 (p. 4).

1-20 Value chain and classification of costs, pharmaceutical company. Merck, a large pharmaceutical company, incurs the following costs:

a. Cost of redesigning blister packs to make drug containers more tamper-proof.

b. Cost of videos sent to doctors to promote sales of a new drug.

c. Cost of a toll-free telephone line used for customer inquiries about usage, side effects of drugs, and so on.

d. Equipment purchased by a scientist to conduct experiments on drugs yet to be approved by the government.

e. Payment to actors on infomercial to be shown on television promoting new hair-growing product for balding men.

f. Labor costs of workers in the packaging area of a production facility.

g. Bonus paid to a salesperson for exceeding monthly sales quota.

h. Cost of Federal Express courier service to deliver drugs to hospitals.

REQUIRED

Classify each of the cost items in parts a–h into a component of the value chain shown in Exhibit 1-1 (p. 4).

1-21 Uses of feedback. Six uses of feedback are described in the chapter (p. 6):

a. Changing goals.

b. Searching for alternative means of operating.

c. Changing methods for making decisions.

d. Making predictions.

e. Changing the operating process.

f. Changing the reward system.

Match the appropriate letters from the preceding list to each of the following items.

1. The California State University system explores subcontracting its gardening operations to a private company instead of hiring its own gardeners.
2. Sales commissions are to be based on total operating income instead of total revenue.
3. The Ford Motor Company adjusts its elaborate way of forecasting demand for its cars by including the effects of expected changes in the price of crude oil.
4. The hiring of new sales personnel will include an additional step: an interview and evaluation by the company psychologist.
5. Quality inspectors at General Motors are now being used in the middle of the production process as well as at the end of the process.
6. Procter & Gamble enters the telecommunications industry.
7. Worker assignments on an assembly line are made by teams instead of directed by a foreman.

1-22 Scorekeeping, attention directing, and problem solving. For each of the following activities, identify the major function (scorekeeping, attention directing, or problem solving) the accountant is performing.
   a. Preparing a monthly statement of Australian sales for the IBM marketing vice president.
   b. Interpreting differences between actual results and budgeted amounts on a performance report for the customer warranty department of General Electric.
   c. Preparing a schedule of depreciation for forklift trucks in the receiving department of a Hewlett Packard plant in Scotland.
   d. Analyzing, for a Mitsubishi international manufacturing manager, the desirability of buying some auto parts made in Korea.
   e. Interpreting why a Birmingham distribution center did not adhere to its delivery costs budget.
   f. Explaining a Xerox shipping department's performance report.
   g. Preparing, for the manager of production control of a U.S. steel plant, a cost comparison of two computerized manufacturing control systems.
   h. Preparing a scrap report for the finishing department of a Toyota parts plant.
   i. Preparing the budget for the maintenance department of Mount Sinai Hospital.
   j. Analyzing, for a General Motors product designer, the impact on product costs of some new headlight lamps.

1-23 Scorekeeping, attention directing, and problem solving. For each of the following activities, identify the major function the accountant is performing—scorekeeping, attention directing, or problem solving.
   a. Interpreting differences between actual results and budgeted amounts on a shipping manager's performance report at a Daewoo distribution center.
   b. Preparing a report showing the benefits of leasing motor vehicles versus owning them.
   c. Preparing adjusting journal entries for depreciation on the personnel manager's office equipment at Citibank.
   d. Preparing a customer's monthly statement for a Sears store.
   e. Processing the weekly payroll for the Harvard University maintenance department.
   f. Explaining the product-design manager's performance report at a Chrysler division.
   g. Analyzing the costs of several different ways to blend materials in the foundry of a General Electric plant.
   h. Tallying sales, by branches, for the sales vice president of Unilever.

i. Analyzing, for the president of Microsoft, the impact of a contemplated new product on net income.

j. Interpreting why an IBM sales district did not meet its sales quota.

1-24 Changes in management and changes in management accounting. A survey on ways organizations are changing their management accounting systems reported the following:

a. Company A now reports a value-chain income statement for each of the brands it sells.

b. Company B now presents in a single report all costs related to achieving high quality levels of its products.

c. Company C now presents estimates of the manufacturing costs of its two most important competitors in its performance reports, in addition to its own internal manufacturing costs.

d. Company D reduces by 1% each month the budgeted labor-assembly cost of a product when evaluating the performance of a plant manager.

e. Company E now reports profitability and satisfaction measures (as assessed by a third party) on a customer-by-customer basis.

REQUIRED

Link each of the above changes to one of the key themes in the new management approach outlined in Exhibit 1-7 (p. 13).

PROBLEMS

1-25 Planning and control, feedback. In April 19_7, Naomi Campbell, editor of *The Daily Sporting News* (DSN), decides to reduce the price per newspaper from $0.70 in April 19_7 to $0.50 starting May 1, 19_7. Actual paid circulation in April is 7.5 million (250,000 per day × 30 days). Campbell estimates that the $0.20 price reduction would increase paid circulation in May to 12.4 million (400,000 × 31 days). The actual May circulation turns out to be 13,640,000 (440,000 × 31 days). Assume that one goal of DSN is to increase operating income. The budgeted increase in circulation would enable DSN to charge higher advertising rates in later months of 19_7 if those budgeted gains actually occur. The actual price paid in May 19_7 was the budgeted $0.50 per newspaper.

REQUIRED

1. Distinguish between planning and control at DSN, giving an example of each.

2. Prepare a newspaper revenue performance report for DSN for May 19_7 showing the actual results, budgeted amounts, and the variance.

3. Give two types of action Campbell might take based on feedback on the May 19_7 circulation revenue.

1-26 Responsibility for analysis of performance. Karen Phillipson is the new corporate controller of a multinational company that has just overhauled its organizational structure. The company is now decentralized. Each division is under an operating vice president who, within wide limits, has responsibilities and authority to run the division like a separate company.

Phillipson has a number of bright staff members. One of them, Bob Garrett, is in charge of a newly created performance-analysis staff. Garrett and staff members prepare monthly division performance reports for the company president. These reports are division income statements, showing budgeted performance and actual results, and they are accompanied by detailed written explanations and appraisals of variances. In the past, each of Garrett's staff members was responsible for analyzing one division; each consulted with division line and staff executives and became generally acquainted with the division's operations.

After a few months, Bill Whisler, vice president in charge of Division C, stormed into the controller's office. The gist of his complaint follows:

"Your staff is trying to take over part of my responsibility. They come in, snoop around, ask hundreds of questions, and take up plenty of our time.

It's up to me, not you and your detectives, to analyze and explain my division's performance to central headquarters. If you don't stop trying to grab my responsibility, I'll raise the whole issue with the president."

REQUIRED
1. What events or relationships may have led to Whisler's outburst?
2. As Phillipson, how would you answer Whisler's contentions?
3. What alternative actions can Phillipson take to improve future relationships?

1-27 Professional ethics and reporting divisional performance. Marcia Miller is division controller and Tom Maloney is division manager of the Ramses Shoe Company. Miller has line responsibility to Maloney, but she also has staff responsibility to the company controller.

Maloney is under severe pressures to achieve budgeted division income for the year. He has asked Miller to book $200,000 of sales on December 31. The customers' orders are firm, but the shoes are still in the production process. They will be shipped on or about January 4. Maloney said to Miller, "The key event is getting the sales order, not shipping of the shoes. You should support me, not obstruct my reaching division goals."

REQUIRED
1. Describe Miller's ethical responsibilities.
2. What should Miller do if Maloney gives her a direct order to book the sales?

1-28 Software procurement decision, ethics. Jorge Michaels is the Chicago-based controller of Fiesta Foods, a rapidly growing manufacturer and marketer of Mexican food products. Michaels is currently considering the purchase of a new cost management package for use by each of its six manufacturing plants and its many marketing personnel. There are four major competing products being considered by Michaels.

Horizon 1-2-3 is an aggressive software developer. It views Fiesta as a target of opportunity. Every 6 months Horizon has a 3-day user's conference in a Caribbean location. Each conference has substantial time left aside for "rest and recreation." Horizon offers Michaels an all-expenses-paid visit to the upcoming conference in Cancun, Mexico. Michaels accepts the offer believing that it will be very useful to talk to other users of Horizon software. He is especially looking forward to the visit as he has close relatives in the Cancun area.

Prior to leaving, Michaels received a visit from the president of Fiesta. She shows him an anonymous letter sent to her. It argues that Horizon is receiving unfair favorable treatment in the Fiesta software decision-making process. The letter specifically mentions Michaels' upcoming "all-expenses-paid trip to Cancun during Chicago's deep winter." Michaels is deeply offended. He says he has made no decision and believes he is very capable of making a software choice on the merits of each product. Fiesta currently does not have a formal written code of ethics.

REQUIRED
1. Do you think Michaels faces an ethical problem as regards his forthcoming visit to the Horizon's user's group meeting? Refer to Exhibit 1-5 (p. 10). Explain.
2. Should Fiesta allow executives to attend user's meetings while negotiating with other vendors about a purchase decision? Explain. If yes, what conditions on attending should apply?
3. Would you recommend Fiesta develop its own code of ethics to handle situations such as this one? What are the pros and cons of having such a written code?

1-29 Professional ethics and end-of-year games. Janet Taylor is the new division controller of the snack foods division of National Foods. National Foods has reported a minimum 15% growth in annual earnings for each of the past five years. The snack foods division has reported annual earnings growth of over 20% each year in this same period. During the current year, the economy went into a recession. The corporate controller estimates a 10% annual earnings growth rate for National Foods in this year. One month before the December 31, fiscal year end of the current year, Taylor estimates the snack foods division will report an annual earnings growth of only 8%. Warren Ryan, the snack foods division president, is less than happy, but he says with a wry smile, "Let the end-of-year games begin."

Taylor makes some inquiries and is able to compile the following list of end-of-year games that were more or less accepted by the prior division controller:

a. Deferring routine monthly maintenance in December on packaging equipment by an independent contractor until January of next year.

b. Extending the close of the current fiscal year beyond December 31 so that some sales of next year are included in the current year.

c. Altering dates of shipping documents of next January's sales to record them as sales in December of the current year.

d. Giving salespeople a double bonus to exceed December sales targets.

e. Deferring the current period's advertising by reducing the number of television spots run in December and running more than planned in January of next year.

f. Deferring the current period's reported advertising costs by having National Food's outside advertising agency delay billing December advertisements until January of next year or having the agency alter invoices to conceal the December date.

g. Persuading carriers to accept merchandise for shipment in December of the current year although they normally would not have done so.

REQUIRED

1. Why might the snack foods division president want to play the end-of-year games described here?

2. The division controller is deeply troubled and reads the *Standards of Ethical Conduct for Management Accountants* in Exhibit 1-5 (p. 10). Classify each of the end-of-year games as (i) acceptable or (ii) unacceptable according to that document.

3. What should Taylor do if Ryan suggests that end-of-year games are played in every division of National Foods and that she would greatly harm the snack foods division if she did not play along and paint the rosiest picture possible of the division's results?

COLLABORATIVE LEARNING PROBLEM

1-30 **Responding to allegations of fraud.** You are the controller of Broad Street Finance (BSF). BSF is an investment banking company that has recently encountered severe financial difficulties and has had to lay off over 200 employees. The only bright spot in this picture is BSF's bond-trading division, but you have just received the following anonymous letter:

Dear Sir,

Last year's reported earnings for the bond-trading division are fictitious. The top three managers of the division recently received bonuses of over $12 million, based on their share of last year's reported earnings. The head of bond trading has been inventing bond trades that are supposed to be highly profitable. They are not. The division profits are like a deck of cards about to collapse. The head of bond trading cares only about "how much you reportedly made" and nothing about how you made it. The auditors don't understand the complexity of today's bond-trading operations. This problem will blow up in your face unless handled quickly and carefully. I am sending a copy of this letter to the Securities & Exchange

Commission, *Business Week*, *Forbes*, *Fortune*, and all members of Broad Street's board of directors.

Sincerely,
Concerned Exemployee

INSTRUCTIONS

Form groups of three or more students. One is to be the chief financial officer, one the president, and one the chairman of the board of directors. Other members are on the board of directors.

REQUIRED

Develop a group consensus on how you should respond to this letter. Should BSF formalize a code of ethics statement? Like many firms in the financial services industry, it has no formal code of ethics.

AN INTRODUCTION TO COST TERMS AND PURPOSES

Many costing systems have multiple cost objects. Managers at a factory can collect costs for their mass-produced products (such as globes), for the assembly plant, and for customers who have globes custom assembled at the plant.

LEARNING OBJECTIVES

After studying this chapter, you should be able to

1. Define and illustrate a cost object
2. Distinguish between direct costs and indirect costs
3. Explain cost drivers, variable costs, and fixed costs
4. Understand why unit costs must be interpreted with caution
5. Distinguish among service-sector, merchandising-sector, and manufacturing-sector companies
6. Differentiate between capitalized costs and noncapitalized costs
7. Describe the three categories of inventories commonly found in many manufacturing-sector companies
8. Explain how different ways of computing product costs are appropriate for different purposes

This chapter explains several widely recognized cost concepts and terms. They will help us demonstrate the multiple purposes of cost accounting systems, which we will stress throughout the book.

Various cost concepts and terms are useful in many contexts, including decision making in all areas of the value chain. They help managers decide such issues as, How much should we spend for research and development? What is the effect of product design changes on manufacturing costs? Should we replace some production assembly workers with a robot? Should we spend more of the marketing budget on sales promotion coupons and less on advertising? Should we distribute from a central warehouse or from regional warehouses? Should we provide a toll-free number for customer inquiries regarding our products?

COSTS IN GENERAL

OBJECTIVE 1

Define and illustrate a cost object

Cost Objects

Accountants usually define **cost** as a resource sacrificed or forgone to achieve a specific objective. Most people consider costs as monetary amounts (such as dollars, pesos, pounds, or yen) that must be paid to acquire goods and services. For now we can think of costs in this conventional way.

To guide their decisions, managers often want to know how much a certain thing (such as a new product, a machine, a service, or a process) costs. We call this "thing" a **cost object,** which is anything for which a separate measurement of costs is desired. Exhibit 2-1 provides examples of several different types of cost objects.

Cost Accumulation and Cost Assignment

A costing system typically accounts for costs in two basic stages:

Stage 1 It *accumulates* costs by some "natural" (often self-descriptive) classification such as materials, labor, fuel, advertising, or shipping.

Stage 2 It *assigns* these costs to cost objects.

Cost accumulation is the collection of cost data in some organized way through an accounting system. **Cost assignment** is a general term that encompasses both (1) tracing accumulated costs to a cost object, and (2) allocating accumulated costs to a cost object. Costs that are traced to a cost object are direct costs, and costs that are allocated to a cost object are indirect costs. Nearly all accounting systems accumulate **actual costs,** which are the costs incurred (historical costs), as distinguished from budgeted or forecasted costs.

EXHIBIT 2-1
Examples of Cost Objects

Cost Object	Illustration
◆ Product	A ten-speed bicycle
◆ Service	An airline flight from Los Angeles to London
◆ Project	An airplane assembled by Boeing for Singapore Airlines
◆ Customer	All products purchased by Safeway (the customer) from General Foods
◆ Brand category	All soft drinks sold by a Pepsi-Cola bottling company with "Pepsi" in their name
◆ Activity	A test to determine the quality level of a television set
◆ Department	A department within a government environmental agency that studies air emissions standards
◆ Program	An athletic program of a university

In some organizations, stage 1 (cost accumulation) and stage 2 (cost assignment) occur simultaneously. Consider the purchase by Boeing of 100 business-class seats to be installed in a 767 airplane to be sold to British Airways. This transaction could be coded to a general ledger account such as materials (the cost accumulation stage) and simultaneously coded to three separate cost objects (the cost assignment stage):

◆ a department (assembly)
◆ a product (767 product line)
◆ a customer (British Airways)

Alternatively, stage 1 (cost accumulation) could occur first, followed by stage 2 (cost assignment). For example, the 100-seat purchase by Boeing could first be coded to the materials account, then subsequently assigned to a department, then reassigned to a product, and finally reassigned to a customer. Advances in information-gathering technology (such as bar coding) are facilitating the simultaneous assignment of costs to more than one cost object at the time costs are incurred.

Remember, managers assign costs to designated cost objects to help decision making. For example, costs may be assigned to a department to facilitate decisions about departmental efficiency. Costs may also be assigned to a product or a customer to facilitate product or customer profitability analysis.

DIRECT COSTS AND INDIRECT COSTS

Cost Tracing and Cost Allocation

A major question concerning costs is whether they have a direct or an indirect relationship to a particular cost object.

OBJECTIVE 2

Distinguish between direct costs and indirect costs

◆ **Direct costs of a cost object** are costs that are related to the particular cost object and that can be traced to it in an economically feasible (cost-effective) way.

◆ **Indirect costs of a cost object** are costs that are related to the particular cost object but cannot be traced to it in an economically feasible (cost-effective) way. Indirect costs are allocated to the cost object using a cost allocation method.

Take a baseball bat as a cost object. The cost of the piece of wood used to make that bat is a direct cost. Why? Because the amount of wood used in making the bat can easily be traced to the bat. The cost of lighting in the factory where the bat was made is an indirect cost of the bat. Why? Because although lighting helped in the making of the bat (the workers needed to see), it is not cost effective to try to determine exactly how much lighting cost was used for a specific bat.

Managers prefer to make decisions on the basis of direct costs rather than indirect costs. Why? Because they know that direct costs are more accurate than indirect costs. In summary, the relationship between these terms is

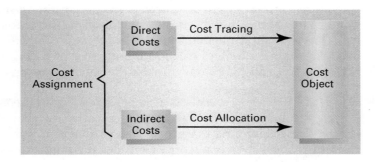

Cost tracing is the assigning of direct costs to the chosen cost object. **Cost allocation** is the assigning of indirect costs to the chosen cost object. *Cost assignment* encompasses both cost tracing and cost allocation.

Factors Affecting Direct/Indirect Cost Classifications

Several factors will affect the classification of a cost as direct or indirect:

1. *The materiality of the cost in question.* The higher the cost in question, the more likely the economic feasibility of tracing that cost to a particular cost object. Consider a mail-order catalog company. It would probably be economically feasible to trace the courier charges for delivering a package directly to each customer. In contrast, the cost of the invoice paper included in the package sent to the customer is likely to be classified as an indirect cost because it is not economically feasible to trace the cost of this paper to each customer. The benefits of knowing the exact number of (say) $0.05 worth of paper included in each package typically do not justify the costs of money and time in tracing the costs to each package.

2. *Available information-gathering technology.* Improvements in this area are enabling an increasing percentage of costs to be classified as direct. Bar codes, for example, allow many manufacturing plants to treat certain materials previously classified as indirect costs as direct costs of products. Bar codes can be read into a manufacturing cost file by waving a "wand" in the same quick and efficient way supermarkets now enter the cost of many items purchased by its customers.

3. *Design of operations.* Facility design can impact cost classification. For example, classifying a cost as direct is helped if an organization's facility (or part thereof) is used exclusively for a specific product or specific cost object, such as a particular customer.

4. *Contractual arrangements.* For example, a contract stating that a given component (an Intel Pentium chip) can be used only in a specific product (an IBM PC) makes it easier to classify the component as a direct cost of the product.

This book examines different ways to assign costs to cost objects. For now, be aware that one particular cost may be both direct and indirect. How? *The direct/indirect classification depends on the choice of the cost object.* For example, the salary of an assembly-department supervisor may be a direct cost of the assembly department at Ford but an indirect cost of a product such as the Ford Taurus.

COST DRIVERS AND COST MANAGEMENT

The continuous cost reduction efforts of competitors create a never-ending need for organizations to reduce their own costs. Cost reduction efforts frequently focus on two key areas:

1. Doing only **value-added activities,** that is, those activities that customers perceive as adding value to the products or services they purchase.
2. Efficiently managing the use of the cost drivers in those value-added activities.

A **cost driver** (also called a *cost generator* or *cost determinant*) is any factor that affects total costs. That is, a change in the level of the cost driver will cause a change in the level of the total cost of a related cost object.

Exhibit 2-2 presents examples of cost drivers in each of the business functions of the value chain. Some cost drivers are financial measures found in accounting systems (such as direct manufacturing labor costs and sales dollars), while others are nonfinancial variables (such as the number of parts per product and the number of service calls). We now discuss the role of cost drivers in describing cost behavior.

Cost management is the set of actions that managers take to satisfy customers while continuously reducing and controlling costs. A caveat on the role of cost drivers in cost management is appropriate. Changes in a particular cost driver do not automatically lead to changes in overall costs. Consider the number of items distributed as a driver of distribution labor costs. Suppose that management reduces the number of items distributed by 25%. This reduction does not automatically translate to a reduction in distribution labor costs. Managers must take steps to reduce distribution labor costs, perhaps by shifting workers out of distribution into other business functions needing additional labor or by laying off some distribution employees.

Business Function	Cost Driver
Research and development	◆ Number of research projects ◆ Personnel hours on a project ◆ Technical complexity of projects
Design of products, services, and processes	◆ Number of products in design ◆ Number of parts per product ◆ Number of engineering hours
Production	◆ Number of units produced ◆ Direct manufacturing labor costs ◆ Number of setups ◆ Number of engineering change orders
Marketing	◆ Number of advertisements run ◆ Number of sales personnel ◆ Sales dollars
Distribution	◆ Number of items distributed ◆ Number of customers ◆ Weight of items distributed
Customer service	◆ Number of service calls ◆ Number of products serviced ◆ Hours spent servicing products

COST BEHAVIOR PATTERNS: VARIABLE COSTS AND FIXED COSTS

Management accounting systems record the cost of resources acquired and track their subsequent use. Tracing these costs allows managers to see how these costs behave. Let us now consider two basic types of cost behavior patterns found in many of these systems—variable costs and fixed costs. A **variable cost** is a cost that changes in total in proportion to changes in a cost driver. A **fixed cost** is a cost that does not change in total despite changes in a cost driver.

◆ *Variable Costs.* If General Motors buys a steering wheel at $60 for each of its Saturn cars, then the total cost of steering wheels should be $60 times the number of cars assembled. This is an example of a variable cost, a cost that changes *in total* in proportion to changes in the cost driver (number of cars). The variable cost per car does not change with the number of cars assembled. Exhibit 2-3 (Panel A) illustrates this variable cost. A second example of a variable cost is a sales commission of 5% of each sales dollar. Exhibit 2-3 (Panel B) shows this variable-cost example.

◆ *Fixed Costs.* General Motors may incur $20 million in a given year for the leasing and insurance of its Saturn plant. Both are examples of fixed costs, costs that are unchanged in total over a designated range of the cost driver during a given time span. Fixed costs become progressively smaller on a per unit basis as the cost driver increases. For example, if General Motors assembles 10,000 Saturn vehicles at this plant in a year, the fixed cost for leasing and insurance per vehicle is $2,000 ($20 million ÷ 10,000). In contrast, if 50,000 vehicles are assembled, the fixed cost per vehicle becomes $400.

Do not assume that individual cost items are inherently variable or fixed. Consider labor costs. An example of purely variable labor costs is the case where workers are paid on a piece-unit basis. Some textile workers are paid on a per shirt sewed basis. In contrast, labor costs are appropriately classified as fixed

EXHIBIT 2-3
Examples of Variable Costs

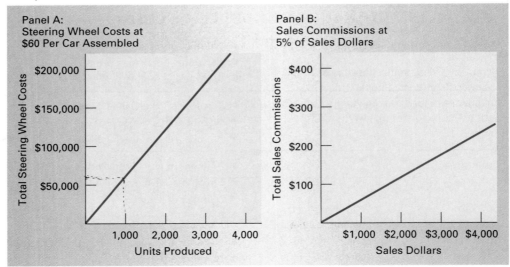

Panel A:
Steering Wheel Costs at
$60 Per Car Assembled

Panel B:
Sales Commissions at
5% of Sales Dollars

when life-time employment exists or where union conditions severely restrict an organization's flexibility to assign workers to any area that has extra labor requirements.

Major Assumptions

The definitions of variable costs and fixed costs have important underlying assumptions:

1. Costs are defined as variable or fixed with respect to a specific cost object.
2. The time span must be specified. Consider the $20 million rent and insurance General Motors pays for its Saturn plant. This amount may be fixed for one year. Beyond that time, the rent and insurance may be renegotiated to be, say, $22 million for a subsequent year.
3. Total costs are linear. That is, when plotted on ordinary graph paper, a total variable-cost or a total fixed-cost relationship to the cost driver will appear as an unbroken straight line.
4. There is only one cost driver. The influences of other possible cost drivers on total costs are held constant or deemed to be insignificant.
5. Variations in the level of the cost driver are within a relevant range (which we discuss in the next section).

Variable costs and fixed costs are the two most frequently recognized cost behavior patterns in existing management accounting systems. Additional cost behavior patterns are discussed in subsequent chapters (see Chapters 5 and 10).

Relevant Range

A **relevant range** is the range of the cost driver in which a specific relationship between cost and driver is valid. A fixed cost is fixed only in relation to a given relevant range (usually wide) of the cost driver and a given time span (usually a particular budget period). Consider the Thomas Transport Company (TTC), which operates two refrigerated trucks that carry agricultural produce to market. Each truck has an annual fixed cost of $40,000 (including an annual insurance cost of $15,000 and an annual registration fee of $8,000) and a variable cost of $1.20 per mile of hauling. TTC has chosen miles of hauling to be the cost driver. The maximum annual usage of each truck is 120,000 miles. In the

Purposes for Distinguishing Between Variable Costs and Fixed Costs

Many chapters in this book illustrate the insights gained from distinguishing between variable costs and fixed costs. One survey* of U.S. companies reported the following ranking of purposes for distinguishing between variable and fixed costs (1 = most important purpose). The relevant chapters refer to where each purpose is extensively discussed in this book.

Rank	Purpose	Relevant Chapters
1 (equal)	Pricing	4, 5, 11, and 12
1 (equal)	Budgeting	6
3	Profitability analysis—existing products	4, 5, 11, and 12
4	Profitability analysis—new products	11 and 12
5	Cost-volume-profit (CVP) analysis	3
6	Variance analysis	7, 8, 16, and 24

Surveys of Australian, Japanese, and United Kingdom companies provide additional evidence on the ranking by managers of the many purposes for distinguishing between variable costs and fixed costs (1 = most important purpose):[†]

Purpose	Ranking by Companies in Australia	Ranking by Companies in Japan	Ranking by Companies in United Kingdom
Pricing decisions	1	5	1
Budgeting2	2	3	
Making profit plans	3	1	2
Cost reduction	6	3	5 (equal)
CVP analysis	4 (equal)	4	4
Cost-benefit analysis	4 (equal)	6	5 (equal)

These surveys highlight the wide range of decisions for which managers feel an understanding of cost behavior is important.

---

*Adapted from Mowen, *Accounting for Costs*.

[†]Blayney and Yokoyama, "Comparative Analysis." Full citations are in Appendix A at the back of the book.

current year (19_7), the predicted combined total hauling of the two trucks is 170,000 miles.

Exhibit 2-4 shows how annual fixed costs behave at different levels of miles of hauling. Up to 120,000 miles, TTC can operate with one truck; from 120,001 to 240,000 miles, it can operate with two trucks; and from 240,001 to 360,000, it can operate with three trucks. This pattern would continue as TTC added trucks to its fleet. The bracketed section from 120,001 to 240,000 is the range at which TTC expects the $80,000 to be valid given the predicted 170,000-mile usage for 19_7.

Fixed costs may change from one year to the next. For example, if the annual registration fee for refrigerated trucks is increased in 19_8, the total level of fixed costs will increase (unless offset by a reduction in other fixed items).[1]

---

[1]Cost behavior questions appear in professional examinations with regularity. For example, see the supplement to this text book: J. K. Harris and D. W. Curry, *Student Guide and Review Manual* (Upper Saddle River, N.J.: Prentice Hall, 1997).

EXHIBIT 2-4
Fixed-Cost Behavior at Thomas Transport Company

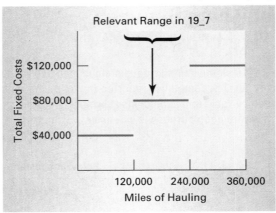

Relationships of Types of Costs

We have introduced two major classifications of costs: direct/indirect and variable/fixed. Costs may simultaneously be

- ◆ direct and variable
- ◆ direct and fixed
- ◆ indirect and variable
- ◆ indirect and fixed

Exhibit 2-5 presents examples of simultaneous cost classifications with each of the four cost types.

EXHIBIT 2-5
Examples of Simultaneous Direct/Indirect and Variable/Fixed Cost Classifications

		Assignment of Costs to Cost Object	
		Direct Cost	**Indirect Cost**
Cost Behavior Pattern	**Variable Cost**	Cost object: Assembled automobile Example: Tires used in assembly of automobile	Cost object: Assembled automobile Example: Power costs where power usage is metered only to the plant
	Fixed Cost	Cost object: Marketing department Example: Annual leasing cost of cars used by sales force representatives	Cost object: Marketing department Example: Monthly charge by corporate computer center for marketing's share of corporate computer costs

TOTAL COSTS AND UNIT COSTS

Meaning of Unit Costs

Accounting systems typically report both total-cost and unit-cost numbers. A **unit cost** (also called an **average cost**) is computed by dividing some total cost by some number of units. Suppose that $980,000 of manufacturing costs were incurred to produce 10,000 units of a finished good. Then the unit cost would be $98:

$$\frac{\text{Total manufacturing costs}}{\text{Number of units manufactured}} = \frac{\$980,000}{10,000} = \$98 \text{ per unit}$$

If 8,000 units are sold and 2,000 units remain in ending inventory, the unit-cost concept helps in the assignment of total costs for the income statement and balance sheet:

Cost of goods sold in the income statement, 8,000 units × $98	$784,000
Ending inventory of finished goods in the balance sheet, 2,000 units × $98	196,000
Total manufacturing costs of 10,000 units	$980,000

Unit costs are found in all areas of the value chain—for example, there are unit costs for product design, sales calls, and customer-service calls.

Use Unit Costs Cautiously

Unit costs are averages. As we shall see, they must be interpreted with caution. For decision making, it is best to think in terms of total costs rather than unit costs. Nevertheless, unit-cost numbers are frequently used in many situations. For example, assume the president of a university social club is deciding whether to hire a musical group for an upcoming party. The group charges a fixed fee of $1,000. The president may intuitively compute a unit cost for the group when thinking about an admission price. Given the fixed fee of $1,000, the unit cost is $10 if 100 people attend, $2 if 500 attend, and $1 if 1,000 attend. Note, however, that with a fixed fee of $1,000 the *total cost* is unaffected by the attendance level, while the *unit cost* is a function of the attendance level. In this example, each attendee is considered to be one unit.

Costs are often neither inherently fixed nor variable. Much depends on the specific context. Consider the $1,000 fixed fee that we assumed was to be paid to the musical group. This is but one way the musical group could be paid. Possible payment schedules that might be considered include

◆ Schedule 1: $1,000 fixed fee
◆ Schedule 2: $1 per person attending + $500 fixed fee
◆ Schedule 3: $2 per person attending

Under schedules 2 and 3, the dollar amount of the payment to the musical group is not known until after the event.

The effects of these three payment schedules on unit costs and total costs for five attendance levels are

	Schedule 1: $1,000 Fixed		Schedule 2: $1 Per Person + $500 Fixed		Schedule 3: $2 Per Person	
Number of Persons Attending	Total Cost	Unit Cost	Total Cost	Unit Cost	Total Cost	Unit Cost
50	$1,000	$20	$ 550	$11	$ 100	$2
100	1,000	10	600	6	200	2
250	1,000	4	750	3	500	2
500	1,000	2	1,000	2	1,000	2
1,000	1,000	1	1,500	1.50	2,000	2

The unit cost under schedule 1 is computed by dividing the fixed cost of $1,000 by the attendance level. For schedule 2, the unit cost is computed by first determining the total cost for each attendance level and then dividing that amount by that attendance level. Thus, for 250 people, schedule 2 has a total cost of $750 ($500 + 250 × $1), which gives a unit cost of $3 per person. Schedule 3 has a unit cost of $2 per person for any attendance level because the musical group is to be paid $2 per person with no fixed payment.

All three payment schedules would yield the same unit cost of $2 per person only if 500 people attend. The unit cost is not $2 per person under schedule 1 or schedule 2 for any attendance level except 500 people. Thus, it would be incorrect to use the $2 per person amount in schedule 1 or 2 to predict what the total costs would be for 1,000 people. Consider what occurs if 250 people attend and the group is paid a fixed fee of $1,000. The unit cost is then $4 per person. *While unit costs are often useful, they must be interpreted with extreme caution if they include fixed costs per unit.* When estimating total cost, think of variable costs as an amount per unit and fixed costs as a lump sum total amount.

The key relationships between total costs and unit costs are summarized in Panel A of Exhibit 2-6. Panel B illustrates these relationships for schedule 3 where the university social club pays the musical group on a variable basis (cost of $2 per person). Panel C illustrates schedule 1 where the musical group is paid a fixed amount (cost of $1,000).

EXHIBIT 2-6
Behavior of Total Costs and Unit Costs when the Level of the Cost Driver Changes with Illustration of Alternate Payment Schedules for Musical Group

PANEL A: SUMMARY OF KEY RELATIONSHIPS

Cost Behavior Pattern	Total Costs	Unit Costs
When item is a variable cost	Total costs change with changes in level of cost driver	Units costs remain the same with changes in level of cost driver
When item is a fixed cost	Total costs remain the same with changes in level of cost driver	Unit costs change with changes in level of cost driver

PANEL B: PAYMENT IS $2 PER ATTENDEE

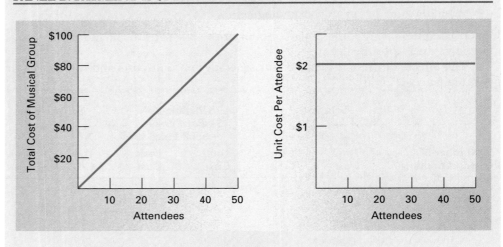

PANEL C: PAYMENT IS A FIXED $1,000

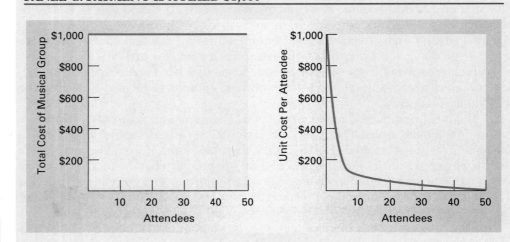

We now consider costs included in the income statements or balance sheets of ser-vice-, merchandising-, and manufacturing-sector companies. One key distinction of costs is their classification as capitalized or noncapitalized when they are incurred:

◆ **Capitalized costs** are first recorded as <u>an asset</u> (capitalized) when they are incurred. These costs are presumed to provide future benefits to the company. Examples are costs to acquire computer equipment and motor vehicles. These costs are written off to those periods assumed to benefit from their incurrence. For example, the cost of acquiring motor vehicles is written off as a depreciation expense that occurs each year of the expected useful life of the vehicle.

◆ **Noncapitalized costs** are recorded as <u>expenses</u> of the accounting period when they are incurred. Examples are salaries paid to marketing personnel and monthly rent paid for administrative offices.

These two categories of costs apply to companies in all three sectors of the economy.

SERVICE-SECTOR COMPANIES

Service-sector companies provide services or intangible products to their customers—for example, legal advice or an audit. These companies do not have any inventory of tangible product at the end of an accounting period. Examples include law firms, accounting firms, advertising agencies, and television stations. Labor costs are typically the most significant cost category, often being as high as 70% of total costs.

Exhibit 2-7 (Panel A) presents an income statement for Elliott & Partners, a law firm specializing in personal-injury litigation. The customers (clients) of this law

OBJECTIVE 5

Distinguish among service-sector, merchandising-sector, and manufacturing-sector companies

EXHIBIT 2-7
Service-Sector Income Statement

**PANEL A: ELLIOTT & PARTNERS INCOME STATEMENT
FOR THE YEAR ENDED DECEMBER 31, 19_7**

Revenues		$1,600,000
Costs:		
Salaries and wages	$970,000	
Rent	180,000	
Depreciation	105,000	
Other costs	187,000	1,442,000
Operating income		$ 158,000

**PANEL B: ELLIOTT & PARTNERS RELATIONSHIP OF CAPITALIZED AND
NONCAPITALIZED COSTS**

firm receive legal advice and representation on their behalf in court and in negotiations. Salaries and wages constitute 67.3% of total operating costs ($970,000 ÷ $1,442,000). The operating-cost line items for service companies will include costs from all areas of the value chain (production of services, marketing, and so on). There is not a line item for cost of goods sold in the income statement of Elliott & Partners. Why? Because the business sells only services or intangible products to its customers.

Exhibit 2-7 (Panel B) shows the relationship between capitalized and noncapitalized costs for service-sector companies. Capitalized costs include the cost of motor vehicles, computers, and similar equipment purchased by Elliott & Partners. These costs are first capitalized and shown in the balance sheet as assets. They are presumed to provide benefits to the company over several periods. Each period part of the cost of these assets is expensed as depreciation—$105,000 in 19_7. Noncapitalized costs of Elliott, such as salaries and wages ($970,000) and rent ($180,000), become expenses immediately as incurred and thus are never shown as assets.

MERCHANDISING- AND MANUFACTURING-SECTOR COMPANIES

Merchandising-sector companies provide tangible products they have previously purchased in the same basic form from suppliers. Merchandise purchased from suppliers but not sold at the end of an accounting period is held as inventory. The merchandising sector includes companies engaged in retailing (such as book stores or department stores), distributing, or wholesaling. **Manufacturing-sector companies** provide tangible products that have been converted to a different form from that of the products purchased from suppliers. At the end of an accounting period, a manufacturer has inventory that can include direct materials, work in process, or finished goods.

Merchandising and manufacturing companies differ from service companies in their holding of inventories. The capitalized costs of merchandising and manufacturing companies can be classified as follows:

OBJECTIVE 6

Differentiate between capitalized costs and noncapitalized costs

◆ **Capitalized inventoriable costs** (also called **inventoriable costs**) are those capitalized costs associated with the purchase of goods for resale (in the costs of merchandise inventory) or costs associated with the acquisition and conversion of materials and all other manufacturing inputs into goods for sale (in the case of manufacturing inventories).

◆ **Capitalized noninventoriable costs** are those capitalized costs associated with any aspect of business other than inventory.

Capitalized inventoriable costs become part of cost of goods sold in the period in which the inventory item is sold. **Operating costs** are all costs associated with generating revenues, other than cost of goods sold.[2] They include (1) the period expensing of capitalized noninventoriable costs, and (2) noncapitalized costs. We now consider Prestige Bathrooms (a merchandiser) and Cellular Products (a manufacturer) to illustrate financial statements in these two sectors.

Merchandising-Sector Example

Exhibit 2-8 (Panel A) presents the income statement of Prestige Bathrooms, a merchandiser of bathroom fixtures and furnishings (showers, sinks, hand towels, and so on). A merchandiser's cost of goods sold consists of the cost of goods purchased for resale adjusted for changes in the level of merchandise inventory:

$$\begin{matrix} \text{Beginning} \\ \text{merchandise} \\ \text{inventory} \end{matrix} + \begin{matrix} \text{Purchases} \\ \text{of merchandise} \end{matrix} - \begin{matrix} \text{Ending} \\ \text{merchandise} \\ \text{inventory} \end{matrix} = \begin{matrix} \text{Cost of} \\ \text{goods} \\ \text{sold} \end{matrix}$$

---

[2]The term *operating costs* is sometimes used to include cost of goods sold. In this book, we do not include cost of goods sold in operating costs.

EXHIBIT 2-8
Merchandising-Sector Income Statement

PANEL A: PRESTIGE BATHROOMS INCOME STATEMENT FOR THE YEAR ENDED DECEMBER 31, 19_7

Revenues		$1,500,000
Cost of goods sold		
Beginning merchandise inventory, January 1, 19_7	$ 95,000	
Purchases of merchandise	1,100,000	
Cost of goods available for sale	1,195,000	
Ending merchandise inventory, December 31, 19_7	130,000	1,065,000
Gross margin (or gross profit)		435,000
Operating costs		315,000
Operating income		$ 120,000

PANEL B: PRESTIGE BATHROOMS RELATIONSHIP OF CAPITALIZED AND NONCAPITALIZED COSTS

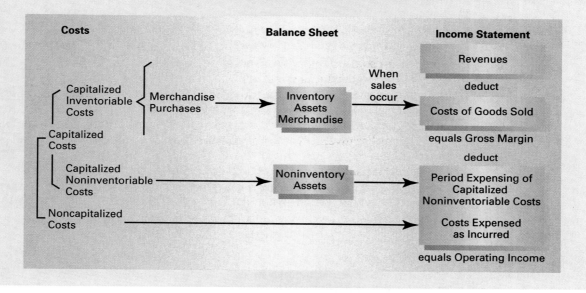

For Prestige Bathrooms in 19_7, the corresponding amounts in Exhibit 2-8 (Panel A) are

$$\$ 95{,}000 + \$1{,}100{,}000 - \$130{,}000 = \$1{,}065{,}000$$

Examples of Prestige's operating costs include the costs of designing the showroom, sales personnel, and advertising.

Exhibit 2-8 (Panel B) shows the relationship between capitalized and noncapitalized costs for merchandising companies. Merchandise purchased for resale is first shown as an asset; its cost is a capitalized inventoriable cost. As the merchandise is sold, its cost becomes an expense of that period in the form of cost of goods sold. Capitalized noninventoriable costs (such as the costs of fixtures, fittings, and computers) are shown on the balance sheet as assets and then become operating cost line items in the form of depreciation (and other forms of asset write-downs) over the useful life of the asset. The $315,000 operating costs of Prestige in Panel A include depreciation on noninventory assets as well as costs expensed to the period as incurred (such as the salaries of checkout staff and monthly cost of electricity).

Subsequent chapters examine merchandising-sector costs in detail. These costs include cost of goods sold, period expensing of capitalized noninventoriable costs, and costs expensed as incurred (noncapitalized costs).

Manufacturing-Sector Example

The manufacturing sector differs from the merchandising sector in that the products sold to customers are converted to a different form from that of the products purchased from suppliers. This distinction results in the manufacturer having one or more of the following types of inventory:

1. **Direct materials inventory.** Direct materials in stock and awaiting use in the manufacturing process.

EXHIBIT 2-9
Income Statement and Schedule of Cost of Goods Manufactured
of Manufacturing-Sector Company

PANEL A: CELLULAR PRODUCTS INCOME STATEMENT FOR THE YEAR ENDED DECEMBER 31, 19_7 (IN THOUSANDS)

Revenues		$210,000
Cost of goods sold		
Beginning finished goods, January 1, 19_7	$ 22,000	
Cost of goods manufactured (see Panel B)	104,000	
Cost of goods available for sale	126,000	
Ending finished goods, December 31, 19_7	18,000	108,000
Gross margin (or gross profit)		102,000
Operating costs		70,000
Operating income		$ 32,000

PANEL B: CELLULAR PRODUCTS SCHEDULE OF COST OF GOODS MANUFACTURED* FOR THE YEAR ENDED DECEMBER 31, 19_7 (IN THOUSANDS)

Direct materials		
Beginning inventory, January 1, 19_7	$ 11,000	
Purchases of direct materials	73,000	
Cost of direct materials available for use	84,000	
Ending inventory, December 31, 19_7	8,000	
Direct materials used		$ 76,000
Direct manufacturing labor		17,750
Indirect manufacturing costs		
Indirect manufacturing labor	4,000	
Supplies	1,000	
Heat, light, and power	1,750	
Depreciation— plant building	1,500	
Depreciation—plant equipment	2,500	
Miscellaneous	500	11,250
Manufacturing costs incurred during 19_7		105,000
Add beginning work in process inventory, January 1, 19_7		6,000
Total manufacturing costs to account for		111,000
Deduct ending work in process inventory, December 31, 19_7		7,000
Cost of goods manufactured (to income statement)		$104,000

*Note that the term *cost of goods manufactured* refers to the cost of goods brought to completion (finished) during the year, whether they were started before or during the current year. Some of the manufacturing costs incurred during the year are held back as costs of the ending work in process inventory; similarly, the costs of the beginning work in process inventory become part of the cost of goods manufactured for the year. Note too that this schedule can become a schedule of cost of goods manufactured and sold simply by including the beginning and ending finished goods inventory figures in the supporting schedule rather than directly in the body of the income statement as in Panel A.

EXHIBIT 2-10
Manufacturing-Sector Income Statement: Relationship of Capitalized and Noncapitalized Costs

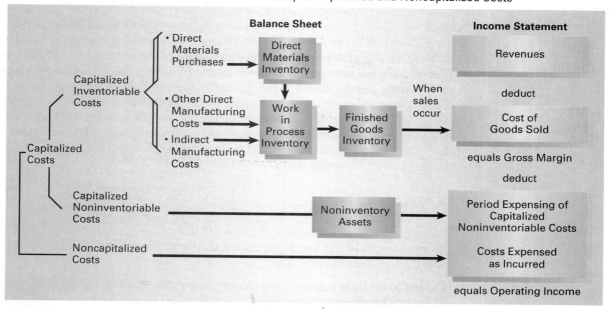

2. **Work-in-process inventory.** Goods partially worked on but not yet fully completed. Also called **work in progress.**
3. **Finished goods inventory.** Goods fully completed but not yet sold.

In this chapter we assume that all manufacturing costs are inventoriable.[3]

The income statement of a manufacturer, Cellular Products, is shown in Exhibit 2-9 (Panel A). This company manufactures telephone systems for large organizations. Cost of goods sold in a manufacturing company is computed as follows:

$$\text{Beginning finished goods inventory} + \text{Cost of goods manufactured} - \text{Ending finished goods inventory} = \text{Cost of goods sold}$$

For Cellular Products in 19_7, the corresponding amounts (in thousands, Panel A) are

$$\$22,000 + \$104,000 - \$18,000 = \$108,000$$

Cost of goods manufactured refers to the cost of goods brought to completion, whether they were started before or during the current accounting period. In 19_7, these costs amount to $104,000 for Cellular Products (see the schedule of cost of goods manufactured in Panel B of Exhibit 2-9). The manufacturing costs incurred during 19_7 ($105,000) is a line item in Panel B. This item refers to the "new" direct manufacturing costs and the "new" manufacturing overhead costs that were incurred during 19_7 for all goods worked on during 19_7, regardless of whether all those goods were fully completed during this year.

Exhibit 2-10 shows cost relationships for a manufacturing-sector company. The manufacturing costs of the finished goods include direct materials, other direct manufacturing costs, and indirect manufacturing costs. All these are capitalized inventoriable costs; they are assigned to work-in-process inventory or finished goods inventory until the goods are sold. Capitalized inventoriable costs include the costs of assets that facilitate the manufacturing process and (typically) become part of indirect

[3]The term *absorption costing* is used to describe the method in which all manufacturing costs are inventoriable. Chapter 9 further discusses this method and two alternative methods—*variable costing*, in which only variable manufacturing costs are inventoriable and *throughput costing*, in which only direct-materials costs are inventoriable.

manufacturing costs in the form of depreciation. For example, the costs of the blast furnace of a steel company are first capitalized at the time of construction. These costs subsequently become part of steel inventory costs as depreciation on the blast furnace is included in indirect manufacturing costs over the useful life of the blast furnace. Newcomers to cost accounting frequently assume that indirect costs such as rent, telephone, and depreciation are always costs of the period in which they are incurred and are unconnected with inventories. However, if these costs are related to manufacturing per se, they are indirect manufacturing costs and are inventoriable. Operating-cost items in the income statement in Panel A of Exhibit 2-9 include (1) the expensing of capitalized noninventoriable costs (such as depreciation on a fleet of delivery vehicles or depreciation on computers purchased for marketing personnel), and (2) the cost of items recorded as an expense as incurred (such as the salaries of customer-service representatives).

MANUFACTURING COSTS

The language of cost accounting has specific terms for manufacturing costs. Three terms in widespread use are direct materials costs, direct manufacturing labor costs, and indirect manufacturing costs.

1. **Direct materials costs** are the acquisition costs of all materials that eventually become part of the cost object (say, units finished or in process), and that can be traced to the cost object in an economically feasible way. Acquisition costs of direct materials include freight-in (inward delivery) charges, sales taxes, and custom duties.

2. **Direct manufacturing labor costs** include the compensation of all manufacturing labor that is specifically identified with the cost object (say, units finished or in process), and that can be traced to the cost object in an economically feasible way. Examples include wages and fringe benefits paid to machine operators and assembly-line workers.

3. **Indirect manufacturing costs** are all manufacturing costs considered to be part of the cost object (say, units finished or in process), but that cannot be individually traced to that cost object in an economically feasible way. Examples include power, supplies, indirect materials, indirect manufacturing labor, plant rent, plant insurance, property taxes on plants, plant depreciation, and the compensation of plant managers. Other terms for this cost category include **manufacturing overhead costs** and **factory overhead costs**. We use *indirect manufacturing costs* and *manufacturing overhead costs* interchangeably in this book.

Three-Part and Two-Part Cost Classifications

Manufacturing-cost accounting systems vary among companies. Some use a three-part classification of manufacturing costs; others use a two-part classification:

THREE-PART CLASSIFICATION	TWO-PART CLASSIFICATION
◆ Direct materials costs	◆ Direct materials costs
◆ Direct manufacturing labor costs	◆ Indirect manufacturing costs
◆ Indirect manufacturing costs	

Accounting systems of organizations often change over time. For example, a company may change from the three-part classification to the two-part classification if direct manufacturing labor costs become immaterial in amount because of increased automation. Other alternatives are also available. A company may change from the three-part classification to one with two direct cost categories and multiple individual manufacturing overhead cost categories. Managers will choose the classification of costs that best helps them in their planning, control, and decision making.

Harley-Davidson Eliminates the Direct Manufacturing Labor Cost Category

For many years, Harley-Davidson's Motorcycle Division used a three-part cost classification in its manufacturing facilities—direct materials, direct manufacturing labor, and manufacturing overhead. In the mid-1980s, a task force of Harley-Davidson managers analyzed how its manufacturing product-cost structure compared with the administrative costs required to collect, inspect, and report data in its accounting system. It found the following information:

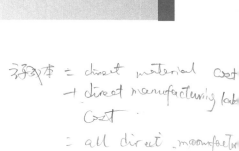

	Manufacturing Product-Cost Structure	Administrative Cost Effort
Direct materials	54%	25%
Manufacturing overhead	36	13
Direct manufacturing labor	10	62

The administrative costs associated with tracking direct manufacturing labor as a separate cost category included:

◆ operators time to fill out labor tickets

◆ supervisors time to review labor tickets

◆ timekeepers time to enter the labor data and review the data output reports for errors

◆ cost accountants time to review the direct labor and variance data

Harley-Davidson concluded that tracing direct labor to products did not meet a cost-benefit test. Direct labor costs were only 10% of total manufacturing costs but required 62% of the administrative effort used to track all manufacturing costs. The company now includes all manufacturing labor costs as part of manufacturing overhead costs. It uses a two-part classification of direct materials and manufacturing overhead.

Source: Adapted from Turk, "Management Accounting Revitalized: The Harley-Davidson Experience." *Journal of Cost Management* (Winter 1990) and conversations with management.

Prime Costs and Conversion Costs

Two terms used in manufacturing-cost systems are prime costs and conversion costs. **Prime costs** are all direct manufacturing costs. In the three-part classification, prime costs would comprise direct materials costs and direct manufacturing labor costs. In the two-part classification, prime costs would include only direct materials costs. As information-gathering technology improves, companies may add additional direct-cost categories. For example, power costs might be metered in specific areas of a plant that are dedicated totally to the assembly of separate products. In this case, prime costs would include direct materials, direct manufacturing labor, and direct metered power. Computer software companies often have a "purchased technology" direct manufacturing-cost item. This item, which covers payments to third parties who develop software algorithms included in a product, would also be included in prime costs. **Conversion costs** are all manufacturing costs other than direct materials costs. These costs are for transforming direct materials into finished goods. In the three-part classification of manufacturing costs, conversion costs would comprise direct manufacturing labor costs and indirect manufacturing costs. In the two-part classification, conversion costs would be only the indirect manufacturing costs.

The components of prime costs and conversion costs for the three-part and two-part classifications can be summarized as follows:

	Three-part Classification	Two-part Classification
Prime costs	Direct materials costs Direct manufacturing labor costs	Direct materials costs
Conversion costs	Direct manufacturing labor costs Indirect manufacturing costs	Indirect manufacturing costs

BENEFITS OF DEFINING ACCOUNTING TERMS

Differences exist across companies in the way accounting terms are defined. Consider a direct laborer, such as a lathe operator or an assembly-line worker, who earns gross wages computed on the basis of a regular wage rate of $20 per hour. This person receives fringe benefits (employer contributions to the employee's social security, life insurance, health insurance, and so on) totaling, say, $8 per hour. Some companies classify the $20 as direct manufacturing labor cost and the $8 as manufacturing overhead cost. Other companies classify the entire $28 as direct manufacturing labor cost. The latter approach is conceptually preferable because these payroll fringe benefit costs are a fundamental part of acquiring manufacturing labor services. The magnitude of fringe benefits makes this issue important. Countries where fringe benefits costs are over 30% of wage rates include Italy (105%), France (90%), Germany (86%), United Kingdom (43%), and the United States (38%).[4]

The problem here is to pinpoint what direct manufacturing labor includes and excludes in a particular situation. Achieving clarity may avoid disputes regarding cost reimbursement contracts, income tax provisions, and labor union matters. For example, some countries offer substantial income tax savings to companies that locate manufacturing plants there. To qualify, the "direct manufacturing labor" costs of these companies in that country must meet a specified minimum percentage of the total manufacturing costs of their products produced there. What incentive does such an income tax provision give managers to classify fringe benefit costs as direct manufacturing labor or manufacturing overhead? Classifying payroll fringe benefit costs as direct manufacturing labor will increase the percentage of direct manufacturing labor costs, thereby making it easier to qualify for the income tax savings. Consider a company with $8 million of payroll fringe benefit costs (figures are assumed to be in millions):

Method A			**Method B**		
Direct materials	$ 40	40%	Direct materials	$ 40	40%
Direct manufacturing labor	20	20	Direct manufacturing labor	28	28
Manufacturing overhead	40	40	Manufacturing overhead	32	32
Total manufacturing costs	$100	100%	Total manufacturing costs	$100	100%

Method A classifies payroll fringe benefit costs as part of manufacturing overhead. In contrast, method B classifies payroll fringe benefit costs as part of direct manufacturing labor. If a country set the minimum percentage of direct manufacturing labor costs at 25%, the company would receive a tax savings using method B, but not using method A. In addition to payroll fringe benefits, other items subject to different possible classifications include compensation for training time, idle time, vacations, sick leave, and extra compensation for overtime. To prevent disputes, contracts and laws should be as specific as feasible regarding definitions and measurements of accounting terms.

[4]H. Salowsky, "Labor Costs in Twenty Industrialized Countries, 1970–1991," Institute of the Germany Economy in Cologne, Germany, 1992.

EXHIBIT 2-11
Different Product Costs for Different Purposes

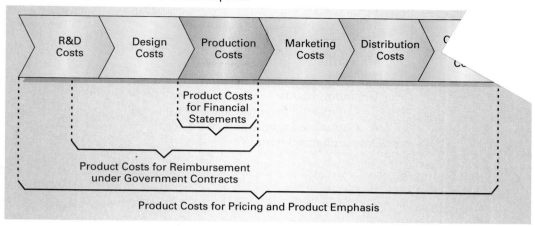

THE MANY MEANINGS OF PRODUCT COSTS

An important theme of this book is "different costs for different purposes." This theme can be illustrated with respect to product costing. A **product cost** is the sum of the costs assigned to a product for a specific purpose. Exhibit 2-11 illustrates three different purposes:

OBJECTIVE 8

Explain how different ways of computing product costs are appropriate for different purposes

1. *Product pricing and product emphasis.* For this purpose, the costs of all those areas of the value chain required to bring a product to a customer should be included.

2. *Contracting with government agencies.* Government agencies frequently provide detailed guidelines on the allowable and nonallowable items in a product-cost amount. For example, some government agencies explicitly exclude marketing costs from reimbursement to contractors and may reimburse only a part of R&D costs. Hence, the bracket in Exhibit 2-11 shows that a specific contract may provide for recovering all design and production costs and part of R&D costs.

3. *Financial statements.* The focus here is on inventoriable costs. For example, under generally accepted accounting principles in manufacturing companies, only manufacturing costs are assigned to products reported in the financial statements.

Exhibit 2-11 illustrates how a product-cost amount may include only inventoriable costs in the financial statements, a broader set of costs for reimbursement under a government contract, and a still broader set of costs for pricing and product emphasis.

CLASSIFICATIONS OF COSTS

This chapter has provided many examples of cost classifications that have various purposes. Classifications can be made on the basis of

1. Business function
   a. Research and development
   b. Design of products, services, and processes
   c. Production
   d. Marketing
   e. Distribution
   f. Customer service
2. Assignment to a cost object
   a. Direct costs
   b. Indirect costs

3. Behavior pattern in relation to changes in the level of a cost driver
   a. Variable costs
   b. Fixed costs

4. Aggregate or average
   a. Total costs
   b. Unit costs

5. Costs in financial statements
   a. Capitalized costs
      i. Capitalized inventoriable costs
      ii. Capitalized noninventoriable costs
   b. Noncapitalized costs

PROBLEM FOR SELF-STUDY

(Try to solve this problem before examining the solution that follows.)

PROBLEM
Campbell Company is a metal and wood cutting manufacturer, selling products to the home construction market. Consider the following data for the year 19_7:

Sandpaper	$ 2,000
Materials-handling costs	70,000
Lubricants and coolants	5,000
Miscellaneous indirect manufacturing labor	40,000
Direct manufacturing labor	300,000
Direct materials, January 1, 19_7	40,000
Finished goods, January 1, 19_7	100,000
Finished goods, December 31, 19_7	150,000
Work in process, January 1, 19_7	10,000
Work in process, December 31, 19_7	14,000
Plant-leasing costs	54,000
Depreciation—plant equipment	36,000
Property taxes on plant equipment	4,000
Fire insurance on plant equipment	3,000
Direct materials purchased	460,000
Direct materials, December 31, 19_7	50,000
Revenue	1,360,000
Marketing promotions	60,000
Marketing salaries	100,000
Shipping costs	70,000
Customer-service costs	100,000

REQUIRED
1. Prepare an income statement with a separate supporting schedule of cost of goods manufactured. For all manufacturing items, indicate by V or F whether each is basically a variable cost or a fixed cost (where the cost object is a product unit). If in doubt, decide on the basis of whether the total cost will change substantially over a wide range of production output.
2. Suppose that both the direct materials and plant-leasing costs are tied to the production of 900,000 units. What is the unit cost for the direct materials assigned to each unit produced? What is the unit cost of the plant-leasing costs? Assume that the plant-leasing costs are a fixed cost.
3. Repeat the computation in requirement 2 for direct materials and plant-leasing costs, assuming that the costs are being predicted for the manufacturing of 1 million units next year. Assume that the implied cost behavior patterns persist.

4. As a management consultant, explain concisely to the president why the unit costs for direct materials did not change in requirements 2 and 3 but the unit costs for plant-leasing costs did.

SOLUTION

1.

CAMPBELL COMPANY
Income Statement for the Year Ended December 31, 19_7

Revenue		$1,360,000
Cost of goods sold		
Beginning finished goods, January 1, 19_7	$ 100,000	
Cost of goods manufactured (see below)	960,000	
Cost of goods available for sale	1,060,000	
Ending finished goods, December 31, 19_7	150,000	910,000
Gross margin (or gross profit)		450,000
Operating costs		
Marketing promotions	60,000	
Marketing salaries	100,000	
Distribution costs	70,000	
Customer-service costs	100,000	330,000
Operating income		$ 120,000

CAMPBELL COMPANY
Schedule of Cost of Goods Manufactured
For the Year Ended December 31, 19_7

Direct materials		
Beginning inventory, January 1, 19_7	$ 40,000	
Purchases of direct materials	460,000	
Cost of direct materials available for use	500,000	
Ending inventory, December 31, 19_7	50,000	
Direct materials used		$450,000 (V)
Direct manufacturing labor		300,000 (V)
Indirect manufacturing costs		
Sandpaper	$ 2,000 (V)	
Materials handling cost	70,000 (V)	
Lubricants and coolants	5,000 (V)	
Miscellaneous indirect manufacturing labor	40,000 (V)	
Plant-leasing costs	54,000 (F)	
Depreciation—plant equipment	36,000 (F)	
Property taxes on plant equipment	4,000 (F)	
Fire insurance on plant equipment	3,000 (F)	214,000
Manufacturing costs incurred during 19_7		964,000
Add beginning work in process inventory, January 1, 19_7		10,000
Total manufacturing costs to account for		974,000
Deduct ending work in process inventory, December 31, 19_7		14,000
Cost of goods manufactured (to income statement)		$960,000

2. Direct materials unit cost = Direct materials used ÷ Units produced
   = $450,000 ÷ 900,000 = $0.50

   Plant-leasing unit cost   = Plant-leasing costs ÷ Units produced
   = $54,000 ÷ 900,000 = $0.06

3. The direct materials costs are variable, so they would increase in total from $450,000 to $500,000 (1,000,000 × $0.50). However, their unit costs would be unaffected: $500,000 ÷ 1,000,000 units = $0.50.

In contrast, the plant-leasing costs of $54,000 are fixed, so they would not increase in total. However, if the plant-leasing costs were assigned to units produced, the unit costs would decline from $0.060 to $0.054: $54,000 ÷ 1,000,000 = $0.054.

4. The explanation would begin with the answer to requirement 3. As a consultant, you should stress that the unitizing (averaging) of costs that have different behavior patterns can be misleading. A common error is to assume that a total unit cost, which is often a sum of variable unit costs and fixed unit costs, is an indicator that total costs change in a wholly variable way as the level of production output changes. The next chapter demonstrates the necessity for distinguishing between cost behavior patterns. You must be especially wary about unit fixed costs. Too often, unit fixed costs are erroneously regarded as being indistinguishable from unit variable costs.

SUMMARY

The following points are linked to the chapter's learning objectives.

1. A cost object is anything for which a separate measurement of costs is desired. Examples include a product, service, project, customer, brand category, activity, department, and program.

2. A direct cost of a cost object is any cost that is related to the cost object and can be traced to that cost object in an economically feasible way. Indirect costs are costs that are related to the cost object but cannot be traced to that cost object in an economically feasible way. A cost may be direct regarding one cost object and indirect regarding other cost objects. This book uses the term *cost tracing* to describe the assignment of direct costs to a cost object and the term *cost allocation* to describe the assignment of indirect costs to a cost object.

3. A cost driver is any factor that affects costs. Examples include the number of set-ups and direct-labor hours in manufacturing and the number of sales personnel and sales dollars in marketing. A variable cost is a cost that does change in total in proportion to changes in a cost driver. A fixed cost is a cost that does not change in total despite changes in a cost driver.

4. Unit costs of a cost object should be interpreted with caution when they include a fixed-cost component. When making total cost estimates, think of variable costs as an amount per unit and fixed costs as a total amount.

5. Service-sector companies provide services or intangible products to their customers. In contrast, merchandising- and manufacturing-sector companies provide tangible products to their customers. Merchandising companies do not change the form of the products they acquire and sell. Manufacturing companies convert materials and other inputs into finished goods for sale. These differences are reflected in both the balance sheets and income statements of companies in these sectors.

6. Capitalized costs are first recorded as an asset (capitalized) when they are incurred. These costs are presumed to provide future benefits to the company. Non-capitalized costs are recorded as expenses when they are incurred.

7. The three categories of inventory found in many manufacturing-sector companies depict stages in the conversion process—direct materials, work in process, and finished goods.

8. Managers may assign different costs to the same cost object depending on their purpose. For example, for financial reporting purposes, the (inventoriable) costs of a product include only manufacturing costs. In contrast, costs from all areas of the value chain can be assigned to a product for decisions on pricing and product emphasis.

▼ TERMS TO LEARN

This chapter contains more basic terms than any other in this book. Do not proceed before you check your understanding of the following terms. You will find definitions of these terms in both this chapter and the Glossary at the end of this book.

actual costs (p. 26)
average cost (32)
capitalized costs (35)
capitalized inventoriable costs (36)
capitalized noninventoriable costs (36)
conversion costs (41)
cost (26)
cost accumulation (26)
cost allocation (27)
cost assignment (26)
cost driver (28)
cost object (26)
cost tracing (27)
direct costs of a cost object (27)
direct manufacturing labor costs (40)
direct materials costs (40)
direct materials inventory (38)
factory overhead costs (40)
finished goods inventory (39)

fixed cost (29)
indirect costs of a cost object (27)
indirect manufacturing costs (40)
inventoriable costs (36)
manufacturing overhead costs (40)
manufacturing-sector company (36)
merchandising-sector company (36)
noncapitalized costs (35)
operating costs (36)
prime costs (41)
product cost (43)
relevant range (30)
service-sector company (35)
unit cost (32)
value-added activities (28)
variable cost (29)
work-in-process inventory (39)
work in progress (39)

▼ ASSIGNMENT MATERIAL

QUESTIONS

2-1 Define *cost object* and give three examples.

2-2 Define *cost assignment*, *cost tracing*, and *cost allocation*. How are these terms related?

2-3 Which costs are considered direct? Indirect? Give an example of each.

2-4 Describe how a given cost item can be both a direct cost and an indirect cost.

2-5 Give three factors that will affect the classification of a cost as direct or indirect.

2-6 Describe two areas that cost reduction efforts frequently focus on.

2-7 What is a *cost driver?* Give one example for each area in the value chain.

2-8 Define *variable cost* and *fixed cost*. Give an example of each.

2-9 What is the *relevant range?* What role does the relevant range concept play in explaining how costs behave?

2-10 Explain why *unit costs* must often be interpreted with caution.

2-11 Describe how service-, merchandising-, and manufacturing-sector companies differ from each other.

2-12 Distinguish between *capitalized costs* and *noncapitalized costs*. Give an example of each from the service, merchandising, and manufacturing sectors.

2-13 What are the three major categories of the inventoriable costs of a manufactured product?

2-14 Define the following: *direct materials costs, direct manufacturing labor costs, indirect manufacturing costs, prime costs*, and *conversion costs*.

2-15 Define *product costs*. Describe three different purposes for computing product costs.

EXERCISES

2-16 **Total costs and unit costs.** A student association has hired a musical group for a graduation party. The cost will be a fixed amount of $4,000.

REQUIRED

1. Suppose 500 people attend the party. What will be the total cost of the musical group? The unit cost per person?
2. Suppose 2,000 people attend. What will be the total cost of the musical group? The unit cost per person?
3. For prediction of total costs, should the manager of the party use the unit cost in requirement 1? The unit cost in requirement 2? What is the major lesson of this problem?

2-17 **Total costs and unit costs.** Nathan Brown is a well-known motivational speaker. The St. George Speaker's Bureau wants Brown to be the sole speaker at an all-day seminar. Brown's agent offers St. George the choice of three possible fee arrangements:

◆ Schedule 1: $8,000 fee
◆ Schedule 2: $20 per person + $2,000 fixed fee
◆ Schedule 3: $50 per person

Each attendee will be charged a $200 fee for the all-day seminar.

REQUIRED

1. What is St. George's fixed cost and variable cost for hiring Brown under each alternative schedule?
2. For each schedule, compute the total cost and unit cost per seminar attendee if (a) 50 attend, (b) 200 attend, and (c) 500 attend. Comment on the results.

2-18 **Total costs and unit costs.** Golden Holidays markets vacation packages to Honolulu from Los Angeles. The package includes a round-trip flight on Global Airways. Golden Holidays pays Global $60,000 for each round-trip flight. The maximum load on a flight is 300 passengers.

REQUIRED

1. What is the unit cost to Golden Holidays of each passenger on a Global Airways round-trip flight if there are (a) 200, (b) 250, or (c) 300 passengers?
2. What role can the unit-cost figures per passenger computed in requirement 1 play when Golden Holidays is predicting the total air-flight costs to be paid next month for Global Airways carrying 4,000 passengers on 15 scheduled round-trip flights?

2-19 **Cost drivers and the value chain.** A Johnson & Johnson analyst is preparing a presentation on cost drivers at its pharmaceutical drug subsidiary. Unfortunately, both the list of its business function areas and the accompanying list of representative cost drivers is accidentally randomized. The two lists now on the computer screen are as follows:

BUSINESS FUNCTION AREA	REPRESENTATIVE COST DRIVER
A. Production	1. Minutes of television advertising time on "60 Minutes"
B. Research and Development	2. Number of calls to toll-free customer phone line

D | C. Marketing ①

3. Hours Tylenol packing line in operation

E | D. Distribution ④

4. Number of packages shipped

B | E. Design of Products/Processes ⑤

5. Hours spent designing tamper-proof bottles

F | F. Customer Service ②

6. Number of patents filed with government agency

REQUIRED

1. Match each business function area with its representative cost driver.
2. Give a second example of a cost driver for each of the business functions of Johnson & Johnson's pharmaceutical drug subsidiary.

2-20 Cost drivers and the value chain. A Toyota analyst is preparing a presentation on cost drivers. Unfortunately, both the list of its business function areas and the accompanying list of representative cost drivers is accidentally randomized. The two lists now on the computer screen are as follows:

BUSINESS FUNCTION AREA	REPRESENTATIVE COST DRIVER
A. Design of Products/Processes	1. Number of cars recalled for defective parts
B. Customer Service	2. Number of machine assembly hours
C. Marketing	3. Number of research scientists
D. Research and Development	4. Hours of computer-aided design (CAD) work
E. Distribution	5. Number of sales personnel
F. Production	6. Weight of cars shipped

REQUIRED

1. Match each business function area with its representative cost driver.
2. Give a second example of a cost driver for each of the business function areas of Toyota.

2-21 Variable costs and fixed costs. Consolidated Minerals (CM) owns the rights to extract minerals from beach sands on Fraser Island. CM has costs in three areas:

a. Payment to a mining subcontractor who charges $80 per ton of beach sand mined and returned to the beach (after being processed on the mainland to extract three minerals—ilmenite, rutile, and zircon).

b. Payment of a government mining and environmental tax of $50 per ton of beach sand mined.

c. Payment to a barge operator. This operator charges $150,000 per month to transport each batch of beach sand—up to 100 tons per batch per day to the mainland and then return to Fraser Island (that is, 0–100 tons per day = $150,000 per month; 101–200 tons = $300,000 per month, and so on). Each barge operates 25 days per month. The $150,000 monthly charge must be paid even if less than 100 tons are transported on any day and even if Consolidated Minerals requires fewer than 25 days of barge transportation in that month.

CM is currently mining 180 tons of beach minerals per day for 25 days per month.

REQUIRED

1. What is the variable cost per ton of beach sand mined? What is the fixed cost to CM per month?

2. Plot one graph of the variable costs and another graph of the fixed costs of CM. Your plots should be similar to Exhibits 2-4 and 2-5. Is the concept of relevant range applicable to your plots?

3. What is the unit cost per ton of beach sand mined (a) if 180 tons are mined each day, or (b) if 220 tons are mined each day? Explain the difference in the unit-cost figures.

2-22 Classification of costs, service sector. Consumer Focus is a marketing research firm that organizes focus groups for consumer product companies. Each focus group has eight individuals who are paid $50 per session to provide comments on new products. These focus groups meet in hotels and are led by a trained independent marketing specialist hired by Consumer Focus. Each specialist is paid a fixed retainer to conduct a minimum number of sessions and a per-session fee of $2,000. A Consumer Focus staff member attends each session to ensure that all the logistical aspects run smoothly.

REQUIRED

Classify each of the following cost items as:
a. Direct or indirect (D or I) costs with respect to each individual focus group.
b. Variable or fixed (V or F) costs with respect to how the total costs of Consumer Focus change as the number of focus groups changes. (If in doubt, select the cost type on the basis of whether the total costs will change substantially if a large number of groups are conducted.)

You will have two answers (D or I; V or F) for each of the following items:

Cost Item	D or I	V or F
A. Payment to individuals in each focus group to provide comments on new products		
B. Annual subscription of Consumer Focus to *Consumer Reports* magazine		
C. Phone calls made by Consumer Focus staff member to confirm individuals will attend a focus group session (Records of individual calls are not kept.)		
D. Retainer paid to focus group leader to conduct 20 focus groups per year on new medical products		
E. Hotel meals provided to participants in each focus group		
F. Lease payment by Consumer Focus for corporate office		
G. Cost of tapes used to record comments made by individuals in a focus group session (These tapes are sent to the company whose products are being tested.)		
H. Gasoline costs of Consumer Focus staff for company-owned vehicles (Staff members submit monthly bills with no mileage breakdowns.)		

2-23 Classification of costs, merchandising sector. Home Entertainment Center (HEC) operates a large store in San Francisco. The store has both a video section and a musical (compact disks, records, and tapes) section. HEC reports revenues for the video section separately from the musical section.

REQUIRED

Classify each of the following cost items as:
a. Direct or indirect (D or I) costs with respect to the video section.
b. Variable or fixed (V or F) costs with respect to how the total costs of the video section change as the number of videos sold changes. (If in doubt, select the cost type on the basis of whether the total costs will change substantially if a large number of videos are sold.)

You will have two answers (D or I; V or F) for each of the following items:

Cost Item	D or I	V or F
A. Annual retainer paid to a video distributor		
B. Electricity costs of HEC store (single bill covers entire store)		
C. Costs of videos purchased for sale to customers		
D. Subscription to *Video Trends* magazine		
E. Leasing of computer software used for financial budgeting at HEC store		
F. Cost of popcorn provided free to all customers of HEC		
G. Earthquake insurance policy for HEC store		
H. Freight-in costs of videos purchased by HEC		

2-24 Classification of costs, manufacturing sector. The Fremont, California, plant of NUMMI (New United Motor Manufacturing, Inc.), a joint venture of General Motors and Toyota, assembles two types of cars (Corollas and Geo Prisms). Separate assembly lines are used for each type of car.

REQUIRED

Classify each of the following cost items as:

a. Direct or indirect (D or I) costs with respect to the type of car assembled (Corolla or Geo Prism).

b. Variable or fixed (V or F) costs with respect to how the total costs of the plant change as the number of cars assembled changes. (If in doubt, select the cost type on the basis of whether the total costs will change substantially if a large number of cars are assembled.)

You will have two answers (D or I; V or F) for each of the following items:

Cost Item	D or I	V or F
A. Cost of tires used on Geo Prisms		
B. Salary of public relations manager for NUMMI plant		
C. Annual awards dinner for Corolla suppliers		
D. Salary of engineer who monitors design changes on Geo Prism		
E. Freight costs of Corolla engines shipped from Toyota City, Japan, to Fremont, California		
F. Electricity costs for NUMMI plant (single bill covers entire plant)		
G. Wages paid to temporary assembly-line workers hired in periods of high production (paid on an hourly basis)		
H. Annual fire insurance policy cost for NUMMI plant		

2-25 Capitalized or Noncapitalized costs. Consider the following ten cost items, three pertaining to the service sector, three to merchandising, and four to manufacturing.

SERVICE (ACCOUNTING FIRM)

1. $200,000—cost of computers purchased
2. $47,560—cost of monthly rental for offices
3. $148,386—wages of secretaries

MERCHANDISING (HOME FURNISHING RETAIL STORE)

4. $6,854—cost of bonuses to salespeople
5. $146,540—cost of merchandise purchased for resale
6. $3,470—electricity cost for showroom lighting

MANUFACTURING (STEEL COMPANY)

7. $14,674,080—cost of new blast furnace
8. $641,030—wages of production workers in steel plant
9. $1,246,031—cost of coal to be used as material input in the manufacture of steel
10. $460,174—cost of vehicles purchased for salespeople

REQUIRED

1. Classify each of the ten items as a capitalized or a noncapitalized cost for balance sheet and income statement reporting purposes.
2. For each capitalized cost item in requirement 1, explain why it is either a capitalized inventoriable cost or a capitalized noninventoriable cost.

2-26 Computing cost of goods manufactured and cost of goods sold. Compute cost of goods manufactured and cost of goods sold from the following account balances relating to 19_7 (in thousands):

Property tax on plant building	$ 3,000
Marketing, distribution, and customer-service costs	37,000
Finished goods inventory, January 1, 19_7	27,000

Plant utilities	17,000
Work in process inventory, December 31, 19_7	26,000
Depreciation of plant building	9,000
General and administrative costs (nonplant)	43,000
Direct materials used	87,000
Finished goods inventory, December 31, 19_7	34,000
Depreciation of plant equipment	11,000
Plant repairs and maintenance	16,000
Work in process inventory, January 1, 19_7	20,000
Direct manufacturing labor	34,000
Indirect manufacturing labor	23,000
Indirect materials used	11,000
Miscellaneous plant overhead	4,000

2-27 Classification of costs, prime and conversion costs. Tanaka Metal Products reports the following components in its manufacturing costs for April 19_7 (in thousands):

Direct costs:		
Direct materials	¥430	
Direct manufacturing labor salaries	110	
Subcontracting	120	¥ 660
Manufacturing overhead:		
Fringe benefits on direct manufacturing labor	40	
Production setup	60	
Other manufacturing overhead	240	340
		¥1,000

Subcontracting costs are treated as a direct-cost item separate from direct materials.

REQUIRED

1. Compute (a) the prime costs and (b) the conversion costs of Tanaka Metal Products using the cost classifications described above.
2. Assume now that Tanaka changes the classification of two items—both fringe benefits on direct manufacturing labor and production setups will now be classified as direct costs. Compute (a) the prime costs and (b) the conversion costs of Tanaka after this change in cost classification, and comment on the results.
3. What information might Tanaka use to change the two items in requirement 2 to be direct-cost items rather than manufacturing overhead cost items?

PROBLEMS

2-28 Cost of goods manufactured. Consider the following account balances (in thousands) for the Canseco Company:

	Beginning of 19_7	End of 19_7
Direct materials inventory	$22,000	$26,000
Work in process inventory	21,000	20,000
Finished goods inventory	18,000	23,000
Purchases of direct materials		75,000
Direct manufacturing labor		25,000
Indirect manufacturing labor		15,000
Plant insurance		9,000
Depreciation—plant building and equipment		11,000
Repairs and maintenance—plant		4,000
Marketing, distribution, and customer-service costs		93,000
General and administrative costs		29,000

REQUIRED

1. Prepare a schedule of cost of goods manufactured for 19_7.
2. Revenues in 19_7 were $300 million. Prepare the 19_7 income statement.

2-29 **Income statement and schedule of cost of goods manufactured.** The Howell Corporation has the following account balances (in millions):

For Specific Date		For Year 19_7	
Direct materials, January 1, 19_7	$15	Purchases of direct materials	$325
Work in process, January 1, 19_7	10	Direct manufacturing labor	100
Finished goods, January 1, 19_7	70	Depreciation—plant building and equipment	80
Direct materials, December 31, 19_7	20	Plant supervisory salaries	5
Work in process, December 31, 19_7	5	Miscellaneous plant overhead	35
Finished goods, December 31, 19_7	55	Revenues	950
		Marketing, distribution, and customer-service costs	240
		Plant supplies used	10
		Plant utilities	30
		Indirect manufacturing labor	60

REQUIRED

Prepare an income statement and a supporting schedule of cost of goods manufactured for the year ended December 31, 19_7. (For additional questions regarding these facts, see the next problem.)

2-30 **Interpretation of statements (continuation of 2-29).** Refer to the preceding problem.

REQUIRED

1. How would the answer to the preceding problem be modified if you were asked for a schedule of cost of goods manufactured and sold instead of a schedule of cost of goods manufactured? Be specific.
2. Would the sales manager's salary (included in marketing, distribution, and customer-service costs) be accounted for differently if the Howell Corporation were a merchandising company instead of a manufacturing company? Using the flow of costs outlined in Exhibit 2-10, describe how the wages of an assembler in the plant would be accounted for in this manufacturing company.
3. Plant supervisory salaries are usually regarded as indirect manufacturing costs. Under what conditions might some of these costs be regarded as direct manufacturing costs? Give an example.
4. Suppose that both the direct materials used and the plant depreciation were related to the manufacture of 1 million units of product. What is the unit cost for the direct materials assigned to those units? What is the unit cost for plant building and equipment depreciation? Assume that yearly plant depreciation is computed on a straight-line basis.
5. Assume that the implied cost behavior patterns in requirement 4 persist. That is, direct materials costs behave as a variable cost and depreciation behaves as a fixed cost. Repeat the computations in requirement 4, assuming that the costs are being predicted for the manufacture of 1.2 million units of product. How would the total costs be affected?
6. As a management accountant, explain concisely to the president why the unit costs differed in requirements 4 and 5.

2-31 **Income statement and schedule of cost of goods manufactured.** The following items (in millions) pertain to the Chan Corporation:

For Specific Date		For Year 19_7	
Work in process, January 1, 19_7	$10	Plant utilities	$ 5
Direct materials, December 31, 19_7	5	Indirect manufacturing labor	20
Finished goods, December 31, 19_7	12	Depreciation—plant, building, and equipment	9
Accounts payable, December 31, 19_7	20		
Accounts receivable, January 1, 19_7	50	Revenues	350
Work in process, December 31, 19_7	2	Miscellaneous manufacturing overhead	10
Finished goods, January 1, 19_7	40		
Accounts receivable, December 31, 19_7	30	Marketing, distribution, and customer-service costs	90
		Purchases of direct materials	80
Accounts payable, January 1, 19_7	40	Direct manufacturing labor	40
Direct materials, January 1, 19_7	30	Plant supplies used	6
		Property taxes on plant	1

Chan's manufacturing cost system uses a three-part classification of direct materials, direct manufacturing labor, and indirect manufacturing costs.

REQUIRED

Prepare an income statement and a supporting schedule of cost of goods manufactured. (For additional questions regarding these facts, see the next problem.)

2-32 Interpretation of statements (continuation of 2-31). Refer to the preceding problem.

REQUIRED

1. How would the answer to the preceding problem be modified if you were asked for a schedule of cost of goods manufactured and sold instead of a schedule of cost of goods manufactured? Be specific.

2. Would the sales manager's salary (included in marketing, distribution, and customer-service costs) be accounted for any differently if the Chan Corporation were a merchandising company instead of a manufacturing company? Using the flow of costs outlined in Exhibit 2-10, describe how the wages of an assembler in the plant would be accounted for in this manufacturing company.

3. Plant supervisory salaries are usually regarded as indirect manufacturing costs. Under what conditions might some of these costs be regarded as direct manufacturing costs? Give an example.

4. Suppose that both the direct materials used and the plant depreciation were related to the manufacture of 1 million units of product. What is the unit cost for the direct materials assigned to those units? What is the unit cost for plant building and equipment depreciation? Assume that yearly depreciation is computed on a straight-line basis.

5. Assume that the implied cost behavior patterns in requirement 4 persist. That is, direct materials costs behave as a variable cost and plant depreciation behaves as a fixed cost. Repeat the computations in requirement 4, assuming that the costs are being predicted for the manufacture of 1.5 million units of product. How would the total costs be affected?

6. As a management accountant, explain concisely to the president why the unit costs differed in requirements 4 and 5.

2-33 Finding unknown balances, merchandising. The following amounts (in thousands) relate to the income statements of two merchandising companies:

	Company M	Company N
Operating costs	$ A	$ 383
Cost of goods available for sale	662	1,238
Gross margin	256	W

	Company M	Company N
Beginning merchandise inventory, January 1, 19_7	B	64
Revenues	C	1,647
Operating income	52	X
Ending merchandise inventory, December 31, 19_7	24	Y
Purchases of merchandise	643	Z
Cost of goods sold	D	1,189

REQUIRED

1. Reconstruct the income statements of the two merchandising companies.
2. Give an example of a cost in each of the following three categories for a merchandiser:
   a. capitalized inventoriable cost
   b. capitalized noninventoriable cost
   c. noncapitalized cost

2-34 Finding unknown balances. An auditor for the Internal Revenue Service is trying to reconstruct some partially destroyed records of two taxpayers. For each of the cases in the accompanying list, find the unknowns designated by capital letters (figures are assumed to be in thousands).

	Case 1	Case 2
Accounts receivable, December 31, 19_7	$ 6,000	$ 2,100
Cost of goods sold	A	20,000
Accounts payable, January 1, 19_7	3,000	1,700
Accounts payable, December 31, 19_7	1,800	1,500
Finished goods inventory, December 31, 19_7	B	5,300
Gross margin	11,300	C
Work in process, January 1, 19_7	0	800
Work in process, December 31, 19_7	0	3,000
Finished goods inventory, January 1, 19_7	4,000	4,000
Direct material used	8,000	12,000
Direct manufacturing labor	3,000	5,000
Indirect manufacturing costs	7,000	D
Purchases of direct material	9,000	7,000
Revenues	32,000	31,800
Accounts receivable, January 1, 19_7	2,000	1,400

2-35 Fire loss, computing inventory costs. A distraught employee, Guy Arson, put a torch to a manufacturing plant on a blustery February 26. The resulting blaze completely destroyed the plant and its contents. Fortunately, certain accounting records were kept in another building. They revealed the following for the period from January 1, 19_7 to February 26, 19_7:

Direct materials purchased	$160,000
Work in process, January 1, 19_7	$ 34,000
Direct materials, January 1, 19_7	$ 16,000
Finished goods, January 1, 19_7	$ 30,000
Indirect manufacturing costs	40% of conversion costs
Revenues	$500,000
Direct manufacturing labor	$180,000
Prime costs	$294,000
Gross margin percentage based on sales	20%
Cost of goods available for sale	$450,000

The loss was fully covered by insurance. The insurance company wants to know the historical cost of the inventories as one factor considered when negotiating a settlement.

REQUIRED

Calculate the cost of

1. finished goods inventory, February 26, 19_7
2. work-in-process inventory, February 26, 19_7
3. direct materials inventory, February 26, 19_7

2-36 **Comprehensive problem on unit costs, product costs.** Tampa Office Equipment manufactures and sells metal shelving. It began operations on January 1, 19_7. Costs incurred for 19_7 (V stands for variable; F stands for fixed) are as follows:

Direct materials used costs	$140,000 V
Direct manufacturing labor costs	30,000 V
Plant energy costs	5,000 V
Indirect manufacturing labor costs	10,000 V
Indirect manufacturing labor costs	16,000 F
Other indirect manufacturing costs	8,000 V
Other indirect manufacturing costs	24,000 F
Marketing, distribution, and customer-service costs	122,850 V
Marketing, distribution, and customer-service costs	40,000 F
Administrative costs	50,000 F

Variable manufacturing costs are variable with respect to units produced. Variable marketing, distribution, and customer-service costs are variable with respect to units sold.

Inventory data are as follows:

	Beginning, January 1, 19_7	Ending, December 31, 19_7
Direct materials	0 pounds	2,000 pounds
Work in process	0 units	0 units
Finished goods	0 units	? units

Production in 19_7 was 100,000 units. Two pounds of direct materials are used to make one unit of finished product.

Revenues in 19_7 were $436,800. The selling price per unit and the purchase price per pound of direct materials were stable throughout the year. The company's ending inventory of finished goods is carried at the average unit manufacturing costs for 19_7. Finished goods inventory, at December 31, 19_7, was $20,970.

REQUIRED

1. Direct materials inventory, total cost, December 31, 19_7.
2. Finished goods inventory, total units, December 31, 19_7.
3. Selling price per unit, 19_7.
4. Operating income, 19_7. Show your computations.

2-37 **Budgeted income statement (continuation of 2-36).** Assume management predicts that the selling price per unit and variable cost per unit will be the same in 19_8 as in 19_7. Fixed manufacturing costs and marketing, distribution, and customer-service costs in 19_8 are also predicted to be the same as in 19_7. Sales in 19_8 are forecast to be 122,000 units. The desired ending inventory of finished goods, December 31, 19_8, is 12,000 units. Assume zero ending inventories of both direct materials and work in process. The company's ending inventory of finished goods is carried at the average unit manufacturing costs for 19_8. The company uses the first-in, first-out inventory method. Management has asked that you prepare a budgeted income statement for 19_8.

REQUIRED

1. Units of finished goods produced in 19_8.
2. Budgeted income statement for 19_8.

2-38 Revenue and cost recording and classifications, ethics. Country Outfitters (C.O.) designs and markets jeans to many retailers and distributors around the globe. Its corporate headquarters is in Los Angeles, California. Manufacturing is done by a subcontractor (Jeans West) on the island state of Caribe. The Caribe government grants locally owned companies a 20% income tax rebate if the ratio of their domestic labor costs to total costs exceeds 25%. Domestic labor costs are defined as the employment costs of all employees who are citizens of Caribe. Nicola Roberts, the newly appointed controller of C.O., has recently been examining payments made to Jeans West. She observes that Jeans West purchases denim from C.O. ($3 million in 19_7). C.O. paid Jeans West $12 million for the jeans manufactured in Caribe in 19_7. Based on her industry experience, the $12 million amount is very low. She was told it was "a great deal" for C.O. There is also a sizable payment by C.O. to the Swiss subsidiary of Jeans West ($4.8 million in 19_7). Roberts is told by the Jeans West president that this payment is for fabric design work that Jeans West does with C.O. C.O. has included the $4.8 million payments in its own product design cost. The director of product design at C.O. told Roberts it is an "off-statement" item that historically he has no responsibility for nor any say about. To his knowledge, Jeans West uses only C.O. designs with either zero or minimal changes.

Jeans West's domestic labor costs in 19_7 were $3.6 million while its total costs were $10 million. Included in this $3.6 million was $1.3 million for labor fringe benefits (for health insurance, etc.). A component of this $1.3 million is $600,000 for life insurance for Jeans West's executives. C.O. helped arrange this life insurance policy. It negotiated with the insurance company managing its own executive life insurance plans to include the Jeans West executives at rates much more favorable than those available in Caribe.

REQUIRED

1. What concerns should Roberts have about the revenue and cost numbers in C.O.'s financial reports?
2. Which (if any) of the concerns in requirement 1 raise ethical issues for Roberts? Explain.
3. What steps should Roberts take to address the ethical issues you identify in requirement 2?

COLLABORATIVE LEARNING PROBLEM

2-39 Defining cost terms. You are the controller of the Heinz potato processing subsidiary in Ireland. This subsidiary processes potatoes for frozen dinners, fast-food restaurants, and other large institutional buyers. Assume that companies setting up manufacturing facilities in Ireland receive an income tax rebate equivalent to the ratio of employment costs of Irish citizens to total manufacturing costs in Ireland. Thus, if the Irish subsidiary has a "pre-rebate" tax bill of $10 million and the ratio of employment costs to total manufacturing costs is 22%, its actual tax bill will be reduced by $2.2 million to $7.8 million.

INSTRUCTIONS

Form groups of two or more students to complete the following requirement.

REQUIRED

Develop guidelines as to how Heinz should define costs at its Irish subsidiary. Assume one aim is to minimize the income taxes that Heinz is legitimately required to pay to the Irish government.

3

COST-VOLUME-PROFIT RELATIONSHIPS

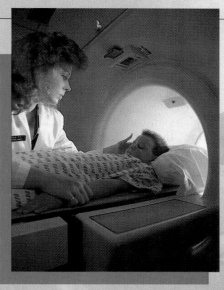

The growing complexity and sophistication of medical testing equipment is increasing the ratio of fixed costs to total costs in many hospitals. Magnetic resonance imaging (MRI) equipment enables hospitals to produce high quality images without exposing patients to ionizing radiation. Obtaining high utilization for this expensive equipment is essential for hospitals justifying investment in MRI technology.

LEARNING OBJECTIVES

After studying this chapter, you should be able to

1. Distinguish between the general case and a special case of CVP
2. Explain the relationship between operating income and net income
3. Describe the assumptions underlying CVP
4. Demonstrate three methods for determining the breakeven point and target operating income
5. Explain how sensitivity analysis can help managers cope with uncertainty
6. Illustrate how CVP can assist cost planning
7. Describe the effect of revenue mix on operating income
8. Illustrate how CVP can incorporate income taxes

Cost-volume-profit analysis provides a sweeping financial overview of the planning process. **Cost-volume-profit (CVP)** analysis examines the behavior of total revenues, total costs, and operating income as changes occur in the output level, selling price, variable costs, or fixed costs. Managers commonly use CVP as a tool to help them answer such questions as, How will revenues and costs be affected if we sell 1,000 more units? If we raise or lower our selling prices? If we expand business into overseas markets? These questions have a common "what-if" theme. CVP is built on simplifying assumptions about revenue and cost behavior patterns. This chapter examines CVP analysis and explains how the reasonableness underlying its assumptions affects the reliability of its results.

REVENUE DRIVERS AND COST DRIVERS: THE GENERAL CASE AND A SPECIAL CASE

OBJECTIVE 1

Distinguish between the general case and a special case of CVP

Revenues are inflows of assets received in exchange for products or services provided to customers. **A revenue driver** is a factor that affects revenues. Examples of revenue drivers are units of output sold, selling prices, and levels of marketing costs. Chapter 2 defined *cost* as a resource sacrificed or forgone to achieve a specific objective and a *cost driver* as any factor that affects cost—that is, a change in the cost driver will cause a change in the total cost of a related cost object. Examples of cost drivers include units of output manufactured, number of sales visits made, and number of packages shipped.

The most detailed way of predicting total revenues and total costs is to consider multiple revenue drivers and multiple cost drivers. We call this the general case. It can require extensive analysis and is likely to be very time-consuming. For now, we focus on a special case where we assume a single revenue driver and a single cost driver. That single driver is units of output (either output units sold or output units manufactured).

We focus on the special case of CVP relationships for two major reasons. First, many companies have found such relationships to be helpful in decisions relating to overall strategies and long-range plans and in decisions such as product and customer emphasis and pricing. Second, the straightforward relationships provide an excellent base for understanding the more complex relationships that exist with multiple revenues and multiple cost drivers:

General Case	Special Case
Many revenue drivers	Single revenue driver (output units)
Many cost drivers	Single cost driver (output units)
Various time spans for decisions (short run, long run, product life cycles)	Short-run decisions (time span, typically less than one year, in which fixed costs do not change within the relevant range)

The term *CVP analysis* is widely used as representing this special case. A single revenue driver and a single cost driver are used in this analysis. In the CVP model, volume (V) refers to units manufactured or units sold.

Our restriction to units of output as the sole revenue or cost driver is important to keep in mind. It means that in the CVP model, changes in the level of revenues and costs arise only because the output level changes. This restriction means that we will not consider a revenue driver such as the number of advertisements for a new product. Nor will we consider a cost driver such as the number of calls a customer makes for after-sales service or service repairs. These factors are examples of revenue or cost drivers that are not a function of units of output.

Keep in mind that our CVP restrictions considerably simplify real-world problems. Managers and accountants must always assess whether the simplified relationships of CVP generate sufficiently accurate predictions of how total revenues and total costs behave. Otherwise, they may be misled into making unwise decisions. In general, the simpler CVP model is preferable as long as management decisions would not be significantly improved using a more complicated decision model.

TERMINOLOGY AND ABBREVIATIONS

Before we can study CVP, we must understand its terminology. In this chapter, we assume total costs (also termed total expenses) are made up of only two categories: variable costs (variable with respect to units of output) and fixed costs.

$$\text{Total costs} = \text{Variable costs} + \text{Fixed costs}$$

Recall from Chapter 2 (Exhibit 2-5) that variable costs include both direct variable costs and indirect variable costs of a chosen cost object. Similarly, fixed costs include both direct fixed costs and indirect fixed costs of a chosen cost object.

Operating income is total revenues from operations minus total costs from operations (excluding income taxes):

$$\text{Operating income} = \text{Total revenues} - \text{Total costs}$$

Net income is operating income plus nonoperating revenues (such as interest revenue) minus nonoperating costs (such as interest cost) minus income taxes. For simplicity, throughout this chapter nonoperating revenues and nonoperating costs are assumed to be zero. Thus, net income will be computed as follows:

$$\text{Net income} = \text{Operating income} - \text{Income taxes}$$

OBJECTIVE 2

Explain the relationship between operating income and net income

In the examples that follow, the measure of output is the number of units manufactured or units sold. Different industries often use different terminology to describe their measure of output. Examples include

Industry	Measure of Output
Airlines	Passenger-miles
Automobiles	Vehicles manufactured
Hospitals	Patient-days
Hotels/motels	Rooms occupied
Universities	Student credit-hours

The following abbreviations are used in this chapter:

- ◆ USP = Unit selling price
- ◆ UVC = Unit variable costs
- ◆ UCM = Unit contribution margin (USP – UVC)
- ◆ FC = Fixed costs
- ◆ Q = Quantity of output units sold (or manufactured)
- ◆ OI = Operating income
- ◆ TOI = Target operating income
- ◆ NI = Net income

CVP ASSUMPTIONS

The CVP analysis that we now discuss is based on the following assumptions:

1. Total costs can be divided into a fixed component and a component that is variable with respect to the level of output.
2. The behavior of total revenues and total costs is linear (straight-line) in relation to output units within the relevant range.[1]

OBJECTIVE 3

Describe the assumptions underlying CVP

[1]For example, one set of conditions in which assumption 2 is descriptive includes the following: Selling prices are constant within the relevant range; productivity is constant; and costs of production inputs are constant within the relevant range. How might nonlinearity arise? On the revenue side, reductions in the selling price may be necessary to spur sales at higher levels of output. On the cost side, variable costs per unit may decline when output increases as employees learn to handle the process more efficiently. The learning curve is discussed in Chapter 10.

3. The unit selling price, unit variable costs, and fixed costs are known. (This assumption is discussed later in the chapter and in the appendix to this chapter.)

4. The analysis either covers a single product or assumes that a given revenue mix of products will remain constant as the level of total units sold changes. (This assumption is also discussed later in the chapter.)

5. All revenues and costs can be added and compared without taking into account the time value of money. (Chapters 22 and 23 relax this assumption.)

These CVP assumptions clearly are extreme in the sense that they would rarely match reality. Managers should always question whether a more complicated approach than CVP is warranted.

THE BREAKEVEN POINT

CVP analysis can be used to examine how various "what-if" alternatives being considered by a decision maker affect operating income. The breakeven point is frequently one point of interest in this analysis. Managers wish to avoid the stigma of making a loss. The **breakeven point** is that quantity of output where total revenues and total costs are equal, that is, where the operating income is zero.

Using the information in the following example, this section examines three methods for determining the breakeven point: the equation method, the contribution margin method, and the graph method.

EXAMPLE: Mary Frost plans to sell Do-All Software, a software package, at a heavily attended two-day computer convention in Chicago. Mary can purchase this software from a computer software wholesaler at $120 per package with the privilege of returning all unsold units and receiving a full $120 rebate per package. The units (packages) will be sold at $200 each. Frost has already paid $2,000 to Computer Conventions, Inc., for the booth rental for the two-day convention. What quantity of units will she need to sell in order to breakeven? Assume there are no other costs.

Equation Method

The first approach for computing the breakeven point is the equation method. Using the terminology in this chapter, the income statement can be expressed in equation form as follows:

$$\text{Revenues} - \text{Variable costs} - \text{Fixed costs} = \text{Operating income}$$

$$(\text{USP} \times Q) - (\text{UVC} \times Q) - \text{FC} = \text{OI}$$

This equation provides the most general and easy-to-remember approach to any CVP situation. Setting operating income equal to zero in the preceding equation, we obtain

$$\$200Q - \$120Q - \$2,000 = \$0$$

$$\$80Q = \$2,000$$

$$Q = \$2,000 \div \$80 = 25 \text{ units}$$

If Frost sells fewer than 25 units, she will have a loss; if she sells 25 units, she will breakeven; and if she sells more than 25 units, she will make a profit. This breakeven point is expressed in units. It can also be expressed in sales dollars: 25 units × $200 selling price = $5,000.

Contribution Margin Method

A second approach is the contribution margin method, which is simply an algebraic manipulation of the equation method. Contribution margin is equal to revenues minus all costs of the output (a product or service) that vary with respect to the units of output. This method uses the fact that

$$(USP \times Q) - (UVC \times Q) - FC = OI$$

$$(USP - UVC) \times Q = FC + OI$$

$$UCM \times Q = FC + OI$$

$$Q = \frac{FC + OI}{UCM}$$

At the breakeven point, operating income is, by definition, zero. Setting OI = 0, we obtain

$$\frac{\text{Breakeven}}{\text{number of units}} = \frac{\text{Fixed costs}}{\text{Unit contribution margin}}$$

$$= \frac{FC}{UCM}$$

The calculations in the equation method and the contribution margin method appear similar because one is merely a restatement of the other. In our example, fixed costs are $2,000 and the unit contribution margin is $80 ($200 – $120). Therefore,

$$\frac{\text{Breakeven}}{\text{number of units}} = \$2,000 \div \$80 = 25 \text{ units}$$

A **contribution income statement** groups line items by cost behavior pattern to highlight the contribution margin. The following such statement confirms the preceding breakeven calculations:

Revenues, $200 × 25	$5,000
Variable costs, $120 × 25	3,000
Contribution margin, $80 × 25	2,000
Fixed costs	2,000
Operating income	$ 0

Graph Method

In the graph method, we plot the total costs line and the total revenues line. Their point of intersection is the breakeven point. Exhibit 3-1 illustrates this method for our Do-All example. We need only two points to plot each line if each is assumed to be linear:

1. *Total costs line.* This line is the sum of the fixed costs and the variable costs. Fixed costs are $2,000 at all output levels within the relevant range. To plot fixed costs, measure $2,000 on the vertical axis (point *A*) and extend a line horizontally. Variable costs are $120 per unit. To plot the total costs line, use as one point the $2,000 fixed costs at 0 output units (point *A*). Select a second point by choosing any other convenient output level (say, 40 units) and determining the corresponding total costs. The total variable costs at this output level are $4,800 (40 × $120). Fixed costs are $2,000 at all output levels within the relevant range. Hence, total costs at 40 units of output are $6,800, which is point *B* in Exhibit 3-1. The total costs line is the straight line from point *A* passing through point *B*.

2. *Total revenues line.* One convenient starting point is zero revenues at the zero output level, which is point *C* in Exhibit 3-1. Select a second point by choosing any other convenient output level and determining its total revenues. At 40 units of output, total revenues are $8,000 (40 × $200), which is point *D* in Exhibit 3-1. The total revenues line is the straight line from point *C* passing through point *D*.

The breakeven point is where the total revenues line and the total costs line intersect. At this point, total revenues equal total costs. But Exhibit 3-1 shows the profit or loss outlook for a wide range of output levels. Many people describe the topics covered in this chapter as break-even analysis. We prefer to use the phrase cost-volume-profit analysis to avoid overemphasizing the single point where total revenues equal total costs. Managers want to know how operating income differs at many different output levels.

EXHIBIT 3-1
Cost-Volume-Profit Graph

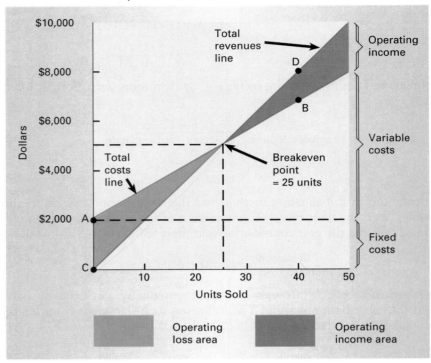

Target Operating Income

Let us introduce a profit element by asking, How many units must be sold to earn an operating income of $1,200? The equation method provides a straightforward way to answer this question:

Let QT = Number of units sold to earn target operating income

Revenues − Variable costs − Fixed costs = Target operating income

$$\$200QT - \$120QT - \$2,000 = \$1,200$$

$$\$80QT = \$2,000 + \$1,200$$

$$\$80QT = \$3,200$$

$$QT = \$3,200 \div \$80 = 40 \text{ units}$$

Alternatively, we could use the contribution margin method. The numerator now consists of fixed costs plus target operating income:

$$QT = \frac{\text{Fixed costs} + \text{Target operating income}}{\text{Unit contribution margin}} = \frac{FC + TOI}{UCM}$$

$$QT = \frac{\$2,000 + \$1,200}{\$80}$$

$$\$80QT = \$3,200$$

$$QT = \$3,200 \div \$80 = 40 \text{ units}$$

Proof:	Revenues, $200 × 40	$8,000
	Variable costs, $120 × 40	4,800
	Contribution margin, $80 × 40	3,200
	Fixed costs	2,000
	Operating income	$1,200

The graph in Exhibit 3-1 indicates that at the 40-unit output level, the difference between total revenues and total costs is the $1,200 operating income.

EXHIBIT 3-2
The Profit-Volume Graph

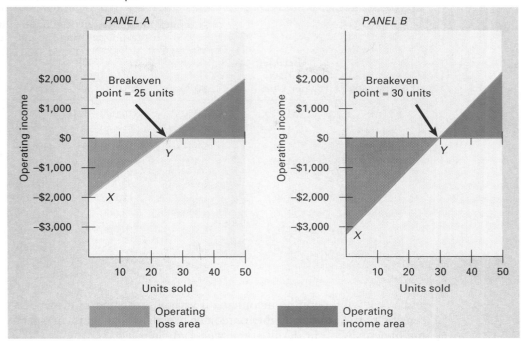

We can recast Exhibit 3-1 in the form of a profit-volume (PV) graph. A **PV graph** shows the impact on operating income of changes in the output level. Exhibit 3-2 (Panel A) presents the PV graph for Do-All (fixed costs of $2,000, selling price of $200, and variable costs per unit of $120). The PV line can be drawn using two points. One convenient point (X) is the level of fixed costs at zero output—$2,000, which is also the operating loss at this output level. A second convenient point (Y) is the breakeven point—25 units in our example (see p. 65). The PV line is drawn by connecting points X and Y and extending the line beyond Y. Each unit sold beyond the breakeven point will add $80 to operating income. At the 35-unit output level, for example, operating income would be $800:

$$(\$200 \times 35) - (\$120 \times 35) - \$2,000 = \$800$$

A comparison of PV charts representing different what-if possibilities can highlight their effects on operating income. Panel B in Exhibit 3-2 shows the PV chart for Do-All assuming fixed costs of $3,300 (compared with $2,000 in Panel A) and variable costs per unit of $90 (compared with $120 in Panel A). The selling price is $200 in both graphs. The unit contribution margin in Panel B is $110. The breakeven point in Panel B is 30 units:

$$\$200Q - \$90Q - \$3,300 = 0$$

$$Q = \$3,300 \div \$110 = 30 \text{ units}$$

Each unit sold beyond the breakeven point will add $110 to operating income. The PV graph in Panel B has a steeper slope for its operating income line, which means that the operating income increases at a faster rate as the level of output increases.

SENSITIVITY ANALYSIS AND UNCERTAINTY

Sensitivity analysis is a what-if technique that examines how a result will change if the original predicted data are not achieved or if an underlying assumption changes. In the context of CVP, sensitivity analysis answers such questions as, What will operating income be if the output level decreases by 5% from the original prediction?

EXHIBIT 3-3
Spreadsheet Analysis of CVP Relationships for Do-All Software

Fixed Costs	Variable Costs per Unit	Revenue Dollars Required at $200 Selling Price to Earn Operating Income of			
		$0	$1,000	$1,500	$2,000
$2,000	$100	$ 4,000	$ 6,000	$ 7,000	$ 8,000
	120	5,000	7,500	8,750	10,000
	140	6,667	10,000	11,667	13,333
$2,500	$100	$ 5,000	$ 7,000	$ 8,000	$ 9,000
	120	6,250	8,750	10,000	11,250
	140	8,333	11,667	13,333	15,000
$3,000	$100	$ 6,000	$ 8,000	$ 9,000	$10,000
	120	7,500	10,000	11,250	12,500
	140	10,000	13,333	15,000	16,667

and What will operating income be if variable costs per unit increase by 10%? The sensitivity to various possible outcomes broadens managers' perspectives as to what might actually occur despite their well-laid plans.

The widespread use of electronic spreadsheets has promoted the use of CVP analysis in many organizations. Using spreadsheets, managers can easily conduct CVP-based sensitivity analyses to examine the effect and interaction of changes in selling prices, unit variable costs, fixed costs, and target operating incomes. Exhibit 3-3 displays a spreadsheet for our Do-All example. Mary Frost can immediately see the revenues that need to be generated to reach particular operating income levels, given alternative levels of fixed costs and variable costs per unit. For example, revenues of $6,000 (30 units at $200 per unit) are required to earn an operating income of $1,000 if fixed costs are $2,000 and variable costs per unit are $100. Frost can also use Exhibit 3-3 to assess whether she wants to sell at the Chicago computer convention if, for example, the booth rental is raised to $3,000 (thus increasing fixed costs to $3,000) or the software supplier raises its price to $140 per unit (thus increasing variable costs to $140 per unit).

One aspect of sensitivity analysis is the **margin of safety,** which is the excess of budgeted revenues over the breakeven revenues. The margin of safety is the answer to the what-if question: If budgeted revenues are above breakeven and drop, how far can they fall below budget before the breakeven point is reached? Such a fall could be due to a competitor having a better product, poorly executed marketing, and so on. Assume that Mary Frost has fixed costs of $3,000, a selling price of $200, and variable costs per unit of $140. For 75 units sold, the budgeted revenues are $15,000 and the budgeted operating income is $1,500. The breakeven point for this set of assumptions is 50 units ($3,000 ÷ $60) or $10,000 ($200 × 50). Hence, the margin of safety is $5,000 ($15,000 – $10,000) or 25 units. ($5000 ÷ 200)

Sensitivity analysis is one approach to recognizing **uncertainty,** which is defined here as the possibility that an actual amount will deviate from an expected amount. Another approach is to compute expected values using probability distributions. The appendix to this chapter illustrates this approach.

COST PLANNING AND CVP

Alternative Fixed-Cost/Variable-Cost Structures

Sensitivity analysis highlights the risks that an existing cost structure poses for an organization. This may lead managers to consider alternative cost structures. CVP helps managers in this task. Consider again Mary Frost and her booth rental agree-

OBJECTIVE 5

Explain how sensitivity analysis can help managers cope with uncertainty

EXHIBIT 3-4
CVP Graphs for Alternative Rental Schedules for Do-All Software

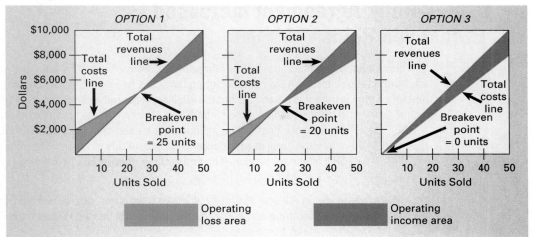

ment with Computer Conventions, Inc. Our original example has Frost paying a $2,000 booth rental fee. Suppose, however, Computer Conventions offers Frost three rental alternatives:

◆ *Option 1:* $2,000 fixed fee

◆ *Option 2:* $1,400 fixed fee plus 5% of the convention revenues from Do-All sales

◆ *Option 3:* 20% of the convention revenues from Do-All sales with no fixed fee

Frost is interested in how her choice of a rental agreement will affect the risks she faces. Exhibit 3-4 presents these options in the CVP format:

◆ *Option 1* exposes her to fixed costs of $2,000 and a breakeven point of 25 units. This option brings $80 additional operating income for each unit sold above 25 units.

◆ *Option 2* exposes her to lower fixed costs of $1,400 and a lower breakeven point of 20 units. There is, however, only $70 in additional operating income for each unit sold above 20 units.

◆ *Option 3* has no fixed costs. Frost makes $40 in additional operating income for each unit sold. This $40 addition to operating income starts from the first unit sold. This option enables Frost to break even if no units are sold.[2]

CVP analysis highlights the different risks and different returns associated with each option. For example, while option 1 has the most downside risk (a $2,000 fixed up-front payment), it also has the highest contribution margin per unit. This $80 contribution margin per unit translates to high upside potential if Frost is able to generate sales above 25 units. By moving from option 1 to option 2, Frost faces less risk (lowers her fixed costs) if demand is low, but she must accept less upside potential (because of the higher variable costs) if demand is high. The choice among options 1, 2, and 3 will be influenced by her confidence in the level of demand for Do-All software and her willingness to risk money.

OBJECTIVE 6

Illustrate how CVP can assist cost planning

[2]The break-even point of 25 units for option 1 was computed earlier in this chapter. The break-even point (Q) for option 2 is calculated as follows:

$$\text{Fixed costs} = \$1,400$$
$$\text{Unit variable costs} = \$120 + 0.05(\$200) = \$130$$
$$\text{Unit contribution margin} = \$200 - \$130 = \$70 \text{ per unit}$$
$$\$200Q - \$130Q - \$1,400 = 0$$
$$Q = \$1,400 \div \$70 = 20 \text{ units}$$

Option 3 has a break-even point of zero units because there are no fixed costs. The variable costs per unit are $160 ($120 + 0.20[$200]). The contribution margin per unit is $40 ($200 − $160).

How a Jobs-Bank Agreement Increased GM's Breakeven Point

The breakeven point of an automotive company is greatly affected by the behavior of manufacturing labor costs. Where manufacturing labor is a fixed cost, the breakeven point will be higher than where it is a variable cost. A 1990 contract between General Motors Corporation (GM) and the United Auto Workers (UAW) resulted in manufacturing labor cost behaving more like a fixed cost than as a variable cost when the level of production declined. In this contract, GM guaranteed $3.3 billion for worker jobs and income guarantees over three years. Provisions of the contract include:

◆ In the first 36 weeks of a layoff, workers receive unemployment insurance and supplemental insurance benefits equal to 95% of take-home pay.

◆ After the 36 weeks of layoff, workers go back on full pay and benefits, either at their old plant or as part of a jobs bank.

This contract was designed, in part, to motivate GM employees to seek new ways to continuously improve quality and reduce costs without their own employment being at risk.

When GM's production output declined in the early 1990s, many workers joined the jobs bank. GM has sought ways to use them productively. One proposal was to have their independent supplier companies use GM workers and facilities when manufacturing parts for GM. This proposal was labeled a "strategic in-sourcing initiative." One commentator noted at the time that the plan met resistance from suppliers who were none too anxious to move into GM's unwanted plants and use GM's highly paid workers.

The result was that GM still had an excessive number of underutilized people who were receiving full pay and benefits. This led to GM having a higher breakeven point than several of its competitors who did not have similar jobs-bank agreements.

Source: Adapted from *The Detroit News* (December 12, 1991) and *Automotive News* (February 1, 1993).

Effect of Time Horizon

A critical assumption of CVP analysis is that costs can be classified as either variable or fixed. This classification can be affected by the time period being considered. The shorter the time horizon we consider, the higher the percentage of total costs we may view as fixed. Consider United Airlines. Suppose a United Airlines plane will depart from its gate in 30 minutes and there are 20 empty seats. A potential passenger arrives bearing a transferable ticket from a competing airline. What are the variable costs to United of placing one more passenger in an otherwise empty seat? Variable costs (such as one more meal) would be negligible. Virtually all the costs in that decision situation are fixed. In contrast, suppose United must decide whether to include another city in its routes. This decision may have a one-year planning horizon. Many more costs would be regarded as variable and fewer as fixed in this decision.

This example underscores the importance of how the time horizon of a decision affects the analysis of cost behavior. In brief, whether costs are really fixed depends heavily on the relevant range, the length of the time horizon in question, and the specific decision situation.

Revenue mix (also called **sales mix**) is the relative combination of quantities of products or services that constitutes total revenues. If the mix changes, overall revenue targets may still be achieved. However, the effects on operating income depend on how the original proportions of lower or higher contribution margin products have shifted.

Suppose Mary Frost in our computer convention example is now budgeting for the next convention. She plans to sell two software products—Do-All and Superword—and budgets the following:

OBJECTIVE 7

Describe the effect of revenue mix on operating income

	Do-All	Superword	Total
Units sold	60	30	90
Revenues, $200 and $130 per unit	$12,000	$ 3,900	$15,900
Variable costs, $120 and $90 per unit	7,200	2,700	9,900
Contribution margin, $80 and $40 per unit	$ 4,800	$ 1,200	6,000
Fixed costs			2,000
Operating income			$ 4,000

What is the breakeven point? Unlike the single product (or service) situation, there is not a unique number of units for a multiple-product situation. This number instead depends on the revenue mix. The following approach can be used when it is assumed that the budgeted revenue mix (2 units of Do-All sold for each unit of Superword sold) will not change at different levels of total revenue:

$$\text{Let } S = \text{Number of units of Superword to break even}$$

$$2S = \text{Number of units of Do-All to break even}$$

$$\text{Revenues} - \text{Variable costs} - \text{Fixed costs} = \text{Operating income}$$

$$[\$200(2S) + \$130S] - [\$120(2S) + \$90S] - \$2,000 = 0$$

$$\$530S - \$330S = \$2,000$$

$$\$200S = \$2,000$$

$$S = 10$$

$$2S = 20$$

The breakeven point is 30 units when the revenue mix is 20 units of Do-All and 10 units of Superword. The total contribution margin of $2,000 (Do-All $80 × 20 = $1,600 plus Superword $40 × 10 = $400) equals the fixed costs of $2,000 at this mix.

Alternative revenue mixes (in units) that have a contribution margin of $2,000 and thus result in breakeven operations include the following:

Do-All	25	20	15	10	5	0
Superword	0	10	20	30	40	50
Total	25	30	35	40	45	50

Other things being equal, for any given total quantity of units sold, if the mix shifts toward units with higher contribution margins, operating income will be higher. Thus, if the mix shifts toward Do-All (say, to 70% Do-All from 60% Do-All) with a contribution margin of twice that of Superword, Frost's operating income will increase.

Despite their desire to maximize revenues from all products, managers must frequently cope with limited (constrained) resources. For instance, additional production capacity may be unavailable. Which products should be produced? As Chapter 11 explains in more detail, the best decision is not necessarily to make the product having the highest contribution margin per unit. Rather, the best decision recognizes the contribution margin per unit of the constraining factor.

ROLE OF INCOME TAXES

When we introduced a target operating income in our earlier Do-All software example, the following income statement was shown (p. 64):

Revenues, $200 × 40	$8,000
Variable costs, $120 × 40	4,800
Contribution margin	3,200
Fixed costs	2,000
Operating income	$1,200

The net income of Do-All is operating income minus income taxes. What number of units must Do-All sell to earn a net income of $1,200, assuming operating income is taxed at a rate of 40%? The only change in the equation method of CVP analysis is to modify the target operating income to allow for income taxes. Recall our previous equation method:

$$\text{Revenues} - \text{Variable costs} - \text{Fixed costs} = \text{Operating income}$$

We now introduce income tax effects:

$$\text{Target net income} = (\text{Operating income}) - [(\text{Operating income}) \times (\text{Tax rate})]$$

$$\text{Target net income} = (\text{Operating income})(1 - \text{Tax rate})$$

$$\text{Operating income} = \frac{\text{Target net income}}{1 - \text{Tax rate}}$$

So, taking income taxes into account, the equation method yields:

$$\text{Revenues} - \text{Variable costs} - \text{Fixed costs} = \frac{\text{Target net income}}{1 - \text{Tax rate}}$$

Substituting numbers from our Do-All example, the equation would now be:

$$\$200Q - \$120Q - \$2,000 = \frac{\text{Target net income}}{1 - \text{Tax rate}}$$

$$\$200Q - \$120Q - \$2,000 = \frac{\$1,200}{1 - 0.40}$$

$$\$200Q - \$120Q - \$2,000 = \$2,000$$

$$\$80Q = \$4,000$$

$$Q = \$4,000 \div \$80 = 50 \text{ units}$$

Proof:

Revenues, $200 × 50	$10,000
Variable costs, $120 × 50	6,000
Contribution margin	4,000
Fixed costs	2,000
Operating income	2,000
Income taxes, $2,000 × 0.40	800
Net income	$ 1,200

Suppose the target net income were set at $1,680 instead of $1,200. The required number of unit sales would rise from 50 to 60 units:

$$\text{Operating income} = \frac{\text{Target net income}}{1 - \text{Tax rate}}$$

$$\$200Q - \$120Q - \$2,000 = \frac{\$1,680}{1 - 0.40}$$

$$\$80Q - \$2,000 = \$2,800$$

$$\$80Q = \$4,800$$

$$Q = \$4,800 \div \$80 = 60 \text{ units}$$

The presence of income taxes will not change the breakeven point. Why? Because, by definition, operating income at the breakeven point is zero, and thus no income taxes will be paid.[3]

NONPROFIT INSTITUTIONS AND CVP

CVP can be readily applied to decisions by both nonprofit and for-profit organizations. Suppose a social welfare agency has a government budget appropriation (revenue) for 19_7 of $900,000. This nonprofit agency's major purpose is to assist handicapped people who are seeking employment. On average, the agency supplements each person's income by $5,000 annually. The agency's fixed costs are $270,000. There are no other costs. The agency manager wants to know how many people could be assisted in 19_7. We can use CVP analysis here by assuming zero operating income. Let Q be the number of people to be assisted:

$$\text{Revenue} - \text{Variable costs} - \text{Fixed costs} = \$0$$

$$\$900,000 - \$5,000Q - \$270,000 = \$0$$

$$\$5,000Q = \$900,000 - \$270,000$$

$$Q = \$630,000 \div \$5,000 = 126 \text{ people}$$

Suppose the manager is concerned that the total budget appropriation for 19_7 will be reduced by 15% to a new amount of $(1 - 0.15) \times \$900,000 = \$765,000$. The manager wants to know how many handicapped people will be assisted. Assume the same amount of monetary assistance per person:

$$\$765,000 - \$5,000Q - \$270,000 = \$0$$

$$\$5,000Q = \$765,000 - \$270,000$$

$$Q = \$495,000 \div \$5,000 = 99 \text{ people}$$

Note the following two characteristics of the CVP relationships in this nonprofit situation:

1. The percentage drop in service, $(126 - 99) \div 126$, or 21.4%, is more than the 15% reduction in the budget appropriation. Why? Because the existence of $270,000 in fixed costs means that the percentage drop in service exceeds the percentage drop in budget appropriation.

2. If the relationships were graphed, the budget appropriation (revenue) amount would be a straight horizontal line of $765,000. The manager could adjust operations to stay within the reduced appropriation in one or more of three major ways: (a) Reduce the number of people assisted; (b) reduce the variable costs (the assistance per person); or (c) reduce the total fixed costs.

CONTRIBUTION MARGIN AND GROSS MARGIN

Contribution margin is a key concept in this chapter. We now consider how it is related to the gross margin concept discussed in Chapter 2. First some definitions:

$$\textbf{Contribution margin} = \text{Revenues} - \frac{\text{All costs that vary with respect}}{\text{to number of output units}}$$

$$\textbf{Gross margin} = \text{Revenues} - \text{Cost of goods sold} \quad (\text{variable cost} + \text{fixed cost})$$

The phrase "all costs that vary" refers to variable costs in each of the business functions of the value chain. Cost of goods sold in the merchandising sector is made up of goods purchased for resale. Cost of goods sold in the manufacturing sector consists entirely of manufacturing costs (including fixed manufacturing costs).

[3]Other types of taxes may affect the breakeven point. For example, a sales tax paid by the seller that is a fixed percentage of revenues can be treated as a variable cost and hence will increase the breakeven point.

Service-sector companies can compute a contribution margin figure but not a gross margin figure. Service-sector companies do not have a cost of goods sold line item in their income statement.

Merchandising Sector

The two areas of difference between contribution margin and gross margin for companies in the merchandising sector are fixed cost of goods sold (such as a fixed annual payment to a supplier to guarantee an exclusive option to purchase merchandise) and variable noncost of goods sold items (such as a salesperson's commission that is a percentage of sales dollars). Contribution margin is computed after all variable costs have been deducted, whereas gross margin is computed by deducting only cost of goods sold from revenues. The following example (figures assumed to be in thousands) illustrates this difference:

Contribution Margin Format			Gross Margin Format		
Revenues		$200	Revenues	VC+FC	$200
Variable cost of goods sold	$120		Cost of goods sold ($120 + $5)		125
Other variable costs	43	163	Gross margin	VC +FC	75
Contribution margin		37	Operating costs ($43 + $19)		62
Fixed costs of goods sold	5		Operating income		$ 13
Other fixed costs	19	24			
Operating income		$ 13			

(VC brackets Variable cost of goods sold and Other variable costs; FC brackets Fixed costs of goods sold and Other fixed costs.)

Fixed cost of goods sold for a merchandiser include only fixed costs directly related to the purchase of merchandise. The preceding example is a fixed annual payment to a supplier of merchandise. It would not include fixed costs (such as fixed salaries) of the purchasing department. These costs would be included in other fixed costs in the contribution margin format.

Manufacturing Sector

The two areas of difference between contribution margin and gross margin for companies in the manufacturing sector are fixed manufacturing costs and variable nonmanufacturing costs. The following example (figures assumed to be in thousands) illustrates this difference:

Revenues		$1,000	Revenues		$1,000
Variable manufacturing costs	$250		Cost of goods sold ($250 + $160)		410
Variable nonmanufacturing costs	270	520	Gross margin		590
Contribution margin		480	Nonmanufacturing costs ($270 + $138)		408
Fixed manufacturing costs	160		Operating income		$ 182
Fixed nonmanufacturing costs	138	298			
Operating income		$ 182			

Fixed manufacturing costs are not deducted from revenues when computing contribution margin but are deducted when computing gross margin. Cost of goods sold in a manufacturing company includes entirely manufacturing costs. Variable nonmanufacturing costs are deducted from revenues when computing contribution margins but are not deducted when computing gross margins.

Both the *contribution margin* and the *gross margin* can be expressed as totals, as an amount per unit, or as percentages. The **contribution margin percentage** is the total contribution margin divided by revenues. The **variable-cost percentage** is the total variable costs (with respect to units of output) divided by revenues. The contribution margin percentage in our manufacturing-sector example is 48% ($480 ÷ $1,000), while the variable-cost percentage is 52% ($520 ÷ $1,000). The **gross margin percentage** is the gross margin divided by revenues—59% ($590 ÷ $1,000) in our manufacturing-sector example.

Wembley Travel is a travel agency specializing in flights between Los Angeles and London. It books passengers on United Airlines. United charges passengers $900 per round-trip ticket. Until last month, United paid Wembley a commission of 10% of the ticket price paid by each passenger. This was Wembley's only source of revenues. Wembley's fixed costs are $14,000 per month (for salaries, rent, etc.), and its variable costs are $20 per ticket purchased for a passenger. This $20 includes a $15 per ticket delivery fee paid to Federal Express. (To keep the analysis simple, we assume each round-trip ticket purchased is delivered in a separate package; thus the $15 delivery fee applies to every ticket.)

United Airlines has just announced a revised payment schedule for travel agents. It will now pay travel agents a 10% commission per ticket up to a maximum of $50. Any ticket costing more than $500 receives only a $50 commission, irrespective of the ticket price.

REQUIRED

1. Under the old 10% commission structure, how many round-trip tickets must Wembley sell each month to (a) breakeven, and (b) earn an operating income of $7,000 per month?
2. How does United's revised payment schedule affect your answers to (a) and (b) in requirement 1?
3. Wembley is approached by DHL Express, who offers to charge $9 per ticket delivered. How would accepting this offer affect your answers to (a) and (b) in requirement 2? (Assume the maximum commission is $50 per ticket.) DHL Express offers next-day service, with reliability comparable to Federal Express.

SOLUTION

1. Wembley receives a 10% commission on each ticket—10% × $900 = $90. Thus,

$$USP = \$90$$

$$UVC = \$20$$

$$UCM = \$90 - \$20 = \$70$$

$$FC = \$14,000 \text{ per month}$$

   a. $Q = \dfrac{FC}{UCM} = \dfrac{\$14,000}{\$70} = 200$ tickets per month

   b. When target operating income (TOI) = $7,000 per month:

$$QT = \frac{FC + TOI}{UCM}$$

$$= \frac{\$14,000 + \$7,000}{\$70} = \frac{\$21,000}{\$70}$$

$$= 300 \text{ tickets per month}$$

2. Wembley receives only $50 on the $900 ticket because it exceeds $500. Thus,

$$USP = \$50$$

$$UVC = \$20$$

$$UCM = \$50 - \$20 = \$30$$

$$FC = \$14,000 \text{ per month}$$

   a. $Q = \dfrac{\$14,000}{\$30} = 467$ tickets (rounded up)

   b. $QT = \dfrac{\$21,000}{\$30} = 700$ tickets

The $50 cap on the commission paid per ticket causes the breakeven point to more than double (from 200 to 467) and the tickets sold to yield $7,000 per month to also more than double (from 300 to 700). Not surprisingly, travel agents reacted very negatively to the United Airlines proposal to change commission payments.

3. The DHL Express offer reduces the variable cost per ticket from $20 to $14 (reflecting the drop in carrier costs from $15 to $9).

$$USP = \$50$$

$$UVC = \$14$$

$$UCM = \$50 - \$14 = \$36$$

$$FC = \$14,000 \text{ per month}$$

a. $Q = \dfrac{\$14,000}{\$36} = 389$ tickets (rounded up)

b. $QT = \dfrac{\$21,000}{\$36} = 584$ tickets (rounded up)

The increase in contribution margin decreases both the breakeven point and the number of tickets required to yield the $7,000 target operating income.

SUMMARY

The following points are linked to the chapter's learning objectives.

1. General profit planning in its full complexity assumes that there are many revenue drivers and many cost drivers. CVP is a special case that, in a restricted number of settings, can assist managers in understanding the behavior of total costs, total revenues, and operating income as changes occur in the output level, selling price, variable costs, or fixed costs.

2. Operating income is computed by subtracting operating costs from operating revenues. Net income is operating income plus nonoperating revenues minus nonoperating costs minus income taxes.

3. Using CVP requires simplifying assumptions, including that costs are either fixed or variable with respect to the number of output units (units manufactured or units sold) and that total sales and total cost relationships are linear.

4. The three methods outlined for computing the breakeven point—the equation method, the contribution margin method, and the graph method—are merely restatements of each other. Managers often select the method they find easiest to use in their specific situation.

5. Sensitivity analysis, a "what-if" technique, can systematically examine the effect on operating income and net income of different levels of fixed costs, variable costs per unit, selling prices, and output.

6. CVP can highlight to managers the downside risk and upside potential reward of alternatives that differ in their fixed costs and variable costs.

7. When CVP is applied to a multiple-product firm, it is assumed that there is a constant sales mix of products as the total quantity of units sold changes.

8. Income taxes can be incorporated into CVP analysis in a straightforward way by adjusting operating income by the income tax rate. The breakeven point is unaffected by the presence of income taxes because no income taxes are paid if there is no operating income.

Managers make predictions and decisions in a world of uncertainty. This appendix explores the characteristics of uncertainty and describes how managers can cope with it. We also illustrate the additional insights gained when uncertainty is recognized in CVP analysis.

Coping with Uncertainty

Role of a Decision Model   *Uncertainty* is the possibility that an actual amount will deviate from an expected amount. For example, marketing costs might be forecast at $400,000 but actually turn out to be $430,000. A **decision model** helps managers deal with uncertainty; it is a formal method for making a choice that often involves quantitative analysis. It usually includes the following elements:

1. A **choice criterion,** which is an objective that can be quantified. This objective can take many forms. Most often the choice criterion is expressed as a maximization of income or a minimization of cost. The choice criterion provides a basis for choosing the best alternative action.

2. A set of the alternative actions being considered.

3. A set of all the relevant **events** that may occur, where an event is a possible occurrence. This set of events should be mutually exclusive and collectively exhaustive. Events are mutually exclusive if they cannot occur at the same time. Events are collectively exhaustive if, taken together, they make up the entire set of possible occurrences (and no other event can occur). Examples are growth or no growth in industry demand and increase, decrease, or no change in interest rates. Only one event in a set of mutually exclusive and collectively exhaustive events will actually occur.

4. A set of probabilities, where a **probability** is the likelihood or chance of occurrence of an event.

5. A set of possible **outcomes** that measures, in terms of the choice criterion, the predicted consequences of the various possible combinations of actions and events.

It is important to distinguish actions from events. Actions are choices made by management—for example, the prices it should charge for the company's products. Events are occurrences that management cannot control—for example, a growing or declining economy. The outcome is the operating income the company makes, which depends both on the action management selects (pricing strategy) and the event that occurs (how the economy performs). Exhibit 3-5 presents an overview of a decision model, the implementation of the chosen action, its outcome, and subsequent performance evaluation.

EXHIBIT 3-5
A Decision Model and Its Link to Performance Evaluation

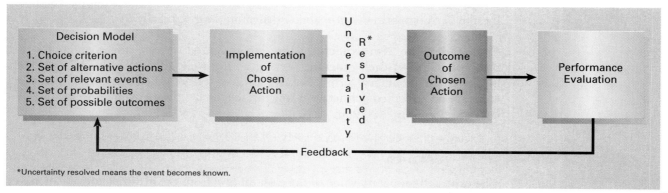

*Uncertainty resolved means the event becomes known.

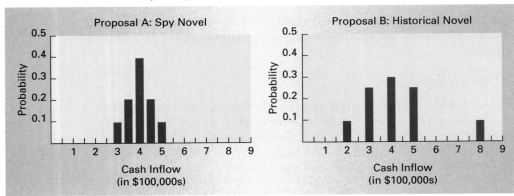

Probabilities Assigning probabilities is a key aspect of the decision model approach to coping with uncertainty. A **probability distribution** describes the likelihood (or probability) of each of the mutually exclusive and collectively exhaustive set of events. The probabilities of these events will add to 1.00 because they are collectively exhaustive. In some cases, there will be much evidence to guide the assignment of probabilities. For example, the probability of obtaining a head in the toss of a fair coin is ½; that of drawing a particular playing card from a standard, well-shuffled deck is ½₂. In business, the probability of having a specified percentage of defective units may be assigned with great confidence, on the basis of production experience with thousands of units. In other cases, there will be little evidence supporting estimated probabilities. For example, how many units of a new pharmaceutical product will be sold next year?

The concept of uncertainty can be illustrated by a decision situation facing a book editor. The editor is deciding between publishing a spy novel and publishing a historical novel. Both book proposals require a $200,000 investment at the beginning of the year. (For simplicity here, we ignore the time value of money, which is covered in Chapters 22 and 23.) On the basis of experience, the editor believes that the following probability distribution (assume that the sales life of each book is one year) describes the relative likelihood of cash inflows for the next year:

Proposal A: Spy Novel		Proposal B: Historical Novel	
Probability	Cash Inflows	Probability	Cash Inflows
0.10	$300,000	0.10	$200,000
0.20	350,000	0.25	300,000
0.40	400,000	0.30	400,000
0.20	450,000	0.25	500,000
0.10	500,000	0.10	800,000
1.00		1.00	

Exhibit 3-6 compares the probability distributions graphically.

Expected Value An **expected value** is a weighted average of the outcomes with the probability of each outcome serving as the weight. Where the outcomes are measured in monetary terms, *expected value* is often called **expected monetary value.** The expected monetary value of the cash inflows from the spy novel—denoted $E(a_1)$—is $400,000:

$$E(a_1) = 0.1(\$300,000) + 0.2(\$350,000) + 0.4(\$400,000) + 0.2(\$450,000) + 0.1(\$500,000)$$

$$= \$400,000$$

The expected monetary value of the cash inflows from the historical novel—denoted $E(a_2)$—is $420,000:

$$E(a_2) = 0.1(\$200,000) + 0.25(\$300,000) + 0.3(\$400,000) + 0.25(\$500,000) + 0.1(\$800,000)$$

$$= \$420,000$$

Expected monetary value is widely used as a decision criterion. For a book editor wanting to maximize the expected monetary value, the historical novel is preferable to the spy novel.

To interpret expected value, imagine that the company publishes many historical novels, each with a probability distribution of cash inflows given in proposal B. The expected value of $420,000 is the average cash inflow per novel that the publisher will receive when averaged across all novels. For a specific novel, the cash inflows will be either $200,000, $300,000, $400,000, $500,000, or $800,000. But if the company publishes 100 such novels, it will expect to receive $42 million in total cash inflows, for an average of $420,000 per novel.

Many statisticians and accountants favor presenting the entire probability distribution to the decision maker. Others present information in three categories: optimistic, most likely, and pessimistic. Either presentation reminds the user that uncertainty exists in the decision at hand.

ILLUSTRATIVE PROBLEM

Reconsider Mary Frost and the booth rental alternatives offered by Computer Conventions, Inc., to sell Do-All software (p. 62):

◆ *Option 1:* $2,000 fixed fee
◆ *Option 2:* $1,400 fixed fee plus 5% of the convention revenues from Do-All sales
◆ *Option 3:* 20% of the convention revenues from Do-All sales (but no fixed fee)

Frost estimates a 0.60 probability that sales will be 40 units and a 0.40 probability that sales will be 70 units. Each Do-All software package will be sold for $200. Frost will purchase the package from a computer software wholesaler at $120 per unit with the privilege of returning all unsold units. Which booth rental alternative should Mary Frost choose?

General Approach to Uncertainty   The construction of a decision model consists of five steps that are keyed to the five characteristics described at the beginning of this appendix.[4]

Step 1   *Identify the choice criterion of the decision maker.* Assume that Mary Frost's choice criterion is to maximize expected net cash inflow at the convention.

Step 2   *Identify the set of alternative actions under consideration.* The notation for an action is a. Mary Frost has three possible actions:

$a_1 = $ Pay $2,000 fixed fee

$a_2 = $ Pay $1,400 fixed fee plus 5% of convention revenues

$a_3 = $ Pay 20% of convention revenues (but no fixed fee)

Step 3   *Identify the set of relevant events that can occur.* Mary Frost's only uncertainty is the number of units of Do-All software that she can sell. Using x as the notation for an event,

$$x_1 = 40 \text{ units}$$

$$x_2 = 70 \text{ units}$$

[4]The presentations here draw (in part) from teaching notes prepared by R. Williamson.

EXHIBIT 3-7
Decision Table for Do-All Software

Actions	Probability of Events	
	$x_1 = 40$ units sold $P(x_1) = 0.60$	$x_2 = 70$ units sold $P(x_2) = 0.40$
a_1: Pay \$2,000 fixed fee	\$1,200[l]	\$3,600[m]
a_2: Pay \$1,400 fixed fee plus 5% of convention revenues	\$1,400[n]	\$3,500[p]
a_3: Pay 20% of convention revenues (but no fixed fee)	\$1,600[q]	\$2,800[r]

[l] Net cash flows = (\$200 − \$120)(40) − \$2,000 = \$1,200
[m] Net cash flows = (\$200 − \$120)(70) − \$2,000 = \$3,600
[n] Net cash flows = (\$200 − \$120 − \$10*)(40) − \$1,400 = \$1,400
[p] Net cash flows = (\$200 − \$120 − \$10*)(70) − \$1,400 = \$3,500
[q] Net cash flows = (\$200 − \$120 − \$40**)(40) = \$1,600
[r] Net cash flows = (\$200 − \$120 − \$40**)(70) = \$2,800
*\$10 = 5% of selling price of \$200
**\$40 = 20% of selling price of \$200

Step 4 *Assign the set of probabilities for the events that can occur.* Frost assesses a 60% chance that she will sell 40 units and a 40% chance that she will sell 70 units. Using $P(x)$ as the notation for the probability of an event, the probabilities are

$$P(x_1) = 0.60$$

$$P(x_2) = 0.40$$

Step 5 *Identify the set of possible outcomes that are dependent on specific actions and events.* The outcomes in this example take the form of six possible net cash flows that are displayed in a decision table in Exhibit 3-7. A **decision table** is a summary of the contemplated actions, events, outcomes, and probabilities of events.

Mary Frost can now use the information in Exhibit 3-7 to compute the expected net cash inflow of each action as follows:

Pay \$2,000 fixed fee: $E(a_1) = 0.60(\$1,200) + 0.40(\$3,600) = \$2,160$

Pay \$1,400 fixed fee plus 5% of revenues: $E(a_2) = 0.60(\$1,400) + 0.40(\$3,500) = \$2,240$

Pay 20% of revenues (but no fixed fee): $E(a_3) = 0.60(\$1,600) + 0.40(\$2,800) = \$2,080$

To maximize expected net cash inflows, Frost should select action a_2—that is, contracting to pay Computer Conventions a \$1,400 fixed fee plus 5% of convention revenues.

Consider the effect of uncertainty on the preferred action choice. If Frost was certain that she would sell only 40 units of Do-All software (that is, $P(x_1) = 1$), she would prefer alternative a_3—pay 20% of revenues and no fixed fee. To follow this reasoning, examine Exhibit 3-7. When 40 units are sold, alternative a_3 yields the maximum net cash inflows of \$1,600. Because fixed costs are zero, booth rental costs are low when sales are low.

However, if Frost was certain that she would sell 70 units of Do-All software (that is, $P(x_2) = 1$), she would prefer alternative a_1—pay a \$2,000 fixed fee. Exhibit 3-7 indicates that when 70 units are sold, alternative a_1 yields the maximum net cash inflows of \$3,600. Rental payments under a_2 and a_3 increase with units sold but are fixed under a_1.

Good Decisions and Good Outcomes   Always distinguish between a good decision and a good outcome. One can exist without the other. By definition, uncertainty rules out guaranteeing, after the fact, that the best outcome will always be obtained. It is possible that bad luck will produce unfavorable consequences even when good decisions have been made.

Suppose you are offered a one-time-only gamble tossing a fair coin. You will win $20 if the event is heads, but you will lose $1 if the event is tails. As a decision maker, you proceed through the logical phases: gathering information, assessing outcomes, and making a choice. You accept the bet. Why? Because the expected value is $9.50 [0.5($20) + 0.5(–$1)]. The coin is tossed and the event is tails. You lose. From your viewpoint, this was a good decision but a bad outcome.

A decision can be made only on the basis of information available at the time of the decision. Hindsight is flawless, but a bad outcome does not necessarily mean that a bad decision was made. Making a good decision is our best protection against a bad outcome.

▼ TERMS TO LEARN

This chapter and the Glossary at the end of the book contain definitions of the following important terms:

breakeven point (p. 62)
choice criterion (75)
contribution income statement (63)
contribution margin (71)
contribution margin percentage (72)
cost-volume-profit (CVP) (60)
decision model (75)
decision table (78)
events (75)
expected monetary value (76)
expected value (76)
gross margin (71)
gross margin percentage (72)
margin of safety (66)

net income (61)
operating income (61)
outcomes (75)
probability (75)
probability distribution (76)
PV graph (65)
revenues (60)
revenue driver (60)
revenue mix (69)
sales mix (69)
sensitivity analysis (65)
uncertainty (66)
variable-cost percentage (72)

▼ ASSIGNMENT MATERIAL

QUESTIONS

Note: To underscore the basic CVP relationships, the assignment material ignores income taxes unless stated otherwise.

3–1 Describe how the special case labeled CVP is different from the general case for predicting total revenues, total costs, and operating income.

3–2 There are many revenue drivers besides units of output sold (or manufactured). Name two.

3–3 There are many cost drivers besides units of output sold (or manufactured). Name two.

3–4 Distinguish between operating income and net income.

3–5 Give three specific ways units of output are measured in different industries.

3–6 Describe the assumptions underlying CVP analysis.

3–7 Why is it more accurate to describe the subject matter of this chapter as CVP analysis rather than as breakeven analysis?

3–8 "CVP is both simple and simplistic. If you want realistic analysis to underpin your decisions, look beyond CVP." Do you agree? Explain.

3–9 Describe *sensitivity analysis.* How has the advent of spreadsheet software affected its use?

3–10 Define contribution margin, gross margin, contribution margin percentage, variable-cost percentage, and margin of safety.

3–11 Give an example of how a manager can decrease variable costs while increasing fixed costs.

3–12 Give an example of how a manager can increase variable costs while decreasing fixed costs.

3–13 "There is no such thing as a fixed cost. All costs can be 'unfixed' given sufficient time." Do you agree? What is the implication of your answer for CVP analysis?

3–14 How can a company with multiple products compute its breakeven point?

3–15 How does an increase in the income tax rate affect the breakeven point?

EXERCISES

3-16 CVP computations. In the following data, fill in the blanks for each of the four independent cases.

Case	Revenues	Variable Costs	Fixed Costs	Total Costs	Operating Income	Contribution Margin Percentage
a	$2000	$500	$300	$ 800	$1,200	25%
b	2,000	1500	300	1800	200	25%
c	1,000	700	300	1,000	0	30%
d	1,500	620	300	900	600	40%

3-17 CVP computations. Fill in the blanks for each of the following independent cases.

Case	Selling Price	Variable Costs Per Unit	Total Units Sold	Total Contribution Margin	Total Fixed Costs	Operating Income
a	$30	$20	70,000	$ 700,000	$ 850,000	-$15,000
b	25	20	180,000	900,000	800,000	100,000
c	12	10	150,000	300,000	220,000	80,000
d	20	14	20,000	120,000	108,000	12,000

3-18 CVP, changing revenues and costs. Sunshine Tours is a travel agency specializing in flights between Toronto and Jamaica. It books passengers on Canadian Air. Canadian Air charges passengers $1,000 per round-trip ticket. Sunshine receives a commission of 8% of the ticket price paid by the passenger. Sunshine's fixed costs are $22,000 per month. Its variable costs are $35 per ticket, including an $18 delivery fee by Emory Express. (Assume each ticket purchased is delivered in a separate package; thus the delivery fee applies to every individual ticket.)

REQUIRED

1. What is the number of tickets Sunshine must sell each month to (a) breakeven, and (b) make a target operating income of $10,000?
2. Assume TNT Express offers to charge Sunshine only $12 per ticket delivered. How would accepting this offer affect your answers to (a) and (b) in requirement 1?

3-19 CVP, changing revenues and costs (continuation of 3-18). Canadian Air changes its commission structure to travel agents. Up to a ticket price of $600, the 8% commission applies. For tickets costing $600 or more, there is a fixed commission of $48. Assume Sunshine Tours has fixed costs of $22,000 per month and variable costs of $29 per ticket (including a $12 delivery fee by TNT).

REQUIRED

1. What is the number of Toronto-to-Jamaica round-trip tickets Sunshine must sell each month to (a) breakeven, and (b) make a target operating income of $10,000? Comment on the results.

2. Sunshine tours decides to charge its customers a delivery fee of $5 per ticket. How would this change affect your answers to (a) and (b) in requirement 1? Comment on the results.

3-20 CVP exercises. The Super Donut owns and operates six donut outlets in and around Kansas City. You are given the following corporate budget data for next year:

Revenues	$10,000,000
Fixed costs	1,700,000
Variable costs	8,200,000

Variable costs change with respect to the number of donuts sold.

REQUIRED

Compute the budgeted operating income for each of the following deviations from the original budget data. (Consider each case independently.)
1. A 10% increase in contribution margin, holding revenues constant
2. A 10% decrease in contribution margin, holding revenues constant
3. A 5% increase in fixed costs
4. A 5% decrease in fixed costs
5. An 8% increase in units sold
6. An 8% decrease in units sold
7. A 10% increase in fixed costs and 10% increase in units sold
8. A 5% increase in fixed costs and 5% decrease in variable costs

3-21 CVP exercises. The Doral Company manufactures and sells pens. Present sales output is 5,000,000 units per year at a selling price of $0.50 per unit. Fixed costs are $900,000 per year. Variable costs are $0.30 per unit.

REQUIRED

(Consider each case separately.)
1. **a.** What is the present operating income for a year?
   b. What is the present breakeven point in revenues?
Compute the new operating income for each of the following changes:
2. A $0.04 per unit increase in variable costs
3. A 10% increase in fixed costs and a 10% increase in units sold
4. A 20% decrease in fixed costs, a 20% decrease in selling price, a 10% decrease in variable costs per unit, and a 40% increase in units sold
Compute the new breakeven point in units for each of the following changes:
5. A 10% increase in fixed costs
6. A 10% increase in selling price and a $20,000 increase in fixed costs

3-22 CVP, changing cost inputs. Maria Montez is planning to sell a vegetable slicer-dicer for $15 per unit at a county fair. She purchases units from a local distributor for $6 each. She can return any unsold units for a full refund. Fixed costs for booth rental, setup, and cleaning are $450.

REQUIRED

1. Compute the breakeven point in units sold.
2. Suppose the unit purchase cost is $5 instead of $6, but the selling price is unchanged. Compute the new breakeven point in units sold.

3-23 CVP, margin of safety. Suppose Lattin Corp's breakeven point is revenues of $1,000,000. Fixed costs are $400,000.

REQUIRED

1. Compute the contribution margin percentage.
2. Compute the selling price if variable costs are $12 per unit.
3. Suppose 80,000 units are sold. Compute the margin of safety.

3-24 CVP, international cost structure differences. Knitwear, Inc., is considering three countries for the sole manufacturing site of its new sweater—Singapore, Thailand, and the United States. All sweaters are to be sold to retail outlets in the United States at $32 per unit. These retail outlets add their own markup when selling to final customers. The three countries differ in their fixed costs and variable costs per sweater.

	Annual Fixed Costs	Variable Manufacturing Costs Per Sweater	Variable Marketing and Distribution Costs Per Sweater
Singapore	$ 6.5 million	$ 8.00	$11.00
Thailand	4.5 million	5.50	11.50
United States	12.0 million	13.00	9.00

REQUIRED

1. Compute the breakeven point of Knitwear, Inc., in both (a) units sold, and (b) revenues for each of the three countries considered for manufacturing the sweaters.
2. If Knitwear, Inc., sells 800,000 sweaters in 19_4, what is the budgeted operating income for each of the three countries considered for manufacturing the sweaters? Comment on the results.

3-25 Revenue mix, new and upgrade customers. Zapo 1-2-3 is a top-selling spreadsheet product. Zapo is about to release version 5.0. It groups its customers into two groups—new customers and upgrade customers (those who previously purchased Zapo 1-2-3 4.0 or earlier versions). Although the same physical product is provided to each customer group, sizable differences exist in their selling prices and variable marketing costs:

	New Customers		Upgrade Customers	
Selling price		$210		$120
Variable cost				
Manufacturing	$25		$25	
Marketing	65	90	15	40

The fixed costs of Zapo 5.0 are $14,000,000.

The planned revenue mix in units is 60% new customers and 40% upgrade customers.

REQUIRED

1. What is the Zapo 1-2-3 5.0 breakeven point in units, assuming that the planned 60%/40% mix is maintained?
2. If the mix is maintained, what is the operating income when 200,000 units are sold?
3. Show how the breakeven point in units changes with the following customer mixes:
   a. New 50%/Upgrade 50%
   b. New 90%/Upgrade 10%

Comment on the results.

3-26 CVP, income taxes. The Bratz Company has fixed costs of $300,000 and a variable-cost percentage of 80%. The company earns net income of $84,000 in 19_4. The income tax rate is 40%.

REQUIRED

Compute (1) operating income, (2) contribution margin, (3) total revenues, and (4) breakeven revenues.

3-27 CVP, income taxes. The Rapid Meal has two restaurants that are open 24 hours a day. Fixed costs for the two restaurants together total $450,000 per year. Service varies from a cup of coffee to full meals. The average sales check for each customer is $8.00. The average cost of food and other variable costs for each customer is $3.20. The income tax rate is 30%. Target net income is $105,000.

REQUIRED

1. Compute the revenues needed to obtain the target net income.
2. How many sales checks are needed to earn net income of $105,000? To breakeven?
3. Compute net income if the number of sales checks is 150,000.

3-28 Appendix, uncertainty, CVP. Angela King is the Las Vegas promoter for Mike Foreman. King is promoting a new world championship fight for Foreman. The key area of uncertainty is the size of the cable pay-per-view TV market. King will pay Foreman a fixed fee of $2 million and 25% of net cable pay-per-view revenue. Every cable TV home receiving the event pays $29.95, of which King receives $16. King pays Foreman 25% of the $16.

King estimates the following probability distribution for homes purchasing the pay-per-view event:

Demand	Probability
100,000	0.05
200,000	0.10
300,000	0.30
400,000	0.35
500,000	0.15
1,000,000	0.05

REQUIRED

1. What is the expected value of the payment King will make to Foreman?
2. Assume the only uncertainty is over cable TV demand for the fight. King wants to know the breakeven point given her own fixed costs of $1 million and her own variable costs of $2 per home. (Also include King's payments to Foreman in your answer).

PROBLEMS

3-29 CVP, executive teaching compensation. Brian Smith is an internationally known American professor specializing in consumer marketing. In 19_2, Smith and the United Kingdom Business School (UKBS) agreed to conduct a one-day seminar at UKBS for marketing executives. Each executive would pay £260 to attend the one-day seminar. The dean at UKBS indicates to Smith that the non-speaker related fixed costs for UKBS conducting the seminar would be

Advertising in magazines	£4,000
Mailing of brochures	£3,000
Administrative labor at UKBS	£2,000
Charge for UKBS lecture auditorium	£1,000

The variable costs to UKBS for each participant attending the seminar would be

Meals and drinks	£25
Binders and photocopying	£35

The dean at UKBS initially offered Smith its regular compensation package of (a) business-class airfare and accommodation (£3,000 maximum) and (b) a £2,000 lecture fee. Smith would qualify for the £3,000 maximum allowance. Smith views the £2,000 lecture fee as providing him no upside potential (that is, no sharing in the potential additional operating income that arises if the seminar is highly attended). He suggests instead that he receive 50% of the operating income to UKBS (if positive) from the one-day seminar and no other payments. The dean of UKBS quickly agrees to Smith's proposal after confirming that Smith is willing to pay his own airfare and accommodation and deliver the seminar irrespective of the number of executives signed up to attend.

REQUIRED

1. What is UKBS's breakeven point (in number of executives attending) if
   a. Smith accepts the regular compensation package of £3,000 expenses and a £2,000 lecture fee.
   b. Smith receives 50% of the operating income to UKBS (if positive) from the one-day seminar and no other payments.
   Comment on the results for (a) and (b).
2. Smith gave the one-day seminar at UKBS in 19_2 (60 attended), 19_3 (90 attended), and 19_4 (180 attended). How much was Smith paid by UKBS for the one-day seminar under the 50% of UKBS's operating income compensation plan in (a) 19_2, (b) 19_3, and (c) 19_4? (Assume that the £260 charge per executive attending and UKBS's fixed and variable costs are the same each year.)
3. After the 19_4 seminar, the dean at UKBS suggested to Smith that the 50%–50% profit-sharing plan was resulting in Smith getting excessive compensation in 19_4 and that a more equitable arrangement to UKBS be used in 19_5. How should Smith respond to this suggestion?

3-30 CVP, movie production. Royal Rumble Productions has just finished production of *Feature Creatures*, the latest action film directed by Tony Savage and starring Ralph Michaels and Sally Martel. The total production cost to Royal Rumble was $5 million. All the production personnel and actors on *Feature Creatures* received a fixed salary (included in the $5 million) and will have no "residual" (equity interest) in the revenues or operating income from the movie. Media Productions will handle the marketing of *Feature Creatures*. Media agrees to invest a minimum $3 million of its own money in marketing the movie and will be paid 20% of the revenues Royal Rumble itself receives from the box-office receipts. Royal Rumble receives 62.5% of the total box-office receipts (out of which comes the 20% payment to Media Productions).

REQUIRED

1. What is the breakeven point to Royal Rumble for *Feature Creatures* expressed in terms of (a) revenues received by Royal Rumble, and (b) total box-office receipts?
2. Assume in its first year of release, the box-office receipts for *Feature Creatures* total $300 million. What is the operating income to Royal Rumble from the movie in its first year?

3-31 CVP, cost structure differences, movie production (continuation of 3-30). Royal Rumble is negotiating for *Feature Creatures 2*, a sequel to its mega-blockbuster *Feature Creatures*. This negotiation is proving more difficult than for the original movie. The budgeted production cost (excluding payments to the director Savage and the stars Michaels and Martel) for *Feature Creatures 2* is $21 million. The agent negotiating for Savage, Michaels, and Martel proposes either of two contracts:

Contract A: Fixed-salary component of $15 million for Savage, Michaels, and Martel (combined) with no residual interest in the revenues from *Feature Creatures 2*.

Contract B: Fixed-salary component of $3 million for Savage, Micheals, and Martel (combined) plus a residual of 15% of the revenues Royal Rumble receives from *Feature Creatures 2*.

Media Productions will market *Feature Creatures 2*. It agrees to invest a minimum of $10 million of its own money. Because of its major role in the success of *Feature Creatures*, Media Productions will now be paid 25% of the revenues Royal Rumble receives from the total box-office receipts. Royal

Rumble receives 62.5% of the total box-office receipts (out of which comes the 25% payment to Media Productions).

REQUIRED
1. What is the breakeven point for Royal Rumble expressed in terms of
    a. revenues received by that company
    b. total box-office receipts for *Feature Creatures 2*
    for contracts A and B? Explain the difference between the breakeven points for contracts A and B.
2. Assume *Feature Creatures 2* achieves the same $300 million in box-office revenues as *Feature Creatures*. What is the operating income to Royal Rumble from *Feature Creatures 2* if it accepts contract B? Comment on the difference in operating income between the two films.

3-32 CVP, sensitivity analysis. Hoot Washington is the newly elected charismatic leader of the Republican Party. He is the darling of the right-wing media. His "take no prisoners" attitude has left many an opponent on a talk show feeling run over by a Mack truck.

Media Publishers is negotiating to publish *Hoot's Manifesto*, a new book that promises to be an instant bestseller. The fixed costs of producing and marketing the book will be $500,000. The variable costs of producing and marketing will be $4.00 per book. These costs are before any payments to Hoot. Hoot negotiates an up-front payment of $3 million plus a 15% royalty rate on the net sales price of each book. The net sales price is the listed bookstore price of $30 minus the margin paid to the bookstore to sell the book. The normal bookstore margin of 30% of the listed bookstore price is expected to apply.

REQUIRED
1. Present a PV graph for Media Publishers.
2. How many copies must Media Publishers sell to (a) breakeven, and (b) earn a target operating profit of $2 million?
3. Examine the sensitivity of the breakeven point to the following changes:
    a. Decreasing the normal bookstore margin to 20% of the listed bookstore price of $30.
    b. Increasing the listed bookstore price to $40 while keeping the bookstore margin at 30%.
    Comment on the results.

3-33 CVP, changing inputs (continuation of 3-32). Hoot Washington's up-front payment of $3 million attracts a lot of negative publicity. His opponents claim he is "in bed" with the right-wing owner of Media Publishers. Congress is considering relaxing some key media ownership restrictions that would expand the opportunities available to many media companies. Hoot and Media Publishers decide to drop the $3 million up-front payment, but make Hoot's royalty rate 20% of the listed bookstore price of $30. The normal bookstore margin of 30% of the listed bookstore price is expected to apply.

REQUIRED
1. Present a PV graph for Media Publishers with the revised contract.
2. How many copies must Media Publishers sell to (a) breakeven, and (b) earn a target operating profit of $2 million? Compare your answers with those in requirement 2 of Problem 3-32.
3. What number of copies must Media Publishers sell for Hoot to be indifferent to receiving either (a) a $3 million up-front payment and a 15% royalty rate, on net sales price, or (b) no up-front payment and a 20% royalty rate on listed bookstore price?

3-34 CVP, shoe stores. The Walk Rite Shoe Company operates a chain of shoe stores. The stores sell ten different styles of inexpensive men's shoes with identical unit costs and selling prices. A unit is defined as a pair of shoes. Each store has a store manager who is paid a fixed salary. Individual salespeople receive a fixed salary and a sales commission. Walk Rite is trying to determine the desirability of opening another store, which is expected to have the following revenue and cost relationships:

	Per Pair
Unit variable data	
Selling price	$30.00
Cost of shoes	$19.50
Sales commissions	1.50
Total variable costs	$21.00
Annual fixed costs	
Rent	$ 60,000
Salaries	200,000
Advertising	80,000
Other fixed costs	20,000
Total fixed costs	$360,000

REQUIRED

(Consider each question independently.)

1. What is the annual breakeven point in (a) units sold, and (b) revenues?
2. If 35,000 units are sold, what will be the store's operating income (loss)?
3. If sales commissions were discontinued for individual salespeople in favor of an $81,000 increase in fixed salaries, what would be the annual breakeven point in (a) units sold, and (b) revenues?
4. Refer to the original data. If the store manager were paid $0.30 per unit sold in addition to his current fixed salary, what would be the annual breakeven point in (a) units sold, and (b) revenues?
5. Refer to the original data. If the store manager were paid $0.30 per unit commission on each unit sold in excess of the breakeven point, what would be the store's operating income if 50,000 units were sold? (This $0.30 is in addition to both the commission paid to the sales staff and the store manager's fixed salary.)

3-35 CVP, shoe stores. Refer to requirement 3 of 3-34.

REQUIRED

1. Calculate the number of units sold where the operating income under (a) a fixed-salary plan, and (b) a lower fixed-salary and commission plan (for salespeople only) would be equal. Above that number of units sold, one plan would be more profitable than the other; below that number of units sold, the reverse would occur.
2. Compute the operating income or loss under each plan in requirement 1 at sales levels of (a) 50,000 units, and (b) 60,000 units.
3. Suppose the target operating income is $168,000. How many units must be sold to reach the target under (a) the fixed-salary plan, and (b) the lower fixed-salary and commission plan?

3-36 Sensitivity and inflation (continuation of 3-35). As president of Walk Rite, you are concerned that inflation may squeeze your profitability. Specifically, you feel committed to the $30 selling price and fear that diluting the quality of the shoes in the face of rising costs would be an unwise marketing move. You expect the cost of shoes to rise by 10% during the coming year. You are tempted to avoid the cost increase by placing a noncancelable order with a large supplier that would provide 50,000 units of the specified quality for each store at $19.50 per unit. (To simplify this analysis, assume that all stores will face identical demands.) These shoes could be acquired and paid for as delivered throughout the year. However, all shoes must be delivered to the stores by the end of the year.

As a shrewd merchandiser, you foresee some risks. If sales were less than 50,000 units, you feel that markdowns of the unsold merchandise would be necessary to sell the goods. You predict that the average selling price of the leftover units would be $18.00. The regular commission of 5% of revenues would be paid to salespeople.

REQUIRED
1. Suppose that actual sales at $30 for the year is 48,000 units and that you contracted for 50,000 units. What is the operating income for the store?
2. If you had perfect forecasting ability, you would have contracted for 48,000 units rather than 50,000 units. What would the operating income have been if you had ordered 48,000 units?
3. Given actual sales of 48,000 units, by how much would the average cost per unit have had to rise before you would have been indifferent between having the contract for 50,000 units and not having the contract?

3-37 **Revenue mix, three products.** The Ronowski Company has three product lines of belts—A, B, and C with contribution margins of $3, $2, and $1, respectively. The president foresees sales of 200,000 units in the coming period, consisting of 20,000 units of A, 100,000 units of B, and 80,000 units of C. The company's fixed costs for the period are $255,000.

REQUIRED
1. What is the company breakeven point in units, assuming that the given revenue mix is maintained?
2. If the mix is maintained, what is the total contribution margin when 200,000 units are sold? What is the operating income?
3. What would operating income become if 20,000 units of A, 80,000 units of B, and 100,000 units of C were sold? What is the new breakeven point in units if these relationships persist in the next period?

3-38 **Revenue mix, three products.** The Mendez Company has three products, tote bags H, J, and K. The president plans to sell 200,000 units during the next period, consisting of 80,000 units of H, 100,000 units of J, and 20,000 units of K. The products have unit contribution margins of $2, $3, and $6, respectively. The company's fixed costs for the period are $406,000.

REQUIRED
1. Compute the budgeted operating income. Compute the breakeven point in units, assuming that the given revenue mix is maintained.
2. Suppose 80,000 units of H, 80,000 units of J, and 40,000 units of K are sold. Compute the budgeted operating income. Compute the new breakeven point in units if these relationships persist in the next period.

3-39 **Revenue mix, two products.** The Goldman Company retails two products, a standard and a deluxe version of a luggage carrier. The budgeted income statement is as follows:

	Standard Carrier	Deluxe Carrier	Total
Units sold	150,000	50,000	200,000
Revenues @ $20 and $30 per unit	$3,000,000	$1,500,000	$4,500,000
Variable costs @ $14 and $18 per unit	2,100,000	900,000	3,000,000
Contribution margins @ $6 and $12 per unit	$ 900,000	$ 600,000	1,500,000
Fixed costs			1,200,000
Operating income			$ 300,000

REQUIRED
1. Compute the breakeven point in units, assuming that the planned revenue mix is maintained.
2. Compute the breakeven point in units (a) if only standard carriers are sold, and (b) if only deluxe carriers are sold.

3. Suppose 200,000 units are sold, but only 20,000 are deluxe. Compute the operating income. Compute the breakeven point if these relationships persist in the next period. Compare your answers with the original plans and the answer in requirement 1. What is the major lesson of this problem?

3-40 CVP, nonprofit event planning. The American-Canadian Chamber of Commerce is planning its July 4 gala ball. There are two possible plans:

   a. Toronto Country Golf Club, which has a fixed rental cost of $2,000 plus a charge of $80 per person for its own catering of meals and serving of drinks and hors d'oeuvres.

   b. Toronto Town Hall, which has a fixed rental cost of $6,600. The Chamber of Commerce can hire a caterer for meals and waiters and waitresses to serve drinks and hors d'oeuvres at $60 per person.

   The Chamber of Commerce budgets $3,500 in costs for administration and marketing. The band will cost a fixed amount of $2,500. Tickets to this prestige event will be $120 per person. All the drinks served and the prizes given away at the ball will be donated by corporate sponsors.

   REQUIRED
   1. Compute the breakeven point for each plan in terms of tickets sold.
   2. Compute the operating income of the ball (a) if 150 people attend, and (b) if 300 people attend. Comment on your results.
   3. At what level of tickets sold will the two plans have the same operating income?

3-41 Nonprofit institution. The City of Little Rock, Arkansas, makes a $400,000 lump-sum budget appropriation to an agency to conduct a counseling program for drug addicts for a year. All of the appropriation is to be spent. The variable costs for drug prescriptions average $400 per patient per year. Fixed costs are $150,000.

   REQUIRED
   1. Compute the number of patients that could be served in a year.
   2. Suppose the total budget for the following year is reduced by 10%. Fixed costs are to remain the same. The same level of service to each patient will be maintained. Compute the number of patients that could be served in a year.
   3. As in requirement 2, assume a budget reduction of 10%. Fixed costs are to remain the same. The drug counselor has discretion as to how much in drug prescriptions to give to each patient. She does not want to reduce the number of patients served. On the average, what is the cost of drugs that can be given to each patient? Compute the percentage decline in the annual average cost of drugs per patient.

3-42 CVP, income taxes. (CMA) The R. A. Ro and Company, a manufacturer of quality handmade walnut bowls, has experienced a steady growth in sales for the past five years. However, increased competition has led Mr. Ro, the president, to believe that an aggressive marketing campaign will be necessary next year to maintain the company's present growth.

   To prepare for next year's marketing campaign, the company's controller has prepared and presented Mr. Ro with the following data for the current year, 19_7:

Variable costs (per bowl)	
Direct manufacturing labor	$ 8.00
Direct materials	3.25
Variable overhead	
(Manufacturing, marketing distribution, customer service, and administration)	2.50
Total variable costs	$13.75

Fixed costs	
Manufacturing	$ 25,000
Marketing, distribution, and customer service	40,000
Administrative	70,000
Total fixed costs	$135,000
Selling price per bowl	$ 25.00
Expected revenues, 19_7 (20,000 units)	$500,000
Income tax rate	40%

REQUIRED

1. What is the projected net income for 19_7?
2. What is the breakeven point in units for 19_7?
3. Mr. Ro has set the revenue target for 19_8 at a level of $550,000 (or 22,000 bowls). He believes an additional marketing cost of $11,250 for advertising in 19_8, with all other costs remaining constant, will be necessary to attain the revenue target. What will be the net income for 19_8 if the additional $11,250 is spent and the revenue target is met?
4. What will be the breakeven point in revenues for 19_8 if the additional $11,250 is spent for advertising?
5. If the additional $11,250 is spent for advertising in 19_8, what is the required 19_8 revenues for 19_8's net income to equal 19_7's net income?
6. At a sales level of 22,000 units, what maximum amount can be spent on advertising if a 19_8 net income of $60,000 is desired?

3-43 Review of Chapters 2 and 3. For each of the following independent cases, find the unknowns designated by the capital letters.

	Case 1	Case 2
Direct materials used	$ H	$ 40,000
Direct manufacturing labor	30,000	15,000
Variable marketing, distribution, customer-service, and administrative costs	K	T
Fixed manufacturing overhead	I	20,000
Fixed marketing, distribution, customer-service, and administrative costs	J	10,000
Gross margin	25,000	20,000
Finished goods inventory, January 1, 19_7	0	5,000
Finished goods inventory, December 31, 19_7	0	5,000
Contribution margin (dollars)	30,000	V
Revenues	100,000	100,000
Direct materials inventory, January 1, 19_7	12,000	20,000
Direct materials inventory, December 31, 19_7	5,000	W
Variable manufacturing overhead	5,000	X
Work in process, January 1, 19_7	0	9,000
Work in process, December 31, 19_7	0	9,000
Purchases of direct materials	15,000	50,000
Breakeven point (in dollars)	66,667	Y
Cost of goods manufactured	G	U
Operating income (loss)	L	(5,000)

3-44 Appendix, CVP under uncertainty. (J. Patell) In your new position as supervisor of product introduction, you have to decide on a pricing strategy for a talking-doll specialty product with the following cost structure:

Variable costs per unit	$ 50
Fixed costs	$200,000

The dolls are manufactured upon receipt of orders, so the inventory levels are insignificant. Your market research assistant is very enthusiastic about probability models and has presented the results of his price analysis in the following form:

a. If you set the selling price at $100 per unit, the probability distribution of revenues is uniform between $300,000 and $600,000. Under this distribution, there is a 0.50 probability of equaling or exceeding revenues of $450,000.

b. If you lower the selling price to $70 per unit, the distribution remains uniform, but it shifts up to the $600,000–$900,000 range. Under this distribution, there is a 0.50 probability of equaling or exceeding revenues of $750,000.

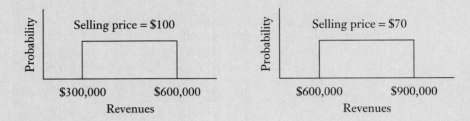

REQUIRED
1. This is your first big contract, and, above all, you want to show an operating income. You decide to select the strategy that maximizes the probability of breaking even or earning a positive operating income.
   a. What is the probability of at least breaking even with a selling price of $100 per unit?
   b. What is the probability of at least breaking even with a selling price of $70 per unit?
2. Your assistant suggests that maximum expected operating income might be a better objective to pursue. Which pricing strategy would result in the higher expected operating income? (Use the expected revenues under each pricing strategy when making expected operating income computations.)

3-45 Appendix, CVP under uncertainty. (R. Jaedicke and A. Robichek, adapted) The Jaro Company is considering two new colors for their umbrella products—emerald green and shocking pink. Either can be produced using present facilities. Each product requires an increase in annual fixed costs of $400,000. The products have the same selling price ($10) and the same variable costs per unit ($8).

Management, after studying past experience with similar products, has prepared the following probability distribution:

	Probability for	
Event (Units Demanded)	**Emerald Green Umbrella**	**Shocking Pink Umbrella**
50,000	0.0	0.1
100,000	0.1	0.1
200,000	0.2	0.1
300,000	0.4	0.2
400,000	0.2	0.4
500,000	0.1	0.1
	1.0	1.0

REQUIRED
1. What is the breakeven point for each product?
2. Which product should be chosen, assuming the objective is to maximize expected operating income? Why? Show your computations.

3. Suppose management is absolutely certain that 300,000 units of shocking pink will be sold, but it still faces the same uncertainty about the demand for emerald green as outlined in the problem. Which product should be chosen? Why? What benefits are available to management from having the complete probability distribution instead of just an expected value?

3-46 Ethics, CVP, cost analysis. Bob Allen is the controller of the Body Products Division of World Wide Drugs (WWD). It is located in Minneapolis, which is also the headquarters of WWD. Allen is helping develop a proposal for a new product to be called "Vital Hair." This product is a cream to be rubbed on the scalp to restore hair growth. Cheryl Kelly, president of the division, and Allen are scheduled to make a presentation to the WWD Executive Committee on the expected profitability of Vital Hair. The fixed costs associated with the development, production, and marketing of Vital Hair are $20,000,000. Each customer will pay a doctor $80 per monthly treatment, of which $55 is paid to WWD. Allen estimates WWD's variable costs per treatment to be $22. Included in this $22 is $8 for potential product litigation costs. Kelly is livid at Allen for including the $8 estimate. She argues that it is imperative to get the R&D funds approved (and quickly) and that any number that increases the breakeven point reduces the likelihood of the Vital Hair project being approved. She notes that WWD has had few successful lawsuits against it, in contrast to some recent "horrendous" experiences of competitors with breast implant products. Moreover, she is furious that Allen put the $8 amount in writing. "How do we know there will be any litigation problem?" She suggests Allen redo the report excluding the $8 litigation risk cost estimate. "Put it on the chalkboard in the executive committee room, if you insist, but don't put it in the report sent to the committee prior to the meeting. You can personally raise the issue at the executive committee meeting and have a full and frank discussion."

Allen takes Kelly's "advice." He reports a variable cost of $14 per treatment in the proposal. While he feels uneasy about this, he is comforted by the fact that he will flag the $8 amount to the executive committee in his forthcoming oral presentation.

One month later, Kelly walks into Allen's office. She is in a buoyant mood and announces she has just come back from an executive committee meeting that approved the Vital Hair proposal. Allen asks why he was not invited to the meeting. Kelly said the meeting was held in New Orleans, and she decided to save the division money by going alone. She then said to Allen that it "was now time to get behind the new venture and help make it the success the committee and her team members believe it will be."

REQUIRED
1. What is the breakeven point (in units of monthly treatments) when WWD's variable costs (a) include the $8 estimate, and (b) exclude the $8 estimate for potential product litigation costs?
2. Should Allen have excluded the $8 estimate in his report to the executive committee of WWD? Explain your answer.
3. What should Allen do in response to Kelly's decision to make the Vital Hair presentation on her own?

COLLABORATIVE LEARNING PROBLEM

3-47 CVP, theater planning. The *New York Herald* has just published a stinging criticism of the inflation in theater ticket prices. The article was titled, "The $75 Price Gouge. Is $100 Next?" This article has increased the concerns of a group planning New York's latest production of *Phantom of the Opera*. It had been planning for a $75 price for all of its seats. The up-front fixed costs to open are $8 million. Production and operating costs are $400,000 per week. The theater has capacity for 2,000 seats with six performances per week planned. Approximately 100 seats per night are held as complementary house seats.

INSTRUCTIONS

Form groups of two or more students to complete the following requirements.

REQUIRED

Your group is charged with exploring ways of improving the profitability of the venture and of reducing its breakeven point. Areas you should explore (but are not restricted to) include the following:

a. Increase the number of shows per week. The cast is under contract for up to eight shows a week for a fixed amount that is included in the $400,000.

b. Provide the two star performers (the Phantom and Christine) with a $25,000 weekly salary and a percentage of revenues or operating income instead of the fixed $50,000 per week each is budgeted to receive.

c. Change the single $75 pricing policy. Whereas all seats in the 2,000-person auditorium have unobstructed views, a recent theater reviewer referred to the back rows of the balcony section as "binocular land."

4

COSTING SYSTEMS AND ACTIVITY-BASED COSTING (I): SERVICE AND MERCHANDISING APPLICATIONS

Retail stores are using activity-based costing to assist in deciding the square footage to allocate to individual products and product areas. ABC cost data, along with information on customer-demand preferences, are enabling many retailers to increase the operating income of the stores they manage.

LEARNING OBJECTIVES

After studying this chapter, you should be able to

1. Describe the building block concept of costing systems
2. Distinguish between job costing and process costing
3. Outline a six-step approach to job costing
4. Distinguish among actual costing, normal costing, and extended normal costing methods
5. Explain undercosting and overcosting of products
6. Describe three guidelines for refining a costing system
7. Describe the distinctive feature of activity-based costing
8. Prepare product-line profitability reports for companies in the merchandising sector

How much does it cost Arthur Andersen to audit Federal Express? How much does it cost Safeway to sell a six-pack of Pepsi-Cola? How much does it cost the Ford Motor Company to manufacture and sell a Ford Bronco to a dealer? Managers ask these questions for many purposes, including formulating overall strategies, product and service emphasis and pricing, cost control and meeting external reporting obligations. Chapters 4 and 5 present concepts and techniques that guide the responses to such questions. Chapter 4 presents examples from the service and merchandising sectors. Examples from the manufacturing sector are presented in Chapter 5.

Before we explore the details of costing systems, three points are worth noting:

1. The cost-benefit approach we discussed in Chapter 1 is essential in designing and choosing costing systems. The costs of elaborate systems, including the costs of educating managers and other personnel, can be quite high. Managers should install a more sophisticated system only if they believe that its benefits will outweigh its costs.

2. Systems should be tailored to the underlying operations, and not vice versa. Any significant change in underlying operations is likely to justify a corresponding change in the accompanying costing systems. The best system's design begins with a careful study of how operations are conducted and a resulting determination of which information to gather and report. The worst systems are those that operating managers perceive as misleading or useless.

3. Costing systems aim to report cost numbers that indicate the manner in which particular cost objects—such as products, services, and customers—use the resources of an organization.

BUILDING BLOCK CONCEPT OF COSTING SYSTEMS

We will now review some terms introduced in Chapter 2 that we will use in discussing costing systems:

◆ *Cost object*—anything for which a separate measurement of costs is desired.
◆ *Direct costs of a cost object*—costs that are related to the particular cost object and can be traced to it in an economically feasible (cost-effective) way.
◆ *Indirect costs of a cost object*—costs that are related to the particular cost object but cannot be traced to it in an economically feasible (cost-effective) way. Indirect costs are allocated to the cost object using a cost-allocation method.

The relationship among these three concepts is as follows:

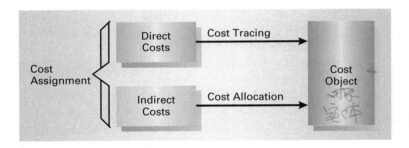

Two concepts not previously defined are also important when discussing costing systems:

◆ **Cost pool**—a grouping of individual cost items. Cost pools can range from the very broad (such as a companywide total-cost pool for telephones and fax machines) to the very narrow (such as the costs of operating a car used by a traveling salesperson).
◆ **Cost-allocation base**—a factor that is the common denominator for systematically linking an indirect cost or group of indirect costs to a cost object. A cost-allocation base can be financial (such as direct labor costs) or nonfinancial (such

as the number of car miles traveled). Companies often seek to use the cost driver of the indirect costs as the cost-allocation base. For example, the number of miles traveled may be used as the base for allocating motor vehicle operating costs among different sales districts.

These five terms constitute the building blocks that we will use to design the costing systems described later in this chapter.

JOB-COSTING AND PROCESS-COSTING SYSTEMS

Companies frequently adopt one of two basic types of costing systems to assign costs to products or services:

OBJECTIVE 2

Distinguish between job costing and process costing

◆ **Job-costing system.** In this system, costs are assigned to a distinct unit, batch, or lot of a product or service. A job is a task for which resources are expended in bringing a distinct product or service to market. The product or service is often custom-made, such as an audit by an accounting firm.

◆ **Process-costing system.** In this system, the cost of a product or service is obtained by using broad averages to assign costs to masses of similar units. Frequently, identical items (such as Barbie dolls or roofing nails) are mass-produced for general sale and not for any specific customer.

These two types of costing systems are best viewed as ends of a continuum:

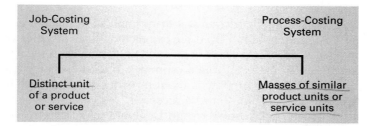

Most companies have costing systems that are neither pure job costing nor pure process costing. Rather, they combine elements of both job costing and process costing. For now, we introduce these two systems by focusing on their pure versions. Exhibit 4-1 presents examples of job and process costing in the service, merchandising, and manufacturing sectors.

The products or services accounted for with job costing can differ greatly. Accounting firms typically define individual audits as jobs, which can differ markedly in

EXHIBIT 4-1

Examples of Job Costing and Process Costing in the Service, Merchandising, and Manufacturing Sectors

	Service Sector	Merchandising Sector	Manufacturing Sector
Job Costing Used	◆ Accounting firm audits ◆ Advertising agency campaigns	◆ Sending a catalog to a mailing list ◆ Special promotion of a new store product	◆ Aircraft assembly ◆ House construction
Process Costing Used	◆ Deposit processing ◆ Postal delivery (standard items)	◆ Grain dealing ◆ Processing new magazine subscriptions	◆ Oil refining ◆ Beverages production

complexity among clients. An aircraft assembly company may define an individual aircraft for a specific customer as a job. Customers usually differ in their specifications about electronic equipment, size of restrooms, and so on. In these examples, the service or product is distinct and identifiable. Job-costing systems are designed to accommodate the cost accounting for these individual services or products.

Companies that use process costing provide similar (in many cases identical) products or services to their customers. For example, a bank provides the same service to all its customers in processing deposits. A magazine publishing company provides the same product (say, a weekly issue of *Newsweek* or *Time*) to each of its customers. The customers of an oil-refining company all receive the same product—crude oil. Process-costing systems average the costs of providing a similar product or service to different customers to obtain a per unit cost. Chapters 17 and 18 discuss process costing in more detail.

JOB COSTING IN SERVICE ORGANIZATIONS USING ACTUAL COSTING

OBJECTIVE 3

Outline a six-step approach to job costing

Service-sector companies provide their customers with services or intangible products. Within the service sector, jobs often differ considerably in terms of their length, complexity, and resources used. Examples include a service call to repair a refrigerator, an audit engagement, the making of a movie, and a university research project for a government agency.

Job Costing of an Audit Engagement

Lindsay & Associates is a public accounting firm. Each audit engagement is viewed as an individual job. Lindsay bids a fixed fee for each audit in advance of doing the work. A key issue for Lindsay is the cost of an audit engagement. A record of costs on previous jobs enables it to make informed estimates of the costs of potential future jobs. The more knowledgeable Lindsay is about its own costs, the more likely it is to price jobs so that it makes a profit on those accepted.

First, consider the actual costing system Lindsay uses to determine the cost of individual jobs. **Actual costing** is a costing method that traces direct costs to a cost object by using the actual direct-cost rate(s) times the actual quantity of the direct-cost input(s) and allocates indirect costs based on the actual indirect-cost rate(s) times the actual quantity of the cost-allocation base. The Tracy Transport audit illustrates actual costing. In November 19_7, Lindsay was awarded the 19_8 Tracy Transport audit job for a fee of $86,000. The 19_8 audit job was done in the January to March 19_8 period and covers Tracy Transport's 19_7 financial year.

General Approach to Job Costing

The six steps taken in assigning costs to individual jobs are presented here. They apply equally to job costing in the service, merchandising, or manufacturing sectors.

Step 1: Identify the Job that Is the Chosen Cost Object   In this example, the job is the annual audit of the financial statements of Tracy Transport.

Step 2: Identify the Direct Costs for the Job   Lindsay identifies only one category of direct costs when costing individual audit jobs—professional labor. Each auditor keeps a daily time record for tracing professional labor-hours to individual audit jobs. These records show that the Tracy Transport job used 800 professional labor-hours. The actual direct-labor cost rate is $51 per hour.[1] Lindsay traces the actual direct-labor costs for the Tracy Transport job as $40,800 ($51 × 800).

---

[1]The actual direct-labor cost rate is the average rate at which professional labor is paid (actual total professional compensation divided by actual total direct labor hours worked) during the period in which the Tracy Transport audit was done.

Step 3: Identify the Indirect-Cost Pools Associated with the Job Lindsay groups all its individual indirect costs into a single cost pool called audit support. This cost pool represents all costs in Lindsay's Audit Support Department. The indirect cost pool consists of a variety of individual costs, such as general audit and secretarial support, that are less predictable and less traceable to jobs than direct labor. Hence, the actual indirect cost rate can often only be computed on an actual basis at the end of the year. In 19_8, indirect costs totaled $12,690,000 ($4,990,000 for "other-labor-related costs" plus $7,700,000 for "nonlabor-related costs").

Step 4: Select the Cost-Allocation Base to Use in Allocating Each Indirect-Cost Pool to the Job The allocation base selected for the audit support indirect-cost pool is professional labor-hours. Total professional labor-hours actually worked in 19_8 were 270,000.

Step 5: Develop the Rate Per Unit of the Cost-Allocation Base Used to Allocate Indirect Costs to the Job The actual indirect-cost rate for Lindsay in 19_8 is $47 per professional labor-hour:

$$\text{Actual indirect-cost rate} = \frac{\text{Actual total costs in indirect-cost pool}}{\text{Actual total quantity of cost-allocation base}}$$

$$= \frac{\$4,990,000 + \$7,700,000}{270,000} = \frac{\$12,690,000}{270,000}$$

$$= \$47 \text{ per professional labor-hour}$$

The actual indirect costs allocated to the Lindsay audit job are $37,600 ($47 × 800).

Step 6: Assign the Costs to the Cost Object by Adding all Direct Costs and All Indirect Costs The information from steps 1 to 5 can now be used to compute the 19_8 actual cost of the Lindsay audit:

Direct job costs traced	
Professional labor, $51 × 800	$40,800
Indirect job costs allocated	
Audit support, $47 × 800	37,600
	$78,400

Recall that Lindsay was paid $86,000 for the 19_8 Tracy Transport audit. Thus, the actual costing system shows a $7,600 operating income ($86,000 − $78,400) on this audit job.

Exhibit 4-2 presents an overview of the Lindsay job-costing system. This exhibit includes the five building blocks of this chapter—cost object, cost pool, direct costs of a cost object, indirect costs of a cost object, and cost-allocation base. Costing-system overviews like Exhibit 4-2 are important learning tools. We urge you to sketch one when you need to understand a costing system. (The symbols in Exhibit 4-2 are used consistently in the costing-system overviews presented in this book. For example, a triangle always identifies a direct cost.)

Source Documents

Managers and accountants gather the information that goes into their cost systems through **source documents,** which are the original records that support journal entries in an accounting system. Time records are Lindsay's main source documents. All professional staff members record how they spend each half-hour of the day. At the end of each week, the number of total professional labor-hours spent on each job (both for the most recent week and the cumulative total since the start of the job) is tabulated. The accuracy of information on how employees spend their time is important, especially in service organizations, where labor costs often make up over *half* of total costs. Accounting and law firms often impose penalties on personnel who do not submit accurate time records when required. Computers ease the recording and preparation of job-cost information.

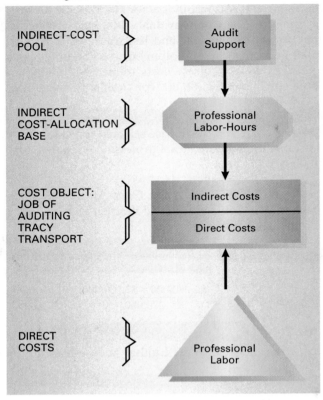

EXHIBIT 4-2
Job-Costing Overview at Lindsay and Associates

INDIRECT-COST POOL	Audit Support
INDIRECT COST-ALLOCATION BASE	Professional Labor-Hours
COST OBJECT: JOB OF AUDITING TRACY TRANSPORT	Indirect Costs / Direct Costs
DIRECT COSTS	Professional Labor

NORMAL COSTING

The difficulty of calculating actual indirect-labor costs for each job means that Lindsay & Associates has to wait until the end of 19_8 to compute the actual costs on individual jobs done in 19_8. Managers often want more timely information about "actual" job costs. This demand for more timely information has prompted the use of alternatives to the actual costing method described earlier in this chapter. The alternatives are practical responses to the desire for a timely approximation of average actual costs of various jobs. Now we discuss normal costing, whereby budgeted rather than actual amounts are used to compute indirect-cost rates. The following 19_8 budgeted data pertain to the *total* operations of Lindsay & Associates:

	Budget
Total professional labor-hours worked	288,000
Direct costs	
Total professional labor costs	$14,400,000
Indirect costs	
Total other labor-related costs	$ 5,328,000
Total non labor-related costs	7,632,000
	$12,960,000

Budg Ind Cost Rate × Actual Qty Cost allocator [handwritten]

Exhibit 4-3 provides details underlying these amounts.

A **normal costing** method traces direct costs to a cost object by using the actual direct-cost rate(s) times the actual quantity of the direct-cost input and allocates indirect costs based on the budgeted indirect-cost rate(s) times the actual quantity of the cost-allocation base(s). Both actual costing and normal costing trace direct costs to jobs in the same way. For the Lindsay & Associates 19_8 audit of Tracy Transport, the actual direct costs traced equal $40,800—the actual direct-cost rate of $51 per professional labor-hour times the actual quantity of 800 hours.

The difference between the actual costing and normal costing methods is that actual costing uses an *actual* indirect-cost rate while normal costing uses a *budgeted* indirect-cost rate to cost jobs. Recall that Lindsay & Associates groups all its individual indirect costs into a single cost pool called audit support. The budgeted amount for audit support in 19_8 is $12,960,000. The allocation base for the audit support indirect-cost pool is professional labor-hours. In 19_8, the budgeted quantity is 288,000 hours. The budgeted indirect-cost rate for 19_8 is $45 per professional labor-hour:

$$\text{Budgeted indirect-cost rate} = \frac{\text{Budgeted total costs in indirect-cost pool}}{\text{Budgeted total quantity of cost-allocation base}}$$

$$= \frac{\$5,328,000 + \$7,632,000}{288,000 \text{ hours}} = \frac{\$12,960,000}{288,000 \text{ hours}}$$

$$= \$45 \text{ per professional labor-hour}$$

Under normal costing, each hour of professional labor on jobs in 19_8 is assigned the actual direct-cost rate of $51 and the budgeted indirect-cost rate of $45. The 19_8 cost of the Tracy Transport audit using normal costing is $76,800:

Direct job costs traced	
Professional labor, $51 × 800	$40,800
Indirect job costs allocated	
Audit support, $45 × 800	36,000
	$76,800

Normal costing uses actual direct costs because these costs are known and can be quickly traced to a job. Indirect costs, by definition, cannot be traced to jobs. Moreover, actual indirect costs are less predictable and not known until the end of the year. Normal costing uses budgeted rates for indirect costs to estimate or approximate the actual indirect costs of a job soon after the job is completed.

EXHIBIT 4-3
Income Statement for Lindsay & Associates: 19_8 Budget and 19_8 Actual Results (in thousands)

	19_8 Budget		19_8 Actual	
Revenues		$33,120		$29,700
Costs				
Professional labor costs		14,400		13,770
Other labor-related costs				
Office staff	$2,030		$1,840	
Information specialists	1,008		1,230	
Administrative	1,252		1,100	
Other	1,038	5,328	820	4,990
Nonlabor related costs				
Professional liability insurance	2,160		2,069	
Professional development	880		540	
Occupancy	2,000		1,913	
Phone/fax/copying	1,430		1,530	
Travel and per diem	770		718	
Other	392	7,632	930	7,700
Total costs		27,360		26,460
Operating income		$ 5,760		$ 3,240

The housing construction industry illustrates the use of normal costing. Here, materials are purchased at a price known at the purchase date, and labor is paid on an hourly rate basis that is set at the time workers are hired. Actual cost information on both major direct-cost categories can thus be computed as construction takes place. Indirect costs are allocated using a budgeted rate.

Note that normal costing uses a predetermined (budgeted) rate for allocating indirect costs, $45 here. In contrast, actual costing used a $47 rate. Chapter 5 discusses alternative approaches to accounting for these differences when reporting individual job costs and when preparing income statements and balance sheets.

TIME PERIOD USED TO COMPUTE INDIRECT-COST RATES

The indirect-cost rates computed for Lindsay & Associates are based on an annual period. Most companies use 6-month or 12-month periods to compute such rates. Few companies use a weekly or monthly period. Why? There are three main reasons.

1. *The numerator reason (budgeted indirect costs).* The shorter the budget period, the greater the influence of seasonal patterns on the level of costs. For example, if a monthly budget period were used, costs of heating (included in the numerator) would be charged only to winter months. The use of an annual period will incorporate the effect of all four seasons into a single indirect-cost rate.

Levels of total indirect costs are also affected by nonseasonal erratic costs. Examples include costs incurred in a particular month that benefit operations during future months: repairs and maintenance of equipment, professional fees, recruiting expenses, and marketing outlays.

2. *The denominator reason (budgeted quantity of the allocation base).* Another rationale for longer budget periods is the spreading of fixed indirect costs over fluctuating activity. Some indirect costs (for example, supplies) may be variable with respect to the cost-allocation base, whereas other indirect costs are fixed (for example, property taxes and rent).

The nonuniform design of the calendar affects the calculation of monthly indirect-cost rates. The number of Monday-to-Friday workdays in a month varies from 20 to 23 during a year. If separate rates are computed each month, jobs undertaken in February, the shortest month, would bear a greater share of indirect costs (such as depreciation and property taxes) than jobs undertaken in March. Many managers believe such results to be unreasonable. Use of an annual budget period reduces the effect that the number of working days per month has on unit costs.

Consider a professional services firm that has a highly seasonal workload. Many firms that provide tax advice and prepare tax returns experience more than 80% of their workload in the 4 months subsequent to the end of the tax year. Assume the following mix of variable indirect costs (such as phone, fax, and photocopying) and fixed indirect costs (insurance and rent):

	Budgeted Indirect Costs			Budgeted Professional Labor-Hours	Allocation Rate per Professional Labor-Hour
	Variable	Fixed	Total		
High-output month	$40,000	$60,000	$100,000	3,200	$31.25
Low-output month	10,000	60,000	70,000	800	87.50

Because of the fixed costs of $60,000, budgeted monthly indirect-cost rates can vary sizably—from $31.25 per hour to $87.50 per hour in our example. Few managers believe that identical jobs done in different months should be allocated indirect-cost charges per hour that differ so significantly ($87.50 ÷ $31.25 = 280%). For the tax season, management has committed itself to a specific level of capacity far beyond a mere 30 days per month. An average, annualized rate based on the relationship of total annual indirect costs to the total annual level of output will smooth out the effect of monthly variations in output levels.

3. *The cost-benefit reason.* Revising indirect-cost rates takes management effort. The shorter the budget period, the more often managers must reestimate the numerator and the denominator. Most managers believe that a budget period shorter than 6 or 12 months provides few—if any—additional benefits to justify the additional management effort.

EXTENDED NORMAL COSTING

Different organizations design their own variations of normal costing systems. These systems primarily aim at obtaining approximations of actual costs of jobs, but they use average costing rates in an assortment of ways. For instance, in the Lindsay & Associates example, actual direct-labor costs may be difficult to trace to jobs as they are completed. Why? Because actual direct-labor costs may include profit-based bonuses that are only known at the end of the year (a numerator reason). Also, the hours worked each period might vary significantly depending on the number of working days each month and the demand from clients (a denominator reason). To factor bonus payments in the calculation of the direct-labor cost rate, Lindsay may choose to use a twelve-month budgeted direct-cost rate rather than an actual direct-cost rate for assigning direct costs to individual jobs.[2]

An **extended normal costing** (also known as **budgeted costing**) method traces direct costs to a cost object by using the budgeted direct-cost rate(s) times the actual quantity of the direct-cost input and allocates indirect costs based on the budgeted indirect-cost rate(s) times the actual quantity of the cost-allocation base(s). The distinctive feature of extended normal costing is that it uses budgeted rates for both direct costs and indirect costs. Both these rates are calculated at the start of the accounting period.

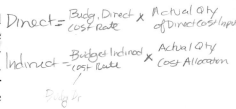

The 19_8 budgeted direct-cost rate for Lindsay & Associates is computed as follows:

$$\text{Budgeted direct-labor cost rate} = \frac{\text{Budgeted total direct-labor costs}}{\text{Budgeted total direct labor-hours to be billed}}$$

$$= \frac{\$14,400,000}{288,000 \text{ hours}} = \$50 \text{ per hour}$$

$$= \$50 \text{ per professional labor-hour}$$

The chapter appendix discusses additional aspects of the budgeted direct labor cost rate calculations.

Under extended normal costing, the 19_8 cost of the Tracy Transport audit is $76,000:

Direct job costs traced	
Professional labor, $50 × 800	$40,000
Indirect job costs allocated	
Audit support, $45 × 800	36,000
	$76,000

The Tracy Transport audit job is finished in March 19_8. Using extended normal costing, Lindsay can compute the $76,000 amount once it knows that 800 professional labor-hours were actually worked on the Tracy audit. This information can be useful when bidding on future audits of Tracy Transport or other similar audits in April 19_8, May 19_8, and so on.

Exhibit 4-4 summarizes the three costing methods described in this chapter. The actual and budgeted rates in Exhibit 4-4 are developed at different points in

[2]Alternatively, as many companies do, Lindsay could simply choose to consider those direct costs, such as bonuses determined only at year-end, as indirect costs to be allocated to jobs under a normal costing system.

> **OBJECTIVE 4**
>
> Distinguish among actual costing, normal costing, and extended normal costing methods

EXHIBIT 4-4
Actual Costing, Normal Costing, and Extended Normal Costing Methods

PANEL A: GENERAL FORMULA

	Actual Costing	Normal Costing	Extended Normal Costing
Direct Costs	Actual direct-cost rate × Actual quantity of direct-cost input	Actual direct-cost rate × Actual quantity of direct-cost input	Budgeted direct-cost rate × Actual quantity of direct-cost input
Indirect Costs	Actual indirect-cost rate × Actual quantity of cost-allocation base	Budgeted indirect-cost rate × Actual quantity of cost-allocation base	Budgeted indirect-cost rate × Actual quantity of cost-allocation base

PANEL B: COSTING OF TRACY TRANSPORT AUDIT JOB

	Actual Costing	Normal Costing	Extended Normal Costing
Direct Costs	$51 × 800 = $40,800	$51 × 800 = $40,800	$50 × 800 = $40,000
Indirect Costs	$47 × 800 = $37,600	$45 × 800 = $36,000	$45 × 800 = $36,000
Total Costs	$78,400	$76,800	$76,000

time. Not surprisingly, they are not the same. For example, the rates used to cost the Tracy Transport audit in 19_8 are

	Actual Rates	Budgeted Rates
Direct-cost rate	$51 per hour	$50 per hour
Indirect-cost rate	$47 per hour	$45 per hour

In practice, costing systems will not always map neatly onto one of the three costing systems described in Exhibit 4-4. For example, an engineering consulting firm may have some actual direct costs traced to jobs as incurred (cost of making blueprints or fees paid to outside experts), other direct costs traced to jobs using a budgeted rate (professional labor costs), and indirect costs allocated to jobs using a budgeted rate (engineering and office support costs).

BROAD AVERAGING VIA PEANUT-BUTTER COSTING APPROACHES

The phrase **peanut-butter costing** describes a costing approach that uses broad averages to uniformly assign (spread or smooth out) the cost of resources to cost objects (such as products, services, or customers) when the individual products, services, or customers in fact use those resources in a nonuniform way.

OBJECTIVE 5

Explain undercosting and overcosting of products

Undercosting and Overcosting

Use of broad averages via a peanut-butter costing approach can lead to undercosting or overcosting of products (services, customers, and so on):

◆ **Product undercosting**—a product consumes a relatively high level of resources but is reported to have a relatively low total cost.

◆ **Product overcosting**—a product consumes a relatively low level of resources but is reported to have a relatively high total cost.

Companies that undercost products may actually make sales that result in losses under the erroneous impression that these sales are profitable. That is, these sales bring in less revenue than the cost of the resources they use. Companies that over-cost products run the risk of losing market share to existing or new competitors. Because these products actually cost less than what is reported to management, the company could cut selling prices to maintain or enhance market shares and still make a profit on each sale.

Product-Cost Cross-Subsidization

Product-cost cross-subsidization means that at least one miscosted product is resulting in the miscosting of other products in the organization. A classic example arises when a cost is uniformly spread (broad averaged or "peanut-buttered") across multiple users without recognition of their different resource demands. Consider the costing of a restaurant bill for four colleagues who meet once a month to discuss business developments. Each diner orders separate entrees, desserts, and drinks. The restaurant bill for the most recent meeting is as follows:

	Entree	Dessert	Drinks	Total
Emma	$11	$ 0	$ 4	$ 15
James	20	8	14	42
Jessica	15	4	8	27
Matthew	14	4	6	24
Total	$60	$16	$32	$108
Average	$15	$ 4	$ 8	$ 27

The $108 total restaurant bill produces a $27 average cost per dinner. This broad-average costing approach treats each diner the same. Emma would probably object to paying $27 because her actual cost is only $15. Indeed, she ordered the lowest-cost entree, had no dessert, and had the lowest drink bill. When costs are averaged across all four diners, both Emma and Matthew are overcosted, James is undercosted, and Jessica is accurately costed.

The restaurant example is both simple and intuitive. The amount of cost cross-subsidization of each diner can be readily computed given that all cost items can be traced as direct costs to each diner. More complex costing issues arise, however, when there are indirect costs. Then resources are used by two or more individual diners. By definition, indirect costs require allocation—for example, the cost of a bottle of wine shared by two or more diners.

We now examine how costing systems can be refined to reduce the miscosting of jobs, products, or customers.

REFINING A COSTING SYSTEM

The costing system for Lindsay & Associates, shown in Exhibit 4-5, Panel A, is based on broad averaging of costs. It has a single direct-cost category and a single indirect-cost pool. Does it provide misleading job cost numbers? The answer depends on whether jobs, services, customers, and so on, are relatively alike (identical, or at least very similar) in the way they use the resources of the organization. If they are not alike, a simple costing system may yield inaccurate cost numbers of jobs, services, customers, and so on. If they are alike, then a simple costing system will suffice for job-costing purposes.

OBJECTIVE 6

Describe three guidelines for refining a costing system

Increasingly, companies are seeking to refine their costing systems. A **refined costing system** is one that often results in a better measure of the nonuniformity in the use of resources by jobs, products, and customers. Increased competition and advances in information technology have accelerated these refinements.

Three guidelines for refining a costing system are

◆ *Guideline 1: Direct-cost tracing.* Classify as many of the total costs as direct costs as is economically feasible.

EXHIBIT 4-5
Alternative Job-Costing Approaches for Lindsay & Associates

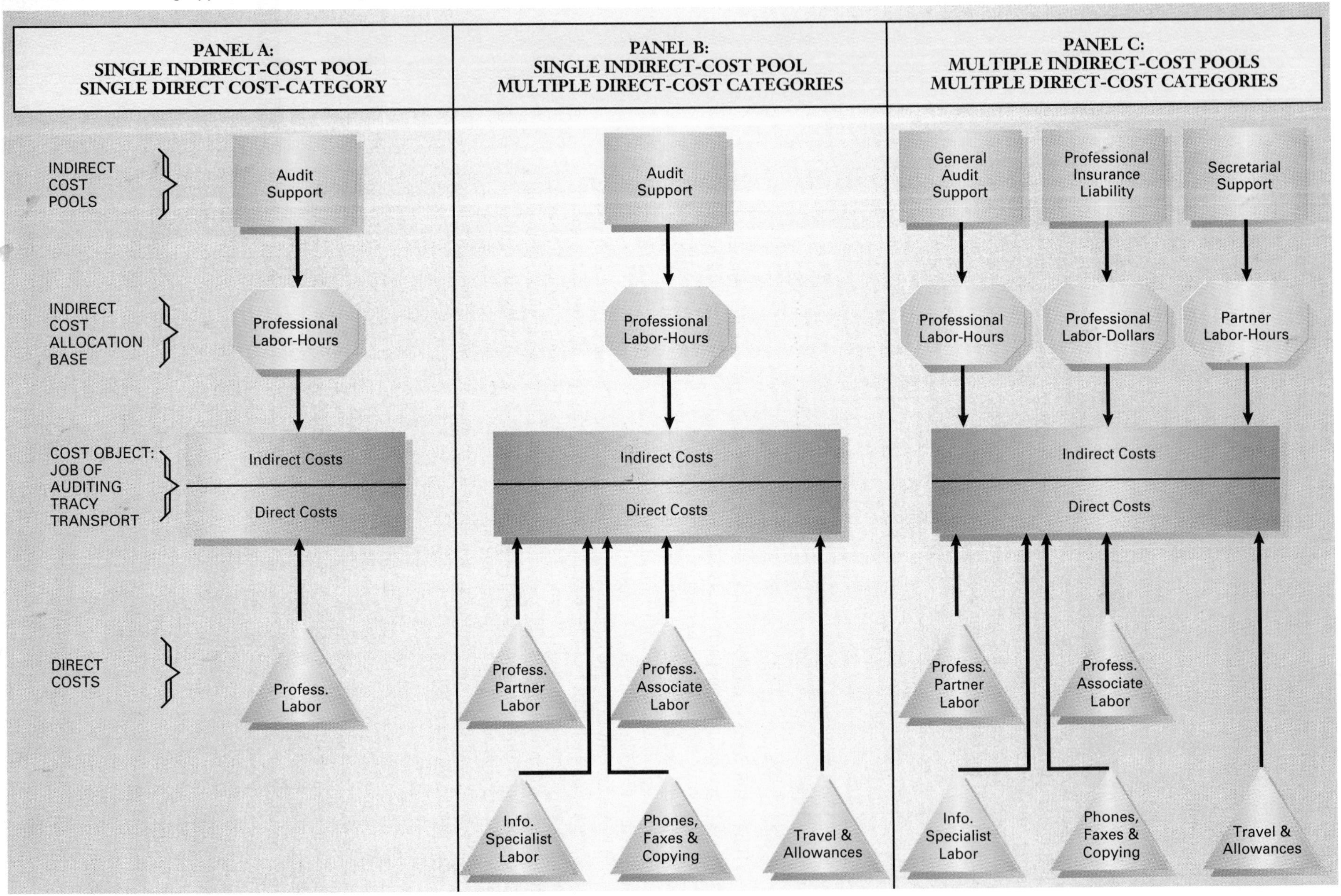
PANEL A:
SINGLE INDIRECT-COST POOL
SINGLE DIRECT COST-CATEGORY
PANEL B:
SINGLE INDIRECT-COST POOL
MULTIPLE DIRECT-COST CATEGORIES
PANEL C:
MULTIPLE INDIRECT-COST POOLS
MULTIPLE DIRECT-COST CATEGORIES
INDIRECT COST POOLS
INDIRECT COST ALLOCATION BASE
COST OBJECT: JOB OF AUDITING TRACY TRANSPORT
DIRECT COSTS
Audit Support
Professional Labor-Hours
Indirect Costs
Direct Costs
Profess. Labor
Audit Support
Professional Labor-Hours
Indirect Costs
Direct Costs
Profess. Partner Labor
Profess. Associate Labor
Info. Specialist Labor
Phones, Faxes & Copying
Travel & Allowances
General Audit Support
Professional Insurance Liability
Secretarial Support
Professional Labor-Hours
Professional Labor-Dollars
Partner Labor-Hours
Indirect Costs
Direct Costs
Profess. Partner Labor
Profess. Associate Labor
Info. Specialist Labor
Phones, Faxes & Copying
Travel & Allowances

- *Guideline 2: Indirect-cost pools.* Expand the number of indirect-cost pools until each of those pools is homogeneous. In a *homogeneous* cost pool, all costs have the same or a similar cause-and-effect or benefits-received relationship with the cost-allocation base; the allocations from this cost pool will not be materially different than allocations from subpools of the cost pool.

- *Guideline 3: Cost-allocation bases.* Identify an appropriate cost-allocation base for each indirect-cost pool. In this chapter we use the cause-and-effect criterion when choosing allocation bases.

COST REFINEMENT IN THE SERVICE SECTOR

Companies in many parts of the service sector are now seeking to refine their costing systems. For example, banks are investing in new costing systems to understand how the costs of their individual products or services differ. The Concepts in Action box (p. 108) discusses this area. We now use the Lindsay & Associates example to illustrate the three guidelines for refining a costing system.

Refinement via Increased Direct-Cost Tracing

Using guideline 1, as many of the total costs as is economically feasible are classified as direct costs. Managers have more confidence in the accuracy of costs traced as direct costs to a job compared to those allocated as indirect costs to the job. Lindsay & Associates examines its activities and concludes that five separate direct-cost categories can be identified. These five categories and their direct-cost rates are

1. Professional partner labor: $100 per partner-hour.
2. Professional associate labor: $40 per associate-hour.
3. Information specialist labor: $35 per specialist-hour.
4. Phone/fax/copying: traced on an as-identified basis, per monthly billings from third parties or internal cost rates.
5. Travel: traced on an as-identified basis, per monthly billings from third parties or internal cost rates.

Lindsay was able to use information in its existing data bases to classify costs in each of these five categories. For example, each auditor has a partner or associate designation. The half-hourly time records for each auditor can be combined with information about their partner/associate status into two separate professional direct-labor categories. (The Problem for Self-Study (pp. 113–114) outlines the computation of the 19_8 direct-cost rates.) Assume that Lindsay uses budgeted direct-cost rates as in an extended normal costing system for the first three direct-cost categories. Why? Because actual cost rates for these categories are not known here until year-end when profit-based bonuses can be determined. In contrast, actual amounts are available for the last two direct-cost categories (phone/fax/copying and travel) on a monthly basis and Lindsay uses these actual amounts in its refined costing system.

An overview of these direct-cost refinements is shown in Exhibit 4-5, Panel B. Having professional partner labor and professional associate labor as separate direct-cost pools recognizes the different total compensation costs of partners and associates; partners average $160,000 total annual compensation, while associates average $64,000 total annual compensation. With professional partners and professional associates as separate direct-cost pools, audit jobs that have the same total professional labor time but different mixes of partner and associate time will be costed differently. Direct-cost categories 3–5 were previously included as indirect costs.

Why might the costing system in Panel B of Exhibit 4-5 provide more accurate job costs than the one in Panel A? The Panel A costing system assumes similarity in the way all jobs use the various resources at Lindsay. It assumes that

1. All jobs use the same mix of partner time and associate time.
2. All jobs use the items of indirect costs (including office staff; information systems; phone, fax, and copy machines; and travel) in the same proportion.

On the basis of interviews with its personnel and analysis of its costing records, Lindsay concludes that neither assumption is valid. The costing system in Exhibit 4-5, Panel B, relaxes both assumptions. Under this system, jobs that differ significantly in their use of resources will be costed differently.

Refinement via Increased Number of Indirect-Cost Pools and Cost Drivers

The job-costing systems in both Panels A and B of Exhibit 4-5 have a single indirect-cost pool. Guideline 2 for refining a costing system is to expand the number of indirect-cost pools until each of those pools is homogeneous. Use of a single indirect-cost pool implicitly assumes that all indirect costs have a single cost driver that is used as the allocation base. After interviews with its professional staff, Lindsay concludes that the following three indirect-cost pools provide increased accuracy in job costing:

Indirect-Cost Pool	Allocation Base
1. General audit support	$25 per professional labor-hour (Same rate for partners and associates)
2. Professional liability insurance	15% of professional labor compensation
3. Secretarial support	$18 per professional partner labor-hour (as in most audit firms, partners have secretaries, while associates do not)

The Problem for Self-Study (pp. 113–114) gives details on the computation of these three indirect-cost rates. The three indirect-cost pools represent separate activity areas whose costs cannot be directly traced to individual audit jobs in an economically feasible way.

The use of three indirect-cost pools results in different job costs when audit jobs utilize support resources differently. For example, audit jobs with the same number of professional labor-hours but with a different number of partner labor-hours will now be costed differently in the refined costing system. Exhibit 4-5, Panel C, presents the overview of this further refined job-costing system. It illustrates the use of different allocation bases for each of the three indirect-cost pools (guideline 3). For example, indirect costs for secretarial support are allocated using partner labor-hours, while general audit support costs are allocated using professional labor-hours.

Exhibit 4-6 shows how Lindsay's refined costing system (shown in Panel C of Exhibit 4-5) can be used to calculate the cost of the Tracy Transport audit as $67,060. Lindsay's management believes this $67,060 cost figure is a more accurate estimate of the resources it uses on the audit than the $76,000 estimate, for example, from the extended normal costing system discussed earlier in this chapter. For example, the Tracy Transport audit actually uses a ratio of 1 partner-hour for every 9 associate-hours. Under the costing system of Panel A of Exhibit 4-5, it was assumed that all audit jobs, including Tracy Transport, used the firmwide ratio of 1 partner-hour for every 5 associate-hours (based on the ratio of 30 partners to 150 associates). Under the new system (Panel C), Lindsay can use the more precise 1 to 9 ratio. The costing format in Exhibit 4-6 is sometimes described as *menu-based costing*, where the direct-cost categories and the indirect-cost pools represent separate items on a restaurant menu. Individual jobs are costed according to what each job orders from the menu.

The refined costing system enables Lindsay & Associates to respond to competitive challenges in a more informed way. Assume that a competing firm (Singleton & Partners) had bid $74,000 for the 19_8 audit of Tracy Transport to be done in 19_9. Using the Panel A system, Lindsay would conclude that it could not quote below $74,000 and cover its $76,000 budgeted cost. With the defined system in Panel C, Lindsay could quote below $74,000 and cover its $67,060 cost plus show a profit.

EXHIBIT 4-6

Job Costing of Tracy Transport Audit Using Multiple Direct-Cost Categories and Multiple Indirect-Cost Pools

Direct costs	
Professional partner labor, $100 × 80	$ 8,000
Professional associate labor, $40 × 720	28,800
Information specialist labor, $35 × 40	1,400
Phone/fax/copying (as identified with this job)	800
Travel and per diem (as identified with this job)	1,100
	40,100
Indirect costs	
General audit support, $25 × 800	20,000
Professional liability insurance $36,800 × 0.15	5,520
Secretarial support, $18 × 80	1,440
	26,960
Total costs	$67,060

ACTIVITY-BASED COSTING IN MERCHANDISING

A specific approach to refining a costing system is **activity-based costing (ABC)**. It focuses on activities as the fundamental cost objects. An **activity** is an event, task, or unit of work with a specified purpose. ABC uses the cost of these activities as the basis for assigning costs to other cost objects such as products, services, or customers.

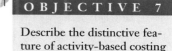

OBJECTIVE 7

Describe the distinctive feature of activity-based costing

ABC uses the cost-driver notion when deciding how many indirect-cost pools to use and the preferred allocation base for each indirect-cost pool.

We now consider a retail application of ABC where a key issue is the profitability (revenues minus costs assigned for each product) of individual products or product lines. A **product line** is a grouping of similar products. For example, the soft-drink product line at a supermarket (a retailer) would include Coca-Cola, Pepsi, and other nonalcoholic beverage products.

For its Memphis store, Family Supermarkets (FS) used a costing system that had a single direct-cost category (goods purchased for sale) and a single indirect-cost category (store support). Store support costs were allocated to products at the rate of 30% of the cost of goods sold. For example, a coffee product costing $6.30 is allocated an indirect-cost charge of $1.89 ($6.30 × 0.30). Exhibit 4-7, Panel A, presents a product-line profitability report from the costing system. A costing overview of the system is shown in Panel B. FS's cost of goods sold makes up 76.92% of total costs ($100,000 ÷ $130,000). This high percentage is typical of many companies in the merchandising sector. The ranking of product lines on the basis of the percentage of operating income to revenues is (1) fresh produce (7.17%); (2) packaged food (3.30%); and (3) soft drinks (1.70%).

EXHIBIT 4-7
Product-Line Profitability at Family Supermarkets with Previous Costing System

PANEL A: MONTHLY PROFITABILITY REPORT FOR DECEMBER 19_7 (IN THOUSANDS)

	Soft Drinks	Fresh Produce	Packaged Food	Total
Revenues	$26,450	$70,020	$40,330	$136,800
Costs				
Cost of goods sold	20,000	50,000	30,000	100,000
Store support	6,000	15,000	9,000	30,000
Total costs	26,000	65,000	39,000	130,000
Operating income	$ 450	$ 5,020	$ 1,330	$ 6,800
Operating income ÷ Revenues	1.70%	7.17%	3.30%	4.97%

PANEL B: JOB-COSTING OVERVIEW

FS has decided to increase the size of its Memphis store. It seeks accurate information about the profitability of individual product lines. It is skeptical about the accuracy of the existing product-line profitability numbers because they are based on broad averaging of store support costs. After observing operations at the Memphis store, its managers conclude that individual product lines differ greatly in their use of FS's support resources.

Managers then decide to introduce an ABC approach to product-line costing. After analyzing its operations and its information systems, they make the following refinements to its costing system:

Guideline 1. Direct-Cost Tracing FS adds an extra direct-cost category—bottle returns. This cost category only applies to the soft-drink product line. It was previously included in the store-support indirect-cost pool.

Guidelines 2 and 3. Indirect-Cost Pools and Cost-Allocation Bases Cost pools representing four separate activity areas were chosen to replace the single store-support indirect-cost pool. Cost drivers are identified and then used as cost-allocation bases.

OBJECTIVE 8

Prepare product-line profitability reports for companies in the merchandising sector

Banks End the "Free Lunch" for Many Services

For many years, retail banks provided their customers a wide range of "free" services. A customer who made a $100 minimum deposit received "free" checking, "free" inquiries about past checks written, "free" money orders, "free" drafts in foreign currencies, and so on. But as a famous economist (Milton Friedman) observed, "there is no such thing as a free lunch." What was occurring was cross-subsidization.

A major source of profitability in retail banks is the interest rate spread (the difference between the rate at which a bank lends or invests money and the rate it pays its depositors). Banks used this interest rate spread to cover the costs of the many "free" services it provided customers. Recently, banks began using activity-based costing (ABC) to determine the costs of their many individual services. This involved examining how each service (such as a checking account) used the resources of the bank. These ABC studies found banks have been losing money on customers who hold small balances and make frequent use of the many "free" services. In contrast, customers holding large balances and making limited use of the "free" services were highly profitable to banks. These customers were cross-subsidizing those with small balance accounts. This situation did not escape the attention of banks.

Many banks responded to increased competition by instituting a detailed set of charges. Consider the following charges by Wells Fargo Bank:

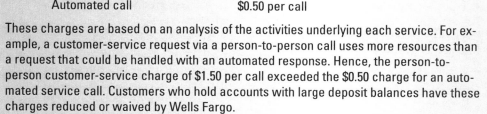

◆ Check deposits	$3 per deposit
◆ Foreign check deposits	$5 per deposit
◆ Special statement requests	$4 per request
◆ Check stop-payment request	$10 per request
◆ 24-hour customer service	
Person-to-person call	$1.50 per call
Automated call	$0.50 per call

These charges are based on an analysis of the activities underlying each service. For example, a customer-service request via a person-to-person call uses more resources than a request that could be handled with an automated response. Hence, the person-to-person customer-service charge of $1.50 per call exceeded the $0.50 charge for an automated service call. Customers who hold accounts with large deposit balances have these charges reduced or waived by Wells Fargo.

Not surprisingly, such bank charges have attracted much attention. Consumer advocacy groups typically express outrage. One group argued that the charge "will particularly disadvantage those groups who can least afford it—namely, older persons, kids, and the poor." In contrast, a management consultant called it "a bold move. They are telling the public what the cost of their interactions will be."

Are there limitations on the extent to which banks are willing to charge for specific services? Yes, for example, ABC studies have documented the costs of having toll-free complaint "hot-lines." However, (to date) banks have refrained from instituting a charge for using these hot-lines. Further, some banks waive customer-service call charges if it is determined that the bank did not deliver on a promised set of commitments.

Source: Conversations with executives implementing activity-based costing at several banks.

1. *Ordering* covers purchasing activities. The cost driver is the number of purchase orders. The 19_7 actual cost rate is $100 per order.
2. *Delivery* covers the physical delivery and receipt of merchandise. The cost driver is the number of deliveries. The 19_7 actual cost rate is $80 per delivery.
3. *Shelf-stocking* covers the stocking of merchandise on store shelves and the ongoing restocking. The cost driver is hours of shelf-stocking time. The 19_7 actual cost rate is $20 per hour.
4. *Customer support* covers assistance provided to customers, including check-out and bagging. The cost driver is the number of items sold. The 19_7 actual cost rate is $0.20 per item sold.

Operating personnel at FS provided the following data for December 19_7:

Activity Area	Cost-Allocation Base	Amount of Driver Used		
		Soft Drinks	Fresh Produce	Packaged Food
Ordering	$100 per purchase order	12	28	12
Delivery	$80 per delivery	10	73	22
Shelf-stocking	$20 per hour	18	180	90
Customer support	$0.20 per item sold	4,200	36,800	10,200

Exhibit 4-8, Panel A, presents a product-line profitability report using the ABC system. A costing overview of the ABC system is shown in Panel B. Managers believe the activity-based system is more credible than the previous system. It better distinguishes the different types of activities at FS. It also better tracks how individual product lines use their resources. Rankings of relative profitability (the percentage of operating income to revenues) of the three product lines under the previous costing system and under the ABC system are as follows:

Previous Costing System		ABC System	
1. Fresh produce	7.17%	1. Soft drinks	10.77%
2. Packaged food	3.30	2. Packaged food	8.75
3. Soft drinks	1.70	3. Fresh produce	0.60

The percentage revenue, cost of goods sold, and activity costs for each product line are as follows:

	Soft Drinks	Fresh Produce	Packaged Food
Revenue	19.34%	51.18%	29.48%
Cost of goods sold	20.00	50.00	30.00
Activity areas			
Ordering	23.08	53.84	27.08
Delivery	9.53	69.52	20.95
Shelf-stocking	6.25	62.50	31.25
Customer support	8.20	71.88	19.92

Soft drinks consume less of all resources. Soft drinks have fewer deliveries and require less shelf-stocking than does either fresh produce or packaged food. Most major soft-drink suppliers deliver merchandise to the store shelves and stock the shelves themselves. In contrast, the fresh produce area has the most deliveries and consumes a large percentage of shelf-stocking time. It also has the highest number of individual sales items. The previous costing system assumed that each product line used the resources in each activity area in the same ratio as their respective individual cost of goods sold to total cost of goods sold. Clearly, this assumption was inappropriate. The previous costing system was a classic example of broad averaging via peanut-butter costing.

EXHIBIT 4-8
Product-Line Profitability at Family Supermarkets with Activity-Based Costing

PANEL A: MONTHLY PROFITABILITY REPORT FOR DECEMBER 19_7 (IN THOUSANDS)

	Soft Drinks	Fresh Produce	Packaged Food	Total
Revenues	$26,450	$70,020	$40,330	$136,800
Costs				
Cost of goods sold	20,000	50,000	30,000	100,000
Bottle returns	400	0	0	400
Ordering	1,200	2,800	1,200	5,200
Delivery	800	5,840	1,760	8,400
Shelf-stocking	360	3,600	1,800	5,760
Customer support	840	7,360	2,040	10,240
Total costs	23,600	69,600	36,800	130,000
Operating income	$ 2,850	$ 420	$ 3,530	$ 6,800
Operating income ÷ Revenues	10.77%	0.60%	8.75%	4.97%

PANEL B: JOB-COSTING OVERVIEW

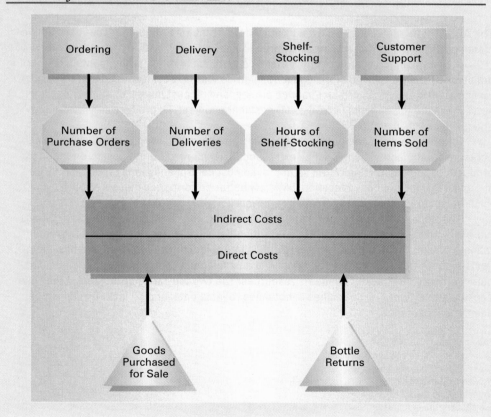

FS managers can use the ABC numbers to guide decisions on how to allocate the planned increase in floor space. An increase in the percentage of space allocated to soft drinks is warranted. Note, however, that ABC numbers should be but one input into decisions about shelf space allocation. FS may have minimum limits on the shelf space allocated to fresh produce because of shoppers' expectations that supermarkets will carry merchandise from this product line.

Growing Interest in Activity-Based Costing

Activity-based costing is being implemented by a growing number of companies around the globe. One study* of 162 U.S.-based companies (including 29 service-sector implementations) reported the following ranking of the primary applications: (1) product/service costing, (2) cost reduction, and (3) process improvement. The rankings for the areas where there were "significant" or "very significant" changes in decisions were (1) pricing strategy, (2) processes, and (3) product mix.

Among Canadian companies, a survey[†] indicates that 14% of the interviewed businesses have implemented ABC, and another 15% are now considering changing to it. What attracts Canadian firms to ABC?

More accurate cost information for product pricing	61%
More accurate profit analysis	61
By product	22
By customer	20
By process	24
By department	43
Improved performance measures	43
Improved insight into cost causation	37

The ABC system replaced the existing system for 24% of the Canadian respondents implementing ABC, while it was a supplementary (off-line) system for 76%.

A United Kingdom survey[‡] found that "just under 20% of 251 respondents had adopted ABC." The ranking of the application areas was (1) cost management, (2) performance measurement, (3) product/service pricing, and (4) cost modeling. A New Zealand survey[§] ranked the benefits of ABC as (1) cost management, (2) product/service pricing, and (3) inventory valuation.

A survey[#] of Irish companies that had implemented ABC reported the following percentages for the actual benefits they experienced: (1) more accurate cost information for product costing and pricing (71%); (2) improved cost control and management (66%); (3) improved insight into cost causation (58%); (4) better performance measures (46%); and (5) more accurate customer profitability analysis (25%).

The Canadian survey reported that the two most common implementation problems were difficulties in defining activities, and difficulties in selecting cost drivers. Implementation problems in the Irish survey were difficulties in identifying activities and assigning costs to those pools; difficulties in identifying and selecting cost drivers; inadequate computer software; and lack of adequate resources. The two top-ranked problems in the New Zealand survey were (1) difficulties in obtaining reliable data, and (2) lack of middle management acceptance.

---

*Adapted from APQC/CAM-I.
[†]Adapted from Armitage and Nicholson.
[‡]Adapted from Innes and Mitchell.
[§]Adapted from Cotton.
[#]Adapted from Clarke.
Full citations are in Appendix A.

Pricing decisions can also be made in a more informed way with the ABC information. For example, suppose a competitor announces a 5% reduction in soft-drink prices. Given the 10.77% margin FS currently earns on its soft-drink product line, it has flexibility to reduce prices and still make a profit on this product line. In contrast, the previous costing system erroneously implied that soft drinks only had a 1.70% margin, leaving little room to counter a competitor's pricing initiatives.

PROBLEM

Lindsay & Associates is refining its existing costing system, which has a single direct-cost pool (professional labor) and a single indirect-cost pool (audit support). It conducts extensive interviews with personnel at all levels and examines past audit working papers. It also notes that recent advances in information-gathering technology (such as codes on its phone, fax, and copy machines) enable it to trace to jobs some items that currently are classified as indirect costs.

The five direct-cost categories in its refined costing system are

◆ Professional partner labor. Average total annual compensation of $160,000 for each of 30 partners, each of whom has 1,600 hours of budgeted billable time.

◆ Professional associate labor. Average total annual compensation of $64,000 for each of 150 associates, each of whom has 1,600 hours of budgeted billable time.

◆ Information specialist labor. Average total annual compensation of $56,000 for each of 18 specialists, each of whom has 1,600 hours of budgeted billable time.

◆ Phone/fax/copying. Costs will be on an as-identified basis per monthly bills from third parties or internal cost rates.

◆ Travel and allowances. Costs will be on an as-identified basis per monthly bills from third parties or internal cost rates.

The three indirect-cost pools and their chosen allocation bases in the refined costing system are

◆ General audit support (Indirect I). The 19_8 budgeted amount is $7,200,000 as shown in column 5 of Exhibit 4-9. The allocation base is budgeted professional labor-hours.

◆ Professional liability insurance (Indirect II). The 19_8 budgeted amount is $2,160,000 as shown in column 6 of Exhibit 4-9. The allocation base is budgeted professional labor-dollars.

◆ Secretarial support (Indirect III). The 19_8 budgeted amount is $864,000, as shown in column 7 of Exhibit 4-9. The allocation base is budgeted partner labor-hours.

REQUIRED

1. Compute the budgeted 19_8 direct-cost rate per hour for (a) professional partner labor, (b) professional associate labor, and (c) information specialist labor.
2. Compute the budgeted 19_8 indirect-cost rate per unit of the allocation base for (a) general audit support, (b) professional liability insurance, and (c) secretarial support.

SOLUTION

1. The formula for computing the 19_8 budgeted direct labor cost rates is

$$\text{Budgeted direct-cost rate} = \frac{\text{Budgeted total setup time for machines}}{\text{Budgeted total manufacturing time}}$$

Lindsay uses budgeted billable time for clients as its denominator.

a. Professional partner labor: $\dfrac{\$160,000 \times 30}{1,600 \times 30} = \$100$ per hour

b. Professional associate labor: $\dfrac{\$64,000 \times 150}{1,600 \times 150} = \$40$ per hour

c. Information specialist labor: $\dfrac{\$56,000 \times 18}{1,600 \times 18} = \$35$ per hour

Column (4) of Exhibit 4-9 shows how $1,008,000 of "other labor-related costs" and $1,728,000 of "nonlabor-related costs" are now direct-cost items in the refined costing system. In the previous costing system, these costs were classified as indirect costs.

2. The formula for computing the 19_8 budgeted indirect-cost rates is

$$\text{Budgeted indirect-cost rate} = \frac{\text{Budgeted total costs in indirect-cost pool}}{\text{Budgeted total quantity of cost-allocation base}}$$

a. General audit support:

$$\frac{\$7,200,000}{288,000 \text{ hours}} = \$25 \text{ per professional labor-hour}$$

b. Professional liability insurance:

$$\frac{\$2,160,000}{\$14,400,000} = 15\% \text{ of professional labor compensation}$$

c. Secretarial support:

$$\frac{\$864,000}{48,000 \text{ hours}} = \$18 \text{ per partner-hour}$$

EXHIBIT 4-9
Budgeted Costing Worksheet for Previous and Refined Costing System of Lindsay & Associates (in thousands)

Cost Line Items (1)	Previous Costing System		Refined Costing System			
					Indirect	
				I	II	III
	Direct (2)	Indirect (3)	Direct (4)	(5)	(6)	(7)
Professional labor costs						
Partners	$14,400	$ 0	$ 4,800	$ 0	$ 0	$ 0
Associates			9,600	0	0	0
Total	14,400	0	14,400	0	0	0
Other labor-related costs						
Office staff	0	2,030	0	1,166	0	864
Information specialists	0	1,008	1,008	0	0	0
Administrative	0	1,252	0	1,252	0	0
Other	0	1,038	0	1,038	0	0
Total	0	5,328	1,008	3,456	0	864
Nonlabor-related costs						
Professional insurance	0	2,160	0	0	2,160	0
Professional liability development	0	880	0	880	0	0
Occupancy	0	2,000	0	2,000	0	0
Phone/fax/copying	0	1,430	1,070	360	0	0
Travel and allowances	0	770	658	112	0	0
Other	0	392	0	392	0	0
Total	0	7,632	1,728	3,744	2,160	0
Total operating costs	$14,400	$12,960	$17,136	$7,200	$2,160	$864

SUMMARY

The following points are linked to the chapter's learning objectives.

1. The building blocks of a costing system are cost object, direct costs, indirect costs, cost pool, and cost-allocation base. Costing-system overview diagrams present

these concepts in a systematic way. Costing systems aim to report cost numbers that reflect the way that chosen cost objects (such as products, services, or customers) use the resources of an organization.

2. Job-costing systems assign costs to a distinct unit of a product or service. In contrast, process-costing systems assign costs to masses of similar units and compute unit costs on an average basis. These two costing systems are best viewed as opposite ends of a continuum. The costing systems of many companies combine some elements of both job costing and process costing.

3. A general approach to job costing involves identifying (a) the job, (b) the direct-cost categories, (c) the indirect-cost categories, (d) the cost-allocation bases, (e) the cost-allocation rates, and (f) adding all direct and indirect costs.

4. Actual costing, normal costing, and extended normal costing differ in their use of actual or budgeted direct- or indirect-cost rates.

	Actual Costing	Normal Costing	Extended Normal Costing
Direct-cost rates	Actual rates	Actual rates	Budgeted rates
Indirect-cost rates	Actual rates	Budgeted rates	Budgeted rates

All three methods use actual quantities of direct-cost inputs and actual quantities of the allocation bases for indirect costs.

5. Product undercosting (or overcosting) occurs when a product or service consumes a relatively high (low) level of resources, but is reported to have a relatively low (high) cost. Peanut-butter costing, a common cause of under- or overcosting, is the result of using broad averages that uniformly assign (spread) the cost of resources to products when the individual products use those resources in a nonuniform way. Product-cost cross-subsidization exists when one or more undercosted (overcosted) products results in one or more other products being overcosted (undercosted).

6. Refining a costing system means making changes that result in cost numbers that better measure the way cost objects (such as jobs) differentially use the resources of the organization. These changes can require additional direct-cost tracing, the choice of more indirect-cost pools, or the use of different cost-allocation bases.

7. Many organizations seeking to refine their costing systems are giving serious consideration to activity-based costing (ABC). A distinctive feature of ABC is the focus on activities as the fundamental cost objects. The costs of these activities are then assigned to other cost objects such as products, services, or customers.

8. A product line is a grouping of similar products. Product profitability statements report the profitability (revenue minus costs assigned to each product) of individual products or product lines. Cost of goods purchased for sale typically is the largest single cost item for companies in the merchandising sector.

APPENDIX: COMPUTATION OF DIRECT LABOR COST RATES

Budgeted direct labor-cost rates can be computed in several ways. They are affected by various choices, such as, number of hours in the denominator. Assume that each professional at Lindsay has 2,000 hours of time available per year, budgeted as follows:

1. Budgeted billable time for clients	1,600 hours
2. Budgeted vacation/sick leave	160 hours
3. Budgeted professional and practice development	240 hours
4. Budgeted unbillable time due to lack of demand	0 hours
Budgeted available time	2,000 hours

For simplicity, we assume there is full demand for the 1,600 hours of billable time of each professional. We defer issues of unused capacity to Chapter 14. Each professional is budgeted to have a total compensation of $80,000 per year (which includes salary, bonus, and fringe benefits).

Different denominators for the professional labor rate computation will affect the budgeted direct-labor cost rate. Consider two alternative approaches:

1. *Billable time as denominator*—1,600 hours, which yields a budgeted direct-labor cost rate of $50 per professional labor-hour ($80,000 ÷ 1,600 hours = $50). The numerator of $80,000 includes compensation earned when the employee is on vacation/sick leave or engaged in professional and practice development. By excluding the 400 (160 + 240) hours for these items from the denominator, every $1 of budgeted direct-labor cost billed to a job implicitly will include an amount to recoup vacation, sick leave, and professional and practice development costs, as well as an amount to recoup the cost of the hours spent on the job. This approach results in the total compensation amount being billed as a direct-labor cost of jobs worked on in the period (assuming full demand for the available billable time). For simplicity, the Lindsay example used this approach. Hence, job costs bore all professional labor costs as direct costs.

2. *Available time as denominator*—2,000 hours, which yields a budgeted direct-cost rate of $40 per professional labor-hour ($80,000 ÷ 2,000 hours = $40). This approach results in the costs of vacation/sick leave component and the professional development component, each having $40 rates per hour being excluded from the direct professional labor rate. Only $64,000 ($40 × 1,600 hours) of the $80,000 total compensation is budgeted to be charged as a direct-labor cost of jobs worked on during the period. The employee compensation for vacation/sick leave and professional or practice development is accounted for as an indirect or overhead cost.

This second approach explicitly recognizes that professional labor surely cannot spend all its time directly on clients jobs. In particular, time must be devoted to other activities such as trying to attract new clients (practice development) and professional training. Total professional compensation is divided into these direct- and indirect-cost categories and the costs of each indirect activity, such as taking a course in new tax laws, are clearly identified (using the $40 rate).

Under either of these two approaches, all professional labor costs are assigned to the various jobs. Under the first approach, all professional labor would be traced as direct-labor costs exclusively. Under the second approach, some professional labor would be allocated as an indirect cost. Moreover, the second approach would systematically tabulate such indirect activities as marketing or professional development—information valuable for the overall management of the firm.

TERMS TO LEARN

This chapter and the Glossary at the end of this book contain definitions of the following important terms:

activity (p. 107)
activity-based costing (ABC) (107)
actual costing (96)
budgeted costing (101)
cost-allocation base (94)
cost pool (94)
extended normal costing (101)
job-costing system (95)
normal costing (98)

peanut-butter costing (102)
process-costing system (95)
product-cost cross-subsidization (103)
product line (107)
product overcosting (102)
product undercosting (102)
refined costing system (103)
source documents (97)

QUESTIONS

4-1 Define cost pool, cost tracing, cost allocation, and cost allocation base.

4-2 "In the production of services, direct materials are usually the major cost." Is this quote accurate? Explain.

4-3 How does a job-costing system differ from a process-costing system?

4-4 Why might an advertising agency use job costing for an advertising campaign for Pepsi while a bank uses process costing for the cost of checking account withdrawals?

4-5 Distinguish among actual costing, normal costing, and extended normal costing.

4-6 Describe two ways in which an accounting firm may use job cost information.

4-7 When might a service company use budgeted costs rather than actual costs to compute direct-labor rates?

4-8 Give two reasons why most organizations use a 6-month or annual period rather than a weekly or monthly period to compute budgeted indirect-cost rates.

4-9 What is the main concern about source documents of the job cost records of accounting and law firms?

4-10 Define peanut-butter costing, and explain how managers can determine whether it occurs with their costing system.

4-11 Why should managers worry about product over- or undercosting?

4-12 What is costing system refinement? Describe three guidelines for such refinement.

4-13 What is an activity-based approach to designing a costing system?

4-14 "Increasing the number of indirect-cost pools is guaranteed to sizably increase the accuracy of product, service, or customer costs." Do you agree? Why?

4-15 The controller of a retailer has just had a $50,000 request to implement an activity-based costing system quickly turned down. A senior vice president, in rejecting the request noted, "Given a choice, I will always prefer a $50,000 investment in improving things a customer sees or experiences, such as our shelves or our store layout. How does a customer benefit by our spending $50,000 on a supposedly better accounting system?" How should the controller respond?

EXERCISES

4-16 Job costing; fill in the blanks. McBain is a management consulting firm. Its job-costing system has a single direct-cost category (consulting labor) and a single indirect-cost pool (consulting support). Consulting support is allocated to individual jobs using actual consulting labor-hours worked on a job. It is currently examining the actual, normal, and extended normal costs of a 19_8 strategy review job for Hogsbreath Cafe that required 70 actual hours of consulting labor. The internal cost expert decides to test your understanding of cost concepts.

REQUIRED

1. Fill in the blanks for the Hogsbreath 19_8 job:

	Actual Costing		Normal Costing		Extended Normal Costing	
Direct job costs	$?	($55 × ?)	$?	($? × ?)	$?	($? × ?)
Indirect job costs	2,660	($? × ?)	2,800	($? × 70)	?	($? × ?)
Total job costs	$?		$?		$7,000	

2. Fill in the blanks for McBain for 19_8:

	Budgeted Amounts for 19_8	Actual Amounts for 19_8
Consulting labor compensation	?	?
Consulting labor-hours	18,000 hours	?
Consulting support costs	?	$798,000

4-17 Job costing; actual, normal, and extended normal. Scandinavian Auto Services (SAS) services and repairs Volvo cars. It employs eight car technicians. SAS prides itself on quick turnaround of cars being serviced. It announced in December 19_6 that in 19_7 it will charge each customer a $100 per hour rate for technician time spent on a job plus a charge at 20% over cost for parts and materials. The $100 per hour charge to customers incorporates (a) technician compensation, (b) the costs of all the support facilities that are allocated to jobs on the basis of actual technician time spent on each job, and (c) a profit component on the job.

Budgeted and actual data for 19_7 are as follows:

Budget for 19_7

Auto-technician compensation	$480,000
Service-area support costs	$560,000
Technician hours billed to jobs	16,000 hours

Actual results for 19_7

Service-area support costs	$512,000
Technician hours billed to jobs	12,800 hours

In April 19_7, the government introduced a 100% increase in duties on imported cars. This change led to a reduction in Volvos being serviced by SAS in the remainder of 19_7. During May 19_7, the actual hourly auto technician compensation was $36.

REQUIRED

An auto repair job done in May 19_7 took 2.5 hours and required parts and materials for which the customer was charged $150.00 (includes 20% charge over cost).

1. Identify the direct-cost rate per auto-technician hour and the indirect-cost rate per auto-technician that SAS would use to cost jobs done in May 19_7 under (a) actual costing, (b) normal costing, and (c) extended normal costing.

2. Compute the 19_7 job cost using (a) actual costing, (b) normal costing, and (c) extended normal costing. Explain any differences. Why might a customer of SAS object to the job being charged at an agreed-upon markup (say 25%) tied to actual cost rates?

4-18 Job costing; actual, normal, and extended normal costing. Chirac & Partners is a Quebec-based public accounting partnership specializing in audit services. Its job-costing system has a single direct-cost category (professional labor) and a single indirect-cost pool (audit support, which contains all the costs in the Audit Support Department). Audit support costs are allocated to individual jobs using actual professional labor-hours. Chirac & Partners employs ten professionals who are involved in their auditing services.

Budgeted and actual amounts for 19_8 are as follows:

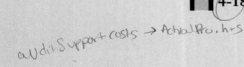

audit Support costs → Actual Pro. hrs

Budget for 19_8

Professional labor compensation	$960,000
Audit Support Department costs	$720,000
Professional labor-hours billed to clients	16,000 hours

Actual Results for 19_8

Audit Support Department costs	$744,000
Professional labor-hours billed to clients	15,500 hours

Actual professional labor cost rate is $58 per hour.

1. Identify the <u>direct-cost</u> rate per <u>professional labor-hour</u> and <u>the indirect-cost rate per professional labor-hour</u> for 19_8 under (a) actual costing, (b) normal costing, and (c) extended normal costing.

2. The audit of the Montreal Expos done in 19_8 was budgeted to take 110 hours of professional labor time. The actual professional labor time on the audit was 120 hours. Compute the 19_8 job cost using (a) actual costing, (b) normal costing, and (c) extended normal costing. Explain any differences.

4-19 Job costing; actual, normal, and extended normal costing. Vista Group provides architectural services for residential and business clients. It employs 25 professionals. Its job-costing system has a single direct-cost category (professional labor) and a single indirect-cost pool (client support, which contains all the costs in the Client Support Department). Client support costs are allocated to individual jobs using actual professional labor-hours.

Budgeted and actual amounts for 19_8 are as follows:

Budget for 19_8

Professional labor compensation	$4,000,000
Client Support Department costs	$2,600,000
Professional labor-hours billed to clients	40,000 hours

Actual Results for 19_8

Client Support Department costs	$2,436,000
Professional labor-hours billed to clients	42,000 hours
Actual professional labor cost rate is $110 per hour.	

REQUIRED

1. Identify the direct-cost rate per professional labor-hour and the indirect-cost rate per professional labor-hour for 19_8 under (a) actual costing, (b) normal costing, and (c) extended normal costing.

2. In 19_8, the Vista Group designed a new retirement village in Tucson, Arizona, for Carefree Years, Inc. Vista budgeted to spend 1,500 professional labor-hours on the project. Actual professional labor-hours spent were 1,720. Compute the job cost of the Carefree Years project using (a) actual costing, (b) normal costing, and (c) extended normal costing. Explain any differences.

4-20 Computing indirect-cost rates, job costing. Mike Rotundo, the president of Tax Assist, is examining alternative ways to compute indirect-cost rates. He collects the following information from the budget for 19_8:

◆ Budgeted variable indirect costs: $10 per hour of professional labor time
◆ Budgeted fixed indirect costs: $50,000 per month

The budgeted billable professional labor-hours per quarter are

January–March	20,000 hours
April–June	10,000 hours
July–September	4,000 hours
October–December	6,000 hours

Rotundo pays all tax professionals employed by Tax Assist on an hourly basis ($30 per hour, including all fringe benefits).

Tax Assist's job-costing system has a single direct-cost category (professional labor at $30 per hour) and a single indirect-cost pool (office support that is allocated using professional labor-hours).

Tax Assist charges clients $65 per professional labor-hour.

REQUIRED

1. Compute budgeted indirect-cost rates per professional labor-hour using:

a. Quarterly budgeted billable hours as the denominator

b. Annual budgeted billable hours as the denominator

2. Compute the operating income for the following four customers using:

   a. Quarterly-based indirect-cost rates

   b. An annual indirect-cost rate

     ◆ Stan Hansen: 10 hours in February

     ◆ Lelani Kai: 6 hours in March and 4 hours in April

     ◆ Ken Patera: 4 hours in June and 6 hours in August

     ◆ Evelyn Stevens: 5 hours in January, 2 hours in September, and 3 hours in November

3. Comment on your results in requirement 2.

4-21 Job costing, consulting firm. Taylor & Associates, a consulting firm, has the following condensed budget for 19_8:

Revenues		$20,000,000
Total costs		
Direct costs		
Professional labor	$ 5,000,000	
Indirect costs		
Audit support	13,000,000	18,000,000
Operating income		$ 2,000,000

Taylor has a single direct-cost category (professional labor) and a single indirect-cost pool (client support). Indirect costs are allocated to jobs on the basis of professional labor costs.

REQUIRED

1. Present an overview diagram of the job-costing system. Compute the 19_8 budgeted indirect-cost rate for Taylor & Associates.

2. The markup rate for pricing jobs is intended to produce a 10% operating income-to-revenue margin. Compute the markup rate as a percentage of professional labor costs.

3. Taylor is bidding on a consulting job for Red Rooster, a fast-food chain specializing in poultry meats. The budgeted breakdown of professional labor on the job is as follows:

Professional Labor Category	Budgeted Rate per Hour	Budgeted Hours
Director	$200	3
Partner	100	16
Associate	50	40
Assistant	30	160

Compute the budgeted cost of the Red Rooster job. How much will Taylor bid for the job if it is to earn its target operating income-to-revenue margin of 10%?

4-22 Computing direct-cost rates, consulting firm. Doherty & Company is an international consulting firm. Its 19_7 annual budget includes the following for each category of professional labor:

Category	Average Salary	Average Fringe Benefits	Billable Time for Clients (hours)	Vacation and Sick Leave (hours)	Professional Development (hours)	Unbilled Time Due to Lack of Demand
Director	$140,000	$60,000	1,600	160	240	0
Partner	105,000	45,000	1,600	160	240	0
Associate	60,000	20,000	1,600	160	240	0
Assistant	38,000	12,000	1,600	160	240	0

1. Compute the budgeted direct-cost rate for professional labor (salary and fringe benefits) per hour for (a) directors, (b) partners, (c) associates, and (d) assistants. Use budgeted billable time for clients as the denominator in these computations.
2. Repeat requirement 1. Use the sum of budgeted billable time, vacation and sick leave time, and professional development time as the denominator in these calculations.
3. Why are the rates different between requirements 1 and 2? How might these differences affect job costing by Doherty & Company?

4-23 Peanut-butter costing, cross-subsidization. For many years, five former classmates—Steve Armstrong, Lola Gonzales, Rex King, Elizabeth Poffo, and Gary Young—have had a reunion dinner at the annual meeting of the American Accounting Association. The bill for the most recent dinner at the Seattle Spaceneedle Restaurant was broken down as follows:

Diner	Entree	Dessert	Drinks	Total
Armstrong	$27	$8	$24	$59
Gonzales	24	3	0	27
King	21	6	13	40
Poffo	31	6	12	49
Young	15	4	6	25

For at least the last ten dinners, King put the total restaurant bill on his American Express card. He then mailed the other four a bill for the average cost. They shared the gratuity at the restaurant by paying cash. King continued this practice for the Seattle dinner. However, just before he sent the bill to the other diners, Young phoned him to complain. He was livid at Poffo for ordering the steak and lobster entree ("She always does that!") and at Armstrong for having three glasses of imported champagne ("What's wrong with domestic beer?").

REQUIRED

1. Why is the average-cost approach in the context of the reunion dinner an example of peanut-butter costing?
2. Compute the average cost to each of the five diners. Who is undercharged and who is overcharged under the average-cost approach? Is Young's complaint justified?
3. Give an example of a dining situation where King would find it more difficult to compute the amount of under- or overcosting. How might the behavior of the diners be affected if each person paid his or her own bill instead of continuing with the average-cost approach?

4-24 ABC, retail product-line profitability. Family Supermarkets (FS) found that its ABC analysis (see p. 110) provided important insights. It extends the analysis to cover three more product lines—baked goods, milk and fruit juice, and frozen foods. The revenues, cost of goods sold, store support costs, and activity area usage of the three product lines is as follows:

	Baked Goods	Milk and Fruit Juice	Frozen Products
Financial data			
Revenues	$57,000	$63,000	$52,000
Cost of goods sold	38,000	47,000	35,000
Store support	11,400	14,100	10,500
Activity area usage (cost driver)			
Ordering (purchase orders)	30	25	13
Delivery (deliveries)	98	36	28
Shelf-stocking (hours)	183	166	24
Customer support (items sold)	15,500	20,500	7,900

There are no bottle returns for any of these three product lines.

REQUIRED

1. Use the previous costing system (support costs allocated to products at the rate of 30% of cost of goods sold) to compute a product-line profitability report for FS.
2. Use the ABC system (ordering at $100 per purchase order, delivery at $80 per delivery, shelf-stacking at $20 per hour, and customer support at $0.20 per item sold) to compute a product-line profitability report for FS.
3. What new insights does the ABC system in requirement 2 provide to FS managers?

4-25 ABC, product-costing at banks, cross-subsidization. First International Bank (FIB) is examining the profitability of its Premier Account, a combined savings and checking account. Depositors receive a 7% annual interest rate on their average deposit. FIB earns an interest rate spread of 3% (the difference between the rate at which it lends money and the rate it pays depositors) by lending money for residential home loan purposes at 10%. Thus, FIB would gain $60 on the interest spread if a depositor has an average Premier Account balance of $2,000 in 19_7 ($2,000 × 3% = $60).

The Premier Account allows depositors unlimited use of services such as deposits, withdrawals, checking account, and foreign currency drafts. Depositors with Premier Account balances of $1,000 or more receive unlimited free use of services. Depositors with minimum balance of less than $1,000 pay $20 a month service fee for their Premier Account.

FIB recently conducted an activity-based costing study of its services. It assessed the following costs for six individual services. The use of these services in 19_7 by three customers is as follows:

	ABC-Based Cost per "Transaction"	Account Usage		
		Robinson	Skerrett	Farrel
Deposit/withdrawal with teller	$ 2.50	40	50	5
Deposit/withdrawal with automatic teller machine	0.80	10	20	16
Deposit/withdrawal on prearranged monthly basis	0.50	0	12	60
Bank checks written	8.00	9	3	2
Foreign currency drafts	12.00	4	1	6
Inquiries about account balance	1.50	10	18	9
Average Premier Account balance for 19_7		$1,100	$800	$25,000

Assume Robinson and Farrel always maintain a balance above $1,000 while Skerrett always had a balance below $1,000 in 19_7.

REQUIRED

1. Compute the 19_7 profitability of the Robinson, Skerrett, and Farrell Premier Accounts at FIB.
2. What evidence is there of cross-subsidization across Premier Accounts? Why might FIB worry about this cross-subsidization if the Premier Account product offering is profitable as a whole?
3. What changes at FIB would you recommend for its Premier Account?

PROBLEMS

4-26 Job costing, engineering consulting firm. Serra & Company, an engineering consulting firm, specializes in analyzing the structural causes of major building catastrophes. Its job-costing system in 19_7 had a single direct-cost category (professional labor) and a single indirect-cost pool (general support). The allocation base for indirect costs is professional labor-costs. Actual costs for 19_7 were

Direct costs	
Professional labor	$10,000,000
Indirect costs	
General support	19,000,000
Total costs	$29,000,000

The following costs were included in the general support indirect-cost pool:

Technical specialists' costs	$ 800,000
Telephone/fax machine	600,000
Computer time	3,700,000
Photocopying	400,000
Total costs	$5,500,000

The firm's data-processing capabilities now make it feasible to trace these costs to individual jobs. The managing partner is considering whether more costs than just professional labor should be traced to each job as a direct cost. In this way, the firm would be better able to justify billings to clients.

In late 19_7, arrangements were made to expand the number of direct-cost categories and to trace them to seven client engagements. Two of the case records showed the following:

	Client Case	
	304	308
Professional labor	$20,000	$20,000
Technical specialists' costs	2,000	6,000
Telephone/fax machine	1,000	2,000
Computer time	2,000	4,000
Photocopying	1,000	2,000
Total direct costs	$26,000	$34,000

REQUIRED

1. Present an overview diagram of the 19_7 Serra job-costing system. What was the actual indirect-cost rate per professional labor-dollar?
2. Assume that the $5.5 million of costs included in the 19_7 general-support indirect-cost pool were reclassified as direct costs. The result is a system with five direct-cost categories. Compute the revised indirect-cost rate as a percentage of
   a. Professional labor-costs
   b. Total direct costs
3. Compute the total costs of jobs 304 and 308 using:
   a. The 19_7 costing system with a single direct-cost category and a single indirect-cost pool (professional labor-costs as the allocation base)
   b. A costing system with five direct-cost categories and a single indirect-cost pool (professional labor-costs as the allocation base)
   c. A costing system with five direct-cost categories and a single indirect-cost pool (total direct costs as the allocation base)
4. Assume that clients are billed at 120% of total job costs (that is, a markup on cost of 20%). Compute the billings in requirement 3 for jobs 304 and 308 for the (a), (b), and (c) costing systems.
5. Which method of job costing in requirement 3 do you favor? Explain.

4-27 Job costing, peanut-butter costing (extension of the Problem for Self-Study). Lindsay & Associates (see pp. 113–114) is examining how the refined costing system in Panel C of Exhibit 4-5 will cost three jobs differently from the costing system outlined in Panel A of Exhibit 4-5. The following information pertains to the 19_8 audit of these three jobs:

	Northern Television	Rooster King	Nambucca Meat, Inc.
Professional partner labor	20 hours	24 hours	58 hours
Professional associate labor	140 hours	76 hours	302 hours
Information specialist labor	8 hours	28 hours	64 hours
Phone/fax/copying	$160	$420	$715
Travel and allowances	$ 0	$180	$340

REQUIRED
1. Use the job-costing system in Exhibit 4-5, Panel A, to cost the 19_8 audits of Northern Television, Rooster King, and Nambucca Meat, Inc. Budgeted direct- and indirect-cost rates are reported on p. 101.
2. Use the job-costing system in Panel C of Exhibit 4-5 to cost the 19_8 audits of Northern Television, Rooster King, and Nambucca Meat. Direct- and indirect-cost rates are reported in the Problem for Self-Study (pp. 113–114).
3. Using the refined costing system from requirement 2 as the benchmark, which 19_8 audit jobs are under- or overcosted when the Exhibit 4-5 (Panel A) job-costing system is used? Explain reasons for this under- or overcosting.
4. How might Lindsay & Associates find the refined costing system in requirement 2 to be more useful than the system in requirement 1 in decisions relating to their audit clients Northern Television, Rooster King, and Nambucca Meat?

4-28 Job costing, law firm. Keating & Associates is a law firm specializing in labor relations and employee-related work. It employs 25 professionals (5 partners and 20 associates) who work directly with its clients. The average budgeted total compensation per professional for 19_6 is $104,000. Each professional is budgeted to have 1,600 billable hours to clients in 19_6. Keating is a highly respected firm, and all professionals work for clients to their maximum 1,600 billable hours available. All professional labor costs are included in a single direct-cost category and are traced to jobs on a per-hour basis.

All costs of Keating & Associates other than professional labor costs are included in a single indirect-cost pool (legal support) and are allocated to jobs using professional labor-hours as the allocation base. The budgeted level of indirect costs in 19_6 is $2.2 million.

REQUIRED
1. Present an overview diagram of Keating's job-costing system.
2. Compute the 19_6 budgeted professional labor-hour direct-cost rate.
3. Compute the 19_6 budgeted indirect-cost rate per hour of professional labor.
4. Keating & Associates is considering bidding on two jobs:
   a. Litigation work for Richardson, Inc., that requires 100 budgeted hours of professional labor
   b. Labor contract work for Punch, Inc., that requires 150 budgeted hours of professional labor
   Prepare a cost estimate for each job.

4-29 Job costing with a refined costing system, law firm (continuation of 4-28). Keating & Associates received feedback from Punch, Inc., that its bid for the labor contract work was too high. This feedback prompted Keating to review its work activities and how they are reflected in its job-costing system. This review included a detailed analysis of how past jobs used the firm's resources and interviews with personnel about what factors drive the level of indirect costs. Management concluded that a system with two direct-cost categories (professional partner labor and professional associate labor) and two indirect-cost categories (general support and secretarial support) would yield more accurate job costs. Budgeted information for 19_6 related to the two direct-cost categories is as follows:

	Professional Partner Labor	Professional Associate Labor
Number of professionals	5	20
Hours of billable time per professional	1,600 per year	1,600 per year
Total compensation (average per professional)	$200,000	$80,000

Budgeted information for 19_6 relating to the two indirect-cost categories is

	General Support	Secretarial Support
Total costs	$1,800,000	$400,000
Cost-allocation base	Professional labor-hours	Partner labor-hours

REQUIRED

1. Present an overview diagram of the refined costing system.
2. Compute the 19_6 budgeted direct-cost rates for (a) professional partners, and (b) professional associates.
3. Compute the 19_6 budgeted indirect-cost rates for (a) general support, and (b) secretarial support.
4. Compute the budgeted job costs for the Richardson and Punch jobs, given the following information:

	Richardson, Inc.	Punch, Inc.
Professional partners	60 hours	30 hours
Professional associates	40 hours	120 hours

5. Comment on the results in requirement 4. Why are the job costs different from those computed in Problem 4-28?

4-30 Job costing with single direct-cost category, single indirect-cost pool, law firm. Wigan Associates is a recently formed law partnership. Ellery Hanley, the managing partner of Wigan Associates, has just finished a tense phone call with Martin Offiah, president of Widnes Coal. Offiah complained about the price Wigan charged for some conveyancing (drawing up property documents) legal work done for Widnes Coal. He requested a breakdown of the charges. He also indicated to Hanley that a competing law firm, Hull & Kingston, was seeking more business with Widnes Coal and that he was going to ask them to bid for a conveyancing job next month. Offiah ended the phone call by saying that if Wigan bid a price similar to the one charged last month, Wigan would not be hired for next month's job.

Hanley is dismayed by the phone call. He is also puzzled because he believes that conveyancing is an area where Wigan Associates has much expertise and is highly efficient. The Widnes Coal phone call is the bad news of the week. The good news is that yesterday Hanley received a phone call from its only other client (St. Helen's Glass) saying it was very pleased with both the quality of the work (primarily litigation) and the price charged on its most recent case.

Hanley decides to collect data on the Widnes Coal and St. Helen's Glass cases. Wigan Associates uses a cost-based approach to pricing (billing) each legal case. Currently it uses a single direct-cost category (for professional labor time) and a single indirect-cost pool (general support). Indirect costs are allocated to cases on the basis of professional labor-hours per case. The case files show the following:

	Widnes Coal	St. Helen's Glass
Professional labor time	104 hours	96 hours

Professional labor costs at Wigan Associates are $70 an hour. Indirect costs are allocated to cases at $105 an hour. Total indirect costs in the most recent period were $21,000.

REQUIRED

1. Why is it important for Wigan Associates to understand the costs associated with individual cases?
2. Present an overview diagram of the existing job-costing system.
3. Compute the costs of the Widnes Coal and St. Helen's Glass cases.

4-31 Job costing with multiple direct-cost categories, single indirect-cost pool, law firm (continuation of 4-30). Hanley speaks to the other partners about the pricing of the two cases. Several believe that the relative prices charged seem out of line with their intuition. One partner observes that a useful approach to obtaining more accurate job costs is to increase direct-cost tracing.

Hanley asks his assistant to collect details on those costs included in the $21,000 indirect-cost pool that can be traced to each individual case. After further analysis, Wigan is able to reclassify $14,000 of the $21,000 as direct costs:

Other Direct Costs	Widnes Coal	St. Helen's Glass
Research support labor	$1,600	$ 3,400
Computer time	500	1,300
Travel and allowances	600	4,400
Telephone/faxes	200	1,000
Photocopying	250	750
Total	$3,150	$10,850

Hanley decides to calculate the costs of each case had Wigan used six direct-cost pools and a single indirect-cost pool. The single indirect-cost pool would have $7,000 of costs and would be allocated to each case using the professional labor-hours base.

REQUIRED

1. Present an overview diagram of the refined job-costing system with its multiple direct-cost categories.
2. What is the revised indirect-cost allocation rate per professional labor-hour for Wigan Associates when total indirect costs are $7,000?
3. Compute the costs of the Widnes and St. Helen's cases if Wigan Associates had used its refined costing system with multiple direct-cost categories and one indirect-cost pool.
4. Compare the costs of the Widnes and St. Helen's cases in requirement 3 with those in requirement 3 of Problem 4-30. Comment on the results.

4-32 Job costing with multiple direct-cost categories, multiple indirect-cost pools, law firm (continuation of 4-30 and 4-31). Hanley examines the job-costing approaches in Problems 4-30 and 4-31. He questions the use of a single cost rate for all professional labor of Wigan Associates. Wigan has two classifications of professional staff—partners and associates. Hanley asks his assistant to examine the relative use of partners and associates on the recent Widnes Coal and St. Helen's cases. The Widnes case used 24 partner-hours and 80 associate-hours. The St. Helen's case used 56 partner-hours and 40 associate-hours.

Hanley decides to examine how the use of separate direct- and indirect-cost pools for partners and associates would have affected the costs of the Widnes and St. Helen's cases. Indirect costs in each cost pool would be allocated on the basis of total hours of that category of professional labor.

The rates per category of professional labor are as follows:

Category of Professional Labor	Direct Cost per Hour	Indirect Cost per Hour
Partner	$100.00	$57.50
Associate	50.00	20.00

These indirect-cost rates are based on a total indirect-cost pool of $7,000; $4,600 of this $7,000 is attributable to the activities of partners, and $2,400 is attributable to the activities of associates. (The indirect cost per hour of $57.50 is calculated by dividing $4,600 by 80 partner-hours; the indirect-cost rate of $20 is calculated by dividing $2,400 by 120 associate-hours.)

REQUIRED

1. Present an overview diagram of the refined job-costing system with its multiple direct-cost categories and its multiple indirect-cost pools.
2. Compute the costs of the Widnes and St. Helen's cases with Wigan Associates further refined system, with multiple direct-cost categories and multiple indirect-cost pools.
3. For what decisions might Wigan Associates find it more useful to use this job-costing approach rather than the approach in Problems 4-30 or 4-31?

4-33 **Activity-based costing, merchandising.** Figure Four, Inc., specializes in the distribution of pharmaceutical products. Figure Four buys from pharmaceutical companies and resells to each of three different markets:

a. General supermarket chains
b. Drugstore chains
c. Ma and Pa single-store pharmacies

Rick Flair, the new controller of Figure Four, reported the following data for August 19_7:

	General Supermarket Chains	Drugstore Chains	Ma and Pa Single Stores
Average revenue per delivery	$30,900	$10,500	$1,980
Average cost of goods sold per delivery	$30,000	$10,000	$1,800
Number of deliveries	120	300	1,000

For many years, Figure Four has used gross margin percentage [(Revenue − Cost of goods sold) ÷ Revenue] to evaluate the relative profitability of its different groupings of customers (distribution outlets).

Flair recently attended a seminar on activity-based costing and decides to consider using it at Figure Four. Flair meets with all the key managers and many staff members. People generally agree that there are five key activity areas at Figure Four:

Activity Area	Cost Driver
1. Customer purchase order processing	Purchase orders by customers
2. Line-item ordering	Line items per purchase order
3. Store delivery	Store deliveries
4. Cartons shipped to stores	Cartons shipped to a store per delivery
5. Shelf-stocking at customer stores	Hours of shelf-stocking

Each customer purchase order consists of one or more line items. A line item represents a single product (such as Extra-Strength Tylenol Tablets). Each store delivery entails delivery of one or more cartons of products to a customer. Each product is delivered in one or more separate cartons. Figure Four staff stack cartons directly onto display shelves in a store. Currently, there is no charge for this service, and not all customers use Figure Four for this activity.

The August 19_7 operating costs (other than cost of goods sold) of Figure Four are $301,080. These operating costs are assigned to the five activity areas. The costs in each area and the amount of the cost drivers units used in that area for August 19_7 are as follows:

Activity Area	Total Costs in August 19_7	Total Units of Cost Driver Used in August 19_7
1. Customer purchase order processing	$ 80,000	2,000 orders
2. Line-item ordering	63,840	21,280 line items
3. Store delivery	71,000	1,420 store deliveries
4. Cartons shipped to stores	76,000	76,000 cartons
5. Shelf-stocking at customer stores	10,240	640 hours
	$301,080	

Other data for August 19_7 include the following:

	General Supermarket Chains	Drugstore Chains	Ma and Pa Single Stores
Total number of orders	140	360	1,500
Average number of line items per order	14	12	10
Total number of store deliveries	120	300	1,000
Average number of cartons shipped per store delivery	300	80	16
Average number of hours of shelf-stocking per store delivery	3.0	0.6	0.1

REQUIRED

1. Compute the August 19_7 gross-margin percentage for each of its three distribution markets. What is the operating income of Figure Four?
2. Compute the August 19_7 per unit cost driver rate for each of the five activity areas.
3. Compute the operating income of each distribution market in August 19_7 using the activity-based costing information. Comment on the results. What new insights are available with the activity-based information?
4. Describe four challenges Flair would face in assigning the total August 19_7 operating costs of $301,080 to the five activity areas.

4-34 **Legal billing practices, ethics.** Rick Adams has just been made managing partner of Smith and Frank, a leading commercial law firm. It should have been the best of times. It was, however, the very worst. Timothy Smith, a founder of the firm, was the subject of an internal review. The findings left Adams feeling betrayed.

◆ Smith had charged clients for 5,000 hours of work in 19_7. Normal annual billing hours at Smith and Frank ranged from 1,700 hours to 2,200 hours. Apart from Smith, the highest number of hours billed by any partner in 19_7 was the 2,800 hours billed by Adams. Smith had the highest hourly billing rate in the firm ($400 per hour). He was their "rainmaker," bringing in the most new business of any partner. The review showed that on at least 20 days in 19_7, Smith billed (in total) 30 hours per day across several clients. Adams previously had great respect for Smith. Clients had always praised Smith's intellectual horsepower and his profound grasp of law and business.

◆ Smith's business expense account for 19_7 totaled $412,867. There was no formal record of approvals. Linda Young, the Smith and Frank accountant, had allowed Smith to submit his monthly American Express Card with lines on those items Smith said were personal. The deleted personal items were 8.7% of the American Express billings in 19_7. Young paid Smith for the 91.3% remaining balance. Young was very conscious of Smith's superstar status ("We all rode on his gravy train") and felt that Smith's time was best spent on billable hours for clients rather than on justifying individual expense account items.

A government auditor will be visiting Smith and Frank next month. The auditor had asked details on Smith's billing of 125 hours to the Department of Commerce at $400 per hour. The auditor accepted the 60% markup on Smith's hourly rate, but wanted details on how the $250 base rate was determined. This $250 rate was based on budgeted 19_7 compensation for Smith of $500,000 divided by 2,000 budgeted hours. Smith's actual compensation (before a $1 million bonus) in 19_7 was $600,000. Only actual costs rather than budgeted costs are reimbursable under government contracting.

REQUIRED

1. If Smith and Frank used an actual cost rate for Smith in 19_7, how much would have they billed the Department of Commerce for the reported 125 hours of work (assuming a 60% markup on cost)?
2. Adams is due to meet Linda Young tomorrow. What issues should Adams raise with her? Refer to the *Standards of Ethical Conduct for Management Accountants* in Exhibit 1-5 (p. 10) in your answer.
3. What advice would you give to Adams when he meets with Timothy Smith in 3 days' time? He is very concerned with the upcoming government auditor visit as well as the general issues raised by Smith's job billing practices.

COLLABORATIVE LEARNING PROBLEM

4-35 **ABC, cross-subsidization.** University Travel (UT) specializes in travel services for college students and university faculty and administrators. For many years, it received a 10% commission on the ticket price paid by each passenger. Thus, when it sold (say) a United Airline ticket for $1,500, it received a $150 commission. Recently, however, airlines have imposed an upper limit of $50 per ticket on the commission to travel agents. These commissions were UT's sole source of revenues. This new limit of $50 per ticket prompted UT to look for other revenue sources. It requested that its personnel make a list of the extra services they had provided to customers at no extra charge. It then hired an activity-based costing consulting firm to determine the cost of providing these individual services.

Three representative customers were selected to determine how this information could be used. Their commission revenues and the total activity in 19_7 were examined under (a) the old 10% plan, and (b) the 10% up to a maximum of $50 plan.

Service	Activity-based Cost	Frequency of Services Used by Representative Customers		
		Tait (Student)	Fallon (Faculty)	Iro (Administrator)
Exchanging tickets	$25 per exchange	0	3	1
Refunding tickets	$15 per refund	0	2	0
Express delivery of tickets	$18 per delivery	0	2	0
Normal delivery of tickets	$5 per delivery	3	6	3
Applying for lost-ticket refunds	$28 per application	0	1	0
Making restaurant reservations	$4 per reservation	0	4	1
Making theater reservations	$4 per reservations	0	3	2
Commission revenues earned on tickets sold				
a. Under old 10% plan		$130	$530	$190
b. 10% plan with $50 limit on each ticket purchased		120	360	140

INSTRUCTIONS

Form groups of two or more students to complete the following requirement.

REQUIRED

Your group is to examine the insights provided by the ABC numbers. What possible strategies should UT consider? Was there cross-subsidization of the costs at UT under the previous 10% plan? Should it now charge for none, some, or all of the services provided? What is the risk of charging for services such as delivery of tickets or making theater reservations?

COSTING SYSTEMS AND ACTIVITY-BASED COSTING (II): MANUFACTURING APPLICATIONS

Inspection and testing of helicopter windshields is an important step in PPG's manufacturing operations. Many activity-costing systems in manufacturing have inspection/ testing activity cost pools with time as a cost driver.

LEARNING OBJECTIVES

After studying this chapter, you should be able to

1. Outline a six-step approach to job costing
2. Describe three key source documents used in job-costing systems
3. Distinguish between the Work-in-Process subsidiary ledger and the Work-in-Process Control account in the general ledger
4. Understand how the steps in the production process are tracked in a job-costing system
5. Describe alternative methods of prorating of period-end under- or overallocated indirect costs
6. Describe how the cost hierarchy notion can be used in manufacturing
7. Distinguish between the traditional and the activity-based costing approaches to designing a costing system in manufacturing

I n Chapter 4 we discussed costing systems in the service and merchandising sectors. We now turn our attention to the manufacturing sector. Costing systems in the manufacturing sector are often more detailed than those in the service and merchandising sectors. Why? Because the production process in manufacturing is more complex. Unlike service and merchandising firms that provide their customers with goods and services that have not been significantly altered from their inputs, manufacturers convert materials into work in process and then into finished goods.

We first discuss job costing in manufacturing. This includes a transaction-by-transaction summary of how a costing system tracks the purchase of manufacturing inputs, their conversion into work in process and then into finished goods, and finally their sale. We then examine the use of activity-based costing in manufacturing.

JOB COSTING IN MANUFACTURING

OBJECTIVE 1

Outline a six-step approach to job costing

The six-step approach to job costing illustrated in Chapter 4 is also applicable to the manufacturing sector. We illustrate this approach using the Robinson Company, which manufactures specialized machinery for the paper-making industry at its Green Bay, Wisconsin, plant. Robinson uses a _normal costing_ method—that is, actual costs for direct-cost items and budgeted costs for indirect-cost items (see Chapter 4, pp. 98–101).

Step 1: Identify the Job That Is the Chosen Cost Object   The job in this case is a pulp machine manufactured for the Western Pulp and Paper Company in 19_7.

Step 2: Identify the Direct Costs for the Job   Robinson identifies two direct manufacturing cost categories—direct materials and direct manufacturing labor.

Step 3: Identify the Indirect-Cost Pools Associated with the Job   For product-costing purposes, Robinson uses a single indirect manufacturing cost pool termed _manufacturing overhead._ This pool represents the indirect costs of the Green Bay Manufacturing Department. It includes items such as depreciation on equipment, energy costs, indirect materials, and indirect manufacturing labor and salaries.

Step 4: Select the Cost-Allocation Base to Use in Allocating Each Indirect-Cost Pool to the Job   Robinson uses machine-hours as the allocation base for manufacturing overhead.

Step 5: Develop the Rate Per Unit of Each Cost-Allocation Base Used to Allocate Indirect Costs to the Job   Robinson budgets 19_7 manufacturing overhead costs to be $1,280,000 and the 19_7 quantity of machine-hours as 16,000. Hence the 19_7 budgeted indirect-cost rate for manufacturing overhead is $80 per machine-hour ($1,280,000 ÷ 16,000 hours).

Step 6: Assign the Costs to the Cost Object by Adding all Direct Costs and all Indirect Costs   The cost of the machine job for Western Pulp is $10,135.

Direct manufacturing costs		
Direct materials	$4,606	
Direct manufacturing labor	1,329	$5,935
Indirect manufacturing costs		
Manufacturing overhead ($80 × 52.5 machine-hours)		4,200
Total manufacturing costs of job		$10,135

Exhibit 5-1 presents an overview of the job-costing system for the manufacturing costs of the Robinson Company.

Robinson uses its job-costing system to help manage the costs in its Green Bay Manufacturing Department as well as to determine the cost of individual jobs such

EXHIBIT 5-1
Job-Costing Overview for Manufacturing Costs at the Robinson Company

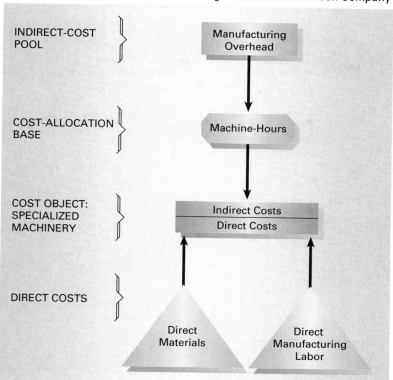

as the Western Pulp and Paper machine. The Manufacturing Department is an important cost object, as is each job manufactured. The relationship between these two important goals of a job-costing system is shown in Exhibit 5-2.

EXHIBIT 5-2
Department and Job Costing at Western Pulp and Paper

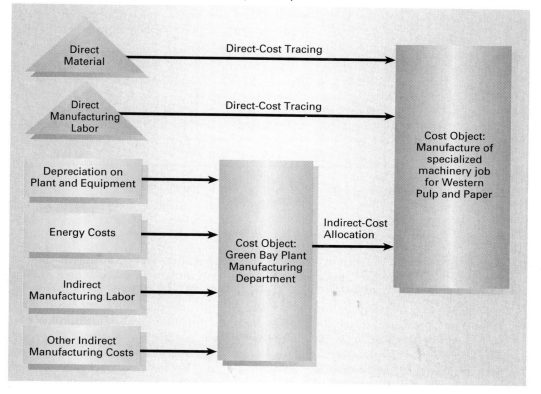

PANEL A

JOB COST RECORD

JOB NO:	WPP298	CUSTOMER:	Western Pulp and Paper
Date Started:	Feb.7,19_7	Date Completed:	April 3,19_7

DIRECT MATERIALS

Materials Requisition No.	Part No.	Date Received	Quantity Used	Unit Cost	Billing Amount
③ 19_7:198	MB 468-A	Feb. 9, 19_7	8	$14	$112
19_7:268	TB 267-F	Feb. 11, 19_7	12	63	756
					•
					•
					•
Total					$4,606

DIRECT MANUFACTURING LABOR

Labor Time Record No.	Employee No.	Period Covered	Hours Used	Hourly Rate	Billing Amount
③ LT 232	551-87-3076	Feb.16–22, 19_7	25	$18	$450
LT 247	287-31-4671	Feb.16–22, 19_7	16	18	288
					•
					•
					•
Total					$1,329

MANUFACTURING OVERHEAD*

Cost Pool Category	Allocation Base	Allocation Base Units Used	Allocation Base Rate	Billing Amount
Manufacturing	Machine-Hours	52.50	$80	$4,200
				•
				•
Total				$4,200
TOTAL BILLABLE JOB COST				$10,135

PANEL B

MATERIALS REQUISITION RECORD

Materials Requisition Record No:				19_7:198
Job No: WPP 298	Date:	Feb. 9, 19_7		

Part No.	Part Description	Quantity	Unit Cost	Total Cost
MB468-A	Metal Brackets	8	$14	$112

Issued By: B. Clyde	Date: Feb. 9, 19_7
Received By: L Daley	Date: Feb. 9, 19_7

PANEL C

LABOR TIME RECORD

Labor Time Record No:		LT 232	
Employee Name: G.L. Cook		Employee No:	551-87-3076
Employee Classification Code:	Grade 3 Machinist		
Week Start: Feb. 16, 19_7		Week End:	Feb. 22, 19_7

Job. No.	M	T	W	Th	F	S	Su	Total
WPP298	4	8	3	6	4	0	0	25

Supervisor: R. Stuart		Date:	Feb. 23, 19_7

* The Robinson Company uses a single manufacturing overhead cost pool. The use of multiple overhead cost pools would mean multiple entries in the "Manufacturing Overhead" section of its job cost record.

Source Documents

OBJECTIVE 2

Describe three key source documents used in job-costing systems

Source documents are the original records that support journal entries in an accounting system. The key source document in a job-costing system is a **job cost record** (also called a **job cost sheet**). This document records and accumulates all the costs assigned to a specific job. Exhibit 5-3, Panel A, shows a typical job cost record at the Robinson Company. Source documents also exist for individual items in a job cost record. Consider direct materials. The basic source document is a **materials requisition record,** which is a form used to charge departments and job cost records for the cost of the materials used on a specific job. Panel B shows a materials requisition record for the Robinson Company. The basic source document for direct manufacturing labor is a **labor time record,** which is used to charge departments and job cost records for labor time used on a specific job. Panel C in Exhibit 5-3 shows a typical labor time record for the Robinson Company. The reliability of job cost records depends on the reliability of the inputs. Problems occurring in this area include materials recorded on one job being "borrowed" and used on other jobs and erroneous job numbers being assigned to material or labor inputs.

In many costing systems, the source documents exist only in the form of computer records. With bar coding and other forms of on-line information recording, the materials and time used on jobs increasingly are being recorded without human intervention.

Cost-Allocation Bases Used for Manufacturing Overhead

How do companies around the world allocate manufacturing overhead costs to products? The percentages in the following table indicate how frequently particular cost-allocation bases are used in management accounting systems in five countries. The reported percentages exceed 100% because many companies surveyed use more than one cost-allocation base.

	United States*	Australia†	Ireland‡	Japan†	United Kingdom†
Direct labor-hours	31%	36%	30%	50%	31%
Direct labor-dollars	31	21	22	7	29
Machine-hours	12	19	19	12	27
Direct materials dollars	4	12	10	11	17
Units of production	5	20	28	16	22
Prime cost (%)	—	1	—	21	10
Other	17	—	9	—	—

*Adapted from Cohen and Paquette, "Management Accounting."
†Blayney and Yokoyama, "Comparative Analysis."
‡Clarke, "Survey."
Full citations are in Appendix A.

AN ILLUSTRATION OF A JOB-COSTING SYSTEM IN MANUFACTURING

We will use the Robinson Company to illustrate how a job-costing system operates in manufacturing. Recall that its job-costing system has two direct-cost categories (direct materials and direct manufacturing labor) and one indirect-cost pool (manufacturing overhead). See Exhibit 5-1. The following example considers events that took place in September 19_7.

General Ledger and Subsidiary Ledgers

As we have noted, a job-costing system has a separate job cost record for each job. This record is typically found in a subsidiary ledger. The general ledger combines these separate job cost records in the Work-in-Process Control account, which pertains to all jobs undertaken.

Exhibit 5-4 shows T-account relationships for the Robinson Company's general ledger and illustrative records in the subsidiary ledgers. Panel A shows the general ledger section that gives a "bird's-eye view" of the costing system; the amounts are based on the illustration that follows. Panel B shows the subsidiary ledgers and

OBJECTIVE 3

Distinguish between the Work-in-Process subsidiary ledger and the Work-in-Process Control account in the general ledger

PANEL A: GENERAL LEDGER

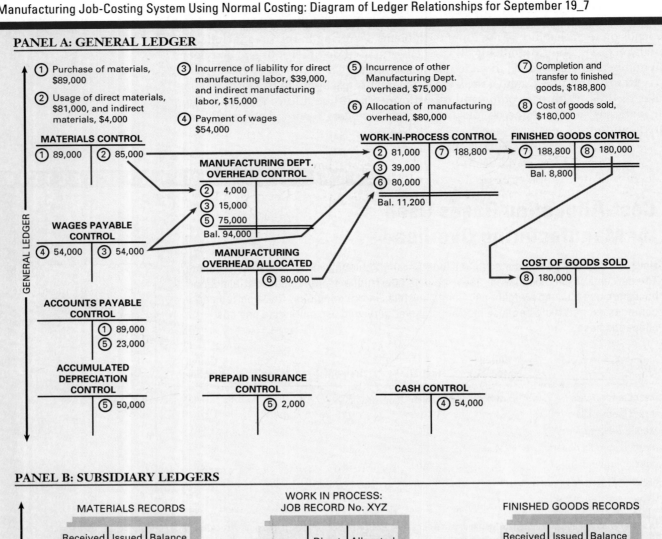

① Purchase of materials, $89,000

② Usage of direct materials, $81,000, and indirect materials, $4,000

③ Incurrence of liability for direct manufacturing labor, $39,000, and indirect manufacturing labor, $15,000

④ Payment of wages $54,000

⑤ Incurrence of other Manufacturing Dept. overhead, $75,000

⑥ Allocation of manufacturing overhead, $80,000

⑦ Completion and transfer to finished goods, $188,800

⑧ Cost of goods sold, $180,000

PANEL B: SUBSIDIARY LEDGERS

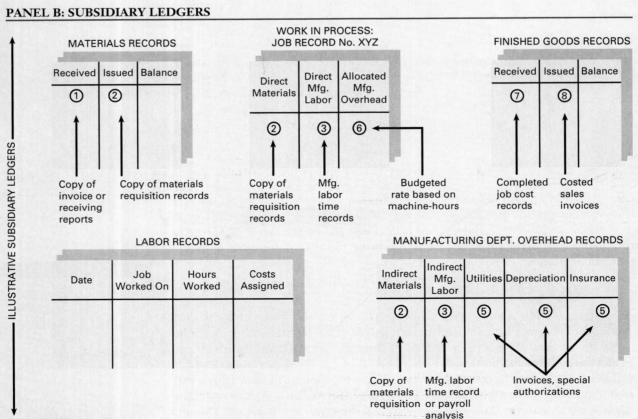

the basic source documents that contain the underlying details—the "worm's-eye view." General ledger accounts with the word *control* in their titles (such as Materials Control and Accounts Payable Control) are supported by underlying subsidiary ledgers.

Software programs guide the processing of transactions in most accounting systems. Some programs make general ledger entries simultaneously with entries in the subsidiary ledger accounts. Other software programs make general ledger entries at, say, weekly or monthly intervals, with entries made in the subsidiary ledger accounts on a more frequent basis. The Robinson Company makes entries in its subsidiary ledger when transactions occur and then makes entries in its general ledger on a monthly basis.

A general ledger should be viewed as only one of many tools that assist management in planning and control. To control operations, managers not only use the source documents in the subsidiary ledgers, they also study nonfinancial variables such as the percentage of jobs requiring rework.

Explanations of Transactions

The following transaction-by-transaction summary analysis explains how a job-costing system serves the twin goals of (1) department responsibility and control, and (2) product costing. These transactions track stages (a) through (d):

OBJECTIVE 4

Understand how the steps in the production process are tracked in a job-costing system

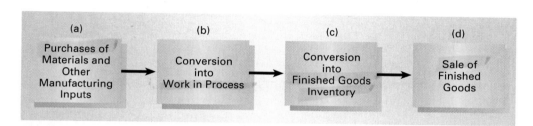

It is the existence of stages (b) and (c) that makes the costing of manufactured products more detailed than the costing of services and merchandise described in Chapter 4.

1. *Transaction:* Purchases of materials (direct and indirect), $89,000 on account.

   Analysis: The asset Materials Control is increased. The liability Accounts Payable Control is increased. Both accounts have the word *control* in their title in the general ledger because they are supported by records in the subsidiary ledger. The subsidiary records for materials at the Robinson Company—called *Materials Records*—maintain a continuous record of additions to, and reductions from, inventory. At a minimum, these records would contain columns for quantity received, issuance to jobs, and balance (see Panel B of Exhibit 5-4). There is a separate subsidiary materials record for each type of material in the subsidiary ledger. The following journal entry summarizes all the September 19_7 entries in the materials subsidiary ledgers:

   Journal Entry: Materials Control   89,000

                    Accounts Payable Control   89,000

   Post to General Ledger:

Materials Control		Accounts Payable Control	
① 89,000			① 89,000

   Materials Control includes all material purchases, whether the items are classified as direct or indirect costs of products.

2. *Transaction:* Materials sent to manufacturing plant floor: direct materials, $81,000, and indirect materials, $4,000.

   Analysis: The accounts Work-in-Process Control and Manufacturing Overhead Control are increased. The account Materials Control is decreased. The assumption is that costs incurred on the work in process "attach" to the work in process, thereby making it a more valuable asset. Responsibility is fixed by using *materials requisitions records* as a basis for charging departments for the materials issued to them. Requisitions are accumulated and posted monthly to the general ledger at the Robinson Company. As direct materials are used, they are charged to individual job records, which are the subsidiary ledger accounts for the Work-in-Process Control account in the general ledger account. Indirect materials are charged to individual Manufacturing Department's overhead cost records, which comprise the subsidiary ledger for Manufacturing Overhead Control at the Robinson Company. The cost of these indirect materials is allocated to individual jobs as a part of the Manufacturing Overhead. The Manufacturing Overhead Control account is the record of the *actual costs* in all the individual overhead categories.

Each indirect-cost pool in a job-costing system will have its own account in the general ledger. Robinson has only one indirect-cost pool—manufacturing overhead.

Journal Entry: Work-in-Process Control   81,000
            Manufacturing Overhead Control   4,000
                 Materials Control   85,000

Post to General Ledger:

Materials Control			
①	89,000	②	85,000

Work-in-Process Control		
②	81,000	

Manufacturing Overhead Control		
②	4,000	

3. *Transaction:* Manufacturing labor wages liability incurred, direct ($39,000) and indirect ($15,000).

Analysis: The accounts Work-in-Process Control and Manufacturing Department Overhead Control are increased. Wages Payable Control is also increased. Labor time records are used to trace direct manufacturing labor to Work-in-Process Control (see Panel B of Exhibit 5-4) and to accumulate the indirect manufacturing labor in Manufacturing Department Overhead Control. The indirect manufacturing labor is, by definition, not being traced to the individual job. Department managers are responsible for making efficient use of available labor.

Journal Entry: Work-in-Process Control   39,000
            Manufacturing Overhead Control   15,000
                 Wages Payable Control   54,000

Post to General Ledger:

Wages Payable Control			
		③	54,000

Work-in-Process Control		
②	81,000	
③	39,000	

Manufacturing Overhead Control		
②	4,000	
③	15,000	

4. *Transaction:* Payment of total manufacturing payroll for the month, $54,000. (For simplicity, payroll withholdings from employees are ignored in this example).

Analysis: The liability Wages Payable Control is decreased. The asset Cash Control is decreased.

Journal Entry: Wages Payable   54,000
            Cash Control   54,000

Wages Payable Control				Cash Control	
④	54,000	③	54,000	④	54,000

For convenience here, wages payable for the month is assumed to be completely paid at month-end.

5. *Transaction:* Additional manufacturing overhead costs incurred during the month, $75,000. These costs consist of utilities and repairs, $23,000; insurance expired, $2,000; and depreciation on equipment, $50,000.

Analysis: The indirect-cost account of Manufacturing Overhead Control is increased. The liability Accounts Payable Control is increased, the asset Prepaid Insurance Control is decreased, and the asset Equipment is decreased by means of a related contra asset account Accumulated Depreciation Control. The detail of these costs is entered in the appropriate columns of the individual manufacturing overhead cost records that make up the subsidiary ledger for Manufacturing Overhead Control. The source documents for these distributions include invoices (for example, a utility bill) and special schedules (for example, a depreciation schedule) from the responsible accounting officer.

Journal Entry:

Manufacturing Overhead Control	75,000	
Accounts Payable Control		23,000
Accumulated Depreciation Control		50,000
Prepaid Insurance Control		2,000

Post to General Ledger:

Accounts Payable Control			Manufacturing Overhead Control		
	①	89,000	②	4,000	
	⑤	23,000	③	15,000	
			⑤	75,000	

Accumulated Depreciation Control			Prepaid Insurance Control		
	⑤	50,000	⑤	2,000	

6. *Transaction:* Allocation of manufacturing overhead to products, $80,000.

Analysis: The asset Work-in-Process Control is increased. The indirect-cost account of Manufacturing Overhead Control is, in effect, decreased by means of its contra account, called Manufacturing Overhead Allocated. **Manufacturing overhead allocated** is the record of manufacturing overhead allocated to individual jobs on the basis of the budgeted rate multiplied by actual units used of the allocation base. It comprises all manufacturing costs that are assigned to a product (or service) using a cost-allocation base because they cannot be traced to it in an economically feasible way. The 19_7 budgeted overhead rate used by Robinson is $80 per machine-hour. The overhead cost allocated to each job depends on the machine-hours used on that job. The job record for each individual job in the subsidiary ledger will include a debit item for manufacturing overhead allocated. It is assumed that 1,000 machine-hours were used for all jobs, resulting in a total manufacturing overhead allocation of 1,000 × $80 = $80,000.

Note that a subsidiary entry is made for Manufacturing Overhead Allocated when machine-hours are used on a job. These entries are made to the individual job records in the subsidiary ledger. In contrast, subsidiary entries are made for Manufacturing Overhead Control when actual transactions occur during the period.

Journal Entry:

Work-in-Process Control	80,000	
Manufacturing Overhead Allocated		80,000

Post to General Ledger:

Manufacturing Overhead Allocated		Work-in-Process Control	
	⑥ 80,000	② 81,000	
		③ 39,000	
		⑥ 80,000	

7. *Transaction:* Completion and transfer to finished goods of eight individual jobs, $188,800.

   Analysis: The asset Finished Goods Control is increased. The asset Work-in-Process Control is decreased. The total costs of each job are computed in the subsidiary ledger as each job is completed. Given Robinson's use of a normal costing method, this total will consist of *actual* direct materials, *actual* direct manufacturing labor, and *budgeted* manufacturing overhead that is allocated to each job.

   Journal Entry: Finished Goods Control   188,800
              Work-in-Process Control   188,800

   Post to General Ledger:

Work-in-Process Control			Finished Goods Control	
② 81,000	⑦ 188,800		⑦ 188,800	
③ 39,000				
⑥ 80,000				

8. *Transaction:* Cost of Goods Sold, $180,000.

   Analysis: The $180,000 amount represents the cost of goods sold in sales transactions with customers during September 19_7. The account Cost of Goods Sold is increased. The asset Finished Goods Control is decreased.

   Journal Entry: Cost of Goods Sold   180,000
              Finished Goods Control   180,000

   Post to General Ledger:

Finished Goods Control			Cost of Goods Sold	
⑦ 188,800	⑧ 180,000		⑧ 180,000	

   At this point, please pause and review all eight entries in the illustration. Be sure to trace each journal entry, step by step, to the general-ledger accounts in the general ledger section in Panel A of Exhibit 5-4.

BUDGETED INDIRECT COSTS AND END-OF-PERIOD ADJUSTMENTS

OBJECTIVE 5

Describe alternative methods of prorating of period-end under- or overallocated indirect costs

Budgeted indirect-cost rates have the advantage of being more timely than actual indirect-cost rates. With budgeted rates, indirect costs can be assigned to individual jobs on an ongoing basis rather than waiting until the end of the accounting period when actual costs will be known. However, the disadvantage of budgeted rates is that they likely will be inaccurate, having been made up to 12 months before actual costs are incurred. We now consider adjustments made when the indirect costs allocated differ from the actual indirect costs incurred.

Underallocated indirect costs occur when the allocated amount of indirect costs in an accounting period is less than the actual (incurred) amount in that period. **Overallocated indirect costs** occur when the allocated amount of indirect costs in an accounting period exceeds the actual (incurred) amount in that period.

$$\text{Under- or overallocated indirect costs} = \text{Indirect costs incurred} - \text{Indirect costs allocated}$$

Equivalent terms are **underapplied** (or **overapplied**) **indirect costs** and **underabsorbed** (or **overabsorbed**) **indirect costs**.

The Robinson Company has a single indirect-cost pool (Manufacturing Overhead) in its job-costing system. There are two indirect-cost accounts in its general ledger that pertain to manufacturing overhead:

◆ Manufacturing Overhead Control, which is the record of the *actual* costs in all the individual overhead categories (such as indirect materials, indirect manufacturing labor, power, and rent).

◆ Manufacturing Overhead Allocated, which is the record of the manufacturing overhead allocated to individual jobs on the basis of the <u>budgeted rate</u> multiplied by <u>actual</u> machine-hours.

Assume the following annual data for the Robinson Company:

Manufacturing Overhead Control		Manufacturing Overhead Allocated	
Bal. Dec. 31, 19_7 1,200,000		Bal. Dec. 31, 19_7 1,000,000	

The $80 budgeted indirect-cost rate is computed by dividing budgeted manufacturing overhead of $1,280,000 (the numerator) by the 16,000 budgeted quantity of machine-hours (the denominator). The $1,200,000 debit balance in Manufacturing Overhead Control is the sum of all the actual costs incurred for manufacturing overhead in 19_7. The $1,000,000 credit balance in Manufacturing Overhead Allocated results from 12,500 actual machine-hours worked on all the jobs in 19_7 times the budgeted rate of $80 per hour.

The $200,000 difference (a net debit) is an underallocated amount because actual manufacturing overhead costs exceed the allocated amount. This $200,000 difference in 19_7 arises from two reasons related to the computation of the $80 budgeted hourly rate:

1. *Numerator reason (budgeted indirect costs).* Actual manufacturing overhead cost of $1,200,000 is less than the budgeted amount of $1,280,000.

2. *Denominator reason (budgeted quantity of allocation base).* Actual machine-hours of 12,500 are fewer than the budgeted amount of 16,000 hours.

There are two main approaches to disposing of this $200,000 underallocation of manufacturing overhead in Robinson's costing system: (1) the adjusted allocation rate approach, and (2) the proration approach.

Adjusted Allocation Rate Approach

The adjusted allocation rate approach, in effect, restates all entries in the general ledger by using actual cost rates rather than budgeted cost rates. First, the actual indirect-cost rate is computed at the end of each period. Then, every job to which indirect costs were allocated during the period has its amount recomputed using the actual indirect-cost rate (rather than the budgeted indirect-cost rate). Finally, end-of-period closing entries are made. The result is that every single job cost record—as well as the ending inventory and cost of goods sold accounts—accurately represents actual indirect costs incurred.

The widespread adoption of computerized accounting systems has greatly reduced the cost of using the adjusted allocated rate approach. Consider the Robinson Company example. The actual manufacturing overhead ($1,200,000) exceeds the manufacturing overhead allocated ($1,000,000) by 20%. The actual 19_7 manufacturing overhead rate was $96 per machine-hour ($1,200,000 ÷ 12,500 machine-hours) rather than the budgeted $80 per machine-hour. At year-end, Robinson could increase the 19_7 manufacturing overhead allocated to each job in that year by 20% using a single software directive. The directive would apply to the subsidiary ledger as well as to the general ledger. This approach increases the accuracy of each individual product cost amount and the accuracy of the end-of-year account balances for inventories and cost of goods sold. This increase in accuracy is an important benefit. After-the-fact analysis of individual product profitability can provide managers with useful insights for future decisions about product pricing and about which products to emphasize. Such decisions are improved by having more accurate product-profitability numbers on prior jobs.

Proration Approach

Proration is the spreading of under- or overallocated overhead among ending inventories and cost of goods sold. Consider the Robinson Company where manufacturing overhead is allocated on the basis of machine-hours. Materials are not allocated any overhead costs. It is not until materials are put into work in process that machining of them commences. Only the ending work-in-process and finished goods inventories will have an allocated manufacturing overhead component. Hence, in our Robinson example, it is only these two Ending Inventory accounts (and Cost of Goods Sold) for which end-of-period proration is an issue. Assume the following actual results for Robinson Company in 19_7:

	End of Year Balances (before Proration)	Manufacturing Overhead Allocated Component of Year-End Balances (before Proration)
Work in Process	$ 50,000	$ 13,000
Finished Goods	75,000	25,000
Cost of Goods Sold	2,375,000	962,000
	$2,500,000	$1,000,000

There are three methods for prorating the underallocated $200,000 manufacturing overhead at the end of 19_7.

Method 1 Proration is based on the <u>total amount of indirect costs allocated</u> (before proration) in the ending balances of Work in Process, Finished Goods, and Cost of Goods Sold. In our Robinson Company example, the $200,000 underallocated overhead is prorated over the three pertinent accounts in proportion to their total amount of indirect costs allocated (before proration) in column 3 in the following table, resulting in the ending balances (after proration) in column 5.

(1)	Account Balance (before Proration) (2)	Indirect Costs Allocated Component in the Balance in Column (2) (3)	Proration of $200,000 Manufacturing Overhead Underallocated (4)	Account Balance (after Proration) (5) = (2) + (4)
Work in Process	$ 50,000	$ 13,000 (1.3%)	0.013 × $200,000 = $ 2,600	$ 52,600
Finished Goods	75,000	25,000 (2.5%)	0.025 × 200,000 = 5,000	80,000
Cost of Goods Sold	2,375,000	962,000 (96.2%)	0.962 × 200,000 = 192,400	2,567,400
	2,500,000	1,000,000 (100.0%)	$200,000	$2,700,000

The journal entry for this proration would be

Work-in-Process Control	2,600	
Finished Goods Control	5,000	
Cost of Goods Sold	192,400	
Manufacturing Overhead Allocated	1,000,000	
Manufacturing Overhead Control		1,200,000

This journal entry results in the 19_7 ending balances for Work in Process, Finished Goods, and Cost of Goods Sold being restated to what they would have been had actual cost rates rather than budgeted cost rates been used. Method 1 reports the same 19_7 ending balances as does the adjusted allocation rate approach.

Method 2 Proration based on <u>total ending balances</u> (before proration) in Work in Process, Finished Goods, and Cost of Goods Sold. In our Robinson Company example, the $200,000 underallocated overhead is prorated over the three pertinent accounts in proportion to their total ending balances (before proration) in column 2 in the following table, resulting in the ending balances (after proration) in column 4:

(1)	Account Balance (before Proration) (2)		Proration of $200,000 Manufacturing Overhead Underallocated (3)		Account Balance (after Proration) (4) = (2) + (3)
Work in Process	$ 50,000	(2%)	0.02 × $200,000 = $ 4,000		$ 54,000
Finished Goods	75,000	(3%)	0.03 × 200,000 = 6,000		81,000
Cost of Goods Sold	2,375,000	(95%)	0.95 × 200,000 = 190,000		2,565,000
	$2,500,000	100%	1.00	$200,000	$2,700,000

% Allocation × 2,500,000

For example, work in process is 2% of the $2,500,000 total, so we allocate 2% of the underallocated amount (0.02 × $200,000 = $4,000) to work in process.

The journal entry for this proration would be

Work-in-Process Control	4,000	
Finished Goods Control	6,000	
Cost of Goods Sold	190,000	
Manufacturing Overhead Allocated	1,000,000	
Manufacturing Overhead Control		1,200,000

Note that if manufacturing overhead had been overallocated, the Work-in-Process, Finished Goods, and Cost of Goods Sold accounts would be decreased (credited) instead of increased (debited).

Method 3 Year-end write-off to Cost of Goods Sold. Here the total under- or overallocated overhead is included in this year's Cost of Goods Sold. In our Robinson Company example, the journal entry would be

Amt Actually underallocated

Cost of Goods Sold	200,000	
Manufacturing Overhead Allocated	1,000,000	
Manufacturing Overhead Control		1,200,000

original Alloatn

Robinson's two Manufacturing Overhead accounts are closed out with all the difference between them now included in cost of goods sold. The Cost of Goods Sold after proration is $2,375,000 before proration + $200,000 underallocated overhead amount = $2,575,000.

Choice among Approaches

Choice among the approaches should be guided by how the resultant information is to be used. The reported account balances under the approaches.

Preferred / *many co.s use*

	Adjusted Allocation Rate Approach	Proration Approach		
		Method 1	Method 2	Method 3
		Proration Based on Indirect Costs Allocated Component of Ending Balances	Proration Based on Total Ending Balances	Write-off to Cost of Goods Sold
Work in Process	$ 52,600	$ 52,600	$ 54,000	50,000
Finished Goods	80,000	80,000	81,000	75,000
Cost of Goods Sold	2,567,400	2,567,400	2,565,000	2,575,000
	$2,700,000	$2,700,000	$2,700,000	$2,700,000

All yield the SAME

If managers wish to develop the most accurate record of individual job costs for profitability analysis purposes, the adjusted allocation rate approach is preferred. The proration approaches do not make any adjustment to individual job cost records.

If the purpose is confined to reporting the most accurate inventory and cost of goods sold figures, either the adjusted allocation rate or the method 1 proration should be used. Both give the same ending balances of Work in Process, Finished Goods, and Cost of Goods Sold that would have been reported had an actual indirect-cost rate been used. Method 2 is frequently justified as being a lower-cost way of approximating the results from method 1. The implicit assumption in method 2 is that the ratio of manufacturing overhead costs allocated to total manufacturing costs is similar in Work in Process, Finished Goods, and Cost of Goods Sold. Where this assumption is not appropriate, method 2 can yield numbers quite different from those of method 1. Many companies use method 3 for several reasons. First, it is the simplest. Second, the three methods often result in similar amounts for ending Work in Process, Finished Goods, and Cost of Goods Sold.

This section has examined end-of-period adjustments for under- or overallocated indirect costs. The same issues also arise when budgeted direct-cost rates are used and end-of-period adjustments must be made.

ACTIVITY-BASED COSTING IN MANUFACTURING

Chapter 4 introduced and illustrated the use of an *activity-based costing (ABC)* approach to designing costing systems in the service and merchandising sectors. ABC focuses on activities as the fundamental cost objects. It uses the cost of these activities as the basis for assigning costs to other cost objects such as products, services, or customers. ABC uses the cost-driver notion when deciding how many indirect-cost pools to use and the preferred allocation base for each indirect-cost pool. We now illustrate the use of ABC in designing costing systems in the manufacturing sector. Instruments, Inc., assembles and tests more than 800 electronic instrument products, including printed-circuit boards. Every board has various parts (diodes, capacitors, and integrated circuits) inserted on it. Consider the previous costing system and the revised ABC system for costing products.

Previous Costing System

The previous job-costing system of Instruments, Inc., was typical of many systems worldwide. Job costing was based on two direct-cost categories and two indirect manufacturing cost pools:

- ◆ Direct manufacturing costs
  Direct materials
  Direct manufacturing labor
- ◆ Indirect manufacturing costs
  Procurement (purchasing) support—allocated to products on the basis of 40% of their direct materials costs
  Production support—allocated to products on the basis of 800% of their direct manufacturing labor costs

A normal costing system was used with actual costs for the two direct-cost categories and budgeted costs for the two indirect-cost categories. Exhibit 5-5, Panel A, shows how products X and Y were costed in the previous costing system. The job-costing overview is in Exhibit 5-5 (Panel B).

As business became increasingly competitive, managers in product design, manufacturing, and marketing became more skeptical about the accuracy of Instruments, Inc.'s costing system. A common complaint was that the system did not produce numbers that reflected the way various products differed in their use of resources. For example, one product designer commented,

> Why is it that when I use a $0.20 capacitor part, the procurement overhead charge is $0.02, but when I use a $100 co-processor part, the procurement overhead charge is $10? Procuring and handling a co-processor does not con-

EXHIBIT 5-5
Manufacturing Product Costs at Instruments, Inc., with Previous Costing System

PANEL A: MANUFACTURING PRODUCT COST REPORTS FOR 19_7

	Board X	Board Y
Direct manufacturing costs		
Direct materials	$ 600	$280
Direct manufacturing labor	32	56
Total	632	336
Indirect manufacturing costs		
Procurement support		
(X, $600; Y, $280) × 40%	240	112
Production support		
(X, $32; Y, $56) × 800%	256	448
Total	496	560
Total manufacturing costs	$1,128	$896

PANEL B: JOB-COSTING OVERVIEW

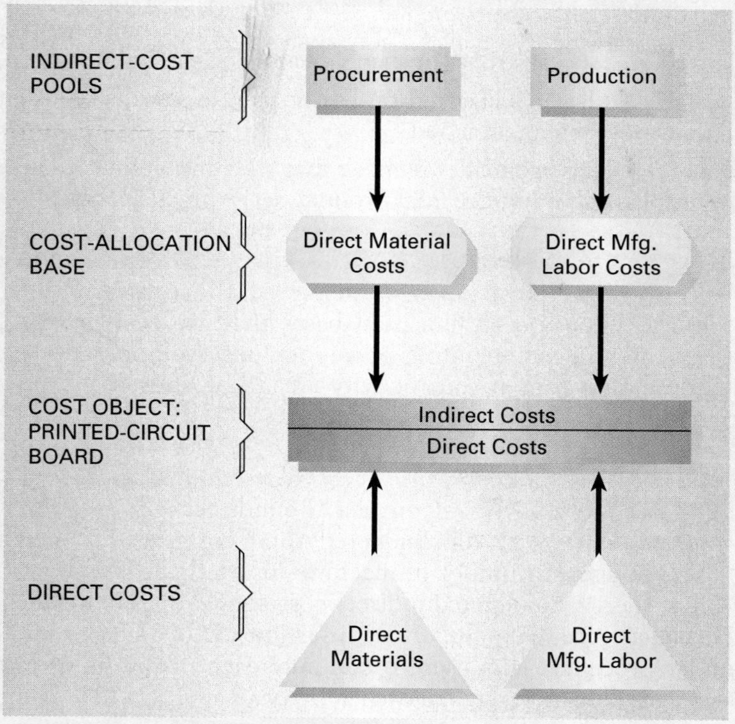

sume 500 times ($10 ÷ $0.02 = 500) the resources used to procure and handle a capacitor. This overhead costing approach is from Looney-toon land.

Managers in manufacturing believed that different factors were causing or driving costs in individual activity areas, but the costing system did not provide information about those differences. These managers found the numbers in the existing costing system to be of limited use or even a detriment in their decisions. Managers in marketing perceived that the costing system tended to "overcost" the intensely competitive high-volume products such as board X. How? By loading too much of the indirect manufacturing costs on high-volume products and too little on low-volume products.

Cost Refinement with Activity-Based Costing

Representatives from product design, manufacturing, and accounting worked as a cross-functional team to refine the normal costing system using an activity-based focus. Our description of Instruments, Inc.'s activity-based job-costing system will follow the six-step general approach to job costing.

Step 1: Identify the Job That Is the Chosen Cost Object   A job at Instruments, Inc., is an order of any size for one of its over 800 electronic instrument products, including 80 different printed-circuit boards.

Step 2: Identify the Direct Costs for the Job   Instruments, Inc., decides to retain its existing two direct-cost categories in its refined job-costing system—direct materials and direct manufacturing labor.

Step 3: Identify the Indirect-Cost Pools Associated with the Job   The refined system has five indirect-cost pools. These indirect-cost pools represent individual activity areas at Instruments, Inc.'s manufacturing facility.

1. *Materials handling.* All the parts necessary for manufacturing the printed-circuit board are combined into a kit.
2. *Machine insertion of parts.* Automated and semiautomated equipment insert components on the board.
3. *Manual insertion of parts.* Skilled workers insert those components that are not machine-inserted (because of their shape, weight, location on the board, and so on).
4. *Wave soldering.* All parts inserted on the board are simultaneously soldered to ensure that they remain attached.
5. *Quality testing.* Tests are made to check that all components are inserted and in the proper place and that the final product performs to specification.

Step 4: Select the Cost-Allocation Base to Use in Allocating Each Indirect-Cost Pool to the Job   Instruments, Inc., used the cause-and-effect criterion central to ABC to choose cost-allocation bases that are cost drivers. The cross-functional team interviewed operating personnel, observed operations at the plant, and analyzed operating data at each activity area. The chosen allocation bases are presented together with their rates in step 5.

Step 5: Develop the Rate Per Unit of Each Cost-Allocation Base Used to Allocate Indirect Costs to the Job   Consider the indirect-cost area for the machine insertion of parts. For 19_8, the budgeted total costs at this activity area are $2,000,000. The budgeted number of machine-inserted parts on boards in 19_8 is 4,000,000. Thus, the 19_8 budgeted indirect cost-allocation rate for the machine insertion of parts activity area is $0.50 per insertion ($2,000,000 ÷ 4,000,000 insertions). A similar procedure was used to compute each of the following 19_8 budgeted indirect cost-allocation rates in each activity area.

Activity Area	Cost Driver Used as Cost-Allocation Base	Indirect Cost-Allocation Rate
1. Materials handling	Parts	$2 per part
2. Machine insertion of parts	Machine-inserted parts	$0.50 per insertion
3. Manual insertion of parts	Manually-inserted parts	$4 per insertion
4. Wave soldering	Boards	$50 per board
5. Quality testing	Test time	$50 per test-hour

Exhibit 5-6, Panel A, shows how products X and Y are costed in the ABC system. The job-costing overview is shown in Panel B. Increasing the number of indirect-cost pools to five results in more homogeneous cost pools. For example, the costs in the quality testing activity area are driven by hours of test time while those in the machine insertion of parts activity area have a different cost driver (machine-inserted parts).

EXHIBIT 5-6
Product Costs at Instruments, Inc., with Activity-Based Costing

PANEL A: PRODUCT COSTS FOR 19_7

	Board X	Board Y
Direct manufacturing costs		
Direct materials	$600	$ 280
Direct manufacturing labor	32	56
Total	632	336
Indirect manufacturing costs		
Materials handling*		
(X, 81 parts; Y, 121 parts) × $2	162	242
Machine insertion of parts		
(X, 70 insertions; Y, 90 insertions) × $0.50	35	45
Manual insertion of parts		
(X, 10 insertions; Y, 30 insertions) × $4	40	120
Wave soldering		
(X, 1 board; Y, 1 board) × $50	50	50
Quality testing		
(X, 1.5 hours; Y, 6.5 hours) × $50	75	325
Total	362	782
Total manufacturing costs	$994	$1,118

*The number of parts includes the raw printed-circuit board (counted as one part) plus the number of component parts to be inserted on the board.

PANEL B: JOB-COSTING OVERVIEW

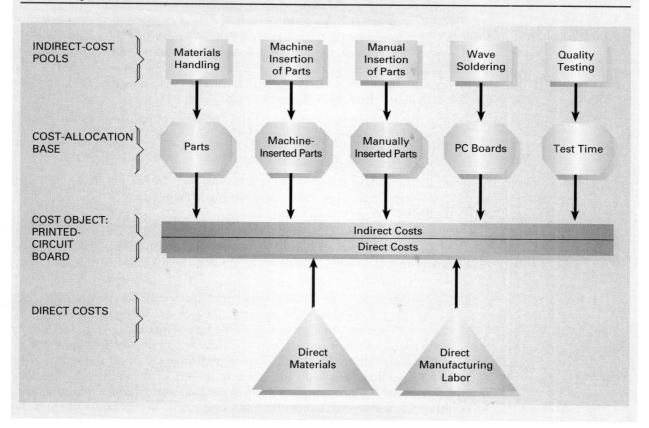

Step 6: Assign the Costs to the Cost Object by Adding all Direct Costs and all Indirect Costs The ABC system results in the following product costs:

	Board X	Board Y
Direct job costs	$632	$ 336
Indirect job costs	362	782
Total job costs	$994	$1,118

Board X has an 11.9% decrease with ABC vis-à-vis its $1,128 cost under the previous system: ($994 – $1,128) ÷ $1,128 = –11.9%. In contrast, board Y has a 24.8% increase with ABC vis-à-vis its $896 cost under the previous system: ($1,118 – $896) ÷ $896 = 24.8%.

Insights Available with ABC

The ABC system provides Instruments, Inc., with a variety of new insights:

1. The differences in the ABC product costs of boards X and Y highlight how these products use different amounts of the resources of each activity area. Consider differences in the relative use of the following four activity areas:

	Board X	Board Y
Materials handling	81 parts	121 parts
Machine insertion of parts	70 insertions	90 insertions
Manual insertion of parts	10 insertions	30 insertions
Quality testing	1.5 hours	6.5 hours

The ABC system, a more refined costing system than the previous system, reports cost numbers that better measure the way jobs, products, customers, and so on, differently use the resources of the organization. These differences help explain how board X was being undercosted while board Y was being overcosted using the previous costing system. Marketing can reduce board X's price and still make a reasonable margin. In recent years, they have been losing market share on this high-volume product.

2. The ABC system pinpoints to product designers opportunities for cost reductions. Managers might ask, why does board X cost less? ABC costing reveals three reasons:
   a. Board X has fewer parts.
   b. Board X has a higher percentage of total insertions made by machine. (These are cheaper than insertions made manually.)
   c. Board X requires less test time.

   The activity-based job-costing system explicitly signals to product designers that (a), (b), and (c) each lead to a lower cost for assembling a printed-circuit board. In fact, board X is a standard, no-frills board that Instruments, Inc., produces in large quantities.

3. Cost reductions efforts by manufacturing personnel at Instruments, Inc., are better focused using the ABC system. The five activity areas have different cost drivers. Cost-reduction targets can now be set that relate to reductions in the costs per driver unit of each activity area. For example, the supervisor of the materials handling area could have a performance target related to reducing the $2 per part handled rate. Note that each of the indirect cost-allocation bases in the ABC system is a nonfinancial variable (number of parts, hours of test time, and so on). Controlling physical items such as hours or parts is often the most fundamental way that operating personnel manage costs.

Activity-Based Costing and End-of-Period Adjustments

The issue of end-of-period adjustments for under- or overallocated indirect costs arises with any costing system using budgeted rates. In the Robinson Company example (pp. 135–144), there was only one budgeted cost rate—manufacturing overhead. In the Instruments, Inc., example, there is a budgeted cost rate for each of the

How Clark-Hurth Implemented Activity-Based Costing

Clark-Hurth (C-H), a division of the Clark Equipment Company, manufactures a broad range of axle and transmission products. As a supplier to many off-highway and equipment manufacturers, C-H has been put under great pressure in recent years to provide ever higher quality products at ever lower costs. To obtain more accurate product cost information, C-H managers believed that they had to abandon their costing system and move to ABC. The company had used direct materials and direct manufacturing labor as direct-cost categories and manufacturing overhead (allocated using direct manufacturing labor-hours) as the indirect-cost pool. But this system, managers felt, provided few insights into how different products were differently using C-H resources. ABC promised to improve C-H's accounting system.

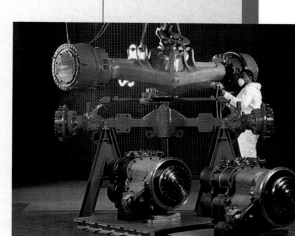

Stage One in implementing ABC at C-H meant surveying every salaried and indirect worker at the company to obtain information on the activities they performed. Over 170 activities were listed. C-H then ranked these activities in order of frequency. Stage Two in the ABC implementation was determining those activities that a C-H customer would view as valuable. This effort led C-H to discontinue several activities. At Stage Three, managers selected cost drivers for the 40 most frequent activities. The cost drivers chosen included both traditional measures (such as direct manufacturing labor-hours and machine-hours) and nontraditional measures (such as the number of parts in a product).

At Stage Four, managers estimated the costs per driver unit at each of the 40 activities. ABC-based product costs were then developed at Stage Five.

The revised product costs showed several patterns. One pattern that emerged was that many products with low sales volume were being undercosted and that C-H was actually losing money on them. Several high-sales-volume products that required no "bells and whistles" on the production line were being significantly overcosted.

C-H has used this revised activity-based product cost information in bidding for work from off-highway companies.

C-H is now using ABC for cost management. For example, in Stage One C-H found that the large number of different parts it purchased was consuming much of its time and other resources. C-H has undertaken a parts deproliferation program. One step is to have a standard part used on many products, which reduces the number of different parts to be purchased. A second step is to require procurement personnel to justify placing an order for a new part when a part on hand at C-H may be adequate.

The president of C-H notes that the company has enjoyed three major benefits from its switch to ABC:

1. A better understanding of what C-H people are doing
2. A better understanding of real costs
3. A better understanding of the opportunities available for reducing costs

Source: Adapted from a presentation by Clark-Hurth at Computer Aided Manufacturing-International (CAM-I).

five activity areas that are indirect costs of the PC boards. Under- or overallocated costs can occur in each activity area. At the end of an accounting period, five adjustments may be required for these under- or overallocated costs.

If the purpose of the end-of-period adjustment is to obtain more accurate individual product costs, then the adjusted allocation rate approach, if economically feasible, should be used for the under- or overallocated costs in each activity area. If the purpose of the end-of-period adjustment is restricted to obtaining the most accurate ending inventory and cost of goods sold figures, proration (based on the costs in each activity area that are allocated to products) should suffice. Note that in the Instruments, Inc., example this proration would include the materials component of ending inventory. Why? Because indirect costs pertaining to materials handling are allocated to all materials. Under- or overallocations of these materials handling indirect costs require end-of-period adjustments to all three components of ending inventory (materials, work in process, and finished goods) as well as to cost of goods sold.

COST HIERARCHIES

The driver of many costs in organizations is units of output (or variables that are a function of units of output). This assumption underlies much of the discussion in this chapter and in earlier chapters. However, not all costs are driven by output units. This has led to the classification of costs into cost hierarchies. A **cost hierarchy** is a categorization of costs into different cost pools on the basis of different classes of cost drivers or different degrees of difficulty in determining cause-and-effect (or benefits received) relationships.

Manufacturing Cost Hierarchy

The cost hierarchy notion is an important part of some ABC applications. This section illustrates a four-part manufacturing cost hierarchy. Chapters 14 and 16 discuss this topic further. The four levels of manufacturing costs we now examine are

1. Output unit-level costs
2. Batch-level costs
3. Product-sustaining costs
4. Facility-sustaining costs

Exhibit 5-7 illustrates these four cost levels.

Output unit-level costs are resources sacrificed on activities performed on each individual unit of product or service. Each product cost item in Exhibit 5-6 for Instruments, Inc., is a linear function of output units of board X or board Y. Consider the indirect manufacturing costs of board X. The total indirect manufacturing costs of the five activity areas for assembling 1, 10, and 100 output units of board X are as follows:

	Total Output Units Assembled		
Indirect Manufacturing	**1**	**10**	**100**
Materials handling			
(81 parts × $2) × 1, 10, 100	$162	$1,620	$16,200
Machine insertion of parts			
(70 × $0.50) × 1, 10, 100	35	350	3,500
Manual insertion of parts			
(10 × $4) × 1, 10, 100	40	400	4,000
Wave soldering			
(1 × $50) × 1, 10, 100	50	500	5,000
Quality testing			
(1.5 × $50) × 1, 10, 100	75	750	7,500
Total indirect manufacturing costs	$362	$3,620	$36,200

EXHIBIT 5-7
Manufacturing Cost Hierarchy

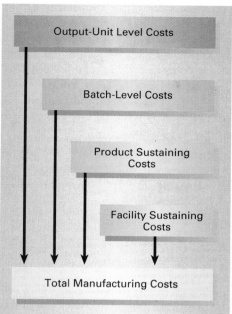

An increase in output units assembled requires (by definition) an increase in total costs if that cost item is classified as an output unit-level cost. In the Instruments, Inc., example, this increase occurs in a linear fashion for each of the five indirect-cost categories. In other cases, the increase may occur in a nonlinear fashion.

Batch-level costs are resources sacrificed on activities that are related to a group of units of product(s) or service(s) rather than to each individual unit of product or service. Setup costs are an example of batch-level costs. Suppose the machine insertion of parts activity area of Instruments, Inc., requires the loading of software programs and the reloading of the parts insertion machine prior to the start of production for board X. These setup tasks take 20 minutes and must be undertaken whether 1 printed-circuit board is assembled or 100 printed-circuit boards are assembled. The actual costs incurred to assemble 100 printed-circuit boards will be the sum of (a) the output-unit level costs of these 100 boards ($35 × 100), and (b) the number of machine setups times the cost per setup. Assume each setup costs $400. Then the batch-level costs in the machine insertion of parts area will be $400 × the number of setups. Thus, the total indirect manufacturing costs of the machine insertion of parts for assembling 100 output units of board X are as follows:

	Number of Setups		
	1	**2**	**20**
Output unit-level costs			
($35 × 100)	$3,500	$3,500	$ 3,500
Batch-level costs			
($400 × 1, 2, 20)	400	800	8,000
Total machine insertion costs	$3,900	$4,300	$11,500
Average unit cost	$ 39	$ 43	$ 115

By having a single setup for assembling 100 units of board X, Instruments, Inc., will have much lower costs than if it has (say) 20 setups with an average of 5 output units being assembled between each setup for board X.

Product-sustaining or **service-sustaining costs** are resources sacrificed on activities undertaken to support specific products or services. Product-sustaining costs cannot be linked in any cause-and-effect way to individual units of products or to individual batches of products. Consider the costs of designing each printed circuit board. These include the labor costs of product designers, the costs of their design equipment, and the costs of materials consumed in exploring alternative designs. These costs are incurred irrespective of the number of output units of (say) board X assembled or the number of any batches in the production area.

Facility-sustaining costs are resources sacrificed on activities that cannot be traced to specific products or services but support the organization as a whole. Examples of facility sustaining costs are the leasehold costs for a manufacturing plant and the plant manager's salary.

Unit Cost Computation

Chapter 2 noted that a unit product cost amount will vary as output units change when a subset of costs is not linearly variable with output units. The cost hierarchy notion provides examples of three categories of costs that do not vary in a linear way with output units. Assume Instruments, Inc., assigns the following costs to board X when 100 output units are assembled:

Output unit-level costs ($994 × 100)	$ 99,400
Batch-level costs	11,716
Product-sustaining costs	6,435
Facility-sustaining costs	16,849
Total manufacturing costs	$134,400

Should costs in all four levels of the cost hierarchy be unitized? The answer is that it depends on the purpose. Consider cost management. For this purpose, expressing all manufacturing costs on a per output unit basis may not be required. The appropriate way to manage costs is typically at the respective hierarchy level. For example, reducing batch-level costs is accomplished by reducing the number of batches or by reducing the cost per batch. No extra insight for cost management is gained by dividing batch level costs by the total number of output units manufactured. For other purposes, however, expressing batch-level, product-sustaining, or facility-sustaining costs on a per output unit level may be required. For example, inventory valuation for financial reporting requires total manufacturing costs be expressed on a per output units manufactured basis. ($134,400 ÷ 100 units) = $1,344.00

TRADITIONAL VERSUS ABC APPROACH TO DESIGNING A COSTING SYSTEM

OBJECTIVE 7

Distinguish between the traditional and the activity-based costing approaches to designing a costing system in manufacturing

The Instruments, Inc., example in Exhibit 5-4 and the Family Supermarkets example in Panel B of Exhibit 4-8 (p. 111) each illustrate how an ABC approach can be used to refine a costing system. The major differences between the so-called "traditional" approach and an ABC approach are as follows:

Traditional Approach	**ABC Approach**
One or a few indirect-cost pools for each department or entire plant, usually with little homogeneity of these cost pools.	Many homogeneous indirect-cost pools because many activity areas are used. Operating personnel play a key role in designating which activity areas to use.
Indirect cost-allocation bases may or may not be cost drivers.	Indirect cost-allocation bases are much more likely to be cost drivers.
Indirect cost-allocation bases are often financial, such as direct labor costs or direct material costs.	Indirect cost-allocation bases are often nonfinancial variables, such as number of parts in a product or hours of test time.

The traditional approach often uses too few pools of indirect costs, so cost allocations are overly broad averages. The resulting costs may lead managers to make erroneous decisions about pricing or product emphasis. For example, a product that is overcosted by the traditional approach may be priced too high, resulting in loss of market share. Similarly, managers may be setting selling prices for some products that are below the cost of the resources used to produce them. The dangers are especially pronounced when hundreds of diverse products are manufactured in various annual output levels ranging from a few units of, say, one or two kinds of motors or computers to thousands of units of other kinds. Case studies have shown that the broad averages in the traditional approach can load indirect manufacturing costs too heavily on high-volume products and too lightly on low-volume products.

Most fundamentally, managers manage costs by overseeing activities rather than products. The pooling of costs by activities or activity areas provides information that may help managers to better plan and control costs throughout the value chain, from R&D to customer service.

Reexamine the Exhibit 5-4 (p. 136) illustration of a job costing system. Then try to solve the following problem, which requires consideration of many of this chapter's important points.

PROBLEM

You are asked to bring the following incomplete accounts of Endeavor Printing, Inc., up to date through January 31, 19_8. Consider the data that appear in the T-accounts as well as the following information in items (a) through (i).

Endeavor's job-costing system, which uses normal costing, has two direct-cost categories (direct materials and direct manufacturing labor) and one indirect-cost pool (manufacturing overhead, which is allocated using direct manufacturing labor costs).

Materials Control		Wages Payable Control	
December 31, 19_7			January 31, 19_8
Balance 15,000			Balance 3,000

Work-in-Process Control		Manufacturing Overhead Control	
		January 19_8	
		Charges 57,000	

		Manufacturing Overhead Allocated	

Finished Goods Control		Cost of Goods Sold	
December 31, 19_7			
Balance 20,000			

ADDITIONAL INFORMATION

a. Manufacturing overhead is allocated using a budgeted rate set every December. Management forecasts next year's manufacturing overhead and next year's direct manufacturing labor costs. The budget for 19_8 is $400,000 of direct manufacturing labor and $600,000 of manufacturing overhead.

b. The only job unfinished on January 31, 19_8, is No. 419, on which direct manufacturing labor costs are $2,000 (125 direct manufacturing labor-hours) and direct materials costs are $8,000.

c. Total materials placed into production during January are $90,000.

d. Cost of goods completed during January is $180,000.

e. Materials inventory as of January 31, 19_8 is $20,000.

f. Finished goods inventory as of January 31, 19_8 is $15,000.

g. All plant workers earn the same wage rate. Direct manufacturing labor-hours used for January total 2,500. Other labor and supervision labor total $10,000.

h. The gross plant payroll on January paydays totals $52,000. Ignore withholdings. All personnel are paid on a weekly basis.

i. All "actual" Manufacturing Department overhead incurred during January has already been posted.

Calculate the following:

1. Materials purchased during January
2. Costs of Goods Sold during January
3. Direct Manufacturing Labor Costs incurred during January
4. Manufacturing Overhead Allocated during January
5. Balance, Wages Payable Control, December 31, 19_7
6. Balance, Work-in-Process Control, January 31, 19_8
7. Balance, Work-in-Process Control, December 31, 19_7
8. Balance, Finished Goods Control, January 31, 19_8
9. Manufacturing Overhead Under- or Overallocated for January

SOLUTION

Amounts from the T-accounts are labeled (T).

1. Materials purchased: $90,000 (c) + $20,000 − $15,000 (T) = $95,000
2. Cost of Goods Sold: $20,000 (T) + $180,000 (d) − $15,000 = $185,000
3. Direct manufacturing wage rate: $2,000 (b) ÷ 125 hours (b) = $16 per hour
   Direct manufacturing labor costs: 2,500 hours (g) × $16 = $40,000
4. Manufacturing overhead rate: $600,000 (a) ÷ $400,000 (a) = 150%
   Manufacturing overhead allocated: 150% × $40,000 (see 3) = $60,000
5. Wages Payable Control, December 31, 19_7: $52,000 (h) + $3,000 (T) − $40,000 (see 3) − $10,000 (g) = $5,000
6. Work-in-Process Control, January 31, 19_8: $8,000 (b) + $2,000 (b) + 150% of $2,000 (b) = $13,000 (This answer is used in item 7.)
7. Work-in-Process Control, December 31, 19_7: $180,000 (d) + $13,000 (see 6) − $90,000 − $40,000 (see 3) − $60,000 (see 4) = $3,000
8. Finished Goods Control, January 31, 19_8: $20,000 (T) + $180,000 (d) − $185,000 (2) = $15,000 (f)
9. Manufacturing overhead overallocated: $60,000 (see 4) − $57,000 (T) = $3,000

Entries in T-accounts are lettered in accordance with the preceding additional information and are numbered in accordance with the requirements.

Materials Control

December 31, 19_7 Bal. (given)	15,000		
(1)	95,000*	(c)	90,000
January 31, 19_8 Bal. (e)	20,000		

Work-in-Process Control

December 31, 19_7 Bal. (7)	3,000	(d)	180,000
Direct materials (c)	90,000		
Direct manufacturing labor (b) (g) (3)	40,000		
Manufacturing overhead allocation (g) (a) (4)	60,000		
January 31, 19_8 Bal. (b) (6)	13,000		

Finished Goods Control

December 31, 19_7 Bal. (given)	20,000		
(d)	180,000	(f) (2)	185,000
January 31, 19_8 Bal. (9)	15,000		

*Can be computed only after all other postings in the account have been found.

Wages Payable Control

(h)	52,000	December 31, 19_7	(5)	5,000
			(g)	{ 40,000
				10,000
		January 31, 19_8 (given)		3,000

Manufacturing Overhead Control

Total January charges (given)	57,000	

Manufacturing Overhead Allocated

		(g) (a) (4)	60,000

Cost of Goods Sold

(f) (2)	185,000	

SUMMARY

The following points are linked to the chapter's learning objectives.

1. Costing systems aim to report cost numbers that reflect the way chosen cost objects (such as products, services, or customers) use the resources of an organization. Designing a job-costing system involves identifying (a) the job, (b) the direct-costs, (c) the indirect-cost categories, (d) the cost-allocation base(s), and (e) the cost-allocation rate(s), and then (f) summing the direct costs and the indirect costs.

2. Three key source documents in a job-costing system are a job cost record, a materials requisition record, and a labor time record.

3. Subsidiary ledgers contain the underlying details of a costing system. The general ledger contains the summary information. The Work-in-Process subsidiary ledger provides a "worm's-eye view" of job costs, while the Work-in-Process Control account in the general ledger provides a "bird's-eye view" of the costing system.

4. The transactions in a job-costing system in manufacturing track include (a) the acquisition of materials and other manufacturing inputs, (b) their conversion into work in process, (c) their eventual conversion into finished goods, and (d) the sale of finished goods. Each of the (a) to (d) stages in the manufacture/sale cycle can be represented by journal entries in the costing system.

5. The theoretically correct alternative to disposing of under- or overallocated indirect costs is to prorate that amount on the basis of the already total amount of the allocated indirect cost in the ending balances of inventories and cost of goods sold. Many organizations simply write off any such amount to cost of goods sold on the basis of simplicity or immateriality.

6. A cost hierarchy is a categorization of costs into different cost pools on the basis of different classes of cost drivers or different degrees of difficulty in determining cause-and-effect (or benefits received) relationships. Four levels of manufacturing costs are output unit-level costs, batch-level costs, product-sustaining costs, and facility-sustaining costs.

7. An ABC approach differs from the traditional approach by its fundamental focus on activities. An ABC approach typically results in (a) more indirect-cost pools than the traditional approach, (b) more cost drivers used as cost-allocation bases, and (c) more frequent use of nonfinancial variables as cost-allocation bases.

This chapter and the Glossary at the end of this book contain definitions of the following important terms:

batch-level costs (151)
cost hierarchy (150)
facility-sustaining costs (152)
job cost record (134)
job cost sheet (134)
labor time record (135)
manufacturing overhead allocated (139)
materials requisition record (134)
output unit-level costs (150)

overabsorbed indirect costs (140)
overallocated indirect costs (140)
overapplied indirect costs (140)
product-sustaining costs (151)
proration (142)
service-sustaining costs (151)
underabsorbed indirect costs (140)
underallocated indirect costs (140)
underapplied indirect costs (140)

▼ ASSIGNMENT MATERIAL

QUESTIONS

5-1 Why are costing systems in the manufacturing sector often more detailed than those in the service and merchandising sectors?

5-2 Give three examples of specific manufacturing overhead cost items allocated to products.

5-3 Describe two source documents used in assigning manufacturing costs to products in a job-costing system.

5-4 What are two major goals of a job-costing system?

5-5 Describe the role of a manufacturing overhead allocation base in job costing.

5-6 Describe two different credit entries to the Materials Control general ledger T-account.

5-7 Describe three different debit entries to the Work-in-Process Control general ledger T-account.

5-8 Give two reasons for under- or overallocation of indirect costs at the end of an accounting period.

5-9 Describe three alternative ways to prorate end-of-period adjustments for under- or overallocated indirect costs.

5-10 Why might a company prefer the adjusted allocation rate approach over a proration approach to under- or overallocated indirect costs?

5-11 What are the most frequently used allocation bases for manufacturing overhead costs?

5-12 Describe four levels of a manufacturing cost hierarchy.

5-13 "The existence of non-output unit-level costs means that managers should not compute unit product costs based on total manufacturing costs in all levels of the cost hierarchy." Do you agree? Explain.

5-14 How is an activity-based approach different from a traditional approach to designing a job-costing system?

5-15 "Activity-based costing is the wave of the present and the future. All companies should adopt it." Do you agree? Explain.

EXERCISES

5-16 Job costing, normal and actual costing. Anderson Construction assembles residential homes. It uses a job-costing system with two direct-cost categories (direct materials and direct labor) and one indirect-cost pool (assembly support). Direct labor-hours is the allocation base for assembly support costs. In December 19_7, Anderson budgets 19_8 assembly support costs to be $8,000,000 and 19_8 direct labor-hours to be 160,000.

At the end of 19_8, Anderson is comparing the costs of several jobs that were started and completed in 19_8.

Construction Period	Laguna Model February–June 19_8	Mission Model May–October 19_8
Direct materials	$106,450	$127,604
Direct labor	$ 36,276	$ 41,410
Direct labor-hours	900	1,010

Direct materials and direct labor are paid for on a contract basis. The costs of each are known when direct materials are used or direct labor-hours are worked. The 19_8 actual assembly support costs were $6,888,000 while the actual direct labor-hours were 164,000

REQUIRED

1. Compute the (a) budgeted and (b) actual indirect-cost rate. Why do they differ?
2. What is the job cost of the Laguna Model and the Mission Model using (a) normal costing, and (b) actual costing?
3. Why might Anderson Construction prefer normal costing over actual costing?

5-17 Job costing, accounting for manufacturing overhead, budgeted rates. The Lynn Company uses a job-costing system at its Minneapolis plant. The plant has a Machining Department and an Assembly Department. Its job-costing system has two direct-cost categories (direct materials and direct manufacturing labor) and two manufacturing overhead cost pools (the Machining Department, allocated using actual machine-hours, and the Assembly Department, allocated using actual direct manufacturing labor cost). The 19_7 budget for the plant is as follows:

	Machining Department	Assembly Department
Manufacturing overhead	$1,800,000	$3,600,000
Direct manufacturing labor cost	$1,400,000	$2,000,000
Direct manufacturing labor-hours	100,000	200,000
Machine-hours	50,000	200,000

The company uses a budgeted overhead rate for allocating overhead to production orders on a machine-hour basis in Machining and on a direct manufacturing labor-cost basis in Assembly.

REQUIRED

1. Present an overview diagram of Lynn's job-costing system. Compute the budgeted manufacturing overhead rate for each department.
2. During February, the cost record for Job 494 contained the following:

	Machining Department	Assembly Department
Direct materials used	$45,000	$70,000
Direct manufacturing labor cost	$14,000	$15,000
Direct manufacturing labor-hours	1,000	1,500
Machine-hours	2,000	1,000

Compute the total manufacturing overhead costs of Job 494.

3. At the end of 19_7, the actual manufacturing overhead costs were $2,100,000 in Machining and $3,700,000 in Assembly. Assume that 55,000 actual machine-hours were used in Machining and that actual direct manufacturing labor costs in Assembly were $2,200,000. Compute the over- or underallocated manufacturing overhead for each department.

5-18 Job costing, journal entries. The University of Chicago Press is wholly owned by the university. It performs the bulk of its work for other university departments, which pay as though the Press were an outside business enterprise. The Press also publishes and maintains a stock of books for general sale. A job-costing system is used to cost each job. There are two direct-cost categories (direct materials and direct manufacturing labor) and one indirect-cost pool (manufacturing overhead, allocated on the basis of direct-labor costs).

The following data (in thousands) pertain to 19_8:

Direct materials and supplies purchased on account	$800
Direct materials used	710
Indirect materials issued to various production departments	100
Direct manufacturing labor	1,300
Indirect manufacturing labor incurred by various departments	900
Depreciation on building and manufacturing equipment	400
Miscellaneous manufacturing overhead* incurred by various departments (ordinarily would be detailed as repairs, photocopying, utilities, etc.)	550
Manufacturing overhead allocated at 160% of direct manufacturing labor costs	?
Cost of goods manufactured	4,120
Revenues	8,000
Cost of goods sold	4,020
Inventories, December 31, 19_7 (not 19_8):	
Materials control	100
Work-in-process control	60
Finished goods control	500

*The term *manufacturing overhead* is not used uniformly. Other terms that are often encountered in printing companies include job overhead and shop overhead.

REQUIRED
1. Present an overview diagram of the job-costing system at the University of Chicago Press.
2. Prepare general journal entries to summarize 19_8 transactions. As your final entry, dispose of the year-end over- or underallocated manufacturing overhead as a direct write-off to Cost of Goods Sold. Number your entries. Explanations for each entry may be omitted.
3. Show posted T-accounts for all inventories, Cost of Goods Sold, Manufacturing Overhead Control, and Manufacturing Overhead Allocated.

For more details concerning these data, see Problem 5-19.

5-19 Job costing, journal entries, and source documents (continuation of 5-18). For each journal entry in your answer to Exercise 5-18, (a) indicate the source document that would most likely authorize the entry, and (b) give a description of the entry into the subsidiary ledgers, if any entry needs to be made there.

5-20 Job costing, journal entries. Donnell Transport assembles prestige mobile homes. Its job-costing system has two direct-cost categories (direct materials and direct manufacturing labor) and one indirect-cost pool (manufacturing overhead allocated at a budgeted $30 per machine-hour in 19_8). The following data (in millions) pertain to operations for the year 19_8:

Materials Control, December 31, 19_7	$ 12
Work-in-Process Control, December 31, 19_7	2
Finished Goods Control, December 31, 19_7	6
Materials and supplies purchased on account	150
Direct materials used	145
Indirect materials (supplies) issued to various production departments	10
Direct manufacturing labor	90
Indirect manufacturing labor incurred by various departments	30
Depreciation on plant and manufacturing equipment	19
Miscellaneous manufacturing overhead incurred (credit Various Liabilities, ordinarily would be detailed as repairs, utilities, etc.)	9
Manufacturing overhead allocated, 2,100,000 actual machine-hours	?
Cost of goods manufactured	294
Revenues	400
Cost of goods sold	292

REQUIRED

1. Present an overview diagram of Donnell Transport's job-costing system.
2. Prepare general journal entries. Number your entries. Post to T-accounts. What is the ending balance of Work-in-Process Control?
3. Show the journal entry for disposing of over- or underallocated manufacturing overhead directly as a year-end write-off to Cost of Goods Sold. Post the entry to T-accounts.

For more details concerning these data, see Exercise 5-21.

5-21 Journal entries and source documents (continuation of 5-20). For each journal entry in your answer to Exercise 5-20, (a) indicate the source documents that would most likely authorize the entry, and (b) give a description of the entry into the subsidiary ledgers, if any.

5-22 Accounting for manufacturing overhead. Consider the following selected cost data for the Pittsburgh Forging Company for 19_7.

Budgeted manufacturing overhead	$7,000,000
Budgeted machine-hours	200,000
Actual manufacturing overhead	$6,800,000
Actual machine-hours	195,000

Pittsburgh's job-costing system has a single manufacturing overhead cost pool (allocated using a budgeted rate based on actual machine-hours). Any amount of under- or overallocation is immediately written off to cost of goods sold.

REQUIRED

1. Compute the budgeted manufacturing overhead rate.
2. Journalize the allocation of manufacturing overhead.
3. Compute the amount of under- or overallocation of manufacturing overhead. Is the amount significant? Journalize the disposition of this amount on the basis of the ending balances in the relevant accounts.

5-23 Proration of overhead. (Z. Iqbal, adapted) The Zaf Radiator Company uses a single manufacturing overhead cost pool in its job-costing system. It uses a normal costing system with actual machine hours as the allocation base. The following data are for 19_8:

Budgeted manufacturing overhead	$4,800,000
Overhead allocation base	Machine-hours
Budgeted machine-hours	80,000
Manufacturing overhead incurred	$4,900,000
Actual machine-hours	75,000

Machine-hours data and the ending balances (before proration of underallocated or overallocated overhead) are as follows:

	Actual Machine-Hours	19_8 End of Year Balance
Cost of Goods Sold	60,000	$8,000,000
Finished Goods	11,000	1,250,000
Work in Process	4,000	750,000

REQUIRED

1. Compute the budgeted manufacturing overhead rate for 19_8.
2. Compute the under- or overallocated manufacturing overhead of Zaf Radiator in 19_8. Prorate this under- or overallocated amount using:
   a. Immediate write-off to Cost of Goods Sold
   b. Proration based on ending balances (before proration) in Work in Process, Finished Goods, and Cost of Goods Sold
   c. Proration based on the allocated overhead amount (before proration) in the ending balances of Work in Process, Finished Goods, and Cost of Goods Sold
3. Which proration method do you prefer in requirement 3? Explain.

5-24 ABC, product cost cross-subsidization. Idaho Potatoes processes potatoes into potato cuts at its highly automated Pocatello plant. For many years, it processed potatoes for only the retail consumer market where it had a superb reputation for quality. Recently, it started selling potato cuts to the institutional market that includes hospitals, cafeterias, and university dormitories. Its penetration into the institutional market has been slower than predicted.

Idaho's existing costing system has a single direct-cost category (direct materials, which are the raw potatoes) and a single indirect-cost pool (production support). Support costs are allocated on the basis of pounds of potato cuts processed. Support costs include packaging material. The 19_7 total actual costs for producing 1,000,000 pounds of potato cuts (900,000 for the retail market and 100,000 for the institutional market) are

Direct materials used	$150,000
Production support	$983,000

The existing costing system does not distinguish between potato cuts produced for the retail or the institutional markets.

At the end of 19_7, Idaho unsuccessfully bid for a large institutional contract. Its bid was reported to be 30% above the winning bid. This came as a shock as Idaho included only a minimum profit margin on its bid. Moreover, the Pocatello plant was widely acknowledged as the most efficient in the industry.

As part of its lost contract bid review process, Idaho decided to explore several ways of refining its costing system. First, it identified that $188,000 of the $983,000 pertains to packaging materials that could be traced to individual jobs ($180,000 for retail and $8,000 for institutional). These will now be classified as a direct material. The $150,000 of direct materials used were classified as $135,000 for retail and $15,000 for institutional. Second, it used activity-based costing (ABC) to examine how the two products (retail potato cuts and institutional potato cuts) used the support area differently. The finding was that three activity areas could be distinguished and that different usage occurred in two of these three areas. The indirect cost per pound of finished product at each activity area is as follows:

Activity Area	Retail Potato Cuts	Institutional Potato Cuts
Cleaning	$0.120	$0.120
Cutting	0.240	0.150
Packaging	0.480	0.120

There was no beginning or ending amount of any inventory (materials, work in process, or finished goods).

REQUIRED

1. Using the current costing system, what is the cost per pound of potato cuts produced by Idaho?
2. Using the refined costing system, what is the cost per pound of (a) retail market potato cuts, and (b) institutional market potato cuts?
3. Comment on the cost differences shown between the two costing systems in requirements 1 and 2. How might Idaho use the information in requirement 2 to make better decisions?

5-25 ABC, activity area cost driver rates (continuation of 5-24). Exercise 5-24 reports ABC data for the three activity areas (cleaning, cutting, and packaging) on a per output unit basis (per pound of potato cut). This format emphasizes product costing. An alternative approach that emphasizes the costs of individual processes (activities) is to identify (a) the costs at each activity area, and (b) the rate per unit of the cost driver at each activity area. The following information pertains to (a) and (b):

◆ Cleaning activity area—Idaho used 1.2 million pounds of raw potatoes to yield 1 million pounds of potato cuts. No distinction is made as to the end product when cleaning potatoes. The cost driver is pounds of raw potatoes cleaned.
◆ Cutting activity area—Idaho processes raw potatoes for the retail market independently of those processed for the institutional market. The production line produces (a) 250 pounds of retail potato cuts per cutting-hour, and (b) 400 pounds of institutional potato cuts per cutting-hour. The cost driver is cutting-hours on the production line.
◆ Packaging activity area—Idaho packages potato cuts for the retail market independently of those packaged for the institutional market. The packaging line packages (a) 25 pounds of retail potato cuts per packaging-hour, and (b) 100 pounds of institutional potato cuts per packaging-hour. The cost driver is packaging-hours on the production line.

REQUIRED

1. What are the total activity costs in the (a) cleaning, (b) cutting, and (c) packaging activity areas?
2. What is the cost rate per unit of the cost driver in the (a) cleaning, (b) cutting, and (c) packaging activity areas?
3. How might Idaho Potato use information about the cost driver rates computed in requirement 2 to better manage the Pocatello plant?

5-26 Cost hierarchies, unit cost analysis. Thirst Quencher operates many bottling plants around the globe. At its Edmonton plant, where nine different brands are bottled, the following costs are incurred in 19_7 to produce 20,000,000 cans of soft drink:

a. New-product development costs—costs of adding new products to those being produced. "Real-Thing Iced Tea" was added in 19_7 at cost of $1,228,000.
b. Incoming material handling costs—costs of inspecting and handling concentrate, bottles, packages, and so on. Driver is hours of materials handling time, which is highly correlated with hours of bottling time ($867,000).

c. Incoming materials purchase costs—can be directly traced to individual products being bottled and packaged. Costs are purely variable with output level ($4,426,000).
d. Production-line labor costs—can be traced directly to (a) individual products being bottled and packaged on an output unit-level basis ($2,421,000), or (b) setups for products when the production line switches to bottling or packaging a different product, such as Diet Quencher instead of Quencher ($795,000).
e. Energy costs—the cost driver is hours of bottling time ($343,000).
f. Plant supervision and safety costs—these costs are for plant infrastructure management, land rates, and plant insurance ($1,246,000).
   Note: Units of output is highly correlated with hours of bottling time.

REQUIRED
1. Classify each of the preceding costs as output unit-level, batch-level, product-sustaining, or facility-sustaining. Explain your answer.
2. Compute unit costs for (a) the output-level costs, and (b) the total costs. Why might Thirst Quencher want to compute both unit costs separately?
3. What benefits might Thirst Quencher management gain by using a cost hierarchy classification of costs?

PROBLEMS

5-27 **Job costing, accounting for manufacturing overhead, budgeted rates.** The Solomon Company uses a job-costing system at its Dover, Delaware, plant. The plant has a Machining Department and a Finishing Department. Its job-costing system has two direct-cost categories (direct materials and direct manufacturing labor) and two manufacturing overhead cost pools (the Machining Department, allocated using actual machine-hours and the Finishing Department, allocated using actual labor cost). The 19_4 budget for the plant is as follows:

	Machining Department	Finishing Department
Manufacturing overhead	$10,000,000	$8,000,000
Direct manufacturing labor cost	$ 900,000	$4,000,000
Direct manufacturing labor-hours	30,000	160,000
Machine-hours	200,000	33,000

REQUIRED
1. Present an overview diagram of Solomon's job-costing system.
2. What is the budgeted overhead rate that should be used in the Machining Department? In the Finishing Department?
3. During the month of January, the cost record for Job 431 shows the following:

	Machining Department	Finishing Department
Direct material used	$14,000	$3,000
Direct manufacturing labor cost	$ 600	$1,250
Direct manufacturing labor-hours	30	50
Machine-hours	130	10

What is the total manufacturing overhead allocated to Job 431?
4. Assuming that Job 431 consisted of 200 units of product, what is the unit product cost of Job 431?

5. Balances at the end of 19_4 are as follows:

	Machining Department	Finishing Department
Manufacturing overhead incurred	$11,200,000	$7,900,000
Direct manufacturing labor cost	$ 950,000	$4,100,000
Machine-hours	220,000	32,000

Compute the under- or overallocated manufacturing overhead for each department and for the Dover plant as a whole.

6. Why might Solomon use two different manufacturing overhead cost pools in its job-costing system?

5-28 Overview of general-ledger relationships. The Blakely Company is a small machine shop that uses highly skilled labor and a job-costing system (using normal costing). The total debits and credits in certain accounts just before year-end are as follows:

	December 30, 19_7	
	Total Debits	Total Credits
Materials Control	$100,000	$ 70,000
Work-in-Process Control	320,000	305,000
Manufacturing Department Overhead Control	85,000	—
Finished Goods Control	325,000	300,000
Cost of Goods Sold	300,000	
Manufacturing Overhead Allocated	—	90,000

All materials purchased are for direct materials. Note that "total debits" in the inventory accounts would include beginning inventory balances, if any.

The preceding accounts *do not* include the following:

a. The manufacturing labor costs recapitulation for the December 31 working day: direct manufacturing labor, $5,000, and indirect manufacturing labor, $1,000.

b. Miscellaneous manufacturing overhead incurred on December 30 and December 31: $1,000.

ADDITIONAL INFORMATION

◆ Manufacturing overhead has been allocated as a percentage of direct manufacturing labor costs through December 30.

◆ Direct materials purchased during 19_7 were $85,000.

◆ There were no returns to suppliers.

◆ Direct manufacturing labor costs during 19_7 totaled $150,000, not including the December 31 working day described previously.

REQUIRED

1. Compute the inventories (December 31, 19_6) of materials control, work-in-process control, and finished goods control. Show T-accounts.

2. Prepare all adjusting and closing journal entries for the preceding accounts. Assume that all under- or overallocated manufacturing overhead is closed directly to Cost of Goods Sold.

3. Compute the ending inventories (December 31, 19_7), after adjustments and closing, of materials control, work-in-process control, and finished goods control.

5-29 Allocation and proration of manufacturing overhead. (SMA, heavily adapted) Nicole Limited is a company that produces machinery to customer order. Its job-costing system (using normal costing) has two direct-cost categories (direct materials and direct manufacturing labor) and one indirect-cost pool (manufacturing overhead, allocated using a budgeted rate based on direct manufacturing labor costs). The budget for 19_8 was

Direct manufacturing labor	$420,000
Manufacturing overhead	$252,000

At the end of 19_8, two jobs were incomplete: No. 1768B (total direct manufacturing labor costs were $11,000) and No. 1819C (total direct manufacturing labor costs were $39,000). Machine time totaled 287 hours for No. 1768B and 647 hours for No. 1819C. Direct materials issued to No. 1768B amounted to $22,000. Direct material for No. 1819C came to $42,000.

Total charges to the Manufacturing Overhead Control account for the year were $186,840. Direct manufacturing labor charges made to all jobs were $400,000, representing 20,000 direct manufacturing labor-hours.

There were no beginning inventories. In addition to the ending work-in-process, the ending finished goods showed a balance of $156,000 (including a direct manufacturing labor cost component of $40,000). Sales for 19_8 totaled $2,700,680, cost of goods sold was $1,600,000, and marketing costs were $857,870. BD prices on a cost-plus basis. It currently uses a cost plus 40% of cost guideline.

REQUIRED

1. Prepare a detailed schedule showing the ending balances in the inventories and cost of goods sold (before considering any under- or overallocated manufacturing overhead). Show also the manufacturing overhead allocated to these ending balances.
2. Compute the under- or overallocated manufacturing overhead for 19_8.
3. Prorate the amount computed in requirement 2 on the basis of
   a. The ending balances (before proration) of work in process, finished goods, and cost of goods sold.
   b. The allocated overhead amount (before proration) in the ending balances of work in process, finished goods, and cost of goods sold.
4. Assume that Nicole decides to immediately write off to cost of goods sold any under- or overallocated manufacturing overhead. Will operating income be higher or lower than the operating income that would have resulted from the proration in requirements 3a and 3b?

5-30 Activity-based costing, product cost cross-subsidization. Baker's Delight (BD) has been in the food-processing business 3 years. For its first 2 years (19_5 and 19_6), its sole product was raisin cake. All cakes were manufactured and packaged in 1-pound units. A normal costing system was used by BD. The two direct-cost categories were direct materials and direct manufacturing labor. The sole indirect manufacturing cost category—manufacturing overhead—was allocated to products using a units of production allocation base.

In its third year, (19_7) BD added a second product—layered carrot cake—that was packaged in 1-pound units. This product differs from raisin cake in several ways:

◆ More expensive ingredients are used.
◆ More direct manufacturing labor time is required.
◆ More complex manufacturing is required.

In 19_7, BD continued to use its existing costing system where a unit of production of either cake was weighted the same.

Direct materials costs in 19_7 were $0.60 per pound of raisin cake and $0.90 per pound of layered carrot cake. Direct manufacturing labor cost in 19_7 was $0.14 per pound of raisin cake and $0.20 per pound of layered carrot cake.

During 19_7, BD sales people reported greater-than-expected sales of layered carrot cake and less-than-expected sales of raisin cake. The budgeted and actual sales volume for 19_7 was as follows:

	Budgeted	Actual
Raisin cake	160,000 pounds	120,000 pounds
Layered carrot cake	40,000 pounds	80,000 pounds

The budgeted manufacturing overhead for 19_7 was $210,800.

At the end of 19_7, Jonathan Davis, the controller of BD, decided to investigate how use of an activity-based costing system would affect the product cost numbers. After consultation with operating personnel, the single manufacturing overhead cost pool was subdivided into five activity areas. These activity areas, their driver, their 19_7 budgeted rate, and the driver units used per pound of each cake are as follows:

Activity	Driver	Budgeted 19_7 Cost per Driver Unit	Driver Units per Pound of Raisin Cake	Driver Units per Pound of Layered Carrot Cake
1. Mixing	Labor time	$0.04	5	8
2. Cooking	Oven time	$0.14	2	3
3. Cooling	Cool room time	$0.02	3	5
4. Creaming/icing	Machine time	$0.25	0	3
5. Packaging	Machine time	$0.08	3	7

REQUIRED

1. Compute the 19_7 unit product cost of raisin cake and layered carrot cake with the normal costing system used in the 19_5 to 19_7 period.
2. Compute the 19_7 unit product cost per cake under the activity-based normal costing system.
3. Explain the differences in unit product costs computed in requirements 1 and 2.
4. Describe three uses Baker's Delight might make of the activity-based cost numbers.

5-31 **Activity-based costing, under- or overallocated indirect costs (continuation of 5-30).** Jonathan Davis, the controller of Baker's Delight, wants to further examine the relative profitability of raisin cake and layered carrot cake in 19_7. He questions the accuracy of the activity-based normal costing numbers. He notes that the 19_7 actual manufacturing indirect cost was $256,256. This differs sizably from the $210,800 budgeted amount. The 19_7 actual indirect costs per activity area were as follows:

Activity Area	19_7 Actual Costs
Mixing	$ 62,400
Cooking	83,840
Cooling	12,416
Creaming/icing	36,000
Packaging	61,600
	$256,256

REQUIRED

1. Compute the under- or overallocated manufacturing indirect costs in 19_7 for
   a. Each of the five activity area indirect-cost pools
   b. The *aggregate* of individual activity area indirect costs
2. Assume that BD allocates under- or overallocated indirect costs to individual accounts based on the allocated overhead component in that account. What are the pros and cons of using:

a. Five separate under- or overallocated adjustments (one for each activity area)

b. One under- or overallocated adjustment for the aggregate of all activity area indirect costs

3. Compute the 19_7 actual unit product cost for raisin cake and layered carrot cake using the information computed in requirement 1a.

4. Comment on the implications of the product cost numbers in requirement 3 for BD's pricing decisions in 19_8.

5-32 Activity-based job-costing system. The Denver Company manufactures and sells packaging machines. It recently used an activity-based approach to refine the job-costing system at its Denver plant. The resulting job-costing system has one direct-cost category (direct materials) and four indirect manufacturing cost pools. These four indirect-cost pools and their allocation bases were chosen by a team of product designers, manufacturing personnel, and marketing personnel:

Indirect Manufacturing Cost Pool	Cost-Allocation Base	Budgeted Cost-Allocation Rate
1. Materials handling	Component parts ~~50parts~~	$8 per part
2. Machining	Machine-hours 12hrs	$68 per hour
3. Assembly	Assembly-line-hours 15hrs	$75 per hour
4. Inspection	Inspection-hours 4hrs	$104 per hour

Cola Supreme recently purchased 50 can-packaging machines from the Denver Company. Each machine has direct materials costs of $3,000, requires 50 component parts, 12 machine-hours, 15 assembly-hours, and 4 inspection-hours.

Denver's prior costing system had one direct-cost category (direct materials) and one indirect-cost category (manufacturing overhead, allocated using assembly-hours).

REQUIRED

1. Present overview diagrams of the prior job-costing system and the refined activity-based job-costing system.

2. Compute the unit manufacturing costs (using ABC) of each machine and the total manufacturing cost of the Cola Supreme job.

3. The activity-based job-costing system of Denver has only one manufacturing direct-cost category—direct materials. A competitor of the Denver Company has two direct-cost categories at its manufacturing plant—direct materials and direct manufacturing labor. Why might Denver not have a direct manufacturing labor costs category in its job-costing system? Where are the manufacturing labor costs included in the Denver costing system?

4. What information might members of the team that refined the prior costing system find useful in the activity-based job-costing system?

5-33 Activity-based costing, job-costing system. The Hewlett-Packard (HP) plant in Roseville, California, assembles and tests printed-circuit (PC) boards. The job-costing system at this plant has two direct-cost categories (direct materials and direct manufacturing labor) and seven indirect-cost pools. These indirect-cost pools represent the seven activity areas that operating personnel at the plant determined were sufficiently different (in terms of cost-behavior patterns or in terms of individual products being assembled) to warrant separate cost pools. The cost-allocation base chosen for each activity area is the cost driver at that activity area.

Debbie Berlant, a newly appointed marketing manager at HP, attends a training session that describes how an activity-based costing approach has been used to design the Roseville plant's job-costing system. Berlant is provided with the following incomplete information for a specific job (an order for a single PC board, No. A82):

Direct materials	$75.00	
Direct manufacturing labor	15.00	$90.00
Manufacturing overhead (see below)		53.30
Total manufacturing cost		$143.30

Manufacturing Overhead Cost Pool	Cost-Allocation Base	Cost-Allocation Rate	Units of Base Used on Job No. A82	Manufacturing Overhead Allocated to Job
1. Axial insertion	Axial insertions	0.08	45	? 3.6
2. Dip insertion	Dip insertions	0.25	? 24	6.00
3. Manual insertion	Manual insertions	? .5	11	5.50
4. Wave solder	Boards soldered	3.50	? 1	3.50
5. Backload	Backload insertions	? .533	6	4.20
6. Test	Budgeted time board is the test activity	90.00	0.25	? 22.5
7. Defect analysis	Budgeted time for defect analysis and repair	? 80	0.10	8.00

53.3

REQUIRED

1. Present an overview exhibit of the activity-based job-costing system at the Roseville plant.
2. Fill in the blanks (signaled by a question mark) in the cost information provided to Berlant for job No. A82.
3. Why might manufacturing managers and marketing managers favor this ABC job-costing system over the prior costing system, which had the same two direct-cost categories but only a single indirect-cost pool (manufacturing overhead allocated using direct-labor cost)?

5-34 Activity-based job costing. The Schramka Company manufactures a variety of prestige boardroom chairs. Its job-costing system was designed using an activity-based approach. There are two direct-cost categories (direct materials and direct manufacturing labor) and three indirect-cost pools. These three cost pools represent three activity areas at the plant.

Manufacturing Activity Area	Budgeted Costs for 19_8	Cost Driver Used as Allocation Base	Cost-Allocation Rate
Materials handling	200,000	Parts	$ 0.25
Cutting	2,160,000	Parts	2.50
Assembly	2,000,000	Direct manufacturing labor-hours	25.00

Two styles of chairs were produced in March, the executive chair and the chairman chair. Their quantities, direct material costs, and other data for March 19_8 are as follows:

	Units Produced	Direct Material Costs	Number of Parts	Direct Manufacturing Labor-Hours
Executive chair	5,000	$600,000	100,000	7,500
Chairman chair	100	25,000	3,500	500

The direct manufacturing labor rate is $20 per hour. Assume no beginning or ending inventory.

1. Compute the March 19_8 total manufacturing costs and unit costs of the executive chair and the chairman chair.
2. Suppose that the upstream activities to manufacturing (R&D and design) and the downstream activities (marketing, distribution, and customer service) were analyzed. The unit costs in 19_8 were budgeted to be as follows:

	Upstream Activities	Downstream Activities
Executive chair	$ 60	$110
Chairman chair	146	236

Compute the full product costs per unit of each line of chairs. (Full product costs are the sum of the costs in all business function areas.)

5-35 Activity-based job costing, unit cost comparisons. The Tracy Corporation has a machining facility specializing in jobs for the aircraft components market. The prior job-costing system had two direct-cost categories (direct materials and direct manufacturing labor) and a single indirect-cost pool (manufacturing overhead, allocated using direct labor-hours). The indirect cost-allocation rate of the prior system for 19_8 would have been $115 per direct manufacturing labor-hour.

Recently, a team with members from product design, manufacturing, and accounting used an activity-based approach to refine its job-costing system. The two direct-cost categories were retained. The team decided to replace the single indirect-cost pool with five indirect-cost pools. These five cost pools represent five activity areas at the facility, each with its own supervisor and budget responsibility. Pertinent data are as follows:

Activity Area	Cost Driver Used as Allocation Base	Cost-Allocation Rate
Materials handling	Parts	$ 0.40
Lathe work	Turns	0.20
Milling	Machine-hours	20.00
Grinding	Parts	0.80
Testing	Units tested	15.00

Information-gathering technology has advanced to the point where all the data necessary for budgeting in these five activity areas are automatically collected.

Two representative jobs processed under the new system at the facility in the most recent period had the following characteristics:

	Job 410	Job 411
Direct materials cost per job	$ 9,700	$59,900
Direct manufacturing labor cost per job	$ 750	$11,250
Direct manufacturing labor-hours per job	25	375
Parts per job	500	2,000
Turns per job	20,000	60,000
Machine hours per job	150	1,050
Units per job	10	200

REQUIRED

1. Compute the per unit manufacturing costs of each job under the prior job-costing system.
2. Compute the per unit manufacturing costs of each job under the activity-based job-costing system.

3. Compare the per unit cost figures for Jobs 410 and 411 computed in requirements 1 and 2. Why do the prior and the activity-based costing systems differ in their job cost estimates for each job? Why might these differences be important to the Tracy Corporation?

5-36 Job costing, contracting, ethics. Jack Halpern is the owner and CEO of Aerospace Comfort, a firm specializing in the manufacture of seats for air transport. He has just received a copy of a letter written to the General Audit Section of the U.S. Navy. He believes it is from an exemployee of Aerospace.

Dear Sir,

Aerospace Comfort in 19_8 manufactured 100 X7 seats for the Navy. You may be interested to know the following:

1. Direct materials costs billed for the 100 X7 seats were $25,000.

2. Direct manufacturing labor costs billed for 100 X7 seats were $6,000. This cost includes 16 hours of setup labor at $25 per hour, an amount included in the manufacturing overhead cost pool as well. The $6,000 also includes 12 hours of design time at $50 an hour. Design time was explicitly identified as a cost the Navy was not to reimburse.

3. Manufacturing overhead costs billed for 100 X7 seats were $9,000 (150% of direct manufacturing labor costs). This amount includes the 16 hours of setup labor at $25 per hour that is incorrectly included as part of direct manufacturing labor costs.

You may also want to know that over 40% of the direct materials is purchased from Frontier Technology, a company that is 51% owned by Jack Halpern's brother.

For obvious reasons, this letter will not be signed.

c.c: *The Wall Street Journal*
Jack Halpern, CEO of Aerospace Comfort

Aerospace Comfort's contract states that the Navy reimburses Aerospace at 130% of manufacturing costs.

REQUIRED

Assume that the facts in the letter are correct as you answer the following questions.

1. What is the cost amount per X7 seat that Aerospace Comfort billed the Navy? Assume that the actual direct materials costs are $25,000.

2. What is the amount per X7 seat that Aerospace Comfort should have billed the Navy? Assume that the actual direct materials costs are $25,000.

3. What should the Navy do to tighten its procurement procedures to reduce the likelihood of such situations recurring?

COLLABORATIVE LEARNING PROBLEM

5-37 Activity-based costing, cost hierarchy. (CMA adapted) Coffee Bean, Inc. (CBI), is a distributor and processor of a variety of different blends of coffee. The company buys coffee beans from around the world and roasts, blends, and packages them for resale. CBI currently offers 15 different coffees to gourmet shops in 1-pound bags. The major cost is raw materials; however, there is a substantial amount of manufacturing overhead in the predominantly automated roasting and packing process. The company uses relatively little direct labor.

Some of the coffees are very popular and sell in large volumes while a few of the newer blends have very low volumes. CBI prices its coffee at budgeted cost, including allocated overhead, plus a markup of 30%. If prices for certain coffees are significantly higher than market, the prices are lowered.

The company competes primarily on the quality of its products, but customers are price conscious as well.

Data for the 19_7 budget include manufacturing overhead of $3 million, which has been allocated in its existing costing system on the basis of each product's budgeted direct-labor cost. The budgeted direct-labor cost for 19_7 totals $600,000. Purchases and use of materials (mostly coffee beans) are budgeted to total $6 million.

The budgeted direct costs for 1-pound bags of two of the company's products are

	Mona Loa	Malaysian
Direct materials	$4.20	$3.20
Direct labor	0.30	0.30

CBI's controller believes the traditional costing system may be providing misleading cost information. She has developed an activity-based analysis of the 19_7 budgeted manufacturing overhead costs shown in the following table:

Activity	Cost Driver	Budgeted Activity	Budgeted Cost
Purchasing	Purchase orders	1,158	$ 579,000
Materials handling	Setups	1,800	720,000
Quality control	Batches	600	144,000
Roasting	Roasting-hours	96,100	961,000
Blending	Blending-hours	33,600	336,000
Packaging	Packaging-hours	26,000	260,000
Total manufacturing overhead cost			$3,000,000

Data regarding the 19_7 production of Mona Loa and Malaysian coffee are presented here. There will be no beginning or ending materials inventory for either of these coffees.

	Mona Loa	Malaysian
Expected sales	100,000 pounds	2,000 pounds
Batch size	10,000 pounds	500 pounds
Setups	3 per batch	3 per batch
Purchase order size	25,000 pounds	500 pounds
Roasting time	1 hour/100 pounds	1 hour/100 pounds
Blending time	0.5 hour/100 pounds	0.5 hour/100 pounds
Packaging time	0.1 hour/100 pounds	0.1 hour/100 pounds

INSTRUCTIONS

Form groups of two or more students to complete the following requirements.

REQUIRED

1. Using Coffee Bean, Inc.'s existing costing system.
   a. Determine the company's 19_7 budgeted manufacturing overhead rate using direct-labor cost as the single allocation base.
   b. Determine the 19_7 budgeted costs and selling prices of 1 pound of Mona Loa coffee and 1 pound of Malaysian coffee.
2. Use the controller's activity-based approach to estimate the 19_7 budgeted cost for 1 pound of
   a. Mona Loa coffee
   b. Malaysian coffee

Allocate all costs to the 100,000 pounds of Mona Loa and the 2,000 pounds of Malaysian. Compare the results with those in requirement 1.

3. Discuss how CBI could use a cost hierarchy approach to better understand its cost structure.

4. Examine the implications of your answers to requirements 2 and 3 for CBI's pricing and product-emphasis strategy.

A WALK THROUGH...

Dell Computer

What role does cost accounting play in a typical manufacturing company? At Dell Computer Corporation, cost accounting is just another component in every computer. **1** Having started in founder Michael Dell's college dorm room, Dell Computer Corporation now has its corporate headquarters in Austin, Texas. The company's products include **2** desktop computers, **3** laptops, and network servers, which, for the most part, are sold directly to consumers. **4** Dell customer service representatives take orders over the phone. Customers can discuss their computing needs with the representatives and can choose the exact specifications of the units they order.

1

2

4

3

Dell Latitude XPi
Dell Computer Corporation

The large, 10.4" TFT display with low-reflection coating improves viewing while black mask technology provides vibrant color. Other features include: Intel's 75MHz or 90MHz Pentium processor, smart Lithium-Ion batteries, up to 1.2 GB hard drives and 256 cache memory. Prices start at $2,999 with a one-year warranty.

Dell Latitude LX
Dell Computer Corporation

The large, 10.4" dual-scan STN display with low-reflection screen coating for easier viewing and fast processor options bring high-performance computing to mobile users looking for best-in-class pricing—prices start at $1,999 with a one-year warranty. Other features include: Intel's 75MHz or 100MHz processors, 128KB L2 cache, up to 810MB hard drives and MiMH batteries that can be easily exchanged with the modular floppy drive to provide longer battery life.

For further information please contact:
Adrianne Mac Pherson
512/728-4100

5 Once a customer order has been placed, the computer units on the order are assembled. Product-assembly manufacturing work cells, called "mods," build the computer as specified by the customer. **6** The direct materials used for assembly, such as this motherboard, are located in the bins behind the assembly employees. Each individual computer is considered a "job" at Dell because each unit is built to the customer's specifications. Therefore, Dell uses a job-costing system to track its costs, such as the direct cost of computer components and assemblers' wages and the indirect costs of customer service representatives' wages and depreciation on the headquarters. **7** Cost information plays an important role in the regular meetings of Dell's managers. As with any manufacturer, cost management is a high priority at Dell. In fact, to better manage its manufacturing costs, Dell is currently developing an activity-based management system for its manufacturing operations. **8** By involving employees in the development of this system, Dell hopes to focus attention on cost reduction to achieve tighter control of product costs. Perhaps Dell will be able to build a costing system as well as it builds computers.

DELL COMPUTER CORPORATION
Cost Accounting Fundamentals and Job Costing

What does it cost to produce a computer for a customer? What are the activity centers for manufacturing, and how well are we managing them? How can we improve corporate performance? These are just a few of the questions managers at Dell Computer Corporation are called upon to answer. In most cases, the source of their replies can be traced back to the company's internal accounting systems, which collect data on the many aspects of Dell's operations and provide information that managers use to answer questions and make decisions.

Dell Computer Corporation, headquartered in Austin, Texas, is a global computer manufacturing company. Dell does not make computer components, such as processor chips or disk drives, but instead focuses on the assembly of the components into computers that are distributed and sold worldwide. Dell produces four categories of personal computers: (1) the Optiplex line of high-end desktop computers, (2) the Dimension line of value-priced computers, (3) notebook computers, and (4) network servers. The company's manufacturing facilities (located in Austin, Texas; Ireland; and Malaysia) serve customers around the globe from these locations. Each computer is built to customer order, so no finished goods inventory exists at Dell. Raw materials inventory is turned over every 30 days.

Dell's goal is to fill each customer's order in an average of 5 to 6 days. Each computer in an order is considered a separate job because the total cost of the components that make up each unit will vary, based on the customer's specifications. For example, costs are tracked to the computer unit level and include direct materials, direct labor, and a standard manufacturing overhead rate. The manufacturing overhead rate is developed in conjunction with Dell's Engineering Group, based upon cost levels in its product manufacturing work cells or "mods." The overhead rates are revised every quarter. Product assembly mods are responsible for computer unit assembly, including putting together individual unit direct materials and testing the components in each computer. Fully assembled and tested units pass out of each assembly mod to the shipping mod, where they are packed and prepared for shipment to the customer.

To remain competitive, Dell maintains a Product Group, which is responsible for research and development of new product ideas. This group works in conjunction with its strategic partners, such as Intel Corporation, a major microprocessor chip manufacturer, to create products that can continue to meet the demands of the marketplace for more processing power and speed. New products that have the latest technology command higher margins, so Dell works hard to minimize the time it takes to develop and produce them. Often, new products are announced the same day component manufacturers unveil their new technological advances.

Dell is implementing an activity-based management system throughout its manufacturing operations. Six cost pools have been identified: receiving, preparation and part kitting, assembly, testing, packaging, and shipping. Managers hope that focusing on these cost pools will increase cost reductions so that even tighter control of product costs can be achieved. Work is underway to identify indirect costs down to a work cell (mod) level. Currently, indirect facility costs are allocated to the facility level, warehousing costs for raw materials are allocated based on the number of component parts in each computer, and engineering costs are allocated on a units of production basis. ◆

QUESTIONS

1. Using the six-step approach to job costing, give an overview of manufacturing costs for Dell Computer Corporation.

2. What kinds of journal entries would you expect Dell to make as part of its job-costing system?

3. Identify the events composing Dell's value chain. In which activities would you expect to find Dell adding the most value? Why?

4. Give examples of Dell's costs that would be considered (1) capitalized inventoriable costs, (2) capitalized noninventoriable costs, and (3) noncapitalized costs.

5. Dell Computer Corporation is implementing an activity-based management system in its manufacturing operations as a step toward activity-based product costing. Cost pools, as described in this case, have been identified. Describe what steps should next be taken by Dell to complete their transition to activity-based costing.

6
C H A P T E R

MASTER BUDGET AND RESPONSIBILITY ACCOUNTING

Media companies focus on a small number of key variables when budgeting for their television operations. Factors such as advertising charges, cable television subscriptions, and programming costs are pivotal to developing budgets at News Corporation.

LEARNING OBJECTIVES

After studying this chapter, you should be able to

1. Define master budget and explain its major benefits to an organization
2. Describe major components of the master budget
3. Prepare the budgeted income statement and its supporting budget schedules
4. Describe the uses of computer-based financial planning models
5. Explain kaizen budgeting and its importance for cost management
6. Illustrate an activity-based budgeting approach
7. Describe responsibility centers and responsibility accounting
8. Explain how controllability relates to responsibility accounting

Budgets are one of the most widely used tools for planning and controlling organizations. Surveys show an almost universal use of budgets by medium or large companies in many parts of the globe. Budgeting systems turn managers' perspectives forward. A forward-looking perspective enables managers to be in a better position to exploit opportunities. It also enables them to anticipate problems and take steps to eliminate or reduce their severity. As one observer said, "Few businesses plan to fail, but many of those that flop failed to plan."

This chapter examines budgeting as a planning and coordinating device. Topics covered in prior chapters are widely used in this discussion. By understanding cost behavior (covered in Chapters 2 and 3), managers can better predict how total budgeted costs are affected by different projected output levels. By understanding cost tracing and cost allocation (covered in Chapters 4 and 5), managers can show how different projected revenue and cost amounts will impact the budgeted income statement and balance sheet.

Chapter 1 (pp. 12–15) described some newly evolving management themes that impact management accounting. Budgets give financial expression to many of these themes. For example, budgets can quantify the planned financial effects of activities aimed at continuous improvement and cost reduction.

The material covered in this chapter is also integral to subsequent chapters. For example, Chapters 7 and 8 examine how the numbers used in budgets assist in evaluating the performance of managers or the business areas where they have responsibility.

MAJOR FEATURES OF BUDGETS

Definition and Role of Budgets

A *budget* is a quantitative expression for a set time period of a proposed future plan of action by management. It can cover both financial and nonfinancial aspects of these plans and acts as a blueprint for the company to follow in the upcoming period. Budgets covering financial aspects quantify management's expectations regarding future income, cash flows, and financial position. Just as individual financial statements are prepared covering past periods, so they can be prepared covering future periods—for example, a budgeted income statement, a budgeted cash-flow statement, and a budgeted balance sheet.

Well-managed organizations usually have the following budgeting cycle:

1. Planning the performance of the organization as a whole as well as its subunits. The entire management team agrees as to what is expected.

2. Providing a frame of reference, a set of specific expectations against which actual results can be compared.

3. Investigating variations from plans. If necessary, corrective action follows investigation.

4. Planning again, considering feedback and changed conditions.

The **master budget** coordinates all the financial projections in the organization's individual budgets in a single organizationwide set of budgets for a set time period. It embraces the impact of both *operating* decisions and *financing* decisions. Operating decisions center on the acquisition and use of scarce resources. Financing decisions center on how to get the funds to acquire resources. This book concentrates on how accounting helps managers make operating decisions, and we emphasize operating budgets in this chapter.

The term *master* in "master budget" refers to it being a comprehensive, organizationwide set of budgets. Consider the News Corporation. Individual product lines such as Fox Television, *TV Guide*, and *The Times/Sunday Times* newspapers each have a separate budgeted income statement, a separate budgeted cash-flow statement, and so on. The master budgeted income statement for the News Corporation is a single income statement that combines information from all these many individual budgeted income statements. Similarly, the master budgeted cash-flow statement is a single cash-flow statement that combines information from all these many individual budgeted cash-flow statements.

Budgets are a major feature of most management control systems. When administered intelligently, budgets (1) compel planning including the implementation of plans, (2) provide performance criteria, and (3) promote communication and coordination within the organization.

Strategy and Plans

Budgeting is most useful when done as an integral part of an organization's strategic analysis. **Strategic analysis** considers how an organization best combines its own capabilities with the opportunities in the market place to accomplish its overall objectives. It includes consideration of such questions as

1. What are the overall objectives of the organization?
2. Are the markets for its product local, regional, national, or global? What trends will affect its markets? How is the organization affected by the economy, its industry, and its competitors?
3. What forms of organizational and financial structures serve the organization best?
4. What are the risks of alternative strategies, and what are the organization's contingency plans if its preferred plan fails?

Consider the diagram in Exhibit 6-1. Strategic analysis underlies both long-run and short-run planning. In turn, these plans lead to the formulation of budgets. The arrows in the diagram are pointing in two directions. Why? Because strategy, plans, and budgets are interrelated and affect one another. Budgets provide feedback to managers about the likely effects of their strategic plans. Managers then use this feedback to revise their strategic plans. Apple Computer's strategic decision to reduce the selling prices of its Power Macintosh computer line provides an example of the interrelation between strategic analysis and budgets. By reducing its prices, the company expected to increase the demand for its computers. The budget, however, indicated that, even at the predicted higher sales quantities, Apple would be unable to meet its financial targets. For the strategy to succeed, Apple would need to reduce operating costs by streamlining operations and moving facilities to lower-cost areas. Apple then used cross-functional teams with members from different parts of the value chain to seek major cost reductions.

A Framework for Judging Performance

Budgeted performance measures can overcome two key limitations of using past performance as a basis for judging actual results. One limitation is that past results incorporate past miscues and substandard performance. Consider a cellular telephone company (Mobile Communications) examining the 19_7 performance of its salesforce. Suppose the past performance in 19_6 incorporates the efforts of many departed salespeople who left because they did not have an understanding of the market place. (As the president of Mobile said, "They could not sell ice cream in a heat wave.") Using the sales record of those departed employees would set the performance bar for new salespeople way too low.

A second limitation of past performance is that the future may be expected to be very different from the past. Consider again our cellular telephone company. Suppose that Mobile Communications had a 20% revenue increase in 19_7 compared to a 10% increase in 19_6. Does this indicate stellar sales performance? Before saying yes, consider two additional facts. Fact one is that in November 19_6, an industry trade association forecast that the 19_7 growth rate in industry revenues would be

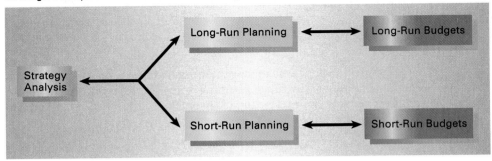

40%. Fact two is that in 19_7, the actual growth rate in industry revenues was 50%. The 20% actual revenue gain in 19_7 takes on a negative connotation given these facts, even though it exceeds the 19_6 actual growth rate of 10%. Use of the 40% figure as the budgeted rate provides a better way to evaluate the 19_7 sales performance than does use of the 19_6 actual rate of 10%. A biking analogy is appropriate here. A budgeted industry growth rate of 40% is equivalent to the biker going downhill on a steep slope. Top management of Mobile Communications expects that good performance will achieve above-average speed compared to other bikers in similar conditions.

Coordination and Communication

Coordination is the meshing and balancing of all factors of production or service and of all the departments and business functions so that the company can meet its objectives. *Communication* is getting those objectives understood and accepted by all departments and functions.

Coordination forces executives to think of relationships among individual operations, departments, and the company as a whole. Coordination implies, for example, that purchasing officers make material purchase plans based on production requirements. Also, production managers plan personnel and machinery needs to produce the number of products necessary to meet revenue forecasts. How does a budget lead to coordination? Consider Snapple Beverage. Production managers who are evaluated on the basis of maximizing output while keeping unit costs per bottle low would prefer long production runs with very few changeovers of flavors. But if the output cannot be sold, Snapple may find itself awash with a costly inventory buildup of Mango Madness. The budget achieves coordination by constraining production managers to produce only what marketing is forecasting it can sell. This may entail doing a changeover from Mango Madness to Lemonade partway into a production shift.

For coordination to succeed, communication is essential. The production manager must know the sales plan. The purchasing manager must know the production plan, and so on. Having a formal document such as the budget is an effective way to communicate a consistent set of plans to the organization as a whole.

Management Support and Administration

Budgets help managers, but budgets need help. Top management has the ultimate responsibility for the budgets of the organization they manage. *Management at all levels, however, should understand and support the budget and all aspects of the management control system.* Top management support is especially critical for obtaining active line participation in the formulation of budgets and for successful administration of the budget. If line managers feel that top management does not "believe" in the budget, these managers are unlikely to be active participants in the budget process. Similarly, a top management that always mechanically institutes "across the board" cost reductions (say, a 10% reduction in all areas) in the face of revenue reductions is unlikely to have line managers willing to be "fully honest" in their budget communications.

Budgets should not be administered rigidly. Changing conditions call for changes in plans. A manager may commit to the budget, but a situation might develop where some special repairs or a special advertising program would better serve the interests of the organization. The manager should not defer the repairs or the advertising in order to meet the budget if such actions will hurt the organization in the long run. Attaining the budget should not be an end in itself.

Time Coverage

The purpose(s) for budgeting should guide the time period chosen for the budget. Consider budgeting for a new Harley-Davidson 500cc motorcycle. If the purpose is to budget for the total profitability of this new model, a 5-year period (or more) may be appropriate (covering design, manufacture, sales, and after-sales support). In contrast, consider budgeting for a Christmas play. If the purpose is to estimate all cash outlays, a 6-month period from the planning to staging of the play may be adequate.

The most frequently used budget period is 1 year. The annual budget is often subdivided by months for the first quarter and by quarters for the remainder of the year. The budgeted data for a year are frequently revised as the year unfolds. For example, at the end of the first quarter, the budget for the next three quarters is changed in light of new information.

Businesses are increasingly using *rolling budgets*. A **rolling budget** is a budget or plan that is always available for a specified future period by adding a month, quarter, or year in the future as the month, quarter, or year just ended is dropped. Thus, a 12-month rolling budget for March 19_7 to February 19_8 period becomes a 12-month rolling budget for the April 19_7 to March 19_8 period the next month, and so on. There is always a 12-month budget in place. Rolling budgets constantly force management to think concretely about the forthcoming 12 months, regardless of the month at hand. The Arizona Public Service Company has a budget that looks ahead 2 years and is updated every month. The NEC Corporation of Japan has a 1-year operating budget that is updated each month. Companies also frequently use rolling budgets when developing 5-year budgets for long-run planning. For example, the NEC Corporation also has a 5-year budget that is updated each year.

Terminology

The terminology used to describe budgets varies among organizations. For example, budgeted financial statements are sometimes called **pro forma statements.** The budgeted financial statements of many companies include the budgeted income statement, the budgeted balance sheet, and the budgeted statement of cash flows. Some organizations, such as Hewlett-Packard, refer to budgeting as *targeting*. Indeed, to give a more positive thrust to budgeting, many organizations—for example, the Nissan Motor Company and Owens-Corning—describe the budget as a *profit plan*.

An Illustration of a Master Budget

A good way to explain the budgeting process is to walk through the development of an actual budget. We shall use a master budget because it provides a comprehensive picture of the entire budgeting process at Halifax Engineering, a manufacturer of aircraft replacement parts. Its job costing system for manufacturing costs has two direct-cost categories (direct materials and direct manufacturing labor) and one indirect-cost pool (manufacturing overhead). Manufacturing overhead (both variable and fixed) is allocated to products using direct manufacturing labor-hours as the allocation base.

Exhibit 6-2 shows a simplified diagram of the various parts of the master budget for Halifax Engineering. The master budget summarizes the financial projections of all the organization's individual budgets. The master budget results in a set of related financial statements for a set time period, usually a year. The bulk of

EXHIBIT 6-2
Overview of the Master Budget for Halifax Engineering

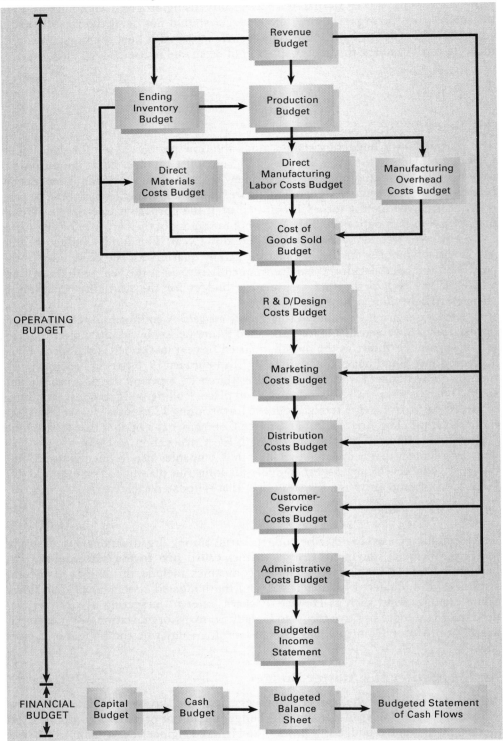

Exhibit 6-2 presents a set of budgets that together is often called the **operating budget**, which is the budgeted income statement and its supporting budget schedules. The supporting budget schedules cut across different categories of the value chain from R&D to customer service. The **financial budget** is that part of the master budget that comprises the capital budget, cash budget, budgeted balance sheet, and budgeted statement of cash flows. It focuses on the impact of operations and planned capital outlays on cash.

The final master budget is often the result of several iterations. Each of its drafts involves interaction across the various business functions of the value chain.

Basic Data and Requirements

Halifax Engineering is a machine shop that uses skilled labor and metal alloys to manufacture two types of aircraft replacement parts—Regular and Heavy-Duty. Halifax managers are ready to prepare a master budget for the year 19_8. To keep our illustration manageable for clarifying basic relationships, we make the following assumptions:

1. The only source of revenues is sales of the two parts. Nonsales-related revenue, such as interest income, is assumed to be zero.

2. Work-in-process inventory is negligible and is ignored.

3. Direct materials inventory and finished goods inventory are costed using the first-in first-out (FIFO) method.

4. Unit costs of direct materials purchased and finished goods sold remain unchanged throughout the budget year (19_8).

5. Variable production costs are variable with respect to direct manufacturing labor hours. Variable nonproduction costs are variable with respect to revenues. Both assumptions are simplifying ones made to keep our example relatively straightforward.

6. For computing inventoriable costs, all manufacturing costs (fixed and variable) are allocated using a single allocation base—direct manufacturing labor-hours.

After carefully examining all relevant factors, the executives of Halifax Engineering forecast the following figures for 19_8:

Direct materials
Material 111 alloy	$ 7 per kilogram
Material 112 alloy	$10 per kilogram
Direct manufacturing labor	$20 per hour

	Product	
Content of Each Product Unit	**Regular Aircraft Part**	**Heavy-Duty Aircraft Part**
Direct materials 111 alloy	12 kilograms	12 kilograms
Direct materials 112 alloy	6 kilograms	8 kilograms
Direct manufacturing labor	4 hours	6 hours

All direct manufacturing costs are variable with respect to the units of output produced. Additional information regarding the year 19_8 is as follows:

	Product	
	Regular	**Heavy-Duty**
Expected sales in units	5,000	1,000
Selling price per unit	$600	$800
Target ending inventory in units*	1,100	50
Beginning inventory in units	100	50
Beginning inventory in dollars	$38,400	$26,200

	Direct Materials	
	111 Alloy	**112 Alloy**
Beginning inventory in kilograms	7,000	6,000
Target ending inventory in kilograms*	8,000	2,000

*Target inventories depend on expected sales, expected variation in demand for products, and management philosophies such as just-in-time inventory management.

At the anticipated output levels for the Regular and Heavy-Duty aircraft parts, management believes the following manufacturing overhead costs will be incurred:

Manufacturing Overhead Costs			
Variable:	Supplies	$ 90,000	
	Indirect manufacturing labor	210,000	
	Direct and indirect manufacturing labor fringe costs	300,000	
	Power	120,000	
	Maintenance	60,000	$ 780,000
Fixed:	Depreciation	220,000	
	Property taxes	50,000	
	Property insurance	10,000	
	Supervision	100,000	
	Power	22,000	
	Maintenance	18,000	420,000
Total			$1,200,000

Other (Nonproduction) Costs			
Variable:	R&D/product design	$ 76,000	
	Marketing	133,000	
	Distribution	66,500	
	Customer service	47,500	
	Administrative	152,000	$ 475,000
Fixed:	R&D/product design	60,000	
	Marketing	67,000	
	Distribution	33,500	
	Customer service	12,500	
	Administrative	222,000	395,000
Total			$ 870,000

Our task at hand is to prepare a budgeted income statement for the year 19_8. As shown in Exhibit 6-2, this is one component of Halifax's master budget. Other components of the master budget—the budgeted balance sheet and the cash budget—are discussed in the Appendix to this chapter.

The following supporting budget schedules will be prepared when developing Halifax's budgeted income statement:

1. Revenue budget
2. Production budget (in units)
3. Direct materials usage budget and direct materials purchases budget
4. Direct manufacturing labor budget
5. Manufacturing overhead budget
6. Ending inventory budget
7. Cost of goods sold budget
8. Other (nonproduction) costs budget

Most organizations have a budget manual, which contains instructions and relevant information for preparing budgets. Although the details differ among organizations, the following basic steps are common for developing a budgeted income statement. Beginning with the revenue budget, each budget follows step by step in logical fashion. In most cases, computer software speeds the budget computations.

Steps in Preparing an Operating Budget

Step 1: Revenue Budget The revenue budget (schedule 1) is the usual starting point for budgeting. Why? Because production (and hence costs) and inventory levels generally depend on the forecasted level of revenue.

Schedule 1: Revenue Budget
for the Year Ended December 31, 19_8

	Units	Selling Price	Total Revenues
Regular	5,000	$600	$3,000,000
Heavy-Duty	1,000	800	800,000
Total			$3,800,000

The $3.8 million is the amount of revenues in the budgeted income statement. The revenue budget is often the outcome of elaborate information gathering and discussions among sales managers and field sales representatives.

Pressures can exist for budgeted revenues to be either over- or underestimates of the expected amounts. Lotus uses the phrase *challenge revenue budget* to describe its revenue budget amount. The term *challenge* signals that well-above-average effort and ingenuity is required to attain the budgeted amount. The challenge targets are used by Lotus as a motivational tool. Employees, however, often view them as overestimates of expected revenues.

Pressure for employees to underestimate budgeted revenues can occur when a company uses the difference between actual and budget amounts to evaluate marketing managers. These managers may respond by giving highly conservative forecasts. **Padding** the budget or introducing **budgetary slack** refers to the practice of underestimating budgeted revenues (or overestimating budgeted costs) in order to make budgeted targets more easily achievable. Introducing budgetary slack makes it more likely that actual revenues will exceed budgeted amounts. From the marketing manager's standpoint, budgetary slack hedges against unexpected adverse circumstances.

Occasionally, revenues are limited by available production capacity. For example, unusually heavy market demand, shortages of personnel or materials, or strikes may cause a company to exhaust its finished goods inventory completely. Additional sales cannot be made because no stock of the product is available. In such cases, the production capacity—the factor that limits revenue—is the starting point for preparing the revenue budget.

Step 2: Production Budget (in Units) After revenues are budgeted, the production budget (schedule 2) can be prepared. The total finished goods units to be produced depends on planned sales and expected changes in inventory levels:

$$\begin{array}{c}\text{Budgeted} \\ \text{production} \\ \text{(units)}\end{array} = \begin{array}{c}\text{Budgeted} \\ \text{sales} \\ \text{(units)}\end{array} + \begin{array}{c}\text{Target ending} \\ \text{finished goods} \\ \text{inventory} \\ \text{(units)}\end{array} - \begin{array}{c}\text{Beginning} \\ \text{finished goods} \\ \text{inventory} \\ \text{(units)}\end{array}$$

Schedule 2: Production Budget (in Units)
for the Year Ended December 31, 19_8

	Product	
	Regular	Heavy-Duty
Budgeted sales (schedule 1)	5,000	1,000
Add target ending finished goods inventory	1,100	50
Total requirements	6,100	1,050
Deduct beginning finished goods inventory	100	50
Units to be produced	6,000	1,000

When unit sales are not stable throughout the year, managers must decide whether (1) to adjust production levels periodically to minimize inventory held, or (2) to maintain constant production levels and let inventory rise and fall. Increasingly, managers are choosing to adjust production. Chapter 20 discusses just-in-time production systems whose objective is to keep extremely low levels of inventories throughout the year.

Step 3: Direct Materials Usage Budget and Direct Materials Purchases Budget   The decision on the number of units to be produced (schedule 2) is the key to computing the usage of direct materials in quantities and in dollars.

Schedule 3A: Direct Materials Usage Budget in Kilograms and Dollars
for the Year Ended December 31, 19_8

| | Material | | |
	111 Alloy	112 Alloy	Total
Direct materials to be used in production of Regular parts (6,000 units × 12 and 6 kilograms—see schedule 2)	72,000	36,000	
Direct materials to be used in production of Heavy-Duty parts (1,000 units × 12 and 8 kilograms—see schedule 2)	12,000	8,000	
Total direct materials to be used (in kilograms)	84,000	44,000	
Direct materials to be used from beginning inventory (under a FIFO cost-flow assumption)	7,000	6,000	
Multiply by cost per kilogram of beginning inventory	$ 7	$ 10	
Cost of direct materials to be used from beginning inventory: (a)	$ 49,000	$ 60,000	$ 109,000
Direct materials to be used from purchases (84,000 – 7,000; 44,000 – 6,000)	77,000	38,000	
Multiply by cost per kilogram of purchased materials	$ 7	$ 10	
Cost of direct materials to be used from purchases: (b)	$539,000	$380,000	$ 919,000
Total costs of direct materials to be used: (a) + (b)	$588,000	$440,000	$1,028,000

Schedule 3B computes the budget for direct materials purchases, which depends on the budgeted direct materials to be used, the beginning inventory of direct materials, and the target ending inventory of direct materials:

$$\begin{array}{l} \text{Purchases} \\ \text{of direct} \\ \text{materials} \end{array} = \begin{array}{l} \text{Usage} \\ \text{of direct} \\ \text{materials} \end{array} + \begin{array}{l} \text{Target ending} \\ \text{inventory} \\ \text{of direct} \\ \text{materials} \end{array} - \begin{array}{l} \text{Beginning} \\ \text{inventory} \\ \text{of direct} \\ \text{materials} \end{array}$$

Schedule 3B: Direct Materials Purchases Budget
for the Year Ended December 31, 19_8

| | Material | | |
	111 Alloy	112 Alloy	Total
Direct materials to be used in production (in kilograms) from schedule 3A	84,000	44,000	
Add target ending direct materials inventory (in kilograms)	8,000	2,000	
Total requirements (in kilograms)	92,000	46,000	
Deduct beginning direct materials inventory (in kilograms)	7,000	6,000	
Direct materials to be purchased (in kilograms)	85,000	40,000	
Multiply by cost per kilogram of purchased materials	$ 7	$ 10	
Total direct materials purchase costs	$595,000	$400,000	$995,000

Step 4: Direct Manufacturing Labor Budget   These costs depend on wage rates, production methods, and hiring plans. The computations of budgeted direct manufacturing labor costs appear in schedule 4.

Schedule 4: Direct Manufacturing Labor Budget
for the Year Ended December 31, 19_8

	Output Units Produced (Schedule 2)	Direct Manufacturing Labor-Hours per Unit	Total Hours	Hourly Wage Rate	Total
Regular	6,000	4	24,000	$20	$480,000
Heavy-Duty	1,000	6	6,000	20	120,000
Total			30,000		$600,000

Step 5: Manufacturing Overhead Budget The total of these costs depends on how individual overhead costs vary with the assumed cost driver, direct manufacturing labor-hours. The calculations of budgeted manufacturing overhead costs appear in schedule 5.

Schedule 5: Manufacturing Overhead Budget*
for the Year Ended December 31, 19_8

	At Budgeted Level of 30,000 Direct Manufacturing Labor-Hours	
Variable manufacturing overhead costs		
Supplies	$ 90,000	
Indirect manufacturing labor	210,000	
Direct and indirect manufacturing labor fringe costs	300,000	
Power	120,000	
Maintenance	60,000	$ 780,000
Fixed manufacturing overhead costs		
Depreciation	220,000	
Property taxes	50,000	
Property insurance	10,000	
Supervision	100,000	
Power	22,000	
Maintenance	18,000	420,000
Total manufacturing overhead costs		$1,200,000

*Data are from p. 182.

Halifax treats both variable and fixed manufacturing overhead as inventoriable costs.[1] It inventories manufacturing overhead at the budgeted rate of $40 per direct manufacturing labor-hour—total manufacturing overhead, $1,200,000 ÷ 30,000 budgeted direct manufacturing labor-hours. It does not use separate variable and fixed manufacturing overhead rates.

Step 6: Ending Inventory Budget Schedule 6A shows the computation of unit costs for the two products. These unit costs are used to calculate the costs of target ending inventories of direct materials and finished goods in schedule 6B.

Schedule 6A: Computation of Unit Costs of Manufacturing Finished Goods in 19_8

		Product			
		Regular		Heavy-Duty	
	Cost per Unit of Input*	Inputs*	Amount	Inputs*	Amount
Material 111 alloy	$ 7	12	$ 84	12	$ 84
Material 112 alloy	10	6	60	8	80
Direct manufacturing labor	20†	4	80	6	120
Manufacturing overhead	40‡	4	160	6	240
Total			$384		$524

*In kilograms or hours. †Data are from p. 181. ‡Direct manufacturing labor-hours is the sole allocation base for manufacturing overhead (both variable and fixed). The budgeted manufacturing overhead rate per direct manufacturing labor-hour of $40 was calculated in step 5.

[1]This inventory costing method is termed *absorption costing;* see Chapter 9 for further discussion.

Schedule 6B: Ending Inventory Budget
December 31, 19_8

	Kilograms	Cost per Kilogram	Total	
Direct materials				
111 alloy	8,000*	$ 7	$ 56,000	
112 alloy	2,000*	10	20,000	$ 76,000
	Units	**Cost per Unit**		
Finished goods				
Regular	1,100†	$384‡	$422,400	
Heavy-Duty	50†	524‡	26,200	448,600
Total ending inventory				$524,600

*Data are from p. 181. †Data are from p. 181. ‡From schedule 6A, this is based on 19_8 costs of manufacturing finished goods because under the FIFO costing method, the units in finished goods ending inventory consist of units that are produced during 19_8.

Step 7: Cost of Goods Sold Budget The information from schedules 3–6 leads to schedule 7:

Schedule 7: Cost of Goods Sold Budget
for the Year Ended December 31, 19_8

	From Schedule		Total
Beginning finished goods inventory, January 1, 19_8	Given*		$ 64,600
Direct materials used	3A	$1,028,000	
Direct manufacturing labor	4	600,000	
Manufacturing overhead	5	1,200,000	
Cost of goods manufactured			2,828,000
Cost of goods available for sale			2,892,600
Deduct ending finished goods inventory, December 31, 19_8	6B		448,600
Cost of goods sold			$2,444,000

*Given in the description of basic data and requirements (Regular $38,400, Heavy-Duty $26,200).

Note that the following holds:

$$\text{Cost of goods sold} = \text{Beginning finished goods inventory} + \text{Cost of goods manufactured} - \text{Ending finished goods inventory}$$

Step 8: Other (Nonproduction) Costs Budget Schedules 2–7 cover budgeting for Halifax's production area of the value chain. For brevity, other areas of the value chain are combined into a single schedule.

Schedule 8: Other (Nonproduction) Costs Budget
for the Year Ended December 31, 19_8

Variable costs		
R&D/product design	$ 76,000	
Marketing	133,000	
Distribution	66,500	
Customer service	47,500	
Administrative	152,000	475,000*
Fixed costs		
R&D/product design	60,000	
Marketing	67,000	
Distribution	33,500	
Customer service	12,500	
Administrative	222,000	395,000
Total costs		$870,000

*Total variable cost for schedule 8 is $0.125 per revenue dollar ($475,000 ÷ $3,800,000).

EXHIBIT 6-3
Budgeted Income Statement for Halifax Engineering for the Year Ended December 31, 19_8

Revenues	Schedule 1		$3,800,000
Costs			
Cost of goods sold	Schedule 7		2,444,000
Gross margin			1,356,000
Operating costs			
R&D/product design costs	Schedule 8	$136,000	
Marketing costs	Schedule 8	200,000	
Distribution costs	Schedule 8	100,000	
Customer service costs	Schedule 8	60,000	
Administration costs	Schedule 8	374,000	870,000
Operating income			$ 486,000

Step 9: Budgeted Income Statement Schedules 1, 7, and 8 provide the necessary information to complete the budgeted income statement, shown in Exhibit 6-3. Of course, more details could be included in the income statement, and then fewer supporting schedules would be prepared.

Top management's strategies for achieving revenue and operating income goals influence the costs planned for the different business functions of the value chain. As strategies change, the budget allocations for different elements of the value chain will also change. For example, a shift in strategy toward emphasizing product development and customer service will result in increased resources being allocated to these parts of the master budget. The actual data resulting from this strategy will be compared to budgeted results. Management can then evaluate whether the focus on product development and customer service has been successful. This feedback is an important input in subsequent plans.

OBJECTIVE 3

Prepare the budgeted income statement and its supporting budget schedules

COMPUTER-BASED FINANCIAL PLANNING MODELS

Exhibit 6-1 (p. 178) shows how strategic analysis, planning, and budgeting are interrelated. The value of budgets to managers in their strategic analysis and planning is enhanced by conducting sensitivity analysis. Sensitivity analysis is a "what-if" technique that examines how a result will change if the original predicted data are not achieved or if an underlying assumption changes. In its simplest form, it can be performed in the straightforward way shown in Chapter 3 (pp. 65–66). Here a handheld calculator would suffice to do the calculations. Commercial software packages are now available for more complex tasks, such as sensitivity analysis for the financial statements found in a master budget. These packages do the calculations for **financial planning models,** which are mathematical representations of the relationships across operating activities, financial activities, and financial statements.

Consider Halifax Engineering. Their financial planning model assumes the following:

OBJECTIVE 4

Describe the uses of computer-based financial planning models

◆ Direct materials and direct manufacturing labor costs vary proportionately with the quantities of Regular and Heavy-Duty parts produced.

◆ Variable manufacturing overhead costs vary with direct manufacturing laborhours.

◆ Variable nonmanufacturing costs vary with revenue dollars.

◆ Target ending inventories remain unchanged.

Exhibit 6-4 presents the budgeted operating income for three what-if scenarios for Halifax Engineering:

Budget Practices Around the Globe

Surveys of companies in the United States, Japan, Australia, the United Kingdom, and Holland indicate some interesting similarities and differences in budgeting practices across countries. The use of master budgets is widespread in all countries. Differences arise with respect to other dimensions of budgeting. U.S. managers prefer more participation and regard return on investment as the most important budget goal. In comparison, Japanese managers prefer less participation and regard sales revenues as the most important budget goal.

	United States	Japan	Australia	United Kingdom	Holland
1. Percentage of firms that prepare a complete master budget	91%	93%	95%	100%	100%
2. Percentage of firms reporting division manager participation in budget committee discussions	78%	67%	—	—	82%
3. Ranking of the most important budget goals for division managers (1 = most important)					
Return on investment	1	3	—	—	—
Operating income	2	2	—	—	—
Sales revenues	3	1	—	—	—

Source: Adapted from Asada, Bailes, and Amano, "An Empirical Study," Blayney and Yokoyama, "Comparative Analysis," and de With and Ijskes "Current Budgeting." Full citations are in Appendix A.

Scenario 1: A 3% decrease in the selling price of the Regular part and a 3% decrease in the selling price of the Heavy-Duty part.

Scenario 2: A 4% decrease in units sold of the Regular part and a 4% decrease in units sold of the Heavy-Duty part.

Scenario 3: A 5% increase in the price per kilogram of 111 alloy and a 5% increase in the price per kilogram of 112 alloy.

EXHIBIT 6-4
Effect of Changes in Budget Assumptions on Budgeted Income for Halifax Engineering

What-If Scenario	Units Sold		Selling Price		Direct Materials Cost*		Budgeted Operating Income	
	Regular	Heavy-Duty	Regular	Heavy-Duty	111 Alloy	112 Alloy	Dollars	Change from Master Budget
Master budget	5,000	1,000	$600	$800	$7.00	$10.00	$486,000	—
Scenario 1	5,000	1,000	582	776	7.00	10.00	386,250	21% decrease
Scenario 2	4,800	960	600	800	7.00	10.00	438,273	10% decrease
Scenario 3	5,000	1,000	600	800	7.35	10.50	448,380	9% decrease

*Per kilogram.

Exhibit 6-4 indicates that, relative to the master budget, budgeted operating income decreases by 21% under scenario 1, by 10% under scenario 2, and by 9% under scenario 3. Managers can use this information to plan actions that they may need to take if faced with these scenarios.

KAIZEN BUDGETING

Chapter 1 (p. 14) noted how continuous improvement is one of the key issues facing management today. The Japanese use the term *kaizen* for continuous improvement. **Kaizen budgeting** is a budgetary approach that explicitly incorporates continuous improvement during the budget period into the resultant budget numbers.

Consider our Halifax Engineering example in schedule 4 (p. 185). The 19_8 budget assumes that it will take 4.0 and 6.0 manufacturing labor-hours, respectively, for each Regular and Heavy-Duty aircraft part. A kaizen budgeting approach would incorporate continuous reduction in these manufacturing labor-hour requirements during 19_8. Assume Halifax budgets the following labor-hour amounts:

	Budgeted Amounts (Labor-Hours)	
	Regular	**Heavy-Duty**
January–March 19_8	4.00	6.00
April–June 19_8	3.90	5.85
July–September 19_8	3.80	5.70
October–December 19_8	3.70	5.55

Unless Halifax meets these continuous improvement goals, unfavorable variances will be reported. Note that in the Halifax budget, the implications of these direct labor-hour reductions would extend to reductions in variable manufacturing overhead costs, given that direct manufacturing labor-hours is the driver of these costs.

Kaizen at Citizen Watch

Citizen Watch is the world's largest manufacturer of watches. The assembly areas at its plants are highly automated. Component part costs for each watch are a sizable percentage of the unit cost of each watch. A central part of Citizen's cost management system is kaizen budgeting. All parts of the entire production area, including component suppliers, are required to continually seek out cost reduction opportunities. For example, at its Tokyo plant, it budgets that all external suppliers will have a steady cost reduction of 3% per annum. Suppliers who exceed this 3% target retain for at least 1 year any cost reductions above the 3% level. Suppliers who do not attain the 3% target receive the "assistance" of Citizen engineers in the following year.[2]

ACTIVITY-BASED BUDGETING

Chapters 4 and 5 explained how activity-based costing systems can lead to improved decision making. Activity-based costing principles extend to budgeting. **Activity-based budgeting** focuses on the cost of activities necessary to produce and sell products and services. It separates indirect costs into separate homogeneous activity cost pools. Management uses the cause-and-effect criterion to identify the cost drivers for each of these indirect-cost pools.

Four key steps in activity-based budgeting are

1. Determine the budgeted costs of performing each unit of activity at each activity area.

2. Determine the demand for each individual activity based on budgeted, production, new product development, and so on.

[2]See R. Cooper, "Citizen Watch Company, Ltd.: Cost Reduction for Mature Products," Harvard Business School, Case No. 9-194-033.

3. Compute the costs of performing each activity.

4. Describe the budget as costs of performing various activities (rather than budgeted costs of functional or conventional value-chain spending categories).

An activity-based budgeting approach is facilitated by adopting activity-based costing as described in Chapters 4 and 5.

Consider activity-based budgeting for the R&D/product design parts of the value chain at Bradford Aerospace. Four activity areas and their cost drivers have been identified. The budgeted 19_7 rates for the costs at each activity area are as follows:

Activity	Cost Driver/ Budgeted Cost Rate
◆ Computer aided design (CAD)—using computer software to design aircraft parts	CAD hours, $80 per hour
◆ Manual design—manually designing aircraft parts	Manual design hours, $50 per hour
◆ Prototyping development—building actual versions of aircraft parts	Protyping hours, $60 per hour
◆ Testing—examining how new aircraft parts "perform" in different operating conditions	Testing hours, $40 per hour
◆ Procurement—purchasing supplies and component parts	Purchase orders, $25 per purchase order

Exhibit 6-5 presents the activity-based budget for January to December 19_7. Bradford budgets usage of the cost driver in each activity area based on budgeted production and new product development. This budgeted usage of the cost driver for each activity is multiplied by the respective budgeted costs rate per activity to obtain the budgeted activity costs. The budgeted total costs for R&D/product design is the sum of the budgeted costs of the individual activities in that part of the value chain.

The activity-based budget in Exhibit 6-5 is for one part of Bradford's value chain. In many cases, the same activity will appear in more than one part of the value chain. For example, procurement activities such as purchase ordering and supplier payment are found in most areas of the value chain. Companies using activity-based budgeting may choose to present their budgets at either the individual value-chain level or at some more basic activity level such as procurement by combining budgeted procurement costs from different parts of the value chain.

A survey of U.K. managers reported the following ranking of the benefits from activity-based budgeting: (1) ability to set more realistic budgets, (2) better identification of resource needs, (3) linking of costs to outputs, (4) clearer linking of costs with staff responsibilities, and (5) identification of budgetary slack.[3]

[3]J. Innes and F. Mitchell, "A Survey of Activity-Based Costing in the U.K.'s Largest Companies," *Management Accounting Research* (Vol. 6), pp. 137–53.

EXHIBIT 6-5
Activity-Based Budget for R&D/Product Design Costs of Bradford Aerospace:
January to December, 19_7

Activity Area	Budgeted Usage of Driver	Budgeted Rate per Cost Driver	Budgeted Costs
Computer-aided design	200 hours	$80	$16,000
Manual design	70 hours	50	3,500
Prototyping development	80 hours	60	4,800
Testing	280 hours	40	11,200
Procurement	120 orders*	25	3,000
Total			$38,500

*purchase orders.

Organizational Structure and Responsibility

Organizational structure is an arrangement of lines of responsibility within the entity. A company such as British Petroleum may be organized primarily by business function: exploration, refining, and marketing. Another company such as Procter & Gamble, a household products giant, may be organized by product or brand line. The managers of the individual divisions (toothpaste, soap, and so on) would each have decision-making authority concerning all the business functions (manufacturing, marketing, and so on) within that division.

To attain the goals described in the master budget, an organization must coordinate the efforts of all its employees—from the top executive through all levels of management to every supervised worker. Coordinating the organization's efforts means assigning responsibility to managers who are accountable for their actions in planning and controlling human and physical resources. Management is essentially a human activity. Budgets exist not for their own sake, but to help managers.

Each manager, regardless of level, is in charge of a responsibility center. A **responsibility center** is a part, segment, or subunit of an organization whose manager is accountable for a specified set of activities. The higher the manager's level, the broader the responsibility center he or she manages and, generally, the larger the number of subordinates who report to him or her. **Responsibility accounting** is a system that measures the plans (by budgets) and actions (by actual results) of each responsibility center. Four major types of responsibility centers are

1. **Cost center**—manager accountable for costs only.
2. **Revenue center**—manager accountable for revenues only.
3. **Profit center**—manager accountable for revenues and costs.
4. **Investment center**—manager accountable for investments, revenues, and costs.

The Maintenance Department of a Marriott hotel would be a cost center because the maintenance manager is responsible only for costs. Hence, the budget would emphasize costs. The Sales Department of the hotel would be a revenue center because the sales manager is responsible only for revenues. Here the budget would emphasize revenues. The hotel manager would be in charge of a profit center because the hotel manager is accountable for both revenues and costs. Here the budget would emphasize both revenues and costs. The regional manager responsible for investments in new hotel projects and for revenues and costs would be in charge of an investment center. Revenue, costs, and the investment base would be emphasized in the budget for this manager.

Responsibility accounting affects behavior. Consider the following incident:

The Sales Department requests a rush production run. The plant scheduler argues that it will disrupt his production and will cost a substantial though not clearly determined amount of money. The answer coming from sales is, "Do you want to take the responsibility of losing the X Company as a customer?" Of course, the production scheduler does not want to take such a responsibility, and he gives up, but not before a heavy exchange of arguments and the accumulation of a substantial backlog of ill feeling. The controller proposes an innovative solution. He analyzes the payroll in the Assembly Department to determine the costs involved in getting out rush orders. This information eliminates the cause for argument. Henceforth, any rush order would be accepted by the production scheduler, "no questions asked." The extra costs would be duly recorded and charged to the Sales Department.

As a result, the tension created by rush orders disappeared, and, somehow, the number of rush orders requested by the Sales Department was progressively reduced to an insignificant level.[4]

[4]R. Villers, "Control and Freedom in a Decentralized Company," *Harvard Business Review* (Vol. 32, No. 2), p. 95.

The responsibility accounting approach traces costs to either (1) the individual who has the best knowledge about why the costs arose, or (2) the activity that caused the costs. In this incident, the cause was the sales activity, and the resulting costs were charged to the Sales Department. If rush orders occur regularly, the Sales Department might have a budget for such costs, and the department's actual performance would then be compared against the budget.

Feedback and Fixing Blame

Budgets coupled with responsibility accounting provide systematic help for managers, particularly if managers interpret the feedback carefully. Managers, accountants, and students of management accounting repeatedly tend to "play the blame game"—using variances (the difference between the actual results and the budgeted results) appearing in the responsibility accounting system to pinpoint fault for operating problems. In looking at variances, managers should focus on whom they should ask and not on whom they should blame. Variances only suggest questions or direct attention to persons who should have the relevant information. Nevertheless, variances, properly used, can be helpful in evaluating managers' performance.

RESPONSIBILITY AND CONTROLLABILITY

Definition of Controllability

Controllability is the degree of influence that a specific manager has over costs, revenues, or other items in question. A **controllable cost** is any cost that is primarily subject to the influence of a given manager of a given responsibility center for a given time span. A responsibility accounting system could either exclude all uncontrollable costs from a manager's performance report or segregate such costs from the controllable costs. For example, a machining supervisor's performance report might be confined to quantities (not costs) of direct materials, direct manufacturing labor, power, and supplies.

In practice, controllability is difficult to pinpoint:

1. Few costs are clearly under the sole influence of one manager. For example, costs of direct materials may be influenced by a purchasing manager, but such costs also depend on market conditions beyond the manager's control. Quantities used may be influenced by a production manager, but quantities used also depend on the quality of materials purchased. Moreover, managers often work in teams. How can individual responsibility be evaluated in a team decision?

2. With a long enough time span, all costs will come under somebody's control. However, most performance reports focus on periods of a year or less. A current manager may have inherited problems and inefficiencies from his or her predecessor. For example, present managers may have to work under undesirable contracts with suppliers or labor unions that were negotiated by their predecessors. How can we separate what the current manager actually controls from the results of decisions made by others? Exactly what is the current manager accountable for? Answers to such questions may not be clear-cut.

Senior managers differ in how they embrace the controllability notion when evaluating those reporting to them. For example, a newly appointed president took his management team on a cruise and commented, "I expect everybody to meet their budget targets no matter what happens, and those who don't should stand a little closer to the railing." Other presidents believe that a more risk-sharing approach with managers is preferable where noncontrollable factors are taken into account when making judgments about the performance of managers who miss their budget.

Emphasis on Information and Behavior

Managers should avoid overemphasizing controllability. Responsibility accounting is more far-reaching. It focuses on *information* and *knowledge*, not control. The key question is, Who is the best informed? Put another way, Who is the person who can tell us the most about the specific item in question, regardless of that person's ability to exert personal control? For instance, purchasing managers may be held accountable for total purchase costs, not because of their ability to affect market prices, but because of their ability to predict uncontrollable prices and explain uncontrollable price changes. Similarly, managers at a Pizza Hut unit may be held responsible for operating income of their units, even though they do not fully control selling prices or the costs for many food items, and have minimal flexibility as to items to sell or their ingredients. Why? Because unit managers are in the best position to explain variances between their actual operating income and their budgeted operating income.

Performance reports for responsibility centers may also include uncontrollable items because this approach could change behavior in the directions top management desires. For example, some companies have changed the accountability of a cost center to a profit center. Why? Because the manager will probably behave differently. A cost-center manager may emphasize production efficiency and deemphasize the pleas of sales personnel for faster service and rush orders. In a profit center, the manager is responsible for both costs and revenues. Thus, even though the manager still has no control over sales personnel, the manager will now more likely weigh the impact of his or her decisions on costs and revenues, rather than solely on costs.

The Budget Games that People Play

Budgets play a key role in how resources are appropriated. Not surprisingly, many budget games are played by those seeking to receive larger rather than smaller appropriations. Labels have been developed to describe some of the "more familiar" budget ploys.* Some examples include the following:

Foot-in-the Door Ploy. This ploy involves obtaining approval for a small project that then expands into a much larger project. Many builders on office extension projects "underbid" on the first set of plans. Once the project is underway, they earn "superprofits" when their clients make the almost inevitable changes to the initial set of plans. The key challenge most builders face is to get the first "foot-in-the-door."

Remove the "White Elephant" Ploy. This ploy involves gaining budget approval for funds by presenting it as "removing a white elephant." One Marketing Department wanted a new training facility. It was informed that top management had an edict that "no new buildings were to be constructed." They then revised their proposal to renovate an existing manufacturing facility. This facility had been idle for a year. The Marketing Department received approval for the project despite it being much cheaper to construct a new facility!

Avoid Lawyers' Dancing on Our Grave Ploy. This ploy involves justifying budget appropriations on the basis that, by not making them, we "guarantee" that many subsequent lawsuits will occur. A heart surgeon wishing to expand his empire successfully argued for the purchase of very expensive equipment. The stated reason was to avoid future litigation about medical malpractice.

We Must Be Up-to-Date Ploy. This ploy for budget appropriations is frequently found with technical people requesting approvals to purchase each new technology. Vendors for engineering software invariably use this pitch to convince product designers to purchase their new products. An inevitable line that peppers the conversation is that the competing design companies have already purchased the new "state of the art" software and that the company will be at a competitive disadvantage by not purchasing it.

* More discussion on budget ploys is in R. Anthony and D. Young, *Management Control in Nonprofit Organizations* (Homewood, Ill.: Irwin, 1994).

HUMAN ASPECTS OF BUDGETING

Why did we cover two major topics, master budgets and responsibility accounting, in the same chapter? Primarily to emphasize that human factors are crucial parts of budgeting. Too often, students study budgeting as though it were a mechanical tool.

The budgeting techniques themselves are free of emotion; however, their administration requires education, persuasion, and intelligent interpretation. Many managers regard budgets negatively. To them, the word *budget* is about as popular as, say, *downsizing, layoff, or strike.* Top managers must convince their subordinates that the budget is a positive tool designed to help them choose and reach goals. But budgets are not cure-alls. They are not remedies for weak management talent, faulty organization, or a poor accounting system.

BUDGETING: A DISCIPLINE IN TRANSITION

Many areas of management accounting are subject to ongoing debate. Budgeting is no exception. Advocates of new proposals invariably include criticisms of so-called "traditional budgeting." These criticisms are often exaggerations of "current worst practice." Exhibit 6-6 summarizes six proposals relating to improving traditional budgeting systems. Few of the negative features cited in the left-hand column are new; they have long been singled out for criticism. Indeed, prior sections of this chapter have mentioned the importance of avoiding many of these problems. Nonetheless, major changes that address these problems are currently being examined by managers.

EXHIBIT 6-6
Criticisms of Traditional Budgeting and Proposals for Change

Criticism of Traditional Budgeting	Proposal for Change
Excessive reliance on extrapolating past trends.	Link budgeting explicitly to strategy.
Make across the board fixed percentage cuts when early iterations of a budget provide "unacceptable results."	Use activity-based budgeting to guide areas for cost reduction.
Budget examines individual functional areas as if they are independent (so-called silos to use a farming analogy).	Explicitly adopt a cross-functional approach where interdependencies across business function areas of the value-chain are recognized.
Budget myopically overemphasizing a fixed time horizon such as a year. Meeting annual cost targets viewed as key task to be accomplished.	Tailor the budget cycle to the purpose of budgeting. Events beyond current period are recognized as important when evaluating current actions. Value creation is given paramount importance.
Budget is preoccupied with financial aspects of events in the budget period.	Balance financial aspects with both non-financial (such as quality and time) aspects.
Budgets are not used until end of budget period to evaluate performance.	Signals to all employees the need for continuous improvement of performance (such as, revenue enhancement and cost reduction) within the budget period.

Source: Adapted from "*Advanced Budgeting Study Group Report* for CAM-I," *Management Accounting* (U.K., Dec. 1994).

Before trying to solve the following problem, review the illustration of the master budget, page 180.

PROBLEM

Prepare a budgeted income statement, including all necessary detailed supporting budget schedules. Use the data given in the illustration of the master budget to prepare your own budget schedules. (See the "Basic Data and Requirements" section on pp. 181–182.)

SUMMARY

The following points are linked to the chapter's learning objectives.

1. The master budget summarizes the financial projections of all the organization's budgets and plans. It expresses management's comprehensive operating and financial plans—the formalized outline of the organization's financial objectives and their means of attainment. Budgets are tools that by themselves are neither good nor bad. How managers administer budgets is the key to their value. When administered wisely, budgets compel management planning, provide definite expectations that are an appropriate framework for judging subsequent performance, and promote communication and coordination among the various subunits of the organization.

2. Two major parts of the master budget are the operating budget, which is the budgeted income statement and its supporting budget schedules, and the financial budget, which comprises the capital budget, cash budget, budgeted balance sheet, and budgeted statement of cash flows.

3. The foundation for the operating budget is generally the revenue budget. The following supporting budget schedules are geared to the revenue budget: production budget, direct materials usage budget, direct materials purchases budget, direct manufacturing labor budget, manufacturing overhead costs budget, ending inventory budget, cost of goods sold budget, R&D/design budget, marketing budget, distribution budget, and customer-service budget. The operating budget ends with the budgeted income statement.

4. Computer-based financial planning models are mathematical statements of the relationships among operating activities, financial activities, and other factors that affect the budget. These models allow management to conduct what-if (sensitivity) analyses of the effects on the master budget of changes in the original predicted data or changes in budget assumptions.

5. Kaizen budgeting captures the continuous improvement notion that is a key management concern. Costs in kaizen budgeting are based on future improvements that are yet to be implemented rather than on current practices or methods.

6. Activity-based budgeting focuses on the costs of activities necessary to produce and sell products and services. It is inherently linked to activity-based costing, but differs in its emphases on future costs and future usage of activity areas.

7. A responsibility center is a part, segment, or subunit of an organization whose manager is accountable for a specified set of activities. Four major types of responsibility centers are cost centers, revenue centers, profit centers, and investment centers. Responsibility accounting systems measure the plans (by budgets) and actions (by actual results) of each responsibility center.

8. Controllable costs are costs that are primarily subject to the influence of a given manager of a given responsibility center for a given time span. Performance reports of responsibility-center managers, however, often include costs, revenues, and investments that the managers cannot control. Responsibility accounting associates financial items with managers on the basis of which manager has the most knowledge and information about the specific items, regardless of the manager's ability to exercise full control. The important question is who should be asked, not who should be blamed.

APPENDIX: THE CASH BUDGET

The major illustration in the chapter features the operating budget. The other major part of the master budget is the **financial budget,** which includes the capital budget, cash budget, budgeted balance sheet, and budgeted statement of cash flows. This Appendix focuses on the cash budget and the budgeted balance sheet. Capital budgeting is covered in Chapters 22 and 23; coverage of the budgeted statement of cash flows is beyond the scope of this book.

Suppose Halifax Engineering in our chapter illustration had the balance sheet for the year ended December 31, 19_7 shown in Exhibit 6-7. The budgeted cash flows for 19_8 are as follows:

| | Quarters | | | |
	1	2	3	4
Collections from customers	$913,700	$984,600	$976,500	$918,400
Disbursements				
Direct materials	314,360	283,700	227,880	213,800
Payroll	557,520	432,080	409,680	400,720
Income taxes	50,000	46,986	46,986	46,986
Other costs	184,000	156,000	151,000	149,000
Machinery purchase	—	—	—	35,080

The quarterly data are based on the cash effects of the operations formulated in schedules 1–8 in the chapter, but the details of that formulation are not shown here in order to keep the illustration relatively brief and focused.

The company wants to maintain a $35,000 minimum cash balance at the end of each quarter. The company can borrow or repay money in multiples of $1,000 at an

EXHIBIT 6-7
Balance Sheet for Halifax Engineering for the Year Ended December 31, 19_7

ASSETS		
Current assets		
Cash	$ 30,000	
Accounts receivable	400,000	
Direct materials	109,000	
Finished goods	64,600	$ 603,600
Property, plant, and equipment:		
Land	200,000	
Building and equipment	2,200,000	
Accumulated depreciation	(690,000)	1,710,000
Total		$2,313,600

LIABILITIES AND STOCKHOLDERS' EQUITY		
Current liabilities		
Accounts payable	$ 150,000	
Income taxes payable	50,000	$ 200,000
Stockholders' equity		
Common stock, no-par,		
25,000 shares outstanding	350,000	
Retained earnings	1,763,600	2,113,600
Total		$2,313,600

interest rate of 12% per year. Management does not want to borrow any more cash than is necessary and wants to repay as promptly as possible. By special arrangement, interest is computed and paid when the principal is repaid. Assume that borrowing takes place at the beginning and repayment at the end of the quarters in question. Interest is computed to the nearest dollar.

Suppose an accountant at Halifax Engineering is given the preceding data and the other data contained in the budgets in the chapter (pp. 181–187). He is instructed as follows:

1. **Prepare a cash budget.** That is, prepare a statement of cash receipts and disbursements by quarters, including details of borrowing, repayment, and interest expense.

2. **Prepare a budgeted balance sheet.**

3. **Prepare a budgeted income statement,** including the effects of interest expense and income taxes. Assume that income taxes for 19_8 (at a tax rate of 40%) are $187,944.

Preparation of Budgets

1. The **cash budget** (Exhibit 6-8) is a schedule of expected cash receipts and disbursements. It predicts the effects on the cash position at the given level of operations. Exhibit 6-8 presents the cash budget by quarters to show the impact of

EXHIBIT 6-8
Cash Budget for Halifax Engineering for the Year Ended December 31, 19_8

| | Quarters | | | | |
	1	2	3	4	Year as a Whole
Cash balance, beginning	$ 30,000	$ 35,820	$ 35,934	$ 35,188	$ 30,000
Add receipts					
Collections from customers	913,700	984,600	976,500	918,400	3,793,200
Total cash available for needs (a)	943,700	1,020,420	1,012,434	953,588	3,823,200
Deduct disbursements					
Direct materials	314,360	283,700	227,880	213,800	1,039,740
Payroll	557,520	432,080	409,680	400,720	1,800,000
Income taxes	50,000	46,986	46,986	46,986	190,958
Other costs	184,000	156,000	151,000	149,000	640,000
Machinery purchase	0	0	0	35,080	35,080
Total disbursements (b)	1,105,880	918,766	835,546	845,586	3,705,778
Minimum cash balance desired	35,000	35,000	35,000	35,000	35,000
Total cash needed (c)	1,140,880	953,766	870,546	880,586	3,740,778
Cash excess (deficiency) (a) – (c)*	$ (197,180)	$ 66,654	$ 141,888	$ 73,002	$ 82,422
Financing					
Borrowing (at beginning)	$ 198,000	$ 0	$ 0	$ 0	$ 198,000
Repayment (at end)	—	(62,000)	(130,000)	(6,000)	(198,000)
Interest (at 12% per year)†	—	(3,720)	(11,700)	(720)	(16,140)
Total effects of financing (d)	$ 198,000	$ (65,720)	$ (141,700)	$ (6,720)	$ (16,140)
Cash balance, ending (a) – (b) + (d)	$ 35,820	$ 35,934	$ 35,188	$101,282	$ 101,282

*Excess of total cash available over total cash needed before current financing.
†Note that the interest payments pertain only to the amount of principal being repaid at the end of a given quarter. The specific computations regarding interest are $62,000 × 0.12 × ¾ = $3,720; $130,000 × 0.12 × ¾ = $11,700; and $6,000 × 0.12 × ¾ = $720. Also note that *depreciation does not require a cash outlay.*

cash-flow timing on bank loans and their repayment. In practice, monthly—and sometimes weekly—cash budgets are very helpful for cash planning and control. Cash budgets help avoid unnecessary idle cash and unexpected cash deficiencies. Cash balances are kept in line with needs. Ordinarily, the cash budget has the following main sections:

a. The beginning cash balance plus cash receipts equals the total cash available before financing. Cash receipts depend on collections of accounts receivable, cash sales, and miscellaneous recurring sources such as rental or royalty receipts. Information on the prospective collectibility of accounts receivable is needed for accurate predictions. Key factors include bad-debt (uncollectible accounts) experience and average time lag between sales and collections.

b. Cash disbursements include the following items:

(i) *Direct materials purchases*—depends on credit terms extended by suppliers and bill-paying patterns of the buyer.

(ii) *Direct labor and other wage and salary outlays*—depends on payroll dates.

(iii) *Other costs*—depends on timing and credit terms. *Be sure to note that depreciation does not require a cash outlay.*

(iv) *Other disbursements*—outlays for property, plant, and equipment, and for long-term investments.

c. Financing requirements depend on how the total cash available for needs, keyed as (a) in Exhibit 6-8, compares with the total cash needed, keyed as (c). Total cash needed includes total disbursements, keyed as (b), plus the minimum ending cash balance desired. The financing plans will depend on the relationship between total cash available for needs and total cash needed. If there is excess cash, loans may be repaid or temporary investments made. The outlays for interest expense are usually shown in this section of the cash budget.

d. The ending cash balance. The total effect of the financing decisions on the cash budget, keyed as (d) in Exhibit 6-8, may be positive (borrowing) or negative (repayment), and the ending cash balance is (a) – (b) + (d).

The cash budget in Exhibit 6-8 shows the pattern of short-term "self-liquidating cash loans." Seasonal peaks of production or sales often result in heavy cash disbursements for purchases, payroll, and other operating outlays as the products are produced and sold. Cash receipts from customers typically lag behind sales. The loan is *self-liquidating* in the sense that the borrowed money is used to acquire resources that are combined for sale, and the proceeds from sales are used to repay the loan. This **self-liquidating cycle**—sometimes called the **working-capital cycle, cash cycle,** or **operating cycle**—is the movement from cash to inventories to receivables and back to cash.

2. The budgeted balance sheet is presented in Exhibit 6-9. Each item is projected in light of the details of the business plan as expressed in all the previous budget schedules. For example, the ending balance of accounts receivable of $406,800 is computed by adding the budgeted revenues of $3,800,000 (from schedule 1) to the beginning balance of $400,000 (given) and subtracting cash receipts of $3,793,200 (given in Exhibit 6-9).

3. The budgeted income statement is presented in Exhibit 6-10. It is merely the budgeted operating income statement in Exhibit 6-3 (p. 187) expanded to include interest expense and income taxes.

For simplicity, the cash receipts and disbursements were given explicitly in this illustration. Frequently, there are lags between the items reported on the accrual basis of accounting in an income statement and their related cash receipts and disbursements. In the Halifax Engineering example, collections from customers are derived under two assumptions: (1) In any month, 10% of sales are cash sales and 90% of sales are on credit, and (2) half the total credit sales are collected in each of the 2 months subsequent to the sale, as the following table shows.

	May	June	July	August	September	Cash Collections in Third Quarter as a Whole
Monthly Revenue Budget for Halifax (Given)						
Credit sales, 90%	$307,800	$307,800	$280,800	$280,800	$280,800	
Cash sales, 10%	34,200	34,200	31,200	31,200	31,200	
Total revenues	$342,000	$342,000	$312,000	$312,000	$312,000	
Cash Collections from						
Cash sales this month			$ 31,200	$ 31,200	$ 31,200	
Credit sales last month			153,900*	140,400‡	140,400§	
Credit sales 2 months ago			153,900†	153,900*	140,400‡	
Total Collections			$339,000	$325,500	$312,000	$976,500

*0.50 × $307,800 (June sales) = $153,900
†0.50 × $307,800 (May sales) = $153,900
‡0.50 × $280,800 (July sales) = $140,400
§0.50 × $280,800 (August sales) = $140,400

EXHIBIT 6-9
Halifax Engineering: Budgeted Balance Sheet for the Year Ended December 31, 19_8

ASSETS

Current assets			
Cash (from Exhibit 6-8)		$ 101,282	
Accounts receivable (1)		406,800	
Direct materials (2)		76,000	
Finished goods (2)		448,600	$1,032,682
Property, plant and equipment			
Land (3)		200,000	
Building and equipment (4)	$2,235,080		
Accumulated depreciation (5)	(920,000)	1,315,080	1,515,080
Total			$2,547,762

LIABILITIES AND STOCKHOLDERS' EQUITY

Current liabilities			
Accounts payable (6)		$ 105,260	
Income taxes payable (7)		46,986	$ 152,246
Stockholders' equity			
Common stock, no-par, 25,000 shares outstanding (8)		350,000	
Retained earnings (9)		2,045,516	2,395,516
Total			$2,547,762

Notes:
Beginning balances are used as the starting point for most of the following computations:
(1) $400,000 + $3,800,000 revenues − $3,793,200 receipts (Exhibit 6-8) = $406,800.
(2) From schedule 6B, p. 186.
(3) From beginning balance sheet, p. 196.
(4) $2,200,000 + $35,080 purchases = $2,235,080.
(5) $690,000 + $230,000 depreciation from schedule 5, p. 185.
(6) $150,000 + $995,000 (schedule 3B) − $1,039,740 (Exhibit 6-8) = $105,260.
There are no wages payable. The detailed payroll consists of $600,000 direct manufacturing labor (schedule 4) + $620,000 manufacturing overhead salaries ($200,000 indirect manufacturing labor + $320,000 direct and indirect manufacturing labor fringe cost + $100,000 supervision from schedule 5) + R&D/design salaries $105,000 (schedule 8) + marketing salaries $130,000 (schedule 8) + distribution salaries and wages $60,000 (schedule 8) + customer-service salaries $40,000 (schedule 8) + administration salaries and clerical wages $245,000 (schedule 8) = $1,800,000, all of which was disbursed per Exhibit 6-8.
(7) $50,000 + $187,944 current year − $190,958 payment = $46,986.
(8) From beginning balance sheet.
(9) $1,763,600 + $281,916 net income per Exhibit 6-10 = $2,045,516.

EXHIBIT 6-10
Budgeted Income Statement for Halifax Engineering for the Year Ended December 31, 19_8

Revenues	Schedule 1		$3,800,000
Costs			
Cost of goods sold	Schedule 7		2,444,000
Gross margin			1,356,000
Operating costs			
R&D/product design costs	Schedule 8	$136,000	
Marketing costs	Schedule 8	200,000	
Distribution costs	Schedule 8	100,000	
Customer-service costs	Schedule 8	60,000	
Administration costs	Schedule 8	374,000	870,000
Operating income			486,000
Interest expense	Exhibit 6-8		16,140
Income before income taxes			469,860
Income taxes	Given		187,944
Net income			$ 281,916

Of course, such schedules of cash collections depend on credit terms, collection histories, and expected bad debts. Similar schedules can be prepared for operating costs and their related cash disbursements.

TERMS TO LEARN

The chapter and the Glossary at the end of this text contain definitions of the following important terms:

activity-based budgeting (p. 189)
budgetary slack (183)
cash budget (197)
cash cycle (198)
controllability (192)
controllable cost (192)
cost center (191)
financial budget (180)
financial planning models (187)
investment center (191)
kaizen budgeting (189)
master budget (176)
operating budget (180)

operating cycle (198)
organizational structure (191)
padding (183)
profit center (191)
pro forma statements (179)
responsibility accounting (191)
responsibility center (191)
revenue center (191)
rolling budget (179)
self-liquidating cycle (198)
strategic analysis (177)
working-capital cycle (198)

ASSIGNMENT MATERIAL

QUESTIONS

6-1 Define master budget.

6-2 What are the elements of the budgeting cycle?

6-3 "Strategy, plans, and budgets are unrelated to one another." Do you agree? Explain.

6-4 "Budgeted performance is a better criterion than past performance for judging managers." Do you agree? Explain.

6-5 "Production and marketing are like oil and water. They just don't mix." How can a budget assist in reducing traditional battles between these two areas?

6-6 "Budgets are wonderful vehicles for communication." Comment.

6-7 "Budgets meet the cost-benefit test. They force managers to act differently." Do you agree? Explain.

6-8 Define rolling budget. Give an example.

6-9 "The revenue budget is the cornerstone for budgeting." Why?

6-10 Give examples where the final amounts in a budget are over- or underestimates of the expected amounts.

6-11 Define kaizen budgeting.

6-12 Cite three benefits companies report from using an activity-based budgeting approach.

6-13 Define responsibility accounting.

6-14 Explain how the choice of the responsibility center type (cost, revenue, profit, or investment) affects budgeting.

6-15 Outline three criticisms of traditional budgeting and a related proposal for change.

EXERCISES

6-16 Production budget (in units), fill in the missing numbers. The following (in units) is taken from the production budget for three models of fax machines in October 19_7:

	Model 101	Model 201	Model 301
1. Beginning finished goods inventory	11	8	?
2. Target ending finished goods inventory	?	6	33
3. Budgeted production	?	?	855
4. Budgeted sales	180	?	867
5. Total required units (2 + 4)	194	199	?

REQUIRED
Fill in the missing numbers.

6-17 Cost of goods sold budget, fill in the missing numbers. Enduro Machining has two direct-cost categories (direct materials and direct manufacturing labor). Its single indirect-cost category (manufacturing overhead) is allocated on the basis of machine-hours. Numbers taken from the monthly budgets for June 19_7 and November 19_7 are as follows:

	June 19_7	November 19_7
Direct materials used	$?	$ 847
Beginning finished goods inventory	87	?
Ending finished goods inventory	?	94
Direct manufacturing labor	481	389
Manufacturing overhead	772	?
Cost of goods manufactured	2,215	1,878
Cost of goods sold	2,189	?
Cost of goods available for sale	?	1,949

REQUIRED
Fill in the missing numbers.

6-18 Sales and production budget. The Mendez Company expects 19_8 sales of 100,000 units of serving trays. Mendez's beginning inventory for 19_8 is 7,000 trays; target ending inventory, 11,000 trays.

REQUIRED
Compute the number of trays budgeted for production in 19_8.

6-19 Sales and production budget. The Gallo Company had a target ending inventory of 70,000 four-liter bottles of burgundy wine. Gallo's beginning inventory was 60,000 bottles, and its budgeted production was 900,000 bottles.

REQUIRED

Compute the budgeted sales in number of bottles.

6-20 Direct materials purchases budget. The Inglenook Company produces wine. The company expects to produce 1.5 million 2-liter bottles of Chablis in 19_9. Inglenook purchases empty glass bottles from an outside vendor. Its target ending inventory of such bottles is 50,000; its beginning inventory is 20,000. For simplicity, ignore breakage.

REQUIRED

Compute the number of bottles to be purchased in 19_9.

6-21 Budgeting material purchases. The Mahoney Company has prepared a sales budget of 42,000 finished units for a 3-month period. The company has an inventory of 22,000 units of finished goods on hand at December 31 and has a target finished goods inventory of 24,000 units at the end of the succeeding quarter.

It takes 3 gallons of direct materials to make 1 unit of finished product. The company has an inventory of 90,000 gallons of direct materials at December 31 and has a target ending inventory of 110,000 gallons.

REQUIRED

How many gallons of direct materials should be purchased during the 3 months ending March 31?

6-22 Budgeting revenue, cost of goods sold, and gross margin. Janet Grossman operates the Centrum Gift Shop. She expects cash sales of $10,000 for October, $11,000 for November, and $16,000 for December. Grossman expects credit card sales of $7,000 during October and $8,000 and $12,000, respectively, during November and December. Sales returns and allowances can be ignored. Credit card companies like VISA and MasterCard charge 4% on credit card sales, so Centrum net sales will be 96%. Cost of goods sold averages 40% of net sales.

REQUIRED

Grossman asks you to prepare a schedule of budgeted revenue, cost of goods sold, and gross margin for each month of the last quarter. She also wants you to show totals for the quarter.

6-23 Revenue, production, and purchases budget. The Suzuki Company in Japan has a division that manufactures two-wheel motorcycles. Its budgeted sales for Model G in 19_9 is 800,000 units. Suzuki's target ending inventory is 100,000 units, and its beginning inventory is 120,000 units. The company's budgeted selling price to its distributors and dealers is 400,000 yen (¥) per motorcycle.

Suzuki buys all its wheels from an outside supplier. No defective wheels are accepted. (Suzuki's needs for extra wheels for replacement parts are ordered by a separate division of the company.) The company's target ending inventory is 30,000 wheels, and its beginning inventory is 20,000 wheels. The budgeted purchase price is ¥16,000 per wheel.

REQUIRED

1. Compute the budgeted revenue in yen.
2. Compute the number of motorcycles to be produced.
3. Compute the budgeted purchases of wheels in units and in yen.

6-24 Budget for production and direct manufacturing labor. (CMA adapted) The Roletter Company makes and sells artistic frames for pictures of weddings, graduations, and other special events. Bob Anderson, controller, is responsible for preparing Roletter's master budget and has accumulated the following information for 19_8:

	19_8				
	January	February	March	April	May
Estimated sales in units	10,000	12,000	8,000	9,000	9,000
Selling price	$54.00	$51.50	$51.50	$51.50	$51.50
Direct manufacturing labor-hours per unit	2.0	2.0	1.5	1.5	1.5
Wage per direct manufacturing labor-hour	$10.00	$10.00	$10.00	$11.00	$11.00

Besides wages, direct manufacturing labor-related costs include pension contributions of $0.50 per hour, worker's compensation insurance of $0.15 per hour, employee medical insurance of $0.40 per hour, and social security taxes. Assume that as of January 1, 19_8, the social security tax rates are 7.5% of wages for employers and 7.5% of wages for employees. The cost of employee benefits paid by Roletter on its employees is treated as a direct manufacturing labor cost.

Roletter has a labor contract that calls for a wage increase to $11.00 per hour on April 1, 19_8. New labor-saving machinery has been installed and will be fully operational by March 1, 19_8.

Roletter expects to have 16,000 frames on hand at December 31, 19_7, and has a policy of carrying an end-of-month inventory of 100% of the following month's sales plus 50% of the second following month's sales.

REQUIRED

Prepare a production budget and a direct manufacturing labor budget for the Roletter Company by month and for the first quarter of 19_8. Both budgets may be combined in one schedule. The direct manufacturing labor budget should include labor-hours and show the detail for each labor cost category.

6-25 **Activity-based budgeting.** Family Supermarkets (FS) is preparing its activity-based budget for January 19_8 for its operating costs (that is, its non-cost of goods purchased for resale costs). Its current concern is with its four activity areas (which are also indirect-cost categories in its product profitability reporting system);

a. *Ordering*—covers purchasing activities. The cost driver is the number of purchase orders.

b. *Delivery*—covers the physical delivery and receipt of merchandise. The cost driver is the number of deliveries.

c. *Shelf stacking*—covers the stacking of merchandise on store shelves and the ongoing restacking before sale.

d. *Customer support*—covers assistance provided to customers, including check-out and bagging.

Assume FS has only three product areas—soft drinks, fresh produce, and packaged food. The budgeted usage of each cost driver in these three areas of the store and the January 19_8 budgeted cost driver rates are as follows:

	Cost Driver Rates		January 19_8 Budgeted Amount of Driver Used		
Activity Area and Driver	19_7 Actual Rate	January 19_8 Budgeted Rate	Soft Drinks	Fresh Produce	Packaged Food
Ordering (per purchase order)	$100	$90	14	24	14
Delivery (per delivery)	$80	$82	12	62	19
Shelf-stacking (per hour)	$20	$21	16	172	94
Customer support (per item sold)	$0.20	$0.18	4,600	34,200	10,750

1. What is the total budgeted cost for each activity area in January 19_8?
2. What advantages might FS gain by using an activity-based budgeting approach over (say) an approach for budgeting operating costs based on a budgeted percentage of cost of goods sold times the budgeted cost of goods sold?

6-26 Kaizen approach to activity-based budgeting (continuation of 6-25). Family Supermarkets (FS) has a kaizen (continuous improvement) approach to budgeting monthly activity area costs for each month of 19_8. February's budgeted cost driver rate is 0.998 times the budgeted January 19_8 rate. March's budgeted cost driver rate is 0.998 times the budgeted February 19_8 rate, and so on. Assume that March 19_8 has the same budgeted amount of cost drivers used as did January 19_8.

REQUIRED

1. What is the total budgeted cost for each activity area in March 19_8?
2. What are the benefits of FS adopting a kaizen budgeting approach? What are the limitations?

PROBLEMS

6-27 Budget schedules for manufacturer. Sierra Furniture is an elite desk manufacturer. It manufactures two products:
♦ Executive desks—3′ × 5′ oak desks
♦ Chairman desks—6′ × 4′ red oak desks

The budgeted direct-cost inputs for each product in 19_8 are as follows:

	Executive Line	Chairman Line
Direct Materials		
Oak top	16 square feet	—
Red oak top	—	25 square feet
Oak legs	4 legs	—
Red oak legs	—	4 legs
Direct manufacturing labor	3 hours	5 hours

Unit data pertaining to the direct materials for March 19_8 are as follows:

Actual Beginning Direct Materials Inventory (March 1, 19_8)

	Product	
	Executive Line	Chairman Line
Oak top	320 square feet	—
Red oak top	—	150 square feet
Oak legs	100 legs	—
Red oak legs	—	40 legs

Target Ending Direct Materials Inventory (March 31, 19_8)

	Product	
	Executive Line	Chairman Line
Oak top	192 square feet	—
Red oak top	—	200 square feet
Oak legs	80 legs	—
Red oak legs	—	44 legs

Unit cost data for direct-cost inputs pertaining to February 19_8 and March 19_8 are

	February 19_8 (Actual)	March 19_8 (Budgeted)
Oak top (per square feet)	$18	$20 ×16
Red oak top (per square feet)	23	25 × 25
Oak legs (per leg)	11	12 × 4
Red oak legs (per leg)	17	18 × 4
Manufacturing labor cost per hour	30	30

Manufacturing overhead (both variable and fixed) is allocated to each desk on the basis of budgeting direct manufacturing labor-hours per desk. The budgeting variable manufacturing overhead rate for March 19_8 is $35 per direct manufacturing labor-hour. The budgeted fixed manufacturing overhead for March 19_8 is $42,500. Both variable and fixed manufacturing overhead cost is allocated to each unit of finished goods.

Data relating to finished goods inventory for March 19_8 are

	Executive Line	Chairman Line
Beginning inventory	20 units	5 units
Beginning inventory in dollars (cost)	$10,480 +	$4,850 = 15330
Target ending inventory	30 units	15 units

Budgeted sales for March 19_8 are 740 units of the Executive Line and 390 units of the Chairman Line. The budgeted selling prices per unit in March 19_8 are $1,020 for an Executive Line desk and $1,600 for a Chairman Line desk.

Assume the following in your answer:

a. Work-in-process inventories are negligible and ignored.

b. Direct materials inventory and finished goods inventory are costed using the FIFO method.

c. Unit costs of direct materials purchased and finished goods are constant in March 19_8.

REQUIRED

Prepare the following budgets for March 19_8:

1. Revenue budget
2. Production budget in units
3. Direct materials usage budget and direct materials purchases budget
4. Direct manufacturing labor budget
5. Manufacturing overhead budget
6. Ending inventory budget
7. Cost of goods sold budget

6-28 **Continuous improvement, budgeting (continuation of 6-27).** Sierra Furniture decides to incorporate continuous improvement into its budgeting process. Describe four areas where Sierra could incorporate continuous improvement into the budget schedules in Problem 6-27. Be explicit as to how the incorporation would occur.

6-29 **Revenue and production budgets.** (CPA adapted) The Scarborough Corporation manufactures and sells two products, Thingone and Thingtwo. In July 19_8, Scarborough's Budget Department gathered the following data in order to prepare budgets for 19_9:

19_9 Projected Sales

Product	Units	Price
Thingone	60,000	$165
Thingtwo	40,000	$250

19_9 Inventories in Units

	Expected	Target
Product	January 1, 19_9	December 31, 19_9
Thingone	20,000	25,000
Thingtwo	8,000	9,000

To produce 1 unit of Thingone and Thingtwo, the following direct materials are used:

		Amount Used per Unit	
Direct Material	Unit	Thingone	Thingtwo
A	pounds	4	5
B	pounds	2	3
C	each	0	1

Projected data for 19_9 with respect to direct materials are as follows:

Direct Material	Anticipated Purchase Price	Expected Inventories January 1, 19_9	Target Inventories December 31, 19_9
A	$12	32,000 pounds	36,000 pounds
B	$5	29,000 pounds	32,000 pounds
C	$3	6,000 units	7,000 units

Projected direct manufacturing labor requirements and rates for 19_9 are as follows:

Product	Hours per Unit	Rate per Hour
Thingone	2	$12
Thingtwo	3	$16

Manufacturing overhead is allocated at the rate of $20 per direct manufacturing labor-hour.

REQUIRED

Based on the preceding projections and budget requirements for Thingone and Thingtwo, prepare the following budgets for 19_9:

1. Revenue budget (in dollars)
2. Production budget (in units)
3. Direct materials purchases budget (in quantities)
4. Direct materials purchases budget (in dollars)
5. Direct manufacturing labor budget (in dollars)
6. Budgeted finished goods inventory at December 31, 19_9 (in dollars)

6-30 Budgeted income statement. (CMA adapted) The Easecom Company is a manufacturer of video-conferencing products. Regular units are manufactured to meet marketing projections, and specialized units are made after an order is received. Maintaining the video-conferencing equipment is an important area of customer satisfaction. With the recent downturn in the computer industry, the video-conferencing equipment segment has suffered, leading to a decline in Easecom's financial performance. The following income statement shows results for the year 19_7:

**Income Statement for the Easecom Company
for the Year Ended December 31, 19_7
(in thousands)**

Revenues		
Equipment	$6,000	
Maintenance contracts	1,800	
Total revenues		$7,800
Cost of goods sold		4,600
Gross margin		3,200
Operating costs		
Marketing	600	
Distribution	150	
Customer maintenance	1,000	
Administration	900	
Total operating costs		2,650
Operating income		$ 550

Easecom's management team is in the process of preparing the 19_8 budget and is studying the following information:

a. Selling prices of equipment are expected to increase by 10% as the economic recovery begins. The selling price of each maintenance contract is unchanged from 19_7.

b. Equipment sales in units are expected to increase by 6%, with a corresponding 6% growth in units of maintenance contracts.

c. The cost of each unit sold is expected to increase by 3% to pay for the necessary technology and quality improvements.

d. Marketing costs are expected to increase by $250,000, but administration costs are expected to be held at 19_7 levels.

e. Distribution costs vary in proportion to the number of units of equipment sold.

f. Two maintenance technicians are to be added at a total cost of $130,000, which covers wages and related travel costs. The objective is to improve customer service and shorten response time.

g. There is no beginning or ending inventory of equipment.

REQUIRED

Prepare a budgeted income statement for 19_8.

6-31 Responsibility of purchasing agent. (Adapted from a description by R. Villers) Mark Richards is the purchasing agent for the Hart Manufacturing Company. Kent Sampson is head of the Production Planning and Control Department. Every 6 months, Sampson gives Richards a general purchasing program. Richards gets specifications from the Engineering Department. He then selects suppliers and negotiates prices. When he took this job, Richards was informed very clearly that he bore responsibility for meeting the general purchasing program once he accepted it from Sampson.

During week 24, Richards was advised that Part No. 1234—a critical part—would be needed for assembly on Tuesday morning of week 32. He found that the regular supplier could not deliver. He called everywhere and finally found a supplier in the Midwest, and accepted the commitment.

He followed up by mail. Yes, the supplier assured him, the part would be ready. The matter was so important that on Thursday of week 31, Richards checked by phone. Yes, the shipment had left in time. Richards was reassured and did not check further. But on Tuesday of week 32, the part had not arrived. Inquiry revealed that the shipment had been misdirected by the railroad and was still in Chicago.

What department should bear the costs of time lost in the plant? Why? As purchasing agent, do you think it fair that such costs be charged to your department?

6-32 Fixing responsibility. (Adapted from a description by H. Bierman, Jr.) The city of Mountainvale hired its first city manager 4 years ago. She favored a "management by objectives" philosophy and accordingly set up many profit responsibility centers, including a Sanitation Department, a Utility Department, and a repair shop.

For many months, the sanitation manager had been complaining to the utility manager about wires being too low at one point in the road. There was barely clearance for large sanitation trucks. The sanitation manager asked the repair shop to make changes in the clearance. The repair shop manager asked, "Should I charge the Sanitation or the Utility Department for the $2,000 cost of making the adjustment?" Both departments refused to accept the charge, so the Repair Department refused to do the work.

Late one day, the top of a sanitation truck caught the wires and ripped them down. The Repair Department made an emergency repair at a cost of $2,600. Moreover, the city lost $1,000 of utility revenues (net of variable costs) because of the disruption of service.

Investigation disclosed that the sanitation truck had failed to clamp down its top properly. The extra 2 inches of height caused the wire to be caught.

Both the sanitation and utility managers argued strenuously about who should bear the $2,600 cost. Moreover, the utility manager demanded reimbursement from the Sanitation Department of the $1,000 of lost utility income.

REQUIRED

As the city controller in charge of the responsibility accounting system, how would you favor accounting for these costs? Specifically, what would you do next? What is the proper role of responsibility accounting in fixing the blame for this situation?

6-33 Traditional budgeting and its critics. Critics of traditional budgeting often make their points in a colorful way. Consider the following comments by the CEO of a multinational with revenues over $30 billion and over 200,000 employees.

We set "stretch" goals for our people. Stretch means that we try for huge gains while having no idea how to get there—but our people figure out ways to get there. To reach these stretch goals, it takes an atmosphere where a goal doesn't become part of the old-fashioned budget. The budget is the bane of corporate America. It never should have existed. A budget is this: If you make it, you generally get a pat on the back and a few bucks. If you miss it, you get a stick in the eye—or worse.

Making a budget is an exercise in minimization. You're always trying to get the lowest out of people, because everyone is negotiating to get a lower number.

If I worked for you, you would come charging into the boardroom and say, "I need four! We'd haggle all day, me making presentations, with 50 charts, saying the right number is two. In the end we'd settle on three. We'd go home and tell our families that we had a helluva day at the office. And what did we do? We ended up minimizing our activity. We weren't dreaming, reaching. I was trying to get the lowest budget number I could sell you. It's all backward.

REQUIRED

1. Do you agree that "The budget is the bane of corporate America. It never should have existed."? Explain.

2. Assume you are the CEO of a television station. Your marketing manager shows you the preceding extract and suggests that "you dispense with the annual budget ritual." How would you respond?

6-34 Comprehensive review of budgeting. British Beverages bottles two soft drinks under license to Cadbury Schweppes at its Manchester plant. Bottling at this plant is a highly repetitive, automated process. Empty bottles are removed from their carton, placed on a conveyor, and cleaned, rinsed, dried, filled, capped, and heated (to reduce condensation). All inventory is in direct materials and finished goods at the end of each working day. There is no work-in-process inventory.

The two soft drinks bottled by British Beverages are lemonade and diet lemonade. The syrup for both soft drinks is purchased from Cadbury Schweppes. Syrup for the regular brand contains a higher sugar content than the syrup for the diet brand.

British Beverages uses a lot size of 1,000 cases as the unit of analysis in its budgeting. (Each case contains 24 bottles.) Direct materials are expressed in terms of lots, where one lot of direct materials is the input necessary to yield one lot (1,000 cases) of beverage. In 19_9, the following purchase prices are forecast for direct materials:

	Lemonade	Diet Lemonade
Syrup	$1,200 per lot	$1,100 per lot
Containers (bottles, caps, etc.)	$1,000 per lot	$1,000 per lot
Packaging	$800 per lot	$800 per lot

The two soft drinks are bottled using the same equipment. The equipment is sanitized daily, but it is only rinsed when a switch is made during the day between diet lemonade and lemonade. Diet lemonade is always bottled first each day to reduce the risk of sugar contamination. The only difference in the bottling process for the two soft drinks is the syrup.

Summary data used in developing budgets for 19_9 are as follows:
a. Sales
- Lemonade, 1,080 lots at $9,000 selling price per lot
- Diet lemonade, 540 lots at $8,500 selling price per lot

b. Beginning (January 1, 19_9) inventory of direct materials
- Syrup for lemonade, 80 lots at $1,100 purchase price per lot
- Syrup for diet lemonade, 70 lots at $1,000 purchase price per lot
- Containers, 200 lots at $950 purchase price per lot
- Packaging, 400 lots at $900 purchase price per lot

c. Beginning (January 1, 19_9) inventory of finished goods
- Lemonade, 100 lots at $5,300 per lot
- Diet lemonade, 50 lots at $5,200 per lot

d. Target ending (December 31, 19_9) inventory of direct materials
- Syrup for lemonade, 30 lots
- Syrup for diet lemonade, 20 lots
- Containers, 100 lots
- Packaging, 200 lots

e. Target ending (December 31, 19_9) inventory of finished goods
- Lemonade, 20 lots
- Diet lemonade, 10 lots

f. Each lot requires 20 direct manufacturing labor-hours at the 19_9 budgeted rate of $25 per hour. Indirect manufacturing labor costs are included in the manufacturing overhead forecast.

g. Variable manufacturing overhead is forecast to be $600 per hour of bottling time; bottling time is the time the filling equipment is in operation. It takes 2 hours to bottle one lot of lemonade and 2 hours to bottle one lot of diet lemonade.

Fixed manufacturing overhead is forecast to be $1,200,000 for 19_9.

h. Hours of budgeted bottling time is the sole allocation base for all fixed manufacturing overhead.

i. Administration costs are forecast to be 10% of the cost of goods manufactured for 19_9. Marketing costs are forecast to be 12% of dollar sales for 19_9. Distribution costs are forecast to be 8% of dollar sales for 19_9.

REQUIRED

Assume British Beverages uses the first-in, first-out method for costing all inventories. On the basis of the preceding data, prepare the following budgets for 19_9:

1. Revenue budget (in dollars)
2. Production budget (in units)
3. Direct materials usage budget (in units and dollars)
4. Direct materials purchases budget (in units and dollars)
5. Direct manufacturing labor budget
6. Manufacturing overhead costs budget
7. Ending finished goods inventory budget
8. Cost of goods sold budget
9. Marketing costs budget
10. Distribution costs budget
11. Administration costs budget
12. Budgeted income statement

6-35 Appendix, collections and disbursements. (CPA) The following accrual accounting information was available from the Montero Corporation's books:

19_8	Purchases (before Discounts)	Sales
January	$42,000	$72,000
February	48,000	66,000
March	36,000	60,000
April	54,000	78,000

Collections from customers are normally 70% in the month of sale, 20% in the month following the sale, and 9% in the second month following the sale. The balance is expected to be uncollectible. Montero takes full advantage of the 2% discount allowed on purchases paid for by the tenth of the following month. Purchases for May are budgeted at $60,000 (before discounts), while sales for May are forecasted at $66,000. Cash disbursements for costs are expected to be $14,400 for the month of May. Montero's cash balance at May 1 was $20,000.

REQUIRED

Prepare the following schedules:

1. Expected cash collections during May
2. Expected cash disbursements during May
3. Expected cash balance at May 31

6-36 Appendix, cash budgeting for distributor. (CMA) Alpha-Tech, a rapidly growing distributor of electronic components, is formulating its plans for 19_7. Carol Jones, the firm's marketing director, has completed the revenue budget presented here.

Alpha-Tech
19_7 Budgeted Revenues (in thousands)

Month	Revenues	Month	Revenues
January	$ 9,000	July	$15,000
February	10,000	August	15,000
March	9,000	September	16,000
April	11,500	October	16,000
May	12,500	November	15,000
June	14,000	December	17,000

Phillip Smith, an accountant in the Planning and Budgeting Department, is responsible for preparing the cash-flow projection. The following information will be used in preparing the cash flow projection:

a. Alpha-Tech's excellent record in accounts receivable collection is expected to continue: 60% of billings are collected the month after the sale and the remaining 40% 2 months after.

b. The purchase of electronic components is Alpha-Tech's largest expenditure and is estimated to be 40% of revenues. Alpha-Tech receives 70% of the parts 1 month prior to sale and 30% during the month of sale.

c. Historically, 75% of accounts payable have been paid 1 month after receipt of the purchased components, and the remaining 25% is paid 2 months after receipt.

d. Hourly wages and fringe benefits, estimated to be 30% of the current month's revenues, are paid in the month incurred.

e. General and administrative expenses are projected to be $15,620,000 for the year. The breakdown of these expenses is as follows:

19_7 Budgeted General and Administrative
Costs (in thousands)

Salaries and fringe benefits	$ 3,200
Promotion	3,800
Property taxes	1,360
Insurance	2,000
Utilities	1,800
Depreciation	3,460
Total	$15,620

All expenditures are paid uniformly throughout the year, except the property taxes, which are paid at the end of each quarter in four equal installments.

f. Income tax payments are made at the beginning of each calendar quarter based on the income of the prior quarter. Alpha-Tech is subject to an effective income tax rate of 40%. Alpha-Tech's operating income for the first quarter of 19_7 is projected to be $3,200,000. The company pays 100% of the estimated tax payment.

g. Alpha-Tech maintains a minimum cash balance of $500,000. If the cash balance is less than $500,000 at the end of each month, the company borrows amounts necessary to maintain this balance. All amounts borrowed are repaid out of subsequent positive cash flow. The projected April 1, 19_7 opening balance is $500,000.

h. Alpha-Tech has no short-term debt as of April 1, 19_7.

i. Alpha-Tech uses a calendar year for both financial reporting and tax purposes.

REQUIRED

1. Prepare a cash budget for Alpha-Tech by month for the second quarter of 19_7. Ignore any interest expense associated with borrowing.

2. Discuss why cash budgeting is important for Alpha-Tech.

6-37 Cash budgeting. On December 1, 19_8, the Itami Wholesale Company is attempting to project cash receipts and disbursements through January 31, 19_9. On this latter date, a note will be payable in the amount of $100,000. This amount was borrowed in September to carry the company through the seasonal peak in November and December.

The trial balance on December 1 shows in part the following information:

Cash	$ 10,000	
Accounts receivable	280,000	
Allowance for bad debts		$15,800
Inventory	87,500	
Accounts payable		92,000

Sales terms call for a 2% discount if payment is made within the first 10 days of the month after purchase, with the balance due by the end of the month after purchase. Experience has shown that 70% of the billings will be collected within the discount period, 20% by the end of the month after purchase, 8% in the following month, and that 2% will be uncollectible. There are no cash sales.

The average selling price of the company's products is $100 per unit. Actual and projected sales are

October actual	$ 180,000
November actual	250,000
December estimated	300,000
January estimated	150,000
February estimated	120,000
Total estimated for year ended June 30, 19_9	1,500,000

All purchases are payable within 15 days. Thus approximately 50% of the purchases in a month are due and payable in the next month. The average unit purchase cost is $70. Target ending inventories are 500 units plus 25% of the next month's unit sales.

Total budgeted marketing, distribution, and customer-service costs for the year are $400,000. Of this amount, $150,000 is considered fixed (and includes depreciation of $30,000). The remainder varies with sales. Both fixed and variable marketing, distribution, and customer-service costs are paid as incurred.

REQUIRED

Prepare a cash budget for December and January. Supply supporting schedules for collections of receivables, payments for merchandise, and marketing, distribution, and customer-service costs.

6-38 **Comprehensive budget; fill in schedules.** The following information is for the Newport Stationery Store.

Balance Sheet Information as of September 30

Current assets	
Cash	$ 12,000
Accounts receivable	10,000
Inventory	63,600
Equipment, net	100,000
Liabilities as of September 30	None

Recent and Anticipated Sales

September	$40,000
October	48,000
November	60,000
December	80,000
January	36,000

Credit sales: Sales are 75% for cash and 25% on credit. Assume that credit accounts are all collected within 30 days from sale. The accounts receivable on September 30 are the result of the credit sales for September (25% of $40,000).

Gross margin averages 30% of sales. Newport treats cash discounts on purchases in the income statement as "other income."

Operating costs: Salaries and wages average 15% of monthly sales; rent, 5%; other operating costs, excluding depreciation, 4%. Assume that these costs are disbursed each month. Depreciation is $1,000 per month.

Purchases: Newport keeps a minimum inventory of $30,000. The policy is to purchase additional inventory each month in the amount necessary to provide for the following month's sales. Terms on purchases are 2/10, n/30;

a 2% discount is available if the payment is made within 10 days after purchase; no discount is available if payment is made beyond 10 days after purchase. Assume that payments are made in the month of purchase and that all discounts are taken.

Light fixtures: The expenditures for light fixtures are $600 in October and $400 in November. These amounts are to be capitalized.

Assume that a minimum cash balance of $8,000 must be maintained. Assume also that all borrowing is effective at the beginning of the month and all repayments are made at the end of the month of repayment. Loans are repaid when sufficient cash is available. Interest is paid only at the time of repaying principal. The interest rate is 18% per year. Management does not want to borrow any more cash than is necessary and wants to repay as soon as cash is available.

REQUIRED

1. On the basis of the preceding facts, complete schedule A.

Schedule A
Budgeted Monthly Cash Receipts

Item	September	October	November	December
Total sales	$40,000	$48,000	$60,000	$80,000
Credit sales	10,000	12,000		
Cash sales				
Receipts				
Cash sales		$36,000		
Collections on accounts receivable		10,000		
Total		$46,000		

2. Complete schedule B. Note that purchases are 70% of next month's sales.

Schedule B
Budgeted Monthly Cash Disbursements for Purchases

Item	October	November	December	4th Quarter
Purchases	$42,000			
Deduct 2% cash discount	840			
Disbursements	$41,160			

3. Complete schedule C.

Schedule C
Budgeted Monthly Cash Disbursements for Operating Costs

Item	October	November	December	4th Quarter
Salaries and wages	$ 7,200			
Rent	2,400			
Other cash operating costs	1,920			
Total	$11,520			

4. Complete schedule D.

Schedule D
Budgeted Total Monthly Cash Disbursements

Item	October	November	December	4th Quarter
Purchases	$41,160			
Cash operating costs	11,520			
Light fixtures	600			
Total	$53,280			

5. Complete schedule E.

Schedule E
Budgeted Cash Receipts and Disbursements

Item	October	November	December	4th Quarter
Receipts	$46,000			
Disbursement	53,280	_____	_____	_____
Net cash increase				
Net cash decrease	$ 7,280	_____	_____	_____

6. Complete schedule F (assume that borrowings must be made in multiples of $1,000).

Schedule F
Financing Required

Item	October	November	December	Total
Beginning cash balance	$12,000	_____	_____	_____
Net cash increase				
Net cash decrease	7,280			
Cash position before borrowing	4,720			
Minimum cash balance required	8,000	_____	_____	_____
Excess/deficiency	(3,280)			
Borrowing required	4,000			
Interest payments				
Borrowing repaid	_____	_____	_____	_____
Ending cash balance	$ 8,720	_____	_____	_____

7. What do you think is the most logical type of loan needed by Newport? Explain your reasoning.

8. Prepare a budgeted income statement for the fourth quarter and a budgeted balance sheet as of December 31. Ignore income taxes.

9. Some simplifications have been introduced in this problem. What complicating factors would be met in a typical business situation?

6-39 Budgetary slack and ethics. (CMA) Marge Atkins, the budget manager at the Norton Company, a manufacturer of infant furniture and carriages, is working on the 19_8 annual budget. In discussions with Scott Ford, the sales manager, Atkins discovers that Ford's sales projections are lower than what Ford believes are actually achievable. When Atkins asked Ford about this, Ford said, "Well, we don't want to fall short of the sales projections, so we generally give ourselves a little breathing room by lowering the sales projections anywhere from 5 to 10%." Atkins also finds that Pete Granger, the production manager, makes similar adjustments. He pads budgeted costs, adding 10% to estimated costs.

REQUIRED

As a management accountant, should Marge Atkins take the position that the behavior described by Scott Ford and Pete Granger is unethical? Refer to the *Standards of Ethical Conduct for Management Accountants* described in Chapter 1 (p. 10).

COLLABORATIVE LEARNING PROBLEM

6-40 Athletic Department of a university, budget revision options. Gary Connolly is the athletic director of Pacific University (PU). He has been director for over 10 years. PU is a men's football and basketball powerhouse. The women's athletic program, however, has had less success. Last year, the women's basketball team finally had more wins than losses.

Connolly has just had a meeting with Laura Reddy, the newly appointed president of PU. It did not go well. Reddy and Connolly discussed what she called "Draft I" of the 19_7 Athletic Department Budget. He had believed it was the final draft. Reddy expressed four grave concerns about Draft I in particular and about the PU athletics program in general:

Concern 1 The Athletic Department was budgeting a loss of over $3 million in 19_7. Given the tight fiscal position of the university, this was unacceptable. A budgeted loss of $1 million was the most she would tolerate for 19_7. Draft II of the 19_7 budget was due in 2 weeks' time. By 19_8, the Athletic Department had to operate with a balanced budget. She told Connolly this was nonnegotiable.

Concern 2 The low allocation of money to the women's athletic program. Frontline, a tabloid television show, recently ran a program titled "It's a Man's World at the Pacific University Athletics Program." Reddy said Connolly was treating woman athletes as "third-class citizens."

Concern 3 The low academic performance of the men's football athletes, many of whom had full scholarships. She noted that the local TV news recently ran an interview with three football-team students, none of whom "exemplified the high academic credentials she wanted Pacific to showcase to the world." She called one student "incoherent" and another "incapable of stringing sentences together."

Concern 4 The outrageous salary paid to Bill Madden, the football coach. She noted it was twice that of the highest paid academic on campus. This academic was a Nobel Prize winner! Moreover, Madden received other payments from his "Football the Pacific Way" summer program for high school students.

Exhibit 6-11 is a summary of the Draft I Athletic Department Budget for 19_7.

EXHIBIT 6-11
Pacific University 19_7 Athletic Department Budget (in millions)

Revenues		
Men's athletic programs	$10.350	
Women's athletic programs	0.780	
Other (endowment income, gifts)	3.400	$14.530
Costs		
Men's athletic programs	$11.040	
Women's athletic programs	2.800	
Other (nonassigned to programs)	3.700	17.540
Operating income		$ (3.010)

Men's Athletic Programs

	Football	Basketball	Swimming	Other	Total
Revenues	$8.600	$1.500	$0.100	$0.150	$10.350
Costs	7.400	2.700	0.300	0.640	11.040
Full student scholarships	37	21	6	4	68

Women's Athletic Programs

	Basketball	Swimming	Other	Total
Revenues	$0.600	$0.080	$0.100	$0.780
Costs	1.800	0.200	0.800	2.800
Full student scholarships	11	4	2	17

INSTRUCTIONS

Form groups of two or more students to complete the following requirement.

REQUIRED

Your group is to prepare Draft II of the Athletic Department's 19_7 Budget. This draft will form the basis of a half-day meeting Connolly will have with key officials of the Athletic Department.

FLEXIBLE BUDGETS, VARIANCES, AND MANAGEMENT CONTROL: I

The manufacturers of pantyhose use large quantities of elastic fibers, such as Dorlastan sold by Bayer A.G. Customers of Bayer are restructuring their procurement relationships with Bayer to reduce the total costs of their elastic fiber and other manufacturing inputs.

LEARNING OBJECTIVES

After studying this chapter, you should be able to

1. Describe the difference between a static budget and a flexible budget

2. Illustrate how a flexible budget can be developed

3. Use the flexible-budget approach to compute flexible-budget and sales-volume variances

4. Interpret the price and efficiency variances for direct-cost input categories

5. Describe two different ways to develop budgeted input prices and budgeted input quantities

6. Explain why purchasing-performance measures should focus on more factors than just price variances for inputs

7. Describe how the continuous improvement theme can be integrated into variance analysis

8. Describe benchmarking and how it can be used by managers in variance analysis

We have learned that managers quantify their plans in the form of budgets. This chapter focuses on how flexible budgets and variances can play a key role in management planning and control. Recall from Chapter 1 that feedback enables managers to compare the actual results with the planned performance. Flexible budgets and variances help managers gain insights into why the actual results differ from the planned performance. It is this insight into "why" that makes the topics covered in this chapter and the next important ones to master.

Each *variance* we compute is the difference between an actual result and a budgeted amount. The budgeted amount is a **benchmark;** that is, it is a point of reference from which comparisons may be made. Companies choose various benchmarks, including

1. Financial variables reported in a company's own accounting system (such as Ford's manufacturing cost for a Bronco wagon).

2. Financial variables not reported in a company's own accounting system (such as when Ford uses the estimated cost Toyota incurs to manufacture a 4 Runner wagon as the benchmark for evaluating the cost competitiveness of its Bronco product line).

3. Nonfinancial variables (such as Ford's assembly-line defect rate).

This chapter emphasizes financial benchmarks reported in a company's own accounting system. Benchmarks related to 2 and 3 above are discussed but covered in less detail.

Organizations differ widely in how they compute and label the budgeted amounts they report in their own accounting system. Some organizations rely heavily on past results when developing budgeted amounts. Other organizations conduct detailed engineering or time-and-motion studies when developing budgeted amounts. The term *standard* is frequently used when such studies underlie the budgeted amounts. A **standard** is a carefully predetermined amount; it is usually expressed on a per unit basis. In practice, there is not a precise dividing line between a *budgeted amount* and a *standard amount*. We use *budgeted amount* as the more general term because some budgeted amounts may not be carefully predetermined amounts. However, all of the variances we discuss can be computed using standard amounts or budgeted amounts.

STATIC BUDGETS AND FLEXIBLE BUDGETS

This chapter illustrates both static budgets and flexible budgets. A **static budget** is a budget that is based on one level of output; it is not adjusted or altered after it is set, regardless of ensuing changes in actual output (or actual revenue and cost drivers). A **flexible budget** is adjusted in accordance with ensuing changes in actual output (or actual revenue and cost drivers). As we shall see, a flexible budget enables managers to compute a richer set of variances than does a static budget. A **favorable variance**—denoted F in the exhibits—is a variance that increases operating income relative to the budgeted amount. An **unfavorable variance**—denoted U—is a variance that decreases operating income relative to the budgeted amount.

Budgets, both static and flexible, can differ in their level of detail. Increasingly, organizations are developing approaches to budgeting that report summary figures with the capability to display more detailed breakdowns of these figures on a computer screen. In this book, the term *level* followed by a number denotes the amount of detail indicated by the variance(s) isolated. Level 0 reports the least detail, Level 1 offers more information, and so on.

The example of the Webb Company illustrates static budgets and flexible budgets. Webb manufactures and sells a single product, a distinctive jacket that requires many materials, tailoring, and hand operations. Sales are made to independent clothing stores and retail chains. Webb sets budgeted revenues (budgeted selling price × budgeted units sold) based on input from its marketing personnel and on an analysis of general and industry economic conditions.

The costing system at Webb includes both manufacturing costs and marketing costs. There are direct and indirect costs in each category:

	Direct Costs	Indirect Costs
Manufacturing	Direct materials	Variable manufacturing overhead
	Direct manufacturing labor	Fixed manufacturing overhead
Marketing	Direct marketing labor	Variable marketing overhead
		Fixed marketing overhead

Webb's manufacturing costs include direct materials (all variable), direct manufacturing labor (all variable), and manufacturing overhead (both variable and fixed). Its marketing costs (which include distribution and customer service costs as well as advertising costs) are made up of direct marketing labor (primarily distribution personnel, which are all variable) and marketing overhead (both variable and fixed). The cost driver for direct materials, direct manufacturing labor, and variable manufacturing overhead is the *number of units manufactured*. The cost driver for direct marketing labor and variable marketing overhead is the *number of units sold*. The revenue driver is the *number of units sold*. The relevant range for the $180 selling price per jacket and for the cost drivers in both manufacturing and marketing is from 8,000 to 16,000 units. All costs at Webb are either driven by output units or are fixed. We make this simplifying assumption to highlight the basic approach to flexible budgeting.

In order to focus on the key concepts, we assume Webb has no beginning or ending inventory. Chapter 9 introduces the complexities that occur when beginning or ending inventory exists.

STATIC-BUDGET VARIANCES

The actual results and the static-budget amounts of Webb for April 19_7 are as follows:

	Actual Results	Static-Budget Amounts
Units sold	10,000	12,000
Revenues	$1,850,000	$2,160,000
Variable costs	1,120,000	1,188,000
Fixed costs	705,000	710,000
Operating income	25,000	262,000

Exhibit 7-1 presents the Level 0 and Level 1 variance analyses for April 19_7. Level 0 gives the least-detailed comparison of the actual and budgeted operating income. The unfavorable variance of $237,000 is simply the result of subtracting the budgeted operating income of $262,000 from the actual operating income of $25,000:

$$\text{Static-budget variance of operating income} = \text{Actual results} - \text{Static-budget amount}$$

$$= \$25,000 - \$262,000$$

$$= \$237,000 \text{ U}$$

This variance is often called a static-budget variance because the number used for the budgeted amount ($262,000) is taken from a static budget.

Level 1 analysis in Exhibit 7-1 provides managers with more detailed information on the static-budget variance of operating income of $237,000 U. The

EXHIBIT 7-1
Static-Budget-Based Variance Analysis for the Webb Company for April 19_7

LEVEL 0 ANALYSIS

Actual operating income	$ 25,000 F*
Budgeted operating income	262,000 F
Static-budget variance of operating income	$237,000 U

LEVEL 1 ANALYSIS

	Actual Results (1)	Static-Budget Variances (2) = (1) – (3)	Static Budget (3)
Units sold	10,000	2,000 U	12,000
Revenues	$1,850,000	$310,000 U	$2,160,000
Variable costs	1,120,000	68,000 F	1,188,000
Contribution margin	730,000	242,000 U	972,000
Fixed costs	705,000	5,000 F	710,000
Operating income	$ 25,000	$237,000 U	$ 262,000

$237,000 U
Total static-budget variance

*F = favorable effect on operating income; U = unfavorable effect on operating income.

additional information added in Level 1 pertains to revenues, variable costs, and fixed costs. The budgeted contribution margin percentage of 45.0% ($972,000 ÷ $2,160,000) decreases to 39.5% ($730,000 ÷ $1,850,000) for the actual results.

While Level 1 contains more information than Level 0, additional insights into the causes of variances can be gained by incorporating a flexible budget into the computation of variances.

STEPS IN DEVELOPING A FLEXIBLE BUDGET

OBJECTIVE 2

Illustrate how a flexible budget can be developed

Webb's five-step approach to developing a flexible budget is relatively straightforward given the assumption that all costs are either variable with respect to output units or fixed. The five steps are as follows:

Step 1: Determine the Budgeted Selling Price per Unit, the Budgeted Variable Costs per Unit, and the Budgeted Fixed Costs   Each output unit (a jacket) has a budgeted selling price of $180. The budgeted variable cost is $99 per jacket. Column 2 of Exhibit 7-2 has a breakdown of this $99 amount. The budgeted fixed costs total $710,000 ($276,000 manufacturing and $434,000 marketing).

Step 2: Determine the Actual Quantity of the Revenue Driver   Webb's revenue driver is the number of units sold. In April 19_7, Webb sold 10,000 jackets.

Step 3: Determine the Flexible Budget for Revenue Based on the Budgeted Unit Revenue and the Actual Quantity of the Revenue Driver

$$\text{Flexible-budget revenues} = \$180 \times 10,000$$
$$= \$1,800,000$$

Step 4: Determine the Actual Quantity of the Cost Driver(s)   Webb's cost driver for manufacturing costs is units produced. The cost driver for marketing costs is units sold. In April 19_7, Webb produced and sold 10,000 jackets.

EXHIBIT 7-2
Flexible-Budget Data for the Webb Company for April 19_7

Line Item (1)	Budgeted Cost Amount per Unit (2)	Flexible Budget Amounts for Alternative Quantities of Output Units Sold			Actual Results for 10,000 Units (6)
		10,000 (3)	12,000 (4)	15,000 (5)	
Revenue	$180	$1,800,000	$2,160,000	$2,700,000	$1,850,000
Variable costs					
Direct materials	60	600,000	720,000	900,000	688,200
Direct manufacturing labor	16	160,000	192,000	240,000	198,000
Direct marketing labor	6	60,000	72,000	90,000	57,600
Variable manufacturing overhead	12	120,000	144,000	180,000	130,500
Variable marketing overhead	5	50,000	60,000	75,000	45,700
Total variable costs	99	990,000	1,188,000	1,485,000	1,120,000
Contribution margin	$ 81	810,000	972,000	1,215,000	730,000
Fixed costs					
Manufacturing overhead		276,000	276,000	276,000	285,000
Marketing overhead		434,000	434,000	434,000	420,000
Total fixed costs	____	710,000	710,000	710,000	705,000
Total costs	____	1,700,000	1,898,000	2,195,000	1,825,000
Operating income	____	$ 100,000	$ 262,000	$ 505,000	$ 25,000

Step 5: Determine the Flexible Budget for Costs Based on the Budgeted Unit Variable Costs and Fixed Costs and the Actual Quantity of the Cost Driver(s).

Flexible-budget variable costs
Manufacturing $= \$88 \times 10,000 = \$880,000$
Marketing $= \$11 \times 10,000 = \underline{110,000}$
$\underline{\$990,000}$

Flexible-budget fixed costs
Manufacturing $= \$276,000$
Marketing $= \underline{434,000}$
$\underline{\$710,000}$

These five steps enable Webb to move to a Level 2 variance analysis, which helps them better explore reasons for the $237,000 unfavorable static-budget variance of operating income. Exhibit 7-2 shows the flexible budget for 10,000 units (column 3) as well as for 12,000 and 15,000 units (columns 4 and 5).

FLEXIBLE-BUDGET VARIANCES AND SALES-VOLUME VARIANCES

Exhibit 7-3 presents the Level 2 flexible-budget-based variance analysis for Webb. Note that the $237,000 unfavorable static-budget variance of operating income is now split into two categories—a flexible-budget variance and a sales-volume variance.

OBJECTIVE 3

Use the flexible-budget approach to compute flexible-budget and sales-volume variances

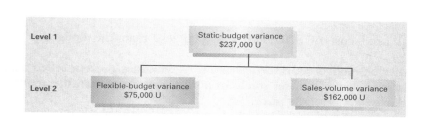

Level 1

Static-budget variance
$237,000 U

Level 2

Flexible-budget variance
$75,000 U

Sales-volume variance
$162,000 U

EXHIBIT 7-3
Flexible-Budget-Based Variance Analysis for the Webb Company for April 19_7

LEVEL 2 ANALYSIS

	Actual Results (1)	Flexible-Budget Variances (2) = (1) – (3)	Flexible Budget (3)	Sales-Volume Variances (4) = (3) – (5)	Static Budget (5)
Units sold	10,000	0	10,000	2,000 U	12,000
Revenues	$1,850,000	$ 50,000 F*	$1,800,000	$360,000 U	$2,160,000
Variable costs	1,120,000	130,000 U	990,000	198,000 F	1,188,000
Contribution margin	730,000	80,000 U	810,000	162,000 U	972,000
Fixed costs	705,000	5,000 F	710,000	0	710,000
Operating income	$ 25,000	$ 75,000 U	$ 100,000	$162,000 U	$ 262,000

$ 75,000 U
Total flexible-budget variance

$162,000 U
Total sales-volume variance

$237,000 U
Total static-budget variance

*F = favorable effect on operating income; U = unfavorable effect on operating income.

The **flexible-budget variance** is the difference between the actual results and the flexible-budget amount for the actual levels of the revenue and cost drivers. The **sales-volume variance** is the difference between the flexible-budget amount and the static-budget amount; unit selling prices, unit variable costs, and fixed costs are held constant. Knowing these variances helps managers better explain the static-budget variance of $237,000 U.

Flexible-Budget Variances

The first three columns of Exhibit 7-3 compare the actual results with the flexible-budget amounts. Flexible-budget variances are reported in column 2 for four line items in the income statement:

$$\text{Flexible-budget variance} = \text{Actual results} - \text{Flexible-budget amount}$$

For the operating income line item, the flexible-budget variance is $75,000 U ($25,000 – $100,000). This variance arises because the actual selling price, unit variable costs, and fixed costs differ from the budgeted amounts. The actual and budgeted unit amounts for the selling price and variable costs are as follows:

	Actual Unit Amount	Budgeted Unit Amount
Selling price	$185	$180
Variable cost	112	99

The actual fixed cost of $705,000 is $5,000 less than the budgeted $710,000 amount.

The flexible-budget variance pertaining to revenues is often called a **selling-price variance** because it arises solely from differences between the actual selling price and the budgeted selling price:

$$\text{Selling-price} = \left(\begin{array}{c} \text{Actual} \\ \text{selling price} \end{array} - \begin{array}{c} \text{Budgeted} \\ \text{selling price} \end{array} \right) \times \begin{array}{c} \text{Actual} \\ \text{units sold} \end{array}$$
$$= (\$185 - \$180) \times 10{,}000$$
$$= \$50{,}000 \text{ F}$$

Webb has a favorable selling-price variance because the actual selling price exceeds the budgeted amount (by $5). Marketing managers typically are best informed as to why this selling price difference arose.

Sales-Volume Variances

The flexible-budget amounts in column 3 of Exhibit 7-3 and the static-budget amount in column 5 are both computed using the budgeted selling prices and budgeted costs. This variance is labeled the "sales-volume variance" because in many contexts the number of units sold is both the revenue driver and the cost driver. For the operating income line item:

$$\text{Sales-volume} \atop \text{variance} = \text{Flexible-budget} \atop \text{amount} - \text{Static-budget} \atop \text{amount}$$
$$= \$100{,}000 - \$262{,}000$$
$$= \$162{,}000 \text{ U}$$

In our Webb example, this sales-volume variance in operating income arises solely because it sold 10,000 units, which was 2,000 less than the budgeted 12,000 units.

PRICE VARIANCES AND EFFICIENCY VARIANCES FOR INPUTS

The flexible-budget variance (Level 2) captures the difference between the actual results and the flexible budget. The sources of this variance (as regards costs) are the individual differences between actual and budgeted prices or quantities for inputs. The next two variances we discuss—price variances and efficiency variances for inputs—analyze such differences. This information helps managers to better understand past performance and to plan for future performance. We call this a Level 3 analysis as it takes a more detailed analysis of the Level 2 variances.

A **price variance** is the difference between the actual price and the budgeted price multiplied by the actual quantity of input in question (such as direct materials purchased or used). *Price variances* are sometimes called **input-price variances** or **rate variances** (especially when those variances are for direct labor). **An efficiency variance** is the difference the actual quantity of input used (such as yards of cloth of direct materials) and the budgeted quantity of input that should have been used, multiplied by the budgeted price. *Efficiency variances* are sometimes called **input-efficiency variances** or **usage variances.**

The relationship of these two variances to those we have already discussed for Webb is as follows:

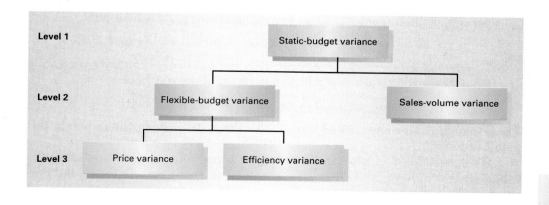

Obtaining Budgeted Input Prices and Input Quantities

Webb's two main sources of information about budgeted input prices and budgeted input quantities are

1. *Actual input data from past periods.* Most companies have past data on actual input prices and actual input quantities. These past amounts could be used for the budgeted amounts in a flexible budget. Past data is typically available at a relatively low cost. The limitations of using this source are (a) past data includes past inefficiencies, and (b) past data does not incorporate any expected changes planned to occur in the budget period.

2. *Standards developed by Webb.* A *standard* is a carefully predetermined amount; it is usually expressed on a per unit basis. Webb uses time-and-motion and engineering studies to determine its standard amounts. For example, it conducts a detailed breakdown of the steps in making a jacket. Each step is then assigned a standard time based on work by a skilled operator using equipment operating in an efficient manner. The advantages of using standard amounts are that (a) they can exclude past inefficiencies, and (b) they can take into account expected changes in the budget period. An example of (a) is a supplier making dramatic improvements in its ability to consistently meet Webb's demanding quality requirements for the cloth material used to make jackets. An example of (b) is the acquisition of new loom machines that operate at a faster speed and that enable work to be done with lower reject rates.

Webb has developed standard inputs and standard costs for each of its variable cost items. A **standard input** is a carefully predetermined quantity of input (such as pounds of materials or hours of labor time) required for one unit of output. A **standard cost** is a carefully predetermined cost. Standard costs can relate to units of inputs or units of outputs. Webb's budgeted cost for each variable cost item is computed using the following formula:

$$\frac{\text{Standard inputs allowed}}{\text{for 1 output unit}} \times \frac{\text{Standard cost}}{\text{per input unit}}$$

And, the variable cost items are

- *Direct materials:* 2.00 square yards of cloth input allowed per output unit (jacket) manufactured, at $30 standard cost per square yard.

    Standard cost = 2.00 × $30 = $60.00 per output unit manufactured

- *Direct manufacturing labor:* 0.80 manufacturing labor-hours of input allowed per output unit manufactured, at $20 standard cost per hour.

    Standard cost = 0.80 × $20 = $16.00 per output unit manufactured

- *Direct marketing labor:* 0.25 marketing labor-hours of input allowed per output unit sold, at $24 standard cost per hour.

    Standard cost = 0.25 × $24 = $6.00 per output unit sold

- *Variable manufacturing overhead:* Allocated on the basis of 1.20 machine-hours per output unit manufactured, at $10 standard cost per machine-hour.

    Standard cost = 1.20 × $10 = $12.00 per output unit manufactured

- *Variable marketing overhead:* Allocated on the basis of 0.125 direct marketing labor-hours per output unit sold, at $40 standard cost per hour.

    Standard cost = 0.125 × $40 = $5.00 per output unit sold

These standard cost computations explain how Webb developed the numbers in column 2 of Exhibit 7-2.

The breakdown of the flexible-budget variance into its price and efficiency components is important when evaluating individual managers. At Webb, the pro-

The Widespread Use of Standard Costs

Surveys of company practice around the globe report widespread use of standard costs by manufacturers. The following data are representative of surveys conducted in five countries:

Country	Respondents Using Standard Costs in Their Accounting System (%)
United States*	86
Ireland[†]	84
United Kingdom[††]	76
Sweden[≈]	73
Japan[#]	65

*Cornick, Cooper, and Wilson, "How Do Companies."
[†]Clarke, "Management Accounting." [††]Drury, Braund, Osborne, and Tayles, *A Survey.* [≈]Ask and Ax, "Trends."
[#]Scarbrough, Nanni, and Sakurai, "Japanese Management."
Full citations are in Appendix A.

The Irish survey reported that standard costs were most frequently used for direct materials (84%), then direct labor (69%), and then manufacturing overhead (59%). The standard costs were most frequently revised on an annual basis (55%).

What explains the popularity of standard costs? Companies based in four countries report the following reasons (ranked 1 for most important, 4 for least important) for using standard costs:

Reason*	United States	Canada	Japan	United Kingdom
Cost management	1	1	1	2
Price making and price policy	2	3	2	1
Budgetary planning and control	3	2	3	3
Financial statement preparation	4	4	4	4

*Inoue, "A Comparative Study."

The materials price and efficiency variances discussed in this chapter illustrate the use of standard costs in promoting cost management.

duction manager is responsible for the efficiency variance, while the purchasing manager is responsible for the price variance. This separate computation of the price variance enables the efficiency variance to be computed using budgeted input prices. Thus, judgments about efficiency (the quantity of inputs used to produce a given level of output) are not affected by whether actual input prices differ from budgeted input prices. A word of caution, however, is appropriate. As will be discussed in following text, the causes of price and efficiency variances can be interrelated. For this reason, do not interpret these variances in isolation from each other.

An Illustration of Price and Efficiency Variances for Inputs

Consider Webb's three direct-cost categories. The actual cost for each of these three categories is

Direct materials purchased and used		
Direct materials costs		$688,200
Square yards of cloth input purchased and used		22,200
Actual price per yard		$31
Direct manufacturing labor		
Direct manufacturing labor costs		$198,000
Manufacturing labor-hours of input		9,000
Actual price per hour		$22
Direct marketing labor		
Direct marketing labor costs		$57,600
Marketing labor-hours of input		2,304
Actual price per hour		$25

For simplicity, we assume here that direct materials used is equal to direct materials purchased.

The actual results and the flexible-budget amounts for each category of direct costs for the 10,000 actual output units in April 19_7 are

	Actual Results	Flexible Budget		Flexible-Budget Variances
Direct materials	$688,200	$600,000	(10,000 × $60)	$ 88,200 U
Direct manufacturing labor	198,000	160,000	(10,000 × $16)	38,000 U
Direct marketing labor	57,600	60,000	(10,000 × $6)	2,400 F
Total	$943,800	$820,000		$123,800 U

We now use this Webb Company data to illustrate the input-price and input-efficiency variances. Consider first the input-price variances.

Price Variances

The formula for computing a price variance is

$$\text{Price variance} = \left(\begin{array}{c}\text{Actual price} \\ \text{of input}\end{array} - \begin{array}{c}\text{Budgeted price} \\ \text{of input}\end{array}\right) \times \begin{array}{c}\text{Actual quantity} \\ \text{of input}\end{array}$$

Price variances for each of Webb's three direct-cost categories are

Direct-Cost Category	$\left(\begin{array}{cc}\text{Actual} & \text{Budgeted} \\ \text{Price} & \text{Price} \\ \text{of Input} & \text{of Input}\end{array}\right)$	×	Actual Quantity of Input	=	Input-Price Variance
Direct materials	($31 – $30)	×	22,200	=	$22,200 U
Direct manufacturing labor	($22 – $20)	×	9,000	=	18,000 U
Direct marketing labor	($25 – $24)	×	2,304	=	2,304 U

All three price variances are unfavorable (they reduce operating income) because the actual price of each direct-cost input exceeds the budgeted price; that is, Webb incurred more cost per input unit than was budgeted.

Always consider a broad range of possible causes for price variances. For example, Webb's unfavorable direct materials price variance could be due to one or more of the following reasons.

◆ Webb's purchasing manager negotiated less skillfully than was assumed in the budget.

◆ Webb's purchasing manager bought in smaller lot sizes than budgeted even though quantity discounts were available for the larger lot sizes.

◆ Materials prices unexpectedly increased because of disruptive weather conditions.

◆ Budgeted purchase prices for Webb's materials were set without careful analysis of the market.

Webb's response to a materials price variance will be vitally affected by the presumed cause of the variance. Assume it decides an unfavorable variance is due to poor negotiating by its purchasing officer. Webb may decide to invest more in training this officer in negotiations, or it may decide to hire a more skillful purchasing officer.

When interpreting materials price variances, Webb's managers should consider any change in the relationship with the company's suppliers. For example, assume that Webb moves to a long-term relationship with a single supplier of material. Webb and the supplier agree to a single purchase price per unit for all material purchases in the next 6 months. It is likely that price variances will be minimal for this material because all purchases will be made from this supplier.

Efficiency Variances

Consider now the efficiency variance. Computation of efficiency variances requires measurement of inputs for a given level of output. For any actual level of output, the efficiency variance is the difference between the input that was actually used and the input that should have been used to achieve that actual output, holding input price constant:

$$\text{Efficiency variance} = \left(\begin{array}{c}\text{Actual quantity} \\ \text{of input used}\end{array} - \begin{array}{c}\text{Budgeted quantity} \\ \text{of input allowed for} \\ \underline{\text{actual output units achieved}}\end{array}\right) \times \begin{array}{c}\text{Budgeted price} \\ \text{of input}\end{array}$$

The idea here is that an organization is inefficient if it uses more inputs than budgeted for the actual output units achieved, and it is efficient if it uses less inputs than budgeted for the actual output units achieved.

The efficiency variances for each of Webb's direct-cost categories are

Direct-Cost Category	$\left(\begin{array}{c}\text{Actual} \\ \text{Input Used}\end{array} - \begin{array}{c}\text{Budgeted Input Allowed} \\ \text{for Actual Output Units}\end{array}\right) \times$	Budgeted Price of Input	= Efficiency Variance
Direct materials	[22,200 yards − (10,000 units × 2.00 yards)] × (22,200 yards − 20,000 yards) ×	$30 $30	 = $66,000 U
Direct manufacturing labor	[9,000 hours − (10,000 units × 0.80 hours)] × (9,000 hours − 8,000 hours) ×	$20 $20	 = $20,000 U
Direct marketing labor	[2,304 hours − (10,000 units × 0.25 hours)] × (2,304 hours − 2,500 hours) ×	$24 $24	 = $ 4,704 F

The two manufacturing efficiency variances (direct materials and direct manufacturing labor) are both unfavorable because more input was used than was budgeted, resulting in a decrease in operating income. The marketing efficiency variance is favorable because less input was used than was budgeted, resulting in an increase in operating income.

As with price variances, Webb's managers need to consider a broad range of possible reasons for efficiency variances arising. For example, Webb's unfavorable direct manufacturing labor variance could be due to one or more of the following reasons.

◆ Webb's personnel manager hired underskilled workers.
◆ Webb's production scheduler inefficiently scheduled work, resulting in more direct manufacturing labor time per jacket.
◆ Webb's maintenance department did not properly maintain machines, resulting in more direct manufacturing labor time per jacket.
◆ Budgeted time standards were set without careful analysis of the operating conditions and the employees' skills.

Suppose Webb determines that the unfavorable variance is due to poor machine maintenance. It may decide to have a team consisting of plant machine engineers and machine operators develop a maintenance schedule so that in the future, jackets can be sewn in shorter times.

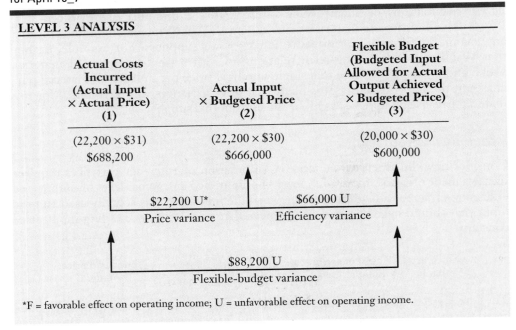

LEVEL 3 ANALYSIS

Actual Costs Incurred (Actual Input × Actual Price) (1)	Actual Input × Budgeted Price (2)	Flexible Budget (Budgeted Input Allowed for Actual Output Achieved × Budgeted Price) (3)
(22,200 × $31) $688,200	(22,200 × $30) $666,000	(20,000 × $30) $600,000

$22,200 U* $66,000 U
Price variance   Efficiency variance

$88,200 U
Flexible-budget variance

*F = favorable effect on operating income; U = unfavorable effect on operating income.

Presentation of Price and Efficiency Variances for Inputs

Note how the sum of the price variance and the efficiency variance equals the flexible-budget variance:

	Price Variance	+ Efficiency Variance	= Flexible-Budget Variance
Direct materials	$22,200 U	$66,000 U	$88,200 U
Direct manufacturing labor	18,000 U	20,000 U	38,000 U
Direct marketing labor	2,304 U	4,704 F	2,400 F

Exhibit 7-4 illustrates a convenient way to integrate the actual and budgeted input information used to compute the price and efficiency variances for direct materials. This exhibit assumes that materials purchased equals materials used.

Overview of Variance Analysis

Exhibit 7-5 presents a comprehensive road map of where we have been. The Level 0 and Level 1 analyses are reproductions of Exhibit 7-1. Level 2 is a reproduction of Exhibit 7-3. We have just discussed price and efficiency variances, which are Level 3.

Some managers refer to proceeding through successively more detailed data as "drilling-down" (or "peeling the onion"). The growing use of on-line data collection is increasing the number of data bases that have this drill-down capability.

PERFORMANCE MEASUREMENT USING VARIANCES

Effectiveness and Efficiency

A key use of variance analysis is in performance evaluation. Two attributes of performance are commonly measured:

◆ **Effectiveness**—the degree to which a predetermined objective or target is met.

◆ **Efficiency**—the relative amount of inputs used to achieve a given level of output.

Be careful to understand the cause(s) of a variance before using it as a performance measure. Assume that a Webb purchasing manager has just negotiated a deal that results in a favorable price variance for materials. The deal could have achieved a favorable variance for any or all of three reasons:

1. The purchasing manager bargained effectively with suppliers.

2. The purchasing manager accepted lower-quality materials at a lower price.

3. The purchasing manager secured a discount for buying in bulk. However, she bought higher quantities than necessary for the short run, which resulted in excessive inventories.

If the purchasing manager's performance is evaluated solely on materials-price variances, then only reason 1 would be considered acceptable, and the evaluation will be positive. Reasons 2 and 3 would be considered unacceptable, and will likely cause the company to incur additional costs, such as higher materials scrap costs and higher storage costs, respectively.

Performance measures increasingly focus on reducing the total costs of the company as a whole. Such a focus is central to the total value-chain-analysis theme in the new management approach. In the purchasing manager example, the company may ultimately lose more money because of reasons 2 and 3 than it gains from reason 1. Conversely, manufacturing costs may be deliberately increased (for example, because higher costs are paid for better materials or more direct manufacturing labor time) in order to obtain better product quality. In turn, the costs of the better product quality may be more than offset by reductions in customer-service costs.

If any single performance measure (for example, a labor efficiency cost variance or a consumer rating report) receives excessive emphasis, managers tend to make decisions that maximize their own reported performance in terms of that single performance measure. Such actions may conflict with the organization's overall goals. This faulty perspective on performance arises because top management has designed a performance measurement and reward system that does not adequately emphasize total organization objectives.

The Concepts in Action box on Parker-Hannifin (p. 231) shows the innovative approach of one company to monitor variables in addition to purchase price when evaluating the performance of the materials procurement function.

Continuous Improvement

Continuous improvement is one of the evolving management themes highlighted in this book. See Exhibit 1-7 (p. 14) and the discussion of kaizen budgeting in Chapter 6 (pp. 188–189). Using **continuous improvement budgeted costs** is yet another way to control variances. This is a budgeted cost that is successively reduced over succeeding time periods. The budgeted direct materials cost for each jacket that Webb Company manufactured in April 19_7 is $60 per unit. The budgeted cost used in variance analysis for subsequent periods could be based on a targeted 1% reduction each period:

Month	Prior Month's Budgeted Amount	Reduction in Budgeted Amount	Revised Budgeted Amount
April 19_7	—	—	$60.00
May 19_7	$60.00	$0.600 (0.01 × $60.00)	59.40
June 19_7	59.40	0.594 (0.01 × $59.40)	58.81
July 19_7	58.81	0.588 (0.01 × $58.81)	58.22

The source of the 1% reduction in budgeted direct materials costs could be efficiency improvements or price reductions. By using continuous improvement budgeted costs, an organization signals the importance of constantly seeking ways to reduce total costs. For example, managers could avoid unfavorable materials-efficiency variances by continuously reducing materials waste.

LEVEL 0 ANALYSIS

Actual operating income	$ 25,000
Budgeted operating income	262,000
Static-budget variance of operating income	$237,000 U*

LEVEL 1 ANALYSIS

	Actual Results (1)	Static-Budget Variances (2) = (1) – (3)	Static Budget (3)
Units sold	10,000	2,000 U	12,000
Revenues (sales)	$1,850,000	$310,000 U	$2,160,000
Variable costs	1,120,000	68,000 F	1,188,000
Contribution margin	730,000	242,000 U	972,000
Fixed costs	705,000	5,000 F	710,000
Operating income	$ 25,000	$237,000 U	$ 262,000

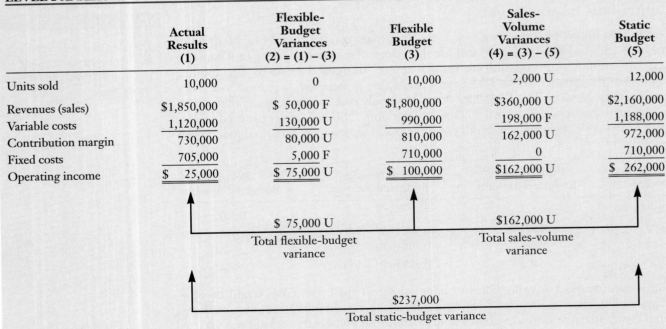

$237,000 U

Total static-budget variance

LEVEL 2 ANALYSIS

	Actual Results (1)	Flexible-Budget Variances (2) = (1) – (3)	Flexible Budget (3)	Sales-Volume Variances (4) = (3) – (5)	Static Budget (5)
Units sold	10,000	0	10,000	2,000 U	12,000
Revenues (sales)	$1,850,000	$ 50,000 F	$1,800,000	$360,000 U	$2,160,000
Variable costs	1,120,000	130,000 U	990,000	198,000 F	1,188,000
Contribution margin	730,000	80,000 U	810,000	162,000 U	972,000
Fixed costs	705,000	5,000 F	710,000	0	710,000
Operating income	$ 25,000	$ 75,000 U	$ 100,000	$162,000 U	$ 262,000

$ 75,000 U

Total flexible-budget
variance

$162,000 U

Total sales-volume
variance

$237,000

Total static-budget variance

Continued

LEVEL 3 ANALYSIS

Revenue Variances by Customers		Cost Variances		Sales-Volume Variances
Retail chains	$ 0 F	**Price Variance**	**Efficiency Variance**	Sales-quantity variances
Independent stores	50,000 F	Direct materials — $22,200 U	$66,000 U	Sales-mix variances
Sales-price variances	50,000 F	Direct Manufacturing Labor — 18,000 U	20,000 U	(These variances are covered in Chapter 16.)
		Direct Marketing Labor — 2,304 U	4,704 F	

(Chapter 8 contains further discussion of Level 3 cost-variance analysis.)

*F = favorable effect on operating income; U = unfavorable effect on operating income.

Total Costs of Materials Ownership at Parker-Hannifin

At Parker-Hannifin's Compumotor Division, materials costs are over 50% of the total manufacturing costs. P-H has developed a supplier cost model that recognizes that the total cost of materials includes many items in addition to materials purchase costs. This model is used to guide supplier-selection decisions and in ongoing cost management of materials-related costs. The supplier cost ratio is the ratio of nonpurchase costs of materials to total supplier costs. P-H uses this supplier cost ratio to examine the performance of each supplier over time. It also uses the ratio to make comparisons across suppliers. P-H can use its model to examine the cause of any change in the supplier cost ratio over time. In Acme's supplier cost ratio, for example, a change could be due to an increase in receiving errors. P-H shares this model with its suppliers so that both the purchaser and the supplier can jointly seek out cost improvements to make the relationship a more productive one for each party. A hypothetical report for a hypothetical supplier (Acme components) is as follows:

Supplier Metric	Output Measure	Number of Output Measures	Cost per Activity	Total Cost
Ordering				
Automatic Purchase	Flat monthly rate	0	$10	$ 0
Manual Purchase	Number of purchase orders	22	2	44
Commodity Complexity	Categories, 1–4 rating	1	16	16
Receiving Inspection	Rate per hour	6	10	60
Receiving Errors	Number of supplier errors	2	25	50
Payment Method				
Automatic Voucher	Number of vouchers	0	1	0
Manual	Number of vouchers	16	3	48
Inventory Carrying	Average balance × Capital costs			940
1. Total nonpurchase costs				1,158
2. Purchase costs				23,842
3. Total supplier costs (1 + 2)				$25,000
Supplier cost ratio (1 ÷ 3)				4.632%

Source: Presentation by Parker-Hannifin at 1995 CAM-I meeting plus discussion with P-H executives.

Products in the initial months of their production may have higher budgeted improvement rates than those that have been in production for, say, 3 years. Improvement opportunities may be much easier to identify when products have just started in production. Once the easy opportunities have been identified ("the low hanging fruit picked"), much more ingenuity may be required to identify successive improvement opportunities.

Value-Chain Explanations of Variances

Organizations adopting a total value-chain approach to analyzing variances are recognizing the diversity of the possible sources of variances. Consider an unfavorable materials-efficiency variance in the production area of an organization. Possible causes of this variance include

◆ Poor design of products or processes
◆ Poor quality or inadequate availability of materials from vendors
◆ Poor work in the manufacturing area
◆ Inadequate training of the labor force
◆ Inappropriate assignment of labor or machines to specific jobs
◆ Congestion due to scheduling a large number of rush orders

This list is far from exhaustive. However, it does indicate that the cause of a variance in one part of the value chain (production in our example) can be actions taken in other parts of the value chain (such as product design or marketing). Note how improvements in early stages of the value chain (such as in product design) can sizably reduce the magnitude of variances in subsequent stages of the value chain. *The most important task in variance analysis is to understand why variances arise and then to use that knowledge to promote learning and continuous improvement.* For instance, in the preceding list of examples, we may seek improvements in product design, in the timeliness of vendor deliveries, in the commitment of the manufacturing labor force to do the job right the first time, and so on. Variance analysis should not be a tool to play the blame game. Rather, it should be an essential ingredient that promotes learning in the organization.

When to Investigate Variances

When should the causes of variances be investigated? Frequently, managers base their answer on subjective judgments, or rules of thumb. For critical items, a small variance may prompt a swift follow-up. For other items, a minimum dollar variance or a certain percentage of variance from budget may be necessary to prompt an in-depth investigation. Of course, a 4% variance in direct materials costs of $1 million may deserve more attention than a 20% variance in repair costs of $10,000. Therefore, rules such as "investigate all variances exceeding $5,000 or 25% of budgeted cost, whichever is lower" are common—see Surveys of Company Practice on "The Decision to Investigate Variances" (p. 233). Variance analysis is subject to the same cost-benefit test as all other phases of a management control system.

Management accounting systems have traditionally implied that a budgeted amount is a single acceptable measure. Practically, managers realize that the budget is a band or range of possible acceptable outcomes and they consequently expect variances to fluctuate randomly within certain normal limits. By definition, a random variance per se is within this band or range and thus calls for no corrective action by managers. Random variances are attributable to chance rather than to management's implementation decisions.

Financial and Nonfinancial Performance Measures

Almost all organizations use a combination of financial and nonfinancial performance measures rather than relying exclusively on either type. Consider our Webb Company illustration. In its cutting room, fabric is laid out and cut into pieces,

The Decision to Investigate Variances

A survey of U.S. managers reported the following approaches to investigating direct materials and direct labor variances:

Approach	Direct Materials (%)	Direct Labor (%)
All variances investigated	6.9	5.3
Variances over prescribed dollar limits investigated	34.8	31.0
Variances over prescribed percentage limits investigated	12.2	14.1
Statistical procedures used to select cases for investigation	0.9	0.0 0.9
Variances never investigated	0.0	0.9
Judgment used to decide if investigation is needed	45.2	47.8
	100.0%	100.0%

Investigating all variances may be justified if the cost of the process being out of control is extremely high. An example is the manufacture of a door lock for a space shuttle.

*Source: Adapted from Gaumnitz and Kollaritsch, "Manufacturing Variances." Full citation is in Appendix A.

which are then matched together and assembled. Control is often exercised at the cutting room level by focusing on nonfinancial measures such as the number of square yards of cloth used to produce 1,000 jackets or the percentage of jackets started and completed without requiring any rework. Production managers at Webb also will likely use financial measures to evaluate the overall cost efficiency with which operations are being run and to help guide decisions about, say, changing the mix of inputs used in manufacturing jackets. Financial measures are often critical in an organization because they summarize the economic impact of diverse physical activities in a way managers readily understand. Moreover, managers are often evaluated on results measured against financial measures.

IMPACT OF INVENTORIES

Our Webb Company illustration assumed the following:

1. All units are manufactured and sold in the same accounting period. There are no work-in-process or finished-goods inventories at either the beginning or the end of the accounting period.

2. All direct materials are purchased and used in the same accounting period. There is no direct materials inventory at either the beginning or the end of the period.

Both assumptions can be relaxed without changing the key concepts introduced in this chapter. However, changes in the computation or interpretation of variances would be required when beginning or ending inventories exist.

Suppose direct materials are purchased sometime prior to their use and that direct materials inventories exist at the beginning or end of the accounting period.

Managers typically want to pinpoint variances at the earliest possible time so that their decisions can be best informed by the variances. For direct materials price variances, the purchase date will almost always be the earliest possible time to isolate them. As a result, many organizations compute direct materials price variances using the quantities purchased in an accounting period. The Problem for Self-Study at the end of this chapter illustrates how to use two different times (purchase time and use time) to pinpoint direct materials variances.

AN ILLUSTRATION OF JOURNAL ENTRIES USING STANDARD COSTS

Control Feature of Standard Costs

We now illustrate journal entries when standard costs are used. For illustrative purposes, we focus on direct materials and direct manufacturing labor.

We will continue with the data in the Webb Company illustration with one exception. Assume that during April 19_7, Webb purchases 25,000 square yards of materials. Recall that the actual quantity used is 22,200 yards and that the standard quantity allowed for the actual output achieved is 20,000 yards. The actual purchase price was $31 per square yard, while the standard price was $30.

Note that in each of the following entries, unfavorable variances are always debits and favorable variances are always credits.

Entry 1a: Isolate the direct materials price variance at the time of purchase by debiting Materials Control at standard prices. This is the earliest date possible to isolate this variance.

1a.	Materials Control	budget		
	(25,000 yards × $30)		$750,000	
	Direct Materials Price Variance			
	(25,000 yards × $1)		25,000	
	Accounts Payable Control			
	(25,000 yards × $31)	actual →		775,000
	To record direct materials purchased.			

Entry 1b: Isolate the direct materials efficiency variance at the time of usage by debiting Work-in-Process Control at standard input quantities allowed for actual output units achieved at standard input prices.

1b.	Work-in-Process Control			
budget →	(20,000 yards × $30)		$600,000	
	Direct Materials Efficiency Variance			
	(2,200 yards × $30)		66,000	
	Materials Control			
actual →	(22,200 yards × $30)			666,000
	To record direct materials used.			

Entry 2: Isolate the direct manufacturing labor price and efficiency variances at the time this labor is used by debiting Work-in-Process Control at standard quantities allowed for actual output units achieved at standard input prices. Note that Wages Payable Control measures the payroll liability and hence is always at actual wage rates.

2.	Work-in-Process Control			
	(8,000 hours × $20)		$160,000	
	Direct Manufacturing Labor Price Variance			
	(9,000 hours × $2)		18,000	
	Direct Manufacturing Labor Efficiency Variance			
	(1,000 hours × $20)		20,000	
	Wages Payable Control			
	(9,000 hours × $22)			198,000
	To record liability for direct manufacturing labor costs.			

A major advantage of this standard costing system is its emphasis on the control feature of standard costs. All variances are isolated at the earliest possible time, when managers can make informed decisions based on those variances.

End-of-Period Adjustments

Chapter 5 discussed two main approaches to recognizing the under- or overallocated manufacturing overhead at the end of a period:

- ◆ The adjusted allocation-rate approach, which adjusts every job cost record for the difference between the allocated and actual indirect cost amounts.
- ◆ The proration approach, which makes adjustments to one or more of the following end-of-period account balances: materials, work in process, finished goods, and cost of goods sold.

Price and efficiency variances can also be disposed of using these same two approaches. The Appendix to Chapter 8 (pp. 273–278) discusses this topic in greater detail.

BENCHMARKING AND VARIANCE ANALYSIS

The budgeted amounts in the variance formulas discussed in this chapter are *benchmarks* (points of reference from which comparisons may be made). The term **benchmarking** is often used to refer to the continuous process of measuring products, services, and activities against the best levels of performance. These best levels of performance may be found in the organization using internal benchmarking information or by using external benchmarks from competing organizations or from other organizations having similar processes. Many consulting firms now offer benchmarking services. Here we discuss information provided by one such service and then note how the variance computations discussed in this chapter can incorporate this information.

Market Insights (MI), based in San Francisco, analyzes cost information submitted by hospitals to various U.S. regulatory bodies. MI develops benchmark reports that show how the cost level at one hospital compares with that at numerous other U.S. hospitals. Reports can be prepared at the total hospital level (for example, cost per patient-day) or at a specific diagnostic-group level (for example, cardiology, orthopedics, or gynecology cost per patient).

Exhibit 7-6 illustrates an MI report for a client hospital. Panel A shows that the client hospital's costs per case is 10% above the average for comparable hospitals. Panel B shows an extract of an MI report at the diagnostic-group level. This report shows that the client hospital has a cost per stroke patient of $33,700 compared with a market average among all hospitals of $31,300. The cost level at this client hospital is well above many hospitals. Cost benchmark reports are attention directing in nature. An individual hospital administrator may well be able to justify an above-average cost level by documenting above-average quality levels or revenue levels. However, in many cases, hospitals with above-average costs have no documentable superiority in their service quality levels, success in surgery operations, or revenue per patient day.

Exhibit 7-6 highlights how hospitals can differ sizably on costs. An administrator of a hospital with above-average costs potentially has much to learn from administrators at hospitals with below-average costs. Be cautious, however, in using benchmark reports such as Exhibit 7-6. The reliability of individual hospital cost data used in benchmark reports varies widely. Many hospitals have not invested heavily in refining their cost accounting systems. In addition, cost figures for individual diagnostic groups require numerous cost allocations, which also vary widely in reliability.

Cost reports like Exhibit 7-6 provide an external benchmark that forces the administrator to ask *why* cost levels differ among hospitals and *how* best practices can be transferred from the more-efficient to the less-efficient hospitals.

PANEL A: COST COMPARISONS AT HOSPITAL LEVEL

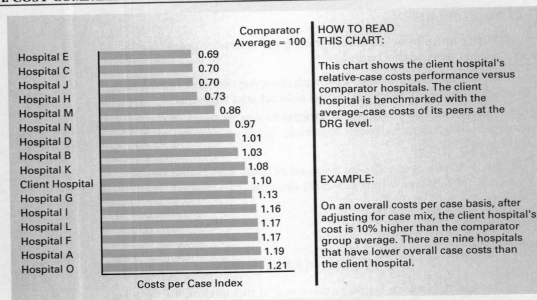

Comparator Average = 100

Hospital	Costs per Case Index
Hospital E	0.69
Hospital C	0.70
Hospital J	0.70
Hospital H	0.73
Hospital M	0.86
Hospital N	0.97
Hospital D	1.01
Hospital B	1.03
Hospital K	1.08
Client Hospital	1.10
Hospital G	1.13
Hospital I	1.16
Hospital L	1.17
Hospital F	1.17
Hospital A	1.19
Hospital O	1.21

Costs per Case Index

HOW TO READ THIS CHART:

This chart shows the client hospital's relative-case costs performance versus comparator hospitals. The client hospital is benchmarked with the average-case costs of its peers at the DRG level.

EXAMPLE:

On an overall costs per case basis, after adjusting for case mix, the client hospital's cost is 10% higher than the comparator group average. There are nine hospitals that have lower overall case costs than the client hospital.

PANEL B: COST COMPARISONS AT DIAGNOSTIC-GROUP LEVEL*

Diagnostic Group	Client Hospital	Market Average	25th Percentile	Average of Lowest Cost Quartile (0–25th)
Stroke	$33,700	$31,300	$21,900	$20,500
Respiratory disorders	66,800	53,700	44,400	38,400
Simple pneumonia	37,100	29,500	23,300	22,000
Heart catherization	24,800	21,200	20,100	17,100

*The cost amounts refer to the insurance premium per month that an insuree would have to pay to the client hospital.
Source: Market Insights (San Francisco, CA).

Evaluating the overall performance of a hospital or hospital personnel requires analyzing other factors in addition to costs. These factors include the perceived quality of service to patients; the success rate of operations (for example, how many patients with strokes survive?); and the morale of the doctors, nurses, and other staff. In many cases, however, cost factors have been given too little weighting in the past, in part because of the lack of reliable information on cost relationships in this sector of the economy.

Benchmark reports based on the costs of other companies can be developed for many activities and products. For example, the Webb Company could estimate (possibly with the aid of consultants) the materials cost of the jackets manufactured by its competitors. The materials cost estimate of the lowest cost competitor could be used as the budgeted amounts in its variance computations. An unfavorable materials efficiency variance would signal that Webb has a higher materials cost than "best cost practice" in its industry. The magnitude of the cost difference would be of great interest to Webb. It could prompt Webb to do an extensive search into how to bring its own cost structure in line with that of the lowest in the industry.

PROBLEM

The O'Shea Company manufactures ceramic vases. It uses its standard costing system when developing its flexible-budget amounts. In April 19_8, 2,000 finished units were produced. The following information is related to its two direct manufacturing cost categories of direct materials and direct manufacturing labor.

Direct materials used were 4,400 pounds. The standard direct materials input allowed for one output unit is 2 pounds at $15 per pound, and 6,000 pounds of materials were purchased at $16.50 per pound, a total of $99,000.

Actual direct manufacturing labor-hours were 3,250 at a total cost of $40,300. Standard manufacturing labor time allowed is 1.5 hours per output unit, and the standard direct manufacturing labor cost is $12 per hour.

REQUIRED

1. Calculate the direct materials price and efficiency variances and the direct manufacturing labor price and efficiency variances. The direct materials price variance will be based on a flexible budget for actual quantities purchased, but the efficiency variance will be based on a flexible budget for actual quantities used.
2. Journal entries for a standard costing system that isolates variances as early as feasible.

SOLUTION

1. Exhibit 7-7 shows how the columnar presentation of variances introduced in Exhibit 7-4 can be adjusted for the difference in timing between the purchase and use of materials. In particular, note the two sets of computations in column 2 for direct materials. The $90,000 pertains to the direct materials purchased; the $66,000 pertains to the direct materials used.

2. Materials Control

(6,000 pounds × $15)	$90,000	
Direct Materials Price Variance		
(6,000 pounds × $1.50)	9,000	
Accounts Payable Control		
(6,000 pounds × $16.50)		$99,000
Work-in-Process Control		
(4,000 pounds × $15)	$60,000	
Direct Materials Efficiency Variance		
(400 pounds × $15)	6,000	
Materials Control		
(4,400 pounds × $15)		$66,000
Work-in-Process Control		
(3,000 hours × $12)	$36,000	
Direct Manufacturing Labor Price Variance		
(3,250 hours × $0.40)	1,300	
Direct Manufacturing Labor Efficiency Variance		
(250 hours × $12)	3,000	
Wages Payable Control		
(3,250 hours × $12.40)		$40,300

EXHIBIT 7-7
Columnar Presentation of Variance Analysis: Direct Materials and Direct Manufacturing Labor*

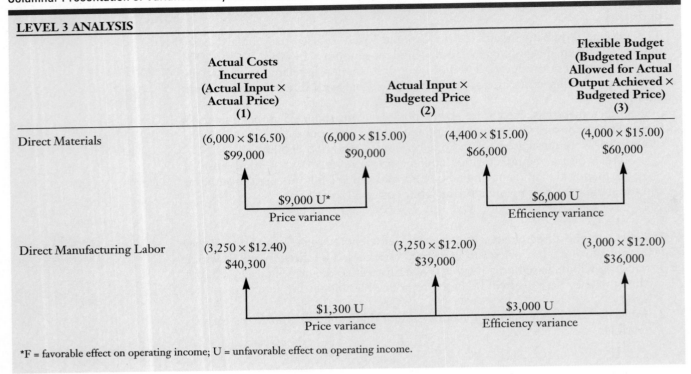

LEVEL 3 ANALYSIS

	Actual Costs Incurred (Actual Input × Actual Price) (1)	Actual Input × Budgeted Price (2)		Flexible Budget (Budgeted Input Allowed for Actual Output Achieved × Budgeted Price) (3)
Direct Materials	(6,000 × $16.50) $99,000	(6,000 × $15.00) $90,000	(4,400 × $15.00) $66,000	(4,000 × $15.00) $60,000
		$9,000 U* Price variance		$6,000 U Efficiency variance
Direct Manufacturing Labor	(3,250 × $12.40) $40,300	(3,250 × $12.00) $39,000		(3,000 × $12.00) $36,000
		$1,300 U Price variance		$3,000 U Efficiency variance

*F = favorable effect on operating income; U = unfavorable effect on operating income.

SUMMARY

The following points are linked to the chapter's learning objectives.

1. A static budget is a budget that is based on one level of output; when variances are computed at the end of the accounting period, no adjustments are made to the amounts in the static budget. A flexible budget is a budget that is developed using budgeted revenue or cost amounts; when variances are computed, the budgeted amounts are adjusted (flexed) to recognize the actual level of output and the actual quantities of the revenue and cost drivers. Flexible budgets help managers gain more insight into the causes of variances than do static budgets.

2. A five-step procedure can be used to develop a flexible budget. Where all costs are either variable with respect to output units or fixed, these five steps require only information about budgeted selling price, budgeted variable cost per output unit, budgeted fixed costs, and the actual quantity of output units achieved.

3. The static-budget variance can be broken into a flexible-budget variance (the difference between the actual result and the flexible-budget amount) and a sales-volume variance. The sales-volume variance arises because the actual output units differ from the budgeted output units.

4. Budgeted input prices and input quantities can be developed from past data (with or without adjustments) or by developing standards based on time and motion studies, engineering studies, and so on. There is much diversity in practice as to how budgeted amounts are obtained.

5. The computation of price variances and efficiency variances helps managers gain insight into two different (but not independent) aspects of performance. Price variances focus on the difference between actual and budgeted input prices. Efficiency variances focus on the difference between actual inputs used and the budgeted inputs allowed for the actual output achieved.

6. Price variances capture only one aspect of a manager's performance. Other aspects include the quality of the inputs the manager purchases and his or her ability to get suppliers to deliver on time.

7. Managers can use continuous improvement budgeted costs in their accounting system to highlight to all employees the importance of continuously seeking ways to reduce total costs.

8. Benchmarking is the continuous process of measuring products, services, and activities against the best levels of performance. Benchmarking enables companies to use the best levels of performance within their organization or by competitors or other external companies to gauge the performance of their own managers.

TERMS TO LEARN

This chapter and the Glossary at the end of this book contain definitions of the following important terms:

benchmark (p. 218)
benchmarking (235)
continuous improvement budgeted
    cost (229)
effectiveness (228)
efficiency (228)
efficiency variance (223)
favorable variance (218)
flexible budget (218)
flexible-budget variance (222)
input-efficiency variance (223)

input-price variance (223)
price variance (223)
rate variance (223)
sales-volume variance (222)
selling-price variance (222)
standard (218)
standard cost (224)
standard input (224)
static budget (218)
unfavorable variance (218)
usage variance (223)

ASSIGNMENT MATERIAL

QUESTIONS

7-1 What is a benchmark? Give an example of three types of benchmarks of interest to managers.

7-2 Distinguish between a *favorable variance* and an *unfavorable variance*.

7-3 What is the key question in deciding which variances should be computed and analyzed?

7-4 Why might managers find a Level 2 flexible-budget analysis more informative than a Level 1 static-budget analysis?

7-5 Describe the steps in developing a flexible budget.

7-6 "Performance may be both effective and efficient, but either condition can occur without the other." Do you agree? Give an example of effectiveness. Give an example of efficiency.

7-7 List four reasons for using standard costs.

7-8 How might a manager gain insight into the causes of a flexible-budget variance for direct materials?

7-9 List three possible causes of a favorable materials efficiency variance.

7-10 Describe why direct materials price and direct materials efficiency variances may be computed with reference to different points in time.

7-11 "There are many costs associated with acquiring and using materials over and above materials purchase costs." Give three examples.

7-12 How might the continuous improvement theme be incorporated into the process of setting budgeted costs?

7-13 Why might an analyst examining variances in the production area look beyond that business function for explanations of those variances?

7-14 Comment on the following statement made by a plant supervisor: "Meetings with my plant accountant are frustrating. All he wants to do is pin the blame for the many variances he reports."

7-15 How might a company obtain information about the costs of competitors and other companies for benchmarking purposes?

EXERCISES

7-16 Flexible budget. Brabham Enterprises manufactures tires for the Formula I motor racing circuit. For August 19_7, Brabham budgeted to manufacture and sell 3,000 tires at a variable cost of $74 per tire and a total fixed cost of $54,000. The budgeted selling price was $110 per tire. Actual results in August 19_7 were 2,800 tires manufactured and sold at a selling price of $112 per tire. The actual total variable costs were $229,600, and the actual total fixed costs were $50,000.

REQUIRED
1. Prepare a performance report (akin to Exhibit 7-3) that uses a flexible budget and a static budget.
2. Comment on the results in requirement 1.

7-17 Flexible budget. The budgeted prices for direct materials, direct manufacturing labor, and direct marketing (distribution) labor per attaché case are $40, $8, and $12, respectively. The president is pleased with the following performance report:

	Actual Costs	Static Budget	Variance
Direct materials	$364,000	$400,000	$36,000 F
Direct manufacturing labor	78,000	80,000	2,000 F
Direct marketing (distribution) labor	110,000	120,000	10,000 F

REQUIRED
Actual output was 8,800 attaché cases. Is the president's pleasure justified? Prepare a revised performance report that uses a flexible budget and a static budget. Assume all three direct costs items are variable costs.

7-18 Price and efficiency variances. Peterson Foods manufactures pumpkin scones. For January 19_8, it budgeted to purchase and use 15,000 pounds of pumpkin at $0.89 a pound; budgeted output was 60,000 scones. Actual purchase and use for January 19_8 was 16,000 pounds at $0.82 a pound; actual output was 60,800 scones.

REQUIRED
1. Compute the flexible-budget variance.
2. Compute the price and efficiency variances.
3. Comment on the results in requirements 1 and 2.

7-19 Materials and manufacturing labor variances. Consider the following data collected for Great Homes, Inc.:

	Direct Materials	Direct Manufacturing Labor
Cost incurred: Actual inputs × Actual prices	$200,000	$90,000
Actual inputs × Standard prices	214,000	86,000
Standard inputs allowed for actual outputs × Standard prices	225,000	80,000

Compute the price, efficiency, and flexible-budget variances for direct materials and direct manufacturing labor.

7-20 Flexible budget, fill in the blanks. Bordeaux Bread operates a bakery that produces French bread. Information pertaining to the first week of July 19_7 is as follows:

	Actual Results	Flexible-Budget Variances	Flexible Budget	Sales-Volume Variances	Static Budget
Units produced and sold	20,000	?	?	?	?
Revenues	?	$1,000 U	?	?	$38,950
Variable costs	?	?	?	?	?
Contribution margin	?	?	?	?	?
Fixed costs	?	?	$9,800	?	?
Operating income	$5,000	?	?	?	?

ADDITIONAL INFORMATION
1. Actual selling price per loaf = $2.00
2. Actual variable cost per loaf = $1.25
3. Budgeted contribution margin per loaf = $0.82

REQUIRED
1. Fill in the missing blanks.
2. Discuss reasons why the actual operating income of $5,000 differed from the budgeted operating income.

7-21 Professional labor variances, efficiency comparisons. Norma Tuck is manager of The Tax Experts, a firm that provides assistance in the preparation of individual tax returns. Because of the highly seasonal nature of her business, Tuck hires staff on a monthly basis from two accounting placement firms—Professional Assist (PA) and Office Support (OS). In February 19_8, The Tax Experts hired 12 staff members from PA and 10 from OS. PA is the prestige firm in its area. OS is a recently formed firm.

Tuck budgets the following for February 19_8:

	PA Staff	OS Staff
Budgeted hourly rate	$45	$40
Budgeted time per tax return in hours	0.40	0.50

Actual results for February 19_8 were as follows:

	PA Staff	OS Staff
Actual hourly rate	$48	$42
Actual time per tax return in hours	0.42	0.46
Number of tax returns completed	4,608	3,600

REQUIRED
1. Compute professional labor price and efficiency variances for (a) the 12 PA staff, and (b) the 10 OS staff hired in February 19_8.
2. Comment on the efficiency of the PA and OS staff The Tax Experts hired.
3. What factors other than efficiency might Tuck consider in deciding whether to hire staff from PA or OS?

7-22 Comprehensive variance analysis. Pacific Furniture is an elite desk manufacturer. At the start of May 19_8, the following budgeted unit amounts (based on a standard costing system) related to its manufacture of executive desks (made out of oak):

◆ Direct materials
   16 square feet of oak per desk
   $20 per square foot
◆ Direct manufacturing labor
   3 hours per desk
   $30 per direct manufacturing labor hour

Budgeted production for May 19_8 was 700 executive desks. There were no beginning inventories of direct materials or finished goods on May 1, 19_8. Work in process is minimal.

Actual results for May 19_8 are as follows:

◆ Direct materials purchased (12,640 square feet) $259,120
◆ Direct materials used (11,850 square feet)   ?
◆ Direct manufacturing labor (2,325 hours at $31.00 per hour)   ?

Actual production in May 19_8 is 750 executive desk units. A constant purchase price for oak wood existed in May 19_8.

REQUIRED

1. Prepare a detailed flexible-budget variance analysis for May 19_8 covering direct materials and direct manufacturing labor.
2. Give two explanations for each of the variances you compute in requirement 1.

7-23 **Flexible budgets, variance analysis.** You have been hired as a consultant by Mary Flanagan, the president of a small manufacturing company that makes automobile parts. Flanagan is an excellent engineer, but she has been frustrated by working with inadequate cost data.

You helped install flexible budgeting and standard costs for Flanagan's company. She has now asked you to consider the following data for May and recommend how variances might be computed and presented in performance reports:

Static budget in output units	20,000
Actual output units produced and sold	23,000
Budgeted selling price per output unit	$40
Budgeted variable costs per output unit	$25
Budgeted total fixed costs per month	$200,000
Actual revenue	$874,000
Actual variable costs	$630,000
Favorable variance in fixed costs	$5,000

Flanagan is disappointed in the May data. Although output units sold exceeded expectations, operating income did not. Assume that there was no beginning or ending inventory.

REQUIRED

1. You decide to present Flanagan with alternative ways to analyze variances so that she can decide what level of detail she prefers. The reporting system can then be designed accordingly. Prepare an analysis similar to Levels 1 and 2 in Exhibit 7-5, (pp. 230–231).
2. What are some likely causes for the variances you report in requirement 1?

7-24 **Flexible budget preparation and analysis.** Bank Management Printers, Inc., produces luxury checkbooks with three checks and stubs per page. Each checkbook is designed for an individual customer and is ordered through the customer's bank. The company's operating budget for September 19_7 included these data:

Number of checkbooks	15,000
Selling price per book	$20
Variable costs per book	$8
Total fixed costs for the month	$145,000

The actual results for September 19_7 were

Number of checkbooks produced and sold	12,000
Average selling price per book	$21
Variable costs per book	$7
Total fixed costs for the month	$150,000

The executive vice president of the company observed that the operating income for September was much less than anticipated, despite a higher-than-budgeted selling price and a lower-than-budgeted variable cost per unit. You have been asked to provide explanations for the disappointing September results.

Bank Management develops its flexible budget on the basis of budgeted revenue per output unit and variable costs per output without a detailed analysis of budgeted inputs.

REQUIRED

1. Prepare a Level 1 analysis of the September performance.
2. Prepare a Level 2 analysis of the September performance.
3. Why might Bank Management find the Level 2 analysis more informative than the Level 1 analysis? Explain your answer.

7-25 Price and efficiency variances, journal entries. Chemical, Inc., has set up the following standards per finished output unit for direct materials and direct manufacturing labor.

◆ Direct materials: 10 pounds at $3.00 per pound $30.00
◆ Direct manufacturing labor: 0.5 hour at $20.00 per hour   10.00

The number of finished output units budgeted for March 19_8 was 10,000; 9,810 units were actually produced.

Actual results in March 19_8 were

| Direct materials: 98,073 pounds used | |
| Direct manufacturing labor: 4,900 hours | $102,900 |

Assume that there was no beginning inventory of either direct materials or finished units.

During the month, materials purchases amounted to 100,000 pounds, at a total cost of $310,000. Price variances are isolated upon purchase. Efficiency variances are isolated at the time of usage.

REQUIRED

1. Compute the March 19_8 price and efficiency variances of direct materials and direct manufacturing labor. Comment on these variances.
2. Prepare journal entries to record the variances in requirement 1.
3. Why might Chemical, Inc., calculate materials price variances and materials efficiency variances with reference to different points in time?

7-26 Continuous improvement (continuation of 7-25). Chemical, Inc., adopts a continuous improvement approach to setting monthly standards' costs. Assume the direct materials standard quantity input of 10 pounds per output unit and the direct manufacturing labor quantity input of 0.5 hours per output unit pertain to January 19_8. The standard amounts for February 19_8 are 0.997 of the January standard amount. The standard amounts for March 19_8 are 0.997 of the February standard amount. Assume the same information for March 19_8 as in Exercise 7-25 except for these revised standard amounts.

REQUIRED
1. Compute the March 19_8 standard quantity input amounts per output unit for direct materials and direct manufacturing labor.
2. Compute the March 19_8 price and efficiency variances of direct materials and direct manufacturing labor.

7-27 Materials and manufacturing labor variances, standard costs. Consider the following selected data regarding the manufacture of a line of upholstered chairs:

	Standards per Chair
Direct materials	2 square yards of input at $10 per square yard
Direct manufacturing labor	0.5 hour of input at $20 per hour

The following data were compiled regarding actual performance: actual output units (chairs) produced, 20,000; square yards of input purchased and used, 37,000; price per square yard, $10.20; direct manufacturing labor costs, $176,400; actual hours of input, 9,000; labor price per hour, $19.60.

REQUIRED
1. Show your computations on the price and efficiency variances for direct materials and for direct manufacturing labor. Give a plausible explanation of why the variances occurred.
2. Suppose 60,000 square yards of materials were purchased (at $10.20 per square yard) even though only 37,000 square yards were used. Suppose further that variances are identified with their most likely control point; accordingly, direct materials price variances are isolated and traced to the purchasing department rather than to the production department. Compute the price and efficiency variances under this approach.

7-28 Journal entries and T-accounts (continuation of 7-27). Prepare journal entries and post them to T-accounts for all transactions in Exercise 7-27, including requirement 2. Summarize in three sentences how these journal entries differ from the normal costing entries described in Chapter 5 (p. 137).

7-29 Flexible budget (continuation of 7-27). Suppose the static budget was for 24,000 units of output. The general manager is thrilled about the following report:

	Actual Results	Static Budget	Variance
Direct materials	$377,400	$480,000	$102,600 F
Direct manufacturing labor	176,400	240,000	63,600 F

REQUIRED
Is the manager's glee warranted? Prepare a report that provides a more detailed explanation of why the static budget was not achieved. Actual output was 20,000 units.

PROBLEMS

7-30 Flexible budget preparation, service sector. Meridian Finance helps prospective homeowners of substantial means to find low-cost financing and assists existing homeowners in refinancing their current loans at lower interest rates. Meridian works only for customers with excellent borrowing capacity. Hence, Meridian is able to obtain a loan for every customer with whom it decides to work.

Meridian charges clients ½% of the loan amount it arranges. In 19_6, the average loan amount per customer was $199,000. In 19_7, the average loan amount was $200,210. In its 19_8 flexible budgeting system, Meridian assumes the average loan amount will be $200,000.

Budgeted cost data per loan application for 19_8 are

◆ Professional labor: 6 budgeted hours at a budgeted rate of $40 per hour
◆ Loan filing fees: budgeted at $100 per loan application
◆ Credit-worthiness checks: budgeted at $120 per loan application
◆ Courier mailings: budgeted at $50 per loan application

Office support (the costs of leases, secretarial workers, and others) is budgeted to be $31,000 per month. Meridian Finance views this amount as a fixed cost.

REQUIRED

1. Prepare a static budget for November 19_8 assuming 90 loan applications.
2. Actual loan applications in November 19_8 were 120. Other actual data for November 19_8 were

◆ Professional labor: 7.2 hours per loan application at $42 per hour
◆ Loan filing fees: $100 per loan application
◆ Credit-worthiness checks: $125 per loan application
◆ Courier mailings: $54 per loan application

Office support costs for November 19_8 were $33,500. The average loan amount for November 19_8 was $224,000. Meridian received its ½% fee on all loans. Prepare a Level 2 variance analysis of Meridian Finance for November 19_8. Meridian's output measure in its flexible budgeting system is the number of loan applications.

7-31 Professional labor efficiency and effectiveness (continuation of 7-30). Meridian Finance is analyzing the efficiency and effectiveness of its professional labor staff.

REQUIRED

1. Compute professional labor price and efficiency variances for November 19_8. (Compute labor price on a per-hour basis.)
2. What factors would you consider in evaluating the effectiveness of professional labor in November 19_8?

7-32 Direct materials variances, long-term agreement with supplier. Yamazaki Mazak manufactures large-scale machining systems that are sold to other industrial companies. Each machining system has a sizable direct materials cost, consisting primarily of the purchase price for a metal compound. For its Lexington, Kentucky, manufacturing facility, Mazak has a long-term contract with Fuji Metals. Fuji will supply to Mazak up to 2,400 pounds of metal per month at a fixed purchase price of $120 per pound for each month in 19_8. For purchases above 2,400 pounds in any month, Mazak renegotiates the price for the additional amount with Fuji Metals (or another supplier). The standard price per pound is $120 for each month in the January to December 19_8 period.

Production data, direct materials actual usage in dollars, and direct materials actual price per pound for the January to May 19_8 period are

	Number of Machining Systems Produced	Total Actual Direct Materials Usage	Average Actual Direct Materials Purchase Price per Pound of Metal
January	10	$242,400	$120
February	12	286,560	120
March	18	442,260	126
April	16	395,264	128
May	11	253,440	120

The average actual direct materials purchase price is for all units purchased in that month. Assume that (a) the direct materials purchased in each month are all used in that month, and (b) each machining system is started and completed in the same month.

The Lexington facility is one of three plants that Mazak operates to manufacture large-scale machining systems. The other plants are in Worcester, the United Kingdom, and Tokyo, Japan.

REQUIRED

1. Assume that Mazak's standard materials input per machining system is 198 pounds of metal. Compute the direct materials price variance and direct materials efficiency variance for each month of the January to May 19_8 period.

2. How does the signing of a long-term agreement with a supplier—an agreement that includes a fixed-purchase-price clause—affect the interpretation of a materials price variance?

7-33 Continuous improvement standards. Assume that in Problem 7-32, Mazak uses the following continuous improvement standards (in pounds of metal) for the direct materials input per machining system:

January	200
February	198
March	196
April	194
May	192

REQUIRED

1. Using these standards, compute the direct materials efficiency variance for each month of the January to May 19_8 period.

2. Outline two basic ways that Mazak might develop continuous improvement standards for the direct materials input per machining system.

7-34 Flexible-budget preparation. The managing partner of Roan Music Box Fabricators has become aware of the disadvantages of static budgets. She asks you to prepare a flexible budget for October 19_7 for the main style of music box. The following partial data are available for the actual operations in August 19_7 (a recent typical month):

Boxes produced and sold	4,500
Direct material costs	$90,000
Direct manufacturing labor costs	$67,500
Depreciation and other fixed manufacturing costs	$50,700
Average selling price per box	$70
Fixed marketing costs	$81,350

Assume no beginning or ending inventory of music boxes.

A 10% increase in the selling price is expected in October. The only variable marketing cost is a commission of $5.50 per unit paid to the manufacturers representatives, who bear all their own costs of traveling, entertaining customers, and so on. A patent royalty of $2 per box manufactured is paid to an independent design firm. Salary increases that will become effective in October are $12,000 per year for the production superintendent and $15,000 per year for the sales manager. A 10% increase in direct materials prices is expected to become effective in October. No changes are expected in direct manufacturing labor wage rates or in the productivity of the direct manufacturing labor personnel. Roan uses a normal costing system and does not have standard costs for any of its inputs.

REQUIRED

1. Prepare a flexible budget for October 19_7, showing budgeted amounts at each of three output levels of music boxes: 4,000, 5,000, and 6,000 units. (Use the flexible-budget approach of developing budgeted revenue and variable costs on a budgeted per output unit basis.)

2. Why might Roan Music Box Fabricators find a flexible budget more useful than a static budget? Explain.

7-35 Flexible and static budgets, service company. Avanti Transportation Company executives have had trouble interpreting operating performance for a number of years. The company has used a budget based on detailed expectations for the forthcoming quarter. For example, the condensed performance report for a midwestern branch for the most recent quarter was as follows:

	Actual Result	Budget	Variance
Revenue	$9,500,000	$10,000,000	$500,000 U*
Variable costs			
Fuel	986,000	1,000,000	14,000 F
Repairs and maintenance	98,000	100,000	2,000 F
Supplies and miscellaneous	196,000	200,000	4,000 F
Variable labor payroll	5,500,000	5,700,000	200,000 F
Total variable costs†	6,780,000	7,000,000	220,000 F
Fixed costs			
Supervision	200,000	200,000	0
Rent	200,000	200,000	0
Depreciation	1,600,000	1,600,000	0
Other fixed costs	200,000	200,000	0
Total fixed costs	2,200,000	2,200,000	0
Total costs	8,980,000	9,200,000	220,000 F
Operating income	$ 520,000	$ 800,000	$280,000 U

*U = unfavorable; F = favorable.
†For purposes of this analysis, assume that all these variable costs are purely variable (in relation to revenue dollars). Also assume that the prices and mix of services sold remain unchanged.

Although the branch manager was upset about the unfavorable revenue variance, he was happy that his cost performance was favorable; otherwise his operating income would have been even lower. His immediate superior, the vice president for operations, was totally unhappy and remarked:

> I can see some merit in comparing actual performance with budgeted performance, because we can see whether actual revenue coincided with our best guess for budget purposes. But I can't see how this performance report helps us evaluate the cost control performance of the branch manager.

REQUIRED

1. Prepare a columnar flexible budget for Avanti at revenue levels of $9 million, $10 million, and $11 million. Use the format of Exhibit 7-2, (p. 221). Assume that the prices and mix of products sold are equal to the budgeted prices and mix.
2. Express the flexible budget for costs in formula form.
3. Prepare a condensed contribution-format income statement showing the static-budget, sales-volume, and flexible-budget variances. Use the format of Exhibit 7-3 (p. 222).

7-36 Direct materials and manufacturing labor variances, solving unknowns. (CPA adapted) On May 1, 19_8, the Bovar Company began the manufacture of a new paging machine known as Dandy. The company installed a standard costing system to account for manufacturing costs. The standard costs for a unit of Dandy are as follows:

Direct materials (3 pounds at $5 per pound)	$15.00
Direct manufacturing labor (0.5 hours at $20 per hour)	10.00
Manufacturing overhead (75% of direct manufacturing labor costs)	7.50
	$32.50

The following data were obtained from Bovar's records for the month of May:

	Debit	Credit
Revenues		$125,000
Accounts payable control (for May's purchases of direct materials)		68,250
Direct materials price variance	$3,250	
Direct materials efficiency variance	2,500	
Direct manufacturing labor price variance	1,900	
Direct manufacturing labor efficiency variance		2,000

Actual production in May was 4,000 units of Dandy, and actual sales in May was 2,500 units. The amount shown for direct materials price variance applies to materials purchased during May. There was no beginning inventory of materials on May 1, 19_8.

REQUIRED

Compute each of the following items for Bovar for the month of May. Show your computations.

1. Standard direct manufacturing labor-hours allowed for actual output achieved.
2. Actual direct manufacturing labor-hours worked.
3. Actual direct manufacturing labor wage rate.
4. Standard quantity of direct materials allowed (in pounds).
5. Actual quantity of direct materials used (in pounds).
6. Actual quantity of direct materials purchased (in pounds).
7. Actual direct materials price per pound.

7-37 **Benchmarking, hospital cost comparisons.** Julie Smith is the newly appointed president of National University. National University Hospital (NUH) is a major problem for her because it is running large deficits. Sam Horn, the chairman of the hospital, tells Smith that he and his staff have cut costs to the bare bone. Any further cost cutting, he argues, would destroy the culture of the hospital. He also argues that the use of detailed cost studies is totally inappropriate for a medical institution because of (a) the inability to have well-defined relationships between inputs and outputs, and (b) the problem of even defining what is a good output for a hospital. He notes that he is "fed up with people equating continuous improvement at NUH with continued cost reduction. This is only a cost accountant's view of the world. Our top priority is to help doctors save lives and to help people recover their health."

Smith hears about a new benchmark cost analysis service offered by Market Insights. She asks Horn to hire Market Insights to provide a benchmark cost report that pertains to NUH. Horn is not enthusiastic about doing so, but he complies with her request. The report includes the following:

a. Aggregate Hospital Cost Comparison (Average = 1.00)

Hospital E	0.69
Hospital C	0.70
Hospital J	0.70
.	.
.	.
.	.
Hospital A	1.19
National University Hospital	1.20
Hospital 0	1.21

b. Diagnostic-Group Cost Comparison

Diagnostic Group	National University Hospital	Market Average	25th Percentile	Average of Best Quartile (0–25th)
Angina, chest pain	$23,000	$20,500	$17,300	$15,300
Asthma, bronchitis	15,400	13,100	10,400	9,000
Skin disorders, cellulitis	9,600	9,200	6,500	5,800
Renal failure and dialysis	7,600	5,500	4,200	3,600
Diabetes	6,700	5,100	3,700	3,100
Gastroenteritis	12,000	18,500	16,000	12,800

REQUIRED

1. Do you agree with Horn that the use of detailed cost studies at NUH is totally inappropriate? Explain your answer and comment on Horn's reasoning.

2. What inferences do you draw from the MI benchmark cost report on NUH?

3. What use might Smith make of the MI benchmark cost report?

4. What criticisms might you anticipate Horn would make of the MI benchmark cost report?

5. What factors other than cost might Smith consider in evaluating Horn's performance and that of NUH?

7-38 **Comprehensive variance analysis.** (CMA adapted) Aunt Molly's Old Fashioned Cookies bakes cookies for retail stores. The company's best-selling cookie is chocolate nut supreme, which is marketed as a gourmet cookie and regularly sells for $8.00 per pound. The standard cost per pound of chocolate nut supreme, based on Aunt Molly's normal monthly production of 400,000 pounds, is calculated as follows:

Cost Item	Quantity	Standard Unit Costs	Total Cost
Direct materials			
Cookie mix	10 ounces	$0.02 per ounce	$0.20
Milk chocolate	5 ounces	0.15 per ounce	0.75
Almonds	1 ounce	0.50 per ounce	0.50
			1.45
Direct labor*			
Mixing	1 minute	14.40 per hour	0.24
Baking	2 minutes	18.00 per hour	0.60
			0.84

*Direct labor rates include employee benefits.

Aunt Molly's management accountant, Karen Blair, prepares monthly budget reports based on these standard costs. Presented here is April's report, which compares budgeted and actual performance.

Performance Report
April 19_7

	Budget	Actual	Variance
Units (in pounds)*	400,000	450,000	50,000 F
Revenue	$3,200,000	$3,555,000	$355,000 F
Direct material	580,000	865,000	285,000 U
Direct labor	336,000	348,000	12,000 U

*Units produced and sold.

Cost Item	Quantity	Actual Cost
Direct materials		
Cookie mix	4,650,000 ounces	$ 93,000
Milk chocolate	2,660,000 ounces	532,000
Almonds	480,000 ounces	240,000
Direct labor		
Mixing	450,000 minutes	108,000
Baking	800,000 minutes	240,000

REQUIRED

1. Compute the following variances
   a. Selling-price variance
   b. Material price variance
   c. Material efficiency variance
   d. Labor price variance
   e. Labor efficiency variance
2. What explanations might exist for the variances in requirement 1?

7-39 Procurement costs, variance analysis, ethics. Rick Daley is the manager of the athletic shoe division of Raider Products. Raider is a U.S.-based company that has just purchased Fastfoot, a leading European shoe company. Fastfoot has long-term production contracts with suppliers in two East European countries—Hergovia and Tanistan. Daley receives a request from Kevin Neal, president of Raider Products. Daley and his controller, Brooke Mullins, are to make a presentation to the next board of director's meeting on the cost competitiveness of its Fastfoot subsidiary. This should include budgeted and actual procurement costs for 19_7 at its Hergovia and Tanistan supply sources.

Mullins decides to visit the two supply operations. The budgeted average procurement cost for 19_7 was $12 per pair of shoes. This includes payments to the shoe manufacturer and all other payments to conduct business in each country. Mullins reports the following to Daley:

◆ *Hergovia.* Total 19_7 procurement costs for 250,000 pairs of shoes was $3,325,000. Payment to the shoe manufacturer was $2,650,000. Very few receipts exist for the remaining $675,000. Kickback payments are viewed as common in Hergovia.

◆ *Tanistan.* Total 19_7 procurement costs for 900,000 pairs of shoes was $10,485,000. Payment to the shoe manufacturer was $8,640,000. Receipts exist for $705,000 of the other costs, but Mullins is skeptical of their validity. Kickback payments are a "way of business" in Tanistan.

At both the Hergovia and Tanistan plants, Mullins is disturbed by the employment of young children (many of them under 15 years). She is told that all major shoe producing companies have similar low-cost employment practices in both countries.

Daley is uncomfortable about the upcoming presentation to the board of directors. He was a leading advocate of the acquisition. A recent business magazine reported that the Fastfoot acquisition would make Raider Products the global low-cost producer in its market lines. The stock price of Raider Products jumped 21% the day the Fastfoot acquisition was announced. Mullins likewise is widely identified as a proponent of the acquisition. She is seen as a "rising star" due for promotion to a division management post in the near future.

REQUIRED

1. What summary procurement cost variances could be reported to the board of directors of Raider Shoes?
2. What ethical issues do (a) Daley and (b) Mullins face when preparing and making a report to the board of directors?
3. How should Mullins address the issues you identify in requirement 2?

COLLABORATIVE LEARNING PROBLEM

7-40 Price and efficiency variances, problems in standard setting, benchmarking. Savannah Fashions manufactures shirts for retail chains. Jorge Rivera, the controller, is becoming increasingly disenchanted with Savannah's 6-month-old standard costing system. The budgeted amounts for both its direct materials and direct manufacturing labor are drawn from its standard costing system. The budgeted and actual amounts for July 19_7 were

	Budgeted	Actual
Shirts manufactured	4,000	4,488
Direct materials cost	$20,000	$20,196
Direct materials units used (rolls of cloth)	400	408
Direct manufacturing labor costs	$18,000	$18,462
Direct manufacturing labor-hours	1,000	1,020

There was no beginning or ending inventory of materials.

Rivera observes that in the last 6 months he has rarely seen an unfavorable variance of any magnitude. The standard costing system is based on a study of the operations conducted by an independent consultant. Rivera decides to play detective and makes some unobtrusive observations of the work force at the plant. He notes that even at their current output levels, the workers seem to have a lot of time to discuss baseball, sitcoms, and the local hot fishing spots.

At a recent industry conference on "Benchmarking and Competitiveness," Mary Blanchard, the controller of Winston Fabrics, told Rivera that Winston had employed the same independent consultant to design a standard costing system. However, the company dismissed him after 2 weeks because Winston employees quickly became aware of the consultant observing their work.

At the industry conference, Rivera participated in seminars on "benchmarking for the fabric industry." A consultant for the Benchmarking Clearing House showed how she could develop 6-month benchmark reports on the estimated costs of Savannah's major competitors. She indicated that she was already examining the estimated cost of shirts manufactured by the four largest importers into the United States. These importers had taken much business from Savannah in recent years. This information would soon be available by subscribing to the Benchmarking Clearing House monthly service.

INSTRUCTIONS

Form groups of two or more students to complete the following requirements.

REQUIRED

1. Compute the price and efficiency variances of Savannah Fashions for direct materials and direct manufacturing labor in July 19_7.
2. Describe the types of actions the employees at Winston Fabrics may have taken to reduce the accuracy of the standards set by the independent consultant. Why would employees take those actions? Is this behavior ethical?
3. Describe how Savannah might use information from the Benchmarking Clearing House when computing the variances in requirement 1.
4. Discuss the pros and cons of Savannah using the Benchmarking Clearing House information to increase its cost competitiveness.

CHAPTER 8

FLEXIBLE BUDGETS, VARIANCES, AND MANAGEMENT CONTROL: II

The planning and control of indirect costs is pivotal in organizations with high investments in plant, equipment, and operating systems. Rank Hovis' flour milling and blending facilities at Manchester, United Kingdom, uses high levels of computer-operated machinery in its operations.

LEARNING OBJECTIVES

After studying this chapter, you should be able to

1. Explain differences in the planning of variable-overhead costs and the planning of fixed-overhead costs

2. Explain the computation and meaning of spending and efficiency variances for variable overhead

3. Illustrate how to compute the budgeted fixed-overhead rate

4. Give two reasons why the production-volume variance may not be a good measure of the opportunity cost of unused capacity

5. Explain how a 4-variance analysis can provide an integrated overview of overhead cost variances

6. Explain the differing roles of cost allocation bases for fixed manufacturing overhead when (a) planning and controlling, and (b) inventory costing

7. Prepare journal entries for variable- and fixed-overhead variances

8. Explain why managers frequently use both financial and nonfinancial variables to plan and control overhead costs

Overhead or indirect costs are a major cost area for many organizations. Chemical, paper, steel, and telecommunications companies, for example, incur sizable costs to construct and maintain their physical plant and equipment and other aspects of their infrastructure. Such costs are included in the indirect costs of the individual products or services they produce and sell. This chapter covers methods of planning and controlling overhead costs, allocating these costs to products, and analyzing overhead variances.

Please proceed slowly as you study this chapter. Trace the data to the analysis in a systematic way. In particular, note how fixed manufacturing overhead is accounted for in one way for the planning and control purpose and in a different way for the inventory costing purpose.

PLANNING OF VARIABLE- AND FIXED-OVERHEAD COSTS

OBJECTIVE 1

Explain differences in the planning of variable-overhead costs and the planning of fixed-overhead costs

We continue the Chapter 7 analysis of the Webb Company. Chapter 7 illustrated how a static-budget variance can be divided into a flexible-budget variance and a sales-volume variance. This chapter focuses on understanding flexible-budget variances for overhead costs and their causes.

Webb's cost structure illustrates why it views the planning of overhead costs as important. The following percentages of total static-budget costs (see column 4 of Exhibit 7-2, p. 221) are based on Webb's budget for 12,000 output units for April 19_7:

	Variable Overhead Costs	Fixed Overhead Costs	Total Overhead Costs
Manufacturing	7.59%	14.54%	22.13%
Marketing	3.16	22.87	26.03
Total	10.75%	37.41%	48.16%

Total overhead costs amount to almost half (48.16%) of Webb's total budgeted costs at 12,000 output units for April 19_7. Clearly, Webb can greatly improve its profitability by effective planning of its overhead costs, both variable and fixed.

Planning Variable-Overhead Costs

Among Webb's variable manufacturing overhead costs are energy, engineering support, indirect materials, and indirect manufacturing labor. Effective planning of variable overhead costs involves undertaking only value-added variable-overhead activities and then managing the cost drivers of those activities in the most efficient way. A **value-added cost** is one that if eliminated, would reduce the value customers obtain from using the product or service. A **nonvalue-added cost** is one that, if eliminated, would not reduce the value customers obtain from using the product or service. Consider the cost of sewing needles used in the sewing of jackets manufactured by Webb. Sewing is an essential element of manufacturing a jacket. Hence, costs associated with sewing (for example, sewing needles) would be classified as adding value. In contrast, consider the cost of a warehouse that stores rolls of cloth to be used in case of an emergency (if, say, a supplier fails to meet the delivery schedule). A jacket sewn from cloth stored in a warehouse is no different from a jacket sewn from cloth delivered by a supplier directly to the production floor. Hence, costs associated with warehousing are likely viewed as "nonvalue adding." There is a continuum between value-added costs and nonvalue-added costs. Many overhead cost items are in a gray, uncertain area between value-adding and nonvalue-adding costs.

Planning Fixed-Overhead Costs

Effective planning of fixed-overhead costs includes undertaking only value-added fixed-overhead activities and then determining the appropriate level for those activities. Webb examples in manufacturing include depreciation or leasing costs on plant and equipment, some administrative costs (for example, the plant manager's salary), and property taxes. Frequently, the most critical issue is how much plant and equipment to acquire. Consider Webb's leasing of weaving machines, each of which has a fixed cost per year. Failure to lease sufficient machine capacity will result in an inability to meet demand and thus in lost sales of jackets. In contrast, if Webb greatly overestimates demand, it will incur additional fixed leasing costs on machines that are not fully utilized during the year.

At the start of an accounting period, management will likely have made most of the key decisions that determine the level of fixed-overhead costs to be incurred. In contrast, day-to-day, ongoing management decisions play a larger role in determining the level of variable-overhead costs incurred in that period.

Manufacturing Overhead Allocation Bases and Rates in the Electronics Industry

Manufacturing overhead costs are the second most important category of manufacturing costs for electronics companies such as Apple Computer, Hewlett-Packard, Hitachi, Philips, Siemens, and Toshiba. Two frequently used allocation bases for manufacturing overhead costs in this industry are direct manufacturing labor dollars (or hours) and direct materials dollars. Many individual companies use both allocation bases (and, in addition, other bases such as hours of equipment testing). Individual segments of this industry differ in their overhead rates, in part, because of differences in their cost structures. The following industry data for four segments of the electronics industry are drawn from companies that are members of the American Electronics Association. The four segments are as follows:

◆ components: includes capacitors, amplifiers, oscillators, and wire and cable
◆ computers: includes mainframes, minicomputers, and microcomputers
◆ peripherals: includes disc drives, printers, and keyboards
◆ instruments: includes test, analytical, and scientific equipment and medical instruments

	Components	Computers	Peripherals	Instruments
Cost Structure				
Revenues	100.0%	100.0%	100.0%	100.0%
Research and development costs	6.3%	11.4%	8.4%	9.6%
Manufacturing costs				
◆ Materials and subcontracts	28.3%	36.5%	40.2%	28.6%
◆ Direct manufacturing labor	10.6	2.8	3.2	4.3
◆ Manufacturing overhead	22.6	10.3	12.2	17.0
Total manufacturing costs	61.5	49.6	55.6	49.9
Marketing costs	12.4	17.9	15.9	20.5
General and administrative costs	11.9	7.8	9.6	11.4
Other costs, taxes, and profits	7.9	13.3	10.5	8.6
	100.0%	100.0%	100.0%	100.0%
Average Manufacturing Overhead Rates				
◆ Allocation base is direct manufacturing labor dollars	214.5%	440.0%	277.0%	262.0%
◆ Allocation base is materials dollars	17.0%	15.5%	12.5%	15.0%

The ratio of manufacturing overhead costs to direct manufacturing labor costs ranges from 3.95 for companies manufacturing instruments (17.0% ÷ 4.3%) to 2.13 for companies manufacturing components (22.6% ÷ 10.6%). Clearly, planning and controlling manufacturing overhead costs is a high priority for managers in the electronics industry.

Source: Adapted from *Operating Ratios Survey,* American Electronics Association. Full citation is in Appendix A.

Webb Company Data

The Webb Company summary information for April 19_7 that we will use in this chapter is as follows:

Overhead Category	Actual Results	Flexible-Budget Amount (for 10,000 Output Units)	Static-Budget Amount (for 12,000 Output Units)
Variable manufacturing overhead	$130,500	$120,000	$144,000
Fixed manufacturing overhead	285,000	276,000	276,000
Variable marketing overhead	45,700	50,000	60,000
Fixed marketing overhead	420,000	434,000	434,000

DEVELOPING BUDGETED VARIABLE-OVERHEAD RATES

Webb uses a three-step approach when developing its variable-overhead rate:

Step 1: Identify the Costs to Include in the Variable-Overhead Cost Pool(s) Webb groups all of its variable manufacturing overhead costs in a single cost pool. Costs in this pool include energy, engineering support, indirect materials, and indirect manufacturing labor.

Step 2: Select the Cost Allocation Base(s) Webb's operating managers believe that machine-hours are an important driver of variable manufacturing overhead costs and decided to use this measure as the cost allocation base.

Step 3: Estimate the Budgeted Variable-Overhead Rate(s) Several approaches can be used in this step. One approach is to adjust the past actual variable-overhead cost rate per unit of the allocation base—for example, an adjustment to take into account expected inflation. A second approach is to use standard costing.

Webb uses the standard costing approach to develop its April 19_7 budgeted variable-overhead cost rate of $30 per machine-hour and also its budgeted machine-hour rate of 0.40 hours per actual output unit. These input amounts are used to compute the budgeted variable manufacturing overhead rate per unit:

$$\text{Budgeted inputs allowed per output unit} \times \text{Budgeted costs per input unit} = 0.40 \times \$30$$

$$= \$12 \text{ per output unit}$$

VARIABLE-OVERHEAD COST VARIANCES

We now illustrate how the budgeted variable manufacturing overhead rate is used in computing Webb's variable manufacturing overhead cost variances. The following data are for April 19_7:

Cost Item/Allocation Base	Actual Results	Flexible-Budget Amount (for 10,000 Output Units)	Static-Budget Amount (for 12,000 Output Units)
1. Variable manufacturing overhead costs	$130,500	$120,000	$144,000
2. Variable manufacturing overhead costs per machine-hour (1 ÷ 5)	29	30	30
3. Variable manufacturing overhead costs per output units (1 ÷ 4)	13.05	12	12
4. Output units (jackets)	10,000	10,000	12,000
5. Machine-hours	4,500	4,000	4,800

EXHIBIT 8-1
Static- and Flexible-Budget Analysis of Variable Manufacturing Overhead Costs for the Webb Company for April 19_7

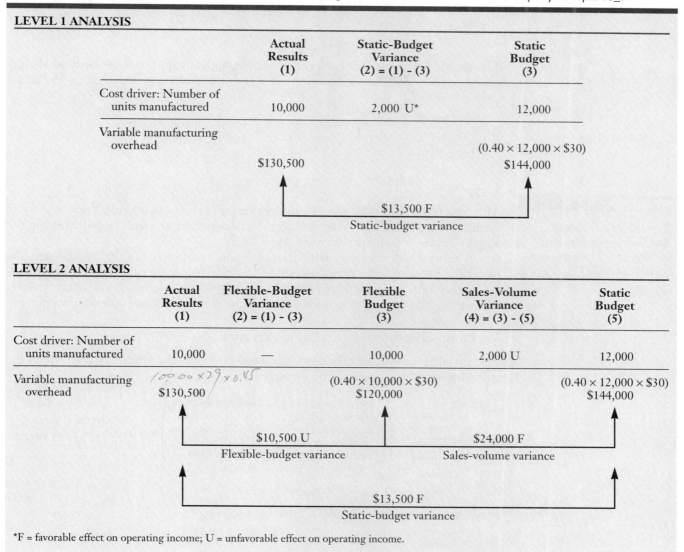

*F = favorable effect on operating income; U = unfavorable effect on operating income.

Static-Budget and Flexible-Budget Analyses

The Level 1 static-budget variance for variable manufacturing overhead cost is shown in Exhibit 8-1:

$$\frac{\text{Variable-overhead}}{\text{static-budget variance}} = \frac{\text{Actual}}{\text{results}} - \frac{\text{Static-budget}}{\text{amount}}$$

$$= \$130,500 - \$144,000$$

$$= \$13,500 \text{ F}$$

Additional insight into the ability of Webb's managers to control variable manufacturing overhead can be gained by moving to the Level 2 flexible-budget analysis also shown in Exhibit 8-1. The budgeted amounts in Level 2 recognize that 10,000 output units were produced instead of the budgeted 12,000 output units. The April 19_7 flexible budget for variable manufacturing overhead is $120,000 ($0.4 × 10,000 × $30).

The variable manufacturing overhead sales-volume variance arises solely because the actual number of output units sold by Webb differs from the budgeted number of output units sold:

$$\text{Variable-overhead sales-volume variance} = \text{Flexible-budget amount} - \text{Static-budget amount}$$

$$= \$120,000 - \$144,000$$

$$= \$24,000 \text{ F}$$

The variable manufacturing overhead flexible-budget variance arises because Webb's actual variable manufacturing overhead cost differs from that budgeted for the actual output units sold:

$$\text{Variable-overhead flexible-budget variance} = \text{Actual results} - \text{Flexible-budget amount}$$

$$= \$130,500 - \$120,000$$

$$= \$10,500 \text{ U}$$

OBJECTIVE 2

Explain the computation and meaning of spending and efficiency variances for variable overhead

This $10,500 unfavorable flexible-budget variance shows that Webb's actual variable manufacturing overhead exceeded the flexible-budget amount by $10,500 for the 10,000 jackets actually produced in April 19_7.

We now discuss how managers can gain additional insight by splitting the Level 2 variable manufacturing overhead flexible-budget variance into its Level 3 efficiency and price (labeled *spending* when dealing with overhead) variances. Exhibit 8-2 is the columnar presentation of these Level 3 efficiency and spending variances.

Variable-Overhead Efficiency Variance

The **variable-overhead efficiency variance** measures the efficiency with which the cost allocation base is used. The formula is

$$\text{Variable-overhead efficiency variance} = \left(\begin{array}{c} \text{Actual units of} \\ \text{variable-overhead} \\ \text{cost allocation base} \\ \text{used for actual} \\ \text{output units} \\ \text{achieved} \end{array} - \begin{array}{c} \text{Budgeted units of} \\ \text{variable-overhead} \\ \text{cost allocation base} \\ \text{allowed for actual} \\ \text{output units} \\ \text{achieved} \end{array} \right) \times \begin{array}{c} \text{Budgeted} \\ \text{variable-overhead} \\ \text{cost allocation rate} \end{array}$$

$$= [4,500 - (10,000 \times 0.40)] \times \$30$$

$$= (4,500 - 4,000) \times \$30 = 500 \times \$30$$

$$= \$15,000 \text{ U}$$

The variable-overhead efficiency variance is computed similarly to the efficiency variance described in Chapter 7 (p. 227) for direct-cost items. But the interpretation of the Chapter 7 and 8 efficiency variances differs. In Chapter 7, input-efficiency variances for direct-cost items are based on differences between actual inputs used and the budgeted inputs allowed for actual outputs achieved. In Chapter 8, efficiency variances for variable-overhead costs are based on the efficiency with which the *cost allocation base* is used. Webb's unfavorable variable-overhead efficiency variance of $15,000 means that actual machine-hours (the cost allocation base) were higher than the budgeted machine-hours allowed to manufacture 10,000 jackets. Possible causes of this higher-than-budgeted machine-hour usage include the following:

◆ Webb's worker's were less skillful in the use of machines than budgeted.
◆ Webb's production scheduler inefficiently scheduled jobs, resulting in higher-than-budgeted machine usage.
◆ Webb's machines were not maintained in good operating condition.
◆ Budgeted machine time standards were set without careful analysis of the operating conditions.

Management's response to this $15,000 unfavorable variance would be guided by which cause(s) best describes the April 19_7 results.

EXHIBIT 8-2
Columnar Presentation of Variance Analysis: Variable Manufacturing Overhead for the
Webb Company

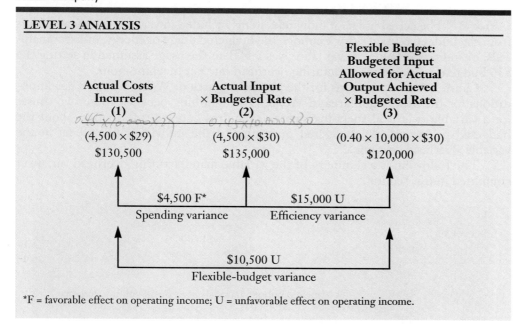

LEVEL 3 ANALYSIS

Actual Costs Incurred (1)	Actual Input × Budgeted Rate (2)	Flexible Budget: Budgeted Input Allowed for Actual Output Achieved × Budgeted Rate (3)
(4,500 × $29)	(4,500 × $30)	(0.40 × 10,000 × $30)
$130,500	$135,000	$120,000

$4,500 F* | $15,000 U
Spending variance | Efficiency variance

$10,500 U
Flexible-budget variance

*F = favorable effect on operating income; U = unfavorable effect on operating income.

The use of cotton thread for sewing jackets illustrates the difference between the efficiency variance for direct-cost inputs and the efficiency variance for variable-overhead cost categories. If Webb classifies cotton thread as a direct-cost item, the direct materials efficiency variance will indicate whether more or less cotton thread per jacket is used than was budgeted for the actual output achieved. In contrast, if Webb classifies cotton thread as an indirect-cost item, the variable manufacturing overhead efficiency variance will indicate whether Webb used more or less machine-hours (the cost allocation base for variable manufacturing overhead) than were budgeted for the actual output achieved. Any variation in cotton thread usage other than that budgeted to vary with respect to machine-hours will be shown in the variable manufacturing overhead spending variance.

Variable-Overhead Spending Variance

The **variable-overhead spending variance** is the difference between the actual amount of variable overhead incurred and the budgeted amount allowed for the actual quantity of the variable-overhead allocation base used for the actual output units achieved. The formula for the variable-overhead spending variance is

$$\begin{matrix} \text{Variable-} \\ \text{overhead} \\ \text{spending} \\ \text{variance} \end{matrix} = \left(\begin{matrix} \text{Actual variable-overhead} \\ \text{cost per unit of} \\ \text{cost allocation base} \end{matrix} - \begin{matrix} \text{Budgeted variable-overhead} \\ \text{cost per unit of} \\ \text{cost allocation base} \end{matrix} \right) \times \begin{matrix} \text{Actual quantity of} \\ \text{variable-overhead} \\ \text{cost allocation base} \\ \text{used for actual} \\ \text{output units achieved} \end{matrix}$$

$$= (\$29 - \$30) \times 4,500$$

$$= -\$1 \times 4,500 = \$4,500 \text{ F}$$

Webb operated in April 19_7 with a lower-than-budgeted variable-overhead cost per machine-hour. Hence, there is a favorable variable-overhead spending variance.

The variable-overhead spending variance is computed similarly to the price variance described in Chapter 7 (p. 226) for direct-cost items such as direct materials. Do not assume, however, that the causes of these two variances are the same. Two main causes could explain a variable-overhead spending variance of $4,500 F at Webb:

Cause A The actual prices of individual items included in variable overhead differ from their budgeted prices—for example, the April 19_7 purchase price of energy, indirect materials, or indirect manufacturing labor was less than budgeted prices.

Cause B The actual usage of individual items included in variable overhead differs from the budgeted usage—for example, the budgeted usage of energy, indirect materials, or indirect manufacturing labor was less than the usage assumed in setting the $30 budgeted variable manufacturing overhead rate per machine-hour.

Cause A has implications for the purchasing area of Webb. Cause B has implications for the production area of Webb. Distinguishing between these two causes for a variable-overhead spending variance requires detailed information about the budgeted prices and the budgeted quantities of the individual line items in the variable-overhead cost pool.

The following is a summary of the variable manufacturing overhead variances computed in this section.

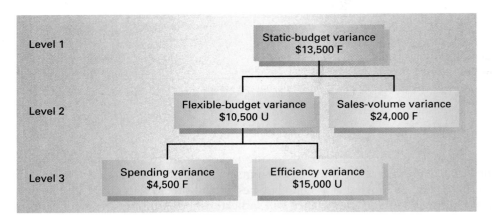

The key cause of Webb's unfavorable flexible-budget variance is that the actual use of machine-hours is higher than budgeted.

DEVELOPING BUDGETED FIXED-OVERHEAD RATES

OBJECTIVE 3

Illustrate how to compute the budgeted fixed-overhead rate

Fixed-overhead costs are, by definition, a lump sum that does not change in total despite changes in a cost driver. While total fixed costs are frequently included in flexible budgets, they remain the same total amount within the relevant range regardless of the output level chosen to "flex" the variable costs and revenues. The three steps in developing Webb Company's budgeted fixed overhead rate are as follows:

Step 1: Identify the Costs in the Fixed Overhead Cost Pool(s) This is the numerator of the budgeted rate computation. For Webb, fixed manufacturing overhead costs include depreciation, plant-leasing costs, property taxes, plant manager's salary, and some administrative costs, all of which are included in a single cost pool. Webb's budget is $276,000 for April 19_7.

Step 2: Estimate the Budgeted Quantity of the Allocation Base(s) This is the denominator of the budgeted rate computation. It is termed the **denominator level.** Webb uses machine-hours as its allocation base. It budgets to manufacture 12,000 jackets in April 19_7. The budgeted machine-hours to manufacture 12,000 jackets is 4,800 (12,000 × 0.40 budgeted machine-hours per output unit).

Step 3: Compute the Budgeted Fixed-Overhead Rate(s)

$$\text{Budgeted fixed-overhead rate per unit of allocation base} = \frac{\text{Budgeted fixed-overhead costs}}{\text{Budgeted quantity of allocation base units}}$$

$$= \frac{\$276,000}{4,800 \text{ machine-hours}}$$

$$= \$57.50 \text{ per machine-hour}$$

In manufacturing settings, the **denominator level** is commonly termed the **production denominator level** or the **production denominator volume**.

FIXED-OVERHEAD COST VARIANCES

The Level 1 static-budget variance for Webb's fixed manufacturing overhead is $9,000 U:

$$\text{Fixed-overhead static-budget variance} = \text{Actual results} - \text{Static-budget amount}$$

$$= \$285,000 - \$276,000$$

$$= \$9,000 \text{ U}$$

The actual results for fixed manufacturing overhead are in Exhibit 7-2 (p. 221). The static-budget amount for fixed manufacturing overhead is based on 12,000 output units. Given that it is for a fixed cost, this same $276,000 would be the budgeted amount for all output levels in the relevant range. There is no "flexing" of fixed costs.

The formula for the fixed manufacturing overhead flexible-budget variance is as follows:

$$\text{Fixed-overhead flexible-budget variance} = \text{Actual results} - \text{Flexible-budget amount}$$

$$= \$285,000 - \$276,000$$

$$= \$9,000 \text{ U}$$

The fixed-overhead flexible-budget variance is the same as the fixed-overhead static-budget variance. Why? Because there is no "flexing" of fixed costs. For Level 3 analysis (decomposing the flexible-budget variance into its efficiency and spending components), all of the flexible-budget variance is attributed to the spending variance because this is precisely why this variance arises for fixed costs.

The $9,000 unfavorable variance simply means that Webb spent more on fixed manufacturing overhead in April 19_7 than it budgeted.

A summary of the Levels 1, 2, and 3 variance analyses for Webb's fixed manufacturing overhead in April 19_7 is as follows:

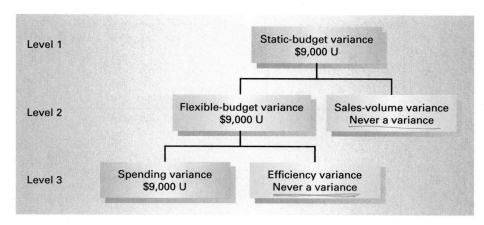

There is never a sales-volume variance in Level 2 for fixed-overhead costs. Why? Because budgeted fixed costs are, by definition, unaffected by sales-volume changes. Similarly, there is never an efficiency variance in Level 3 for fixed-overhead costs. After all, a manager cannot be more or less efficient in dealing with a given amount of fixed costs.

PRODUCTION-VOLUME VARIANCE

The variances discussed so far in this chapter are presented in Exhibit 8-3—Panel A for variable costs and the first three columns of Panel B for fixed costs. We now discuss a new variance for fixed-overhead costs (shown on the right-hand side of Ex-

EXHIBIT 8-3
Variance Analysis: Variable and Fixed Manufacturing Overhead for the Webb Company

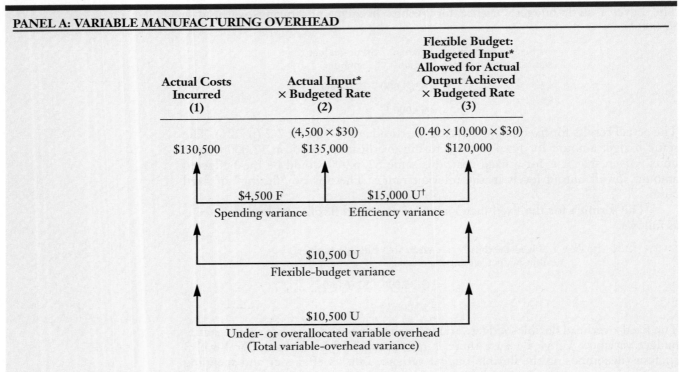

PANEL A: VARIABLE MANUFACTURING OVERHEAD

Actual Costs Incurred (1)	Actual Input* × Budgeted Rate (2)	Flexible Budget: Budgeted Input* Allowed for Actual Output Achieved × Budgeted Rate (3)
	(4,500 × $30)	(0.40 × 10,000 × $30)
$130,500	$135,000	$120,000

$4,500 F — Spending variance
$15,000 U† — Efficiency variance

$10,500 U — Flexible-budget variance

$10,500 U — Under- or overallocated variable overhead (Total variable-overhead variance)

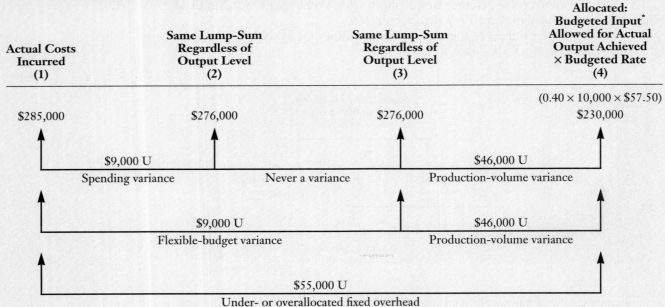

PANEL B: FIXED MANUFACTURING OVERHEAD

Actual Costs Incurred (1)	Same Lump-Sum Regardless of Output Level (2)	Same Lump-Sum Regardless of Output Level (3)	Allocated: Budgeted Input* Allowed for Actual Output Achieved × Budgeted Rate (4)
			(0.40 × 10,000 × $57.50)
$285,000	$276,000	$276,000	$230,000

$9,000 U — Spending variance
Never a variance
$46,000 U — Production-volume variance

$9,000 U — Flexible-budget variance
$46,000 U — Production-volume variance

$55,000 U — Under- or overallocated fixed overhead (Total fixed-overhead variance)

*For overhead costs, input refers to units of cost allocation base.
†F = favorable effect on operating income; U = unfavorable effect on operating income.

hibit 8-3, Panel B). The **production-volume variance** is the difference between budgeted fixed overhead and the fixed overhead allocated. Fixed overhead is allocated based on the budgeted fixed overhead rate times the budgeted quantity of the fixed-overhead allocation base for the actual output units achieved. Other terms for this variance include **denominator-level variance** and **output-level overhead variance.**

The formula for the production-volume variance, expressed in terms of allocation base units (machine-hours for Webb), is

$$\begin{array}{l}\text{Production-} \\ \text{volume} \\ \text{variance}\end{array} = \begin{array}{l}\text{Budgeted} \\ \text{fixed} \\ \text{overhead}\end{array} - \left(\begin{array}{l}\text{Fixed overhead allocated using} \\ \text{budgeted input allowed for} \\ \text{actual output units achieved}\end{array} \times \begin{array}{l}\text{Budgeted fixed} \\ \text{overhead rate}\end{array} \right)$$

$$= \$276,000 - (0.40 \times 10,000 \times \$57.50)$$

$$= \$276,000 - (4,000 \times \$57.50)$$

$$= \$276,000 - \$230,000$$

$$= \$46,000 \text{ U}$$

The amount used for budgeted fixed overhead will be the same lump sum shown in the static budget and also in any flexible budget within the relevant range. Fixed-overhead costs allocated is the sum of the individual fixed-overhead costs allocated to each of the products manufactured during the accounting period.

Panel A of Exhibit 8-3 does not have the column 4 shown for Panel B. Why? Because column 4 does not apply to variable-overhead costs. The amount of variable overhead allocated is always the same as the flexible-budget amount.

Interpreting the Production-Volume Variance

The production-volume variance arises whenever actual production differs from the denominator level used to calculate the budgeted fixed-overhead rate. We compute this rate because inventory costing and some types of contracts require fixed-overhead costs to be expressed on a unit-of-output basis. The production-volume variance results from "unitizing" fixed costs. Be careful not to attribute much economic significance to this variance. The most common misinterpretation is to assume this variance measures the economic cost of producing and selling 10,000 units rather than the 12,000 budgeted for April. This assumption does not consider why Webb sold only 10,000 units. Assume that a new competitor had gained market share by pricing below what Webb charged its customers. To sell the budgeted 12,000 units, Webb may have had to reduce its own selling price on all 12,000 units. Suppose it decided that selling 10,000 units at a higher price yielded higher operating income than selling 12,000 units at a lower price. The production-volume variance does not take into account such information. Hence, it would be misleading to interpret the $46,000 unfavorable amount as Webb's economic cost of selling 2,000 units less than budgeted quantity of 12,000 units for April.

OBJECTIVE 4

Give two reasons why the production-volume variance may not be a good measure of the opportunity cost of unused capacity

INTEGRATED ANALYSIS OF OVERHEAD COST VARIANCES

Exhibit 8-3 illustrates the four variances explained in this chapter. When all four variances are presented, it is called a 4-variance analysis.

OBJECTIVE 5

Explain how a 4-variance analysis can provide an integrated overview of overhead cost variances

4-Variance Analysis

	Spending Variance	Efficiency Variance	Production-Volume Variance
Variable Manufacturing Overhead	$4,500 F	$15,000 U	Never a variance
Fixed Manufacturing Overhead	$9,000 U	Never a variance	$46,000 U

FLEXIBLE BUDGETS, VARIANCES, AND MANAGEMENT CONTROL **263**

The four variances in this presentation are the two variable manufacturing overhead variances and the two fixed manufacturing overhead variances. Note also that there are two boxes showing "Never a variance." Why? The efficiency variance pertains only to variable manufacturing overhead. There can be no efficiency for fixed manufacturing overhead because this amount is a lump sum regardless of the output level. The production-volume variance pertains only to fixed manufacturing overhead. It arises because lump sum is required to be allocated to individual output units for inventory costing (and, in some cases, for contract reimbursement).

3-Variance Analysis

	Spending Variance	Efficiency Variance	Production-Volume Variance
Total Manufacturing Overhead	$4,500 U	$15,000 U	$46,000 U

The two spending variances from the 4-variance analysis have been combined in the 3-variance analysis. The only loss of information in the 3-variance analysis is the overhead spending variance area—only one spending variance is reported instead of separate variable- and fixed-overhead spending variances. 3-variance analysis is sometimes called **combined variance analysis,** because it combines variable- and fixed-cost variances when reporting overhead cost variances.

2-Variance Analysis

	Flexible-Budget Variance	Production-Volume Variance
Total Manufacturing Overhead	$19,500 U	$46,000 U

The spending and efficiency variances from the 3-variance analysis have been combined under the 2-variance analysis.

1-Variance Analysis

	Total Overhead Variance
Total Manufacturing Overhead	$65,500 U

The single variance of $65,500 U in 1-variance analysis is the sum of the flexible-budget variance and the production-volume variance under 2-variance analyses. Using figures from Exhibit 8-3, the total overhead variance is the difference between the total actual manufacturing overhead incurred ($130,500 + $285,000 = $415,500) and the manufacturing overhead allocated ($120,000 + $230,000 = $350,000) to the actual output units produced. The $65,500 unfavorable total manufacturing overhead variance for the Webb Company in April 19_7 is largely the result of the $46,000 unfavorable production-volume variance. Using the 4-variance analysis presentation, the next largest amount (after the $46,000) is the $15,000 unfavorable variable-overhead efficiency variance. This variance arises from the additional 500 machine-hours used in April 19_7 above the 4,000 machine-hours allowed to manufacture the 10,000 jackets. The two spending variances ($4,500 F and $9,000 U) partially offset each other.

The variances in Webb's 4-variance analysis are not necessarily independent of each other. For example, Webb may purchase lower-quality machine fluids (giving rise to a favorable spending variance); this results in the machines taking longer to operate than budgeted (giving rise to an unfavorable efficiency variance).

OVERHEAD COST VARIANCES IN NONMANUFACTURING SETTINGS

Our Webb Company example examines variable and fixed manufacturing overhead costs. Under generally accepted accounting principles, both variable and fixed manufacturing overhead costs are inventoriable costs for financial reporting purposes. In

Baxter Corporation Reduces Emphasis on Individual Variances as Independent Performance Measures

The Baxter Corporation manufactures sterile plastic bags for medical applications at its Lessines, Belgium, plant. It uses a standard costing system in which both variable and fixed costs are inventoried. For many years, performance reviews focused on individual variances as if they were independent of each other. The Baxter Corporation eventually concluded that this approach led managers to take actions that sometimes resulted in minimum variances being reported but did not necessarily promote its long-run interests.

Baxter now recognizes that interdependencies exist across variance. A key performance figure is the difference between the plant's output at standard costs (with all manufacturing costs inventoried) and actual costs. A detailed variance statement is reported each month, but managers are not held accountable for unfavorable variances that are offset by related favorable variances elsewhere. Thus, an unfavorable fixed-overhead spending variance due to an upgrading plant and equipment maintenance would not be considered in isolation of a favorable variable-overhead efficiency variance due to machines making the plastic bags at a faster rate with equivalent (or even higher) conformance to quality specifications.

Source: Discussions with management and E. Noreen, D. Smith, and J. Mackey, *The Theory of Constraints and Its Implication for Management Accounting* (Great Barrington, Ma.: North River Press, 1995).

contrast, the overhead costs of nonmanufacturing areas of the value chain (such as R&D and marketing) are not inventoriable costs under generally accepted accounting principles; they either are capitalized noninventoriable costs or are immediately expensed to the period in which they are incurred. Should the overhead costs of nonmanufacturing areas be examined using the variance analysis framework discussed in this chapter?

Variable-cost information pertaining to nonmanufacturing as well as manufacturing costs is used for pricing decisions and for decisions about which products to emphasize. Variance analysis of all variable-overhead costs is important when analyzing such decisions. For example, managers in industries with high distribution costs may invest in accounting systems that give reliable and timely information on spending and efficiency variances for variable distribution costs.

Variance analysis of fixed nonmanufacturing overhead costs is important where a company is doing work on a full-actual-cost-plus basis—that is, where it is reimbursed for its full actual costs plus an additional percentage of those costs. Here, information on these variances enables more accurate estimates of actual costs to be computed. In many other cases, however, managers do not conduct detailed variance analysis of fixed nonmanufacturing costs. Most believe little information is gained by computing spending or efficiency variances for these fixed nonmanufacturing costs.

OBJECTIVE 6

Explain the differing roles of cost allocation bases for fixed manufacturing overhead when (a) planning and controlling, and (b) inventory costing

DIFFERENT PURPOSES OF MANUFACTURING OVERHEAD COST ANALYSIS

Different types of cost analysis may be appropriate for different purposes. Consider the planning and control purpose and the inventory costing for financial reporting purpose. Panel A of Exhibit 8-4 depicts variable manufacturing overhead for each purpose; Panel B depicts fixed manufacturing overhead for each purpose.

EXHIBIT 8-4
Behavior of Variable and Fixed Manufacturing Overhead Costs for Planning and Control and for Inventory Costing

PANEL A: VARIABLE MANUFACTURING OVERHEAD COSTS

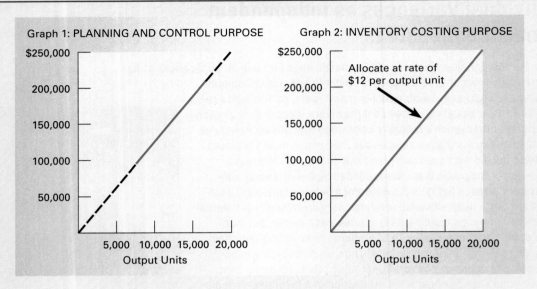

PANEL B: FIXED MANUFACTURING OVERHEAD COSTS

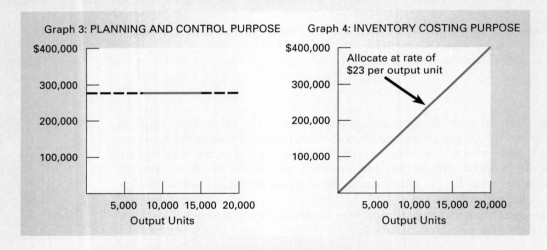

Variable Manufacturing Overhead Costs

Webb's variable manufacturing overhead is shown in Panel A of Exhibit 8-4 as being variable with respect to output units (jackets) produced for both the planning and control purpose (graph 1) and the inventory costing purpose (graph 2). The greater the number of output units manufactured, the higher the budgeted total variable manufacturing overhead costs and the higher the total variable manufacturing overhead costs allocated to output units.

Graph 1 of Exhibit 8-4 presents an overall picture of how total variable overhead might behave. Of course, variable overhead consists of many items, including energy costs, repairs, indirect labor, and so on. Managers help control variable overhead costs by budgeting each line item and then investigating possible causes for any significant variances.

Fixed Manufacturing Overhead Costs

Panel B of Exhibit 8-4 (graph 3) shows that for the planning and control purpose, fixed overhead costs do not change in the 8,000- to 16,000-unit output range. Consider a monthly leasing cost of $20,000 for a building under a 3-year leasing agreement. Managers control this fixed leasing cost at the time the lease is signed. During any month in the leasing period, management can do little to change this $20,000 lump-sum payment. Contrast this description of fixed overhead with how these costs are depicted for the inventory costing purpose, graph 4 of Panel B. Under generally accepted accounting principles, fixed manufacturing costs are capitalized as part of inventory on a unit-of-output basis. Every output unit that Webb manufactures will increase the fixed overhead allocated to products by $23 ($57.50 per machine-hour × 0.40 machine-hours per output unit). Managers should not use this unitization of fixed manufacturing overhead costs for their planning and control.

The denominator level in each graph in Exhibit 8-4 is expressed in output units produced. Alternatively, we could also have expressed this denominator in terms of input units. For Webb, machine-hours would be the chosen denominator, as this is the allocation base for both variable and fixed manufacturing overhead costs.

JOURNAL ENTRIES FOR OVERHEAD COSTS AND VARIANCES

Recording Overhead Costs

The Robinson Company job-costing example (Chapter 5, p. 132) used a single manufacturing overhead control account. This chapter illustrates separate variable and fixed manufacturing overhead control accounts. Each overhead control account requires its own overhead allocated account.

Consider the following journal entries for the Webb Company. Recall that for April 19_7,

	Actual Results	Flexible-Budget Amount (10,000 Units)	Allocated Amount
Variable manufacturing overhead	$130,500	$120,000*	$120,000*
Fixed manufacturing overhead	285,000	276,000†	230,000‡

*0.40 × 10,000 × $30 = $120,000
†$276,000 is the budgeted fixed manufacturing overhead.
‡0.40 × 10,000 × $57.50 = $230,000

The budgeted variable-overhead rate is $30 per machine-hour. The denominator level for fixed manufacturing overhead is 4,800 machine-hours of input with a budgeted rate of $57.50 per machine-hour. Webb uses 4-variance analysis.

During the accounting period, actual variable-overhead and actual fixed-overhead costs are accumulated in separate control accounts. As each unit is manufactured, the budgeted variable- and fixed-overhead rates are used to record the amounts in the respective overhead allocated accounts.

Entries for variable manufacturing overhead for April 19_7 are

1. Variable Manufacturing Overhead Control   130,500
       Accounts Payable Control and other accounts   130,500
      To record actual variable manufacturing overhead costs incurred.

2. Work in Process Control   120,000
       Variable Manufacturing Overhead Allocated   120,000
      To record variable manufacturing overhead cost allocated,
         (0.40 × 10,000 × $30).

3. Variable Manufacturing Overhead Allocated	120,000	
Variable Manufacturing Overhead Efficiency Variance	15,000	
Variable Manufacturing Overhead Control		130,500
Variable Manufacturing Overhead Spending Variance		4,500
To isolate variances for the accounting period.		

Entries for fixed manufacturing overhead are

1. Fixed Manufacturing Overhead Control	285,000	
Wage Payable, Accumulated Depreciation, etc.		285,000
To record actual fixed-overhead costs incurred.		
2. Work in Process Control	230,000	
Fixed Manufacturing Overhead Allocated		230,000
To record fixed manufacturing overhead costs allocated,		
($0.40 \times 10,000 \times \$57.50$).		
3. Fixed Manufacturing Overhead Allocated	230,000	
Fixed Manufacturing Overhead Spending Variance	9,000	
Fixed Manufacturing Production-Volume Variance	46,000	
Fixed Manufacturing Overhead Control		285,000
To isolate variances for the accounting period.		

The end-of-period adjustments for these variances are now discussed.

Overhead Variances and End-of-Period Adjustments

Chapter 5 (pp. 140–144) outlined the adjusted allocation rate approach and the pro-ration approach to handling the end-of-period difference between manufacturing overhead incurred and manufacturing overhead allocated. Consider Webb's variable manufacturing overhead. The budgeted rate was $30 per machine-hour. The actual rate is $29 per machine-hour.

Under the adjusted allocation rate approach, Webb would adjust the job record of every job worked on during the year. This adjustment, in effect, would entail using the actual rate per machine-hour of $29 instead of the budgeted rate of $30. Then, Webb would accordingly recompute the ending inventory and cost of goods sold for the accounting period. This approach has several benefits. Individual job records are restated to show actual costs accurately. Also, ending inventory and cost of goods sold would accurately show actual variable overhead incurred. A similar approach could be used to restate the fixed manufacturing overhead in job records. Providing all accounting records are on compatible computer systems, the adjusted allocation rate approach can often be done in a low-cost timely manner.

The proration approach is used where managers view the adjusted allocation rate approach as not being cost-effective. The three main options for disposing of variances under this approach are

♦ Proration based on the allocated overhead amount (before proration) in the ending balances of Inventory and Cost of Goods Sold.

♦ Proration based on total ending balances (before proration) in Inventory and Cost of Goods Sold.

♦ Immediate writeoff to Cost of Goods Sold.

OBJECTIVE 8

Explain why managers frequently use both financial and nonfinancial variables to plan and control overhead costs

Webb could use any one of these options when prorating the $10,500 of underallocated variable manufacturing overhead (and the $55,000 of underallocated fixed manufacturing overhead).

FINANCIAL AND NONFINANCIAL PERFORMANCE MEASURES

The overhead variances discussed in this chapter are examples of financial performance measures. Managers also find that nonfinancial measures provide useful information. Examples of such measures that Webb would likely find useful in planning and controlling its overhead costs are

1. Actual indirect materials usage in yards per machine-hour, compared to budgeted indirect materials usage in yards per machine-hour.

2. Actual energy usage per machine-hour, compared to budgeted energy usage per machine-hour.

3. Actual machining time per job, compared to budgeted machining time per job.

These performance measures, like the variances discussed in this chapter, are best viewed as attention directors, not problem solvers. These performance measures would probably be reported on the manufacturing floor on a daily, or even hourly, basis. The manufacturing overhead variances we discussed in this chapter capture the financial effects of items such as 1, 2, and 3, which in many cases first appear as nonfinancial performance "flags."

Both financial and nonfinancial performance measures are key inputs when evaluating the performance of managers. Exclusive reliance on either one is nearly always simplistic.

ACTUAL, NORMAL, EXTENDED-NORMAL, AND STANDARD COSTING

Chapter 4 presented three possible combinations of actual and budgeted direct-cost rates and actual and budgeted indirect-cost rates. Exhibit 8-5 presents these three costing systems along with a fourth system—**standard costing**—discussed in Chapters 7 and 8. Standard costing is a costing method that traces direct costs to a cost object by multiplying the standard price(s) or rate(s) times the standard inputs allowed for actual outputs achieved and allocates indirect costs on the basis of the standard indirect rate(s) times the standard inputs allowed for the actual outputs achieved.

With a standard costing system, the costs of every product or service planned to be worked on during that period can be computed at the start of that period. This feature enables a simplified recording system to be used. No record need be kept of the actual costs of items used or of the actual quantity of the cost allocation base used on individual products or services worked on during the period. Once standards have been set, the costs of operating a standard costing system can be low relative to an actual, normal, or extended-normal costing system. Appendix A to this chapter illustrates a standard costing system as well as how proration of variances can occur in that system.

EXHIBIT 8-5
Actual, Normal, Extended-Normal, and Standard Costing Methods

	Actual Costing	Normal Costing	Extended-Normal Costing	Standard Costing
Direct Costs	Actual direct price/rate × Actual quantity of direct cost input	Actual direct price/rate × Actual quantity of direct cost input	Budgeted direct price/rate × Actual quantity of direct cost input	Standard direct price/rate × Standard inputs allowed for actual outputs achieved
Overhead (Indirect) Costs	Actual indirect rate × Actual quantity of cost allocation base	Budgeted indirect rate × Actual quantity of cost allocation base	Budgeted indirect rate × Actual quantity of cost allocation base	Standard indirect rate × Standard inputs allowed for actual outputs achieved

PROBLEM

The Webb Company is analyzing its marketing overhead costs. It uses a 4-variance analysis of its marketing overhead costs. The following information was collected for April 19_7.

a. Variable marketing overhead is allocated to products using budgeted direct marketing labor-hours per jacket. Fixed marketing overhead is allocated to products on a per jacket basis.

b. Budgeted amounts for April 19_7 are
  - (i)   Direct marketing labor-hours: 0.25 hours per jacket
  - (ii) Variable marketing overhead rate: $20 per direct marketing labor-hour
  - (iii) Fixed marketing overhead: $434,000
  - (iv) Output, which is used as the denominator level of output: 12,000 jackets

c. Actual results for April 19_7 are
  - (i)   Variable marketing overhead: $45,700
  - (ii) Fixed marketing overhead: $420,000
  - (iii) Direct marketing labor-hours: 2,304
  - (iv) Actual output: 10,000 jackets

REQUIRED

1. Present an analysis of the April 19_7 marketing overhead costs using the format shown in both panels of Exhibit 8-3.

2. Provide at least one possible explanation for each of the variances in Webb's 4-variance analysis of its marketing overhead costs.

3. Describe how the Webb Company might plan and control (a) its variable marketing overhead costs, and (b) its fixed marketing overhead costs.

SOLUTION

1. Exhibit 8-6 is the columnar presentation of variances. The budgeted fixed marketing overhead rate is $36.1667 (rounded) per jacket. These variances can be summarized as follows:

	Spending Variance	Efficiency Variance	Production-Volume Variance
Variable Marketing Overhead	$380 F	$3,920 F	Never a variance
Fixed Marketing Overhead	$14,000 F	Never a variance	$58,333 U

2. *Variable marketing overhead spending variance* ($380 F). The reasons for this variance include

  a. Lower-than-expected prices for line items in the variable marketing overhead budget, such as lower wage rates for marketing support staff, lower prices for long-distance phone calls, and lower prices for gasoline used by salespeople.

  b. Lower-than-expected usage of line items in the variable marketing overhead budget, such as fewer marketing support staff, fewer long-distance phone calls, and fewer gallons of gasoline per direct marketing labor-hour.

Variable marketing overhead efficiency variance ($3,920 F). The reason for this variance is more productive use of the cost allocation base (direct marketing labor-hours); 2,304 direct marketing labor-hours were used, compared with a budgeted 2,500 hours. Perhaps marketing personnel classified as direct labor were more efficient, maybe because of a new incentive plan, a better training program, or greater-than-expected continuous improvement.

EXHIBIT 8-6
Variance Analysis: Variable and Fixed Marketing Overhead for the Webb Company

PANEL A: VARIABLE MARKETING OVERHEAD

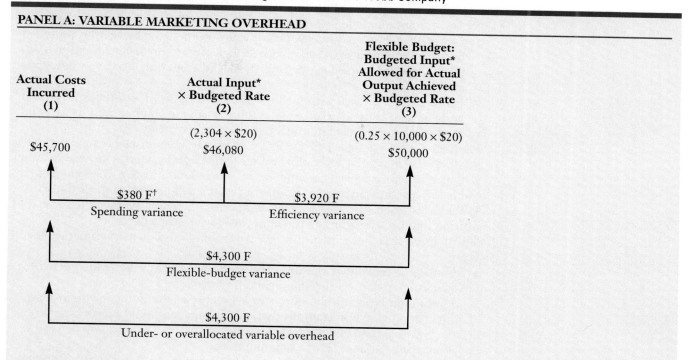

Actual Costs Incurred (1)	Actual Input* × Budgeted Rate (2)	Flexible Budget: Budgeted Input* Allowed for Actual Output Achieved × Budgeted Rate (3)
$45,700	(2,304 × $20) $46,080	(0.25 × 10,000 × $20) $50,000

$380 F† $3,920 F
Spending variance   Efficiency variance

$4,300 F
Flexible-budget variance

$4,300 F
Under- or overallocated variable overhead

PANEL B: FIXED MARKETING OVERHEAD

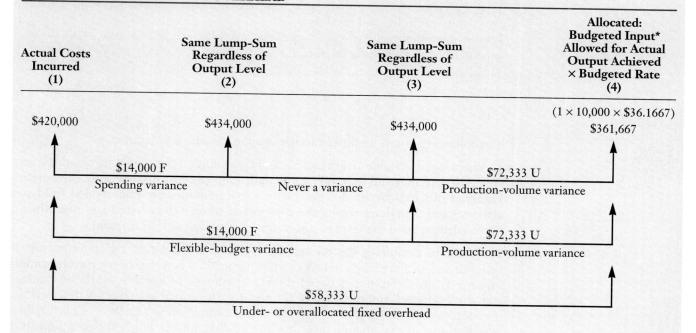

Actual Costs Incurred (1)	Same Lump-Sum Regardless of Output Level (2)	Same Lump-Sum Regardless of Output Level (3)	Allocated: Budgeted Input* Allowed for Actual Output Achieved × Budgeted Rate (4)
$420,000	$434,000	$434,000	(1 × 10,000 × $36.1667) $361,667

$14,000 F $72,333 U
Spending variance   Never a variance   Production-volume variance

$14,000 F $72,333 U
Flexible-budget variance   Production-volume variance

$58,333 U
Under- or overallocated fixed overhead

*For overhead costs, input refers to units of cost allocation base.
†F = favorable effect on operating income; U = unfavorable effect on operating income.

Fixed marketing overhead spending variance ($14,000 F). The possible reasons for this variance include

    a. Lower-than-expected prices for line items in the fixed marketing overhead budget. Perhaps a marketing department supervisor resigned and was replaced by a lower-paid supervisor, or maybe a building lease was renegotiated at a lower-than-budgeted amount.

    b. Lower-than-expected usage of line items in the fixed marketing overhead budget, such as the marketing sales force leasing five rather than six cars and thus reducing the fixed monthly auto-leasing payment.

Production-volume variance ($72,333 U). This variance arises because the output level (sales) was 10,000 jackets rather than 12,000 jackets. One explanation is that marketing sales personnel were much less effective than budgeted. Other explanations include a downturn in the economy, poor-quality work at Webb's manufacturing plant, a new competitor entering the market, and a reduction in tariffs, resulting in the import of lower-cost jackets.

3. The main approaches to planning and controlling variable marketing overhead costs are

    a. Working creatively at the design stage to avoid nonvalue-added activities (for example, double-checking marketing mailings).

    b. Working on reducing the rate per cost driver or the number of cost driver units per output. For example, marketing managers could exert tighter control over the price of department purchases.

    c. Monitoring variances on an ongoing basis.

    d. Assigning responsibilities for the marketing variance to managers who will promote the productivity of the marketing staff.

4. The main approaches to planning and controlling fixed marketing overhead costs are

    a. Planning capacity needs in detail, including providing incentives for managers to estimate their budgeted usage in an unbiased way.

    b. Having marketing managers make careful, cost-conscious planning decisions on individual line items.

Day-to-day monitoring of variances is likely to play a relatively minor role in the control of fixed marketing overhead costs.

SUMMARY

The following points are linked to the chapter's learning objectives.

1. Planning of variable-overhead costs involves undertaking only value-added variable-cost activities and then efficiently managing the cost drivers of those activities. Planning of fixed-overhead costs includes undertaking only value-added fixed-cost activities and then determining the appropriate level of those activities, given the expected demand and the level of uncertainty pertaining to that demand.

2. When the flexible budget for variable overhead is developed, a spending overhead variance and an efficiency variance can be computed. The variable-overhead spending variance is the difference between the actual amount of variable overhead incurred and the budgeted amount that is allowed for the actual quantity of the variable-overhead allocation base used for the actual output units achieved. The variable-overhead efficiency variance measures the efficiency with which the cost allocation base is used; this is a different type of efficiency variance than that calculated in Chapter 7 for direct-cost items, such as direct materials.

3. The budgeted fixed-overhead rate is calculated by dividing the budgeted fixed-overhead costs by the budgeted quantity of allocation base units. This rate is calculated for inventory costing and, in some cases, for contract reimbursement.

4. Production-volume variances are rarely a good measure of the opportunity cost of unused capacity. For example, the plant capacity level may exceed the budgeted level; hence, some unused capacity may not be included in the denominator. Moreover, the production-volume variance focuses only on costs. It does not take into account any price changes necessary to spur extra demand that would in turn make use of any idle capacity.

5. A 4-variance analysis presents spending and efficiency variances for variable-overhead costs and spending and production-volume variances for fixed-overhead costs. By analyzing these four variances together, managers can consider possible interrelationships among them. These variances collectively measure differences between actual and budgeted amounts for output level, selling prices, variable costs, and fixed costs.

6. For planning and control, fixed manufacturing overhead is a lump sum that is unaffected by the budgeted quantity of the fixed-overhead allocation base. In contrast, for inventory costing the unitized fixed manufacturing overhead rate will be affected by the budgeted quantity of the fixed-overhead allocation base.

7. The separate analysis of variable- and fixed-overhead costs requires the use of separate variable- and fixed-overhead control accounts and separate variable- and fixed-overhead allocated accounts. At the end of each accounting period, any variances for variable- or fixed-overhead costs can be disposed as illustrated in Chapter 5.

8. Managers use both financial and nonfinancial measures to plan and control overhead costs. In many cases, overhead variances initially appear as nonfinancial measures. Expressing these measures in financial terms can highlight the relative importance of different types of nonfinancial performance gaps.

APPENDIX A: PRORATION OF MANUFACTURING VARIANCES USING STANDARD COSTS

This appendix explores the proration of variances in a standard costing system. We also illustrate how the proration approach discussed in Chapter 5 (pp. 142–143) can be refined by a more detailed analysis of direct materials price variances.

The Morales Company makes one uniform product, a specialty plastic container. The company uses a standard costing system. Both variable and fixed manufacturing costs are inventoried. Morales distributes monthly income statements to its internal managers. The following results pertain to October 19_7. (To keep the calculations manageable, the following numbers are deliberately small.)

Direct materials purchased (charged to Materials Control at standard prices):	
200,000 pounds × $0.50	$100,000
Direct materials price variance: 200,000 pounds × $0.05	10,000 U
Direct materials, assigned at standard prices: 160,000 pounds × $0.50	80,000
Direct materials efficiency variance: 8,000 pounds × $0.50	4,000 U
Direct manufacturing labor costs incurred: 2,200 hours × $20.4545	45,000
Direct manufacturing labor costs, assigned at standard rate:	
2,000 hours × $20.00	40,000
Direct manufacturing labor price variance: 2,200 hours × $0.4545	1,000 U
Direct manufacturing labor efficiency variance: 200 hours × $20.00	4,000 U
Manufacturing overhead allocated: At budgeted rate per machine-hour	70,000
Manufacturing overhead incurred	75,000
Underallocated manufacturing overhead	5,000
Revenues	273,000
Marketing, distribution, and customer-service costs	130,000

Materials price variances are measured when the material is purchased rather than when it is used.

Assume that 40% of the October 19_7 production is in the ending inventory of finished goods and that 60% of the October production has been sold in that month. There is no ending work in process on October 31, 19_7. All manufacturing variances are unfavorable. There were no beginning inventories on October 1, 19_7. There were no variances for marketing, distribution, and customer-service costs. The following account balances (before proration) at the end of the month are based on the previous data:

	Dollars	Percentage
Work in process	$ 0	0%
Finished goods, 40% of the total standard manufacturing costs assigned for direct materials, direct manufacturing labor, and manufacturing overhead ($80,000 + $40,000 + $70,000): 40% of $190,000	76,000	40
Cost of goods sold, 60% of $190,000	114,000	60
Total	$190,000	100%

Morales purchases 200,000 pounds of direct materials, of which 160,000 pounds is the standard amount used for October's production. The standard amounts of direct materials in ending work in process, ending finished goods, and cost of goods sold in October are 0 pounds (0% × 160,000), 64,000 pounds (40% × 160,000), and 96,000 pounds (60% × 160,000), respectively. Given purchases of 200,000 pounds, standard usage in production of 160,000 pounds, and an unfavorable direct materials efficiency quantity of 8,000 pounds, there are 32,000 pounds in ending direct materials inventory:

	Pounds	Total Costs at $0.50 Standard Cost per Pound	Percentage
To account for	200,000	$100,000	100%
Now present in:			
Direct materials efficiency variance	8,000	$ 4,000	4%
Work in process	0	0	0
Finished goods	64,000	32,000	32
Cost of goods sold	96,000	48,000	48
Remainder, in direct materials inventory	32,000	16,000	16
Accounted for	200,000	$100,000	100%

Management is considering two different approaches to handling end-of-period accounting variances:

1. Prorate direct manufacturing labor and manufacturing overhead variances based on the total end-of-period account balances of Work in Process, Finished Goods, and Cost of Goods Sold. The proration of direct materials variances is based on the total end-of-period account balances of Direct Materials, Work in Process, Finished Goods, and Cost of Goods Sold.

2. Immediately write off any end-of-period account balances to Cost of Goods Sold. What effect does each approach have on operating income for October 19_7?

Proration of Direct Manufacturing Labor and Manufacturing Overhead Variances

We will present the analysis using T-accounts. The following entries are numbered in accordance with the logical flow of the amounts through the accounts for direct manufacturing labor and manufacturing overhead.

Work in Process

① Direct manufac- turing labor	40,000	③ Transferred*	110,000
② Manufacturing over- head allocated	70,000		

Finished Goods

③	110,000	④ Sold†	66,000

Cost of Goods Sold

④	66,000

Manufacturing Overhead Control

⑤ Incurred	75,000

Manufacturing Overhead Allocated

	②	70,000

Direct Manufacturing Labor Price Variance

①	1,000

Cash, Current Liabilities, etc.

	① Direct manufac- turing labor	45,000
	⑤ Manufacturing overhead	75,000

Direct Manufacturing Labor Efficiency Variance

①	4,000

*Transferred as a part of the total standard costs transferred; direct manufacturing labor of $40,000 + manufacturing overhead allocated of $70,000 = $110,000.
†Sixty percent of $110,000.

In our example, there is a zero ending Work in Process balance. Finished Goods in ending inventory represents 40% of total manufacturing costs, and Cost of Goods Sold, 60%. All direct manufacturing labor and manufacturing overhead variances may be prorated accordingly. See the final three prorations in Exhibit 8-7.

	Total Variance	Work in Process 0%	Finished Goods 40%	Cost of Goods Sold 60%
Direct manufacturing labor price variance	$ 1,000 U	$0	$ 400	$ 600
Direct manufacturing labor efficiency variance	4,000 U	0	1,600	2,400
Manufacturing overhead variance	5,000 U	0	2,000	3,000
Totals	$10,000 U	$0	$4,000	$6,000

EXHIBIT 8-7
Comprehensive Schedule of Proration of Variances for the Morales Company for October 19_7 (All Manufacturing Variances Are Unfavorable)

Type of Variance	Total Variance (1)	To Direct Materials Inventory (2)	To Direct Materials Efficiency Variance (3)	To Work in Process (4)	To Finished Goods (5)	To Cost of Goods Sold (6)
Direct materials price	$10,000*	$1,600	$ 400	$0	$3,200	$ 4,800
Direct materials efficiency						
Balance before proration	4,000		4,000			
Balance after proration			$4,400†	0	1,760	2,640
Direct manufacturing labor price	1,000†			0	400	600
Direct manufacturing labor efficiency	4,000†			0	1,600	2,400
Manufacturing overhead	5,000†			0	2,000	3,000
Total variances prorated	$24,000	$1,600		$0	$8,960	$13,440
*Percentage used for proration	100%	16%	4%	0%	32%	48%
†Percentage used for proration	100%			0%	40%	60%

For simplicity, the manufacturing overhead variance of $5,000 has not been subdivided into spending, efficiency, or production-volume variances.

Based on the proration of these variances, the following journal entry would be made:

Finished goods	4,000	
Cost of goods sold	6,000	
Manufacturing overhead allocated	70,000	
Direct manufacturing labor price variance		1,000
Direct manufacturing labor efficiency variance		4,000
Manufacturing overhead control		75,000

Proration of Direct Materials Variances

Direct materials is inventoried when purchased. In contrast, other manufacturing costs are not inventoried until used. This difference requires an extra step when prorating direct materials variances (assuming that materials price variances are measured when the material is purchased rather than when it is used). Some key T-accounts regarding the flow of the direct materials cost (only) through the accounts are as follows:

Direct Materials Inventory					Work in Process*			
① Purchased	100,000	② Used	84,000		②	80,000	③ Transferred*	80,000

Finished Goods*					Cost of Goods Sold*		
③	80,000	④ Sold†	48,000		④	48,000	
Balance	32,000						

Accounts Payable				Direct Materials Price Variance		
		110,000		①	10,000	

				Direct Materials Efficiency Variance		
				②	4,000	

*Direct materials cost component only; standard cost of direct materials in cost of goods sold is $48,000 (96,000 pounds × $0.50 standard cost per pound).
†Transferred as a part of the total standard costs transferred.

The most complex proration is the direct materials price variance. To be most accurate, its proration in our illustration should be traced at $10,000 ÷ 200,000 = $0.05 per pound to wherever the 200,000 pounds have been charged at standard cost. The pounds are not only in Work in Process, Finished Goods, and Cost of Goods Sold. They are also in Direct Materials Inventory and in the Direct Materials Input-Efficiency Variance accounts. Hence, we begin with a proration of the materials input-price variance to five accounts, using the percentages shown for direct materials in the Morales data (p. 274).

	%	
Direct material price variance		$10,000
Allocated to:		
Direct materials efficiency variance	4	$ 400
Work in process inventory	0	0
Finished goods inventory	32	3,200
Cost of goods sold	48	4,800
Direct materials inventories	16	1,600
Total allocated	100	$10,000

The following journal entry prorates the direct materials input-price variance:

Direct materials efficiency variance	400	
Finished goods	3,200	
Cost of goods sold	4,800	
Direct materials inventory	1,600	
Direct materials price variance		$10,000

After the proration of the direct materials price variance is posted, the Direct Materials Efficiency Variance account will be as follows:

Direct Materials Efficiency Variance

Balance before proration	4,000
Proration of unfavorable direct materials	
price variance	400
Balance after proration	4,400

In turn, the direct materials efficiency variance after proration is allocated to

Work in process inventory, 0%	$ 0
Finished goods inventory, 40%	1,760
Cost of goods sold, 60%	2,640
Total allocated	$4,400

The following journal entry prorates the direct materials efficiency variance:

Finished goods	1,760	
Cost of goods sold	2,640	
Direct materials efficiency variance		4,400

Exhibit 8-7 is a comprehensive schedule of all the variance prorations explained here. The T-accounts for inventories and cost of goods sold after proration are as follows:

Direct Materials Inventory					Work in Process			
Purchased	100,000	Used	84,000		Direct materials	80,000	Transferred	190,000
Proration of direct					Direct manufacturing			
materials price					labor	40,000		
variance	1,600				Manufacturing over-			
					head allocated	70,000		
Balance	17,600							

Finished Goods					Cost of Goods Sold		
Transferred	190,000	Sold	114,000		Sold	114,000	
Proration of direct					Proration of direct		
manufacturing					manufacturing		
labor and manufac-					labor and manufac-		
turing overhead					turing overhead		
variances	4,000				variances	6,000	
Proration of direct					Proration of direct		
materials price					materials price		
variance	3,200				variance	4,800	
Proration of direct					Proration of direct		
materials effi-					materials effi-		
ciency variance	1,760				ciency variance	2,640	
Balance	84,960				Balance	127,440	

EXHIBIT 8-8
Effects of Disposal of Manufacturing Variances on Operating Income for the Morales Company for October 19_7

	Standard Absorption Costing	
	All Variances Cost of Goods Sold	Variance Proration
Sales	$273,000	$273,000
Cost of goods sold (at standard costs)	114,000	114,000
Gross margin (at standard costs)	159,000	159,000
Total variances (from column 1, Exhibit 8-7)	24,000	0
Prorated variances (from column 6, Exhibit 8-7)	0	13,440
Gross margin	135,000	145,560
Marketing, distribution, and customer-service costs	130,000	130,000
Operating income	$ 5,000	$ 15,560

Exhibit 8-8 compares how immediate write-off and proration affect operating income. All the variances are unfavorable, so an immediate writing off to cost of goods sold reduces operating income by $24,000. When prorated, however, the variances reduce income by only $13,440. The difference between these two approaches—$10,560—is the difference in the operating income amounts. Immediately writing off all the variance to cost of goods sold will result in operating income of $5,000; prorating the variances will result in operating income of $15,560. Managers at Morales are likely very interested in these differences, especially if operating income is used as one of their performance measures.

Alternative Views on Proration

Accountants who support proration of variances among end-of-period account balances frequently view the method as a means of approximating the actual costs, which are assumed to be the most accurate costs to report. An alternative viewpoint is that actual costs are not the appropriate costs to report in a balance sheet for inventories. For example, with proration, an unfavorable materials efficiency variance is treated as a capitalized inventoriable cost even though that variance may be due to poor work or inadequate maintenance of plant and equipment. Advocates of writing off all variances to cost of goods sold typically argue that standard costs best represent the appropriate cost for an inventory asset item in a balance sheet.

Generally accepted accounting principles and income tax laws typically require that financial statements show actual costs, not standard costs, of inventories and cost of goods sold. Consequently, proration of manufacturing variances is required if it results in a material change in inventories or operating income.

APPENDIX B: ENGINEERED, DISCRETIONARY, AND INFRASTRUCTURE COSTS

From a planning and control standpoint, managers often find it useful to classify costs in general, and overhead costs in particular, into three main categories—engineered, discretionary, and infrastructure.

◆ **Engineered costs** result specifically from a clear cause-and-effect relationship between costs and output. In the Webb Company example, direct materials and direct manufacturing labor are examples of engineered direct costs, while energy, indirect materials, and indirect support labor are examples of engineered overhead costs. Each of these costs increases in a specific way as the units manufactured (jackets) increase. Consider, in particular, the costs of leasing machines (p. 255). This is a fixed cost in the short run, but it is also an example of an engineered cost. Why? Because, over time, there is a clear cause-and-effect relationship between output, machine-hours of capacity required, and machine leasing costs. Thus, engineered costs can be variable or fixed costs.

◆ **Discretionary costs** have two important features: (1) They arise from periodic (usually yearly) decisions regarding the maximum outlay to be incurred, and (2) they have no clearly measurable cause-and-effect relationship between costs and outputs. There is often a delay between the acquisition of a resource and its eventual use. Examples of discretionary costs include advertising, executive training, R&D, health care, and management consulting, and corporate staff department costs such as legal, human resources, and public relations. The most noteworthy aspect of discretionary costs is that managers are seldom confident that the "correct" amounts are being spent. The founder of Lever Brothers, an international consumer-products company, once noted, "Half the money I spend on advertising is wasted; the trouble is, I don't know which half."

◆ **Infrastructure costs** arise from having property, plant and equipment, and a functioning organization. Examples are depreciation, long-run lease rental, and the acquisition of long-run technical capabilities. The time period between when infrastructure costs are committed to and acquired and when they are eventually used is very long. Careful long-range planning, rather than day-to-day monitoring, is the key to managing infrastructure costs. Frequently, there is also a high level of uncertainty about the outputs (cash inflows) resulting from the capital-expenditure decisions.

This chapter has focused almost exclusively on engineered costs, not on discretionary or infrastructure costs. Chapters 22 and 23 outline the formal decision models (such as discounted cash flow) that managers use in making choices about infrastructure costs. This appendix examines the differences that arise in planning and control methods when overhead costs are classified as either discretionary or engineered.

Relationships between Inputs and Outputs

Engineered costs differ from discretionary costs along two key dimensions: the type of process and the level of uncertainty. Engineered overhead costs describe processes that are detailed, physically observable, and repetitive, such as shipping activity. In contrast, discretionary overhead costs are associated with processes that are sometimes called *black boxes*. Managers are unsure about what is the "right" amount of discretionary costs. For example, the process relating advertising costs to output is sketchy and not well understood.

Uncertainty refers to the possibility that an actual amount will deviate from an expected amount. The higher the level of uncertainty about the relationship between inputs and outputs, the less likely a cause-and-effect relationship will exist, leading the cost to be classified as a discretionary cost. Advertising costs have an uncertain effect on output because other factors such as overall market conditions, competitors' reactions, and new product introductions also affect output. In contrast, there is a low level of uncertainty about the effect of output on shipping costs because other factors do not affect this relationship. As output levels change, a company adjusts its shipping activity (for example, batches delivered) and shipping costs to the change. Uncertainty is greater in the case of discretionary costs such as advertising and R&D because, in most cases, these costs are incurred well before any output is realized. Exhibit 8-9 summarizes these key distinctions between engineered and discretionary costs.

The presence or absence of a cause-and-effect relationship between inputs (activities and costs) and outputs has a significant influence on the planning and control techniques used to manage engineered and discretionary overhead costs. Planning and control for engineered overhead costs can be done effectively by analyzing activities using *work-measurement* methods. These techniques are unsuitable for discretionary overhead costs, and companies use other techniques such as *negotiated static budgets* to manage these costs.

EXHIBIT 8-9
Differences between Engineered and Discretionary Costs

	Engineered Costs	**Discretionary Costs**
1. Process or activity	a. Detailed and physically observable	a. Black box (knowledge of process is sketchy or unavailable)
	b. Repetitive	b. Nonrepetitive or nonroutine
2. Level of uncertainty	Moderate or small (shipping or manufacturing settings)	Great (R&D or advertising settings)

Source: This exhibit is a modification of one suggested by H. Itami.

Work Measurement and Engineered Costs

Work measurement is the careful analysis of a task, its size, the method used in its performance, and the efficiency with which it is performed. The objective of work measurement is to determine the workload in an operation and the number of workers needed to perform that work efficiently. It is ideally suited for measuring the cause-and-effect relationships of engineered costs.

Work-measurement techniques include the following:[1]

◆ *Micromotion study.* Film or videotape records of what a job entails and how long it takes. This technique is used most frequently in studying high-volume settings, for example, to establish the relationship between activities and output of the distribution center.

◆ *Work sampling.* A large number of random observations on output and activity levels are made of the job. These observations are used to determine the number and type of steps for the job in its *normal* operating mode.

Dayton-Hudson, a U.S. retailer, is an enthusiastic advocate of work-measurement techniques. This company measures cartons handled, invoices processed, and store items ticketed on a per hour basis. Productivity programs in its administrative and distribution areas have been aided by detailed work measures.

By relating output to costs, work measurement analysis results in standard costs per output unit. These standards can then be used to control engineered costs by calculating flexible budgets (in the case of variable engineered costs) and absorbed costs (in the case of fixed engineered costs) for the actual output achieved. Comparing the flexible budget to actual performance results in prompt feedback for control. Work measurement also provides nonfinancial benchmarks, for example, by monitoring packing and shipping time per unit of output.

Negotiated Static Budgets and Discretionary Costs

A **negotiated static budget** is a budget that establishes a fixed amount of costs through negotiations before the start of a budget period. As in the case of all static budgets, negotiated static budgets are not adjusted after they are set, regardless of changes in the level of output. This is an important aspect of planning and control of discretionary costs because these costs bear no cause-and-effect relationship to output. Senior management recognizes that discretionary overhead costs run the risk of earning a low return. They exercise control over these costs through careful scrutiny of the budget.

Companies use three basic approaches to determining a negotiated static budget:

Ordinary incremental budgets consider the previous period's budget and actual results as well as expectations for the new period to determine the budget for the current period. For instance, a budget for a research department might be increased because of salary raises, the addition of personnel, or the introduction of a new project.

[1]For an extensive discussion of the subject, see R. Failing, J. Janzen, and L. Blevins, *Improving Productivity Through Work Measurement: A Cooperative Approach* (New York: AICPA, 1988).

Priority incremental budgets are ordinary incremental budgets that include a description of incremental changes if the budget were increased or decreased by, say, 10%. For example, a university sports department may decide that if its budget is cut by 10%, it will drop scholarships for sports that do not attract large numbers of spectators. The budget explicitly forces a manager and his or her superiors to establish priorities.

Zero-base budgeting (ZBB) is budgeting from the ground up, as though the budget were being prepared for the first time. Every proposed expenditure comes under review. ZBB requires managers to rank objectives, operations, and activities; to explore alternative means of conducting each activity; and to determine activity costs. Consequently, it requires much more extensive work than other forms of budgeting. ZBB forces managers to better justify their outlays on a more regular and a more systematic basis.

Most firms use ordinary incremental or priority incremental budgets on an annual basis. To the extent that zero-base budgeting is undertaken, it is generally used on a less regular basis and for only a subset of responsibility centers or departments at any one time.

Variance Analysis for Engineered and Discretionary Overhead Costs

When budgeting for engineered overhead costs, managers use work measurement, flexible budgets, and allocated fixed costs to cost output. In contrast, the negotiated static-budgets process for discretionary costs often treats those costs as fixed. This leads to differences in calculating overhead variances.

Assume that Family Farm employs five people (called customer representatives) to process orders for its mail-order catalog business. Each employee earns a budgeted amount of $1,800 per month and should, if operating efficiently, process 1,000 orders per month. The planning and control decision is how many customer-order personnel to hire and then how to control personnel resources effectively and efficiently. In June, Family Farm processed 4,700 individual orders. Actual costs were $9,300.

Variance Analysis Assuming Customer-Order Payroll Costs Are Engineered Overhead Costs The engineered-cost approach to control of customer-order payroll costs is exactly as described in this chapter. A budgeted cost rate of $1.80 per order is calculated based on the cause-and-effect relationship between the $1,800 per month that each employee earns and the 1,000 orders each employee is expected to process each month ($1,800 ÷ 1,000 = $1.80). Therefore, the allocated costs for the actual number of orders processed is $8,460 (4,700 × $1.80). The following performance report would be prepared (exactly as in Exhibit 8-3):

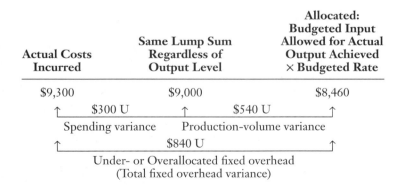

Actual Costs Incurred	Same Lump Sum Regardless of Output Level	Allocated: Budgeted Input Allowed for Actual Output Achieved × Budgeted Rate
$9,300	$9,000	$8,460

↑ $300 U ↑ $540 U ↑
Spending variance Production-volume variance
↑ $840 U ↑
Under- or Overallocated fixed overhead
(Total fixed overhead variance)

Exhibit 8-10 (left graph) shows the variance analysis of the engineered-cost approach. It is similar to Exhibit 8-4, Panel B, except that there are many levels of fixed costs. Note also that as in Exhibit 8-4, Panel B, the allocated cost line on the engineered-cost graph in Exhibit 8-10 is purely variable, even though the budgeted costs are actually incurred in steps.

EXHIBIT 8-10
Comparison of the Engineered-Cost and Discretionary-Cost Approaches at Family Farm

	Engineered-Cost Approach	Discretionary-Cost Approach
Budgeted costs	$9,000	$9,000
Allocated costs	8,460*	9,000
Production-volume variance	540 U	0

*Rate = $1,800 ÷ 1,000 orders = $1.80 per order. Total = 4,700 orders × $1.80 per order = $8,460.

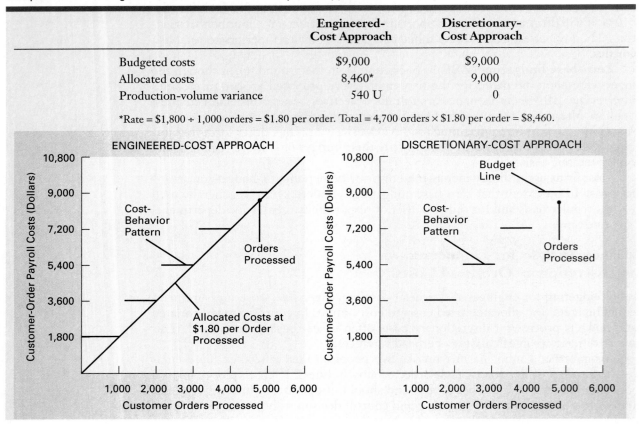

The production-volume variance of $540 U alerts management to the possibilities of overstaffing and unused capacity. The step of the cost-behavior pattern from $7,200 to $9,000 on the graph in Exhibit 8-10 was only partially utilized. The workload capability was 5,000 customer orders, in contrast to the 4,700 actually processed. The spending variance of $300 U indicates additional costs incurred perhaps because of higher wage rates paid to customer representatives or due to inefficiencies.

Variance Analysis Assuming Customer-Order Payroll Costs Are Discretionary Overhead Costs The budget line in the discretionary-cost approach in Exhibit 8-10 is flat from 4,000 to 5,000 customer orders. Why? Because discretionary costs imply the absence of a cause-and-effect relation between costs and output that can be approximated by a budgeted cost rate. This also means that we cannot determine allocated costs for the actual number of orders processed as we did in the case of engineered costs. The production-volume variance is therefore $0, because we cannot tell what, if any, capacity is unutilized between 4,000 and 5,000 customer orders. The spending variance is $300 U as in the case of engineered costs.

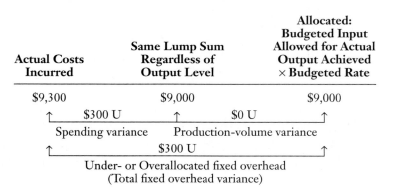

Looking at the right-hand graph of Exhibit 8-10 provides no insight into how to control costs between 4,000 and 5,000 customer orders processed. The primary means of control with a discretionary-cost approach is personal observation. That is, the department manager uses his or her experience to judge the size of the work force needed to carry out the department's functions. Occasional peak loads are often met by hiring temporary workers or by having the regular employees work overtime.

Finally, note that managers enjoy some discretion in classifying costs as engineered or discretionary. The classification is affected by attitudes toward how costs should be managed. Where good cost drivers for overhead costs exist, managers generally prefer the engineered-cost approach because it provides more information about resources utilized and unused capacity (as represented by the production-volume variance). As with all cost accounting methods, however, the choice is affected by executives' predictions about the technique's impact on operating decisions throughout the organization.

TERMS TO LEARN

This chapter and the Glossary at the end of this book contain definitions of the following important terms:

combined variance analysis (p. 264)
denominator-level (261)
denominator-level variance (263)
discretionary costs (279)
engineered costs (278)
infrastructure costs (279)
negotiated static budget (280)
nonvalue-added cost (254)
ordinary incremental budgets (280)
output-level overhead variance (263)
priority incremental budgets (281)
production denominator level (261)

production denominator volume (261)
production-volume variance (263)
standard costing (269)
value-added cost (254)
variable-overhead efficiency variance (258)
variable-overhead spending variance (259)
work measurement (280)
zero-based budgeting (ZBB) (281)

ASSIGNMENT MATERIAL

QUESTIONS

8-1 What are the steps in planning variable-overhead costs?

8-2 How does the planning of fixed-overhead costs differ from the planning of variable-overhead costs?

8-3 What are the steps in developing a budgeted variable-overhead cost rate?

8-4 Budgeting for variable manufacturing overhead requires a knowledge of cost drivers. Name three possible cost drivers.

8-5 Both financial and nonfinancial measures are used to control variable manufacturing overhead. Give two examples of each type of measure.

8-6 The spending variance for variable manufacturing overhead is affected by several factors. Explain.

8-7 Assume variable manufacturing overhead is allocated using machine-hours. Give three possible reasons for a $25,000 favorable variable-overhead efficiency variance.

8-8 Describe the difference between a direct materials efficiency variance and a variable manufacturing overhead efficiency variance.

8-9 What are the steps in developing a budgeted fixed-overhead rate?

8-10 Why is the flexible-budget variance the same amount as the spending variance for fixed manufacturing overhead?

8-11 Explain how 4-variance analysis differs from 1-, 2-, and 3-variance analyses.

8-12 The 4-variance analysis format shows "never a variance" for two areas. Which two areas? Why?

8-13 "Overhead variances should be viewed as interdependent rather than independent." Give an example.

8-14 Explain how the analysis of fixed-overhead costs differs for (a) planning and control on the one hand, and (b) inventory costing for financial reporting on the other.

8-15 How does a standard costing system differ from (a) actual, (b) normal and (c) extended-normal costing systems?

EXERCISES

8-16 Variable manufacturing overhead, variance analysis. Esquire Clothing is a manufacturer of designer suits. The cost of each suit is the sum of three variable costs (direct material costs, direct manufacturing labor costs, and manufacturing overhead costs) and one fixed-cost category (manufacturing overhead costs). Variable manufacturing overhead cost is allocated to each suit on the basis of budgeted direct manufacturing labor-hours per suit. For June 19_7, each suit is budgeted to take 4 labor-hours. Budgeted variable manufacturing overhead costs per labor-hour is $12. The budgeted number of suits to be manufactured in June 19_7 is 1,040.

Actual variable manufacturing overhead costs in June 19_7 were $52,164 for 1,080 suits started and completed. There was no beginning or ending inventory of suits. Actual direct manufacturing labor-hours for June were 4,536.

REQUIRED
1. Compute the static-budget variance, the flexible-budget variance, and the sales-volume variance for variable manufacturing overhead.
2. Comment on the results.

8-17 Fixed manufacturing overhead, variance analysis (continuation of 8-16). Esquire Clothing allocates fixed manufacturing overhead to each suit using budgeted direct manufacturing labor-hours per suit. Data pertaining to fixed manufacturing overhead costs for June 19_7 are budgeted, $62,400, and actual, $63,916.

REQUIRED
1. Compute the spending variance and the flexible-budget variance for fixed manufacturing overhead. Comment on these results.
2. Compute the production-volume variance for June 19_7. What inferences can Esquire Clothing draw from this variance?

8-18 Manufacturing overhead, variance analysis. Zyton assembles its CardioX product at its Scottsdale plant. Manufacturing overhead (both variable and fixed) is allocated to each CardioX unit using budgeted assembly-time hours. Budgeted assembly time per CardioX product is 2 hours. The budgeted variable manufacturing overhead cost per assembly time hour is $40. The budgeted number of CardioX units to be assembled in March 19_7 is 8,000. Budgeted fixed manufacturing overhead costs are $480,000.

Actual variable manufacturing overhead costs for March 19_7 were $610,500 for 7,400 units actually assembled. Actual assembly-time hours were 16,280. Actual fixed manufacturing overhead costs were $503,420.

REQUIRED
1. Conduct a 4-variance analysis (Exhibit 8-3) for Zyton's Scottsdale plant.
2. Comment on the results in requirement 1.
3. How does the planning and control of variable manufacturing overhead costs differ from that of fixed manufacturing overhead costs?

8-19 Spending and efficiency overhead variances, service sector. Meals on Wheels (MOW) operates a home meal delivery service. It has agreements with 20 restaurants to pick up and deliver meals to customers who phone or fax in orders. MOW is currently examining its overhead costs for May 19_8.

Variable-overhead costs for May 19_8 were budgeted at $2 per hour of home delivery time. Fixed-overhead costs were budgeted at $24,000. The budgeted number of home deliveries in May 19_8 was 8,000. Delivery time, the allocation base for variable- and fixed-overhead costs, is budgeted to be 0.80 hour per delivery.

Actual results for May 19_8 were

Variable overhead	$14,174
Fixed overhead	$27,600
Number of home deliveries	7,460
Hours of delivery time	5,595

Customers are charged $12 per delivery. The delivery driver is paid $7 per delivery. MOW receives a 10% commission on the meal costs that the restaurants charge the customers who use MOW.

REQUIRED

1. Compute spending and efficiency variances for MOW's variable and fixed overhead in May 19_8. Comment on the results.
2. How might MOW manage its variable-overhead costs differently from the way it manages its fixed-overhead costs?

8-20 Spending and efficiency overhead variances, distribution. Package Postal Service (PPS) operates a parcel delivery service. PPS's costing system has one direct cost category (delivery driver payments) and two overhead categories—variable delivery overhead and fixed delivery overhead. In 19_7 it charged retail companies and mail-order catalog companies $15 per delivery. Delivery drivers in 19_7 were contracted at $5 per delivery. Variable delivery overhead for September 19_7 was budgeted at $2 per hour of delivery time. Budgeted fixed delivery overhead in September 19_7 was $120,000. PPS budgeted 100,000 deliveries for September 19_7. Delivery time, the allocation base for variable and fixed overhead costs, is budgeted to be 0.25 hours per delivery.

Actual results for September 19_7 were

Variable delivery overhead	$ 60,000
Fixed delivery overhead	$128,400
Number of deliveries	96,000
Hours of delivery time	28,800

REQUIRED

1. Compute the spending and efficiency variances for PPS's variable delivery overhead costs in September 19_7. Compute the spending and production-volume variances for PPS's fixed delivery overhead costs in September 19_7. Comment on the results.
2. What problems might PPS face in managing (a) its direct costs, (b) its variable delivery overhead costs, and (c) its fixed delivery overhead costs?

8-21 Manufacturing overhead, under- or overallocated amounts. (Z. Iqbal) The Peach Company estimated variable manufacturing overhead of $800,000 and fixed manufacturing overhead of $500,000 for the year. The company uses a standard costing system. It allocates manufacturing overhead on the basis of standard machine-hours. The denominator level is the budgeted usage of 100,000 machine-hours. During the time period in question, Peach used 110,000 machine-hours.

According to the standard costing system, 95,000 machine-hours should have been used for actual output achieved. Actual costs incurred for variable and fixed manufacturing overhead were $815,000 and $470,000, respectively.

REQUIRED

1. Compute the under- or overallocated variable manufacturing overhead amount.
2. Compute the under- or overallocated fixed manufacturing overhead amount.
3. Compute the under- or overallocated total manufacturing overhead amount.

8-22 4-variance analysis, fill in the blanks. Use the given manufacturing overhead data to fill in the blanks.

	Variable	Fixed
Actual costs incurred	$11,900	$6,000
Allocated to products	9,000	4,500
Flexible budget: Budgeted input allowed for actual output achieved × Budgeted rate	9,000	5,000
Actual input × Budgeted rate	10,000	5,000

Use F for favorable and U for unfavorable:

	Variable	Fixed
1. Spending variance	$_____	$_____
2. Efficiency variance	_____	_____
3. Production-volume variance	_____	_____
4. Flexible-budget variance	_____	_____
5. Underallocated (overallocated) manufacturing overhead	_____	_____

8-23 Straightforward 4-variance overhead analysis. The Lopez Company uses a standard cost system in its manufacturing plant for auto parts. Its standard cost of an auto part, based on a denominator level of 4,000 output units per year, included 6 machine-hours of variable manufacturing overhead at $8 per hour and 6 machine-hours of fixed manufacturing overhead at $15 per hour. Actual output achieved was 4,400 units. Variable manufacturing overhead incurred was $245,000. Fixed manufacturing overhead incurred was $373,000. Actual incurred machine-hours were 28,400.

REQUIRED

1. Prepare an analysis of all variable manufacturing overhead and fixed manufacturing overhead variances, using the 4-variance analysis (p. 263).
2. Prepare journal entries using the 4-variance analysis.
3. Describe how individual variable manufacturing overhead items are controlled from day to day. Also, describe how individual fixed manufacturing overhead items are controlled.

8-24 Straightforward coverage of manufacturing overhead, standard cost system. The Singapore division of a Canadian telecommunications company uses a standard cost system for its machine-paced production of telephone equipment. Data regarding production during June are

Variable manufacturing overhead costs incurred:	$155,100
Variable manufacturing overhead costs allocated (per standard machine-hour allowed for actual output achieved):	$12
Fixed manufacturing overhead costs incurred:	$401,000
Fixed manufacturing overhead budgeted:	$390,000
Denominator level in machine-hours:	13,000
Standard machine-hours allowed per unit of output:	0.30
Units of output:	41,000
Actual machine-hours used:	13,300
Ending work in process inventory:	0

REQUIRED

1. Prepare an analysis of all manufacturing overhead variances. Use the 4-variance analysis framework illustrated in Exhibit 8-3, (p. 262).
2. Prepare journal entries for manufacturing overhead without explanations.
3. Describe how individual variable manufacturing overhead items are controlled from day to day. Also, describe how individual fixed manufacturing overhead items are controlled.

8-25 Total overhead, 3-variance analysis. The Wright-Patterson Air Force Base has an extensive repair facility for jet engines. It developed standard costing and flexible budgets to account for this activity. Budgeted variable overhead at a level of 8,000 standard monthly direct labor-hours was $64,000; budgeted total overhead at 10,000 standard direct labor-hours was $197,600. The standard cost allocated to repair output included a total overhead rate of 120% of standard direct labor cost.

Total overhead incurred for October was $249,000. Direct labor costs incurred were $202,440. The direct labor price variance was $9,640 U. The direct labor flexible-budget variance was $14,440 U. The standard labor price was $16 per hour. The production-volume variance was $14,000 F.

REQUIRED

1. Compute the direct labor efficiency variance and the spending, efficiency, and production-volume variances for overhead. Also, compute the denominator level.
2. Describe how individual variable manufacturing overhead items are controlled from day to day. Also, describe how individual fixed manufacturing overhead items are controlled.

8-26 Comprehensive review of Chapters 7 and 8, static budget. *The Monthly Herald* budgets to produce 300,000 copies of its monthly newspaper for August 19_7. It is budgeted to run 15,000,000 print pages in August with 50 print pages per newspaper. Actual production in August 19_7 was 320,000 copies with 17,280,000 print pages run. Each paper was only 50 print pages, but quality problems with paper led to many pages being unusable.

Variable costs comprise direct materials, direct labor, and variable indirect costs. Variable and fixed indirect costs are allocated to each copy on the basis of print pages. The driver for all variable costs is the number of print pages. Data pertaining to August 19_7 are

	Budgeted	Actual
Direct materials	$180,000	$224,640
Direct labor costs	45,000	50,112
Variable indirect costs	60,000	63,936
Fixed indirect costs	90,000	97,000

Data pertaining to revenues for *The Monthly Herald* in August 19_7 are

	Budgeted	Actual
Circulation revenue	$140,000	$154,000
Advertising revenue	360,000	394,600

The Monthly Herald sells for $0.50 per copy in 19_7. No change from this budgeted price of $0.50 per copy occurred in August 19_7. The actual direct labor rate in August 19–7 was $29.00 per hour. Actual and budgeted pages produced per direct labor hour in August 19–7 was 10,000 print pages. Copies produced but not sold have no value. Advertising revenue covers payments from all advertising sources.

REQUIRED

1. Present a static-budget variance (Level 1) report for *The Monthly Herald*.
2. Comment on the results in requirement 1.

8-27 Comprehensive review of Chapters 7 and 8, flexible budget (continuation of 8-26).

REQUIRED

1. Prepare a comprehensive set of variances for each of the four categories of cost of *The Monthly Herald*.
2. Comment on the results in requirement 1. What extra insights are available with a flexible-budget analysis over that of a static-budget analysis?

8-28 Engineered and discretionary overhead costs. Susan Brand manages the warehouse of Quickserve, a mail-order firm. Brand is concerned about controlling the fixed costs of the 20 workers who collect merchandise in the warehouse and bring it to the area where orders are assembled for shipment. Each employee works 180 hours per month at a budgeted cost of $15 per hour. Studies show that it takes an average of 12 minutes for a worker to locate an article of merchandise and move it to the order assembly area, and that the average order is for two different articles. In August, Quickserve processed 8,500 orders. Actual costs were $56,000.

REQUIRED

1. Calculate the spending and production-volume variances for Quickserve using an engineered overhead cost approach.
2. Calculate the spending and production-volume variances for Quickserve using a discretionary overhead cost approach.
3. Comment on the differences in the approaches to controlling costs under requirements 1 and 2.

PROBLEMS

8-29 Graphs and overhead variances. The Carvelli Company is a manufacturer of housewares. In its job-costing system, manufacturing overhead (both variable and fixed) is allocated to products on the basis of budgeted machine-hours. The budgeted amounts are taken from Carvelli's standard costing system. The budget for 19_7 included

Variable manufacturing overhead	$9 per machine-hour
Fixed manufacturing overhead	$72,000,000
Denominator level	4,000,000 machine-hours

REQUIRED

1. Prepare four graphs, two for variable manufacturing overhead and two for fixed manufacturing overhead. Each pair of graphs should display how total manufacturing overhead costs of Carvelli will be depicted for the purpose of (a) planning and control, and (b) inventory costing.
2. Suppose that 3,500,000 machine-hours were allowed for actual output achieved in 19_7, but 3,800,000 machine-hours were used. Actual manufacturing overhead was variable, $36,100,000; fixed, $72,200,000. Compute (a) variable manufacturing overhead spending and efficiency variances, and (b) the fixed manufacturing overhead spending and production-volume variances. Use the columnar presentation illustrated in Exhibit 8-2 (p. 259).
3. What is the amount of the under- or overallocated variable manufacturing overhead? Of the under- or overallocated fixed manufacturing overhead? Why are the flexible-budget variance and the under- or overallocated overhead amount always the same for variable manufacturing overhead but rarely the same for fixed manufacturing overhead?
4. Suppose the denominator level was 3,000,000 rather than 4,000,000 machine-hours. What variances in requirement 2 would be affected? Recompute them.

8-30 Journal entries (continuation of 8-29). Refer to requirement 2. Consider variable manufacturing overhead and then fixed manufacturing overhead. Prepare the journal entries for (a) the incurrence of overhead, (b) the allocation of overhead, and (c) the isolation and closing of overhead variances to Cost of Goods Sold for the year.

8-31 4-variance analysis, find the unknowns. Consider each of the following situations—cases A, B, and C—independently. Data refer to operations of April 19_8. For each situation, assume a standard cost system. Also assume the use of a flexible budget for control of variable and fixed manufacturing overhead based on machine-hours.

		Cases	
	A	B	C
1. Fixed manufacturing overhead incurred	$10,600	—	$12,000
2. Variable manufacturing overhead incurred	7,000	—	—
3. Denominator level in machine-hours	500	—	1,100
4. Standard machine-hours allowed for actual output achieved	—	$650	—
Flexible-budget data:			
5. Fixed manufacturing overhead	—	—	—
6. Variable manufacturing overhead (per standard machine-hour)	—	8.50	5.00
7. Budgeted fixed manufacturing overhead	10,000	—	11,000
8. Budgeted variable manufacturing overhead*	—	—	—
9. Total budgeted manufacturing overhead*	—	12,525	—
Additional data:			
10. Standard variable manufacturing overhead allocated	7,500	—	—
11. Standard fixed manufacturing overhead allocated	10,000	—	—
12. Production-volume variance	—	500 U	500 F
13. Variable manufacturing overhead spending variance	950 F	0	350 U
14. Variable manufacturing overhead efficiency variance	—	0	100 U
15. Fixed manufacturing overhead spending variance	—	300 F	—
16. Actual machine-hours used	—	—	—

*For standard machine-hours allowed for actual output achieved.

REQUIRED
Fill in the blanks under each case. (*Hint:* Prepare a worksheet similar to that in Exhibit 8-3, p. 262. Fill in the knowns and then solve for the unknowns.)

8-32 Working backward from given variances. The Mancusco Company uses a flexible budget and standard costs to aid planning and control of its machining manufacturing operations. Its normal costing system for manufacturing has two direct-cost categories (direct materials and direct manufacturing labor—both variable) and two indirect-cost categories (variable manufacturing overhead and fixed manufacturing overhead, both allocated using direct manufacturing labor hours).

At the 40,000 budgeted direct manufacturing labor-hour level for August, budgeted direct manufacturing labor is $800,000, budgeted variable manufacturing overhead is $480,000, and budgeted fixed manufacturing overhead is $640,000. The following actual results are for August:

Direct materials price variance (based on purchases)	$176,000 F
Direct materials efficiency variance	69,000 U
Direct manufacturing labor costs incurred	522,750
Variable manufacturing overhead flexible-budget variance	10,350 U
Variable manufacturing overhead efficiency variance	18,000 U
Fixed manufacturing overhead incurred	597,460
Fixed manufacturing overhead spending variance	42,540 F

The standard cost per pound of direct materials is $11.50. The standard allowance is 3 pounds of direct materials for each unit of product. Thirty thousand units of product were produced during August. There was no beginning inventory of direct materials. There was no beginning or ending work in process. In August, the direct materials price variance was $1.10 per pound.

In July, labor troubles caused a major slowdown in the pace of production, resulting in an unfavorable direct manufacturing labor efficiency variance of $45,000. There was no manufacturing labor price variance. These troubles persisted into August. Some workers quit. Their replacements had to be hired at higher rates, which had to be extended to all workers. The actual average wage rate in August exceeded the standard average wage rate by $0.50.

REQUIRED

1. Compute the following for August.
   a. Total pounds of direct materials purchased.
   b. Total number of pounds of excess direct materials used.
   c. Variable manufacturing overhead spending variance.
   d. Total number of actual hours of direct manufacturing labor-hours used.
   e. Total number of standard direct manufacturing labor-hours allowed for the units produced.
   f. Production-volume variance.
2. Describe how Mancusco's control of variable manufacturing overhead items differs from its control of fixed manufacturing overhead items.

8-33 Flexible budgets, 4-variance analysis. (CMA, adapted) Nolton Products uses a standard costing system. It allocates manufacturing overhead (both variable and fixed) to products on the basis of standard direct manufacturing labor-hours (DLH). Nolton develops its manufacturing overhead rate from the current annual budget. The manufacturing overhead budget for 19_7 is based on budgeted output of 720,000 units requiring 3,600,000 direct manufacturing labor-hours. The company is able to schedule production uniformly throughout the year.

A total of 66,000 output units requiring 315,000 direct labor-hours was produced during May 19_7. Manufacturing overhead (MOH) costs incurred for May amounted to $375,000. The actual costs as compared with the annual budget and ¹⁄₁₂ of the annual budget are shown below.

Annual Manufacturing Overhead Budget 19_7

	Total Amount	Per Output Unit	Per DLH Input Unit	Monthly MOH Budget May 19_7	Actual MOH Costs for May 19_7
Variable MOH					
Indirect manufacturing labor	$ 900,000	$1.25	$0.25	$ 75,000	$ 75,000
Supplies	1,224,000	1.70	0.34	102,000	111,000
Fixed MOH					
Supervision	648,000	0.90	0.18	54,000	51,000
Utilities	540,000	0.75	0.15	45,000	54,000
Depreciation	1,008,000	1.40	0.28	84,000	84,000
Total	$4,320,000	$6.00	$1.20	$360,000	$375,000

REQUIRED

Calculate the following amounts for Nolton Products for May 19_7:
1. Total manufacturing overhead costs allocated.
2. Variable manufacturing overhead spending variance.

3. Fixed manufacturing overhead spending variance.

4. Variable manufacturing overhead efficiency variance.

5. Production-volume variance.

Be sure to identify each variance as favorable (F) or unfavorable (U).

8-34 Review of Chapters 7 and 8, 3-variance analysis. (CPA, adapted) The Beal Manufacturing Company's job-costing system has two direct-cost categories—direct materials and direct manufacturing labor. Manufacturing overhead (both variable and fixed) is allocated to products on the basis of standard direct manufacturing labor-hours (DLH). At the beginning of 19_8, Beal adopted the following standards for its manufacturing costs:

	Input	Cost Per Output Unit
Direct materials	3 pounds at $5.00 per pound	$ 15.00
Direct manufacturing labor	5 hours at $15.00 per hour	75.00
Manufacturing overhead:		
Variable	$6.00 per DLH	30.00
Fixed	$8.00 per DLH	40.00
Standard manufacturing cost per output unit		$160.00

The denominator level for total manufacturing overhead per month in 19_8 is 40,000 direct manufacturing labor-hours. Beal's flexible budget for January 19_8 was based on this denominator level. The records for January indicate the following:

Direct materials purchased	25,000 pounds at $5.20 per pound
Direct materials used	23,100 pounds
Direct manufacturing labor	40,100 hours, at $14.60 per hour
Total actual manufacturing overhead (variable and fixed)	$600,000
Actual production	7,800 output units

REQUIRED

1. Prepare a schedule of total standard manufacturing costs for the 7,800 output units in January, 19_8.

2. For the month of January 19_8, compute the following variances, indicating whether each is favorable (F) or unfavorable (U):

a. Direct materials price variance, based on purchases

b. Direct materials efficiency variance

c. Direct manufacturing labor price variance

d. Direct manufacturing labor efficiency variance

e. Total manufacturing overhead spending variance

f. Variable manufacturing overhead efficiency variance

g. Production-volume variance

8-35 Working backward, comprehensive variance analysis. (H. Hoverland) The Durrell Company manufactures a single product name, Preston. It uses a standard costing system for both its two direct costs (direct materials and direct manufacturing labor) and its variable manufacturing overhead costs. The standard variable cost for one unit of Preston in 19_7 is

Direct materials (10 pounds at $0.50 per pound)	$ 5
Direct manufacturing labor (2 hours at $10 per hour)	20
Variable manufacturing overhead (3 machine-hours at $5 per hour)	15
Total variable cost per unit	$40

Fixed manufacturing costs for 19_7 are budgeted to be $400,000.
Selected actual results and variances for 19_7 are

Production output	100,000 units
Direct materials inventory, 1/1/19_7	0
Direct materials inventory, 12/31/19_7	100,000 pounds
Materials price variance (MPV)	$24,000 U
Materials efficiency variance (MEV)	$50,000 U
Manufacturing labor price variance	$50,000 F
Manufacturing labor efficiency variance	$100,000 U
Variable manufacturing overhead spending variance (VMOSV)	$50,000 F
Variable manufacturing overhead efficiency variance (VMOEV)	$150,000 U
Fixed manufacturing overhead spending variance (FMOSV)	$30,000 U
Production-volume variance	$0

REQUIRED
Compute the following items:
1. Direct materials purchased ($). *1,200,000*
2. Direct materials purchased (pounds). *1,200,000*
3. Average price paid per pound of direct material. *1*
4. Direct materials used ($). *1,100,000*
5. Direct materials used (pounds). *1,100,000*
6. Direct manufacturing labor used ($). *2,050,000*
7. Direct manufacturing labor used (DLH). *2.1*
8. Average rate paid per DLH. *9.??*
9. Actual variable overhead ($). *500,000*
10. Machine-hours used. *330,000*
11. Average variable manufacturing overhead rate per machine-hour. *3.3*
12. Actual fixed manufacturing overhead ($). *270,000*
13. Planned production level (units).
14. Planned production level (machine-hours). *300,000*

8-36 Appendix, straightforward proration of manufacturing variances. Consider the following balances of standard costs before proration at the end of the year: work in process, $180,000; finished goods, $720,000; cost of goods sold, $900,000. The production-volume variance was $50,000 F. All other manufacturing variances were $330,000 U. Management has decided to prorate all variances in proportion to the ending balances in work in process, finished goods, and cost of goods sold before proration.

REQUIRED
1. Prepare a schedule that prorates the manufacturing variances.
2. Prepare a journal entry that closes all variance accounts.
3. Assume that the major justification for proration is the attempt to approximate the actual cost of the units produced. Name two likely sources of inaccuracy in the proration here. Explain.

8-37 Appendix, proration of manufacturing variances and income effects of standard costs. The Stefano Company uses a standard costing system, which shows the following account balances (before proration of any variances) at December 31, 19_7:

Direct materials, ending inventory	$175,000
Work in process, ending inventory	100,000
Finished goods, ending inventory	300,000
Cost of goods sold	600,000
Direct materials price variance	64,000
Direct materials efficiency variance	25,000
Direct manufacturing labor price variance	5,000

Direct manufacturing labor efficiency variance	25,000
Manufacturing overhead incurred	210,000
Manufacturing overhead allocated, at standard rate	170,000
Sales	900,000
Marketing and administrative costs	180,000

Materials price variances are measured when the material is purchased rather than when it is used. Assume that Work in Process, Finished Goods, and Cost of Goods Sold contain standard costs in uniform proportions of direct materials, direct manufacturing labor, and manufacturing overhead. The direct materials component represented 60% of the ending balance in Work in Process, Finished Goods, and Cost of Goods Sold. All manufacturing variances are unfavorable. There are no beginning inventories. There are no variances for marketing and administrative costs. Both variable and fixed manufacturing costs are inventoried.

REQUIRED

1. Prepare a comprehensive schedule showing the proration of all manufacturing variances.
2. Prepare a journal entry for the proration.
3. Prepare comparative summary income statements based on a standard costing system:
    a. Without proration of any manufacturing variances (all variances written off to Cost of Goods Sold)
    b. With proration of all manufacturing variances based on total ending balances
4. Compute the amount of direct manufacturing labor cost included in the balance of Finished Goods ending inventory (before proration).

8-38 Engineered and discretionary overhead costs, customer service. Cable Galore, the largest cable television operator in California, had 120,000 subscribers, many of whom were not happy with their service. To eliminate the causes of their customers' concerns, Cable Galore hired eight special troubleshooters at a fixed budgeted salary of $3,000 per month. The budget for the next two months (April and May) assumed that each troubleshooter would service 5 calls a day for 20 working days per month. The actual number of calls in the April to May period was 1,460 (810 in April, 650 in May); actual costs in each month were $24,600.

REQUIRED

1. Calculate the spending and production-volume variances for each month using an engineered overhead cost approach.
2. Calculate the spending and production-volume variances for each month using a discretionary overhead cost approach.
3. On the basis of your answers to requirements 1 and 2, would you recommend that Cable Galore use the engineered overhead cost of the discretionary overhead cost approach to controlling the overhead costs of troubleshooters? Explain your answer briefly.

8-39 Hospital overhead variances, 4-variance analysis. The Sharon Hospital, a large metropolitan health-care complex, has had difficulty controlling its accounts receivable. Bills for patients, various government agencies, and private insurance companies have frequently been inaccurate and late. This situation has led to intolerable levels of bad debts and investments in receivables.

In conjunction with the billing department, a set of standard costs and standard amounts was developed for 19_7. These standard costs can be used in a flexible budget with separate variable-cost and fixed-cost categories. The output unit is defined to be a single bill.

The accountant to Sharon Hospital provides you with the following for April 19_7:

Variable overhead costs, allowance per standard hour	$10
Fixed overhead flexible-budget variance	$200 F
Total budgeted overhead costs for the bills prepared	$22,500
Production-volume variance	$900 F
Variable-cost spending variance	$2,000 U
Variable-cost efficiency variance	$2,000 F
Standard hours allowed for the bills prepared	1,800 labor-hours

REQUIRED

1. Actual hours of input used.
2. Fixed overhead budget.
3. Fixed overhead allocated.
4. Budgeted fixed overhead rate per hour.
5. Denominator level in hours.

8-40 Standard setting, benchmarking, ethics (continuation of 8-39). Ira Stone, the president of Sharon Hospital, has a meeting with the Medical Economics Group (MEG). MEG is a consulting firm in the health services sector. It reports that Sharon's billing operations are grossly inefficient. Its standard costing per bill is above 90% of the 130 hospitals MEG tracks in its benchmarking data base.

Stone suspects the billing group deliberately "padded" its standard costs and standard amounts. Despite large investment in new information systems, the standards for 19_7 were not below actual results for 19_6. Stone does not want to institute a witch-hunt, but he does want to eliminate the fat in Sharon's cost structure.

REQUIRED

1. How might Sharon's billing operations group have "padded" its standard costs and standard amounts? Why might they do this padding?
2. What steps should Stone take to "reduce the fat" in the overhead costs of the billing operations at Sharon Hospital?

COLLABORATIVE LEARNING PROBLEM

8-41 Manufacturing overhead variance analysis, cost classifications. Kylee Hutchinson is the newly appointed president of Laser Products. She is examining the November 19_7 results for the Aerospace Products division. This division manufactures wing parts for satellites. Hutchinson's current concern is with manufacturing overhead costs at the Aerospace Products division. Both variable and fixed manufacturing overhead costs are allocated to the wing parts on the basis of laser cutting hours. The budgeted rates are variable manufacturing overhead of $200 an hour and fixed manufacturing overhead of $240 an hour. The budgeted laser cutting time per wing part is 1.50 hours. Budgeted production and sales for 19_7 is 5,000 wing parts. Budgeted fixed manufacturing overhead for November 19_7 is $1,800,000.

Actual results for November 19_7 are

Wing parts produced and sold	4,800 units
Laser cutting hours used	8,400 hours
Variable manufacturing overhead costs	$1,478,400
Fixed manufacturing overhead costs	$1,832,200

Hutchinson asks Michael Minogue, her financial analyst, to give her a report on the November 19_7 manufacturing overhead results.

As part of his research, Minogue analyzes individual items in the variable- and fixed-overhead cost pools. He observes that depreciation on machines had traditionally been classified as a variable cost. The rationale was that usage of the laser cutting machines is the key variable affecting machine wear and tear and replacement. However, in 19_7, the former manager of the Aerospace Division had reclassified depreciation on machines as a fixed cost. For November 19_7, budgeted depreciation on machines was $825,000. Based on his own study of machine purchases and wear and tear, Minogue estimates actual depreciation in November 19_7 to be $882,000.

Laser Products has long held division managers responsible for only variable-cost variances in its monthly performance reviews. Hutchinson wondered if this is still appropriate (if it ever was). Fixed-cost variances are only considered in the annual performance reviews of division managers.

INSTRUCTIONS

Form groups of two or more students to complete the following requirements.

REQUIRED

1. Your group is to help Minogue develop a comprehensive variance analysis of the manufacturing overhead costs of the Aerospace Products division for November 19_7. Use Exhibit 8-3 as a guideline. Assume depreciation is a fixed cost in your answer to this requirement.

2. Outline possible explanations for each of the variances you compute in requirement 1.

3. How would your analysis be affected by the classification of depreciation as a variable manufacturing overhead cost as opposed to a fixed manufacturing overhead cost?

4. Should Laser Products continue its policy of not using fixed manufacturing overhead costs in its monthly performance reviews of division managers?

9 CHAPTER

INCOME EFFECTS OF ALTERNATIVE INVENTORY-COSTING METHODS

The bottling lines at the Salem, New Hampshire, 7-Up bottling plant can operate at varying degrees of speed. Management considers these different operating speeds, as well as demand factors, when determining the denominator level to use in setting fixed overhead cost rates.

LEARNING OBJECTIVES

After studying this chapter, you should be able to

1. Identify the fundamental feature that distinguishes variable costing from absorption costing

2. Construct income statements using absorption costing and variable costing

3. Explain differences in operating income under absorption costing and variable costing

4. Describe the effects of absorption costing on computing the breakeven point

5. Differentiate throughput costing from variable costing and absorption costing

6. Understand how absorption costing influences performance evaluation decisions

7. Describe the various denominator-level concepts that can be used in absorption costing

8. Explain how the choice of denominator level affects reported operating income and inventory costs

The reported income number captures the attention of managers in a way few other numbers do. Consider three examples:

◆ Planning decisions typically include an analysis of how the considered options affect future reported income.

◆ Increases in reported income is the object of many decisions related to cost reduction.

◆ Reported income is a key number in the performance evaluation of managers.

The reported income number of manufacturing companies is affected by cost accounting choices related to inventories. In this chapter we examine two such choices:

1. **Inventory-costing choices**—the choices here relate which costs are to be recorded as an inventory asset when they are incurred. We discuss three alternatives: variable costing, absorption costing, and throughput costing.

2. **Denominator-level choices**—the choices here relate to the preselected level of the cost allocation base used to set budgeted fixed manufacturing cost rates. We discuss four alternatives: theoretical capacity, practical capacity, normal utilization, and master-budget utilization.

◆ PART ONE: INVENTORY-COSTING METHODS

The two most commonly encountered methods of costing inventories are variable costing and absorption costing. We discuss these two first and then cover throughput costing.

VARIABLE COSTING AND ABSORPTION COSTING

These two methods differ in only one conceptual respect: whether fixed manufacturing costs (both direct and indirect) are inventoriable costs. Recall from Chapter 2 that *inventoriable costs* for a manufacturing company are costs associated with the acquisition and conversion of materials and all other manufacturing inputs into goods for sale; these costs are first recorded as an asset and then subsequently become an expense when the goods are sold. **Variable costing** is a method of inventory costing in which all variable manufacturing costs are included as inventoriable costs. All fixed manufacturing costs are excluded from inventoriable costs; they are costs of the period in which they are incurred. **Absorption costing** is a method of inventory costing in which all variable manufacturing costs and all fixed manufacturing costs are included as inventoriable costs. That is, inventory "absorbs" all manufacturing costs. Throughout this chapter, to emphasize underlying concepts, we assume that the chosen denominator level for computing the variable and fixed manufacturing overhead allocation rates is a production, output-related variable. Examples include direct labor-hours, direct machine-hours, and units of production output.

We will use the Radius Company, which manufactures specialty clothing belts, to illustrate the difference between variable costing and absorption costing.[1] Radius uses a normal costing system. That is, its direct costs are traced to products using actual prices and the actual inputs used, and its indirect (overhead) costs are allocated using budgeted indirect cost rate(s) times actual inputs used. The allocation base for all indirect manufacturing costs is units produced. The allocation base for all variable indirect marketing costs is units sold. (Only manufacturing costs are included in inventoriable costs.)

[1] The variable- versus absorption-costing choice is but one of several pertaining to inventory costing. For example, decisions related to cost flows (FIFO, LIFO, weighted-average, and so on) must also be made.

To keep our focus on variable- versus absorption-costing issues, we assume the following for 19_7:

◆ The budgeted number and actual number of units produced are equal (1,100,000 units).

◆ The budgeted number and actual number of units sold are equal (1,000,000 units).

◆ The budgeted and actual fixed costs are equal.

◆ Work in process is minimal.

◆ No beginning inventory on January 1, 19_7.

◆ All variable costs are driven by an output-unit-related variable. (We assume, for example, batch-level and product-sustaining costs are zero.)

With 19_7 production of 1,100,000 units and sales of 1,000,000 units, the ending inventory on December 31, 19_7 is 100,000 units.

The per unit and total actual costs for 19_7 are

	Per Unit	Total Costs
Variable costs		
Direct materials	$3.50	$3,850,000
Direct manufacturing labor	1.60	1,760,000
Indirect manufacturing costs	0.90	990,000
Manufacturing costs	6.00	6,600,000
Direct marketing costs	0.80	800,000
Indirect marketing costs	1.60	1,600,000
Marketing costs	2.40	2,400,000
Total variable costs	$8.40	$9,000,000
Fixed costs		
Direct manufacturing costs	$0.30	$ 330,000
Indirect manufacturing costs	1.70	1,870,000
Manufacturing costs	2.00	2,200,000
Direct marketing costs	2.10	2,100,000
Indirect marketing costs	3.40	3,400,000
Marketing costs	5.50	5,500,000
Total fixed costs	$7.50	$7,700,000

The heart of the difference between variable and absorption costing for financial reporting is accounting for fixed manufacturing costs:

	Direct	Indirect
Same under Both methods { Variable	Direct manufacturing cost	Indirect manufacturing
Differs under Both methods { Fixed	Direct manufacturing cost	Indirect manufacturing

For inventory valuation under both methods, all variable manufacturing costs (both direct and indirect) are capitalizable costs. That is, they are first recorded as an asset when they are incurred. Under variable costing, fixed manufacturing costs (both direct and indirect) are deducted as a period cost in the period in which they are incurred. Examples of variable direct manufacturing costs are direct materials and direct manufacturing labor. An example of a fixed direct manufacturing cost is the annual lease cost of a machine dedicated exclusively to the assembly of a single product. The annual lease cost of a building in which multiple products are assembled illustrates a fixed indirect manufacturing cost. Under absorption costing, fixed manufacturing costs are initially capitalized as an inventoriable cost. They then become expenses in the form of cost of goods sold when sales occur. The unit inventoriable costs for Radius under the two methods are

	Variable Costing		Absorption Costing	
Variable manufacturing costs				
Direct materials	$3.50		$3.50	
Direct manufacturing labor	1.60		1.60	
Indirect manufacturing costs	0.90	6.00	0.90	6.00
Fixed manufacturing costs				
Direct manufacturing costs			0.30	
Indirect manufacturing costs			1.70	2.00
Total inventoriable costs		$6.00		$8.00

OBJECTIVE 2

Construct income statements using absorption costing and variable costing

Exhibit 9-1 presents the variable-costing and absorption-costing income statements for the Radius Company in 19_7. The variable-costing income statement uses the contribution approach format introduced in Chapter 3. The absorption-costing income statement uses the gross margin format, also introduced in Chapter 3. Why these differences in format? The distinction between variable and fixed costs is central to variable costing; the contribution format highlights this distinction. The distinction between manufacturing and nonmanufacturing costs is central to absorption costing; the gross margin format highlights this distinction. Many companies using absorption costing do not make any distinction between variable and fixed costs in their accounting system.

Trace the fixed manufacturing costs of $2,200,000 in Exhibit 9-1. The income statement under variable costing deducts the $2,200,000 lump sum as a period cost in 19_7. In contrast, the income statement under absorption costing regards each finished unit as absorbing $2 of fixed manufacturing costs. Under absorption costing the $2,200,000 is initially capitalized as an inventoriable cost in 19_7. Given the preceding data for Radius, $2,000,000 subsequently becomes an expense in 19_7, and $200,000 remains an asset—part of ending finished goods inventory, 100,000 units × $2—at December 31, 19_7. The variable manufacturing costs are accounted for in the same way in both income statements in Exhibit 9-1.

Never overlook the heart of the matter. The difference between variable costing and absorption costing centers on accounting for fixed manufacturing costs. If inventory levels change, operating income will differ between the two methods because of the difference in accounting for fixed manufacturing overhead. Compare sales of 900,000, 1,000,000, and 1,100,000 units by the Radius Company in 19_7. Fixed manufacturing costs would be included in the 19_7 expense as follows:

	Fixed Manufacturing Costs Treated as an Expense in 19_7
Variable costing, whether	
◆ sales are 900,000, 1,000,000, or 1,100,000 units	$2,200,000
Absorption costing, where	
◆ sales are 900,000 units, $400,000 (200,000 × $2) held back in inventory	$1,800,000
◆ sales are 1,000,000 units, $200,000 (100,000 × $2) held back in inventory	$2,000,000
◆ sales are 1,100,000 units, $0 held back in inventory	$2,200,000

Some companies use the term **direct costing** to describe the inventory costing method we call *variable costing*. Direct costing is an unfortunate choice of terms for two reasons: (1) Variable costing does not include all direct costs as inventoriable costs. Only direct variable manufacturing costs are included. Any direct fixed manufacturing costs and any direct nonmanufacturing costs (such as marketing) are excluded from inventoriable costs. (2) Variable costing includes as inventoriable costs not only direct manufacturing costs, but also some indirect costs (variable indirect manufacturing costs).

EXHIBIT 9-1
Comparison of Variable-Costing and Absorption-Costing Income Statements for the Year Ended December 31, 19_7 for the Radius Company (in thousands)

PANEL A: VARIABLE COSTING

① Revenues: $17.00 × 1,000,000 units			$17,000
② Variable costs			
Beginning inventory		$ 0	
Variable cost of goods manufactured:			
$6.00 × 1,100,000		6,600	
Cost of goods available for sale		6,600	
Ending inventory: $6.00 × 100,000		600	
Variable manufacturing cost of goods sold		6,000	
Variable marketing costs		2,400	
Adjustment for variable cost variances		0	
Total variable costs			8,400
③ Contribution margin			8,600
④ Fixed costs			
Fixed manufacturing costs		2,200	
Fixed marketing costs		5,500	
Adjustment for fixed cost variances		0	
Total fixed costs			7,700
⑤ Operating income			$ 900

PANEL B: ABSORPTION COSTING

① Revenues: $17.00 × 1,000,000 units			$17,000
② Cost of goods sold			
Beginning inventory		$ 0	
Variable manufacturing costs:			
$6.00 × 1,100,000		6,600	
Fixed manufacturing costs:			
$2.00 × 1,100,000		2,200	
Cost of goods available for sale		8,800	
Ending inventory: $8.00 × 100,000		800	
Adjustment for manufacturing variances		0	
Cost of goods sold			8,000
③ Gross margin			9,000
④ Marketing costs			
Variable marketing costs		2,400	
Fixed marketing costs		5,500	
Adjustment for marketing variances		0	
Total marketing costs			7,900
⑤ Operating income			$ 1,100

COMPARISON OF STANDARD VARIABLE COSTING AND STANDARD ABSORPTION COSTING

Our next example explores the implications of accounting for fixed manufacturing costs in more detail. The Stassen Company manufactures and markets telescopes. It uses a standard costing system for both its manufacturing and marketing costs.[2] It

[2] For ease of exposition, we assume that the Stassen Company uses a standard costing system for all its operating costs—that is, it uses standards for both variable and fixed costs in both its manufacturing and marketing.

began business on January 1, 19_7, and it is now March 19_7. The president asks you to prepare comparative income statements for January 19_7 and February 19_7. The following simplified data in units are available:

Unit Data	January 19_7	February 19_7
Beginning inventory	0	200
Production	600	650
Sales	400	750
Ending inventory	200	100

Other data

Selling price	$99
Standard variable manufacturing costs per unit	$20
Standard variable marketing costs per unit	$19
Standard fixed manufacturing costs per month	$12,800
Standard fixed marketing costs per month	$10,400
Budgeted denominator level of production per month	800 output units

The standard variable manufacturing costs per unit of $20 includes $11 for direct materials. For simplicity, we assume all fixed manufacturing costs are indirect product costs.

We assume work in process is minimal. There were no beginning or ending inventories of materials. On January 1, 19_7, there was no beginning inventory of finished goods. In order to highlight the effect of the production-volume variance, we assume there were no price, efficiency, or spending variances for any costs in either January or February of 19_7. The standard fixed manufacturing cost per unit is $16 ($12,800 ÷ 800). Thus the key standard cost data per unit are

Variable costs	
Standard variable manufacturing costs	$20
Standard variable marketing costs	19
Total variable costs	$39

Manufacturing costs	
Standard variable manufacturing costs	$20
Standard fixed manufacturing costs	16
Total manufacturing costs	$36

Stassen expenses all variances to cost of goods sold in the accounting period in which they occur.

Assume that managers at Stassen receive a bonus based on reported monthly income. The following points illustrate how the choice between variable and absorption costing will affect Stassen's reported monthly income and hence the bonuses their managers will receive.

Comparative Income Statements

Exhibit 9-2 contains the comparative income statements under variable costing (Panel A) and absorption costing (Panel B) for the Stassen Company in January 19_7 and February 19_7. The operating income numbers are

	January 19_7	February 19_7
1. Absorption costing	$4,000	$20,200
2. Variable costing	800	21,800
3. Difference (1) – (2)	$3,200	$ (1,600)

EXHIBIT 9-2

Stassen Company: Comparison of Variable Costing and Absorption Costing Income Statements for January 19_7 and February 19_7

PANEL A: VARIABLE COSTING

	January 19_7	February 19_7
Revenue*	$39,600	$74,250
Variable costs		
Beginning inventory	0	4,000
Variable cost of goods manufactured[†]	12,000	13,000
Cost of goods available for sale	12,000	17,000
Ending inventory[††]	4,000	2,000
Variable manufacturing cost of goods sold	8,000	15,000
Variable marketing costs[≈]	7,600	14,250
Total variable costs (at standard)	15,600	29,250
Contribution margin (at standard)	24,000	45,000
Adjustment for variable-cost variances	0	0
Contribution margin	24,000	45,000
Fixed costs		
Fixed manufacturing costs	12,800	12,800
Fixed marketing costs	10,400	10,400
Total fixed costs (at standard)	23,200	23,200
Adjustment for fixed cost variances	0	0
Total fixed costs	23,200	23,200
Operating income	$ 800	$21,800

*400 × $99 = $39,600; 750 × $99 = $74,250. [†]600 × $20 = $12,000; 650 × $20 = $13,000. [††]200 × $20 = $4,000; 100 × $20 = $2,000. [≈]400 × $19 = $7,600; 750 × $19 = $14,250

PANEL B: ABSORPTION COSTING

	January 19_7	February 19_7
Revenue*	$39,600	$74,250
Cost of goods sold		
Beginning inventory	0	7,200
Variable manufacturing costs[†]	12,000	13,000
Fixed manufacturing costs[††]	9,600	10,400
Cost of goods available for sale	21,600	30,600
Ending inventory[≈]	7,200	3,600
Total cost of goods sold (at standard)	14,400	27,000
Gross margin (at standard costs)	$25,200	47,250
Adjustment for manufacturing variances[#]	3,200 U	$ 2,400 U
Gross margin	22,000	44,850
Marketing costs		
Variable marketing costs[∥]	7,600	14,250
Fixed marketing costs	10,400	10,400
Total marketing (at standard)	18,000	24,650
Adjustment for marketing variances	0	0
Total marketing	18,000	24,650
Operating income	$ 4,000	$20,200

[*]400 × $99 = $39,600; 750 × $99 = $74,250. [†]600 × $20 = $12,000; 650 × $20 = $13,000. [††]600 × $16 = $9,600; 650 × $16 = $10,400. [≈]200 × ($20 + $16) = $7,200; 100 × ($20 + $16) = $3,600. [#]January, 19_7 has $3,200 unfavorable (U) production-volume variance (600 − 800) × $16 = $3,200 unfavorable. February, 19_7 has $2,400 unfavorable production-volume variance (650 − 800) × $16.00 = $2,400 unfavorable. [∥]400 × $19 = $7,600; 750 × $19 = $14,250

In Panel A, Variable Costing, all variable-cost line items are at standard cost except the last line item, "Adjustment for variances." This line item would include all price, spending, and efficiency variances related to variable-cost items (which are zero in our Stassen example). In Panel B, Absorption Costing, all cost of goods sold line items are at standard cost except the last line item, "Adjustment for variances." This line item would include all manufacturing cost variances—price, spending, efficiency, and production-volume variances. Only the production-volume variance is nonzero in our Stassen example.

Keep the following points in mind about absorption costing as you study Panel B of Exhibit 9-2:

1. The inventoriable costs are $36 per unit, not $20, because fixed manufacturing costs ($16) as well as variable manufacturing costs ($20), are assigned to each unit of product.

2. The $16 fixed manufacturing costs rate were based on a denominator level of 800 units per month ($12,800 ÷ 800 = $16). Whenever *production* (not sales) deviates from the denominator level, a production-volume variance arises. The amount of the variance is $16 multiplied by the difference between the actual level of production and the denominator level.

3. The production-volume variance, which relates to fixed manufacturing overhead, exists only under absorption costing and not under variable costing. All other variances exist under both absorption costing and variable costing.

4. The absorption-costing income statement classifies costs primarily by *business function*, such as manufacturing and marketing. In contrast, the variable-costing income statement features *cost behavior* (variable or fixed) as the basis of classification. Absorption-costing income statements need not differentiate between the variable and fixed costs. Exhibit 9-2 does make this differentiation for the Stassen Company in order to highlight how individual line items are classified differently under variable- and absorption-costing formats.

Explaining Differences in Operating Income

OBJECTIVE 3

Explain differences in operating income under absorption costing and variable costing

If the inventory level increases during an accounting period, variable costing will generally report less operating income than absorption costing; when the inventory level decreases, variable costing will generally report more operating income than absorption costing. These differences in operating income are due solely to moving fixed manufacturing costs into inventories as inventories increase and out of inventories as they decrease.

The difference between operating income under absorption costing and variable costing can be computed by formula 1, which is illustrated with Exhibit 9-2 data:[3]

Formula 1

$$\begin{pmatrix} \text{Absorption-costing} \\ \text{operating} \\ \text{income} \end{pmatrix} - \begin{pmatrix} \text{Variable-costing} \\ \text{operating} \\ \text{income} \end{pmatrix} = \begin{pmatrix} \text{Fixed manufacturing} \\ \text{costs in} \\ \text{ending inventory} \end{pmatrix} - \begin{pmatrix} \text{Fixed manufacturing} \\ \text{costs in} \\ \text{beginning inventory} \end{pmatrix}$$

January 19_7 $4,000 - \$800 = (200 \times \$16) - (0 \times \$16)$

$$\$3,200 = \$3,200$$

February 19_7 $20,200 - \$21,800 = (100 \times \$16) - (200 \times \$16)$

$$-\$1,600 = -\$1,600$$

Fixed manufacturing costs in ending inventory are a current-period expense under variable costing that absorption costing defers to future period.

Two alternative formulas can be used if we assume that all manufacturing variances are written off as period costs, that no change occurs in work in process inventory, and that no change occurs in the budgeted fixed manufacturing overhead rate between accounting periods:

[3]This formula assumes that the amounts used for beginning and ending inventory are after proration of manufacturing overhead variances.

Formula 2

$$\begin{pmatrix} \text{Absorption-costing} \\ \text{operating} \\ \text{income} \end{pmatrix} - \begin{pmatrix} \text{Variable-costing} \\ \text{operating} \\ \text{income} \end{pmatrix} = \begin{pmatrix} \text{Units} \\ \text{produced} - \text{Units} \\ \text{sold} \end{pmatrix} \times \begin{pmatrix} \text{Budget fixed} \\ \text{manufacturing} \\ \text{cost rate} \end{pmatrix}$$

January 19_7 $\qquad$ $\$4{,}000 - \$800 = (600 - 400) \times \$16$

$$\$3{,}200 = \$3{,}200$$

February 19_7 $\qquad$ $\$20{,}200 - \$21{,}800 = (650 - 750) \times \$16$

$$-\$1{,}600 = -\$1{,}600$$

Formula 3

$$\begin{pmatrix} \text{Absorption-costing} \\ \text{operating} \\ \text{income} \end{pmatrix} - \begin{pmatrix} \text{Variable-costing} \\ \text{operating} \\ \text{income} \end{pmatrix} = \begin{pmatrix} \text{Ending} \\ \text{inventory} - \begin{array}{c}\text{Beginning} \\ \text{inventory}\end{array} \\ \text{in units} \quad \text{in units} \end{pmatrix} \times \begin{pmatrix} \text{Budget fixed} \\ \text{manufacturing} \\ \text{cost rate} \end{pmatrix}$$

January 19_7 $\qquad$ $\$4{,}000 - \$800 = (200 - 0) \times \$16$

$$\$3{,}200 = \$3{,}200$$

February 19_7 $\qquad$ $\$20{,}200 - \$21{,}800 = (100 - 200) \times \$16$

$$-\$1{,}600 = -\$1{,}600$$

Effect of Sales and Production on Operating Income

The period-to-period change in operating income under variable costing is driven solely by changes in the unit level of sales, given a constant contribution margin per unit. Consider for Stassen the variable-costing operating income in February 19_7 versus that in January 19_7:

$$\begin{array}{c}\text{Change in} \\ \text{operating income}\end{array} = \begin{array}{c}\text{Contribution} \\ \text{margin}\end{array} \times \begin{array}{c}\text{Change in unit} \\ \text{sales level}\end{array}$$

$$\$21{,}800 - \$800 = (\$99 - \$39) \times (750 - 400)$$

$$\$21{,}000 = \$60 \times 350$$

$$\$21{,}000 = \$21{,}000$$

Note that under variable costing, Stassen managers cannot increase operating income (and hence their bonuses) by producing for inventory.

Under absorption costing, however, period-to-period change in operating income is driven by variations in *both* the unit level of sales and the unit level of production. Exhibit 9-3 illustrates this point. The exhibit shows how absorption-costing operating income for February 19_7 changes as the production level in February 19_7 changes. This exhibit assumes that all variances (including the production-volume variance) are written off to cost of goods sold at the end of each accounting period. The beginning inventory in February 19_7 of 200 units and the February sales of 750 units are unchanged. Exhibit 9-3 shows that production of only 550 units meets February 19_7 sales of 750. Operating income at this production level is $18,600. By producing more than 550 units in February 19_7, Stassen increases absorption-costing operating income. Each unit in February 19_7 ending inventory will increase February operating income by $16. For example, if 800 units are produced, ending inventory will be 250 units and operating income will be $22,600. This amount is $4,000 more than what operating income is with zero ending inventory (250 units × $16 = $4,000) on February 28, 19_7. Recall that Stassen's managers receive a bonus based on monthly operating income. Absorption costing enables them to increase operating income (and hence their bonuses) by producing for inventory. A subsequent section of this chapter (p. 310) on "Performance Measures" discusses the undesirable effects of this behavior.

Exhibit 9-4 compares the key differences between variable and absorption costing.

EXHIBIT 9-3
Stassen Company: Effect on Absorption-Costing Operating Income of Different Production Levels Holding the Unit Sales Level Constant, Data for February 19_7 with Sales of 750 Units

	February 19_7 Production Level				
	550	650	700	800	850
Unit Data					
Beginning inventory	200	200	200	200	200
Production	550	650	700	800	850
Goods available for sale	750	850	900	1,000	1,050
Sales	750	750	750	750	750
Ending inventory	0	100	150	250	300
Income Statement					
Revenues	$74,250	$74,250	$74,250	$74,250	$74,250
Beginning inventory	7,200	7,200	7,200	7,200	7,200
Variable manufacturing costs*	11,000	13,000	14,000	16,000	17,000
Fixed manufacturing costs†	8,800	10,400	11,200	12,800	13,600
Cost of goods available for sale	27,000	30,600	32,400	36,000	37,800
Ending inventory††	0	3,600	5,400	9,000	10,800
Cost of goods sold (at standard cost)	27,000	27,000	27,000	27,000	27,000
Adjustment for manufacturing variances=	4,000 U	2,400 U	1,600 U	0	800 F
Total cost of goods sold	31,000	29,400	28,600	27,000	26,200
Gross margin	43,250	44,850	45,650	47,250	48,050
Total marketing and administrative costs	24,650	24,650	24,650	24,650	24,650
Operating income	$18,600	$20,200	$21,000	$22,600	$23,400

*$20 per unit.
†Assigned at $16 per unit.
††$36 per unit.
=(Production in units − 800) × $16. All written off to cost of goods sold at end of the accounting period.

BREAKEVEN POINTS IN VARIABLE AND ABSORPTION COSTING

OBJECTIVE 4

Describe the effects of absorption costing on computing the breakeven point

Chapter 3 introduced cost-volume-profit analysis. If variable costing is used, the breakeven point (reported operating income of zero) is computed in the usual manner. It is unique; there is only one breakeven point. It is a function of (1) fixed costs, (2) unit contribution margin, and (3) sales level in units. Holding (1) and (2) constant, operating income rises as the sales level in units rises, and vice versa. As the level of sales in units rises, operating income rises, and vice versa. In our Stassen illustration for February 19_7, the following holds:

$$\frac{\text{Breakeven}}{\text{number of units}} = \frac{\text{Total fixed costs}}{\text{Unit contribution margin}}$$

Let Q = Number of units sold to break even

$$Q = \frac{\$12,800 + \$10,400}{\$99 - (\$20 + \$19)} = \frac{\$23,200}{\$60}$$

Q = 387 units (rounded)[4]

If absorption costing is used, the breakeven point (reported operating income of zero) is not unique. The following formula, which can be used to compute the

[4]Proof of breakeven point:
Revenues: $99 × 387	$38,313
Costs: $39 × 387	15,093
Contribution margin	23,220
Fixed costs	23,200
Operating income	$ 20 (rounding error)

EXHIBIT 9-4
Comparative Income Effects of Variable Costing and Absorption Costing

Question	Variable Costing	Absorption Costing	Comment
Are fixed manufacturing costs inventoried?	No	Yes	Basic theoretical question when these costs should be expensed as period costs.
Is there a production volume variance?	No	Yes	Choice of denominator level affects measurement of operating income under absorption costing only.
How are the other variances treated?	Same	Same	Highlights that the basic difference is the accounting for fixed manufacturing costs, not the accounting for any variable manufacturing costs.
Are classifications between variable and fixed costs routinely made?	Yes	Not always	Absorption costing can be easily modified to obtain subclassifications for variable and fixed costs, if desired (for example, see Exhibit 9-1, Panel B).
How do changes in unit inventory levels affect operating income?			Differences are attributable to the timing of when fixed manufacturing costs become period costs.
Production = sales	Equal	Equal	
Production > sales	Lower*	Higher†	
Production < sales	Higher	Lower	
What are the effects on CVP relationships?	Driven by unit sales level	Driven by unit sales level and unit production level	Management control benefit: Effects of changes in production level on operating income are easier to understand under variable costing.

*That is, lower operating income than under absorption costing.
†That is, higher operating income than under variable costing.

breakeven point under absorption costing, highlights several factors that will affect the breakeven point:

$$\text{Breakeven number of units} = \frac{\text{Total fixed costs} + \left[\text{Fixed manufacturing cost rate} \left(\text{Breakeven sales in units} - \text{Units produced} \right) \right]}{\text{Unit contribution margin}}$$

Let N = the number of units sold to break even. Consider the Stassen Company in February 19_7:

$$Q = \frac{\$12,800 + \$10,400 + [\$16 \, (Q - 650)]}{\$99 - (\$20 + \$19)}$$

$$Q = \frac{\$23,200 + \$16Q - \$10,400}{\$60}$$

$$\$60Q = \$12,800 + \$16Q$$

$$\$44Q = \$12,800$$

$$Q = 291 \text{ units (rounded)}[5]$$

[5]Proof of breakeven point:

Revenues: $99 × 291		$28,809
Cost of goods sold		
Cost of goods sold (standard): $36 × 291	$10,476	
Production-volume variance: (800 − 650) × $16	2,400	12,876
Gross margin		15,933
Marketing costs		
Variable marketing: $19 × 291	5,529	
Fixed marketing	10,400	15,929
Operating income		$ 4
(rounding error)		

The breakeven point under absorption costing depends on (1) fixed costs, (2) unit contribution margin, (3) sales level in units, (4) production level in units, and (5) the denominator level chosen to set the fixed manufacturing costs rate. For Stassen in February 19_7, a combination of fixed costs of $23,200, unit contribution margin of $60, units sold of 291 (rounded), 650 units produced, and an 800-unit denominator level would result in an operating income of zero. Note, however, there are many combinations of these five factors that would give an operating income of zero.

We see that variable costing dovetails with cost-volume-profit analysis. Managers using variable costing can easily compute the breakeven point or any effects that changes in the sales level in units may have on operating income. In contrast, managers using absorption costing must also consider the unit production level, and the denominator level before making such computations.

Suppose in our illustration that actual production in February 19_7 was equal to the denominator level, 800 units. Also suppose that there were no sales and no fixed marketing costs. All the production would be placed in inventory, and so all the fixed manufacturing overhead would be included in inventory. There would be no production-volume variance. Thus, the company could break even with no sales whatsoever! In contrast, under variable costing the operating loss would be equal to the fixed costs of $12,800.

THROUGHPUT COSTING

OBJECTIVE 5

Differentiate throughput costing from variable costing and absorption costing

Some critics of existing costing systems maintain that even variable costing promotes an excessive amount of costs being inventoried. They argue that only direct materials are "truly variable" and propose the use of throughput costing instead. **Throughput costing** (also called **super-variable costing**) treats all costs except those related to variable direct materials as costs of the period in which they are incurred; only variable direct materials costs are inventoriable. This method is a very recent proposal and currently is not yet widely used.

Exhibit 9-5 is the throughput costing income statement for the Stassen Company. Compare the operating income amounts reported with those for absorption and variable costing:

	Absorption Costing	Variable Costing	Throughput Costing
January 19_7	$ 4,000	$ 800	$ (1,000)
February 19_7	20,200	21,800	22,700

Only the $11 direct materials cost per unit is inventoriable under throughput costing (compared to $36 for absorption costing and $20 for variable costing). Where production exceeds sales (as in January 19_7), throughput costing results in the largest amount of costs being expensed to the current period. Throughput contribution in Exhibit 9-5 is revenues minus all variable direct materials costs.

Advocates of throughput costing maintain there is reduced incentive for building up excess inventories vis-à-vis the case when variable or (especially) absorption costing is used. Reducing inventory levels means less funds are tied up in inventory and hence there are more funds available to invest in productive outlets. Moreover, reducing inventory levels typically means reducing inventory spoilage and obsolescence costs.

CAPSULE COMPARISON OF INVENTORY-COSTING METHODS

Variable costing, absorption costing, or throughput costing may be combined with actual, normal, extended-normal, or standard costing. Exhibit 9-6 presents a capsule comparison of a job-costing record under 12 alternative inventory-costing systems:

EXHIBIT 9-5
Throughput Costing for Stassen Company

	January 19_7	February 19_7
Unit Data		
Production	600	650
Sales	400	750
Income Statement		
Revenues*	$39,600	$74,250
Variable direct materials costs		
Beginning inventory	0	2,200
Direct materials in goods manufactured[†]	6,600	7,150
Cost of goods available for sale	6,600	9,350
Ending inventory[††]	2,200	1,100
Direct materials costs (at standard)	4,400	8,250
Adjustment for direct materials variances	0	0
Total variable direct materials costs	4,400	8,250
Throughput contribution[~]	35,200	66,000
Other costs		
Manufacturing[#]	18,200	18,650
Marketing[‖]	18,000	24,650
Adjustment for variances	0	0
Total other costs	36,200	43,300
Operating income	$ (1,000)	$22,700

Handwritten annotations: "99 × 400" by Revenues; "250 × 99" by $74,250; "600 × 11" by Direct materials in goods manufactured; "650 × 11"; "200 × 11" by Ending inventory; "100 × 11"; "200 × 11" in right margin.

*400 × $99 = $39,600; 750 × $99 = $74,250
[†]600 × $11 = $6,600; 650 × $11 = $7,150
[††]200 × $11 = $2,200; 100 × $11 = $1,100
[~]Throughput contribution is the difference between revenues and variable direct materials costs.
[#](600 × $9) + $12,800 = $18,200; (650 × $9) + $12,800 = $18,650
[‖](400 × $19) + $10,400 = $18,000; (750 × $19) + $10,400 = $24,650

Variable Costing	Absorption Costing	Throughput Costing
1. Actual costing	5. Actual costing	9. Actual costing
2. Normal costing	6. Normal costing	10. Normal costing
3. Extended-normal costing	7. Extended-normal costing	11. Extended-normal costing
4. Standard costing	8. Standard costing	12. Standard costing

The data in Exhibit 9-6 represent the debits to job costing account (that is, the amounts assigned to product) under alternative inventory-costing systems.

Variable costing has been a controversial subject among accountants—not so much because there is disagreement about the need for delineating between variable and fixed costs for management planning and control, but because there is a question about using variable costing for *external* reporting. Those favoring variable costing for external reporting maintain that the fixed portion of manufacturing costs is more closely related to the capacity to produce than to the production of specific units. Supporters of absorption costing maintain that inventories should carry a fixed manufacturing cost component. Why? Because both variable and fixed manufacturing costs are necessary to produce goods, both types of costs should be inventoriable, regardless of their having different behavior patterns.

Absorption costing (or variants close to it) is the method most commonly used for the external regulatory purpose of accounting systems. For example, for reporting to the U.S. Internal Revenue Service, all manufacturing costs plus some product design and administrative costs (such as legal) must be included as inventoriable costs. Legal department costs must be allocated between those costs related to

			Actual Costing	Normal Costing	Extended-Normal Costing	Standard Costing
Absorption Costing	**Variable Costing**	**Throughput Costing**				
		Variable Direct Materials Costs	Actual prices × Actual inputs used	Actual prices × Actual inputs used	Budgeted prices × Actual inputs used	Standard prices × Standard inputs allowed for actual output achieved
		Variable Direct Conversion Costs*	Actual prices × Actual inputs used	Actual prices × Actual inputs used	Budgeted prices × Actual inputs used	Standard prices × Standard inputs allowed for actual output achieved
		Variable Indirect Manufacturing Costs	Actual variable indirect rates × Actual inputs used	Budgeted variable indirect rates × Actual inputs used	Budgeted variable indirect rates × Actual inputs used	Standard variable indirect rates × Standard inputs allowed for actual output achieved
		Fixed Direct Manufacturing Costs	Actual prices × Actual inputs used	Actual prices × Actual inputs used	Budgeted prices × Actual inputs used	Standard prices × Standard inputs allowed for actual output achieved
		Fixed Indirect Manufacturing Costs	Actual fixed indirect rates × Actual inputs used	Budgeted fixed indirect rates × Actual inputs used	Budgeted fixed indirect rates × Actual inputs used	Standard fixed indirect rates × Standard inputs allowed for actual output achieved

*Conversion costs are all manufacturing costs minus direct materials costs.

manufacturing activities (inventoriable costs) and those not related to manufacturing activities. For external reporting to shareholders, companies around the globe tend to follow the generally accepted accounting principle that all manufacturing overhead is inventoriable.

Throughput costing is not permitted for the external regulatory purpose of accounting systems if it results in materially different numbers to those reported by absorption costing. Advocates of throughput costing emphasize the internal purposes of management accounting data.

PERFORMANCE MEASURES AND ABSORPTION COSTING

Undesirable Buildups of Inventories

OBJECTIVE 6

Understand how absorption costing influences performance evaluation decisions

Absorption costing enables managers to increase operating income in the short run by increasing the production schedule independent of customer demand for products. Exhibit 9-3 shows how a Stassen manager could increase February 19_7 operating income from $18,600 to $22,600 by producing an additional 250 units for inventory. Such an increase in the production schedule can increase the costs of doing business without any attendant increase in sales. For example, a manager whose performance is evaluated on the basis of absorption-costing income may increase production at the end of a review period solely to increase reported income. Each additional unit produced absorbs fixed manufacturing costs that would otherwise have been written off as a cost of the period.

The undesirable effects of such an increase in production may be sizable, and they can arise in several ways as the following examples show:

1. A plant manager may switch production to those orders that absorb the highest amount of fixed manufacturing costs, irrespective of the customer demand for these products (called "cherry picking" the production line). Some difficult-to-manufacture items may be delayed, resulting in failure to meet promised customer delivery dates.

Nothing Beats a Great Deduction: The IRS and Packaging Design Costs

Where does the U.S. Internal Revenue Service draw the line on inventoriable line items? Cost accounting issues arise in many areas of tax reporting. The IRS requires firms to use absorption costing when computing inventoriable costs, but just what are inventoriable costs?

As a general rule, taxpayers want to have as few line items in inventoriable costs as the tax laws permit and to claim as many deductions in the current period as possible. The higher the deductions, the lower the taxable income. Conversely, in this tax tug-of-war, the more line items the IRS classifies as inventoriable costs, the more its tax receipts will increase.

One group of taxpayers—consumer-products companies—can spend sizable amounts on package design. Consider the container of L'Eggs panty hose, manufactured by Sara Lee. The cost of designing this package included the costs of materials, labor, and overhead at each step of its development, from preliminary designs, to prototypes, and on to the working models that Sara Lee tests. Any work that an independent design company or consumer-testing firm conducted would also be design costs for Sara Lee. The question is, Just how much of this cost can L'Eggs deduct and how much must it absorb as inventoriable costs? Are package design costs that are spent before production begins allowable as inventoriable costs?

Although many companies do not share this view, the IRS requires companies to capitalize as inventoriable line items the costs incurred in designing packages. Companies must then amortize these costs over a six-year period. The IRS does, however, permit early write-off of any unamortized design costs if the company abandons the use of the design in its products. In other words, companies may write off in the current period only those costs incurred in designing a package that was not a success in the marketplace.

Source: Adapted from Ochsenchlager, "IRS Rules on Package Design Costs."

---

2. A plant manager may accept a particular order to increase production even though another plant in the same company is better suited to handle that order.

3. To meet increased production, a manager may defer maintenance beyond the current accounting period. Although operating income may increase now, future operating income will probably decrease because of increased repairs and less efficient equipment.

Early criticisms of absorption costing concentrated on whether fixed manufacturing overhead qualified as an asset under generally accepted accounting principles. However, current criticisms of absorption costing have increasingly emphasized its potentially undesirable incentives for managers. Indeed, one critic labels absorption costing as "one of the black holes of cost accounting," in part because it may induce managers to make decisions "against the long-run interests" of the company.

Proposals for Revising Performance Evaluation

Critics of absorption costing have made a variety of proposals for revising how managers are evaluated. Their proposals include the following:

1. *Change the accounting system.* As discussed previously in this chapter, both variable and throughput costing reduce the incentives of managers to build for inventory. An alternative approach is to incorporate into the accounting system a charge for managers who tie up funds in inventory. The higher the amount of inventory held, the higher the inventory holding charge.

2. *Change the time period used to evaluate performance.* Critics of absorption costing give examples where managers take actions that maximize quarterly or annual income at the potential expense of long-run income. By evaluating performance over a three- to five-year period, the incentive to take short-run actions that reduce long-term income is lessened.

3. *Include nonfinancial as well as financial variables in the measures used to evaluate performance.* Companies currently are using nonfinancial variables, such as the following, to monitor managers' performance in key areas:

A. $\dfrac{\text{Ending inventory in units this period}}{\text{Ending inventory in units last period}}$

B. $\dfrac{\text{Sales in units this period}}{\text{Ending inventory in units this period}}$

SURVEYS OF COMPANY PRACTICE

Company Usage of Variable Costing

Surveys of company practice in many countries report that approximately 30–50% of companies use variable costing in their internal accounting system:

	United States*	Canada*	Australia[†]	Japan[†]	Sweden[††]	United Kingdom[†]
Variable costing used	31%	48%	33%	31%	42%	52%
Absorption costing used	65	52	}67	}69	}58	}48
Other	4	0				

A survey of Irish companies[≈] reported predominant use of absorption costing. Only 19% of respondents used variable costing as the primary format in their internal reports to top management. A further 31% used it as a supplementary format in their internal reports. Surveys to date have not examined usage of throughput costing.

Many companies use some version of variable costing for internal reporting but use absorption costing for external reporting or tax reporting. How do companies using some version of variable costing treat fixed manufacturing overhead (MOH) in their internal reporting system?

	Australia[†]	Japan[†]	United Kingdom[†]
Prorate fixed MOH to inventory/ cost of goods sold at period end	41%	39%	25%
Use variable costing for monthly costing, and convert to absorption costing once a year	11	8	4
Use both variable costing and absorption costing as dual systems	23	33	31
Treat fixed MOH as a period cost	25	3	35
Other	0	17	4

The most common problem reported by companies using variable costing was the difficulty of classifying costs into fixed or variable categories.

*Adapted from Inoue, "A Comparative Study."
[†]Adapted from Blayney and Yokoyama, "A Comparative Analysis."
[††]Adapted from Ask and Ax, "Trends."
[≈]Adapted from Clarke, "Management Accounting Systems."
Full citations are in Appendix A.

Any buildup of inventory at the end of the year would be signaled by tracking the month-to-month behavior of these two nonfinancial inventory measures (where a company manufactures or sells several products, the two measures could be reported on a product-by-product basis).

◆ PART TWO: DENOMINATOR-LEVEL CONCEPTS AND ABSORPTION COSTING

Now we examine how alternative denominator-level concepts affect fixed manufacturing overhead rates and operating income under absorption costing. Reported cost numbers can be sizably affected by the choice of a denominator level. This can be important in many contexts, such as pricing and contracting based on reported cost numbers.

ALTERNATIVE DENOMINATOR-LEVEL CONCEPTS

We use an iced-tea bottling plant to illustrate several alternative denominator-level concepts. The Bushells Company produces 12-ounce bottles of iced tea. The variable manufacturing costs of each bottle are $0.35. The fixed monthly manufacturing costs of the bottling plant are $50,000. Bushells uses absorption costing for its monthly internal reporting system and for financial reporting to shareholders. Bushells could use any one of at least four different denominator-level concepts for computing the fixed manufacturing overhead rate—theoretical capacity, practical capacity, normal utilization, and master-budget utilization. Whichever the denominator-level concept, Bushells defines its denominator in output units (12-ounce bottles of iced tea).

> **OBJECTIVE 7**
>
> Describe the various denominator-level concepts that can be used in absorption costing

Theoretical Capacity and Practical Capacity

The term *capacity* means constraint, an upper limit. **Theoretical capacity** is the denominator-level concept that is based on the production of output at full efficiency for all of the time. Bushells can produce 2,400 bottles an hour when the bottling lines are operating at full speed. There is a maximum of two 8-hour shifts per day due to a labor union agreement. Thus, the theoretical monthly capacity would be

$$2,400 \text{ per hour} \times 16 \text{ hours} \times 30 \text{ days} = 1,152,000 \text{ bottles}$$

Theoretical capacity is theoretical in the sense that it does not allow for any plant maintenance, any interruptions because of bottle breakages on the filling lines, or a host of other factors. While it is a rare plant that is able to operate at theoretical capacity, it can represent a goal or target level of usage.

Practical capacity is the denominator-level concept that reduces theoretical capacity for unavoidable operating interruptions such as scheduled maintenance time, shutdowns for holidays and other days, and so on. Assume that the practical hourly production rate is 2,000 bottles an hour and that the plant can operate 25 days a month. The practical monthly capacity is thus:

$$2,000 \text{ per hour} \times 16 \text{ hours} \times 25 \text{ days} = 800,000 \text{ bottles}$$

Engineering, economic and human factors are important to consider when estimating theoretical or practical capacity. Engineers at the Bushells' plant can provide input on the technical capabilities of machines for filling bottles. In some cases, however, an increase in capacity may be technically possible but not economically sound. For example, the labor union may actually permit a third shift per day but only at unusually high wage rates that clearly do not make financial sense in the iced-tea market. Human-safety factors, such as increased injury risk when the line operates at faster speeds, are also important to consider.

Normal Utilization and Master-Budget Utilization

Both theoretical capacity and practical capacity measure the denominator level in terms of what a plant can supply. In contrast, normal utilization and master-budget utilization measure the denominator level in terms of demand for the output of the plant. In many cases, budgeted demand is well below the supply available (productive capacity).

Normal utilization is the denominator-level concept based on the level of capacity utilization that satisfies average customer demand over a period (say, of two to three years) that includes seasonal, cyclical, or other trend factors. **Master-budget utilization** is the denominator-level concept based on the anticipated level of capacity utilization for the next budget period. These two denominator levels can differ—for example, when an industry has cyclical periods of high and low demand or when management believes that the budgeted production for the coming period is unrepresentative of "long-term" demand.

Consider our Bushells example of iced-tea production. The master budget for 19_8 is based on production of 400,000 bottles per month. Hence the master-budget denominator level is 400,000 bottles. However, Bushells senior management believes that over the next one to three years the normal monthly production level will be 500,000 bottles. These people view the 19_8 budgeted production level of 400,000 bottles to be "abnormally" low. Why? A major competitor has been sharply reducing its iced-tea selling prices and has also been spending enormous amounts on advertising. Bushells expects that the lower prices and advertising blitz will be a short-run phenomenon and that in 19_9 the market share it has lost to this competitor will be regained.

A major reason for choosing master-budget utilization over normal utilization is the difficulty of forecasting normal utilization in many industries with long-run cyclical patterns. For example, many U.S. steel companies in the 1980s believed that they were in a downturn of the demand cycle and that there would be an upturn shortly. Unfortunately, the cycle did not turn up for years, and many plants closed. A similar problem occurs when estimating "normal" demand. Some marketing managers are prone to overestimating their ability to regain lost market share. Their estimate of "normal" demand for their product may be based on an overly optimistic outlook ("anticipating roses when all that exists are thorns").

EFFECT ON FINANCIAL STATEMENTS

OBJECTIVE 8

Explain how the choice of denominator level affects reported operating income and inventory costs

Bushells has budgeted fixed manufacturing costs of $50,000 per month. Assume that actual costs are also $50,000. To keep this example simple, we assume all fixed manufacturing costs are indirect. The budgeted fixed manufacturing overhead rates in May 19_8 for the four alternative denominator-level concepts discussed are

Denominator-Level Concept (1)	Budgeted Fixed Manufacturing Overhead per Month (2)	Budgeted Denominator Level (in bottles) (3)	Budgeted Fixed Manufacturing Overhead Cost Rate (4) = (2) ÷ (3)
Theoretical capacity	$50,000	1,152,000	$0.0434
Practical capacity	50,000	800,000	0.0625
Normal utilization	50,000	500,000	0.1000
Master-budget utilization	50,000	400,000	0.1250

The budgeted fixed manufacturing overhead rate based on master-budget utilization ($0.1250) is more than 180% above the rate based on theoretical capacity ($0.0434).

Assume now that Bushells' actual production in May 19_8 is 460,000 bottles of iced tea. Actual sales are 420,000 bottles. Also assume no beginning inventory on May 1, 19_8 and no price, spending, or efficiency variances in manufacturing for May 19_8. The manufacturing plant sells bottles of iced tea to another division for $0.50 per bottle. Its only costs are variable manufacturing costs of $0.35 per bottle and \$50,000 per month for fixed manufacturing overhead. Bushells writes off all variances to cost of goods sold on a monthly basis.

The budgeted manufacturing costs per bottle of iced tea for each denominator-level concept is the sum of \$0.35 in variable manufacturing costs and the budgeted fixed manufacturing overhead costs (shown from the preceding table).

Denominator-Level Concept (1)	Variable Manufacturing Costs (2)	Budgeted Fixed Manufacturing Overhead Cost Rate (3)	Total Manufacturing Costs (4) = (2) + (3)
Theoretical capacity	\$0.3500	\$0.0434	\$0.3934
Practical capacity	0.3500	0.0625	0.4125
Normal utilization	0.3500	0.1000	0.4500
Master-budget utilization	0.3500	0.1250	0.4750

Each denominator-level concept will result in a different production-volume variance.

$$\text{Production-volume variance} = \left(\begin{array}{c} \text{Denominator} \\ \text{level in} \\ \text{output units} \end{array} - \begin{array}{c} \text{Actual} \\ \text{output} \\ \text{units} \end{array} \right) \times \begin{array}{c} \text{Budgeted fixed} \\ \text{manufacturing} \\ \text{overhead rate} \\ \text{per output unit} \end{array}$$

Theoretical capacity
$$= (1,152,000 - 460,000) \times \$0.0434$$
$$= \$30,033 \text{ U (rounded up)}$$

Practical capacity
$$= (800,000 - 460,000) \times \$0.0625$$
$$= \$21,250 \text{ U}$$

Normal utilization
$$= (500,000 - 460,000) \times \$0.1000$$
$$= \$4,000 \text{ U}$$

Master-budget utilization $= (400,000 - 460,000) \times \$0.1250$
$$= \$7,500 \text{ F}$$

Exhibit 9-7 shows how the choice of a denominator affects Bushell's operating income for May 19_8. Using the master-budget denominator results in assigning the highest amount of fixed manufacturing overhead costs per bottle to the 40,000 bottles in ending inventory. Accordingly, operating income is highest using the master-budget utilization denominator. Recall that Bushells had no beginning inventory on May 1, 19_8, production in May of 460,000 bottles, and sales in May of 420,000 bottles. Hence, the ending inventory on May 31 is 40,000 bottles. The differences among the operating income for the four denominator-level concepts in Exhibit 9-7 are due to different amounts of fixed manufacturing overhead being inventoried:

Denominator-Level Concept	Fixed Manufacturing Overhead in May 31, 19_8 Inventory
Theoretical capacity	40,000 × \$0.0434 = \$1,736
Practical capacity	40,000 × 0.0625 = 2,500
Normal utilization	40,000 × 0.1000 = 4,000
Master-budget utilization	40,000 × 0.1250 = 5,000

Thus, in Exhibit 9-7 the difference in operating income between the master-budget utilization concept and the normal utilization concept of \$1,000 (\$8,000 − \$7,000) is due to the difference in fixed manufacturing overhead inventoried (\$5,000 − \$4,000).

There is no requirement that U.S. companies use the same denominator-level concept for internal reporting, financial reporting, and income tax purposes. Nevertheless, the costs of recordkeeping and the desire for simplicity often lead companies to choose the same denominator level for internal reporting and tax purposes. Income tax rulings by the U.S. Internal Revenue Service effectively prohibit use of the

EXHIBIT 9-7

Bushells Company: Income Statement Effects of Alternative Denominator-Level Concepts for May 19_8

	Theoretical Capacity	Practical Capacity	Normal Utilization	Master-Budget Utilization
Sales, $0.50 × 420,000	$210,000	$210,000	$210,000	$210,000
Cost of goods sold				
Beginning inventory	0	0	0	0
Variable manufacturing costs*	161,000	161,000	161,000	161,000
Fixed manufacturing overhead costs†	19,964	28,750	46,000	57,500
Cost of goods available for sale	180,964	189,750	207,000	218,500
Ending inventory††	15,736	16,500	18,000	19,000
Total COGS (at standard costs)	165,228	173,250	189,000	199,500
Adjustment for manufacturing variances˜	30,033 U	21,250 U	4,000 U	7,500 F
Total COGS	195,261	194,500	193,000	192,000
Gross margin	14,739	15,500	17,000	18,000
Marketing costs	10,000	10,000	10,000	10,000
Operating income	$ 4,739	$ 5,500	$ 7,000	$ 8,000

*$0.35 × 460,000 = $161,000
†Fixed manufacturing overhead costs:
  $0.0434 × 460,000 = $19,964
  $0.0625 × 460,000 = $28,750
  $0.1000 × 460,000 = $46,000
  $0.1250 × 460,000 = $57,500
††Ending inventory costs
  ($0.3500 + $0.0434) × (460,000 − 420,000) = $15,736
  ($0.3500 + $0.0625) × (460,000 − 420,000) = $16,500
  ($0.3500 + $0.1000) × (460,000 − 420,000) = $18,000
  ($0.3500 + $0.1250) × (460,000 − 420,000) = $19,000
˜ The only variance for Bushells in May 19_8 is the production-volume variance.
  See text (p.315) for the computations.

theoretical capacity or practical capacity denominator-level concepts. Both these concepts typically result in companies taking write-offs of fixed manufacturing overhead as tax deductions more quickly than the IRS wants. The IRS requires companies to use the master-budget denominator level (along with full proration of variances between inventories and cost of goods sold) for income tax reporting.

PROBLEM FOR SELF-STUDY

PROBLEM

Suppose that the Bushells Company in our example is computing the operating income for May 19_9. This month is identical to May 19_8, the results of which are in Exhibit 9-7, except that master-budget utilization for 19_9 is 600,000 bottles per month instead of 400,000 bottles. There was no beginning inventory on May 1, 19_9, and no variances other than the production-volume variance. Bushells writes off this variance to cost of goods sold on a monthly basis.

REQUIRED

How would the results in Exhibit 9-7 for Bushells Company be different if the month is May 19_9 rather than May 19_8? Show your computations.

SOLUTION

The only change in the Exhibit 9-7 results will be for the master-budget utilization level. The budgeted fixed manufacturing overhead cost rate in May 19_9 is

$$\frac{\$50,000}{600,000 \text{ bottles}} = \$0.0833 \text{ per bottle}$$

The manufacturing cost per bottle becomes $0.4333 ($0.3500 + $0.0833). In turn, the production-volume variance for May 19_9 becomes

$$(600,000 - 460,000) \times (\$0.0833) = \$11,662 \text{ U}$$

The income statement for May 19_9 is now:

Revenues	$210,000
Cost of goods sold	
Beginning inventory	0
Variable manufacturing costs:	
$0.35 × 460,000	161,000
Fixed manufacturing costs:	
$0.0833 × 460,000	38,318
Cost of goods available for sale	199,318
Ending inventory:	
$0.4333 × (460,000 − 420,000)	17,332
Total cost of goods sold (at standard costs)	181,986
Adjustment for variances	11,662 U
Total cost of goods sold	193,648
Gross margin	16,352
Other costs	0
Operating income	$ 16,352

The higher denominator level in the 19_9 master budget means that less fixed manufacturing overhead costs are inventoried in May 19_9 than in May 19_8 given identical sales and production levels.

SUMMARY

The following points are linked to this chapter's learning objectives.

1. Variable costing and absorption costing differ in only one respect—how to account for fixed manufacturing overhead costs. Under variable costing, fixed manufacturing overhead costs are excluded from inventoriable costs and are a cost of the period in which they are incurred. Under absorption costs, these costs are inventoriable and become expenses only when a sale occurs.

2. The variable-costing income statement is based on the contribution margin format. The absorption-costing income statement is based on the gross margin format.

3. Under variable costing, reported operating income is driven by variations in unit sales levels. Under absorption costing, reported operating income is driven by variations in unit production levels as well as by variations in unit sales levels.

4. There is only one breakeven point with a variable-costing income statement. In contrast, there can be multiple breakeven points with an absorption-costing income statement; there are multiple combinations of fixed costs, unit contribution margin, unit sales, unit production, and the denominator level that yield an operating income of zero.

5. Throughput costing treats all costs except those related to variable direct materials as costs of the period in which they are incurred. It results in a lower percentage of manufacturing costs being inventoried than does either variable or absorption costing.

6. Managers can increase operating income when absorption costing is used by producing for inventory even when there is no immediate demand for the extra production. Critics of absorption costing label this as the major negative consequence of treating fixed manufacturing overhead as an inventoriable cost. Such negative consequences can be highlighted by using nonfinancial as well as financial variables for performance evaluation.

7. The denominator level chosen for fixed manufacturing overhead can greatly affect reported inventory and operating income amounts. In some cases it can also affect pricing and contract reimbursement. Denominator levels focusing on the capacity of a plant to supply product are theoretical capacity and practical capacity. Denominator levels focusing on the demand for the products a plant can manufacture are normal utilization and master-budget utilization.

8. The smaller the denominator level chosen, the higher the fixed manufacturing overhead cost per output unit that is inventoriable. The IRS's requirement that the master-budget utilization concept be used typically results in higher operating income amounts being reported compared with the operating income reported using the practical capacity or theoretical capacity denominator-level concepts.

▼ TERMS TO LEARN

This chapter and the Glossary at the end of the book contain definitions of the following important terms:

absorption costing (p. 298)	super-variable costing (308)
direct costing (300)	theoretical capacity (313)
master-budget utilization (314)	throughput costing (308)
normal utilization (314)	variable costing (298)
practical capacity (313)	

▼ ASSIGNMENT MATERIAL

QUESTIONS

9-1 Differences in operating income between variable and absorption costing are due solely to accounting for fixed costs. Do you agree? Explain.

9-2 Why is the term *direct costing* a misnomer?

9-3 The term *variable costing* could be improved by calling it variable manufacturing costing. Do you agree? Why?

9-4 Explain the main conceptual issue under variable and absorption costing regarding the proper timing for the release of fixed manufacturing overhead as expense.

9-5 "Companies that make no variable-cost/fixed-cost distinctions must use absorption costing and those that do make variable-cost/fixed-cost distinctions must use variable costing." Do you agree? Explain.

9-6 "The main trouble with variable costing is that it ignores the increasing importance of fixed costs in modern manufacturing." Do you agree? Why?

9-7 Give an example of how, under absorption costing, operating income could fall even though the unit sales level rises.

9-8 What are the factors that affect the breakeven point under variable costing?

9-9 What are the factors that affect the breakeven point under absorption costing?

9-10 Why might *throughput costing* be also called *super-variable costing?*

9-11 Critics of absorption costing have increasingly emphasized its potential for promoting undesirable incentives for managers. Give an example.

9-12 What are two ways of reducing the negative aspects associated with using absorption costing to evaluate the performance of a plant manager?

9-13 What is the costing method most frequently used by companies in their internal accounting system—throughput costing, variable costing, or absorption costing?

9-14 Which denominator-level concepts emphasize what a plant can supply? Which denominator-level concepts emphasize what customers demand for products produced by a plant?

9-15 Name one reason why many companies prefer the master-budget utilization-level concept rather than the normal utilization-level concept.

EXERCISES

9-16 **Variable and absorption costing, explaining operating income differences.** Nascar Motors assembles and sells motor vehicles. It uses an actual costing system, in which unit costs are calculated on a monthly basis. Data relating to April and May of 19_7 are

	April	May
Unit data		
Beginning inventory	0	150
Production	500	400
Sales	350	520
Variable-cost data		
Manufacturing costs per unit produced	$10,000	$10,000
Marketing costs per unit sold	3,000	3,000
Fixed-cost data		
Manufacturing costs	$2,000,000	$2,000,000
Marketing costs	600,000	600,000

The selling price per motor vehicle is $24,000.

REQUIRED
1. Present income statements for Nascar Motors in April and May of 19_7 under (a) variable costing, and (b) absorption costing.
2. Explain any differences between (a) and (b) for April and May.

9-17 **Throughput costing (continuation of 9-16).** The unit variable manufacturing costs of Nascar Motors are

	April	May
Direct materials	$6,700	$6,700
Direct manufacturing labor	1,500	1,500
Manufacturing overhead	1,800	1,800

1. Present income statements for Nascar Motors in April and May of 19_7 under throughput costing.

2. Contrast the results in requirement 1 with those in requirement 1 of Exercise 9-16.

3. Give one motivation for Nascar Motors adopting throughput costing.

9-18 Variable and absorption costing, explaining operating income differences. BigScreen Corporation manufactures and sells 50-inch television sets. It uses an actual costing system, in which unit costs are calculated on a monthly basis. Data relating to January, February and March of 19_8 are

	January	February	March
Unit data			
Beginning inventory	0	300	300
Production	1,000	800	1,250
Sales	700	800	1,500
Variable-cost data			
Manufacturing costs per unit produced	$900	$900	$900
Marketing costs per unit sold	600	600	600
Fixed-cost data			
Manufacturing costs	$400,000	$400,000	$400,000
Marketing costs	140,000	140,000	140,000

The selling price per unit is $2,500.

REQUIRED

1. Present income statements for BigScreen in January, February, and March of 19_8 under (a) variable costing, and (b) absorption costing.

2. Explain any differences between (a) and (b) for January, February, and March.

9-19 Throughput costing (continuation of 9-18). The unit variable manufacturing costs of BigScreen Corporation are

	January	February	March
Direct materials	$500	$500	$500
Direct manufacturing labor	100	100	100
Manufacturing overhead	300	300	300
	$900	$900	$900

REQUIRED

1. Present income statements for BigScreen in January, February, and March of 19_8 under throughput costing.

2. Contrast the results in requirement 1 with those in requirement 1 of Exercise 9-18.

3. Give one motivation for BigScreen adopting throughput costing.

9-20 Absorption and variable costing. (CMA) Osawa, Inc., planned and actually manufactured 200,000 units of its single product in 19_8, its first year of operation. Variable manufacturing costs were $20 per unit produced. Variable marketing and administrative costs were $10 per unit sold. Planned and actual fixed manufacturing costs were $600,000. Planned and actual marketing and administrative costs totaled $400,000 in 19_8. Osawa sold 120,000 units of product in 19_8 at a selling price of $40 per unit.

REQUIRED

1. Osawa's 19_8 operating income using absorption costing is (a) $440,000, (b) $200,000, (c) $600,000, (d) $840,000, (e) none of these.

2. Osawa's 19_8 operating income using variable costing is (a) $800,000, (b) $440,000, (c) $200,000, (d) $600,000, (e) none of these.

9-21 Comparison of actual costing methods. The Rehe Company sells its razors at $3 per unit. The company uses a first-in, first-out actual-costing system. A new fixed manufacturing overhead allocation rate is computed each year by dividing the actual fixed manufacturing overhead cost by the actual production units. The following simplified data are related to its first two years of operation:

	Year 1	Year 2
Unit data		
Sales	1,000	1,200
Production	1,400	1,000
Cost		
Variable manufacturing	$ 700	$ 500
Fixed manufacturing	700	700
Variable marketing and administration	1,000	1,200
Fixed marketing and administration	400	400

REQUIRED

1. Prepare income statements based on (a) variable costing and (b) absorption costing for each year.

2. Prepare a reconciliation and explanation of the difference in the operating income for each year resulting from the use of absorption costing and variable costing.

3. Critics have claimed that a widely used accounting system has led to undesirable buildups of inventory levels. (a) Is variable costing or absorption costing more likely to lead to such buildups? Why? (b) What can be done to counteract undesirable inventory buildups?

9-22 Income statements. (SMA) The Mass Company manufactures and sells a single product. The following data cover the two latest years of operations:

	19_6	19_7
Unit data		
Sales	25,000	25,000
Beginning inventory	1,000	1,000
Ending inventory	1,000	5,000
Selling price per unit	$40	$40
Cost data		
Standard fixed costs		
Manufacturing overhead	$120,000	$120,000
Marketing and administrative	$190,000	$190,000
Standard variable costs per unit:		
Direct materials	$10.50	
Direct manufacturing labor	$9.50	
Manufacturing overhead	$4.00	
Marketing and administrative	$1.20	

The denominator level is 30,000 output units per year. The Mass Company's accounting records produce variable-costing information, and year-end adjustments are made to produce external reports showing absorption-costing information. All variances are charged to cost of goods sold.

REQUIRED

1. Prepare two income statements for 19_7, one under variable costing and one under absorption costing.

2. Explain briefly why the operating income figures computed in requirement 1 agree or do not agree.

3. Give two advantages and two disadvantages of using variable costing for internal reporting.

PROBLEMS

9-23 **Variable costing versus absorption costing.** The Mavis Company uses an absorption-costing system based on standard costs. Total variable manufacturing costs, including direct materials costs, were $3 per unit; the standard production rate was 10 units per machine-hour. Total budgeted and actual fixed manufacturing overhead costs were $420,000. Fixed manufacturing overhead was allocated at $7 per machine-hour ($420,000 ÷ 60,000 machine-hours of denominator level). The selling price is $5 per unit. Variable marketing and administrative costs, which are driven by units sold, were $1 per unit. Fixed marketing and administrative costs were $120,000. Beginning inventory in 19_8 was 30,000 units; ending inventory was 40,000 units. Sales in 19_8 were 540,000 units. The same standard unit costs persisted throughout 19_7 and 19_8. For simplicity, assume that there were no price, spending, or efficiency variances.

REQUIRED

1. Prepare an income statement for 19_8 assuming that all under- or overallocated overhead is written off directly at year-end as an adjustment to cost of goods sold.

2. The president has heard about variable costing. She asks you to recast the 19_8 statement as it would appear under variable costing. Explain the difference in operating income as calculated in requirements 1 and 2.

3. Graph how fixed manufacturing overhead is accounted for under absorption costing. That is, there will be two lines, one for the budgeted fixed overhead (which is equal to the actual fixed manufacturing overhead in this case) and one for the fixed overhead allocated. Show how the over- or underallocated manufacturing overhead might be indicated on the graph.

9-24 **Breakeven under absorption costing (continuation of 9-23).**

REQUIRED

1. Compute the breakeven point in units under variable costing.

2. Compute the breakeven point in units under absorption costing.

3. Suppose that production was exactly equal to the denominator level, but no units were sold. Fixed manufacturing costs are unaffected. Assume, however, that all marketing and administrative costs were avoided. Compute operating income under (a) variable costing and (b) absorption costing. Explain the difference between your answers.

9-25 **Alternative denominator-level concepts.** Lucky Lager recently purchased a brewing plant from a bankrupt company. The brewery is in Austin, Texas. It was constructed only two years ago. The plant has budgeted fixed manufacturing overhead of $42 million ($3.5 million each month) in 19_8. Paul

Vautin, the controller of the brewery, must decide on the denominator-level concept to use in its absorption costing system for 19_8. The options available to him are

a. Theoretical capacity: 600 barrels an hour for 24 hours a day × 365 days = 5,256,000 barrels

b. Practical capacity: 500 barrels an hour for 20 hours a day × 350 days = 3,500,000 barrels

c. Normal utilization for 19_8: 400 barrels an hour for 20 hours a day × 350 days = 2,800,000 barrels

d. Master-budget utilization for 19_8 (separate rates computed for each half-year):

◆ January to June 19_8 budget—320 barrels an hour for 20 hours a day × 175 days = 1,120,000 barrels

◆ July to December 19_8 budget—480 barrels an hour for 20 hours a day × 175 days = 1,680,000 barrels

Variable standard manufacturing costs per barrel are $45 (variable direct materials, $32; variable manufacturing labor, $6; and variable manufacturing overhead, $7). The Austin brewery "sells" its output to the sales division of Lucky Lager at a budgeted price of $68 per barrel.

REQUIRED

1. Compute the budgeted fixed manufacturing overhead rate using each of the four denominator-level concepts for (a) beer produced in March 19_8, and (b) beer produced in September 19_8. Explain why any differences arise.

2. Explain why the theoretical capacity and practical capacity concepts are different.

3. Which denominator-level concept would the plant manager of the Austin brewery prefer when senior management of Lucky Lager is judging plant manager performance during 19_8? Explain.

9-26 **Operating income effects of alternative denominator-level concepts (continuation of 9-25).** In 19_8, the Austin brewery of Lucky Lager showed these results:

Unit data in barrels	
Beginning inventory, January 1, 19_8	0
Production	2,600,000
Ending inventory, December 31, 19_8	200,000

The Austin brewery had actual costs of:

Cost data	
Variable manufacturing	$120,380,000
Fixed manufacturing overhead	$ 40,632,000

The sales division of Lucky Lager purchased 2,400,000 barrels in 19_8 at the $68 per barrel rate.

All manufacturing variances are written off to cost of goods sold in the period in which they are incurred.

REQUIRED

1. Compute the operating income of the Austin brewery using the following: (a) theoretical capacity, (b) practical capacity, and (c) normal utilization denominator-level concepts. Explain any differences among (a), (b), and (c).

2. What denominator-level concept would Lucky Lager prefer for income tax reporting? Explain.

3. Explain the ways in which the Internal Revenue Service might restrict the flexibility of a company like Lucky Lager, which uses absorption costing, to reduce its reported taxable income.

9-27 Standard absorption, variable and throughput costing (CMA). The Byrd Company is a manufacturer of appliances for both residential and commercial use. The company's accounting and financial reporting system is primarily designed to meet external reporting requirements in accordance with generally accepted accounting principles. For inventory costing purposes, Byrd uses the absorption-costing method in conjunction with a standard costing system. Normal activity is used as the denominator level. Costs are allocated to products on a units produced basis. The denominator of fixed manufacturing costs is normal activity in production units. Relevant information on Byrd's steam cooker appliance is provided below for the last two years.

Unit Data	19_7	19_8
Beginning inventory	900	1,400
Production	2,000	400
Sales	1,500	1,700
Normal activity	2,000	2,000

The standard costs for this product are the same in (19_6), 19_7, and 19_8:

Financial Data	19_7	19_8
Selling price per unit	$ 100.00	$ 100.00
Standard variable direct manufacturing costs per unit*	40.00	40.00
Standard variable indirect manufacturing cost per unit	15.00	15.00
Variable marketing costs per unit sold	1.00	1.00
Total budgeted (and actual) fixed manufacturing costs	10,000	10,000
Total fixed marketing costs	3,000	3,000
Net unfavorable variance** pertaining to variable manufacturing costs	1,000	1,000

*Standard variable direct materials costs are $23.00 per unit
**All variances are written off to cost of goods sold in the period incurred

Currently, Byrd evaluates the performance of its product line managers and calculates the bonus on the basis of operating income computed on an absorption-costing basis. It has been suggested that the use of variable costing for internal reporting purposes would more accurately reflect the performance of each product line manager.

REQUIRED
1. Calculate the Byrd Company's operating income on its steam cooker appliance line for 19_7 and 19_8 using (a) absorption costing, (b) variable costing, and (c) throughput costing.
2. Discuss the features of variable costing that allow it to more accurately reflect the performance of Byrd's product line managers. Be sure to include in your discussion how absorption costing may influence a product line manager's behavior differently from variable costing.

3. What are the pros and cons of adopting throughput costing?

9-28 The All-Fixed Company in 19_9. (R. Marple, adapted) It is the end of 19_9. The All-Fixed Company began operations in January 19_8. The company is so named because it has no variable costs. All its costs are fixed; they do not vary with output.

All-Fixed is located on the bank of a river and has its own hydroelectric plant to supply power, light, and heat. The company manufactures a synthetic fertilizer from air and river water and sells its product at a price that is not expected to change. It has a small staff of employees, all hired on a fixed annual salary. The output of the plant can be increased or decreased by adjusting a few dials on a control panel.

The following are data regarding the operations of the All-Fixed Company:

	19_8	19_9*
Sales (units)	10,000	10,000
Production (units)	20,000	—
Selling price per ton	$30	$30
Costs (all fixed):		
Manufacturing	$280,000	$280,000
Marketing and administrative	$40,000	$40,000

*Management adopted the policy, effective January 1, 19_9, of producing only as much product as was needed to fill sales orders. During 19_9, sales were the same as for 19_8 and were filled entirely from inventory at the start of 19_9.

REQUIRED

1. Prepare income statements with one column for 19_8, one column for 19_9, and one column for the two years together, using (a) variable costing, and (b) absorption costing.

2. What is the break-even point under (a) variable costing, and (b) absorption costing?

3. What inventory costs would be carried on the balance sheets at December 31, 19_8 and 19_9, under each method?

4. Assume that the performance of the top manager of the company is evaluated and rewarded largely on the basis of reported operating income. Which costing method would the manager prefer? Why?

9-29 The Semi-Fixed Company in 19_9. The Semi-Fixed Company began operations in 19_8 and differs from the All-Fixed Company (described in Problem 9-28) in only one respect: It has both variable and fixed manufacturing costs. Its variable manufacturing costs are $7 per ton, and its fixed manufacturing costs are $140,000 per year. The denominator level is 20,000 tons per year.

REQUIRED

1. Using the same data as in Problem 9-28 except for the change in manufacturing cost behavior, prepare income statements with adjacent columns for 19_8, 19_9, and the two years together, under (a) variable costing, and (b) absorption costing.

2. Why did the Semi-Fixed Company have operating income for the two-year period when the All-Fixed Company in Problem 9-28 suffered an operating loss?

3. What inventory costs would be carried on the balance sheets at December 31, 19_8 and 19_9, under each method?

4. Assume that the performance of the top manager of the company is evaluated and rewarded largely on the basis of reported operating income. Which costing method would the manager prefer? Why?

9-30 Comparison of variable costing and absorption costing. Consider the following data:

Hinkle Company
Income Statements for the Year Ended December 31, 19_8

	Variable Costing	Absorption Costing
Revenues	$7,000,000	$7,000,000
Costs of goods sold (at standard)	3,660,000	4,575,000
Fixed manufacturing overhead	1,000,000	—
Manufacturing variances (all unfavorable):		
Direct materials price and efficiency	50,000	50,000
Direct manufacturing labor price and efficiency	60,000	60,000
Variable manufacturing overhead spending and efficiency	30,000	30,000
Fixed manufacturing overhead:		
Spending	100,000	100,000
Production volume	—	400,000
Total marketing costs (all fixed)	1,000,000	1,000,000
Total administrative costs (all fixed)	500,000	500,000
Total costs	6,400,000	6,715,000
Operating income	$ 600,000	$ 285,000

The inventories, carried at standard costs, were

	Variable Costing	Absorption Costing
December 31, 19_7	$1,320,000	$1,650,000
December 31, 19_8	60,000	75,000

REQUIRED

1. Tim Hinkle, president of the Hinkle Company, has asked you to explain why the operating income for 19_8 is less than for 19_7, even though sales have increased 40% over last year. What will you tell him?

2. At what percentage of denominator level was the plant operating during 19_8?

3. Prepare a numerical reconciliation and explanation of the difference between the operating incomes under absorption costing and variable costing.

4. Critics have claimed that a widely used accounting system has led to undesirable buildups of inventory levels. (a) Is variable costing or absorption costing more likely to lead to such buildups? Why? (b) What can be done to counteract undesirable inventory buildups?

9-31 Inventory costing and management planning. It is November 30, 19_7. Consider the income statement for the operations of Industrial Products, Inc., for January through November, 19_7.

Industrial Products, Inc.
Income Statement for 11 Months Ended November 30, 19_7

	Units	Dollars	
Revenues @ $1,000	1,000		$1,000,000
Cost of goods sold			
Beginning inventory, December 31, 19_6, @ $800	50	$ 40,000	
Manufacturing costs @ $800, including $600 per unit for fixed manufacturing overhead	1,100	880,000	
Total standard cost of goods available for sale	1,150	920,000	
Ending inventory, November 30, 19_7, @ $800	150	120,000	
Standard cost of goods sold*	1,000		800,000
Gross margin			200,000
Marketing, distribution and customer-service costs			
Variable, 1,000 units @ $50		50,000	
Fixed, @ $10,000 monthly		110,000	160,000
Operating income			$ 40,000

*There are no variances for the 11-month period considered as a whole.

Production in the past three months has been 100 units monthly. Practical capacity is 125 units monthly. To retain a stable nucleus of key employees, management never schedules monthly production at less than 40 units.

Maximum available storage space for inventory is regarded as 200 units. The sales outlook for the next four months is 70 units monthly. Inventory is never to be less than 50 units.

The company uses a standard absorption-costing system. The denominator production level is 1,200 units annually. All variances are disposed of at year-end as an adjustment to cost of goods sold.

REQUIRED

1. The division manager is given an annual bonus that is geared to operating income. Assume that the manager wants to maximize the company's operating income for 19_7. How many units should the manager schedule for production in December? Note that you do not have to (nor should you) compute the operating income for 19_7 in this or in subsequent parts of this problem.

2. Assume that standard variable costing is in use rather than standard absorption costing. Would variable-costing operating income for 19_7 be higher, lower, or the same as standard absorption-costing income, assuming that production for December is 80 units and sales are 70 units? Why?

3. If standard variable costing were used, what production schedule should the division manager set? Why?

4. Assume that the manager is interested in maximizing his performance over the long run and that performance is being judged on the basis of net income. Assume that the company's income tax rate will be cut in half in 19_8 and that the year-end write-offs of variances are acceptable for income tax purposes. Assume that standard absorption costing is used. How many units should be scheduled for production in December? Why?

5. Assume that the total production and total sales for 19_7 and 19_8, taken together, will be unchanged by the specific decision in requirement 4. Assume also that the standards will be unchanged in 19_8. Suppose the decision in requirement 4 is to schedule 50 units instead of an originally scheduled 120 units. By how much will operating income in 19_8 be affected by the decision to schedule 50 units in December 19_7? (That is, how much operating income is shifted from 19_7 to 19_8?)

9-32 Some additional requirements to Problem 9-31; absorption costing and output-level variances.

REQUIRED

1. What operating income will be reported for 19_7 as a whole, assuming that the implied cost behavior patterns will continue in December as they did in January through November and assuming without regard to your answer to requirement 1 in Problem 9-31 that production for December is 80 units and sales are 70 units?

2. Assume the same conditions as in requirement 1 except that a monthly denominator level of 125 units (practical capacity) was used in setting fixed manufacturing overhead rates for inventory costing throughout 19_7. What production-volume variance would be reported for 19_7?

9-33 Effects of denominator-level concept choice. The Wong Company installed standard costs and a flexible budget on January 1, 19_7. The president had been pondering how fixed manufacturing overhead should be allocated to products. Machine-hours had been chosen as the allocation base. Her remaining uncertainty was the denominator-level concept for machine-hours. She decided to wait for the first month's results before making a final choice of what denominator-level concept should be used from that day forward.

In January 19_7, the actual units of output had a standard of 70,000 machine-hours allowed. If the company used practical capacity as the denominator-level concept, the fixed manufacturing overhead spending variance would be $10,000, unfavorable, and the production-volume variance would be $36,000, unfavorable. If the company used normal utilization as the denominator-level concept, the production-volume variance would be $20,000, favorable. Budgeted fixed manufacturing overhead was $120,000 for the month.

REQUIRED

1. Compute the denominator level, assuming that the normal utilization concept is chosen.

2. Compute the denominator level, assuming that the practical capacity concept is chosen.

3. Suppose you are the executive vice-president. You want to maximize your 19_7 bonus, which depends on 19_7 operating income. Assume that the production-volume variance is charged or credited to income at year-end. Which denominator-level concept would you favor? Why?

9-34 Absorption costing, standard costs, management ethics. Industrial Equity Company (IEC) is a multinational business selling metal products used in the assembly of many cars, trucks, and planes. IEC has over 50 manufacturing divisions worldwide and is listed on the New York Stock Exchange. IEC has consistently reported annual earnings growth rates of 15% or more for each of the last ten years.

Division managers at IEC receive an annual bonus of 30% of their annual salary if the plant operating income increases 15% or more over the previous years operating income. Division managers who increase operating income more than 10% but less than 15% receive a bonus of 5% of their annual salary. Division managers who do not achieve a 10% increase in operating income receive no bonus. Instead, they receive a visit from the IEC corporate consulting team.

Bob Wood is manager of the Flint, Michigan, division, which manufactures crankshafts for sale to automobile manufacturers. Wood has just received a 30% bonus for 19_7. Mary Easson, head of the IEC corporate consulting team, is less than impressed by Wood's performance. She suspects him of producing for inventory and collects the following information on the Flint division for 19_7:

Unit data in crankshafts	
Beginning inventory	0
Production	480,000
Ending inventory	30,000
Sales	450,000
Selling price per unit	$66
Cost data	
Standard variable costs per crankshaft	
Direct materials	$20
Direct manufacturing labor	5
Manufacturing overhead	12
Variable marketing	4
Standard fixed costs	
Manufacturing overhead	$9,000,000
Marketing	1,000,000

Manufacturing overhead is allocated to each crankshaft on the basis of standard machine-hours. Each crankshaft has a standard machining time of 30 minutes. The denominator level in 19_7 was the master-budget utilization for the Flint plant, 500,000 crankshafts. A standard absorption-costing system is used for each IEC plant. All variances are recorded as a cost of the period in which they are incurred.

All auto companies require suppliers to deliver on a just-in-time basis (that is, just before the crankshafts are required for assembly). The last four months of 19_7 saw a reduction in the orders auto companies placed for crankshafts.

The price, spending, and efficiency manufacturing variances for 19_7 were $300,000, unfavorable. The total marketing variances were $156,000, favorable (variable $130,000 favorable and fixed $26,000 favorable).

Operating income for the Flint division in 19_6 was $1,427,010.

REQUIRED
1. Compute the absorption-costing operating income for the Flint division in 19_7.
2. Why might Easson believe that in 19_7 Wood engaged in behavior not in the best interests of IEC? How might Wood respond to any charges Easson might make about producing for inventory?
3. Is the problem Easson raised likely to be eliminated by her talking to Wood about management ethics? Explain.

9-35 **Absorption costing, management ethics (continuation of 9-34).** Mary Easson decides to undertake a systematic investigation of how the combination of the existing division manager bonus plan and absorption costing may be causing division managers to make decisions not in the best interests of Industrial Equity Company (IEC). She will first visit the Morristown division of IEC, which manufactures more than 100 different metal products.

1. Name three types of behavior that Easson should look for that would suggest problems for IEC with the existing bonus plan and accounting system.

2. What possible changes might Easson consider if her investigation produces widespread evidence of systematic poor decision making by division managers at IEC?

COLLABORATIVE LEARNING PROBLEM

9-36 Absorption, variable, and throughput costing. The Waterloo, Ontario, plant of Maple Leaf Motors assembles the Icarus motor vehicle. The standard unit manufacturing cost per vehicle in 19_7 is

◆ Direct materials	$6,000
◆ Direct manufacturing labor	1,800
◆ Variable manufacturing overhead	2,000
◆ Fixed manufacturing overhead	?

The Waterloo plant is highly automated. Maximum productive capacity per month is 4,000 vehicles. Variable manufacturing overhead is allocated to vehicles on the basis of assembly time on the line. The standard assembly time per vehicle is 20 hours. Fixed manufacturing overhead in 19_7 is allocated on the basis of the standard assembly time for the budgeted normal utilization of the plant. In 19_7, the budgeted normal utilization is 3,000 vehicles per month. The budgeted monthly fixed manufacturing overhead is $7,500,000.

On January 1, 19_7, there is zero beginning inventory of Icarus vehicles. The actual unit production and sales figures for the first three months of 19_7 are

	January	February	March
Production	3,200	2,400	3,800
Sales	2,000	2,900	3,200

Assume no direct materials variances, no direct manufacturing labor variances, and no manufacturing overhead spending or efficiency variances in the first three months of 19_7.

Pierre Rougeau, a vice president of Maple Leaf Motors, is the manager of the Waterloo plant. His compensation includes a monthly bonus that is 0.5% of quarterly operating income. Operating income is calculated using absorption costing. Maple Leaf Motors reports monthly absorption costing income statements. Each month an adjustment to cost of goods sold is made for the total manufacturing variances occurring in that month.

The Waterloo plant "sells" each Icarus to Maple Leaf's marketing subsidiary at $16,000 per vehicle. No marketing costs are incurred by the Waterloo plant.

INSTRUCTIONS

Form groups of two or more students to complete the following requirements.

REQUIRED

1. Compute (a) the unit fixed manufacturing overhead cost, and (b) the unit total manufacturing cost.

2. Compute the monthly operating income for January, February, and March under absorption costing. What bonus is paid each month to Rougeau?

3. How much would the use of variable costing change the bonus paid each month to Rougeau if the same 0.5% figure is applied to variable-costing operating income?

4. Explain the differences in the bonuses paid each month to Rougeau in requirements 2 and 3.

5. How much would the use of throughput costing change the bonus paid each month to Rougeau if the same 0.5% figure is applied to throughput-costing operating income?

6. Describe different approaches Maple Leaf Motors could use to reduce the dysfunctional aspects associated with absorption costing at its Waterloo plant.

Ritz-Carlton

When traveling, many people will budget how much it will cost them to stay at a hotel. Interestingly enough, the hotels also budget how much that stay will cost the hotels. Take Ritz-Carlton for example. The company operates thirty-one luxury hotels and resorts in different locations around the world, and each one is responsible for preparing its own operating budget. The operating budget at the hotel in Scottsdale, Arizona, starts with sales director Sharon Alexander. **1** Sharon prepares the sales budget based on projections from all the various sources of hotel revenue. These include revenues from rooms as well as revenues from **2** The Sundry (the hotel's gift shop), dining facilities, **3** room service, and banquet and meeting facilities. After all revenues have been projected, Sharon passes the sales budget on to controller Lydia Frank. **4** In preparing the annual operating budget, Lydia must weigh expected revenues from the sales budget against expected costs. Guest room costs, as well as costs for housekeeping, banquet and meeting facilities **5**, and **6** food and bever-

1

3

2

4

5

6

7

8

9

age services, are based on standard costs. To calculate these standards, Lydia seeks input from all hotel employees. **7** For example, in determining the standard costs for housekeeping, she would speak not only to the manager of housekeeping about specific estimates and figures, **8** but also to several of the housekeepers themselves to determine if these estimates are accurate. Once all of the standard costs are determined, Lydia seeks out information on all other costs for the coming year, including special events, payroll changes, and promotional events. **9** Assistant controller Tom Milton then helps Lydia calculate the operating budget, which they then pass on to corporate headquarters in Atlanta, Georgia. Actual performance is then closely monitored and evaluated against budget. And you can rest assured that managers at Ritz-Carlton don't like surprises in their actual costs any more than their guests do.

RITZ-CARLTON HOTEL COMPANY
Budgets and Responsibility Accounting

adies and gentlemen serving ladies and gentlemen."
That's the motto of the Ritz-Carlton, based in Atlanta, Georgia, a region known for southern hospitality and old-fashioned elegance. It may seem a bit indis-
creet, then, to talk about such mundane topics as costs
and budgets when referring to the activities of the hotel.
Yet it is precisely the attention given to these items that
helps make the company so successful.

Each hotel's performance is the responsibility of the
general manager and controller at each of thirty-one
worldwide locations. Local forecasts and budgets are prepared annually and are the basis of subsequent performance evaluation. Preparation of the annual budget begins with the sales budget, prepared by the hotel's sales
director. Budgeted sources of revenue include hotel
rooms; convention, wedding, and meeting facilities; merchandise; and food and beverage. The controller then
seeks input from all employees, from maintenance staff to
kitchen workers, about anticipated payroll changes, operating expenses, and planned events or promotions that
might affect costs. Standard costs, based on cost per occupied room, are used to build the budget for guest room
stays. Other standards are used for meeting rooms and
food and beverage. After employee input is provided, the
completed sales budget and annual operating budget are
sent to corporate headquarters. From there, actual
monthly performance against plan is monitored. Each
property is allowed a five percent variance in profitability
goals each month and must provide explanations when
targets are not met.

On the twenty-fifth of each month, budgets for the
next three months are reviewed to be sure goals are still
accurate. Accuracy can be critical for a business whose occupancy can fluctuate significantly from day to day, depending on group or company bookings, special events,
or changes in local competition. The changes are communicated to corporate headquarters, with explanations of
revisions provided as needed. Local hotel managers also
meet daily to review performance to date and have the
ability to adjust prices in the reservation system at any
time to make sure profitability targets are met. Adjusting
prices can be particularly important if a large group can-
cels at the last minute, or if other unforeseen events cause
occupancy to drop suddenly.

Meeting the monthly budgeted goals is primarily
the responsibility of each hotel's controller. The controller at each location receives a monthly report from
corporate headquarters that shows how all thirty-one hotels performed against their goals. Controllers compare
their performance against their own budgets, as well as
comparing actual performance against the other hotel
properties. Ideas for boosting revenues and reducing costs
are regularly shared among the company's controllers,
who recognize the value of contributing to the entire organization's success, not just their own. ◆

QUESTIONS

1. How would you expect the Ritz-Carlton to develop its standard costs per occupied room? How would these standards
differ among locations?

2. The Ritz-Carlton recently started giving all employees the
chance to meet with the controller to review budgets and
reports on actual performance, as a form of participatory
budgeting. What advantages or disadvantages do you see
with this approach?

3. How might the Ritz-Carlton use benchmarking within its own
chain to improve efficiency?

4. What factors might affect the Ritz-Carlton's annual sales
forecast for room occupancy? For restaurants? For use of
meeting rooms and conference facilities?

5. How is uncertainty handled in the budget process?

6. The Ritz-Carlton uses responsibility accounting for its worldwide hotel and resort operations. What levels of responsibility reports would you expect to see throughout the company?

DETERMINING HOW COSTS BEHAVE

Speedboat assembly companies report reductions in unit variable costs as the number of speedboats assembled increases because of learning-curve effects. Regal Marine has observed such learning curve effects when assembling boats at its plant.

After studying this chapter, you should be able to

1. Explain the two assumptions frequently used in cost-behavior estimation
2. Describe linear cost functions and three common ways in which they behave
3. Recognize various approaches to cost estimation
4. Outline six steps in estimating a cost function on the basis of current or past cost relationships
5. Describe three criteria to evaluate and choose cost drivers
6. Explain and give examples of nonlinear cost functions
7. Distinguish between the cumulative average-time learning model and incremental unit-time learning model
8. Understand data problems encountered in estimating cost functions

This chapter focuses on how to determine cost behavior—that is, on understanding how costs change with changes in activity levels, units of products produced, and so on. Knowing how costs vary by identifying the drivers of costs and by distinguishing fixed from variable costs are frequently the keys to making good management decisions. Many managerial functions such as planning and control rely on knowing how costs will behave. For example, consider the questions, What price should we charge? Should we make the item or buy it? What effect will a 20% increase in units sold have on operating income? Decisions in the control area, such as the interpretation of some variances, similarly rely heavily on knowledge of cost behavior. Determining and understanding how costs behave are among the most important functions of the cost accountant.

GENERAL ISSUES IN ESTIMATING COST FUNCTIONS

Basic Assumptions and Examples of Cost Functions

OBJECTIVE 1

Explain the two assumptions frequently used in cost-behavior estimation

A cost function is a mathematical function describing cost behavior patterns—how costs change with changes in the cost driver. Cost functions can be plotted on graph paper by measuring the cost driver on the *x*-axis and the corresponding amount of total costs on the *y*-axis.

Two assumptions are frequently made when estimating cost functions.

1. Variations in the total costs of a cost-object are explained by variations in a single cost driver.
2. Cost behavior is adequately approximated by a *linear cost function* of the cost driver within the relevant range. A **linear cost function** is a cost function where, within the relevant range, the graph of total costs versus a single cost driver forms a straight line.

OBJECTIVE 2

Describe linear cost functions and three common ways in which they behave

We use these assumptions throughout much of this chapter. Later sections give examples of nonlinear cost behavior patterns in which the plot of the relationship between the cost driver and total costs is not a straight line. The last section in the Appendix describes how changes in two or more cost drivers can explain changes in the level of total costs. We illustrate cost functions in the context of negotiations between Cannon Services and World Wide Communications (WWC) for exclusive use of a telephone line between New York and Paris. WWC offers Cannon Services three alternative cost structures.

◆ *Alternative 1:* $5 per minute of phone use. As we saw in Chapter 2, this is a *strictly variable cost* for Cannon Services. The number of phone-minutes used is the cost driver; that is, the number of phone-minutes used is the factor whose change causes a change in total costs.

Graph 1 in Exhibit 10-1 presents the *strictly variable* or *proportionately variable* cost. Total costs (measured along the vertical *y*-axis) change in proportion to the number of phone-minutes used (measured along the horizontal *x*-axis) within the relevant range. The *relevant range*, described in Chapter 2, is the range of the cost driver where the relationship between total costs and the driver is valid. There are no fixed costs. Every additional minute adds $5 to total costs. Graph 1 of Exhibit 10-1 illustrates the $5 **slope coefficient,** the amount by which total costs change for a unit change in the cost driver within the relevant range.

We can write the cost function in Graph 1 of Exhibit 10-1 as

$$y = \$5X$$

where *X* measures the number of phone-minutes used and *y* measures the total costs of the phone-minutes determined from the cost function.

◆ *Alternative 2:* $10,000 per month. Under this alternative, Cannon Services has a fixed cost of $10,000. Graph 2 in Exhibit 10-1 presents the *fixed cost.* The

EXHIBIT 10-1
Examples of Linear Cost Functions

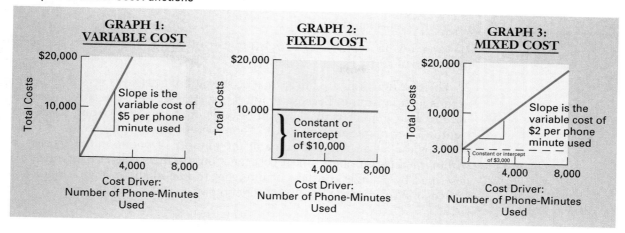

total costs will be $10,000 per month regardless of the number of phone-minutes used. (We use the same cost driver, the number of phone-minutes used, to compare cost-behavior patterns under various alternatives.)

Graph 2 in Exhibit 10-1 refers to the fixed cost of $10,000 as a **constant** or **intercept,** the component of total costs that, within the relevant range, does not vary with changes in the level of the cost driver. Under alternative 2, the constant or intercept accounts for all the costs, since there are no variable costs. The slope is zero. We can write the cost function in Graph 2 of Exhibit 10-1 as

$$y = \$10,000$$

showing that total costs will be $10,000, regardless of the number of phone-minutes used by Cannon Services.

◆ *Alternative 3:* $3,000 per month plus $2 per minute of phone use. This is an example of a *mixed* cost. A **mixed cost** (or **semivariable cost**) is a cost that has both fixed and variable elements. Graph 3 in Exhibit 10-1 presents the mixed cost. It has one component that is fixed regardless of the number of phone-minutes used ($3,000 per month) and another component that is variable with respect to the number of phone-minutes used ($2 per minute of phone use). In this example, the constant or intercept is $3,000 and the slope coefficient is $2.

We can write the cost function in Graph 3 of Exhibit 10-1 as

$$y = \$3,000 + \$2X.$$

In the case of mixed costs, the total costs in the relevant range increase as the number of phone-minutes used increases in the relevant range. *However, total costs do not change in proportion to the change in the number of phone-minutes used in the relevant range.* For example, when 4,000 phone-minutes are used, the total costs are [$3,000 + ($2 × 4,000)] = $11,000, but when 8,000 phone-minutes are used, the total costs are [$3,000 + ($2 × 8,000)] = $19,000. Although the number of phone-minutes used has doubled, the total costs have increased to only 1.73 ($19,000 ÷ $11,000) times the original costs.

Understanding cost-behavior patterns is a crucial input in choosing among the alternatives. Suppose Cannon Services expects to use at least 4,000 phone-minutes per month. Its costs for 4,000 phone-minutes under the three alternatives would be: alternative 1, $20,000 ($5 × 4,000); alternative 2, $10,000; alternative 3, $11,000 [$3,000 + ($2 × 4,000)]. Alternative 2 is the least costly. Moreover, if Cannon used more than 4,000 phone-minutes, alternatives 1 and 3 would be even more costly than alternative 2. Cannon would prefer alternative 2.

Basic Terms

Note two features of the cost functions in the Cannon Services/WWC example. For specificity, consider graph 3.

1. Variations in a *single* cost driver (number of phone-minutes used) explain variations in total costs.

2. The cost functions are linear; that is, the plot of total costs versus phone-minutes used is a straight line. Because graph 3 is a straight line, the only information we need to draw graph 3 is the constant or intercept term ($3,000) and the slope coefficient ($2 per phone-minute used). These two pieces of information describe total costs for the entire relevant range of the number of phone-minutes used. That is, within the relevant range, linear cost functions (in the single cost driver case) can be described by a single constant or intercept (called a) and a single slope coefficient (called b). We write the linear cost function as

$$y = a + bX$$

Under alternative 1, $a = \$0$ and $b = \$5$ per phone-minute used; under alternative 2, $a = \$10,000$, $b = \$0$ per phone-minute used; and under alternative 3, $a = \$3,000$, $b = \$2$ per phone-minute used.

The Cannon Services/WWC example illustrates variable, fixed, and mixed cost functions using information about future cost structures proposed to Cannon by WWC. Often, however, cost functions are estimated from past cost data. **Cost estimation** is the attempt to measure *past* cost relationships between total costs and the drivers of those costs. For example, managers could use cost estimation to understand what causes marketing costs to change from year to year (the number of cars sold or the number of new models introduced), and its fixed and variable cost components. Managers are interested in estimating past cost-behavior patterns primarily because these estimates can help them make more accurate **cost predictions,** or forecasts, about future costs. Better cost predictions help managers make more informed planning and control decisions, such as the marketing costs budget for next year.

Chapter 2 outlined three other specifications necessary to classify costs into their variable and fixed cost components. We review them briefly here.

Choice of Cost Object   A particular cost item could be variable with respect to one cost object and fixed with respect to another. For example, annual van registration and license costs would be a variable cost with respect to the number of vans owned and operated by SuperShuttle, an airport transportation company, but registration and license costs for a particular van is a fixed cost with respect to the number of miles that the van covered during the year.

Time Span   *Whether a cost is variable or fixed with respect to a particular driver depends on the time span considered in the decision situation. The longer the time span, other things being equal, the more likely that the cost will be variable.* For example, inspection salaries and costs at the Boeing Company are typically fixed in the short run with respect to hours of inspection activity. But in the long run, Boeing's total inspection costs will vary with the inspection time required: More inspectors will be hired if more inspection is needed, while some inspectors will be reassigned to other tasks if less inspection is needed.

Relevant Range   Accountants and managers use linear cost functions to approximate the relation of total costs to cost drivers within a relevant range. Exhibit 10-2 plots the relationship over several years between total direct manufacturing labor costs and the number of valves produced each year by AMC, Inc., at its Cleveland plant. Costs are nonlinear outside the relevant range. In this case, nonlinearities occur when the valve output is low because of inefficiencies in using manufacturing labor. Nonlinearities occur at very high levels of production because of greater congestion in the plant and the need for more coordination.

EXHIBIT 10-2
Linearity within Relevant Range

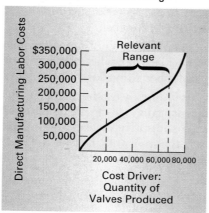

THE CAUSE-AND-EFFECT CRITERION IN CHOOSING COST DRIVERS

The most important issue in estimating a cost function is to determine whether a cause-and-effect relationship exists between the cost driver and the resulting costs. The cause-and-effect relationship might arise in several ways.

SURVEYS OF COMPANY PRACTICE

International Comparison of Cost Classification by Companies

Organizations differ in classifying individual costs. A variable cost item in one organization can be a fixed cost item in another organization. Consider labor costs. Home construction companies often classify labor cost as a variable cost. These companies rapidly adjust their labor force in response to changes in the demand for housing construction. In contrast, oil-refining companies often classify labor cost as a fixed cost. The labor force is stable even when sizable changes occur in the volume or type of oil products refined.

Surveys indicate significant differences in the percentage of companies in various countries classifying individual cost categories as variable, fixed, or mixed. A lower percentage of U.S. and Australian companies treat labor costs as a fixed cost compared with Japanese companies.

Cost Category	U.S. Companies			Japanese Companies			Australian Companies		
	Variable	Mixed	Fixed	Variable	Mixed	Fixed	Variable	Mixed	Fixed
Production labor	86%	6%	8%	52%	5%	43%	70%	20%	10%
Setup labor	60	25	15	44	6	50	45	33	22
Materials-handling labor	48	34	18	23	16	61	40	30	30
Quality-control labor	34	36	30	13	12	75	21	27	52
Tooling	32	35	33	31	26	43	25	28	47
Energy	26	45	29	42	31	27	—	—	—
Building occupancy	1	6	93	0	0	100	—	—	—
Depreciation	1	7	92	0	0	100	—	—	—

Source: Adapted from the NAA Tokyo Affiliate, "Management Accounting in the Advanced Manufacturing," and Joye and Blayney, "Cost and Management Accounting." Full citations are in Appendix A.

1. It may be due to a physical relationship between costs and the cost driver. An example of a physical relationship is when units of production is used as the cost driver of materials costs. To produce more units requires more materials, which results in higher materials costs.

2. Cause and effect can arise from a contractual arrangement, as in the Cannon Services example described earlier, where the number of phone-minutes used is the cost driver of the telephone line costs.

3. Cause and effect can be implicitly established by logic and knowledge of operations. An example is when number of component parts is used as a cost driver of design costs. It seems intuitively clear that a complex product design with many component parts that must fit together precisely will incur higher design costs than a simple product with few parts.

Be careful not to interpret a high correlation, or connection, between two variables to mean that either variable causes the other. A high correlation between two variables, u and v, indicates merely that the two variables move together. It is possible that u may cause v; v may cause u; u and v may interact; both may be affected by a third variable z; or the correlation may be due to chance. No conclusions about cause and effect are warranted by high correlations. For example, higher production generally results in higher materials costs and higher labor costs. Materials costs and labor costs are highly correlated, but neither causes the other.

Consider another example. Over the past 28 years, the New York Stock Exchange index has almost always increased during the year in which an original National Football League team (such as the San Francisco 49ers) has won the Super Bowl, and almost always decreased in the year in which an original American Football League team (such as the Miami Dolphins) has won.[1] There is, however, no plausible cause-and-effect explanation for this high correlation.

Only a true cause-and-effect relationship, not merely correlation, establishes an economically plausible relationship between costs and their cost drivers. Economic plausibility gives the analyst confidence that the estimated relationship will appear again and again in other similar sets of data. Establishing economic plausibility is a vital aspect of cost estimation.

COST ESTIMATION APPROACHES

OBJECTIVE 3

Recognize various approaches to cost estimation

There are four approaches to cost estimation:

1. Industrial engineering method
2. Conference method
3. Account analysis method
4. Quantitative analysis of current or past cost relationships

These approaches differ in the costs of conducting the analysis, the assumptions they make, and the evidence they provide about the accuracy of the estimated cost function. They are not mutually exclusive. Many organizations use a combination of these approaches.

Industrial Engineering Method

The **industrial engineering method,** also called the **work-measurement method,** estimates cost functions by analyzing the relationship between inputs and outputs in physical terms. This method has its roots in studies and techniques developed by Frank and Lillian Gilbreth in the early twentieth century. Consider, for example, a carpet manufacturer that uses inputs of cotton, wool, dyes, direct labor, machine time, and power. Production output is square yards of carpet. Time-and-motion studies analyze the time and materials required to perform the various operations to

[1] J. Granelli and T. Petruno, "You can Take Heart from the January Gain or You can Punt," *Los Angeles Times* (Feb. 1, 1993).

produce the carpet. For example, a time-and-motion study may conclude that to produce 20 square yards of carpet requires 2 bales of cotton and 3 gallons of dye. Standards and budgets transform these physical input and output measures into costs. The result is an estimated cost function relating total manufacturing costs to the cost driver, square yards of carpet.

The industrial engineering method can be very time-consuming. Some government contracts mandate its use. Many organizations, however, find it too costly for analyzing their entire cost structure. More frequently, organizations use this approach for direct-cost categories such as materials and labor but not for indirect-cost categories such as manufacturing overhead. Physical relationships between inputs and outputs may be difficult to specify for individual overhead cost items.

Conference Method

The **conference method** estimates cost functions on the basis of analysis and opinions about costs and their drivers gathered from various departments of an organization (purchasing, process engineering, manufacturing, employee relations, and so on). The Co-operative Bank in the United Kingdom has a cost-estimating department that develops cost functions for its retail banking products (current account, VISA cards, mortgages, and so on) on the basis of a consensus of estimates from the relevant departments. The Bank uses this information to price products, to adjust its product mix to the products that are most profitable, and to monitor and measure cost improvements over time.

The conference method allows cost functions and cost estimates to be developed quickly. The pooling of expert knowledge from each value-chain area gives the conference method credibility. The accuracy of the cost estimates largely depends on the care and detail taken by the people providing the inputs.[2]

Account Analysis Method

The **account analysis method** estimates cost functions by classifying cost accounts in the ledger as variable, fixed, or mixed with respect to the identified cost driver. Typically, managers use qualitative rather than quantitative analysis when making these cost-classification decisions. The account analysis approach is widely used.[3]

Consider indirect manufacturing labor costs for a small production area (or cell) at Elegant Rugs, which weaves carpets for homes and offices and uses state-of-the-art automated weaving machines. These costs include maintenance, quality control and setup costs for the machines. During the most recent 12-week period, Elegant Rugs worked the machines in the cell for a total of 862 hours and incurred total indirect manufacturing labor costs of $12,501. Management wants the cost analyst to use the account analysis method to estimate a linear cost function for indirect manufacturing labor costs with machine-hours as the cost driver.

The cost analyst decides to separate total indirect manufacturing labor costs ($12,501) into costs that are fixed ($2,157) and costs that are variable ($10,344) with respect to the number of machine-hours worked. Variable costs per machine hour are $10,344 \div 862 = 12. The general cost equation, $y = a + bX$, is Indirect manufacturing labor costs = $2,157 + ($12 \times$ Number of machine-hours). The indirect manufacturing labor costs per machine-hour is $12,501 \div 862 = 14.50.

Management at Elegant Rugs can use the cost function to estimate the indirect manufacturing labor costs of using 950 machine-hours to produce carpet in the next 12-week period. Using the cost function, estimated costs = $2,157 + (950 \times 12) = $13,557$. The indirect manufacturing labor costs per machine-hour decrease to $13,557 \div 950 = 14.27, as fixed costs are spread over a greater number of units.

Organizations differ with respect to the care taken in implementing account analysis. In some organizations, individuals thoroughly knowledgeable about the

[2]The conference method is further described in W. Winchell, *Realistic Cost Estimating for Manufacturing*, 2nd ed. (Dearborn, Mich.: Society for Manufacturing Engineers, 1991).
[3]Survey evidence appears in M. M. Mowen, *Accounting for Costs as Fixed and Variable* (Montvale, N.J.: National Association of Accountants, 1986).

Week	Indirect Manufacturing Labor Costs (1)	Cost Driver: Machine-Hours (2)	Alternative Cost Driver: Direct Manufacturing Labor-Hours (3)
1	$1,190	68	30
2	1,211	88	35
3	1,004	62	36
4	917	72	20
5	770	60	47
6	1,456	96	45
7	1,180	78	44
8	710	46	38
9	1,316	82	70
10	1,032	94	30
11	752	68	29
12	963	48	38

operations make the cost-classification decisions. For example, manufacturing personnel may classify costs such as machine lubricants and materials-handling labor, while marketing personnel may classify costs such as advertising brochures and sales salaries. In other organizations, only cursory analysis is conducted, sometimes by individuals with limited knowledge of operations, before cost-classification decisions are made. Clearly, the former approach would provide more reliable cost classifications, and hence estimates of the fixed and variable components of the cost, than the latter. Supplementing the account analysis method by the conference method improves its credibility.

Quantitative Analyses of Cost Relationships

Quantitative analyses of cost relationships are formal methods to fit linear cost functions to past data observations. Columns 1 and 2 of Exhibit 10-3 break down the $12,501 of total indirect manufacturing labor costs and the 862 total machine-hours for the most recent 12-week period into weekly data. Note that the data are paired. For example, week 12 shows indirect manufacturing labor costs of $963 and 48 machine-hours. The next section uses the data in Exhibit 10-3 to illustrate two different quantitative ways to estimate a cost function: the high-low method and regression analysis.

STEPS IN ESTIMATING A COST FUNCTION

There are six steps in estimating a cost function on the basis of an analysis of current or past cost relationships: (1) Choose the dependent variable (the variable to be predicted, which is some type of cost); (2) identify the cost driver(s) (independent variable(s)); (3) collect data on the dependent variable and the cost driver(s); (4) plot the data; (5) estimate the cost function; and (6) evaluate the estimated cost function. As we discussed earlier in this chapter, choosing a cost driver is not always straightforward. Frequently, the cost analyst will cycle through these steps several times trying alternative economically plausible cost drivers to see which cost driver best fits the data.

Step 1: Choose the Dependent Variable Choice of the **dependent variable** (the cost variable to be predicted) will depend on the purpose for estimating a cost function. For example, if the purpose is to determine indirect manufacturing costs for a production line, then the dependent variable should incorporate all costs that are classified as indirect with respect to the production line.

Step 2: Identify the Cost Driver(s)   The chosen cost driver should have an economically plausible relationship with the dependent variable and be accurately measurable. Ideally, all the individual items included in the dependent variable should have the same cost driver(s). Where a single relationship does not exist, the cost analyst should investigate the possibility of estimating more than one cost function.

Consider several types of fringe benefits paid to employees and their cost drivers:

Fringe Benefit	Cost Driver
Health benefits	Number of employees
Cafeteria meals	Number of employees
Pension benefits	Salaries of employees
Life insurance	Salaries of employees

The costs of health benefits and cafeteria meals can be combined into one cost pool because they both have the same cost driver, number of employees. Pension benefits and life insurance costs have a different cost driver, salaries of employees, and hence should not be combined with health benefits and cafeteria meals. Instead, they should be combined into a separate cost pool and estimated using salaries of employees receiving the benefits as the cost driver.

Step 3: Collect Data on the Dependent Variable and the Cost Driver(s)   This step is usually the most difficult one in cost analysis. Cost analysts obtain data from company documents, from interviews with managers, and through special studies. These data may be time-series data or cross-sectional data. *Time-series data* pertain to the same entity (organization, plant, activity area, and so on) over a sequence of past time periods. Weekly observations of indirect manufacturing labor costs and machine-hours in the Elegant Rugs illustration are an example of time-series data. The ideal time-series data base would contain numerous observations for a firm whose operations have not been affected by economic or technological change. Stable technology ensures that data collected in the estimation period represent the same underlying relationship between the dependent variable and the cost driver(s). Moreover, the time periods (for example, daily, weekly, or monthly) used to measure the dependent variable and the cost driver(s) should be identical. *Cross-sectional data* pertain to different entities for the same time period. For example, studies of personnel costs and loans processed at 50 individual branches of a bank during March would produce cross-sectional data for March. A later section of this chapter describes problems that arise in data collection.

Step 4: Plot the Data   This step is important. The expression "a picture is worth a thousand words" conveys the benefits of plotting the data. The general relation between the dependent variable and the cost driver can readily be observed in a plot of the data. Moreover, the plot highlights extreme observations that analysts should check. Was there an error in recording the data or an unusual event, such as a labor strike, that makes these observations unrepresentative of the normal relationship between the dependent variable and the cost driver? Plotting the data can also provide insight into whether the relation is approximately linear and what the relevant range of the cost function is.

Exhibit 10-4 plots the weekly data from columns 1 and 2 of Exhibit 10-3. There is strong visual evidence of a positive relation between indirect manufacturing labor costs and machine-hours (that is, when machine-hours go up, so do costs). There do not appear to be any extreme observations in Exhibit 10-4. The relevant range is from 46 to 96 machine-hours per week.

Step 5: Estimate the Cost Function   We show how to estimate the cost function for our Elegant Rugs data using the high-low method and regression analysis.

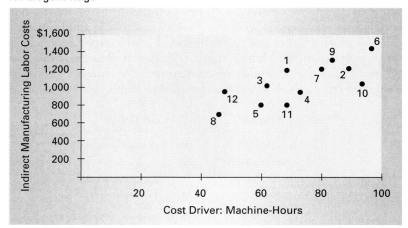

EXHIBIT 10-4
Plot of Weekly Indirect Manufacturing Labor Costs and Machine-Hours
for Elegant Rugs

Step 6: Evaluate the Estimated Cost Function We describe criteria for evaluating a cost function after illustrating the high-low method and regression analysis.

High-Low Method

Managers, at times, use very simple methods to estimate cost functions. An example is the **high-low method,** which entails using only the highest and lowest observed values of the *cost driver* within the relevant range. The line connecting these two points becomes the estimated cost function.

We illustrate the high-low method using data from Exhibit 10-3.

	Cost Driver: Machine-Hours	Indirect Manufacturing Labor Costs
Highest observation of cost driver (week 6)	96	$1,456
Lowest observation of cost driver (week 8)	46	710
Difference	50	$ 746

$$\text{Slope coefficient } b = \frac{\text{Difference between costs associated with highest and lowest observations of the cost driver}}{\text{Difference between highest and lowest observations of the cost driver}}$$

$$= \$746 \div 50 = \$14.92 \text{ per machine-hour}$$

To compute the constant, we can use either the highest or the lowest observation of the cost driver. Both calculations yield the same answer (because the solution technique solves two linear equations with two unknowns, the slope coefficient and the constant).

$$\text{Since} \quad y = a + bX, \quad a = y - bX$$

At the highest observation of the cost driver,

$$\text{Constant } a = \$1,456 - (\$14.92 \times 96) = \$23.68$$

At the lowest observation of the cost driver,

$$\text{Constant } a = \$710 - (\$14.92 \times 46) = \$23.68$$

Therefore, the high-low estimate of the cost function is

$$y = a + bX$$

$$= \$23.68 + (\$14.92 \times \text{Machine-hours})$$

EXHIBIT 10-5

High-Low Method for Weekly Indirect Manufacturing Labor Costs and Machine-Hours for Elegant Rugs

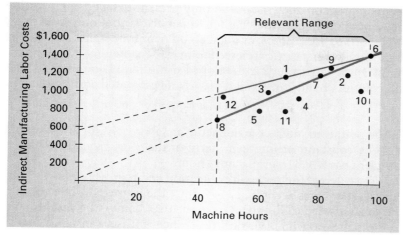

The blue line in Exhibit 10-5 shows the estimated cost function using the high-low method. The estimated cost function is a straight line joining the observations with the highest and lowest values of the cost driver (machine-hours). The constant, or intercept, term does not serve as an estimate of the fixed costs of Elegant Rugs if no machines were run. Why? Because running no machines and shutting down the plant is outside the relevant range. The intercept term is the constant component of the equation that provides the best (linear) approximation of how a cost behaves within the relevant range.

Suppose indirect manufacturing labor costs in week 6 were $1,280 instead of $1,456 while 96 machine-hours were worked. In this case, the highest observation of the cost driver (machine-hours of 96 in week 6) will not coincide with newly highest observation of the dependent variable (costs of $1,316 in week 9). Given that causality runs from the cost driver to the dependent variable in a cost function, choosing the highest and lowest observation of the cost driver is appropriate. The high-low method would estimate the new cost function still using data from weeks 6 and 8.

There is an obvious danger of relying on only two observations. Suppose that because of certain provisions in the labor contract that guarantee certain minimum payments, indirect manufacturing labor costs in week 8 were $1,000 instead of $710 when only 46 machine-hours were worked. The green line in Exhibit 10-5 shows the revised estimated cost function using the high-low method. It lies above the data. In this case, picking the highest and lowest observations for the machine-hours variable can result in an estimated cost function that poorly describes the underlying (linear) cost relationship between indirect manufacturing labor costs and machine-hours.

Sometimes the high-low method is modified so that the two observations chosen are a representative high and a representative low. The reason is that management wants to avoid having extreme observations, which arise from abnormal events, affect the cost function. Even with such a modification, this method ignores information from all but two observations when estimating the cost function.

Regression Analysis Method

Unlike the high-low method, regression analysis uses all available data to estimate the cost function. **Regression analysis** is a statistical method that measures the *average* amount of change in the dependent variable that is associated with a unit change in one or more independent variables. In the Elegant Rugs example, the dependent variable is total indirect manufacturing labor costs. The independent variable, or cost driver, is machine-hours. **Simple regression** analysis estimates the relationship between the dependent variable and one independent variable; **multiple regression** analysis estimates the relationship between the dependent variable and multiple independent variables.

We emphasize the interpretation and use of output from computer software programs for regression analysis and so only present detailed computations for deriving the regression line in the chapter Appendix. Commonly available programs (for example, SPSS, SAS, Lotus, and Excel) on mainframes and personal computers calculate almost all the statistics referred to in this chapter.

Exhibit 10-6 shows the line developed using regression analysis that best fits the data in columns 1 and 2 of Exhibit 10-3. The estimated cost function is

$$y = \$300.98 + \$10.31X$$

where y is the predicted indirect manufacturing labor costs for any level of machine-hours (X). The constant, or intercept, term of the regression a is \$300.98, and the slope coefficient b is \$10.31 per machine-hour.

How do we derive the regression equation and regression line in Exhibit 10-6? We use the least-squares technique. We draw the regression line to minimize the sum of the squared vertical distances from the data points (the various points on the graph) to the regression line. Vertical differences measure distance between actual cost and the estimated cost for each observation. The difference between actual and predicted cost is called the **residual term.** The smaller the residual terms, the better the fit between predicted costs and actual cost observations. Goodness of fit indicates the strength of the relationship between the cost driver and costs. The regression line in Exhibit 10-6 rises reasonably steeply from left to right. The positive slope of this line indicates that, on average, indirect manufacturing labor costs increase as machine-hours increase.

The vertical dashed lines in Exhibit 10-6 indicate the relevant range. As discussed previously, the estimated cost function only applies to cost driver levels *within the relevant range*, not to cost driver levels outside the relevant range.

The estimate of the slope coefficient b indicates that the average indirect manufacturing labor costs vary at the rate of \$10.31 for every machine-hour within the relevant range. Management can use this equation when budgeting for future indirect manufacturing labor costs. For instance, if 90 machine-hours are budgeted for the upcoming week, the predicted indirect manufacturing labor costs would be

$$y = \$300.98 + (\$10.31 \times 90) = \$1,228.88$$

Compare the regression equation with the high-low equation in the preceding section, which was \$23.68 + \$14.92 per machine-hour. For 90 machine-hours, the predicted cost based on the high-low equation is \$23.68 + (\$14.92 × 90) = \$1,366.48. Suppose that for 3 weeks over the next 12-week period, Elegant Rugs runs its

EXHIBIT 10-6
Regression Model for Weekly Indirect Manufacturing Labor Costs and
Machine-Hours for Elegant Rugs

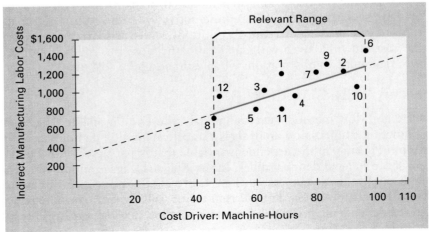

machines for 90 hours each week. Assume average indirect manufacturing labor costs for those 3 weeks is $1,300. Based on the high-low prediction of $1,366.48, Elegant Rugs would conclude it has performed well. But comparing the $1,300 performance with the $1,228.88 prediction of the regression model tells a different story, and would probably prompt Elegant Rugs to search for ways to improve its cost performance.

Intelligent application of regression analysis requires knowledge of both operations and cost accounting. Consider the costs to maintain and repair metal cutting machines at Helix Corporation, a manufacturer of filing cabinets. Helix schedules repairs and maintenance when production is at a low level to avoid having to take machines out of service when they are needed most. A plot and regression analysis of the monthly data will then show high repair costs in months of low production and low repair costs in months of high production. The engineering link between units of production and repair costs, however, is usually clear-cut. Over time there is a cause-and-effect relation: The higher the level of production, the higher the repair costs. To estimate the relation correctly, a thoughtful analyst will recognize that repair costs will tend to lag behind periods of high production, and use *lagged* production as the cost driver.

EVALUATING AND CHOOSING COST DRIVERS

Correctly identifying the cost driver and separating fixed costs from variable costs are important inputs for many management decisions. Suppose management at Elegant Rugs is thinking of introducing a new style of carpet. Sales of 650 square yards of this carpet are expected each week at a price of $12 per square yard. To make this decision, management needs to estimate costs. The key to doing so is identifying the correct cost drivers and cost functions. Consider, in particular, indirect manufacturing labor costs. Management believes that both machine-hours and direct manufacturing labor-hours are plausible cost drivers of indirect manufacturing labor costs. It estimates 72 machine-hours and 21 direct manufacturing labor-hours would be required to produce the square yards of carpet it needs.

What guidance do the different cost estimation methods provide for choosing among cost drivers? The industrial engineering method relies on analyzing physical relationships between costs and cost drivers, which are difficult to specify in this case. The conference method and the account analysis method use subjective assessments to choose a cost driver and to estimate the fixed and variable components of the cost function. In these cases, management must go with its best judgment. Management cannot use these methods to test and try alternative cost drivers. The major advantage of quantitative methods is that managers can use these methods to evaluate different cost drivers. We illustrate how using the regression analysis approach.

Suppose Elegant Rugs wants to evaluate whether direct manufacturing labor-hours is a better cost driver than machine-hours for indirect manufacturing labor costs. The cost analyst at Elegant Rugs inputs the data in columns 1 and 3 of Exhibit 10-3 into a computer program and estimates the cost function:

$$y = \$744.67 + \$7.72X$$

Exhibit 10-7 shows the plots for indirect manufacturing labor costs and direct manufacturing labor-hours, and the regression line that best fits the data.

Which cost driver should Elegant Rugs choose? We consider three of the most important criteria.

1. *Economic plausibility.* Both cost drivers are economically plausible. However, in the state-of-the-art, highly automated production environment of Elegant Rugs, costs are likely to be more closely related to machine-hours than to direct manufacturing labor-hours.

2. *Goodness of fit.* Compare Exhibits 10-6 and 10-7. The vertical differences between actual and predicted costs are much smaller for machine-hours than for direct manufacturing labor-hours—machine-hours has a stronger relationship with indirect manufacturing labor costs.

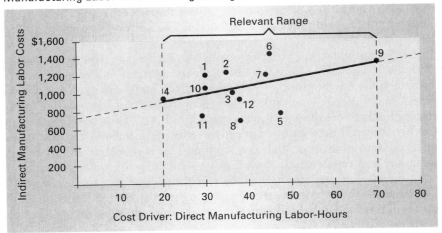

3. *Slope of regression line*. Again compare Exhibits 10-6 and 10-7. The machine-hours regression line has a relatively steep slope while the direct manufacturing labor hours regression line is relatively flat (small slope). A relatively flat regression line indicates a weak or no relationship between indirect manufacturing labor costs and direct manufacturing labor-hours since, on average, changes in direct manufacturing labor-hours appear to have a minimal effect on indirect manufacturing labor costs.

Elegant Rugs should choose machine-hours as the cost driver and use the cost function $y = \$300.98 + (\$10.31 \times \text{Machine-hours})$ to predict future indirect manufacturing labor costs. Using this model, Elegant Rugs would predict costs of $y = \$300.98 + (\$10.31 \times 72) = \$1,043.30$. Had it used direct manufacturing labor-hours as the cost driver, it would have incorrectly predicted costs of $\$744.67 + (\$7.72 \times 21) = \$906.79$. If Elegant Rugs systematically underestimates costs and chooses incorrect cost drivers for other indirect costs as well, it would conclude that the costs of manufacturing the new style of carpet are quite low and essentially fixed (the regression line is relatively flat). But the actual costs driven by machine-hours would prove to be much higher. Without identifying the correct cost drivers, management would be misled into believing the new style of carpets are more profitable than they actually are.

Incorrectly estimating the cost function will also have repercussions for cost management and cost control. Suppose direct manufacturing labor-hours was used as the cost driver, and actual indirect manufacturing labor costs were $970. Actual costs would then be higher than the predicted costs of $906.79. Management would feel compelled to find ways to cut costs. In fact, on the basis of the preferred machine-hour cost driver, the plant has actual costs lower than the predicted amount ($1,043.30)—a performance that management should seek to replicate, not change.

NONLINEARITY AND COST FUNCTIONS

In practice, cost functions are not always linear. A **nonlinear cost function** is a cost function where, within the relevant range, the graph of total costs versus a single cost driver does not form a straight line. Exhibit 10-2 graphically illustrated a cost function that is nonlinear over the range from 0 to 80,000 valves produced. Consider another example. Economies of scale in advertising may enable an advertising agency to double the number of advertisements for less than double the costs. Even direct materials costs are not always linear variable costs. Consider quantity discounts on direct materials purchases. As shown in Exhibit 10-8, the total direct materials costs

Activity-Based Costing and Cost Estimation

Cost estimation in activity-based costing (ABC) systems blend the various methods presented in this chapter. ABC systems exploit managers' knowledge of operations via in-depth interviews (as well as company records) to identify key activities and the cost drivers and costs of each activity at the output-unit level, batch-level and product-sustaining level. To determine the cost of an activity, ABC systems often rely on expert analyses and opinions gathered from operating personnel (the conference method). For example, loan department staff at the Co-operative Bank in the United Kingdom subjectively estimates the costs of the loan processing activity and the cost driver of loan processing costs (the number of loans processed, a batch-level cost driver, rather than the value of the loans, an output unit-level cost driver), to derive the cost of processing a loan. ABC systems sometimes use input-output relationships (the industrial engineering method) to identify cost drivers and the cost of an activity. For example, John Deere and Company uses work-measurement methods to identify a batch-level cost driver (the number of standard loads moved) and the cost per load moved within its components plant.

In complex, manufacturing environments, multiple cost drivers are necessary for accurate product costing. Consider heavy equipment manufacturer Caterpillar Inc.'s method of identifying the cost driver for receiving costs in its ABC system. Three plausible cost drivers were the weight of parts received, the number of parts received, or the number of shipments received. The weight of parts and number of parts are output unit-level cost drivers, while the number of shipments is a batch-level cost driver. Caterpillar uses the weight of parts as the basis for cost assignment because a regression analysis showed that it is the primary driver of the costs of receiving material. Caterpillar also uses a variety of other cost drivers in assigning costs to its products.

Source: Based on the Co-operative Bank, Harvard Business School Case No. N9-195-196, John Deere Component Works (A), Harvard Business School Case 9-187-107, and discussions with the company managements.

rise, but they rise more slowly as the cost driver increases because of quantity discounts. The cost function in Exhibit 10-8 has $b = \$25$ for 1–1,000 units purchased; $b = \$15$ for 1,001–2,000 units purchased; and $b = \$10$ for 2,000 or more units purchased ($a = \$0$ for all ranges of the units purchased). The cost per unit falls at each price break; that is, the cost per unit decreases with larger orders.

EXHIBIT 10-8
Effects of Quantity Discounts on Slope of
Direct Materials Cost Function

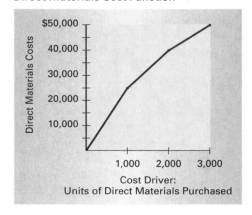

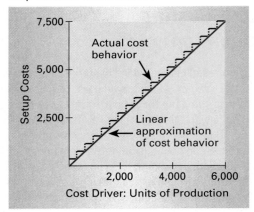

EXHIBIT 10-9
Step Variable-Cost Function

Step cost functions are also examples of nonlinear cost functions. A **step cost function** is a cost function in which the cost is constant over various ranges of the cost driver, but the cost increases by discrete amounts (that is, in steps) as the cost driver moves from one range to the next. The graph in Exhibit 10-9 shows a *step variable-cost function*, a step-cost function in which cost is constant over narrow ranges of the cost driver in each relevant range. Exhibit 10-9 shows the relationship between setup costs and units of production. The pattern is a stepcost function because setup costs are incurred only when each production batch is started. This step-pattern behavior also occurs when inputs such as production scheduling, product design labor, and process engineering labor are acquired in discrete quantities but used in fractional quantities. As shown in Exhibit 10-9, management often approximates step variable costs with a variable cost function.

The graph in Exhibit 10-10 shows a *step fixed-cost function* for Crofton Steel, a company that operates large heat-treatment furnaces to harden steel parts. The main difference relative to Exhibit 10-9 is that the cost in a step-fixed cost function is constant over large ranges of the cost driver in each relevant range. The ranges indicate the number of furnaces being used (each furnace costing $300,000). The cost changes from one range to the next higher range when the hours of furnace time demanded require the use of another furnace. The relevant range indicates that the company expects to operate with two furnaces at a cost of $600,000. Management considers the cost of operating furnaces as a fixed cost within the relevant range of operation.

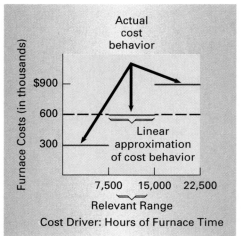

EXHIBIT 10-10
Step Fixed-Cost Function

Learning curves also result in cost functions being nonlinear. A **learning curve** is a function that shows how labor-hours per unit decline as units of production increase and workers learn and become better at what they do. Managers use learning curves to predict how labor-hours (or labor costs) will change as more units are produced.

The aircraft-assembly industry first documented the effect that learning has on efficiency. As workers become more familiar with their tasks, their efficiency improves. Managers learn how to improve the scheduling of work shifts. Plant operators learn how best to operate the facility. Unit costs decrease as productivity increases, which means that the unit-cost function behaves nonlinearly.

Managers are now extending the learning-curve notion to include other cost areas in the value chain, such as marketing, distribution, and customer service. The term *experience curve* describes this broader application of the learning curve. An **experience curve** is a function that shows how full product costs per unit (including manufacturing, marketing, distribution, and so on) decline as units of output increase.

We now describe two learning-curve models: the cumulative average-time learning model and the incremental unit-time learning model.[4]

Cumulative Average-Time Learning Model

OBJECTIVE 7

Distinguish between the cumulative average-time learning model and incremental unit-time learning model

In the **cumulative average-time learning model,** the cumulative average time per unit declines by a constant percentage each time the cumulative quantity of units produced doubles. Exhibit 10-11 illustrates the cumulative average-time learning model with an 80% learning curve. The 80% means that when the quantity of units produced is doubled from X to $2X$, the cumulative average time *per unit* for the $2X$ units is 80% of the cumulative average time *per unit* for the X units. In other words, average time per unit has dropped by 20%. Graph 1 in Exhibit 10-11 shows the cumulative average time *per unit* as a function of units produced. Graph 2 in Exhibit 10-11 shows the cumulative *total* labor-hours as a function of units produced. The data points underlying Exhibit 10-11, and the details of their calculation, are presented in Exhibit 10-12. To obtain the cumulative total time, multiply the cumulative average time per unit by the cumulative number of units produced. For example, to produce 4 cumulative units would require 256.00 labor-hours (4×64).

Incremental Unit-Time Learning Model

In the **incremental unit-time learning model,** the incremental unit time (the time needed to produce the last unit) declines by a constant percentage each time the cumulative quantity of units produced doubles. Exhibit 10-13 illustrates the incremental unit-time learning model with an 80% learning curve. The 80% here means that when the quantity of units produced is doubled from X to $2X$, the time needed to produce the *last unit* at the $2X$ production level is 80% of the time needed to produce the *last unit* at the X production level. Graph 1 in Exhibit 10-13 shows the cumulative average time *per unit* as a function of cumulative units produced. Graph 2 in Exhibit 10-13 shows the cumulative *total* labor-hours as a function of units produced. The data points underlying Exhibit 10-13, and the details of their calculation, are presented in Exhibit 10-14. We obtain the cumulative total time by summing the individual unit times. For example, to produce 4 cumulative units would require 314.21 labor-hours ($100.00 + 80.00 + 70.21 + 64.00$).

The incremental unit-time model predicts that a higher cumulative total time is required to produce two or more units than does the cumulative average-time model, assuming the same learning rate for the two models (compare results in Exhibit 10-12 with results in Exhibit 10-14). For example, to produce 4 cumulative units, the 80% incremental unit-time learning model predicts 314.21 labor-hours

[4]For further discussion, see J. Chen and R. Manes, "Distinguishing the Two Forms of the Constant Percentage Learning Curve Model," *Contemporary Accounting Research* (Spring 1985), pp. 242–252. See also the Northern Aerospace Manufacturing case study in A. A. Atkinson, *Cost Estimation in Management Accounting—Six Case Studies* (Hamilton, Ontario: Society of Management Accountants of Canada, 1987).

EXHIBIT 10-11
Plots for Cumulative Average-Time Learning Model

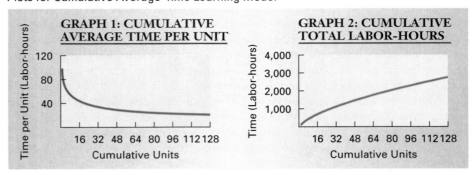

EXHIBIT 10-12
Cumulative Average-Time Learning Model

Cumulative Number of Units (1)	Cumulative Average Time per Unit (y): Labor-Hours (2)	Cumulative Total Time: Labor-Hours (3) = (1) × (2)	Individual Unit Time for Xth Unit: Labor-Hours (4)
1	100.00	100.00	100.00
2	80.00 (100 × 0.8)	160.00	60.00
3	70.21	210.63	50.63
4	64.00 (80 × 0.8)	256.00	45.37
5	59.57	297.85	41.85
6	56.17	337.02	39.17
7	53.45	374.15	37.13
8	51.20 (64 × 0.8)	409.60	35.45
•	•	•	•
•	•	•	•
•	•	•	•
16	40.96 (51.2 × 0.8)	655.36	28.06

NOTE: The mathematical relationship underlying the cumulative average-time learning model is

$$y = p\,X^q$$

where y = Cumulative average time (labor-hours) per unit
  X = Cumulative number of units produced
  p = Time (labor-hours) required to produce the first unit
  q = Rate of learning

The value of q is calculated as

$$q = \frac{\ln\,(\%\ \text{learning})}{\ln 2}$$

For an 80% learning curve,

$$q = \frac{-0.2231}{0.6931} = -0.3219$$

As an illustration, when $X = 3$, $p = 100$, and $q = -0.3219$

$$y = 100 \times 3^{-0.3219} = 70.21 \text{ labor-hours}$$

The cumulative total time when $X = 3$ is $70.21 \times 3 = 210.63$ labor-hours.
  The individual unit times in column 4 are calculated using the data in column 3. For example, the individual unit time of 50.63 labor-hours for the third unit is calculated as $210.63 - 160.00$.

versus 256.00 labor-hours predicted by the 80% cumulative average-time learning model.

Which of these two models is preferable? The one that more accurately approximates the behavior of manufacturing labor-hour usage as production levels increase. The choice can be decided only on a case-by-case basis. Engineers, plant

EXHIBIT 10-13

Plots for Incremental Unit-Time Learning Model

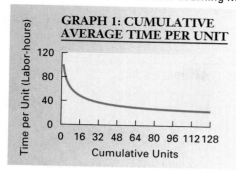

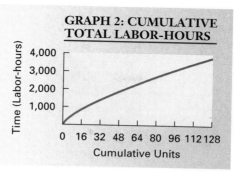

EXHIBIT 10-14

Incremental Unit-Time Learning Model

Cumulative Number of Units (1)	Individual Unit Time for Xth Unit (m): Labor-Hours (2)	Cumulative Total Time: Labor-Hours (3)	Cumulative Average Time per Unit: Labor-Hours (4) = (3) ÷ (1)
1	100.00	100.00	100.00
2	80.00 (100 × 0.8)	180.00	90.00
3	70.21	250.21	83.40
4	64.00 (80 × 0.8)	314.21	78.55
5	59.57	373.78	74.76
6	56.17	429.95	71.66
7	53.45	483.40	69.06
8	51.20 (64 × 0.8)	534.60	66.82
•	•	•	•
•	•	•	•
•	•	•	•
16	40.96 (51.2 × 0.8)	892.00	55.75

NOTE: The mathematical relationship underlying the incremental unit-time learning model is

$$m = pX^q$$

where m = Time (labor-hours) taken to produce the last single unit
X = Cumulative number of units produced
p = Time (labor-hours) required to produce the first unit
q = Rate of learning

The value of q is calculated as

$$q = \frac{\ln (\% \text{ learning})}{\ln 2}$$

For an 80% learning curve,

$$q = \frac{-0.2231}{0.6931} = -0.3219$$

As an illustration, when $X = 3$, $p = 100$, and $q = -0.3219$

$$m = 100 \times 3^{-0.3219} = 70.21 \text{ labor-hours}$$

The cumulative total time when $X = 3$ is $100 + 80 + 70.21 = 250.21$ labor-hours.

managers, and workers are good sources of information on the amount and type of learning actually occurring as production increases. Plotting this information is helpful in selecting the appropriate model.

The Problem for Self-Study that follows this section illustrates the cumulative average-time learning model and the incremental unit-time learning model in a job-costing situation.

EXHIBIT 10-15
Predicting Costs Using Learning Curves

Cumulative Number of Units	Cumulative Total Labor–Hours*	Cumulative Costs	Additions to Cumulative Costs
1	100.00	$ 5,000 (100.00 × $50)	$ 5,000
2	160.00	8,000 (160.00 × $50)	3,000
4	256.00	12,800 (256.00 × $50)	4,800
8	409.60	20,480 (409.60 × $50)	7,680
16	655.36	32,768 (655.36 × $50)	12,288

*Based on the cumulative average-time learning model. See Exhibit 10-12 for the computation of these amounts.

Setting Prices, Budgets, and Standards

Predictions of costs should allow for learning. Consider the data in Exhibit 10-12 for the cumulative average-time learning model. Suppose the variable costs subject to learning effects consist of direct manufacturing labor ($20 per hour) and related overhead ($30 per hour). Management should predict the costs shown in Exhibit 10-15.

These data show that the effects of the learning curve could have a major influence on decisions. For example, a company might set an extremely low selling price on its product in order to generate high demand. As the company's production increases to meet this growing demand, costs per unit drop. The company rides the product down the learning curve as it establishes a higher market share. Although the company may have earned little on its first unit sold—it may actually have lost money—the company earns more profit per unit as output increases.

Alternatively, subject to legal and other considerations, the company might set a low price on just the final 8 units. After all, the labor and related overhead costs per unit are predicted to be only $12,288 for these final 8 units ($32,768 – $20,480). The per unit costs of $1,536 on these final 8 units ($12,288 ÷ 8) are much lower than the $5,000 costs per unit of the first unit produced.

Many companies incorporate learning-curve effects when evaluating performance. For example, the Nissan Motor Company sets assembly-labor efficiency standards for new models of cars after taking into account the learning that will occur as more units are produced.

The learning-curve models examined in Exhibits 10-11 to 10-14 assume that learning is driven by a single variable (production output). Other models of learning have been developed by companies such as Analog Devices and Yokogowa Hewlett-Packard that focus on how quality (rather than manufacturing labor-hours) will change over time (rather than as more units are produced). Some recent studies suggest that factors other than production output—such as job rotation and organizing workers into teams—contribute to learning that improves quality.

DATA COLLECTION AND ADJUSTMENT ISSUES

OBJECTIVE 8

Understand data problems encountered in estimating cost functions

The ideal data base for estimating cost functions quantitatively has two characteristics:

1. It contains numerous reliably measured observations of the cost driver(s) and the dependent variable. Errors in measuring the costs and cost driver(s) are particularly serious. They result in inaccurate estimates of the effect of the cost driver(s) on costs.

2. It considers many values for the cost driver over a wide range. Using only a few values that are grouped closely together considers too small a segment of the relevant range and reduces the confidence in the estimates obtained.

Unfortunately, cost analysts typically do not have the advantage of working with a data base having both characteristics. This section outlines some frequently encountered data problems, and steps the analyst can take to overcome these problems.

1. The time period for measuring the dependent variable (for example, indirect manufacturing labor costs) does not properly match the period for measuring the cost driver(s). This problem often arises when accounting records are not kept on an accrual basis. Consider a cost function with machine-lubricant costs as the dependent variable and machine-hours as the cost driver. Assume that the lubricant is purchased sporadically and stored for later use. Records maintained on a cash basis will indicate no lubricant consumption in many months and sizable lubricant consumption in other months. This is an obviously inaccurate picture of what is actually taking place. The analyst should use accrual accounting to measure consumption of machine lubricants to better match costs with the cost driver in this example.

2. Fixed costs are allocated as if they are variable. For example, costs such as depreciation, insurance, or rent may be allocated to products to calculate costs per unit of output. *The danger is to regard these costs as variable rather than as fixed. They seem to be variable because of the allocation methods used.* To avoid this problem, the analyst should distinguish carefully between fixed and variable costs, and not treat allocated fixed costs per unit as a variable cost.

3. Data are either not available for all observations or are not uniformly reliable. Missing cost observations often arise from a failure to record a cost or from classifying a cost incorrectly. Data on cost drivers often originate outside the internal accounting system. For example, the accounting department may get data on testing times for medical instruments from the company's manufacturing department and data on the number of items shipped to customers from the distribution department. The reliability of such data varies greatly among organizations. In some systems, data are still recorded manually rather than electronically. Manually recorded data typically have a higher percentage of missing observations and erroneously entered observations than electronically entered data. To minimize this problem, the cost analyst should design data collection reports that regularly and routinely obtain the required data, and should follow up immediately whenever data is missing.

4. Extreme values of observations occur from errors in recording costs (for example, a misplaced decimal point); from nonrepresentative time periods (for example, from a period in which a major machine breakdown occurred or from a period in which delay in delivery of materials from an international supplier curtailed production); or from observations being outside the relevant range. Analysts should adjust or eliminate unusual observations before estimating a cost relationship; otherwise, an incorrect estimate would result.

5. There is no homogeneous relationship between the individual cost items in the dependent variable pool and the cost driver. A homogeneous relationship exists when each activity whose costs are included in the dependent variable has the same cost driver. Consider materials procurement overhead costs. This overhead cost account can include a diverse set of activities (for example, new vendor negotiations, materials ordering, incoming inspection, and materials handling). If each activity has the same cost driver, the homogeneous relationship principle suggests that a single cost function can be estimated for the entire cost pool. Where the cost driver for each activity is different, separate cost functions, each with its own cost driver, would be estimated for each activity.

6. The relationship between cost and the cost driver is not stationary; that is, the underlying process that generated the observations has not remained stable over time. For example, the relationship between manufacturing overhead costs and machine-hours is unlikely to be stationary if the data covers a period in which new technology was introduced. One way to test for stationarity in this case is to split the sample into two parts and estimate separate cost relationships for the before- and after-technology change periods. Then, if the estimated coefficients for the two periods are similar, the analyst can pool all the data together to estimate a single cost relationship. Pooling data provides a larger data set for the estimation, which increases the confidence in the cost predictions being made.

7. Inflation has affected the dependent variable, the cost driver, or both. For example, inflation may cause costs to change even when there is no change in the cost driver. To study the underlying cause-and-effect relationship between the cost driver and costs, the analyst should remove purely inflationary price effects from the data.

In many cases, a cost analyst must expend much effort to reduce the effect of these problems before estimating a cost function on the basis of past data.

PROBLEM FOR SELF-STUDY

PROBLEM

The Helicopter Division of Aerospatiale is examining helicopter assembly costs at its plant in Marseilles, France. It has received an initial order for eight of its new land-surveying helicopters. Aerospatiale can adopt one of two methods of assembling the helicopters:

	Labor-Intensive Assembly Method	Machine-Intensive Assembly Method
Direct materials costs per helicopter	$40,000	$36,000
Direct assembly labor time for first helicopter	2,000 labor-hours	800 labor-hours
Learning curve for assembly labor time per helicopter	85% cumulative average time*	90% incremental unit time†
Direct assembly labor costs	$30 per hour	$30 per hour
Equipment-related indirect manufacturing costs	$12 per direct-assembly labor-hour	$45 per direct-assembly labor-hour
Materials-handling-related indirect manufacturing costs	50% of direct materials costs	50% of direct materials costs

*An 85% learning curve is expressed mathematically as $q = -0.2345$.
†A 90% learning curve is expressed mathematically as $q = -0.1520$.

REQUIRED

1. How many direct-assembly labor-hours are required to assemble the first eight helicopters under (a) the labor-intensive method, and (b) the machine-intensive method?
2. What is the cost of assembling the first eight helicopters under (a) the labor-intensive method, and (b) the machine-intensive method?

SOLUTION

1a. Labor-intensive assembly method based on cumulative average-time learning model (85% learning).

Cumulative Number of Units (1)	Cumulative Average Time per Unit (y): Labor-Hours (2)	Cumulative Total Time: Labor-Hours (3) = 1 × (2)	Individual Unit Time for Xth Unit: Labor-Hours (4)
1	2,000	2,000	2,000
2	1,700 (2,000 × 0.85)	3,400	1,400
3	1,546	4,638	1,238
4	1,445 (1,700 × 0.85)	5,780	1,142
5	1,371	6,855	1,075
6	1,314	7,884	1,029
7	1,267	8,869	985
8	1,228.25 (1,445 × 0.85)	9,826	957

The cumulative average-time per unit for the Xth unit in column 2 is calculated as $y = pX^q$; see Exhibit 10-12 (p. 352). For example, when $X = 3$, $y = 2,000 \times 3^{-0.2345} = 1,546$ labor-hours.

1b. Machine-intensive assembly method based on incremental unit-time learning model (90% learning).

Cumulative Number of Units (1)	Individual Unit Time for Xth Unit (m): Labor-Hours (2)	Cumulative Total Time: Labor-Hours (3)	Cumulative Average Time per Unit: Labor-Hours (4) = (3) ÷ (1)
1	800	800	800
2	720 (800 × 0.9)	1,520	760
3	677	2,197	732
4	648 (720 × 0.9)	2,845	711
5	626	3,471	694
6	609	4,080	680
7	595	4,675	668
8	583 (648 × 0.9)	5,258	657

The individual unit time for the Xth unit in column 2 is calculated as $m = pX^q$; see Exhibit 10-14 (p. 353). For example, when $X = 3$, $m = 800 \times 3^{-0.1520} = 677$ labor-hours

2. Costs of assembling the first eight helicopters are

	Labor-Intensive Assembly Method	Machine-Intensive Assembly Method
Direct materials: 8 × $40,000; 8 × $36,000	$320,000	$288,000
Direct assembly labor: 9,826 × $30; 5,258 × $30	294,780	157,740
Indirect manufacturing costs Equipment-related: 9,826 × $12; 5,258 × $45	117,912	236,610
Materials-handling-related: 0.50 × $320,000; 0.50 × $288,000	160,000	144,000
Total assembly costs	$892,692	$826,350

The machine-intensive method has assembly costs that are $66,342 lower than the labor-intensive method ($892,692 – $826,350).

SUMMARY

The following points are linked to the chapter's learning objectives.

1. Two assumptions frequently made in cost-behavior estimation are (a) that changes in total costs can be explained by changes in the level of a single cost driver, and (b) that cost behavior can adequately be approximated by a linear function of the cost driver within the relevant range.

2. A linear cost function is a cost function where, within the relevant range, the graph of total costs versus a single cost driver forms a straight line. Linear cost functions can be described by a single constant (a), which represents the estimate of the total cost component that does not vary with changes in the level of the cost driver, and a slope coefficient (b), which represents the estimate of the amount by which total costs change for each unit change in the level of the cost driver. Three types of linear cost functions are variable, fixed, and mixed (or semivariable).

3. Four broad approaches to estimating cost functions are the industrial engineering method, the conference method, the account analysis method, and quantitative analysis of cost relationships (the high-low method and regression analysis method). Regression analysis is a systematic approach to estimating a cost function on the basis of identified cost drivers. Ideally, the cost analyst applies more than one approach; each approach serves as a check on the others.

4. The six steps in estimating a cost function on the basis of an analysis of current or past cost relationships are (a) choose the dependent variable; (b) identify the cost driver(s); (c) collect data on the dependent variable and the cost driver(s); (d) plot the data; (e) estimate the cost function; and (f) evaluate the estimated cost function. In most situations, the cost analyst will cycle through these steps several times before identifying an acceptable cost function.

5. Three criteria for evaluating and choosing cost drivers are (a) economic plausibility, (b) goodness of fit, and (c) the slope of the regression line.

6. A nonlinear cost function is a cost function where, within the relevant range, the graph of total costs versus a single cost driver does not form a straight line. Nonlinear costs can arise due to economies of scale, quantity discounts, step cost functions, and learning-curve effects.

7. The learning curve is an example of a nonlinear cost function. Labor-hours per unit decline as units of production increase. In the cumulative average-time learning model, the cumulative average-time per unit declines by a constant percentage each time the cumulative quantity of units produced doubles. In the incremental unit-time learning model, the incremental unit time (the time needed to produce the last unit) declines by a constant percentage each time the cumulative quantity of units produced doubles.

8. The most difficult task in cost estimation is collecting high-quality, reliably measured data on the dependent variable and the cost driver(s). Common problems include missing data, extreme values of observations, changes in technology, and distortions resulting from inflation.

APPENDIX: REGRESSION ANALYSIS

This Appendix describes formulas for estimating the regression equation and several commonly used statistics. We use the data for Elegant Rugs presented in Exhibit 10-3. The Appendix also discusses goodness of fit, significance of independent variables, and specification analysis of estimation assumptions for regression analysis.

Estimating the Regression Line

The least-squares technique for estimating the regression line minimizes the sum of the squares of the vertical deviations (distances) from the data points to the estimated regression line.

The object is to find the values of a and b in the predicting equation $y = a + bX$, where y is the predicted cost value as distinguished from the observed cost value, which we denote by Y. We wish to find the numerical values of a and b that minimize $\Sigma(Y-y)^2$. This calculation is accomplished by using two equations, usually called the normal equations:

$$\Sigma Y = na + b(\Sigma X)$$

$$\Sigma XY = a(\Sigma X) + b(\Sigma X^2)$$

where n is the number of data points; ΣX and ΣY are, respectively, the sums of the given X and Y values; ΣX^2 is the sum of squares of the X values; and ΣXY is the sum of the amounts obtained by multiplying each of the given X values by the associated observed Y value.

Exhibit 10-16 shows the calculations required for obtaining the line that best fits the data of indirect manufacturing labor costs and machine-hours for Elegant Rugs. Substituting into the two normal equations simultaneously, we obtain

EXHIBIT 10-16
Computation for Least-Squares Regression between Indirect Manufacturing Labor Costs and Machine-Hours for Elegant Rugs

Week (1)	Machine-Hours* X (2)	Indirect Manufacturing Labor Costs* Y (3)	X^2 (4)	XY (5)	y (6)	Variance of Y $(Y-\bar{Y})^2$ (7)	Unexplained Variance $(Y-y)^2$ (8)	Variance of X $(X-\bar{X})^2$ (9)
1	68	1,190	4,624	80,920	1,002.06	21,978	35,321	15
2	88	1,211	7,744	106,568	1,208.26	28,646	8	261
3	62	1,004	3,844	62,248	940.20	1,425	4,070	97
4	72	917	5,184	66,024	1,043.30	15,563	15,952	0
5	60	770	3,600	46,200	919.58	73,848	22,374	140
6	96	1,456	9,216	139,776	1,290.74	171,603	27,311	584
7	78	1,180	6,084	92,040	1,105.16	19,113	5,601	38
8	46	710	2,116	32,660	775.24	110,058	4,256	667
9	82	1,316	6,724	107,912	1,146.40	75,213	28,764	103
10	94	1,032	8,836	97,008	1,270.12	95	56,701	491
11	68	752	4,624	51,136	1,002.06	83,955	62,530	15
12	48	963	2,304	46,224	795.86	6,202	27,936	568
Total	862	12,501	64,900	928,716	≈12,501	607,699	290,824	2,979

*Same data as in columns 1 and 2 of Exhibit 10-3.

$$12{,}501 = 12a + 862b$$

and

$$928{,}716 = 862a + 64{,}900b$$

The solution is $a = \$300.98$ and $b = \$10.31$, which can be obtained by direct substitution if the normal equations are reexpressed symbolically as follows:

$$a = \frac{(\Sigma Y)(\Sigma X^2) - (\Sigma X)(\Sigma XY)}{n(\Sigma X^2) - (\Sigma X)(\Sigma X)} \quad \text{and} \quad b = \frac{n(\Sigma XY) - (\Sigma X)(\Sigma Y)}{n(\Sigma X^2) - (\Sigma X)(\Sigma X)}$$

For our illustration, we now have

$$a = \frac{(12{,}501)(64{,}900) - (862)(928{,}716)}{12(64{,}900) - (862)(862)} = \$300.98$$

$$b = \frac{12(928{,}716) - (862)(12{,}501)}{12(64{,}900) - (862)(862)} = \$10.31$$

Placing the amounts for a and b in the equation of the least-squares line, we have

$$y = \$300.98 + \$10.31X$$

where y is the predicted indirect manufacturing labor costs for any specified number of machine-hours within the relevant range. Generally, these computations are done using software packages such as SPSS, SAS, Lotus, and Excel.

Goodness of Fit

Goodness of fit measures how well the predicted values, y, based on the cost driver, X, match actual cost observations, Y. The regression analysis method computes a formal measure of goodness of fit, called the coefficient of determination. The **coefficient of determination, r^2,** measures the percentage of variation in Y explained by X (the independent variable). The coefficient of determination (r^2) indicates the proportion of the variance of Y, $(Y - \bar{Y})^2 \div n$, that is explained by the independent variable X (where $\bar{Y} = \Sigma Y \div n$). It is more convenient to express the coefficient of determination as 1 minus the proportion of total variance that is *not* explained by the independent variable. The unexplained variance arises because of differences between the actual values of Y and the predicted values of y:

$$r^2 = 1 - \frac{\text{Unexplained variation}}{\text{Total variation}} = 1 - \frac{\Sigma(Y-y)^2}{\Sigma(Y-\overline{Y})^2}$$

From Exhibit 10-16, $\Sigma Y = 12{,}501$ and $\overline{Y} = 12{,}501 \div 12 = 1{,}041.75$. Therefore, to obtain the total variation,

$$\Sigma(Y-\overline{Y})^2 = (1{,}190 - 1{,}041.75)^2 + (1{,}211 - 1{,}041.75)^2 + \cdots + (963 - 1{,}041.75)^2$$

$$= 607{,}699$$

Each value of X generates a prediction y. For example, in week 1, $y = \$300.98 + (\$10.31 \times 68) = \$1002.06$. Therefore, to obtain the unexplained variation,

$$\Sigma(Y-y)^2 = (1{,}190 - 1{,}002.06)^2 + (1{,}211 - 1{,}208.26)^2 + \cdots + (963 - 795.86)^2$$

$$= 35{,}321 + 8 + \cdots + 27{,}936 = 290{,}824$$

$$r^2 = 1 - \frac{290{,}824}{607{,}699} = 0.52$$

The calculations indicate that r^2 increases as the predicted values y more closely approximate the actual observations Y. The range of r^2 is from 0 (implying no explanatory power) to 1 (implying perfect explanatory power). When $r^2 = 1$, the predicted cost values exactly equal actual cost values; that is, the independent variable X has perfectly explained variations in actual costs Y. Generally, an r^2 of 0.30 or higher passes the goodness-of-fit test. Do not rely exclusively on goodness of fit. It can lead to the indiscriminate inclusion of independent variables that increase r^2 but have no economic plausibility as cost driver(s). Goodness of fit has meaning only if the relationship between costs and the drivers is economically plausible.

Significance of Independent Variables

A key question that managers ask is, Do changes in the economically plausible independent variable result in significant changes in the dependent variable, or alternatively, is the slope b of the regression line significant? Recall, for example, that in the regression of machine-hours on indirect manufacturing labor costs in the Elegant Rugs illustration, b is estimated from a sample of 12 observations. The estimate b is subject to random factors, as are all sample statistics. That is, a different sample of 12 data points will give a different estimate of b. The **standard error of the estimated coefficient** indicates how much the estimated value b is likely to be affected by random factors. The t-value of the b coefficient measures how large the value of the estimated coefficient is relative to its standard error. A t-value with an absolute value greater than 2.00 suggests that the b coefficient is significantly different from zero.[5] In other words, a relationship exists between the independent variable and the dependent variable that cannot be attributed to chance alone.

Exhibit 10-17 presents a convenient format for summarizing the regression results for indirect manufacturing labor costs and machine-hours. The t-value for the

[5]The benchmark for inferring that a b coefficient is significantly different from zero is a function of the degrees of freedom in a regression. The benchmark of 2.00 assumes a sample size of 60 observations. The number of degrees of freedom is calculated as the sample size minus the number of a and b parameters estimated in the regression. For a simple regression, the benchmark values for the t-values are

Sample Size	Benchmark*
12	$\lvert t \rvert > 2.23$
15	$\lvert t \rvert > 2.16$
20	$\lvert t \rvert > 2.10$
30	$\lvert t \rvert > 2.05$
60	$\lvert t \rvert > 2.00$

*$\lvert t \rvert$ denotes the absolute value of the t-value.

For simplicity, we use a cut-off t-value of 2.00 throughout this chapter.

EXHIBIT 10-17

Simple Regression Results with Indirect Manufacturing Labor Costs as Dependent Variable
and Machine-Hours as Independent Variable for Elegant Rugs

Variable	Coefficient (1)	Standard Error (2)	t-Value (3) = (1) ÷ (2)
Constant	$300.98	$229.75	1.31
Independent variable 1: Machine-hours	$ 10.31	$ 3.12	3.30

$r^2 = 0.52$; Durbin–Watson statistic $= 2.05$

slope coefficient b is $10.31 ÷ $3.12 = 3.30, which exceeds the benchmark of 2.00. Therefore, the coefficient of the machine-hours variable is significantly different from zero. The probability is low (less than 5%) that random factors could have caused the coefficient b to be positive. Alternatively, we can restate our conclusion in terms of a "confidence interval"—there is less than a 5% chance that the true value of the machine-hours coefficient lies outside the range $10.31 ± (2.00 × $3.12) or $10.31 ± $6.24, or from $4.07 and $16.55. Therefore, we can conclude that changes in machine-hours do affect indirect manufacturing labor costs. Similarly, using data from Exhibit 10-17, the t-value for the constant term a is $300.98 ÷ $229.76 = 1.31, which is less than 2.00. This value indicates that, within the relevant range, the constant term is not significantly different from zero.

Specification Analysis of Estimation Assumptions

Specification analysis is the testing of the assumptions of regression analysis. If the assumptions of (1) linearity within the relevant range, (2) constant variance of residuals, (3) independence of residuals, and (4) normality of residuals hold, the simplest regression procedures give reliable estimates of unknown coefficient values. This section provides a brief overview of specification analysis. When these assumptions are not satisfied, more complex regression procedures are necessary to obtain the best estimates.[6]

1. Linearity within the relevant range. A common assumption is that a linear relationship exists between the independent variable X and the dependent variable Y within the relevant range. If a linear regression model is used to estimate a fundamentally nonlinear relationship, however, the coefficient estimates obtained will be inaccurate.

Where there is only one independent variable, the easiest way to check for linearity is by studying the data on a scatter diagram, a step that often is unwisely skipped. Exhibit 10-6 (p. 346) presents a scatter diagram for the indirect manufacturing labor costs and machine-hours variables of Elegant Rugs shown in Exhibit 10-3 (p. 342). The scatter diagram reveals that linearity appears to be a reasonable assumption for these data.

The learning-curve models discussed in the chapter (pp. 351–354) are examples of nonlinear cost functions; costs increase when the level of production increases, but by lesser amounts than would occur with a linear cost function. In this case, the analyst should estimate a nonlinear cost function that explicitly incorporates learning effects.

2. Constant variance of residuals. The vertical deviation of the *observed* value Y from the regression line estimate y is called the *residual term, disturbance term,* or *error term, $u = Y - y$.* The assumption of constant variance implies that the residual terms are unaffected by the level of the independent variable. The assumption also implies that there is a uniform scatter, or dispersion, of the data points about the regression line. The scatter diagram is the easiest way to check for *constant variance.* This

[6]For details see, for example, C. J. Watson, P. Billingsley, D. J. Croft and D. V. Huntsberger, *Statistics for Management and Economics* 5th ed. (Needham Heights: Allyn and Bacon, 1993), and W. H. Greene, *Econometric Analysis* 2nd ed. (New York: Macmillan, 1993).

EXHIBIT 10-18
Constant Variance of Residuals Assumption

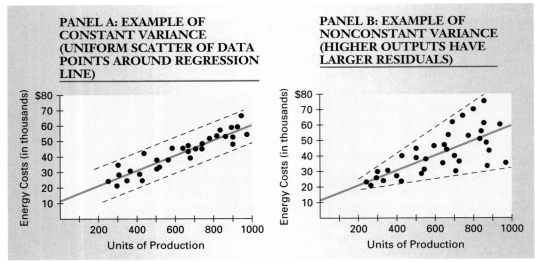

PANEL A: EXAMPLE OF CONSTANT VARIANCE (UNIFORM SCATTER OF DATA POINTS AROUND REGRESSION LINE)

PANEL B: EXAMPLE OF NONCONSTANT VARIANCE (HIGHER OUTPUTS HAVE LARGER RESIDUALS)

assumption holds for Panel A of Exhibit 10-18 but not for Panel B. Constant variance is also known as *homoscedasticity*. Violation of this assumption is called *heteroscedasticity*.

Heteroscedasticity does not affect the accuracy of the regression estimates *a* and *b*. It does, however, reduce the reliability of the estimates of the standard errors, and thus affects the precision with which inferences can be drawn.

3. Independence of residuals. The assumption of the independence of residuals is that the residual term for any one observation is not related to the residual term for any other observation. The problem of *serial correlation* in the residuals (also called *autocorrelation*) arises when the residuals are not independent. Serial correlation means that there is a systematic pattern in the sequence of residuals such that the residual in observation n conveys information about the residuals in observation $n + 1$, $n + 2$, and so on. In time-series data, inflation is a common cause of autocorrelation because it causes costs (and hence residuals) to be related over time. Autocorrelation can also occur in cross-sectional data as, for example, in Exhibit 10-19. The scatter

EXHIBIT 10-19
Independence of Residuals Assumption

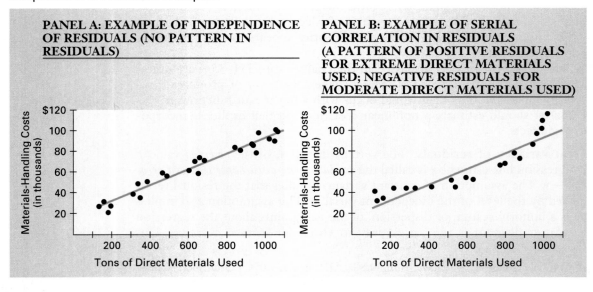

PANEL A: EXAMPLE OF INDEPENDENCE OF RESIDUALS (NO PATTERN IN RESIDUALS)

PANEL B: EXAMPLE OF SERIAL CORRELATION IN RESIDUALS (A PATTERN OF POSITIVE RESIDUALS FOR EXTREME DIRECT MATERIALS USED; NEGATIVE RESIDUALS FOR MODERATE DIRECT MATERIALS USED)

diagram helps in identifying autocorrelation. Autocorrelation does not exist in Panel A of Exhibit 10-19 but does exist in Panel B. Observe the systematic pattern of the residuals in Panel B—positive residuals for extreme quantities of direct materials used and negative residuals for moderate quantities of direct materials used. No such systematic pattern prevails for Panel A.

Like nonconstant variance in residuals, serial correlation does not affect the accuracy of the regression estimates *a* and *b*. It does, however, affect the standard errors of the coefficients, which in turn affect the precision with which inferences about the population parameters can be drawn from the regression estimates.

The Durbin–Watson statistic is one measure of serial correlation in the estimated residuals. For samples of 10–20 observations, a Durbin–Watson statistic in the 1.10–2.90 range suggests that the residuals are independent. The Durbin–Watson statistic for the regression results of Elegant Rugs in Exhibit 10-17 is 2.05. Therefore, an assumption of independence in the estimated residuals seems reasonable for this regression model.

4. Normality of Residuals. The normality of residuals assumption means that the residuals are distributed normally around the regression line. This assumption is necessary for making inferences about *y*, *a*, and *b*.

Using Regression Output to Choose Among Cost Functions

Consider the two cost functions we had described earlier:

$$y = a + (b \times \text{Machine-hours})$$

$$y = a + (b \times \text{Direct manufacturing labor-hours})$$

Exhibits 10-6 and 10-7 present plots of the data for the two regressions. Exhibit 10-17 reports regression results for the cost function using machine-hours as the independent variable. Exhibit 10-20 presents comparable regression results for the cost function using direct manufacturing labor-hours as the independent variable.

On the basis of the material in this Appendix, which regression is better? Exhibit 10-21 compares these two cost functions in a systematic way. For several criteria, the cost function based on machine-hours is preferable to the cost function based on direct manufacturing labor-hours. The economic plausibility criterion is especially important.

Do not always assume that any one cost function will perfectly satisfy all the criteria in Exhibit 10-21. A cost analyst must often make a choice among "imperfect" cost functions, in the sense that the data of any particular cost function will not perfectly meet one or more of the assumptions underlying regression analysis.

Multiple Regression and Cost Hierarchies

In some cases, a satisfactory estimation of a cost function may be based on only one independent variable, such as machine-hours. In many cases, however, basing the estimation on more than one independent variable is more economically plausible and improves accuracy. The most widely used equations to express relationships between two or more independent variables and a dependent variable are linear in the form

$$Y = a + b_1 X_1 + b_2 X_2 + \cdots + u$$

where

Y = cost variable to be predicted

$X_1, X_2, \ldots$ = independent variables on which the prediction is to be based

$a, b_1, b_2, \ldots$ = estimated coefficients of the regression model

u = residual term that includes the net effect of other factors not in the model and measurement errors in the dependent and independent variables

EXHIBIT 10-20

Simple Regression Results with Indirect Manufacturing Labor Costs as Dependent Variable and Direct Manufacturing Labor-Hours as Independent Variable for Elegant Rugs

Variable	Coefficient (1)	Standard Error (2)	t-Value (3) = (1) ÷ (2)
Constant	$744.67	$217.61	3.42
Independent variable 1: Direct manufacturing labor-hours	$ 7.72	$ 5.40	1.43

$r^2 = 0.17$; Durbin–Watson statistic = 2.26

EXAMPLE: Consider the Elegant Rugs data in Exhibit 10-22 (p. 365). Indirect manufacturing labor costs include sizable costs incurred for setup and changeover costs when production on one carpet batch is stopped and production on another batch is started. Management believes that in addition to machine-hours (an output-unit level cost driver), indirect manufacturing labor costs are also affected by the number of different batches of carpets produced during each week (a batch-level driver). Elegant Rugs estimates the relation between two independent variables, machine-hours and number of separate carpet jobs worked on during the week, and indirect manufacturing labor costs.

Exhibit 10-23 presents results for the following multiple regression model, using data in columns 1, 2, and 4 of Exhibit 10-22:

$$y = \$42.58 + \$7.60X_1 + \$37.77X_2$$

where X_1 is the number of machine-hours and X_2 is the number of production batches. It is economically plausible that both machine-hours and production batches would help explain variations in indirect manufacturing labor costs at Elegant Rugs. The r^2 of 0.52 for the simple regression using machine-hours (Exhibit

EXHIBIT 10-21

Comparison of Alternative Cost Functions for Indirect Manufacturing Labor Costs Estimated with Simple Regression for Elegant Rugs

Criterion	Cost Function 1: Machine-Hours as Independent Variable	Cost Function 2: Direct Manufacturing Labor-Hours as Independent Variable
Economic plausibility	A positive relationship between indirect manufacturing labor costs (technical support labor) and machine-hours is economically plausible in a highly automated plant.	A positive relationship between indirect manufacturing labor costs and direct manufacturing labor-hours is economically plausible, but less so than machine-hours in a highly automated plant on a week-to-week basis.
Goodness of fit	$r^2 = 0.52$ Excellent goodness of fit.	$r^2 = 0.17$ Poor goodness of fit.
Significance of independent variable(s)	The t-Value of 3.30 is significant.	The t-Value of 1.43 is not significant.
Specification analysis of estimation assumptions	Plot of the data indicates that assumptions of linearity, constant variance, independence of residuals, and normality of residuals hold, but inferences drawn from only 12 observations are not reliable; Durbin–Watson statistic = 2.05.	Plot of the data indicates that assumptions of linearity, constant variance, independence of residuals, and normality of residuals hold, but inferences drawn from only 12 observations are not reliable; Durbin–Watson statistic = 2.26.

EXHIBIT 10-22

Weekly Indirect Manufacturing Labor Costs, Machine-Hours, Direct Manufacturing Labor-Hours, and Number of Production Batches for Elegant Rugs

Week	Indirect Manufacturing Labor Costs (1)	Machine-Hours (2)	Direct Manufacturing Labor-Hours (3)	Number of Production Batches (4)
1	$1,190	68	30	12
2	1,211	88	35	15
3	1,004	62	36	13
4	917	72	20	11
5	770	60	47	10
6	1,456	96	45	12
7	1,180	78	44	17
8	710	46	38	7
9	1,316	82	70	14
10	1,032	94	30	12
11	752	68	29	7
12	963	48	38	14

10-17) increases to 0.72 with the multiple regression in Exhibit 10-23. The t-values suggest that the independent variable coefficients of both machine-hours and production batches are significantly different from zero ($t = 2.74$ for the coefficient on machine-hours, and $t = 2.48$ for the coefficient on production batches). The multiple regression model in Exhibit 10-23 satisfies both economic and statistical criteria, and it explains much greater variation in indirect manufacturing labor costs than does the simple regression model using only machine-hours as the independent variable. The information in Exhibit 10-23 indicates that both machine-hours and production batches are important cost drivers of monthly indirect manufacturing labor costs at Elegant Rugs.

In Exhibit 10-23, the slope coefficients—$7.60 for machine-hours and $37.77 for production batches—measure the change in indirect manufacturing labor costs associated with a unit change in an independent variable (assuming that the other independent variable is held constant). For example, indirect manufacturing labor costs increase by $37.77 when one more production batch is added, assuming that the number of machine-hours is held constant.

EXHIBIT 10-23

Multiple Regression Results with Indirect Manufacturing Labor Costs and Two Independent Variables (Machine-Hours and Production Batches) for Elegant Rugs

Variable	Coefficient (1)	Standard Error (2)	t-Value (3) = (1) ÷ (2)
Constant	$42.58	$213.91	0.20
Independent variable 1: Machine-hours	$ 7.60	$ 2.77	2.74
Independent variable 2: Production batches	$37.77	$ 15.25	2.48

$r^2 = 0.72$; Durbin–Watson statistic = 2.49

An alternative approach would create two separate cost pools—one for costs tied to machine-hours and another for costs tied to production batches. Elegant Rugs would then estimate the relationship between the cost driver and overhead costs separately for each cost pool. The difficult task under that approach would be properly dividing overhead costs into the two cost pools.

Multicollinearity

A major concern that arises with multiple regression is multicollinearity. **Multicollinearity** exists when two or more independent variables are highly correlated with each other. Generally, users of regression analysis believe that a coefficient of correlation between independent variables greater than 0.70 indicates multicollinearity. Multicollinearity increases the standard errors of the coefficients of the individual variables. The result is that there is greater uncertainty about the underlying value of the coefficients of the individual independent variables. That is, variables that are economically and statistically significant will appear insignificant.

The coefficients of correlation between the potential independent variables for Elegant Rugs in Exhibit 10-22 are

Pairwise Combinations	Coefficient of Correlation
Machine-hours and direct manufacturing labor-hours	0.12
Machine-hours and production batches	0.40
Direct manufacturing labor-hours and production batches	0.31

These results indicate that multiple regressions using any pair of the independent variables in Exhibit 10-23 are not likely to encounter multicollinearity problems.

If severe multicollinearity exists, try to obtain new data that does not suffer from multicollinearity problems. Do not drop an independent variable (cost driver) that should be included in a model because it is correlated with another independent variable. Omitting such a variable will cause the estimated coefficient of the independent variable included in the model to be biased away from its true value.

TERMS TO LEARN

This chapter and the Glossary at the end of this book contain definitions of the following important terms:

QUESTIONS

10-1 Describe three alternative linear cost functions.

10-2 What two assumptions are frequently made when estimating a cost function?

10-3 What is the difference between a linear and a nonlinear cost function? Give an example of each type of cost function.

10-4 "High correlation between two variables means that one is the cause and the other is the effect." Do you agree? Explain.

10-5 Name four approaches to estimating a cost function.

10-6 Describe the conference method for estimating a cost function. What are two advantages of this method?

10-7 Describe the account analysis method for estimating a cost function.

10-8 List the six steps in estimating a cost function on the basis of an analysis of current or past cost relationships. Which step is typically the most difficult for a cost analyst?

10-9 When using the high-low method, should you base the high and low observations on the dependent variable or on the cost driver?

10-10 Describe three criteria for evaluating cost functions and choosing cost drivers.

10-11 Discuss four frequently encountered problems when collecting cost data on variables included in a cost function.

10-12 Define learning curve. Outline two models that can be used when incorporating learning into the estimation of cost functions.

10-13 What are the four key assumptions examined in specification analysis in the case of simple regression?

10-14 "All the independent variables in a cost function estimated with regression analysis are cost drivers." Do you agree? Explain.

10-15 "Multicollinearity exists when the dependent variable and the independent variable are highly correlated." Do you agree? Explain.

EXERCISES

10-16 Estimating a cost function. The controller of the Ijiri Company wants you to estimate a cost function from the following two observations in a general-ledger account called Maintenance:

Month	Machine-Hours	Maintenance Costs Incurred
January	4,000	$3,000
February	7,000	3,900

REQUIRED
1. Estimate the cost function for maintenance.
2. Can the constant in the cost function be used as an estimate of fixed maintenance cost per month? Explain.

10-17 Identifying variable, fixed, and mixed cost functions. The Pacific Corporation operates car rental agencies at over 20 airports. Customers can choose from one of three contracts for car rentals of one day or less:
◆ Contract 1: $50 for the day
◆ Contract 2: $30 for the day plus $0.20 per mile traveled
◆ Contract 3: $1.00 per mile traveled

REQUIRED
1. Present separate plots for each of the three contracts, with costs on the vertical axis and miles traveled on the horizontal axis.

2. Describe each contract as a linear cost function of the form $y = a + bX$.
3. Describe each contract as a variable, fixed, or mixed cost function.

10-18 Various cost-behavior patterns. (CPA, adapted) Select the graph that matches the numbered manufacturing-cost data. Indicate by letter which of the graphs best fits each of the situations or items described.

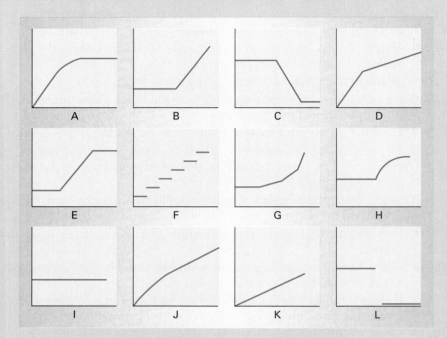

The vertical axes of the graphs represent *total* dollars of cost, and the horizontal axes represent production output during a calendar year. In each case, the zero point of dollars and production is at the intersection of the two axes. The graphs may be used more than once.

1. Annual depreciation of equipment, where the amount of depreciation charged is computed by the machine-hours method.
2. Electricity bill—a flat fixed charge, plus a variable cost after a certain number of kilowatt-hours are used, where the quantity of kilowatt-hours used varies proportionately with quantity of production output.
3. City water bill, which is computed as follows:

First 1,000,000 gallons or less	$1,000 flat fee
Next 10,000 gallons	$0.003 per gallon used
Next 10,000 gallons	$0.006 per gallon used
Next 10,000 gallons	$0.009 per gallon used
and so on	and so on

The gallons of water used vary proportionately with the quantity of production output.

4. Cost of lubricant for machines, where cost per unit decreases with each pound of lubricant used (for example, if 1 pound is used, the cost is $10; if 2 pounds are used, the cost is $19.98; if 3 pounds are used, the cost is $29.94) with a minimum cost per pound of $9.20.
5. Annual depreciation of equipment, where the amount is computed by the straight-line method. When the depreciation rate was established, it was anticipated that the obsolescence factor would be greater than the wear-and-tear factor.
6. Rent on a manufacturing plant donated by the city, where the agreement calls for a fixed-fee payment unless 200,000 labor-hours are worked, in which case no rent need be paid.

7. Salaries of repair personnel, where one person is needed for every 1,000 machine-hours or less (that is, 0–1,000 hours requires one person, 1,001–2,000 hours requires two people, etc.).

8. Cost of direct materials used (assume no quantity discounts).

9. Rent on a manufacturing plant donated by the county, where the agreement calls for rent of $100,000 reduced by $1 for each direct manufacturing labor-hour worked in excess of 200,000 hours, but a minimum rental fee of $20,000 must be paid.

10-19 Matching graphs with descriptions of cost behavior. (D. Green) Given below are a number of charts, each indicating some relationship between cost and a cost driver. No attempt has been made to draw these charts to any particular scale; the absolute numbers on each axis may be closely or widely spaced.

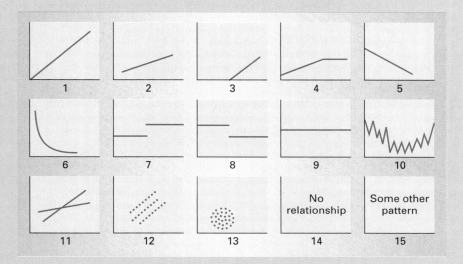

Indicate by number which one of the charts best fits each of the situations or items described. Each situation or item is independent of all the others; all factors not stated are assumed to be irrelevant. Some charts will be used more than once; some may not apply to any of the situations. Note that category 14, "No relationship," is not the same as 15, "Some other pattern."

If the horizontal axis represents the production output over the year and the vertical axis represents *total cost* or *revenue*, indicate the one best pattern or relationship for:

1. Direct materials costs.

2. Supervisors' salaries.

3. A breakeven chart.

4. Mixed costs—for example, fixed electrical power *demand* charge plus variable usage rate.

5. Depreciation of plant, computed on a straight-line basis.

6. Data supporting the use of a variable cost rate, such as manufacturing labor cost of $14 per unit produced.

7. Incentive bonus plan that pays managers $0.10 for every unit produced above some level of production.

8. Interest charges on money borrowed at a fixed rate of interest to finance the acquisition of a plant, before any payments on principal.

10-20 Account analysis method. Lorenzo operates a brushless car wash. Incoming cars are put on an automatic, continuously moving conveyor belt. Cars are washed as the conveyor belt carries the car from the start station to the finish station. After the car moves off the conveyor belt, the car is dried manually. Workers then clean and vacuum the inside of the car. Workers are managed by a single supervisor. Lorenzo serviced 80,000 cars in 19_8. Lorenzo reports the following costs for 19_8.

Account Description	Costs
Car wash labor	$240,000
Soap, cloth, and supplies	32,000
Water	28,000
Power to move conveyor belt	72,000
Depreciation	64,000
Supervision	30,000
Cashier	16,000

REQUIRED

1. Classify each account as variable or fixed with respect to cars washed. Explain.
2. Lorenzo expects to wash 90,000 cars in 19_9. Use the cost classification you developed in requirement 1 to estimate Lorenzo's total costs in 19_9.
3. Calculate the average cost of washing a car in 19_8 and 19_9. (Use the expected 90,000 car wash level for 19_9.)

10-21 Account analysis method. Gower, Inc., a manufacturer of plastic products, reports the following manufacturing costs and account analysis classification for the year ended December 31, 19_8.

Account	Classification	Amount
Direct materials	All variable	$300,000
Direct manufacturing labor	All variable	225,000
Power	All variable	37,500
Supervision labor	20% variable	56,250
Materials-handling labor	50% variable	60,000
Maintenance labor	40% variable	75,000
Depreciation	0% variable	95,000
Rent, property taxes, and administration	0% variable	100,000

Gower, Inc., produced 75,000 units of product in 19_8. Gower's management is estimating costs for 19_9 on the basis of 19_8 numbers. The following additional information is available for 19_9.

a. Direct materials prices in 19_9 are expected to increase by 5% compared with 19_8.
b. Under the terms of the labor contract, direct manufacturing labor wage rates are expected to increase by 10% in 19_9 compared with 19_8.
c. Power rates and wage rates for supervision, materials handling, and maintenance are not expected to change from 19_8 to 19_9.
d. Depreciation costs are expected to increase by 5%, and rent, property taxes, and administration costs are expected to increase by 7%.
e. Gower, Inc., expects to manufacture and sell 80,000 units in 19_9.

REQUIRED

1. Prepare a schedule of variable, fixed, and total manufacturing costs for each account category in 19_9. Estimate total manufacturing costs for 19_9.
2. Calculate Gower's total manufacturing cost per unit in 19_8 and estimate total manufacturing cost per unit in 19_9.
3. How can you get better estimates of fixed and variable costs? Why would these better estimates be useful to Gower?

10-22 Estimating a cost function, high-low method. Laurie Daley is examining customer-service costs in the Southern Region of Capitol Products. Capitol Products has over 200 separate electrical products that are sold with a

6-month guarantee of full repair or replacement with a new product. When a product is returned by a customer, a service report is made. This service report includes details of the problem and the time and cost of resolving the problem.

Weekly data for the most recent 10-week period are

Week	Customer-Service Department Costs	Number of Service Reports
1	$13,845	201
2	20,624	276
3	12,941	122
4	18,452	386
5	14,843	274
6	21,890	436
7	16,831	321
8	21,429	328
9	18,267	243
10	16,832	161

REQUIRED
1. Plot the relationship between customer-service costs and number of service reports. Is the relationship economically plausible?
2. Use the high-low method to compute the cost function, relating customer-service costs to the number of service reports.
3. What variables, in addition to number of service reports, might be cost drivers of monthly customer-service costs of Capitol Products?

10-23 **Linear cost approximation.** Terry Lawler, managing director of the Memphis Consulting Group, is examining how overhead costs behave with variations in monthly professional labor-hours billed to clients. Assume the following historical data:

Total Overhead Costs	Professional Labor-Hours Billed to Clients
$340,000	3,000
400,000	4,000
435,000	5,000
477,000	6,000
529,000	7,000
587,000	8,000

REQUIRED
1. Compute the linear cost function, relating total overhead cost to professional labor-hours, using the representative observations of 4,000 and 7,000 hours. Plot the linear cost function. Does the constant component of the cost function represent the fixed overhead costs of the Memphis Consulting Group? Why?
2. What would be the predicted total overhead costs for (a) 5,000 hours, and (b) 8,000 hours using the cost function estimated in requirement 1? Plot the predicted costs and actual costs for 5,000 and 8,000 hours.
3. Lawler had a chance to accept a special job that would have boosted professional labor-hours from 4,000 to 5,000 hours. Suppose Lawler, guided by the linear cost function, rejected this job because it would have brought a total increase in contribution margin of $38,000, before deducting the predicted increase in total overhead cost, $43,000. What is the total contribution margin actually forgone?

10-24 **Regression analysis, service company.** (CMA, adapted) Bob Jones owns a catering company that prepares banquets and parties for both individual and business functions throughout the year. Jones's business is seasonal, with a heavy schedule during the summer months and the year-end holidays and a light schedule at other times. During peak periods there are extra costs.

One of the major events Jones's customers request is a cocktail party. He offers a standard cocktail party and has developed the following cost structure on a per person basis.

Food and beverages	$15.00
Labor (0.5 hour × $10 per hour)	5.00
Overhead (0.5 hour × $14 per hour)	7.00
Total costs per person	$27.00

Jones is quite certain about his estimates of the food, beverages, and labor costs but is not as comfortable with the overhead estimate. This estimate was based on the actual data for the past 12 months presented here. These data indicate that overhead expenses vary with the direct labor-hours expended. The $14 estimate was determined by dividing total overhead expended for the 12 months by total labor-hours.

Month	Labor-Hours	Overhead Costs
January	2,500	$ 55,000
February	2,700	59,000
March	3,000	60,000
April	4,200	64,000
May	4,500	67,000
June	5,500	71,000
July	6,500	74,000
August	7,500	77,000
September	7,000	75,000
October	4,500	68,000
November	3,100	62,000
December	6,500	73,000
Total	57,500	$805,000

Jones has recently become aware of regression analysis. He estimated the following regression equation with overhead costs as the dependent variable and labor-hours as the independent variable.

$$y = \$48,271 + \$3.93X$$

REQUIRED

1. Plot the relationship between overhead costs and labor-hours. Draw the regression line and evaluate it using the criteria of economic plausibility, goodness of fit, and slope of the regression line.
2. Using data from the regression analysis, what is the variable cost per person for a cocktail party.
3. Bob Jones has been asked to prepare a bid for a 200-person cocktail party to be given next month. Determine the minimum bid price that Jones would be willing to submit to earn a positive contribution margin.

10-25 **Regression analysis, activity-based costing, choosing cost drivers.** Larry Chu, the plant controller at Rohan Plastics has been concerned about correctly identifying cost drivers ever since the plant began implementing activity-based costing a year or so ago. Correctly identifying cost drivers is important for bidding and pricing of jobs and for managing costs within the plant.

The cost drivers for support overhead has been a particular problem. Rohan has eliminated many job categories, so indirect support consists of skilled staff responsible for the efficient functioning of all aspects (setup, production, maintenance, and quality control) of the plastic injection molding facility. In talking to the support staff, Chu has the impression that they spend a good portion of their time ensuring that the equipment is set up correctly and checking that the first units of production in each batch are of good quality.

Chu has collected the following monthly data for the past 12 months:

Month	Support Overhead	Machine-Hours	Number of Batches
January	$ 57,000	2,000	106
February	41,000	2,400	128
March	33,000	1,850	147
April	44,000	2,100	159
May	46,000	3,600	162
June	48,000	2,250	174
July	66,000	3,800	264
August	44,000	2,700	216
September	63,000	2,850	249
October	66,000	3,300	219
November	81,000	3,750	303
December	84,000	2,250	309
Total	$673,000	32,850	2,436

Chu estimates the following regression equations:

$$y = \$28{,}089 + (\$10.23 \times \text{Machine-hours})$$

and $\quad y = \$16{,}031 + (\$197.30 \times \text{Number of batches})$

where y is the monthly support overhead.

REQUIRED

1. Present plots of the monthly data and the regression lines underlying each of the following cost functions:
   a. Support overhead costs $= a + (b \times \text{Machine-hours})$
   b. Support overhead costs $= a + (b \times \text{Number of batches})$
   Which cost driver for support overhead costs would you choose?
2. Chu anticipates 2,600 machine-hours and 300 batches will be run next month. Using the cost driver you chose in requirement 1, what support overhead costs should Chu budget?
3. (a) Chu adds 20% to costs as a first cut for determining target revenues (and hence prices). Costs other than support overhead are expected to equal $125,000 next month. Compare the target revenue numbers obtained if (i) machine-hours, and (ii) number of batches is used as the cost driver. Discuss what would happen if Chu picked the "wrong" cost driver—the cost driver other than the one you chose in requirement 1—to set target revenues and prices. (b) Describe any other implications of choosing the "wrong" cost driver and cost function.

10-26 High-low method, cost estimation, cost management. Refer to the information and data in Exercise 10-25. Chu decides to use the high-low method to estimate the relation between support overhead costs and number of batches.

REQUIRED

1. (a) Estimate the cost function for support overhead costs and number of batches using the high-low method. (b) Present plots of the monthly data and the cost function estimated using the high-low method for support overhead costs and the number of batches. (c) The regression cost estimates for support overhead and number of batches is

$$y = \$16{,}031 + (\$197.30 \times \text{Number of batches})$$

On the plots drawn for requirement 1b, draw the regression line. Evaluate the high-low cost function and the regression cost function. Which cost function would you choose? Why?

2. Chu anticipates 300 batches will be run next month. Estimate the support overhead costs that Chu should budget for the month based on the high-low cost function and the regression cost function.

3. (a) Chu adds 20% to costs as a first cut for determining target revenues (and hence prices). Costs other than support overhead are expected to equal $125,000 next month. Compare the revenues Chu would target next month using (i) the high-low cost function, and (ii) the regression cost function. Discuss what would happen if Chu picked the "wrong" cost function—the cost function other than the one you chose in requirement 3—to set target revenues and prices. (b) Discuss any other implications of choosing the "wrong" cost function.

10-27 Learning curve, cumulative average-time learning curve. Global Defense manufactures radar systems. It has just completed the manufacture of its first newly designed system, RS-32. It took 3,000 direct manufacturing labor-hours (DMLH) to produce this one unit. Global believes that a 90% cumulative average-time learning model for direct manufacturing labor-hours applies to RS-32. (A 90% learning curve implies $q = -0.1520$). The variable costs of producing RS-32 are

Direct materials costs	$80,000 per RS-32
Direct manufacturing labor costs	$25 per DMLH
Variable manufacturing overhead costs	$15 per DMLH

REQUIRED
Calculate the total variable costs of producing 2, 4, and 8 units.

10-28 Learning curve, incremental unit-time learning curve. Assume the same information for Global Defense as in Exercise 10-27 except that Global Defense uses a 90% incremental unit-time learning curve as a basis for forecasting direct manufacturing labor-hours. (A 90% learning curve implies $q = -0.1520$.)

REQUIRED
1. Calculate the total variable costs of producing 2, 3, and 4 units.
2. If you solved Exercise 10-27, compare your cost predictions in the two exercises for 2 and 4 units. Why are the predictions different?

PROBLEMS

10-29 Cost estimation, cumulative average-time learning curve. The Nautilus Company, which is under contract to the U.S. Navy, assembles troop deployment boats. As part of its research program, it completes the assembly of the first of a new model (PT109) of deployment boats. The Navy is impressed with the PT109. It requests that Nautilus submit a proposal on the cost of producing another seven PT109s.

The accounting department at Nautilus reports the following cost information for the first PT109 assembled by Nautilus:

Direct materials	$100,000
Direct manufacturing labor (10,000 labor-hours × $30)	300,000
Tooling cost*	50,000
Variable manufacturing overhead†	200,000
Other manufacturing overhead‡	75,000
	$725,000

*Tooling can be reused at no extra cost, since all of its cost has been assigned to the first deployment boat.
†Variable overhead incurred is directly affected by direct manufacturing labor-hours; a rate of $20 per hour is used for purposes of bidding on contracts.
‡Other overhead is allocated at a flat rate of 25% of direct manufacturing labor costs for purposes of bidding on contracts.

Nautilus uses an 85% cumulative average-time learning curve as a basis for forecasting direct manufacturing labor-hours on its assembling operations. (An 85% learning curve implies $q = -0.2345$.)

REQUIRED

1. Prepare a prediction of the total costs for producing the seven PT109s for the Navy. (Nautilus will keep the first deployment boat assembled, costed at $725,000, as a demonstration model for other potential customers.)

2. What is the difference between (a) the predicted total costs for producing the seven PT109s in requirement 1, and (b) the predicted total costs for producing the seven PT109s assuming that there is no learning curve for direct manufacturing labor—that is, for (b) assume a linear function for direct labor-hours and units produced.

10-30 Cost estimation, incremental unit-time learning curve. Assume the same information for the Nautilus Company as that in requirement 1 of Problem 10-29 with one exception. This exception is that Nautilus uses an 85% incremental unit-time learning curve as a basis for forecasting direct manufacturing labor-hours on its assembling operations. (An 85% learning curve implies $q = -0.2345$.)

REQUIRED

1. Prepare a prediction of the total expected costs for producing the seven PT109s for the Navy.

2. If you solved requirement 1 of Problem 10-29, compare your cost prediction there with the one you made here. Why are the predictions different?

10-31 Cost estimation, cumulative average-time learning model. (CMA, adapted) The Cooper Corporation has received a contract to supply 240 units of new telecommunication equipment. The direct materials costs are $60,000 per unit. The average direct manufacturing labor costs for each unit (in the first lot of 30 units) was estimated to be $40,000. Direct manufacturing labor on a per lot basis is subject to a 90% cumulative average-time learning model. (A 90% learning curve implies $q = -0.1520$.) Variable manufacturing overhead was estimated to be 60% of direct manufacturing labor cost. Cooper's price includes a markup of 25% on total variable manufacturing costs.

REQUIRED

1. Determine the Cooper Corporation's cumulative average unit cost of manufacturing labor for producing the 240 units.

2. Determine the total variable manufacturing costs for producing the 240 units.

3. Assume that the Cooper Corporation is asked to produce additional telecommunication equipment beyond the 240 units currently under contract. Cooper anticipates that the expected average cost incurred to produce the last 120 units is the expected manufacturing cost per unit for each additional unit after 240 units. Calculate the unit price Cooper should bid, employing the same markup used in the original bid.

10-32 Cost estimation, incremental unit-time learning curve. Assume the same information for Cooper Corporation as that in requirement 1 of Problem 10-31 with one exception. This exception is that Cooper uses a 90% incremental unit-time learning curve as a basis for forecasting direct manufacturing labor-hours. (A 90% learning curve implies $q = -0.1520$.)

REQUIRED

Determine the total variable manufacturing costs for producing the 240 units of the new telecommunication equipment. If you solved requirement 2 of Problem 10-31, compare your cost prediction there with the one you make here. Why are the predictions different?

10-33 Data collection issues, use of high-low method. Robin Green, financial analyst at Central Railroad, is examining the behavior of monthly transportation costs for budgeting purposes. Transportation costs at Central Railroad are the sum of two types of costs: (a) operating costs (labor, fuel, and so on), and (b) maintenance costs (overhaul of engines and track, and so on). Green collects monthly data on (a), (b), and track-miles hauled. Track-miles hauled are the miles clocked by the engine that pulls the rail cars. Monthly observations for the most recent year are

Month	Operating Costs (1)	Maintenance Costs (2)	Total Transportation Costs (3) = (1) + (2)	Track-Miles Hauled (4)
January	$471	$437	$ 908	3,420
February	504	388	892	5,310
March	609	343	952	5,410
April	690	347	1,037	8,440
May	742	294	1,036	9,320
June	774	211	985	8,910
July	784	176	960	8,870
August	986	210	1,196	10,980
September	895	282	1,177	4,980
October	651	394	1,045	5,220
November	481	381	862	4,480
December	386	514	900	2,980

Central Railroad earns its greatest revenues carrying agricultural commodities such as wheat and barley.

REQUIRED
1. Present plots of the monthly data underlying each of the following cost functions:
   a. Operating costs = $a + (b \times$ Track-miles hauled)
   b. Maintenance costs = $a + (b \times$ Track-miles hauled)
   c. Total transportation costs = $a + (b \times$ Track-miles hauled)
   Comment on the patterns in the three plots.
2. Estimate the three cost functions in requirement 1 using the high-low method. Comment on the estimated cost functions.
3. Green anticipates 6,000 track-miles hauled each month next year. What total transportation costs should Green budget for next year?
4. Outline three limitations of the high-low method for estimating a cost function.

10-34 High-low and regression approaches. (Chapter Appendix) The Campi Corporation wishes to set a flexible budget for its power costs, which are primarily a function of machine-hours worked. Data for the first four periods follows:

Period	Power Costs (Y)	Machine-Hours (X)
1	$350	200
2	450	300
3	300	100
4	500	400

REQUIRED
1. Plot the relationship between power costs and machine-hours.
2. Compute the constant a and slope coefficient b of the function $y = a + bX$ using (i) the high-low approach, and (ii) the regression approach. Comment on the results.
3. For the regression approach, compute the coefficient of determination, r^2. Comment on the result.

10-35 Evaluating alternative simple regression models, not for profit. (Chapter Appendix) Kathy Hanks, executive assistant to the president of Southwestern University is concerned about the overhead costs at her university. Cost pressures are severe, so controlling and reducing overheads is very important. Hanks believes overhead costs incurred are generally a function of the number of different academic programs (including different specializations, degrees, and majors) that the university has and the number of enrolled students. Both have grown significantly over the years. She collects the following data:

Year	Overhead Costs (in thousands)	Number of Academic Programs	Number of Enrolled Students
1	$13,500	29	3,400
2	19,200	36	5,000
3	16,800	49	2,600
4	20,100	53	4,700
5	19,500	54	3,900
6	23,100	58	4,900
7	23,700	88	5,700
8	20,100	72	3,900
9	22,800	83	3,500
10	29,700	73	3,700
11	31,200	101	5,600
12	38,100	103	7,600

She finds the following results for two separate simple regression models:

Regression 1: Overhead Costs $= a + (b \times$ Number of academic programs$)$

Variable	Coefficient	Standard Error	t-Value
Constant	$7,127.75	$3,335.34	2.14
Independent variable 1: Number of academic programs	$ 240.64	$ 47.33	5.08

$r^2 = 0.72$; Durbin–Watson statistic $= 1.81$

Regression 2: Overhead Costs $= a + (b \times$ Number of enrolled students$)$

Variable	Coefficient	Standard Error	t-Value
Constant	$5,991.75	$5,067.88	1.18
Independent variable 1: Number of enrolled students	$ 3.78	$ 1.07	3.53

$r^2 = 0.55$; Durbin–Watson statistic $= 0.77$

REQUIRED

1. Plot the relationship between overhead costs and each of the following variables: (a) number of academic programs, and (b) number of enrolled students.
2. Compare and evaluate the two simple regression models estimated by Hanks. Use the comparison format employed in Exhibit 10-21 (p. 364).
3. What insights do the analyses provide about controlling and reducing overhead costs at the University?

10-36 Evaluating multiple regression models, not for profit (continuation of Problem 10-35). (Chapter Appendix)

REQUIRED

1. Given your findings in Problem 10-35, should Hanks use multiple regression analysis to better understand the cost drivers of overhead costs? Explain your answer.
2. Hanks decides that the simple regression analysis in Problem 10-35 should be extended to a multiple regression analysis. She finds the following result:

Regression 3: Overhead Costs = $a + (b_1 \times$ Number of academic programs) + $(b_2 \times$ Number of enrolled students)

Variable	Coefficient	Standard Error	t-Value
Constant	$2,779.62	$3,620.05	0.77
Independent variable 1: Number of academic programs	$ 178.37	$ 51.54	3.46
Independent variable 2: Number of enrolled students	$ 1.87	$ 0.92	2.03

$r^2 = 0.81$; Durbin–Watson statistic = 1.84

The coefficient of correlation between number of academic programs and number of students is 0.60. Use the format in Exhibit 10-21 (p. 364) to evaluate the multiple regression model. (Assume linearity, and constant variance and normality of residuals.) Should Hanks choose the multiple regression model over the two simple regression models of Problem 10-35?

3. How might the president of Southwestern University use these regression results to manage overhead costs?

10-37 Purchasing department cost drivers, activity-based costing, simple regression analysis. (Chapter Appendix) Fashion Flair operates a chain of 10 retail department stores. Each department store makes its own purchasing decisions. Barry Lee, assistant to the president of Fashion Flair, is interested in better understanding the drivers of purchasing department costs. For many years, Fashion Flair has allocated purchasing department costs to products on the basis of the dollar value of merchandise purchased. An item costing $100 is allocated 10 times as much overhead costs associated with the purchasing department as an item costing $10 is allocated.

Lee recently attended a seminar titled "Cost Drivers in the Retail Industry." In a presentation at the seminar, Couture Fabrics, a leading competitor that has implemented activity-based costing, reported the number of purchase orders and the number of suppliers to be the two most important cost drivers of purchasing department costs. The dollar value of merchandise purchased on each purchase order was not found to be a significant cost driver by Couture Fabrics. Lee interviewed several members of the purchasing department at the Fashion Flair store in Miami. These people told Lee that they believed that Couture Fabric's conclusions also applied to their purchasing department.

Lee collects the following data for the most recent year for the 10 retail department stores of Fashion Flair:

Department Store	Purchasing Department Costs (PDC)	Dollar Value of Merchandise Purchased (MP$)	Number of Purchase Orders (No. of PO's)	Number of Suppliers (No. of S's)
Baltimore	$1,523,000	$ 68,315,000	4,357	132
Chicago	1,100,000	33,456,000	2,550	222
Los Angeles	547,000	121,160,000	1,433	11
Miami	2,049,000	119,566,000	5,944	190
New York	1,056,000	33,505,000	2,793	23
Phoenix	529,000	29,854,000	1,327	33
Seattle	1,538,000	102,875,000	7,586	104
St. Louis	1,754,000	38,674,000	3,617	119
Toronto	1,612,000	139,312,000	1,707	208
Vancouver	1,257,000	130,944,000	4,731	201

Lee decides to use simple regression analysis to examine whether one or more of three variables (the last three columns in the table) are cost drivers of purchasing department costs. Summary results for these regressions are as follows:

Regression 1: PDC = a + (b × MP$)

Variable	Coefficient	Standard Error	t-Value
Constant	$1,039,061	$343,439	3.03
Independent variable 1: MP$	0.0031	0.0037	0.84

$r^2 = 0.08$; Durbin–Watson statistic = 2.41

Regression 2: PDC = a + (b × No. of PO's)

Variable	Coefficient	Standard Error	t-Value
Constant	$730,716	$265,419	2.75
Independent variable 1: No. of PO's	$ 156.97	$ 64.69	2.43

$r^2 = 0.42$; Durbin–Watson statistic = 1.98

Regression 3: PDC = a + (b × No. of S's)

Variable	Coefficient	Standard Error	t-Value
Constant	$814,862	$247,821	3.29
Independent variable 1: No. of S's	$ 3,875	$ 1,697	2.28

$r^2 = 0.39$; Durbin–Watson statistic = 1.97

REQUIRED

1. Compare and evaluate the three simple regression models estimated by Lee. Graph each one. Also, use the format employed in Exhibit 10-21 (p. 364) to evaluate the information.
2. Do the regression results support the Couture Fabrics presentation about purchasing department cost drivers? Which of these cost drivers would you recommend in designing an activity-based cost system?
3. How might Lee gain additional evidence on drivers of purchasing department costs at each store of Fashion Flair?

10-38 **Purchasing department cost drivers, multiple regression analysis (continuation of 10-37).** (Chapter Appendix) Barry Lee decides that the simple regression analysis reported in Problem 10-37 could be extended to a multiple regression analysis. He finds the following results for several multiple regressions:

Regression 4: PDC = a + (b₁ × No. of PO's) + (b₂ × No. of S's)

PDC = a + (b_1 × No. of PO's) + (b_2 × No. of S's)

Variable	Coefficient	Standard Error	t-Value
Constant	$485,384	$257,477	1.89
Independent variable 1: No. of PO's	$ 123.22	$ 57.69	2.14
Independent variable 2: No. of S's	$ 2,952	$ 1,476	2.00

$r^2 = 0.63$; Durbin–Watson statistic = 1.90

Regression 5: PDC = a + (b_1 × No. of PO's) + (b_2 × No. of S's) + (b_3 × MP$)

Variable	Coefficient	Standard Error	t-Value
Constant	$494,684	$310,205	1.59
Independent variable 1: No. of PO's	$ 124.05	$ 63.49	1.95
Independent variable 2: No. of S's	$ 2,984	$ 1,622	1.84
Independent variable 3: MP$	−0.0002	0.0030	−0.07

$r^2 = 0.63$; Durbin–Watson statistic = 1.90

The coefficients of correlation between pairwise combinations of the variables are

	PDC	MP$	No. of PO's
MP$	0.29		
No. of PO's	0.65	0.27	
No. of S's	0.63	0.34	0.29

REQUIRED

1. Evaluate regression 4 using the economic plausibility, goodness of fit, significance of independent variables, and specification analysis criteria. Compare regression 4 with regressions 2 and 3 in Problem 10-37. Which model would you recommend that Lee use? Why?
2. Compare regression 5 with regression 4. Which model would you recommend that Lee use? Why?
3. Lee estimates the following data for the Baltimore store for next year: dollar value of merchandise purchased, $75,000,000; number of purchase orders, 3,900; number of suppliers, 110. How much should Lee budget for purchasing department costs for the Baltimore store for next year?
4. What difficulties may arise in multiple regressions that do not arise in simple regressions? Is there evidence of such difficulties in either of the multiple regressions presented in this problem?
5. Give two examples of decisions where the regression results reported here (and in Problem 10-37) could be informative.

10-39 **Data analysis and ethics.** Comdex Electronics makes video cassette recorders (VCRs). Sales of VCRs have been very steady over the last 10 years. Helen Gibbs, the manager of the department that makes the head mechanism for the VCR, is keen on introducing robots into the department to improve VCR quality. To obtain funding, Gibbs knows that she will need to justify the investment in terms of labor cost savings. Gibbs estimates average annual labor costs in the department of $1,200,000 over the last 10 years. Labor costs over the last 3 years have averaged $800,000. If robots are introduced, labor costs would decrease to $550,000 per year. Average savings in labor costs of at least $400,000 per year are needed to justify the investment in robots. Gibbs uses the $1,200,000 number in her analysis. She then asks Joan Hansen, the management accountant, to review her calculations before she submits the robot proposal to senior management.

Hansen has a problem with Gibbs's analysis. She feels that by using a long time period of 10 years, Gibbs was able to show larger labor cost savings than was justified. Hansen knew that Gibbs would be unhappy with these findings.

Hansen also felt that the robot investment was good for the company. She tried to redo the analysis in a way that might show larger cost savings, even though she knew that the assumptions she was using were not appropriate. Nothing she tried could change the conclusion that the cost savings were not large enough to justify the investment in robots. Gibbs is upset when she sees Hansen's report. She tells Hansen, "Try something else. I am sure you can come up with a set of assumptions under which this investment can be justified. You and I both know this is a good investment for the company to make. Quality is essential if we are to compete."

REQUIRED

1. Calculate the labor cost savings if Gibbs uses average labor costs incurred (a) over the past 10 years and (b) over the past 3 years. Does it make a difference in terms of justifying the robot investment?
2. Why do you think the average labor costs over the past 10 years differ significantly from the average labor costs over the past 3 years?
3. Referring to the *Standards of Ethical Conduct for Management Accountants* described in Chapter 1 (pp. 10–11), explain whether Joan Hansen's initial attempts to redo the data analysis to justify the robot investment were ethical.

4. Identify the steps that Joan Hansen should follow in attempting to resolve this situation.

COLLABORATIVE LEARNING PROBLEM

10-40 High-low method, alternative regression functions, accrual accounting adjustments. Trevor Kennedy, the cost analyst at a can manufacturing plant of United Packaging, is seeking to examine the relationship between total engineering support costs reported in the plant records and machine-hours. These costs have two components: (1) labor (which is paid monthly), and (2) materials and parts (which are purchased from an outside vendor every 3 months). After further discussion with the operating manager, Kennedy discovers that the materials and parts numbers reported in the monthly records are on an "as purchased" basis and not on an "as used" or accrual accounting basis. By examining materials and parts usage records, Kennedy is able to restate the materials and parts costs to an "as used" basis. (No restatement of the labor costs was necessary.) The reported and restated costs are as follows:

Month	Labor: Reported Costs (1)	Materials and Parts: Reported Costs (2)	Materials and Parts: Restated Costs (3)	Total Engineering Support: Reported Costs (4) = (1) + (2)	Total Engineering Support: Restated Costs (5) = (1) + (3)	Machine-Hours (6)
March	$347	$847	$182	$1,194	$529	30
April	521	0	411	521	932	63
May	398	0	268	398	666	49
June	355	961	228	1,316	583	38
July	473	0	348	473	821	57
August	617	0	349	617	966	73
September	245	821	125	1,066	370	19
October	487	0	364	487	851	53
November	431	0	290	431	721	42

The regression results, when total engineering support reported costs (column 4) are used as the dependent variable, are

Regression 1: Engineering support reported costs = $a + (b \times \text{Machine-hours})$

Variable	Coefficient	Standard Error	t-Value
Constant	$1,393.20	$305.68	4.56
Independent variable 1: Machine-hours	$ −14.23	$ 6.15	−2.31

$r^2 = 0.43$; Durbin–Watson statistic = 2.26

The regression results, when total engineering support restated costs (column 5) are used as the dependent variable, are

Regression 2: Engineering support restated costs = $a + (b \times \text{Machine-hours})$

Variable	Coefficient	Standard Error	t-Value
Constant	$176.38	$53.99	3.27
Independent variable 1: Machine-hours	$ 11.44	$ 1.08	10.59

$r^2 = 0.94$; Durbin–Watson statistic = 1.31

INSTRUCTIONS

Form groups of two or more students to complete the following requirements.

REQUIRED

1. Present a plot of the data for the cost function relating the *reported costs* for total engineering support to machine-hours. Present a plot of the data for the cost function relating the *restated costs* for total engineering support to machine-hours. Comment on the plots.

2. Compute estimates of the cost functions $y = a + bX$ for reported engineering support costs and machine-hours and restated engineering support costs and machine-hours using the high-low method.

3. Contrast and evaluate the cost function estimated with regression using restated data for materials and parts with the cost function estimated with regression using the data reported in the plant records. Use the comparison format employed in Exhibit 10-21 (p. 364).

4. Of all the cost functions estimated in requirements 2 and 3, which one would you choose to best represent the relationship between engineering support costs and machine-hours? Why?

5. Kennedy expects 50 machine-hours to be worked in December. What engineering support costs should Kennedy budget for December?

6. What problems might Kennedy encounter when restating the materials and parts costs recorded to an "as used" or accrual accounting basis?

7. Why is it important for Kennedy to pick the correct cost function? That is, illustrate two potential problems Kennedy could run into, by choosing a cost function other than the one you chose in requirement 4.

RELEVANT REVENUES, RELEVANT COSTS, AND THE DECISION PROCESS

Grocery stores, such as Krogers must decide how to allocate limited shelf space among different products. An analysis of relevant revenues, relevant costs, and contribution margin per unit of the limited resource is useful in making informed decisions.

LEARNING OBJECTIVES

After studying this chapter, you should be able to

1. Describe a five-step sequence in the decision process
2. Outline the meaning of relevant cost and relevant revenue and describe its two key aspects
3. Distinguish between quantitative factors and qualitative factors in decisions
4. Indicate two ways in which per unit cost data can mislead decision makers
5. Identify two common pitfalls in relevant-cost analysis
6. Describe the opportunity cost concept; explain why it is used in decision making
7. Describe the key concept in choosing which among multiple products to produce when there are capacity constraints
8. Explain why the book value of equipment is irrelevant in equipment-replacement decisions
9. Explain how conflicts can arise between the decision model used by a manager and the performance model used to evaluate the manager

Working with managers to make decisions is one of the main functions of the management accountant and an important thrust of this book. The use of accounting information for decision making has been a consistent theme in earlier chapters. In this chapter, we focus on decisions such as accepting or rejecting a one-time-only special order, insourcing or outsourcing products or services, and replacing or keeping equipment. We especially stress the importance of distinguishing between relevant and irrelevant items in making these decisions.

INFORMATION AND THE DECISION PROCESS

Each manager has a method, often called a decision model, for deciding among different courses of action. A **decision model** is a formal method for making a choice, frequently involving quantitative and qualitative analyses. Accountants serve as technical experts supplying managers with relevant data to guide their decisions.

Predictions and Models

Consider a decision that Home Appliances, a manufacturer of vacuum cleaners, faces: Should it rearrange a manufacturing assembly line to reduce manufacturing labor costs? For simplicity, assume that the only alternatives are "do not rearrange" and "rearrange." The rearrangement will eliminate all manual handling of materials. The current manufacturing line uses 20 workers—15 workers operate machines, and 5 workers handle materials. Each worker puts in 2,000 hours annually. The rearrangement is predicted to cost $90,000. The predicted production output of 25,000 units for the next year will be unaffected by the decision. Also unaffected by the decision are the predicted selling price per unit of $250, direct materials costs per unit of $50, other manufacturing overhead of $750,000, and marketing costs of $2,000,000. The cost driver is units of production.

To make the decision, management proceeds in a sequence of steps. The first step is to gather more information about manufacturing labor costs. The historical manufacturing labor rate of $14 per hour is the starting point for predicting total manufacturing labor costs under both alternatives. The manufacturing labor rate is expected to increase to $16 per hour following a recently negotiated increase in employee benefits.

The second step is to predict future costs under the two alternatives. Predicted manufacturing labor costs under the "do not rearrange" alternative are 20 workers × 2,000 hours × $16 per hour = $640,000. Predicted manufacturing labor costs under the "rearrange" alternative are 15 workers × 2,000 hours × $16 per hour = $480,000. Predicted costs of rearrangement are $90,000.

As the third step, Home Appliances' management compares the predicted savings from eliminating materials handling labor costs (5 workers × 2,000 hours × $16 per hour) = $160,000 to the costs of rearrangement of $90,000. It also takes into account other qualitative considerations such as the effect that reducing the number of workers will have on employee morale. After weighing the costs and benefits, management chooses the "rearrange" alternative. Management next implements the decision in the fourth step by rearranging the manufacturing assembly line.

Models and Feedback

As the fifth and final step, management gathers information about the actual results of the plant rearrangement to evaluate performance and to provide feedback. Actual results show that the new manufacturing labor costs are $550,000 (due to, say, lower-than-expected manufacturing labor productivity) rather than the predicted $480,000. This feedback may lead to better implementation through, for example, a change in supervisory behavior, employee training, or personnel so that the $480,000 target is achieved in subsequent periods. However, the feedback may convince the decision maker that the prediction method, rather than the implementation, was faulty. Perhaps the prediction method for similar decisions in the future should be modified to allow for worker training or learning time.

EXHIBIT 11-1
Accounting Information and the Decision Process

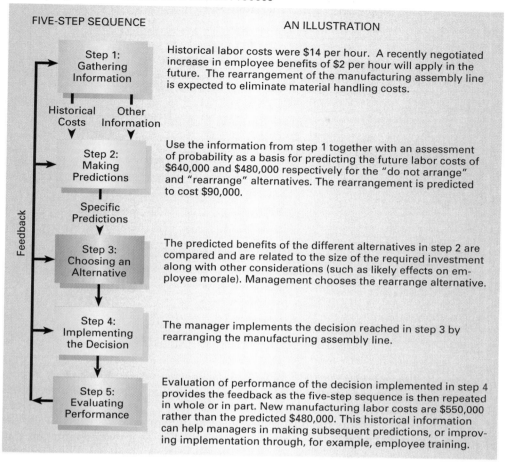

FIVE-STEP SEQUENCE — AN ILLUSTRATION

Step 1: Gathering Information
Historical labor costs were $14 per hour. A recently negotiated increase in employee benefits of $2 per hour will apply in the future. The rearrangement of the manufacturing assembly line is expected to eliminate material handling costs.

Historical Costs → Other Information

Step 2: Making Predictions
Use the information from step 1 together with an assessment of probability as a basis for predicting the future labor costs of $640,000 and $480,000 respectively for the "do not arrange" and "rearrange" alternatives. The rearrangement is predicted to cost $90,000.

Specific Predictions

Step 3: Choosing an Alternative
The predicted benefits of the different alternatives in step 2 are compared and are related to the size of the required investment along with other considerations (such as likely effects on employee morale). Management chooses the rearrange alternative.

Step 4: Implementing the Decision
The manager implements the decision reached in step 3 by rearranging the manufacturing assembly line.

Step 5: Evaluating Performance
Evaluation of performance of the decision implemented in step 4 provides the feedback as the five-step sequence is then repeated in whole or in part. New manufacturing labor costs are $550,000 rather than the predicted $480,000. This historical information can help managers in making subsequent predictions, or improving implementation through, for example, employee training.

Feedback

Exhibit 11-1 summarizes the five-step decision process that we just described—gathering information, making predictions, choosing an alternative, implementing the decision, and evaluating actual performance to provide feedback. The feedback, in turn, might affect future predictions, the prediction method itself, the decision model, or the implementation.

THE MEANING OF RELEVANCE

Relevant Costs and Relevant Revenues

The most important decision-making concepts in this chapter are relevant costs and relevant revenues. **Relevant costs** are those *expected future costs* that differ among alternative courses of action. The two key aspects to this definition are that the costs must occur in the future and that they must differ among the alternative courses of action. We focus on the future because *every decision deals with the future*—whether it be 20 seconds ahead (the decision to adjust a dial) or 20 years ahead (the decision to plant and harvest pine trees). The function of decision making is to select courses of action for the future. *Nothing can be done to alter the past.* Also, the future costs must differ among the alternatives because if they do not, there will be no difference in costs no matter what decision is made. Likewise, **relevant revenues** are those expected future revenues that differ among alternative courses of action.

In Exhibit 11-2, the $640,000 and $480,000 manufacturing labor costs are relevant costs—they are expected future costs that differ between the two alternatives. The past manufacturing labor rate of $14 per hour and total past manufacturing labor costs of $560,000 (2,000 hours × 20 workers × $14 per hour) are not relevant, even though they may play a role in preparing the $640,000 and $480,000 labor cost

O B J E C T I V E 2

Outline the meaning of relevant cost and relevant revenue and describe its two key aspects

	All Data		Relevant Data	
	Alternative 1: Do Not Rearrange	**Alternative 2: Rearrange**	**Alternative 1: Do Not Rearrange**	**Alternative 2: Rearrange**
Revenues*	$6,250,000	$6,250,000	—	—
			—	—
Costs:				
Direct materials†	1,250,000	1,250,000	—	—
Manufacturing labor	640,000‡	480,000§	$ 640,000‡	$ 480,000§
Manufacturing overhead	750,000	750,000	—	—
Marketing	2,000,000	2,000,000	—	—
Rearrangement costs	—	90,000	—	90,000
Total costs	4,640,000	4,570,000	640,000	570,000
Operating income	$1,610,000	$1,680,000	$(640,000)	$(570,000)

$70,000 Difference $70,000 Difference

*25,000 × $250 = $6,250,000   ‡20 × 2,000 × $16 = $640,000
†25,000 × $50 = $1,250,000   §15 × 2,000 × $16 = $480,000

predictions. *Although they may be a useful basis for making informed judgments for predicting expected future costs, historical costs in themselves are irrelevant to a decision.* Why? Because they deal strictly with the past, not the future.

Exhibit 11-2 presents the quantitative data underlying the choice between the "do not rearrange" and the "rearrange" alternatives. The first two columns present *all data*. The last two columns present only relevant costs or revenues. The revenues, direct materials, manufacturing overhead, and marketing items can be ignored. Why? Because although they are expected future costs, they do not differ between the alternatives. They are thus irrelevant. The data in Exhibit 11-2 indicate that rearranging the production line will increase next year's predicted operating income by $70,000. Note that we reach the same conclusion whether we use all data or include only the relevant data in the analysis. By confining the analysis to only the relevant data, managers can clear away related but irrelevant data that might confuse them.

The difference in total cost between two alternatives is a **differential** or **net relevant cost.** The differential cost between alternatives 1 and 2 in Exhibit 11-2 is $70,000.

Qualitative Factors Can Be Relevant

OBJECTIVE 3

Distinguish between quantitative factors and qualitative factors in decisions

We divide the consequences of alternatives into two broad categories: *quantitative and qualitative*. **Quantitative factors** are outcomes that are measured in numerical terms. Some quantitative factors are financial—that is, they can be easily expressed in financial terms. Examples include the costs of direct materials, direct manufacturing labor, and marketing. Other quantitative factors are nonfinancial—that is, they can be measured numerically, but they are not expressed in financial terms. Reduction in product-development time for a manufacturing company and the percentage of on-time flight arrivals for an airline company are examples of quantitative, nonfinancial factors. **Qualitative factors** are outcomes that cannot be measured in numerical terms. Employee morale is an example.

Cost analysis generally emphasizes quantitative factors that can be expressed in financial terms. But just because qualitative factors and nonfinancial quantitative factors cannot be easily measured in financial terms does not make them unimportant. Managers must at times give more weight to qualitative or nonfinancial quantitative factors. For example, Home Appliances may find that it can purchase a part from an outside supplier at a price that is lower than what it costs to manufacture the part in-house. Home Appliances may still choose to make the part in-house because it feels that the supplier is unlikely to meet the demanding delivery schedule—a quantitative nonfinancial factor—and because purchasing the part from outside may adversely affect employee morale—a qualitative factor. Trading off nonfinancial and financial considerations, however, is seldom easy.

AN ILLUSTRATION OF RELEVANCE: CHOOSING OUTPUT LEVELS

Managers often make decisions that affect output levels. For example, managers must choose whether to introduce a new product or sell more units of an existing product. When changes in output levels occur, managers are interested in the effect it has on the organization and on operating income. Why? Because maximizing organizational objectives (typically operating income in our illustrations) also increases managers' rewards.

One-Time-Only Special Orders

Management sometimes faces the decision of accepting or rejecting one-time-only special orders when there is idle production capacity and where the order has no long-run implications. We assume that all costs can be classified as either variable with respect to a single driver (units of output) or fixed. The following example illustrates how focusing on revenues, variable costs, and contribution margins can provide key information for decisions about the choice of output level. The example also indicates how reliance on unit-cost numbers calculated after allocating fixed costs can mislead managers about the effect that increasing output has on operating income.

EXAMPLE: Fancy Fabrics manufactures quality bath towels at its highly automated Charlotte, North Carolina, plant. The plant has a production capacity of 48,000 towels each month. Current monthly production is 30,000 towels. Retail department stores account for all existing sales. Expected results for the coming month (August) are shown in Exhibit 11-3. (Note that these amounts are predictions.) The manufacturing costs per unit of $12 consist of direct materials $6 (all variable), direct manufacturing labor $2 ($0.50 of which is variable), and manufacturing overhead $4 ($1 of which is variable). The marketing costs per unit are $7 ($5 of which is variable). Fancy Fabrics has no R&D costs or product-design costs. Marketing costs include distribution costs and customer-service costs.

A luxury hotel chain offers to buy 5,000 towels per month at $11 a towel for each of the next 3 months. No subsequent sales to this customer are anticipated. No marketing costs will be necessary for the 5,000-unit one-time-only special order. The acceptance of this special order is not expected to affect the selling price or the quantity of towels sold to regular customers. Should Fancy Fabrics accept the hotel chain's offer?

Exhibit 11-3 presents data in an absorption-costing format: Fixed manufacturing costs are included as product costs (see Chapter 9). The manufacturing cost per unit is $12 ($7.50 of which is variable and $4.50 of which is fixed), which is above the $11 price offered by the hotel chain. Using the $12 absorption cost as a guide in decision making, a manager might reject the offer.

EXHIBIT 11-3
Budgeted Income Statement for August, Absorption-Costing Format for Fancy Fabrics

	Total	Per Unit
Sales (30,000 towels × $20)	$600,000	$20
Cost of goods sold	360,000	12
Gross margin (gross profit)	240,000	8
Marketing costs	210,000	7
Operating income	$ 30,000	$ 1

Exhibit 11-4 presents data in a contribution income statement format. The relevant costs are the expected future costs that differ between the alternatives—the variable manufacturing costs of $37,500 ($7.50 per unit × 5,000 units). The fixed manufacturing costs and all marketing costs (including variable marketing costs) are irrelevant in this case; they will not change in total whether or not the special order is accepted. Therefore, the only relevant items here are sales revenues and variable manufacturing costs. Given the $11 relevant revenue per unit (the special-order price) and the $7.50 relevant costs per unit, Fancy Fabrics would gain an additional $17,500 [($11.00 − $7.50) × 5,000] in operating income per month by accepting the special order. In this example, comparisons based on either total amounts or relevant amounts (Exhibit 11-4) avoid the misleading implication of the absorption cost per unit (Exhibit 11-3).

The additional costs of $7.50 per unit that Fancy Fabrics will incur if it accepts the special order for 5,000 towels are sometimes called incremental costs, outlay costs, or out-of-pocket costs. **Incremental, outlay,** or **out-of-pocket costs** are additional costs to obtain an additional quantity, over and above existing or planned quantities, of a cost object. Fancy Fabrics could avoid these costs if it did not accept the special order. Fancy Fabrics incurs no incremental fixed manufacturing costs if it accepts the special order; those costs will not change whether or not the special order is accepted. Fixed manufacturing costs do not change because the analysis in Exhibit 11-4 assumes that the 5,000-towel special order will use already acquired capacity that will otherwise remain idle for each of the next 3 months.

The assumption of no long-run implications is crucial in the analysis we present for the one-time-only special order decision. Suppose, for example, that Fancy Fabrics is concerned that the retail department stores (its regular customers) will de-

EXHIBIT 11-4
Comparative Income Statements for August, Contribution Income Statement Format for Fancy Fabrics

	Without One-Time-Only Special Order, 30,000 Units		With One-Time-Only Special Order, 35,000 Units	Difference, 5,000 Units
	Per unit	Total	Total	Total
Sales	$20.00	$600,000	$655,000	$55,000‡
Variable costs:				
Manufacturing	7.50*	225,000	262,500	37,500$
Marketing	5.00	150,000	150,000	— #
Total variable costs	12.50	375,000	412,500	37,500
Contribution margin	7.50	225,000	242,500	17,500
Fixed Costs:				
Manufacturing	4.50†	135,000	135,000	— ‖
Marketing	2.00	60,000	60,000	— ‖
Total fixed costs	6.50	195,000	195,000	—
Operating income	$ 1.00	$ 30,000	$ 47,500	$17,500

*Variable manufacturing costs = Direct materials, $6 + Direct manufacturing labor, $0.50 + Manufacturing overhead, $1 = $7.50
†Fixed manufacturing costs = Direct manufacturing labor, $1.50 + Manufacturing overhead, $3 = $4.50
‡5,000 × $11.00 = $55,000
$5,000 × $7.50 = $37,500
#No variable marketing costs would be incurred for the 5,000-unit one-time-only special order.
‖Fixed manufacturing costs and fixed marketing costs are also unaffected by the special order.

mand a lower price if it sells towels at $11 a towel to the luxury hotel chain. In this case, the analysis of the luxury hotel chain order must be modified to consider both the short-term benefits from accepting the order and the long-term consequences on Fancy Fabrics' business and profitability.

How Unit Costs Can Mislead

OBJECTIVE 4

Indicate two ways in which per unit cost data can mislead decision makers

Unit-cost data can often help in the cost analysis. Nevertheless, they can also mislead decision makers in two major ways:

1. *When irrelevant costs are included.* Consider the $4.50 per unit allocation of fixed direct manufacturing labor and manufacturing overhead costs in the one-time-only special-order decision for Fancy Fabrics (see Exhibit 11-4). This $4.50 per unit cost is irrelevant given the assumptions of our example and therefore should be excluded.

2. *When unit costs at different output levels are compared.* Generally, use total costs rather than unit costs. Then, if desired, the total costs can be unitized. Machinery sales personnel, for example, may brag about the low unit costs of using their new machines. However, they sometimes neglect to say that the unit costs are based on outputs far in excess of their prospective customer's current or anticipated production levels. Consider, for example, a new machine that costs $100,000, is capable of producing 100,000 units over its useful life, and has a zero terminal disposal price. The salesperson may represent the machine-related costs per unit to be $1. This amount is incorrect if the company anticipates a total demand of say, only 50,000 units over the useful life of the machine (unit cost would be $100,000 ÷ 50,000 = $2). Unitizing fixed costs over different production levels can be particularly misleading.

Pitfalls in Relevant-Cost Analysis

OBJECTIVE 5

Identify two common pitfalls in relevant-cost analysis

One pitfall in relevant-cost analysis is to assume that all variable costs are relevant. In the Fancy Fabrics example, the marketing costs of $5 per unit are variable but not relevant. Why? Because for the special-order decision, Fancy Fabrics incurs no extra marketing costs.

A second pitfall is to assume that all fixed costs are irrelevant. Consider fixed manufacturing costs. In our example, we assume that the extra production of 5,000 towels per month does not affect fixed manufacturing costs. That is, we assume that the relevant range is at least from 30,000 to 35,000 towels per month. In some cases, however, the extra 5,000 towels might increase fixed manufacturing costs. Assume that Fancy Fabrics would have to run three shifts of 16,000 towels per shift to achieve full capacity of 48,000 towels per month. Increasing the monthly production from 30,000 to 35,000 would require a partial third shift because two shifts alone could produce only 32,000 towels. This extra shift would probably increase fixed manufacturing costs, thereby making any partial additional fixed manufacturing costs relevant for this decision.

The best way to avoid these two pitfalls is to focus first and foremost on the relevance concept. Always require each item included in the analysis *both* (1) to be an expected future revenue or cost, and (2) to differ among the alternatives.

Confusing Terminology

Many different terms are used to describe the costs of specific products and services. Exhibit 11-5 presents several different unit-cost numbers using the data from column 1 of Exhibit 11-4. **Business function costs** are the sum of all the costs (variable costs and fixed costs) in a particular business function in the value chain. For example, manufacturing costs are $12 per unit, and marketing costs are $7 per unit. For inventory costing purposes, absorption costs are often used as a synonym for manufacturing costs.

EXHIBIT 11-5
Variety of Cost Terms for Fancy Fabrics* Using Unit Cost Data from Exhibit 11-4

	Variable Product Costs	Fixed Product Costs	Manufacturing (Absorption) Costs	Marketing Costs	Full Product Costs
Variable manufacturing costs	$ 7.50		$ 7.50		$ 7.50
Variable marketing costs	5.00			$5.00	5.00
Fixed manufacturing costs		$ 4.50	4.50		4.50
Fixed marketing costs		2.00		2.00	2.00
	$12.50	$ 6.50	$12.00†	$7.00†	$19.00

*In this example, marketing costs include distribution costs and customer-service costs, and there are no R&D or product-design costs.
†Business function costs.

Full product costs refer to the sum of all the costs in all the business functions in the value chain (R&D, design, production, marketing, distribution, and customer service). Full product costs in Exhibit 11-5 are $19 per unit.

Managers use terms such as *business function costs* and *full product costs* differently. In a given situation, be sure to understand their exact meaning.

OUTSOURCING AND MAKE-VERSUS-BUY DECISIONS

We now consider the decision of whether a company should make a part or buy it. As in the previous section, we retain the assumption of idle capacity.

Outsourcing and Idle Facilities

Outsourcing is the process of purchasing goods and services from outside vendors rather than producing the same goods or providing the same services within the organization, which is called **insourcing.** For example, Kodak prefers to manufacture its own films (insourcing) but has IBM do its data-processing (outsourcing). Toyota relies on outside vendors to supply some parts and components but chooses to manufacture other parts internally. In making decisions about outsourcing and insourcing, cost is a major factor.

Decisions about whether a producer of goods or services will insource or outsource are also called **make-or-buy decisions.** Sometimes qualitative factors dictate management's make-or-buy decision. For example, Dell Computers must buy the Pentium chip for its personal computers from Intel because it does not have the know-how and technology to make the chip itself. Sometimes, a company may prefer to make the product in-house to retain control of the product and technology. For example, in order to safeguard Coca Cola's formula, the company does not outsource the manufacture of its concentrate. What are the most important factors in the make-or-buy decision? Surveys of company practices indicate they are quality, dependability of supplies, and cost.

In the El Cerrito Company example described here, assume that financial factors predominate in the make-or-buy decision. The question we address is, What financial factors are relevant?

The El Cerrito Company manufactures thermostats for home and industrial use. Thermostats consist of relays, switches, and valves. El Cerrito makes its own switches. Columns (1) and (2) of the following table report the current costs for its heavy-duty switch (HDS) based on an analysis of its various manufacturing activities:

	Total Current Costs of Producing 10,000 Units (1)	Current Cost per Unit (2) = (1) ÷ 10,000	Expected Total Costs of Producing 10,000 Units Next Year (3)	Expected Cost per Unit (4) = (3) ÷ 10,000
Direct materials	$ 80,000	$ 8.00	$ 80,000	$ 8
Direct manufacturing labor	10,000	1.00	10,000	1
Variable manufacturing overhead costs for power and utilities	40,000	4.00	40,000	4
Mixed overhead costs of purchasing, receiving, and setups	17,500	1.75	20,000	2
Fixed overhead costs of plant depreciation, insurance, and administration	30,000	3.00	30,000	3
Total manufacturing costs	$177,500	$17.75	$180,000	$18

Purchasing, receiving, and setup activities occur each time a batch of HDS is made. El Cerrito produces the 10,000 units of HDS in 25 batches of 400 units each. The cost driver for mixed overhead costs is number of batches. Mixed overhead costs of purchasing, receiving, and setup consist of fixed costs of $5,000 plus variable costs of $500 per batch giving total costs of $5,000 + 25 × $500 = $17,500. El Cerrito only commences production after it receives a firm customer order. El Cerrito's customers are pressuring the company to supply thermostats in smaller batch sizes. El Cerrito anticipates that next year, the 10,000 units of HDS will be manufactured in 50 batches of 200 units each. Through continuous improvement, El Cerrito expects to reduce purchasing, receiving, and setup costs to $300 per batch. No other changes in fixed costs or unit variable costs are anticipated.

Another manufacturer offers to sell El Cerrito 10,000 units of HDS next year for $16 per unit on whatever delivery schedule El Cerrito wants. Should El Cerrito make or buy the part?

Columns (3) and (4) of the preceding table indicate the expected total costs and the expected per unit cost of producing 10,000 units of HDS next year. Direct materials, direct manufacturing labor, and variable manufacturing overhead costs that vary with units produced are not expected to change since El Cerrito plans to continue to produce 10,000 units next year at the same variable costs per unit as this year. The costs of purchasing, receiving, and setups are expected to increase even though there is no expected change in the total production quantity. Why? Because these costs vary with the number of batches started, not the quantity of production. Expected total purchasing, receiving, and setup costs = $5,000 + 50 batches × the cost per batch of $300 = $5,000 + $15,000 = $20,000. El Cerrito expects fixed overhead costs to remain the same. The expected manufacturing cost per unit equals $18. At this cost, it seems that the company should buy HDS from the outside supplier because making the part appears to be more costly than the $16 per unit to buy it. A make-or-buy decision, however, is rarely obvious. A key question for management is, What is the difference in relevant costs between the alternatives?

For the moment, suppose the capacity now used to make HDS will become idle if HDS is purchased. Assume that the $5,000 in fixed clerical salaries to support setup, receiving, and purchasing will not be incurred if the manufacture of HDS is completely shut down. Further suppose that the $30,000 in plant depreciation, insurance, and administration costs represent fixed manufacturing overhead that will not vary regardless of the decision made.

Exhibit 11-6 presents the relevant cost computations. El Cerrito saves $10,000 by making HDS rather than buying it from the outside supplier. Alternatively stated, purchasing HDS costs $160,000 but saves only $150,000 in manufacturing costs. Making HDS is thus the preferred alternative. Exhibit 11-6 excludes the $30,000 of

EXHIBIT 11-6
Relevant (Incremental) Items for Make-or-Buy Decision for HDS at the El Cerrito Company

Relevant Items	Total Relevant Costs		Per Unit Relevant Costs	
	Make	Buy	Make	Buy
Outside purchase of parts		$160,000		$16
Direct materials	$ 80,000		$ 8	
Direct manufacturing labor	10,000		1	
Variable manufacturing overhead	40,000		4	
Fixed purchasing, receiving, and setup overhead*	20,000		2	
Total relevant costs	$150,000	$160,000	$15	$16
Difference in favor of making HDS	$10,000		$1	

*Alternatively, the $30,000 of depreciation, plant insurance, and plant administration costs could be included under both alternatives. These would be irrelevant to the decision.

plant depreciation, insurance, and administration costs under both the make and the buy alternatives. Why? Because these costs are irrelevant; they do not differ between the two alternatives. Alternatively, the $30,000 could be included under both alternatives since the $30,000 will continue to be incurred whether HDS is bought or made. Exhibit 11-6 includes the $20,000 of purchasing, receiving, and setup costs under the make alternative but not under the buy alternative. Why? Because buying HDS and not having to manufacture it saves both the variable costs per batch and the avoidable fixed costs. The $20,000 of costs differ between the alternatives and hence are relevant to the make-or-buy decision.

The figures in Exhibit 11-6 are valid only if the released facilities remain idle. If the component part is bought from the outside supplier, the released facilities can potentially be used for other, more profitable purposes. More generally, then, the choice in our example is not fundamentally whether to make or buy; it is how best to use available facilities.

The use of otherwise idle resources can often increase profitability. For example, consider the machine-repair plant of Beijing Engineering, where the decision was whether to drop or keep a product. The *China Daily* noted that workers were "busy producing electric plaster-spraying machines" even though the unit cost exceeded the selling price. According to the prevailing method of calculating its cost, each sprayer costs 1,230 yuan to make. However, each sprayer sells for only 985 yuan, resulting in a loss of 245 yuan per sprayer. Still, to meet market demand, the plant continues to produce sprayers. Workers and machines would otherwise be idle, and the plant would still have to pay 759 yuan even if no sprayers were made. In the short run, the production of sprayers, even at a loss, actually helps cut the company's operating loss.

OPPORTUNITY COSTS, OUTSOURCING, AND CAPACITY CONSTRAINTS

OBJECTIVE 6

Describe the opportunity cost concept; explain why it is used in decision making

Reconsider the El Cerrito Company example where we assumed that the capacity currently used to make HDS became idle if the parts were purchased. Suppose instead that El Cerrito has alternative uses for the extra capacity. The best available alternative is for El Cerrito to use the capacity to produce 5,000 units each year of a regular switch (RS) that the Terrence Corporation wants. John Marquez, the accountant at El Cerrito, estimates the following future revenues and future costs if RS is manufactured and sold:

Chevron and British Petroleum— Rivals in the Oil Patch but Partners in Outsourcing Distribution

Chevron and British Petroleum, competitors in the oil industry, have joined together to outsource their logistics function. They have entered into a strategic alliance with GATX Logistics to supply tires, batteries, and accessories (TBA) to the 6,500 Chevron and BP service stations throughout the United States. The team effort has enabled Chevron and BP to reduce their TBA distribution centers by more than 60% and to achieve efficiencies in transportation, personnel, and other distribution-related activities. The outsourcing arrangement has both reduced cost and improved service.

When a British Petroleum or Chevron service station needs tires, batteries, or accessories, it places an order with its respective company. The company electronically downloads the order to GATX's systems each afternoon. GATX uses sophisticated truck-routing software to determine distribution routes and electronically transmits the order to one of five distribution centers spread throughout the United States. The next day, the center shrink-wraps and loads the order onto one of GATX's 100 trucks. The trucks deliver the orders to appropriate service stations the following day, according to the route schedule.

What's the payoff to Chevron and BP? Chevron and BP managers argue that using a firm specializing in logistics and distribution is more efficient and economical because of GATX's access to better systems and its economies of scale. Consensus is that the outsourcing arrangement has reduced transportation costs by at least 25%, running into several tens of millions of dollars. It has also led to faster delivery and response times.

Source: Adapted from *Purchasing*, Nov. 24, 1994, pp. 41–42.

Expected additional future revenues		$80,000
Expected additional future costs		
Direct materials	$30,000	
Direct manufacturing labor	5,000	
Variable overhead (power, utilities)	15,000	
Purchasing, receiving, and setup overheads	5,000	
Total expected additional future costs		55,000
Expected additional operating income		$25,000

Since El Cerrito cannot make both HDS and RS, the three alternatives available to management are as follows:

1. Make HDS and do not make RS for Terrence.

2. Buy HDS and do not make RS for Terrence.

3. Buy HDS and use excess capacity to make and sell RS to Terrence.

Exhibit 11-7, Panel A, summarizes the "total-alternatives" approach—the incremental expected future costs and expected future revenues for *all* alternatives. Buying HDS and using the excess capacity to make RS and sell it to Terrence is the preferred

EXHIBIT 11-7
Total-Alternatives Approach and Opportunity-Costs Approach to Make-or-Buy Decisions for El Cerrito

PANEL A: TOTAL-ALTERNATIVES APPROACH TO MAKE-OR-BUY DECISIONS

	Choices for El Cerrito		
Relevant Items	**Make HDS and Do Not Make RS**	**Buy HDS and Do Not Make RS**	**Buy HDS and Make RS**
Total incremental costs of making/buying HDS (from Exhibit 11-6)	$150,000	$160,000	$160,000
Excess of future revenues over future costs from RS	0	0	(25,000)
Total relevant costs	$150,000	$160,000	$135,000

PANEL B: OPPORTUNITY-COSTS APPROACH TO MAKE-OR-BUY DECISIONS

	Choices for El Cerrito	
Relevant Items	**Make HDS**	**Buy HDS**
Total incremental costs of making/buying HDS (from Exhibit 11-6)	$150,000	$160,000
Opportunity cost: Profit contribution forgone because capacity cannot be used to make RS, the next-best alternative	25,000	0
Total relevant costs	$175,000	$160,000
Difference in favor of buying HDS	$15,000	

alternative. The incremental costs of buying HDS from an outside supplier is more than the incremental costs of making HDS in-house ($160,000 to buy versus $150,000 to make). But the capacity freed up by buying HDS from the outside supplier enables El Cerrito to gain $25,000 in operating income (expected additional future revenues of $80,000 minus expected additional future costs of $55,000) by making RS and selling to Terrence. The total relevant costs of buying HDS (and making and selling RS) is $160,000 – $25,000 = $135,000.

Deciding to use a resource in a particular way causes a manager to give up the opportunity to use the resource in alternative ways. The lost opportunity is a cost that the manager must take into account when making a decision. **Opportunity cost** is the contribution to income that is forgone (rejected) by not using a limited resource in its next-best alternative use.

Exhibit 11-7, Panel B, displays the opportunity-costs approach for analyzing the alternatives faced by El Cerrito. Management focuses on the two alternatives before it—whether to make or buy HDS. It does not explicitly include RS in the analysis. Focus first on the make HDS column and ask, What are all the costs of choosing this alternative? Certainly, El Cerrito incurs $150,000 of incremental costs to make HDS. But is this the entire cost? No, because by using limited manufacturing resources to make HDS, El Cerrito gives up the opportunity to earn $25,000 from not using these resources to make RS. Therefore, the relevant costs of making HDS are the incremental costs of $150,000 plus the opportunity cost of $25,000. Next consider the buy alternative. The incremental costs are $160,000. The opportunity cost is zero because choosing this alternative does not require the use of a limited resource—El Cerrito's manufacturing capacity is still available to make and sell RS. Panel B leads management to the same conclusion as Panel A does—buying HDS is the preferred alternative by an amount of $15,000.

Panels A and B of Exhibit 11-7 describe two consistent approaches to decision making with capacity constraints. The total-alternatives approach in Panel A includes only incremental costs and benefits and no opportunity costs. Why? Because the incremental benefit from making RS when HDS is bought is explicitly considered under the alternatives. Panel B does not explicitly consider the incremental benefits from selling RS. Instead, it factors in the forgone benefit as a cost of the make alternative. Panel B highlights the idea that when capacity is constrained, relevant costs equal the incremental costs plus the opportunity cost.

Opportunity costs are seldom incorporated into formal financial accounting reports because these costs do not entail cash receipts or disbursements. Accountants usually confine their systematic recording to costs that require cash disbursements currently or in the near future. Historical recordkeeping is limited to alternatives selected rather than those rejected, because once rejected, there are no transactions to record. For example, if El Cerrito makes HDS, it would not make RS, and it would not record any accounting entries for RS. Yet the opportunity cost of making HDS, which equals the profit contribution that El Cerrito forgoes by not making RS, is a crucial input into the make-versus-buy decision. Consider again Exhibit 11-7, Panel B. On the basis of incremental costs alone, the costs systematically recorded in the accounting system, it is less costly for El Cerrito to make rather than buy HDS. Recognizing the opportunity cost of $25,000 leads to a different conclusion. It is preferable to buy HDS.

Suppose El Cerrito has sufficient excess capacity to make RS (and indeed any other part) even if it makes HDS. Under this assumption, the opportunity cost of making HDS is zero. Why? Because El Cerrito gives up nothing even if it chooses to manufacture HDS. It follows from Panel B (substituting opportunity costs equal to zero) that, under these conditions, El Cerrito would prefer to make HDS.

Our analysis emphasizes purely quantitative considerations. The final decision, however, should consider qualitative factors as well. For example, before deciding to buy HDS from an outside supplier, El Cerrito management will consider such qualitative factors as the supplier's reputation for quality and the supplier's dependability for on-time delivery.

Carrying Costs of Inventory

The notion of opportunity cost can also be illustrated for the Garvey Corporation's direct-materials purchase-order decision. Garvey has enough cash to pay for whatever quantity of direct materials it buys.

Annual estimated direct-materials requirements for the year	120,000 pounds
Cost per pound for purchase orders below 120,000 pounds	$10.00
Cost per pound for purchase orders equal to or greater than 120,000 pounds; $10.00 minus 2% discount	$9.80
Alternatives under consideration:	
A. Buy 120,000 pounds at start of year	
B. Buy 10,000 pounds per month	
Average investment in inventory:	
A. (120,000 pounds × $9.80) ÷ 2*	$588,000
B. (10,000 pounds × $10.00) ÷ 2*	$50,000
Annual interest rate for investment in government bonds	6%

*The example assumes that the direct materials purchased will be used up uniformly at the rate of 10,000 pounds per month. If direct materials are purchased at the start of the year (month), the average investment in inventory during the year is the cost of the inventory at the beginning of the year (month) plus the cost of inventory at the end of the year (month) divided by 2.

The following table presents the two alternatives.

	Alternative A: Purchase 120,000 Pounds at Beginning of Year (1)	Alternative B: Purchase 10,000 Pounds at Beginning of Each Month (2)	Difference (3) = (1) - (2)
Annual purchase (incremental) costs (120,000 × $9.80; 120,000 × $10)	$1,176,000	$1,200,000	$(24,000)
Annual interest income that could be earned if investment in inventory were invested in government bonds (opportunity cost) (6% × $588,000; 6% × $50,000)	35,280	3,000	32,280
Relevant costs	$1,211,280	$1,203,000	$ 8,280

The opportunity cost of holding inventory is the income forgone from not investing this money elsewhere. These opportunity costs would not be recorded in the accounting system because they are not incremental or outlay costs. Column (3) indicates that, consistent with the trends toward holding smaller inventories as in JIT systems, purchasing 10,000 pounds per month is preferred relative to purchasing 120,000 pounds at the beginning of the year because the lower opportunity cost of holding smaller inventory exceeds the higher purchase cost. If other incremental benefits of holding lower inventory such as lower insurance, materials handling, storage, obsolescence, and breakage costs were considered, alternative B would be preferred even more.

PRODUCT-MIX DECISIONS UNDER CAPACITY CONSTRAINTS

Companies with capacity constraints, such as El Cerrito, must also often decide which products to make and in what quantities. When a multiple-product plant operates at full capacity, managers must often make decisions regarding which products to emphasize. These decisions frequently have a short-run focus. For example, General Mills must continually adapt the mix of its different products to short-run fluctuations in materials costs, selling prices, and demand. Throughout this section, we assume that as short-run changes in product mix occur, the only costs that change are those that are variable with respect to the number of units produced (and sold).

Analysis of individual product contribution margins provides insight into the product mix that maximizes operating income. Consider Power Recreation, a company that manufactures engines for a broad range of commercial and consumer products. At its Lexington, Kentucky, plant, it assembles two engines—a snowmobile engine and a boat engine. Information on these products is as follows:

	Snowmobile Engine	Boat Engine
Selling price	$800	$1,000
Variable costs per unit	560	625
Contribution margin per unit	$240	$ 375
Contribution margin ratio	30%	37.5%

At first glance, boat engines appear more profitable than snowmobile engines. The product to be emphasized, however, is not necessarily the product with the higher individual contribution margin per unit or contribution margin percentage. Rather, managers should aim for the *highest contribution margin per unit of the constraining factor*—that is, the scarce, limiting, or critical factor. The constraining factor restricts or limits the production or sale of a given product. (See also Chapter 19, the theory of constraints, pp. 698–701.)

Assume that only 600 machine-hours are available daily for assembling engines. Additional capacity cannot be obtained in the short run. Power Recreation can sell as many engines as it produces. The constraining factor, then, is machine-hours. It takes

Contracting and Opportunity Costs

Opportunity costs are a central feature of the damages that companies seek when there is litigation regarding a breach of contract or the violation of a patent. Inter-Power Development Corporation builds power plants and sells the power it generates under power purchase contracts to companies that have distribution and transmission capabilities. Inter-Power and Niagara Mohawk are locked in a contract dispute relating to Niagara Mohawk's cancellation of a power purchase contract on Inter-Power's 200-megawatt coal-fired project in upstate New York.* Inter-Power is claiming damages in the $50 million range for development costs incurred on the stalled power plant plus opportunity costs equal to profits that Inter-Power would have made over the term of the contract, had it built the plant. Niagara Mohawk argues it was within its rights to cancel the contract. The case has yet to be heard.

The Intel Corporation designs and makes computer chips (microprocessors) that are used to run personal computers. The AMD Corporation also makes similar chips (clones) to Intel's 80386 and I486 chips under a technology-sharing agreement with Intel. In 1987, Intel terminated the agreement and asked AMD to stop making the clones using Intel's design. AMD refused. Intel filed a law suit against AMD for $1 billion—the profits Intel claimed it lost because AMD cloned its chips. AMD also sued Intel for breach of the original agreement. Recently, the two companies settled the suit with AMD agreeing to pay Intel $40 million net for the right to clone Intel's 80386 and I486 chips but not its newer Pentium chip.†

Suppliers' contracts almost always attempt to exclude any liability for opportunity costs. For example, suppliers of semiconductor furnaces, such as Semitherm, make clear that they are not responsible for the opportunity cost of lost profits that may result if the furnaces malfunction and the buyers' plants have to be shut down.

Beyond legal and contractual dimensions, however, opportunity cost is a potent cost for any business. Opportunity cost concerns are primary drivers of quality and timeliness—an important cost of poor quality and slow response time is the opportunity cost of lost profits from dissatisfied customers and lost sales.

---

* Adapted from *Northeast Power Report,* August 4, 1995.
† Adapted from *Computerworld,* March 14, 1994, p. 10, and January 16, 1995, p. 4.

2 machine-hours to produce one snowmobile engine and 5 machine-hours to produce one boat engine.

	Snowmobile Engine	Boat Engine
Contribution margin per engine	$240	$375
Machine-hours required to produce one engine	2 machine-hours	5 machine-hours
Contribution margin per machine-hour (240 ÷ 2; 375 ÷ 5)	$120	$75
Total contribution margin for 600 machine-hours ($120 × 600; $75 × 600)	$72,000	$45,000

Producing snowmobile engines contributes more margin per machine-hour, which is the constraining factor in this example. Therefore, choosing to emphasize snowmobile engines is the correct decision. Other constraints in manufacturing settings can be the availability of direct materials, components, or skilled labor, as well as financial and sales considerations. In a retail department store, the constraining factor may be linear feet of display space. The greatest possible contribution margin per unit of the constraining factor yields the maximum operating income.

As you can imagine, in many cases, a manufacturer or retailer must meet the challenge of trying to maximize total operating income for a variety of products, each with more than one constraining factor. The problem of formulating the most profitable production schedules and the most profitable product mix is essentially that of maximizing the total contribution margin in the face of many constraints. Optimization techniques, such as the linear-programming technique discussed in the Appendix to this chapter, help solve these complicated problems.

CUSTOMER PROFITABILITY, ACTIVITY-BASED COSTING, AND RELEVANT COSTS

In addition to making choices among products, companies must often decide about whether they should add some customers and drop others. This section illustrates relevant-revenue and relevant-cost analysis when different cost drivers are identified for different activities in activity-based costing. The cost object in our example is customers. The analysis focuses on customer profitability at Allied West, the West Coast sales office of Allied Furniture, a wholesaler of specialized furniture.

Allied West supplies furniture to three local retailers, Vogel, Brenner, and Wisk. Exhibit 11-8 presents representative revenues and costs of Allied West by customers for the year 19_8. Additional information on Allied West's costs for different activities at various levels of the cost hierarchy is as follows:

1. Materials handling labor costs vary with the number of units of furniture shipped to customers.

2. Different areas of the warehouse stock furniture for different customers. Materials handling equipment in an area and depreciation costs on the equipment are identified with individual customer accounts. Any equipment not used remains idle. The equipment has a 1-year useful life and zero disposal price.

3. Allied West allocates rent to each customer account on the basis of the amount of warehouse space occupied by the products to be shipped to that customer.

4. Marketing costs vary with the number of sales visits made to customers.

5. Purchase-order costs vary with the number of purchase orders received; delivery-processing costs vary with the number of shipments made.

6. Allied West allocates fixed general administration costs to customers on the basis of dollar sales made to each customer.

Relevant-Cost Analysis of Dropping a Customer

Exhibit 11-8 indicates a loss of $23,000 on sales to Wisk. Allied West's manager believes this loss occurred because Wisk places many low-volume orders with Allied, resulting in high purchase-order and delivery-processing, and materials handling, and marketing activity. Allied West is considering several possible actions with respect to the Wisk account—reducing its own costs of supporting Wisk by becoming more efficient, cutting back on some of the services it offers Wisk, charging Wisk higher prices, or dropping the Wisk account. The following analysis focuses on the operating income effect of dropping the Wisk account.

The key question is, What are the relevant costs and relevant revenues? The following information about the effect of reducing various activities related to the Wisk account is available.

1. Dropping the Wisk account will save cost of goods sold, materials handling labor, marketing support, purchase-order, and delivery-processing costs incurred on the Wisk account.

2. Dropping the Wisk account will mean that the warehouse space currently occupied by products for Wisk and the materials handling equipment used to move them will become idle.

3. Dropping the Wisk account will have no effect on fixed general administration costs.

EXHIBIT 11-8
Customer Profitability Analysis for Allied West

	Vogel	Brenner	Wisk	Total
Sales	$500,000	$300,000	$400,000	$1,200,000
Cost of goods sold	370,000	220,000	330,000	920,000
Materials handling labor	41,000	18,000	33,000	92,000
Materials handling equipment cost written off as depreciation	10,000	6,000	8,000	24,000
Rent	14,000	8,000	14,000	36,000
Marketing support	11,000	9,000	10,000	30,000
Purchase orders and delivery processing	13,000	7,000	12,000	32,000
General administration	20,000	12,000	16,000	48,000
Total operating costs	479,000	280,000	423,000	1,182,000
Operating income	$ 21,000	$ 20,000	$ (23,000)	$ 18,000

Exhibit 11-9 presents the relevant-cost computations. Allied West's operating income will be $15,000 lower if it drops the Wisk account, so Allied decides to keep the Wisk account. The last column in Exhibit 11-9 shows that the cost savings from dropping the Wisk account, $385,000, is not enough to offset the loss of $400,000 in revenue. The key reason is that depreciation, rent, and general administration costs will not decrease if the Wisk account is dropped.

Now suppose that if Allied drops the Wisk account, it could lease the extra warehouse space to the Sanchez Corporation, which has offered $20,000 per year for it. Then the $20,000 that Allied would receive would be the opportunity cost of continuing to use the warehouse to service Wisk. Allied would gain $5,000 by dropping the Wisk account ($20,000 from lease revenue minus lost operating income of $15,000). Before reaching a final decision, however, Allied must examine whether Wisk can be made more profitable so that supplying products to Wisk earns more than the $20,000 from leasing to Sanchez. Allied must also consider qualitative factors such as the effect of the decision on Allied's reputation for developing stable, long-run business relationships.

EXHIBIT 11-9
Relevant-Cost Analysis for Allied West Dropping the Wisk Account

	Amount of Total Revenues and Total Costs		Difference: Incremental (Loss in Revenue) and Savings in Costs from Dropping Wisk Account
	Keep Wisk Account	Drop Wisk Account	
Sales	$1,200,000	$800,000	$(400,000)
Cost of goods sold	920,000	590,000	330,000
Materials handling labor	92,000	59,000	33,000
Materials handling equipment cost written off as depreciation	24,000	24,000	0
Rent	36,000	36,000	0
Marketing support	30,000	20,000	10,000
Purchase orders and delivery processing	32,000	20,000	12,000
General administration	48,000	48,000	0
Total operating costs	1,182,000	797,000	385,000
Operating income (loss)	$ 18,000	$ 3,000	$ (15,000)

EXHIBIT 11-10
Relevant-Cost Analysis for Adding the Loral Account

	Amount of Total Revenues and Total Costs		Difference: Incremental Revenue and (Incremental Costs) from Adding Loral Account
	Do Not Add Loral Account	Add Loral Account	
Sales	$1,200,000	$1,600,000	$400,000
Cost of goods sold (variable)	920,000	1,250,000	(330,000)
Materials handling labor	92,000	125,000	(33,000)
Materials handling equipment cost written off as depreciation	24,000	32,000	(8,000)
Rent	36,000	36,000	0
Marketing support	30,000	40,000	(10,000)
Purchase orders and delivery processing	32,000	44,000	(12,000)
General administration	48,000	48,000	0
Total operating costs	1,182,000	1,575,000	393,000
Operating income	$ 18,000	$ 25,000	$ 7,000

Relevant-Cost Analysis of Adding a Customer

Suppose that in addition to Vogel, Brenner, and Wisk, Allied is evaluating the profitability of adding a fourth customer, Loral. Allied is already paying rent of $36,000 for the warehouse and is incurring general administration costs of $48,000. These costs will not change if Loral is added as a customer. Loral is a customer with a profile much like Wisk's. Suppose Allied predicts other revenues and costs of doing business with Loral to be the same as those described under the Wisk column of Exhibit 11-8. Should Allied add Loral as a customer? Exhibit 11-10 shows incremental revenues exceed incremental costs by $7,000. Allied would prefer to add Loral as a customer. The key point is that the cost of acquiring new equipment to support the Loral order (written off as depreciation of $8,000 in Exhibit 11-10) is included as a relevant cost. Why? Because this cost can be avoided if Allied decides not to do business with Loral. Note the critical distinction here. Depreciation cost is irrelevant in deciding whether to drop Wisk as a customer (because it is a past cost), but the purchase cost of the new equipment that will then be written off as depreciation in the future is relevant in deciding whether to add Loral as a new customer.

IRRELEVANCE OF PAST COSTS AND EQUIPMENT-REPLACEMENT DECISIONS

OBJECTIVE 8

Explain why the book value of equipment is irrelevant in equipment-replacement decisions

The illustrations in this chapter have shown that expected future costs that do not differ among alternatives are irrelevant. Now we return to the idea that all past costs are irrelevant.

Consider an example of equipment replacement. The irrelevant cost illustrated here is the **book value** (original cost minus accumulated depreciation) of the existing equipment. Assume that the Toledo Company is considering replacing a metal-cutting machine for aircraft parts with a more technically advanced model. The new machine has an automatic quality-testing capability and is more efficient than the old machine. The new machine, however, has a shorter life. The Toledo Company uses the straight-line depreciation method. Sales from aircraft parts ($1.1 million per year) will be unaffected by the replacement decision. Summary data on the existing machine and the replacement machine are as follows:

	Existing Machine	Replacement Machine
Original cost	$1,000,000	$600,000
Useful life in years	5 years	2 years
Current age in years	3 years	0 years
Useful life remaining in years	2 years	2 years
Accumulated depreciation	$600,000	Not acquired yet
Book value	$400,000	Not acquired yet
Current disposal price (in cash)	$40,000	Not acquired yet
Terminal disposal price (in cash 2 years from now)	$0	$0
Annual operating costs (maintenance, energy, repairs, coolants, and so on)	$800,000	$460,000

To focus on the main concept of relevance, we ignore the time value of money in this illustration.

Exhibit 11-11 presents a cost comparison of the two machines. Some managers would not replace the old machine because it would entail recognizing a $360,000 "loss on disposal" ($400,000 book value minus $40,000 current disposal price); retention would allow spreading the $400,000 book value over the next 2 years in the form of "depreciation expense" (a term more appealing than "loss on disposal").

We can apply our definition of relevance to four commonly encountered items in equipment-replacement decisions such as the one facing Toledo Company:

1. *Book value of old machine.* Irrelevant, because it is a past (historical) cost. All past costs are "down the drain." Nothing can change what has already been spent or what has already happened.

2. *Current disposal price of old machine.* Relevant, because it is an expected future cash inflow that differs between alternatives.

3. *Gain or loss on disposal.* This is the algebraic difference between items 1 and 2. It is a meaningless combination blurring the distinction between the irrelevant book value and the relevant disposal price. Each item should be considered separately.

4. *Cost of new machine.* Relevant, because it is an expected future cash outflow that will differ between alternatives.

EXHIBIT 11-11
Cost Comparison—Replacement of Machinery, Including Relevant and Irrelevant Items for the Toledo Company

	Two Years Together		
	Keep	Replace	Difference
Sales	$2,200,000	$2,200,000	—
Operating costs			
Cash-operating costs	1,600,000	920,000	$680,000
Old machine book value			
Periodic write-off as depreciation or	400,000	—	—
Lump-sum write-off	—	400,000*	
Current disposal price of old machine	—	(40,000)*	40,000
New machine cost, written off periodically as depreciation	—	600,000	(600,000)
Total operating costs	2,000,000	1,880,000	120,000
Operating income	$ 200,000	$ 320,000	$120,000

*In a formal income statement, these two items would be combined as "loss on disposal of machine" of $360,000.

EXHIBIT 11-12
Cost Comparison—Replacement of Machinery, Relevant Items Only for the Toledo Company

	Two Years Together		
	Keep	Replace	Difference
Cash-operating costs	$1,600,000	$ 920,000	$680,000
Current disposal price of old machine	—	(40,000)	40,000
New machine, written off periodically as depreciation	—	600,000	(600,000)
Total relevant costs	$1,600,000	$1,480,000	$120,000

Exhibit 11-11 should clarify these four assertions. The difference column in Exhibit 11-11 shows that the book value of the old machine is not an element of difference between alternatives and could be completely ignored for decision-making purposes. No matter what the timing of the charge against revenue, the amount charged is still $400,000 regardless of the alternative chosen because it is a past (historical) cost. Note that the advantage of replacing is $120,000 for the 2 years together.

In either event, the undepreciated cost will be written off with the same ultimate effect on operating income. The $400,000 enters into the income statement either as a $400,000 offset against the $40,000 proceeds to obtain the $360,000 loss on disposal in the current year or as $200,000 depreciation in each of the next 2 years. But how it appears in the income statement is irrelevant to the replacement decision. In contrast, the $600,000 cost of the new machine is relevant because it can be avoided by deciding not to replace.

Past costs that are unavoidable because they cannot be changed, no matter what action is taken, are sometimes described as **sunk costs.** In our example, old equipment has a book value of $400,000 and a current disposal price of $40,000. What are the sunk costs in this case? The entire $400,000 is sunk and down the drain because it represents an outlay made in the past that cannot be changed. Thus, past costs and sunk costs are synonyms.

Exhibit 11-12 concentrates on relevant items only. Note that the same answer (the $120,000 net difference) will be obtained even though the book value is completely omitted from the calculations. The only relevant items are the cash-operating costs, the disposal price of the old machine, and the cost of the new machine (represented as depreciation in Exhibit 11-12).

Decision makers vary in their preference between the formats presented in Exhibits 11-11 and 11-12. Some prefer the format used in Exhibit 11-11 because it illustrates why some items are irrelevant to the decision. Other managers prefer the format used in Exhibit 11-12 because it is concise.

DECISIONS AND PERFORMANCE EVALUATION

Consider our equipment-replacement example in light of the five-step sequence in Exhibit 11-1 (p. 385).

OBJECTIVE 9

Explain how conflicts can arise between the decision model used by a manager and the performance model used to evaluate the manager

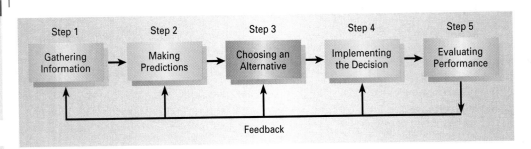

If the decision model (step 3) demands choosing the alternative that will minimize total costs over the life span of the equipment, then the analysis in Exhibits 11-11 and 11-12 dictates replacing rather than keeping. In the real world, however, would the manager replace? The answer depends on the manager's perceptions of whether the decision model is consistent with the performance-evaluation model (step 5). The performance-evaluation model describes the basis on which the manager's performance is judged.

Managers tend to favor the alternative that makes their performance look best. If the performance-evaluation model conflicts with the decision model, the performance-evaluation model often prevails in influencing a manager's behavior. For example, the decision model in Exhibit 11-11, based on a relevant-cost analysis over the life of the two machines, favors replacing the machine. But if the manager's promotion or bonus hinges on the first year's operating income performance under accrual accounting, the manager's temptation *not* to replace will be overwhelming. Why? Because the accrual accounting model for measuring performance will show a higher first-year operating income if the old machine is kept than if it is replaced (as the following table shows):

	First Year Results: Accrual Accounting			
	Keep		Replace	
Sales		$1,100,000		$1,100,000
Operating costs				
Cash-operating costs	$800,000		$460,000	
Depreciation	200,000		300,000	
Loss on disposal	—		360,000	
Total operating costs		1,000,000		1,120,000
Operating income		$ 100,000		$ (20,000)

Even if top management's goals are long-run (and consistent with the decision model), the subordinate manager's concern is more likely to be short-run if his or her evaluation is based on short-run measures such as operating income.

Resolving the conflict between the decision model and the performance-evaluation model is frequently a baffling problem in practice. In theory, resolving the difficulty seems obvious—merely design consistent models. Consider our replacement example. Year-by-year effects on operating income of replacement can be budgeted over the planning horizon of 2 years. The manager would be evaluated on the understanding that the first year would be expected to be poor, the next year much better.

The practical difficulty is that accounting systems rarely track each decision separately. Performance evaluation focuses on responsibility centers for a specific time period, not on projects or individual items of equipment for their entire useful lives. Therefore, the impacts of many different decisions are combined in a single performance report. Top management, through the reporting system, is rarely aware of particular desirable alternatives that were not chosen by subordinate managers.

Consider another conflict between the decision model and the performance evaluation model. Suppose a manager buys a particular machine only to discover that a better machine could have been purchased in its place. The decision model may suggest replacing the existing machine with the better machine, but the manager may be reluctant to do so. Why? Because replacing the machine so soon after its purchase may reflect badly on the manager's capabilities and performance. If the manager's superiors have no knowledge of the better machine, the manager may prefer to keep, rather than replace, the existing machine.

PROBLEM

Wally Lewis is manager of the engineering development division of Goldcoast Products, Inc. Lewis has just received a proposal signed by all ten of his engineers to replace the existing mainframe computing system with ten workstations. Lewis is not enthusiastic about the proposal.

Summary data on the mainframe and workstation machines are as follows:

	Mainframe	Workstations
Original cost	$300,000	$135,000
Useful life in years	5 years	3 years
Current age in years	2 years	0 years
Useful life remaining in years	3 years	3 years
Accumulated depreciation	$120,000	Not acquired yet
Current book value	$180,000	Not acquired yet
Current disposal price (in cash)	$95,000	Not acquired yet
Terminal disposal price (in cash 3 years from now)	$0	$0
Annual computer-related cash-operating costs	$40,000	$10,000
Annual revenues	$1,000,000	$1,000,000
Annual noncomputer-related operating costs	$880,000	$880,000

Lewis's annual bonus includes a component based on division operating income. He has a promotion possibility next year that would make him a group vice-president of Goldcoast Products.

REQUIRED

1. Compare the costs of the mainframe and workstation options. Consider the cumulative results for the 3 years together, ignoring the time value of money.
2. Why might Lewis be reluctant to purchase the ten workstations?

SOLUTION

1. The following table considers all cost items when comparing future costs of the mainframe and workstation options:

	Three Years Together		
All Items	**Mainframe**	**Workstations**	**Difference**
Revenues	$3,000,000	$3,000,000	—
Operating costs			
Noncomputer-related operating costs	2,640,000	2,640,000	—
Computer-related cash-operating costs	120,000	30,000	$ 90,000
Mainframe book value			
Periodic write-off as depreciation or	180,000	—	
Lump-sum write-off	—	180,000 }	
Current disposal price of mainframe	—	(95,000)	95,000
Workstations, written off periodically as depreciation		135,000	(135,000)
Total operating costs	2,940,000	2,890,000	50,000
Operating income	$ 60,000	$ 110,000	$ 50,000

Alternatively, the analysis could focus on only those items in the preceding table that differ across the alternatives.

Relevant Items	Three Years Together		
	Mainframe	Workstations	Difference
Computer-related cash-operating costs	$120,000	$ 30,000	$ 90,000
Current disposal price of mainframe	—	(95,000)	95,000
Workstations, written off periodically as depreciation	—	135,000	(135,000)
Total relevant costs	$120,000	$ 70,000	$ 50,000

The analysis suggests that it is cost-effective to replace the mainframe with the workstations.

2. The accrual accounting operating incomes for the first year under the "keep mainframe" versus the "buy workstations" alternatives are as follows:

	Keep Mainframe		Buy Workstations	
Revenues		$1,000,000		$1,000,000
Operating costs				
Noncomputer-related operating costs	$880,000		$880,000	
Computer-related cash-operating costs	40,000		10,000	
Depreciation	60,000		45,000	
Loss on disposal of mainframe	—		85,000*	
Total operating costs		980,000		1,020,000
Operating income		$ 20,000		$ (20,000)

*85,000 = Book value of mainframe, $180,000 – Current disposal price, $95,000

Lewis would probably react negatively to the expected operating loss of $20,000 if the workstations are replaced as compared to an operating income of $20,000 if the mainframe is kept. The decision would eliminate the component of his bonus based on operating income. He might also perceive the $20,000 operating loss as reducing his chances of being promoted to a group vice president.

SUMMARY

The following points are linked to the chapter's learning objectives.

1. The five steps in a decision process are (a) obtaining information, (b) making predictions, (c) building decision models, (d) implementing decisions, and (e) evaluating performance.

2. To be relevant to a particular decision, a revenue or cost must meet two criteria: (a) It must be an expected future revenue or cost, and (b) it must differ among alternative courses of action.

3. The consequences of alternative actions can be quantitative and qualitative. Quantitative factors are outcomes that are measured in numerical terms. Some quantitative factors can be easily expressed in financial terms, others cannot. Qualitative factors, such as employee morale, cannot be measured in numerical terms. Due consideration must be given to both financial and nonfinancial factors in making decisions.

4. Unit-cost data can mislead decision makers in two major ways: (a) when costs that are irrelevant to a particular decision are included in unit costs, and (b) when unit costs that are computed at different output levels are used to choose among alternatives. Unitized fixed costs are often erroneously interpreted as if they behave like unit variable costs. Generally, use total costs rather than unit costs in relevant-cost analysis.

5. There are two common pitfalls in relevant-cost analysis, (a) assuming all variable costs are relevant, and (b) assuming all fixed costs are irrelevant.

6. Opportunity cost is the maximum available contribution to income that is forgone (rejected) by not using a limited resource in its next-best alternative use. The idea of an opportunity cost arises when there are multiple uses for resources and some alternatives are not selected. Opportunity cost is included in decision making because it represents the best alternative way in which an organization may have used its resources had it not made the decision it did.

7. In choosing among multiple products when resource capacity is constrained, managers should emphasize the product that yields the highest contribution margin per unit of the constraining or limiting factor.

8. Past revenues and costs, though irrelevant for decision making, can be useful in predicting future relevant revenues and relevant costs. Expected future revenues and costs are the only revenues and costs relevant in any decision model. The book value of existing equipment in equipment-replacement decisions represents past (historical) cost and therefore is irrelevant.

9. Top management faces a persistent challenge—that is, making sure that the performance-evaluation model is consistent with the decision model. A common inconsistency is to tell subordinate managers to take a multiple-year view in their decision making but then judge their performance only on the basis of the current year's operating income.

APPENDIX: LINEAR PROGRAMMING

Linear programming (LP) is an optimization technique used to maximize total contribution margin (the objective function), given multiple constraints. LP models typically assume that all costs can be classified as either variable or fixed with respect to a single driver (units of output). LP models also require certain other linear assumptions to hold. When these assumptions fail, other decision models should be considered.[1]

Consider the Power Recreation example described earlier in the chapter (pp. 396–397). Suppose that both the snowmobile and boat engines must be tested on a very expensive machine before they are shipped to customers. The available testing-machine time is limited. Production data are as follows:

Department	Available Daily Capacity in Hours	Use of Capacity in Hours per Unit of Product		Daily Maximum Production in Units	
		Snowmobile Engine	Boat Engine	Snowmobile Engine	Boat Engine
Assembly	600 machine-hours	2.0	5.0	300*	120
Testing	120 testing-hours	1.0	0.5	120	240

*For example, 600 machine-hours ÷ 2.0 machine-hours per snowmobile engine = 300, the maximum number of snowmobile engines that the Assembly Department can make if it works exclusively on snowmobile engines.

Exhibit 11-13 summarizes these and other relevant data. Note that snowmobile engines have a contribution margin of $240 and that boat engines have a contribution margin of $375. Material shortages for boat engines will limit production to 110 boat engines per day. How many engines of each type should be produced daily to maximize operating income?

Steps in Solving an LP Problem

We use the data in Exhibit 11-13 to illustrate the three steps in solving an LP problem. Throughout this discussion, S equals the number of units of snowmobiles produced and B equals the number of units of boat engines produced.

---

[1]Other decision models are described in G. Eppen, F. Gould, and C. Schmidt, *Quantitative Concepts for Management* (Englewood Cliffs, N.J.: Prentice-Hall, 1991); and S. Nahmias, *Production and Operations Analysis* (Homewood, Ill.: Irwin, 1993).

EXHIBIT 11-13
Operating Data for Power Recreation

Product	Department Capacity (per Day) in Product Units		Selling Price	Variable Cost per Unit	Contribution Margin per Unit
	Assembly	Testing			
Only snowmobile engines	300	120	$ 800	$560	$240
Only boat engines	120	240	$1,000	$625	$375

Step 1: Determine the Objective The **objective function** of a linear program expresses the objective or goal to be maximized (for example, operating income) or minimized (for example, operating costs). In our example, the objective is to find the combination of products that maximizes total contribution margin in the short run. Fixed costs remain the same regardless of the product mix chosen and are therefore irrelevant. The linear function expressing the objective for the total contribution margin (TCM) is

$$TCM = \$240S + \$375B$$

Step 2: Specify the Constraints A **constraint** is a mathematical inequality or equality that must be satisfied by the variables in a mathematical model. The following linear inequalities depict the relationships in our example:

Assembly Department constraint $\qquad$ $2S + 5B \leq 600$

Testing Department constraint $\qquad$ $1S + 0.5B \leq 120$

Material shortage constraint for boat engines $\qquad$ $B \leq 110$

Negative production is impossible $\qquad$ $S \geq 0 \text{ and } B \geq 0$

The coefficients of the constraints are often called technical coefficients. For example, in the Assembly Department, the technical coefficient is 2 machine-hours for snowmobile engines and 5 machine-hours for boat engines.

The three solid lines on the graph in Exhibit 11-14 show the existing constraints for Assembly and Testing and the material shortage constraint.[2] The feasible alternatives are those combinations of quantities of snowmobile engines and boat engines that satisfy all the constraining factors. The shaded "area of feasible solutions" in Exhibit 11-14 shows the boundaries of those product combinations that are feasible, or technically possible.

Step 3: Compute the Optimal Solution We present two approaches for finding the optimal solution: the trial-and-error approach and the graphic approach. These approaches are easy to use in our example because there are only two variables in the objective function and a small number of constraints. An understanding of these two approaches provides insight into LP modeling. In most real-world LP applications, however, managers use computer software packages to calculate the optimal solution.[3]

---

[2] As an example of how the lines are plotted in Exhibit 11-14, use equal signs instead of inequality signs and assume for the Assembly Department that B = 0; then S = 300 (600 machine-hours ÷ 2 machine-hours per snowmobile engine). Assume that S = 0; then B = 120 (600 machine-hours ÷ 5 machine-hours per boat engine). Connect those two points with a straight line.

[3] Although the trial-and-error and graphic approaches can be useful for two or possibly three variables, they are impractical when many variables exist. Standard computer software packages rely on the simplex method. The *simplex method* is an iterative step-by-step procedure for determining the optimal solution to an LP problem. It starts with a specific feasible solution and then tests it by substitution to see whether the result can be improved. These substitutions continue until no further improvement is possible and the optimal solution is obtained.

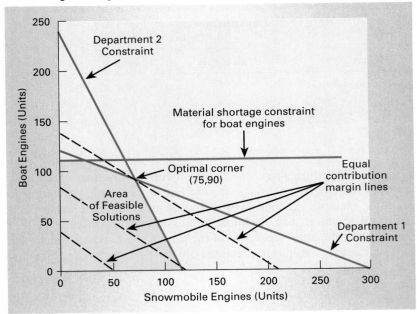

EXHIBIT 11-14
Linear Programming—Graphic Solution for Power Recreation

Trial-and-Error Approach   The optimal solution can be found by trial and error, by working with coordinates of the corners of the area of feasible solutions. The approach is simple.

First, select any set of corner points and compute the total contribution margin. Five corner points appear in Exhibit 11-14. It is helpful to use simultaneous equations to obtain the exact graph coordinates. To illustrate, the point ($S = 75$; $B = 90$) can be derived by solving the two pertinent constraint inequalities as simultaneous equations:

$$2S + 5B = 600 \qquad (1)$$

$$1S + 0.5B = 120 \qquad (2)$$

Multiplying (2) by 2.0, we get $\qquad 2S + 1B = 240 \qquad (3)$

Subtracting (3) from (1): $\qquad 4B = 360$

Therefore, $\qquad B = 360 \div 4 = 90$

Substituting for B in (2): $\qquad 1S + 0.5(90) = 120$

$$S = 120 - 45 = 75$$

Given $S = 75$ and $B = 90$, TCM = $240(75) + $375(90) = $51,750.

Second, move from corner point to corner point, computing the total contribution margin at each corner point. The total contribution margin, at each corner point is as follows:

Trial	Corner Point ($S; B$)	Snowmobile Engines (S)	Boat Engines (B)	Total Contribution Margin
1	(0; 0)	0	0	$240(0) + $375(0) = $ 0
2	(0; 110)	0	110	$240(0) + $375(110) = 41,250
3	(25; 110)	25	110	$240(25) + $375(110) = 47,250
4	(75; 90)	75	90	$240(75) + $375(90) = 51,750*
5	(120; 0)	120	0	$240(120) + $375(0) = 28,800

*Indicates the optimal solution.

The optimal product mix is the mix that yields the highest total contribution—75 snowmobile engines and 90 boat engines.

Graphic Approach Consider all possible combinations that will produce an equal total contribution margin of, say, $12,000. That is,

$$\$240S + \$375B = \$12,000$$

This set of $12,000 contribution margins is a straight dashed line in Exhibit 11-14 through ($S = 50$; $B = 0$) and ($S = 0$; $B = 32$). Other equal total contribution margins can be represented by lines parallel to this one. In Exhibit 11-14, we show three dashed lines. The equal total contribution margins increase as the lines get farther from the origin because lines drawn farther from the origin represent more sales of both snowmobile and boat engines.

The optimal line is the one farthest from the origin but still passing through a point in the area of feasible solutions. This line represents the highest contribution margin. The optimal solution is the point at the corner ($S = 75$; $B = 90$). This solution will become apparent if you put a ruler on the graph and move it outward from the origin and parallel with the $12,000 line. The idea is to move the ruler as far away from the origin as possible (that is, to increase the total contribution margin) without leaving the area of feasible solutions. In general, the optimal solution in a maximization problem lies at the corner where the dashed line intersects an extreme point of the area of feasible solutions. Moving the ruler out any further puts it outside the feasible region.

The key to the optimal solution is exchanging a given contribution margin per unit of scarce resource for some other contribution margin per unit of scarce resource. Examine Exhibit 11-14 and consider moving from corner ($S = 25$; $B = 110$) to corner ($S = 75$; $B = 90$). In the Assembly Department, each machine-hour devoted to 1 unit of boat engines (B) may be given up (sacrificed or traded) for 2.5 units of snowmobile engines (S) (5 hours required for 1 boat engine ÷ 2 hours required for 1 snowmobile engine). Will this exchange add to profitability? Yes, as shown here:

Total contribution margin at ($S = 25$; $B = 110$): $240 × 25 + $375 × 110		$47,250
Added contribution margin from product S by moving to corner ($S = 75$; $B = 90$): (75 – 25) × $240	$12,000	
Lost contribution margin from product B by moving to corner ($S = 75$; $B = 90$): (110 – 90) × $375	7,500	
Net additional contribution margin		4,500
Total contribution margin at ($S = 75$; $B = 90$): $240 × 75 + $375 × 90		$51,750

As we move from corner ($S = 25$; $B = 110$) to corner ($S = 75$; $B = 90$), we are contending with the Assembly Department constraint. In this department, there is a net advantage of trading 1 unit of B for 2.5 units of S. At corner ($S = 25$; $B = 110$), the Testing Department constraint comes into effect. Should we move to corner ($S = 120$; $B = 0$) along the Testing Department constraint? No, an analysis (not presented) similar to the one here will show that such a move is not worthwhile.

Sensitivity Analysis

What are the implications of uncertainty about the accounting or technical coefficients used in the LP model? Changes in coefficients affect the slope of the objective function (the equal contribution margin lines) or the area of feasible solutions. Consider how a change in the contribution margin of snowmobile engines from $240 to $300 per unit might affect the optimal solution. Assume the contribution margin for boat engines remains unchanged at $375 per unit. The revised objective function will be

$$TCM = \$300S + \$375B$$

Using the trial-and-error approach, calculate the total contribution margin for each of the five corner points described in the table on p. 408. The optimal solution is still ($S = 75$; $B = 90$).

Now suppose the contribution margin of snowmobile engines is lower than $240 per unit. By repeating the preceding steps, you will find that the optimal solution will not change so long as the contribution margin of the snowmobile engine does not fall below $150. *Big changes in the contribution margin per unit of snowmobile engines have no effect on the optimal solution.*

What happens if the contribution margin falls below $150? The optimal solution will then shift to the corner ($S = 25$; $B = 110$). Snowmobile engines now generate so little contribution margin per unit that Power Recreation will choose to shift its mix in favor of boat engines.

▼ TERMS TO LEARN

This chapter and the Glossary at the end of this book contain definitions of the following important terms:

book value (p. 400)	objective function (407)
business function costs (389)	opportunity cost (394)
constraint (407)	outlay costs (388)
decision model (384)	out-of-pocket costs (388)
differential cost (386)	outsourcing (390)
full product costs (390)	qualitative factors (386)
incremental costs (388)	quantitative factors (386)
insourcing (390)	relevant costs (385)
make-or-buy decisions (390)	relevant revenues (385)
net relevant cost (386)	sunk costs (402)

▼ ASSIGNMENT MATERIAL

QUESTIONS

11-1 Outline the five-step sequence in a decision process.

11-2 Define *relevant cost.* Why are historical costs irrelevant?

11-3 "All future costs are relevant." Do you agree? Why?

11-4 Distinguish between *quantitative* and *qualitative* factors in decision making.

11-5 Describe two ways in which unit-cost data can mislead a decision maker.

11-6 "Variable costs are always relevant, and fixed costs are always irrelevant." Do you agree? Why?

11-7 "A component part should be purchased whenever the purchase price is less than its total unit manufacturing cost." Do you agree? Why?

11-8 Define *opportunity cost.*

11-9 "Managers should always buy inventory in quantities that result in the lowest purchase cost per unit." Do you agree? Why?

11-10 "Management should always maximize sales of the product with the highest contribution margin per unit." Do you agree? Why?

11-11 "Cost written off as depreciation is always irrelevant." Do you agree? Why?

11-12 "Managers will always choose the alternative that maximizes operating income or minimizes costs in the decision model." Do you agree? Why?

11-13 Explain why book value of the old machine is irrelevant in a machine replacement decision.

11-14 Describe the three steps in solving a linear programming problem.

11-15 How might the optimal solution of a linear programming problem be determined?

EXERCISES

11-16 Disposal of assets.

1. A company has an inventory of 1,000 assorted parts for a line of missiles that has been discontinued. The inventory cost is $80,000. The parts can be either (a) remachined at total additional costs of $30,000 and then sold for $35,000, or (b) sold as scrap for $2,000. Which action should be taken?

2. A truck, costing $100,000 and uninsured, is wrecked its first day in use. It can be either (a) disposed of for $10,000 cash and replaced with a similar truck costing $102,000, or (b) rebuilt for $85,000 and thus be brand-new as far as operating characteristics and looks are concerned. What should be done?

11-17 The careening personal computer. (W. A. Paton) An employee in the Accounting Department of a certain business was moving a personal computer from one room to another. As he came alongside an open stairway, he carelessly slipped and let the computer get away from him. It went careening down the stairs with a great racket and wound up at the bottom, completely wrecked. Hearing the crash, the office manager came rushing out and turned rather pale when he saw what had happened. "Someone tell me quickly," the manager yelled, "if that is one of our fully depreciated items." A check of the accounting records showed that the smashed computer was, indeed, one of those items that had been written off. "Thank God!" said the manager.

REQUIRED

Explain and comment on the point of this anecdote.

11-18 Multiple choice. (CPA) Choose the best answer.

1. The Woody Company manufactures slippers and sells them at $10 a pair. Variable manufacturing costs are $4.50 a pair, and allocated fixed manufacturing costs are $1.50 a pair. It has enough idle capacity available to accept a one-time-only special order of 20,000 pairs of slippers at $6 a pair. Woody will not incur any marketing costs as a result of the special order. What would the effect on operating income be if the special order could be accepted without affecting normal sales? (a) $0, (b) $30,000 increase, (c) $90,000 increase, (d) $120,000 increase.

2. The Reno Company manufactures Part No. 498 for use in its production line. The manufacturing costs per unit for 20,000 units of Part No. 498 are as follows:

Direct materials	$ 6
Direct manufacturing labor	30
Variable manufacturing overhead	12
Fixed manufacturing overhead allocated	16
	$64

The Tray Company has offered to sell 20,000 units of Part No. 498 to Reno for $60 per unit. Reno will make the decision to buy the part from Tray if there is an overall savings of at least $25,000 for Reno. If Reno accepts Tray's offer, $9 per unit of the fixed overhead allocated would be totally eliminated. Furthermore, Reno has determined that the released facilities could be used to save relevant costs in the manufacture of Part No. 575. For Reno to have an overall savings of $25,000, the amount of relevant costs that would have to be saved by using the released facilities in the manufacture of Part No. 575 would be (a) $80,000, (b) $85,000, (c) $125,000, (d) $140,000.

11-19 Special order, activity-based costing. (CMA, adapted) The Award Plus Company manufactures medals for winners of athletic events and other contests. Its manufacturing plant has the capacity to produce 10,000 medals each month; current production and sales are 7,500 medals per month. The company normally charges $150 per medal. Cost information for the current activity level is as follows:

Variable costs that vary with units produced	
Direct materials	$ 262,500
Direct manufacturing labor	300,000
Variable costs (for setups, materials handling, quality control, and so on) that vary with number of batches, 150 batches × $500 per batch	75,000
Fixed manufacturing costs	275,000
Fixed marketing costs	175,000
Total costs	$1,087,500

Award Plus has just received a special one-time-only order for 2,500 medals at $100 per medal. Award Plus makes medals for its existing customers in batch sizes of 50 medals (150 batches × 50 medals per batch = 7,500 medals). The special order requires Award Plus to make the medals in 25 batches of 100 each.

REQUIRED

1. Should Award Plus accept this special order? Why? Explain briefly.
2. Suppose plant capacity was only 9,000 medals instead of 10,000 medals each month. The special order must either be taken in full or rejected totally. Should Award Plus accept the special order?
3. As in requirement 1, assume that monthly capacity is 10,000 medals. Award Plus is concerned that if it accepts the special order, its existing customers will immediately demand a price discount of $10 in the month in which the special order is being filled. They would argue that Award Plus's capacity costs are now being spread over more units, and that existing customers should get the benefit of these lower costs. Should Award Plus accept the special order under these conditions? Show all calculations.

11-20 Make versus buy, activity-based costing. The Svenson Corporation manufactures cellular modems. It manufactures its own cellular modem circuit boards (CMCB), an important part of the cellular modem. It reports the following cost information about the costs of making CMCBs in 19_7 and the expected costs in 19_8:

	Current Costs in 19_7	Expected Costs in 19_8
Variable manufacturing costs		
Direct materials costs per CMCB	$ 180	$ 170
Direct manufacturing labor costs per CMCB	50	45
Variable manufacturing costs per batch for setups, material handling, and quality control	1,600	1,500
Fixed manufacturing costs		
Fixed manufacturing overhead costs that can be avoided if CMCBs are not made	320,000	320,000
Fixed manufacturing overhead costs of plant depreciation, insurance, and administration that cannot be avoided even if CMCBs are not made	800,000	800,000

Svenson manufactured 8,000 CMCBs in 19_7 in 40 batches of 200 each. In 19_8, Svenson anticipates needing 10,000 CMCBs. The CMCBs would be needed in 80 batches of 125 each.

The Minton Corporation has approached Svenson about supplying CMCBs to Svenson in 19_8 at $300 per CMCB on whatever delivery schedule Svenson wants.

REQUIRED

1. Calculate the total expected manufacturing (absorption) cost per unit of making CMCBs in 19_8.

2. Suppose the capacity currently used to make CMCBs will become idle if Svenson purchases CMCBs from Minton. Should Svenson make CMCBs or buy them from Minton?

3. Now suppose that if Svenson purchases CMCBs from Minton, its best alternative use of the capacity currently used to make CMCBs is to make and sell special circuit boards (CB3s) to the Essex Corporation. Svenson estimates the following incremental revenues and costs from CB3s:

Total expected incremental future revenues	$2,000,000
Total expected incremental future costs	$2,150,000

Should Svenson make CMCBs or buy them from Minton?

11-21 Which bases to close, relevant-cost analysis, opportunity costs. The U.S. Defense Department has the difficult decision of deciding which military bases to close down. Military and political factors obviously matter, but cost savings are also an important factor. Consider two naval bases located on the West Coast—one in Alameda, California, and the other in Everett, Washington. The Navy has decided that it needs only one of those two bases permanently, so one must be shut down. The decision regarding which base to shut down will be made on cost considerations alone. The following information is available:

a. The Alameda base was built at a cost of $10 million. The operating costs of the base are $400 million per year. The base is built on land owned by the Navy, so the Navy pays nothing for the use of the property. If the base is closed, the land will be sold to developers for $500 million.

b. The Everett base was built at a cost of $15 million on land leased by the Navy from private citizens. The Navy can choose to lease the land permanently for an annual lease payment of $3 million per year. If it decides to keep the Everett base open, the Navy plans to invest $60 million in a fixed income note, which at 5% interest will earn the $3 million the government needs for the lease payments. The land and buildings will immediately revert back to the owner if the base is closed. The operating costs of the base, excluding lease payments, are $300 million per year.

c. If the Alameda base is closed down, the Navy will have to transfer some personnel to the Everett facility. As a result, the yearly operating costs at Everett will increase by $100 million per year. If the Everett facility is closed down, no extra costs will be incurred to operate the Alameda facility.

REQUIRED

The California delegation in Congress argues that it is cheaper to close down the Everett base for two reasons: (1) It would save $100 million per year in additional costs required to operate the Everett base, and (2) it would save $3 million dollars per year in lease payments. (Recall that the Alameda base requires no cash payments for use of the land because the land is owned by the Navy.) Do you agree with the California delegation's arguments and conclusions? In your answer, identify and explain all costs that you consider relevant and all costs that you consider irrelevant for the base-closing decision.

11-22 Inventory decision, opportunity cost. Lawnox, a manufacturer of lawn mowers, predicts that 240,000 spark plugs will have to be purchased during the next year. The manufacturer estimates that 20,000 spark plugs will be required each month. A supplier quotes a price of $8 per spark plug. The supplier also offers a special discount option: If all 240,000 spark plugs are purchased at the start of the year, a discount of 5% off the $8 price will be given. Lawnox can invest its cash at 8% per year.

REQUIRED

1. What is the opportunity cost of interest forgone from purchasing all 240,000 units at the start of the year instead of in 12 monthly purchases of 20,000 units per order?

2. Would this opportunity cost ordinarily be recorded in the accounting system? Why?

3. Should Lawnox purchase 240,000 units at the start of the year or 20,000 units each month?

11-23 Relevant costs, contribution margin, product emphasis. The Beach Comber is a take-out food store at a popular beach resort. Susan Sexton, owner of the Beach Comber, is deciding how much refrigerator space to devote to four different drinks. Pertinent data on these four drinks are as follows:

	Cola	Lemonade	Punch	Natural Orange Juice
Selling price per case	$18.00	$19.20	$26.40	$38.40
Variable costs per case	$13.50	$15.20	$20.10	$30.20
Cases sold per foot of shelf space per day	25	24	4	5

Sexton has a maximum front shelf space of 12 feet to devote to the four drinks. She wants a minimum of 1 foot and a maximum of 6 feet of front shelf space for each drink.

REQUIRED

1. What is the contribution margin per case of each type of drink?

2. A co-worker of Sexton's recommends that she maximize the shelf space devoted to those drinks with the highest contribution margin per case. Evaluate this recommendation.

3. What shelf-space allocation for the four drinks would you recommend for the Beach Comber?

11-24 Selection of most profitable product. Body-Builders, Inc., produces two basic types of weight-lifting equipment, Model 9 and Model 14. Pertinent data are as follows:

	Per Unit	
	Model 9	Model 14
Sales price	$100.00	$70.00
Costs		
Direct materials	$ 28.00	$13.00
Direct manufacturing labor	15.00	25.00
Variable manufacturing overhead*	25.00	12.50
Fixed manufacturing overhead*	10.00	5.00
Marketing costs (all variable)	14.00	10.00
Total costs	$ 92.00	$65.50
Operating income	$ 8.00	$ 4.50

*Allocated on the basis of machine-hours.

The weight-lifting craze is such that enough of either Model 9 or Model 14 can be sold to keep the plant operating at full capacity. Both products are processed through the same production departments.

REQUIRED

Which product should be produced? If both should be produced, indicate the proportions of each. Briefly explain your answer.

11-25 Adding and dropping business segments (continuation of the Allied West example described in the chapter). Refer to the information in Exhibit 11-8 (p. 399) and the information on Allied West's costs on p. 398. Further assume these facts:

a. General administration costs at Allied West of $48,000 include depreciation of $10,000 on furniture and office equipment that has zero terminal disposal price.

b. Allied Furniture has decided to allocate corporate-office costs to all its warehouse locations, including $25,000 to Allied West. Corporate-office costs consist of top management salaries and corporate-image advertising costs. Allied West shows a loss of $7,000 after corporate-office allocations—$18,000 operating income (Exhibit 11-8) minus $25,000 corporate-office costs. Because Allied West's operating income does not cover corporate-office costs, Allied Furniture is contemplating closing Allied West.

REQUIRED

Show the relevant revenues and relevant costs that help answer the following questions:

1. Should Allied West be shut down?
2. Suppose Allied Furniture had the opportunity to open a new office whose revenues and costs were identical to Allied West. Should Allied Furniture open such an office?

11-26 Customer profitability, choosing customers. Broadway Printers operates a printing press with a monthly capacity of 2,000 machine hours. Broadway has two main customers, Taylor Corporation and Kelly Corporation. Data on each customer for January follows:

	Taylor Corporation	Kelly Corporation	Total
Revenues	$120,000	$80,000	$200,000
Variable costs	42,000	48,000	90,000
Fixed costs (allocated on the basis of revenues)	60,000	40,000	100,000
Total operating costs	102,000	88,000	190,000
Operating income	$ 18,000	$ (8,000)	$ 10,000
Machine hours required	1,500 hours	500 hours	2,000 hours

Each of the following requirements refers only to the preceding data; there is *no connection* between the requirements.

REQUIRED

1. Should Broadway drop the Kelly Corporation business? If Broadway drops the Kelly Corporation business, its total fixed costs will decrease by 20%.
2. Kelly Corporation indicates that it wants Broadway to do an *additional* $80,000 worth of printing jobs during February. These jobs are identical to the existing business Broadway did for Kelly in January in terms of variable costs and machine hours required. Broadway anticipates that the business from Taylor Corporation in February would be the same as that in January. Broadway can choose to accept as much of the Taylor and Kelly business for February as it wants. Assume that total fixed costs for February will be the same as the fixed costs in January. What should Broadway do? What will Broadway's operating income be in February?

11-27 Relevance of equipment costs. The Auto Wash Company has just today paid for and installed a special machine for polishing cars at one of its several outlets. It is the first day of the company's fiscal year. The machine cost $20,000. Its annual operating costs total $15,000, exclusive of depreciation. The machine will have a 4-year useful life and a zero terminal disposal price.

After the machine has been used for a day, a machine salesperson offers a different machine that promises to do the same job at a yearly operating cost of $9,000, exclusive of depreciation. The new machine will cost $24,000 cash, installed. The "old" machine is unique and can be sold outright for only $10,000, minus $2,000 removal cost. The new machine, like the old one, will have a 4-year useful life and zero terminal disposal price.

Sales, all in cash, will be $150,000 annually, and other cash costs will be $110,000 annually, regardless of this decision.

For simplicity, ignore income taxes, interest, and present-value considerations.

REQUIRED

1. (a) Prepare a statement of cash receipts and disbursements for each of the 4 years under both alternatives. What is the cumulative difference in cash

flow for the 4 years taken together? (b) Prepare income statements for each of the 4 years under both alternatives. Assume straight-line depreciation. What is the cumulative difference in operating income for the 4 years taken together? (c) What are the irrelevant items in your presentations in requirements a and b? Why are they irrelevant?

2. Suppose the cost of the "old" machine was $1 million rather than $20,000. Nevertheless, the old machine can be sold outright for only $10,000, minus $2,000 removal cost. Would the net differences in requirements 1 and 2 change? Explain.

3. "To avoid a loss, we should keep the old machine." What is the role of book value in decisions about replacement of machines?

11-28 Equipment upgrade versus replacement. (A. Spero, adapted) The Pacifica Corporation makes steel table lamps. It is considering either upgrading its existing production line or replacing it. The production equipment was purchased 2 years ago for $600,000. It has an expected useful life of 5 years, a terminal disposal price of $0, and is depreciated on a straight-line basis at the rate of $120,000 per year. It has a current book value of $360,000 and a current disposal price of $90,000. The following table presents expected costs under the upgrade and replace alternatives:

	Upgrade	Replace
Expected one-time-only capital costs	$300,000	$750,000
Variable manufacturing costs per unit	$12	$9
Expected production and sales per year	60,000 units	60,000 units
Selling price per unit	$25	$25

The expected useful life after the machine is upgraded or replaced is 3 years, and the expected terminal disposal price is $0. If the machine is upgraded, the $300,000 would be added to the current book value of $360,000 and depreciated on a straight-line basis. The new equipment, if purchased, will also be depreciated on a straight-line basis.

For simplicity, ignore income taxes, interest, and present-value considerations.

REQUIRED

1. Should Pacifica upgrade its production line or replace it?

2. (a) Now suppose the capital expenditure needed to replace the production line is not known. All other data are as given previously. What is the maximum price that Pacifica would be willing to pay for the new line to prefer replacing the existing line over upgrading it? (b) Assume that the capital expenditure needed to replace the production line is $750,000. Now suppose the expected production and sales quantity is not known. For what production and sales quantity would Pacifica prefer to (a) replace the line, (b) upgrade the line?

3. Consider again the basic information given in this exercise. Suppose John Azinger, the manager of the Pacifica Corporation, is evaluated on operating income. The upcoming year's operating income is crucial to Azinger's bonus. What alternative would Azinger choose?

PROBLEMS

11-29 Special-order decision. The Modern Packing Corporation (MPC) specializes in the manufacture of 1-liter plastic bottles. The plastic molding machines are capable of producing 100 bottles per hour. The firm estimates that the variable cost of producing a plastic bottle is 25 cents. The bottles are sold for 55 cents each.

Management has been approached by a local toy company that would like the firm to produce a molded plastic toy for them. The toy company is willing to pay $3.00 per unit for the toy. The unit variable cost to manufacture the toy will be $2.40. In addition, MPC would have to incur a cost of $20,000 to construct the mold required exclusively for this order. Because the toy uses more plastic and is of a more intricate shape than a bottle, a molding machine can produce only 40 units per hour. The customer wants 100,000 units. Assume that MPC has a total capacity of 10,000 machine-hours available during the period in which the toy company wants delivery of the toys. The firm's fixed costs, *excluding* the costs to construct the toy mold, during the same period will be $200,000.

REQUIRED

1. Suppose the demand for its bottles is 750,000 units, and the special toy order has to be either taken in full or rejected totally. Should MPC accept the special toy order? Explain your answer.

2. Suppose the demand for its bottles is 850,000 units, and the special toy order has to be either taken in full or rejected totally. Should MPC accept the special toy order? Explain your answer.

3. Suppose the demand for its bottles is 850,000 units, and MPC can accept any quantity of the special toy order. How many bottles and toys should it manufacture?

4. Suppose the demand for its bottles is 900,000 units, and the special toy order has to be either taken in full or rejected totally. Should MPC accept the special toy order? Explain your answer.

5. Suppose the demand for its bottles is 900,000 units, and MPC can accept any quantity of the special toy order. How many bottles and toys should it manufacture?

6. Suppose the demand for its bottles is 950,000 units and MPC can accept any quantity of the special toy order. How many bottles and toys should it manufacture?

7. The management has located a firm that has just entered the molded plastic business. This firm has considerable excess capacity and more efficient molding machines, and is willing to subcontract the toy job, or any portion of it, for $2.80 per unit. It will construct its own toy mold. Suppose the demand for its bottles is 900,000 units, and MPC can accept any quantity of the special toy order. How many bottles and toys should MPC manufacture? How many toys should it subcontract out?

11-30 Opportunity cost. (H. Schaefer) The Wolverine Corporation is working at full production capacity producing 10,000 units of a unique product, Rosebo. Manufacturing costs per unit for Rosebo are as follows:

Direct materials	$ 2
Direct manufacturing labor	3
Manufacturing overhead	5
	$10

The unit manufacturing overhead cost is based on a variable cost per unit of $2 and fixed costs of $30,000 (at full capacity of 10,000 units). The selling costs, all variable, are $4 per unit, and the selling price is $20 per unit.

A customer, the Miami Company, has asked Wolverine to produce 2,000 units of Orangebo, a modification of Rosebo. Orangebo would require the same manufacturing processes as Rosebo. The Miami Company has offered to pay Wolverine $15 for a unit of Orangebo and half the selling costs per unit.

REQUIRED

1. What is the opportunity cost to Wolverine of producing the 2,000 units of Orangebo? (Assume that no overtime is worked.)

2. The Buckeye Corporation has offered to produce 2,000 units of Rosebo for Wolverine so that Wolverine may accept the Orangebo offer. That is, if Wolverine accepts the Buckeye offer, Wolverine would manufacture

8,000 units of Rosebo and 2,000 units of Orangebo and purchase 2,000 units of Rosebo from Buckeye. Buckeye would charge Wolverine $14 per unit to manufacture Rosebo. Should Wolverine accept the Buckeye offer? (Support your conclusions with specific analysis.)

3. Suppose Wolverine had been working at less than full capacity, producing 8,000 units of Rosebo at the time the Orangebo offer was made. What is the minimum price Wolverine should accept for Orangebo under these conditions? (Ignore the previous $15 unit price.)

11-31 Contribution approach, relevant costs. Air Frisco owns a single jet aircraft and operates between San Francisco and the Fiji Islands. Flights leave San Francisco on Mondays and Thursdays and depart from Fiji on Wednesdays and Saturdays. Air Frisco cannot offer any more flights between San Francisco and Fiji. Only tourist-class seats are available on its planes. An analyst has collected the following information:

Seating capacity per plane	360 passengers
Average number of passengers per flight	200 passengers
Flights per week	4 flights
Flights per year	208 flights
Average one-way fare	$500
Variable fuel costs	$14,000 per flight
Food and beverage service cost (no charge to passenger)	$20 per passenger
Commission to travel agents paid by Air Frisco (all tickets are booked by travel agents)	8% of fare
Fixed annual lease costs allocated to each flight	$53,000 per flight
Fixed ground services (maintenance, check in, baggage handling) cost allocated to each flight	$7,000 per flight
Fixed flight crew salaries allocated to each flight	$4,000 per flight

For simplicity, assume that fuel costs are unaffected by the actual number of passengers on a flight.

REQUIRED
1. What is the operating income that Air Frisco makes on each one-way flight between San Francisco and Fiji?
2. The Market Research Department of Air Frisco indicates that lowering the average one-way fare to $480 will increase the average number of passengers per flight to 212. Should Air Frisco lower its fare?
3. Travel International, a tour operator, approaches Air Frisco on the possibility of chartering (renting out) its jet aircraft twice each month, first to take Travel International's tourists from San Francisco to Fiji and then to bring the tourists back from Fiji to San Francisco. If Air Frisco accepts Travel International's offer, Air Frisco will be able to offer only 184 (208 − 24) of its own flights each year. The terms of the charter are as follows: (a) For each one-way flight, Travel International will pay Air Frisco $75,000 to charter the plane and to use its flight crew and ground service staff; (b) Travel International will pay for fuel costs; and (c) Travel International will pay for all food costs. On purely financial considerations, should Air Frisco accept Travel International's offer? What other factors should Air Frisco consider in deciding whether or not to charter its plane to Travel International?

11-32 Make or buy, unknown level of volume. (A. Atkinson) Oxford Engineering manufactures small engines. The engines are sold to manufacturers who install them in such products as lawn mowers. The company currently manufactures all the parts used in these engines but is considering a proposal from an external supplier who wishes to supply the starter assembly used in these engines.

The starter assembly is currently manufactured in Division 3 of Oxford Engineering. The costs relating to Division 3 for the last 12 months were as follows:

Direct materials	$200,000
Direct manufacturing labor	150,000
Manufacturing overhead	400,000
Total	$750,000

Over the last year, Division 3 manufactured 150,000 starter assemblies; the average cost for the starter assembly is computed as $5 ($750,000 ÷ 150,000).

Further analysis of manufacturing overhead revealed the following information. Of the total manufacturing overhead reported, only 25% is considered variable. Of the fixed portion, $150,000 is an allocation of general overhead that would remain unchanged for the company as a whole if production of the starter assembly is discontinued. A further $100,000 of the fixed overhead is avoidable if self-manufacture of the starter assembly is discontinued. The balance of the current fixed overhead, $50,000, is the division manager's salary. If self-manufacture of the starter assembly is discontinued, the manager of Division 3 will be transferred to Division 2 at the same salary. This move will allow the company to save the $40,000 salary that would otherwise be paid to attract an outsider to this position.

REQUIRED

1. Tidnish Electronics, a reliable supplier, has offered to supply starter assembly units at $4 per unit. Since this price is less than the current average cost of $5 per unit, the vice president of manufacturing is eager to accept this offer. Should the outside offer be accepted? (*Hint:* Production output in the coming year may be different from production output in the last year.)

2. How, if at all, would your response to requirement 1 change if the company could use the vacated plant space for storage and, in so doing, avoid $50,000 of outside storage charges currently incurred? Why is this information relevant or irrelevant?

11-33 **Make versus buy, activity-based costing, opportunity costs.** (N. Melumad and S. Reichelstein, adapted) The Ace Bicycle Company produces bicycles. This year's expected production is 10,000 units. Currently, Ace makes the chains for its bicycles. Ace's accountant reports the following costs for making the 10,000 bicycle chains:

	Costs per Unit	Costs for 10,000 Units
Direct materials	$4.00	$ 40,000
Direct labor	2.00	20,000
Variable manufacturing overhead (power and utilities)	1.50	15,000
Inspection, setup, material handling		2,000
Machine rent		3,000
Allocated fixed costs of plant administration, taxes, and insurance		30,000
Total costs		$110,000

Ace has received an offer from an outside vendor to supply any number of chains Ace requires at $8.20 per chain. The following additional information is available:

a. Inspection, setup, and materials handling costs vary with the number of batches in which the chains are produced. Ace produces chains in batch sizes of 1,000 units. Ace estimates that it will produce the 10,000 units in ten batches.

b. Ace rents the machine used to make the chains. If Ace buys all its chains from the outside vendor, it does not need to pay rent on this machine.

REQUIRED

1. Assume that if Ace purchases the chains from the outside supplier, the facility where the chains are currently made will remain idle. Should Ace accept the outside supplier's offer at the anticipated production (and sales) volume of 10,000 units?

2. For this question, assume that if the chains are purchased outside, the facilities where the chains are currently made will be used to upgrade the bicycles by adding mud flaps and reflectors. As a consequence, the selling price on bicycles will be raised by $20. The variable per unit cost of the upgrade would be $18, and additional tooling costs of $16,000 would be incurred. Should Ace make or buy the chains, assuming that 10,000 units are produced (and sold)?

3. The sales manager at Ace is concerned that the estimate of 10,000 units may be high and believes that only 6,200 units will be sold. Production will be cut back, and this opens up work space, which can be used to add the mud flaps and reflectors whether Ace goes outside for the chains or makes them in-house. At this lower output, Ace will produce the chains in eight batches of 775 units each. Should Ace purchase the chains from the outside vendor?

11-34 Relevant cost of materials. The Hernandez Corporation is bidding on a new construction contract, here called Contract No. 1. If the bid is accepted, work will begin in a few days on January 1, 19_7. Contract No. 1 requires a special cement. Hernandez has already purchased 10,000 pounds of the special cement for $20,000. The current purchase cost of the cement is $2.40 per pound. The company could sell the cement now for $1.60 per pound after all selling costs.

Hernandez will also bid on Contract No. 2 one month from now. If Contract No. 1 is not landed, the special cement will be available for Contract No. 2. If Contract No. 1 is landed, Hernandez will need to buy 10,000 pounds of another grade of cement for $2.10 per pound to fulfil Contract No. 2.

If it is not used in either of these two ways, the special cement would be of no use to the company and would be sold a little more than a month from now for $1.50 per pound after all selling costs.

The president of Hernandez, Julio Gomez, is puzzled about the appropriate total cost of the special cement to be used in bidding on Contract No. 1. Competition is intense and markups are very thin, so determining the relevant material costs when bidding on Contract No. 1 is crucial.

REQUIRED

1. Suppose Gomez is certain that Hernandez would land Contract No. 2, what (relevant) cost figure should Gomez use for the special cement when bidding on Contract No. 1?

2. This part requires knowledge of the material on decision making under uncertainty in the Appendix to Chapter 3. Suppose Gomez estimates a probability of 0.7 that Hernandez would land Contract No. 2. What (relevant) cost figure should Gomez use for the special cement when bidding on Contract No. 1?

3. Suppose Hernandez could sell the special cement now for $2.30 per pound after all selling costs (instead of $1.60 per pound described in paragraph 1). Suppose Gomez is certain that Hernandez would land Contract No. 2. What (relevant) cost figure should Gomez use for the special cement when preparing a bid on Contract No. 1?

11-35 Discontinuing a product line, selling more product, activity-based costing. Home Furnishings makes bookshelves, tables, and beds. The following sales and cost information is available about the profitability of each of these lines:

	Bookshelves	Tables	Beds	Total
Revenues	$750,000	$500,000	$1,000,000	$2,250,000
Direct materials	300,000	220,000	400,000	920,000
Direct manufacturing labor	75,000	60,000	80,000	215,000
Setups and materials handling	45,000	40,000	60,000	145,000
Depreciation on tools and fixtures	50,000	48,000	72,000	170,000
Marketing and distribution	75,000	60,000	120,000	255,000
General administration and facilities	150,000	100,000	200,000	450,000
Total costs	695,000	528,000	932,000	2,155,000
Operating income (loss)	$ 55,000	$ (28,000)	$ 68,000	$ 95,000

Home Furnishings uses an activity-based cost system to assign costs to products. The following additional information is available:

a. Direct materials and direct manufacturing labor costs vary with the number of units of products manufactured.

b. Setups and materials handling costs vary with the number of batches made.

c. Tools and fixtures have 1-year lives and zero disposal prices.

d. Of the total marketing and distribution costs, $112,500 are fixed costs allocated to product lines on the basis of sales revenue. Fixed marketing and distribution costs allocated to a product line can be avoided if the line is discontinued. The remaining marketing costs vary with the number of shipments made.

e. General administration and facilities costs are fixed costs that will not change if sales of individual product lines are increased or decreased or if product lines are added or dropped. These costs are allocated to product lines on the basis of sales revenues.

REQUIRED

In answering the following requirements, assume that prices of the various products do not change.

1. Should Home Furnishings discontinue the tables product line assuming the released facilities remain idle? Assume Home Furnishings has already acquired the tools and fixtures it needs to manufacture tables.

2. Suppose that if Home Furnishings discontinues the tables product line, the released facilities could be used to sell beds worth an additional $250,000. This would require Home Furnishings to purchase tools and fixtures for $4,000. Assume that there will be no change in either the number of batches in which beds are made or the number of shipments.

   a. On the basis of your calculations, should Home Furnishings discontinue the tables product line?

   b. What is the opportunity cost of continuing the tables product line?

   c. What other factors should Home Furnishings consider before making a decision?

3. What would be the effect on operating income if Home Furnishings could double its sales of tables? Assume that at the higher sales, both the number of batches and shipments would be three times and purchases of tools and fixtures would be twice the current levels.

11-36 **Considering three alternatives.** (CMA) The Auer Company had just completed an order for a special machine from the Jay Company when the Jay Company declared bankruptcy, defaulted on the order, and forfeited the 10% deposit paid on the selling price of $72,500. Auer's manufacturing manager identified the costs already incurred in the production of the special machine for Jay as follows:

Direct materials used		$16,600
Direct manufacturing labor incurred		21,400
Overhead allocated		
Manufacturing		
Variable	$10,700	
Fixed	5,350	16,050
Fixed marketing and administrative		5,405
Total costs		$59,455

Another company, the Kaytell Corporation, would be interested in buying the special machine if it is reworked to Kaytell's specifications. Auer offered to sell the reworked machine to Kaytell as a special order for a net price (price minus cash discount, if any) of $68,400. Kaytell has agreed to pay the net price when it takes delivery in 2 months. The additional traceable costs to rework the machine to Kaytell's specifications are as follows:

Direct materials	$ 6,200
Direct manufacturing labor	4,200
	$10,400

A second alternative available to Auer is to convert the special machine to the standard model. The standard model lists for $62,500. The additional incremental costs to convert the special machine to the standard model are

Direct materials	$2,850
Direct manufacturing labor	3,300
	$6,150

A third alternative for the Auer Company is to sell, as a special order, the machine as is (that is, without modification) for a net price of $52,000. However, the potential buyer of the unmodified machine does not want it for 60 days. The buyer offers a $7,000 down payment with final payment upon delivery.

The following additional information is available regarding Auer's operations:

◆ The sales commission rate is 2% on sales of standard models and 3% on special orders. All sales commissions are calculated on net selling price (that is, list price minus cash discount, if any).

◆ Normal credit terms for sales of standard models are 2/10, n/30 (2/10 means a discount of 2% is given if payment is made within 10 days; n/30 means full amount is due within 30 days). Customers take the discounts except in rare instances. Credit terms for special orders are negotiated with the customer.

◆ The allocation rates for manufacturing overhead and the fixed marketing and administrative costs are

Manufacturing	
Variable	50% of direct manufacturing labor costs
Fixed	25% of direct manufacturing labor costs
Marketing and administration	
Fixed	10% of the total of direct materials, direct manufacturing labor costs, and manufacturing overhead costs

◆ Normal time required for rework is 1 month.
◆ A surcharge of 5% of the selling price is placed on all customer requests for minor modifications of standard models.
◆ Auer normally sells a sufficient number of standard models for the company to operate at a volume in excess of the breakeven point.

Auer does not consider the time value of money in their analyses of special orders whenever the time period is less than 1 year because the effect is not significant.

REQUIRED

1. Determine the dollar contribution that each of the three alternatives will add to the Auer Company's operating income.

2. If Kaytell makes Auer a counteroffer, what is the lowest price Auer should accept from Kaytell for the reworked machine? Explain your answer.

3. Discuss the influence that fixed manufacturing overhead costs should have on the selling prices Auer quotes for special orders when (a) the firm is operating at or below the breakeven point; and (b) the firm's special orders constitute efficient utilization of unused capacity above the breakeven point.

11-37 **Multiple choice, comprehensive problem on relevant costs.** The following are the Class Company's *unit* costs of manufacturing and marketing a high-style pen at a level of 20,000 units per month:

Manufacturing costs	
Direct materials	$1.00
Direct manufacturing labor	1.20
Variable manufacturing indirect costs	0.80
Fixed manufacturing indirect costs	0.50
Marketing costs	
Variable	1.50
Fixed	0.90

REQUIRED

The following situations refer only to the preceding data; there is *no connection* between the situations. Unless stated otherwise, assume a regular selling price of $6 per unit.

Choose the best answer to each of the seven questions. Support each answer with summarized computations.

1. In an inventory of 10,000 units of the high-style pen presented on the balance sheet, the unit cost used is (a) $3.00, (b) $3.50, (c) $5.00, (d) $2.20, (e) $5.90.

2. The pen is usually produced and sold at the rate of 240,000 units per year (an average of 20,000 per month). The selling price is $6 per unit, which yields total annual sales of $1,440,000. Total costs are $1,416,000, and operating income is $24,000, or $0.10 per unit. Market research estimates that unit sales could be increased by 10% if prices were cut to $5.80. Assuming the implied cost-behavior patterns to be correct, this action, if taken, would

   a. Decrease operating income by a net of $7,200.
   b. Decrease operating income by $0.20 per unit ($48,000) but increase operating income by 10% of sales ($144,000) for a net increase of $96,000.
   c. Decrease unit fixed costs by 10%, or $0.14, per unit, and thus decrease operating income by $0.06 ($0.20 – $0.14) per unit.
   d. Increase unit sales to 264,000 units, which at the $5.80 price would give total sales of $1,531,200; costs of $5.90 per unit for 264,000 units would be $1,557,600, and a loss of $26,400 would result.
   e. None of these.

3. A cost contract with the government for 5,000 units of the pens calls for the reimbursement of all manufacturing costs plus a fixed fee of $1,000. No variable marketing costs are incurred on the government contract. You are required to compare the following two alternatives:

Sales Each Month to	Alternative A	Alternative B
Regular customers	15,000 units	15,000 units
Government	0 units	5,000 units

Operating income under alternative B is greater than that under alternative A by (a) $1,000, (b) $2,500, (c) $3,500, (d) $300, (e) none of these.

4. Assume the same data with respect to the government contract as in requirement 3 except that the two alternatives to be compared are

Sales Each Month to	Alternative A	Alternative B
Regular customers	20,000 units	15,000 units
Government	0 units	5,000 units

Operating income under alternative B relative to that under alternative A is (a) $4,000 less, (b) $3,000 greater, (c) $6,500 less, (d) $500 greater, (e) none of these.

5. The company wants to enter a foreign market in which price competition is keen. The company seeks a one-time-only special order for 10,000 units on a minimum-unit-price basis. It expects that shipping costs for this order will amount to only $0.75 per unit, but the fixed costs of obtaining the contract will be $4,000. The company incurs no variable marketing costs other than shipping costs. Domestic business will be unaffected. The selling price to break even is (a) $3.50, (b) $4.15, (c) $4.25, (d) $3.00, (e) $5.00.

6. The company has an inventory of 1,000 units of pens that must be sold immediately at reduced prices. Otherwise, the inventory will be worthless. The unit cost that is relevant for establishing the minimum selling price is (a) $4.50, (b) $4.00, (c) $3.00, (d) $5.90, (e) $1.50.

7. A proposal is received from an outside supplier who will make and ship these high-style pens directly to the Class Company's customers as sales orders are forwarded from Class's sales staff. Class's fixed marketing costs will be unaffected, but its variable marketing costs will be slashed by 20%. Class's plant will be idle, but its fixed manufacturing overhead will continue at 50% of present levels. How much per unit would the company be able to pay the supplier without decreasing operating income? (a) $4.75, (b) $3.95, (c) $2.95, (d) $5.35, (e) none of these.

11-38 Make or buy (continuation of 11-37). Assume that, as in requirement 7 of Problem 11-37, a proposal is received from an outside supplier who will make and ship high-style pens directly to the Class Company's customers as sales orders are forwarded from Class's sales staff. If the supplier's offer is accepted, the present plant facilities will be used to make a new pen whose unit costs will be

Variable manufacturing costs	$5.00
Fixed manufacturing costs	1.00
Variable marketing costs	2.00
Fixed marketing costs for the new pen	0.50

Total fixed manufacturing overhead will be unchanged from the original level given at the beginning of Problem 11-37. Fixed marketing costs for the new pens are over and above the fixed marketing costs incurred for marketing the high-style pens at the beginning of Problem 11-37. The new pen will sell for $9. The minimum desired operating income on the two pens taken together is $50,000 per year.

REQUIRED

What is the maximum purchase cost per unit that the Class Company should be willing to pay for subcontracting the production of the high-style pens?

11-39 Optimal production plan, computer manufacturer. (Chapter Appendix) Information Technology, Inc., assembles and sells two products: printers and desktop computers. Customers can purchase either (a) a computer, or (b) a computer plus a printer. The printers are *not* sold without the computer. The result is that the quantity of printers sold is equal to or less than the quantity of desktop computers sold. The contribution margins are $200 per printer and $100 per computer.

Each printer requires 6 hours assembly time on production line 1 and 10 hours assembly time on production line 2. Each computer requires 4 hours assembly time on production line 1 only. (Many of the components of each computer are preassembled by external vendors.) Production line 1 has 24 hours of available time per day. Production line 2 has 20 hours of available time per day.

Let X represent units of printers and Y represent units of desktop computers. The production manager must decide on the optimal mix of printers and computers to manufacture.

REQUIRED

1. Express the production manager's problem in an LP format.
2. Which combination of printers and computers will maximize the operating income of Information Technology? Use both the trial-and-error and the graphic approaches.

11-40 **Optimal sales mix for a retailer, sensitivity analysis.** (Chapter Appendix) Always Open, Inc., operates a chain of food stores open 24 hours a day. Each store has a standard 40,000 square feet of floor space available for merchandise. Merchandise is grouped in two categories: grocery products and dairy products. Always Open requires each store to devote a minimum of 10,000 square feet to grocery products and a minimum of 8,000 square feet to dairy products. Within these restrictions, each store manager can choose the mix of products to carry.

The manager of the Winnipeg store estimates the following weekly contribution margins per square foot: grocery products, $10; dairy products, $3.

REQUIRED

1. Formulate the decision facing the store manager as an LP model. Use G to represent square feet of floor space for grocery products and D to represent square feet of floor space for dairy products.
2. Why might Always Open set minimum bounds on the floor space devoted to each line of products?
3. Compute the optimal mix of grocery products and dairy products for the Winnipeg store.
4. Will the optimal mix determined in requirement 3 change if the contribution margins per square foot change to grocery products, $8, and dairy products, $5?

11-41 **Ethics and relevant costs.** The Pastel Company must reach a make-or-buy decision with respect to a high-volume, easily made metal tool, RG1. Sean Gray, the cost analyst, estimates the following costs and production information for the 50,000 units of RG1 that are expected to be started into production.

Total direct materials costs	$600,000
Direct manufacturing labor costs (all variable)	$200,000
Manufacturing overhead costs (all fixed)	$400,000
Good units of RG1 manufactured and sold	40,000 units
Units of RG1 scrapped for zero revenue	10,000 units

York Corporation has offered to supply as many units of RG1 as Pastel needs for $21 per unit. If Pastel buys RG1 from York instead of manufacturing it in-house, Pastel would be able to save $239,500 of the $400,000 fixed manufacturing overhead costs. (There is no alternative use for the capacity currently used to make RG1.)

Gray shows his analysis to Jim Berry, the controller. Berry does not like what he sees. He asks Gray to review all his assumptions and calculations with the comment, "The yield assumptions you made are very low. I think this plant can achieve much better quality than we have in the past. Better quality will reduce our costs and make them competitive with the outside purchase price." Gray knows that Berry is very concerned about purchasing RG1 from an outside supplier because it will mean that some of his close friends who work on the RG1 line will be laid off. Berry had played a key role in convincing management to produce RG1 in-house.

Gray rechecks his calculations. He believes it is unlikely that the plant can achieve the quality levels it would take for the make alternative to be superior to the buy alternative.

REQUIRED

1. On the basis of the information Gray obtains, should Pastel make-or-buy RG1?
2. For what levels of scrap would the make alternative be preferred to purchasing from outside?
3. Evaluate whether Jim Berry's suggestion to Gray to review his estimates is unethical. Will it be unethical for Gray to change his analysis to support the make alternative? What steps should Gray take next?

COLLABORATIVE LEARNING PROBLEM

11-42 **Relevant costs, opportunity costs.** Larry Miller, the general manager of Basil Software, scheduled a meeting on June 2, 19_8 with Sally Shields, sales manager, Andy Ashby, accountant, and Ellen Eisner, software operations manager, to discuss the development and release of Basil Software's new version of its spreadsheet package, Easyspread 2.0. It is only a question of time before other software firms have a package that matches Easyspread 2.0. Sally Shields, the sales manager, could hardly control her enthusiasm for the new product.

> **Sally Shields:** "This product is exactly what the market has been waiting for. We should not delay, by even a single day, the introduction of this product. Let's make July 1, 19_8, the sales release date."

> **Ellen Eisner:** "I don't disagree with Sally's assessment of the market potential for this product, but I have a problem. The threatened strike by our printers caused us to purchase large quantities of User Manuals for Easyspread 1.0. We don't like to store the manuals separately, so we also got extra diskettes duplicated. The manuals and diskettes were then packaged and shrink-wrapped. We are currently holding 60,000 completed packages, which equals the expected sales for July, August, and September 19_8 of Easyspread 1.0. I think we should make October 1, 19_8, the expected release date of Easyspread 2.0. This date would enable us to sell all of our inventory of Easyspread 1.0."

> **Larry Miller:** "Sally, do you see any problem with Ellen's suggestion? Our inventory of Easyspread 1.0 seems rather large for us to ignore. If we introduce Easyspread 2.0 on July 1, what would we do with the inventory of Easyspread 1.0 that we currently hold?"

> **Sally Shields:** "We currently sell Easyspread 1.0 to our wholesalers and distributors for $150 each. The additional optimization features in Easyspread 2.0 means that we should be able to sell Easyspread 2.0 to our distributors for about $185. We should not ignore the higher profit margins from Easyspread 2.0. It is true, though, that each time we sell 1 unit of Easyspread 2.0, we forgo the sale of 1 unit of Easyspread 1.0. Since the expected demand for Easyspread 2.0 is at least as large as the demand for Easyspread 1.0, we may have to throw away the existing inventory of Easyspread 1.0 once we introduce Easyspread 2.0."

> **Larry Miller:** "Andy, you've heard what Sally and Ellen have to say. I would like you to do a detailed analysis of the alternatives, and let me know within a week what you come up with. We need to make a decision on this one way or another, and we need to do so soon."

When Ashby returned to his office, he pulled out the cost records he had developed for Easyspread 1.0 and Easyspread 2.0. The unit costs for the two products are summarized as follows:

	Easyspread 1.0	Easyspread 2.0
Manuals, diskettes	$ 20	$ 25
Development costs	75	105
Marketing and administration costs	25	30
Total cost per unit	$120	$160

The following additional facts are available:

a. Basil contracts with outside vendors to print manuals and duplicate diskettes.
b. Development costs are allocated on the basis of the total costs of developing the software and the anticipated unit sales over the life of the software.
c. Marketing and administration costs are fixed costs in 19_8, incurred to support all activities of Basil Software. Marketing and administration costs are allocated to products on the basis of the budgeted revenues from each of the products. The preceding unit costs assume Easyspread 2.0 will be introduced on July 1, 19_8.

INSTRUCTIONS

Form groups of three students to complete the following requirements. To answer requirement 2, each of three students should play the role of Larry Miller, Sally Shields, and Ellen Eisner.

REQUIRED

1. On the basis of financial considerations only, is Basil Software better off introducing Easyspread 2.0 immediately instead of waiting? Explain your conclusion, clearly identifying relevant and irrelevant costs.
2. What other factors might Sally Shields and Ellen Eisner raise? What factors might Larry Miller consider as important?

PRICING DECISIONS, PRODUCT PROFITABILITY DECISIONS, AND COST MANAGEMENT

Computer component manufacturers recognize that the key to managing manufacturing costs is at the product design stage before costs get locked in. Tatung at its Taipei plant uses multi-function teams to design new color monitors that both satisfy customers on quality and are competitive on cost.

LEARNING OBJECTIVES

After studying this chapter, you should be able to

1. Discuss the three major influences on pricing decisions
2. Distinguish between short-run and long-run pricing decisions
3. Describe the target-costing approach to pricing
4. Distinguish between cost incurrence and locked-in costs
5. Describe the cost-plus approach to pricing
6. Describe two pricing practices in which noncost reasons are important when setting price
7. Explain how life-cycle product budgeting and costing assist in pricing decisions
8. Explain the effects of antitrust laws on pricing

Pricing decisions are decisions that managers make about what to charge for the products and services they deliver. For brevity, we use the term *pricing decision* in this chapter to include decisions about the profitability of products. These decisions impact the revenues a company earns, which must exceed total costs if profits are to be achieved. Consequently, determining product costs is important for pricing decisions. There is, however, no single way of computing a product cost that is universally relevant for all pricing decisions. Why? Because pricing decisions differ greatly in both their time horizons and their contexts. We emphasize how an understanding of cost-behavior patterns and cost drivers can lead to better pricing decisions and also apply the relevant-revenue and relevant-cost framework described in Chapter 11.

Economic theory indicates that companies acting optimally should produce and sell units until the marginal revenue (the additional revenue from selling an additional unit based on the demand for a product) equals the marginal or variable cost (the additional cost of supplying an additional unit). The market price is the price that creates a demand for these optimal numbers of units. This chapter describes how managers evaluate demand at different prices, manage their costs to influence supply, and earn a profit.

MAJOR INFLUENCES ON PRICING

There are three major influences on pricing decisions: customers, competitors, and costs.

Customers Managers must always examine pricing problems through the eyes of their customers. A price increase may cause customers to reject a company's product and choose a competing or substitute product.

Competitors Competitors' reactions influence pricing decisions. At one extreme, a rival's prices and products may force a business to lower its prices to be competitive. At the other extreme, a business without a rival in a given situation can set higher prices. A business with knowledge of its rivals' technology, plant capacity, and operating policies is able to estimate its rivals' costs, which is valuable information in setting competitive prices.

Competitor analysis takes different forms. Many companies, inlcuding Ford, General Motors, Nutrasweet, PPG Industries, and Raychem have established departments to search out information on their competitors' financial performance, patents, technologies, revenue and cost structures, and strategic alliances. Competitors themselves and their customers, suppliers, and former employees are important sources of information. Another form of obtaining information is via reverse engineering—a process of analyzing and tearing down competitors' products—to incorporate the best features, materials, and technology in a company's own designs.

Competition spans international borders. For example, when companies have excess capacity in their domestic markets, they often take an aggressive pricing policy in their export markets. Today, managers often take a global viewpoint, and it is increasingly common for them to consider both domestic and international rivals in making pricing decisions.

Costs Companies price products to exceed the costs of making them. The study of cost-behavior patterns gives insight into the income that results from different combinations of price and output quantities sold for a particular product.

Economic theory and surveys of how executives make pricing decisions reveal that companies weigh customers, competitors, and costs differently. Companies selling commodity-type products in highly competitive markets must accept the price determined by market forces. For example, sellers of wheat, rice, and soybeans have many competitors, each offering the identical product at the same price. The market sets the price, but cost data can help these sellers to decide, say, on the output level that best meets a company's particular objective.

In less competitive markets, managers have some discretion in setting prices. The pricing decision depends on how much customers value the product, the pricing strategies of competitors, and the costs of the product. The price of a product or service is the outcome of the interaction between *demand* for the product or service and its *supply*. Customers influence prices through their effect on demand. Costs influence prices because they affect supply. Competitors offer alternative or substitute products and so affect demand and price.

Chapter 1 described customer satisfaction, continuous improvement, and the dual internal/external focus as important, newly evolving themes in management. Pricing is an area where many of these themes explicitly come together. For example, charging lower prices for high-quality products is important for customer satisfaction, an external focus. But when prices are lower, costs must be reduced as well. Continuous improvement, an internal focus, is the key to keeping costs down.

PRODUCT-COST CATEGORIES AND TIME HORIZON

When reducing costs, a company must consider costs in all six value-chain business functions, from R&D to customer service. In computing the costs within these functions that are relevant in a pricing decision, the time horizon of the decision is critical. Most pricing decisions are either short run or long run. Short-run decisions include (1) pricing for a one-time-only special order with no long-term implications, and (2) adjusting product mix and output volume in a competitive market. The time horizon used to compute those costs that differ among the alternatives for short-run decisions is typically 6 months or less but sometimes as long as a year. Long-run decisions include pricing a product in a major market where price setting has considerable leeway. A time horizon of a year or longer is used when computing relevant costs for these long-run decisions. Many pricing decisions have both short-run and long-run implications. We next examine short-run pricing decisions.

OBJECTIVE 2

Distinguish between short-run and long-run pricing decisions

COSTING AND PRICING FOR THE SHORT RUN

A One-Time-Only Special Order

Consider a one-time-only special order from a customer to supply products for the next 4 months. Acceptance or rejection of the order will not affect the revenues (units sold or the selling price per unit) from existing sales outlets. The customer is unlikely to place any future sales orders.

EXAMPLE: The National Tea Corporation (NTC) operates a plant with a monthly capacity of 1 million cases (each case consisting of 200 cans) of iced tea. Current production and sales are 600,000 cases per month. The selling price is $90 per case. Costs of R&D and product and process design at NTC are negligible. Customer-service costs are also small and are included in marketing costs. All variable costs vary with respect to output units (cases), and production is equal to sales. The variable cost per case and the fixed cost per case (based on a production quantity of 600,000 cases per month) are as follows:

	Variable Cost per Case	Fixed Cost per Case	Variable and Fixed Cost per Case
Manufacturing costs			
Direct materials costs	$ 7	—	$ 7
Packaging costs	18	—	18
Direct manufacturing labor costs	4	—	4
Manufacturing overhead costs	6	$13	19
Manufacturing costs	35	13	48
Marketing costs	5	16	21
Distribution costs	9	8	17
Full product costs	$49	$37	$86

Variable manufacturing overhead of $6 per case is the cost of power and utilities. Details of the fixed manufacturing overhead costs and their per case unitized costs (based on a production quantity of 600,000 cases per month) are as follows:

	Total Fixed Manufacturing Overhead Costs	Fixed Manufacturing Overhead Cost per Case
Depreciation and production support costs	$3,000,000	$ 5
Materials procurement costs	600,000	1
Salaries paid for process changeover	1,800,000	3
Product and process engineering costs	2,400,000	4
Total fixed manufacturing overhead costs	$7,800,000	$13

Canadian Tea (CT) is constructing a new plant to make iced tea in Toronto. The plant will not open for 4 months. CT's management, however, wants to start selling 250,000 cases of iced tea each month for the next 4 months in Canada. CT has asked NTC and two other companies to bid on this special order. From a manu-facturing-cost viewpoint, the iced tea to be made for CT is identical to that currently made by NTC.

If NTC makes the extra 250,000 cases, the existing total fixed manufacturing overhead ($7,800,000 per month) would continue to be incurred. In addition, NTC would incur a further $300,000 in fixed manufacturing overhead costs (materials procurement costs of $100,000 and process-changeover costs of $200,000) each month. No additional costs will be required for R&D, design, marketing, distribu-tion, or customer service. The 250,000 cases will be marketed by CT in Canada, where NTC does not sell its iced tea.

A vice president of CT notifies each potential bidder that a bid above $45 per case will probably be noncompetitive. NTC knows that one of its competitors, with a highly efficient plant, has sizable idle capacity and will definitely bid for the con-tract. What price should NTC bid for the 250,000-case contract?

To compute the relevant costs for the price-bidding decision, NTC systemati-cally analyzes the costs in each business function of the value chain. In this example, only manufacturing costs are relevant. All other costs in the value chain will be unaf-fected if the special order is accepted, so they are irrelevant.

Exhibit 12-1 presents an analysis of the relevant costs. They include all manu-facturing costs that will change in total if the special order is obtained: all direct and indirect variable manufacturing costs plus materials procurement costs and process-changeover salaries related to the special order. *Existing* fixed manufacturing over-head costs are irrelevant. Why? Because these costs will not change if the special order is accepted. But the *additional* materials procurement and process-changeover salaries of $300,000 per month for the special order are relevant because these addi-tional fixed manufacturing costs will only be incurred if the special order is accepted.

EXHIBIT 12-1
Monthly Relevant Costs for NTC: The 250,000-Case One-Time-Only Special Order

Direct materials (250,000 cases × $7)		$1,750,000
Packaging (250,000 cases × $18)		4,500,000
Direct manufacturing labor (250,000 cases × $4)		1,000,000
Variable manufacturing overhead (250,000 × $6)		1,500,000
Fixed manufacturing overhead		
Materials procurement	$100,000	
Salaries paid for process changeover	200,000	
Total fixed manufacturing overhead		300,000
Total relevant costs		$9,050,000

Per case relevant costs: $9,050,000 ÷ 250,000 cases = $36.20

Exhibit 12-1 shows the total relevant costs of $9,050,000 per month (or $36.20 per case) for the 250,000-case special order. Any bid above $36.20 per case will improve NTC's profitability. For example, a successful bid of $40 per case, well under CT's ceiling of $45 per case, will add $950,000 to NTC's monthly operating income: 250,000 × ($40 − $36.20) = $950,000. Note again how unit costs can mislead. The table on p. 431 reports total manufacturing costs to be $48 per case. The $48 cost might erroneously suggest that a bid of $45 per case for the Canadian Tea special order will result in NTC sustaining a $3 per case loss on the contract. Why erroneous? Because total manufacturing cost per case includes $13 of fixed manufacturing cost per case that will not be incurred on the 250,000-case special order. These costs are hence irrelevant for the special-order bid.

Cost data, though key information in NTC's decision on the price to bid, are not the only inputs. NTC must also consider business rivals and their likely bids. For example, if NTC knows that its under-capacity rival plans to bid $39 per case, NTC will bid $38 per case instead of $40 per case.

COSTING AND PRICING FOR THE LONG RUN

Many pricing decisions are made for the long run. Buyers—whether a person buying a box of Wheaties, a construction company, such as Bechtel Corporation, buying a fleet of tractors, or General Foods Corporation buying audit services—prefer stable prices over an extended time horizon. A stable price reduces the need for continuous monitoring of suppliers' prices. Greater price stability also improves planning and builds long-run buyer-seller relationships.

Calculating Product Costs

Obtaining accurate product-cost information is essential to a manager making a pricing decision. In industries such as oil and gas and mining, competitive forces set the price for a product, and knowledge of long-run product costs can guide decisions about entering or remaining in the market. In other industries such as specialized machines, appliances, and automobiles, managers have some control over the price charged for a product, and long-run product costs can be used as a base for setting that price.

Consider the Astel Computer Corporation. Astel manufactures two brands of personal computers (PCs)—Deskpoint and Provalue. Deskpoint is Astel's top-of-the-line product, a Pentium chip-based PC sold through computer dealers to large organizations and government accounts. Our analysis focuses on pricing Provalue, a less powerful 486 DX chip-based machine sold through catalogs and mass merchandisers to individual consumers and small organizations.

The manufacturing costs of Provalue are calculated using the activity-based costing (ABC) approach described in Chapters 4 and 5. Astel has three direct manufacturing cost categories (direct materials, direct manufacturing labor, and direct machining costs) and three indirect manufacturing cost pools (ordering and receiving, testing and inspection, and rework) in its accounting system. Astel treats machining costs as a direct cost of Provalue because it is manufactured on machines that are used for no other products. The following table summarizes the activity cost pools, the cost driver for each activity, and the cost per unit of cost driver Astel uses to allocate manufacturing overhead costs to products.

Manufacturing Activity	Description of Activity	Cost Driver	Cost per Unit of Cost Driver
1. Ordering and receiving	Placing orders, receiving, and paying for components	Number of orders	$80 per order
2. Testing and inspection	Testing components and final product	Testing-hours	$2 per testing-hour
3. Rework	Correcting and fixing errors and defects	Units reworked	$100 per unit reworked

Astel uses a long-run time horizon to price Provalue. Over this horizon, Astel's management views direct materials costs and direct manufacturing labor costs as variable with respect to the units of Provalue produced, and manufacturing overhead costs as variable with respect to their chosen cost drivers. For example, ordering and receiving costs vary with the number of orders. Staff members responsible for placing orders can be reassigned or laid off in the long run if fewer orders need to be placed. Direct machining costs (rent paid on leased machines) do not vary over this time horizon for the relevant range of production; they are fixed long-run costs.

Astel has no beginning or ending inventory of Provalue in 19_7 and manufactures and sells 150,000 units. How does Astel calculate Provalue's manufacturing costs? It uses the following information, which indicates the resources used to manufacture Provalue in 19_7:

1. Direct materials costs per unit of Provalue are $460.
2. Direct manufacturing labor costs per unit of Provalue are $64.
3. Direct fixed costs of machines used exclusively for the manufacture of Provalue are $11,400,000.
4. Number of orders placed to purchase components required for the manufacture of Provalue is 22,500. (We assume for simplicity that Provalue has 450 components supplied by different suppliers, and that 50 orders are placed for each component to match Provalue's production schedule.)
5. Number of testing-hours used for Provalue is 4,500,000 (150,000 Provalue units are tested for 30 hours per unit).
6. Number of units of Provalue reworked during the year is 12,000 (8% of the 150,000 units manufactured).

The detailed calculations underlying each of these numbers are shown in Exhibit 12-2. This exhibit indicates that the total costs of manufacturing Provalue are $102 million, and the manufacturing cost per unit of Provalue is $680. Manufacturing, however, is just one business function in the value chain. For setting long-run prices and for managing costs, Astel determines the full product costs of Provalue.

For brevity, we do not present any detailed analyses or calculations for the other value-chain functions. Astel chooses cost drivers and cost pools in each

EXHIBIT 12-2
Manufacturing Costs of Provalue in 19_7 Based on an Activity Analysis

	Total Manufacturing Costs for 150,000 Units (1)	Manufacturing Cost per Unit (2) = (1) ÷ 150,000
Direct manufacturing costs		
Direct materials costs (150,000 units × $460)	$ 69,000,000	$460
Direct manufacturing labor costs (150,000 units × $64)	9,600,000	64
Direct machining costs (fixed costs of $11,400,000)	11,400,000	76
Direct manufacturing costs	90,000,000	600
Manufacturing overhead costs		
Ordering and receiving costs (22,500 orders × $80)	1,800,000	12
Testing and inspection costs (4,500,000 hours × $2)	9,000,000	60
Rework costs (12,000 units × $100)	1,200,000	8
Manufacturing overhead costs	12,000,000	80
Total manufacturing costs	$102,000,000	$680

value-chain function to measure the cause-and-effect relationship between the activities and costs within each activity's cost pool. Costs are allocated to Provalue on the basis of the quantity of cost driver units that Provalue requires. Exhibit 12-3 summarizes the product operating income statement for Provalue for the year 19_7 based on an activity analysis of costs in all value-chain functions (supporting calculations for nonmanufacturing value-chain functions are not given). Astel earned $15 million from Provalue, or $100 per unit sold. We next consider the role of costs in long-run pricing decisions.

Alternative Long-Run Pricing Approaches

The starting point for pricing decisions can be

1. Market-based
2. Cost-based (also called cost-plus)

The market-based approach to pricing *starts* by asking, Given what our customers want and how our competitors will react to what we do, what price should we charge? The cost-based approach to pricing *starts* by asking, What does it cost us to make this product, and hence what price should we charge that will recoup our costs and produce a desired profit? Both approaches consider customers, competitors, and costs. Only their starting points differ.

In very competitive markets (for example, oil and gas, and airlines) the market-based approach is logical. The items produced or services provided by one company are very similar to those produced or provided by others, so companies have no influence over the prices to charge. In other industries, where there is more product differentiation (for example, automobiles, management consulting, and legal services) firms have some discretion over prices, products, and services. Companies choose prices and product and service features on the basis of anticipated customer and competitor reactions. A final decision on price, product, and service is made after evaluating these external influences on pricing along with the costs to produce and sell the product.

EXHIBIT 12-3

Product Profitability of Provalue in 19_7 Based on Value-Chain Activity Analysis

	Total for 150,000 Units (1)	Per Unit (2) = (1) ÷ 150,000
Revenues	$150,000,000	$1,000
Cost of goods sold* (from Exhibit 12-2)		
Direct materials costs	69,000,000	460
Direct manufacturing labor costs	9,600,000	64
Direct machining costs	11,400,000	76
Manufacturing overhead costs	12,000,000	80
Cost of goods sold	102,000,000	680
Operating Costs		
R&D costs	5,400,000	36
Design costs of products and processes	6,000,000	40
Marketing costs	15,000,000	100
Distribution costs	3,600,000	24
Customer-service costs	3,000,000	20
Operating costs	33,000,000	220
Full product costs	135,000,000	900
Operating income	$ 15,000,000	$ 100

*Cost of goods sold = Total manufacturing costs since there is no beginning or ending inventory of Provalue in 19_7.

Under the cost-plus approach, price is first computed on the basis of the costs to produce and sell a product. Typically, a markup, representing a reasonable return, is added to cost. Often, the price is then modified on the basis of anticipated customer reaction to alternative price levels and the prices charged by competitors for similar products. In short, market forces dictate the eventual size of the markup and thus the final price.

TARGET COSTING FOR TARGET PRICING

An important form of market-based price is the *target price*. A **target price** is the estimated price for a product (or service) that potential customers will be willing to pay. This estimate is based on an understanding of customers' perceived value for a product and competitors' responses. A **target operating income per unit** is the operating income that a company wants to earn on each unit of a product (or service) sold. The target price leads to a *target cost*. A **target cost per unit** is the estimated long-run cost per unit of a product (or service) that, when sold at the target price, enables the company to achieve the target operating income per unit. Target cost per unit is derived by subtracting the target operating income per unit from the target price.

What relevant costs should we include in the target cost calculations? *All* costs, both variable and fixed. Why? Because in the long run, a company's prices and revenues must recover all its costs. If not, the company's best alternative is to shut down. Relative to the shutting-down alternative, all costs, whether fixed or variable, are relevant.

Target cost per unit is often lower than the existing full product cost per unit. To achieve the target cost per unit and the target operating income per unit, the organization must improve its products and processes. Target costing is widely used among different industries around the world. Ford, General Motors, Mercedes, Toyota, and Daihatsu in the automobile industry; Matsushita, Panasonic, and Sharp in the electronics industry; and Compaq and Toshiba in the personal computer industry are examples of companies that use target pricing and target costing.

Implementing Target Pricing and Target Costing

Developing target prices and target costs requires the following four steps:

Step 1: Develop a product that satisfies the needs of potential customers.

Step 2: Choose a *target price* based on customers' perceived value for the product and the prices competitors charge, and a *target operating income per unit*.

Step 3: Derive a *target cost per unit* by subtracting the target operating income per unit from the target price.

Step 4: Perform *value engineering* to achieve target costs. **Value engineering** is a systematic evaluation of all aspects of the value-chain business functions, with the objective of reducing costs while satisfying customer needs. Value engineering can result in improvements in product designs, changes in materials specifications, or modifications in process methods.

We illustrate the four steps for target pricing and target costing using the Astel Computer's example introduced earlier in the chapter.

Step 1: Product Planning for Provalue Astel is in the process of planning design modifications for Provalue. Astel is very concerned about severe price competition from several competitors.

Step 2: Target Price of Provalue Astel expects its competitors to lower the prices of PCs that compete against Provalue by 15%. Astel's management believes that it must respond aggressively by reducing Provalue's price by 20%, from $1,000 per unit to $800 per unit. At this lower price, Astel's marketing manager forecasts an increase in annual sales from 150,000 to 200,000 units.

Step 3: Target Cost per Unit of Provalue
Astel's management wants a 10% target operating income on sales revenues.

Total target sales revenues	= $800 × 200,000 units = $160,000,000
Total target operating income	= 10% × $160,000,000 = $16,000,000
Target operating income per unit	= $16,000,000 ÷ 200,000 units = $80 per unit
Target cost per unit	= Target price − Target operating income per unit
	= $800 − $80 = $720
Total current costs of Provalue	= $135,000,000 (from Exhibit 12-3)
Current cost per unit of Provalue	= $135,000,000 ÷ 150,000 units = $900 per unit

The target cost per unit of $720 is substantially lower than Provalue's existing unit cost of $900. The goal is to find ways to reduce the cost per unit of Provalue by $180, from $900 to $720. The challenge in step 4 is to achieve the target cost through value engineering.

Step 4: Value Engineering for Provalue
An important element of Astel's value engineering is determining the kind of low-end PC that will meet the needs of potential customers. For example, the existing Provalue design accommodates various upgrades that can make the PC run faster and perform calculations more quickly. It also comes with special audio features. An essential first step in the value-engineering process is to determine whether potential customers are willing to pay the price for these features. Customer feedback indicates that customers do not value Provalue's extra features. They want Astel to redesign Provalue into a no-frills PC and sell it at a much lower price. Value engineering at Astel then proceeds with cross-functional teams consisting of marketing managers, product designers, manufacturing engineers, and production supervisors making suggestions for design improvements and process modifications. Cost accountants estimate the savings in costs that would result from the proposed changes.

Managers often find the distinction between value-added and nonvalue-added activities and costs introduced in Chapter 2 useful in value engineering. A *value-added cost* is a cost that customers perceive as adding value, or utility (usefulness), to a product or service. Determining value-added costs requires identifying attributes that customers perceive to be important. For Provalue, these attributes include the PC's features and its price. Activities undertaken within the company (such as the manufacturing line) influence the attributes that customers value. Astel assesses whether each activity adds value or not. Activities and the costs of these activities do not always fall neatly into value-added or nonvalue-added categories. Some costs fall in the gray area in between, and include both value-added and nonvalue-added components. The following examples are drawn from classifications made by operating personnel at a General Electric medical equipment assembly plant:

Category	Examples
Value-added costs	Costs of assembly, design, tools, and machinery
Nonvalue-added costs	Costs of rework, expediting, special delivery, and obsolete inventory
Gray area	Costs of testing, materials movement, and ordering

In the Provalue example, direct materials, direct manufacturing labor, and machining costs are value-added costs, ordering and testing costs fall in the gray area (customers perceive some portion but not all of these costs as necessary for adding value), while rework costs are nonvalue-added costs.

Value engineering seeks to reduce or eliminate nonvalue-added activities and hence nonvalue-added costs by reducing the cost drivers of the nonvalue-added activities. For example, to reduce rework costs, Astel must reduce rework-hours. Value engineering also focuses on achieving greater efficiency in value-added activities to reduce value-added costs. For example, to reduce direct manufacturing labor costs, Astel must reduce the time it takes to make Provalue. But how should Astel reduce rework time and direct manufacturing labor time? We focus on these issues next.

Cost Incurrence and Locked-in Costs

Two key concepts in value engineering and in managing value-added and nonvalue-added costs are *cost incurrence* and *locked-in costs*. **Cost incurrence** occurs when a resource is sacrificed or used up. Costing systems emphasize cost incurrence. They recognize and record costs only when costs are incurred. Astel's costing system, for example, recognizes the direct materials costs of Provalue as each unit of Provalue is assembled and sold. But Provalue's direct materials costs per unit are determined much earlier when designers finalize the components that will go into Provalue. Direct materials costs per unit of Provalue are *locked in* (or *designed in*) at the product-design stage. **Locked-in costs (designed-in costs)** are those costs that have not yet been incurred but that will be incurred in the future on the basis of decisions that have already been made.

Why is it important to distinguish between when costs are locked in and when costs are incurred? Because it is difficult to alter or reduce costs that have already been locked in. For example, if Astel experiences quality problems during manufacturing, its ability to improve quality and reduce scrap may be limited by Provalue's design. Scrap costs are incurred during manufacturing, but they may be locked in by a faulty design. Similarly, in the software industry, costs of producing software are often locked in at the design and analysis stage. Costly and difficult-to-fix errors that appear during coding and testing are frequently locked in by bad designs.

Other examples of how Astel's design decisions affect costs include the following:

1. Design decisions influence direct materials costs through the choices of printed circuit boards and add-on features used in Provalue. Better designs also reduce both product failures in the plant and the time it takes to rework defective products.

2. Designing Provalue so that it is easy to manufacture and easy to assemble decreases direct manufacturing labor costs. For example, designing Provalue so that various parts snap-fit together (rather than having various parts soldered together) saves manufacturing labor time.

3. Designing Provalue with fewer components reduces ordering and materials handling costs.

4. Simplifying the Provalue design decreases the time required for testing and inspection.

5. Designing Provalue to reduce the need for repairs as well as the time it takes to service and repair Provalue at customer sites reduces customer-service costs.

Exhibit 12-4 illustrates how the locked-in cost curve and the cost-incurrence curve might appear in the case of Provalue. (The numbers underlying the graph are assumed.) The bottom curve plots the cumulative costs per unit incurred in different business functions. The top curve plots the cumulative costs locked in. Both curves deal with the same total cumulative costs per unit. The graph emphasizes the wide divergence between the time when costs are locked in and the time when those costs are incurred. In our example, once the product and processes are designed, more than 86% (say, $780 \div $900) of the unit costs of Provalue are locked in when only about 8% (say, $76 \div $900) of the unit costs are actually incurred. For example, at the end of the design stage, costs such as direct materials; direct manufacturing labor; direct machining; and many manufacturing, marketing, distribution, and customer-service overheads are all locked in. To reduce total costs, Astel must act to modify the design before costs get locked in.

We caution that it is not always the case that costs are locked in early in the design stage as was the case with Provalue. In some industries, such as mining, costs are locked in and incurred at about the same time. When costs are not locked in early,

EXHIBIT 12-4
Pattern of Cost Incurrence and Locked-in Costs for Provalue

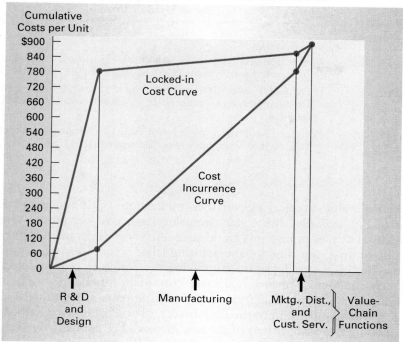

cost-reduction activities can be successful right up to the time that costs are incurred. In these industries, the key to lowering costs is improved operational efficiency and productivity rather than better design.

ACHIEVING THE TARGET COST PER UNIT FOR PROVALUE

Astel's value-engineering teams focus their cost-reduction efforts on analyzing the Provalue design. Their goal? To design a high-quality, highly reliable machine with fewer features that meets customers' price expectations and achieves target cost.

Provalue is discontinued. In its place, Astel introduces Provalue II. Provalue II has fewer components than does Provalue and is easier to manufacture and test. The following tables compare the direct costs and the manufacturing overhead costs and cost drivers of Provalue and Provalue II. In place of the 150,000 Provalue units manufactured and sold in 19_7, Astel expects to make and sell 200,000 Provalue II units in 19_8.

Direct Costs

Cost Category	Costs per Unit		Explanation of Costs for Provalue II
	Provalue	**Provalue II**	
1. Direct materials	$460	$385	The Provalue II design will use a simplified main printed circuit board, fewer components, and no audio features.
2. Direct manufacturing labor	$ 64	$ 53	Provalue II will require less assembly time
3. Direct machining costs	$ 76	$ 57	Machining costs are fixed at $11,400,000. Astel can use the machine capacity to produce 200,000 units of Provalue II. The new design will enable Astel to manufacture each unit of Provalue II in less time than a unit of Provalue. Direct machining costs per unit of Provalue II will equal $57 ($11,400,000 ÷ 200,000).

Manufacturing Overhead Costs

Cost Driver	Quantity of Cost Driver		Explanation for Quantity of Cost Driver Used by Provalue II
	Provalue*	Provalue II	
1. Number of orders	22,500	21,250	Astel will place 50 orders for each of the 425 components in Provalue II. Total orders for Provalue II will equal 21,250 (425 × 50).
2. Testing-hours	4,500,000	3,000,000	Provalue II is easier to test and will require 15 testing-hours per unit. Total number of expected testing-hours will equal 3,000,000 (15 × 200,000).
3. Units reworked	12,000	13,000	Provalue II will have a lower rework rate of 6.5% because it is easier to manufacture. Total units reworked will equal 13,000 (6.5% × 200,000).

*From Exhibit 12-2.

Note that value-engineering activities reduce both value-added and nonvalue-added costs. For example, direct manufacturing labor cost per unit, a value-added cost, is reduced by designing a product that requires less direct manufacturing labor hours (the cost driver for direct manufacturing labor costs). Rework cost per unit, a nonvalue-added cost, is reduced by simplifying the design to reduce defects during manufacturing and hence rework-hours (the cost driver for rework costs).

Exhibit 12-5 presents the target manufacturing costs of Provalue II, assuming no change in the cost per unit of the cost drivers. (The Problem for Self-Study considers changes in the cost per unit of the cost drivers.) For comparison, Exhibit 12-5 also reproduces the manufacturing costs per unit of Provalue from Exhibit 12-2. Exhibit 12-5 shows that the new design is expected to reduce the manufacturing cost per unit by $140 to $540 from $680. A similar analysis (not presented) estimates the expected effect of the new design on costs in other value-chain business functions. Exhibit 12-6 shows that the estimated full product cost per unit equals $720—the target cost per unit for Provalue II. Astel's goal is to sell Provalue II at the target price, achieve target cost, and earn the target operating income.[1]

EXHIBIT 12-5
Target Manufacturing Costs of Provalue II

	PROVALUE II		PROVALUE
	Estimated Manufacturing Costs for 200,000 Units (1)	Estimated Manufacturing Costs per Unit (2) = (1) ÷ 200,000	Manufacturing Costs per Unit (Exhibit 12-2, Column 2) (3)
Direct manufacturing costs			
Direct materials costs (200,000 units × $385)	$ 77,000,000	$385.00	$460.00
Direct manufacturing labor costs (200,000 units × $53)	10,600,000	53.00	64.00
Direct machining costs (fixed costs of $11,400,000)	11,400,000	57.00	76.00
Direct manufacturing costs	99,000,000	495.00	600.00
Manufacturing overhead costs			
Ordering and receiving costs (21,250 orders × $80)	1,700,000	8.50	12.00
Testing and inspection costs (3,000,000 hours × $2)	6,000,000	30.00	60.00
Rework costs (13,000 units × $100)	1,300,000	6.50	8.00
Manufacturing overhead costs	9,000,000	45.00	80.00
Total manufacturing costs	$108,000,000	$540.00	$680.00

[1]For a description of target pricing, target costing, and value engineering in the automobile industry, see R. Cooper, "Nissan Motor Company, Ltd: Target Costing System," Harvard Business School Case N9-194-040.

EXHIBIT 12-6
Target Product Profitability of Provalue II in 19_8

	Total for 200,000 Units (1)	Per Unit (2) = (1) ÷ 200,000
Revenues	$160,000,000	$800
Cost of goods sold* (from Exhibit 12-5)		
Direct materials costs	77,000,000	385
Direct manufacturing labor costs	10,600,000	53
Direct machining costs	11,400,000	57
Manufacturing overhead costs	9,000,000	45
Cost of goods sold	108,000,000	540
Operating costs		
R&D costs	4,000,000	20
Design of products and processes costs	6,000,000	30
Marketing costs	18,000,000	90
Distribution costs	5,000,000	25
Customer-service costs	3,000,000	15
Operating costs	36,000,000	180
Full product costs	144,000,000	720
Operating income	$ 16,000,000	$ 80

*Cost of goods sold = Total manufacturing costs (since we assume no beginning or ending inventory for Provalue II in 19_8).

Target Costing at CFM International, Toyota, and Nissan

CFM International (CFMI),* a joint company of General Electric of the United States and SNECMA of France, manufactures aircraft engines. In negotiations with the Boeing company, CFMI established a lower market-based price for its CFM56-7 engine, which is used in Boeing's 737-600, -700, and -800 aircraft. To support the pricing of the CFM56-7, CFMI has identified target costs for each of the engine's top 50 parts. CFMI achieves these target costs by using value engineering at the design stage. Drawings for manufacturing a part are issued only after target costs are achieved.

The Toyota and Nissan Motor Companies[†] are also enthusiastic advocates of target pricing and target costing. Toyota and Nissan believe that a substantial fraction of their costs are locked in at the design stage. Design engineers at these companies are trained to recognize the influence that design choices have on materials consumption, yield, and machining methods. Specially trained cost estimators then estimate the manufacturing costs of alternative designs. Toyota often simultaneously designs a family of cars to take advantage of common parts and processes. Cars in the Celica line, consisting of the Celica itself, the Corona Exsiv, and the Carina ED, have much in common in the engine and chassis but are differentiated along external styling dimensions.

*"CFM International Locks in 737-X Engine Prices," *Aerospace Propulsion* (September 1, 1994); T. Smart and Z. Schiller, "Just Imagine if Time Were Good," *Business Week* (April 17, 1995).
[†]T. Tanaka, "Target Costing at Toyota," *Journal of Cost Management* (Spring 1993), pp. 4–11; and R. Cooper, "Nissan Motor Company Ltd.: Target Costing System," Harvard Business School Case N9-194-040.

COST-PLUS PRICING

OBJECTIVE 5

Describe the cost-plus approach to pricing

As illustrated in the last section, Astel uses an external market-based approach in its long-run pricing decisions. An alternative approach is to determine a cost-based price. Managers can turn to numerous pricing formulas based on cost. The general formula for setting a price adds a markup to the cost base:

Cost base	$X
Markup component	$\underline{Y}$
Prospective selling price	$\underline{\underline{X + Y}}$

Cost-Plus Target Rate of Return on Investment

Consider a cost-based pricing formula that Astel could use for Provalue II. Assume that Astel's engineers have redesigned Provalue into Provalue II as described earlier and that Astel uses a 12% markup on the full product cost per unit in developing the prospective selling price.

Cost base (full product cost per unit, from Exhibit 12-6)	$720.00
Markup component (12% × $720)	$\underline{86.40}$
Prospective selling price	$\underline{\underline{\$806.40}}$

How is the markup percentage of 12% determined? One approach is to choose a markup to earn a *target rate of return on investment*. The **target rate of return on investment** is the target operating income that an organization must earn divided by invested capital. Invested capital can be defined in many ways. In this chapter, we define it as total assets (long-term or fixed assets plus current assets). Companies usually specify the target rate of return required on investments. Suppose Astel's (pretax) target rate of return on investment is 18%. Assume that the capital investment needed for Provalue II is $96 million. The target operating income that Astel must earn from Provalue II can then be calculated as follows:

Invested capital	$96,000,000
Target rate of return on investment	18%
Total target operating income (18% × $96,000,000)	$17,280,000
Target operating income per unit of Provalue II ($17,280,000 ÷ 200,000 units)	$ 86.40

The calculation indicates that Astel would like to earn a target operating income of $86.40 on each unit of Provalue II. What markup does this return amount to? Expressed as a percentage of the full product cost per unit of $720, the markup is equal to 12% ($86.40 ÷ $720). Do not confuse the 18% target rate of return on investment with the 12% markup percentage. The 18% target rate of return on investment expresses Astel's expected operating income as a percentage of investment. The 12% markup expresses operating income per unit as a percentage of the full product cost per unit. Astel first calculates the target rate of return on investment, and then determines the markup percentage.

Companies sometimes find it difficult to determine the capital invested to support a product. Computing invested capital requires allocations of investments in equipment and buildings (used for design, production, marketing, distribution, and customer service) to individual products—a difficult and sometimes arbitrary task. Some companies therefore prefer to use alternative cost bases and markup percentages that do not require calculations of invested capital to set price.

Alternative Cost-Plus Methods

We illustrate these alternatives using the Astel example. Exhibit 12-7 separates the cost per unit for each value-chain business function into its variable and fixed components (without providing details of the calculations). The following table illustrates some alternative cost bases and markup percentages.

Cost Base	Estimated Cost per Unit of Provalue II (1)	Markup Percentage (2)	Markup Component for Provalue II (3) = (1) × (2)	Prospective Selling Price for Provalue II (4) = (1) + (3)
Variable manufacturing costs	$483.00	65%	$313.95	$796.95
Variable product costs	547.00	45	246.15	793.15
Manufacturing function costs	540.00	50	270.00	810.00
Full product cost	720.00	12	86.40	806.40

To illustrate the markup calculations, we have assumed (but not derived) the markup percentages in the table. The different cost bases and markup percentages that we use in the table give prospective selling prices that are relatively close to one another. In practice, a company will choose a cost base that it regards as reliable, and a markup percentage on the basis of its experience in pricing products to recover its costs and earn a desired return on investment. For example, a company may choose a full product cost base if it is unsure about variable- and fixed-cost distinctions.

The markup percentages in the table vary a great deal, from a high of 65% on variable manufacturing costs to a low of 12% on full product costs. Why? Because the markup based on variable manufacturing costs takes into account the need to earn a profit, and to recoup fixed manufacturing costs and other business function costs such as R&D, marketing, and distribution. The greater these costs relative to variable manufacturing costs, the higher the markup percentage. The markup percentage on full product costs is much lower. Why? Because full product costs already include all costs incurred to sell the product. The precise markup percentage also depends on the competitiveness of the product market. Markups and profit margins tend to be lower the more competitive the market.

EXHIBIT 12-7
Estimated Cost Structure for Provalue II

Business Function	Variable Cost per Unit	Fixed Cost per Unit*	Business Function Cost per Unit
R&D	$ 8.00	$ 12.00	$ 20.00
Design of product/process	10.00	20.00	30.00
Manufacturing	483.00	57.00	540.00
Marketing	25.00	65.00	90.00
Distribution	15.00	10.00	25.00
Customer service	6.00	9.00	15.00
Product costs	$547.00	$173.00	$720.00
	↑ Variable product cost per unit	↑ Fixed product cost per unit	↑ Full product cost per unit

*Based on budgeted annual production of 200,000 units.

Surveys indicate that most managers use full product costs (see Surveys of Company Practice on p. 445)—that is, they include both fixed costs per unit and variable costs per unit in the cost base when making their pricing decisions. The advantages cited for including fixed costs per unit for pricing decisions include the following:

1. *Full product cost recovery.* For long-run pricing decisions, full product costs inform managers of the bare minimum costs they need to recover to continue in business rather than shut down. Using variable costs as a base does not give managers this information. There is then a temptation to engage in excessive long-run price cutting as long as prices give a positive contribution margin. Long-run price cutting, however, may result in long-run revenues being less than long-run (full product) costs, resulting in the company going out of business.

2. *Price stability.* Managers believe that full-cost formula pricing promotes price stability, because it limits the ability of managers to cut prices. Managers prefer price stability because it facilitates planning.

3. *Simplicity.* A full-cost formula for pricing does not require a detailed analysis of cost-behavior patterns to separate costs into fixed and variable components for each product. Calculating variable costs for each product is expensive and prone to errors. For these reasons, many managers believe that full-cost formula pricing meets the cost-benefit test.

Including unit fixed costs when pricing is not without its problems. Allocating fixed costs to products can be somewhat arbitrary. Calculating fixed cost per unit requires an estimate of expected future sales quantities. If actual sales fall short of this estimate, the actual full product cost per unit could exceed price.

Cost-Plus Pricing and Target Pricing

The selling prices computed under cost-plus pricing are *prospective* prices. For example, suppose Astel's initial product design results in a $750 cost for Provalue II. Assuming a 12% markup, Astel sets a prospective price of $840 [$750 + (12% × $750)]. Since the personal computer market is reasonably competitive, customer and competitor reactions to this price may force Astel to reduce the markup percentage, and the price to $800. Alternatively, Astel may redesign Provalue II to reduce cost to $720 per unit, as in our example, and achieve a markup of $80 per unit. The eventual design and cost-plus price balance the conflicting tensions among costs, markup, and customer reactions.

The target pricing approach eliminates the need to go back and forth among cost-plus prospective prices, customer reactions, and design and cost modifications. Instead, the target pricing approach first determines product characteristics and price on the basis of customer preferences and competitor responses. The target price then serves to focus and motivate managers to achieve the target cost to earn the target operating income. Sometimes the target cost is not achieved. Managers must then redesign the product, adjust the price, or work with a smaller margin.

Suppliers who provide relatively unique products and services—accountants and management consultants, for example—frequently use cost-plus pricing. Professional service firms set prices based on hourly cost-plus billing rates of partners, managers, and associates. These prices are, however, reduced in competitive situations. Professional service firms also consider a multiyear client perspective when choosing prices. Certified public accountants, for example, sometimes charge a client a low price initially and higher prices later.

Refined cost driver and cost information play an important role in both cost-plus pricing and target costing and pricing. The identification of cost drivers is critical as managers do value engineering to "cost down" their products. *Cost down* refers to reducing the cost of a product while still satisfying customer expectations.

Differences in Pricing Practices and Cost Management Methods in Various Countries

Surveys* of financial officers of the largest industrial companies in several countries indicate similarities and differences in pricing practices across the globe. The use of cost-based pricing appears to be more prevalent in the United States than in Ireland, Japan, and the United Kingdom.

Some Japanese survey data indicate that market-based target pricing practices vary considerably among industries. While a majority of Japanese companies in assembly-type operations (for example, electronics and automobiles) use target costing for pricing, it is far less prevalent in Japanese process-type industries (for example, chemicals, oil, and steel). Japanese companies use value engineering more frequently and involve designers more often when estimating costs. When costs are used for pricing decisions, the pattern is consistent—overwhelmingly, companies across the globe use full costs rather than variable costs.

Ranking of Factors Primarily Used to Price Products (1 is Most Important)

	United States	Japan	Ireland	United Kingdom
Market based	2	1	1	1
Cost based	1	2	2	2

Use of Value Engineering and Designers in Cost Management

	Australia	Japan	United Kingdom
Percentage of companies that use value engineering or analysis for cost reduction	24	58	29
Percentage of companies in which designers are involved in estimating costs	25	46	32

Ranking of Cost Methods Used in Pricing Decisions (1 is Most Important)

	United States	United Kingdom	Ireland
Full product cost based	1	1	1
Variable cost based	2	2	2

*Adapted from Management Accounting Research Group, "Investigation"; Blayney and Yokoyama, "Comparative Analysis"; *Grant Thornton Survey;* Cornick, Cooper, and Wilson, "How Do Companies"; Mills and Sweeting, "Pricing Decisions"; and Drury, Braund, Osborne, and Tayles, *A Survey.* Full citations are in Appendix A.

CONSIDERATIONS OTHER THAN COSTS IN PRICING DECISIONS

Consider the prices airlines charge for a round-trip flight from San Francisco to Chicago. A coach-class ticket for the flight is $400 if the passenger stays in Chicago over a Saturday night. It is $1,500 if the passenger returns without staying over a Saturday night. Can this price difference be explained by the difference in the cost to the airlines of these round-trip flights? No, it costs the airline the same amount of money to transport the passenger from San Francisco to Chicago and back regardless of whether the passenger stays in Chicago over a Saturday night. How then can we explain this difference in price? We must recognize the potential for price discrimination.

Price discrimination is the practice of charging some customers a higher price than is charged to other customers. How does price discrimination work in our airline example? The demand for airline tickets comes from two main sources: business travelers and pleasure travelers. Business travelers need to travel in order to conduct business on behalf of their companies. They generally travel to their destinations and return home within the same week immediately after completing their work because time is very important to them. These aspects make business travelers' demand for air travel relatively insensitive to prices. The insensitivity of demand to price changes is called *demand inelasticity*. Airlines can charge business travelers higher fares because the higher fares have little effect on demand and earn higher operating income for the airlines.

Pleasure travelers have a less pressing need to return home during the week—in fact, they generally prefer to spend weekends at their destinations. Since they pay for their tickets themselves, they are much more sensitive to price than the business traveler (demand is more price-elastic). For pleasure travelers, it is profitable for the airlines to keep fares low to stimulate demand. Requiring a Saturday night stay distinguishes between the two customer segments. The airline company price-discriminates between the two market segments to take advantage of the different sensitivities to prices exhibited by the business and pleasure travelers. Price differences exist even though there is no cost difference in serving the two segments.

In addition to price discrimination, pricing decisions also consider other noncost considerations such as capacity constraints. **Peak-load pricing** is the practice of charging a higher price for the same product or service when demand approaches physical capacity limits. That is, the prices charged during busy periods (when loads on the system are high) are greater than the prices charged when slack or excess capacity is available. Peak-load pricing can be found in the telephone, telecommunication, hotel, car rental, and electric utility industries. The following are the daily rental rates charged by the Avis Corporation in October 1995 for mid-sized cars rented at the Detroit Metropolitan Airport:

Weekdays (Monday through Thursday)	$55 per day
Weekends (Friday through Sunday)	$26 per day

Avis' incremental costs of renting a car are the same whether the car is rented on a weekday or a weekend. What then explains the difference in prices? We offer two separate, but related, explanations. One explanation is that there is a greater demand for cars during weekdays because of business activity. Faced with capacity limits, Avis raises rental rates to levels that the market will bear.

A second explanation is that the rental rates are a form of price discrimination. During weekdays, the demand for cars comes largely from business travelers who need to rent cars to conduct their business and who are relatively insensitive to prices. Charging higher rental rates during weekdays is profitable because it has little effect on demand. In contrast, the demand for weekend rentals comes largely from nonbusiness or pleasure travelers who are more price-sensitive. Lower rates stimulate demand from these individuals and increase Avis' operating income. Under either explanation, the pricing decision is not driven by cost considerations.

LIFE-CYCLE PRODUCT BUDGETING AND COSTING

The **product life cycle** spans the time from initial R&D to the time at which support to customers is withdrawn. For motor vehicles, this time span may range from 5 to 10 years. For some pharmaceutical products, the time span may be 3–5 years. For fashion clothing products, the time span may be less than 1 year.

Using **life-cycle budgeting**, managers estimate the revenues and costs attributable to each product from its initial R&D to its final customer servicing and support in the marketplace. **Life-cycle costing** tracks and accumulates the actual costs attributable to each product from start to finish. The terms "cradle-to-grave costing" and "womb-to-tomb costing" convey the sense of fully capturing all costs associated with the product.

EXHIBIT 12-8

Budgeted Life-Cycle Revenues and Costs for "General Ledger" Software Package of Insight, Inc.*

	Alternative Selling Price/ Sales-Quantity Combinations		
	1	**2**	**3**
Selling price per package	$400	$480	$600
Sales quantity in units	5,000	4,000	2,500
Life-cycle revenues ($400 × 5,000; $480 × 4,000; $600 × 2,500)	$2,000,000	$1,920,000	$1,500,000
Life-cycle costs			
R&D costs	240,000	240,000	240,000
Design costs of product/process	160,000	160,000	160,000
Production costs			
$100,000 + ($25 × 5,000); $100,000 + ($25 × 4,000); $100,000 + ($25 × 2,500)	225,000	200,000	162,500
Marketing costs			
$70,000 + ($24 × 5,000); $70,000 + ($24 × 4,000); $70,000 + ($24 × 2,500)	190,000	166,000	130,000
Distribution costs			
$50,000 + ($16 × 5,000); $50,000 + ($16 × 4,000); $50,000 + ($16 × 2,500)	130,000	114,000	90,000
Customer-service costs			
$80,000 + ($30 × 5,000); $80,000 + ($30 × 4,000); $80,000 + ($30 × 2,500)	230,000	200,000	155,000
Total life-cycle costs	1,175,000	1,080,000	937,500
Life-cycle operating income	$ 825,000	$ 840,000	$ 562,500

*This exhibit does not take into consideration the time value of money when computing life-cycle revenues or life-cycle costs. Chapters 22 and 23 outline how this important factor can be incorporated into such calculations.

Life-Cycle Budgeting and Pricing Decisions

Life-cycle budgeted costs can provide important information for pricing decisions. For some products, the development period is relatively long, and many costs are incurred prior to manufacturing. Consider Insight, Inc., a computer software company developing a new accounting package, "General Ledger." Assume the following budgeted amounts for General Ledger over a 6-year product life cycle:

Years 1 and 2	
R&D costs	$240,000
Design costs	160,000

Years 3 to 6	One-Time Setup Costs	Costs per Package
Production costs	$100,000	$25
Marketing costs	70,000	24
Distribution costs	50,000	16
Customer-service costs	80,000	30

To be profitable, Insight must generate revenues to cover costs in all six business functions. A product life-cycle budget highlights the importance of setting prices and budgeting revenues to recover costs in *all* the value-chain business functions rather than costs in only some of the functions (such as production). The life-cycle budget also indicates the costs to be incurred over the life of the product. Exhibit 12-8 presents the life-cycle budget for General Ledger.

Three combinations of the selling price per package and predicted demand are shown. The high nonproduction costs at Insight are readily apparent in Exhibit 12-8. For example, R&D and product-design costs constitute over 30% of total costs for each of the three combinations of selling price and predicted sales quantity. Insight should put a premium on having as accurate a set of revenue and cost predictions for General Ledger as possible, given the high percentage of total life-cycle costs incurred before any production begins and before any revenue is received.

Exhibit 12-8 assumes that the selling price per package is the same over the entire life cycle. For strategic reasons, however, Insight may choose to "skim the market" by charging higher prices to customers eager to try General Ledger when it first comes out, and lower prices to customers who are willing to wait. The life-cycle budget will then express this strategy.

Developing Life-Cycle Reports

Most accounting systems emphasize reporting on a calendar basis—monthly, quarterly, and annually. In contrast, product life-cycle reporting does not have this calendar-based focus. Consider the life spans of four Insight products:

	Year 1	Year 2	Year 3	Year 4	Year 5	Year 6
General Ledger Package						
Law Package						
Payroll Package						
Engineering Package						

Each product spans more than 1 calendar year.

Developing life-cycle reports for each product requires tracking costs and revenues on a product-by-product basis over several calendar periods. For example, the R&D costs included in a product life-cycle cost report are often incurred in different calendar years. When R&D costs are tracked over the entire life cycle, the total magnitude of these costs for each individual product can be computed and analyzed.

A product life-cycle reporting format offers at least three important benefits:

1. The full set of revenues and costs associated with each product becomes visible. Manufacturing costs are highly visible in most accounting systems. However, the costs associated with upstream areas (for example, R&D) and downstream areas (for example, customer service) are frequently less visible on a product-by-product basis.

2. Differences among products in the percentage of their total costs incurred at early stages in the life cycle are highlighted. The higher this percentage, the more important it is for managers to develop, as early as possible, accurate predictions of the revenues for that product.

3. Interrelationships among business function cost categories are highlighted. For example, companies that cut back their R&D and product-design costs may experience major increases in customer-service costs in subsequent years. Those costs arise because products fail to meet promised quality-performance levels. A life-cycle revenue and cost report prevents such causally related changes among business function costs from being hidden (buried) as they are in calendar income statements.

Life-cycle costs further reinforce the importance of locked-in costs, target costing, and value engineering in pricing and cost management. For products with long life cycles, a very small fraction of the total life-cycle costs are actually incurred at the time when costs are locked in. But locked-in costs will determine how costs will be incurred over several years. Automobile companies combine target costing with life-cycle budgeting. For example, Chrysler, Ford, General Motors, Mercedes, Nissan, and Toyota determine target prices and target costs for their car models on the basis of estimated costs and revenues over a multiyear horizon.

Management of environmental costs provides another example of life-cycle budgeting. The enactment of strict environmental laws (for example, the Clean Air Act and the Superfund Amendment and Reauthorization Act) has introduced tougher environmental standards and increased the penalties and fines for polluting the air and contaminating subsurface soil and groundwater. Environmental costs are often locked in at the product and process design stage itself. To avoid these environmental liabilities, companies design products, processes, and procedures to prevent and reduce pollution over the product's life cycle. The computer manufacturers Compaq and Apple, for example, have recently introduced costly recycling programs to ensure that nickel-cadmium batteries (used to run laptop computers) are disposed of in an environmentally safe way at the end of the product's life.

A different notion of life-cycle costs is customer life-cycle costs. **Customer life-cycle costs** focus on the total costs to a customer of acquiring and using a product or service until it is replaced. Customer life-cycle costs for a car, for example, include the cost of the car itself plus the costs of operating and maintaining the car minus the disposal price of the car. Customer life-cycle costs can be an important consideration in the pricing decision. The Ford Motor Company's goal is to design cars that require minimal maintenance for 100,000 miles. Ford expects to charge a higher price and/or gain greater market share by selling these cars.

EFFECTS OF ANTITRUST LAWS ON PRICING

OBJECTIVE 8

Explain the effects of antitrust laws on pricing

Under the U.S. Robinson-Patman Act, a manufacturer cannot price-discriminate between two customers if the intent is to lessen or prevent competition among customers. Three key features of the price discrimination laws are (1) they apply to manufacturers and not service providers; (2) price discrimination is permissible if differences in prices can be justified by differences in costs, and (3) price discrimination is illegal only if the intent is to destroy competition. The price discrimination by airlines and car rental companies described earlier in the chapter is legal because these companies are service companies and because their practices do not hinder competition.

To comply with U.S. antitrust laws, such as the Sherman Act, the Clayton Act, the Federal Trade Commission Act, and the Robinson-Patman Act, pricing must not be predatory.[2] A business engages in **predatory pricing** when it deliberately prices below its costs in an effort to drive out competitors and restrict supply and then raises prices rather than enlarge demand or meet competition.[3]

The U.S. Supreme Court has established the following conditions to prove that predatory pricing has occurred: (1) the predator company charges a price that is below an appropriate measure of its costs, and (2) the predator company has a reasonable prospect of recovering in the future (through larger market share or higher prices) the money it lost by pricing below cost. The Supreme Court has not specified the "appropriate measure of costs."[4]

---

[2]Discussion of the Sherman Act and the Clayton Act is in A. Barkman and J. Jolley, "Cost Defenses for Antitrust Cases," *Management Accounting* **67**, no. 10, pp. 37–40.

[3]See W. Viscusi, J. Vernon, and J. Harrington, *Economics of Regulation and Antitrust* (Lexington, Mass.: D. C. Heath, 1992), p. 213; and J. L. Goldstein, "Single Firm Predatory Pricing in Antitrust Law: The Rose Acre Recoupment Test and the Search for an Appropriate Judicial Standard," *Columbia Law Review* **91**(1991), pp. 1757–92.

[4]*Brooke Group v. Brown & Williamson Tobacco*, 113 S. Ct. (1993); T. J. Trujillo, "Predatory Pricing Standards under Recent Supreme Court Decisions and Their Failure to Recognize Strategic Behavior as a Barrier to Entry," *Iowa Journal of Corporation Law* (Summer 1994), pp. 809–31.

Most courts in the United States have defined the "appropriate measure of costs" as the short-run marginal and average costs.[5] In *Adjustor's Replace-a-Car v. Agency Rent-a-Car*,[6] Adjustor's (the plaintiff) claimed that it was forced to withdraw from the Austin and San Antonio, Texas, markets because Agency had engaged in predatory pricing. To prove predatory pricing, Adjustor pointed to "the net loss from operations" on Agency's income statement, calculated after allocating Agency's headquarters overhead. The judge, however, ruled that Agency had not engaged in predatory pricing because the price it charged for a rental car never dropped below its average variable cost.

Managers and accountants who are concerned with their conformance to antitrust laws would be prudent to have a system that incorporates the following procedures:

1. Collect data in a manner that permits relatively easy compilation of variable costs.

2. Keep detailed records of variable costs for all value-chain business functions and review all proposed prices below variable costs in advance, with a presumption of claims of predatory intent.

The Supreme Court decision in *Brooke Group v. Brown & Williamson Tobacco* (BWT) illustrates that, for predatory pricing to occur, the company pricing below cost must have a reasonable chance of later increasing prices or market share to recover its losses.[7] The defendant, BWT, a cigarette manufacturer, sold "brand name" cigarettes and had 12% of the cigarette market. The introduction of generic cigarettes threatened BWT's market share. BWT responded by introducing its own version of generics priced below average variable cost, thereby making it difficult for generic manufacturers to continue in business. The Supreme Court ruled that BWT's action was a competitive response and not predatory pricing. Why? Because, given BWT's current small (12%) market share and the existing competition within the industry, it would not be able to later charge a monopoly price to recoup its losses.

Closely related to predatory pricing is dumping. Under U.S. laws, **dumping** occurs when a non-U.S. company sells a product in the United States at a price below the market value in the country of its creation, and this action materially injures or threatens to materially injure an industry in the United States. If dumping is proven, an antidumping duty can be imposed under U.S. tariff laws equal to the amount by which the foreign market value exceeds the U.S. price. Cases related to dumping have occurred in the cement, steel, semiconductor, and sweater industries. For example, in 1990, the U.S. International Trade Commission ruled that Cementos Mexicanos, S.A. (Cemex) had dumped cement in the southern and southwestern United States. The Commission levied an antidumping tariff of 58% on all subsequent Cemex imports.[8]

Another violation of antitrust laws is collusive pricing. **Collusive pricing** occurs when companies in an industry conspire in their pricing and output decisions to achieve a price above the competitive price. Collusive pricing violates the antitrust laws of the United States because it restrains trade. In 1990, for example, the Justice Department charged that the use of a common computer reservation system enabled airlines to collude on maintaining noncompetitive prices. The airlines involved—American, Continental, Delta, Midway, Northwest, PanAm, TWA, United, and USAir—have reimbursed customers under the terms of the settlement.

---

[5]An exception is *McGahee v. Northern Propane Gas Co.* [858 F. 2d 1487 (1988)] where the Eleventh Circuit Court held that prices below average total cost constitute evidence of predatory intent. For more discussion, see P. Areeda and D. Turner, "Predatory Pricing and Related Practices under Section 2 of the Sherman Act," *Harvard Law Review* **88**(1975), pp. 697–733. For an overview of case law, see W. Viscusi, J. Vernon, and J. Harrington, *Economics of Regulation and Antitrust* (Lexington, Mass.: D. C. Heath, 1992). See also the "Legal Developments" section of the *Journal of Marketing* for summaries of court cases.

[6]*Adjustor's Replace-a-Car, Inc. v. Agency Rent-a-Car*, 735 2d 884 (1984).

[7]*Brooke Group v. Brown & Williamson Tobacco*, 113 S. Ct. (1993).

[8]"Cemex and Antidumping," Graduate School of Business, Stanford University Case S-P-4, 1994.

PROBLEM

Consider again the Astel Computer example described earlier (pp. 439–441). Astel's marketing manager realizes that a further reduction in price is necessary to sell 200,000 units of Provalue II. To maintain a target profitability of $16 million, or $80 per unit on Provalue II (the same figure shown in Exhibit 12-6), Astel will need to reduce costs of Provalue II by $6 million or $30 per unit. The new version is called Modified Provalue II. Astel targets a reduction of $4 million or $20 per unit in manufacturing costs, and the rest in marketing, distribution, and customer-service costs. The cross-functional team assigned to this task proposes the following changes in the manufacture of Modified Provalue II:

1. Purchase some subassembled components that combine the functions performed by individual components. This change will not affect Modified Provalue II's quality or performance but will reduce direct materials costs from $385 to $375 per unit.

2. Reengineer processes to reduce ordering and receiving costs per order from $80 to $60. Using component subassemblies will reduce the number of purchased components in Modified Provalue II from 425 to 400. As in the chapter example, Astel will place 50 orders per year for each component.

3. Reduce the labor and power required per hour of testing. This will decrease testing and inspection costs for Modified Provalue II from $2 to $1.70 per testing-hour. Under the new proposal, each Modified Provalue II will be tested for 14 hours rather than 15 hours.

4. Develop new rework procedures that will reduce the rework cost of Modified Provalue II from $100 to $80 for each of the 13,000 units (6.5% of 200,000) expected to be reworked.

No changes are proposed in direct manufacturing labor costs per unit and in total machining costs.

REQUIRED

Will the proposed changes achieve Astel's targeted reduction of $4 million (or $20 per unit) in manufacturing costs? Show your computations.

SOLUTION

Exhibit 12-9 presents the manufacturing costs for Modified Provalue II. The proposed changes will reduce manufacturing costs from $108 million or $540 per unit (see Exhibit 12-5) to $104 million or $520 per unit (Exhibit 12-9), and will thus achieve the target reduction of $4 million or $20 per unit.

SUMMARY

The following points are linked to the chapter's learning objectives.

1. Three major influences on pricing decisions are customers, competitors, and costs.

2. Short-run pricing decisions focus on a period of a year or less and have no long-run implications. Long-run pricing decisions focus on a product in a major market with a time horizon of longer than 1 year. The time horizon appropriate to a decision on pricing dictates which costs are relevant.

3. One approach to pricing is to use a target price. Target price is the estimated price that potential customers are willing to pay for a product (or service). A target

EXHIBIT 12-9
Target Manufacturing Costs of Modified Provalue II in 19_8

	Estimated Manufacturing Costs for 200,000 Units (1)	Estimated Manufacturing Cost per Unit (2) = (1) ÷ 200,000
Direct manufacturing costs		
Direct materials costs (200,000 units × $375)	$ 75,000,000	$375.00
Direct manufacturing labor costs (200,000 units × $53)	10,600,000	53.00
Direct machining costs (fixed costs of $11,400,000)	11,400,000	57.00
Direct manufacturing costs	97,000,000	485.00
Manufacturing overhead costs		
Ordering and receiving costs (20,000* orders × $60)	1,200,000	6.00
Testing and inspection costs (2,800,000[†] hours × $1.70)	4,760,000	23.80
Rework costs (13,000 units × $80)	1,040,000	5.20
Manufacturing overhead costs	7,000,000	35.00
Total manufacturing costs	$104,000,000	$520.00

*400 components × 50 orders per component = 20,000 orders.
[†]200,000 units × 14 testing-hours per unit = 2,800,000 testing-hours.

operating profit per unit is subtracted from the target price to determine the target cost per unit. The target cost per unit is the estimated long-run cost of a product (or service) that when sold enables the firm to achieve the targeted income. The challenge for the organization is to make the cost improvements necessary through value-engineering methods to achieve the target cost.

4. Cost incurrence arises when resources are actually sacrificed or used up. Locked-in costs refer to costs that have not yet been incurred but which, based on decisions that have already been made, will be incurred in the future.

5. The cost-plus approach to pricing chooses prospective prices by using a general formula that adds a markup to a cost base. Many different costs (such as full product costs or manufacturing costs) can serve as the cost base in applying the cost-plus formula. Prices are then modified on the basis of customers' reactions and competitors' responses.

6. Price discrimination is the practice of charging some customers a higher price than is charged to other customers. Peak-load pricing is the practice of charging a higher price for the same product or service when demand approaches physical capacity limits. Under price discrimination and peak-load pricing, prices differ among market segments even though the outlay costs of providing the product or service are approximately the same.

7. Life-cycle budgeting and life-cycle costing estimate, track, and accumulate the costs (and revenues) attributable to each product from its initial R&D to its final customer service and support in the marketplace. Life-cycle costing offers three important benefits: (a) the full set of costs associated with each product become visible; (b) differences among products in the percentage of their total costs incurred at early stages in the life cycle are highlighted; and (c) interrelationships among value-chain business function costs are emphasized. Companies choose prices to maximize the profits earned over a product's life cycle.

8. To comply with antitrust laws, a company must not engage in predatory pricing, dumping, or collusive pricing, which lessens competition or puts another company at a competitive disadvantage.

This chapter and the Glossary at the end of the book contain definitions of the following important terms:

collusive pricing (p. 450)
cost incurrence (438)
customer life-cycle costs (449)
designed-in costs (438)
dumping (450)
life-cycle budgeting (446)
life-cycle costing (446)
locked-in costs (438)
peak-load pricing (446)
predatory pricing (449)

price discrimination (445)
product life cycle (446)
target cost per unit (436)
target operating income per unit (436)
target price (436)
target rate of return on investment (442)
value engineering (436)

QUESTIONS

12-1 What are the three major influences on pricing decisions?

12-2 "The relevant costs for pricing decisions are full product costs." Comment.

12-3 Give two examples of pricing decisions with a short-run focus.

12-4 How is activity-based costing useful for pricing decisions?

12-5 Describe two alternative approaches to long-run pricing decisions.

12-6 What is a *target cost per unit?*

12-7 Describe *value engineering* and its role in target costing.

12-8 Give two examples each of a *value-added cost* and a *nonvalue-added cost.*

12-9 "It is not important for a firm to distinguish between cost incurrence and locked-in costs." Do you agree? Explain.

12-10 What is *cost-plus pricing?*

12-11 Describe three alternative cost-plus methods.

12-12 Give two examples where the difference in the costs of two products or services is much smaller than the difference in their prices.

12-13 What is *life-cycle budgeting?*

12-14 What are three benefits of using a product life-cycle reporting format?

12-15 Define predatory pricing, dumping, and collusive pricing.

EXERCISES

12-16 Relevant-cost approach to pricing decisions, special order. The following financial data apply to the videotape production plant of the Dill Company for October 19_7:

	Budgeted Manufacturing Costs per Video Tape
Direct materials	$1.50
Direct manufacturing labor	0.80
Variable manufacturing overhead	0.70
Fixed manufacturing overhead	1.00
Total manufacturing costs	$4.00

Variable manufacturing overhead varies with respect to units produced. Fixed manufacturing overhead of $1 per tape is based on budgeted fixed manufacturing overhead of $150,000 per month and budgeted production of 150,000 tapes per month. The Dill Company sells each tape for $5.

Marketing costs have two components:
◆ Variable marketing costs (sales commissions) of 5% of dollar sales
◆ Fixed monthly costs of $65,000

During October 19_7, Lyn Randell, a Dill Company salesperson, asked the president for permission to sell 1,000 tapes at $3.80 per tape to a customer not in its normal marketing channels. The president refused this special order on the grounds that the order would show a loss because the selling price was below the total budgeted manufacturing cost.

REQUIRED
1. What would have been the effect on monthly operating income of accepting the special order?
2. Comment on the president's "below manufacturing costs" reasoning for rejecting the special order.
3. What factors would you recommend that the president consider when deciding whether to accept or reject the special order?

12-17 Relevant-cost approach to short-run pricing decisions. The San Carlos Company is an electronics business with eight product lines. Income data for one of the products (XT-107) for the month just ended (June 19_8) are as follows:

Sales, 200,000 units at average price of $100		$20,000,000
Variable costs		
Direct materials at $35 per unit	$7,000,000	
Direct manufacturing labor at $10 per unit	2,000,000	
Variable manufacturing overhead at $5 per unit	1,000,000	
Sales commissions at 15% of sales	3,000,000	
Other variable costs at $5 per unit	1,000,000	
Total variable costs		14,000,000
Contribution margin		6,000,000
Fixed costs		5,000,000
Operating income		$ 1,000,000

Abrams, Inc., an instruments company, has a problem with its preferred supplier of XT-107 component products. This supplier has had a 3-week labor strike and will not be able to supply Abrams 3,000 units next month. Abrams approaches the sales representative, Sarah Holtz, of the San Carlos Company about providing 3,000 units of XT-107 at a price of $80 per unit. Holtz informs the XT-107 product manager, Jim McMahon, that she would accept a flat commission of $6,000 rather than the usual 15% if this special order were accepted. San Carlos has the capacity to produce 300,000 units of XT-107 each month, but demand has not exceeded 200,000 units in any month in the last year.

REQUIRED
1. If the 3,000-unit order from Abrams is accepted, what will be the effect on monthly operating income? (Assume the same cost structure as occurred in June 19_8.)
2. McMahon ponders whether to accept the 3,000-unit special order. He is afraid of the precedent that might be set by cutting the price. He says, "The price is below our full cost of $95 per unit. I think we should quote a full price, or Abrams will expect favored treatment again and again if we continue to do business with them." Do you agree with McMahon? Explain.

12-18 Short-run pricing, capacity constraints. Boutique Chemicals makes a specialized chemical product, Bolzene, from a specially imported material, Pyrone. To make 1 kilogram of Bolzene requires 1.5 kilograms of Pyrone.

Bolzene has a contribution margin of $6 per kilogram. Boutique has just received a request to manufacture 3,000 kilograms of Seltium that also requires Pyrone as the material input. Boutique calculates the following costs of making 1 kilogram of Seltium:

Pyrone (2 kilograms × $4 per kilogram)	$ 8
Direct manufacturing labor	4
Variable manufacturing overhead costs	3
Fixed manufacturing overhead costs allocated	5
Total manufacturing costs	$20

Boutique has adequate excess plant capacity to make Seltium.

REQUIRED

1. Suppose Boutique has adequate Pyrone available to make Seltium. What is the minimum price per kilogram that Boutique should charge to manufacture Seltium?
2. Now suppose Pyrone is in short supply. The Pyrone used to make Seltium will reduce the Bolzene that Boutique can make and sell. What is the minimum price per kilogram that Boutique should charge to manufacture Seltium?

12-19 Value-added, nonvalue-added costs. The Marino Repair Shop repairs and services machine tools. A summary of its costs (by activity) for 19_8 is as follows:

a. Materials and labor for servicing machine tools	$800,000
b. Rework costs	75,000
c. Expediting costs caused by work delays	60,000
d. Materials handling costs	50,000
e. Materials procurement and inspection costs	35,000
f. Preventive maintenance of equipment	15,000
g. Breakdown maintenance of equipment	55,000

REQUIRED

1. Classify each of the seven costs as value-added, nonvalue-added, or in the gray area in between.
2. For any costs classified in the gray area, assume 65% of the costs are value-added and 35% are nonvalue-added. How much of the total costs are value-added and how much are nonvalue-added?
3. Marino is considering the following changes at the shop: (a) introducing quality improvement programs whose net effect will be to reduce rework and expediting costs by 75% and materials and labor costs by 5%, (b) working with suppliers to reduce materials procurement and inspection costs by 20% and materials handling costs by 25%, and (c) increasing preventive maintenance costs by 50% to reduce breakdown maintenance costs by 40%. What effect would each of these programs have on value-added costs, nonvalue-added costs, and total costs? Comment briefly.

12-20 Value-added versus nonvalue-added cost classifications. Olivia Johns is manager of the Home Appliance plant of Newton Products. Johns decides to experiment with the value-added/nonvalue-added classification of costs in the accounting records. She selects the clothes dryer product line for her test. She asks your advice on classifying items of labor time (and cost) in the plant for this product:

a. Moving component parts from warehouse to assembly line.
b. Assembling the tumbler unit.
c. Expediting materials to the door-assembly area because of stock-balance error.
d. Assembling the control panel.
e. Inserting the owner's manual and instruction guide in the dryer package.
f. Reworking faulty latches on clothes-dryer doors.
g. Testing the operating capabilities of the assembled unit.
h. Packaging the clothes dryer in a breakage-resistant box.

REQUIRED

1. What is the distinction between a value-added cost and a nonvalue-added cost? Classify each of the eight items (a–h) as (i) a value-added cost, (ii) in the gray area, or (iii) a nonvalue-added cost.
2. How can Johns use your classifications in requirement 1 in making decisions at the plant?
3. Johns attends a conference where a well-known cost accounting writer expresses a great deal of cynicism about the value-added/nonvalue-added distinction. He calls it a "fad with a shelf life shorter than freshly cut roses." Johns has the chance to meet the cost accounting writer. What question should she pose to him about her proposed experiment with the value-added/nonvalue-added cost distinction?

12-21 Target prices, target costs, activity-based costing systems. Snappy Tiles is a small distributor of marble tiles. Snappy identifies its three major activities and cost pools as ordering, receiving and storage, and shipping, and reports the following details for 19_7:

Activity	Cost Driver	Quantity of Cost Driver	Cost per Unit of Cost Driver
1. Placing and paying for orders of marble tiles	Number of orders	500	$50 per order
2. Receiving and storage	Number of loads moved	4,000	$30 per load
3. Shipping of marble tiles to retailers	Number of shipments	1,500	$40 per shipment

Snappy buys 250,000 marble tiles at an average cost of $3 per tile and sells them to retailers at an average price of $4 per tile. Fixed costs are $40,000.

REQUIRED

1. Calculate Snappy's operating income for 19_7.
2. For 19_8, retailers are demanding a 5% discount off the 19_7 price. Snappy's suppliers are only willing to give a 4% discount. Snappy expects to sell the same quantity of marble tiles in 19_8 as it did in 19_7. If all other costs and cost driver information remain the same, what will Snappy's operating income be in 19_8?
3. Suppose further that Snappy decides to make changes in its ordering, and receiving and storing practices. By placing long-term orders with its key suppliers, it expects to reduce the number of orders to 200 and the cost per order to $25 per order. By redesigning the layout of the warehouse and reconfiguring the crates in which the marble tiles are moved, Snappy expects to reduce the number of loads moved to 3,125 and the cost per load moved to $28. Will Snappy achieve its target operating income of $0.30 per tile in 19_8? Show your calculations.

12-22 Cost-plus target return on investment pricing. John Beck is the managing partner of a partnership that has just finished building a 60-room motel. Beck anticipates that he will rent these rooms for 16,000 nights next year (or 16,000 room-nights). All rooms are similar and will rent for the same price. Beck estimates the following operating costs for next year:

Variable operating costs	$3 per room-night
Fixed costs	
Salaries and wages	$175,000
Maintenance of building and pool	37,000
Other operating and administration costs	140,000
Total fixed costs	$352,000

The capital invested in the motel is $960,000. The partnership's target return on investment is 25%. Beck expects demand for rooms to be about uniform throughout the year. He plans to price the rooms at cost plus a markup to earn the target return on investment.

1. What price should Beck charge for a room-night? What is the markup over the full cost of a room-night?
2. Beck's market research indicates that if the price of a room-night determined in requirement 1 was reduced by 10%, the expected number of room-nights Beck could rent would increase by 10%. Should Beck make the 10% cut?

12-23 Cost-plus and market-based pricing. California Temps, a large labor contractor, supplies contract labor to building construction companies. For 19_8, California Temps has budgeted to supply 80,000 hours of contract labor. Its variable cost is $12 per hour and its fixed costs are $240,000. Roger Mason, the general manager, has proposed a cost-plus approach for pricing labor at full cost plus 20%.

REQUIRED
1. Calculate the price per hour that California Temps should charge based on Mason's proposal.
2. Sheila Woods, the marketing manager, has supplied the following information on demand levels at different prices:

Price per Hour	Demand (Hours)
$16	120,000
17	100,000
18	80,000
19	70,000
20	60,000

California Temps can meet any of these demand levels. Fixed costs will remain unchanged for all the preceding demand levels. On the basis of this additional information, what price per hour should California Temps charge?
3. Comment on your answers to requirements 1 and 2. Why are they the same or not the same?

12-24 Considerations other than cost in pricing. Examples of round-trip ticket prices on the London Underground are as follows:

	Piccadilly to Wembley Park	Heathrow to Trafalgar Square	Edgware to Wimbledon
Peak hours (for travel starting between 5:30 A.M. and 9:30 A.M. Monday through Friday)	£4.80	£6.40	£5.80
Off-peak hours	£3.50	£3.90	£3.90

REQUIRED
1. Are there differences in incremental or outlay costs for the London Underground for trips starting in peak hours versus off-peak hours?
2. Why do you think the London Underground charges different rates for peak-hour and off-peak-hour travel?

12-25 Considerations other than cost in pricing. Examples of prices charged per minute by AT&T for long-distance telephone calls within the United States at different times of the day and week are as follows:

	Washington, D.C. to Philadelphia	Washington, D.C. to St. Louis	Washington, D.C. to Los Angeles
Peak period (8 A.M. to 5 P.M., Monday through Friday)	$0.21	$0.22	$0.24
Evenings (5 P.M. to 11 P.M., Monday through Friday)	$0.13	$0.13	$0.14
Nights and weekends	$0.11	$0.11	$0.12

1. Are there differences in incremental or outlay costs per minute for AT&T for telephone calls made during peak hours compared to telephone calls made at other times of the day?

2. Why do you think AT&T charges different prices per minute for telephone calls made during peak hours compared to telephone calls made at other times of the day?

12-26 Life-cycle product costing, product emphasis. Decision Support Systems (DSS) is examining the profitability and pricing policies of its software division. The DSS software division develops software packages for engineers. DSS has collected data on three of its more recent packages:

◆ EE-46: package for electrical engineers
◆ ME-83: package for mechanical engineers
◆ IE-17: package for industrial engineers

Summary details on each package over their 2-year "cradle-to-grave" product lives are as follows:

		Number of Units Sold	
Package	Selling Price	Year 1	Year 2
EE-46	$250	2,000	8,000
ME-83	300	2,000	3,000
IE-17	200	5,000	3,000

Assume that no inventory remains on hand at the end of year 2.

DSS is deciding which product lines to emphasize in its software division. In the past 2 years, the profitability of this division has been mediocre. DSS is particularly concerned with the increase in R&D costs in several of its divisions. An analyst at the software division pointed out that for one of its most recent packages (IE-17), major efforts had been made to cut back R&D costs.

Last week Nancy Sullivan, the software division manager, attended a seminar on product life-cycle management. The topic of life-cycle reporting was discussed. Sullivan decides to use this approach in her own division. She collects the following life-cycle revenue and cost information for the EE-46, ME-83, and IE-17 packages:

	EE-46		ME-83		IE-17	
	Year 1	Year 2	Year 1	Year 2	Year 1	Year 2
Revenues	$500,000	$2,000,000	$600,000	$900,000	$1,000,000	$600,000
Costs						
R&D	700,000	0	450,000	0	240,000	0
Design of product	185,000	15,000	110,000	10,000	80,000	16,000
Manufacturing	75,000	225,000	105,000	105,000	143,000	65,000
Marketing	140,000	360,000	120,000	150,000	240,000	208,000
Distribution	15,000	60,000	24,000	36,000	60,000	36,000
Customer service	50,000	325,000	45,000	105,000	220,000	388,000

1. How does a product life-cycle income statement differ from an income statement that is calendar-based? What are the benefits of using a product life-cycle reporting format?

2. Present a product life-cycle income statement for each software package. Which package is the most profitable, and which is the least profitable?

3. How do the three software packages differ in their cost structure (the percentage of total costs in each cost category)?

PROBLEMS

12-27 Pricing of hotel rooms on weekends. Paul Diamond is the owner of the Galaxy chain of four-star prestige hotels. These hotels are in Chicago, London, Los Angeles, Montreal, New York, Seattle, San Francisco, and Tokyo. Diamond is currently struggling to set weekend rates for the San Francisco hotel (the San Francisco Galaxy). From Sunday through Thursday, the Galaxy has an average occupancy rate of 90%. On Friday and Saturday nights, however, average occupancy declines to less than 30%. Galaxy's major customers are business travelers who stay mainly Sunday through Thursday.

The current room rate at the Galaxy is $150 a night for single occupancy and $180 a night for double occupancy. These rates apply 7 nights a week. For many years, Diamond has resisted having rates for Friday and Saturday nights that are different from those for the remainder of the week. Diamond has long believed that price reductions convey a "nonprestige" impression to his guests. The San Francisco Galaxy highly values its reputation for treating its guests as "royalty."

Most room costs at the Galaxy are fixed on a short-stay (per night) basis. Diamond estimates the variable costs of servicing each room to be $20 a night per single occupancy and $22 a night per double occupancy.

Many prestige hotels in San Francisco offer special weekend rate reductions (Friday and/or Saturday) of up to 50% of their Sunday-through-Thursday rates. These weekend rates also include additional items such as a breakfast for two, a bottle of champagne, and discounted theater tickets.

REQUIRED

1. Would you recommend that Diamond reduce room rates at the San Francisco Galaxy on Friday and Saturday nights? What factors should be considered in his decision?
2. In 6 months' time, the Super Bowl is to be held in San Francisco. Diamond observes that several four-star prestige hotels have already advertised a Friday-through-Sunday rate for Super Bowl weekend of $300 a night. Should Diamond charge extra for the Super Bowl weekend? Explain.

12-28 Relevant-cost approach to pricing decisions. Stardom, Inc., cans peaches for sale to food distributors. All costs are classified as either manufacturing or marketing. Stardom prepares monthly budgets. The March 19_8 budgeted absorption-costing income statement is as follows:

Revenues (1,000 crates × $100 a crate)	$100,000	100%
Cost of goods sold	60,000	60
Gross margin	40,000	40
Marketing costs	30,000	30
Operating income	$ 10,000	10%

Normal markup percentage:
$40,000 ÷ $60,000 = 66.7% of absorption cost

Monthly costs are classified as fixed or variable (with respect to the cans produced for manufacturing costs and with respect to the cans sold for marketing costs):

	Fixed	Variable
Manufacturing	$20,000	$40,000
Marketing	16,000	14,000

Stardom has the capacity to can 1,500 crates per month. The relevant range in which monthly fixed manufacturing costs will be "fixed" is from 500 to 1,500 crates per month.

REQUIRED

1. Calculate the normal markup percentage based on total variable costs.
2. Assume that a new customer approaches Stardom to buy 200 crates at $55 per crate. The customer does not require additional marketing effort. Additional manufacturing costs of $2,000 (for special packaging) will be required. Stardom believes that this is a one-time-only special order because the customer is discontinuing business in 6 weeks' time. Stardom is reluctant to accept this 200-crate special order because the $55 per crate price is below the $60 per crate absorption cost. Do you agree with this reasoning? Explain.
3. Assume that the new customer decides to remain in business. How would this longevity affect your willingness to accept the $55 per crate offer? Explain.

12-29 Target prices, target costs, value engineering, cost incurrence, locked-in cost, activity-based costing. Cutler Electronics makes a radio-cassette player, CE100, which has 80 components. Cutler sells 7,000 units each month for $70 each. The costs of manufacturing CE100 are $45 per unit, or $315,000 per month. Monthly manufacturing costs incurred are as follows:

Direct materials costs	$182,000
Direct manufacturing labor costs	28,000
Machining costs (fixed)	31,500
Testing costs	35,000
Rework costs	14,000
Ordering costs	3,360
Engineering costs (fixed)	21,140
Total manufacturing costs	$315,000

Cutler's management identifies the activity cost pools, the cost drivers for each activity, and the cost per unit of cost driver for each overhead cost pool as follows:

Manufacturing Activity	Description of Activity	Cost Driver	Cost per Unit of Cost Driver
1. Machining costs	Machining components	Fixed costs	No cost driver
2. Testing costs	Testing components and final product (Each unit of CE100 is tested individually.)	Testing-hours	$2 per testing-hour
3. Rework costs	Correcting and fixing errors and defects	Units of CE100 reworked	$20 per unit
4. Ordering costs	Ordering of components	Number of orders	$21 per order
5. Engineering costs	Designing and managing of products and process	Fixed costs	No cost driver

Over a long-run time horizon, Cutler's management views direct materials costs and direct manufacturing labor costs as variable with respect to the units of CE100 manufactured. Each of the overhead costs described in the preceding table varies, as described, with the chosen cost drivers.

The following additional information describes the existing design:
a. Testing and inspection time per unit is 2.5 hours.
b. Ten percent of the CE100s manufactured are reworked.
c. Cutler places two orders with each component supplier each month. Each component is supplied by a different supplier. It takes 1 hour to place an order.

To respond to competitive pressures, Cutler must reduce its price to $62 per unit and reduce its costs by $8 per unit. No additional sales are anticipated at this lower price. However, Cutler stands to lose significant sales if it does not cut its price. Manufacturing has been asked to reduce its costs by $6 per unit. Improvements in manufacturing efficiency are expected to yield net savings of $1.50 per radio-cassette player, but that is not enough. The chief engineer has proposed a new modular design that reduces the number of components to 50 and also simplifies testing. The newly designed radio-cassette player, called "New CE100" will replace CE100.

The expected effects of the new design are as follows:

a. Direct materials costs for the New CE100 are expected to be lower by $2.20 per unit.

b. Direct manufacturing labor costs for the New CE100 are expected to be lower by $0.50 per unit.

c. Machining time required to manufacture the New CE100 is expected to be 20% less. It currently takes 1 hour to manufacture 1 unit of CE100.

d. Time required for testing the New CE100 is expected to be lower by 20%.

e. Rework is expected to decline to 4% of New CE100s manufactured.

Assume that the cost per unit of the cost driver for CE100 continues to apply to New CE100.

REQUIRED

1. Calculate Cutler's manufacturing cost per unit of New CE100.
2. Will the new design achieve the per unit cost-reduction targets that have been set for the manufacturing costs of New CE 100?
3. The problem describes two strategies to reduce costs: (a) improving manufacturing efficiency, and (b) modifying the design. Which strategy has a bigger impact on costs? Why? Explain briefly.

12-30 Product costs, activity-based costing systems. Executive Power (EP) manufactures and sells computers and computer peripherals to several nationwide retail chains. John Farnham is the manager of the printer division. Its two largest selling printers are P-41 and P-63.

The manufacturing cost of each printer is calculated using EP's activity-based costing system. EP has one direct-manufacturing cost category (direct materials) and the following five indirect-manufacturing cost pools:

Indirect-Manufacturing Cost Pool	Allocation Base	Allocation Rate
1. Materials handling	Number of parts	$1.20 per part
2. Assembly management	Hours of assembly time	$40 per hour of assembly time
3. Machine insertion of parts	Number of machine-inserted parts	$0.70 per machine-inserted part
4. Manual insertion of parts	Number of manually inserted parts	$2.10 per manually inserted part
5. Quality testing	Hours of quality testing time	$25 per testing-hour

Product characteristics of P-41 and P-63 are as follows:

	P-41	P-63
Direct materials costs	$407.50	$292.10
Number of parts	85 parts	46 parts
Hours of assembly time	3.2 hours	1.9 hours
Number of machine-inserted parts	49 parts	31 parts
Number of manually inserted parts	36 parts	15 parts
Hours of quality testing	1.4 hours	1.1 hours

REQUIRED

What is the manufacturing cost of P-41? Of P-63?

12-31 Target cost, activity-based costing systems (continuation of 12-30). Assume all the information in Problem 12-30. Farnham has just received some bad news. A foreign competitor has introduced products very similar to P-41 and P-63. Given their announced selling prices, Farnham estimates the P-41 clone to have a manufacturing cost of approximately $680 and the P-63 clone to have a manufacturing cost of approximately $390. He calls a meeting of product designers and manufacturing personnel at the printer division. They all agree to have the $680 and $390 figures become target costs for redesigned versions of EP's P-41 and P-63, respectively. Product designers examine alternative ways of designing printers with comparable performance but lower cost. They come up with the following revised designs for P-41 and P-63 (termed P-41 REV and P-63 REV, respectively):

	P-41 REV	P-63 REV
Direct materials costs	$381.20	$263.10
Number of parts	71 parts	39 parts
Hours of assembly time	2.1 hours	1.6 hours
Number of machine-inserted parts	59 parts	29 parts
Number of manually inserted parts	12 parts	10 parts
Hours of quality testing	1.2 hours	0.9 hours

REQUIRED
1. What is a target cost per unit?
2. Using the activity-based costing system outlined in Problem 12-30, compute the manufacturing costs of P-41 REV and P-63 REV. How do they compare with the $680 and $390 target costs per unit?
3. Explain the differences between P-41 and P-41 REV and between P-63 and P-63 REV.
4. Assume now that John Farnham has achieved major cost reductions in one of the activity areas. As a consequence, the allocation rate in the assembly-management activity area will be reduced from $40 to $28 per assembly-hour. How will this activity-area cost reduction affect the manufacturing costs of P-41 REV and P-63 REV? Comment on the results.

12-32 Cost-plus pricing. (CMA, adapted) Marcus Fibers, Inc., specializes in manufacturing synthetic fibers, which the company uses in many products, such as blankets. The company uses a standard costing system and allocates overhead costs on the basis of direct manufacturing labor-hours.

Marcus has recently received a request from Thermco, Inc., to bid on the manufacture of 800,000 blankets. The bid must be stated at full cost per unit plus a return on full cost of no more than 9% after income taxes. Full cost has been defined as including all variable costs of manufacturing the product, a reasonable amount of fixed manufacturing overhead, and a reasonable amount of incremental administrative costs associated with the manufacture and sale of the product. Thermco has indicated that bids in excess of $25 per blanket are not likely to be considered.

In order to prepare the bid for the 800,000 blankets, Andrea Lightner, cost accountant, has gathered the following information about the costs associated with blanket production:

Direct materials costs	$1.50 per pound of fibers
Direct manufacturing labor costs	$7.00 per hour
Direct machine costs*	$10 per blanket
Variable manufacturing overhead costs	$3.00 per direct manufacturing labor-hour

Fixed manufacturing overhead costs	$8.00 per direct manufacturing labor-hour
Incremental administrative costs	$2,500 per 1,000 blankets
Special fee[†]	$0.50 per blanket
Materials usage	6 pounds per blanket
Production rate	4 blankets per direct manufacturing labor-hour
Effective tax rate	40%

*Direct machine costs consist of items such as special lubricants, replacement of needles used in stitching, and maintenance costs. These costs are not included in the budgeted overhead rates.
[†]Marcus recently developed a new blanket fiber at a cost of $750,000. In an effort to recover this cost, Marcus has instituted a policy of adding a $0.50 fee to the cost of each blanket that uses the new fiber. To date, the company has recovered $125,000. Lightner knows that this fee does not fit within the definition of full cost because it is not a cost of manufacturing the product.

REQUIRED

1. Calculate the minimum price per blanket that Marcus Fibers, Inc., could bid without changing the company's net income.
2. Using the full cost criterion and the maximum allowable return specified, calculate Marcus Fibers' bid price per blanket.
3. Without considering your answer to requirement 2, assume that the price per blanket that Marcus Fibers calculated using the cost-plus criterion is greater than the maximum bid of $25 per blanket allowed. Discuss the factors that Marcus Fibers should consider before deciding whether or not to submit a bid at the maximum acceptable price of $25 per blanket.

12-33 Cost-plus target rate of return on investment pricing. Brighton Paints is a paint retailer. Brighton's variable cost per can is $7 per can. Brighton expects to sell 100,000 cans next year. Fixed costs are expected to equal $200,000. Expected capital investment is $350,000 in fixed assets plus 15% of sales dollars in current assets.

REQUIRED

1. Calculate the price per can that Brighton should charge next year to earn a 20% rate of return on its investment in fixed and current assets. (*Hint:* Express Brighton's operating profit in two ways—as sales dollars minus total costs and as 20% of investment—and solve for the unknown sales price.)
2. Suppose Brighton's management has just obtained market research information that indicates that a 10% increase in the price per can calculated in requirement 1 will result in a 10% decrease in paint cans sold. Should Brighton increase the price per can by 10%?

12-34 Airline pricing, considerations other than cost in pricing. Air Americo is about to introduce a daily round-trip flight from New York (NY) to Los Angeles (LA). Air Americo offers only one class of seats—Comfort Class, which allows more leg room for passengers—on all its flights. No other airline offers this kind of seat. Air Americo is in the process of determining how it should price its round-trip tickets. The following information is available:

Seating capacity per plane	360
Maximum demand for seats on any flight	300
Food and beverage service cost for a round-trip (no charge to passenger)	$40 per passenger
Commission to travel agents paid by Air Americo on each ticket booked on Air Americo (Assume all of Air Americo's tickets are booked by travel agents.)	8% of fare
Fuel costs for a round-trip flight	$24,000
Fixed annual lease costs allocated to a round-trip flight	$100,000
Fixed ground services (maintenance, check in, baggage-handling) costs allocated to a round-trip flight	$10,000
Fixed flight crew salaries allocated to a round-trip flight	$8,000

For simplicity, assume that fuel costs are not affected by the actual number of passengers on a flight.

The market research group at Air Americo segments the market into business and pleasure travelers and provides the following information on the effect of two different prices on the estimated number of seats sold:

	Price Charged	Number of Seats Expected to Be Sold
Business travelers	$500	200
	$2,000	190
Pleasure travelers	$500	100
	$2,000	20

Assume these prices are the only choices available to Air Americo. The market research team offers one additional fact. Pleasure travelers start their travel in 1 week, spend at least 1 weekend at their destination, and return in some following week. Business travelers usually start and complete their travel within the week. They do not stay over weekends.

REQUIRED

1. If you could charge different prices to business travelers and pleasure travelers, would you? Show all your computations.
2. Explain the key factor (or factors) that drives your answer in requirement 1.
3. How might Air Americo implement price discrimination? That is, what scheme could the airline devise so that business travelers pay the price the airline would like business travelers to pay, and pleasure travelers pay the price the airline would like pleasure travelers to pay?

12-35 Life-cycle product costing, activity-based costing. Destin Products makes digital watches. Destin is preparing a product life-cycle budget for a new watch, MX3. Development on the new watch with features such as a calculator and a daily diary is to start shortly. Destin expects the watch to have a product life cycle of 3 years. Estimates about MX3 are as follows:

	Year 1	Year 2	Year 3
Units manufactured and sold	50,000	200,000	150,000
Price per watch	$45	$40	$35
R&D and design costs	$900,000	$100,000	—
Manufacturing			
Variable cost per watch	$16	$15	$15
Variable cost per batch	$700	$600	$600
Watches per batch	400	500	500
Fixed costs	$600,000	$600,000	$600,000
Marketing			
Variable cost per watch	$3.60	$3.20	$2.80
Fixed costs	$400,000	$300,000	$300,000
Distribution			
Variable cost per watch	$1	$1	$1
Variable cost per batch	$120	$120	$100
Watches per batch	200	160	120
Fixed costs	$240,000	$240,000	$240,000
Customer service costs per watch	$2	$1.50	$1.50

Ignore the time value of money in your answers.

REQUIRED

1. Calculate the budgeted life-cycle operating income for the new watch.
2. What percentage of the budgeted product life-cycle costs will be incurred at the end of the R&D and design stages?

3. An analysis reveals that 80% of the total product life-cycle costs of the new watch will be locked in at the end of the R&D and design stages. What implications would this finding have on managing MX3's costs?

4. Destin's Market Research Department estimates that reducing MX3's price by $3 each year will increase sales by 10% each year. If sales increase by 10%, Destin plans to increase manufacturing and distribution batch sizes by 10% as well. Assume that all variable costs per watch, variable costs per batch, and fixed costs will remain the same. Should Destin reduce MX3's price by $3?

12-36 Ethics and pricing. Baker, Inc., manufactures ball bearings. Baker is preparing to submit a bid for a new ball-bearings order. Greg Lazarus, controller of the Bearings Division of Baker, Inc., has asked John Decker, the cost analyst, to prepare the bid. Baker determines price on the basis of full product costs plus a markup of 10%. Lazarus tells Decker that he is keen on winning the bid and that the price he calculates should be competitive.

Decker prepares the following costs for the bid:

Direct materials costs	$40,000
Direct manufacturing labor costs	10,000
Design and parts administration overhead costs	4,000
Production-order overhead costs	5,000
Setup overhead costs	5,500
Materials-handling overhead costs	6,500
General and administration overhead costs	9,000

All direct costs and 30% of overhead costs are incremental costs of the order.

Lazarus reviews the numbers and says, "As usual your costs are way too high. You have allocated a lot of overhead costs to this job. You know our fixed overhead is not going to change if we win this order and manufacture the bearings. Ever since we installed this new activity-based costing system, we never seem to be able to come up with reasonable product and job costs. Rework your numbers. You have got to make the costs lower."

On returning to his office, Decker rechecks his numbers. He knows that Lazarus wants this order because the additional revenue from the order would lead to a big bonus for Lazarus and the senior division managers. Decker wonders if he can adjust the costs downward. He knows that if he does not come up with a lower bid, Lazarus will be very upset.

REQUIRED

1. Using Baker's pricing policy and based on Decker's estimates, what price should Baker bid for the ball-bearings order?
2. Calculate the incremental costs of the ball-bearings order. Why do you think Baker uses full product costs rather than incremental costs in its pricing decisions?
3. Evaluate whether Lazarus' suggestion to Decker to use lower cost numbers is unethical. Will it be unethical for Decker to change his analysis so that a lower price can be bid? What steps should Decker take to resolve this situation?

COLLABORATIVE LEARNING PROBLEM

12-37 Target prices, target costs, value engineering. Avery, Inc., manufactures two component parts for the television industry:

◆ *Tvez:* Annual production and sales of 50,000 units at a selling price of $40.60 per unit.
◆ *Premia:* Annual production and sales of 25,000 units at a selling price of $60 per unit.

Avery includes all R&D and design costs in engineering costs. Assume that Avery has no marketing, distribution, or customer-service costs.

The direct and overhead costs incurred by Avery on Tvez and Premia are described as follows:

	Tvez	Premia	Total
Direct materials costs (variable)	$850,000	$600,000	$1,450,000
Direct manufacturing labor costs (variable)	300,000	200,000	500,000
Direct machining costs (fixed)	150,000	100,000	250,000
Manufacturing overhead costs			
Machine setup costs			86,250
Testing costs			487,500
Engineering costs			450,000
Manufacturing overhead costs			1,023,750
Total costs			$3,223,750

Avery's management identifies the following activity cost pools, cost drivers for each activity, and the costs per unit of cost driver for each overhead cost pool:

Manufacturing Activity	Description of Activity	Cost Driver	Cost per Unit of Cost Driver
1. Setup	Preparing machine to manufacture a new batch of products	Setup-hours	$25 per setup-hour
2. Testing	Testing components and final product (Avery tests each unit of Tvez and Premia individually)	Testing-hours	$2 per testing-hour
3. Engineering	Designing products and processes and ensuring their smooth functioning	Complexity of product and process	Costs assigned to products by special study

Over a long-run time horizon, Avery's management views direct materials costs and direct manufacturing labor costs as variable with respect to the units of Tvez and Premia produced. Direct machining costs for each product do not vary over this time horizon and are fixed long-run costs. Overhead costs vary with respect to their chosen cost drivers. For example, setup costs vary with the number of setup-hours. Additional information is as follows:

	Tvez	Premia
1. Production batch sizes	500 units	200 units
2. Setup time per batch	12 hours	18 hours
3. Testing and inspection time per unit of product produced	2.5 hours	4.75 hours
4. Engineering costs incurred on each product	$170,000	$280,000

Avery is facing competitive pressure to reduce the price of Tvez and has set a target price of $34.80, well below its current price of $40.60. The challenge for Avery is to reduce the cost of Tvez. Avery's engineers have proposed a new product design and process improvements for the "New Tvez" to replace Tvez. The new design would improve product quality, and reduce scrap and waste. The reduction in prices will not enable Avery to increase its current sales. (However, if Avery does not reduce prices, it will lose sales.)

The expected effects of the new design relative to Tvez are as follows:

1. Direct materials costs for New Tvez are expected to decrease by $2.00 per unit.
2. Direct manufacturing labor costs for New Tvez are expected to decrease by $0.50 per unit.
3. Time required for testing each unit of New Tvez is expected to be reduced by 0.5 hours.
4. Machining time required to make New Tvez is expected to decrease by 20 minutes. It currently takes 1 hour to manufacture 1 unit of Tvez. The machines are dedicated to the production of New Tvez.
5. New Tvez will take 7 setup-hours for each setup.
6. Engineering costs are unchanged.

Assume that the batch sizes are the same for New Tvez as for Tvez. If Avery requires additional resources to implement the new design, it can acquire these additional resources in the quantities needed. Further assume the costs per unit of cost driver for the New Tvez are the same as those described for Tvez.

INSTRUCTIONS

Form groups of two students to complete the following requirements.

REQUIRED

1. Develop full product costs per unit for Tvez and Premia using an activity-based product costing approach.
2. What is the markup on the full product cost per unit for Tvez?
3. What is Avery's target cost per unit for New Tvez if it is to maintain the same markup percentage on the full product cost per unit as it had for Tvez?
4. Will the New Tvez design achieve the cost-reduction targets that Avery has set?
5. What price will Avery charge for New Tvez if it used the same markup percentage on the full product cost per unit for New Tvez as it did for Tvez?
6. What price should Avery charge for New Tvez, and what next steps should Avery take regarding New Tvez?

Grand Canyon Railway

How do you set a price on experiencing a little bit of American history? It may be a tough job, but the Grand Canyon Railway has to do it. The railway, originally established in 1901, offers classic steam engine rides from Williams, Arizona, to the southern rim of the Grand Canyon. **1** Trains depart from the railway's Williams Depot, originally built in 1908 and now restored. The trains travel 65 miles at an average speed of 35 mph. **2** Seen here is Engine 18, built in 1910, steaming through the desert. **3** Old Number 18's destination, and the end of the line, is the railway's Grand Canyon Depot. **4** From the depot, passengers make their way to their final destination—the Grand Canyon. The Grand Canyon Railway offers passengers three price levels of service.

5

6

7

8

5 The basic level of service is Coach Class seating, aboard fully re-stored 1923 Harriman coaches. **6** Club Class seating is the next level of service. Passengers in Club cars receive upgraded service from Coach Class, including such amenities as this mahogany bar. The highest and most elegant level of service is, of course, First Class. **7** Passengers choosing to travel first class ride in the Chief Keokuck car—a fully restored 1927 Pullman parlor car that features lounge furniture and an open-air platform. Because seating capacity in each class is fixed, pricing decisions take on extra importance at the railway. Maintenance costs are not insignificant on such vintage equipment, and neither are the depreciation costs on the more re-cently acquired engines, coaches, and tracks. Managers at the Grand Canyon Railway must consider these and all other costs when deter-mining a pricing structure. Managers must also consider the profits from the company's gift shop, museum, and hotel. **8** The Fray Mar-cos Hotel, opened in 1996, is located directly in the company's Williams Depot; it provides accommodations for both passengers and nonpassengers alike. Passengers and hotel guests may find it hard to put a price on history, but for the Grand Canyon Railway, it's all in a day's work.

GRAND CANYON RAILWAY
Pricing

In the high mountain country of Arizona, you can travel back to a time when the West was wild and adventure ruled the day. The Grand Canyon Railway, originally established in 1901 and re-established in 1989, offers visitors to Northern Arizona a chance to relive a piece of history aboard its vintage train. Departing once a day from the historic depot in Williams, Arizona, the train transports travelers to the south rim of the Grand Canyon, one of nature's most incredible natural landmarks. At the canyon, visitors are free to explore. They then board the train in the afternoon for the return trip to the depot.

Riders have a choice of three classes of service aboard the Grand Canyon Railway: Coach class—which features travel in fully-restored 1923 Harriman coaches, the Club car—which includes bar service, and the Chief car—offering elegant first class service. The railway also operates a gift shop, a museum, and an upscale hotel located in the historic Williams Depot complex. Because capacity in each railcar is fixed, managers rely on a wide range of information to determine the best mix of prices to charge in filling seats. For instance, data are gathered regularly about operating costs such as fuel costs, labor costs, food and beverage costs, and maintenance costs. Indirect costs, such as those for administration and the reservation center, are also captured. Peak-load pricing is practiced during the summer season (April to September), when demand for travel approaches capacity.

The railway's cost structure is heavily weighted toward fixed costs, such as depreciation on railroad track, engines, physical facilities, and administrative salaries. Pricing must cover variable costs to make a contribution toward covering these fixed costs. Costs can be driven by a number of factors. For example, unit passenger-driven costs would include those for food and beverage; unit trip-driven costs would include those for fuel, engineer, and entertainment; and facility-sustaining costs encompass advertising and railroad track costs. Understanding how costs are affected by different cost drivers is useful for making future cost predictions and setting prices.

In addition to historical costs and sales data, managers rely on monthly reports of future bookings and past travel patterns for predicting expected future behaviors. Managers analyze gross margins and look at demographic data to determine where customers come from. They also analyze data on pricing promotions to determine which offers are best received in the marketplace and most profitable for the railway. Based on this information, managers at the Grand Canyon Railway recently reduced the number of discounts and packages offered to travelers. Although the number of passengers traveling the railway decreased by 12% from 1994 to 1995, profitability increased 67%, attributable to better management of costs and pricing. ◆

QUESTIONS

1. What environmental and market factors might affect the Grand Canyon Railway's pricing decisions?
2. What are the implications of the Grand Canyon Railway's cost structure?
3. Because capacity on the railway is fixed each trip, what ways might managers try to fill empty seats in the Club and Chief cars on the day of departure?
4. How does offering fewer pricing packages affect Grand Canyon Railway's costs?
5. Why might it make sense for Grand Canyon Railway to attempt to increase revenues through booking tour packages including transportation, hotels, and meals?

COST ALLOCATION: I

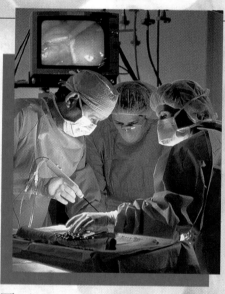

The increasing use of sophisticated medical technology, such as new laparoscopic instruments, is leading to much concern about medical costs. Hospital administrators are now examining how different cost-allocation approaches can better prompt doctors to balance cost factors with health considerations in their patient decisions.

LEARNING OBJECTIVES

After studying this chapter, you should be able to

1. Describe how a costing system can have multiple cost objects

2. Outline four purposes for allocating costs to cost objects

3. Describe alternative criteria used to guide decisions related to cost allocations

4. Discuss key decisions faced when collecting costs in indirect cost pools

5. Describe how the single-rate cost-allocation method differs from the dual-rate method

6. Explain how the choice of budgeted versus actual allocation rates changes the risks managers face

7. Distinguish among direct allocation, step-down, and reciprocal methods of allocating support department costs

8. Distinguish between the incremental and stand-alone cost-allocation methods

Cost allocation is an inescapable problem in nearly every organization and in nearly every facet of accounting. How should the airline costs of a recruiting trip from Seattle to Boston to Chicago and then return to Seattle be allocated among the prospective employers in Boston and Chicago? How should university costs be allocated among undergraduate programs, graduate programs, and research? How should the costs of expensive medical equipment, facilities, and staff be allocated in a hospital? How should manufacturing overhead be allocated to individual products in a multiple-product company such as Heinz?

Finding answers to cost-allocation questions is difficult. The answers are seldom clearly right or clearly wrong. Nevertheless, in this chapter and in Chapter 14, we will try to obtain some insight into cost allocation and to understand the dimensions of the questions, even if the answers seem elusive. Regardless of your profession, you will undoubtedly be faced with many cost-allocation questions in your career. The emphasis in Chapter 13 is on the allocation of costs to departments. Chapter 14 extends the coverage to specific topics related to the allocation of costs to individual products, services, customers, or jobs.

THE TERMINOLOGY OF COST ALLOCATION

Key terms used in this chapter include the following:

◆ *Cost object*—anything for which a separate measurement of costs is desired.
◆ *Direct costs of a cost object*—costs that are related to the particular cost object and can be traced to it in an economically feasible way. The term *cost tracing* describes assigning direct costs to the chosen cost object.
◆ *Indirect costs of a cost object*—costs that are related to the particular cost object but cannot be traced to it in an economically feasible way. The term *cost allocation* describes assigning indirect costs to the chosen cost object.

Examples of direct costs and indirect costs for a product and for an activity area include the following:

OBJECTIVE 1

Describe how a costing system can have multiple cost objects

Cost Object	Example of a Direct Cost	Example of an Indirect Cost
Product: Microwave oven manufactured by a home appliance company	Materials assembled to make the microwave oven	Rent for manufacturing plant. Rent is paid by the company, which manufactures 200 different products.
Activity area: Document-photocopying by a law firm	Paper and liquids used in photocopying machine	Electricity used to run machine. Electricity metered to firm but not to individual machines.

Organizations differ in how they classify costs. A direct-cost item in one organization, such as assembly labor or energy, can be an indirect-cost item in another organization.

PURPOSES OF COST ALLOCATION

OBJECTIVE 2

Outline four purposes for allocating costs to cost objects

Indirect costs often comprise a sizable percentage of the costs assigned to cost objects such as products, distribution channels, and customers. Exhibit 13-1 illustrates four purposes for allocating indirect costs to such cost objects:

1. To provide information for economic decisions
2. To motivate managers and employees
3. To justify costs or compute reimbursement
4. To measure income and assets for reporting to external parties

EXHIBIT 13-1
Purposes of Cost Allocation

Purpose	Illustrations
1. To provide information for economic decisions	◆ To decide whether to add a new airline flight ◆ To decide whether to make a component part of a television set or to purchase it from another manufacturer ◆ To decide on the selling price for a customized product or service
2. To motivate managers and employees	◆ To encourage the design of products that are simpler to manufacture or less costly to service ◆ To encourage sales representatives to push high-margin products or services
3. To justify costs or compute reimbursement	◆ To cost products at a "fair" price, often done with government defense contracts ◆ To compute reimbursement for a consulting firm that is paid a percentage of the cost savings resulting from the implementation of its recommendations
4. To measure income and assets for meeting external regulatory and legal reporting obligations	◆ To cost inventories for financial reporting to stockholders, bondholders, and so on. (Under generally accepted accounting principles, inventoriable costs include manufacturing costs but exclude R & D, marketing, distribution, and customer-service costs.) ◆ To cost inventories for reporting to tax authorities

The allocation of one particular cost need not satisfy all purposes simultaneously. Consider the salary of an aerospace scientist in a central research department of Boeing or Airbus. This salary cost may be allocated as part of central research costs to satisfy purpose 1 (economic decisions); it may or may not be allocated to satisfy purpose 2 (motivation); it may or may not be allocated to a government contract to justify a cost to be reimbursed to satisfy purpose 3 (cost reimbursement); and it must not be allocated (under generally accepted accounting principles) to inventory to satisfy purpose 4 (income and asset measurement).

Different costs are appropriate for different purposes. Consider product costs of the following business functions in the value chain:

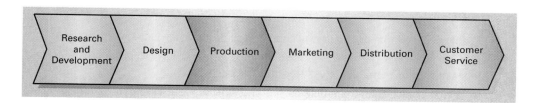

The same combination of costs in these six business functions typically will not satisfy each of the four purposes in Exhibit 13-1. For the economic-decision purpose (for example, product pricing), the costs in all six functions should be included. For the motivation purpose, costs from more than one function are often included to emphasize to managers how costs in different functions are related to each other. For example, some Japanese companies require product designers to incorporate costs further down the chain than design (such as distribution and customer service, as well as manufacturing) into their product-cost estimates. The aim is to focus attention on how different product-design options affect the total costs of the organization. For the cost-reimbursement purpose, the particular contract will often stipulate whether all six of the business functions or only a subset of them are to be reimbursed. For instance, cost-reimbursement rules governing U.S. government contracts explicitly excludes marketing costs. For the purpose of income and asset measurement for reporting to external parties, inventoriable costs under generally accepted accounting principles include only manufacturing costs (and product-design costs in some cases). In the United States, R&D costs are expensed to the accounting period in which they are incurred, as are marketing, distribution, and customer-service costs.

Why Allocate Corporate and Other Support Costs to Divisions and Departments?

Extensive survey evidence exists on the reasons why managers allocate corporate and other support costs to divisions and departments. A survey* of U.S. managers revealed the following purposes, ranked by frequency:

1. To remind profit-center managers that indirect costs exist and that profit-center earnings must be adequate to cover some share of those costs
2. To encourage the use of central services that would otherwise be underutilized
3. To stimulate profit-center managers to put pressure on central managers to control service costs

Canadian executives[†] cited the following objectives, ranked in order of importance, for allocating costs to divisions and departments:

1. To determine costs
2. To evaluate profit centers
3. To fix accountability
4. To allocate costs per usage
5. To promote more effective resource usage
6. To foster cost awareness

These executives encountered the following difficulties in implementing their cost-allocation programs: making the allocations result in losses being reported, friction arises among managers, market prices are unstable, allocations are perceived as arbitrary, usage is hard to monitor, agreement on the allocation method is difficult to obtain, and the allocation process is time-consuming.

A similar survey was conducted among Australian[‡] and U.K.[§] managers. The two sets of managers gave the same ranking of the following reasons for allocating corporate costs to divisions (in order of importance):

1. To acknowledge that divisions would incur such costs if they were independent units or if the services were not provided centrally
2. To make division managers aware that central costs exist
3. To stimulate divisional managers to put pressure on central support managers to control costs
4. To stimulate divisional managers to economize in usage of central services

---

*Fremgen and Liao, *The Allocation;* [†]Atkinson, *Intrafirm Cost;* [‡]Ramadan, "The Rationale"; [§]Dean, Joye, and Blayney, *Strategic Management.* Full citations are in Appendix A.

CRITERIA FOR GUIDING COST-ALLOCATION DECISIONS

The Role of Dominant Criteria

Exhibit 13-2 presents four criteria used to guide decisions related to cost allocations. These decisions include both the number of indirect-cost pools and the cost allocation base for each indirect cost pool. Managers must first choose the primary

EXHIBIT 13-2
Criteria for Guiding Cost-Allocation Decisions

1. **CAUSE AND EFFECT.** Using this criterion, managers identify the variable or variables that cause resources to be consumed. For example, managers may use hours of testing as the variable when allocating the costs of a quality-testing area to products. Cost allocations based on the cause-and-effect criterion are likely to be the most credible to operating personnel.

2. **BENEFITS RECEIVED.** Using this criterion, managers identify the beneficiaries of the outputs of the cost object. The costs of the cost object are allocated among the beneficiaries in proportion to the benefits each receives. For example, consider a corporatewide advertising program that promotes the general image of the corporation rather than any individual product. The costs of this program may be allocated on the basis of division sales; the higher the sales, the higher the division's allocated cost of the advertising program. The rationale behind this allocation is the belief that divisions with higher sales levels apparently benefited from the advertising more than did divisions with lower sales levels and therefore ought to be allocated more of the advertising costs.

3. **FAIRNESS OR EQUITY.** This criterion is often cited in government contracts when cost allocations are the basis for establishing a price satisfactory to the government and its supplier. The cost allocation here is viewed as a "reasonable" or "fair" means of establishing a selling price in the minds of the contracting parties. For most allocation decisions, fairness is a lofty objective rather than an operational criterion.

4. **ABILITY TO BEAR.** This criterion advocates allocating costs in proportion to the cost object's ability to bear them. An example is the allocation of corporate executive salaries on the basis of divisional operating income; the presumption is that the more profitable divisions have a greater ability to absorb corporate headquarters' costs.

purpose for a particular cost allocation and then select the appropriate criterion to implement the allocation. This book emphasizes the superiority of the cause-and-effect and the benefits-received criteria, especially when the purpose for cost allocation is related to economic decisions or motivation.

OBJECTIVE 3

Describe alternative criteria used to guide decisions related to cost allocations

The benefits-received criterion and fairness-or-equity criterion are sometimes cited in regulations governing U.S. federal government procurement. The Federal Acquisition Regulation (FAR) includes the following definition of "allocability" (in FAR 31.201-4):

> A cost [is] allocable if it is assignable or chargeable to one or more cost objectives in accordance with the relative benefits received or other equitable relationship. Subject to the foregoing, a cost is allocable to a government contract if it:
>
> ◆ Is incurred specifically for the contract;
>
> ◆ Benefits both the contract and other work, . . . and can be distributed to them in reasonable proportion to the benefits received; or
>
> ◆ Is necessary to the overall operation of the business, although a direct relationship to any particular cost objective cannot be shown.[1]

Further discussion of the contract reimbursement purpose of cost allocation is presented in Chapter 14.

[1]F. Alston, M. Worthington, and L. Goldsman, *Contracting with the Federal Government*, 3rd ed. (New York: Wiley, 1993) p. 136. This book contains extensive discussion of the use of cost data in government contracting.

The feasibility of using an individual criterion in Exhibit 13-2 varies according to the context of the cost allocation. Consider using the cause-and-effect criterion for allocating indirect costs to individual products in a multiple-product company. Where the indirect costs are variable and each product is assembled sequentially, the cause-and-effect criterion can guide the choice of a cost-allocation base. In contrast, where the indirect costs are fixed and two or more products are jointly assembled, it is not possible to identify specific cause-and-effect relationships between work on an individual product and the total costs incurred.

THE COST-BENEFIT CONSIDERATION

Many companies place great importance on cost-benefit consideration when designing their cost-allocation systems. Companies incur costs not only in gathering data, but also in taking the time necessary to educate management about the chosen system. The more sophisticated the system, in general, the higher these education costs.

The costs of designing and implementing sophisticated cost-allocation systems are highly visible, and most companies work to reduce them. In contrast, the benefits from using a well-designed cost-allocation system—being able to make better-informed make-or-buy decisions, pricing decisions, cost-control decisions, and so

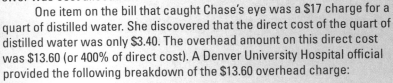

CONCEPTS IN ACTION

How a Quart of Distilled Water Cost Cindy Chase $17

Cost allocation is an inescapable aspect of life. Cindy Chase discovered this after breaking a leg while skiing in the Rocky Mountains. A 4-day stay in Denver University Hospital cost her over $10,000. Cindy was covered by her health insurance plan, but she was still puzzled by how a bill for only 4 days could possibly reach $10,000. The answer was cost allocation.

One item on the bill that caught Chase's eye was a $17 charge for a quart of distilled water. She discovered that the direct cost of the quart of distilled water was only $3.40. The overhead amount on this direct cost was $13.60 (or 400% of direct cost). A Denver University Hospital official provided the following breakdown of the $13.60 overhead charge:

◆ $ 4.25	Salaries and equipment of people handling the distilled water at the hospital
◆ 3.40	Malpractice insurance, teaching, and administrative costs
◆ 5.10	Cost of treating uninsured patients
◆ 0.85	Profit component
◆ $13.60	

The $5.10 overhead charge for Denver University Hospital treatment of uninsured patients means that Chase is subsidizing those patients who have no insurance. A Denver University hospital administrator admitted that the cost-allocation rate involved cross-subsidization. He noted, "We are moving some of the costs of caring for uninsured patients onto people who do have insurance or who pay out of their own pocket. Nobody likes that. It is not rational. But it is just the way the system has evolved over the years."

Ability to bear is the cost-allocation criterion that best explains Denver University Hospital's inclusion of the $5.10 amount in the $13.40 overhead allocated to Chase's $3.40 bottle of distilled water.

Source: Adapted from "ABC World News."

on—are difficult to measure and are frequently less visible. Still, designers of cost-allocation systems should consider these benefits as well as costs.

Spurred by rapid reductions in the costs of collecting and processing information, organizations today are moving toward more detailed cost-allocation systems. Many companies have now developed manufacturing or distribution overhead costing systems that use more than ten different cost-allocation bases. Also, some businesses have state-of-the-art information technology already in place for operating their plants or distribution networks. Applying this existing technology to the development and operation of a cost-allocation system is less expensive—and thus more inviting—than starting up such a system from scratch.

COST ALLOCATION AND COSTING SYSTEMS

We will use Computer Horizons to illustrate how costs incurred in different parts of an organization can be assigned and then reassigned when costing products, services, customers, or contracts. Computer Horizons has two manufacturing divisions. The MicroComputer Division manufactures its Plum, Plum Laptop, and Super Plum products. The Plum and Plum Laptop are assembled at its St. Louis, Birmingham, and Singapore plants. The Super Plum is assembled at its Vancouver plant. The Peripheral Equipment Division manufactures printers, cables, and other items used with its computer products. It has plants in St. Louis and Monterey.

Exhibit 13-3 presents an overview of the costing system at the St. Louis assembly plant of the MicroComputer Division. This plant assembles the Plum line and

EXHIBIT 13-3
Cost Tracing and Cost Allocation at the St. Louis Assembly Plant of Computer Horizons

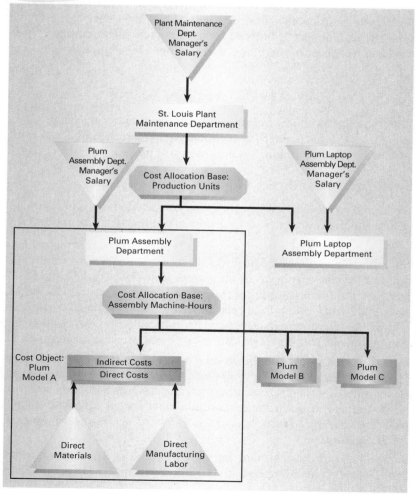

the Laptop Plum line. The area within the box in Exhibit 13-3 shows a costing system overview for the Model A version of the Plum. This costing overview is similar to that presented in earlier chapters. See, for example, Exhibit 4-2 (p. 98) and Exhibit 5-1 (p. 133).

The product costing overviews presented in earlier chapters (and, indeed, in this chapter) are typically only parts of larger costing systems. This larger costing system can be for a plant, a division, or even a whole company with multiple plants and divisions in many countries. Computer Horizons has manufacturing plants located in the United States, Canada, Mexico, Singapore, and the United Kingdom. It has marketing operations in more than 20 countries. Every month it consolidates accounting information from each of its operations to use in its planning and control decisions. A detailed costing overview of this companywide system would be sizably more complex than that in Exhibit 13-3.

The costing system for the St. Louis plant portrayed in Exhibit 13-3 highlights two important points. First, it highlights how there are multiple cost objects in most costing systems. Examples at the St. Louis plant include the Plant Maintenance Department, the Plum Assembly Department, the Laptop Plum Assembly Department, and the separate products in the Plum Assembly Department—for example, Plum Models A, B, and C. Note, however, that Exhibit 13-3 presents only a small subset of the separate cost objects at the St. Louis plant. Other examples include the Procurement Department, the Energy Department, and the various Plum Laptop products.

Exhibit 13-3 also highlights how an individual cost item can be simultaneously a direct cost of one cost object and an indirect cost of another cost object. Consider the salary of the Plant Maintenance Department manager. This salary is a direct cost traced to the Plant Maintenance Department. Computer Horizons then allocates the costs of this department to the two Assembly Departments at the St. Louis plant using units produced as the allocation base. In turn, the costs of the two Assembly Departments are allocated to individual products, such as the Plum Model A, using assembly machine-hours as the allocation base. Thus, the salary of the Plant Maintenance Department manager is both an indirect cost of each computer assembled at the plant and a direct cost of the Plant Maintenance Department.

INDIRECT COST POOLS AND COST ALLOCATION

The indirect costs of products assembled at the manufacturing plants of Computer Horizons include (1) costs incurred at corporate headquarters, and (2) costs incurred at the manufacturing plants. Exhibit 13-4 illustrates cost pools at both the (1) and (2) levels.

Choices Related to Indirect Costs

Computer Horizons has several key choices to make when accumulating and subsequently allocating the indirect costs to products of the MicroComputer Division:

- ◆ Which cost categories from Corporate Headquarters and the other divisions should be included in the indirect costs of the MicroComputer Division? Should all of the corporate headquarters cost pools in Exhibit 13-4 be allocated, or should only a subset of them be allocated? For example, some companies exclude corporate public relations from any corporate cost allocations to the divisions; division managers have little say in corporate public relations decisions and would object to allocations as "taxation without representation."

- ◆ How many cost pools should be used when allocating corporate costs to the MicroComputer Division? A *cost pool* is a grouping of individual cost items. One extreme is to aggregate all corporate costs into a single cost pool. The other extreme is to have numerous individual corporate cost pools. The concept of homogeneity (described in the following section) is important in making this decision.

- ◆ Which allocation base should be used for each of the corporate cost pools when allocating corporate costs to the MicroComputer Division? Examples include the following:

EXHIBIT 13-4
Indirect Cost Pools (when the Cost Object Is an Individual Product) of Computer Horizons

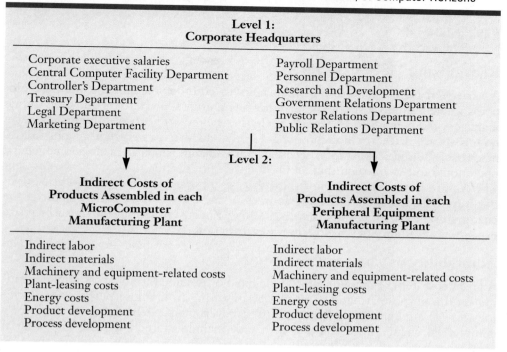

Cost Pool	Possible Allocation Bases
Corporate executive salaries	Sales; assets employed; operating income
Treasury Department	Sales; assets employed; estimated time or usage
Legal Department	Estimated time or usage; sales; assets employed
Marketing Department	Sales; number of sales personnel
Payroll Department	Number of employees; payroll dollars
Personnel Department	Number of employees; payroll dollars; number of new hires

◆ Which allocation base should be used when allocating the indirect-cost pools at each manufacturing plant to the products assembled in those plants? Examples include number of parts assembled in each product, direct manufacturing labor-hours, machining-hours, and testing-hours.

These allocation bases for both corporate and plant indirect costs are illustrative only. Managers' choices of allocation bases depend on the purpose served by the cost allocation (see Exhibit 13-1), the criteria used to guide the cost allocation (see Exhibit 13-2), and the costs of implementing the different allocation bases.

Homogeneity of Cost Pools

A **homogeneous cost pool** is one in which all the activities whose costs are included in the pool have the same or a similar cause-and-effect relationship or benefits-received relationship between the cost allocator and the costs of the activity. Why is homogeneity important? Because using homogeneous indirect-cost pools enables more accurate product, service, and customer costs to be obtained. A consequence of using a homogeneous cost pool is that the cost allocations using that pool will be the same as would be made if costs of each individual activity in that pool were allocated separately. The greater the degree of homogeneity, the fewer cost pools required to explain accurately the differences in how products use resources of the organization.

Assume that Computer Horizons wishes to use the cause-and-effect criterion to guide cost-allocation decisions. The company should aggregate only those cost pools that have the same cause-and-effect relationship to the cost object. For example, if the number of employees in a division is the cause for incurring both corporate

Payroll Department costs and corporate Personnel Department costs, the payroll cost pool and the personnel cost pool could be aggregated before determining the combined payroll and personnel cost rate per unit of the allocation base. That is, the combined rate per unit of the allocation base is the same as the sum of the rates if the individual cost pools were allocated separately.

Recognizing More Cost Pools

A variety of factors may prompt managers to consider recognizing multiple cost pools where a single cost pool is currently being used. One factor is the views of line managers and personnel. For example, do they believe important differences exist in how costs are driven or how products use the facilities not currently being recognized using a single cost pool? A second factor is changes made in plant layout, general operations, and so on such that all products do not use the facility in an equivalent way. A third factor is changes in the diversity of products (or services) produced or in the way those products use the resources in the cost pool. A fourth factor is the changes in information-gathering technology. Improvements in this technology are expanding the ability to develop multiple cost pools.

Allowability of Costs in Cost Pools

A given cost item or amount may be included or excluded from a cost pool depending on the purpose at hand. Consider a consulting firm whose purpose is to price jobs for (1) a commercial client, and (2) a government client. When pricing for a commercial client, the consulting firm may include the cost of beer and wine at meals that have a clear business-related rationale. In contrast, when billing the U.S. government under a contract, no cost amount for any alcoholic beverage is permitted to enter the cost pools from which costs are allocated to the government. The U.S. government requires all alcohol costs be excluded from the cost pools before any allocation is made.

ALLOCATING COSTS FROM ONE DEPARTMENT TO ANOTHER

In many cases, the costs of a department will include costs allocated from other departments. Three key issues that arise when allocating costs from one department to another are (1) whether to use a single-rate method or a dual-rate method, (2) whether to use budgeted rates or actual rates, and (3) whether to use budgeted quantities or actual quantities.

OBJECTIVE 5

Describe how the single-rate cost-allocation method differs from the dual-rate method

Single-Rate and Dual-Rate Methods

A **single-rate cost-allocation method** pools all costs in one cost pool and allocates them to cost objects using the same rate per unit of the single allocation base. There is no distinction between costs in the cost pool in terms of cost variability (such as fixed costs versus variable costs). A **dual-rate cost-allocation method** first classifies costs in one cost pool into two subpools (typically into a variable-cost subpool and a fixed-cost subpool). Each subpool has a different allocation rate or a different allocation base.

Consider the Central Computer Department at the corporate headquarters of Computer Horizons (shown in Exhibit 13-4). For simplicity, assume that the only users of this facility are the MicroComputer Division and the Peripheral Equipment Division. The following data apply to the coming budget year:

Fixed costs of operating the facility	$300,000 per year
Total capacity available	1,500 hours
Budgeted long-term usage (quantity) in hours	
MicroComputer Division	800
Peripheral Equipment Division	400
Total	1,200
Budgeted variable costs per hour in the 1,000- to 1,500-hour relevant range	$200 per hour used

Under the single-rate method, the costs of the Central Computer Department (assuming budgeted usage is the allocation base and budgeted rates are used) would be allocated as follows:

Total cost pool: $300,000 + (1,200 budgeted hours × $200) $540,000 per year
Budgeted usage   1,200 hours
Budgeted total rate per hour rate: $540,000 ÷ 1,200 hours $450 per hour used
Allocation rate for MicroComputer Division $450 per hour used
Allocation rate for Peripheral Equipment Division $450 per hour used

The rate of $450 per hour differs sizably from the $200 budgeted variable cost per hour. The $450 rate includes an allocated amount of $250 per hour ($300,000 ÷ 1,200 hours) for the fixed costs of operating the facility. These fixed costs will be incurred whether the computer runs its 1,500-hour capacity, its 1,200-hour budgeted usage, or even, say, only 600 hours usage.

Using the $450 per hour single-rate method (combined with the budgeted usage allocation base) transforms what is a fixed cost to the Central Computer Department (and to Computer Horizons) into a variable cost to users of that facility. This approach could lead internal users to purchase computer time outside the company. Consider an external vendor that charges less than $450 per hour but more than $200 per hour. A division of Computer Horizons that uses this vendor rather than the Central Computer Department may decrease its own division costs, but the overall costs to Computer Horizons are increased. For example, suppose the Micro-Computer Division uses an external vendor that charges $360 per hour when the Central Computer Department has excess capacity. In the short-run, Computer Horizons incurs an extra $160 per hour because this external vendor is used ($360 external purchase price per hour minus the $200 internal variable costs per hour) instead of its own Central Computer Department.

When the dual-rate method is used, allocation bases for each different subcost pool must be chosen. Assume that the budgeted rates are used. The allocation quantities chosen are budgeted usage for fixed costs and actual usage for variable costs. The total budgeted usage of 1,200 hours comprises 800 hours for the MicroComputer Division and 400 hours for the Peripheral Equipment Division. The costs allocated to the MicroComputer Division would be as follows:

Fixed-cost function: (800 hours ÷ 1,200 hours) × $300,000 $200,000 per year
Variable-cost function $200 per hour used

The costs allocated to the Peripheral Equipment Division would be

Fixed-cost function: (400 hours ÷ 1,200 hours) × $300,000 $100,000 per year
Variable-cost function $200 per hour used

Assume now that during the coming year the MicroComputer Division actually uses 900 hours but the Peripheral Equipment Division uses only 300 hours. The costs allocated to these two divisions would be computed as follows.

Under the Single-Rate Method
MicroComputer Division   900 × $450 = $405,000
Peripheral Equipment Division   300 × $450 = $135,000
Under the Dual-Rate Method
MicroComputer Division $200,000 + (900 × $200) = $380,000
Peripheral Equipment Division $100,000 + (300 × $200) = $160,000

One obvious benefit of using the single-rate method is the low cost of implementation. It avoids the often expensive analysis necessary to classify the individual cost items of a department into fixed and variable categories. However, a single-rate method may lead divisions to take actions that appear to be in their own best interest but are not in the best interest of the organization as a whole.

An important benefit of the dual-rate method is that it signals to division managers how variable costs and fixed costs behave differently. This important information could steer division managers into making decisions that benefit the corporation as well as each division. For example, it would signal that using a third-party computer provider who charges more than $200 per hour could result in Computer Horizons being worse off than if it had used its own Central Computer Department, which has a variable cost of $200 per hour.

Budgeted versus Actual Rates

OBJECTIVE 6

Explain how the choice of budgeted versus actual allocation rates changes the risks managers face

The decision on whether to use budgeted cost rates or actual cost rates affects the level of uncertainty user departments face. Budgeted rates let the user departments know the cost rates they will be charged in advance. Users are then better equipped to determine the amount of the service to request and—if the option exists—whether to use the internal department source or an external vendor. In contrast, when actual rates are used, the user department will not know the rates charged until the end of the period.

Budgeted rates also help motivate the manager of the support department (for example, the Central Computer Department) to improve efficiency. During the budget period, the support department, not the user departments, bears the risk of any unfavorable cost variances. Why? Because the user department does not pay for any costs that exceed the budgeted rates. The manager of the support department would likely view this as a con of using budgeted rates, especially when unfavorable cost variances occur because of price increases outside the department's control.

Some organizations recognize that it may not always be best to impose all the risks of variances from budgeted amounts completely on the support department (as when costs are allocated using budgeted rates) or completely on the user departments (as when costs are allocated using actual rates). For example, the two departments may agree to share the risk (through an explicit formula) of a large, uncontrollable increase in the price of materials used by the support department.

Budgeted versus Actual Usage Allocation Bases

The choice between actual usage and budgeted usage for allocating department fixed costs also can affect a manager's behavior. Consider the budget of $300,000 fixed costs at the Central Computer Department of Computer Horizons. Assume that actual and budgeted fixed costs are equal. Assume also that the actual usage by the MicroComputer Division is always equal to the budgeted usage. We now look at the effect on allocating the $300,000 in total fixed costs when actual usage by the Peripheral Equipment Division equals (case 1), is greater than (case 2), and is less than (case 3) than the budgeted usage. Recall that the budgeted usage is 800 hours for the MicroComputer Division and 400 hours for the Peripheral Equipment Division. Exhibit 13-5 presents the allocation of total fixed costs of $300,000 to each division for these three cases.

In case 1, the fixed-cost allocation equals the expected amount. In case 2, the fixed-cost allocation is $40,000 less to the MicroComputer Division than expected ($160,000 vs. $200,000). In case 3, the fixed-cost allocation is $40,000 more than expected ($240,000 vs. $200,000). Consider case 3. Why is there an increase of $40,000 even though the MicroComputer Division's actual and budgeted usage are exactly equal? Because the fixed costs are spread over fewer hours of usage. Variations in usage in another division will affect the fixed costs allocated to the MicroComputer Division when fixed costs are allocated on the basis of actual usage. When actual usage is the allocation base, user divisions will not know how much cost is allocated to them until the end of the budget period.

When budgeted usage is the allocation base, user divisions will know their allocated costs in advance. This information helps the user divisions with both short-run and long-run planning. The main justification given for the use of budgeted usage to allocate fixed costs relates to long-run planning. Organizations commit to infrastructure costs (such as the fixed costs of a support department) on the basis of a

	Actual Usage		Budgeted Usage as Allocation Base		Actual Usage as Allocation Base	
Case	MicroComputer Division	Peripheral Equipment Division	MicroComputer Division	Peripheral Equipment Division	MicroComputer Division	Peripheral Equipment Division
1	800 hours	400 hours	$200,000*	$100,000†	$200,000*	$100,000†
2	800 hours	700 hours	$200,000*	$100,000†	$160,000‡	$140,000‖
3	800 hours	200 hours	$200,000*	$100,000†	$240,000§	$ 60,000#

$* \dfrac{800}{(800 + 400)} \times \$300{,}000$ $\dagger \dfrac{400}{(800 + 400)} \times \$300{,}000$ $\ddagger \dfrac{800}{(800 + 700)} \times \$300{,}000$

$\S \dfrac{800}{(800 + 200)} \times \$300{,}000$ $\| \dfrac{700}{(800 + 700)} \times \$300{,}000$ $\# \dfrac{200}{(800 + 200)} \times \$300{,}000$

long-run planning horizon; the use of budgeted usage to allocate these fixed costs is consistent with this long-run horizon.

If fixed costs are allocated on the basis of estimated long-run use, some managers may be tempted to underestimate their planned usage. In this way, they will bear a lower fraction of the total costs (assuming all other managers do *not* similarly underestimate). Some organizations offer rewards in the form of salary increases and promotions to managers who make accurate forecasts of long-run usage. (This is the carrot approach.) Alternatively, some organizations impose cost penalties for under-predicting long-run usage. For instance, a higher cost rate may be charged after a division exceeds its budgeted usage. (This is the stick approach.)

ALLOCATING COSTS OF SUPPORT DEPARTMENTS

Operating Departments and Support Departments

Many organizations distinguish between operating departments and support departments. An **operating department** (also called a **production department** in manufacturing companies) adds value to a product or service that is observable by a customer. A **support department** (also called a **service department**) provides the services that maintain other internal departments (operating departments and other support departments) in the organization. Support departments at Computer Horizons include the Legal Department and the Personnel Department at corporate headquarters.

Support departments create special accounting problems when they provide reciprocal support to each other as well as support to operating departments. An example of reciprocal support at Computer Horizons would be the Legal Department providing services to the Personnel Department (such as advice on compliance with labor laws) and the Personnel Department providing support to the Legal Department (such as advice about the hiring of attorneys and secretaries). To obtain accurate product, service, and customer costs at Computer Horizons requires inclusion of support department costs as well as operating department costs. This section illustrates alternative ways to recognize support department costs. More accurate support department cost allocations results in more accurate product, service, and customer costs.

Be cautious here for several reasons. First, organizations differ in the departments located at the corporate and division levels. Some departments located at corporate headquarters of Computer Horizons (for example, R&D) are located at the division level in other organizations. Second, organizations differ in their definitions of *operating department* and *support department*. Always try to ascertain the precise meaning of these terms when analyzing data that include allocations of operating department costs and support department costs. Third, organizations differ in the percentage of total support costs allocated using the methods described in this section. Some companies allocate all support department costs using one of the methods outlined in this section. Other companies only allocate *indirect* support department costs using these methods, with all *direct* support costs traced to the appropriate operating department.

OBJECTIVE 7

Distinguish among direct allocation, step-down, and reciprocal methods of allocating support department costs

Support Department Cost-Allocation Methods

We now examine three methods of allocating the costs of support departments: *direct*, *step-down*, and *reciprocal*. To focus on concepts, we use the single-rate method to allocate the costs of each support department. The Problem for Self-Study at the end of this chapter illustrates the use of the dual-rate method for allocating support department costs.

Consider Castleford Engineering, which manufactures engines used in electric power generating plants. Castleford has two support departments and two operating departments in its manufacturing facility:

Support Departments	Operating Departments
Plant maintenance	Machining
Information systems	Assembly

Costs are accumulated in each department for planning and control purposes. For inventory costing, however, the support department costs of Castleford must be allocated to the operating departments. The data for our example are listed in Exhibit 13-6. The percentages in this table can be illustrated by reference to the Plant Maintenance Department. This support department provides a total of 8,000 hours of support work: 20% (1,600 ÷ 8,000) goes to the Information Systems support department; 30% (2,400 ÷ 8,000) to the Machining Department; and 50% (4,000 ÷ 8,000) to the Assembly Department.

Direct Allocation Method

The **direct allocation method** (often called the **direct method**) is the most widely used method of allocating support department costs. This method allocates each support department's costs directly to the operating departments. Exhibit 13-7 illustrates this method using the data in Exhibit 13-6. Note how this method ignores both the 1,600 hours of support time rendered by the Plant Maintenance Department to the Information Systems Department and the 200 hours of support time rendered by Information Systems to Plant Maintenance. The base used to allocate Plant Maintenance is the budgeted total maintenance labor-hours worked in the operating departments: 2,400 + 4,000 = 6,400 hours. This amount excludes the 1,600 hours of support time provided by Plant Maintenance to Information Systems. Similarly, the base used for allocation of Information Systems costs is 1,600 + 200 = 1,800 hours of computer time, which excludes the 200 hours of support time provided by Information Systems to Plant Maintenance.

The benefit of the direct method is its simplicity. There is no need to predict the usage of support department resources by other support departments.

Step-Down Allocation Method

Some organizations use the **step-down allocation method** (sometimes called the **step allocation method,** or **sequential allocation method**), which allows for *partial* recognition of the services rendered by support departments to other support departments. This method requires the support departments to be ranked (sequenced) in the order which the step-down allocation is to proceed. The costs in the first-ranked support department are allocated to the other support departments

EXHIBIT 13-6
Data for Allocating Support Department Costs at Castleford Engineering for 19_7

	Support Departments		Operating Departments		
	Plant Maintenance	Information Systems	Machining	Assembly	Total
Budgeted manufacturing overhead costs before any interdepartment cost allocations	$600,000	$116,000	$400,000	$200,000	$1,316,000
Support work furnished					
By Plant Maintenance					
Budgeted labor-hours	—	1,600	2,400	4,000	8,000
Percentage	—	20%	30%	50%	100%
By Information Systems					
Budgeted computer time	200	—	1,600	200	2,000
Percentage	10%	—	80%	10%	100%

EXHIBIT 13-7
Direct Method of Allocating Support Department Costs for 19_7 at Castleford Engineering

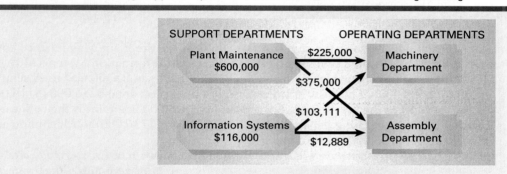

	Support Departments		Operating Departments		
	Plant Maintenance	Information Systems	Machining	Assembly	Total
Budgeted manufacturing overhead costs before any interdepartment cost allocations	$600,000	$116,000	$400,000	$200,000	$1,316,000
Allocation of Plant Maintenance (³⁄₈, ⁵⁄₈)*	(600,000)		225,000	375,000	
	$ 0				
Allocation of Information Systems (⁸⁄₉, ¹⁄₉)†		(116,000)	103,111	12,889	
		$ 0			
Total budgeted manufacturing overhead of operating departments			$728,111	$587,889	$1,316,000

*Base is (2,400 + 4,000), or 6,400 hours; 2,400÷6,400 = ³⁄₈; 4,000÷6,400 = ⁵⁄₈.
†Base is (1,600 + 200), or 1,800 hours; 1,600÷1,800 = ⁸⁄₉; 200÷1,800 = ¹⁄₉.

and to the operating departments. The costs in the second-ranked department are allocated to those support departments not yet allocated and to the operating departments. This procedure is followed until the costs in the last-ranked support department have been allocated to the operating departments. Two ways to determine the sequence to allocate support department costs are as follows:

Approach A Rank support departments on the percentage of the support department's total support provided to other support departments. The support department with the highest percentage is allocated first. The support department with the lowest percentage is allocated last. In our Castleford Engineering example, the chosen order would be

	Percentage of Total Service Provided to Other Support Departments
1. Plant Maintenance	20%
2. Information Systems	10%

Approach B Rank support departments on the total dollars of service provided to other support departments. In our Castleford Engineering example, the chosen order would be

	Dollar Amount of Total Service Provided to Other Support Departments
1. Plant Maintenance (0.20 × $600,000)	$120,000
2. Information Systems (0.10 × $116,000)	11,600

Exhibit 13-8 shows the step-down method where the Plant Maintenance costs of $600,000 is allocated first; $120,000 is allocated to Information Systems (20% of $600,000); $180,000 to Machining (30% of $600,000); and $300,000 to Assembly (50% of $600,000). The costs in Information Systems now total $236,000 ($116,000 + $120,000 from the first-round allocation). This $236,000 amount is then allocated among the two operating departments—$209,778 (8⁄9 × $236,000) to Machining and $26,222 (1⁄9 × $236,000) to Assembly.

Under the step-down method, once a support department's costs have been allocated, no subsequent support department costs are allocated or circulated back to it. Thus, once the Plant Maintenance department costs are allocated, they receive no further allocation from other (lower ranked) support departments.

Reciprocal Allocation Method

The **reciprocal allocation method** allocates costs by explicitly including the mutual services provided among all support departments. Theoretically, the direct method and the step-down method are less accurate when support departments provide services to one another reciprocally. For example, the Plant Maintenance Department maintains all the computer equipment in the Information Systems Department. Similarly, Information Systems provides data-base support for Plant Maintenance. The reciprocal allocation method enables us to incorporate interdepartmental relationships *fully* into the support department cost allocations. That is, Plant Maintenance is allocated to Information Systems, and Information Systems is allocated to Plant Maintenance; each is allocated to the operating departments as well. Implementing the reciprocal allocation method requires three steps.

Step 1: Express Support Department Costs and Reciprocal Relationships in Linear Equation Form Let PM be the *complete reciprocated costs* of Plant Maintenance and IS be the complete reciprocated costs of Information Systems. We then express the data in Exhibit 13-6 as follows:

$$(1)\ \ PM = \$600{,}000 + 0.1IS$$

$$(2)\ \ IS = \$116{,}000 + 0.2PM$$

EXHIBIT 13-8
Step-Down Method of Allocating Support Department Costs for 19_7 at Castleford Engineering

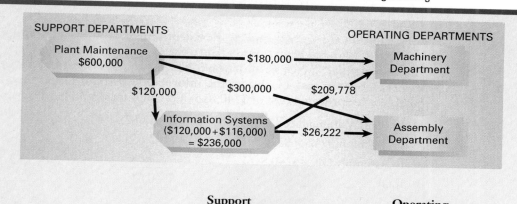

	Support Departments		Operating Departments		
	Plant Maintenance	Information Systems	Machining	Assembly	Total
Budgeted manufacturing overhead costs before any interdepartment cost allocations	$600,000	$116,000	$400,000	$200,000	$1,316,000
Allocation of Plant Maintenance ($\frac{2}{10}, \frac{3}{10}, \frac{5}{10}$)*	(600,000)	120,000	180,000	300,000	
	$ 0	236,000			
Allocation of Information Systems ($\frac{8}{9}, \frac{1}{9}$)†		(236,000)	209,778	26,222	
		$ 0			
Total budgeted manufacturing overhead of operating departments			$789,778	$526,222	$1,316,000

*Base is (1,600 + 2,400 + 4,000), or 8,000 hours; 1,600÷8,000 = $\frac{2}{10}$; 2,400÷8,000 = $\frac{3}{10}$; 4,000 ÷ 8,000 = $\frac{5}{10}$.
†Base is (1,600 + 200), or 1,800 hours; 1,600÷1,800 = $\frac{8}{9}$; 200÷1,800 = $\frac{1}{9}$.

The 0.1IS term in equation (1) is the percentage of the Information Systems work used by Plant Maintenance. The 0.2PM term in equation (2) is the percentage of the Plant Maintenance work used by Information Systems.

By **complete reciprocated cost** in equations (1) and (2), we mean the actual costs incurred by a support department plus a part of the costs of the other support departments that provide service to it. This complete reciprocated costs figure is sometimes called the **artificial costs** of the support department; it is always larger than the actual costs.

Step 2: Solve the System of Simultaneous Equations to Obtain the Complete Reciprocated Costs of Each Support Department Where there are two support departments, the following substitution approach can be used. Substituting equation (2) into equation (1),

$$PM = \$600,000 + [0.1(\$116,000 + 0.2PM)]$$

$$PM = \$600,000 + \$11,600 + 0.02PM$$

$$0.98PM = \$611,600$$

$$PM = \$624,082$$

Substituting into equation (2),

$$IS = \$116,000 + 0.2(\$624,082) = \$240,816$$

Where there are more than two support departments with reciprocal relationships, computer programs can be used to calculate the complete reciprocated costs of each support department.

Step 3: Allocate the Complete Reciprocated Costs of Each Support Department to All other Departments (Both Support and Operating Departments) on the Basis of the Usage Proportions (Based on Total Units of Service Provided to All Departments) / Consider the Information Systems Department, which has a complete reciprocated cost of $240,816. This amount would be allocated as follows:

◆ To Plant Maintenance (⅒ × $240,816) = $ 24,082
◆ To Machining (⁸⁄₁₀ × $240,816) = 192,653
◆ To Assembly (⅒ × $240,816) = 24,082
◆ Total $240,817

Exhibit 13-9 presents summary data pertaining to the reciprocal method.

    One source of confusion to some managers using the reciprocal cost-allocation method is why the complete reciprocated costs of the support departments $864,898

EXHIBIT 13-9
Reciprocal Method of Allocating Support Department Costs for 19_7 at Castleford Engineering

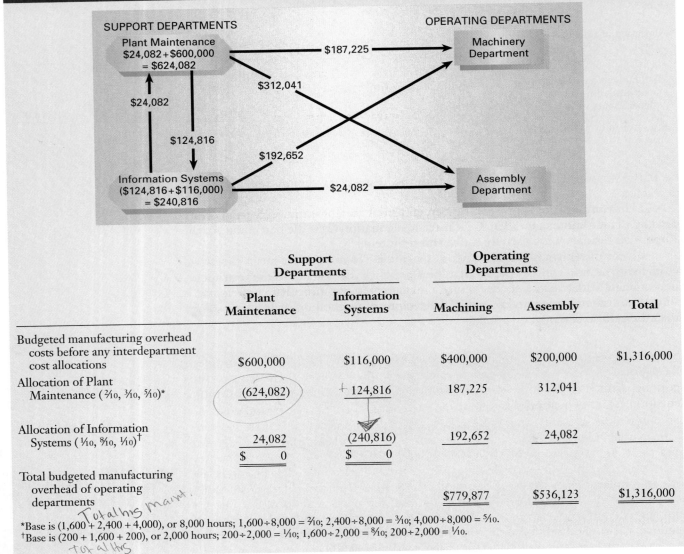

| | Support Departments | | Operating Departments | | |
	Plant Maintenance	Information Systems	Machining	Assembly	Total
Budgeted manufacturing overhead costs before any interdepartment cost allocations	$600,000	$116,000	$400,000	$200,000	$1,316,000
Allocation of Plant Maintenance (²⁄₁₀, ³⁄₁₀, ⁵⁄₁₀)*	(624,082)	+ 124,816	187,225	312,041	
Allocation of Information Systems (⅒, ⁸⁄₁₀, ⅒)†	24,082	(240,816)	192,652	24,082	
	$ 0	$ 0			
Total budgeted manufacturing overhead of operating departments			$779,877	$536,123	$1,316,000

*Base is (1,600 + 2,400 + 4,000), or 8,000 hours; 1,600÷8,000 = ²⁄₁₀; 2,400÷8,000 = ³⁄₁₀; 4,000÷8,000 = ⁵⁄₁₀.
†Base is (200 + 1,600 + 200), or 2,000 hours; 200÷2,000 = ⅒; 1,600÷2,000 = ⁸⁄₁₀; 200÷2,000 = ⅒.

($624,082 and $240,816 in Exhibit 13-9) exceed their budgeted amount of $716,000 ($600,000 and $116,000 in Exhibit 13-6). The excess of $148,898 ($24,082 for Plant Maintenance and $124,816 for Information Systems) is the total costs that are allocated among support departments. The total costs allocated to the operating departments under the reciprocal allocation method are still only $716,000.

Overview of Methods

Assume that the total budgeted overhead costs of each operating department in the example in Exhibits 13-7 to 13-9 are allocated to individual products on the basis of budgeted machine-hours for the Machining Department (4,000 hours) and budgeted direct labor-hours for the Assembly Department (3,000 hours). The budgeted overhead allocation rates associated with each support department allocation method (rounded to the nearest dollar) are

| Support Department Cost-Allocation Method | Total Budgeted Overhead Costs after Allocation of All Support Department Costs | | Budgeted Overhead Rate per Hour for Product-Costing Purposes | |
	Machining	Assembly	Machining (4,000 Machine-hours)	Assembly (3,000 Labor-hours)
Direct	$728,111	$587,889	$182	$196
Step-down	789,778	526,222	197	175
Reciprocal	779,877	536,123	195	179

These differences in budgeted overhead rates with alternative support department cost-allocation methods can be important to managers. For example, consider a cost-reimbursement contract that uses 100 machine-hours and 15 assembly labor-hours. The support department costs allocated to this contract would be

Direct:	$21,140	($182 × 100 + $196 × 15)
Step-down:	22,325	($197 × 100 + $175 × 15)
Reciprocal:	22,185	($195 × 100 + $179 × 15)

Use of the step-down method would result in the highest cost reimbursement to the contractor.

The reciprocal method, while conceptually preferable, is not widely used. The advantage of the direct and step-down methods is that they are relatively simple to compute and understand. However, with the ready availability of computer software to solve sets of simultaneous equations, the extra costs of using the reciprocal method will, in most cases, be minimal. The more likely roadblocks to the reciprocal method being widely adopted are (1) many managers find it difficult to understand, and (2) the numbers obtained by using the reciprocal method differ little, in some cases, from those obtained by using the direct or step-down method.

ALLOCATING COMMON COSTS

We next consider two methods used to allocate common costs. A **common cost** is a cost of operating a facility, operation, activity, or like cost object that is shared by two or more users. Consider Jason Stevens, a senior student in Seattle who has been invited to an interview with an employer in Boston. The round-trip Seattle–Boston airfare costs $1,200. A week prior to leaving, Stevens is also invited to an interview with an employer in Chicago. The round-trip Seattle–Chicago airfare costs $800. Stevens decides to combine the two recruiting steps into a Seattle–Boston–Chicago trip that will cost $1,500 in airfare. The $1,500 is a common cost that benefits both employers. Two methods for allocating this common cost between the two potential employers are now discussed: the stand-alone method and the incremental method.

Allocation of Support Department Costs

Use of the direct method of allocating support department costs is widespread. Systematic surveys of support department cost-allocation methods are available for Australia, Japan, and the United Kingdom.

Support Department Cost-Allocation Method	Australia	Japan	United Kingdom
1. Direct method	43%	58%	64%
2. Step-down method	3	27	6
3. Reciprocal method	5	10	14
4. Other method	15	1	8
5. Not allocated	34	4	8
	100%	100%	100%

Source: From Blayney and Yokoyama, "Comparative Analysis." Full citation is in Appendix A.

Stand-Alone Cost-Allocation Method

The **stand-alone cost-allocation method** uses information pertaining to each cost object as a separate operating entity to determine the cost-allocation weights. For the airfare common cost of $1,500, information about the separate (stand-alone) return airfares ($1,200 and $800) is used to determine the allocation weights:

Boston employer: $\dfrac{\$1,200}{\$1,200 + \$800} \times \$1,500 = 0.60 \times \$1,500 = \$900$

Chicago employer: $\dfrac{\$800}{\$800 + \$1,200} \times \$1,500 = 0.40 \times \$1,500 = \$600$

Advocates of this method often emphasize an equity or fairness rationale. That is, fairness occurs because each employer bears a proportionate share of total costs in relation to their individual stand-alone costs. This method is analogous to the stand-alone revenue-allocation method discussed in Chapter 16 (pp. 579–580).

Incremental Cost-Allocation Method

The **incremental cost-allocation method** ranks the individual cost objects and then uses this ranking to allocate costs among those cost objects. The first-ranked cost object is termed the *primary party* and is allocated costs up to its cost as a stand-alone entity. The second-ranked cost object is termed the *incremental party* and is allocated the additional cost that arises from there being two users instead of only the primary user. If there are more than two parties, the nonprimary parties will need to be ranked. The method is analogous to the incremental revenue-allocation method discussed in Chapter 16 (pp. 580–581).

Consider Jason Stevens and his $1,500 airfare cost. Assume that the Boston employer is viewed as the primary party. Stevens' rationale was that he had already committed to go to Boston. The cost allocations would then be

Party	Costs Allocated	Costs Remaining to Be Allocated to Other Parties
Boston (primary)	$1,200	$300 ($1,500 – $1,200)
Chicago (incremental)	300	0

The Boston employer is allocated the full Seattle–Boston airfare. The nonallocated part of the total airfare is allocated to the Chicago employer. Had the Chicago employer been chosen as the primary party, the cost allocations would have been Chicago, $800 (the stand-alone Seattle–Chicago return airfare), and Boston, $700 ($1,500 − $800). Where there are more than two parties, this method requires them to be ranked and the common costs allocated to those parties in the ranked sequence.

Under the incremental method, the primary party typically receives the highest allocation of the common costs. Not surprisingly, most users in common cost situations propose themselves as the incremental party. In some cases, the incremental party is a newly formed "organization" such as a new product line or a new sales territory. Chances for its short-term survival may be enhanced if it bears a relatively low allocation of common costs.

A caution is appropriate here as regards Stevens' cost-allocation options. His chosen method must be acceptable to each prospective employer. Indeed, some prospective employers may have guidelines that recruiting candidates must follow. For example, the Boston employer may have a policy that the maximum reimbursable airfare is a 7-day advance booking price in economy class. If this amount is less than the amount that Stevens would receive under (say) the stand-alone method, then the employer's upper limit guideline would govern how much could be allocated to that interviewer. Stevens' should obtain approval before he purchases his ticket as to what cost-allocation method(s) each potential employer views as acceptable.

PROBLEM

This problem illustrates how support department cost-allocation methods can be used in a setting different from the manufacturing example examined earlier in the chapter (Exhibits 13-6 to 13-9). In this problem, the costs of central corporate support departments are allocated to operating divisions. The corporate departments provide services to each other as well as to the operating divisions. Also, this problem illustrates the use of the dual-rate method of allocating support department costs. (The dual-rate method can also be used in manufacturing support department cost allocations.)

Computer Horizons budgets the following amounts for its two central corporate support departments (Legal and Personnel) in supporting each other and the two manufacturing divisions—the MicroComputer Division (MCD) and the Peripheral Equipment Division (PED):

To Be Supplied by	Budgeted Capacity				
	Legal	Personnel	MCD	PED	Total
Legal (hours)	—	250	1,500	750	2,500
Legal (percentages)	—	10%	60%	30%	100%
Personnel (hours)	2,500	—	22,500	25,000	50,000
Personnel (percentages)	5%	—	45%	50%	100%

Details on actual usage are as follows:

To Be Supplied by	Actual Usage by				
	Legal	Personnel	MCD	PED	Total
Legal (hours)	—	400	400	1,200	2,000
Legal (percentages)	—	20%	20%	60%	100%
Personnel (hours)	2,000	—	26,600	11,400	40,000
Personnel (percentages)	5%	—	66.5%	28.5%	100%

The actual costs were

	Fixed	Variable
Legal	$360,000	$200,000
Personnel	$475,000	$600,000

Fixed costs are allocated on the basis of budgeted capacity. Variable costs are allocated on the basis of actual usage.

REQUIRED

What support department costs for Legal and Personnel will be allocated to MCD and PED using (a) the direct method, (b) the step-down method (allocating the Legal Department costs first), and (c) the reciprocal method?

SOLUTION

Exhibit 13-10 presents the computations for allocating the fixed and variable support department costs. A summary of these costs is as follows:

	MicroComputer Division	Peripheral Equipment Division
A. Direct Method		
Fixed costs	$465,000	$370,000
Variable costs	470,000	330,000
	$935,000	$700,000
B. Step-Down Method		
Fixed costs	$458,053	$376,947
Variable costs	488,000	312,000
	$946,053	$688,947
C. Reciprocal Method		
Fixed costs	$462,513	$372,487
Variable costs	476,364	323,636
	$938,877	$696,123

The simultaneous equations for the reciprocal method are

Fixed Costs
$L = \$360,000 + 0.05P$
$P = \$475,000 + 0.10L$
$L = \$360,000 + 0.05(\$475,000 + 0.10L) = \$385,678$
$P = \$475,000 + 0.10(\$385,678) = \$513,568$

Variable Costs
$L = \$200,000 + 0.05P$
$P = \$600,000 + 0.20L$

SUMMARY

The following points are linked to the chapter's learning objectives.

1. A *cost object* is anything for which a separate measurement of costs is desired. Costing systems in organizations have multiple cost objects (departments, products, services, and customers) meaning many individual costs are allocated and reallocated several times before becoming an indirect cost of a specific cost object.

2. The four purposes of cost allocation are to provide information for economic decisions, to motivate managers and employees, to justify costs or compute reimbursement, and to measure income and assets for meeting external regulatory and legal

EXHIBIT 13-10
Alternative Methods of Allocating Corporate Support Department Costs to Operating
Divisions of Computer Horizons: Dual-Rate Method

Allocation Method	Corporate Support Department		Manufacturing Divisions	
	Legal	Personnel	MCD	PED
A. Direct Method				
Fixed Costs	$360,000	$475,000		
Legal (⅔, ⅓)	(360,000)		$240,000	$120,000
Personnel ($^{225}/_{475}$, $^{250}/_{475}$)	$ 0	(475,000)	225,000	250,000
		$ 0	$465,000	$370,000
Variable Costs	$200,000	$600,000		
Legal (0.25, 0.75)	(200,000)		$ 50,000	$150,000
Personnel (0.7, 0.3)	$ 0	(600,000)	420,000	180,000
		$ 0	$470,000	$330,000
B. Step-Down Method				
(Legal Department first)				
Fixed Costs	$360,000	$475,000		
Legal (0.10, 0.60, 0.30)	(360,000)	36,000	$216,000	$108,000
Personnel ($^{225}/_{475}$, $^{250}/_{475}$)	$ 0	(511,000)	242,053	268,947
		$ 0	$458,053	$376,947
Variable Costs	$200,000	$600,000		
Legal (0.20, 0.20, 0.60)	(200,000)	40,000	$ 40,000	$120,000
Personnel (0.05, 0.45, 0.50)	$ 0	(640,000)	448,000	192,000
		$ 0	$488,000	$312,000
C. Reciprocal method				
Fixed Costs	$360,000	$475,000		
Legal (0.10, 0.60, 0.30)	(385,678)	(38,568)	$231,407	$115,703
Personnel (0.05, 0.45, 0.50)	25,678	513,568	231,106	256,784
	$ 0	$ 0	$462,513	$372,487
Variable Costs	$200,000	$600,000		
Legal (0.20, 0.20, 0.60)	(232,323)	46,465	$ 46,465	$139,393
Personnel (0.05, 0.665, 0.285)	32,323	(646,465)	429,899	184,243
	$ 0	$ 0	$476,364	$323,636

reporting obligations. Different cost allocations may be appropriate depending on the specific purpose.

3. The cause-and-effect and the benefits-received criteria guide most decisions related to cost allocations. Other criteria found in practice include fairness or equity and ability to bear.

4. A cost pool is a grouping of individual cost items. Two key decisions related to indirect-cost pools are the number of indirect-cost pools and the allowability of individual cost items to be included in those cost pools.

5. A single-rate cost-allocation method pools all costs in one cost pool and allocates them to cost objects using the same rate per unit of the single allocation base. In the dual-rate method, costs are grouped in two separate cost pools, each of which has a different allocation rate and which may have a different allocation base.

6. When cost allocations are made using budgeted rates, managers of divisions to which costs are allocated face no uncertainty about the rates to be used in that period. In contrast, when actual rates are used for cost allocation, managers do not know the rates to be used until the end of the accounting period.

7. The three main methods of allocating support department costs to operating departments are the direct, step-down, and reciprocal. The last is conceptually preferable, but the direct and step-down methods are more widely used. The direct method ignores any reciprocal support among support departments. The step-down method allows for partial recognition while the reciprocal method provides full recognition of support among support departments.

8. Common costs are the costs of operating a facility, operation, or activity area that are shared by two or more users. The stand-alone cost-allocation method uses information pertaining to each operating entity to determine how to allocate the common costs. The incremental cost-allocation method ranks cost objects and allocates common costs first to the primary cost object and then to the other remaining (incremental) cost objects.

▼ TERMS TO LEARN

This chapter and the Glossary at the end of this book contain definitions of the following important terms:

artificial costs (p. 487)
common cost (489)
complete reciprocated cost (487)
direct allocation method (484)
direct method (484)
dual-rate cost-allocation method (480)
homogeneous cost pool (479)
incremental cost-allocation method (490)
operating department (483)

production department (483)
reciprocal allocation method (486)
sequential allocation method (484)
service department (483)
single-rate cost-allocation method (480)
stand-alone cost-allocation method (490)
step allocation method (484)
step-down allocation method (484)
support department (483)

▼ ASSIGNMENT MATERIAL

QUESTIONS

13-1 Why might the classification of a cost as a direct cost or an indirect cost of a cost object change over time?

13-2 How can an individual cost item, such as the salary of a plant security guard, be both a direct cost and an indirect cost at the same time?

13-3 A given cost may be allocated for one or more purposes. List four purposes.

13-4 What criteria might be used to guide cost-allocation decisions? Which are the dominant criteria?

13-5 What are three justifications for a cost to be allocable to a government contract?

13-6 How do cost-benefit considerations affect choices by a company about the allocation of indirect costs to products, services, or customers?

13-7 What is a cost pool? Give an example.

13-8 Name three decisions managers face when designing the cost-allocation component of an accounting system.

13-9 What is a support department? What is another term for a support department?

13-10 Give examples of bases used to allocate corporate cost pools to the operating divisions of an organization.

13-11 Why might a manager prefer that budgeted rather than actual indirect cost-allocation rates be used for costs being allocated to her department from another department?

13-12 "To ensure unbiased cost allocations, fixed indirect costs should be allocated on the basis of estimated long-run use by user department managers." Do you agree? Why?

13-13 Distinguish among the three methods of allocating the costs of service departments to production departments.

13-14 What is the theoretically most defensible method for allocating service department costs?

13-15 Distinguish between two methods of allocating common costs.

EXERCISES

13-16 Cost allocation in hospitals, alternative allocation criteria. Dave Meltzer went to Lake Tahoe for his annual winter vacation. Unfortunately, he suffered a severe break in his ankle while skiing and had to spend 2 days at the Sierra University Hospital. Meltzer's insurance company received a $4,800 bill for his 2-day stay. One item that caught Meltzer's eye was an $11.52 charge for a roll of cotton. Meltzer was a salesman for Johnson & Johnson and knew that the cost to the hospital of the roll of cotton would be in the $2.20 to $3.00 range. He asked for a breakdown of how the $11.52 charge was derived. The accounting office of the hospital sent him the following information:

a. Invoiced cost of cotton roll	$ 2.40
b. Processing of paperwork for purchase	0.60
c. Supplies room management fee	0.70
d. Operating-room and patient-room handling charge	1.60
e. Administrative hospital costs	1.10
f. University teaching-related recoupment	0.60
g. Malpractice insurance costs	1.20
h. Cost of treating uninsured patients	2.72
i. Profit component	0.60
Total	$11.52

Meltzer believes the overhead charge is obscene. He comments, "There was nothing I could do about it. When they come in and dab your stitches, it's not as if you can say, 'Keep your cotton roll. I brought my own.'"

REQUIRED
1. Compute the overhead rate Sierra University Hospital charged on the cotton roll.
2. What criteria might Sierra use to justify allocation of each of the overhead items b through i in the preceding list? Examine each item separately, and use the allocation criteria listed in Exhibit 13-2 (p. 475) in your answer.
3. What should Meltzer do about the $11.52 charge for the cotton roll?

13-17 Single-rate versus dual-rate cost-allocation methods. (W. Crum, adapted) The Carolina Company has a power plant designed and built to serve its three factories. Data for 19_7 are as follows:

	Usage in Kilowatt-Hours	
Factory	Budget	Actual
Durham	100,000	80,000
Charlotte	60,000	120,000
Raleigh	40,000	40,000

Actual fixed costs of the power plant were $1 million in 19_7; actual variable costs, $2 million.

REQUIRED

1. Compute the amount of power costs that would be allocated to Charlotte using a single-rate method.
2. Compute the amount of power costs that would be allocated to Charlotte using a dual-rate method.

13-18 Single-rate versus dual-rate allocation methods, support department. The Chicago power plant that services all manufacturing departments of MidWest Engineering has a budget for the coming year. This budget has been expressed in the following terms on a monthly basis:

Manufacturing Departments	Needed at Practical Capacity Production Level* (Kilowatt-Hours)	Average Expected Monthly Usage (Kilowatt-Hours)
Rockford	10,000	8,000
Peoria	20,000	9,000
Hammond	12,000	7,000
Kankakee	8,000	6,000
Totals	50,000	30,000

*This factor was the most influential in planning the size of the power plant.

The expected monthly costs for operating the department during the budget year are $15,000: $6,000 variable and $9,000 fixed.

REQUIRED

1. Assume that a single-cost pool is used for the power plant costs. What dollar amounts will be allocated to each manufacturing department? Use (a) practical capacity, and (b) average expected monthly usage as the allocation bases.
2. Assume a dual-rate method; separate cost pools for the variable and fixed costs are used. Variable costs are allocated on the basis of expected monthly usage. Fixed costs are allocated on the basis of practical capacity. What dollar amounts will be allocated to each manufacturing department? Why might you prefer the dual-rate method?

13-19 Single-rate cost-allocation method, budgeted versus actual costs and quantities. Fruit Juice, Inc., processes orange juice at its East Miami plant and grapefruit juice at its West Miami plant. It purchases oranges and grapefruit from growers' cooperatives in the Orlando area. It owns its own trucking fleet. It takes the same mileage to go to each Miami plant from Orlando. The trucking fleet is run as a cost center. Each Miami plant is billed for the direct costs and the indirect costs of each return trip.

The trucking fleet costs include direct costs (labor costs of drivers, fuel, and toll charges) and indirect costs. Indirect costs include wear and tear on tires and the vehicle, leasing costs, insurance, and state registration fees.

At the start of 19_7, the Orange Juice Division budgeted for 150 Orlando to East Miami truck trips while the Grapefruit Juice Division budgeted for 100 Orlando to West Miami truck trips. Based on these 250 budgeted trips, the Trucking Fleet Division budgeted trucking fleet indirect costs of $575,000. The following actual results occurred for 19_7:

Trucking fleet indirect costs	$645,000
Trips to East Miami plant	200
Trips to West Miami plant	100

The Trucking Fleet Division uses a single-rate method when allocating indirect trucking costs. The costs charged to each plant equal this rate times the actual number of trips made.

REQUIRED

1. What is the indirect cost rate per truck trip when (a) budgeted costs and budgeted quantities (trips) are used, and (b) actual costs and actual quantities (trips) are used?

2. From the viewpoint of the Orange Juice Division, what are the effects of using budgeted costs/quantities rather than actual costs/quantities?

13-20 Dual-rate cost-allocation method, budgeted versus actual costs and quantities (continuation of 13-19). Fruit Juice, Inc., decides to examine the effect of using a dual-rate method for allocating indirect trucking costs to each truck trip. At the start of 19_7, the budgeted indirect costs were

Variable indirect costs per trip	$1,500
Fixed indirect costs	$200,000

The actual results for the 300 round-trips made in 19_7 were

Variable indirect costs	$465,000
Fixed indirect costs	180,000
	$645,000

Assume all other information to be the same as in Exercise 13-19.

REQUIRED

1. What is the indirect cost per truck trip with a dual-rate method when (a) variable indirect costs are allocated using the budgeted variable indirect rate times actual trips made, and (b) fixed indirect costs are allocated using the budgeted fixed indirect cost rate times budgeted trips to be made?

2. Compare the results for requirement 1 with that in requirement 1(a) and (b) for Exercise 13-19. From the viewpoint of the Orange Juice Division, what are the effects of using a dual-rate method rather than a single-rate method?

13-21 Allocation of common costs. Sam, Sarah, and Tony are members of the New Orleans Fire Brigade. They share a penthouse apartment that has a lounge room with the latest 50″ TV. Tony owns the apartment, its furniture, and the 50″ TV. He can subscribe to a cable television company that has the following packages available:

Package	Rate Per Month
A. Basic news	$32
B. Premium movies	25
C. Premium sports	30
D. Basic news and premium movies	50
E. Basic news and premium sports	54
F. Premium movies and premium sports	48
G. Basic news, premium movies, and premium sports	70

Sam is a TV news junkie, has average interest in movies and zero interest in sports ("they are overpaid jocks"). Sarah is a movie buff, likes sports, and avoids the news ("it's all depressing anyway"). Tony is into sports in a big way, has average interest in news, and zero interest in movies ("he always falls asleep before the end"). They all agree that the purchase of the $70 total package is a "win-win-win" situation.

Each works on a different 8-hour shift at the fire station, so conflicts in viewing are minimal.

REQUIRED

1. What criteria might be used to guide the choice about how to allocate the $70 monthly cable fee among Sam, Sarah and Tony?

2. Outline two methods of allocating the $70 among Sam, Sarah, and Tony.

13-22 Allocation of travel costs. Joan Ernst, a graduating senior at a university near San Francisco, received an invitation to visit a prospective employer in New York. A few days later, she received an invitation from a prospective employer in Chicago. She decided to combine her visits, traveling from San Francisco to New York, New York to Chicago, and Chicago to San Francisco.

Ernst received job offers from both companies. Upon her return, she decided to accept the offer in Chicago. She was puzzled about how to allocate her travel costs between the two employers. She gathered the following data:

Regular round-trip fares with no stopovers

San Francisco to New York	$1,400
San Francisco to Chicago	$1,100

Ernst paid $1,800 for her three-leg flight (San Francisco to New York, New York to Chicago, Chicago to San Francisco). In addition, she paid $30 for a limousine from her home to San Francisco Airport and another $30 for a limousine from San Francisco Airport to her home when she returned.

REQUIRED

1. How should Ernst allocate the $1,800 airfare between the employers in New York and Chicago? Show the actual amounts you would allocate, and give reasons for your allocations.
2. Repeat requirement 1 for the $60 limousine charges at the San Francisco end of her travels.

13-23 Support department cost allocation; direct and step-down methods. Phoenix Consulting provides outsourcing services and advice to both government and corporate clients. For costing purposes, Phoenix classifies its departments into two support departments (Administrative/Human Resources and Information Systems) and two operating departments (Government Consulting and Corporate Consulting). For the first quarter of 19_7, Phoenix incurs the following costs in its four departments:

Administrative/Human Resources (A/H)	$600,000
Information Systems (IS)	$2,400,000
Government Consulting (GOVT)	$8,756,000
Corporate Consulting (CORP)	$12,452,000

The actual level of support relationships among the four departments for the first quarter of 19_7 was

		Used by			
		A/HR	IS	GOVT	CORP
Supplied	A/HR	—	25%	40%	35%
by	IS	10%	—	30%	60%

The Administrative/Human Resource support percentages are based on headcount. The Information Systems support percentages are based on actual hours of computer time used.

REQUIRED

1. Allocate the two support department costs to the two operating departments using the following methods.
   a. Direct method
   b. Step-down method (allocate Administrative/Human Resources first)
   c. Step-down method (allocate Information Systems first)
2. Compare and explain differences in the support department costs allocated to each operating department.
3. What criteria could determine the sequence for allocating support departments using the step-down method? What criterion should Phoenix use if government consulting jobs require the step-down method?

13-24 Support department cost allocation, reciprocal method (continuation of 13-23). Assume the same facts as in Exercise 13-23.

REQUIRED

1. Allocate the two support department costs to the two operating departments using the reciprocal method.
2. Compare and explain differences in requirement 1 with those in requirement 1 of Exercise 13-23. Which method do you prefer?

13-25 Support department cost allocation. (CMA) Computer Information Services is a computer software consulting company. Its three major functional areas are computer programming, information systems consulting, and software training. Carol Birch, a pricing analyst in the Accounting Department, must develop total costs for the functional areas. These costs will guide pricing for new contracts. In computing these costs, Birch is considering two different methods of allocating support department costs—the direct method and the step-down method. Birch assembled the following data on budgeted costs from its two support departments, the Information Systems Department and the Facilities Department.

	Support Departments		Operating Departments			
	Information Systems	Facilities	Computer Programming	Consulting	Software Training	Total
Budgeted costs	$50,000	$25,000	$75,000	$110,000	$85,000	$345,000
Information Systems (hours)	—	300	1,200	600	900	3,000
Facilities (thousand square feet)	200	—	400	600	800	2,000

REQUIRED

1. Allocate the support department costs in Information Systems and Facilities using the
   a. Direct method
   b. Step-down method (Information Systems first)
2. Explain to Birch any differences across the methods. Which method should she use?

PROBLEMS

13-26 Allocation of central corporate costs to divisions. Dusty Rhodes, the corporate controller of the Richfield Oil Company, is about to make a presentation to the senior corporate executives and the top managers of its four divisions. These divisions are
   a. Oil & Gas Upstream (the exploration, production, and transportation of oil and gas)
   b. Oil & Gas Downstream (the refining and marketing of oil and gas)
   c. Chemical Products
   d. Copper Mining
Under the existing internal accounting system, costs incurred at central corporate headquarters are collected in a single pool and allocated to each division on the basis of the actual revenues of each division. The central corporate costs (in millions) for the most recent year are as follows:

Interest on debt	$2,000
Corporate salaries	100
Accounting and control	100
General marketing	100
Legal	100
R&D	200
Public affairs	208
Personnel and payroll	192
	$3,000

Public affairs includes the public relations staff, the lobbyists, and the sizable donations Richfield makes to numerous charities and nonprofit institutions.

Summary data (in millions) related to the four divisions for the most recent year are as follows:

	Oil and Gas Upstream	Oil and Gas Downstream	Chemical Products	Copper Mining	Total
Revenue	$7,000	$16,000	$4,000	$3,000	$30,000
Operating costs	$3,000	$15,000	$3,800	$3,200	$25,000
Operating income	$4,000	$1,000	$200	$(200)	$5,000
Identifiable assets	$14,000	$6,000	$3,000	$2,000	$25,000
Number of employees	9,000	12,000	6,000	3,000	30,000

The top managers of each division share in a divisional income bonus pool. Divisional income is defined as operating income less allocated central corporate costs.

Rhodes is about to propose a change in the method used to allocate central corporate costs. He favors collecting these costs in four separate pools:

◆ *Cost Pool 1:* Allocated using identifiable assets of division
  Cost Item: Interest on debt
◆ *Cost Pool 2:* Allocated using revenue of division
  Cost Items: Corporate salaries, accounting and control, general marketing, legal, R&D
◆ *Cost Pool 3:* Allocated using operating income (if positive) of division, with only divisions with positive operating income included in the allocation base
  Cost Item: Public affairs
◆ *Cost Pool 4:* Allocated using number of employees in division
  Cost Item: Personnel and payroll

REQUIRED

1. What purposes might be served by the allocation of central corporate costs to each division at Richfield Oil?
2. Compute the divisional income of each of the four divisions when central corporate costs are allocated using revenue of each division.
3. Compute the divisional income of each of the four divisions when central corporate costs are allocated through the four cost pools.
4. What are the strengths and weaknesses of Rhodes' proposal relative to the existing single-pool method?

13-27 Division managers' reactions to the allocation of central corporate costs to divisions (continuation of 13-26). Dusty Rhodes presents his proposal for the use of four separate cost pools to allocate central corporate costs to the divisions. The comments of the top managers of each of the four divisions include the following:

a. By the top manager of the Oil & Gas Upstream Division: "The multiple-pool method of Rhodes is absurd. We are the only division generating a substantial positive cash flow, and this is ignored in the proposed (and indeed the existing) system. We could pay off any debt very quickly if we were not a cash cow for the rest of the dog divisions in Richfield Oil."

b. By the top manager of the Oil & Gas Downstream Division: "Rhodes' proposal is the first sign that the money we spend in the accounting and control function at corporate headquarters is justified. The proposal is fair and equitable."

c. By the top manager of the Chemical Products Division: "I oppose any cost-allocation method. Last year I was the only major player in the chemical industry to show a positive operating income. We are operating at the bare-bones level. Last year I saved $300,000 by making everyone travel economy class. This policy created a lot of dissatisfaction, but we finally managed to get it accepted. Then at the end of the year we get a charge of $400 million for corporate central costs. What's the point of our division economy drives when they get swamped by allocations of corporate fat?"

d. By the top manager of Copper Mining Division: "I should probably get concerned, but frankly I view it all as bookkeeping entries. If we were in the black, certain aspects would really infuriate me. For instance, why should corporate R&D costs be allocated to the Copper Division? The only research corporate does for us is how to best prepare our division for divestiture."

REQUIRED

How should Rhodes respond to these comments?

13-28 Departmental cost allocation, university computer-service center. A computer-service center of National University serves two major users, the College of Engineering and the College of Humanities and Sciences (H&S).

REQUIRED

1. When the computer equipment was initially installed, the procedure for cost allocation was straightforward. The actual monthly costs were compiled and divided between the two colleges on the basis of the computer time used by each. In October, the costs were $100,000. H&S used 100 hours and Engineering used 100 hours. How much cost should be allocated to each college? Suppose costs were $110,000 because of various inefficiencies in the operation of the computer center. How much cost would then be allocated? Does such an allocation seem justified? If not, what improvement would you suggest?

2. Use the same approach as in requirement 1. The actual cost-behavior pattern of the computer center was $80,000 fixed cost per month plus $100 variable cost per hour used. In November, H&S used 50 hours and Engineering used 100 hours. How much cost would be allocated to each college? Use a single-rate method.

3. As the computer-service center developed, a committee was formed that included representatives of H&S and Engineering. This committee determined the size and composition of the center's equipment. The committee based its planning on the long-run average utilization of 180 monthly hours for H&S and 120 monthly hours for Engineering. Suppose the $80,000 fixed costs are allocated through a budgeted monthly lump sum based on long-run average utilization. Variable costs are allocated through a budgeted unit rate of $100 per hour. How much cost should be allocated to each college? What are the advantages of this dual-rate allocation method over other methods?

4. What are the likely behavioral effects of lump-sum allocations of fixed costs? For example, if you were the representative of H&S on the facility planning committee, what would your biases be in predicting long-run usage? How would top management counteract the bias?

13-29 Allocating costs of support departments; step-down and direct methods. The Central Valley Company has prepared departmental overhead budgets for normal-volume levels before allocations, as follows:

Support departments		
Building and grounds	$10,000	
Personnel	1,000	
General factory administration	26,090	
Cafeteria (subsidy for operating loss)	1,640	
Storeroom	2,670	
Total support departments		$ 41,400
Operating departments		
Machining	$34,700	
Assembly	48,900	
Total operating departments		83,600
Total for both departments		$125,000

Management has decided that the most sensible inventory costs are achieved by using individual departmental overhead rates. These rates are developed after appropriate support department costs are allocated to operating departments. Bases for allocation are to be selected from the following:

Department	Manufacturing Labor-Hours	Direct Number of Employees	Square Feet of Floor Space Occupied	Manufacturing Labor-Hours	Total Number of Requisitions
Building and grounds	0	0	0	0	0
Personnel*	0	0	2,000	0	0
General plant administration	0	35	7,000	0	0
Cafeteria	0	10	4,000	1,000	0
Storeroom	0	5	7,000	1,000	0
Machining	5,000	50	30,000	8,000	2,000
Assembly	15,000	100	50,000	17,000	1,000
Total	20,000	200	100,000	27,000	3,000

*Basis used is number of employees.

REQUIRED

1. Using a worksheet, allocate support department costs by the step-down method. Develop overhead rates per direct manufacturing labor-hour for machining and assembly. Allocate the support departments in the order given in this problem. Use the allocation base for each support department you think is most appropriate.
2. Using the direct method, rework requirement 1.
3. Based on the following information about two jobs, determine the total overhead costs for each job by using rates developed in requirements 1 and 2.

	Direct Manufacturing Labor-Hours	
	Machining	Assembly
Job 88	18	2
Job 89	3	17

13-30 Support department cost allocations; single-department cost pools; direct, step-down, and reciprocal methods. The Manes Company has two products. Product 1 is manufactured entirely in Department X. Product 2 is manufactured entirely in Department Y. To produce these two products, the Manes Company has two support departments: A (a materials handling department) and B (a power-generating department).

An analysis of the work done by Departments A and B in a typical period is as follows:

		Used by		
Supplied by	A	B	X	Y
A		100	250	150
B	500		100	400

The work done in Department A is measured by the direct labor-hours of materials handling time. The work done in Department B is measured by the kilowatt-hours of power.

The budgeted costs of the support departments for the coming year are

	Department A	Department B
Variable indirect labor and indirect materials costs	$ 70,000	$10,000
Supervision	10,000	10,000
Depreciation	20,000	20,000
	$100,000	$40,000
	+ Power costs	+ Materials handling costs

The budgeted costs of the operating departments for the coming year are $1,500,000 for Department X and $800,000 for Department Y.

Supervisory costs are salary costs. Depreciation in B is the straight-line depreciation of power-generation equipment in its nineteenth year of an estimated 25-year useful life; it is old but well-maintained equipment.

REQUIRED

1. What are the allocations of costs of support Departments A and B to operating Departments X and Y using the direct method, two different sequences of the step-down method, and the reciprocal method of reallocation?
2. The power company has offered to supply all the power needed by the Manes Company and to provide all the services of the present Power Department. The cost of this service will be $40 per kilowatt-hour of power. Should Manes accept? Explain.

13-31 Allocating costs of support departments; dual rates; cost justification. Lindsay Transport Enterprises (LTE) operates an integrated transportation network that includes both rail operations and road operations. LTE has two support departments and two transportation departments:

Support Departments	Transportation Departments
Equipment and Maintenance (EM)	Rail (train) Operations
Information Systems (IS)	Road (truck) Operations

The budgeted level of service relationships at the start of the year was

		Used by			
		EM	**IS**	**Rail**	**Road**
Supplied	EM	—	0.10	0.30	0.60
by	IS	0.20	—	0.50	0.30

The actual level of service relationships for the year was

		Used by			
		EM	**IS**	**Rail**	**Road**
Supplied	EM	—	0.20	0.40	0.40
by	IS	0.25	—	0.55	0.20

LTE collects fixed costs and variable costs of each service department in separate cost pools. The actual costs (in thousands) in each pool for the year were

	Fixed-Cost Pool	Variable-Cost Pool
EM	$300	$540
IS	80	75

Fixed costs are allocated on the basis of the budgeted level of service. Variable costs are allocated on the basis of the actual level of service.

LTE monitors the cost per track-mile for the Rail Department and the cost per road-mile for the Road Department. These cost figures include costs allocated from the support departments to the transportation departments. During the year, the actual transportation miles were

◆ Rail operations   15,000,000 miles
◆ Road operations   12,000,000 miles

REQUIRED

1. Allocate the support department costs to the two transportation departments using the following three methods:

a. Direct method

b. Step-down method (allocate EM first)

c. Reciprocal method

Show full details of your calculations. Present your results in a format similar to Exhibit 13-10 (p. 493). Allocate the variable and fixed service department costs separately.

2. Compare the service department total costs per transportation mile for the rail and road operations under each of the three methods in requirement 1. (Round to four decimal places.)

3. The prices LTE charges for rail are regulated by a government agency and set on a full-cost basis. Full costs includes allocations of service department costs. The road rates LTE sets are unregulated, and competition among road transportation operators is intense. What advice would you give the government regulatory agency about how to minimize the ability of rail transportation operators to overstate the service department costs included in their submissions to the agency about the full costs of their rail operations? Be specific.

13-32 Allocating costs of support departments; dual rates; direct, step-down, and reciprocal methods. Magnum T.A., Inc., specializes in the assembly and installation of high-quality security systems for the home and business segments of the market. The four departments at its highly automated state-of-the-art assembly plant are as follows:

Service Departments	Assembly Departments
Engineering Support	Home Security Systems
Information Systems Support	Business Security Systems

The budgeted level of service relationships at the start of the year was

		Used by		
Supplied by	Engineering Support	Information Systems Support	Home Security Systems	Business Security Systems
Engineering Support	—	0.10	0.40	0.50
Information Systems Support	0.20	—	0.30	0.50

The actual level of service relationships for the year was

		Used by		
Supplied by	Engineering Support	Information Systems Support	Home Security Systems	Business Security Systems
Engineering Support	—	0.15	0.30	0.55
Information Systems Support	0.25	—	0.15	0.60

Magnum collects fixed costs and variable costs of each department in separate cost pools. The actual costs (in thousands) in each pool for the year were

	Fixed-Cost Pool	Variable-Cost Pool
Engineering Support	$2,700	$8,500
Information Systems Support	8,000	3,750

Fixed costs are allocated on the basis of the budgeted level of service. Variable costs are allocated on the basis of the actual level of service.

The support department costs allocated to each assembly department are allocated to products on the basis of units assembled. The units assembled in each department during the year were

Home Security Systems	7,950 units
Business Security Systems	3,750 units

REQUIRED

1. Allocate the support department costs to the assembly departments using a dual-rate system and (a) the direct method, (b) the step-down method (allocate Information Systems Support first), (c) the step-down method (allocate Engineering Support first), and (d) the reciprocal method. Present results in a format similar to Exhibit 13-10.
2. Compare the support department costs allocated to each Home Security Systems unit assembled and each Business Security Systems unit assembled under a, b, c, and d in requirement 1.
3. What factors might explain the very limited adoption of the reciprocal method by many organizations?

13-33 Cost allocation for all cost categories in the value chain, different costs for different purposes. Laser Technologies develops, assembles, and sells two product lines:

◆ Product Line A (laser scanning systems)
◆ Product Line B (laser cutting tools)

Product Line A is sold exclusively to the Department of Defense under a cost-plus reimbursement contract. Product Line B is sold to commercial organizations.

Laser Technologies classifies costs in each of its six value-chain business functions into two cost pools; direct product-line costs (separately traced to Product Line A or B) and indirect product-line costs. The indirect product-line costs are grouped into a single cost pool for each of the six functions of the value-chain cost structure:

Value-Chain Indirect Product-Line Cost Function	Base for Allocating Indirect Costs to Each Product Line
1. R&D	Hours of R&D time identifiable with each product line
2. Product design	Number of new products
3. Production	Hours of machine assembly time
4. Marketing	Number of salespeople
5. Distribution	Number of shipments
6. Customer service	Number of customer visits

Summary data in 19_7 are:

	Product Line A: Direct Costs (millions)	Product Line B: Direct Costs (millions)	Total Indirect Costs (millions)	Product Allocation Base for Indirect Costs	Product Line A Units of Allocation Base	Line B Units of Allocation Base
R&D	$10.0	$ 5.0	$20.0	R&D time	6,000 hours	2,000 hours
Product design	2.0	3.0	6.0	New products	8 new products	4 new products
Production	15.0	13.0	24.0	Machine-hours	70,000 machine-hours	50,000 machine-hours
Marketing	6.0	5.0	7.0	Salespeople	25 people	45 people
Distribution	2.0	3.0	2.0	Shipments	600 shipments	1,400 shipments
Customer service	5.0	3.0	1.0	Customer visits	1,000 visits	4,000 visits

REQUIRED

1. For product pricing on its Product Line B, Laser Technologies sets a preliminary selling price of 140% of full cost (made up of both direct costs and the allocated indirect costs for all six of the value-chain cost categories). What is the average full cost per unit of the 2,000 units of Product Line B produced in 19_7?

2. For motivating managers, Laser Technologies separately classifies costs into three groups:
   ◆ Upstream (R&D and product design)
   ◆ Manufacturing
   ◆ Downstream (marketing, distribution, and customer service)
   Calculate the costs (direct and indirect) in each of these three groups for Product Lines A and B.

3. For the purpose of income and asset measurement for reporting to external parties, inventoriable costs under generally accepted accounting principles for Laser Technologies include manufacturing costs and product design costs (both direct and indirect costs of each category). At the end of 19_7, what is the average inventoriable cost for the 300 units of Product Line B on hand? (Assume zero beginning inventories.)

4. The Department of Defense purchases all Product Line A units assembled by Laser Technologies. Laser is reimbursed 120% of allowable costs. Allowable cost is defined to include all direct and indirect costs in the R&D, product design, manufacturing, distribution, and customer-service functions. Laser Technologies employs a marketing staff that makes many visits to government officials, but the Department of Defense will not reimburse Laser for any marketing costs. What is the 19_7 allowable cost for Product Line A?

5. "Differences in the costs appropriated for different decisions, such as pricing and cost reimbursement, are so great that firms should have multiple accounting systems rather than a single accounting system." Do you agree?

13-34 Division cost allocation, R&D, ethics. World Semiconductor (WS) has eight divisions. It has a central R&D group in San Diego that conducts contract research for each of these eight divisions. At the start of each year, each division estimates the hours of research scientist time at the San Diego group it will use in the coming year. These estimates are summed for WS as a whole. Each division is charged for budgeted overhead costs incurred at the San Diego facility on the basis of its relative budgeted percentage use of research scientist time in the coming year. Central R&D bears the risk of any overruns on overhead costs during the year. Each division also pays (in 19_7) the San Diego facility $100 per hour of research scientist time and the actual costs of any materials used on the project.

Toni Goodwin is the controller of the Applied Semiconductor Division (ASD), which is based in Tuscon, Arizona. She notes that in the first 9 months of 19_7, ASD was charged $12.597 million for contract research at the San Diego facility:

Research scientist time	$ 2,564,000
Materials and other direct charges	2,883,000
Overhead cost charge (22% of $32,500,000)	7,150,000
	$12,597,000

The $32,500,000 amount represents WS's budgeted overhead costs for the first 9 months of 19_7.

It is now time to prepare the 19_8 budget. Goodwin estimates that ASD will have a 19_8 budget of 30,000 hours of research scientist time at the San Diego facility. This estimate is based on detailed interviews she has had with operating managers at ASD and on a recent ASD retreat, at which the strategy and operations for 19_8 were finalized. Roy Masters, the new president of ASD, is less than pleased with the 30,000 budget number. Goodwin and Masters have the following conversation.

GOODWIN: But Roy, you were at the retreat where we all signed off on the 30,000 number.

MASTERS: I was there, but I think "signed off" is too strong a phrase. By all means use the 30,000 number in our internal planning and budgeting at ASD. However, I want you to tell San Diego that we are budgeting for only 25,000 hours in 19_8.

GOODWIN: But . . .

MASTERS: But nothing, Toni. Everyone plays games in this company. This is the fourth division of World Semiconductor I have worked in. I know for a fact that in all my three prior divisions, we deliberately understated budgeted usage of research scientists to the San Diego people at the start of each year. Anyway, San Diego always artificially inflates its estimate of overhead costs for the coming year. They do it every year. Anyone who thinks this is a level playing field is more naive than my dog.

GOODWIN: Roy, I have to think about this.

MASTERS: Don't think too long Toni. I want the senior managers on my team to be team players. The issue you face, Toni, is whether you want to remain on the team.

REQUIRED

1. Why might Masters want Goodwin to report 25,000 budgeted hours rather than 30,000 budgeted hours to San Diego?
2. What steps might San Diego take to reduce WS divisions' understating their budgeted usage of San Diego research scientist time?
3. What should Goodwin do? In your answer, refer to *Standards of Ethical Conduct for Management Accountants* (p. 10).

COLLABORATIVE LEARNING PROBLEM

13-35 **Cost allocation for car pool, common costs.** Jeannette Smith, a recent law school graduate, works at Prescott & Partners in downtown San Francisco. She drives her Volvo from Los Altos to San Francisco each working day. It is a 40-mile trip each way. She is approached by Scott Gibbs, a fellow associate in her law firm, about car pooling. Smith responds that they should try it for a week. Then, if it works out schedule-wise, they could agree on how to share the costs of the car travel. Gibbs lives at San Mateo, which is nearly midway on Smith's drive to San Francisco. On the third day of their car pooling, Gibbs suggests they approach Robbie Goulding, another associate working for a different law firm in the same building as Prescott. Goulding lives in Palo Alto, which is between Los Altos and San Mateo. Gibbs wants to invite Goulding so that they can travel in the special express lane. The drive between San Mateo and San Francisco in the peak-hour times they travel is bumper to bumper unless they satisfy the "3 in a car pool" requirement for the express lane.

Goulding said yes on a trial basis with one provision. This proviso was that her commuting cost had to be very "competitive" with her current alternative of commuting by train. She liked to travel by train because she could read the newspaper and also meet "nonlawyer types."

Smith discusses with her fiancé how much to charge Gibbs and Goulding. He collects the following for her:

a. Distances traveled:

Los Altos (Smith)	Palo Alto (Goulding)	San Mateo (Gibbs)	Downtown San Francisco Law Offices
10 miles	12 miles	18 miles	

All three live very close to the freeway, so the distances traveled by Smith to pick up or drop Goulding or Gibbs are minimal.

b. Smith's Volvo has a variable cost of $0.15 per mile. The fixed cost per month is $100. She makes minimal use of the Volvo outside of travel to work. She prefers to use her fiancé's Jaguar sports car.

c. Smith pays $100 per month for parking at the law firm's offices. Prescott & Partners subsidizes this rate. The commercial rate is $250 per month.

d. Monthly train passes with unlimited use at any time of day are
   ◆ Los Altos–San Francisco $200
   ◆ Palo Alto–San Francisco   170
   ◆ San Mateo–San Francisco   145

   The monthly bus pass with unlimited use at any time of day for the bus between the San Francisco train depot and the downtown Prescott law office is $40.

e. The average number of commuting days per month is 20.

INSTRUCTIONS

Form groups of two or more students to complete the following requirements.

REQUIRED

1. Describe the alternative methods of allocating Smith's monthly commuting costs among Smith, Goulding, and Gibbs.

2. What cost-allocation method do you prefer? Use Exhibit 13-2 (p. 475) to guide your choice.

3. What noncost-related factors should Smith consider in deciding how much to suggest Goulding and Gibbs contribute to her monthly commuting costs?

COST ALLOCATION: II

Information technology-related costs (such as computers and software) are an important component of indirect costs in many print-media and book publishing companies.

LEARNING OBJECTIVES

After studying this chapter, you should be able to

1. Explain how the "different costs for different purposes" notion applies to cost allocations
2. Describe reasons why companies make changes in their costing systems
3. Understand when department overhead rates give more accurate product costs than a plantwide rate
4. Outline the consequences of the inappropriate use of an allocation base
5. Explain the importance of explicit agreement between parties when reimbursement is based on costs incurred
6. Describe the two main ways the U.S. government reimburses contractors
7. Describe how different ways of accounting for the costs of unused capacity can affect reported product costs
8. Explain how attempts to recover fixed costs may lead to a downward demand spiral
9. Describe why managers may find cost hierarchy-based reports useful in their decisions

C hapter 13 introduced four purposes of cost allocation and discussed the allocation of costs to departments. Chapter 14 continues our exploration of cost allocation. We now examine the allocation of costs to individual products, services, customers, or jobs (for example, a government contract). Topics related to both cost pools and cost allocation bases are examined. Costs we discuss include those incurred on the production or service line and those already allocated into these cost pools (such as allocations from corporate headquarters, as discussed in Chapter 13).

COST TRACING AND COST ALLOCATION

We will use the costing of a deluxe refrigerator model built by Consumer Appliances, Inc. (CAI), to continue our illustration of cost allocation issues. CAI assembles this refrigerator, along with eight other products, at its Windsor, Ontario, plant. It uses its own sales force to sell refrigerators to retail department stores. CAI employs the six-step approach to costing outlined in Chapter 4 (p. 96) and Chapter 5 (p. 132).

Step 1: Identify the Product that Is the Chosen Cost Object The cost object in this example is a deluxe refrigerator model called the Arctic.

Step 2: Identify the Direct-Costs for the Product CAI identifies three categories of direct costs. At CAI's Windsor manufacturing plant, there are two direct manufacturing costs—direct materials and direct manufacturing labor. CAI subcontracts customer service to a separate electrical goods repair company. It pays this company $75 per Arctic unit sold. The repair company handles all customer requests for service during the 24-month warranty period. Amounts traced to each Arctic unit are

Direct materials	$140
Direct manufacturing labor	35
Customer service	75
Total direct costs	$250

Step 3: Identify the Indirect-Cost Pools Associated with the Product CAI identifies six indirect-cost pools associated with the manufacturing and sale of the Arctic. These six pools are listed in step 5.

Step 4: Select the Cost Allocation Base to Use in Allocating Each Indirect-Cost Pool to the Product The chosen cost allocation bases are also listed in step 5.

Step 5: Develop the Rate Per Unit of the Cost Allocation Base Used to Allocate Indirect Costs to the Product The allocation base and rate for each indirect-cost pool in the January to June 19_8 period are

Indirect-Cost Pool	Allocation Base	Allocation Rate
Procurement	Number of parts	$0.50 per part
Production:	Direct manufacturing	
Labor-paced assembly	labor-hours	$20 per hour
Machine-paced assembly	Machine-hours	$16 per hour
Quality testing	Testing-hours	$30 per hour
Distribution	Cubic feet	$2 per cubic foot
Marketing	Units sold	$70 per unit

These allocation rates are used in the costing of all products assembled at the Windsor plant. The rates are revised every 6 months. The allocation rate for each indirect cost pool is calculated as

$$\text{Budgeted indirect-cost rate} = \frac{\text{Budgeted total costs in indirect-cost pool}}{\text{Budgeted total quantity of cost allocation base}}$$

For example, the procurement allocation rate of $0.50 per part in each product assembled at the Windsor plant is computed as follows:

$$\frac{\$2,000,000}{4,000,000 \text{ parts}} = \$0.50 \text{ per part}$$

The budgeted total costs for procurement at the Windsor plant in the January to June 19_8 period are $2 million. This amount includes costs for labor in the procurement department, for the equipment (for example, computers), and for the handling and inspection of incoming materials. The budgeted total quantity of the allocation base is 4 million parts. This figure is the budgeted number of parts for all products assembled at the Windsor plant in the January to June 19_8 period. It includes a budget of 252,000 parts for the deluxe refrigerator model (84 parts per refrigerator × 3,000 budgeted production units of refrigerators). The remaining 3,748,000 parts included in the denominator are for other products.

Step 6: Assign the Costs to the Product by Adding All Direct Costs and All Indirect Costs Exhibit 14-1 presents the product-cost buildup for the Arctic refrigerator model. The full product costs are $608, consisting of $250 direct costs and $358 indirect costs. The $358 amount includes $150 indirect costs for distribution and marketing. Only manufacturing costs are included when computing the inventoriable product costs (for financial reporting to external parties). The inventoriable product costs are $383 per Arctic model.

Exhibit 14-1 reinforces the *different costs for different purposes* notion. The $608 figure captures the full set of business function costs that CAI must cover in its pricing if it is to remain a profitable organization. For financial reporting, however, generally accepted accounting principles prohibit the inclusion of nonmanufacturing costs (distribution, marketing, and customer service) in the inventoriable product-cost figure. Note that this exclusion pertains to both direct costs and indirect non-manufacturing costs.

EXHIBIT 14-1
Costing of the Arctic Refrigerator Model

	Manufacturing Costs	Non-manufacturing Costs	Total Costs
Direct product costs			
Direct materials costs	$140	—	$140
Direct manufacturing labor	35	—	35
Customer service	—	$ 75	75
	$175	$ 75	$250
Indirect product costs			
Procurement, 84 × $0.50	$ 42	—	42
Production: labor-paced, 0.6 × $20	12	—	12
Production: machine-paced, 4.0 × $16	64	—	64
Production: quality-testing, 3.0 × $30	90	—	90
Distribution, 40 × $2	—	$ 80	80
Marketing, 1 × $70	—	70	70
	208	150	358
Full product costs	$383	$225	$608

CHOOSING INDIRECT-COST POOLS AND DETERMINING COST RATES

Indirect costs allocated to individual products, services, or customers are a function of

◆ *Cost pool choices*—how many cost pools and what costs in each pool.
◆ *Cost allocation base choices*—what allocation bases and what quantity of the allocation base.

This section discusses issues related to the choice of cost pools. Subsequent sections discuss the choice of cost allocation bases.

The concept of *cost pool homogeneity*, discussed in Chapter 13, is central to the issues raised in this section. A cost pool is homogeneous if all activities whose costs are included in it have the same or a similar cause-and-effect or benefits-received relationship between the cost driver and the costs of the activity. As an illustration, we consider the issue of plantwide versus department overhead cost rates.

Plantwide Rates versus Department Rates

If a company produces many products, should it use a single plantwide manufacturing overhead rate or individual department manufacturing overhead rates for product costing? Two important questions arise:

1. Do individual departments *differ* in the cause-and-effect or benefits-received relationship of the department's manufacturing overhead costs and the driver of these costs?

2. Do individual products *differ* in the way they are handled by individual departments in the plant?

If these differences are sizable, department overhead rates will provide more accurate product-cost figures than plantwide overhead rates. When these differences are minimal, the use of plantwide overhead rates will result in similar product-cost numbers as department overhead rates with the benefit of having fewer cost pools to track.

Consider product costing at CAI's Windsor production plant. This production plant has three individual departments:

For many years, Consumer Appliances used a single plantwide overhead rate, based on direct manufacturing labor-hours in the labor-paced assembly department. When the plant was first built, labor-paced assembly was the largest department of the plant. In recent years, the size of the labor-paced assembly department has decreased as machine-paced assembly lines have grown, and CAI has responded by changing its costing system. The existing product-costing system has three department overhead rates for the production plant:

Production Cost Pool	Cost Allocation Rate
Labor-paced assembly	$20 per direct manufacturing labor-hour
Machine-paced assembly	$16 per machine-hour
Quality testing	$30 per testing-hour

The plantwide overhead rate for the current period would have been $100 per direct manufacturing labor-hour in the previous costing system.

The effect of using three department cost pools, compared with a single plantwide cost pool, can be illustrated with the example of two products—the Arctic refrigerator model and the Sunshine clothes dryer model. These two products use the following resources from the three departments:

Department	Cost Allocation Base	Arctic Refrigerator Model	Sunshine Clothes Dryer Model
Labor-paced assembly	Direct manufacturing labor-hours	0.6 hour	0.8 hour
Machine-paced assembly	Machine-hours	4.0 hours	1.5 hours
Quality-testing	Testing-hours	3.0 hours	0.4 hour

The manufacturing overhead costs allocated to these two products using the plantwide rate and the department rates are as follows:

	Arctic Refrigerator	Sunshine Clothes Dryer
Plantwide manufacturing overhead rate		
0.6 direct manufacturing labor-hour, $100	$ 60	
0.8 direct manufacturing labor-hour, $100		$80
Department manufacturing overhead rates		
Labor-paced assembly department		
0.6 direct manufacturing labor-hour, $20	$ 12	
0.8 direct manufacturing labor-hour, $20		$16
Machine-paced assembly department		
4.0 machine-hours, $16	64	
1.5 machine-hours, $16		24
Quality-testing department		
3.0 testing-hours, $30	90	
0.4 testing-hour, $30		12
	$166	$52

The manufacturing overhead costs allocated to each Arctic refrigerator are $166 with department rates and $60 with a plantwide rate. Why the large difference? Because the department rates capture the Arctic's relatively high use of the machine-paced assembly and quality-testing departments. In contrast, the manufacturing overhead costs allocated to each Sunshine clothes dryer are $52 with department rates and $80 with a plantwide rate. This product makes relatively low use of the machine-paced assembly and quality-testing departments. Note, however, that each Sunshine clothes dryer has 0.8 hour use of the labor-paced assembly (compared to 0.6 for the Arctic). Recall that labor-hours was the allocation base for the plantwide rate. Indeed, one of the reasons CAI recently adopted department overhead rates was a complaint from the Sunshine products manager. She argued that the plantwide rate penalized her product line, making it appear that CAI was losing money on a product line she believed was a "winner." Top management accepted her argument and directed operating personnel to analyze the cause-and-effect cost relationships in the production plan. The use of different allocation bases in the three departments—manufacturing labor-hours, machine-hours, and testing-hours—resulted from that effort.

The plantwide versus department cost allocation discussion illustrates two guidelines for refining a costing system that were first introduced in Chapter 4 (p. 105):

1. Expand the number of indirect-cost pools until each pool is homogeneous.
2. Identify an appropriate cost allocation base for each indirect-cost pool.

The use of department cost pools results in more accurate cost rates when individual departments differ in their cause-and-effect (or benefits-received) relationships and individual products differ in the way they draw upon the resources of the individual departments. This case occurs with the Arctic and Sunshine products of Consumer Appliances. The guidelines used by Consumer Appliances are consistent with activity-based costing (ABC), which was discussed in Chapters 4 and 5. For example, Consumer Appliances identified separate activity areas in the product plant, and it used the cause-and-effect criterion to guide its choice of cost allocation bases.

OBJECTIVE 3

Understand when department overhead rates give more accurate product costs than a plantwide rate

CHANGES IN COST ALLOCATION BASES

Companies make changes in their costing systems at varying degrees of regularity. The prompts to these changes vary. In some cases, it is a change in the operations (for example, an increase in automation or a change in the products manufactured).

It can also be a change in information-gathering technology. Another prompt is a change in the products or services offered by competitors (for example, a competitor separately selling as individual products items that were previously sold as a bundle for a single price).

Chapters 4 and 5 illustrated how companies are using ABC to make better product emphasis, pricing, and cost management decisions. The adoption of ABC is leading to increases in the number of cost pools and in the number of cost-driver-related allocation bases in costing systems. In one study[1] of 166 ABC implementations, the distribution of the number of activities was

Less than 25	26–100	101–250	Above 250
19.4%	28.1%	34.4%	18.1%

The distribution of the number of separate cost drivers used as allocation bases in these 166 ABC implementations were

Less than 5	6–10	11–25	26–50	Above 50
8.1%	26.1%	27.3%	20.5	18.0%

In many companies, the same cost driver is used for more than one activity area, although the rate per cost-driver unit in each activity using the same driver can vary. The median number of activity-area-based cost pools in this study is over 100, whereas the median number of cost drivers is over 10. These numbers well exceed that in many existing (non-ABC) costing systems.

As companies change from labor-paced to machined-paced operations, they increase their use of machine-hours-related allocation bases. In **labor-paced operations,** worker dexterity and productivity determine the speed of production. Machines function as tools that aid production workers. Direct manufacturing labor costs or direct manufacturing labor-hours may still capture cause-and-effect relationships here, even if operations are highly automated. In contrast, in **machine-paced operations,** machines conduct most (or all) phases of production, such as movement of materials to the production line, assembly and other activities on the production line, and shipment of finished goods to the delivery dock areas. Machine operators in such environments may simultaneously operate more than one machine. Workers focus their efforts on supervising the production line and general troubleshooting rather than on operating the machines. Computer specialists and industrial engineers are the real controllers of the speed of production. In machine-paced operations, machine-hours will likely better capture cause-and-effect relationships than the direct labor-hours allocation base.

Increasingly, companies are turning to nonfinancial allocation bases. For example, several companies are now experimenting with manufacturing lead time as an allocation base. **Manufacturing lead time** is the time from when an order is ready to start on the production line to when it becomes a finished good. Any time delays, either at the start of production or during production, are included in the manufacturing lead time measure. The rationale for using this allocation base is that steps that lengthen manufacturing lead time frequently add to the indirect costs at the plant. For example, moving partly assembled products into and out of a work-in-process inventory area increases lead time and increases materials-handling costs. By using this allocation base, management signals to operating personnel that reported product costs can be reduced by shortening the lead time of products being assembled. The Problem for Self-Study at the end of this chapter illustrates use of the lead time allocation base for a medical instruments company.

OBJECTIVE 4

Outline the consequences of the inappropriate use of an allocation base

Consequences of an Inappropriate Allocation Base

Cost figures play a key role in many important decisions. If these figures result from allocation bases that fail to capture cause-and-effect relationships, managers may

---

[1] *American Productivity and Quality Center and CAM-I*, ABM Best Practices Study, 1995.

make decisions that conflict with maximizing long-run company net income. Consider the use of direct manufacturing labor costs as an allocation base in machine-paced manufacturing settings. In this environment, indirect-cost rates of 500% of direct manufacturing labor costs (or more) may be encountered. Thus, every $1 of indirect manufacturing labor costs has a $6 impact ($1 in direct costs + 500% per $1 in indirect costs) on reported product costs. Possible negative consequences include the following points:

1. Product managers may make excessive use of external vendors for parts that have a high direct manufacturing labor content.

2. Manufacturing managers may pay excessive attention to controlling direct manufacturing labor-hours relative to the attention paid to controlling the more costly categories of materials and machining. By eliminating $1 of direct manufacturing labor costs when the indirect-cost rate is 500% of these costs, $6 of reported product cost can be eliminated. When the indirect-cost rate is 500% of these costs, managers can control much of the accounting amounts allocated to products by controlling direct labor use. However, this action does not control the actual incurrence of the larger materials and machining costs.

3. Managers may attempt to classify shop-floor personnel as indirect labor rather than as direct labor. As a result, part of these labor costs will be allocated (inappropriately) to other products.

4. Products may be under- or overcosted. The danger then arises that a company will push to gain market share on products that it believes are profitable when in fact they are unprofitable. Similarly, the company may neglect products that are profitable because it believes they are unprofitable.

Cost Drivers and Allocation Bases

When a cause-and-effect criterion is used, the chosen allocation bases are cost drivers. Because a change in the level of a cost driver causes a change in the total cost of a related cost object, the use of cost drivers as allocation bases increases the accuracy of reported product costs. However, not all chosen cost-allocation bases are cost drivers. Consider the following reasons for using bases that are not cost drivers.

1. Improving the accuracy of individual product costs may be less important to a company than other goals. Think about the goal of restraining the growth in headcount (the number of employees on a company's payroll). Several Japanese companies use direct manufacturing labor-hours as the cost allocation base, while acknowledging that such labor-hours are not the most important driver of their manufacturing overhead costs. The purpose of this choice is to send a clear signal to all managers that reduction in headcount is a key goal.

Managers may also prefer direct manufacturing labor-hours as an allocation base so as to promote increased levels of automation. Using this allocation base, product designers are motivated to decrease the direct manufacturing labor content of the products they design. Management may view increased automation as a strategic necessity to remain competitive in the long run.

2. Information about cost-driver variables may not be reliably measured on an ongoing basis. For example, managers often view the number of machine setups as a driver of indirect manufacturing costs, but some companies do not systematically record this information.

3. Accounting systems with many indirect-cost pools and allocation bases are more expensive to use than systems with few cost pools and allocation bases. The investment required to develop and implement a system with many indirect-cost pools—and to educate users about it—can be sizable. Unfortunately, some firms place a low priority on investments in their internal accounting systems, given that the benefits from such investments are frequently difficult to quantify.

Is the Product-Costing System Broken?

A viewer knows when a television set no longer works. A driver knows when a motor vehicle no longer starts. The breakdown of many products is easy to detect. The breakdown of a product-costing system is not. Nonetheless, guidelines for assessing whether a product-costing system is broken do exist. Robin Cooper of the Claremont Graduate School offers such a set of guidelines.* Although no one individual guideline is conclusive, collectively they can flag the need for a detailed review of an existing product-costing system. The following four questions focus on these guidelines. The responses are from a sample of Dutch companies: [†]

Guideline	Yes	No
1. Can managers easily explain changes in profit margins from one period to the next? (If they cannot, one explanation is that the existing system is broken.)	70%	30%
2. Can managers easily explain why their bids for business are successful or unsuccessful? (If they cannot, one explanation is that the costing system is broken.)	64	36
3. Does the costing system have a small number of cost pools, and are the items in each cost pool heterogeneous? (Reducing heterogeneity will require an increase in the number of cost pools.)	56	44
4. Are competitors pricing their high-volume products comparable to ours at prices substantially lower than our cost figure? (One explanation is that we are overcosting these products.)	54	46

The responses indicate a sizable percentage of companies saying no to questions 1 and 2 and yes to questions 3 and 4. These are the red-flag responses to the overall question of whether a product-costing system is broken. An individual company that gave a red-flag response to all four of these questions should quickly examine whether its existing costing system should be significantly changed.

*Cooper, "Does Your Company."
[†]Boons and Roozen, "Symptoms." Full citations are in Appendix A.

CONTRACT COST JUSTIFICATION AND REIMBURSEMENT

Cost data are frequently key items in many contracting situations. Examples include

OBJECTIVE 5

Explain the importance of explicit agreement between parties when reimbursement is based on costs incurred

1. A contract between the Department of Defense and a company designing and assembling a new fighter plane; the price paid for the plane is based on the contractor's costs plus a preset fixed fee.

2. A research contract between a university and a government agency; the university is reimbursed its direct costs plus an overhead rate that is a percentage of direct costs.

3. A contract between two oil companies in a joint venture; the operating costs of a shared oil-refining facility are allocated between the companies on the basis of expected usage of the refinery.

4. A contract between an energy-consulting firm and a hospital; the consulting firm receives a fixed fee plus a share of the energy-cost savings arising from the consulting firm's recommendations.

Contracting disputes arise with some regularity, often with respect to cost allocation. The areas of dispute between parties can be reduced by making the "rules of the game" explicit (and preferably written) and well understood at the time the contract is signed. Such rules include the definition of cost items allowed, the cost pools, and the permissible cost allocation bases.

Contracting with the U.S. Government

The U.S. government reimburses most contractors in one of two ways:[2]

1. The *contractor is paid a preset price without analysis of actual contract cost data.* This approach is used, for example, where there is competitive bidding, where there is adequate price competition, or where there is an established catalog with prices quoted for items sold in substantial quantities to the general public.

2. The *contractor is paid after analysis of actual contract cost data.* In some cases, the contract will explicitly state that reimbursement is based on actual allowable costs plus a fixed fee. This arrangement is a **cost-plus contract.** In other cases, the contractor is paid a preset fixed price, provided that a government contracting officer views this price as reasonable (that is, close to actual costs).

All contracts with any U.S. government agency must comply with cost accounting standards issued by the **Cost Accounting Standards Board (CASB).** The CASB has the exclusive authority to make, promulgate, amend, and rescind cost accounting standards and interpretations thereof designed to achieve *uniformity* and *consistency* in the cost accounting standards governing measurement, assignment, and allocation of costs to contracts within the United States.

CASB Standards and Interpretations

Several CASB standards cover general issues related to the definition of cost items, consistency, and the prohibition of double-counting. **Double-counting** occurs when a cost item is included both as a direct-cost item and as part of an indirect-cost pool allocated to the contract using a budgeted rate. Other standards cover the allocation of indirect costs to government contracts. For example, Standard 403, "Allocation of Home Office Expenses to Segments," illustrates the CASB approach to determining cost pools and the allocation bases for these pools. The thrust of the standard requires home-office expenses to be allocated on the basis of the beneficial or causal relationship between supporting and receiving activities. The standard sets forth the following hierarchy of allocation techniques for centralized services:

- ◆ *Preferred*—a measure of the activity of the organization performing the function. Supporting functions are usually labor-, machine-, or space-oriented.
- ◆ *First alternative*—a measure of the output of the supporting function.

Exhibit 14-2 gives examples of the allocation bases provided in Standard 403 for individual home-office expense cost pools.

Fairness of Pricing

Negotiated contracts often attempt to use *cost assignment*—which includes both the *cost tracing* and *cost allocation*—as a means for establishing a mutually satisfactory price. A cost allocation may be difficult to defend on the basis of any cause-and-effect reasoning, but it may be a "reasonable" or "fair" means to help establish a contract price in the minds of the appropriate parties. Some costs become "allowable," but others are "nonallowable." An **allowable cost** is a cost that the parties to a contract agree to include in the costs to be reimbursed. Some contracts identify cost categories that are nonallowable. For example, the costs of lobbying activities and the costs of alcoholic beverages are not allowable costs on U.S. government contracts. Other contracts specify how allowable costs are to be determined. For example, only economy-class airfares are allowable for many contracts. Making the cost assignment rules as explicit as possible (and in writing) reduces argument and litigation when costs are to be used for establishing a contract price.

[2]For a detailed discussion of the issues in this section see F. Alston, M. Worthington, and L. Goldsman, *Contracting with the Federal Government*, 3d ed. (New York: Wiley, 1993).

EXHIBIT 14-2

Illustrative Allocation Bases Suggested by CASB for Centralized Home-Office Service Functions in Cost Accounting Standard 403

Service Rendered	Cost Allocation Bases
1. Personnel administration	1. Number of personnel, labor-hours, payroll, number of hires
2. Data-processing services	2. Machine time, number of reports
3. Centralized purchasing and subcontracting	3. Number of purchase orders, value of purchases, number of items
4. Centralized warehousing	4. Square footage, value of materials, volume
5. Company aircraft service	5. Actual or standard rate per hour, mile, passenger-mile, or similar unit
6. Central telephone service	6. Usage costs, number of telephones

COST ALLOCATIONS AND USED/UNUSED CAPACITY DISTINCTIONS

Cost allocation for fixed indirect costs has an extra dimension to that discussed previously in this book when unused capacity exists. **Unused capacity** (also called **excess capacity**) is the difference between the productive capacity available and the productive capacity required to meet consumer demand in the current period. Resource allocation decisions can be affected by how the costs associated with unused capacity are taken into account when computing indirect-cost rates. An example from the roadfreight industry illustrates this point.

Capacity's Effect on Indirect-Cost Rates

Rightway Foodmarkets is a national chain of supermarkets. For many years, it has used Barton Transport, an independent company, to distribute refrigerated produce from its warehouses to each of its supermarkets. In 19_7, Barton Transport charged Rightway (and other comparable supermarket chains) $4 per ton-mile of distributed produce. (A "ton-mile" is a measure of 1 ton moved 1 mile.) In July 19_7, Barton drivers went on strike for 3 weeks. One result was that Rightway had smaller amounts of produce delivered to each of its supermarkets.

Rightway decided to provide its own distribution. It had two options:

1. Develop its own distribution network (drivers, trucks, and so on) from the "ground up."

2. Acquire an existing trucking company.

Rightway opted for (2). In November 19_7, it acquired National Roadfreight, a superbly run trucking company.

Rightway's budgeted distribution requirements for 19_8 are 5 million ton-miles. Rightway's National Roadfreight subsidiary has the practical capacity to transport 8 million ton-miles in 19_8. Rightway expects to grow and thereby use the full 8 million ton-miles capacity by 19_9. Budgeted 19_8 distribution costs for Rightway's National Roadfreight subsidiary are

◆ Variable operating costs are $2.10 per ton-mile.

◆ Fixed costs are $12 million.

Each supermarket in the Rightway chain is charged for the cost of produce delivered to it. How should Rightway compute this cost? The main debate at Rightway is over the choice of the denominator to use for allocating the fixed costs. The two alternatives considered are

◆ *Budgeted utilization*—the level of capacity required to meet expected demand. For Rightway, expected demand is 5 million ton-miles. The budgeted fixed-cost allocation rate would be $2.40 per ton-mile ($12,000,000 ÷ 5,000,000).

OBJECTIVE 7

Describe how different ways of accounting for the costs of unused capacity can affect reported product costs

◆ *Practical capacity*—the level of capacity available, taking into account scheduled maintenance, and so on. For Rightway, practical capacity is 8 million ton-miles. The budgeted fixed-cost allocation rate would be $1.50 per ton-mile ($12,000,000 ÷ 8,000,000).

The effect on budgeted costs per ton-mile are

	Approach 1: Budgeted Utilization as Denominator Level	Approach 2: Practical Capacity as Denominator Level
Variable costs	$2.10	$2.10
Fixed costs	2.40	1.50
Total	$4.50	$3.60

The difference between the two approaches results from the 3 million ton-miles of budgeted unused capacity in 19_8.

In approach 1, this 3 million ton-miles of unused capacity is excluded from the fixed costs per ton-mile computation. Hence, the fixed costs of $12 million are fully charged out to the supermarkets in 19_8 as distribution costs of that period. The manager of a supermarket would see distribution costs increase from $4 per ton-mile in 19_7 (using Barton Transport) to $4.50 in 19_8 (using Rightway's trucking subsidiary).

In approach 2, the 3 million ton-mile unused capacity is included in the fixed costs per ton-mile computation. This approach results in only $7.5 million of the 19_8 fixed costs of $12 million being allocated to existing supermarkets as distribution cost in 19_8. Because the remaining $4.5 million of fixed costs is excluded, the distribution costs that the Rightway Foodmarket managers face drops to $3.60 per ton-mile. Where does the remaining $4.5 million of 19_8 fixed costs appear in the accounting system? One answer is to have a line item in the income statement for the fixed costs allocated to unused capacity:

Fixed costs	
Used capacity	$ 7,500,000
Unused capacity	4,500,000
	$12,000,000

Senior managers of Rightway made the strategic decision to acquire a trucking company with capacity well above its 19_8 internal requirements. Reporting the $4.5 million amount separately highlights that Rightway has this sizable excess capacity in its trucking subsidiary.

Many organizations have excess capacity in their manufacturing plants, their distribution networks, their sales forces, and elsewhere. Separate tracking of the costs of used capacity and unused capacity leads to a better understanding of operations. Moreover, this separate tracking assists in evaluating managers at different levels who have different areas of responsibility. The decision to acquire Rightway was a strategic one, made with the full knowledge that 3 million ton-miles of unused capacity would exist in 19_8. The separate tracking of this $4.5 million unused-capacity cost might prompt senior managers to seek ways for using this capacity.

Recall that Rightway has a national chain of supermarkets. Individual store managers will face different freight costs of acquiring food they sell to customers depending on how the accounting of the costs of unused trucking capacity is done. These different freight costs will affect the reported profitability of its many individual products. Burdening individual products with the costs of unused freight capacity can lead managers to inappropriately deemphasize products that have a relatively high freight cost component.

Unused Capacity Costs and the Downward Demand Spiral

Organizations that use a cost-based approach to pricing face difficult issues when capacity costs are high and sizable excess capacity exists. Consider again our Rightway example. Assume now that each supermarket manager has the option to use the

Rightway trucking subsidiary or the Barton Transport. In 19_8, the Barton Transport rate is $4.10 per ton-mile. If Rightway computes its internal cost with budgeted usage as the denominator for fixed costs, the quoted price will be $4.50 per ton-mile. Suppose now that some supermarket managers decide to use Barton Transport. As a result, the budgeted denominator in the following year drops from 5 million to 4 million ton-miles. The total cost per ton-mile would increase from $4.50 to $5.10, as shown in the following table. This increase in total cost may spur more Rightway managers to shift to Barton, which has a $4.10 per ton-mile rate. Again the total cost per ton-mile increases as the denominator level (budgeted usage) is reduced, as shown by the following numbers:

Budgeted Denominator (Ton-Miles) (1)	Variable Costs per Ton-Mile (2)	Fixed Costs Allocated per Ton-Mile [$12,000,000 ÷ (1)] (3)	Total Costs per Ton-Mile (4)
8 million	$2.10	$1.50	$3.60
5 million	2.10	2.40	4.50
4 million	2.10	3.00	5.10
3 million	2.10	4.00	6.10
2 million	2.10	6.00	8.10

As Rightway revises its total costs per ton-mile to allocate the fixed costs over a smaller and smaller number of ton-miles, a higher revised costs per ton-mile occurs. More and more supermarkets likely would turn to Barton Transport rather than use the Rightway subsidiary.

The **downward demand spiral** (also called the **black hole demand spiral**) refers to the continuing reduction in demand that occurs when prices are raised and then raised again in an attempt to recover fixed costs from an ever-decreasing customer base (in our example, the Rightway managers of individual supermarkets).

CHALLENGES IN MEASURING CAPACITY

While the term *capacity* has an intuitive meaning (a "constraint" or an "upper limit"), there is much debate about how it is to be measured. This section discusses several related issues in this area. In many organizations, the available capacity is well above the *just right* capacity. "Just right" in its narrowest sense is often interpreted to mean that capacity required to produce a given output level, assuming certainty (about demand, suppliers, distribution, and so on) and maximum efficiency for 100% of the time.

Exhibit 14-3 shows how a research group of company representatives distinguished between just right (A) and other classifications of "total capacity available." The waste box (B) represents capacity currently used on nonvalue-added activities such as waste, spoilage, and rework. The sum of (A) and (B) represents currently used capacity. Boxes dealing with customers (C) and suppliers (D) highlight how companies provide capacity in anticipation of coordination problems with these two external parties. The growth area (E) represents management acquiring capacity it does not currently require but which it anticipates using in future years.

Exhibit 14-3 makes visible the potential amount of unused capacity. Organizations can use this information either to seek better utilization of the current level of capacity or to reduce the available capacity and thus save unused-capacity carrying costs.

Much current work in operations management centers on eliminating bottlenecks—see Chapter 19 for discussion. Dramatic changes in available capacity levels can occur by redesigning key aspects of an organization (such as customer order-taking, plant layout, or product design). These changes obviously have implications for how capacity costs are estimated and how unitized fixed costs are interpreted.

EXHIBIT 14-3
Analyzing Difference between Total Capacity Available
and Capacity Used

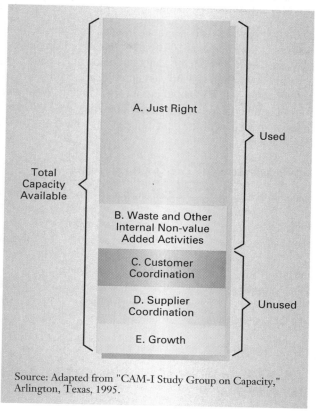

Source: Adapted from "CAM-I Study Group on Capacity,"
Arlington, Texas, 1995.

COST ASSIGNMENT AND COST HIERARCHIES

One extreme approach to cost assignment is to fully assign every cost to each individual unit of a product or service. There is growing interest in cost hierarchy systems that stop short of this full assignment of costs. A *cost hierarchy* is a categorization of costs into different cost pools on the basis of either different classes of cost drivers or different degrees of difficulty in determining cause-and-effect relationships. Not all costs in a cost hierarchy are driven by unit-level product or unit-level service-related variables. Chapter 5 (p. 150) introduced the cost hierarchy notion where the focal cost object was a product. The four levels of costs in the product-based cost hierarchy are (1) output unit-level costs, (2) batch-level costs, (3) product-sustaining costs, and (4) facility-sustaining costs. The Concepts in Action box (p. 522) illustrates this four-tier cost hierarchy for a cattle ranch. Only output unit-level costs are allocated to individual products using this hierarchy. Chapter 16 (p. 596) discusses the customer-cost hierarchy, including GM's hierarchy for its Service Parts Operation.

We now discuss two additional cost hierarchies and how they result in different types of cost allocations: (1) an organization-structure cost hierarchy, and (2) a brand cost hierarchy. Note that all of these approaches are illustrations of the contribution approach to the measurement of profitability.

OBJECTIVE 9

Describe why managers may
find cost hierarchy-based
reports useful in their
decisions

Organization-Structure Cost Hierarchy

A frequently encountered cost hierarchy classifies costs along the organizations structural lines (plants, divisions, corporate headquarters, and so on). We illustrate this approach with divisions and corporate headquarters. Within each division, costs are classified as variable (with respect to output units) or fixed. Finally, fixed costs are classified into those controllable within the division and those controllable outside the division. *Controllability* is the degree of influence that a specific manager has over the costs (revenues or other items in question) within a particular time span.

Cost Hierarchies Down on the Farm

The Canadian Valley Cattle Ranch (CVCR) is a family-owned business in Seminole, Oklahoma. It owns 1,000 acres of land and over 600 head of registered Limousin cattle (so named because they were originally from the Limoges region of France). In its operations, CVCR makes decisions about when to sell individual cattle, about where to feed herds of cattle, about its Limousin cattle line, and about corporate planning. What would a product-based cost hierarchy model look like? The CVCR cost hierarchy, along with examples of the cost items at each level and their cost drivers, is as follows:

Cost Hierarchy Level	Cost Items Included	Cost Drivers
Output unit-level costs	Semen costs	Number of artificial inseminations
Feeding costs	Age and sex of animal	
Batch-level costs	Seeding, spraying of pastures	Acreage of pastures
Weaning costs	Number of labor-hours	
Product-sustaining costs	Consultation on new Limousin strains	Number of visits by consultant
Promotion at agriculture fairs	Number of shows attended	
Facility-sustaining costs	Property taxes	

The different groupings of costs in this cost hierarchy help CVCR managers make more informed decisions at all levels.

Source: C. Fulkerson, A. Lau, and H. Pourjalali, "Applying Activity-Based Costing to the Canadian Valley Cattle Ranch: A Case Study," *Advanced Management Accounting*, Vol. 3 (Greenwich, Conn.: JAI Press, 1994).

Exhibit 14-4 presents an income statement for Newcastle Machining, which has a corporate headquarters and two divisions (A and B). This income statement stresses cost-behavior patterns in relation to output levels at each of its two divisions or segments. The assigning of revenues and variable costs to segments is usually straightforward. The result is line item 1, contribution margin. Line item 2 in Exhibit 14-4 is a measure of the manager's controllable contribution, and it is often used as a measure of the manager's performance. Line item 3 describes the performance of the segment as an economic investment. A **segment** is an identifiable part or subunit of an organization. For example, the Division A manager's objective for the forthcoming month may be to increase the division's contribution in line item 2 from $10,000 to $30,000. If this objective is attained, the manager may subsequently be judged successful by corporate management. However, using line item 3, top management may continue to regard the division as a poor investment. Distinguishing between line items 2 and 3 can be difficult. There is often a gray area between cost items that segment managers control and those they do not control.

The income statement in Exhibit 14-4 shows that $135,000 is not allocated to divisions. Examples of unallocated costs in many organizations are corporate income taxes and interest on company debt.

Brand Cost Hierarchy

Brand names such as Coca-Cola, Nestlé, and Sony are valuable assets to the companies that own them. Managers in these companies frequently make decisions that focus on brand categories. Cost hierarchies have been developed to support these decisions. Consider the Swiss-based Nestlé Company. A brand cost hierarchy for its Nestlé brand would include the following:

EXHIBIT 14-4

Monthly Income Statement of Newcastle Machining: Organization
Division/Controllability-Based Cost Hierarchy (all figures in thousands)

		Total	Division A		Division B
Revenues		$1,500	$500		$1,000
Variable manufacturing costs	$780		$250	$530	
Variable marketing costs	220		100	120	
Total variable costs		1,000	350		650
1. Contribution margin		500	150		350
Fixed division costs controllable by division managers*		190	140		50
2. Contribution controllable by division		310	10		300
Fixed division costs controllable outside division†		70	20		50
3. Contribution by divisions		240	$ (10)		$ 250
Corporate costs unallocated		135			
4. Operating income		$ 105			

*Examples include division-related advertising, sales promotion, salespersons' salaries, and engineering research.
†Examples include property taxes and the division manager's salary.

1. Individual product-level costs. These costs pertain to each unit of a single product, such as a 1-pound block of Nestlé milk chocolate or a Nestlé can of sweetened condensed milk.

2. Related product-line costs. These costs support the manufacture and marketing of a general product group (such as the Nestlé chocolate product line or the Nestlé dairy products line). The cost of a TV advertisement that includes several different Nestlé chocolate products would fall into this category.

3. Brand-level costs. These costs pertain to the general support of all products using the Nestlé brand. These costs are not assigned to individual product lines, individual products, or units of a product. The cost of a Nestlé-sponsored hot-air balloon that carries only the Nestlé name would fall into this category.

By making cost assignments at these different levels, a brand cost hierarchy can assist managers faced with challenging decisions at each level. For example, consider a proposal for Nestlé to be a major sponsor for the Year 2000 Olympic Games. Sponsorship would cost $25 million. All Nestlé brand products will benefit from the prestigious exposure associated with this event. Individual product managers (such as the product manager for Nestlé Chocolate Quik Drink), however, would not have any control over the $25 million cost for Olympic sponsorship. Not allocating the $25 million beyond the brand-level increases the ability of Nestlé to evaluate how individual product managers perform vis-a-vis the cost areas they can control or at least sizably affect.

PROBLEM FOR SELF-STUDY

PROBLEM

In 19_7, Medical Instruments changed the costing system at its manufacturing plant. The prior system had two direct product-cost categories (direct materials and direct manufacturing labor) and one indirect-cost category (manufacturing overhead). Indirect costs were allocated to products on the basis of direct labor manufacturing costs.

The new costing system retains the same two direct product-cost categories. Now, however, indirect manufacturing costs are collected into two cost pools:

1. Materials handling overhead allocated on the basis of the budgeted number of parts in a product. (When the individual parts in a product are all different, the number of parts and the number of individual parts in the product will be equal. When the same part number is used multiple times in a product, the number of parts will exceed the number of separate parts in that product.)

2. Production overhead allocated on the basis of the budgeted manufacturing lead time for each product. Manufacturing lead time is the time from when a product is ready to start on the production line to when it becomes a finished good.

Management made the following assumptions in developing the 19_7 budgeted indirect-cost allocation rates:

Materials Handling Overhead

Budgeted total materials handling overhead costs	$8,000,000
Budgeted number of separate part numbers	5,000
Budgeted average usage per separate part number	800
Budgeted total number of parts (5,000×800)	4,000,000

$$\text{Budgeted materials handling overhead cost allocation rate} = \frac{\$8,000,000}{4,000,000 \text{ parts}}$$

$$= \$2 \text{ per part}$$

Production Overhead

Budgeted total production overhead costs	$12,000,000
Budgeted number of individual products	400
Budgeted average production output per product	100 units
Budgeted average manufacturing lead time per product	6 hours
Budgeted total manufacturing lead time (400×100×6 hours)	240,000 hours

$$\text{Budgeted production overhead cost allocation rate} = \frac{\$12,000,000}{240,000 \text{ hours}}$$

$$= \$50 \text{ per hour}$$

Curt Henning is examining how the new costing system affects the reported costs of three products. Details of these products in 19_7 are as follows:

	Product A	Product B	Product C
Direct materials costs	$1,680	$1,250	$2,070
Direct manufacturing labor-hours	7.2	4.3	6.1
Number of parts	128	86	260
Manufacturing lead time in hours	4.8	3.9	18.5

The direct manufacturing labor rate in 19_7 is $30 per hour. Under the prior product-costing system (with one indirect-cost category), an indirect-cost allocation rate of 300% of direct manufacturing labor costs would have been used in 19_7.

REQUIRED
1. What characteristics of a product will lead to its having a much higher cost under the 19_7 costing system, than it would have had under the prior costing system?

2. Compute the manufacturing costs of products A, B, and C using (a) the prior product-costing system, and (b) the product-costing system introduced in 19_7.

3. Why might there be a cause-and-effect relationship between actual manufacturing lead time and production overhead costs?

SOLUTION

1. The characteristics of a product that will lead to its having a much higher cost under the new costing system are (a) low direct manufacturing labor cost content, (b) high number of parts, and (c) long manufacturing lead time.

2a.

	Product A	Product B	Product C
Direct manufacturing unit cost			
Direct materials *Given*	$1,680	$1,250	$2,070
Direct manufacturing labor *Given*			
(7.2; 4.3; 6.1×$30)	216	129	183
	$1,896	$1,379	$2,253
Indirect manufacturing unit costs			
($216; $129; $183×300%)	648	387	549 ← Old
Total manufacturing unit costs	$2,544	$1,766	$2,802

2b.

	Product A	Product B	Product C
Direct manufacturing unit cost			
Direct materials *Given*	$1,680	$1,250	$2,070
Direct manufacturing labor *Given*			
(7.2; 4.3; 6.1×$30)	216	129	183
	$1,896	$1,379	$2,253
Indirect manufacturing unit cost			
Materials handling			
(128; 86; 260×$2) *Alloc Rate*	$ 256	$ 172	$ 520
Production			
(4.8; 3.9; 18.5×$50) *Alloc Rate*	240	195	925
	496	367	1,445
Total manufacturing unit cost	$2,392	$1,746	$3,698
	lower	*lower*	*higher*

3. The actions required to reduce manufacturing lead time will probably reduce the activities that drive production overhead costs. For example, many firms achieving dramatic reductions in manufacturing lead times also achieve

♦ Lower inventory levels (meaning lower materials-handling costs)
♦ Higher quality levels (meaning reduced rework activities)
♦ Reduced complexity in scheduling (meaning lower manufacturing administrative costs)

The following points are linked to the chapter's learning objectives.

1. The purpose for computing costs guides the costs to be assigned to a chosen cost object. For example, many marketing costs cannot be allocated to U.S. government contracts. In contrast, the costing of products sold to other customers should include any marketing costs associated with doing business with those companies.

2. Department overhead rates will provide more accurate product-cost figures than plantwide overhead rates when the individual departments differ in their cost drivers and when the individual products differ in the way they use individual departments in the plant.

3. Companies make changes in their accounting systems for a variety of reasons, including changes in their operations, changes in their information-gathering technology, and changes in the behavior of their competitors.

4. The use of an inappropriate cost allocation base can cause products to be manufactured less efficiently, management to be misfocused, and products to be mispriced in the marketplace.

5. Contract disputes over costs incurred often can be reduced by making the cost assignment rules as explicit as possible (and in writing). These rules should include details such as the allowable cost items, the acceptable cost allocation bases, and how differences between budgeted and actual costs are to be handled.

6. The U.S. government pays contractors in some cases with, and in other cases without, any analysis of their cost data. Even if the contract has a set price, there frequently is a provision that the set price must bear a reasonable relationship to the actual costs the contractor incurs.

7. Unused capacity is the difference between the productive capacity available and the productive capacity required to meet consumer demand in the current period. Companies can spread the costs of unused capacity across all units produced in the current period, or they can keep these costs in total as a separate category.

8. Companies with high fixed costs and unused capacity may encounter ongoing and increasingly greater reductions in demand if they continue to raise selling prices to fully recover fixed costs from a declining sales base. This has been termed the *downward demand spiral.*

9. There is growing interest in cost hierarchies, which are categorizations of costs into different cost pools based on either different classes of cost drivers or different degrees of difficulty in determining cause-and-effect relationships. Examples include product, customer, organization, and brand-level cost hierarchies.

▼ TERMS TO LEARN

This chapter and the Glossary at the end of this book contain definitions of the following important terms:

allowable cost (p. 517)	excess capacity (518)
black hole demand spiral (520)	labor-paced operations (514)
Cost Accounting Standards Board (CASB) (517)	machine-paced operations (514)
cost-plus contract (517)	manufacturing lead time (514)
double-counting (517)	segment (522)
downward demand spiral (520)	unused capacity (518)

▼ ASSIGNMENT MATERIAL

QUESTIONS

14-1 Different costs for different purposes means that a cost allocated for one purpose is not allocated for another purpose. Do you agree?

14-2 Name two factors that affect the indirect costs allocated to individual products, services, or customers.

14-3 When are department overhead rates generally preferable to plantwide overhead rates?

14-4 "To obtain higher homogeneity, have more rather than fewer cost pools." Do you agree? Why?

14-5 How is the debate over plantwide versus departmentwide overhead rates related to the growing use of activity-based costing to refine costing systems?

14-6 Why is the distinction between labor-paced and machine-paced operations important when selecting indirect-cost allocation bases?

14-7 Manufacturing firms that make extensive use of machines should abandon the use of direct manufacturing labor cost as an allocation base. Do you agree? Why?

14-8 Describe two consequences of using direct manufacturing labor-hours as an allocation base in a machine-paced work environment.

14-9 Explain why some firms have adopted manufacturing lead time as the allocation base for manufacturing overhead.

14-10 Name two ways that firms are reimbursed under government contracts.

14-11 Define double-counting. Give an example.

14-12 Define *unused capacity*. What role does it play in the setting of indirect-cost rates?

14-13 What factors might explain differences between total capacity of a plant and the "just right" capacity?

14-14 Explain why and how the downward demand spiral can occur when a company has a high level of fixed costs.

14-15 What is a cost hierarchy? Give two examples. Why might managers find the cost hierarchy notion useful in analyzing costs?

EXERCISES

14-16 Alternative allocation bases for a professional services firm. The Wolfson Group (WG) provides tax advice to multinational firms. WG charges clients for (a) direct professional time (at an hourly rate), and (b) support services (at 30% of the direct professional costs billed). The three professionals in WG and their rates per professional hour are

Professional	Billing Rate per Hour
Myron Wolfson	$500
Ann Brown	120
John Anderson	80

WG has just prepared the May 19_7 bills for two clients. The hours of professional time spent on each client are as follows:

	Hours per Client	
Professional	Seattle Dominion	Tokyo Enterprises
Wolfson	15	2
Brown	3	8
Anderson	22	30
Total	40	40

REQUIRED
1. What amounts did WG bill to Seattle Dominion and Tokyo Enterprises for May 19_7?
2. Suppose support services were billed at $50 per professional labor-hour (instead of 30% of professional labor costs). How would this change

affect the amounts WG billed to the two clients for May 19_7? Comment on the differences between the amounts billed in requirements 1 and 2.

3. How would you determine whether professional labor costs or professional labor-hours is the more appropriate allocation base for WG's support services?

14-17 Plantwide indirect-cost rates. Automotive Products (AP) designs, manufactures, and sells automotive parts. It has three main operating departments: design, engineering, and production.

◆ *Design*—the design of parts, using state of the art, computer-aided design (CAD) equipment.
◆ *Engineering*—the prototyping of parts and testing of their specifications.
◆ *Production*—the manufacture of parts.

For many years, AP had long-term contracts with major automobile assembly companies. These contracts had large production runs. AP's costing system allocates variable manufacturing overhead on the basis of machine-hours. Actual variable manufacturing overhead costs for 19_7 were $308,600. AP had three contracts in 19_7, and its machine-hours used in 19_7 were assigned as follows:

United Motors	120
Holden Motors	2,800
Leland Vehicle	1,080
Total	4,000

REQUIRED

1. Compute the plantwide variable manufacturing overhead rate for 19_7.
2. Compute the variable manufacturing overhead allocated to each contract in 19_7.
3. What conditions must hold for machine-hours to provide an accurate estimate of the variable manufacturing overhead incurred on each individual contract at AP in 19_7?

14-18 Department indirect cost rates (continuation of 14-17). The controller of Automotive Parts (AP) decides to interview key managers of the Design, Engineering, and Production Departments. Each manager is to indicate the consensus choice among department personnel as to the cost driver of variable manufacturing overhead costs at that department. Summary data are

	19_7 Variable Manufacturing Overhead	Cost Driver
Design	$ 39,000	CAD design-hours
Engineering	29,600	Engineering-hours
Production	240,000	Machine-hours
	$308,600	

Details pertaining to usage of these cost drivers for each of the three 19_7 contracts are

Operating Area	Cost Driver	United Motors	Holden Motors	Leland Vehicle
Design	CAD design-hours	110	200	80
Engineering	Engineering-hours	70	60	240
Production	Machine-hours	120	2,800	1,080

REQUIRED

1. What is the variable manufacturing overhead rate for each department in 19_7?

2. What is the variable manufacturing overhead allocated to each contract in 19_7 using department variable manufacturing overhead rates?

3. Compare your answer in requirement 2 to that in requirement 2 of Exercise 14-17. Comment on the results.

14-19 Cost allocation, use of a separate machining cost pool category. Mahitsu Motors is a manufacturer of motorcycles. Production and cost data for 19_7 are as follows:

	500 CC Brand	1,000 CC Brand
Units produced	10,000	20,000
Direct manufacturing labor-hours per unit	2	4
Machine-hours per unit	8	8

A single cost pool is used for manufacturing overhead. For 19_7, manufacturing overhead was $6.4 million. Mahitsu allocates manufacturing overhead costs to products on the basis of direct manufacturing labor-hours per unit.

Mahitsu's accountant now proposes that two separate pools be used for manufacturing overhead costs:
◆ Machining cost pool ($3.6 million in 19_7)
◆ General plant overhead cost pool ($2.8 million in 19_7)

Machining costs are to be allocated using machine-hours per unit. General plant overhead costs are to be allocated using direct manufacturing labor-hours per unit.

REQUIRED

1. Compute the overhead costs allocated per unit to each brand of motorcycle in 19_7 using the current single-cost-pool approach of Mahitsu.

2. Compute the machining costs and general plant overhead costs allocated per unit to each brand of motorcycle assuming that the accountant's proposal for two separate cost pools is used in 19_7.

3. What benefits might arise from the accountant's proposal for separate pools for machining costs and general plant costs?

14-20 Cost allocation with a nonfinancial variable, retailing. Best for Less is a retail chain of supermarkets. For many years, it has used gross margin (selling price minus cost of goods sold) to guide it in deciding on which products to emphasize or deemphasize. And, for many years, it has not allocated any costs to products. It changed its internal reporting system recently, and goods handling costs are now allocated to individual products on the basis of cubic volume. (Most products are delivered to the shelves in cartons. A detailed study showed that cubic volume was the major driver of Best for Less goods handling costs. These costs make up over 30% of noncost of goods sold costs of Best for Less.) The following data focus on four products in April 19_7:

Product	Revenue per Carton	Cost of Goods Purchased per Carton	Volume (Cubic Feet)
Breakfast cereal	$ 82	$56	24
Cheese product	64	52	12
Paper towels	36	26	24
Toothpaste	100	74	12

Each supermarket has a weekly report on product contribution:

Revenue	$ R
Cost of goods sold	C
Gross margin (GM)	R – C
Goods handling costs	D
Product contribution (PC)	$GM – D

The April 19_7 goods-handling cost allocation rate is $0.50 per cubic foot.

REQUIRED

1. Compute the gross margin for each of the four products. Rank these four products using their gross margin percentage.
2. Compute the product contribution for each of the four products. Rank these four products using the product contribution to revenue percentage.
3. Compare your ranking in requirement 2 with that in requirement 1. How is the requirement 2 analysis useful to Best for Less management?

14-21 Manufacturing cost allocation, use of a conversion cost pool category, automation. Medical Technology Products manufactures a wide range of medical instruments. Two testing instruments (101 and 201) are produced at its highly automated Quebec City plant. Data for December 19_7 are as follows:

	Instrument 101	Instrument 201
Direct materials	$100,000	$300,000
Direct manufacturing labor	$ 20,000	$ 10,000
Units produced	5,000	20,000
Actual direct labor-hours	1,000	500

Manufacturing overhead is allocated to each instrument product on the basis of actual direct manufacturing labor-hours per unit for that month. Manufacturing overhead cost for December 19_7 is $270,000. The production line at the Quebec City plant is a machine-paced one. Direct manufacturing labor is made up of costs paid to workers minimizing machine problems rather than actually operating the machines. The machines in this plant are operated by computer specialists and industrial engineers.

REQUIRED

1. Compute the cost per unit in December 19_7 for instrument 101 and instrument 201 under the existing cost accounting system.
2. The accountant at Medical Technology proposes combining direct manufacturing labor costs and manufacturing overhead costs into a single conversion costs pool. These conversion costs would be allocated to each unit of product on the basis of direct materials costs. Compute the cost per unit in December 19_7 for instrument 101 and instrument 201 under the accountant's proposal.
3. What are the benefits of combining direct manufacturing labor costs and manufacturing overhead costs into a single conversion costs pool?

14-22 Overhead disputes. (Suggested by Howard Wright) The Azure Ship Company works on U.S. Navy vessels and commercial vessels. General yard overhead (for example, the cost of the purchasing department) is allocated to the jobs on the basis of direct labor costs.

In 19_3, Azures total $150 million of direct labor cost consisted of $50 million Navy and $100 million commercial. The general yard overhead was $30 million.

Navy auditors periodically examine the records of defense contractors. The auditors investigated a nuclear submarine contract, which was based on cost-plus-fixed-fee pricing. The auditors claimed that the Navy was entitled to a refund because of double-counting of overhead in 19_3.

The government contract included the following provision:

Par. 15-202. Direct Costs.

(a) A direct cost is any cost which can be identified specifically with a particular cost object. Direct costs are not limited to items which are incorporated in the end product as material or labor. Costs identified specifically with the contract are direct costs of the contract and are to be charged directly thereto. Costs identified specifically with other work of the contractor are direct costs of that work and are not to be charged to the contract directly or indirectly. When items ordinarily chargeable as indirect costs are charged to the contract as direct costs, the cost of like items applicable to other work must be eliminated from indirect costs allocated to the contract.

Azure had formed a special expediting purchasing group, the SE group, to join with the central purchasing group to obtain materials for the nuclear submarine only. Their direct costs, $5 million, had been included as direct labor of the nuclear work. Accordingly, overhead was allocated to the contracts in the usual manner. The SE costs of $5 million were not included in the general yard overhead. The auditors claimed that no overhead should have been allocated to these SE costs.

REQUIRED

1. Compute the amount of the refund that the Navy would claim.
2. Suppose the Navy also discovered that $4 million of general yard overhead was devoted exclusively to commercial engine-room purchasing activities. Compute the additional refund that the Navy would probably claim. (*Note:* This $4 million was never classified as direct labor. Furthermore, the Navy would claim that it should be reclassified as a direct cost but not as direct labor.)

14-23 Contract reimbursement for a university. Cardinal University conducts federal government-sponsored research for the Department of Health. Government contract guidelines permit universities to recover direct costs of each project plus an indirect cost amount that is 70% of the "allowable direct cost base for computing indirect costs." Some direct costs (travel) are recoverable without any associated indirect cost rate being chargeable to the project.

The University Provost is currently examining three government-sponsored projects (each labeled by the name of its research head):

Direct Costs, 19_7	Chen	Adams	Porras
Salary & wages	$146,000	$97,000	$183,000
Direct materials	39,000	2,000	85,000
Travel	11,000	18,000	6,000

The 70% indirect cost rate applies only to the salary and wages and direct materials.

REQUIRED

1. What amount should the provost of Cardinal University bill the federal government for the Chen, Adams, and Porras projects?
2. Suppose Chen inappropriately included $8,000 for a library research associate in its $146,000 salary and wages figure. The $8,000 salary was already included in the indirect cost pool used to calculate the 19_7 rate of 70%. What effect would correcting this inappropriate inclusion have on the contract reimbursement amount?
3. Why might the federal government preclude the indirect cost rate being applied to travel costs?

14-24 Downward demand spiral, pricing, cost hierarchy. Francoise Le May is the new president (as of August 1, 19_7) of Sky Shuttle, a commuter airline that flies between San Francisco and Los Angeles. Sky Shuttle is a division of Global Shuttle, which operates more than 20 subsidiaries around the globe. Le May previously was president of Alliance Shuttle, which operates a commuter airline between Paris and Marseilles. Alliance Shuttle has the dominant market share on this air corridor because of its ownership of extensive gate slots at each airport.

The financial results of Sky Shuttle for July 19_7 were

Revenues

    150 round-trip flights
    100 passengers per round-trip (average)
    $150 per round-trip passenger (average)

Cost data
> $20 variable costs per round-trip passenger
> $6,000 variable costs per round-trip flight
> $1,200,000 monthly fixed costs

Each flight has a maximum capacity of 160 passengers.

Le May is depressed by these July 19_7 results. She expresses concerns about the $150 round-trip price. She tells the director of marketing and the controller that a Paris-to-Marseilles round-trip ticket on Alliance Shuttle averaged $360. "How can you possibly recover all those fixed costs when you price at $150 per round-trip?" The controller agrees with her. Unfortunately, the marketing director is in a quandary. He was about to ask Le May to approve a special $120 per round-trip price in September to match a price promotion by Pacific West Airlines on its San Francisco-to-Los Angeles route.

REQUIRED

1. Compute the July 19_7 operating income of Sky Shuttle using a cost hierarchy that is based on cost variability at different levels of drivers. How might Le May find this cost hierarchy useful in her decision making?
2. Compute the operating income to Sky Shuttle if, in August 19_7,
   a. Le May increases the round-trip price to $180 and the 150 scheduled flights average 90 passengers.
   b. Le May increases the round-trip price to $200 and the 150 scheduled flights average 75 passengers.
   Does the (a) or (b) pricing strategy enable Le May to recover Sky Shuttle's fixed costs? Explain.
3. Should Le May approve the special $120 per round-trip price in September? Explain.

14-25 Segment reporting and cost hierarchies. (Z Iqbal) The AB Company has only two divisions: A and B. The following data apply to Division A.

Fixed costs controllable outside division	$ 100,000
Net revenues	1,500,000
Variable marketing and administrative exp.	200,000
Total traceable costs	1,000,000
Total variable costs	600,000

REQUIRED

1. Prepare a segment report for Division A that differentiates between the performance of the manager and the performance of the division.
2. Division B's net revenue is $3 million, and its contribution margin is $1.2 million. The segment margin (contribution by division of Division B is $700,000.
   a. Determine fixed costs traceable to Division B.
   b. Determine variable costs of Division B.
3. AB Company's corporate costs unallocated to divisions are $400,000. Determine AB's income.

PROBLEMS

14-26 Cost allocation for financial institution. The Florida Police and Fireman's Credit Union (FPFCU) is a credit union providing financial services for police and firemen and their families. Individuals eligible to join can deposit money with the FPFCU and earn a "dividend" payment on their money. Deposits are the largest source of funds. Because FPFCU is a credit union owned by its members, the payment to depositors is labeled a dividend rather than interest. The second source of funds is borrowing from other financial institutions (typically banks or savings and loans). All sources of funds are put into a common pool of funds available to use. The main use of funds held by FPFCU is consumer loans to its members.

EXHIBIT 14-5
Florida Fireman and Police Credit Union

Sources of Funds	19_4	19_5	19_6
Average Balance			
Deposits	$10.5 mill.	$11.6 mill.	$12.8 mill.
Borrowings	0.4	1.9	0.6
Average dividend/interest paid			
Deposits (dividend)	7.8%	4.9%	6.1%
Borrowings (interest)	8.3	5.7	7.4
Uses of Funds			
Average Balance			
Consumer Loans	$9.1 mill.	$12.6 mill.	$10.7 mill.
Investments	1.8	0.9	2.7
Average "interest" received			
Consumer loans	10.3%	7.4%	8.6%
Investments	8.1	5.6	7.2
Number of consumer loans	455	492	392
Number of investments	11	7	23

Where the funds available from deposits and other sources exceed the consumer loans outstanding, FPFCU invests money in minimal risk government securities. Exhibit 14-5 presents summary information on FPFCU in the 19_4 to 19_6 period. The nondividend and noninterest costs of the credit union (for buildings, personnel, legal, regulatory, marketing, and so on) are

	19_4	19_5	19_6
Costs traceable to loans	$ 82,700	$ 91,500	$ 86,700
Costs traceable to investments	6,100	4,500	8,900
Other costs	97,800	133,500	137,600
	$186,600	$229,500	$233,200

The other costs include facilities-related costs, general marketing and administrative costs, and costs traceable to the sources (rather than the uses) of money.

Alondra Micelli, the president of FPFCU, seeks your help on two issues relating to product line profitability of consumer loans and investments. Micelli wants to compare the relative profitability of consumer loans and investments with that of other financial institutions. She wants you to prepare product line profitability statements assuming the following:

a. Cost of money is recognized as a cost. The same rate is used for consumer loans and for investments. The rate is the weighted average cost of funds from all sources.

b. Where possible, trace costs directly to each product line.

c. For costs not included in (a) and (b), allocate to consumer loans and investments based on their relative percentage of total "earning assets" (defined as the sum of consumer loans and investments).

REQUIRED

1. Compute annual product-line profitability statements for 19_4, 19_5, and 19_6 following the given assumptions.

2. Critically evaluate assumptions (a) to (c). Outline possible alternative ways of assigning costs to product lines.

3. What use can Micelli make of the product line profitability reports in requirement 1?

14-27 Plantwide versus department overhead cost rates. (CGA, adapted) The Sayther Company manufactures and sells two products, A and B. Manufacturing overhead costs at its Portland plant are allocated to each product using a plantwide rate of $17 per direct manufacturing labor-hour. This rate is based on budgeted manufacturing overhead of $340,000 and 20,000 budgeted direct labor-hours:

Manufacturing Department	Budgeted Manufacturing Overhead	Budgeted Direct Manufacturing Labor-Hours
1	$240,000	10,000
2	100,000	10,000
Total	$340,000	20,000

The number of direct manufacturing labor-hours required to manufacture each product is

Manufacturing Department	Product A	Product B
1	4	1
2	1	4
Total	5	5

Per unit costs for the two categories of direct manufacturing costs are

Direct Manufacturing Costs	Product A	Product B
Direct materials costs	$120	$150
Direct manufacturing labor costs	80	80

At the end of the year, there was no work in process. There were 200 finished units of product A and 600 finished units of product B on hand. Assume that the budgeted production level of the Portland plant was exactly attained.

Sayther sets the listed selling price of each product by adding 120% to its unit manufacturing costs; that is, if the unit manufacturing costs are $100, the listed selling price is $220 ($100 + $120). This 120% markup is designed to cover costs upstream to manufacturing (for example, product design) and costs downstream from manufacturing (for example, marketing and customer service) as well as to provide an operating income.

REQUIRED

1. What is the effect on the inventoriable costs for products A and B of using a plantwide overhead rate instead of department overhead rates?
2. What difference would result in the per unit selling prices of product A and product B from using a plantwide overhead rate instead of department overhead rates?
3. Should Sayther Company prefer plantwide or department manufacturing overhead rates?

14-28 Plantwide versus department overhead cost rates. (CMA) The MumsDay Corporation manufactures a complete line of fiberglass attaché cases and suitcases. MumsDay has three manufacturing departments (molding, component, and assembly) and two support departments (maintenance and power).

The sides of the cases are manufactured in the Molding Department. The frames, hinges, locks, and so on are manufactured in the Component Department. The cases are completed in the Assembly Department. Varying amounts of materials, time, and effort are required for each of the various cases. The Maintenance and Power Departments provide services to the three manufacturing departments.

MumsDay has always used a plantwide overhead rate. Direct manufacturing labor-hours are used to allocate the overhead to each product. The budgeted rate is calculated by dividing the company's total budgeted overhead cost by the total budgeted direct labor-hours to be worked in the three manufacturing departments.

Whit Portlock, manager of Cost Accounting, has recommended that MumsDay use department overhead rates. Portlock has projected operating costs and production levels for the coming year. They are presented (in thousands) by department in the following tables:

| | Manufacturing Department | | |
	Molding	Component	Assembly
Department operating data			
Direct manufacturing labor-hours	500	2,000	1,500
Machine-hours	875	125	
Department costs			
Direct manufacturing materials	$12,400	$30,000	$ 1,250
Direct manufacturing labor	3,500	20,000	12,000
Variable manufacturing overhead	3,500	10,000	16,500
Fixed manufacturing overhead	17,500	6,200	6,100
Total departmental costs	$36,900	$66,200	$35,850
Use of support departments			
Maintenance			
Estimated usage in labor-hours for coming year	90	25	10
Power (in kilowatt-hours)			
Estimated usage for coming year	360	320	120
Maximum allotted capacity	500	350	150

(handwritten: 4,000 beside labor-hours row; 30,000 and 29,800 / 59,800 beside overhead rows; 950, 695, 280 below Maximum allotted capacity)

| | Support Department | |
	Maintenance	Power
Department operating data		
Maximum capacity	Adjustable	1,000 kWh
Budgeted usage in coming year	125 hours	800 kWh
Department costs		
Materials and supplies	$1,500	$ 5,000
Variable labor	2,250	1,400
Fixed overhead	250	12,000
Total support department costs	$4,000	$18,400

(handwritten: 12,250 / 72,050)

REQUIRED

1. Calculate the plantwide overhead rate for the MumsDay Corporation for the coming year using the same method as used in the past.
2. Whit Portlock has been asked to develop department overhead rates for comparison with the plantwide rate. Follow these steps in developing the department rates:
   a. Allocate the Maintenance Department costs to the three manufacturing departments using a single rate.
   b. Allocate the Power Department costs to the three manufacturing departments using a dual-rate method; allocate fixed costs according to maximum capacity and variable costs according to budgeted usage in the coming year.

c. Calculate department overhead rates for the three manufacturing departments using a machine-hour allocation base for the Molding Department and a direct manufacturing labor-hour allocation base for the Component and Assembly Departments.

3. Should the MumsDay Corporation use a plantwide rate or department rates to allocate overhead to its products? Explain your answer.

14-29 Effect of overhead cost allocation rate changes and product-design changes on reported product costs. (Extension of Problem for Self-Study, pp. 523–525) In 19_7, Medical Instruments adopted an accounting system with two direct product-cost categories (direct materials costs and direct manufacturing labor costs) and two indirect manufacturing product-cost categories:

a. Materials-handling overhead allocated on the basis of budgeted number of parts in a product

b. Production overhead allocated on the basis of budgeted average manufacturing lead time for each product

It is now 19_8. Curt Henning makes the following assumptions when developing the 19_8 cost allocation rates for materials handling overhead and production overhead:

Budgeted total materials handling overhead costs	$ 7,695,000
Budgeted number of separate part numbers	4,500 part numbers
Budgeted average usage per separate part number	900 hours
Budgeted total production overhead costs	$12,240,000
Budgeted number of individual products	425 products
Budgeted average production output per product	120 hours
Budgeted average manufacturing lead time per product	5 hours

Henning is now examining the reported costs of products A and C in 19_8. (Product B has been discontinued.) Product designers at Medical Instruments made several changes in these two products at the end of 19_7 that reduced both the direct manufacturing labor-hours content and the number of parts in each product. The 19_8 direct manufacturing labor rate is $32 per hour. Manufacturing has made substantial progress in reducing the manufacturing lead time for each product. Details of these two products in 19_7 and 19_8 are as follows:

	Product A		Product C	
	19_7	19_8	19_7	19_8
Direct materials dollars	$1,680	$1,618	$2,070	$2,027
Direct manufacturing labor-hours	7.2	6.9	6.1	5.2
Number of parts	128	116	260	224
Manufacturing lead time in hours	4.8	4.2	18.5	14.8

REQUIRED

1. Compute the 19_8 budgeted materials handling overhead cost allocation rate per part and the 19_8 budgeted production overhead cost allocation rate per hour of manufacturing lead time.

2. Compute the 19_8 manufacturing costs of products A and C using the 19_8 indirect-cost allocation rates computed in requirement 1.

3. Compare the manufacturing cost figures for products A and C in 19_7 (see the Problem for Self-Study) and 19_8. Explain any differences between 19_7 and 19_8 costs for each product.

4. Assume that Medical Instruments uses actual rather than budgeted manufacturing lead time (at the budgeted rate per manufacturing lead time hour) when allocating production overhead costs to products. The plant is operating at full capacity. A special customer purchases 20 units of product C on the condition that they be rushed (say, at 10.8 hours per unit) through the production line. The customer will pay the listed price in the catalog. How should Medical Instruments compute the gross margin (selling price minus manufacturing costs) on this sale of 20 units of product C? Is the reported product cost of product C accurate for products sold to this customer?

14-30 Single versus multiple indirect-cost pools, behavior change or accuracy in product costing (continuation of 14-29). Medical Instruments uses one indirect-cost pool for production overhead. Several companies with production facilities similar to those at Medical Instruments use more than ten separate production overhead cost pools, each with a different allocation base or rate. A manufacturing manager at Medical Instruments made the following observation:

> Our objective in using a single production overhead cost pool based on manufacturing lead time is to signal to a broad set of people (in product design, process engineering, and manufacturing) the strategic importance of Medical Instruments reducing manufacturing lead time. The system is designed to cause behavioral change at Medical Instruments. A single production overhead rate based on manufacturing lead time sends a clear and unambiguous signal to reduce manufacturing lead time. Personally, I do not see the need to adopt a system using six or eight production overhead cost pools, each with their own allocation base. That would be overly complex and complete overkill.

REQUIRED

Comment on the manufacturing manager's rationale for allocating production overhead costs using a single indirect-cost rate.

14-31 Product-line and territorial income statements. The Delvin Company shows the following results for the year 19_7:

Revenues	$1,000,000	100.0%
Cost of goods sold	$ 675,000	67.5%
Marketing*	220,000	22.0%
Administrative (all fixed)	35,000	3.5%
Total costs	$ 930,000	93.0%
Operating income	$ 70,000	7.0%

*All fixed except for $40,000 freight-out cost.

The sales manager has asked you to prepare statements that will help him assess the company efforts by product line and by territories. You have gathered the following information:

	Product			Territory		
	A	**B**	**C**	**North**	**Central**	**Eastern**
Revenues*	25%	40%	35%			
Product A				50%	20%	30%
Product B				15%	70%	15%
Product C				14/35	8/35	13/35
Variable manufacturing and packaging costs[†]	68%	55%	60%			
Fixed separable costs						
Manufacturing	$15,000	$14,000	$21,000		(not allocated)	
Marketing	40,000	18,000	42,000	$48,000	$32,000	$40,000
Freight-out		(not allocated)		13,000	9,000	18,000

Note: All items not directly allocated were considered common costs.
*Percent of company revenues.
[†]Percent of product revenues.

1. Prepare a product-line income statement, showing the results for the company as a whole in the first column, costs not allocated in the second column, and the results for the three products in adjoining columns. Show a contribution margin and a product margin, as well as operating income.
2. Repeat requirement 1 on a territorial basis. Show a contribution margin and a territory margin.
3. Should salespeople's commissions be based on contribution margins, product margins, territorial margins, operating income, or dollar sales? Explain.

14-32 Cost allocation, brand cost hierarchies. The Heinz U.S.A. division of H. J. Heinz is currently reexamining its management accounting system. Donna Fargo, the controller, recently heard a presentation on product-cost hierarchies. The presenter spent a great deal of time outlining output unit-level, batch-level, product-sustaining-level, and facility-sustaining costs. The Heinz controller asked the presenter, "How can this cost hierarchy be applied to companies where the focus is on brands rather than individual products?" After much silence, the presenter said, "That's a good question. Let's talk about it later."

Fargo was intrigued by the cost hierarchy approach. The manager of the Heinz brand of products, Bob Rau, had long argued against fully allocating all the Heinz costs to every individual item of product sold. Currently, all costs are allocated to individual items of product using revenues as the allocation base. Rau recently commented, "The only reason I can see to fully allocate all costs to individual products is to demonstrate that our people can divide and then add up."

Fargo decided to pursue the brand cost hierarchy notion herself. She developed the following hierarchy for the Heinz brand family of products:

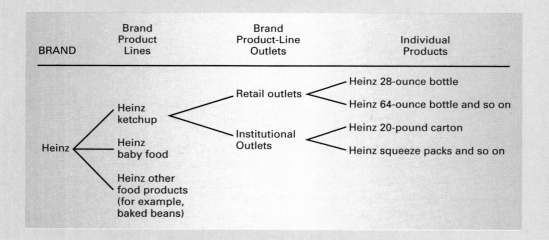

REQUIRED

1. Why might Rau be against fully allocating all the Heinz costs to every individual item of product sold?
2. Describe two specific cost items that would be included in the following categories:
   a. Individual product-level costs for the Heinz ketchup 28-ounce plastic bottle
   b. Related product-line costs for the Heinz ketchup product line
   c. Brand-level costs for the Heinz brand name
3. How might Rau find a cost hierarchy based on (a), (b), and (c) in requirement 2 useful for decision making?

14-33 Cost allocation, downward demand spiral. Western Health Maintenance (WHM) operates a chain of ten hospitals in the Los Angeles area. For many years, it has operated a central food-catering facility in Santa Monica, which delivers meals to the ten hospitals. The Santa Monica facility has the capacity to serve 3,650,000 meals a year (10,000 meals a day). In 19_7 it budgeted for 2,920,000 meals (8,000 meals a day), based on demand estimates from each hospital controller. The budgeted variable costs per meal in 19_7 are $3.80, which includes delivery to the hospital. Budgeted fixed costs for 19_7 are $4,380,000.

In July 19_7, the new WHM president announces that each hospital is to be a profit center. In addition, the head of each hospital can purchase services from outside WHM, providing those services meet the WHM quality requirements. The president gives catering as an example. Roy Jenkins, the head of the Santa Monica catering facility, is less than pleased. This facility also will become a profit center (it has been a cost center for many years) under the reorganization.

Jenkins charged each hospital $5.30 per meal in 19_7—comprising $3.80 variable cost + $1.50 allocation of budgeted fixed costs. Several hospitals complained about the $5.30 cost as well as the quality of the food. (Jenkins sarcastically labels the quality complaints as "recycled mystery meat stories.") Indeed, the cost rose from $4.90 in 19_3 to $5.30 in 19_7. Jenkins defended the increase, claiming he needed to spread the same fixed costs over a smaller number of patient-days in 19_7. WHM experienced negative press on a local TV station in 19_3 and early 19_7, and local doctors are referring fewer patients to the WHM hospitals.

In October 19_7, Jenkins started to prepare the 19_8 budget, including the new cost to be charged per meal. He estimated that the total annual demand for meals at all ten WHM hospitals will be 2,550,000. Then he learned that three of the ten hospitals will use an outside canteen service, which reduces the 19_8 budgeted demand at the Santa Monica facility to 2 million meals. No change in total fixed costs or variable costs per meal are expected in 19_8.

REQUIRED

1. How did Jenkins compute the budgeted fixed costs per meal in 19_7?
2. What alternative cost-per-meal figures might Jenkins compute for meals delivered to WHM hospitals in 19_8? Which cost figure should Jenkins use?
3. What factors should Jenkins consider in pricing meals the Santa Monica facility prepares for the WHM hospitals?

14-34 Cost allocation, budgeted rates, ethics (continuation of 14-33). The actual meal counts used in 19_7 by all of WHM's hospitals were less than the budgeted amounts each hospital controller provided Jenkins at the start of 19_7. Jenkins suspects collusion on the part of the hospital controllers. He is concerned that the 19_8 budgeted meal counts from the individual hospitals will likewise turn out to be way too optimistic about actual demand.

REQUIRED

1. Why might the individual hospital administrators deliberately overestimate the 19_7 budgeted meal count demand?
2. Jenkins decides to approach the WHM corporate controller to discuss his concerns about individual hospital controller's colliding about budgeted meal count demand. What evidence should the corporate controller seek to investigate Jenkins's concerns?
3. What steps should the corporate controller take to reduce any incentives individual hospital controllers have to deliberately mis-estimate meal count demand for 19_8?

COLLABORATIVE LEARNING PROBLEM

14-35 Allocating materials handling costs, government contracts, ethics. (CMA) Grand-Mark Industries was found by Mark Preston in 1950 as a small machine shop producing machined parts for the aircraft industry. The

Korean War brought rapid growth to Grand-Mark. By the end of the war, Grand-Mark's annual sales had reached $15 million, almost exclusively under government contracts. The next 30 years brought slow but steady growth as cost-reimbursement government contracts continued to be the main source of revenue.

Realizing that Grand-Mark could not depend on government contracts for long-term growth and stability. Drew Preston, son of the founder and now president of the company, began planning for diversified commercial growth in the mid-1980s. By the end of 1994, Grand-Mark had succeeded in reducing the ratio of government contract sales to 50% of total sales.

Traditionally, the costs of the Materials Handling Department have been allocated to direct materials as a percentage of direct materials dollar costs. This was adequate when the majority of the manufacturing was homogenous and related to government contracts. Recently, however, auditors from the Government Contract Audit Agency have rejected some proposals stating, "The amount of Materials Handling Department costs allocated to these proposals is disproportionate to the total effort involved."

Kara Lindley, the newly hired cost accounting manager, has been asked by the manager of the Government Contracts Unit, Paul Anderson, to find a more equitable method of allocating Materials Handling Department costs to the user departments. Her review reveals the following information:

◆ The majority of the direct materials purchases for government contracts are high-dollar, low-volume purchases. All other users of the Materials Handling Department involve only low-dollar, high-volume purchases.

◆ Administrative departments (marketing, finance, administration, human resources, and maintenance) also use the services of the Materials Handling Department on a limited basis but have never been charged in the past for materials handling costs.

◆ Several costs can be 100% traced to the government contracts. One purchasing agent with a direct phone line is assigned exclusively to purchasing high-dollar, low-volume material for government contracts at an annual salary of $36,000. Employee benefits are estimated to be 20% of the annual salary. The annual dedicated phone line costs are $2,800.

The components of the Materials Handling Department's budget for 1995 (including those traceable to government contracts), as proposed by Lindley's predecessor are as follows:

Payroll	$ 181,000
Employee benefits	36,200
Telephones	38,000
Other utilities	20,800
Materials and supplies	7,000
Depreciation	5,000
Direct materials budget	
Government contracts	2,006,000
Commercial products	874,000

Lindley has estimated the number of low-dollar, high-volume purchase orders to be processed in 1995 to be as follows:

Government contracts	80,000
Commercial products	156,000
Marketing	1,800
Finance and administration	2,700
Human resources	500
Maintenance	1,000

Lindley recommended to Anderson that Grand-Mark (a) assign to government contracts all materials handling costs traceable to high-dollar, low-volume material for government contracts, and (b) allocate all other materials handling costs to all users on a per low-dollar high-volume purchase order basis. Anderson realizes and accepts that the company probably has been allocating to government contracts more materials handling costs than can be justified. However, the implication of Lindley's analysis could be a decrease in his unit's earnings and, consequently, a cut in his annual bonus. Anderson told Lindley to "adjust" her numbers and modify her recommendation so that the results will be more favorable to the Government Contracts Unit.

Being new in her position, Lindley is not sure how to proceed. She feels ambivalent about Anderson's instructions and suspects his motivation. To complicate matters for Lindley, Preston has asked her to prepare a 3-year forecast of the Government Contracts Unit's results, and she believes that the newly recommended allocation method would provide the most accurate data. However, this would put her in direct opposition to Anderson's directives.

Lindley has assembled the following data to project the direct materials handling costs:

◆ Total direct materials costs increase 2.5% per year.
◆ Direct materials handling costs remain the same percent of direct material costs.
◆ Direct government costs (payroll, employee benefits, and the direct phone line) remain constant.
◆ The number of purchase orders increases 5% per year.
◆ The ratio of government purchase orders to total purchase orders remains at 33%.
◆ In addition, she has assumed that government material in the future will be 70% of total material costs.

INSTRUCTIONS

Form groups of two or more students to complete the following requirements.

REQUIRED

1. Calculate the materials handling rate per dollar of direct material costs that would have been used by Kara Lindley's predecessor at Grand-Mark Industries.

2. **a.** Calculate the revised materials handling costs at Grand-Mark Industries to be allocated on a per low-dollar, high-volume purchase order basis.

   b. Discuss why purchase orders might be a more reliable cost driver than the dollar amount of direct materials.

3. Calculate the difference in materials handling costs charged to government contracts due to the change to the new method of allocating materials handling costs of Grand-Mark Industries.

4. Prepare a forecast of the cumulative dollar impact over a 3-year period from 1995–1997 of Kara Lindley's recommended change for allocating Materials Handling Department costs to the Government Contracts Unit. Round all calculations to the nearest whole number.

5. Referring to the specific standards (competence, confidentiality, integrity, and objectivity) and recommendations made in the *Standards of Ethical Conduct for Management Accountants* (Exhibit 1-5, p. 10).

   a. Discuss why Kara Lindley has an ethical conflict.

   b. Identify the steps that Lindley should take to resolve the ethical conflict.

15

COST ALLOCATION: JOINT PRODUCTS AND BYPRODUCTS

Joint cost issues often arise in extractive industries, such as petroleum, where hydrocarbons are processed to yield crude oil, gas, and raw LPG simultaneously.

LEARNING OBJECTIVES

After studying this chapter, you should be able to

1. Identify the splitoff point(s) in a joint-cost situation
2. Distinguish between joint products and byproducts
3. Provide several reasons for allocating joint costs to individual products
4. Explain alternative methods of allocating joint costs
5. Identify the criterion used to support market-based joint cost allocation methods
6. Describe the irrelevance of joint costs in deciding to sell or further process
7. Distinguish alternative methods of accounting for byproducts

Handwritten margin notes:
Focus on: Joint costs
→ Allocation
  * Unit based
  * Rev based
→ By Product costing

Prior chapters have emphasized costing for either single-product companies or for companies in which individual products are separately produced. We now consider costing for the more complex case where two or more products are simultaneously produced with each other. Costs incurred in this more complex case are termed *joint costs*. A **joint cost** is the cost of a single process that yields multiple products simultaneously. This chapter examines methods for allocating joint costs to products and services. Some of the topics discussed in this chapter are related to issues already covered in Chapters 13 and 14. Before reading on, be sure you are comfortable with pages 472–477 of Chapter 13.

MEANING OF TERMS

OBJECTIVE 1

Identify the splitoff point(s) in a joint-cost situation

Consider a single process that yields two or more products (or services) simultaneously. The distillation of coal, for example, gives us coke, gas, and other products. The cost of this distillation process would be called a joint cost. The juncture in the process when one or more products in a joint-cost setting become separately identifiable is called the **splitoff point**. An example is the point where coal becomes coke, gas, and other products. **Separable costs** are costs incurred beyond the splitoff point that are assignable to one or more individual products. At or beyond the splitoff point, decisions relating to sale or further processing of individual products can be made independently of decisions about other products.

OBJECTIVE 2

Distinguish between joint products and byproducts

Various terms have arisen in conjunction with production processes. A **product** is any output that has a positive sales value (or an output that enables an organization to avoid incurring costs). **Joint products** all have relatively high sales value but are not separately identifiable as individual products until the splitoff point. When a single process yielding two or more products yields only one product with a relatively high sales value, that product is termed a **main product.** A **byproduct** has a low sales value compared with the sales value of the main or joint product(s). **Scrap** has a minimal sales value. The classification of products as main, joint, byproduct, or scrap can change over time, especially for products (such as tin) whose market price can increase or decrease by, say, 30% or more in any one year.

Exhibit 15-1 shows the relationship between the terms defined in the preceding paragraph. Be careful. These distinctions are not firm in practice. The variety of terminology and accounting practice is bewildering. Always gain an understanding of the terms as used by the particular organization with which you are dealing.

Industries abound in which single processes simultaneously yield two or more products. Exhibit 15-2 presents examples of joint-cost situations in diverse industries. In each example in Exhibit 15-2, no individual product can be produced without the accompanying products appearing, although sometimes the proportions can

EXHIBIT 15-1
Joint Products, Main Product, Byproduct, and Scrap

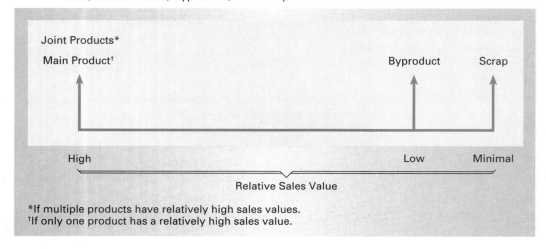

*If multiple products have relatively high sales values.
†If only one product has a relatively high sales value.

EXHIBIT 15-2
Examples of Joint-Cost Situations

Industry	Separable Products at the Splitoff Point
Agriculture	
Lamb	Lamb cuts, tripe, hides, bones, fat
Raw milk	Cream, liquid skim
Turkey farm	Breasts, wings, thighs, drumsticks, digest, feathermeal, and poultrymeal
Extractive industries	
Coal	Coke, gas, benzole, tar, ammonia
Copper ore	Copper, silver, lead, zinc
Petroleum	Crude oil, gas, raw LPG
Salt	Hydrogen, chlorine, caustic soda
Chemical industries	
Raw LPG (liquefied petroleum gas)	Butane, ethane, propane
Semiconductor industry	
Fabrication of silicon-wafer chips	Memory chips of different quality (as to capacity), speed, life expectancy, and temperature tolerance

be varied. A poultry farm cannot kill a turkey wing; it has to kill a whole turkey, which yields breasts, thighs, drumsticks, digest, feathermeal, and poultrymeal in addition to wings. In this example, the focus is on building up costs of individual products as disassembly occurs. This focus contrasts with prior chapters that emphasize building up costs of individual products as assembly occurs.

In some joint-cost settings, the number of outputs produced exceed the number of products. This situation can occur where an output, produced as an inherent part of the joint production process, is recycled without any value being added by its production. For example, the offshore processing of hydrocarbons to yield oil and gas also yields water as an output, which is recycled back into the ocean. Similarly, the processing of mineral ore to yield gold and silver also yields dirt as an output, which is recycled back into the ground. The water and dirt in these examples typically are not classified as products, but they are outputs. No entries are made in the accounting system to record their processing. The physical quantity of these outputs can be large relative to the physical quantity of outputs that are recorded in the accounting system as products. It is only those outputs that have a positive sales value that are typically labeled products.

WHY ALLOCATE JOINT COSTS?

There are many contexts that require the allocation of joint costs to individual products or services. Examples include

1. Inventory costing and cost-of-goods-sold computations for external financial statements and reports for income tax authorities.

2. Inventory costing and cost-of-goods-sold computations for internal financial reporting. Such reports are used in division profitability analysis when determining compensation for division managers.

3. Cost reimbursement under contracts when only a portion of a business's products or services is sold or delivered to a single customer (such as a government agency).

4. Customer profitability analysis where individual customers purchase varying combinations of joint products or byproducts as well as other products of the company.

OBJECTIVE 3

Provide several reasons for allocating joint costs to individual products

5. Insurance settlement computations when damage claims made by businesses with joint products, main products, or byproducts are based on cost information.

6. Rate regulation when one or more of the jointly produced products or services are subject to price regulation.[1]

These six areas are illustrative rather than exhaustive. Their wide-ranging natures illustrate why it is important to master methods for allocating joint costs.

APPROACHES TO ALLOCATING JOINT COSTS

OBJECTIVE 4

Explain alternative methods of allocating joint costs

There are two basic approaches to allocating joint costs:

◆ *Approach 1.* Allocate costs using market-based data (for example, revenues). Three methods that can be used in applying this approach are
The sales value at splitoff method
The estimated net realizable value (NRV) method
The constant gross-margin percentage NRV method

◆ *Approach 2.* Allocate costs using physical measure-based data such as weight or volume.

In prior chapters we have emphasized both the cause-and-effect and benefits-received criteria (see Exhibit 13-2, p. 475) for guiding cost-allocation decisions. In joint-cost settings, it is not feasible to use the cause-and-effect criterion to guide individual product-cost allocations. Joint costs, by definition, cannot be the subject of cause-and-effect analysis at the individual product level. The cause-and-effect relationship exists only at the joint process level. The benefits-received criterion leads to a preference for methods under approach 1. Revenues, in general, are a better indicator of benefits received than are physical measures such as weight or volume.

In the simplest situation, the joint products are sold at the splitoff point without further processing. We use this case first (termed Example 1) to illustrate the sales value at splitoff method and the physical measures method using volume as the metric. Then we consider situations involving further processing beyond the splitoff point (termed Example 2) to illustrate the estimated NRV method and the constant gross-margin percent NRV method.

To highlight each joint-cost example, we make extensive use of exhibits in this chapter. We use the following notation:

Joint Product or Main Product   Byproduct or Scrap

To enable comparisons across the methods, we report for each method individual gross-margin percentages for individual products.

EXAMPLE 1: Farmers' Dairy purchases raw milk from individual farms and processes it up to the splitoff point, where two products (cream and liquid skim) are obtained. These two products are sold to an independent company, which markets and distributes them to supermarkets and other retail outlets.

[1]See J. Crespi and J. Harris, "Joint Cost Allocation under the Natural Gas Act: An Historical Review," *Journal of Extractive Industries Accounting* 2, no. 2, pp. 133–142.

EXHIBIT 15-3

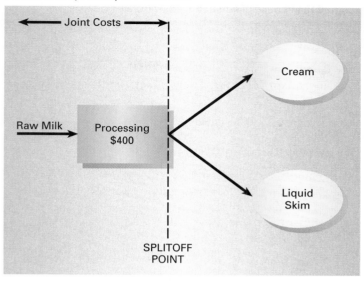

Farmers Dairy: Example 1 Overview

Exhibit 15-3 presents an overview of the basic relationships in this example. Summary data for May 19_7 are as follows:

- Raw milk processed: 110 gallons (110 gallons of raw milk yield 100 gallons of good product with a 10-gallon shrinkage)

	Production	Sales
◆ Cream	25 gallons	20 gallons at $8 per gallon
◆ Liquid skim	75 gallons	30 gallons at $4 per gallon

- ◆ Inventories

	Beginning Inventory	Ending Inventory
Raw milk	0 gallons	0 gallons
Cream	0 gallons	5 gallons
Liquid skim	0 gallons	45 gallons

- ◆ Cost of purchasing 110 gallons of raw milk and processing it up to the splitoff point to yield 25 gallons of cream and 75 gallons of liquid skim: $400

How much of the joint costs of $400 should be allocated to the ending inventory of 5 gallons of cream and 45 gallons of liquid skim? The joint production costs of $400 cannot be uniquely identified with or traced to either product. Why? Because the products themselves were not separated before the splitoff point. The joint-cost-allocation methods we now discuss can be used for costing the inventory of cream and liquid skim as well as determining cost of goods sold.

Sales Value at Splitoff Method

The **sales value at splitoff method** allocates joint costs on the basis of the relative sales value at the splitoff point of the total production in the accounting period of each product. In Example 1, the sales value at splitoff of the May 19_7 production is $200 for cream and $300 for liquid skim. We then assign a weighting to each

EXHIBIT 15-4
Farmers' Dairy Product-Line Income Statement for May 19_7:
Joint Costs Allocated Using Sales Value at Splitoff Method

	Cream	Liquid Skim	Total
Sales (cream, 20 gallons × $8; liquid skim, 30 gallons × $4)	$160	$120	$280
Joint costs			
Production costs (cream, 0.4 × $400; liquid skim, 0.6 × $400)	160	240	400
Deduct ending inventory (cream, 5 gallons × $6.40; liquid skim, 45 gallons × $3.20)	32	144	176
Cost of goods sold	128	96	224
Gross margin	$ 32	$ 24	$ 56
Gross-margin percentage	20%	20%	20%

product, which is a percentage of total sales value. Using this weighting, we allocate the joint costs to the individual products:

	Cream	Liquid Skim	Total
1. Sales value at splitoff point (cream, 25 gallons × $8; liquid skim, 75 gallons × $4)	$200	$300	$500
2. Weighting ($200 ÷ $500; $300 ÷ $500)	0.40	0.60	
3. Joint costs allocated (cream, 0.40 × $400; liquid skim, 0.60 × $400)	$160	$240	$400
4. Joint production costs per gallon (cream, $160 ÷ 25 gallons; liquid skim, $240 ÷ 75 gallons)	$6.40	$3.20	

Note that this method uses the sales value of the *entire production* of the accounting period. The joint costs were incurred on all units produced and not just those sold. Exhibit 15-4 presents the product-line income statement, using the sales value at splitoff method of joint-cost allocation. Use of this method has enabled us to obtain individual product costs and gross margins. Both cream and liquid skim have gross-margin percentages of 20%.[2]

The sales value at splitoff point method exemplifies the benefits-received criterion of cost allocation. Costs are allocated to products in proportion to their ability to contribute revenue. This method is both straightforward and intuitive. The cost-allocation base (sales value at splitoff) is expressed in terms of a common denominator (dollars) that is systematically recorded in the accounting system and well understood by all parties.

Physical Measure Method

The **physical measure method** allocates joint costs on the basis of their relative proportions at the splitoff point, using a common physical measure such as weight or volume of the total production of each product. In Example 1, the $400 joint costs produced 25 gallons of cream and 75 gallons of liquid skim. Joint costs using these quantities are allocated as follows:

---

[2]The equality of the gross-margin percentages for the two products is a mechanical result reached with the sales value at splitoff method when there are no beginning inventories and all products are sold at the splitoff point.

	Cream	Liquid Skim	Total
1. Physical measure of production (gallons)	25	75	100
2. Weighting (25 gallons ÷ 100 gallons; 75 gallons ÷ 100 gallons)	0.25	0.75	
3. Joint costs allocated (cream, 0.25 × $400; liquid skim, 0.75 × $400)	$100	$300	$400
4. Joint production costs per gallon (cream, $100 ÷ 25 gallons; liquid skim, $300 ÷ 75 gallons)	$4	$4	

Exhibit 15-5 presents the product-line income statement using this method of joint-cost allocation. The gross-margin percentages are 50% for cream and 0% for liquid skim.

The physical weights used for allocating joint costs may have no relationship to the revenue-producing power of the individual products. Using the benefits-received criterion, the physical measure method is less preferred than the sales value at splitoff method. Consider a mine that extracts ore containing gold, silver, and lead. Use of a common physical measure (tons) would result in almost all the costs being allocated to the product that weighs the most—lead, which has the lowest revenue-producing power. As a second example, if the joint cost of a hog were assigned to its various products on the basis of weight, center-cut pork chops would have the same cost per pound as pigs feet, lard, bacon, bones, and so forth. In a product-line income statement, the pork products that have a high sales value per pound (for example, center-cut pork chops) would show a fabulous "profit," and products that have a low sales value per pound (for example, bones) would show consistent losses.

Obtaining comparable physical measures for all products is not always straight-forward. Consider oil and gas joint-cost settings, where oil is a liquid and gas is a vapor. A standard physical measure, the British Thermal Unit (BTU), is often used here. However, this physical measure can vary with the temperature of the gas. Technical personnel outside of accounting may be required when using some physical measures in joint-cost-allocation situations.

EXAMPLE 2: Assume the same situation as in Example 1 except that both cream and liquid skim can be processed further:

◆ Cream → Butter cream: 25 gallons of cream are further processed to yield 20 gallons of butter cream at additional processing (separable) costs of $280. Butter cream is sold for $25 per gallon.

EXHIBIT 15-5
Farmers' Dairy Product-Line Income Statement for May 19_7:
Joint Costs Allocated Using Physical Measure Method

	Cream	Liquid Skim	Total
Sales (cream, 20 gallons × $8; liquid skim, 30 gallons × $4)	$160	$120	$280
Joint costs			
Production costs (cream, 0.25 × $400; liquid skim, 0.75 × $400)	100	300	400
Deduct ending inventory (cream, 5 gallons × $4; liquid skim, 45 gallons × $4)	20	180	200
Cost of goods sold	80	120	200
Gross margin	$ 80	$ 0	$ 80
Gross-margin percentage	50%	0%	28.6%

EXHIBIT 15-6
Farmers Dairy: Example 2 Overview

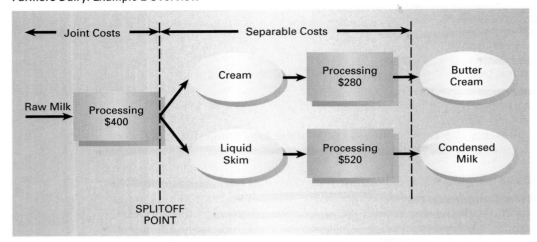

◆ Liquid skim → Condensed milk: 75 gallons of liquid skim are further processed to yield 50 gallons of condensed milk at additional processing costs of $520. Condensed milk is sold for $22 per gallon.

Sales during the accounting period were 12 gallons of butter cream and 45 gallons of condensed milk. Exhibit 15-6 presents an overview of the basic relationships. Inventory information is as follows:

	Beginning Inventory	Ending Inventory
Raw milk	0 gallons	0 gallons
Cream	0 gallons	0 gallons
Liquid skim	0 gallons	0 gallons
Butter cream	0 gallons	8 gallons
Condensed milk	0 gallons	5 gallons

Example 2 will be used to illustrate the estimated net realizable value (NRV) method and the constant gross-margin percentage NRV method.

Estimated Net Realizable Value Method

The **estimated net realizable value (NRV) method** allocates joint costs on the basis of the *relative estimated net realizable value* (expected final sales value in the ordinary course of business minus the expected separable costs of production and marketing of the total production of the period). Joint costs would be allocated as follows:

	Butter Cream	Condensed Milk	Total
1. Expected final sales value of production (butter cream, 20 gallons × $25; condensed milk, 50 gallons × $22)	$ 500	$1,100	$1,600
2. Deduct expected separable costs to complete and sell	280	520	800
3. Estimated net realizable value at splitoff point	$ 220	$ 580	$ 800
4. Weighting ($220 ÷ $800; $580 ÷ $800)	0.275	0.725	
5. Joint costs allocated (butter cream, 0.275 × $400; condensed milk, 0.725 × $400)	$ 110	$ 290	$ 400
6. Production costs per gallon [butter cream, ($110 + $280) ÷ 20 gallons; condensed milk, ($290 + $520) ÷ 50 gallons]	$19.50	$16.20	

TC/yield ↓

EXHIBIT 15-7
Farmers' Dairy Product-Line Income Statement for May 19_7:
Joint Costs Allocated Using Estimated NRV Method

	Butter Cream	Condensed Milk	Total
Sales (butter cream, 12 gallons × $25; condensed milk, 45 gallons × $22)	$300	$990	$1,290
Cost of goods sold			
Joint costs (butter cream, 0.275 × $400; condensed milk, 0.725 × $400)	110	290	400
Separable processing costs *Given*	280	520	800
Cost of goods available for sale	390	810	1,200
Deduct ending inventory (butter cream, 8 gallons × $19.50; condensed milk, 5 gallons × $16.20)	156	81	237
Cost of goods sold	234	729	963
Gross margin	$ 66	$261	$ 327
Gross-margin percentage *Gm/Sales*	22.0%	26.4%	25.3%

(handwritten annotations: "Sales" and "SP/gallon" above Butter Cream column)

Exhibit 15-7 presents the product-line income statement using the estimated NRV method. The gross-margin percentages are 22.0% for butter cream and 26.4% for condensed milk.

Estimating the net realizable value of each product at the splitoff point requires information about the subsequent processing steps to be taken (and their expected separable costs).[3] In some plants, such as in petrochemicals, there may be many possible subsequent steps. Companies may frequently change further processing to exploit fluctuations in the separable costs of each processing stage or in the selling prices of individual products. Under the estimated NRV method, each such change would affect the joint-cost-allocation percentages. (In practice, a set of standard subsequent steps is assumed at the start of the accounting period when using the estimated NRV method.)

The sales value at splitoff method is less complex than the estimated NRV method as it does not require knowledge of the subsequent steps in processing. However, it is not always feasible to use the sales value at splitoff method. Why? Because, there may not be any market prices at the splitoff point for one or more individual products. Market prices may not first appear until after processing beyond the splitoff point has occurred.

Constant Gross-Margin Percentage NRV Method

The **constant gross-margin percentage NRV method** allocates joint costs in such a way that the overall gross-margin percentage is identical for all the individual products. This method entails three steps:

Step 1: Compute the overall gross-margin percentage.

Step 2: Use the overall gross-margin percentage and deduct the gross margin from the final sales values to obtain the total costs that each product should bear.

Step 3: Deduct the expected separable costs from the total costs to obtain the joint-cost allocation.

[3] The estimated NRV method is clear-cut when there is only one splitoff point. When there are multiple splitoff points, however, additional allocations may be required if processes subsequent to the initial splitoff point remerge with each other to create a second joint-cost situation.

EXHIBIT 15-8
Farmers' Dairy for May 19_7:
Joint Costs Allocated Using Constant Gross-Margin Percentage NRV Method

	Butter Cream	Condensed Milk	Total
Step 1			
Expected final sales value of production: (20 gallons × $25) + (50 gallons × $22)		$1,600	
Deduct joint and separable costs ($400 + $280 + $520)		1,200	
Gross margin		$ 400	
Gross-margin percentage ($400 ÷ $1,600)		25%	
Step 2			
Expected final sales value of production (butter cream, 20 gallons × $25; condensed milk, 50 gallons × $22)	$500	$1,100	$1,600
Deduct gross margin, using overall gross-margin percentage (25%)	125	275	400
Cost of goods sold	375	825	1,200
Step 3			
Deduct separable costs to complete and sell	280	520	800
Joint costs allocated	$ 95	$ 305	$ 400

Exhibit 15-8 presents these three steps for allocating the $400 joint costs between butter cream and condensed milk. To determine the joint-cost allocation, Exhibit 15-8 uses the expected final sales value of the *total production* of the period ($1,600) and *not* the actual sales of the period. The joint costs allocated to each product need not always be positive under this method. Some products may receive negative allocations of joint costs to bring their gross-margin percentages up to the overall company average. The overall gross-margin percentage is 25%. A product-line income statement for the constant gross-margin percentage NRV method is presented in Exhibit 15-9.

EXHIBIT 15-9
Farmers' Dairy Product-Line Income Statement for May 19_7:
Joint Costs Allocated Using Constant Gross-Margin Percentage NRV Method

	Butter Cream	Condensed Milk	Total
Sales (butter cream, 12 gallons × $25; condensed milk, 45 gallons × $22)	$300.0	$990.0	$1,290.0
Cost of goods sold			
Joint costs (from Exhibit 15-8)	95.0	305.0	400.0
Separable costs to complete and sell	280.0	520.0	800.0
Cost of goods available for sale	375.0	825.0	1,200.0
Deduct ending inventory (butter cream, 8 × $18.75*; condensed milk, 5 × $16.50†)	150.0	82.5	232.5
Cost of goods sold	225.0	742.5	967.5
Gross margin	$ 75.0	$247.5	$ 322.5
Gross-margin percentage	25%	25%	25%

*$375 ÷ 20 gallons = $18.75.
†$825 ÷ 50 gallons = $16.50.

Chicken Processing: Costing on the Disassembly Line

Chicken processing operations provide many examples where joint and byproduct costing issues can arise. Each chicken is killed and then "disassembled" into many products. Every effort is made to obtain revenue from each disassembled item.

White breast meat, the highest revenue generating product, is obtained from the front end of the bird. Dark meat is obtained from the back end of the bird. Other edible products include chicken wings, giblets, and kidneys. There are many non-edible products including feathers and blood, the head, feet, and intestines. The non-edible products have a diverse set of uses. Examples include: poultry feathers (used in bedding and sporting goods); poultry leftover parts such as bones, beaks, and feet (ground into livestock pellets and fertilizer); and poultry fat (used in animal feed and pet food).

Poultry companies use individual product cost information for several purposes. One purpose is in customer profitability analysis. Customers (such as supermarkets and fast food restaurants) differ greatly in the mix of products purchased. Individual product cost data enable companies to determine differences in individual customer profitability. A subset of products is placed into frozen storage, which creates a demand for individual product cost information for inventory valuation.

Companies differ in how they cost individual products. Consider two of the largest U.S. companies—Southern Poultry and Golden State Poultry (disguised names).

Southern Poultry classifies white breast meat as the single main product in its costing system. All other products are classified as byproducts. Market selling prices of the many byproducts are used to reduce the chicken processing costs that are allocated to the main product. The white breast meat is often further processed into many individual products (such as trimmed chicken and marinated chicken). The separable cost of this further processing is added to the cost per pound of deboned white breast meat to obtain the cost of further processed products.

Golden State Poultry classifies any product sold to a retail outlet as a joint product. Such products include breast fillets, half breasts, drummettes, thighs, and whole legs. All other products are classified as byproducts. Revenue from byproducts is offset against the chicken processing cost before that cost is allocated amongst the joint products. The average selling prices of products sold to its retail outlets are used to allocate the net chicken processing cost among the individual joint products. The distribution costs of transporting the chicken products from the processing plants to retail outlets are not taken into account when determining the joint cost allocation weights.

Source: Adapted from conversations with executives of Southern Poultry and Golden State Poultry.

The tenuous assumption underlying the constant gross-margin percentage NRV method is that all the products have the same ratio of cost to sales value. A constant ratio of cost to sales value across products is rarely seen in companies that produce multiple products but have no joint costs.

Comparison of Methods

Which method of allocating joint costs should be chosen? Because the costs are joint in nature, managers cannot use the cause-and-effect criterion in making this choice. Managers cannot be sure what causes what cost when examining joint costs. The benefits-received criterion leads to a preference for the sales value at splitoff point method (or other related revenue or market-based methods). Additional benefits of this method include:

OBJECTIVE 5

Identify the criterion used to support market-based joint cost allocation methods

1. *No anticipation of subsequent management decisions.* The sales value at splitoff method does not presuppose an exact number of subsequent steps undertaken for further processing.

2. *Availability of a meaningful common denominator to compute the weighing factors.* The denominator of the sales value at splitoff method (dollars) is a meaningful one. In contrast, the physical measure method may lack a meaningful common denominator for all the separable products (for example, when some products are liquids and other products are solids).

3. *Simplicity.* The sales value at splitoff method is simple. In contrast, the estimated NRV method can be very complex in operations with multiple products and multiple splitoff points. The total sales value at splitoff is unaffected by any change in the production process after the splitoff point.

The purpose of the joint-cost allocation is important. Consider rate regulation. Market-based measures are difficult to use in this context. It is circular to use selling prices as a basis for setting prices (rates) and at the same time use selling prices to allocate the costs on which prices (rates) are based. Physical measures represent one joint-cost-allocation approach available in rate regulation.[4]

NO ALLOCATION OF JOINT COSTS

All of the preceding methods of allocating joint costs to individual products are subject to criticism. As a result, some companies refrain from joint-cost allocation entirely. Instead, they carry all inventories at estimated net realizable value. Income on each product is recognized when production is completed. Industries that use variations of this approach include meatpacking, canning, and mining.

Accountants ordinarily criticize carrying inventories at estimated net realizable values. Why? Because income is recognized *before* sales are made. Partly in response to this criticism, some companies using this no-allocation approach carry their inventories at estimated net realizable values minus a normal profit margin.

Exhibit 15-10 presents the product-line income statement with no allocation of joint costs for Example 2. The separable costs are assigned first, which highlights for

[4]An alternative is to use the stand-alone method described in Chapter 13 (pp. 489–490) and Chapter 16 (pp. 579–580). Consider rate regulation for gas that is jointly produced with oil. With the stand-alone method, an estimate would be made of A, the stand-alone cost of producing the designated gas output, and B, the stand-alone cost of producing the designated oil output. Then the total joint cost of production would be allocated using a $[A/(A + B)]$ weight for gas and a $[B/(A + B)]$ weight for oil.

EXHIBIT 15-10
Farmers' Dairy Product-Line Income Statement for May 19_7:
No Allocation of Joint Costs

	Butter Cream	Condensed Milk	Total
Produced and sold (butter cream, 12 gallons × $25; condensed milk, 45 gallons × $22)	$300	$ 990	$1,290
Produced but not sold (butter cream, 8 gallons × $25; condensed milk, 5 gallons × $22)	200	110	310
Total sales value of production	500	$1,100	1,600
Separable costs	280	520	800
Contribution to joint costs and operating income	$220	$ 580	800
Joint costs			400
Gross margin			$ 400
Gross-margin percentage			25%

Joint-Cost-Allocation Methods Used by U.K. Companies

Systematic survey evidence on company use of joint-cost-allocation methods is available for Australia, Japan, and the United Kingdom. The reported percentage use by companies exceeds 100% because some companies use more than one method.

	Australia	Japan	United Kingdom
Physical measure method	60%	45%	76%
Sales value method	6	28	5
Negotiated basis	10	10	19
Not allocated	8	0	10
Other	27	10	14

The most detailed study reports joint-cost-allocation methods used by chemical and oil-refining companies in the United Kingdom.

Type of Company	Predominant Joint-Cost-Allocation Method Used
Petrochemicals	Sales value at splitoff or estimated NRV
Coal processing	Physical measure
Coal chemicals	Physical measure
Oil refining	No allocation of joint cost

The authors of the survey noted that it was considered by the majority of oil refineries that the complex nature of the process involved and the vast number of joint product outputs made it impossible to establish any meaningful cost apportionment between products. In addition, market prices for many partly processed products at one or more of the splitoff points are typically not available.

Source: Adapted from Blayney and Yokoyama, "A Comparative Analysis," and Slater and Wooton, A Study. Full citation is in Appendix A.

managers the cause-and-effect relationship between individual products and the costs incurred on them. The joint costs are not allocated to butter cream and condensed milk as individual products.

IRRELEVANCE OF JOINT COSTS FOR DECISION MAKING

No technique for allocating joint-product costs should guide management decisions regarding whether a product should be sold at the splitoff point or processed beyond splitoff. When a product is an inevitable result of a joint process, the decision to further process should not be influenced either by the size of the total joint costs or by the portion of the joint costs allocated to particular products. Instead, managers should use the relevant-cost concepts introduced in Chapter 11.

Sell or Process Further

The decision to incur additional costs beyond splitoff should be based on the incremental operating income attainable beyond the splitoff point. Example 2 assumed that it was profitable for both cream and liquid skim to be further processed into

OBJECTIVE 6

Describe the irrelevance of joint costs in deciding to sell or further process

butter cream and condensed milk, respectively. The incremental analysis for these decisions to further process is as follows:

Further Processing Cream into Butter Cream

Incremental revenue ($500 − $200)	$300
Incremental processing costs	280
Incremental operating income	$ 20

Further Processing Liquid Skim into Condensed Milk

Incremental revenue ($1,100 − $300)	$800
Incremental processing costs	520
Incremental operating income	$280

The amount of joint costs incurred up to splitoff ($400)—and how it is allocated—is irrelevant in deciding whether to process further cream or liquid skim. Why? Because the joint costs of $400 are the same whether or not further processing is done.

Many manufacturing companies constantly face the decision of whether to further process a joint product. Meat products may be sold as cut or may be smoked, cured, frozen, canned, and so forth. Petroleum refiners are perpetually trying to adjust to the most profitable product mix. The refining process necessitates separating all products from crude oil, even though only two or three may have high revenue potential. The refiner must decide what combination of processes to use to get the most profitable mix of crude oil, gas, butane, ethane, propane, and the like.

In designing reports for managers' decisions of this nature, the accountant must concentrate on incremental costs rather than on how historical joint costs are to be allocated among various products. The only relevant items are incremental revenue and incremental costs. This next example illustrates the importance of the incremental cost viewpoint.

EXAMPLE 3: Fragrance, Inc., jointly processes a specialty chemical that yields two perfumes: 50 ounces of Mystique and 150 ounces of Passion. The sales values per ounce at splitoff are $6 for Mystique and $4 for Passion. The joint costs incurred up to the splitoff point are $880. The manager has the option of further processing 150 ounces of Passion to yield 100 ounces of Romance. The total additional costs of converting Passion into Romance would be $160, and the selling price per ounce of Romance would be $8. Exhibit 15-11 summarizes the relationships in this example.

The correct approach in deciding whether to further process Passion into Romance is to compare the incremental revenue with the incremental costs, if all other

EXHIBIT 15-11
Fragrance, Inc.: Example 3 Overview

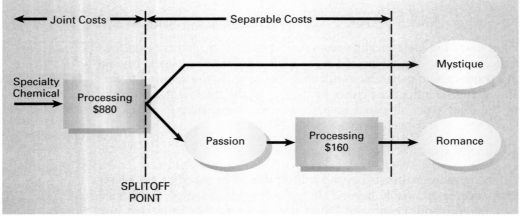

556

factors such as invested capital and the time period are held constant:

Incremental revenue of Romance (100 × $8) – (150 × $4)	$200
Incremental costs of Romance, further processing	160
Incremental operating income from converting Passion into Romance	$ 40

The following is a total income computation of each alternative:[5]

	Alternative 1: Sell Mystique and Passion		Alternative 2: Sell Mystique and Romance		Difference
Total revenues	($300 + $600)	$900	($300 + $800)	$1,100	$200
Total processing costs		880	($880 + $160)	1,040	160
Operating income		$ 20		$ 60	$ 40

As we can see from our example, it is profitable to extend processing and to incur additional costs on a joint product as long as the incremental revenue exceeds incremental costs.

Conventional methods of joint-cost allocation may mislead managers who rely on unit-cost data to guide their sell-or-further-process decisions. For example, the physical measure method (ounces in our example) would allocate the $880 joint costs as follows:

Product	Ounces Produced	Weighting	Allocation of Joint Costs
Mystique	50	50 ÷ 200 = 0.25	0.25 × $880 = $220
Passion	150	150 ÷ 200 = 0.75	0.75 × $880 = 660
	200		$880

The resulting product-line income statement for the alternative of selling Mystique and Romance would erroneously imply that the company would suffer a loss by selling Romance:

	Mystique	Romance
Revenues	$300	$800
Costs		
Joint costs allocated	220	660
Separable costs	—	160
Cost of goods sold	220	820
Operating income	$ 80	$ (20)

ACCOUNTING FOR BYPRODUCTS

Processes that yield joint products often also yield what are frequently referred to as byproducts—products that have relatively low sales value compared with the sales value of the main or joint product(s). We now discuss accounting for byproducts. To simplify the discussion, consider a two-product example consisting of a main product and a byproduct. (In many cases, there are several joint products and several byproducts as well as scrap. The accounting alternatives for scrap are discussed in Chapter 18.[6])

OBJECTIVE 7

Distinguish alternative methods of accounting for byproducts

[5]The revenues reported for each product are Mystique (50 ounces at $6 per ounce = $300), Passion (150 ounces at $4 per ounce = $600), and Romance (100 ounces at $8 per ounce = $800).

[6]Further discussion on byproduct accounting methods is in C. Cheatham and M. Green, "Teaching Accounting for Byproducts," *Management Accounting News & Views* (Spring 1988), pp. 14–15; and D. Stout and D. Wygal, "Making By-Products a Main Product of Discussion: A Challenge to Accounting Educators," *Journal of Accounting Education* (1989), pp. 219–233.

EXAMPLE 4: The Meatworks Group processes meat from slaughterhouses. One of its departments cuts lamb shoulders and generates two products:

◆ Shoulder meat (the main product)—sold for $60 per pack
◆ Hock meat (the byproduct)—sold for $4 per pack

Both products are sold at the splitoff point without further processing, as Exhibit 15-12 shows. Data (number of packs) for this department in July 19_7 are as follows:

	Production	Sales	Beginning Inventory	Ending Inventory
Shoulder meat	500	400	0	100
Hock meat	100	30	0	70

Total manufacturing costs of these products were $25,000.

Accounting methods for byproducts address two major questions:

◆ *When are byproducts first recognized in the general ledger?* The two basic choices are (1) at the time of production, or (2) at the time of sale.
◆ *Where do byproduct revenues appear in the income statement?* The two basic choices are (1) as a cost reduction of the main or joint product(s), or (2) as a separate item of revenue or other income.

Combining these two questions and choices gives four possible ways of accounting for byproducts:

Byproduct Accounting Method	When Byproducts Are Recognized in General Ledger	Where Byproduct Revenues Appear in Income Statement	Where Byproduct Inventories Appear on Balance Sheet
A	Production	Reduction of cost	Byproduct inventory reported at (unrealized) selling prices
B	Production	Revenue or other income item	
C	Sale	Reduction of cost	Byproduct inventory not recognized
D	Sale	Revenue or other income item	

Exhibit 15-13 presents the income statement figures and inventory figures that the Meatworks Group would report under each method. Methods A and B recognize the byproduct inventory at the time of production. Note, however, that byproduct inventories are reported on the balance sheet at selling prices rather than at a cost amount. (One variation of methods A and B is to report byproduct inventories at

EXHIBIT 15-12
Meatworks Group: Example 4 Overview

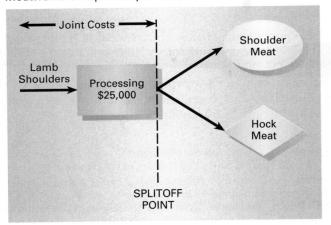

EXHIBIT 15-13
Meatworks Group: Income Statement for July 19_7

	Byproduct Accounting Method			
	A	**B**	**C**	**D**
When byproducts recognized in general ledger	At production	At production	At sale	At sale
Where byproduct revenues appear in income statement	Reduction of cost	Revenue item	Reduction of cost	Revenue item
Revenues				
Main product: shoulder meat (400 × $60)	$24,000	$24,000	$24,000	$24,000
Byproduct: hock meat (30 × $4)	—	120	—	120
Total revenue	24,000	24,120	24,000	24,120
Cost of goods sold				
Total manufacturing costs	25,000	25,000	25,000	25,000
Deduct byproduct net revenue (30 × $4)	120	—	120	—
Net manufacturing costs	24,880	25,000	24,880	25,000
Deduct main product inventory*	4,976	5,000	4,976	5,000
Deduct byproduct inventory (70 × $4)	280	280	—	—
Total cost of goods sold	19,624	19,720	19,904	20,000
Gross margin	$ 4,376	$ 4,400	$ 4,096	$ 4,120
Gross-margin percentage	18.23%	18.24%	17.07%	17.08%
Inventoriable costs (end of period)				
Main product: shoulder meat	$ 4,976	$ 5,000	$ 4,976	$ 5,000
Byproduct: hock meat[†]	280	280	0	0

*(100 ÷ 500) × net manufacturing costs.
[†]Shown at selling prices.

selling price minus a "normal profit margin." This variation avoids including unrealized gains as an offset to cost of goods sold in the period of production.[7])

Methods C and D are rationalized in practice primarily on grounds of the relative insignificance of byproducts. Byproducts are sometimes viewed as incidental. Methods C and D permit managers to "manage" reported earnings by timing when they sell byproducts. Managers may stockpile byproducts so that they have flexibility to give revenue a "boost" when most propitious for them.

Meatworks uses method B in its accounting system. This method highlights how each salable product contributes to its total revenues. Over time, the revenues contributed by individual products can vary. Method B enables managers to track these changing contributions easily.

Alternative Approach

The accounting methods outlined in Exhibit 15-13 are based on one or more products being classified as byproducts, while the others are classified as joint products. An alternative approach is to consistently use the same joint-cost-allocation method for *all* products. Suppose the estimated NRV method is used. It is straightforward to compute the estimated NRV for every product. Those with low estimated NRVs would be given low weights (be it 15%, 5%, or 0.5%). This approach would make the distinction between joint products and byproducts unnecessary. This alternative approach would make the costing of all joint and byproducts consistent. Moreover, consistent use of a market-based method would mean the resultant allocations reflect the benefits-received criterion.

[7]One version of method A deducts the estimated NRV of the byproduct(s) from the joint costs before the remainder is allocated to individual joint products. Another version of method A deducts the estimated NRV of the byproduct(s) from the total production costs (joint costs plus separable costs).

PROBLEM

Inorganic Chemicals purchases salt and processes it into more-refined products such as caustic soda, chlorine, and PVC (polyvinyl chloride). In the most recent month (July), Inorganic Chemicals purchased salt for $40,000. Conversion costs of $60,000 were incurred up to the splitoff point, at which time two salable products were produced: caustic soda and chlorine. Chlorine can be further processed into PVC. The July production and sales information are as follows:

	Production	Sales	Sales Price per Ton
Caustic soda	1,200 tons	1,200 tons	$ 50
Chlorine	800 tons		
PVC	500 tons	500 tons	$200

All 800 tons of chlorine were further processed, at an incremental cost of $20,000, to yield 500 tons of PVC. There were no byproducts or scrap from this further processing of chlorine. There were no beginning or ending inventories of caustic soda, chlorine, or PVC in July.

There is an active market for chlorine. Inorganic Chemicals could have sold all its July production of chlorine at $75 a ton.

REQUIRED

1. Calculate how the joint costs of $100,000 would be allocated between caustic soda and chlorine under each of the following methods: (a) sales value at splitoff, (b) physical measure (tons), and (c) estimated net realizable value.
2. What is the gross-margin percentage of (a) caustic soda and (b) PVC under the three methods cited in requirement 1?
3. Lifetime Swimming Pool Products offers to purchase 800 tons of chlorine in August at $75 a ton. This sale would mean that no PVC would be produced in August. How would accepting this offer affect August operating income?

SOLUTION

1. a. Sales value at splitoff method

	Caustic Soda	Chlorine	Total
1. Sales value at splitoff (caustic, 1,200 × $50; chlorine, 800 × $75)	$60,000	$60,000	$120,000
2. Weighting ($60,000 ÷ $120,000; $60,000 ÷ $120,000)	0.5	0.5	
3. Joint costs allocated (caustic, 0.5 × $100,000; chlorine, 0.5 × $100,000)	$50,000	$50,000	$100,000

   b. Physical measure method

	Caustic Soda	Chlorine	Total
1. Physical measure (tons)	1,200	800	2,000
2. Weighting (1,200 ÷ 2,000; 800 ÷ 2,000)	0.6	0.4	
3. Joint costs allocated (caustic, 0.6 × $100,000; chlorine, 0.4 × $100,000)	$60,000	$40,000	$100,000

c. Estimated NRV method

	Caustic Soda	Chlorine	Total
1. Expected final sales value of production (caustic, 1,200 × $50; PVC from chlorine, 500 × $200)	$60,000	$100,000	$160,000
2. Expected separable costs		20,000	20,000
3. Estimated NRV at splitoff point	$60,000	$ 80,000	$140,000
4. Weighting ($60,000 ÷ $140,000; $80,000 ÷ $140,000)	$\frac{3}{7}$	$\frac{4}{7}$	
5. Joint costs allocated (caustic, $\frac{3}{7}$ × $100,000; chlorine, $\frac{4}{7}$ × $100,000)	$42,857	$ 57,143	$100,000

2. a. Caustic soda

	Sales Value at Splitoff Point	Physical Measure	Estimated Net Realizable Value
Sales	$60,000	$60,000	$60,000
Joint costs	50,000	60,000	42,857
Gross margin	$10,000	$ 0	$17,143
Gross-margin percentage	16.67%	0%	28.57%

b. PVC

	Sales Value at Splitoff Point	Physical Measure	Estimated Net Realizable Value
Sales	$100,000	$100,000	$100,000
Joint costs	50,000	40,000	57,143
Separable costs	20,000	20,000	20,000
Gross margin	$ 30,000	$ 40,000	$ 22,857
Gross-margin percentage	30.00%	40.00%	22.86%

3. Incremental revenue from further processing of chlorine into PVC:

(500 × $200) − (800 × $75)	$40,000
Incremental costs of further processing chlorine into PVC	20,000
Incremental operating income from further processing	$20,000

The operating income of Inorganic Chemicals would be reduced by $20,000 if it sold 800 tons of chlorine to Lifetime Swimming Pool Products instead of further processing the chlorine into PVC for sale.

SUMMARY

The following points are linked to the chapter's learning objectives.

1. A joint cost is the cost of a single process that yields multiple products. The *splitoff point* is the juncture in the process when the products become separately identifiable.

2. Joint products have relatively high sales value and are not separately identifiable as individual products until the splitoff point. A byproduct has a low sales value compared with the sales value of a joint product. Individual products can change from being a byproduct or a joint product when their market prices move sizably in one direction.

3. The purposes for allocating joint costs to products include inventory costing for external financial reporting, internal financial reporting, cost reimbursement under contracts, customer profitability analysis, insurance settlements, and rate regulation.

4. The accounting methods available for allocating joint costs include using market selling price (either sales value at splitoff or estimated net realizable value) or using a physical measure. Choosing not to allocate is also an option.

5. The benefits-received criterion leads to a preference for revenue or market-based methods such as the sales value at splitoff point method. Additional pros of this method include not anticipating subsequent management decisions on further processing, using a meaningful common denominator, and being simple.

6. The incremental-cost analysis emphasized elsewhere in this book applies equally to joint-cost situations. No techniques for allocating joint-product costs should guide decisions about whether a product should be sold at the splitoff point or processed beyond splitoff because joint costs are irrelevant.

7. Byproduct accounting is an area where there is much inconsistency in practice and where some methods used are justified on the basis of expediency rather than theoretical soundness. Byproducts can be recognized at production or at the point of sale. Byproduct revenues can appear as a separate revenue item or an offset to other costs.

TERMS TO LEARN

This chapter and the Glossary at the end of this book contain definitions of the following important terms:

byproduct (p. 544)
constant gross-margin percentage
  NRV method (551)
estimated net realizable value (NRV)
  method (550)
joint cost (544)
joint products (544)

main product (544)
physical measure method (548)
product (544)
sales value at splitoff method (547)
scrap (544)
separable costs (544)
splitoff point (544)

ASSIGNMENT MATERIAL

QUESTIONS

15-1 What is a joint cost?

15-2 Define separable costs.

15-3 Give two examples of industries in which joint costs are found. For each example, what are the individual products at or beyond the splitoff point?

15-4 Distinguish between a joint product and a byproduct.

15-5 Why might the number of products in a joint-cost setting differ from the number of outputs? Give an example.

15-6 Provide three reasons for allocating joint costs to individual products or services.

15-7 Name two methods of allocating joint costs to joint products.

15-8 Why does the sales value at splitoff method use the sales value of the total production in the accounting period and not just the sales value of the products sold?

15-9 Distinguish between the sales value at splitoff method and the estimated NRV method.

15-10 Give two limitations of the physical measure method of joint-cost allocation.

15-11 Which joint-cost-allocation method is supported by the cause-and-effect criterion for choosing among allocation methods?

15-12 "Managers must decide whether a product should be sold at splitoff or processed further. The sales value at splitoff method of joint-cost allocation is the best method for generating the information managers need." Do you agree? Why?

15-13 "Managers should consider only additional revenues and separable costs when making decisions about selling now or processing further." Do you agree? Why?

15-14 Describe two major questions addressed by methods to account for byproducts.

15-15 Describe an accounting method that would eliminate some key inconsistencies that often arise in byproduct reporting.

EXERCISES

15-16 Matching terms with definitions.

Terms
a. Splitoff point
b. Joint cost
c. Separable cost
d. Byproduct
e. Joint product
f. Product

Definition
1. Product with low sales value compared with the sales value of the main or joint product(s).
2. Any output that has a positive sales value.
3. Junction in the process when one or more products in a joint-cost setting become separately identifiable.
4. Costs of a single process that yields multiple products simultaneously.
5. Costs incurred beyond the splitoff point that are assignable to one or more individual products.
6. Product that is one of two or more products with relatively high sales value but not separately identifiable until the splitoff point.

REQUIRED
Match the terms with their appropriate definition.

15-17 Joint-cost allocation, insurance settlement. Chicken Little grows and processes chickens. Each chicken is disassembled into five main parts. Information pertaining to production in July 19_8 is as follows:

Parts	Pounds of Product	Wholesale Selling Price per Pound at End of Production Line
Breasts	100	$1.10
Wings	20	0.40
Thighs	40	0.70
Bones	80	0.20
Feathers	10	0.10

Joint costs of production in July 19_8 were $100.

A special shipment of 20 pounds of breasts and 10 pounds of wings has been destroyed in a fire. Chicken Little's insurance policy provides for reimbursement for the cost of the items destroyed. The insurance company permits Chicken Little to use a joint-cost-allocation method. The splitoff point is assumed to be at the end of the production line.

REQUIRED

1. Compute the cost of the special shipment destroyed using (a) the sales value at splitoff point method, and (b) the physical measure method using pounds of finished product?
2. Which joint-cost-allocation method would you recommend that Chicken Little use?

15-18 Estimated net realizable value method. Illawara, Inc., produces two joint products, cooking oil and soap oil, from a single vegetable oil refining process. In July 19_7, the joint costs of this process were $24,000,000. Separable processing costs beyond the splitoff point were cooking oil, $30,000,000; and soap oil, $7,500,000. Cooking oil sells for $50 per drum. Soap oil sells for $25 per drum. Illawara produced and sold 1,000,000 drums of cooking oil and 500,000 drums of soap oil. There are no beginning or ending inventories of cooking oil or soap oil.

REQUIRED

Allocate the $24,000,000 joint costs using the estimated NRV method.

15-19 Joint-cost allocation, process further. The Sinclair Refining Company (SRC) is a 100% owned subsidiary of Sinclair Oil & Gas. SRC operates a refinery that processes hydrocarbons sold to it by the Sinclair Production Company, another 100% owned subsidiary of Sinclair Oil & Gas. SRC's refinery has three outputs from its processing of hydrocarbons—crude oil, natural gas liquids, and gas. The first two outputs are liquids, while gas is a vapor. However, gas can be expressed as a liquid equivalent using a standard industry conversion factor. For costing purposes, SRC assumes all three outputs are jointly produced until a single splitoff point where each output separately appears and is then further processed individually.

For August, 19_6, the following data (in millions) apply:

◆ Crude oil—150 barrels produced and sold at $18 per barrel. Separable costs beyond the splitoff point are $175.
◆ Natural gas liquids—50 barrels produced and sold at $15 per barrel. Separable costs beyond the splitoff point are $105.
◆ Gas—800 equivalent barrels produced and sold at $1.30 per equivalent barrel. Separable costs beyond the splitoff point are $210.

SRC paid the Sinclair Production Company $1,400 for hydrocarbons delivered to it from its offshore platform in August 19_6. The costs of operating the refinery in August up to the splitoff point was $400, including $100 of gas charges from Deadhorse Utilities, an independent utility company. Deadhorse signed a long-term contract with SRC several years ago when gas prices were much lower than in 19_6.

A new federal law has recently been passed that taxes crude oil at 30% of operating income. No new tax is to be paid on natural gas liquid or natural gas. Starting in August 19_6, SRC must report a separate product-line income statement for crude oil. One challenge facing SRC is how to allocate the joint cost of producing the three separate salable outputs. Assume no beginning or ending inventory.

REQUIRED

1. Draw an exhibit showing the joint-cost situation for SRC.
2. Allocate the August 19_6 joint cost among the three salable products using (a) the physical measures method, and (b) the estimated NRV method. Compute the operating income for each product using each of these methods.
3. Discuss the pros and cons of each method for Sinclair product emphasis decisions.

15-20 Joint-cost allocation, physical measures method (continuation of 15-19). Assume that SRC is not able to sell its gas output. The refinery is located in a remote area and a terrorist group has just destroyed major sections of the gas pipeline used to transport the gas to market. The pipeline that carries the crude oil and natural gas liquid is still operational. The Sinclair Production Company must now reinject the gas into the offshore field. The costs of the hydrocarbons to SRC will not be reduced, but Sinclair Production (not SRC) will bear the cost of gas reinjection. No separable costs of gas production beyond the splitoff point will now be incurred.

REQUIRED

1. Assume that the same data for all three outputs for August 19_6 apply to the new set of facts. Show the operating income for each salable product using the estimated NRV method of joint-cost allocation.
2. Assume the taxation authorities argue that, for crude oil income tax determination, the physical measures method should be used to allocate joint costs and that all outputs (including gas, whether sold or reinjected) should be used in deciding the cost allocation weights. Do you agree with this argument? Explain your position.

15-21 Alternative methods of joint-cost allocation, ending inventories. The Darl Company operates a simple chemical process to reduce a single material into three separate items, here referred to as X, Y, and Z. All three end products are separated simultaneously at a single splitoff point.

Products X and Y are ready for sale immediately upon splitoff without further processing or any other additional costs. Product Z, however, is processed further before being sold. There is no available market price for Z at the splitoff point.

The selling prices quoted below have not changed for 3 years, and no changes are foreseen for the coming year. During 19_5, the selling prices of the items and the total amounts sold were as follows:

◆ X—120 tons sold for $1,500 per ton
◆ Y—340 tons sold for $1,000 per ton
◆ Z—475 tons sold for $700 per ton

The total joint manufacturing costs for the year were $400,000. An additional $200,000 was spent in order to finish product Z.

There were no beginning inventories of X, Y, or Z. At the end of the year, the following inventories of completed units were on hand: X, 180 tons; Y, 60 tons; Z, 25 tons. There was no beginning or ending work in process.

REQUIRED

1. What will be the cost of inventories of X, Y, and Z for balance sheet purposes and what will be the cost of goods sold for income statement purposes as of December 31, 19_5, using (a) the estimated NRV method of joint-cost allocation, and (b) the constant gross-margin percentage NRV method of joint-cost allocation?
2. Compare the gross-margin percentages for X, Y, and Z using the two methods given in requirement 1.

15-22 Net realizable value cost-allocation method, further process decision. (W. Crum) The Tuscania Company crushes and refines mineral ore into three products in a joint-cost operation. Costs and production for 19_4 were as follows:

◆ *Department 1*, at initial joint costs of $420,000, produces 20,000 pounds of Alco, 60,000 pounds of Devo, 100,000 pounds of Holo.
◆ *Department 2* processes Alco further at a cost of $100,000.
◆ *Department 3* processes Devo further at a cost of $200,000.

Results for 19_4 are

◆ *Alco:* 20,000 pounds completed; 19,000 pounds sold for $20 per pound; ending inventory, 1,000 pounds.
◆ *Devo:* 60,000 pounds completed; 59,000 pounds sold for $6 per pound; ending inventory, 1,000 pounds.
◆ *Holo:* 100,000 pounds completed; 99,000 pounds sold for $1 per pound; ending inventory, 1,000 pounds; Holo required no further processing.

REQUIRED

1. Use the estimated NRV method to allocate the joint costs of the three products. Compute the total costs and unit costs of ending inventories.
2. Compute the individual gross-margin percentages of the three products.
3. Suppose Tuscania receives an offer to sell all of its Devo product for a price of $2 per pound at the splitoff point before going through Department 3, just as it comes off the production line in Department 1. Using last year's figures, would Tuscania be better off by selling Devo that way or processing it through Department 3 and selling it? Show computations to support your answer. Disregard all other factors not mentioned in the problem.

15-23 Accounting for a main product and a byproduct. (Cheatham and Green, adapted) Bill Dundee is the owner and operator of Louisiana Bottling, a bulk soft-drink producer. A single production process yields two bulk soft drinks, Rainbow Dew (the main product) and Resi-Dew (the byproduct). Both products are fully processed at the splitoff point, and there are no separable costs.

Summary data for September 19_5 are as follows:

◆ Cost of soft-drink operations = $120,000
◆ Production and sales data

	Production (in gallons)	Sales (in gallons)	Selling Price per Gallon	
Main product (Rainbow Dew)	10,000	8,000	$20.00	2,000
Byproduct (Resi-Dew)	2,000	1,400	2.00	600

There were no beginning inventories on September 1, 19_5. The following is an overview of operations:

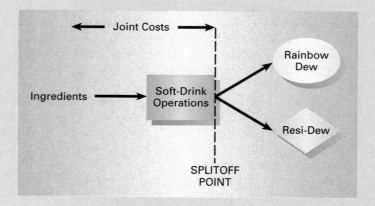

1. What is the gross margin for Louisiana Bottling under methods A, B, C, and D of byproduct accounting described on p. 559 of this chapter?
2. What are the inventory amounts reported in the balance sheet on September 30, 19_5, for Rainbow Dew and Resi-Dew under each of the four methods of byproduct accounting cited in requirement 1?
3. Which method would you recommend Louisiana Bottling use? Explain.

15-24 Joint costs and byproducts. (W. Crum) The Caldwell Company processes an ore in Department 1, out of which come three products, L, W, and X. Product L is processed further through Department 2. Product W is sold without further processing. Product X is considered a byproduct and is processed further through Department 3. Costs in Department 1 are $800,000 in total; Department 2 costs are $100,000; and Department 3 costs are $50,000. Processing 600,000 pounds in Department 1 results in 50,000 pounds of product L, 300,000 pounds of product W, and 100,000 pounds of product X.

   Product L sells for $10 per pound. Product W sells for $2 per pound. Product X sells for $3 per pound. The company wants to make a gross margin of 10% of sales on product X and also allow 25% for marketing costs on product X.

REQUIRED

1. Compute unit costs per pound for products L, W, and X, treating X as a byproduct. Use the estimated NRV method for allocating joint costs. Deduct the estimated NRV of the byproduct produced from the joint cost of products L and W.
2. Compute unit costs per pound for products L, W, and X, treating all three as joint products and allocating costs by the estimated NRV method.

PROBLEMS

15-25 Alternative joint-cost-allocation methods, further process decision. The Wood Spirits Company produces two products, turpentine and methanol (wood alcohol), by a joint process. Joint costs amount to $120,000 per batch of output. Each batch totals 10,000 gallons: 25% methanol and 75% turpentine. Both products are processed further without gain or loss in volume. Separable processing costs include: methanol, $3 per gallon; and turpentine, $2 per gallon. Methanol sells for $21 per gallon; turpentine sells for $14 per gallon.

REQUIRED

1. What joint costs per batch should be allocated to the turpentine and methanol, assuming that joint costs are allocated on a physical measure (number of gallons at splitoff point) basis?
2. If joint costs are to be assigned on an estimated NRV basis, what amounts of joint cost should be assigned to the turpentine and to the methanol?
3. Prepare product-line income statements per batch for requirements 1 and 2. Assume no beginning or ending inventories.
4. The company has discovered an additional process by which the methanol (wood alcohol) can be made into a pleasant tasting alcoholic beverage. The new selling price would be $60 a gallon. Additional processing would increase separable costs $9 (in addition to the $3 separable cost required to yield methanol). The company would have to pay excise taxes of 20% on the new selling price. Assuming no other changes in cost, what is the joint cost applicable to the wood alcohol (using the estimated NRV method)? Should the company use the new process?

15-26 Alternative methods of joint-cost allocation, product-mix decisions.

The Sunshine Oil Company buys crude vegetable oil. Refining this oil results in four products at the splitoff point: A, B, C, and D. Product C is fully processed at the splitoff point. Products A, B, and D can be individually further refined into Super A, Super B, and Super D. In the most recent month (December), the output at the splitoff point was

Product A	300,000 gallons
Product B	100,000 gallons
Product C	50,000 gallons
Product D	50,000 gallons

The joint costs of purchasing the crude vegetable oil and processing it were $100,000.

Sunshine had no beginning or ending inventories. Sales of product C in December were $50,000. Total output of products A, B, and D was further refined and then sold. Data related to December are as follows:

	Separable Processing Costs to Make Super Products	Sales
Super A	$200,000	$300,000
Super B	80,000	100,000
Super D	90,000	120,000

Sunshine had the option of selling products A, B, and D at the splitoff point. This alternative would have yielded the following sales for the December production:

Product A	$50,000
Product B	30,000
Product D	70,000

REQUIRED

1. What is the gross-margin percentage for each product sold in December, using the following methods for allocating the $100,000 joint costs: (a) sales value at splitoff, (b) physical measure, and (c) estimated NRV?
2. Could Sunshine have increased its December operating income by making different decisions about the further refining of products A, B, or D? Show the effect on operating income of any changes you recommend.

15-27 Comparison of alternative joint-cost allocation methods, further process decision, chocolate products.

Roundtree Chocolates manufactures and distributes chocolate products. It purchases cocoa beans and processes them into two intermediate products:

◆ Chocolate-powder liquor base
◆ Milk-chocolate liquor base

These two intermediary products become separately identifiable at a single splitoff point. Every 500 pounds of cocoa beans yields 20 gallons of chocolate-powder liquor base and 30 gallons of milk-chocolate liquor base.

The chocolate-powder liquor base is further processed into chocolate powder. Every 20 gallons of chocolate-powder liquor base yields 200 pounds of chocolate powder. The milk-chocolate liquor base is further processed into milk chocolate. Every 30 gallons of milk-chocolate liquor base yields 340 pounds of milk chocolate.

The following is an overview of the manufacturing operations at Roundtree Chocolates:

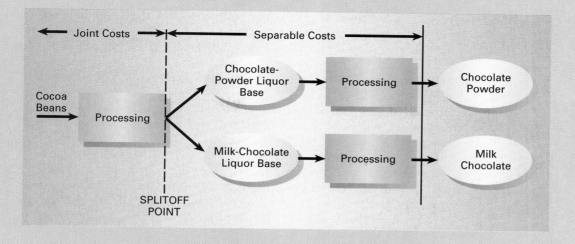

Production and sales data for August 19_7 are as follows:

◆ Cocoa beans processed, 5,000 pounds
◆ Costs of processing cocoa beans to splitoff point (including purchase of beans) = $10,000

	Production	Sales	Unit Selling Price
Chocolate powder	2,000 pounds	2,000 pounds	$4 per pound
Milk chocolate	3,400 pounds	3,400 pounds	$5 per pound

The August 19_7 separable costs of processing chocolate-powder liquor base into chocolate powder are $4,250. The August 19_7 separable costs of processing milk-chocolate liquor base into milk chocolate are $8,750.

Roundtree fully processes both of its intermediate products into chocolate powder or milk chocolate. There is an active market for these intermediate products. In August 19_7, Roundtree could have sold chocolate-powder liquor base for $21 a gallon and milk-chocolate liquor base for $26 a gallon.

REQUIRED

1. Calculate how the joint costs of $10,000 would be allocated between chocolate-powder liquor base and milk-chocolate liquor base under each of the following methods: (a) sales value at splitoff, (b) physical measure (gallons), (c) estimated NRV, and (d) constant gross-margin percentage NRV.
2. What is the gross-margin percentage of chocolate-powder liquor base and milk-chocolate liquor base under methods a, b, c, and d in requirement 1?
3. Could Roundtree Chocolates have increased its operating income by a change in its decision to fully process both of its intermediate products?

15-28 Alternative methods of joint-cost allocation, further process decision, memory chips. AMC is a semiconductor firm that specializes in memory chips. In the first stage of the manufacturing operation, raw silicon wafers are photolithographed and then baked at high temperatures. This process yields three individual products at a common splitoff point. For each batch of 1,600 raw silicon wafers, these products are

a. 300 high-density (HD) memory chips
b. 900 low-density (LD) memory chips
c. 400 defective memory chips

The density of a memory chip is based on the number of good memory bits on each chip, with HD chips having more memory bits per chip than LD chips. The 400 defective memory chips from each batch have a zero disposal price. The joint costs of purchasing and processing the 1,600 raw silicon wafers up to the splitoff point are $5,000.

AMC has two options for each grade of good memory chip at the splitoff point:

◆ Sell immediately. The selling price for each HD chip is $10. The selling price for each LD chip is $5.
◆ Process further into extended-life memory chips. This processing step further exposes the chips to extreme temperatures, and the chips that survive are sold as extended-life memory chips. Data pertaining to this further processing stage are as follows.

Extended-life high-density (EL-HD) chips. From a batch of 300 HD chips, the yield is 200 EL-HD chips. The 100 defective chips from this further processing step have a zero disposal price. The separable costs to further process the 300 HD chips are $1,000. The selling price for each EL-HD chip is $30.

Extended-life low-density (EL-LD) chips. From a batch of 900 LD chips, the yield is 500 EL-LD chips. The 400 defective chips from this further processing step have a zero disposal price. The separable cost to further process the 900 LD chips is $3,000. The selling price for each EL-LD chip is $18.

AMC has consistently followed the policy of further processing the entire output of both the HD and LD chips into their EL-HD and EL-LD forms. Separable costs are equal to incremental costs.

REQUIRED

1. Compute how the joint costs of $5,000 would be allocated between HD and LD chips under each of the following methods: (a) sales value at splitoff, (b) physical measure (number of good chips at splitoff point), (c) estimated NRV, and (d) constant gross-margin percentage NRV. Assume that AMC has no beginning or ending inventories.
2. What is the gross-margin percentage of EL-HD and EL-LD chips under methods a, b, c, and d in requirement 1?
3. Peach Computer Systems offers to buy 900 LD memory chips from AMC at $5 a chip. What would be the effect on operating income of accepting this offer rather than pursuing the current policy of further processing the LD chips into EL-LD form?

15-29 Joint and byproducts, estimated net realizable value method. (CPA) The Harrison Corporation produces three products—Alpha, Beta, and Gamma. Alpha and Gamma are joint products, and Beta is a byproduct of Alpha. No joint costs are to be allocated to the byproduct. The production processes for a given year are as follows:

a. In Department 1, 110,000 pounds of direct material, Rho, are processed at a total cost of $120,000. After processing in Department 1, 60% of the units are transferred to Department 2, and 40% of the units (now Gamma) are transferred to Department 3.
b. In Department 2, the material is further processed at a total additional cost of $38,000. Seventy percent of the units (now Alpha) are transferred to Department 4, and 30% emerge as Beta, the byproduct, to be sold at $1.20 per pound. Separable marketing costs for Beta are $8,100.
c. In Department 4, Alpha is processed at a total additional cost of $23,660. After this processing, Alpha is ready for sale at $5 per pound.
d. In Department 3, Gamma is processed at a total additional cost of $165,000. In this department, a normal loss of units of Gamma occurs, which equals 10% of the good output of Gamma. The remaining good output of Gamma is then sold for $12 per pound.

REQUIRED

1. Prepare a schedule showing the allocation of the $120,000 joint costs between Alpha and Gamma using the estimated NRV method. The esti-

mated NRV of Beta should be treated as an addition to the sales value of Alpha.

2. Independent of your answer to requirement 1, assume that $102,000 of total joint costs were appropriately allocated to Alpha. Assume also that there were 48,000 pounds of Alpha and 20,000 pounds of Beta available to sell. Prepare an income statement through gross margin for Alpha using the following facts:

   a. During the year, sales of Alpha were 80% of the pounds available for sale. There was no beginning inventory.

   b. The estimated NRV of Beta available for sale is to be deducted from the cost of producing Alpha. The ending inventory of Alpha is to be based on the net costs of production.

   c. All other cost and selling price data are listed in a–d.

15-30 Estimated net realizable value method, byproducts. (CMA, adapted) The Princess Corporation grows, processes, packages, and sells three joint apple products: (a) sliced apples that are used in frozen pies, (b) applesauce, and (c) apple juice. The outside skin of the apple, processed as animal feed, is treated as a byproduct. Princess uses the estimated NRV method to allocate costs of the joint process to its joint products. The byproduct is inventoried at its selling price when produced; the net realizable value of the byproduct is used to reduce the joint production costs before the splitoff point. Details of Princess production process are presented here:

◆ The apples are washed and the outside skin is removed in the Cutting Department. The apples are then cored and trimmed for slicing. The three joint products and the byproduct are recognizable after processing in the Cutting Department. Each product is then transferred to a separate department for final processing.

◆ The trimmed apples are forwarded to the Slicing Department, where they are sliced and frozen. Any juice generated during the slicing operation is frozen with the slices.

◆ The pieces of apple trimmed from the fruit are processed into applesauce in the Crushing Department. The juice generated during this operation is used in the applesauce.

◆ The core and any surplus apple pieces generated from the Cutting Department are pulverized into a liquid in the Juicing Department. There is a loss equal to 8% of the weight of the good output produced in this department.

◆ The outside skin is chopped into animal feed and packaged in the Feed Department. It can be kept in cold storage until needed.

A total of 270,000 pounds of apples were entered into the Cutting Department during November. The following schedule shows the costs incurred in each department, the proportion by weight transferred to the four final processing departments, and the selling price of each end product.

Processing Data and Costs
November 19_7

Department	Costs Incurred	Proportion of Product by Weight Transferred to Departments	Selling Price per Pound of Final Product
Cutting	$60,000		
Slicing	11,280	33%	$0.80
Crushing	8,550	30	0.55
Juicing	3,000	27	0.40
Feed	700	10	0.10
Total	$83,530	100%	

1. The Princess Corporation uses the estimated NRV method to determine inventory cost of its joint products; byproducts are reported on the balance sheet at their selling price when produced. For the month of November 19_7, calculate the following:

    a. The output for apple slices, applesauce, apple juice, and animal feed, in pounds.
    b. The estimated NRV at the splitoff point for each of the three joint products.
    c. The amount of the cost of the Cutting Department assigned to each of the three joint products and the amount assigned to the byproduct in accordance with corporate policy.
    d. The gross margins in dollars for each of the three joint products.

2. Comment on the significance to management of the gross-margin dollar information by joint product for planning and control purposes, as opposed to inventory costing purposes.

15-31 Joint product/byproduct distinctions, ethics (continuation of 15-30). The Princess Corporation classifies animal feed as a byproduct. The byproduct is inventoried at its selling price when produced; the net realizable value of the product is used to reduce the joint production costs before the splitoff point. Prior to 19_7, Princess classified both apple juice and animal feed as byproducts. These byproducts were not recognized in the accounting system until sold. Revenues from their sale were treated as a revenue item at the time of sale.

The Princess Corporation uses a "management by objectives" basis to compensate its managers. Every 6 months, managers are given "stretch" operating-income-to-revenue ratio targets. They receive no bonus if the target is not met and a fixed amount if the target is met or exceeded.

1. Assume that Princess managers aim to maximize their bonuses over time. What byproduct method (the pre-19_7 method or the 19_7 method) would the manager prefer?
2. How might a controller gain insight into whether the manager of the Apple Products division is "abusing" the accounting system in an effort to maximize his bonus?
3. Describe an accounting system for the Princess Corporation that would reduce "gaming" behavior by managers with respect to accounting rules for byproducts.

COLLABORATIVE LEARNING PROBLEM

15-32 Joint-cost allocation, process further or sell byproducts. (CMA) The Goodson Pharmaceutical Company manufactures three joint products from a joint process: Altox, Lorex, and Hycol. Data regarding these products for the fiscal year ended May 31, 1993 are as follows:

	Altox	Lorex	Hycol
Units produced	170,000	500,000	330,000
Selling price per unit at splitoff	$3.50	—	$2.00
Separable costs	—	$1,400,000	—
Final selling price per unit	—	$5.00	—

The joint production cost up to the splitoff point where Altox, Lorex, and Hycol become separable products is $1,800,000 (which includes the $17,500 disposal costs for Dorzine as described below).

The president of Goodson, Arlene Franklin, is reviewing an opportunity to change the way in which these three products are processed and sold.

Proposed changes for each product are as follows:

◆ Altox is currently sold at the splitoff point to a manufacturer of vitamins. Altox can also be refined for use as a medication to treat high blood pressure; however, this additional processing would cause a loss of 20,000 units of Altox. The separable costs to further process Altox are estimated to be $250,000 annually. The final product would sell for $5.50 per unit.

◆ Lorex is currently processed further after the splitoff point and sold by Goodson as a cold remedy. The company has received an offer from another pharmaceutical company to purchase Lorex at the splitoff point for $2.25 per unit.

◆ Hycol is an oil produced from the joint process and is currently sold at the splitoff point to a cosmetics manufacturer. Goodson's Research Department has suggested that the company process this product further and sell it as an ointment to relieve muscle pain. The additional processing would cost $75,000 annually and would result in 25% more units of product. The final product would be sold for $1.80 per unit.

The joint process currently used by Goodson also produces 50,000 units of Dorzine, a hazardous chemical waste product. The company pays $0.35 per unit to dispose of the Dorzine properly. Dietriech Mills, Inc., is interested in using the Dorzine as a solvent; however, Goodson would have to refine the Dorzine at an annual cost of $43,000. Dietriech would purchase all the refined Dorzine produced by Goodson and is willing to pay $0.75 for each unit.

INSTRUCTIONS

Form groups of two or more students to complete the following requirements.

REQUIRED

1. Allocate the $1,800,000 joint production cost to Altox, Lorex, and Hycol using the estimated NRV method.

2. Identify which of the three joint products Goodson should sell at the splitoff point in the future and which of the three main products the company should process further in order to maximize profits. Support your decisions with appropriate calculations.

3. Assume that Goodson has decided to refine the waste product Dorzine for sale to Dietriech Mills, Inc., and will treat Dorzine as a byproduct of the joint process in the future.

   a. Evaluate whether Goodson made the correct decision regarding Dorzine. Support your answer with appropriate calculations.

   b. Explain whether the decision to treat Dorzine as a byproduct will affect the decisions reached in requirement 2.

16

REVENUES, REVENUE VARIANCES, AND CUSTOMER-PROFITABILITY ANALYSIS

The revenues of most large soft-drink companies—such as Cott, Coca-Cola, Pepsi-Cola, and Schweppes—come from many countries. Revenue analysis that highlights sales mix, sales quantity, market size, and market share is a key input to decisions regarding product and country emphasis.

LEARNING OBJECTIVES

After studying this chapter, you should be able to

1. Distinguish between revenue tracing and revenue allocation

2. Show how broad averaging of revenue adjustments can result in misstatement of product, service, or customer revenues

3. Describe two methods of allocating the revenues of a bundled package to the individual products in that package

4. Describe the insight gained from dividing the sales-volume variance into the sales-mix and sales-quantity variances

5. Explain how market-size and market-share variances provide different explanations for a sales-quantity variance

6. Discuss why explicitly recording the amount of price discounting provides insight into customer revenue and customer profitability

7. Show how customer-profitability reports can be prepared to highlight differences across customers in their profitability

8. Explain how the cost hierarchy notion can be applied to customer costing

P revious chapters have highlighted how a detailed understanding of costs is essential when making decisions related to, for example, products, services, customers, or departments. This chapter highlights the importance of having a detailed understanding of revenues. Revenues are the lifeblood of most organizations. Companies that prosper make revenue planning and revenue analysis center stage in how managers allocate their energies. We cover three revenue-related topics:

Part One: Revenue Analysis   Discusses revenue tracing and revenue-allocation issues when assigning revenues to products, services, customers, or departments.

Part Two: Revenue and Sales-Mix Analysis   Discusses revenue and sales-mix analysis for companies with multiple products or for companies with single products sold in different countries.

Part Three: Customer-Profitability Analysis   Covers issues in collecting and analyzing customer revenues and customer costs.

Many of the concepts already introduced in previous chapters covering costs carry over to revenues. For example, Chapter 2 discussed cost tracing and cost allocation. We now cover revenue tracing and revenue allocation. Chapters 4 and 5 discussed how overaveraging of costs can lead to peanut-butter costing. Here we look at how similar problems arise with revenues. Chapter 7 showed how detailed variance analysis can provide insight into why actual results differ from budgeted amounts. Now we focus on how a detailed variance analysis of the revenues of companies with multiple products or the same product in multiple countries can provide additional insights into why actual results differ from those budgeted.

◆ PART ONE
REVENUE ANALYSIS

Revenues are inflows of assets received in exchange for products or services provided to customers. In this part, we discuss issues related to the tracing and allocation of revenue to products, services, customers, or departments. **Revenue tracing** occurs where revenues can be identified with an individual product (service, customer, and so on) in an economically feasible (cost-effective) way. **Revenue allocation** occurs when revenues, related but not traceable to individual products (services, customers, and so on), are assigned to those individual products. Revenue tracing results in a more accurate assignment of revenues to products than does revenue allocation. Just as with cost data, more accurate information is believed to result in better decisions.

The Superhighway Application Group (SAG), a computer software company, is used to illustrate the issues discussed. Superhighway develops, sells, and supports three software packages:

1. WordMaster—current version is WordMaster 5.0, which was released 36 months ago. WordMaster was the company's initial product.
2. SpreadMaster—current version is SpreadMaster 3.0, which was released 18 months ago.
3. FinanceMaster—current version is FinanceMaster 2.0. This product, the company's most recent, has been its most successful. The 2.0 version was released 6 months ago.

REVENUE TRACING

Revenue Tracing and Sales Returns

The broad averaging of revenue-related items across individual products can result in inaccurate revenue amounts being assigned to individual products. By investing in information systems that trace as many revenue items as possible to individual products, managers are able to increase the accuracy of reported product revenues and hence the accuracy of reported product profits. More accurate product profits can, in turn, lead to more accurate customer profitability figures.

Consider sales returns. Many companies permit dissatisfied customers to return products previously purchased and to receive a refund of the purchase price (or a credit toward future purchases). At the time the original sale is made, it is not known which specific customer will return a product. However, based on past returns, companies often assume that a percentage of actual sales will subsequently be returned.

Companies that make sales-return adjustments based on broad averaging across the returns for many products potentially reduce the accuracy of the individual product revenue amounts they report. The current sales-return reporting approach of Superhighway illustrates broad averaging. It assumes that 3% of gross revenues will be returned when sales are made. This 3% return provision applies to each of its three products. Returned products are assumed to have zero value. Superhighway records revenues for each month to be 97% of the gross revenues when sales are made. Assume the following sales to new customers were made in 19_7:

	WordMaster	SpreadMaster	FinanceMaster	Total
Actual units sold	6,000	9,000	4,000	
Actual selling price	$ 250	$ 300	$ 450	
Gross revenues	$1,500,000	$2,700,000	$1,800,000	$6,000,000
Deduct sales return provision (3%)	45,000	81,000	54,000	180,000
Net revenues	$1,455,000	$2,619,000	$1,746,000	$5,820,000

Superhighway's policy is to permit sales returns within 1 month of the sale. One month after the end of the 19_7 year, it knows the actual sales return amounts for 19_7.

Broad Averaging Via Peanut-Butter Revenue Adjustments

The current approach of Superhighway is to accumulate the actual sales returns in a single account. At the end of the reporting period, it makes a single adjustment to the 19_7 revenue. Assume that Superhighway has actual sales returns of $249,000 that pertain to the 19_7 sales of $6 million. Its 3% assumption underestimated the actual sales returns by $69,000. Its actual sales-return percentage was 4.15% ($249,000 ÷ 6,000,000) as opposed to the budgeted 3.00% ($180,000 ÷ $6,000,000).

At the end of 19_7, Superhighway makes a uniform adjustment to the net revenues of each product. An additional 1.15% of gross revenues is deducted, making the actual sales-return adjustment 4.15%:

OBJECTIVE 2

Show how broad averaging of revenue adjustments can result in misstatement of product, service, or customer revenues

	WordMaster	SpreadMaster	FinanceMaster	Total
Gross revenues	$1,500,000	$2,700,000	$1,800,000	$6,000,000
Sales-return adjustment (4.15% × gross revenues)	62,250	112,050	74,700	249,000
Net revenues	$1,437,750	$2,587,950	$1,725,300	$5,751,000

The use of the uniform 4.15% across all products is a peanut-butter approach to revenue adjustment for sales returns. It is analogous to the peanut-butter approach to costing discussed in Chapter 4 (pp. 102–103). If there are differences across products in their sales return percentages, more accurate individual product net revenue amounts can be obtained by tracing actual returns to the appropriate product lines.

Assume that Superhighway had the following actual sales returns for 19_7:

	WordMaster	SpreadMaster	FinanceMaster	Total
Gross revenues	$1,500,000	$2,700,000	$1,800,000	$6,000,000
Actual sales returns	15,000	108,000	126,000	249,000
Net revenues	$1,485,000	$2,592,000	$1,674,000	$5,751,000

The actual sales-return percentages are

- ◆ WordMaster   1.0% ($15,000 ÷ $1,500,000)
- ◆ SpreadMaster   4.0% ($108,000 ÷ $2,700,000)
- ◆ FinanceMaster 7.0% ($126,000 ÷ $1,800,000)

Use of the 4.15% uniform adjustment results in the following under- and over-statements of net revenues:

	Actual Net Revenues	Assumed Net Revenues with 4.15% Return Assumption	Difference
WordMaster	$1,485,000	$1,437,750	$47,250 Understatement
SpreadMaster	2,592,000	2,587,950	4,050 Understatement
FinanceMaster	1,674,000	1,725,300	51,300 Overstatement
	$5,751,000	$5,751,000	

These under- or overstatements of actual net revenues will result in under- or overstatements of individual product profitability. For example, WordMaster is actually more profitable than is reported when the 4.15% average adjustment is made.

Collecting reliable product-by-product sales-return data is now more feasible with recent advances in information technology. In the past, many companies used broad averaging for sales returns because of the difficulty of collecting reliable return data for many individual products returned to many different stores. It is only in recent years that retailers have had extensive information systems where all stores can enter product-by-product sales-return information into a common data base.

REVENUE ALLOCATION

Managers increasingly face challenging revenue-allocation issues. One such issue stems from the sale of bundled products. A **bundled product** is a package of two or more products or services, sold for a single price, where the individual components of the bundle may also be sold as separate items, each with their own stand-alone prices. The single price for the bundled product is typically less than the sum of the prices of two or more products if purchased separately. For example, banks often provide their customers with a bundle of services from different departments (checking, security deposit, and investment advisory) for a single fee. A resort hotel may offer, for a single amount, a weekend package that includes services from its lodging (the room), food (the restaurant), and recreational (golfing) divisions. Where individual department or division managers have revenue or profit responsibilities, the issue thus becomes how to allocate the single bundled revenue amount among the individual products in that bundle.

The Superhighway Application Group encounters revenue-allocation decisions with its bundled product sales (termed "suite sales"). Here, two or more of the software products are sold as a single package. Managers at Superhighway are keenly interested in individual product-profitability figures. There are separate managers for each product who are responsible for the operating income of that product. Moreover, its Software Department engineers are organized on a product-by-product basis and receive a percentage of product profitability as part of their bonus. How should Superhighway allocate suite revenues to individual products? Information pertaining to its three suite sales and the stand-alone prices of its individual products is as follows:

Suites	Stand-Alone Sales Price			Suite Sales Price
	WordMaster	SpreadMaster	FinanceMaster	
Word and Spread	$250	$300	—	$440
Word and Finance	$250	—	$450	$560
Word, Spread, and Finance	$250	$300	$450	$760

The unit manufacturing costs of each software product are WordMaster, $36; SpreadMaster, $40; and FinanceMaster, $50.

The two main classes of revenue-allocation methods are the stand-alone method and the incremental method. We now discuss each in turn. Both methods have analogues for cost allocation as discussed in Chapter 13 (pp. 489–491).

Stand-Alone Revenue-Allocation Methods

The **stand-alone revenue-allocation method** uses product-specific information pertaining to products in the bundle to determine the weights used to allocate the bundled revenues to those individual products. The term *stand-alone* refers to the product as a separate (nonsuite) item. Consider the Word and Finance suite, which sells for $560. Three stand-alone sources of weights are as follows.

1. *Unit selling prices.* The individual selling prices are $250 for WordMaster and $450 for FinanceMaster. The weights for allocating the $560 between the two products are

$$\text{Word:} \quad \frac{\$250}{\$250 + 450} \times \$560 = 0.36 \times \$560 = \$202$$

$$\text{Finance:} \quad \frac{\$450}{\$250 + 450} \times \$560 = 0.64 \times \$560 = \$358$$

2. *Unit costs.* This method uses costs of individual products to determine the weights to allocate revenues. Assume unit manufacturing costs are used to determine the weights to allocate the $560 and Word and Finance suite revenues.

$$\text{Word:} \quad \frac{\$36}{\$36 + \$50} \times \$560 = 0.42 \times \$560 = \$235$$

$$\text{Finance:} \quad \frac{\$50}{\$36 + \$50} \times \$560 = 0.58 \times \$560 = \$325$$

This method does not recognize differences across products in the willingness of customers to purchase individual products.

3. *Unit based.* This method gives each product unit in the suite the same weight when allocating suite revenue to individual products. Thus, with two products in the Word plus Finance suite, each product gets 50% of the suite revenues allocated to it.

$$\text{Word:} \quad \frac{1}{1+1} \times \$560 = 0.50 \times \$560 = \$280$$

$$\text{Finance:} \quad \frac{1}{1+1} \times \$560 = 0.50 \times \$560 = \$280$$

These three approaches to determining weights with the stand-alone method yield the following revenue allocations to individual products:

Revenue-Allocation Weights	WordMaster	FinanceMaster
Unit selling prices	$202	$358
Unit manufacturing costs	235	325
Units	280	280

The unit selling-price weights are advantageous in that they frequently are the best available external indicator of the benefits companies receive from selling products. Market-based weighting schemes that are closer to the customer better capture a benefits-received notion in a bundled product allocation setting than do cost-based or unit-based weights. Unit-based revenue allocation is typically rationalized on the basis of ease of use or on limitations of alternative methods (such as unit selling prices are unstable, or unit manufacturing costs are difficult to calculate at the individual product level).[1]

Incremental Revenue-Allocation Method

The **incremental revenue-allocation method** ranks the individual products in a bundle and then uses this ranking to allocate the bundled revenues to these individual products. The first-ranked product is termed the *primary product* in the bundle. The second-ranked product is termed the *incremental product*.

Consider again the Word and Finance suite of Superhighway. Assume Finance-Master is designated as the primary product. If the suite revenue exceeds the stand-alone revenue of the primary product, the primary product is allocated 100% of its stand-alone revenue. This is the case for the Word and Finance suite. The suite revenue of $560 exceeds the stand-alone revenue of $450 for Finance. Thus, Finance is allocated $450 revenues and the $110 ($560 – $450) remaining revenue is allocated to Word:

Product	Revenue Allocated	Revenue Remaining to Be Allocated to Other Products
Finance	$450	$110 ($560 – $450)
Word	110	0

If the suite revenue is less than or equal to the stand-alone revenue of the primary product, the primary product is allocated 100% of the suite revenue. All other products in the suite would receive zero allocation of revenues.

Where there are more than two products in the suite, the suite revenue is allocated sequentially. Consider the Word, Spread, and Finance suite, which sells for $760. Assume Superhighway ranks Finance as the primary product, Spread as the first incremental product, and Word as the second incremental product. The allocation of the $760 suite revenue proceeds as follows:

Product	Revenue Allocated	Revenue Remaining to Be Allocated to Other Products
Finance	$450	$310 ($760 – $450)
Spread	300	10 ($760 – $450 – $300)
Word	10	0

Clearly, the ranking of the individual products in the suite is a key factor in determining the revenues allocated to individual products.

Who decides the ranking of products in the incremental revenue-allocation method? One approach is to survey customers on the relative importance of individual products in their decision to purchase the bundled products. A second approach is to use data on recent stand-alone performance of the individual products in the bundle. A third approach is for top management at Superhighway to make the rankings.

Product managers at Superhighway would likely differ on how they believe their individual products contribute to sales of the suite products. It is possible that each individual product manager would claim to be responsible for the primary

---

[1]An alternative weighting scheme uses the stand-alone revenues. This approach recognizes differences in units sold as well as unit selling prices across items in the bundle. Managers are less able to affect these weights by setting "artificially high" unit selling prices. One approach that reduces the incentives of managers to set "artificially high" unit selling prices is to use actual average selling prices rather than listed selling prices. Actual unit prices often differ from listed unit prices because of discounts or price rebates.

product in the Word + Spread + Finance suite! The stand-alone revenue-allocation method does not require rankings of individual products in the suite. It is therefore less likely to place product managers in highly acrimonious debates.

◆ PART TWO
REVENUE AND SALES VARIANCES

Part One of this chapter highlighted several issues in obtaining reliable information on the revenues of individual products or services. We now examine how variances that use revenue information as a key output can be computed. Special attention is paid to companies with multiple products or services and to companies selling the same product or service in multiple countries.

The revenue variances we discuss are most frequently called sales variances, in large part because sales are the single largest component of revenue for many companies. For example, sales of new or used motor vehicles in an automobile dealership are typically a larger source of revenues than are after-sales revenue items such as servicing and repairs.

The levels approach introduced in Chapter 7 shows how the variances we now discuss are linked to each other:

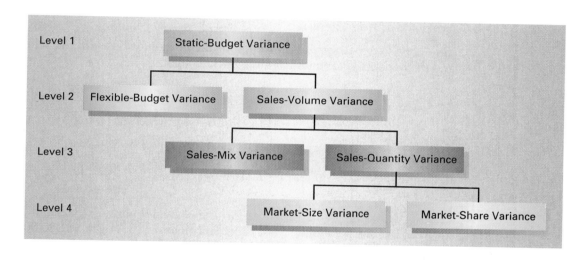

We first discuss how each variance can be computed for the revenues of Global Air, which has multiple classes of air service on its flights. Then we discuss how each variance can be computed for the multinational operations of Superhighway Application Group's (SAG), where the same product is sold in different countries. The variances in this section could be computed for any line item in the income statement. For exposition purposes, we compute variances for the revenue line item of Global Air. Airlines face many challenges in increasing their revenues, such as the level of price discounting and the special mileage club promotions to use. The variances discussed in the next section help managers to evaluate how well budgeted revenue targets are met. A second reason for Global Air's emphasis on revenues (as opposed to, say, contribution margin per passenger) is that variable costs per passenger are minimal. A third reason is that many marketing or sales divisions are run as revenue centers.

VARIANCE ANALYSIS FOR MULTIPLE PRODUCTS

Global Air operates flights between New York and London. It has three classes of service—first class, business class, and economy class. It is currently examining results for August 19_7. Unit volume is measured in terms of a round-trip ticket (one-way tickets are converted into equivalent round-trip tickets). Budgeted and actual results for August 19_7 are as follows:

	Budget for August 19_7				Actual for August 19_7			
	Selling Price per Unit	Unit Volume	Sales Mix	Revenue	Selling Price per Unit	Unit Volume	Sales Mix	Revenue
First class	$3,200	1,000	5%	$ 3,200,000	$2,600	2,400	10%	$ 6,240,000
Business class	2,400	3,000	15%	7,200,000	1,600	6,000	25%	9,600,000
Economy class	900	16,000	80%	14,400,000	700	15,600	65%	10,920,000
Total		20,000	100%	$24,800,000		24,000	100%	$26,760,000

In July 19_7, PanAir, a major competitor of Global, went bankrupt. It was acquired by Laker Travel, a low-cost economy travel operator. PanAir had a sizable presence in the first- and business-class markets. Laker Travel immediately offered deep price discounts for all classes of travel. Its reputation among first-class and business-class travelers, however, was poor (it "reset global minimums in customer-service" to use an expression in a travel magazine). Global Air dropped all its fares in late July (after its budget was prepared) to meet the new competition.

Static-Budget Variance

The *static-budget variance* for revenues is the difference between the actual revenues and the budgeted revenues from the static budget.

$$\text{Static-budget variance of revenues} = \text{Actual results} - \text{Static-budget amount}$$

First class = $6,240,000 − $3,200,000 = $3,040,000 F

Business class = $9,600,000 − $7,200,000 = $2,400,000 F

Economy class = $10,920,000 − $14,400,000 = $3,480,000 U

Total $1,960,000 F

Global Air has favorable variances for first class and business class and an unfavorable variance for economy class. More information about the $1,960,000 favorable total variance can be gained by examining the flexible-budget variance and the sales-volume variance:

Flexible-Budget and Sales-Volume Variances

The *flexible-budget variance* for revenues is the difference between the actual revenues and the flexible-budget amount for the actual unit volume of sales.

OBJECTIVE 4

Describe the insight gained from dividing the sales-volume variance into the sales-mix and sales-quantity variances

$$\text{Flexible-budget variance of revenues} = \text{Actual results} - \text{Flexible-budget amount}$$

First class = $6,240,000 − ($3,200 × 2,400)

= $6,240,000 − $7,680,000 = $1,440,000 U

Business class = $9,600,000 − ($2,400 × 6,000)

= $9,600,000 − $14,400,000 = $4,800,000 U

Economy class = $10,920,000 − ($900 × 15,600)

= $10,920,000 − $14,040,000 = $3,120,000 U

Total $9,360,000 U

The $9,360,000 unfavorable total variance arises because Global Air sizably reduced the price for each class of travel relative to the budgeted price.

The *sales-volume variance* shows the effect of the difference between the actual and budgeted quantity of the variable used to "flex" the flexible budget. For the revenues of Global Air, this variable is units sold. This variance can be computed for each class of service of Global Air:

$$\begin{array}{l} \text{Sales-volume} \\ \text{variance of} \\ \text{revenues} \end{array} = \left(\begin{array}{c} \text{Actual sales} \\ \text{quantity} \\ \text{in units} \end{array} - \begin{array}{c} \text{Budgeted sales} \\ \text{quantity} \\ \text{in units} \end{array} \right) \times \begin{array}{c} \text{Budgeted} \\ \text{selling price} \\ \text{per unit} \end{array}$$

First class	$= (2,400 - 1,000) \times \$3,200 =$	\$ 4,480,000 F
Business class	$= (6,000 - 3,000) \times \$2,400 =$	\$ 7,200,000 F
Economy class	$= (15,600 - 16,000) \times \$900 =$	\$ 360,000 U
Total		\$11,320,000 F

While the total sales-volume variance for revenues is \$11,320,000 favorable, there is a combination of favorable variances for first class and business class and an unfavorable variance for economy class. Managers can gain additional insight into sales-volume changes by separating the sales-volume variance into a sales-quantity variance and a sales-mix variance.

Sales-Quantity Variance

The **sales-quantity variance** is the difference between two amounts: (1) the budgeted amount based on actual quantities sold of all products and the budgeted mix, and (2) the amount in the static budget (which is based on the budgeted quantities to be sold of all products and the budgeted mix). The formula for computing the sales-quantity variance in terms of revenues and the amounts for Global Air is

$$\begin{array}{l} \text{Sales-quantity} \\ \text{variance of} \\ \text{revenues} \end{array} = \left(\begin{array}{c} \text{Actual units} \\ \text{of all products} \\ \text{sold} \end{array} - \begin{array}{c} \text{Budgeted units} \\ \text{of all products} \\ \text{sold} \end{array} \right) \times \begin{array}{c} \text{Budgeted} \\ \text{sales-mix} \\ \text{percentage} \end{array} \times \begin{array}{c} \text{Budgeted} \\ \text{selling price} \\ \text{per unit} \end{array}$$

First class	$= (24,000 - 20,000) \times 0.05 \times \$3,200 =$	\$ 640,000 F
Business class	$= (24,000 - 20,000) \times 0.15 \times \$2,400 =$	\$1,440,000 F
Economy class	$= (24,000 - 20,000) \times 0.80 \times \$900 =$	\$2,880,000 F
Total		\$4,960,000 F

This variance is favorable when the actual units of product sold exceed the budgeted units of product sold. Global sold 4,000 more round-trip tickets than was budgeted. Hence, its sales-quantity variance for revenues is favorable.

Sales-Mix Variance

The **sales-mix variance** is the difference between two amounts: (1) the budgeted amount for the actual sales mix, and (2) the budgeted amount if the budgeted sales mix had been unchanged. The formula for computing the sales-mix variance in terms of revenue and the amounts for Global Air is

$$\begin{array}{l} \text{Sales-mix} \\ \text{variance of} \\ \text{revenues} \end{array} = \begin{array}{c} \text{Actual units} \\ \text{of all} \\ \text{products sold} \end{array} \times \left(\begin{array}{c} \text{Actual} \\ \text{sales mix} \\ \text{percentage} \end{array} - \begin{array}{c} \text{Budgeted} \\ \text{sales-mix} \\ \text{percentage} \end{array} \right) \times \begin{array}{c} \text{Budgeted} \\ \text{selling price} \\ \text{per unit} \end{array}$$

First class	$= 24,000 \times (0.10 - 0.05) \times \$3,200 =$	\$3,840,000 F
Business class	$= 24,000 \times (0.25 - 0.15) \times \$2,400 =$	\$5,760,000 F
Economy class	$= 24,000 \times (0.65 - 0.80) \times \$900 =$	\$3,240,000 U
Total		\$6,360,000 F

A favorable sales-mix variance arises at the individual product level when the actual sales-mix percentage exceeds the budgeted sales-mix percentage. This situation applies to both first class (10% actual versus 5% budgeted) and business class (25% actual versus 15% budgeted). In contrast, economy class has an unfavorable variance because the actual sales mix percentage (65%) is less than the budgeted sales-mix percentage (80%).

The concept behind the sales-mix variance for revenues of $6,360,000 F is best explained in terms of the budgeted selling prices per composite unit of the sales mix. A **composite product unit** is a hypothetical unit with weights related to the individual products of the company. The weights for the revenue-based variances are computed as follows in column 3 for the actual mix and column 5 for the budgeted mix:

	Budgeted Selling Price per Unit (1)	Actual Sales-Mix Percentage (2)	Budgeted Selling Price per Composite Unit for Actual Mix (3) = (1) × (2)	Budgeted Sales-Mix Percentage (4)	Budgeted Selling Price per Composite Unit for Budgeted Mix (5) = (1) × (4)
First class	$3,200	0.10	$ 320	0.05	$ 160
Business class	2,400	0.25	600	0.15	360
Economy class	900	0.65	585	0.80	720
Total			$1,505		$1,240

The actual sales mix has a budgeted selling price per composite unit of $1,505 (where the composite unit comprises 0.10 of first class, 0.25 of business class, and 0.65 of economy class). The budgeted sales mix had a budgeted selling price per composite unit of $1,240 (where the composite unit comprises 0.05 of first, 0.15 of business, and 0.80 of economy). Thus, the effect of the 19_7 sales-mix shift for Global Air is to increase the budgeted selling price per composite unit by $265 ($1,505 − $1,240). For the 24,000 units actually sold, this increase translates to a favorable sales-mix variance of $6 million.

Exhibit 16-1 shows how both the sales-mix and sales-quantity variances can be computed using the columnar approach introduced in Chapter 7. Exhibit 16-1 highlights the revenue effect of the shift toward a mix with higher revenue generating units (first class and business class) and the revenue effect of the 20% increase in total units sold (actual of 24,000 round-trips versus 20,000 budgeted).

Market-Size and Market-Share Variances

Sales depend on overall market demand as well as the company's ability to maintain its share of the market. Assume that the budgeted unit sales of 20,000 units (round-trip tickets) came from a management estimate of a 50% market share on the New York to London route in August 19_7 and an industry sales forecast by the Travel Information Group (TIG) of 40,000 round-trip tickets for the route. In September, TIG reported the following:

	Budgeted Industry Volume for August 19_7	Actual Industry Volume for August 19_7
First class	1,500	3,000
Business class	6,000	9,000
Economy class	32,500	38,000
Total	40,000	50,000

Global Air's actual market share was 48% of unit volume (24,000 ÷ 50,000) in contrast to its budgeted share of 50%. TIG noted that Laker Travel was highly successful in generating economy travel but had been unsuccessful in attracting first- and business-class travelers. In contrast, it noted Global Air's great success in expanding its first- and business-class presence.

EXHIBIT 16-1
Sales-Mix and Sales-Quantity Variance Analysis for Revenues of Global Air for New York to London Route for August 19_7

	Flexible Budget: Actual Units of All Products Sold × Actual Sales Mix × Budgeted Selling Price per Unit	Actual Units of All Products Sold × Budgeted Sales Mix × Budgeted Selling Price per Unit	Static Budget: Budgeted Units of All Products Sold × Budgeted Sales Mix × Budgeted Selling Price per Unit
First class	24,000 × 0.10 × $3,200 = $ 7,680,000	(24,000 × 0.05 × $3,200) = $ 3,840,000	(20,000 × 0.05 × $3,200) = $ 3,200,000
Business class	24,000 × 0.25 × $2,400 = $14,400,000	(24,000 × 0.15 × $2,400) = $ 8,640,000	(20,000 × 0.15 × $2,400) = $ 7,200,000
Economy class	24,000 × 0.65 × $900 = $14,040,000	(24,000 × 0.80 × $900) = $17,280,000	(20,000 × 0.80 × $900) = $14,400,000
	$36,120,000	$29,760,000	$24,800,000

$6,360,000 F
Total sales-mix variance

$4,960,000 F
Total sales-quantity variance

$11,320,000 F
Total sales-volume variance

F = favorable effect on revenue; U = unfavorable effect on revenue.

Global Air can use this industry information from TIG to get further insight into the sales-quantity variance by dividing it into a market-size variance and a market-share variance. The **market-size variance** is the difference between two amounts: (1) the budgeted amount based on the *actual market size in units* and the budgeted market share, and (2) the static-budget amount based on the *budgeted market size in units* and the budgeted market share. The formula and the 19_7 amount for Global Air for revenues is

$$\begin{array}{c} \text{Market-size} \\ \text{variance} \\ \text{in revenues} \end{array} = \left(\begin{array}{c} \text{Actual} \\ \text{market size} \\ \text{in units} \end{array} - \begin{array}{c} \text{Budgeted} \\ \text{market size} \\ \text{in units} \end{array} \right) \times \begin{array}{c} \text{Budgeted} \\ \text{market} \\ \text{share} \end{array} \times \begin{array}{c} \text{Budgeted average} \\ \text{selling price} \\ \text{per unit} \end{array}$$

$$= (50{,}000 - 40{,}000) \times 0.50 \times \$1{,}240$$

$$= \$6{,}200{,}000 \text{ F}$$

The budgeted average selling price per (composite) unit is computed by dividing the total budgeted revenues of $24,800,000 by the total budgeted units of 20,000. The $6,200,000 market-size variance for revenues is favorable because it is the additional revenue expected as a result of the 25% increase in market size (50,000 ÷ 40,000 = 125%), provided Global Air maintains both its budgeted market share of 50% and its budgeted average selling price of $1,240.

The **market-share variance** is the difference between two amounts: (1) the budgeted amount at budgeted mix based on the actual market size in units and the actual market share, and (2) the budgeted amount at budgeted mix based on actual market size in units and the *budgeted market share*. The formula and the 19_7 amounts for Global Air for revenues is

$$\begin{array}{c} \text{Market-share} \\ \text{variance for} \\ \text{revenues} \end{array} = \begin{array}{c} \text{Actual} \\ \text{market size} \\ \text{in units} \end{array} \times \left(\begin{array}{c} \text{Actual} \\ \text{market} \\ \text{share} \end{array} - \begin{array}{c} \text{Budgeted} \\ \text{market} \\ \text{share} \end{array} \right) \times \begin{array}{c} \text{Budgeted average} \\ \text{selling price} \\ \text{per unit} \end{array}$$

$$= 50{,}000 \times (0.48 - 0.50) \times \$1{,}240$$

$$= \$1{,}240{,}000 \text{ U}$$

Global Air lost total market share from that budgeted—from the 50% budgeted to the actual of 48%. The $1,240,000 unfavorable variance highlights the revenue impact of this 2 percentage-point decline in market share.

Exhibit 16-2 shows both the market-share and market-size variances using the columnar approach introduced in Chapter 7. Exhibit 16-3 presents an overview of the Level 1 to Level 4 variances computed for Global Air. Note how offsetting variances occur in both Levels 2 and 4. In some cases, these offsetting variances may be causally related. The $9,360,000 unfavorable flexible-budget variance arises because of the decline in actual ticket prices from that budgeted. The $11,320,000 favorable sales-volume variance reflects the unit-volume increase stimulated by this decrease in selling prices.

The phrase "drilling down" or "peeling the onion" is sometimes used to describe starting at the most aggregate level (Level 1) and then progressively seeking more detail on the factors underlying specific variance amounts. Managers are increasingly able to access software programs that start at Level 1 and then proceed to Levels 2, 3, and 4.

Is dividing the sales-quantity variance into the market-size and market-share variances useful for evaluating the marketing manager's performance? Suppose market size and the demand for an industry's products are largely influenced by factors such as growth and interest rates in the economy. Then the market-size variance does not tell us much about the marketing manager's performance because it is largely determined by factors outside the manager's control. Top management may therefore put greater weight on the market-share variance in their evaluation of the marketing manager.

A caution when computing market-size and market-share variances is appropriate. Reliable information on market size and market share is available for some, but not all, industries. For example, the soft-drink and television industries are ones

EXHIBIT 16-2

Market-Share and Market-Size Variance Analysis for Revenues of Global Air on New York to London Route for August 19_7

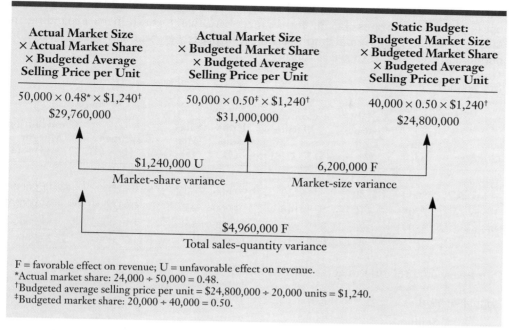

Actual Market Size × Actual Market Share × Budgeted Average Selling Price per Unit	Actual Market Size × Budgeted Market Share × Budgeted Average Selling Price per Unit	Static Budget: Budgeted Market Size × Budgeted Market Share × Budgeted Average Selling Price per Unit
$50,000 \times 0.48^* \times \$1,240^\dagger$	$50,000 \times 0.50^\ddagger \times \$1,240^\dagger$	$40,000 \times 0.50 \times \$1,240^\dagger$
$29,760,000	$31,000,000	$24,800,000

$1,240,000 U
Market-share variance

6,200,000 F
Market-size variance

$4,960,000 F
Total sales-quantity variance

F = favorable effect on revenue; U = unfavorable effect on revenue.
*Actual market share: 24,000 ÷ 50,000 = 0.48.
†Budgeted average selling price per unit = $24,800,000 ÷ 20,000 units = $1,240.
‡Budgeted market share: 20,000 ÷ 40,000 = 0.50.

EXHIBIT 16-3

Overview of Revenue Variances for Global Air on New York to London Route for August 19–7

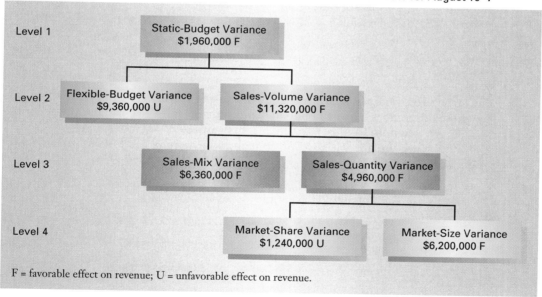

Level 1 — Static-Budget Variance $1,960,000 F

Level 2 — Flexible-Budget Variance $9,360,000 U | Sales-Volume Variance $11,320,000 F

Level 3 — Sales-Mix Variance $6,360,000 F | Sales-Quantity Variance $4,960,000 F

Level 4 — Market-Share Variance $1,240,000 U | Market-Size Variance $6,200,000 F

F = favorable effect on revenue; U = unfavorable effect on revenue.

where market size and share statistics are widely available. In other industries such as management consulting, information about market size and market share is far less reliable and is usually not published on a regular basis.

VARIANCE ANALYSIS FOR MULTIPLE COUNTRIES

The Global Air example used the revenue line item to illustrate variance analysis. Our next example (SAG) uses the contribution margin line item to further illustrate variance analysis. The emphasis here is variance analysis of a single product or service sold in different countries. These countries can differ in the selling prices and costs of this product, as well as in the degree of competition in their markets.

Consider the Superhighway Application Group (SAG) discussed earlier in this chapter (pp. 576–581). Its SpreadMaster software product is sold in three countries—the United States, Japan, and France. SAG has recently been expanding its sales base beyond its original emphasis on the U.S. market. Summary data relating to budgeted results for 19_8 are as follows:

Budget for 19_8

Country	Selling Price per Unit (1)	Variable Cost per Unit (2)	Contrib. Margin per Unit (3) = (1) – (2)	Units Sold (4)	Sales Mix (5)	Revenues (6) = (1) × (4)	Contribution Margin (7) = (3) × (4)
United States	$300	$ 80	$220	9,600	60%	$2,880,000	$2,112,000
Japan	270	130	140	4,000	25	1,080,000	560,000
France	350	120	230	2,400	15	840,000	552,000
				16,000	100%	$4,800,000	$3,224,000

Summary data relating to actual results for 19_8 are as follows:

Actual for 19_8

Country	Selling Price per Unit (1)	Variable Cost per Unit (2)	Contrib. Margin per Unit (3) = (1) – (2)	Units Sold (4)	Sales Mix (5)	Revenues (6) = (1) × (4)	Contribution Margin (7) = (3) × (4)
United States	$295	$ 85	$210	9,000	50%	$2,655,000	$1,890,000
Japan	285	125	160	5,400	30	1,539,000	864,000
France	340	95	245	3,600	20	1,224,000	882,000
				18,000	100%	$5,418,000	$3,636,000

The structured variance analysis framework (using Levels 1–3) can be used to analyze these differences between budgeted and actual results. We will use the contribution margin line item to illustrate the insights gained.

The static-budget variance of contribution margin for SAG's SpreadMaster product is

$$\text{Static-budget variance of contribution margin} = \text{Actual results} - \text{Static-budget amount}$$

United States = $1,890,000 – $2,112,000 = $222,000 U

Japan   = $864,000 – $560,000 = $304,000 F

France   = $882,000 – $552,000 = $330,000 F

Total $412,000 F

The $222,000 unfavorable variance for the United States is more than offset by the favorable variances in Japan and France.

The flexible-budget variance shows the following:

$$\text{Flexible-budget variance of contribution margin} = \text{Actual results} - \text{Flexible-budget amount}$$

United States = $1,890,000 – ($220 × 9,000) = $ 90,000 U

Japan   = $864,000 – ($140 × 5,400) = $108,000 F

France   = $882,000 – ($230 × 3,600) = $ 54,000 F

Total $ 72,000 F

The sales-volume variance shows the following:

$$\text{Sales-volume variance of contribution margin} = \left(\begin{array}{c}\text{Actual sales}\\\text{quantity}\\\text{in units}\end{array} - \begin{array}{c}\text{Budgeted sales}\\\text{quantity}\\\text{in units}\end{array}\right) \times \begin{array}{c}\text{Budgeted}\\\text{contribution}\\\text{margin per unit}\end{array}$$

United States = (9,000 − 9,600) × $220 = $132,000 U

Japan = (5,400 − 4,000) × $140 = $196,000 F

France = (3,600 − 2,400) × $230 = $276,000 F

Total $340,000 F

The U.S. market had an actual contribution margin below that budgeted ($210 versus $220) and actual units sold below that budgeted (9,000 units versus 9,600). This results in unfavorable flexible-budget and sales-volume variances for the U.S. market. In contrast, the reverse holds for both the Japanese and French markets. Here, the actual contribution margin exceeds the budgeted amount ($160 versus $140 for Japan and $245 versus $230 for France), and the actual units sold exceeds that budgeted (5,400 units versus 4,000 for Japan and 3,600 units versus 2,400 for France). This results in favorable flexible-budget and sales-volume variances for both the Japanese and French markets.

The total favorable sales-volume variance of $340,000 can be further subdivided into a sales-quantity variance and a sales-mix variance. The sales-quantity variance for SpreadMaster is

$$\begin{array}{c}\text{Sales-quantity}\\\text{variance of}\\\text{contribution margin}\end{array} = \left(\begin{array}{c}\text{Actual units}\\\text{of all products}\\\text{sold}\end{array} - \begin{array}{c}\text{Budgeted units}\\\text{of all products}\\\text{sold}\end{array}\right) \times \begin{array}{c}\text{Budgeted}\\\text{sales-mix}\\\text{percentage}\end{array} \times \begin{array}{c}\text{Budgeted}\\\text{contribution}\\\text{margin per unit}\end{array}$$

United States = (18,000 − 16,000) × 0.60 × $220 = $264,000 F

Japan = (18,000 − 16,000) × 0.25 × $140 = $ 70,000 F

France = (18,000 − 16,000) × 0.15 × $230 = $ 69,000 F

Total $403,000 F

The sales-mix variance for SpreadMaster is

$$\begin{array}{c}\text{Sales-mix}\\\text{variance of}\\\text{contribution margin}\end{array} = \begin{array}{c}\text{Actual units}\\\text{of all}\\\text{products sold}\end{array} \times \left(\begin{array}{c}\text{Actual}\\\text{sales mix}\\\text{percentage}\end{array} - \begin{array}{c}\text{Budgeted}\\\text{sales-mix}\\\text{percentage}\end{array}\right) \times \begin{array}{c}\text{Budgeted}\\\text{contribution}\\\text{margin per unit}\end{array}$$

United States = 18,000 × (0.50 − 0.60) × $220 = $396,000 U

Japan = 18,000 × (0.30 − 0.25) × $140 = $126,000 F

France = 18,000 × (0.20 − 0.15) × $230 = $207,000 F

Total $ 63,000 U

Exhibit 16-4 presents a summary of the variances for the SpreadMaster product computed in this section. Note how the Level 2 sales-volume variance of $340,000 F is primarily attributable to the 2,000 units sold increase over that budgeted (18,000 units actually sold versus the 16,000 units budgeted). The Level 3 sales-quantity variance is $403,000 F, while the sales-mix variance is $63,000 U. The budgeted contribution margin per composite unit for the actual mix is $198 [($220 × 0.50) + ($140 × 0.30) + ($230 × 0.20)] compared to $201.50 [($220 × 0.60) + ($140 × 0.25) + ($230 × 0.15)] for the budgeted mix. This $3.50 decline in budgeted contribution margin per composite unit for the 18,000 actual units sold translates to the unfavorable sales-mix variance of $63,000 U ($3.50 × 18,000). The decline in sales mix for the United States (0.50 actual versus 0.60 budgeted) is an important contributor to this unfavorable sales-mix variance.[2]

---

[2]Our SAG example expressed all the analysis in U.S. dollars. One extension would be to introduce currency differences so that the effect of movements in the Japanese yen or the French franc relative to the U.S. dollar is made explicit in the comparison.

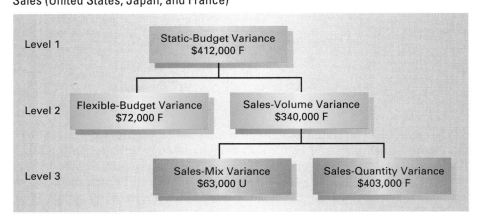

EXHIBIT 16-4
Overview of Variances for the SpreadMaster Product's Contribution Margin for Total Sales (United States, Japan, and France)

Our SAG example in Exhibit 16-4 could be extended to incorporate market-size and market-share variances as was done for the Global Air example in Exhibit 16-3. Note that obtaining reliable market size or market share is often difficult, especially when the analysis is conducted at the multiple-country level. The market-size and market-share variances can be computed at several line-item levels in the income statement, such as at the revenue line-item level and at the contribution-margin line-item level if the company makes a distinction between variable costs and fixed costs.

◆ PART THREE
CUSTOMER PROFITABILITY ANALYSIS

Customer-profitability analysis examines how individual customers, or groupings of customers, differ in their profitability. It is a relatively new topic in management accounting, but a vitally important one. Managers need to ensure that customers contributing sizably to the profitability of an organization receive a comparable level of attention from the organization. An accounting system that reports customer profitability helps managers in this task.

The marketing efforts of companies aim to attract and retain profitable customers. This section examines the reporting and analysis of customer revenues and customer costs. We will discuss the Spring Distribution Company, a distributor of water bottled by Spring Products. Spring Distribution buys bottled water from Spring Products at $0.50 a bottle. It sells to wholesale customers at a list price of $0.60 a bottle. Customers range from large supermarkets, hospitals, and university eating clubs to "Ma and Pa" corner stores. It does not sell to final end-point consumers.

CUSTOMER REVENUES

Customer revenues are inflows of assets from customers received in exchange for products or services being provided to those customers. Part One of this chapter illustrated how more accurate product revenues can be obtained by tracing sales returns and other revenue offsets to individual products rather than by using broad averaging across many products. More accurate customer revenues can likewise be obtained by tracing as many revenue items (such as sales returns and coupons) as possible to individual customers.

The analysis of customer profitability is enhanced by retaining as much detail as possible about revenue. A key concern here is **price discounting,** which is the reduction of selling prices below listed levels in order to encourage an increase in purchases by customers. Accounting systems differ with respect to how details on discounting are recorded. Spring Distribution offers price discounts below its $0.60 list price per bottle to key customers. Individual sales representatives have discretion as to the amount of discounting. Its largest customer is SuperMart, to which it sold 1 million bottles at $0.56 per bottle in November 19_7. The two main revenue recording options are

OBJECTIVE 6

Discuss why explicitly recording the amount of price discounting provides insight into customer revenue and customer profitability

Option A: Recognize the list price ($0.60 per bottle) and the discount ($0.04 per bottle) from this list price as separate line items.

Revenues at list prices, $0.60 × 1,000,000	$600,000
Deduct revenue discounting, $0.04 × 1,000,000	40,000
Reported revenues	$560,000

Option B: Record only the actual price when reporting revenues.

Reported revenues, $0.56 × 1,000,000	$560,000

Option A has the benefit of highlighting the extent of price discounting. It facilitates further analysis that could examine which customers had price discounting and which sales representatives at Spring Distribution most frequently resorted to price discounting. Option B effectively precludes such systematic analysis of price discounting.

Studies on customer profitability in companies have found large price discounting to be an important explanation for a subset of customers being below their expected profitability. Sales representatives may have given these customers large price discounts that are unrelated to their current or potential future value to a company.

CUSTOMER COSTS

We discuss two approaches to customer costing. The first approach is to allocate all costs to individual customers. The second approach is to allocate only some costs to individual customers. A customer-cost hierarchy is used to illustrate this second approach.

Allocate All Costs to Individual Customers

In this approach, the sum of customer profits will be the same as the total profitability of the company. Spring Distribution uses an activity-based costing system when determining the profitability of individual customers. The five activity areas and their cost drivers are

Activity Area	Cost Driver and Rate
Order taking	$100 per purchase order
Sales visits	$80 per sales visit
Delivery vehicles	$2 per delivery mile traveled
Product handling	$0.02 per bottle sold
"Hot-hot runs"	$300 per hot-hot run

A "hot-hot run" is an emergency delivery outside the scheduled delivery pattern. Exhibit 16-5 shows a customer-profitability analysis for four customers. Data underlying this exhibit are as follows:

	Customer			
	A	B	G	J
Bottles sold	1,000,000	800,000	70,000	60,000
List selling price	$0.60	$0.60	$0.60	$0.60
Actual selling price	$0.56	$0.59	$0.55	$0.60
Number of purchase orders	30	25	15	10
Number of sales visits	6	5	4	3
Number of deliveries	60	30	20	15
Miles traveled per delivery	5	12	20	6
Number of hot-hot runs	1	0	2	0

Customers A, B, and J are profitable while customer G is unprofitable. Exhibit 16-5 shows how differences across customers in both revenues and costs explain these profitability differences. Consider the profitability differences between customers A and B. Other things being equal, the higher the volume, the more profitable the customer is expected to be. However, customer A (with higher volume) receives a $0.04 price discount per bottle, while customer B receives only a $0.01 price discount per bottle. This difference in selling-price discount is a major factor explaining why customer B is more profitable than customer A. A similar situation exists between customer G and J. Customer J receives no price discount while G receives a $0.05 per bottle price discount. There may be compelling reasons for customer G's large discount. For example, customer G may be expected to grow rapidly, or it may be a highly prestigious very visible account that enhances the general marketing efforts of Spring Distribution. Alternatively, there may be little or no rationale for the price discount. In this case, Spring Distribution should explore restructuring customer G's contract. Customers often talk among each other about the prices they are paying. A policy of inconsistent price discounting can lead to pressure from customers for equivalent price reductions.

Differences in cost structure also explain how customers with similar volume can have differences in profitability. Customer G has more purchase orders than J (15 versus 10), more sales visits (4 versus 3), more deliveries (20 versus 15), requires more travel miles per delivery (20 versus 6), and has more hot-hot (rush) runs (2 versus 0). Note how an activity-based customer-costing system provides Spring Distributors with a road map as to how to reduce costs on each customer account. For example, by encouraging customer G to consolidate its orders, it can reduce purchase

EXHIBIT 16-5
Customer-Profitability Analysis for Four Customers of Spring Distribution

	Customer			
	A	B	G	J
Revenues at list prices	$600,000	$480,000	$42,000	$36,000
Discount	40,000	8,000	3,500	0
Net revenues	560,000	472,000	38,500	36,000
Cost of goods sold	500,000	400,000	35,000	30,000
Gross margin	60,000	72,000	3,500	6,000
Operating costs				
Order taking	3,000	2,500	1,500	1,000
Sales visits	480	400	320	240
Delivery vehicles	600	720	800	180
Product handling	20,000	16,000	1,400	1,200
Hot-hot runs	300	0	600	0
Total	24,380	19,620	4,620	2,620
Operating income	$ 35,620	$ 52,380	$ (1,120)	$ 3,380

order costs. Similarly, by persuading customer G to order in sufficient quantities, which eliminates the need for hot-hot runs, it can reduce rush order costs.

CUSTOMER-PROFITABILITY PROFILES

Exhibit 16-6 shows two approaches to presenting customer-profitability profiles. For simplicity, we assume Spring Distribution has only ten customers. Panel A ranks customers on operating income. Column 4 shows the cumulative operating income for these customers. This column is computed by cumulatively adding up the individual customer incomes. For example, row three for customer C has a cumulative income of $108,650 in column 4. This is the sum of $52,380 for customer B, $35,620 for customer A, and $20,650 for customer C. Column 5 shows what percentage this

EXHIBIT 16-6
Customer-Profitability Analysis for Spring Distribution

PANEL A: CUSTOMERS RANKED ON 19_7 OPERATING INCOME

Customer Code (1)	Customer Operating (2)	Customer Revenue* (3)	Cumulative Operating Income (4)	Percentage of Cumulative Operating Income to Total Operating Income (5)
B	$ 52,380	$ 480,000	$ 52,380	39%
A	35,620	600,000	88,000	66
C	20,650	247,000	108,650	81
D	16,840	227,000	125,490	94
F	6,994	99,000	132,484	99
J	3,380	36,000	135,864	101
E	3,176	193,000	139,040	104
G	-1,120	42,000	137,920	103
H	-1,760	39,000	136,160	102
I	-2,160	37,000	$134,000	100%
	$134,000	$2,000,000		

PANEL B: CUSTOMERS RANKED ON 19_7 REVENUES

Customer Code (1)	Customer Revenue* (2)	Customer Operating Income (3)	Operating Income Revenues (4)	Cumulative Revenues (5)	Percentage of Cumulative Revenue to Total Revenues (6)
A	$ 600,000	$ 35,620	0.059	$ 600,000	30%
B	480,000	52,380	0.109	1,080,000	54
C	247,000	20,650	0.084	1,327,000	66
D	227,000	16,840	0.074	1,554,000	78
E	193,000	3,176	0.016	1,747,000	87
F	99,000	6,994	0.071	1,846,000	92
G	42,000	-1,120	(0.027)	1,888,000	94
H	39,000	-1,760	(0.045)	1,927,000	96
I	37,000	-2,160	(0.058)	1,964,000	98
J	36,000	3,380	0.094	$2,000,000	100%
	$2,000,000	$134,000			

*Customer revenue is gross revenue prior to price offset items such as a price discount.

$108,650 amount is of the total operating income of $134,000. Thus, the three most profitable customers contribute 81% of total operating income. This high percentage contribution by a small number of customers is a common finding in many studies. It highlights the importance of Spring Distribution maintaining good relations with this pivotal set of customers.

Exhibit 16-6, Panel B, ranks customers on revenue (before price discounts). Three of the four smallest customers (based on revenue) are unprofitable. Moreover, customer E, with revenues of $193,000, is only marginally profitable. Further analysis revealed that a former sales representative gave customer E an excessively high price discount in an attempt to meet a monthly sales-volume target.

Managers often find the bar chart presentation in Exhibit 16-7 to be the most intuitive way to analyze customer profitability. The highly profitable customers clearly stand out. Moreover, the number of loss-customers and the magnitude of their losses are apparent.

Managers find customer-profitability analysis useful for several reasons. First, it frequently highlights how vital a small set of customers is to total profitability. Managers need to ensure that the interests of these customers receive high priority. Microsoft uses the phrase "not all revenue dollars are endowed equally in profitability" to stress this key point. Second, when a customer is ranked in the loss category, managers can focus on ways to make future business with this customer more profitable.

Several caveats on the customer-profitability information in Exhibits 16-5 through 16-7 are necessary. First, this information relates to profitability in a single accounting period. An unprofitable customer in one period may be highly profitable in subsequent future periods. Managers give high priority to maintaining long-term relationships with customers. Exhibits 16-5 through 16-7 could be extended to incorporate a longer time horizon when making profitability computations. Second, the cost information does not distinguish between different levels of variability or the time period over which that variability occurs. In many cases, not all costs assigned to a customer are purely variable with respect to short-run reductions in purchases by customers. It is typically not the case that a policy of dropping any customer currently unprofitable (sometimes called "revenue shedding") will eliminate in the short run all the costs assigned to that customer.

EXHIBIT 16-7
Bar Chart Presentation of Customer Profitability for Spring Distribution

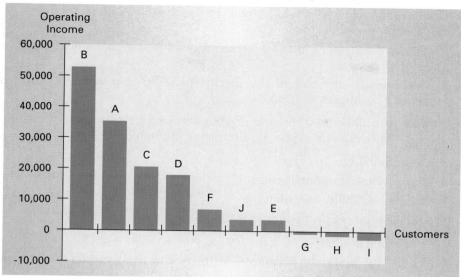

CUSTOMER-COST HIERARCHY

In the Spring Distribution example, all costs are assigned to individual customers. An alternative approach is to use the cost hierarchy approach introduced in Chapter 5 (p. 150). This section illustrates how General Motors Service Parts Operations (GMSPO) has developed a customer hierarchy.[3] A **customer-cost hierarchy** categorizes costs related to customers into different cost pools on the basis of either different classes of cost drivers or different degrees of difficulty in determining the cause-and-effect (or benefits received) relationships. GMSPO provides replacement parts to four major distribution channels:

◆ GM dealers

◆ Non-GM distributors

◆ Auto parts stores

◆ Mass-market retailers

GMSPO buys parts from other GM divisions. These parts may be shipped directly to distribution outlets or shipped first to one of GM's part warehouses. GMSPO has operations similar in many ways to the Spring Distribution example discussed previously as well as to the Hewlett-Packard distribution center described in the Concepts in Action box (p. 597).

Exhibit 16-8 presents the cost hierarchy used by GMSPO to analyze profitability. The aim of this cost hierarchy is to assign costs to the lowest level of the hierarchy at which they can be identified. The seven levels of the customer-cost hierarchy in Exhibit 16-8 are

1. *Enterprise-related activities*—the most aggregate level; includes security of the plant, employee training, and new initiatives in data processing.

2. *Market-related activities*—includes costs for general promotional expenditures (for example, sponsorship of motor car sporting events).

3. *Channel-related activities*—includes the costs of managing receivables and the cost of export sales staff.

> **OBJECTIVE 8**
>
> Explain how the cost hierarchy notion can be applied to customer costing

[3]The work of Ron Bellow and his team at GMSPO is gratefully acknowledged.

4. *Customer-related activities*—includes price discounts to specific customers, customer contacts, and materials return.

5. *Order-related activities*—includes pick-and-pack labor, outbound freight, and customer invoicing.

6. *Parts-related activities*—includes receiving, carloading, inbound freight, and scrap/obsolescence.

7. *Direct materials*—the cost of the specific parts being distributed (such as a fender or a dashboard display).

Exhibit 16-8 illustrates how the revenues for service parts can be combined with costs at different levels to provide alternative profitability figures:

1. Total profitability
2. Market profitability contribution
3. Channel profitability contribution
4. Customer-segment profitability contribution
5. Gross margin on parts

The GMSPO cost hierarchy enables GM to look at their profitability through several different lenses. For example, channel profitability, customer profitability, and product profitability can each be separately examined. Thus, for example, the relative profitability of the four major distribution channels (GM dealers, non-GM distributors, auto parts stores, and mass-market retailers) can be examined independently of the profitability of specific accounts within any of those channels. When analyzing individual customer profitability, GM does not allocate costs in the channel, market, and enterprise levels. These costs are not viewed as being assignable to any specific customer. In this case, the sum of individual customer profits is more than the total profits of GMSPO. Customers unprofitable under the GMPSO approach fail to contribute to the recovery of the many infrastructure costs related to the enterprise-related, market-related, and channel-related levels.

EXHIBIT 16-8
General Motors Service Parts: Alternative Profitability Measures Based on Cost Hierarchy ABC Model

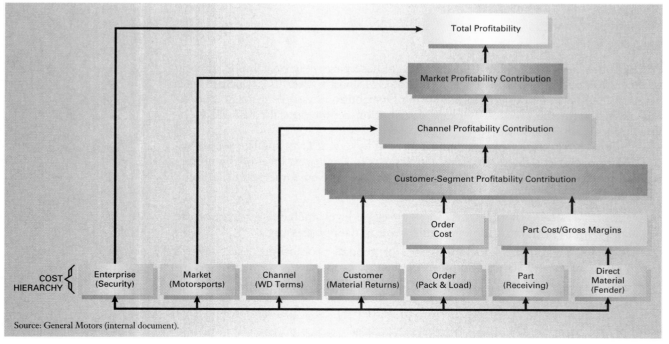

Source: General Motors (internal document).

Hewlett-Packard Adopts Customer-Profitability Analysis

Hewlett-Packard's North American Distribution Organization (HP-NADO) is one of four HP distribution organizations worldwide. NADO is the contact point between HP and its customers. It is always the information node between HP's production plants and its reseller channels. In many cases, their product also physically passes through the distribution depot, where any specific customization (such as product combinations and packaging) is undertaken.

The previous costing system at HP-NADO was typical of many existing systems. It focused on costs at a single function (distribution) and concentrated on the costs of distributing products. The most telling criticism of the system was that it did not assist managers in making many of their key decisions—for example, what channels to push and what individual customers to emphasize.

HP decided to use activity-based costing to develop a "data warehouse." This data warehouse is based on the activities undertaken by HP in linking a product from its manufacturing to its delivery to customers. Each activity is assigned a cost. Then the cost of a chosen focal object (be it a reseller channel, customer, or product) is determined by examining how that focal object uses the activities of the organization. Different focal objects are costed by slicing and dicing data in the warehouse in different ways. A key aspect here is the flexibility that the data warehouse concept provides to managers. What occurs at NADO can always be expressed in terms of its usage of one or more activity areas.

The customer-based profitability reports facilitate decisions in key areas. From a strategic perspective, the customer profile reveals the importance of a small set of customers. Less than 25% of customers account for over 85% of all HP revenues. By cutting across the diverse product lines, the NADO data base facilitates a customer focus that was not previously possible. The data base profiles the specific mix of revenue and cost activities that individual customers utilize. This information can be very insightful in explaining differences in customer profitability. Customer-price discounting policies are an important concern here. Customers with relatively low revenues or relatively low profitability but relatively frequent and large price discounting are highlighted. The onus is on marketing personnel to reduce these price discounts unless compelling reasons exist for keeping them.

Source: Based on discussions with management.

PROBLEM

Business Horizons (BH) produces and markets videos for sale to the business community. It hires well-known business speakers to present new developments in their area in video format. The compensation paid to each speaker is individually negotiated. It always has a component based on the percentage of revenues from the sale of the video, but that percentage is not uniform across speakers. Moreover, some speakers negotiate separate fixed-dollar payments or multiple-video deals.

BH sells most videos as separate items. However, there is a growing trend for videos also to be sold as part of bundled packages. BH offered bundled packages of its three best-selling videos in 19_7. Individual and bundled sales of these three videos for 19_7 are

Individual Sales

Speaker	Title	Units Sold	Selling Price	Speaker Royalty
Jeannett Smith	Negotiating for Win-Win	25,000	$150	24%
Paul Newlove	Marketing for 2,000	17,000	$120	16%
Ikram Butt	Reengineering for Success	8,000	$130	19%

Bundled Product Sales

Title	Units Sold	Selling Price
Negotiating for Win-Win + Marketing	12,000	$210
Negotiating for Win-Win + Reengineering	5,000	$220
Marketing + Reengineering	4,000	$140
Negotiating + Marketing + Reengineering	11,000	$280

REQUIRED

1. Allocate the bundled product revenues to the individual videos using the stand-alone revenue-allocation method (using unit selling prices).
2. What total royalty payments are made to Smith, Newlove, and Butt using the stand-alone revenue-allocation method?
3. Describe an alternative method of allocating the bundled product revenues to that in requirement 1.

SOLUTION

1. The weights in the stand-alone method are based on the unit selling prices of the videos in the bundled package. The footnotes in the following table detail these weights, which are then used to allocate the revenues of each bundled package to the three individual videos.

Allocation Formula		Negotiating	Marketing	Reengineering
N + M:	$0.56^* \times \$210 \times 12{,}000$	$1,411,200		
N + R:	$0.54^\dagger \times \$220 \times 5{,}000$	594,000		
N + M + R:	$0.375^\ddagger \times \$280 \times 11{,}000$	1,155,000		
Total		$3,160,200		
M + N:	$0.44^\S \times \$210 \times 12{,}000$		$1,108,800	
M + R:	$0.48^\# \times \$190 \times 4{,}000$		364,800	
M + N + R:	$0.30^\parallel \times \$280 \times 11{,}000$		924,000	
Total			$2,397,600	
R + N:	$0.46^\# \times \$220 \times 5{,}000$			$ 506,000
R + M:	$0.52^{\dagger\dagger} \times \$190 \times 4{,}000$			395,200
R + N + M:	$0.325^{\ddagger\ddagger} \times \$280 \times 11{,}000$			1,001,000
Total				$1,902,200

*$150/$270
†$150/$280
‡$150/$400
§$120/$270
$^\#$$120/$250
$^\parallel$$120/$400
**$130/$280
††$130/$250
‡‡$130/$400

2.

		Negotiating	Marketing	Reengineering
A:	Individual Sales			
	$150 × 25,000	$3,750,000		
	$120 × 17,000		$2,040,000	
	$130 × 8,000			$1,040,000
B:	Bundled Sales			
	(from requirement			
	1's solution)	3,160,200	2,397,600	1,902,200
C = A + B:	Total revenues	$6,910,200	$4,437,600	$2,942,200
D:	Royalty Rate	24%	16%	19%
E = C × D:	Royalty payment	$1,658,448	$ 710,016	$ 559,018

3. An alternative approach to allocating the bundled product revenues is the incremental revenue-allocation method. Here the individual videos in the bundle are ranked in order of importance and the revenues allocated to each product using stand-alone selling prices until all the bundled revenue has been fully allocated. Use of this approach would likely create some friction among the three business speakers. It would be in each speaker's interest to claim to be the primary speaker driving sales of the bundle. The actual 19_7 units sold figures would enable Business Horizons to give a market-success-based ranking of individual business speakers if it used the incremental revenue-allocation method.

SUMMARY

The following points are linked to the chapter's learning objectives.

1. Revenue tracing occurs where revenues can be identified with an individual product (services, customer, and so on) in an economically feasible (cost-effective) way. Revenue allocation occurs when revenues, related but not traceable to individual products, are assigned to those individual products.

2. Individual products can differ sizably in their percentage revenue adjustments for such items as sales returns and price offset coupon usage. Companies that use broad averages to adjust revenues can cause the actual revenues of individual products to be misstated. Advances in information technology are making it possible to trace revenue adjustments to individual products (or customers) and thus avoid the inaccuracies arising from peanut-butter broad averaging of revenue restatements and offsets.

3. Companies are increasingly packaging two or more products that are sold independently into a bundled product that sells for a single price. Two methods for allocating the revenue of the bundled product to the individual products are the stand-alone revenue-allocation method and the incremental revenue-allocation method.

4. A sales-volume variance can occur because of (a) a change in the actual unit sales from the budgeted unit sales (a sales-quantity variance), and (b) a change in the actual sales mix from the budgeted sales mix (a sales-mix variance). Sales-quantity and sales-mix variances can be computed for companies selling multiple products or services or the same product or service in multiple markets.

5. The sales-quantity variance can occur because of (a) a change in the actual market size in units from that budgeted (the market-size variance), and (b) a change in the actual share of the market compared to its budgeted share (the market-share variance).

6. Price discounting is the practice of reducing selling prices below listed levels to encourage increased purchases. Separate tracking of price discounting across individual customers enables managers to determine whether price discounting is an important reason for customer differences in revenues and profitability.

7. Customer-profitability reports, shown in a cumulative form, often reveal that a small percentage of customers contributes a large percentage of profits. It is important that companies devote sufficient resources to maintaining and expanding relationships with these key contributors to profitability.

8. Customer-cost hierarchies are being used by companies such as General Motors and Hewlett-Packard to determine how some costs can be reliably assigned to individual customers while others can only be reliably assigned to distribution channels or to general corporatewide efforts. The result is that not all costs are "fully loaded" onto each individual customer.

▼ TERMS TO LEARN

This chapter and the Glossary at the end of this book contain definitions of the following important terms:

bundled product (p. 578)	market-size variance (586)
composite product unit (584)	price discounting (591)
customer-cost hierarchy (595)	revenue allocation (576)
customer-profitability analysis (590)	revenue tracing (576)
customer revenues (590)	sales-mix variance (583)
incremental revenue-allocation	sales-quantity variance (583)
method (580)	stand-alone revenue-allocation
market-share variance (586)	method (579)

▼ ASSIGNMENT MATERIAL

QUESTIONS

16-1 Distinguish between revenue tracing and revenue allocation.

16-2 Why do companies make provisions for sales returns and how might these provisions be determined?

16-3 "Broad averaging via peanut-butter revenue adjustments is equivalent to broad averaging via peanut-butter costing." Do you agree?

16-4 Describe how companies are increasingly facing revenue-allocation decisions.

16-5 Distinguish between the stand-alone revenue-allocation method and the incremental revenue-allocation method.

16-6 Show how managers can gain insight into the causes of a sales-volume variance by drilling down into the components of this variance.

16-7 How can the concept of a composite unit be used to explain why an unfavorable total sales-mix variance for revenues occurs?

16-8 Explain why a favorable sales-quantity variance occurs.

16-9 Distinguish between a market-size variance and a market-share variance.

16-10 Why might some companies not compute market-size and market-share variances?

16-11 Why is customer-profitability analysis a vitally important topic to managers?

16-12 How can the extent of price discounting be tracked on a customer-by-customer basis?

16-13 How can differences across companies in their profitability be highlighted?

16-14 "A customer-profitability profile highlights those customers that should be dropped to improve profitability." Do you agree?

16-15 Give an example of three types of different levels of costs in a customer-cost hierarchy.

EXERCISES

16-16 Revenue tracing, sales returns. Southern Business (SB) publishes three textbook study guides used in college courses. Sales of these study guides in 19_7 were

Title	Gross Unit Sales	% Unit Returns	Wholesale Selling Price	Author Royalty
◆ Introduction to Marketing	22,000	3%	$20.00	17%
◆ Principles of Economics	17,000	22%	20.00	15%
◆ Corporate Finance	11,000	12%	20.00	15%

Returned study guides cannot be resold. Authors are paid a royalty on the dollar amount of net revenues (gross wholesale revenues minus returns).

Up to 19_6, SB did not have reliable information on individual title sales returns. Books could be returned to any university book store, not all of whom kept detailed records on the titles of returns. Up to 19_6, SB used an average return percentage of gross revenues on all its titles when computing the net revenues on each study guide.

Starting in 19_6, SB required all its sales outlets to detail sales returns by individual title. The result was that SB is now able to compute more accurate net revenue figures for each individual title it sells.

REQUIRED

1. What is the actual average return percentage of gross revenues for the three titles sold by SB in 19_7?
2. Why is the use of an actual average return percentage on all titles an example of peanut-butter revenue adjustments? Why might companies adopt this approach?
3. Compute the royalties paid to each author by SB in 19_7 using
   a. The actual average sales return on all three titles
   b. The actual sales return applicable to that title
   Comment on the results.

16-17 Revenue allocation, bundled products. Pebble Resorts operates a five-star hotel with a world-recognized championship golf course. It has a decentralized management structure. There are three divisions:

◆ Lodging (rooms, conference facilities)
◆ Food (restaurants and in-room service)
◆ Recreation (the golf course, tennis courts, and so on)

Starting next month, Pebble will offer a two-day, two-person "getaway package" deal for $700. This deal includes

◆ Two nights' stay for two in an ocean view room—separately priced at $640 ($320 per night for two).
◆ Two rounds of golf separately priced at $300 ($150 per round). One person can do two rounds, or two can do one round each.
◆ Candlelite dinner for two at the exclusive Pebble Pacific Restaurant— separately priced at $80 per person.

Samantha Lee, president of the Recreation Division, recently asked the CEO of Pebble Resorts how her division would share in the $700 revenue from the package. The golf course was operating at 100% capacity (and then some). Under the "getaway package" rules, participants who booked one week in advance were guaranteed access to the golf course. Lee noted that every "getaway" booking would displace a $150 booking. She stressed that the high demand reflected the devotion of her team to keeping the golf course rated in the "Best 10 Courses in the World" listings in *Golf Monthly*. As an aside she also noted that the Lodging and Food divisions only had to turn away customers on "peak season events such as the New Year's period."

REQUIRED

1. Allocate the $700 "getaway package" revenue to the three divisions using
   a. The stand-alone revenue-allocation method
   b. The incremental revenue-allocation method (with recreation first, then lodging, and then food)
   Use unit selling prices as the weights in a. and b.
2. What are the pros and cons of (a) and (b) in requirement 1?

16-18 **Revenue allocation, bundled products, additional complexities (continuation of 16-17).** The individual items in the "getaway package" deal at Pebble Resorts are not fully used by each guest. Assume that 10% of the "getaway package" users in its first month do not use the golfing option, while 5% do not use the food option. The lodging option has a 100% usage rate.

REQUIRED

How should Pebble Resorts recognize this nonuse factor in its revenue sharing of the $700 package across the Lodging, Food, and Recreation Divisions?

16-19 **Variance analysis of revenues, multiple products.** The Detroit Penguins play in the American Ice Hockey League. The Penguins play in the Downtown Arena (owned and managed by the City of Detroit), which has a capacity of 30,000 seats (10,000 lower-tier seats and 20,000 upper-tier seats). The Downtown Arena charges the Penguins a per-ticket charge for use of their facility. All tickets are sold by the Reservation Network, which charges the Penguins a reservation fee per ticket. The Penguins budgeted net revenue for each type of ticket in 19_7 is computed as follows:

	Lower-Tier Tickets	Upper-Tier Tickets
Selling price	$35	$14
Downtown Arena fee	10	6
Reservation Network fee	5	3
Net revenue per ticket	20	5

The budgeted and actual average attendance figures per game in the 19_7 season are

	Budgeted Seats Sold	Actual Seats Sold
Lower-tier	8,000	6,600
Upper-tier	12,000	15,400
Total	20,000	22,000

There was no difference between the budgeted and actual net revenue for lower-tier or upper-tier seats.

The manager of the Penguins was delighted that actual attendance was 10% above budgeted attendance per game, especially given the depressed state of the local economy in the past 6 months.

REQUIRED

1. Compute the sales-volume variance for individual "product" net revenues and total net revenues for the Detroit Penguins in 19_7.
2. Compute the sales-quantity and sales-mix variances for individual "product" net revenues and total net revenues in 19_7.

3. Present a summary of the variances in requirements 1 and 2. Comment on the results.

16-20 Variance analysis of contribution margin, multiple products; working backward. The Jinwa Corporation sells two brands of wine glasses—Plain and Chic. Jinwa provides the following information for sales in the month of June 19_7:

Static-budget total contribution margin	$5,600
Budgeted units to be sold of all glasses in June 19_7	2,000 units
Budgeted contribution margin per unit of Plain	$2 per unit
Budgeted contribution margin per unit of Chic	$6 per unit
Total sales-quantity variance	$1,400 U
Actual sales-mix percentage of Plain	60%

All variances are to be computed in contribution-margin terms.

REQUIRED

1. Calculate the sales-quantity variances for each product for June 19_7.
2. Calculate the individual product and total sales-mix variances for June 19_7. Calculate the individual product and total sales-volume variances for June 19_7.
3. Briefly describe the conclusions you would draw from the variances.

16-21 Variance analysis of revenues, multiple countries. Cola-King manufactures and sells cola soft drinks in three countries—Canada, Mexico, and the United States. The same product is sold in each market. Budgeted and actual results for 19_8 (all in U.S. dollars) are as follows:

	Budget for 19_8			Actual for 19_8		
Country	Selling Price per Carton	Variable Cost per Carton	Units Sold (Cartons in thousands)	Selling Price per Carton	Variable Cost per Carton	Units Sold (Cartons in thousands)
Canada	$6.00	$4.00	400,000	$6.20	$4.50	480,000
Mexico	$4.00	$2.80	600,000	$4.25	$2.75	900,000
United States	$7.00	$4.50	1,500,000	$6.80	$4.60	1,620,000

REQUIRED

1. Compute a Level 1 to Level 3 variance analysis (Exhibit 16-4) for the revenues of Cola-King. Show results for each country in your computations.
2. What inferences do you make from the variances computed in requirement 1?

16-22 Variance analysis of contribution margin, multiple countries (continuation of 16-21). Repeat Exercise 16-21 for contribution margin. What differences are inferred when the focus is on contribution margin as opposed to revenues?

16-23 Customer profitability, service company. Instant Service (IS) is a repair-service company specializing in the rapid repair of photocopying machines. Each of its ten clients pays a fixed monthly service fee (based on the type of photocopying machines owned by that client and the number of employees at that site). IS keeps records of the time technicians spend at each client as well as the cost of the equipment used to repair each photocopying machine. IS recently decided to compute the profitability of each customer. The following data (in thousands) pertain to May 19_7:

	Customer Revenues	Customer Costs
Avery Group	$260	$182
Duran Systems	180	184
Retail Systems	163	178
Wizard Partners	322	225
Santa Clara College	235	308
Grainger Services	80	74
Software Partners	174	100
Problem Solvers	76	108
Business Systems	137	110
Okie Enterprises	373	231

REQUIRED

1. Compute the operating income of each customer. Prepare exhibits for Instant Service that are similar to Exhibits 16-6 and 16-7. Comment on the results.
2. What options regarding individual customers should Instant Service consider in light of your customer-profitability analysis in requirement 1?
3. What problems might Instant Service encounter in accurately estimating the operating cost of each customer?

16-24 **Customer profitability, distribution.** Figure Four is a distributor of pharmaceutical products. Its activity-based costing system has five activity areas:

Activity Area	Cost Driver and 19_7 Rate
1. Order processing	$40 per order
2. Line item ordering	$3 per line item
3. Store deliveries	$50 per store delivery
4. Carton deliveries	$1 per carton
5. Shelf-stocking	$16 per stocking-hour

Rick Flair, the controller of Figure Four, wants to use this activity-based costing system to examine individual customer profitability within each distribution market. He focuses first on the Ma and Pa single-store distribution market. Two customers are used to exemplify the insights available with the activity-based costing approach. Data pertaining to these two customers in August 19_7 are as follows:

	Charleston Pharmacy	Chapel Hill Pharmacy
Total orders	12	10
Average line items per order	10	18
Total store deliveries	6	10
Average cartons shipped per store delivery	24	20
Average hours of shelf-stocking per store delivery	0	0.5
Average revenue per delivery	$2,400	$1,800
Average cost of goods sold per delivery	$2,100	$1,650

REQUIRED

1. Use the activity-based costing information to compute the operating income of each customer in August 19_7. Comment on the results.

2. Flair ranks the individual customers in the Ma and Pa single-store distribution market on the basis of operating income. The cumulative operating income of the top 20% of customers is $55,680. Figure Four reports negative operating income of $21,247 for the bottom 40% of its customers. Make four recommendations that you think Figure Four should consider in light of this new customer-profitability information.

PROBLEMS

16-25 Revenue tracing, sales returns. Celebrity Posters sells its lines of posters of high-profile sporting celebrities to major sporting stores. Celebrity hires separate photographers for each of five sports. Each photographer is paid a percentage of the net revenues from the sale of the company's posters. Each poster is sold to a sporting store for $12.00. Stores receive a rebate of the $12.00 if one of their customers returns a poster. Prior to the current year, each sporting store reported to Celebrity Posters only a total sales return amount. Posters returned to a sporting store were not resold and were disposed of at no value. Several photographers complained that they were disadvantaged by Celebrity Posters not knowing the actual sales return percentage by individual sport. The hockey photographer claimed his photos were classics and that his sales return percentage "had to be trivial." He made derogatory comments about "the predictability of the basketball poster line" and claimed Celebrity Posters should use him to take both the hockey and basketball photos next year. He argued that the wrestling photos "looked as fake as the sport itself, if you could even call it a sport."

Summary information for 19_7 is:

Sport	Gross Unit Sales	Actual Unit Returns	Photographer Royalty Percentage
Basketball	32,000	1,600	18
Football	25,000	3,000	20
Hockey	20,000	5,000	14
Tennis	12,000	1,200	12
Wrestling	11,000	2,200	12

REQUIRED

1. What is the unit sales return percentage for (a) the average for all five sports in 19_7, and (b) each individual sport?
2. Compute the 19_7 payment to the photographer of each sporting line of posters (a) using the average return percentage for all five sports, and (b) using the actual return percentage for each sport. Comment on your results.
3. Why might Celebrity Posters have used the average return percentage approach in prior years?

16-26 Revenue allocation, bundled products. Athletic Programs (AP) sells exercise videos through television infomercials. It uses a well-known sporting celebrity in each video. Each celebrity receives a share (typically varying between 10% and 25%) of the revenues from sale of that video.

In recent months, AP has started selling their exercise videos in bundled form as well as in individual form. Typically, the bundled products are offered to people who telephone for a specific video after watching an infomercial. Each infomercial is for a specific exercise tape. As a marketing experiment, AP has begun advertising the bundled product at the end of some infomercials in a select set of markets.

Sales in 19_7 of three products that have been sold individually, as well as in bundled form, are as follows:

	Average Retail Price	Net Units Sold	Royalty Paid to Celebrity
Individual Sales			
SuperAbs	$40	27,000	15%
SuperArms	$35	53,000	25%
SuperLegs	$25	20,000	18%
Bundled Product Sales			
SuperAbs + SuperArms	$60	18,000	?
SuperAbs + SuperLegs	$52	6,000	?
SuperArms + SuperLegs	$42	11,000	?
SuperAbs + SuperArms + SuperLegs	$65	22,000	?

The AP infomercials have received widespread recognition.

REQUIRED

1. What royalty would be paid to the celebrity on each tape for the individual sales in 19_7?
2. What royalty would be paid to each celebrity for the bundled product sales in 19_7 using
   a. The stand-alone revenue-allocation method (with average retail price as the weight)?
   b. The incremental revenue-allocation method (with SuperArms ranked 1, SuperAbs 2, and SuperLegs 3)?
3. Discuss the relative merits of the two revenue-allocation methods in requirement 2.
4. Assume the incremental revenue-allocation method is used. What alternative approaches could be used to determine the sequence in which the bundled revenue could be allocated to individual products?

16-27 Variance analysis of contribution margin, multiple products. Debbie's Delight, Inc., operates a chain of cookie stores. Budgeted and actual operating data of its three Chicago stores for August 19_7 are as follows:

Budget for August

	Selling Price per Pound	Variable Costs per Pound	Contribution Margin per Pound	Sales Volume in Pounds
Chocolate chip	$4.50	$2.50	$2.00	45,000
Oatmeal raisin	5.00	2.70	2.30	25,000
Coconut	5.50	2.90	2.60	10,000
White chocolate	6.00	3.00	3.00	5,000
Macadamia nut	6.50	3.40	3.10	15,000
				100,000

Actual for August

	Selling Price per Pound	Variable Costs per Pound	Contribution Margin per Pound	Sales Volume in Pounds
Chocolate chip	$4.50	$2.60	$1.90	57,600
Oatmeal raisin	5.20	2.90	2.30	18,000
Coconut	5.50	2.80	2.70	9,600
White chocolate	6.00	3.40	2.60	13,200
Macadamia nut	7.00	4.00	3.00	21,600
				120,000

Debbie's Delight focuses on contribution margin in its variance analysis.

REQUIRED

1. Compute the individual product and total sales-volume variances for August 19_7.
2. Compute the individual product and total sales-quantity variances for August 19_7.
3. Compute the individual product and total sales-mix variances for August 19_7.
4. Comment on your results in requirements 1, 2, and 3.

16-28 Market-size and market-share variances (continuation of 16-27). Debbie's Delight assumes a 10% market share of the Chicago market and a budgeted total Chicago market for August 19_7 of 1,000,000 sales volume in pounds. The actual total Chicago market for August 19_7 was 960,000 sales volume in pounds.

REQUIRED

Compute the market-size and market-share variances for Debbie's Delight in August 19_7. Report all variances in contribution-margin terms. Comment on the results.

16-29 Variance analysis of contribution margin, multiple products. Computer Horizons manufactures and sells three related microcomputer products:
  a. Plum, sold mostly to college students.
  b. Portable Plum, a smaller version of the Plum that can be carried in a briefcase.
  c. Super Plum, with a larger memory and more capabilities than the Plum and which is targeted at the business market.
  Budgeted and actual operating data for 19_7 are as follows:

Budget for 19_7

	Selling Price per Unit	Variable Costs per Unit	Contribution Margin per Unit	Sales Volume in Units
Plum	$1,200	$ 700	$ 500	700,000
Portable Plum	800	500	300	100,000
Super Plum	5,000	3,000	2,000	200,000
				1,000,000

Actual for 19_7

	Selling Price per Unit	Variable Costs per Unit	Contribution Margin per Unit	Sales Volume in Units
Plum	$1,100	$ 500	$ 600	825,000
Portable Plum	650	400	250	165,000
Super Plum	3,500	2,500	1,000	110,000
				1,100,000

During 19_7, competition sparked by overseas suppliers drove the cost of computer chips down, allowing Computer Horizons to buy key components at bargain prices. Computer Horizons had budgeted for a major expansion into the lucrative microcomputer business market in 19_7. Unfortunately, it underestimated the marketing power of its rival, the Big Blue Company.

Computer Horizons focuses on contribution-margin in its variance analysis.

REQUIRED

1. Compute the individual product and total sales-volume variances for Computer Horizons in 19_7.
2. Compute the individual product and total sales-quantity variances for 19_7.
3. Compute the individual product and total sales-mix variances for 19_7.
4. Comment on your results in requirements 1, 2, and 3.

16-30 Market-size and market-share variances (continuation of 16-29). Computer Horizons derived its total unit sales budget for 19_7 from an internal management estimate of a 20% market share and an industry sales forecast by Micro-Information Services of 5,000,000 units. At the end of 19_7, Micro-Information reported actual industry sales of 6,875,000 units.

REQUIRED

Compute the market-size and market-share variances for Computer Horizons. Report all variances in contribution-margin terms.

16-31 Variance analysis of revenues, multiple countries. Vista Productions markets movies on behalf of independent production companies. It is currently examining the results for Road Warrior, an action movie made in Australia. Vista has marketing rights in five countries. The budgeted and actual results for these five countries for 19_8 are as follows:

	Budget for 19_8		Actual for 19_8	
Country	Revenue per Person	Tickets Sold	Revenue per Person	Tickets Sold
United States	$2.50	5,500,000	$2.40	5,400,000
Canada	2.00	1,800,000	2.05	2,160,000
Japan	2.80	1,200,000	3.10	6,300,000
United Kingdom	2.20	1,000,000	2.10	2,700,000
New Zealand	1.80	500,000	1.90	1,440,000

REQUIRED

1. Conduct a Level 1 to Level 3 variance analysis (see Exhibit 16-4) of the 19_8 revenues for Vista Productions from marketing Road Warrior. Show computations for each country and for the total of all five countries.
2. What conclusions do you draw from your analysis in requirement 1?

16-32 Customer profitability, distribution. Spring Distribution has decided to analyze the profitability of another five customers (see pp. 590-594 of the text). It buys bottled water at $0.50 per bottle and sells to wholesale customers at a list price of $0.60 per bottle. Data pertaining to five customers are:

	Customer				
	P	Q	R	S	T
Bottles sold	50,000	210,000	1,460,000	764,000	94,000
List selling price	$0.60	$0.60	$0.60	$0.60	$0.60
Actual selling price	$0.60	$0.59	$0.55	$0.58	$0.54
Number of purchase orders	15	25	30	25	30
Number of sales visits	2	4	6	2	3
Number of deliveries	10	30	60	40	20
Miles traveled per delivery	14	4	3	8	40
Number of hot-hot runs	0	0	0	0	1

Its five activity areas and their cost drivers are:

Activity Area	Cost Driver and Rate
Order taking	$100 per purchase order
Sales visits	$80 per sales visit
Delivery vehicles	$2 per delivery mile traveled
Product handling	$0.02 per bottle sold
"Hot-hot runs"	$300 per hot-hot run

1. Compute the operating income of each of the five customers now being examined (P, Q, R, S, and T). Comment on the results.
2. What insights are gained by reporting both the list selling price and the actual selling price for each customer?
3. What factors should Spring Distribution consider in deciding whether to drop one or more of customers P, Q, R, S, or T?

16-33 Customer profitability, responsibility for environmental clean-up, ethics. Industrial Fluids, Inc. (IF), manufactures and sells fluids used by metal-cutting plants. These fluids enable metal cutting to be done more accurately and more safely.

IF has over 1,000 customers. It is currently undertaking a customer-profitability analysis. Ariana Papandopolis, a newly hired MBA, is put in charge of the project. One issue in this analysis is IF's liability for its customers' fluid disposal.

Papandopolis discovers that IF may have a responsibility under U.S. environmental legislation for the disposal of toxic waste by its customers. Moreover, she visits ten customer sites and finds dramatic differences in their toxic-waste-handling procedures. She describes one site owned by Acme Metal as an "environmental nightmare about to become a reality." She tells the IF Controller that even if they have only one-half of the responsibility for the clean-up at Acme's site, they will still be facing very high damages. He is displeased at the news. Acme Metal has not paid its account to IF for the last 3 months and has formally announced bankruptcy. He cautions Papandopolis to be careful in her written report. He notes that, "IF does not want any smoking guns in its files in the case of subsequent litigation."

REQUIRED

1. As Papandopolis prepares IF's customer-profitability analysis, how should she handle any estimates of litigation and clean-up costs that IF may be held responsible for?
2. How should Papandopolis handle the Acme Metal situation when she prepares a profitability report for that customer?

COLLABORATIVE LEARNING PROBLEM

16-34 Customer profitability, credit card operations. The Freedom Card is a credit card that competes with national credit cards such as Visa and Master Card. Freedom Card is marketed by the Bay Bank. Mario Verdolini is manager of the Freedom Card division. He is seeking to develop a customer-profitability reporting system. He collects the following information on four users of the Freedom Card:

	Customer			
	A	**B**	**C**	**D**
Annual purchases at retail merchants	$80,000	$26,000	$34,000	$8,000
Customer transactions at retail merchants	800	520	272	200
Membership fee paid	$50	$0	$50	$0
Average annual outstanding balance on credit card on which interest is paid to Bay Bank	$6,000	0	$2,000	$100
Inquiries to Bay Bank	6	12	8	2
Credit card replacement due to loss or theft	0	2	1	0

Customer B pays no membership fee as his card was issued under a special "lifetime promotion program" in which annual fees are waived as long as the card is used at least once a year. Customer D is a student. Bay Bank does not charge a membership fee to student credit card holders at select universities.

Bay Bank has an activity-based costing system that Verdolini can use in his analysis. The following data apply to 19_7:

a. Each customer transaction with a retail merchant costs Bay Bank $0.50 to process.
b. Each customer inquiry to Bay Bank costs $5.
c. Replacing a lost card costs $120.
d. Annual cost to Bay Bank of maintaining a credit card account is $108 (includes sending out monthly statements).

Bay Bank receives 2.0% of the purchase amount from retail merchants when the Freedom Card is used. Bad debts of the Freedom Card in 19_7 were 0.5% of the purchase amounts. Thus, Bay Bank nets 1.5% revenue when its credit card holders use the Freedom Card at retail merchants.

Bay Bank had an interest spread of 9% in 19_7 on the average outstanding balances on which interest is paid by its credit card holders. An interest spread is the difference between what Bay Bank receives from card holders on outstanding balances and what it pays to obtain the funds so used. Thus, on a $500 average annual outstanding balance in 19_7, Bay Bank would receive $45 in interest payment revenues (9% × $500).

INSTRUCTIONS

Form groups of two or more students to complete the following requirements.

REQUIRED

1. Compute the 19_7 customer profitability of the four representative credit card users of The Freedom Card.
2. Develop profiles of (a) profitable card holders, and (b) unprofitable card holders for Bay Bank.
3. Should Bay Bank charge its card holders for making inquiries (such as outstanding balances) or for replacing lost or stolen cards? At present, no such charges are made.
4. Verdolini has an internal proposal that Bay Bank discontinue a sizable number of the low-volume credit card customers. What factors should he consider in evaluating and responding to this proposal?
5. Verdolini seeks your group's advice on an ethical issue he is facing. A chain of gambling casinos (Lucky Roller) has offered to provide Freedom Card holders with money advances of up to $500 at its casinos. Verdolini observes that from a strict financial perspective, providing money advances to its customers was highly profitable in 19_7. Should Freedom Card holders be able to obtain money advances at Lucky Roller gambling casinos?

Milk is processed in a series of standard production steps, and like or similar bottles of milk are mass produced. To compute the cost per bottle of milk, Dean Foods Company uses process costing systems at its various production plants.

LEARNING OBJECTIVES

After studying this chapter, you should be able to

1. Recognize when process-costing systems are used
2. Describe four key steps in process costing
3. Explain equivalent units
4. Prepare journal entries for process-costing systems
5. Demonstrate the weighted-average method of process costing
6. Demonstrate the first-in, first-out (FIFO) method of process costing
7. Show how standard costs simplify process costing
8. Explain weighted-average process-costing with transferred-in costs
9. Explain FIFO process-costing with transferred-in costs

A *process-costing system* is a costing system in which the cost of a product or service is obtained by assigning costs to masses of like or similar units. Unit costs are then computed on an average basis. Process-costing systems are used in industries that cost like or similar units of products, which are often mass produced. In these industries, relatively homogeneous products are processed in a very similar manner and are hence assumed to receive the same amount of direct materials, direct manufacturing labor costs, and manufacturing overhead costs. Industries using process costing in their manufacturing area include chemical processing, oil refining, pharmaceuticals, plastics, brick and tile manufacturing, semiconductor chips, beverages, and breakfast cereals.

The principal difference between process costing and job costing is the extent of averaging used to compute unit costs of products or services. The cost object in a job-costing system is a job that constitutes a distinctly identifiable product or service. Individual jobs use different quantities of manufacturing resources, so it would be incorrect to cost each job at the same average manufacturing cost. In contrast, when like or similar units are mass produced, and not processed as individual jobs, process costing averages manufacturing costs over all units produced.

Knowing what products cost is important information for inventory valuation, pricing decisions, and product profitability analysis. Companies also use product costs to measure how well they are doing in managing and reducing costs. As we examine process costing in this chapter, we will be concerned only incidentally with *planning and control*, which are discussed in other chapters and are applicable to *all* product-costing systems regardless of whether process costing, job costing, or some hybrid system is used.

ILLUSTRATING PROCESS COSTING

The easiest way to learn process costing is by example. Let us consider the following illustration.

EXAMPLE: Global Defense, Inc., manufactures thousands of components for missiles and military equipment. We will focus on the production of one of these components, DG-19. The product-costing system for DG-19 has a single direct-cost category (direct materials) and a single indirect-cost category (conversion costs). Each DG-19 unit passes through two departments—the Assembly Department and the Testing Department. Every effort is made to ensure that all DG-19 units are identical and meet a set of demanding performance specifications. Direct materials are added at the beginning of the process in Assembly. Additional direct materials are added at the end of processing in the Testing Department where final assembly of the DG-19 component occurs. Conversion costs are added evenly during both processes. *Conversion costs* are all manufacturing costs other than direct materials costs. Conversion costs include manufacturing labor, indirect materials, energy, plant depreciation, and so on. When the Testing Department finishes work on each DG-19 component, it is immediately transferred to Finished Goods. The following graphic summarizes these facts:

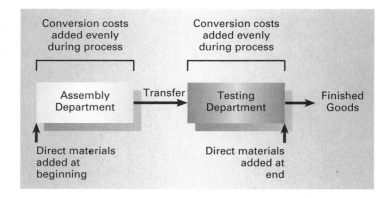

Process Costing in Different Industries

A survey of cost accounting practices in Australian manufacturing companies indicates the widespread use of process-costing systems for product costing across a variety of industries. The reported percentages exceed 100% because several companies surveyed use more than one product costing system.

	Food	Textiles	Primary Metals	Chemicals	Refining
Process costing	96%	91%	92%	75%	100%
Job-order costing	4	18	25	25	25
Other	—	—	8	12	—

	Printing and Publishing	Furniture and Fixtures	Machinery and Computers	Electronics
Process costing	20%	38%	43%	55%
Job-order costing	73	63	65	58
Other	13	—	9	10

The survey data indicate that the use of process costing varies considerably among industries. Process costing is widely used in mass production industries that manufacture homogeneous products—food, textiles, primary metals, chemicals, and refining. In contrast, as we move across the spectrum to industries that produce many distinct and different products, job-order costing is favored over process costing as, for example, in industries like printing and publishing, furniture and fixtures, machinery and computers, and electronics.

Source: Adapted from Joye and Blayney, "Cost and Management Accounting Practices." Full citation is in Appendix A.

We will use the manufacture of the DG-19 component to illustrate three cases:

◆ **Case 1**   Process costing with no beginning or ending work-in-process inventory of DG-19—that is, all units are started and fully completed by the end of the accounting period. *This case illustrates the basic averaging of costs idea that is a key feature of process-costing systems.*

◆ **Case 2**   Process costing with no beginning work-in-process inventory but an ending work-in-process inventory of DG-19—that is, some units of DG-19 started during the accounting period are incomplete at the end of the period. *This case introduces the concept of equivalent units.*

◆ **Case 3**   Process costing with both beginning and ending work-in-process inventory of DG-19. *This case describes the effect of weighted-average and first-in, first-out (FIFO) cost flow assumptions on cost of units completed and cost of work-in-process inventory.*

CASE 1: PROCESS COSTING WITH NO BEGINNING OR ENDING WORK-IN-PROCESS INVENTORY

On January 1, 19_7, there was no beginning inventory of DG-19 units. During January 19_7, Global Defense started, completed assembly, and transferred out to the Testing Department 400 DG-19 units.

Data for the Assembly Department for January 19_7 are

◆ **Physical Units for January 19_7**

Work in process, beginning inventory (January 1)	0 units
Started during January	400 units
Completed and transferred out during January	400 units
Work in process, ending inventory (January 31)	0 units

◆ **Total Costs for January 19_7**

Direct materials costs added during January	$32,000
Conversion costs added during January	24,000
Total Assembly Department costs added during January	$56,000

Global Defense records direct materials and conversion costs in the Assembly Department as these costs are incurred. By averaging, the assembly cost per unit of DG-19 would simply be $56,000 ÷ 400 units = $140, itemized as follows:

Direct materials cost per unit ($32,000 ÷ 400)	$ 80
Conversion costs per unit ($24,000 ÷ 400)	60
Assembly Department cost per unit	$140

This case shows that in a process-costing system, unit costs can be averaged by dividing total costs in a given accounting period by total units produced in that period. Because each unit is identical, we assume that all units receive the same amount of direct materials and conversion costs. This approach can be used by organizations that mass-produce standard units and have no incomplete units when each accounting period ends. This situation frequently occurs in service-sector organizations. For example, banks can adopt this process-costing approach to compute the unit cost of 100,000 similar customer deposits made in a month.

CASE 2: PROCESS COSTING WITH NO BEGINNING BUT AN ENDING WORK-IN-PROCESS INVENTORY

In February 19_7, Global Defense places another 400 units of DG-19 into production. Since the assembly of all units placed into production in January 19_7 had been fully completed, there is no beginning inventory of partially completed units in the Assembly Department on February 1, 19_7. Customer delays in placing orders for DG-19 prevented the complete assembly of all units started in February. Only 175 units were completed and transferred out to the Testing Department.

Data for the Assembly Department for February 19_7 are

◆ **Physical Units for February 19_7**

Work in process, beginning inventory (February 1)	0 units
Started during February	400 units
Completed and transferred out	175 units
Work in process, ending inventory (February 28)	225 units

The 225 partially assembled units as of February 28, 19_7, were fully processed with respect to direct materials. Why? Because all direct materials in the Assembly Department are added at the beginning of the assembly process. Conversion costs are added evenly during the assembly process. Based on the work completed relative to the total work required to be done, an Assembly Department supervisor estimates that the partially assembled units were, on average, 60% complete as to conversion costs.

The accuracy of the completion percentages depends on the care and skill of the estimator and the nature of the process. Estimating the degree of completion is usually easier for direct materials than for conversion costs. The conversion sequence usually consists of a number of basic operations or a specified number of hours, days, weeks, or months for various steps in machining, assembling, testing, and so forth. Thus, the degree of completion for conversion costs depends on what proportion of the total effort needed to complete one unit or one batch has been devoted to units still in process. In industries where no exact estimate is possible or, as in the textile industry, where vast quantities in process prohibit making costly physical estimates, all work in process in every department is assumed to be complete to some reasonable degree (for example, one-third, one-half, or two-thirds complete).

Total Costs for February 19_7

Direct materials costs added during February	$32,000
Conversion costs added during February	18,600
Total Assembly Department costs added during February	$50,600

The key point in this example is that a partially assembled unit is not the same as a fully assembled unit. Faced with some fully assembled and some partially assembled units, how should Global Defense calculate (1) the cost of fully assembled units in February 19_7, and (2) the cost of the partially assembled units still in process at the end of February 19_7?

We can find the answers to these two questions using a process-costing system and the following four steps:

◆ **Step 1** Summarize the flow of physical units of output.
◆ **Step 2** Compute output in terms of equivalent units.
◆ **Step 3** Compute equivalent unit costs.
◆ **Step 4** Summarize total costs to account for and assign these costs to units completed and to units in ending work in process.

Physical Units and Equivalent Units (Steps 1 and 2)

Step 1 tracks the physical units of output. Where did the units come from and how many units are there to account for? Where did they go and how are they accounted for? The physical units column of Exhibit 17-1 tracks where the physical units went—175 units completed and transferred out, and 225 units in ending inventory, and where they came from—400 units started.

In step 2, how should the output for February be measured? The output was 175 fully assembled units plus 225 partially assembled units. Since all physical units of output are not uniformly completed, output in step 2 is stated in *equivalent units*, not in physical units.

Equivalent units measure output in terms of the physical quantities of each of the inputs (factors of production) that have been consumed when producing the units. For example, each equivalent unit of DG-19 is comprised of the physical quantities of direct materials and the conversion costs inputs necessary to produce output of one fully complete unit of DG-19.

Process-costing systems separate costs into cost categories according to the timing of when costs are introduced into the process. Often, only two cost classifications, direct materials and conversion costs, are necessary to assign costs to products, since all conversion costs are generally added to the process at about the same time. If, however, manufacturing labor is added to the process at different times than other conversion costs, an additional cost category (direct manufacturing labor costs) would be used for separately assigning these costs to products. Equivalent units are calculated separately for each cost category. Instead of thinking of output in terms of physical units, think of output in terms of the quantities of completed units that can be made from inputs of direct materials and conversion costs. *Disregard dollar amounts until equivalent units are computed.*

All 400 units, the 175 fully assembled ones and the 225 partially assembled ones, are complete in terms of equivalent units of direct materials. Why? Because all direct materials are added in the Assembly Department at the initial stage of the process. Exhibit 17-1 shows output as 400 *equivalent* units of direct materials because all 400 units are fully complete with respect to materials.

The 175 fully assembled units are completely processed with respect to conversion costs. The partially assembled units in ending work in process are 60% complete (on average). Therefore, the conversion costs in the 225 partially assembled

EXHIBIT 17-1

Steps 1 and 2: Summarize Output in Physical Units and Compute Equivalent Units, Assembly Department of Global Defense, Inc., for February 19_7

		(Step 2) Equivalent Units	
Flow of Production	(Step 1) Physical Units	Direct Materials	Conversion Costs
Completed and transferred out during current period	175	175	175
Add work in process, ending* 225 × 100%; 225 × 60%	225	225	135
Total accounted for	400	400	310
Deduct work in process, beginning	0	0	0
Started during current period	400		
Work done in current period only		400	310

*Degree of completion in this department: direct materials, 100%; conversion costs, 60%.

units is *equivalent* to conversion costs in 135 (60% of 225) fully assembled units. Hence, Exhibit 17-1 shows output as 310 *equivalent* units of conversion costs—175 equivalent units assembled and transferred out and 135 equivalent units in ending work-in-process inventory.

Calculation of Product Costs (Steps 3 and 4)

Exhibit 17-2 shows step 3: computing equivalent unit costs. Step 3 calculates equivalent unit costs by dividing direct materials and conversion costs added during February by the related quantity of equivalent units of work done in February calculated in Exhibit 17-1.

We can see the importance of using equivalent units in unit cost calculations by comparing conversion costs for the months of January and February 19_7. Observe that the total conversion costs of $18,600 for the 400 units worked on during February are less than the conversion costs of $24,000 for the 400 units worked on in January. However, the conversion costs to fully assemble a unit are $60 in both January and February. Total conversion costs are lower in February because fewer equivalent units of conversion costs work were completed in February (310) than in January (400). If, however, we had used physical units instead of equivalent units in the per unit calculation, we would have erroneously concluded that conversion costs per unit declined from $60 in January to $46.50 ($18,600 ÷ 400) in February. This incorrect costing might have prompted Global Defense, for example, to inappropriately lower the price of DG-19.

Exhibit 17-3 presents step 4: summarizing total costs to account for, and assigning these costs to units completed and transferred out and to units still in process at the end of February 19_7. Panel A of Exhibit 17-3 summarizes the total costs to be

EXHIBIT 17-2

Step 3: Compute Equivalent Unit Costs, Assembly Department of Global Defense, Inc., for February 19_7

	Direct Materials	Conversion Costs
Costs added during February (given, p. 615)	$32,000	$18,600
Divide by equivalent units of work done in February 19_7 (from Exhibit 17-1)	÷ 400	÷ 310
Cost per equivalent unit of work done in February 19_7	$ 80	$ 60

EXHIBIT 17-3
Step 4: Summarize Total Costs to Account for and Assign These Costs to Units Completed
and to Units in Ending Work in Process, Assembly Department of Global Defense, Inc.,
for February 19_7

	Direct Materials			**Conversion Costs**			**Total Prod. Costs**
	Equiv. Units (1)	Cost per Equiv. Unit (2)	Total Costs (3)= (1)×(2)	Equiv. Units (4)	Cost per Equiv. Unit (5)	Total Costs (6)= (4)×(5)	(7)= (3)+(6)
PANEL A: **TOTAL COSTS TO ACCOUNT FOR**							
Work done in February (from Exhibit 17-2)	400	$80	$32,000	310	$60	$18,600	$50,600
PANEL B: **ASSIGNMENT OF COSTS**							
Completed and transferred out (175 physical units)	175*	$80	$14,000	175*	$60	$10,500	$24,500
Work in process, ending (225 physical units)	225*	$80	18,000	135*	$60	8,100	26,100
Accounted for	400		$32,000	310		$18,600	$50,600

*From Exhibit 17-1.

accounted for (that is, the total charges or debits to Work in Process) in February 19_7. Since the beginning balance of the work-in-process inventory is zero, total costs to account for consist of the costs added during February: direct materials, $32,000 and conversion costs, $18,600.

Panel B of Exhibit 17-3 shows how costs are assigned to units completed and transferred out and to units in ending inventory. For example, the 225 physical units in work in process are completely processed with respect to direct materials. Therefore, direct materials costs are 225 equivalent units times $80, which equals $18,000. In contrast, the 225 physical units are 60% complete with respect to conversion costs. Therefore, the conversion costs are 135 equivalent units (60% of 225 physical units) times $60, which equals $8,100. The total cost of ending work in process equals $26,100 ($18,000 + $8,100).

Journal Entries

OBJECTIVE 4

Prepare journal entries for process-costing systems

Process-costing journal entries are basically like those made in the job-costing system. That is, direct materials and conversion costs are accounted for as in job-costing systems. The main difference is that, in process costing, there is often more than one Work-in-Process account—in our example, Work in Process—Assembly and Work in Process—Testing. Global Defense purchases direct materials as needed. These materials are delivered directly to the Assembly Department. Using dollar amounts from Exhibit 17-3, summary journal entries for the month of February at Global Defense, Inc., are

1. Work in Process—Assembly   32,000
       Accounts Payable   32,000
   To record direct materials purchased and
   used in production during February.

2. Work in Process—Assembly   18,600
       Various accounts   18,600
   To record Assembly Department conversion costs
   for February; examples include energy,
   manufacturing supplies, all manufacturing
   labor, and plant depreciation.

3. Work in Process—Testing   24,500
       Work in Process—Assembly   24,500
   To record cost of goods completed and transferred from
   Assembly to Testing during February.

Exhibit 17-4 shows a general sketch of the flow of costs through the T-accounts. The key T-account, Work in Process—Assembly, shows an ending balance of $26,100.

EXHIBIT 17-4
Flow of Costs in a Process-Costing System, Assembly Department of Global Defense, Inc., for February 19_7

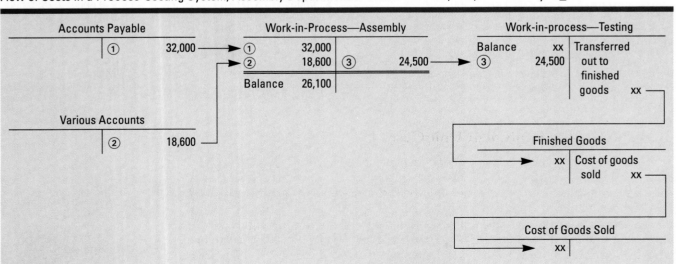

CASE 3: PROCESS COSTING WITH BOTH BEGINNING AND ENDING WORK-IN-PROCESS INVENTORY

At the beginning of March 19_7, Global Defense had 225 partially assembled DG-19 units in the Assembly Department. During March 19_7, Global Defense placed another 275 units into production. Data for the Assembly Department for March 19_7 are

Physical Units for March 19_7

Work in process, beginning inventory (March 1)	225 units
Direct materials (100% complete)	
Conversion costs (60% complete)	
Started during March	275 units
Completed and transferred out during March	400 units
Work in process, ending inventory (March 31)	100 units
Direct materials (100% complete)	
Conversion costs (50% complete)	

Total Costs for March 19_7

Work in process, beginning inventory		
Direct materials	$18,000	
Conversion costs	8,100	$26,100
Direct materials costs added during March		19,800
Conversion costs added during March		16,380
Total costs to account for		$62,280

We follow the four steps introduced earlier in Case 2. However, we now have incomplete units of beginning work-in-process inventory to account for.

Step 1: Summarize the Flow of Physical Units

Step 1 traces the physical units of production. The physical units column of Exhibit 17-5 shows where the units went—400 units completed and transferred out and 100 units in ending inventory, and where they came from—225 units from beginning inventory and 275 units started during the current period.

Step 2: Compute Output in Terms of Equivalent Units

As we saw in Case 2, even partially assembled units are complete in terms of direct materials since direct materials are introduced at the beginning of the process. For conversion costs, the fully assembled physical units transferred out are fully completed. The Assembly Department supervisor estimates the partially assembled physical units in March 31 work in process to be 50% complete (on average). Recall from Case 2 that the partially assembled physical units on February 28, 19_7, which is the beginning work-in-process inventory for March, had been estimated to be 60% complete on average. Exhibit 17-5 shows equivalent units of work done in March to equal 275 equivalent units of direct materials and 315 equivalent units of conversion costs.

Step 3: Compute Equivalent Unit Costs

Exhibit 17-6 shows the computation of equivalent unit costs for the units in beginning work-in-process inventory and for the work done in the current period. It also calculates equivalent unit costs separately for direct materials and conversion costs. You can see that the equivalent unit assembly costs for work done in February (that is, on units currently in beginning work in process) are slightly higher than the equivalent unit assembly costs for work done in March. Global Defense has reduced costs by becoming more efficient. Costs in March are also lower because of a decline in the prices of direct materials and conversion costs inputs.

EXHIBIT 17-5

Steps 1 and 2: Summarize Output in Physical Units and Compute Equivalent Units, Assembly Department of Global Defense, Inc., for March 19_7

| | | (Step 2) Equivalent Units | |
| | (Step 1) Physical Units | Direct Materials | Conversion Costs |
Flow of Production			
Completed and transferred out during current period	400	400	400
Add work in process, ending* 100 × 100%; 100 × 50%	100	100	50
Total accounted for	500	500	450
Deduct work in process, beginning† 225 × 100%; 225 × 60%	225	225	135
Started during current period	275		
Work done in current period only		275	315

* Degree of completion in this department: direct materials, 100%; conversion costs, 50%.
† Degree of completion in this department: direct materials, 100%; conversion costs, 60%.

EXHIBIT 17-6

Step 3: Compute Equivalent Unit Costs, Assembly Department of Global Defense, Inc., for March 19_7

	Direct Materials	Conversion Costs
Equivalent unit costs of beginning work in process		
Work in process, beginning (given, p. 619)	$18,000	$ 8,100
Divide by equivalent units of beginning work in process (from Exhibit 17-5)	÷ 225	÷ 135
Cost per equivalent unit of beginning work in process	$ 80	$ 60
Equivalent unit costs of work done in current period only		
Costs added in current period (given, p. 619)	$19,800	$16,380
Divide by equivalent units of work done in current period (from Exhibit 17-5)	÷ 275	÷ 315
Cost per equivalent unit of work done in current period only	$ 72	$ 52

Step 4: Summarize Total Costs to Account for, and Assign These Costs to Units Completed and to Units in Ending Work in Process

The key points in this step (also called prepare a production cost report) are to calculate (1) the cost of units completed and transferred out, and (2) the cost of ending work in process. The costs that get assigned to each of these categories depend, *as in all inventory accounting*, on the specific assumptions regarding the flow of costs. We next describe two alternative methods—the weighted-average method and the first-in, first-out method.

WEIGHTED-AVERAGE METHOD

The **weighted-average process-costing method** assigns the average equivalent unit cost of all work done to date (regardless of when it was done) to equivalent units completed and transferred out, and to equivalent units in ending inventory. The weighted-average cost is simply the average of various equivalent unit costs entering the Work in Process account.

Exhibit 17-7 presents step 4 using the weighted-average method. The total costs columns in Panel A of Exhibit 17-7 summarize the total costs to be accounted

EXHIBIT 17-7

Step 4: Summarize Total Costs to Account for, and Assign These Costs to Units Completed and to Units in Ending Work in Process Using the Weighed Average Method, Assembly Department of Global Defense, Inc., for March 19_7

	Direct Materials			Conversion Costs			Total Prod. Costs
	Equiv. Units (1)	Cost per Equiv. Unit (2)	Total Costs (3) = (1)×(2)	Equiv. Units (4)	Cost per Equiv. Unit (5)	Total Costs (6) = (4)×(5)	(7) = (3)+(6)
PANEL A: **TOTAL COSTS TO ACCOUNT FOR**							
Work in process, beginning (from Exhibit 17-6)	225	$80.00	$18,000	135	$60.00	$ 8,100	$26,100
Work done in current period only (from Exhibit 17-6)	275	$72.00	19,800	315	$52.00	16,380	36,180
To account for	500	$75.60*	$37,800	450	$54.40[†]	$24,480	$62,280
PANEL B: **ASSIGNMENT OF COSTS**							
Completed and transferred out (400 physical units)	400[‡]	$75.60	$30,240	400[‡]	$54.40	$21,760	$52,000
Work in process, ending (100 physical units)	100[‡]	$75.60	7,560	50[‡]	$54.40	2,720	10,280
Accounted for	500		$37,800	450		$24,480	$62,280

*Weighted-average cost per equivalent unit of direct materials = Total direct materials costs divided by total equivalent units of direct materials: $37,800 ÷ 500 = $75.60.

[†]Weighted-average cost per equivalent unit of conversion costs = Total conversion costs divided by total equivalent units of conversion costs: $24,480 ÷ 450 = $54.40.

[‡]From Exhibit 17-5.

for in March 19_7 as described in the example data on p. 619—beginning work in process, $26,100 (direct materials, $18,000; conversion costs, $8,100); direct materials costs added during March, $19,800; and conversion costs added during March, $16,380 for a total of $62,280.

The weighted-average calculation has two main components: (1) the calculation of the weighted-average cost per equivalent unit described in Panel A and (2) the assignment of costs to units completed (and transferred out) and to units in ending work in process. The calculations in Panel A of Exhibit 17-7 demonstrate the heart of the weighted-average method.

The weighted-average method takes into account all work done to date by totaling costs for beginning work in process and costs for work done in the current period, and totaling equivalent units for beginning work in process and for work done in the current period. The weighted-average cost per equivalent unit is obtained by dividing total costs by the total equivalent units. For example, the weighted-average cost per equivalent unit of conversion costs in Exhibit 17-7 equals:

◆ Total conversion costs (beginning WIP, $8,100 plus
  work done in current period, $16,380) $24,480
◆ Divided by total equivalent units of conversion costs
  (beginning WIP, 135 units plus work done in current period, 315 units)   ÷ 450
◆ Weighted-average cost per equivalent unit of conversion costs $ 54.40

Panel B of Exhibit 17-7 uses the weighted-average cost per equivalent unit as the key to assigning direct materials costs and conversion costs to equivalent units of all products, whether they have been fully assembled or are partially assembled and remain in work in process. For example, note that the total cost of the 100 physical units in ending work in process consists of

Direct materials
    100 equivalent units × weighted-average cost per equivalent unit, $75.60 $ 7,560
Conversion costs
    50 equivalent units × weighted-average cost per equivalent unit, $54.40   2,720
Total costs of ending work in process $10,280

Note also that the total costs accounted for, $62,280 in Panel B of Exhibit 17-7 equals the total costs to account for in Panel A.

Before proceeding, please pause and review Exhibit 17-7 carefully to check your understanding of the weighted-average method.

Using dollar amounts from Exhibit 17-7, summary journal entries for the month of March at Global Defense, Inc., are

1. Work in Process—Assembly	19,800	
Accounts Payable		19,800
To record direct materials purchased and used in production during March.		
2. Work in Process—Assembly	16,380	
Various accounts		16,380
To record Assembly Department conversion costs for March; examples include energy, manufacturing supplies, all manufacturing labor, and plant depreciation.		
3. Work in Process—Testing	52,000	
Work in Process—Assembly		52,000
To record cost of goods completed and transferred from Assembly to Testing during March.		

The key T-account, Work in Process—Assembly, would show the following:

Work in Process—Assembly

Beginning inventory, March 1	26,100	③ Transferred out to Work in Process—Testing	52,000
① Direct materials	19,800		
② Conversion costs	16,380		
Ending inventory, March 31	10,280		

The **first-in, first-out (FIFO) process-costing method** assigns the cost of the earliest equivalent units available (starting with the equivalent units in beginning work-in-process inventory) to units completed and transferred out, and the cost of the most recent equivalent units worked on during the period to ending work-in-process inventory. This method assumes that the earliest equivalent units in Work in Process—Assembly account are completed first.

Exhibit 17-8 presents step 4—summarizing total costs to account for, and assigning costs to units completed and to ending work in process—using the FIFO method. The total costs columns in Panel A of Exhibit 17-8 summarize the total costs to be accounted for in March 19_7 of $62,280 as described in the Example data (p. 619).

Panel B of Exhibit 17-8 describes the assignment of costs under FIFO. The FIFO method assigns the costs of the beginning work-in-process inventory to the first units completed and transferred out. The costs of work done in the current period are first assigned to the additional work done to complete the beginning work in process, then to the work done on units started and completed during the current period, and finally to the ending work in process. Follow these computations in Panel B of Exhibit 17-8. For example, consider conversion costs. The costs of the 135 equivalent units of beginning inventory at $60 per unit are assigned to the first units completed and transferred out. The costs of the 315 equivalent units of work done in March 19_7 at $52 per unit are assigned as follows: (1) The first 90 units to the work done to complete the beginning work in process, (2) the next 175 units to the work done on units started and completed during the current period, and (3) the final 50 units to ending work in process.

[handwritten margin note: *Costs of wk in current period are 1st assigned to addtl. wk done to complete BI-WIP]

Under FIFO, the ending work-in-process inventory comes from units that were started but not fully completed during the current period. The total cost of the 100 partially assembled physical units in ending work in process consists of

Direct materials: 100 equivalent units × cost per equivalent unit in March, $72	$7,200
Conversion costs: 50 equivalent units × cost per equivalent unit in March, $52	2,600
Total costs of work in process on March 31	$9,800

Note that the total costs accounted for in Panel B of Exhibit 17-8, $62,280, equal the total costs to account for in Panel A.

Before proceeding, please pause and review Exhibit 17-8 carefully to check your understanding of the FIFO method. The journal entries and flow of costs through the T-accounts under the FIFO method parallel the journal entries and flow of costs under the weighted-average method and are not repeated here.

The average cost of units transferred out is $52,480 ÷ 400 units = $131.20 per DG-19 unit. The Assembly Department uses FIFO to distinguish between monthly batches of production. The succeeding department, Testing, however, costs these units at one average unit cost ($131.20 in this illustration). If this averaging were not done, the attempt to track costs on a pure FIFO basis throughout a series of processes would be unduly cumbersome.

Only rarely is an application of pure FIFO ever encountered in process costing. It should really be called a *modified* or *departmental* FIFO method. Why? Because FIFO is applied within a department to compile the cost of units transferred *out*, but the units transferred *in* during a given period usually are carried at a single average unit cost as a matter of convenience.

COMPARISON OF WEIGHTED-AVERAGE AND FIFO METHODS

The following table summarizes the costs assigned to units completed and those still in process under the weighted-average and FIFO process-costing methods for our example:

EXHIBIT 17-8
Step 4: Summarize Total Costs to Account for, and Assign These Costs to Units Completed and to Units in Ending Work in Process Using the FIFO Method, Assembly Department of Global Defense, Inc., for March 19_7

(handwritten:)
Units
WIP 225
Started 275
        500
Comp/Trans 400
End WIP 100

	Direct Materials			Conversion Costs			Total Prod. Costs
	Equiv. Units (1)	Cost per Equiv. Unit (2)	Total Costs (3) = (1)×(2)	Equiv. Units (4)	Cost per Equiv. Unit (5)	Total Costs (6) = (4)×(5)	(7) = (3)+(6)
PANEL A: **TOTAL COSTS TO ACCOUNT FOR**							
Work in process, beginning (from Exhibit 17-6)	225	$80	$18,000	135	$60	$ 8,100	$26,100
Work done in current period only (from Exhibit 17-6)	275	$72	19,800	315	$52	16,380	36,180
To account for	500		$37,800	450		$24,480	$62,280
PANEL B: **ASSIGNMENT OF COSTS**							
Completed and transferred out (400 physical units)							
Work in process, beginning (225 physical units)	225	$80	$18,000	135	$60	$ 8,100	$26,100
Work done in current period to complete beginning work in process	0*	$72	0	90†	$52	4,680	4,680
Total from beginning inventory	225		18,000	225		12,780	30,780
Started and completed (175 physical units)	175‡	$72	12,600	175‡	$52	9,100	21,700
Total completed and transferred out (400 physical units)	400		30,600	400		21,880	52,480
Work in process, ending (100 physical units)	100§	$72	7,200	50§	$52	2,600	9,800
Accounted for	500		$37,800	450		$24,480	$62,280

(handwritten annotations near Panel A:) Dm+EU Bea'n WIP ; DM+EU ; Dm+ EU Started ; Dm+ EU Started

(handwritten annotations near Panel B:) 100% complete ; [225−(.60×225)] ; (400 compl. Tran out −225) ; (100 units ×100%) ; (100 units ×50%)

*Beginning work in process is 100% complete as to direct materials so zero equivalent units of direct materials need to be added to complete beginning work in process.
†Beginning work in process is 60% complete, which equals 135 equivalent units of conversion costs. To complete the 225 physical units of beginning work in process, 90 (225 − 135) equivalent units of conversion costs need to be added.
‡400 total equivalent units completed and transferred out (Exhibit 17-5) minus 225 equivalent units completed and transferred from beginning inventory equals 175 equivalent units.
§From Exhibit 17-5.

(handwritten at bottom of page:)
Costs
WIP Begin   18000
  Dm
  cc   8100   26000
Costs Added
  Dm   19800
  cc   16380
Total costs   62280

	Weighted Average (from Exhibit 17-7)	FIFO (from Exhibit 17-8)	Difference
Cost of units completed and transferred out	$52,000	$52,480	+$480
Work in process, ending	10,280	9,800	−$480
Total costs accounted for	$62,280	$62,280	

The weighted-average ending inventory is higher than the FIFO ending inventory by $480, or 4.9% ($480 ÷ $9,800). This is a significant difference when aggregated over the many thousands of components that Global Defense makes. The weighted-average method in our example also results in lower cost of goods sold and hence higher operating income and higher tax payments than the FIFO method. Differences in equivalent unit costs of beginning inventory and work done during the current period account for the differences in weighted-average and FIFO costs. Recall from Exhibit 17-6 that the cost per equivalent unit of beginning work in process was greater than the cost per equivalent unit of work done during the period.

For the Assembly Department, FIFO assumes that all the higher-cost prior-period units in beginning work in process are the first to be completed and transferred out while ending work in process consists of only the lower-cost current-period units. The weighted-average method, however, smoothes out cost per equivalent unit by assuming that more of the lower-cost units are completed and transferred out, while some of the higher-cost units are placed in ending work in process. Hence, in this example, the weighted-average method results in a lower cost of units completed and transferred out and a higher ending work-in-process inventory relative to FIFO.

Unit costs can differ materially between the weighted-average and FIFO methods when (1) the direct materials or conversion costs per unit vary from period to period, and (2) the physical inventory levels of work in process are large in relation to the total number of units transferred out.

Managers need feedback about their most recent performance (March in this illustration) in order to plan and improve their future performance. A major advantage of FIFO is that it gives managers information from which they can judge their performance in the current period independently from that in the preceding period. Work done during the current period is vital information for these planning and control purposes.

STANDARD COSTS AND PROCESS COSTING

This section assumes that you have already studied Chapters 7 and 8. If you have not, proceed to the next major section, Transferred-in Costs in Process Costing (p. 629).

OBJECTIVE 7

Show how standard costs simplify process costing

As we have mentioned, companies that use process-costing systems produce numerous like or similar units of output. Setting standard quantities for inputs is often relatively straightforward in such companies. Standard costs per input unit may then be assigned to the physical standards to develop standard costs.

Weighted-average and FIFO methods become very complicated when used in industries that produce a variety of products. For example, a steel-rolling mill uses various steel alloys and produces sheets of various sizes and of various finishes. The items of direct materials are not numerous; neither are the operations performed. But used in various combinations, they yield too great a variety of products that inaccurate costs for each product result if the broad averaging procedure of historical process costing is used. Similarly complex conditions are frequently found, for example, in plants that manufacture rubber products, textiles, ceramics, paints, and packaged food products. As we shall see, standard costing is especially useful in these situations. The intricacies of weighted-average and FIFO historical costing methods and the conflicts between them are also eliminated by using standard costs.

Computations under Standard Costing

We again use the Assembly Department of Global Defense, Inc., as an example, except this time we assign standard costs to the process. The same standard costs apply in February and March of 19_7:

Direct materials	$ 74 per unit
Conversion costs	54 per unit
Total standard manufacturing costs	$128 per unit

Data for the Assembly Department are

Physical Units for March 19_7

Work in process, beginning inventory (March 1)	225 units
Direct materials (100% complete)	
Conversion costs (60% complete)	
Started during March	275 units
Completed and transferred out during March	400 units
Work in process, ending inventory (March 31)	100 units
Direct materials (100% complete)	
Conversion costs (50% complete)	

Total Costs for March 19_7

Work in process, beginning inventory at standard costs		
Direct materials: 225 equivalent units × $74 per unit	$16,650	
Conversion costs: 135 equivalent units × $54 per unit	7,290	$23,940
Actual direct materials costs added during March		19,800
Actual conversion costs added during March		16,380

We follow the four steps introduced earlier in Case 2. Steps 1 and 2 for standard costing are identical to the steps described for the weighted-average and FIFO methods in Exhibit 17-5. Steps 1 and 2 are the same as before because they measure the same physical and equivalent unit quantities of work done in March. Work done in the current period equals direct materials, 275 equivalent units, and conversion costs, 315 equivalent units.

Step 3 is easier under standard costing than under the weighted-average and FIFO methods. Why? Because the cost per equivalent unit does not have to be computed, as was done for the weighted-average and FIFO methods. Instead, the costs per equivalent unit are the standard costs: direct materials, $74, and conversion costs, $54. Using standard costs simplifies the computations for assigning total costs to account for, costs completed and transferred out, and ending work-in-process inventory. Exhibit 17-9 describes step 4.

Panel A of Exhibit 17-9 summarizes the total costs to account for—that is, the total debits in Work in Process. The debits differ from the debits to Work in Process—Assembly under the actual cost-based weighted-average and FIFO methods explained earlier in the chapter. Why? Because *in standard costing systems* (see Chapters 7 and 8) the debits to the Work in Process account are at standard costs rather than actual costs. These standard costs total $61,300.

Panel B of Exhibit 17-9 assigns total costs to units completed and to units in ending work-in-process inventory. All equivalent units are costed at standard costs. Note how the total costs accounted for in Panel B of Exhibit 17-9, $61,300, equal the total costs to account for in Panel A. If standard costs had changed between February and March 19_7, these costs would be assigned to units completed and to ending work-in-process inventory using the FIFO method described in Exhibit 17-8.

Accounting for Variances

Process-costing systems using standard costs usually accumulate actual costs separately from the inventory accounts. The following is an example. The actual data are recorded in the first two entries. Recall that Global Defense purchases direct

EXHIBIT 17-9

Step 4: Summarize Total Costs to Account for and Assign These Costs to Units Completed and to Units in Ending Work in Process Using Standard Costs, Assembly Department of Global Defense, Inc., for March 19_7

	Direct Materials			**Conversion Costs**			**Total Prod. Costs**
	Equiv. Units (Exh. 17-5) (1)	Cost per Equiv. Unit (2)	Total Costs (3) = (1) × (2)	Equiv. Units (Exh. 17-5) (4)	Cost per Equiv. Unit (5)	Total Costs (6) = (4) × (5)	(7) = (3) + (6)
PANEL A: **TOTAL COSTS TO ACCOUNT FOR**							
Work in process, beginning	225	$74	$16,650	135	$54	$ 7,290	$23,940
Work done in current period only	275	$74	20,350	315	$54	17,010	37,360
To account for	500		$37,000	450		$24,300	$61,300
PANEL B: **ASSIGNMENT OF COSTS**							
Completed and transferred out (400 physical units)	400	$74	$29,600	400	$54	$21,600	$51,200
Work in process, ending (100 physical units)	100	$74	7,400	50	$54	2,700	10,100
Accounted for	500		$37,000	450		$24,300	$61,300

materials as needed and that these materials are delivered directly to the Assembly Department. The total variances are recorded in the next two entries. The final entry transfers out the completed goods at standard costs.

1. Assembly Department Direct Materials Control (at actual)   19,800
    Accounts Payable   19,800
    To record direct materials purchased and used in
    production during March. This cost control
    account is debited with actual costs and credited
    later with standard costs assigned to the units worked on.

2. Assembly Department Conversion Costs Control (at actual)   16,380
    Various accounts   16,380
    To record Assembly Department conversion costs for March.

(*Entries 3, 4, and 5 use standard cost dollar amounts from Exhibit 17-9.*)

3. Work in Process—Assembly (at standard costs)   20,350
    Direct Materials Variances   550
    Assembly Department Direct Materials Control   19,800
    To record actual direct materials used and total direct materials variances.

4. Work in Process—Assembly (at standard costs)   17,010
    Conversion Costs Variances   630
    Assembly Department Conversion Costs Control   16,380
    To record actual conversion costs and total conversion costs variances.

5. Work in Process—Testing (at standard costs)   51,200
    Work in Process—Assembly (at standard costs)   51,200
    To record cost of units completed and transferred
    at standard cost from Assembly to Testing.

Variances arise under the standard costing method, as in entries 3 and 4 above, because the standard costs assigned to products on the basis of work done in the current period do not usually equal the actual costs incurred in the current period. Variances can be measured and analyzed in little or great detail for feedback, control, and decision-making purposes, in the same manner as described in Chapters 7 and 8. Exhibit 17-10 shows how the costs flow through the accounts.

EXHIBIT 17-10
Flow of Standard Costs in a Process-Costing System, Assembly Department of Global Defense, Inc., for March 19_7

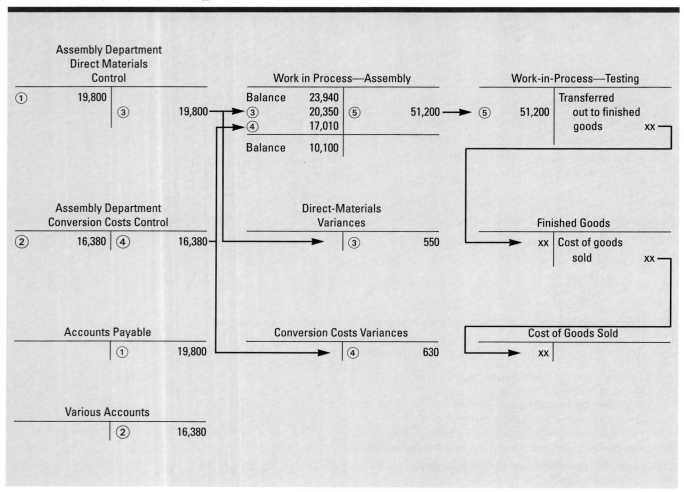

We conclude by explaining the comment we made at the beginning of this section—that standard costs are particularly helpful when a process produces a variety of products. In these situations, historical-cost FIFO and weighted-average methods calculate a *single* average cost for all products produced resulting in inaccurate product costs. Under standard costing, teams of design and process engineers, operations personnel and cost accountants, determine *separate* standard or equivalent unit costs on the basis of the different technical processing specifications for each product. Identifying standard costs for each product overcomes the disadvantage of costing all products at a single average amount as in historical-cost methods.

TRANSFERRED-IN COSTS IN PROCESS COSTING

Many process-costing systems have two or more departments or processes in the production cycle. Ordinarily, as units move from department to department, related costs are also transferred by monthly journal entries. If standard costs are used, the accounting for such transfers is relatively simple. However, if weighted average or FIFO is used, the accounting can become more complex. We now extend our Global Defense, Inc., example to encompass the Testing Department. The Assembly Department of Global Defense transfers DG-19 units to its Testing Department. Here the units receive additional direct materials, such as crating and other packing materials, to prepare the units for shipment, at the *end* of the process. Conversion costs are added evenly during the Testing Department's process. As the process in Assembly is completed, units are immediately transferred to Testing; as units are completed in Testing, they are immediately transferred to Finished Goods.

Data for the Testing Department for the month of March 19_7 are

Physical Units for March 19_7

Work in process, beginning inventory (March 1)	240 units
Transferred-in costs (100% complete)	
Direct materials (0% complete)	
Conversion costs (⅝ or 62.5% complete)	
Transferred-in during March	400 units
Completed during March	440 units
Work in process, ending inventory (March 31)	200 units
Transferred-in costs (100% complete)	
Direct materials (0% complete)	
Conversion costs (80% complete)	

Costs of Testing Department for March 19_7

Work in process, beginning inventory[1]		
Transferred-in costs	$33,600	
Direct materials	0	
Conversion costs	18,000	$51,600
Transferred-in during March		
Weighted average (from Exhibit 17-7)		52,000
FIFO (from Exhibit 17-8)		52,480
Direct materials costs added during March		13,200
Conversion costs added during March		48,600

Transferred-in costs (or **previous department costs**) are costs incurred in a previous department that are carried forward as part of the product's cost as it moves to a subsequent department for processing. That is, as the units move from one department to the next, their costs move with them. Thus, computations of Testing costs must include transferred-in costs, as well as any additional direct materials costs and conversion costs added in Testing.

We use the four-step procedure described earlier (p. 615) to account for the costs of a subsequent department that has transferred-in costs. Exhibit 17-11 shows steps 1 and 2 for Testing: summarize output in physical units and compute equivalent units. Units are fully completed as to transferred-in costs because these costs are just carried forward from the previous process. Direct materials costs, however, have a zero degree of completion in both beginning and ending work-in-process inventories, because in Testing, direct materials are introduced at the end of the process.

[1] The work-in-process beginning inventory is the same under both the weighted-average and FIFO inventory methods because we assumed costs per equivalent unit to be the same in both January and February. If the cost per equivalent unit had been different in February compared to January, the work-in-process inventory at the end of February (beginning of March) would be costed differently under the weighted-average and FIFO methods. If this were the case, the basic approach to process costing with transferred-in costs would still be the same as what we describe in this section. Only the beginning balances of work in process would be different.

Note that the numbers in steps 3 and 4 will differ between the weighted-average and FIFO methods with transferred-in costs. Why? Because differences in transferred-in costs under the two methods result in different debits to Work in Process.

Transferred-in Costs and the Weighted-Average Method

OBJECTIVE 8

Explain weighted-average process-costing with transferred-in costs

Exhibit 17-12 describes step 3, the computation of equivalent unit costs. Exhibit 17-13 presents step 4. Panel A of Exhibit 17-13 summarizes the total costs to account for—that is, the total debits to Work in Process under the weighted-average method. These costs total $165,400. Panel B of Exhibit 17-13 shows how these costs are assigned to units completed and to units in ending work-in-process inventory. Note how beginning work in process and work done in the current period are totaled and merged together for purposes of computing weighted-average costs.

EXHIBIT 17-11

Steps 1 and 2: Summarize Output in Physical Units and Compute Equivalent Units, Testing Department of Global Defense, Inc., for March 19_7

Flow of Production	(Step 1) Physical Units	(Step 2) Equivalent Units		
		Transferred-in Costs	Direct Materials	Conversion Costs
Completed and transferred out during current period	440	440	440	440
Add work in process, ending* (200 × 100%; 200 × 0%; 200 × 80%)	200	200	0	160
Total accounted for	640	640	440	600
Deduct work in process, beginning† (240 × 100%; 240 × 0%; 240 × 62.5%)	240	240	0	150
Transferred in during current period	400			
Work done in current period only		400	440	450

*Degree of completion in this department: transferred-in costs, 100%; direct materials, 0%; conversion costs, 80%.
†Degree of completion in this department: transferred-in costs, 100%; direct materials, 0%; conversion costs, 62.5%.

EXHIBIT 17-12

Step 3: Compute Equivalent Unit Costs under the Weighted-Average Method, Testing Department of Global Defense, Inc., for March 19_7

	Transferred-in Costs	Direct Materials	Conversion Costs
Equivalent unit costs of beginning work in process			
Work in process, beginning (given, p. 630)	$33,600	—	$18,000
Divide by equivalent units of beginning work in process (from Exhibit 17-11)	÷ 240	—	÷ 150
Cost per equivalent unit of beginning work in process	$ 140	—	$ 120
Equivalent unit costs of work done in current period only			
Costs added in current period (given, p. 630)	$52,000	$13,200	$48,600
Divide by equivalent units of work done in current period (from Exhibit 17-11)	÷ 400	÷ 440	÷ 450
Cost per equivalent unit of work done in current period only	$ 130	$ 30	$ 108

EXHIBIT 17-13

Step 4: Summarize Total Costs to Account for, and Assign These Costs to Units Completed and to Units in Ending Work in Process Using the Weighted-Average Method, Testing Department of Global Defense, Inc., for March 19_7

PANEL A:
TOTAL COSTS TO ACCOUNT FOR

	Transferred-in Costs			Direct Materials			Conversion costs			Total Production Costs
	Equivalent Units (1)	Cost per Equivalent Unit (2)	Total Costs (3) = (1) × (2)	Equivalent Units (4)	Cost per Equivalent Unit (5)	Total Costs (6) = (4) × (5)	Equivalent Units (7)	Cost per Equivalent Unit (8)	Total Costs (9) = (7) × (8)	(10) = (3) + (6) + (9)
Work in process, beginning (from Exhibit 17-12)	240	$140.00	$33,600	0	—	$ 0	150	$120	$18,000	$ 51,600
Work done in current period only (from Exhibit 17-12)	400	$130.00	52,000	440	$30	13,200	450	$108	48,600	113,800
To account for	640	$133.75*	$85,600	440	$30†	$13,200	600	$111‡	$66,600	$165,400

PANEL B:
ASSIGNMENT OF COSTS

Completed and transferred out (440 physical units)	440§	$133.75	$58,850	440§	$30	$13,200	440§	$111	$48,840	$120,890
Work in process, ending (200 physical units)	200§	$133.75	26,750	0§	—	0	160§	$111	17,760	44,510
Accounted for	640		$85,600	440		$13,200	600		$66,600	$165,400

*Weighted-average cost per equivalent unit of transferred-in costs = Total transferred-in costs divided by total equivalent units of transferred-in costs = $85,600 ÷ 640 = $133.75.
†Weighted-average costs per equivalent unit of direct materials = Total direct materials costs divided by total equivalent units of direct materials = $13,200 ÷ 440 = $30.
‡Weighted-average cost per equivalent unit of conversion costs = Total conversion costs divided by total equivalent units of conversion costs = $66,600 ÷ 600 = $111.
§From Exhibit 17-11.

Using the dollar amount from Exhibit 17-13 (column 10), the journal entry for the transfer out of Testing to finished goods inventory is

Finished Goods	120,890	
Work in Process—Testing		120,890
To transfer units to finished goods.		

Entries to the key T-account, Work in Process—Testing follow (from Exhibit 17-13).

Work in Process—Testing

Beginning inventory, March 1	51,600	Transferred out	120,890
Transferred-in-costs	52,000		
Direct materials	13,200		
Conversion costs	48,600		
Ending inventory, March 31	44,510		

A company may split the Work in Process account into Work in Process—Testing, Transferred-in Costs, Work in Process—Testing, Direct Materials, and Work in Process—Testing, Conversion Costs. The journal entries would contain this detail, though the underlying reasoning and techniques would be unaffected.

Transferred-in Costs and the FIFO Method

Exhibit 17-14 (p. 634) describes Step 3, the computation of equivalent unit costs. The costs transferred-in from the Assembly Department are different when the weighted-average rather than the FIFO method is used. Exhibit 17-15 (p. 635) presents Step 4. Panel A of Exhibit 17-15 summarizes the total costs to account for, consisting of the beginning inventory plus costs added during the current period, under the FIFO method. These costs totaling $165,880 differ from the total debits to Work in Process under the weighted-average method of $165,400 because of the different costs of completed units transferred-in from the Assembly Department under the weighted-average and FIFO methods. Panel B of Exhibit 17-15 shows how these costs are assigned to units completed and to units in ending work in process inventory. When assigning costs, the FIFO method keeps the beginning inventory separate and distinct from the work done during the current period.

EXHIBIT 17-14

Step 3: Compute Equivalent Unit Costs under the FIFO Method, Testing Department of Global Defense, Inc., for March 19_7

	Transferred-in Costs	Direct Materials	Conversion Costs
Equivalent unit costs of beginning work in process			
Work in process, beginning (given, p. 630)	$33,600	—	$18,000
Divide by equivalent units of beginning work in process (from Exhibit 17-11)	÷ 240	—	+ 150
Cost per equivalent unit of beginning work in process	$ 140	—	$ 120
Equivalent unit costs of work done in current period only			
Costs added in current period (given, p. 630)	$52,480	$13,200	$48,600
Divide by equivalent units of work done in current period (from Exhibit 17-11)	÷ 400	÷ 440	÷ 450
Cost per equivalent unit of work done in current period only	$131.20	$ 30	$ 108

EXHIBIT 17-15 Step 4: Summarize Total Costs to Account for and Assign These Costs to Units Completed and to Units in Ending Work in Process Using the FIFO Method, Testing Department of Global Defense, Inc., for March 19_7

	Transferred-in Costs			Direct Materials			Conversion Costs			Total Production Costs
	Equivalent Units (1)	Cost per Equivalent Unit (2)	Total Costs (3)=(1)×(2)	Equivalent Units (4)	Cost per Equivalent Unit (5)	Total Costs (6)=(4)×(5)	Equivalent Units (7)	Cost per Equivalent Unit (8)	Total Costs (9)=(7)×(8)	(10)=(3)+(6)+(9)
PANEL A:										
TOTAL COSTS TO ACCOUNT FOR										
Work in process, beginning (from Exhibit 17-14)	240	$140.00	$33,600	0	—	$ 0	150	$120	$18,000	$ 51,600
Work done in current period only (from Exhibit 17-14)	400	$131.20	52,480	440	$30	13,200	450	$108	48,600	114,280
To account for	640		$86,080	440		$13,200	600		$66,600	$165,880
PANEL B:										
ASSIGNMENT OF COSTS										
Completed and transferred out (440 physical units)										
Work in process, beginning (240 physical units)	240	$140.00	$33,600	0	—	$ 0	150	$120	$18,000	$ 51,600
Work done in current period to complete beginning work in process	0*		0	240†	$30	7,200	90‡	$108	9,720	16,920
Total from beginning inventory	240		33,600	240		7,200	240		27,720	68,520
Started and completed (200 physical units)	200§	$131.20	26,240	200§	$30	6,000	200§	$108	21,600	53,840
Total completed and transferred out (440 physical units)	440**		59,840	440**		13,200	440**		49,320	122,360
Work in process, ending (200 physical units)	200**	$131.20	26,240	0**	$30	0	160**	$108	17,280	43,520
Accounted for	640		$86,080	440		$13,200	600		$66,600	$165,880

*Beginning work in process is 100% complete as to transferred-in costs so zero equivalent units of transferred-in costs need to be added to complete beginning work in process.   †Beginning work in process is 0% complete, which equals zero equivalent units of direct materials. To complete the 240 physical units of beginning work in process, 240 equivalent units of direct materials need to be added.   ‡Beginning work in process is 62.5% complete, which equals 150 equivalent units of conversion costs.   §440 total equivalent units completed and transferred out (Exhibit 17-11) minus 240 equivalent units completed and transferred from equivalent units of conversion costs need to be added. $ 440 total equivalent units completed and transferred out (Exhibit 17-11) minus 240 equivalent units completed and transferred from beginning inventory equals 200 equivalent units.   **From Exhibit 17-11.

Using the dollar amount from Exhibit 17-15 (column 10) the journal entry for the transfer out to finished goods inventory is

Finished Goods	122,360	
Work in Process—Testing		122,360
To transfer units to finished goods.		

Entries to the key T-account, Work in Process—Testing follow, using information from Exhibit 17-15.

Work in Process—Testing			
Beginning inventory, March 1	51,600	Transferred out	122,360
Transferred-in costs	52,480		
Direct materials	13,200		
Conversion costs	48,600		
Ending inventory, March 31	43,520		

Remember that in a series of interdepartmental transfers, each department is regarded as being separate and distinct for accounting purposes. All costs transferred in during a given accounting period are carried at one unit cost figure, as described when discussing modified FIFO (p. 623), regardless of whether previous departments used the weighted-average or the FIFO method.

Common Mistakes with Transferred-in Costs

Here are some common pitfalls to avoid when accounting for transferred-in costs:

1. Remember to include transferred-in costs from previous departments in your calculations. Such costs should be treated as if they were another kind of direct material added at the beginning of the process. In other words, when successive departments are involved, transferred units from one department become all or a part of the direct materials of the next department; however, they are called transferred-in costs, not direct materials costs.

2. In calculating costs to be transferred on a FIFO basis, do not overlook the costs assigned at the beginning of the period to units that were in process but are now included in the units transferred. For example, do not overlook the $51,600 in Exhibit 17-15.

3. Unit costs may fluctuate between periods. Therefore, transferred units may contain batches accumulated at different unit costs. For example, the 400 units transferred in at $52,480 in Exhibit 17-15 using the FIFO method consist of units that have different unit costs for direct materials and conversion costs when these units were worked on in the Assembly Department (see Exhibit 17-8). Remember, however, that when these units are transferred in to the Testing Department, they are costed at *one* average unit cost of $131.20 ($52,480 ÷ 400) as in Exhibit 17-15.

4. Units may be measured in different terms in different departments. Consider each department separately. Unit costs could be based on kilograms in the first department and liters in the second, so as units are received by the second department, their measurements must be converted to liters.

Process Costing in the Ceramics Industry

Ceramics, Inc., produces ceramic products (such as, multilayer packages for integrated circuits) in a batch flow manufacturing process. Forming and finishing are the two major production stages.

◆ *Forming.* Ceramic material is mixed, forced through an extruder, and sent to a dryer.

◆ *Finishing.* The products are fired in a kiln, cut, ground, and packaged.

For many years Ceramics, Inc., has manufactured like or similar products in large production runs for industrial customers (termed "original equipment manufacturers," or OEMs) such as computer companies and defense companies.

Ceramics, Inc., costs individual products using standard costs in a process-costing system. Cost data are accumulated and tracked for the forming and finishing operations. Conversion costs are allocated to departments using standard (scheduled) hours of production time in each department. Depreciation on plant and equipment is included in this conversion cost. The controller at Ceramics believes that this system "accurately measures the cost of manufacturing OEM products." These products are manufactured in large batches in a highly standardized way.

Ceramics, Inc., recently added a "custom production line" at its plant. This line manufactures ceramic products that vary greatly in production volume and frequently are tailored to each individual customer's needs. For example, custom-designed nozzles used for pollution control are being manufactured for one customer who needs to rid its flue gas of sulfur.

The controller is skeptical about the accuracy of product costs for these custom products based on the existing process-costing system. She believes that the costs of these products are driven by more variables than standard hours in production at each department. For example, many custom jobs require specialized finishing steps that are undertaken in a job shop adjoining the main production area. Currently she is keeping a separate, largely manual job-costing system that uses some data from the main system and some separately maintained cost data.

The controller is now exploring ways to adapt the formal process-costing system to incorporate some elements of a job-costing system. Her point is that custom jobs put different demands on the resources of Ceramics, Inc., than does the average large production run job. For these custom jobs, a hybrid costing system with elements of both process costing and job costing may be appropriate.

Source: Adapted from U. Karmarkar, P. Lederer, and J. Zimmerman, "Choosing Manufacturing Production Control and Cost Accounting Systems," in R. Kaplan, *Measures For Manufacturing Excellence* (Boston, Mass.: Harvard Business School Press, 1990). Ceramics, Inc., is a fictitious name for the actual company.

PROBLEM

Allied Chemicals operates a thermoassembly process as the second of three processes at its plastics plant. Direct materials in thermoassembly are added at the end of the process. The following data pertain to the Thermoassembly Department for June 19_7:

Work in process, beginning inventory	50,000 units
Transferred-in costs (100% complete)	
Direct materials (0% complete)	
Conversion costs (80% complete)	
Transferred in during current period	200,000 units
Completed and transferred out during current period	210,000 units
Work in process, ending inventory	? units
Transferred-in costs (100% complete)	
Direct materials (0% complete)	
Conversion costs (40% complete)	

REQUIRED

Compute the equivalent units for work done in the current period.

SOLUTION

		(Step 2) Equivalent Units		
Flow of Production	(Step 1) Physical Units	Transferred-in Costs	Direct Materials	Conversion Costs
Completed and transferred out during current period	210,000	210,000	210,000	210,000
Add work in process, ending* (40,000 × 100%; 40,000 × 0%; 40,000 × 40%)	40,000	40,000	0	16,000
Total accounted for	250,000			
Deduct work in process, beginning† (50,000 × 100%; 50,000 × 0%; 50,000 × 80%)	50,000	250,000 50,000	210,000 0	226,000 40,000
Transferred in during current period	200,000			
Work done in current period only		200,000	210,000	186,000

*Degree of completion in this department: transferred-in costs, 100%; direct materials, 0%; conversion costs, 40%.

†Degree of completion in this department: transferred-in costs, 100%; direct materials, 0%; conversion costs, 80%.

SUMMARY

The following points are linked to the chapter's learning objectives.

1. Process-costing systems are used in industries like chemical processing, oil refining, and breakfast cereals to cost like or similar products or services. The key feature of process costing is the averaging of costs over a quantity (often large) of these like or similar units.

2. The four key steps in a process-costing system using equivalent units are (a) summarize flow of physical units of output, (b) compute output in terms of equivalent units, (c) compute equivalent unit costs, and (d) summarize total costs to account for, and assign these costs to units completed and to units in ending work in process.

3. An equivalent unit measures output in terms of the physical quantities of inputs necessary to produce one fully complete unit of the product or service. Equivalent unit calculations are necessary when all physical units of output are not uniformly completed.

4. Journal entries in a process-costing system are similar to entries in a job-costing system. The main difference is that in a process-costing system, there is a separate work-in-process account for each department rather than for each job.

5. The weighted-average method of process costing computes unit costs by focusing on the total costs and the total equivalent units completed to date and assigns this average cost to units completed and to units in ending work-in-process inventory.

6. The first-in, first-out (FIFO) method of process costing assigns unit costs of the earliest equivalent units available to units completed, and the unit costs of the most recent equivalent units worked on during the period to ending work-in-process inventory.

7. The use of standard costs simplifies process costing because standard costs directly serve as the costs per equivalent unit when assigning costs to units completed and to units in ending work-in-process inventory.

8. The weighted-average process-costing system for transferred-in costs computes weighted-average costs for transferred-in costs by merging beginning work in process and work done in the current period.

9. The FIFO process-costing system for transferred-in costs assigns transferred-in costs in beginning work in process to units completed, and the costs transferred in during the current period to ending work-in-process inventory.

▼ TERMS TO LEARN

This chapter and the Glossary at the end of this book contain definitions of the following important terms:

equivalent units (p. 615)
first-in, first-out (FIFO) process-
    costing method (623)
previous department costs (630)

transferred-in costs (630)
weighted-average process-costing
    method (620)

▼ ASSIGNMENT MATERIAL

QUESTIONS

17-1 Give three examples of industries that often use process-costing systems.

17-2 In process costing, why are costs often divided into two main classifications?

17-3 Explain equivalent units. Why are equivalent-unit calculations necessary for process costing?

17-4 What problems might arise in estimating the degree of completion of an aircraft blade in a machining shop?

17-5 Name the four key steps in process costing when equivalent units are computed.

17-6 Name the three inventory methods commonly associated with process costing.

17-7 Describe the distinctive characteristic of weighted-average computations in assigning costs to units completed and ending work in process.

17-8 Describe the distinctive characteristic of FIFO computations in assigning costs to units completed and ending work in process.

17-9 Why should the FIFO method be called a modified or departmental FIFO method?

17-10 Identify a major advantage of the FIFO method for purposes of planning and control.

17-11 Identify the main difference between journal entries in process costing and the ones in job costing.

17-12 "Standard cost procedures are particularly applicable to process-costing situations." Do you agree? Why?

17-13 Why should the accountant distinguish between transferred-in costs and additional direct materials costs for a particular department?

17-14 "Previous department costs are those incurred in the preceding accounting period." Do you agree? Explain.

17-15 "There's no reason for me to get excited about the choice between the weighted-average and FIFO methods in my process-costing system. I have long-term contracts with my materials suppliers at fixed prices." State the conditions under which you would (a) agree and (b) disagree with this statement, made by a plant controller. Explain.

EXERCISES

17-16 No beginning inventory. International Electronics manufactures microchips in large quantities. Each microchip undergoes assembly and testing. The total assembly costs during January 19_7 were

Direct materials used	$ 720,000
Conversion costs	760,000
Total manufacturing costs	$1,480,000

REQUIRED

1. Assume there was no beginning inventory on January 1, 19_7. During January, 10,000 microchips were placed into production and all 10,000 microchips were fully completed at the end of January. What is the unit cost of an assembled microchip in January 19_7?

2. Assume that during February 10,000 microchips were placed into production. Further assume the same total assembly costs for January are also incurred in February 19_7, but only 9,000 microchips are fully completed at the end of February. All direct materials had been added to the remaining 1,000 microchips. However, on average, these remaining 1,000 microchips were only 50% complete as to conversion costs. (a) What are the equivalent units for direct materials and conversion costs and their respective equivalent unit costs for February? (b) What is the unit cost of an assembled microchip in February 19_7?

3. Explain the difference in your answers to requirements 1 and 2.

17-17 Journal entries (continuation of 17-16). Refer to requirement 2 of Exercise 17-16.

REQUIRED

Prepare summary journal entries for the use of direct materials and conversion costs. Also prepare a journal entry to transfer out the cost of goods completed. Show the postings to the Work in Process account.

17-18 No beginning inventory, materials introduced in middle of process. Vaasa Chemicals has a mixing department and a refining department. Its process-costing system in the mixing department has two direct materials cost categories (chemical P and chemical Q) and one conversion costs pool. The following data pertain to the mixing department for July 19_7:

Units	
Work in process, July 1	0
Units started	50,000
Completed and transferred to refining department	35,000

Costs	
Chemical P	$250,000
Chemical Q	70,000
Conversion costs	135,000

Chemical P is introduced at the start of operations in the mixing department, and chemical Q is added when the product is three-fourths completed in the mixing department. Conversion costs are added uniformly during the process. The ending work in process in the mixing department is two-thirds completed.

REQUIRED

1. Compute the equivalent units in the mixing department for July 19_7 for each cost element.
2. Compute (a) the cost of goods completed and transferred to the refining department during July, and (b) the cost of work in process as of July 31, 19_7.

17-19 Journal entries (continuation of 17-18). Refer to requirement 2 of Exercise 17-18.

REQUIRED

Prepare journal entries. Assume that the completed goods are transferred to the refining department.

17-20 Equivalent units and equivalent unit costs. Consider the following data for the satellite assembly division of Aerospatiale:

	Physical Units (Satellites)	Direct Materials	Conversion Costs
Beginning work in process, (May 1)*	8	$ 4,968,000	$ 928,000
Started in May 19_7	50		
Completed during May 19_7	46		
Ending work in process (May 31)†	12		
Costs added during May 19_7		$32,200,000	$13,920,000

*Degree of completion: direct materials, 90%; conversion costs, 40%.
†Degree of completion: direct materials, 60%; conversion costs, 30%.

REQUIRED

1. Compute equivalent units of work done in the current period for direct materials and conversion costs. Show physical units in the first column.
2. Calculate cost per equivalent unit of beginning work in process and of work done in the current period for direct materials and conversion costs.

17-21 Weighted-average method. The Chatham Company makes chemical compounds in a single processing department. The following information about equivalent units and actual costs for July 19_7 is available.

	Direct Materials		Conversion Costs	
	Equivalent Units	Total Costs	Equivalent Units	Total Costs
Work in process, July 1*	20,000	$120,000	14,000	$140,000
Work done during July 19_7	30,000	210,000	28,000	301,000
To account for	50,000	$330,000	42,000	$441,000
Completed during July 19_7	34,000		34,000	
Work in process, July 31†	16,000		8,000	

*Degree of completion: direct materials, 100%; conversion costs, 70%.
†Degree of completion: direct materials, 100%; conversion costs, 50%.

Summarize total costs to account for, and assign these costs to units completed (and transferred out) and to units in ending work in process using the weighted-average method.

17-22 FIFO method. Refer to the information in Exercise 17-21.

REQUIRED

Do Exercise 17-21 using the FIFO method.

17-23 Standard costing method. Refer to the information in Exercise 17-21. Suppose Chatham determines standard costs of $6.10 per (equivalent) unit for direct materials and $10.20 per (equivalent) unit for conversion costs for both beginning work in process and work done in the current period.

REQUIRED

1. Do Exercise 17-21 using the standard costing method.
2. Provide journal entries for the total direct materials and conversion costs variances for July 19_7.

17-24 Transferred-in costs, equivalent unit costs, working backwards. Bangkok Plastics has two processes—extrusion and thermoassembly. Consider the June 19_7 data for physical units in the thermoassembly process of Bangkok Plastics: beginning work in process, 15,000 units; transferred in from the Extruding Department during September, 9,000; ending work in process, 5,000. Direct materials are added when the process in the Thermoassembly Department is 80% complete. Conversion costs are added evenly during the process. Bangkok Plastics uses the weighted-average process-costing method. The following information is available.

	Transferred-in Costs	Direct Materials	Conversion Costs
Beginning work-in-process cost	$90,000	—	$45,000
Cost per equivalent unit of beginning work in process	$ 6	—	$ 5
Costs added in current period	$58,500	$57,000	$57,200
Cost per equivalent unit of work done in current period	$ 6.50	$ 3	$ 5.20

REQUIRED

1. For each cost element, compute equivalent units of (a) beginning work in process, and (b) work done in the current period.
2. For each cost element, compute the equivalent units in ending work in process.
3. (a) For each cost element, calculate the percentage of completion of beginning work-in-process inventory, and (b) for each cost element, calculate the percentage of completion of ending work-in-process inventory.

17-25 Transferred-in costs, weighted-average method. Hideo Chemicals manufactures an industrial solvent in two departments—mixing and cooking. This question focuses on the Cooking Department. During June 19_7, 90 tons of solvent were completed and transferred out from the Cooking Department. Direct materials are added at one point in time during the process. Conversion costs are added uniformly during the process. Hideo Chemicals uses the weighted-average process-costing method. The following information about the actual costs for June 19_7 is available.

	Transferred-in Costs		Direct Materials		Conversion Costs	
	Equivalent Tons	Total Costs	Equivalent Tons	Total Costs	Equivalent Tons	Total Costs
Work in process, June 1	40	$40,000	0	$ 0	30	$18,000
Work done in June 19_7	80	$87,200	90	$36,000	75	$49,725
Completed in June 19_7	?	?	?	?	?	?
Work in process, June 30	?	?	?	?	?	?

1. Calculate the equivalent tons of solvent completed and transferred out, and in ending work in process for each cost element.
2. Compute cost per equivalent unit for beginning work in process and work done in current period.
3. Summarize total costs to account for, and assign these costs to units completed (and transferred out) and to units in ending work in process using the weighted-average method.

17-26 Transferred-in costs, FIFO method. Refer to the information in Exercise 17-25. Suppose that Hideo uses the FIFO method instead of the weighted-average method in all its departments. The only changes under the FIFO method are that the total transferred-in cost of beginning work in process is $39,200 and that the cost of work done in the current period is $85,600.

REQUIRED

Do Exercise 17-25 using the FIFO method.

17-27 Transferred-in costs, standard costing method. Refer to the information in Exercise 17-25. Suppose Hideo determines standard costs of $1,050 per (equivalent) ton of transferred-in costs, $390 per (equivalent) ton of direct materials, and $640 per (equivalent) ton of conversion costs for both beginning work in process and work done in the current period.

REQUIRED

Do Exercise 17-25 using the standard costing method.

PROBLEMS

17-28 Weighted-average method. Global Defense, Inc., is a manufacturer of military equipment. Its Santa Fe plant manufactures the Interceptor missile under contract to the U.S. government and friendly countries. All Interceptors go through an identical manufacturing process. Every effort is made to ensure that all Interceptors are identical and meet many demanding performance specifications. The product-costing system at the Santa Fe plant has a single direct-cost category (direct materials) and a single indirect-cost category (conversion costs). Each Interceptor passes through two departments—the Assembly Department and the Testing Department. Direct materials are added at the beginning of the process in Assembly. Conversion costs are added evenly throughout the two departments. When the Assembly Department finishes work on each Interceptor, it is immediately transferred to Testing.

Global Defense uses the weighted-average method of process costing. Data for the Assembly Department for October 19_7 are

	Physical Units (Missiles)	Direct Materials	Conversion Costs
Work in process, October 1*	20	$ 460,000	$120,000
Started during October 19_7	80		
Completed during October 19_7	90		
Work in process, October 31†	10		
Costs added during October 19_7		$2,000,000	$935,000

*Degree of completion: direct materials, ?%; conversion costs, 60%.
†Degree of completion: direct materials, ?%; conversion costs, 70%.

REQUIRED

1. For each cost element, compute equivalent units of work done in October 19_7 in the Assembly Department. Show physical units in the first column.
2. For each cost element, calculate cost per equivalent unit of beginning work in process and of work done in October 19_7.

3. Summarize the total Assembly Department costs for October 19_7, and assign these costs to units completed (and transferred out) and to units in ending work in process using the weighted-average method.

17-29 Journal entries (continuation of 17-28).

REQUIRED

Prepare a set of summarized journal entries for all October 19_7 transactions affecting Work in Process—Assembly. Set up a T-account for Work in Process—Assembly, and post the entries to it.

17-30 FIFO method (continuation of 17-28 and 17-29).

REQUIRED

Do Problem 17-28 using the FIFO method of process costing. Explain any difference between the cost of work completed and transferred out and cost of ending work in process in the Assembly Department under the weighted-average method and the FIFO method.

17-31 Transferred-in costs, weighted average (related to 17-28 to 17-30). Global Defense, Inc., as you know, manufactures the Interceptor missile at its Santa Fe plant. It has two departments—Assembly Department and Testing Department. This problem focuses on the Testing Department. (Problems 17-28 to 17-30 focused on the Assembly Department.) Direct materials are added at the end of the Testing Department. Conversion costs are added evenly during the Testing Department's process. As work in Assembly is completed, each unit is immediately transferred to Testing. As each unit is completed in Testing, it is immediately transferred to Finished Goods.

Global Defense uses the weighted-average method of process costing. Data for the Testing Department for October 19_7 are

	Physical Units (Missiles)	Transferred-in Costs	Direct Materials	Conversion Costs
Work in process, October 1*	30	$ 985,800	$ 0	$ 331,800
Transferred-in during October 19_7	?			
Completed during October 19_7	105			
Work in process, October 31†	15			
Costs added during October 19_7		$3,192,866	$3,885,000	$1,581,000

*Degree of completion: transferred-in costs, ?%; direct materials, ?%; conversion costs, 70%.
†Degree of completion: transferred-in costs, ?%; direct materials, ?%; conversion costs, 60%.

REQUIRED

1. What is the percentage of completion for (a) transferred-in costs and direct materials in beginning work-in-process inventory, and (b) transferred-in costs and direct materials in ending work-in-process inventory?
2. For each cost element, compute equivalent units of work done in October 19_7 in the Testing Department. Show physical units in the first column.
3. For each cost element, calculate the cost per equivalent unit of beginning work in process and of work done in October 19_7.
4. Summarize total Testing Department costs for October 19_7, and assign these costs to units completed (and transferred out) and to units in ending work in process using the weighted-average method.
5. Prepare journal entries for October transfers from the Assembly Department to the Testing Department and from Testing to Finished Goods.

17-32 Transferred-in costs, FIFO costing (continuation of 17-31).

REQUIRED

Using the FIFO process-costing method, do the requirements of Problem 17-31. The transferred-in costs from the Assembly Department for the beginning work in process on October 1 are $980,060. During October, costs transferred in to the Testing Department are $3,188,000. All other data are unchanged.

17-33 Weighted-average method. Star Toys manufactures one type of wooden toy figure. It buys wood as its direct material for the Forming Department of its Madison plant. The toys are transferred to the Finishing Department, where they are hand shaped and metal is added to them.

Star Toys uses the weighted-average method of process costing. Consider the following data for the Forming Department in April 19_7:

	Physical Units (Toys)	Direct Materials	Conversion Costs
Work in process, April 1*	300	$ 7,500	$ 2,125
Started during April 19_7	2,200		
Completed during April 19_7	2,000		
Work in process, April 30†	500		
Costs added during April 19_7		$70,000	$42,500

*Degree of completion: direct materials, 100%; conversion costs, 40%.
†Degree of completion: direct materials, 100%; conversion costs, 25%.

REQUIRED

Summarize the total Forming Department costs for April 19_7, and assign these costs to units completed (and transferred out) and to units in ending work in process using the weighted-average method.

17-34 Journal entries (continuation of 17-33).

REQUIRED

Prepare a set of summarized journal entries for all April transactions affecting Work in Process—Forming. Set up a T-account for Work in Process—Forming, and post the entries to it.

17-35 FIFO computations (continuation of 17-33 and 17-34).

REQUIRED

Do Problem 17-33, using FIFO and four decimal places for unit costs. Explain any difference between the cost of work completed and transferred out and cost of ending work in process in the Forming Department under the weighted-average method and the FIFO method.

17-36 Transferred-in costs, weighted-average (related to 17-33 through 17-35). Star Toys manufactures wooden toy figures at its Madison plant. It has two departments—the Forming Department and the Finishing Department. (Problems 17-33 to 17-35 focused on the Forming Department.) Consider now the Finishing Department, which processes the formed toys through hand shaping and the addition of metal. For simplicity here, suppose all additional direct materials are added at the end of the process. Conversion costs are added evenly during Finishing operations.

Star Toys uses the weighted-average method of process costing. The following is a summary of the April 19_7 operations in the Finishing Department:

	Physical Units (Toys)	Transferred-in Costs	Direct Materials	Conversion Costs
Work in process, April 1*	500	$ 17,750	$ 0	$ 7,250
Transferred-in during April 19_7	2,000			
Completed during April 19_7	2,100			
Work in process, April 30†	400			
Costs added during April 19_7		$104,000	$23,100	$38,400

*Degree of completion: transferred-in costs, 100%; direct materials, 0%; conversion costs, 60%.
†Degree of completion: transferred-in costs, 100%; direct materials, 0%; conversion costs, 30%.

1. Summarize the total Finishing Department costs for April 19_7, and assign these costs to units completed (and transferred out) and to units in ending work in process using the weighted-average method.
2. Prepare journal entries for April transfers from the Forming Department to the Finishing Department and from the Finishing Department to Finished Goods.

17-37 Transferred-in costs, FIFO costing (continuation of 17-36).

REQUIRED

1. Using the FIFO process-costing method, do the requirements of Problem 17-36. The transferred-in costs from the Forming Department for the April beginning work in process are $17,520. During April, the costs transferred in are $103,566. All other data are unchanged.
2. Explain any difference between the cost of work completed and transferred out and cost of ending work in process in the Finishing Department under the weighted-average method and the FIFO method.

17-38 Transferred-in costs, weighted-average and FIFO. Frito-Lay, Inc., manufactures convenience foods, including potato chips and corn chips. Production of corn chips occurs in four departments: cleaning, mixing, cooking, and drying and packaging. Consider the Drying and Packaging Department, where direct materials (packaging) is added at the end of the process. Conversion costs are added evenly during the process. Suppose the accounting records of a Frito-Lay plant provided the following information for corn chips in its Drying and Packaging Department during a weekly period (week 37):

	Physical Units (Cases)	Transferred-in Costs	Direct Materials	Conversion Costs
Beginning work in process, week 37*	1,250	$29,000	$ 0	$ 9,060
Transferred-in during week 37 from Cooking Department	5,000			
Completed during week 37	5,250			
Ending work in process, week 37†	1,000			
Costs added during week 37		$96,000	$25,200	$38,400

*Degree of completion: transferred-in costs, 100%; direct materials, ?%; conversion costs, 80%.
†Degree of completion: transferred-in costs, ?%; direct materials, ?%; conversion costs, 40%.

REQUIRED

1. For each cost element, compute equivalent units of work done in week 37 in the Drying and Packaging Department. Show physical units in the first column.
2. Summarize the total Drying and Packaging Department costs for week 37, and assign these costs to units completed (and transferred out) and to units in ending work in process using the weighted-average method.
3. Assume that the FIFO method is used for the Drying and Packaging Department. The transferred-in costs for work-in-process beginning inventory are $28,920. The transferred-in costs during the week from the Cooking Department are $94,000. All other data are unchanged. Summarize the total Drying and Packaging Department costs for week 37 and assign these costs to units completed (and transferred out) and to units in ending work in process using the FIFO method.

17-39 Standard costing with beginning and ending work in process. The Victoria Corporation uses a standard costing system for its manufacturing operations. Standard costs for the cooking process are $6 per unit for direct materials and $3 per unit for conversion costs. All direct materials are introduced at the beginning of the process, but conversion costs are added uniformly during the process. The operating summary for May 19_7 included the following data for the cooking process:

Work-in-process inventories
   May 1: 3,000 units*
      (direct materials $18,000; conversion costs $5,400)
   May 31: 5,000 units†
Units started in May: 20,000
Units completed and transferred out of cooking in May: 18,000
Additional actual costs incurred for cooking during May
   Direct materials: $125,000
   Conversion cost: $57,000

*Degree of completion: direct materials, 100%; conversion costs, 60%.
†Degree of completion: direct materials, 100%; conversion costs, 50%.

REQUIRED

1. Compute the total standard costs of units transferred out in May and the total standard costs of the May 31 inventory of work in process.
2. Compute the total May variances for direct materials and conversion costs.

17-40 Equivalent unit computations, benchmarking, ethics. Margaret Major is the corporate controller of Leisure Suits. Leisure Suits has 20 plants worldwide that manufacture basic suits for retail stores. Each plant uses a process-costing system. At the end of each month, each plant manager submits a production report and a production-cost report. The production report includes the plant manager's estimate of the percentage of completion of the ending work in process as to direct materials and conversion costs. Major uses these estimates to compute the equivalent units of work done in each plant and the cost per equivalent unit of work done for both direct materials and conversion costs in each month. Plants are ranked from 1 to 20 in terms of (a) cost per equivalent unit of direct materials, and (b) cost per equivalent unit of conversion costs. Each month Major publishes a report that she calls "Benchmarking for Efficiency Gains at Leisure Suits." The top three ranked plants on each category receive a bonus and are written up as the best in their class in the company newsletter.

Major has been pleased with the success of her benchmarking program. However, she has heard some disturbing news. She has received some unsigned letters stating that two plant managers have been manipulating their monthly estimates of percentage of completion in an attempt to obtain best in class status.

REQUIRED

1. How and why might plant managers "manipulate" their monthly estimates of percentage of completion?
2. Major's first reaction is to contact each plant controller and discuss the problem raised by the unsigned letters. Is that a good idea?
3. Assume that the plant controller's primary reporting responsibility is to the plant manager and that each plant controller receives the phone call from Major mentioned in requirement 2. What is the ethical responsibility of each plant controller (a) to Margaret Major, and (b) to Leisure Suits in relation to the equivalent unit information each plant provides for the "Benchmarking for Efficiency" report?

4. How might Major gain some insight into whether the equivalent unit figures provided by particular plants are being manipulated?

COLLABORATIVE LEARNING PROBLEM

17-41 Weighted-average, FIFO, standard costs methods, working backwards. "I am astounded that we cannot find the cost records for the month of July 19_7," said Greg Andrews, plant manager of Detroit Component Works (DCW). "I have a division meeting to attend where I will be asked about the plant's July performance compared to June. All I have now are the weighted-average cost figures, but those numbers are hardly helpful in answering the question of whether we have improved our performance this month compared to the previous months. I think we have improved the efficiency of our operations, and direct materials prices have also been lower, so I was expecting to report some good news at the division meeting. I need those July numbers and I need them now." DCW makes complex aircraft engine components in two operations—machining and assembly. The following is a summary of the Assembly operations in July 19_7.

	Physical Units	Transferred-in Costs	Direct Materials	Conversion Costs
Work in process, July 1*	120	$16,800	$ 0	$9,000
Transferred-in during July 19_7	200			
Completed during July 19_7	220			
Work in process, July 31†	100			
Costs added during July		?	?	?
Weighted-average cost per equivalent unit		$ 131.25	$20	$ 114

*Degree of completion: transferred-in costs, 100%; direct materials, 0%; conversion costs, 5/8 or 62.5%.
†Degree of completion: transferred-in costs, 100%; direct materials, 0%; conversion costs, 80%.

INSTRUCTIONS
Form groups of two or three students. Compute the missing numbers. Then discuss requirements 4, 5, and 6 among yourselves to prepare for class discussion.

REQUIRED
1. For each cost element, compute the equivalent units of work done in the current period.
2. For each cost element, calculate the cost per equivalent unit of beginning work in process.
3. Calculate the total Assembly Department costs to account for in July 19_7 for each cost element.
4. For each cost element, calculate the cost per equivalent unit of work performed in the current period. These are the numbers that Greg Andrews wants for the division meeting. Prepare a brief report comparing and commenting on the cost per equivalent unit of work done in the current period with the cost per equivalent unit of beginning inventory.
5. Without doing any further calculations, do you think the cost of units completed and transferred out in July 19_7 would have been lower or higher if DCW had used the FIFO rather than the weighted-average method? Why? Explain briefly.

6. DCW is looking to add more variations of the components it currently manufactures to its product line. Gina Davis, the plant controller, believes that if it does so, DCW should consider implementing a standard costing system. The assistant controller, Tom Rogers, however, feels that a job-costing system might be more appropriate. What do you think DCW should do—maintain its current system, adopt a standard costing system, or switch to a job-costing system?

Nally & Gibson Georgetown, Inc.

When Nally & Gibson Georgetown, Inc., was founded in 1955, business was, so to speak, rocky—and it has stayed that way ever since. Why? Because Nally & Gibson mines and supplies limestone rock from its 200-acre quarry. **1** Having fully mined the quality limestone from the surface, Nally & Gibson's mining operations take place 350 feet underneath their quarry. **2** The underground rock must first be loosened by carefully placed dynamite charges. **3** It is then loaded into trucks and transported to the surface, where it is taken to a rock crushing plant. Here the limestone is broken into smaller pieces. **4** These pieces are then carried by a conveyor belt to a second crushing plant. **5** By using filtering screens, rocks in the second crusher are separated by size. Because size is the main and sometimes only difference among Nally & Gibson's different rock products, the second crushing plant is considered the split-off point for many of those products.

1

2

4

5

3

6 Once the rocks are separated by size, each grouping leaves the second crushing unit on its own conveyer belt. These conveyers transport the rocks to various stockpiles, **7** from which they can be loaded onto trucks for customers **8** or moved to storage piles farther away from the crushing plants. Although the company sells rocks of all different sizes, certain sizes are more popular and, therefore, command higher prices. **9** Rocks that are either too large or too small to sell are used to fill reclaimed land on the quarry's surface. Because its products come from the same source, are processed in the same way, and vary only in size, Nally & Gibson uses a process costing system. **10** One of the biggest costs this system must track is the depreciation on equipment such as the rock crushers and company trucks. By appropriately tracking and allocating this and all other costs, Nally & Gibson's cost accounting system helps keep the company rock solid.

NALLY & GIBSON GEORGETOWN, INC.
Cost Allocation and Process Costing

You drive on it, walk on it, wear it, and even brush your teeth with it. For 3 cents, you can buy 10 pounds of it. What is it? Limestone. It's a versatile natural resource found in asphalt highways, concrete sidewalks, cosmetics, and toothpaste, to name a few. Nally & Gibson Georgetown, Inc., in central Kentucky, has been a primary supplier of quality limestone products since 1955. Over the years, the company has seen many changes as its business and its local economy have matured. Its rock quarry operations are a good example of the role cost accounting can play in a process-based business.

Considered a commodity, limestone rock is extracted from Nally & Gibson's underground mine located 350 feet below the original 200-acre surface of the quarry. Limestone used to be mined on the surface, but the supply of quality surface rock has been exhausted. Engineers estimate that close to 40 million tons of good quality limestone rock still remain to be mined underground. The production process involves three primary stages. First, the rock is blasted with dynamite charges to loosen it. The large limestone rocks are loaded into 35-ton capacity trucks for transport to one of two rock-crushing plants located at the quarry. Next, the rock is dumped into a crusher, which breaks the rocks into smaller pieces. These pieces then travel by conveyer to a second crusher, where the split-off point for various sizes of rock occurs. Finally, the rocks are separated into different sizes. Filtering screens are used to separate the pieces into their respective size groupings. The different sizes of rock are carried by multiple conveyers to various stockpiles, where they can be loaded onto trucks for customers or moved to a storage pile away from the crushing plant. Nally & Gibson uses process costing to determine the cost per ton of limestone rock processed. All rock is processed in a relatively homogeneous way, and all costs are placed into a single cost pool. By this use of a single cost pool, the company can calculate an equivalent cost per ton of limestone rock.

Pricing of the quarry's thirty-six different sizes of rock is largely driven by market conditions and competitive forces. The most popular rock sizes are those with diameters of 1/4 to 3/8 inch, and they command a higher per-ton price. While the rock-crushing process produces varying sizes of rock, nothing goes to waste. Rocks that are too large to be crushed and the fine sand produced in crushing are used to fill in reclaimed surface land at the quarry. Byproducts, such as unpopular rock sizes that are unavoidable in the crushing process, are sold at lower prices as dictated by the market.

Within a 25-mile radius of Nally & Gibson are six other quarries that offer the same products. Because pricing is so competitive, managers at Nally & Gibson keep a close eye on costs to ensure operations remain profitable. Major costs for the business include depreciation on $5 million worth of equipment; labor, repair, and maintenance; fuel; transportation; and safety and environmental protection costs. The results of operations are reviewed weekly by the company's management team. The cost data have been particularly useful for identifying whether certain expenditures are within expected ranges and have given managers better information with which to maximize the quarry's profitability. ◆

QUESTIONS

1. Which costing system would you suggest Nally & Gibson use to determine product costs?

2. Because the mining of limestone rock has an effect on the surrounding environment, what costs would you expect Nally & Gibson to incur related to maintaining and preserving the environment?

3. What quality issues might be associated with the mining and production of different rock sizes? How are costs and prices affected by these issues?

4. If Nally & Gibson called the processing plant a joint cost area, how would it use an estimated net realizable value joint costing method?

5. How might Nally & Gibson use a revenue mix variance analysis to examine profitability changes over time?

18

SPOILAGE, REWORKED UNITS, AND SCRAP

Reducing spoilage, reworked units, and scrap is an important aspect of cost management. Motorola monitors both financial and nonfinancial variables in its efforts to minimize reworked units and scrap, and to improve quality. Motorola estimates that these initiatives have resulted in billions of dollars of cost savings.

LEARNING OBJECTIVES

After studying this chapter, you should be able to

1. Distinguish among spoilage, reworked units, and scrap
2. Describe the general accounting procedures for normal and abnormal spoilage
3. Account for spoilage in process costing using the weighted-average method
4. Account for spoilage in process costing using the first-in, first-out method
5. Account for spoilage in process costing using the standard costs method
6. Account for spoilage in job costing
7. Account for reworked units
8. Account for scrap

The emphasis on quality, and the high costs of spoilage, reworked units, and scrap, has resulted in managers paying close attention to these costs. **Spoilage** refers to unacceptable units of production that are discarded or are sold for net disposal proceeds. Partially completed or fully completed units of output may be spoiled. Examples are defective shirts, jeans, shoes and carpets sold as "seconds," and defective aluminum cans sold to aluminum manufacturers for remelting and production of aluminum foils. **Reworked units** are unacceptable units of production that are subsequently reworked and sold as acceptable finished goods. For example, defective units of products such as pagers, computer disk drives, computers, and telephones can sometimes be repaired and sold as good products. Scrap is material left over when making a main or joint product. *Scrap* is defined in Chapter 15 as a product that has minimal (frequently zero) sales value compared with the sales value of the main or joint product(s). Examples are shavings and short lengths from woodworking operations, steel edges left over from stamping operations, and frayed cloth and end cuts from suit-making operations.

Recording and identifying the costs of spoilage, rework, and scrap helps managers make more informed decisions, especially concerning production systems. For example, major reductions in these costs might help managers justify investments in cutting-edge production systems such as just-in-time (JIT) and computer-integrated manufacturing (CIM). This chapter concentrates on how spoilage, rework, and scrap are recorded in management accounting systems.

MANAGEMENT EFFORT AND CONTROL

Some amount of spoilage, rework, or scrap appears to be an inherent part of many production processes. One example is semiconductor manufacturing, where the products are so complex and delicate that some spoiled units are invariably produced. In this case, the spoiled units cannot be reworked. An example involving spoilage and rework occurs in the manufacture of high-precision machine tools that must be built to very demanding tolerances. In this case, spoiled units can be reworked to meet standards but only at a considerable cost. And in the mining industry, companies process ore that contains varying amounts of valuable metals and rock. Some amount of rock, which is scrap, is inevitable, but its volume can often be decreased. Managers in all industries must strive to reduce costly spoilage, rework, and scrap. For example, managers can take steps to improve quality and reduce costs by designing better products and processes, training and motivating workers, and properly maintaining machines.

In many cases, growing competition in the global market place has forced managers to focus on improving quality. Executives have learned that a rate of defects regarded as normal in the past is no longer tolerable. Consider these words from a speech by George Fisher, the former chief executive officer of Motorola, an electronics manufacturer:

> We want to improve our quality in everything we do by ten times in two years, by a hundred times in four years, and in six years . . . three and a half defects for every million operations, whether typing, manufacturing, or serving a customer.

SPOILAGE IN GENERAL

Two key objectives when accounting for spoilage are determining the magnitude of the costs of spoilage and distinguishing between the costs of normal and abnormal spoilage. Managers use this information both to cost products and to control and reduce costs by improving the quality of the product and process.

There is an unmistakable trend in manufacturing to increase quality. Why? Because managers at companies, such as AT&T, IBM, and Milliken Corporation have found that improved quality and intolerance for high spoilage have lowered overall costs and increased sales. The accounting procedures in this section highlight spoilage costs so that they are not ignored or buried as an unidentified part of the costs of good units manufactured.[1]

Normal Spoilage

Normal spoilage is spoilage that arises under efficient operating conditions; it is an inherent result of the particular production process. For a given production process, management must decide the rate of spoilage it is willing to accept as normal. Costs of normal spoilage are typically viewed as a part of the costs of good units manufactured, when good units cannot be made without the simultaneous appearance of spoiled units.

Normal spoilage rates should be computed using the total *good* units completed as the base, not the total *actual* units started. Why? Because total actual units started also include any abnormal spoilage in addition to normal spoilage.

Abnormal Spoilage

Abnormal spoilage is spoilage that is not expected to arise under efficient operating conditions; it is not an inherent part of the chosen production process. Most abnormal spoilage is usually regarded as avoidable and controllable. Line operators and other plant personnel can generally decrease abnormal spoilage by minimizing machine breakdowns, accidents, and the like. Abnormal spoilage costs are written off as losses of the accounting period in which detection of the spoiled units occurs. For the most informative feedback, the Loss from Abnormal Spoilage account should appear in a detailed income statement as a separate line item and not be buried as an indistinguishable part of the cost of goods manufactured.

Many companies such as the Toyota Motor Corporation adhere to a perfection standard as a part of their emphasis on total quality control. Their ideal goal is zero defects. Hence, all spoilage would be treated as abnormal.

Count All Spoilage

Spoiled units can either be recognized (approach A) or not counted (approach B) when computing output units—actual or equivalent—in a process-costing system. Approach A makes visible the costs associated with spoilage. Approach B spreads the spoilage costs over good units, potentially resulting in less accurate product costs.

Spoilage is typically assumed to occur at the stage of completion where inspection takes place. Why? Because spoilage is not detected until that point.

EXAMPLE 1 Chipmakers, Inc., manufactures computer chips for television sets. All direct materials are added at the beginning of the chipmaking process. To highlight issues that arise with spoilage, we assume no beginning inventory. In May 19_7, $270,000 in direct materials were introduced. Production data for May indicate that 10,000 units were started, 5,000 good units were completed, 1,000 units were spoiled (all normal spoilage). Ending work in process had 4,000 units (each 100% complete as to direct materials costs). Spoilage is detected upon completion of the process.

The direct materials unit costs are computed and assigned using approaches A and B as shown in Exhibit 18-1. Not counting the equivalent units for spoilage decreases equivalent units, resulting in a higher cost of each good unit. A $30 equivalent unit cost (instead of a $27 equivalent unit cost) is assigned to work in process that has not reached the inspection point. Simultaneously, the direct materials costs assigned to good units completed, which include the cost of normal spoilage, are too low ($150,000 instead of $162,000). Consequently, the 4,000 units in ending work in process contain costs of spoilage of $12,000 ($120,000 – $108,000) that do not

---

[1]The helpful suggestions of Samuel Laimon, University of Saskatchewan, are gratefully acknowledged.

	Approach A: Recognizing Spoiled Units When Computing Output in Equivalent Units	Approach B: Not Counting Spoiled Units When Computing Output in Equivalent Units
Costs to account for	$270,000	$270,000
Divide by equivalent units	÷ 10,000	÷ 9,000
Cost per equivalent unit	$ 27	$ 30
Assigned to		
Good units transferred out		
Good units completed: 5,000 × $27; 5,000 × $30	$135,000	$150,000
Add normal spoilage: 1,000 × $27	27,000	0
Good units transferred out	162,000	150,000
Work in process, ending: 4,000 × $27; 4,000 × $30	108,000	120,000
Costs accounted for	$270,000	$270,000

pertain to those units and that, in fact, belong with the good units completed and transferred out. The 4,000 units in ending work in process undoubtedly include some units that will be detected as spoiled in the subsequent accounting period. In effect, under approach B, these units will bear two charges for spoilage. The ending work in process is being charged for spoilage in the current period, and it will be charged again when inspection occurs as the units are completed. Such cost distortions do not occur when spoiled units are recognized in the computation of equivalent units. Approach A has a further advantage. It highlights the cost of normal spoilage to management and thereby focuses management's attention on reducing spoilage. Therefore, we will use approach A to present process costing with spoilage.

EXAMPLE 2 The Anzio Company manufactures a wooden recycling container in its Processing Department. Direct materials for this product are introduced at the beginning of the production cycle. At the start of production, all direct materials required to make one output unit are bundled together in a single kit. Conversion costs are added evenly during the cycle. Some units of this product are spoiled as a result of defects only detectable at inspection of finished units. Normally, the spoiled units are 10% of the good output. Summary data for July 19_7 are

Physical Units for July 19_7

Work in process, beginning inventory (July 1)	1,500 units
Direct materials (100% complete)	
Conversion costs (60% complete)	
Started during July	8,500 units
Completed and transferred out in July (good units)	7,000 units
Work in process, ending inventory (July 31)	2,000 units
Direct materials (100% complete)	
Conversion costs (50% complete)	

Total Costs for July 19_7

Work in process, beginning inventory		
Direct materials	$12,000	
Conversion costs	9,000	$ 21,000
Direct materials costs added during July		76,500
Conversion costs added during July		89,100
Total costs to account for		$186,600

Computing Spoiled Units

The number of total spoiled units is computed as follows:

$$\text{Total spoiled units} = \left(\begin{array}{c}\text{Beginning} \\ \text{units}\end{array} + \begin{array}{c}\text{Units} \\ \text{started}\end{array}\right) - \left(\begin{array}{c}\text{Good units} \\ \text{transferred out}\end{array} + \begin{array}{c}\text{Ending} \\ \text{units}\end{array}\right)$$

$$= (1,500 + 8,500) - (7,000 + 2,000)$$

$$= 10,000 - 9,000$$

$$= 1,000 \text{ units}$$

Normal spoilage at Anzio's Processing Department is 10% of the 7,000 units of good output, or 700 units. Thus,

$$\text{Abnormal spoilage} = \text{Total spoilage} - \text{Normal spoilage}$$

$$= 1,000 - 700$$

$$= 300 \text{ units}$$

We now illustrate how the weighted-average, FIFO, and standard costing methods of process costing discussed in Chapter 17 can incorporate both normal and abnormal spoilage in their computations.

Follow the Four-Step Approach

The basic four-step approach used in Chapter 17 needs only slight modification to accommodate spoilage. The following observations pertain to the weighted-average, FIFO, and standard costing methods:

Step 1 Summarize the flow of physical units of output. Identify both normal and abnormal spoilage.

Step 2 Compute output in terms of equivalent units. Compute equivalent units for spoilage in the same way as for good units. Because Anzio inspects at the completion point, the same amount of work will be done on each spoiled unit and each completed good unit.

Step 3 Compute equivalent unit costs. The details of this step do not differ from those in Chapter 17. We assume that spoiled units are included in the computation of output units.

Step 4 Summarize total costs to account for, and assign these costs to units completed, spoiled units, and to units in ending work in process. This step now includes computation of the cost of spoiled units and the cost of good units.

Exhibit 18-2 presents steps 1 and 2 and includes calculations of equivalent units of normal and abnormal spoilage. Exhibit 18-3 computes the equivalent unit costs for beginning work in process and work done in the current period (step 3).

EXHIBIT 18-2

Steps 1 and 2. Summarize Output in Physical Units and Compute Equivalent Units, Processing Department of the Anzio Company for July 19_7

Flow of Production	(Step 1) Physical Units	(Step 2) Equivalent Units	
		Direct Materials	Conversion Costs
Good units completed and transferred out during current period	7,000	7,000	7,000
Normal spoilage* 700 × 100%; 700 × 100%	700	700	700
Abnormal spoilage† 300 × 100%; 300 × 100%	300	300	300
Work in process, ending‡ 2,000 × 100%; 2,000 × 50%	2,000	2,000	1,000
Total Accounted For	10,000	10,000	9,000
Deduct work in process, beginning§ 1,500 × 100%; 1,500 × 60%	1,500	1,500	900
Started during current period	8,500		
Work done in current period only		8,500	8,100

*Normal spoilage is 10% of good units transferred out: 10% × 7,000 = 700 units. Degree of completion of normal spoilage in this department: direct materials, 100%; conversion costs, 100%.
†Abnormal spoilage = Actual spoilage – Normal spoilage = 1,000 – 700 = 300 units. Degree of completion of abnormal spoilage in this department: direct materials, 100%; conversion costs, 100%.
‡Degree of completion in this department: direct materials, 100%; conversion costs, 50%.
§Degree of completion in this department: direct materials, 100%; conversion costs, 60%.

EXHIBIT 18-3

Step 3. Compute Equivalent Unit Costs, Processing Department of the Anzio Company for July 19_7

	Direct Materials	Conversion Costs
Equivalent unit costs of beginning work in process		
Work in process, beginning (given, p. 655)	$12,000	$ 9,000
Divide by equivalent units of beginning work in process (from Exhibit 18-2)	÷ 1,500	÷ 900
Cost per equivalent unit of beginning work in process	$ 8	$ 10
Equivalent unit costs of work done in current period only		
Costs added in current period (given, p. 655)	$76,500	$89,100
Divide by equivalent units of work done in current period (from Exhibit 18-2)	÷ 8,500	÷ 8,100
Cost per equivalent unit of work done in current period only	$ 9	$ 11

Weighted-Average Method and Spoilage

Exhibit 18-4 presents step 4 using the weighted-average method. The total costs columns in Panel A of Exhibit 18-4 summarize the costs to account for. Note how, for each cost category, the costs of beginning work in process and costs of work done in the current period are totaled and divided by the sum of the equivalent units in beginning work in process and equivalent units of work done in the current period to calculate the weighted-average cost. The costs of abnormal spoilage of $5,925 are

EXHIBIT 18-4

Step 4: Summarize Total Costs to Account for, and Assign These Costs to Units Completed, Units Spoiled and Units in Ending Work in Process Using the Weighted-Average Method, Processing Department of Anzio Company for July 19_7

	Direct Materials			Conversion Costs			Total Prod. Costs
	Equiv. Units (1)	Cost per Equiv. Unit (2)	Total Costs (3) = (1) × (2)	Equiv. Units (4)	Cost per Equiv. Unit (5)	Total Costs (6) = (4) × (5)	(7) = (3) + (6)

PANEL A:
TOTAL COSTS TO ACCOUNT FOR

Work in process, beginning (from Exhibit 18-3)	1,500	$8.00 *	$12,000	900	$10.00 **	$ 9,000	$ 21,000
Work done in current period only (from Exhibit 18-3)	8,500	$9.00	76,500	8,100	$11.00	89,100	165,600
To account for	10,000	$8.85 *	$88,500	9,000	$10.90 †	$98,100	$186,600

WA = Total cost + DM / Total EQ Units

WA = Total CC / Total EQ Units

PANEL B:
ASSIGNMENT OF COSTS

		Direct Materials			Conversion Costs			
	Good units completed and transferred (out 7,000 units)		WA COST			WA COSTS		
	Costs before adding normal spoilage Given	7,000‡	$8.85	$61,950	7,000‡	$10.90	$76,300	$138,250
	Normal spoilage 10% 7000	700‡	$8.85	+ 6,195	700‡	$10.90	+ 7,630	13,825
(A)	Total costs of good units transferred out			68,145			83,930	152,075
(B)	Abnormal spoilage Spoilage − Norm = 300‡	300‡	$8.85	2,655	300‡	$10.90	3,270	5,925
(C)	Work in process, ending Given	2,000‡	$8.85	17,700	1,000‡	$10.90	10,900	28,600
(A) + (B) + (C)	Accounted for	10,000		$88,500	9,000		$98,100	$186,600

100% WRT DM

50% of 2000 WRT CC

*Weighted-average cost per equivalent unit of direct materials = Total costs of direct materials divided by total equivalent units = $88,500 ÷ 10,000 = $8.85.

†Weighted-average cost per equivalent unit of conversion costs = Total conversion costs divided by total equivalent units = $98,100 ÷ 9,000 = $10.90.

‡From Exhibit 18-2.

assigned to the Loss from Abnormal Spoilage account. The costs of normal spoilage, $13,825, are added to the costs of their related good units. Hence, the cost per good unit completed and transferred out equals the total costs transferred out (including the costs of normal spoilage) divided by the number of good units produced, $152,075 ÷ 7,000 = $21.725. It is not equal to $19.75, the sum of the costs per equivalent unit of direct materials, $8.85 and conversion costs, $10.90. Why? Because the cost per good unit is equal to the total cost of an equivalent unit, $19.75 *plus* a share of the normal spoilage, $1.975 ($13,825 ÷ 7,000), or $21.725.

This illustration assumes inspection upon completion. In contrast, inspection may take place at some other stage—say, at the halfway point in the production cycle. In such a case, normal spoilage costs would be added to completed goods and to the units in process that are at least 50% completed.

Having early and frequent inspections in production processes reduces the amount of material and conversion costs wasted on units that are already spoiled. Thus, in the Exhibit 18-4 example, suppose inspection can occur when units are 80% complete as to conversion costs and 100% complete as to direct materials, and spoilage occurs before this point. Then the company would avoid incurring the final 20% of conversion costs on the spoiled units.

OBJECTIVE 4

Account for spoilage in process costing using the first-in, first-out method

FIFO Method and Spoilage

Exhibit 18-5 presents step 4 using the FIFO method. The total costs columns in Panel A of Exhibit 18-5 summarize the costs to account for. Note how the FIFO method keeps the costs of the beginning work-in-process inventory separate and distinct from the costs of work done in the current period when assigning costs. All spoilage costs are assumed to be related to units completed during this period, using the unit costs of the current period.[2] With the exception of accounting for spoilage, the FIFO method is the same as presented in Chapter 17.

Journal Entries

The information in Exhibits 18-4 and 18-5 supports the following journal entries:

	Weighted Average		FIFO	
1. Finished Goods	152,075		151,600	
Work in Process—Processing		152,075		151,600
To transfer good units completed in July.				
2. Loss from Abnormal Spoilage	5,925		6,000	
Work in Process—Processing		5,925		6,000
To recognize abnormal spoilage detected in July.				

OBJECTIVE 5

Account for spoilage in process costing using the standard costs method

Standard Costs and Spoilage

This section assumes you have studied Chapters 7 and 8 and the standard costs method in Chapter 17 (pp. 625–629). Otherwise, omit this section.

Standard costing methods can also be used to account for normal and abnormal spoilage. We illustrate how much simpler the calculations become by continuing our Anzio Company example.

---

[2]If the FIFO method were used in its purest form, normal spoilage costs would be split between the goods started and completed during the current period and those completed from beginning work in process—using the appropriate unit costs of the period in which the units were worked on. The simpler, modified FIFO method, as illustrated in Exhibit 18-5, in effect uses the unit costs of the current period for assigning normal spoilage costs to the goods completed from beginning work in process. This modified FIFO method assumes that all normal spoilage traceable to the beginning work in process was started and completed during the current period, an obvious contradiction to the pure FIFO method.

EXHIBIT 18-5
Step 4: Summarize Total Costs to Account for, and Assign These Costs to Units Completed, Units Spoiled and Units in Ending Work in Process Using the FIFO Method, Processing Department of Anzio Company for July 19_7

	Direct Materials			Conversion Costs			Total Prod. Costs
	Equiv. Units (1)	Cost per Equiv. Unit (2)	Total Costs (3) = (1) × (2)	Equiv. Units (4)	Cost per Equiv. Unit (5)	Total Costs (6) = (4) × (5)	(7) = (3) + (6)
PANEL A:							
TOTAL COSTS TO ACCOUNT FOR							
Work in process, beginning (from Exhibit 18-3)	1,500	$8.00	$12,000	900	$10.00	$ 9,000	$ 21,000
Work done in current period only (from Exhibit 18-3)	8,500	$9.00	76,500	8,100	$11.00	89,100	165,600
To account for	10,000		$88,500	9,000		$98,100	$186,600
PANEL B:							
ASSIGNMENT OF COSTS							
Good units completed and transferred out (7,000 physical units)							
Work in process, beginning(1,500 physical units)	1,500	$8.00	$12,000	900	$10.00	$ 9,000	$ 21,000
Work done in current period to complete beginning work in process	0*	$9.00	0	600†	$11.00	6,600	6,600
Total from beginning inventory before normal spoilage	1,500		12,000	1,500		15,600	27,600
Started and completed before normal spoilage (5,500 units)	5,500‡	$9.00	49,500	5,500‡	$11.00	60,500	110,000
Normal spoilage (700 units)	700§	$9.00	6,300	700§	$11.00	7,700	14,000
(A) Total costs of good units transferred out			67,800			83,800	151,600
(B) Abnormal spoilage (300 units)	300§	$9.00	2,700	300§	$11.00	3,300	6,000
(C) Work in process, ending (2,000 units)	2,000§	$9.00	18,000	1,000§	$11.00	11,000	29,000
(A) + (B) + (C) Accounted for	10,000		$88,500	9,000		$98,100	$186,600

*Beginning work in process is 100% complete as to direct materials so zero equivalent units of direct materials need to be added to complete beginning work in process.
†Beginning work in process is 60% complete, which equals 900 equivalent units of conversion costs. To complete the 1,500 physical units of beginning work in process, 600 (1,500 – 900) equivalent units of conversion costs need to be added.
‡7,000 total equivalent units completed and transferred out (Exhibit 18-2) minus 1,500 equivalent units completed and transferred out from beginning inventory equal to 5,500 equivalent units.
§From Exhibit 18-2.

Suppose the Anzio Company develops standard costs for the Processing Department. Assume the same standard costs apply to the beginning inventory and to work done in July 19_7.

Standard Costs for Processing Department for July 19_7

Direct materials	$ 8.50 per unit
Conversion costs	10.50 per unit
Total production costs	$19.00 per unit

Steps 1 and 2 for standard costing are the same as for the weighted-average and FIFO methods described in Exhibit 18-2. Step 3, the cost per equivalent unit is simply the standard cost: direct materials $8.50, and conversion costs, $10.50. Standard costing makes calculating equivalent unit costs unnecessary and so simplifies process costing. Exhibit 18-6 presents step 4. The costs to account for in Panel A of Exhibit 18-6 are at *standard* costs and hence differ from the costs to account for under the weighted-average and FIFO methods, which are at *actual* costs. Step 4 uses standard costs to assign costs to units completed, to normal and abnormal spoilage, and to ending work-in-process inventory. Variances can be measured and analyzed in the manner described in Chapters 7 and 8.

Assumptions for Allocating Normal Spoilage

Spoilage might actually occur at various points or stages of the production cycle, but spoilage is typically not detected until one or more specific points of inspection. The cost of spoiled units is assumed to be all costs incurred by spoiled units prior to inspection. When spoiled goods have a disposal value, the net cost of spoilage is computed by deducting disposal value from the costs of the spoiled goods accumulated to the point of inspection. The unit costs of abnormal and normal spoilage are the same when the two are detected simultaneously. However, situations might arise when abnormal spoilage is detected at a different point than normal spoilage. In such cases, the unit cost of abnormal spoilage would differ from the unit cost of normal spoilage.

Costs of abnormal spoilage are separately accounted for as losses for the period. Recall, however, that normal spoilage costs are added to costs of good units. Accounting for normal spoilage, therefore, raises an additional issue: Should normal spoilage costs be allocated between completed units and ending work-in-process inventory? One approach is to presume that normal spoilage occurs at the inspection point in the production cycle and to allocate its cost over all units that have passed that point. In the Anzio Company example, spoilage is assumed to occur when finished units are inspected, so no cost of normal spoilage is allocated to ending work in process.

Whether the cost of normal spoilage is allocated to the units in ending work-in-process inventory, in addition to completed units, depends strictly on whether they have passed the point of inspection. For example, if the inspection point is presumed to be the halfway stage of the production cycle, work in process that is more than 50% completed would be allocated a full measure of normal spoilage costs, calculated on the basis of all costs incurred prior to the point of inspection. But work in process that is under 50% completed would not be allocated any normal spoilage costs. The appendix to this chapter contains additional discussion concerning various assumptions about spoilage.

SPOILAGE, REWORK, AND SCRAP IN JOB-COSTING SYSTEMS

The concepts of normal and abnormal spoilage also apply to job-costing systems. Abnormal spoilage is usually regarded as controllable by the manager. It is separately identified with the goal of eliminating it altogether. Costs of abnormal spoilage are not considered as product manufacturing costs and are written off as costs of the period in which detection occurs. Normal or planned spoilage in job-costing systems, however, are considered part of normal manufacturing costs, although increasingly, managements are tolerating only small amounts of spoilage as normal. The costs are

EXHIBIT 18-6

Step 4: Summarize Total Costs to Account for and Assign These Costs to Units Completed, Units Spoiled and Units in Ending Work in Process Using Standard Costs, Processing Department of Anzio Company for July 19_7

	Direct Materials			Conversion Costs			Total Prod. Costs
	Equiv. Units (Exh. 8-2) (1)	Cost per Equiv. Unit (2)	Total Costs (3) = (1) × (2)	Equiv. Units (Exh. 18-2) (4)	Cost per Equiv. Unit (5)	Total Costs (6) = (4) × (5)	(7) = (3) + (6)
PANEL A: **TOTAL COSTS TO ACCOUNT FOR**							
Work in process, beginning	1,500	$8.50	$12,750	900	$10.50	$ 9,450	$ 22,200
Work done in current period only	8,500	$8.50	72,250	8,100	$10.50	85,050	157,300
To account for	10,000	$8.50	$85,000	9,000	$10.50	$94,500	$179,500
PANEL B: **ASSIGNMENT OF COSTS**							
Good units completed and transferred out (7,000 units)							
Costs before adding normal spoilage	7,000	$8.50	$59,500	7,000	$10.50	$73,500	$133,000
Normal spoilage	700	$8.50	5,950	700	$10.50	7,350	13,300
(A) Total costs of good units transferred out			65,450			80,850	146,300
(B) Abnormal spoilage	300	$8.50	2,550	300	$10.50	3,150	5,700
(C) Work in process, ending	2,000	$8.50	17,000	1,000	$10.50	10,500	27,500
(A) + (B) + (C) Accounted for	10,000		$85,000	9,000		$94,500	$179,500

then assigned to individually distinct jobs, a step unnecessary in process costing since masses of similar units are manufactured. When assigning costs, job-costing systems generally distinguish normal spoilage attributable to a specific job from normal spoilage common to all jobs.

We also use the job-costing context to illustrate the accounting for rework and scrap. For rework, we again distinguish (1) abnormal rework, (2) normal rework attributable to a specific job, and (3) normal rework common to all jobs. Scrap accounting follows the accounting for a by-product described in Chapter 15. No distinctions are made between normal and abnormal scrap, but scrap attributable to a specific job is distinguished from scrap common to all jobs.

JOB COSTING AND SPOILAGE

OBJECTIVE 6

Account for spoilage in job costing

We illustrate the accounting for spoilage in job costing using the following example.

EXAMPLE 3 In the Hull Machine Shop, 5 aircraft parts out of a job lot of 50 aircraft parts are spoiled. Costs assigned up to the point of inspection are $100 per unit. Hull calculates these costs on the basis of its inventory costing assumptions—weighted average, FIFO, or standard costs. We do not, however, emphasize cost-flow assumptions in our presentation here or in subsequent sections. The current disposal price of the spoiled parts is estimated to be $30 per part. When the spoilage is detected, the spoiled goods are inventoried at $30 per unit.

Normal Spoilage Attributable to a Specific Job When normal spoilage occurs because of the specifications of a specific job, that job bears the cost of the spoilage reduced by the current disposal value of that spoilage. The journal entry to recognize the disposal value of the salvage (items in parentheses indicate subsidiary postings) is as follows:

Materials Control (spoiled goods at current disposal value): 5 × $30	150	
Work-in-Process Control (specific job): 5 × $30		150

The effect of this accounting is that the net cost of the normal spoilage, $350 ($500 − $150) becomes a direct cost of the 45 (50 − 5) good units produced.

Normal Spoilage Common to All Jobs In some cases, spoilage may be considered a normal characteristic of a given production cycle. The spoilage inherent in the process only coincidentally occurs when a specific job is being worked on. The spoilage then is not attributable, and hence is not charged, to the specific job. Instead, it is costed as manufacturing overhead. The budgeted manufacturing overhead allocation rate includes a provision for normal spoilage cost. Therefore, normal spoilage cost is spread, through overhead allocation, over all jobs rather than loaded on particular jobs only.[3]

Materials Control (spoiled goods at current disposal value): 5 × $30	150	
Manufacturing Department Overhead Control (normal spoilage): 5 × $70	350	
Work-in-Process Control (specific job): 5 × $100		500

Abnormal Spoilage If the spoilage is abnormal, the net loss is highlighted to management by charging the loss to an abnormal loss account:

Materials Control (spoiled goods at current disposal value): 5 × $30	150	
Loss from Abnormal Spoilage: 5 × $70	350	
Work-in-Process Control (specific job): 5 × $100		500

---

[3]Note that costs *already assigned to products* are being charged back to Manufacturing Department Overhead Control, which generally accumulates only *costs incurred*, not both costs incurred and costs assigned.

Reworked units are unacceptable units of production that are subsequently reworked into good units and sold.

Consider the Hull Machine Shop data (Example 3). Assume that the five spoiled parts used in our Hull Machine Shop illustration are reworked. The journal entry for the $500 of total costs (details of costs assumed) assigned to the five spoiled units before considering rework costs are as follows:

Work-in-Process Control	500	
Materials Control		200
Wages Payable		200
Manufacturing Overhead Allocated		100

Assume that rework costs equal $190 (direct materials, $40; direct labor, $100; manufacturing overhead, $50).

Normal Rework Attributable to a Specific Job   If the rework is normal but occurs because of the requirements of a specific job, the rework costs are charged to that job. The journal entry is as follows:

Work-in-Process Control (specific job)	190	
Materials Control		40
Wages Payable		100
Manufacturing Overhead Allocated		50

Normal Rework Common to All Jobs   When rework is normal and not attributable to any specific job, the costs of rework are charged to manufacturing overhead and spread, through overhead allocation, over all jobs.

Manufacturing Department Overhead Control (rework)	190	
Materials Control		40
Wages Payable		100
Manufacturing Overhead Allocated		50

Abnormal Rework   If the rework is abnormal, it is highlighted to management by charging abnormal rework to a separate loss account.

Loss from Abnormal Rework	190	
Materials Control		40
Wages Payable		100
Manufacturing Overhead Allocated		50

Accounting for rework in process costing only requires abnormal rework to be distinguished from normal rework. Abnormal rework is accounted for as in job costing. Since masses of similar units are manufactured, accounting for normal rework follows the accounting described for normal rework common to all jobs.

Costing rework highlights the resources wasted on activities that would not have to be undertaken if the product were made correctly. It prompts management to seek ways to reduce rework, for example, by designing new products or processes, training workers, or investing in new machines. Calculating rework costs helps management perform cost-benefit analyses for various alternatives. To emphasize the importance of eliminating rework and to simplify the accounting, some companies expense all rework, including the costs of normal rework, as an expense of the current period.

Scrap was defined in Chapter 15 in conjunction with the discussion of byproducts. Scrap is a product that has minimal (frequently zero) sales value compared with the sales value of the main or joint product(s).

There are two major aspects of accounting for scrap:

1. Planning and control, including physical tracking.
2. Inventory costing, including when and how to affect operating income.

Initial entries to scrap records are most often in physical or nonfinancial terms such as in pounds or units. In various industries, items such as stamped-out metal

Rejection in the Electronics Industry

From country to country and from industry to industry, the rates of rejected and reworked units vary tremendously. The data in the following table focus on different segments of the U.S. electronics industry. The data reported are median numbers drawn from companies that are members of the American Electronics Association. The reject rate is the rejects as a percentage of items checked by quality control. The rework rate is reworked items as a percentage of rejects and returns. The scrap rate reports scrap as a percentage of all materials and products purchased. Also reported is the operating income to net sales figure for each segment of the electronics industry.

Segment of Electronics Industry	Reject Rate (% rejects)	Rework Rate (% rework)	Scrap Rate (% scrap)	Operating Income to Net Sales
1. Computers and office equipment (includes mainframes, minicomputers, microcomputers, printers, and point-of-sale equipment)	2.55%	6.50%	0.62%	5.33%
2. Electronic components and accessories (includes printed circuit boards and semiconductors)	1.55	2.00	1.63	4.53
3. Specialized production equipment (includes semiconductor production equipment)	7.50	10.00	0.43	5.67
4. Telecommunications equipment (includes telephone, radio, and TV apparatus)	1.00	2.00	1.29	4.73
5. Aerospace, nautical, and military equipment (includes aircraft manufacture and guided missiles)	—	1.50	0.52	6.52
6. Laboratory and measurement devices (includes optical instruments and process control equipment)	4.90	3.30	0.66	3.89
7. Prepackaged software	1.00	0.80	0.06	4.02
8. Computer-related services (includes data processing and computer systems design)	5.00	N/A	N/A	7.78

The reject rate for specialized production equipment is five times as great as that for electronic components and semiconductors. Electronic components and semiconductors show a low percentage of rework (in part because rework is not always possible when defects arise). Scrap rates are reasonably small across all industry segments. The operating income to net sales ratio ranges from 3.89% for laboratory and measurement devices to 6.52% for aerospace, nautical, and military equipment. Given these profitability percentages, reductions in reject and rework rates can markedly increase the profitability of many companies in the electronics industry.

Source: Adapted from American Electronics Association, *Operating Ratios Survey.* Full citation is in Appendix A.

sheets are quantified by weighing, counting, or some other expedient means. Scrap records not only help measure efficiency, but also often focus on a tempting source for theft. Scrap reports are prepared as source documents for periodic summaries of the amount of actual scrap compared with budgeted norms or standards. Scrap is either sold or disposed of quickly, or stored in some routine way for later sale, disposal, or reuse.

The tracking of scrap often extends into the financial records. For example, in one survey, 60% of the companies maintained a distinct cost for scrap somewhere in their cost accounting system.[4] The issues here are similar to those discussed in Chapter 15 regarding the accounting for byproducts:

1. When should any value of scrap be recognized in the accounting records: at the time of production of scrap or at the time of sale of scrap?
2. How should revenue from scrap be accounted for?

To illustrate, we extend our Hull Machine Shop example by assuming that the manufacture of aircraft parts generates scrap. We further assume that the normal scrap from a job lot has a total sales value of $45.

Recognizing Scrap at the Time of Sale of Scrap

Scrap Attributable to a Specific Job Job-costing systems sometimes trace the sales of scrap to the jobs that yielded the scrap. This method is used only when the tracing can be done in an economically feasible way. For example, the Hull Machine Shop and particular customers, such as the U.S. Department of Defense, may reach an agreement that provides for charging specific jobs with all rework or spoilage costs and for crediting these jobs with all scrap sales that arise from them. The journal entry is

Scrap returned to storeroom:	No journal entry. [Memo of quantity received and related job is entered in the inventory record.]	
Sale of scrap:	Cash or Accounts Receivable	45
	Work in Process Control	45
	Posting made to specific job record.	

Unlike spoilage and rework, there is no cost attached to the scrap, and hence no normal or abnormal scrap. All scrap sales, whatever the amount, are credited to the specific job. Scrap sales reduce the materials' costs of the job.

Scrap Common to All Jobs The journal entry in this case is

Scrap returned to storeroom:	No journal entry. [Memo of quantity received and related job is entered in the inventory record.]	

When scrap is sold, the simplest accounting is to regard scrap sales as a separate line item of other revenues. The journal entry is

Sale of scrap:	Cash or Accounts Receivable	45
	Sales of Scrap	45

However, many companies account for the sales as offsets against manufacturing overhead. The journal entry is

Sale of scrap:	Cash or Accounts Receivable	45
	Manufacturing Department Overhead Control	45
	Posting made to subsidiary record—"Sales of Scrap" column on department cost record.	

[4]Price Waterhouse, *Survey of the Cost Management Practices of Selected Midwest Manufacturers* (Cleveland: Price Waterhouse, 1989), p. 10.

Managing Waste and Environmental Costs at the DuPont Corporation

The DuPont Corporation manufactures a wide range of chemicals and chemical products. DuPont classifies the spoilage and scrap it generates as waste. Besides the cost of lost materials, chemical waste is a particular problem because of its impact on the environment. Strict environmental laws require that chemical waste be disposed of in an environmentally safe way, further adding to the cost of generating waste.

DuPont calculates the full cost of waste to include (1) the costs of materials lost in the chemical process minus their scrap value; (2) the full costs of semifinished and finished products spoiled; (3) the full cost of disposing of or treating the waste, such as site charges for hazardous waste, or costs of scrubbers and biotreatment plants to treat the waste; and (4) the cost of any solvents used to clean plant and equipment as a result of generating waste.

DuPont believes that calculating the total costs of waste helps businesses understand the operational and environmental costs of waste. This motivates individual plants to take actions such as redesigning products, reconfiguring processes, or investing in capital equipment to reduce these costs.

DuPont's acrylonitrile process at Beaumont, Texas, is a good example of how DuPont reduces waste costs. This plant generated more than 110 million pounds of ammonium sulfate waste, which was disposed of by injecting the waste in deep wells. While DuPont considered the disposal of the waste environmentally safe, the U.S. Environmental Protection Agency included ammonium sulfate in its figures of the toxic releases generated by DuPont. To improve its environmental performance and to reduce its waste costs, a team of DuPont engineers began modifying the reactor operating conditions for producing acrylonitrile. By changing the process, the team improved the yields of acrylonitrile and reduced ammonium sulfate waste by 70 million pounds. By altering its acrylonitrile process, DuPont saved a million dollars a year in lower waste and waste disposal costs.

Source: Adapted from 1990 Environmental Respect Awards, DuPont Corporation and based on discussions with Dale Martin, Manager, Environmental Effectiveness.

This method does not link scrap with any particular physical product. Instead, all products bear regular production costs without any credit for scrap sales except in an indirect manner: The sales of scrap are considered when setting budgeted manufacturing overhead rates. Thus, the budgeted overhead rate is lower than it would be if no credit for scrap sales were allowed in the overhead budget. This accounting for scrap is used in both process-costing and job-costing systems.

Recognizing Scrap at the Time of Production of Scrap

Our preceding illustrations assume that scrap returned to the storeroom is sold or disposed of quickly and hence not assigned an inventory cost figure. Scrap, however, sometimes has a significant market value, and the time between storing it and selling or reusing it can be quite long. Under these conditions, the company is justified in inventorying scrap at a conservative estimate of net realizable value so that production costs and related scrap recovery may be recognized in the same accounting period. Some companies tend to delay sales of scrap until the market price is most attractive. Volatile price fluctuations are typical for scrap metal. If scrap inventory becomes significant, it should be inventoried at some "reasonable value"—a difficult task in the face of volatile market prices.

Scrap Attributable to a Specific Job   The journal entry in the Hull Machine Shop example is

Scrap returned to storeroom:	Materials Control	45	
	Work in Process Control		45

Scrap Common to All Jobs   The journal entry in this case is

Scrap returned to storeroom:	Materials Control	45	
	Manufacturing Department Overhead Control		45

Observe that Materials Control account is debited in place of Cash or Accounts Receivable.

When this scrap is sold, the journal entry is

Sale of scrap:	Cash or Accounts Receivable	45	
	Materials Control		45

Scrap is sometimes reused as direct materials rather than sold as scrap. Then it should be debited to Materials Control as a class of direct materials and carried at its estimated net realizable value. For example, the entries when the scrap generated is common to all jobs are

Scrap returned to storeroom:	Materials Control	45	
	Manufacturing Department Overhead Control		45
Reuse of scrap:	Work in Process Control	45	
	Materials Control		45

The accounting for scrap under process costing follows the accounting for jobs when scrap is common to all jobs since process costing is used to cost the mass manufacture of similar units. The high cost of scrap focuses management's attention on ways to reduce scrap and to use it more profitably. For example, General Motors has redesigned its plastic injection molding processes to reduce the scrap plastic that must be broken away from its molded products. General Motors also regrinds and reuses the plastic scrap as direct materials, saving substantial input costs.

PROBLEM FOR SELF-STUDY

PROBLEM

Burlington Textiles has some spoiled goods that had an assigned cost of $4,000 and zero net disposal value.

REQUIRED

Prepare a journal entry for each of the following conditions under both (a) process costing (Department A) and (b) job costing:
1. Abnormal spoilage of $4,000.
2. Normal spoilage of $4,000 related to general plant operations.
3. Normal spoilage of $4,000 related to specifications of a particular job.

SOLUTION

(a) Process Costing			(b) Job Costing		
1. Loss from Abnormal Spoilage	4,000		Loss from Abnormal Spoilage	4,000	
Work in Process—Dept. A		4,000	Work in Process Control (job)		4,000
2. No entry until units are transferred. Then the normal spoilage costs are transferred along with the other costs:			Manufacturing Dept. Overhead Control	4,000	
			Work in Process Control (job)		4,000
Work in Process—Dept. B	4,000				
Work in Process—Dept. A		4,000			
3. Not applicable			No entry. Spoilage cost remains in Work in Process Control (job)		

The following points are linked to the chapter's learning objectives.

1. Spoilage is unacceptable units of production that are discarded or are sold for net disposal proceeds. Reworked units are unacceptable units that are subsequently reworked and sold as acceptable finished goods. Scrap is a product that has minimal sales value compared with the sales value of the main or joint product(s).

2. Normal spoilage is spoilage that arises under <u>efficient</u> operating conditions. Abnormal spoilage is spoilage that is not expected to arise under efficient operating conditions. Many accounting systems explicitly recognize both forms of spoilage when computing output units. Normal spoilage is typically included in the cost of good output units, while abnormal spoilage is recorded as a loss for the period.

3. Under the weighted-average method of process costing, costs in beginning inventory are pooled with costs in the current period when determining the costs of good units (which includes a normal spoilage amount) and the costs of abnormal spoilage.

4. Under the FIFO method of process costing, costs in beginning inventory are kept separate from the costs in the current period when determining the cost of good units (which includes a normal spoilage amount). The cost of abnormal spoilage is kept separate from the cost of good units.

5. Under the standard costing method of process costing, standard costs are used to determine the cost of good units (which includes a normal spoilage amount) and the costs of abnormal spoilage.

6. With a job-costing system, companies can decide to assign spoilage to specific jobs. Alternatively, they can allocate spoilage to all jobs as part of manufacturing overhead. Loss from abnormal spoilage is recorded as a period cost.

7. Reworked units should be indistinguishable from nonreworked good units when completed, and hence the two are assigned the same costs. Normal rework can be assigned to a specific job, or if common, to all jobs as part of manufacturing overhead. Abnormal rework is written off as a period cost.

8. Accounting for scrap is similar to the accounting for byproducts discussed in Chapter 15. Companies differ as to both when and how scrap is recognized in the accounting records.

APPENDIX: INSPECTION AND SPOILAGE AT INTERMEDIATE STAGES OF COMPLETION IN PROCESS COSTING

Consider how the timing of inspection at various stages of completion affects the amount of normal and abnormal spoilage. Assume that normal spoilage is 10% of the good units passing inspection in the Forging Department of the Dana Corporation, a manufacturer of automobile parts. Direct materials are added at the start of production in the Forging Department. Conversion costs are allocated evenly during the process.

Suppose inspection had occurred at the 20%, 50%, or 100% completion stage. A total of 8,000 units are spoiled in all cases. Note how the number of units of normal spoilage and abnormal spoilage change. Normal spoilage is computed on the number of *good units* that pass the inspection point *in the current period*. The following data are for October.

Flow of Production	**Physical Units:** Inspection at Stage of Completion at 20%	at 50%	at 100% *(at the end of period)*
Work in process, beginning (25%)*	11,000	11,000	11,000
Started during October	74,000	74,000	74,000
To account for	85,000	85,000	85,000
Good units completed and transferred out (85,000 – 8,000 spoiled – 16,000 ending)	61,000	61,000	61,000
Normal spoilage	6,600[†]	7,700[‡]	6,100[§]
Abnormal spoilage (8,000 – normal spoilage)	1,400	300	1,900
Work in process, ending (75%)*	16,000	16,000	16,000
Accounted for	85,000	85,000	85,000

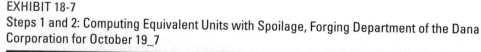

*Degree of completion for conversion costs of this department at the dates of the work-in-process inventories.
[†]10% × (74,000 units started – 8,000 units spoiled), since only the units started passed the 20% completion inspection point in the current period. Beginning work in process is excluded from this calculation since it is 25% complete.
[‡]10% × (85,000 units – 8,000 units spoiled), since *all* units passed the 50% completion inspection point in the current period.
[§]10% × 61,000, since 61,000 units were fully completed and inspected in the current period.

Exhibit 18-7 shows the computation of equivalent units assuming inspection at the 50% completion stage. The calculations depend on how much direct materials and conversion costs were incurred to get the units to the point of inspection. In Exhibit 18-7 the spoiled units have a full measure of direct materials and a 50% measure of conversion costs. The computations of equivalent unit costs and the assignments of total costs to units completed and in ending work in process would be similar to those in previous illustrations. Since ending work in process has passed the inspection point in this example, these units would bear normal spoilage costs, just like the units that have been completed and transferred out.

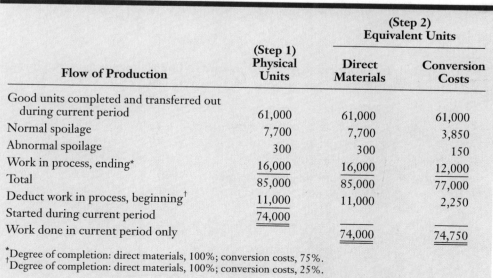

EXHIBIT 18-7

Steps 1 and 2: Computing Equivalent Units with Spoilage, Forging Department of the Dana Corporation for October 19_7

Flow of Production	(Step 1) Physical Units	(Step 2) Equivalent Units Direct Materials	Conversion Costs
Good units completed and transferred out during current period	61,000	61,000	61,000
Normal spoilage	7,700	7,700	3,850
Abnormal spoilage	300	300	150
Work in process, ending*	16,000	16,000	12,000
Total	85,000	85,000	77,000
Deduct work in process, beginning[†]	11,000	11,000	2,250
Started during current period	74,000		
Work done in current period only		74,000	74,750

*Degree of completion: direct materials, 100%; conversion costs, 75%.
[†]Degree of completion: direct materials, 100%; conversion costs, 25%.

This chapter and the Glossary at the end of this book contain definitions of the following important terms:

abnormal spoilage (p. 653)
normal spoilage (653)

reworked units (652)
spoilage (652)

ASSIGNMENT MATERIAL

QUESTIONS

18-1 Why is there an unmistakable trend in manufacturing to improve quality?

18-2 Distinguish among spoilage, reworked units, and scrap.

18-3 "Normal spoilage is planned spoilage." Discuss.

18-4 "Costs of abnormal spoilage are lost costs." Explain.

18-5 "What has been regarded as normal spoilage in the past is not necessarily acceptable as normal in the present or future." Explain.

18-6 "Abnormal units are inferred rather than identified." Explain.

18-7 "In accounting for spoiled goods, we are dealing with cost assignment rather than cost incurrence." Explain.

18-8 "Total input includes abnormal as well as normal spoilage and is therefore irrational as a basis for computing normal spoilage." Do you agree? Why?

18-9 "The point of inspection is the key to the allocation of spoilage costs." Do you agree? Explain.

18-10 "The unit cost of normal spoilage is the same as the unit cost of abnormal spoilage." Do you agree? Explain.

18-11 "In job-order costing, the costs of specific normal spoilage are charged to specific jobs." Do you agree? Explain.

18-12 "The costs of reworking defective units are always charged to the specific jobs where the defects were originally discovered." Do you agree? Explain.

18-13 "Abnormal rework costs should be charged to a loss account, not to manufacturing overhead." Do you agree? Explain.

18-14 When is a company justified in inventorying scrap?

18-15 How do company managements use information about scrap?

EXERCISES

18-16 **Normal and abnormal spoilage in units.** The following data, in physical units, describe a grinding process for January:

Work process, beginning	19,000
Started during current period	150,000
To account for	169,000
Spoiled units	12,000
Good units completed and transferred out	132,000
Work in process, ending	25,000
Accounted for	169,000

Inspection occurs at the 100% conversion stage. Normal spoilage is 5% of the good units passing inspection.

REQUIRED

1. Compute the normal and abnormal spoilage in units.
2. Assume that the equivalent unit cost of a spoiled unit is $10. Compute the amount of potential savings if all spoilage were eliminated, assuming that all other costs would be unaffected. Comment on your answer.

18-17 Equivalent units, equivalent unit costs, spoilage. (CMA adapted) Consider the following data for November 19_7 from the Gray Manufacturing Company, which makes silk pennants and operates a process-costing system. All direct materials are added at the beginning of the process and conversion costs are added evenly during the process. Spoilage is detected upon inspection at the completion of the process. Spoiled units are disposed of at zero net disposal price.

	Physical Units (Pennants)	Direct Materials	Conversion Costs
Work in process, November 1*	1,000	$ 1,300	$ 1,250
Started in November 19_7	?		
Good units completed and transferred out during November 19_7	9,000		
Normal spoilage	100		
Abnormal spoilage	50		
Work in process, November 30†	2,000		
Costs added during November 19_7		$12,180	$27,750

*Degree of completion: direct materials, 100%; conversion costs, 50%.
†Degree of completion: direct materials, 100%; conversion costs, 30%.

REQUIRED

1. Compute the equivalent units of work done in the current period for direct materials and conversion costs. Show physical units in the first column.
2. Calculate the cost per equivalent unit of beginning work in process and of work done in the current period for direct materials and conversion costs.

18-18 Weighted-average method, spoilage. Anderson Plastics makes plastic rear lamps for cars using an injection molding process. Spoiled units are detected upon inspection at the end of the process and are disposed of at zero net disposal price. Assume normal spoilage is 15% of the good output produced. Anderson Plastics uses the weighted-average method of process costing. The following information about actual costs for April 19_8 is available.

	Direct Materials		Conversion Costs	
	Equivalent Units	Total Costs	Equivalent Units	Total Costs
Work in process, April 1 (15,000 units)	15,000	$120,000	14,000	$140,000
Work done during April 19_8	25,000	210,000	28,000	301,000
To account for	40,000	$330,000	42,000	$441,000
Good units completed and transferred out during April 19_8	20,000	?	20,000	?
Normal and abnormal spoilage	4,000		4,000	
Work in process, April 30 (20,000 units)	16,000	?	18,000	?

REQUIRED

1. Calculate the cost per equivalent unit of beginning work in process and of work done in the current period for direct materials and conversion costs.
2. Summarize total costs to account for, and assign these costs to units completed (and transferred out), normal spoilage, abnormal spoilage, and ending work in process using the weighted-average method.
3. What is the cost of a good unit completed and transferred out under the weighted-average method?

18-19 FIFO method. Refer to the information in Exercise 18-18.

Do Exercise 18-18 using the FIFO method.

18-20 Standard costing method. Refer to the information in Exercise 18-18. Suppose Anderson determines standard costs of $8.20 per (equivalent) unit for direct materials and $10.20 per (equivalent) unit for conversion costs for both beginning work in process and work done in the current period.

REQUIRED
Do Exercise 18-18 using the standard costing method.

18-21 Weighted-average method, spoilage. Superchip specializes in the manufacture of microchips for aircraft. Direct materials are added at the start of the production process. Conversion costs are added evenly during the process. Some units of this product are spoiled as a result of defects not detectable before inspection of finished goods. Normally, the spoiled units are 15% of the good units transferred out. Spoiled units are disposed of at zero net disposal price.

Superchip uses the weighted-average method of process costing. Summary data for September 19_7 are

	Physical Units (Microchips)	Direct Materials	Conversion Costs
Work in process, September 1*	400	$ 64,000	$ 10,200
Started in September 19_7	1,700		
Good units completed and transferred out during September 19_7	1,400		
Work in process, September 30†	300		
Costs added during September 19_7		$378,000	$153,600

*Degree of completion: direct materials, 100%; conversion costs, 30%.
†Degree of completion: direct materials, 100%; conversion costs, 40%.

REQUIRED
1. For each cost element, compute the equivalent units of work done in September 19_7. Show physical units in the first column.
2. For each cost element, calculate the cost per equivalent unit of beginning work in process and of work done in September 19_7.
3. Summarize the total costs to account for, and assign these costs to units completed (and transferred out), normal spoilage, abnormal spoilage, and ending work in process using the weighted-average method.

18-22 FIFO method, spoilage. Refer to the information in Exercise 18-21.
REQUIRED
Do Exercise 18-21 using the FIFO method of process costing.

18-23 Standard costing method, spoilage. Refer to the information in Exercise 18-21. Suppose Superchip determines standard costs of $205 per (equivalent) unit for direct materials and $80 per (equivalent) unit for conversion costs for both beginning work in process and work done in the current period.

REQUIRED
Do Exercise 18-21 using standard costs.

18-24 Spoilage and job costing. (L. Bamber) Bamber Kitchens produces a variety of items in accordance with special job orders from hospitals, plant cafeterias, and university dormitories. An order for 2,500 cases of mixed vegetables costs $6 per case: direct materials, $3; direct manufacturing labor, $2; and manufacturing overhead allocated, $1. The manufacturing overhead rate includes a provision for normal spoilage. Consider each requirement independently. Omit explanations of journal entries.

1. Assume that a laborer dropped 200 cases. Suppose that part of the 200 cases could be sold to a nearby prison for $200 cash. Prepare a journal entry to record this event. Calculate and explain briefly the unit cost of the remaining 2,300 cases.
2. Refer to the original data. Tasters at the company reject 200 of the 2,500 cases. The 200 cases are disposed of for $400. Assume that this rejection rate is considered normal. Prepare a journal entry to record this event, and calculate the unit cost if
   a. The rejection is attributable to exacting specifications of this particular job.
   b. The rejection is characteristic of the production process and is not attributable to this specific job.
   Are unit costs the same in requirements 2a and 2b? Explain your reasoning briefly.
3. Refer to the original data. Tasters rejected 200 cases that had insufficient salt. The product can be placed in a vat, salt added, and reprocessed into jars. This operation, which is considered normal, will cost $200. Prepare a journal entry to record this event, and calculate the unit cost of all the cases if
   a. This additional cost was incurred because of the exacting specifications of this particular job.
   b. This additional cost occurs regularly because of difficulty in seasoning.
   Are unit costs the same in requirements 3a and 3b? Explain your reasoning briefly.

18-25 Reworked units, costs of rework. White Goods assembles washing machines at its Auburn plant. In February 19_8, 60 tumbler units that cost $44 each from a new supplier were defective and had to be disposed of at zero disposal price. White Goods was able to rework all 60 washing machines by substituting new tumbler units purchased from one of its existing suppliers. Each replacement tumbler cost $50.

1. What alternative approaches are there to account for the materials costs of reworked units?
2. Should White Goods use the $44 or $50 amount as the costs of materials reworked? Explain.
3. What other costs might White Goods include in its analysis of the total costs of rework due to the tumbler units purchased from the (now) bankrupt supplier?

18-26 Scrap, job-order costing. The Mendoza Company has an extensive job-costing facility that uses a variety of metals. Consider each requirement independently. Omit explanations of journal entries.

1. Job 372 uses a particular metal alloy that is not used for any other job. Assume that scrap is accounted for at the time of sale of scrap. The scrap is sold for $490. Prepare the journal entry.
2. The scrap from Job 372 consists of a metal used by many other jobs. No record is maintained of the scrap generated by individual jobs. Assume that scrap is accounted for at the time of its sale. Scrap totaling $4,000 is sold. Prepare two journal entries that could be used to account for the sale of scrap.
3. Suppose the scrap generated in requirement 2 is returned to the storeroom for future use and a journal entry is made to record the scrap. A month later, the scrap is reused as direct material on a subsequent job. Prepare the journal entries to record these transactions.

18-27 Physical units, inspection at various stages of completion. (Chapter Appendix) Normal spoilage is 6% of the good units passing inspection in a forging process. In March, a total of 10,000 units were spoiled. Other data include units started during March, 120,000; work in process, beginning, 14,000 units (20% completed for conversion costs); work in process, ending, 11,000 units (70% completed for conversion costs).

REQUIRED

In columnar form, compute the normal and abnormal spoilage in units, assuming inspection at 15%, 40%, and 100% stages of completion.

PROBLEMS

18-28 Weighted-average method, spoilage. Spicer uses the weighted-average method of process costing. Consider the following data for the Cooking Department of Spicer, Inc., for the month of January

	Physical Units	Direct Materials	Conversion Costs
Work in process, January 1*	11,000	$ 220,000	$ 30,000
Started in January	74,000		
Good units completed and transferred out during January	61,000		
Spoiled units	8,000		
Work in process, January 31†	16,000		
Costs added during January		$1,480,000	$942,000

*Degree of completion: direct materials, 100%; conversion costs, 25%.
†Degree of completion: direct materials, 100%; conversion costs, 75%.

Inspection occurs when production is 100% completed. Normal spoilage is 11% of good units completed and transferred out during the current period. Spoiled units are disposed of at zero net disposal price.

REQUIRED

1. Summarize total costs to account for, and assign these costs to units completed (and transferred out), normal spoilage, abnormal spoilage, and ending work in process using the weighted-average method.
2. What is the cost of a good unit completed and transferred out under the weighted-average method?

18-29 FIFO method, spoilage. Refer to the information in Problem 18-28.

REQUIRED

Do Problem 18-28 using the FIFO method of process costing. If you did Problem 18-28, comment on the cost differences under the weighted-average and FIFO methods.

18-30 Standard costing method, spoilage. Refer to the information in Problem 18-28. Suppose Superchip determines standard costs of $20 per (equivalent) unit for direct materials and $11 per (equivalent) unit for conversion costs for both beginning work in process and work done in the current period.

REQUIRED

Do Problem 18-28 using the standard costing method of process costing.

18-31 Weighted-average method, spoilage. The Alston Company operates under a weighted-average method of process costing. It has two departments, Cleaning and Milling. For both departments, conversion costs are added uniformly throughout the processes. However, direct materials are added at the beginning of the process in the Cleaning Department, and additional direct materials are added at the end of the milling process. The costs and unit production statistics for May follow. All unfinished work at the end of May is 25% completed as to conversion costs. The beginning inventory (May 1) was 80% completed as to conversion costs as of May 1. All completed work is transferred to the next department.

	Cleaning	Milling
Beginning Inventories		
Cleaning: $1,000 direct materials, $800 conversion costs	$1,800	
Milling: $6,450 previous department cost (transferred-in cost) and $2,450 conversion costs		$8,900
Costs Added during Current Period		
Direct materials	$9,000	$ 640
Conversion costs	$8,000	$4,950
Physical Units		
Units in beginning inventory	1 ,000	3,000
Units started this month	9,000	7,400
Good units completed and transferred out	7,400	6,000
Normal spoilage	740*	300†
Abnormal spoilage	260	100

*Normal spoilage in the Cleaning Department is 10% of good units completed and transferred out.
†Normal spoilage in the Milling Department is 5% of good units completed and transferred out.

ADDITIONAL INFORMATION

1. Spoilage is assumed to occur at the end of each of the two processes when the units are inspected. Spoiled units are disposed of at zero net disposal price.
2. Assume that there is no shrinkage, evaporation, or abnormal spoilage other than that indicated in the information given.
3. Carry unit cost calculations to three decimal places where necessary. Calculate final totals to the nearest dollar.

REQUIRED

Using the weighted-average method, summarize total costs to account for, and assign these costs to units completed (and transferred out), normal spoilage, abnormal spoilage, and ending work in process for the Cleaning Department. (Problem 18-33 explores additional facets of this problem.)

18-32 FIFO method, spoilage. Refer to the information in Problem 18-31.

REQUIRED

Do Problem 18-31 using the FIFO method of process costing. (Problem 18-34 explores additional facets of this problem.)

18-33 Weighted-average method, Milling Department (continuation of 18-31). Refer to the information in Problem 18-31.

REQUIRED

Use the weighted-average method to summarize total costs to account for, and assign these costs to units completed (and transferred out), normal spoilage, abnormal spoilage, and ending work in process for the Milling Department.

18-34 FIFO method, Milling Department (continuation of 18-32). Refer to the information in Problem 18-31.

REQUIRED

Use the FIFO method to summarize total costs to account for, and assign these costs to units completed (and transferred out), normal spoilage, abnormal spoilage, and ending work in process for the Milling Department.

18-35 Job-cost spoilage and scrap. (F. Mayne) Santa Cruz Metal Fabricators, Inc., has a large job, No. 2734, that calls for producing various ore bins, chutes, and metal boxes for enlarging a copper concentrator. The following charges were made to the job in November 19_8:

Direct materials	$26,951
Direct manufacturing labor	15,076
Manufacturing overhead	7,538

The contract with the customer called for the total price to be based on a cost-plus approach. The contract defined cost to include direct materials, direct manufacturing labor costs, and manufacturing overhead to be allocated at 50% of direct manufacturing labor costs. The contract also provided that the total costs of all work spoiled were to be removed from the billable cost of the job and that the benefits from scrap sales were to reduce the billable cost of the job.

REQUIRED

1. In accordance with the stated terms of the contract, prepare journal entries for the following two items:
   a. A cutting error was made in production. The up-to-date job-cost record for the batch of work involved showed materials of $650, direct manufacturing labor of $500, and allocated overhead of $250. Because fairly large pieces of metal were recoverable, the company believed that the scrap value was $600 and that the materials recovered could be used on other jobs. The spoiled work was sent to the warehouse.
   b. Small pieces of metal cuttings and scrap in November 19_8 amounted to $1,250, which was the price quoted by a scrap dealer. No journal entries have been made with regard to the scrap until the price was quoted by the scrap dealer. The scrap dealer's offer was immediately accepted.
2. Consider normal and abnormal spoilage. Suppose the contract described above had contained the clause "a normal spoilage allowance of 1% of the job costs will be included in the billable costs of the job."
   a. Is this clause specific enough to define exactly how much spoilage is normal and how much is abnormal? Explain.
   b. Repeat requirement 1a with this "normal spoilage of 1%" clause in mind. You should be able to provide two slightly different journal entries.

18-36 Job costing, rework. The Bristol Corporation manufactures two brands of motors, SM-5 and RW-8. The costs of manufacturing each SM-5 motor, excluding rework costs, are direct materials, $300; direct manufacturing labor, $60; and manufacturing overhead, $190. Defective units are sent to a separate rework area. Rework costs per SM-5 motor are direct materials, $60; direct manufacturing labor, $45; and manufacturing overhead, $75.

In February 19_8, Bristol manufactured 1,000 SM-5 and 500 RW-8 motors, and 80 of the SM-5 motors required rework. Bristol classifies 50 of these motors as normal rework for SM-5 and RW-8, and not specifically attributable to SM-5. None of the RW-8 motors required rework. Bristol allocates manufacturing overhead on the basis of machine-hours required to manufacture SM-5 and RW-8. Each SM-5 and RW-8 motor requires the same number of machine-hours.

REQUIRED

1. Prepare journal entries to record the accounting for rework.
2. What were the total rework costs charged to SM-5 motors in February 19_8?

18-37 Job costing, scrap. The Wong Corporation makes two different types of hubcaps for cars—models HM3 and JB4. Circular pieces of metal are stamped out of steel sheets (leaving the edges as scrap), formed, and finished. The stamping operation is identical for both types of hubcaps. During March, Wong manufactured 20,000 units of HM3 and 10,000 units of JB4. In March, manufacturing costs per unit of HM3 and JB4 before accounting for the scrap are as follows:

	HM3	JB4
Direct materials	$10	$15
Direct manufacturing labor	3	4
Materials-related manufacturing overhead (materials handling, storage, etc.)	2	3
Other manufacturing overhead	6	8
Unit manufacturing costs	$21	$30

Materials-related manufacturing costs are allocated to products at 20% of direct materials costs. Other manufacturing overhead is allocated to products at 200% of direct manufacturing labor costs. Since the same metal sheets are used to make both types of hubcaps, Wong maintains no records of the scrap generated by the individual products. Scrap generated during manufacturing is accounted for at the time it is returned to the storeroom as an offset to materials-related manufacturing overhead. The value of scrap generated during March and returned to the storeroom was $7,000.

REQUIRED

1. Prepare a journal entry to summarize the accounting for scrap during March.
2. Suppose the scrap generated in March was sold in April for $7,000. Prepare a journal entry to account for this transaction.
3. What is the manufacturing cost per unit for HM3 and JB4 in March after accounting for scrap? Explain.

18-38 **Weighted-average, inspection at 80% completion.** (A. Atkinson) (Chapter Appendix) Ottawa Manufacturing produces a plastic toy in a two-stage manufacturing operation. The company uses a weighted-average process-costing system. During the month of June, the following data were recorded for the Finishing Department:

Units of beginning inventory	10,000
Percentage of beginning units completed	25%
Cost of direct materials in beginning work in process	$ 0
Units started	70,000
Units completed	50,000
Units in ending inventory	20,000
Percentage of ending units completed	95%
Spoiled units	10,000
Costs added during current period	
Direct materials	$655,200
Direct manufacturing labor	$635,600
Manufacturing overhead	$616,000
Work in process, beginning	
Conversion costs	$ 42,000
Transferred-in costs	$ 82,900
Cost of units transferred in during current period	$647,500

Conversion costs are incurred evenly throughout the process. Direct materials costs are incurred when production is 90% complete. Inspection occurs when production is 80% complete. Normal spoilage is 10% of all good units that pass inspection. Spoiled units are disposed of at zero net disposal price.

REQUIRED

For the month of June, summarize total costs to account for, and assign these costs to units completed (and transferred out), normal spoilage, abnormal spoilage, and ending work in process.

18-39 Process versus job costing, spoilage, ethics. Chip Contractors assembles high-performance microchips for two customers—Prestige Jets and the U.S. Air Force. The emphasis the Air Force places on quality helps Chip impress potential customers about the quality of its chips. Kelly Gillis, the president of Chip Contractors, decides to use a double-testing procedure for chips sold to the U.S. Air Force. Tom Sanders, the controller of Chip Contractors, asks Gillis how she wants the cost of this extra testing shown in the accounting records. Each month Sanders compiles a production-cost report that he sends to Prestige Jets. Prestige pays Chip the actual production cost per chip purchased plus a 20% profit margin. The U.S. Air Force contract is for a fixed price per good chip.

Gillis tells Sanders to follow the normal practice of computing the cost of good chips at the total plant level rather than for each customer. Sanders strongly objects to this approach. He believes it will result in Chip Contractors overcharging Prestige Jets. Gillis believes that they should wait until Prestige Jets complains before they make any adjustments. She is adamant that no internal spoilage data should be shown to Prestige Jets.

Sanders decides to privately track cost and spoilage data in May 19_7 for Chip's two product lines. This tracking is relatively easy because a separate production line is used for each customer:

	Prestige Jets	U.S. Air Force	Total Plant
Physical Units for May			
Work in process, beginning inventory	0	0	0
Started during May	6,000	4,000	10,000
Good units completed and transferred out during May	4,000	2,000	6,000
Work in process, ending inventory	1,500	1,100	2,600
Direct materials (both 100% complete)			
Conversion costs (both 70% complete)			
Normal spoilage (% of good units transferred out)	7.5%	25%	?
Costs for May			
Work in process, beginning inventory	$0	$0	$0
Direct materials added during May	$12,750,000	$8,500,000	$21,250,000
Conversion costs added during May	$ 7,834,000	$6,327,080	$14,161,080

All direct materials are introduced at the beginning of the production process. Conversion costs are assigned evenly during the process. Inspection occurs at the end of the production process. Spoiled chips are disposed of at zero net disposal price. Chip Contractors uses the weighted-average method of process costing.

REQUIRED
1. Compute the actual cost per good chip transferred out in May for (a) Prestige Jets, (b) the U.S. Air Force, and (c) the total plant. Chip Contractors includes both normal and abnormal spoilage costs when computing actual costs for Prestige Jets.
2. Explain any differences between (a) and (b) in requirement 1.
3. What cost number per good chip sold in May 19_7 should Sanders report to Prestige Jets? Explain any ethical dilemmas that he might face.
4. Suppose the purchasing officer of Prestige Jets receives the May 19_7 bill based on the plant unit cost per good output unit. He immediately requests that Sanders provide full details on how the May unit cost amount was determined. What should Sanders do?

COLLABORATIVE LEARNING PROBLEM

18-40 Job costing, spoilage. (CMA adapted) The Richport Company manufactures products that often require specification changes or modifications to meet its customers' needs. Still, Richport has been able to establish a normal spoilage rate of 2.5% of *normal input*. Normal spoilage is recognized during the budgeting process and classified as a component of manufacturing overhead when determining the overhead rate.

Rose Duncan, one of Richport's inspection managers, obtains the following information for Job No. N1192-122 that was recently completed. A total of 122,000 units were started, and 5,000 units were rejected at final inspection yielding 117,000 good units. Duncan noted that 900 of the first units produced were rejected because of a design defect that was considered very unusual; this defect was corrected immediately, and no further units were rejected for this reason. These units were disposed of after incurring an additional cost of $1,200. Duncan was unable to identify a rejection pattern for the remaining 4,100 rejected units. These units can be sold at $7 per unit.

The total costs for all 122,000 units of Job No. N1192-122 are presented here. The job has been completed, but the costs have yet to be transferred to finished goods.

Direct materials	$2,196,000
Direct manufacturing labor	1,830,000
Manufacturing overhead	2,928,000
Total manufacturing costs	$6,954,000

INSTRUCTIONS

Form groups of two or more students to complete the following requirements.

REQUIRED

1. Calculate the unit quantities of normal and abnormal spoilage.
2. Prepare the appropriate journal entry (or entries) to properly account for Job No. N1192-122 including spoilage, disposal, and transfer of costs to finished goods control.
3. How would the information in requirement 2 be useful to Richport?
4. How well do you think Richport is managing spoilage?

COST MANAGEMENT: QUALITY, TIME, AND THE THEORY OF CONSTRAINTS

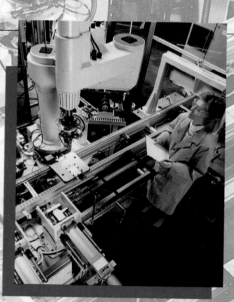

Customers are requiring companies to meet demanding quality levels and delivery schedules while maintaining competitive prices. To achieve these multiple goals, companies such as Hansford Manufacturing Company use sophisticated flexible robotic systems in their manufacturing operations and monitor performance using both financial and nonfinancial measures of quality and time.

LEARNING OBJECTIVES

After studying this chapter, you should be able to

1. Explain four cost categories in a cost of quality program
2. Describe three methods that companies use to identify quality problems
3. Identify the relevant costs and benefits of quality improvements
4. Provide examples of nonfinancial quality measures of customer satisfaction and internal performance
5. Understand why companies use both financial and nonfinancial measures of quality
6. Describe customer-response time, and explain the reasons for and the cost of lines and delays
7. Define the three main measurements in the theory of constraints
8. Describe four steps in managing bottlenecks

As we stated in Chapter 1, global competition and demanding customers have forced managers to improve the quality of their products and to deliver them to customers faster. But achieving higher quality and faster delivery requires managers to identify and overcome a variety of organizational constraints. This chapter examines how management accounting can assist managers in taking initiatives in the quality and time areas, and in making decisions under many constraints.

QUALITY AS A COMPETITIVE WEAPON

Many companies throughout the world—for example, Hewlett-Packard and Ford Motor Company in the United States and Canada; British Telecom in the United Kingdom; Fujitsu and Toyota in Japan; Crysel in Mexico; and Samsung in Korea—view total-quality management as one of the most important success factors of the 1990s because it reduces costs and increases customer satisfaction. Several prestigious, high-profile awards—for example, the Malcolm Baldrige Quality Award in the United States, the Deming Prize in Japan, and the Premio Nacional de Calidad in Mexico—have been instituted to recognize exceptional quality.

International quality standards have emerged. For example, ISO 9000, developed by the International Organization for Standardization, is a set of five international standards for quality management adopted by more than 60 countries. ISO 9000 was created to enable companies to effectively document and certify their quality system elements. Some companies, such as DuPont and General Electric, are increasingly requiring their suppliers to obtain ISO 9000 certification. Why? To reduce their own costs by evaluating, assessing, and working to improve the quality of their suppliers' products. Thus, certification and an emphasis on quality are rapidly becoming conditions for competing in the global market.

Why this emphasis on quality? Because quality costs can be as much as 10% to 20% of sales revenue for many organizations. Quality-improvement programs can result in substantial savings and higher revenues. Motorola, the telecommunications and electronics manufacturer, estimates that it saved $2 billion in 1994 from quality programs. This amounts to savings of 9% on annual revenues of $22.2 billion in 1994. Motorola's 1994 operating income was $2.4 billion. Without the savings from its quality programs, Motorola's income would be considerably lower.[1]

Consider a general effect that quality has on revenues. If competitors are improving quality, then a company that does not invest in quality improvement will likely suffer a decline in its market share and revenues. In this case, the benefit of better quality is in preventing lower revenues, not in generating higher revenues.

Quality improvement also has nonfinancial and qualitative effects that improve a company's long-term performance. For example, managers and workers focusing on quality gain expertise about product and process. This knowledge may lead to lower costs in the future. Manufacturing a product of high quality can enhance a company's reputation and increase customer goodwill, which may lead to higher future revenues. Motorola believes that its quality initiatives, which have increased customer satisfaction, also fueled its 380% increase in revenues, 800% increase in profits, and 600% increase in stock price over the last 8 years.

As corporations' responsibilities toward the environment grow, many managers are paying increasing attention to environmental quality and the problems of air pollution, waste water, oil and chemical spills, hazardous waste, and waste management. The costs of environmental damage (failure costs) can be extremely high to corporations under the 1990 amendments to the Clean Air Act. Companies can be charged multimillion dollar fines. For example, Exxon paid $125 million in fines and restitution on top of $1 billion in civil payments for the Exxon Valdez oil spill, which harmed the Alaskan coast. In 1994, the International Organization for Standardization announced ISO 14000, an environmental management standard. The standard's goal is to nudge organizations to pursue environmental goals vigorously by developing (1) environmental management systems to improve the environmental impact of

---

[1]Based on discussions with Richard Buetow, Director of Quality, Motorola, Inc.

an organization's activities, products, and services, and (2) environmental auditing and performance evaluation systems to review and provide feedback on how well an organization has achieved its environmental goals.

TWO ASPECTS OF QUALITY

The term *quality* refers to a wide variety of factors—fitness for use, the degree to which a product satisfies the needs of a customer, and the degree to which a product conforms to design specification and engineering requirements.[2] We discuss two basic aspects of quality—*quality of design* and *conformance quality*.[3]

Quality of design measures how closely the characteristics of products or services match the needs and wants of customers. Suppose customers of photocopying machines want copiers that combine copying, faxing, scanning, and electronic printing. Photocopying machines that fail to meet these customer needs fail in the quality of their design. Similarly, if customers of a bank want an automated payment system for their monthly bills, not providing this facility would be a quality of design failure.

Conformance quality is the performance of a product or service according to design and production specifications. For example, if a photocopying machine mishandles paper or breaks down, it will have failed to satisfy conformance quality. Products not conforming to specifications must be repaired, reworked, or scrapped at an additional cost to the organization. If nonconformance errors are not corrected within the plant and the product breaks down at the customer site, even greater repair costs as well as the loss of customer goodwill—often the highest quality cost of all—may result. In the banking industry, depositing a customer's check into the wrong bank account is an example of conformance quality failure.

The following diagram illustrates our framework:

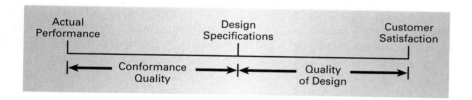

To travel the road from actual performance to customer satisfaction, companies must meet design specifications through conformance quality, but they must also design products to satisfy customers through quality of design.

COSTS OF QUALITY

The **costs of quality (COQ)** are costs incurred to prevent or rectify the production of a low-quality product. These costs focus on conformance quality and are incurred in all areas of the value chain. They are classified into four categories:

1. **Prevention costs**—costs incurred in precluding the production of products that do not conform to specifications.

2. **Appraisal costs**—costs incurred in detecting which of the individual units of products do not conform to specifications.

[2]The American Society for Quality Control defines *quality* as the totality of features and characteristics of a product made or a service performed according to specifications, to satisfy customers at the time of purchase and during use. ANSI/ASQC A3-1978, *Quality Systems Terminology* (Milwaukee, Wis.: American Society for Quality Control, 1978).
[3]See R. DeVor, T. Chang, and J. Sutherland, *Statistical Quality Design and Control* (New York: Macmillan, 1992); and J. Evans and W. Lindsay, *The Management and Control of Quality* (St. Paul: West, 1993).

EXHIBIT 19-1

Items Pertaining to Costs of Quality Reports

Prevention Costs	Appraisal Costs	Internal Failure Costs	External Failure Costs
Design engineering	Inspection	Spoilage	Customer support
Process engineering	On-line product	Rework	Transportation costs
Quality engineering	manufacturing and	Scrap	Manufacturing/process
Supplier evaluations	process inspection	Breakdown maintenance	engineering
Preventive equipment	Product testing	Manufacturing/process	Warranty repair costs
maintenance		engineering on	Liability claims
Quality training		internal failure	
New materials used			
to manufacture products			

3. **Internal failure costs**—costs incurred when a nonconforming product is detected before it is shipped to customers.

4. **External failure costs**—costs incurred when a nonconforming product is detected after it is shipped to customers.

Exhibit 19-1 presents examples of individual cost of quality items in each of these four categories reported on COQ reports. Note that the items included in Exhibit 19-1 come from all value-chain business functions and are broader than the internal failure costs of spoilage, rework, and scrap in manufacturing considered in Chapter 18.

We illustrate the various issues in managing quality—from computing the costs of quality, to identifying quality problems, to taking actions to improve quality—using the Photon Corporation as example. Photon makes many products. Our presentation focuses on Photon's photocopying machines, which earned an operating income of $24 million on sales of $300 million (20,000 copiers) in 19_8. Photon determines its costs of quality using an activity-based approach with five steps.

Step 1: Identify All Quality-Related Activities and Activity Cost Pools   Column 1 of Exhibit 19-2, Panel A, classifies costs into prevention, appraisal, internal failure, and external failure categories, and indicates the value-chain functions in which the costs occur. One such activity is inspecting (including testing) the photocopying machines.

Step 2: Determine the Quantity of the Cost-Allocation Base for Each Quality-Related Activity   (See Exhibit 19-2, Panel A, column 2.) For example, Photon identifies inspection hours, the primary cost driver, as the cost-allocation base of the inspection activity. Assume that photocopying machines use 240,000 hours (12 hours per copier × 20,000 copiers) of the cost-allocation base.

Step 3: Compute the Rate per Unit of Each Cost-Allocation Base   (See Exhibit 19-2, Panel A, column 3.) Due to space considerations, we do not provide details of the calculations.[4] In the Photon example, the total (fixed and variable) costs of inspection are $40 per hour.

Step 4: Compute the Costs of Each Quality-Related Activity for Photocopying Machines by Multiplying the Quantity of the Cost-Allocation Base Determined in Step 2 by the Rate per Unit of the Cost-Allocation Base Computed in Step 3   (See Exhibit 19-2, Panel A, column 4.) In our example, quality-related inspection costs are $9,600,000 (240,000 hours × $40 per hour).

[4]Allocation rates are computed using methods described in Chapter 4 (p. 96–97), Chapter 5 (p. 146), and Chapter 14 (p. 510–511).

EXHIBIT 19-2
Activity-Based COQ Analysis for the Photon Corporation

PANEL A: COQ REPORT

Costs of Quality and Value-Chain Category (1)	Allocation Base or Cost Driver		Total Costs (4) = (2) × (3)	Percentage of Sales (5) = (4) ÷ $300,000,000
	Quantity (2)	Rate (Number Assumed) (3)		
Prevention costs				
Design engineering (R&D/Design)	40,000* hours	$80 per hour	$ 3,200,000	1.07%
Process engineering (R&D/Design)	45,000* hours	$60 per hour	2,700,000	0.90
Total prevention costs			5,900,000	1.97
Appraisal costs				
Inspection (Manufacturing)	240,000† hours	$40 per hour	9,600,000	3.20
Total appraisal costs			9,600,000	3.20
Internal failure costs				
Rework (Manufacturing)	2,500‡ copiers reworked	$4,000 per copier reworked	10,000,000	3.33
Total internal failure costs			10,000,000	3.33
External failure costs				
Customer support (Marketing)	3,000§ copiers repaired	$200 per copier repaired	600,000	0.20
Transportation costs (Distribution)	3,000 copiers repaired	$240 per copier repaired	720,000	0.24
Warranty repair (Customer service)	3,000 copiers repaired	$4,400 per copier repaired	13,200,000	4.40
Total external failure costs			14,520,000	4.84
Total costs of quality			$40,020,000	13.34%

PANEL B: OPPORTUNITY COST ANALYSIS

Costs of Quality Category (1)	Quantity of Lost Sales (2)	Contribution Margin per Copier (Number Assumed) (3)	Total Estimated Contribution Margin Lost (4) = (2) × (3)	Percentage of Sales (5) = (4) ÷ $300,000,000
External failure costs				
Estimated forgone contribution margin and income on lost sales	2,000# copiers	$6,000	$12,000,000	4.00%
Total costs of quality			$12,000,000	4.00%

*Based on special studies.
†12 hours per copier × 20,000 copiers.
‡12.5% of 20,000 copiers manufactured required rework.
§15% of 20,000 copiers manufactured required warranty repair service.
#Estimated by Photon's Market Research Department.

Step 5: Obtain the Total Costs of Quality by Adding the Costs of all Quality-Related Activities for Photocopying Machines in All Value-Chain Business Functions Exhibit 19-2, Panel A, shows Photon's total costs of quality reported on the COQ report for photocopying machines at $40.02 million, of which the largest categories are $14.52 million in total external failure costs and $10 million in total internal failure costs—a sum of $24.52 million. Total reported costs of quality are 13.34% of current sales.

Do not assume, however, that costs reported on COQ reports represent the total costs of quality for a company. COQ reports typically exclude opportunity costs, such as forgone contribution margins and income from lost sales, lost production, or lower prices, that result from poor quality. Why? Because opportunity costs are difficult to estimate and generally not recorded in accounting systems. Nevertheless, opportunity costs can be substantial and important driving forces in quality-improvement programs. Exhibit 19-2, Panel B, presents the analysis of the opportunity costs of poor quality at Photon. Photon Corporation's Market Research Department estimates lost sales of 2,000 photocopying machines because of external failures. The forgone contribution and operating income of $12 million measures the financial costs from dissatisfied customers who have returned machines to Photon and from sales lost because of quality problems. Total costs of quality (including opportunity costs) equal $52.02 million (Panel A, $40.02 million + Panel B, $12 million), or 17.34% of current sales. Opportunity costs account for 23% ($12 million ÷ $52.02 million) of Photon's total costs of quality.

The COQ report and the opportunity cost analysis highlight Photon's high internal and external failure costs. To reduce costs of quality, Photon must identify and reduce failures caused by quality problems.

METHODS USED TO IDENTIFY QUALITY PROBLEMS

Control Charts

Statistical quality control (SQC) or statistical process control (SPC) is a formal means of distinguishing between random variation and nonrandom variation in an operating process. A key tool in SQC is a control chart. A **control chart** is a graph of a series of successive observations of a particular step, procedure, or operation taken at regular intervals of time. Each observation is plotted relative to specified ranges that represent the expected distribution. Only those observations outside the specified limits are ordinarily regarded as nonrandom and worth investigating.

Exhibit 19-3 presents control charts for the daily defect rates observed at Photon's three production lines. Defect rates in the prior 60 days for each plant were assumed to provide a good basis from which to calculate the distribution of daily defect rates. The arithmetic mean (μ, read mu) and standard deviation (σ, read sigma) are the two parameters of the distribution that are used in the control charts in Exhibit 19-3. On the basis of experience, the company decides that any observation outside the $\mu \pm 2\sigma$ range should be investigated.

For production line A in Exhibit 19-3, all observations are within the range of $\pm 2\sigma$ from the mean. Management, then, believes no investigation is necessary. For

EXHIBIT 19-3
Statistical Quality-Control Charts: Daily Defect Rate at the Photon Corporation

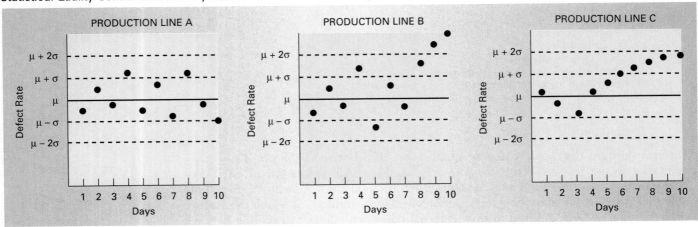

production line B, the last two observations signal that an out-of-control occurrence is highly likely. Given the ±2σ rule, both observations would lead to an investigation. Production line C illustrates a process that would not prompt an investigation under the ±2σ rule but may well be out of control. Note that the last eight observations show a clear direction and that the direction by day 5 (the third point in the last eight) is away from the mean. Statistical procedures have been developed using the trend as well as the level of the variable in question to evaluate whether a process is out of control.

Pareto Diagrams

Observations outside control limits serve as inputs to *Pareto diagrams*. A **Pareto diagram** indicates how frequently each type of failure (defect) occurs. Exhibit 19-4 presents a Pareto diagram for Photon's quality problems. Fuzzy and unclear copies are the most frequently recurring problem.

The fuzzy copy problem results in high rework costs because, in many cases, Photon discovers the fuzzy image problem only after the copier has been built. Sometimes fuzzy images occur at customer sites, resulting in high warranty and repair costs.

Cause-and-Effect Diagrams

The most frequently occurring problems identified by the Pareto diagram are analyzed using *cause-and-effect diagrams*. A **cause-and-effect diagram** identifies potential causes of failures or defects. As a first step, Photon analyzes the causes of the most frequently occurring failure, fuzzy and unclear copies. Exhibit 19-5 presents the cause-and-effect diagram for this problem. The exhibit identifies four major categories of potential causes of failure—human factors, methods and design factors, machine-related factors, and materials and components factors. As additional arrows are added for each cause, the general appearance of the diagram begins to resemble a fishbone (hence, cause-and-effect diagrams are also called *fishbone diagrams*).[5]

[5] Managers in U.S. electronics companies consider the following factors (ranked in order of importance with 1 = most important) as contributing to improvements in quality:
1. Better product design
2. Improved process design
3. Improved training of operators
4. Improved products from suppliers
5. Investments in technology and equipment

See G. Foster and L. Sjoblom, "Survey of Quality Practices in the U.S. Electronics Industry," Working Paper, Stanford University, 1993.

EXHIBIT 19-4
Pareto Diagram for the Photon Corporation

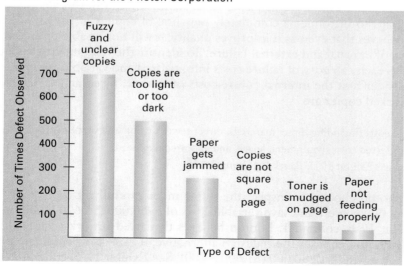

EXHIBIT 19-5
Cause-and-Effect Diagram for Fuzzy and Unclear Copies at the Photon Corporation

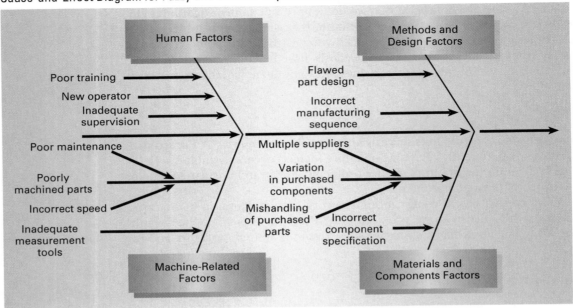

RELEVANT COSTS AND BENEFITS OF QUALITY IMPROVEMENT

Careful analysis of the cause-and-effect diagram reveals that the steel frame (or chassis) of the copier is often mishandled as it travels from the suppliers' warehouses to Photon's plant. The frame must satisfy very precise specifications and tolerances; otherwise, various copier components (such as drums, mirrors, and lenses) attached to the frame will be improperly aligned. Mishandling causes the dimensions of the frame to vary from specifications, resulting in fuzzy images.

Suppose the team of engineers working to solve the fuzzy image problem offers two alternative solutions: (1) to improve the inspection of the frame immediately upon delivery, or (2) to redesign and strengthen the frame and the containers used to transport them to better withstand mishandling during transportation.

OBJECTIVE 3

Identify the relevant costs and benefits of quality improvements

Should Photon inspect incoming frames more carefully or redesign them and their containers? Exhibit 19-6 shows the costs and benefits of each choice. Management estimates that additional inspection will cost $400,000 ($40 per hour × 10,000 hours). Redesign will cost an additional $460,000 (design engineering, $80 per hour × 2,000 hours; process engineering, $60 per hour × 5,000 hours). The potential benefits of incurring these costs are lower internal and external failure costs. The key question here is, What are the relevant cost savings and other relevant benefits? Photon considers only a 1-year time horizon for analyzing this decision because Photon plans to introduce a completely new line of copiers at the end of the year. Photon believes that even as it improves quality, it will not be able to save any of the fixed costs of internal and external failure. To identify the relevant cost savings, Photon divides each category of failure costs into its fixed and variable components.

Consider first the internal failure costs of rework. Fixed and variable costs for each reworked copier are

Variable costs (including direct materials, direct rework labor, and supplies)	$1,600
Allocated fixed costs (equipment, space, and allocated overhead)	2,400
Total costs (Exhibit 19-2, Panel A, column 3)	$4,000

If Photon chooses to inspect the frame more carefully, it expects to eliminate rework on 600 copiers and save variable costs of $960,000 ($1,600 × 600) in rework. See Exhibit 19-6, column 1. Photon believes that fixed rework costs will be unaffected. If Photon chooses the redesign alternative, it expects to eliminate rework on 800 copiers, saving $1,280,000 ($1,600 × 800). See Exhibit 19-6, column 2.

EXHIBIT 19-6
Estimated Effect of Quality-Improvement Actions on Costs of Quality for the Photon Corporation

Description	Incremental Costs and Benefits of	
	Further Inspecting Incoming Frame (1)	Redesigning Frame (2)
Costs of Quality Items		
Additional design engineering costs		
$80 × 2,000 hours	—	$ 160,000
Additional process engineering costs		
$60 × 5,000 hours	—	300,000
Additional inspection and testing costs		
$40 × 10,000 hours	$ 400,000	—
Savings in rework costs		
$1,600 × 600 fewer copiers reworked	(960,000)	
$1,600 × 800 fewer copiers reworked		(1,280,000)
Savings in customer-support costs		
$80 × 500 fewer copiers repaired	(40,000)	
$80 × 700 fewer copiers repaired		(56,000)
Savings in transportation costs for repair parts		
$180 × 500 fewer copiers repaired	(90,000)	
$180 × 700 fewer copiers repaired		(126,000)
Savings in warranty repair costs		
$1,800 × 500 fewer copiers repaired	(900,000)	
$1,800 × 700 fewer copiers repaired		(1,260,000)
Opportunity Costs		
Contribution margin from increased sales		
$6,000 × 250 additional copiers sold	(1,500,000)	
$6,000 × 300 additional copiers sold		(1,800,000)
Net cost savings and additional contribution margin	$(3,090,000)	$(4,062,000)
Difference in favor of redesigning frame	$972,000	

Next consider external failure costs. Photon currently repairs 3,000 copiers at customer sites. If incoming frames are inspected more carefully, Photon estimates that 500 fewer copiers will require warranty repair and that it will be able to sell 250 additional copiers. If the frame is redesigned, Photon estimates that 700 fewer copiers will require warranty repair and that it will be able to sell 300 additional copiers.

Variable and fixed costs per copier repaired of individual external failure COQ items described in Exhibit 19-2 (Panel A, column 4) are as follows:

	Variable Costs	Fixed Costs	Total Costs
Customer-support costs	$ 80	$ 120	$ 200
Transportation costs	180	60	240
Warranty repair costs	1,800	2,600	4,400

As Photon eliminates repair work on copiers, it expects to save only the variable costs of customer support, transportation, and warranty repair.

Crysel Wins Premio Nacional de Calidad—Mexico's Premier Quality Award

Crysel, a member of the Mexican industrial group CYDSA *(Celulosa y Derivados Society Anonimos)*, is the largest producer of acrylic fiber in Latin America and among the top-ten producers of acrylic fiber in the world. In 1991, Crysel was awarded the Premio Nacional de Calidad, Mexico's equivalent of the Malcolm Baldrige quality award.

One element of the Premio Nacional de Calidad's evaluation criteria is a company's costs of quality reporting. Companies vary as to which items they include in their COQ reports, choosing those cost categories that management feels warrant the greatest emphasis. Crysel classifies its costs of failure into six main classes:

1. *Consumption factors*—excess or wasted direct materials, steam, or energy.

2. *Maintenance*—costs of repairing machines that break down.

3. *Human resources*—costs of extra workers and staff, such as a rework crew employed to correct quality problems.

4. *Accounts receivable*—finance costs of not receiving money from customers on time.

5. *Substandard quality*—contribution margin lost from selling inferior-grade rather than top-grade fiber.

6. *Sales volume*—contribution margin lost from selling less than the available plant capacity because of quality problems.

The first three classes appear in the COQ reports that most companies prepare. Crysel's innovation in quality reporting is to include the last three classes: accounts receivable, substandard quality, and sales volume. Each of these three classes measures an opportunity cost of poor quality, a cost not generally found in COQ reports. The following table indicates that these opportunity costs are a significant percentage of Crysel's total costs of failure. Including them in the COQ reports signals to all employees that top management believes these classes deserve close attention.

Costs of Quality as a Percentage of Sales

	1985	1989	1992
Items Generally Recorded in COQ Reports			
Consumption factors	3.8%	4.1%	2.6%
Maintenance	0.8	0.9	0.8
Human resources	0.6	0.5	0.4
Total	5.2%	5.5%	3.8%
Opportunity Cost Items Generally Not Recorded in COQ Reports			
Accounts receivable	3.7%	0.9%	0.5%
Substandard quality	1.0	0.4	0.8
Sales volume	8.5	2.4	1.6
Total	13.2	3.7	2.9
Total costs of quality as a percentage of sales	18.4%	9.2%	6.7%

An important component of the Premio Nacional de Calidad is a company's safety record. Crysel's safety index, measured by the number of accidents per million labor-hours, declined from 6.3 in 1986 to 3.0 in 1992. Crysel eliminated accidents by redesigning machines, training operators in safety practices, and implementing safe operating procedures.

Source: Based on a presentation by Raul Gil Dufoo, Director General of Crysel, and discussions with company management.

Note that the savings per copier in rework costs, customer-support costs, transportation costs, and warranty repair costs in Exhibit 19-6 differ from the costs per copier for each of these items in Exhibit 19-2. Why? Because Exhibit 19-6 shows only the variable costs that Photon expects to save. Exhibit 19-2 shows the *total* (fixed and variable) costs of each of these items. Also note that Exhibit 19-6 includes the incremental contribution margin from the estimated increases in sales due to the improved quality and performance of Photon's copiers.

Photon's management chooses to redesign the frame since Exhibit 19-6 indicates that the net estimated cost savings are $972,000 greater under this alternative. The costs of a poorly designed frame appear in the form of higher manufacturing, marketing, distribution, and customer-service costs, as internal and external failures begin to mount. But these costs are locked in when the frame is designed. Thus, it is not surprising that redesign will yield significant savings.

In the Photon example, lost contribution margin occurs because Photon's repeated external failures damage its reputation for quality, resulting in lost sales. Lost contribution margin can also occur as a result of internal failures. Suppose Photon's manufacturing capacity is fully used. In this case, rework uses up valuable manufacturing capacity and causes the company to forgo contribution margin from producing and selling additional copiers. Suppose Photon could produce (and subsequently) sell an additional 600 copiers by improving quality and reducing rework. The costs of internal failure would then include lost contribution margin of $3,600,000 ($6,000 contribution margin per copier × 600 copiers). This $3,600,000 is the opportunity cost of poor quality.

Photon can use its COQ report to examine interdependencies across the four categories of quality-related costs. In our example, redesigning the frame increases costs of prevention activities (design and process engineering), decreases costs of internal failure (rework), and decreases costs of external failure (warranty repairs). Costs of quality give more insight when managers compare trends over time. (See Concepts in Action, p. 690). In successful quality programs, the costs of quality as a percentage of sales and the costs of internal and external failure as a percentage of total costs of quality should decrease over time. Many companies, for example, Digital Equipment Corporation, Solectron, and Toyota, believe they should eliminate all failure costs and have zero defects.

QUALITY AND CUSTOMER-SATISFACTION MEASURES

Even if products and services are defect-free and fully satisfy conformance quality, they will not be effective or sell well unless they also have design quality—that is, unless they satisfy customer needs. Yet there is more to customer satisfaction than just design quality. Motorola describes its program of total customer satisfaction as

◆ Giving the customer product-performance features that are perceived by the customer as providing fair value.

◆ Delivering the product when promised.

◆ Delivering the product with no defects.

◆ Ensuring that the product will not experience early failure.

◆ Ensuring that the product will not fail excessively in service.

To evaluate how well they are doing, Motorola and other companies track customer-satisfaction trends over time. Customer satisfaction is difficult to measure precisely, but companies can choose among many indicators in their search for answers.

Financial Measures of Customer Satisfaction

Costs of external failures—such as warranty repair costs, liability claims, forgone contribution margin on lost sales, and lower prices for products sold—are all financial indicators of poor customer satisfaction. But financial measures do not indicate the specific areas that need improvement, nor do they reveal the future needs and preferences of customers. For these reasons, most companies also use nonfinancial measures. Cost and management accountants are often responsible for maintaining and presenting these nonfinancial measures.

Nonfinancial Measures of Customer Satisfaction

Nonfinancial measures of customer satisfaction include

◆ The number of defective units shipped to customers as a percentage of total units of products shipped

◆ The number of customer complaints (Companies estimate that for every customer who actually complains, there are 10–20 others who have had bad experiences with the product but have not complained.)

◆ Excessive customer-response time (the difference between scheduled delivery date and date requested by the customer)

◆ On-time delivery (percentage of shipments made on or before the scheduled delivery date)

Federal Express tracks similar measures for customer satisfaction in its overnight delivery business. Management steps in and investigates if these numbers deteriorate over time.

In addition to these routine nonfinancial measures, many companies such as Xerox conduct surveys to measure customer satisfaction. Surveys serve two objectives. First, they provide a deeper perspective into customer experiences and preferences. Second, they provide a glimpse into features that customers would like future products to have.

QUALITY AND INTERNAL PERFORMANCE MEASURES

Prevention costs, appraisal costs, and internal failure costs are examples of financial measures of quality performance inside the company. Most companies monitor both financial and nonfinancial measures of internal quality.

What nonfinancial measures might a business use? Analog Devices, a semiconductor manufacturer, follows trends in these gauges of quality:

◆ The number of defects for each product line

◆ Process yield (ratio of good output to total output)

◆ Manufacturing lead time (the time taken to convert direct materials into finished output)

◆ Employee turnover (ratio of the number of employees who left the company to the total number of employees)

By themselves, nonfinancial measures of quality have limited meaning. They are more informative when management examines trends over time. To prepare this report, the management accountant must review the numbers to ensure that nonfinancial measures are calculated accurately and consistently, and must then present the information to help management evaluate internal quality performance. Management accountants help companies improve quality in multiple ways—they compute the costs of quality, assist in developing cost-effective solutions to quality problems, and provide feedback about quality improvement.

EVALUATING QUALITY PERFORMANCE

Measuring the financial costs of quality and the nonfinancial aspects of quality have distinctly different advantages.

Advantages of the Costs of Quality (COQ) Measures

1. COQ focuses attention on how costly poor quality can be.

2. Financial COQ measures are a useful way of comparing different quality-improvement programs and setting priorities for achieving maximum cost reduction.

3. Financial COQ measures serve as a common denominator for evaluating trade-offs among prevention and failure costs. COQ provides a single, summary measure of quality performance.

Advantages of Nonfinancial Measures of Quality

1. Nonfinancial measures of quality are often easy to quantify and easy to understand.

2. Nonfinancial measures direct attention to physical processes and hence focus attention on the precise problem areas that need improvement.

3. Nonfinancial measures provide immediate short-run feedback on whether quality improvement efforts have, in fact, succeeded in improving quality.

The advantages cited for COQ are disadvantages of nonfinancial measures, and vice versa. Most organizations use both financial and nonfinancial quality measures to measure quality performance.

Management accountants at some companies (for example, Analog Devices, Milliken, and Octel) present both financial and nonfinancial measures of quality performance in a single report, sometimes called a *balanced scorecard*.[6] The balanced scorecard helps top management evaluate whether lower-level managers have improved one area at the expense of others. For example, a manager at risk of not meeting operating income goals may start to ship high-margin products and delay deliveries of low-margin products. The balanced scorecard will recognize the improvement in financial performance but will also reveal that operating income targets were achieved by sacrificing on-time performance. Moreover, corporations often use multiple measures of quality in managers' bonus plans. For example, Motorola explicitly ties employee bonuses to improvements in customer satisfaction, yield, and cycle time.

TIME AS A COMPETITIVE WEAPON

Companies increasingly view time as a key variable in competition.[7] Doing things faster helps to increase revenues and decrease costs. For example, a moving company such as United Van Lines will be able to generate more revenues if it can move goods from one place to another faster and on time. Companies such as AT&T and Texas Instruments also report lower costs from their emphasis on time. They cite, for example, the need to carry less inventory because of their ability to respond rapidly to customer demands.

In this chapter, we focus on *operational measures of time*, which reveal how quickly companies respond to customers' demands for their products and services and the reliability with which these companies meet scheduled delivery dates. Another important aspect of time is *new product development time* and the financial success a company derives from bringing new products to market quickly. We discuss capital budgeting for new products and *breakeven time*, the time it takes to recover investments in new products, in Chapter 22.

OPERATIONAL MEASURES OF TIME

Companies need to measure time in order to manage it properly. Two common operational measures of time are customer-response time and on-time performance.

Customer-Response Time

Customer-response time is the amount of time from when a customer places an order for a product or requests a service to when the product or service is delivered to the customer. A timely response to customer requests is a key competitive factor

[6]See R. Kaplan and D. Norton, "Using the Balanced Scorecard as a Strategic Management System," *Harvard Business Review* (Jan.–Feb. 1996).
[7]See G. Stalk and T. Hout, *Competing Against Time* (New York: Free Press, 1990).

OBJECTIVE 6

Describe customer-response time, and explain the reasons for and the cost of lines and delays

in many industries. Consider a manufacturer of custom machine tools such as Yamazaki Mazak. Yamazaki's customers value faster delivery because it enables them to produce and sell products made using the new machine tools sooner. Customer-response time is critical in many other industries, especially service industries such as banking, car-rental, and fast-food.

The following diagram describes components of customer-response time.

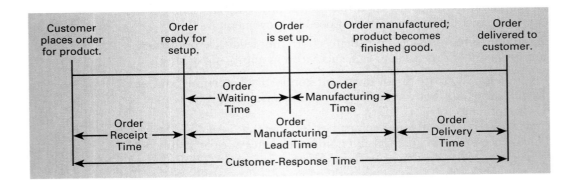

In the Yamazaki Mazak example, *order receipt time* is the time it takes Mazak's Marketing Department to describe the customer's exact specifications and to place an order with manufacturing. **Manufacturing lead (or cycle) time** is the time when the order is ready to start on the production line (ready to be set up) to when it becomes a finished good. Manufacturing lead time includes waiting time plus manufacturing time for the order. An order for machine tools, in the Mazak example, may need to wait and be delayed because the equipment the order requires is busy processing orders that arrived earlier. *Order delivery time* is the time it takes distribution to pick up the order from manufacturing and deliver it to the customer.

Several companies have adopted manufacturing lead time as the base for allocating indirect manufacturing costs to products. The Zytec Corporation, a manufacturer of computer equipment, believes that using manufacturing lead time motivates managers to reduce the time taken to manufacture products. In turn, total overhead costs decrease and operating income rises.

Effects of Uncertainty and Bottlenecks on Delays

A **time driver** is any factor where change in the factor causes a change in the speed with which an activity is undertaken. What are the drivers of time? We consider two of the most important: (1) Uncertainty about when customers will order products or services. For example, the more randomly Mazak receives orders for its machine tools, the more likely that queues will form and delays will occur. (2) Limited capacity and bottlenecks. A **bottleneck** is an operation where the work required to be performed approaches or exceeds the available capacity. For example, a bottleneck is created when products that need to be processed at a particular machine arrive while the machine is busy processing other products. The demand for time on the machine exceeds available capacity, and delays occur.

The management accountant is frequently called upon to evaluate the profitability of a new product given capacity constraints (Chapter 11, p. 396–398). In some instances, introducing a new product causes delays in the delivery of all products. When time is a key dimension of competitiveness, the management accountant must recognize and consider the costs of delays when calculating the costs and benefits of introducing a new product. To calculate the costs of delays, the management accountant must first understand the reasons for, and the magnitude of, the resulting delays. We illustrate these ideas using the Falcon Works example.

Falcon Works (FW) uses one turning machine to convert steel bars into one specialty component, A22. FW makes this component only after FW's customers order the component. To focus on manufacturing lead time, we assume that FW's order receipt time and order delivery time are minimal.

FW expects it will receive 30 orders, but it could actually receive 10, 20, or 50 orders of A22. Each order is for 1,000 units. Each order will take 100 hours of manufacturing time (8 hours of setup time to clean and prepare the machine, and 92 hours of processing time). The annual capacity of the machine is 4,000 hours. If FW receives the number of orders it expects, the total amount of manufacturing time required on the machine will be 3,000 (100×30) hours, which is within the available machine capacity of 4,000 hours. Even though expected capacity utilization is not strained, queues and delays will still occur. Why? Because uncertainty about when FW's customers will place an order may cause the order to be received while the machine is processing another order.

In the single-product case, under certain assumptions about the pattern of customer orders and how orders will be processed,[8] the **average waiting time,** the average amount of time that an order will wait in line before it is set up and processed, equals

$$\frac{\text{Average number of orders of A22} \times \left(\text{Manufacturing time for A22}\right)^2}{2 \times \left[\text{Annual machine capacity} - \left(\text{Average number of orders of A22} \times \text{Manufacturing time for A22}\right)\right]}$$

$$= \frac{30 \times (100)^2}{2 \times [4,000 - (30 \times 100)]} = \frac{30 \times 10,000}{2 \times (4,000 - 3,000)} = \frac{300,000}{2 \times 1,000} = \frac{300,000}{2,000} = 150 \text{ hours}$$

The denominator in this formula measures excess capacity or cushion. The smaller the cushion, the greater the delays. Manufacturing time enters the numerator in the formula as a squared term. The longer the manufacturing time, the greater the chance that the machine will be busy when an order arrives, and the longer the delays.

Our formula describes only the average waiting time. A particular order may happen to arrive when the machine is free, in which case manufacturing will start immediately. In other situations, FW may receive an order while two other orders are waiting to be processed. In this case, the delay will be longer than 150 hours. The average manufacturing lead time for an order of A22 is 250 hours (150 hours of average waiting time + 100 hours of manufacturing time). Throughout this section, we use manufacturing lead time to refer to manufacturing lead time for an order.

FW is considering whether to introduce a new product, C33. FW expects to receive ten orders of C33 (each order for 800 units) in the coming year. Each order will take 50 hours of manufacturing time (4 hours of setup time and 46 hours of processing time). The expected demand for A22 will be unaffected whether or not FW introduces C33.

The average waiting time *before* an order is set up and processed is given by the following formula, which is an extension of the formula described earlier for the single-product case.

$$\frac{\left[\text{Average number of orders of A22} \times \left(\text{Manufacturing time for A22}\right)^2\right] + \left[\text{Average number of orders of C33} \times \left(\text{Manufacturing time for C33}\right)^2\right]}{2 \times \left[\text{Annual machine capacity} - \left(\text{Average number of orders of A22} \times \text{Manufacturing time for A22}\right) - \left(\text{Average number of orders of C33} \times \text{Manufacturing time for C33}\right)\right]}$$

$$= \frac{[30 \times (100)^2] + [10 \times (50)^2]}{2 \times [4,000 - (30 \times 100) - (10 \times 50)]} = \frac{(30 \times 10,000) + (10 \times 2,500)}{2 \times (4,000 - 3,000 - 500)}$$

$$= \frac{300,000 + 25,000}{2 \times 500} = \frac{325,000}{1,000} = 325 \text{ hours}$$

Introducing C33 causes average waiting time to more than double from 150 hours to 325 hours. To understand why, think of excess capacity as a cushion for

[8]The precise technical assumptions are that customer orders for the product follow a Poisson distribution with a mean equal to the expected number of orders (30 in the case of A22) and that orders are processed on a first-in first-out (FIFO) basis. The Poisson arrival pattern for customer orders has been found to be reasonable in many real-world settings. The FIFO assumption can be modified. The basic queuing and delay effects will still occur, but the precise formulas will be different.

absorbing the shocks of variability and uncertainty in the arrival of customer orders. Introducing C33 causes excess capacity to shrink, increasing the chance that at any point in time, new orders will arrive while existing orders are being manufactured.

Average manufacturing lead time for A22 is 425 hours (325 hours of average waiting time + 100 hours of manufacturing time), and for C33 it is 375 hours (325 hours of average waiting time + 50 hours of manufacturing time). Note that C33 spends 86.67% (325 ÷ 375) of its manufacturing lead time just waiting for manufacturing to start!

On-Time Performance

On-time performance refers to situations in which the product or service is actually delivered at the time it is scheduled to be delivered. Customer orders for products or services generally specify quantity, cost, and delivery time. For example, Federal Express specifies a price per package and a next-day delivery time for its overnight courier service. Delivering packages early the next day, say by 9 A.M. rather than 10:30 A.M., would decrease customer-response time. On-time performance, on the other hand, measures how often Federal Express meets its stated delivery time of 10:30 A.M. There is a trade-off, however, between customer-response time and on-time performance. Simply scheduling longer customer-response times, say, delivery by 1 P.M. the next day, makes achieving on-time performance easier.

On-time performance is an important element of customer satisfaction because customers want and expect to receive things when they are supposed to. An airline that gets passengers to their destination on time is likely to enjoy competitive advantage. On-time performance in the airline industry is becoming increasingly prominent. For example, on the basis of statistics maintained by the Department of Transportation, Northwest Airlines reported that it was rated the number one U.S. airline for on-time performance in December 1994 (84.7% of its daily flights arrived within 15 minutes of the scheduled time). Management accountants track information on customer-response time and on-time performance because companies use these measures to evaluate managers.

COSTS OF TIME

Relevant Revenues and Relevant Costs

Should FW introduce product C33? Consider the following information:

Product	Average Number of Orders	Average Selling Price per Order If Average Manufacturing Lead Time		Direct Material Costs per Order	Inventory Carrying Costs per Order per Hour
		Less than 300 Hours	More than 300 Hours		
A22	30	$22,000	$21,500	$16,000	$1.00
C33	10	10,000	9,600	8,000	0.50

Note that manufacturing lead times affect both revenues and costs in our example. Revenues are affected because customers are willing to pay a slightly higher price for faster delivery. Direct materials costs and inventory carrying costs are the only costs affected by the decision to introduce C33. Inventory carrying costs usually consist of the opportunity costs of investment tied up in inventory (see Chapter 11, p. 395–396) and the relevant costs of storage such as space rental, spoilage, deterioration, and materials handling. Companies usually calculate inventory carrying costs on a per order per year basis. To simplify computations, we express inventory carrying costs on a per order per hour basis. FW incurs inventory carrying costs for the duration of the wait time and manufacturing time.

Exhibit 19-7 presents relevant revenues and relevant costs that the management accountant would calculate for this decision. The preferred alternative is not to introduce C33. Note that C33 is rejected despite having a positive contribution

EXHIBIT 19-7
Determining Expected Relevant Revenues and Expected Relevant Costs for Falcon Works'
Decision to Introduce C33

Relevant Items	Alternative 1: Introduce C33 (1)	Alternative 2: Do Not Introduce C33 (2)	Difference (3) = (1) – (2)
Expected revenues	$741,000*	$660,000[†]	$81,000
Expected variable costs	560,000[‡]	480,000[§]	80,000
Expected inventory carrying costs	14,625[#]	7,500[‖]	7,125
Expected costs	574,625	487,500	87,125
Expected revenues minus expected costs	$166,375	$172,500	$ (6,125)

*($21,500 × 30) + ($9,600 × 10) = $741,000; average manufacturing lead times will be more than 300 hours.
[†]$22,000 × 30 = $660,000; average manufacturing lead times will be less than 300 hours.
[‡]($16,000 × 30) + ($8,000 × 10) = $560,000.
[§]$16,000 × 30 = $480,000.
[#](A22's average manufacturing lead time × A22's unit carrying costs per order × A22's expected number of orders) + (C33's average manufacturing lead time × C33's unit carrying costs per order × C33's expected number of orders) = (425 × $1.00 × 30) + (375 × $0.50 × 10) = $12,750 + 1,875 = $14,625.
[‖]A22's average manufacturing lead time hours × A22's unit carrying costs per order × A22's expected number of orders = 250 × $1.00 × 30 = $7,500.

margin of at least $1,600 ($9,600 – $8,000) per order. Recall, too, that FW's machine has the capacity to process C33 because the machine will, on average, use only 3,500 of the available 4,000 hours. Why is C33 rejected? *The key is to recognize the negative effects of C33 on the existing product A22.* The following table presents the expected loss in revenues and expected increase in costs of using up extra capacity on the turning machine to manufacture C33.

Product	Effect of Increasing Average Manufacturing Lead Times		Expected Loss in Revenues plus Expected Increase in Costs of Introducing C33 (3) = (1) + (2)
	Expected Loss in Revenues for A22 (1)	Expected Increase in Carrying Costs for All Products (2)	
A22	$15,000*	$5,250[†]	$20,250
C33	—	1,875[‡]	1,875
Total	$15,000	$7,125	$22,125

*($22,000 – $21,500) × 30 expected orders = $15,000.
[†](425 hours – 250 hours) × $1.00 × 30 expected orders = $5,250.
[‡](375 hours – 0) × $0.50 × 10 expected orders = $1,875.

Introducing C33 causes the average manufacturing lead time of A22 to increase from 250 hours to 425 hours. This increases inventory carrying costs. Introducing C33 also causes A22's revenues to decrease because it would, on average, take more than 300 hours to manufacture A22. The expected costs of introducing C33 equal $22,125, which exceeds C33's expected contribution margin of $16,000 ($1,600 per order × 10 expected orders). FW should choose not to produce C33.

We have described a simple setting to explain the effects of uncertainty and capacity constraints and the relevant revenues and relevant costs of time.[9] How can delays be reduced? Increasing the capacity of the bottleneck resource can reduce lines, delays, and inventories. When demand uncertainty is high, *some* excess capacity is desirable. Companies can increase capacity in several ways. One way, for example, is

[9]Other complexities such as analyzing a network of machines, priority scheduling, and allowing for uncertainty in processing times are beyond the scope of this book. In these cases, the basic queuing and delay effects persist, but the precise formulas are different.

to reduce the time required for setups and processing by doing these activities more efficiently. Another is to invest in new equipment. Many companies are investing in flexible manufacturing systems that can be programmed to quickly switch from producing one product to producing another. Delays can also be reduced through careful scheduling of orders on machines—for example, by batching similar jobs together for processing.

THEORY OF CONSTRAINTS AND THROUGHPUT CONTRIBUTION ANALYSIS

OBJECTIVE 7

Define the three main measurements in the theory of constraints

We now expand the discussion of the previous section by considering products that are made from multiple parts and processed on different machines. With multiple parts and multiple machines, dependencies arise among operations; some operations cannot be started until parts from a previous operation are available. Some operations are bottlenecks; others are not.

The **theory of constraints (TOC)** describes methods to maximize operating income when faced with some bottleneck and some nonbottleneck operations.[10] It defines three measurements:

1. **Throughput contribution,** equal to sales revenue minus direct materials costs.

2. **Investments (inventory),** equal to the sum of materials costs of direct materials inventory, work-in-process inventory, and finished goods inventory; R&D costs; and costs of equipment and buildings.

3. **Operating costs,** equal to all operating costs (other than direct materials) incurred to earn throughput contribution. Operating costs include salaries and wages, rent, utilities, and depreciation.

OBJECTIVE 8

Describe four steps in managing bottlenecks

The objective of TOC is to increase throughput contribution while decreasing investments and operating costs. *The theory of constraints considers short-run time horizons and assumes other current operating costs to be fixed costs.* The key steps in managing bottleneck resources are as follows:

Step 1   Recognize that the bottleneck resource determines throughput contribution of the plant as a whole.

Step 2   Search and find the bottleneck resource by identifying resources with large quantities of inventory waiting to be worked on.

Step 3   Keep the bottleneck operation busy and subordinate all nonbottleneck resources to the bottleneck resource. That is, the needs of the bottleneck resource determine the production schedule of nonbottleneck resources.

Step 3 represents a key notion described in Chapter 11: To maximize overall contribution margin, the plant must maximize contribution margin (in this case, throughput contribution) of the constrained or bottleneck resource (see pp. 396–398). For this reason, step 3 suggests that the bottleneck machine always be kept running, not waiting for jobs. To achieve this, companies often maintain a small buffer inventory of jobs waiting for the bottleneck machine. The bottleneck machine sets the pace for all nonbottleneck machines. That is, the output at the nonbottleneck operations are tied or linked to the needs of the bottleneck machine. For example, workers at nonbottleneck machines are not motivated to improve their productivity if the additional output cannot be processed by the bottleneck machine. Producing more nonbottleneck output only creates excess inventory; it does not increase throughput contribution.

[10]See E. Goldratt and J. Cox, *The Goal* (New York: North River Press, 1986); E. Goldratt, *The Theory of Constraints* (New York: North River Press, 1990); E. Noreen, D. Smith, and J. Mackey, *The Theory of Constraints and Its Implications for Management Accounting* (New York: North River Press, 1995).

Step 4 Take actions to increase bottleneck efficiency and capacity—the objective is to increase throughput contribution minus the incremental costs of taking such actions. The management accountant plays a key role in step 4 by calculating throughput contribution, identifying relevant and irrelevant costs, and doing a cost-benefit analysis of alternative actions to increase bottleneck efficiency and capacity.

We illustrate step 4 using the example of Cardinal Industries (CI). CI manufactures car doors in two operations—stamping and pressing. Additional information is as follows:

	Stamping	Pressing
Capacity per hour	20 units	15 units
Annual capacity (6,000 hours of capacity available in each of stamping and pressing)	120,000 units	90,000 units
Annual production	90,000 units	90,000 units
Fixed operating costs (excluding direct materials)	$720,000	$1,080,000
Fixed operating costs per unit produced ($720,000 ÷ 90,000; $1,080,000 ÷ 90,000)	$8 per unit	$12 per unit

Each door sells for $100 and has direct materials costs of $40. Variable costs in other functions of the value chain—R&D, design of products and processes, marketing, distribution, and customer service—are negligible. CI's output is constrained by the capacity of 90,000 units at the pressing operation. What can CI do to relieve the bottleneck constraint at the pressing operation?

a. *Eliminate idle time (time when the pressing machine is neither being set up to process products nor actually processing products) at the bottleneck operation.* CI is considering permanently positioning two workers at the pressing operation. Their sole responsibility would be to unload finished units as soon as one batch of units is processed and to set up the machine to process the next batch. Suppose the annual cost of this action is $48,000 and the effect of this action is to increase bottleneck output by 1,000 units per year. Should CI incur the additional costs? Yes, because CI's relevant throughput contribution increases by $60,000 [1,000 units × (selling price, $100 – direct materials costs, $40)], which exceeds the additional cost of $48,000. All other costs are irrelevant.

b. *Process only those parts or products that increase sales and throughput contribution, not parts or products that remain in finished goods or spare parts inventory.* Manufacturing products that sit in inventory does not increase throughput contribution.

c. *Shift products that do not have to be made on the bottleneck machine to nonbottleneck machines or to outside facilities.* Suppose the Spartan Corporation, an outside contractor, offers to press 1,500 doors at $15 per door from direct materials that CI supplies. Spartan's quoted price is greater than CI's own operating costs in the Pressing Department of $12 per door. Should CI accept the offer? Yes, because pressing is the bottleneck operation. Getting additional doors pressed from outside increases throughput contribution by $90,000 [($100 – $40) × 1,500 doors], while relevant costs increase by $22,500 ($15 × 1,500). The fact that CI's unit cost is less than Spartan's quoted price is irrelevant.

Suppose Gemini Industries, another outside contractor, offers to stamp 2,000 doors from direct materials that CI supplies at $6 per door. Gemini's price is lower than CI's operating cost of $8 per door in the Stamping Department. Should CI accept the offer? Since other operating costs are fixed costs, CI will not save any costs by subcontracting the stamping operations. Total costs will be greater by $12,000 ($6 × 2,000) under the subcontracting alternative. Stamping more doors will not increase throughput contribution, which is constrained by pressing capacity. CI should not accept Gemini's offer.

d. *Reduce setup time and processing time at bottleneck operations (for example, by simplifying the design or reducing the number of parts in the product).* Suppose CI can reduce setup time at the pressing operation by incurring additional costs of $55,000 a year. Suppose further that reducing setup time enables CI to press

Throughput Accounting at Allied-Signal Skelmersdale, United Kingdom

Allied-Signal in Skelmersdale, United Kingdom, manufactures turbochargers for the automotive industry. In the late 1980s and early 1990s, the Skelmersdale plant was forced to change from producing few products in large quantities to producing many products in small quantities in a very competitive market. The plant also had to cope with frequent changes in its sales mix. The plant often missed delivery dates and incurred high transportation costs to ship via air those parts urgently needed by its automotive customers. John Darlington, the controller of the Skelmersdale plant, recognized the important role finance and accounting could play in this environment, but "we were just not supporting, communicating with, and complementing shop-floor management—not until we began emphasizing throughput contributions."

The format designed by the Allied-Signal accountants for the throughput contribution-based operating income statement is as follows:

Throughput Operating Income Statement (in thousands)		
Sales revenues		£50,000
Direct materials costs		28,500
Throughput contribution		21,500
Operating costs		
Direct manufacturing labor	£ 4,275	
Engineering costs	1,767	
Other manufacturing costs	11,585	
Marketing costs	1,873	
Total operating costs		19,500
Operating income		£ 2,000

The Skelmersdale management viewed operating costs, other than direct materials costs, as fixed in the short-run. The key to improving profitability was maximizing throughput contribution by identifying and optimizing the use of bottleneck resources. Management reduced the load on the bottleneck machines by shifting operations performed there onto other machines. New investments to improve efficiency at nonbottleneck machines were turned down because greater efficiency at nonbottleneck machines did nothing to improve throughput contribution. Instead, Allied-Signal made additional investments to increase bottleneck capacity.

To motivate workers to improve throughput, Allied-Signal managers designed new performance measures. Instead of measuring localized efficiency such as direct labor efficiency at various operations, management introduced "adherence to schedule" as the key performance measure. Workers at nonbottleneck operations were asked not to produce more than what was required according to the bottleneck schedule. In the surplus time available to these workers, they received training in TQM practices and in improving operator skills. The Skelmersdale plant also introduced four other performance measures—costs of quality, customer due-date delivery, days inventory on hand, and manufacturing lead time—all with the objective of satisfying customers and maximizing throughput contribution. Over a 4-year period, the Skelmersdale plant showed dramatic increases in each of these measures and in profitability, cash flow, and return on investment.

Source: Adapted from J. Darlington, J. Innes, F. Mitchell, and J. Woodward, "Throughput Accounting: The Garrett Automotive Experience," *Management Accounting* (April 1992); P. Coughlan and J. Darlington, "As Fast as the Slowest Operation: The Theory of Constraints," *Management Accounting* (June 1993); and discussions with Allied-Signal, Skelmersdale, management.

2,500 more doors a year. Should CI incur the costs to reduce setup time? Yes, because throughput contribution increases by $150,000 [($100 − $40) × 2,500], which exceeds the additional costs incurred of $55,000. Will CI find it worthwhile to incur costs to reduce machining time at the stamping operation? No. Other operating costs will increase, but throughput contribution will remain unaffected. Throughput contribution increases only by increasing bottleneck output; increasing nonbottleneck output has no effect.

e. *Improve the quality of parts or products manufactured at the bottleneck operation.* Poor quality is often more costly at a bottleneck operation than it is at a nonbottleneck operation. The cost of poor quality at a nonbottleneck operation is the cost of materials wasted. If CI produces 1,000 defective doors at the stamping operation, the cost of poor quality is $40,000 (direct materials cost per unit, $40 × 1,000 doors). No throughput contribution is forgone because stamping has excess capacity. Despite the defective production, stamping can produce and transfer 90,000 doors to the pressing operation. At a bottleneck operation, the cost of poor quality is the cost of materials wasted *plus* the opportunity cost of lost throughput contribution. Bottleneck capacity not wasted in producing defective units could be used to generate additional sales and throughput contribution. If CI produces 1,000 defective units at the pressing operation, the cost of poor quality is $100,000: direct materials cost of $40,000 (direct materials cost per unit, $40 × 1,000 units) plus forgone throughput contribution of $60,000 [($100 − $40) × 1,000 doors].

The high costs of poor quality at the bottleneck operation means that bottleneck time should not be wasted processing units that are defective. That is, inspection should be done before processing parts at the bottleneck to ensure that only good-quality units are transferred to the bottleneck operation. Also, quality-improvement programs should focus on ensuring that bottlenecks produce minimal defects.

The theory of constraints emphasizes the management of bottlenecks as the key to improving the performance of the system as a whole. It focuses on the short-run maximization of throughput contribution—revenues minus materials costs. It is less useful for the long-run management of costs because it does not model the behavior of costs or identify individual activities and cost drivers. Instead, it regards operating costs as given and fixed.

PROBLEM

Let us revisit the Falcon Works (FW) example. FW has convinced all its customers to place orders for A22 in order sizes of 500 units. FW expects to receive and manufacture 60 orders of A22. Each order will take 54 hours of manufacturing time (8 hours of setup time plus 46 hours of processing time). Assume the following with respect to A22: Average selling price per order, if average manufacturing lead time is less than 300 hours, is $11,000; average selling price per order, if average manufacturing lead time is greater than 300 hours, is $10,750; direct materials costs per order are $8,000; and inventory carrying costs per order are $0.50 per order per hour. Assume the same data for C33 as in the chapter example (p. 695). Given this new information, FW is reconsidering whether it should introduce C33. What should FW do?

SOLUTION

Average waiting time for A22 if C33 is not introduced (using the formula from p. 695) is

$$\frac{60 \times (54)^2}{2 \times [4,000 - (60 \times 54)]} = \frac{60 \times 2,916}{2 \times (4,000 - 3,240)} = \frac{174,960}{2 \times 760} = \frac{174,960}{1,520} = 115 \text{ hours}$$

Average waiting time for A22 if C33 is introduced (using the formula from p. 695) is

$$\frac{[60 \times (54)^2] + [10 \times (50)^2]}{2 \times [4{,}000 - (60 \times 54) - (10 \times 50)]} = \frac{(60 \times 2{,}916) + (10 \times 2{,}500)}{2 \times (4{,}000 - 3{,}240 - 500)}$$

$$= \frac{174{,}960 + 25{,}000}{2 \times 260} = \frac{199{,}960}{520} = 385 \text{ hours}$$

Average manufacturing lead time for A22 = 385 + 54 = 439 hours

Average manufacturing lead time for C33 = 385 + 50 = 435 hours

The following table describes the expected loss in revenues and expected increase in costs from introducing C33.

Product	Effect of Increasing Average Manufacturing Lead Times		Expected Loss in Revenues plus Expected Increase in Costs of Introducing C33 (3) = (1) + (2)
	Expected Loss in Revenues for A22 (1)	Expected Increase in Carrying Costs for All Products (2)	
A22	$15,000*	$ 9,720†	$24,720
C33	—	2,175‡	2,175
Total	$15,000	$11,895	$26,895

*($11,000 − $10,750) × 60 orders = $15,000.
†(439 hours − 115 hours) × $0.50 × 60 orders = $9,720.
‡(435 hours − 0) × $0.50 × 10 orders = $2,175.

FW is better off not introducing C33. The additional costs of $26,895 exceed C33's expected contribution of $16,000 ($1,600 per order × 10 orders).

SUMMARY

The following points are linked to the chapter's learning objectives.

1. Four cost categories in a costs of quality program are *prevention costs* (costs incurred in precluding the manufacture of products that do not conform to specifications), *appraisal costs* (costs incurred in detecting which of the individual products produced do not conform to specifications), *internal failure costs* (costs incurred when a nonconforming product is detected before its shipment to customers), and *external failure costs* (costs incurred when a nonconforming product is detected after its shipment to customers).

2. Three methods that companies use to improve quality are *control charts*, to distinguish random variations from other sources of variation in an operating process; *Pareto diagrams*, which indicate how frequently each type of failure occurs; and *cause-and-effect diagrams*, which identify potential factors or causes of failure.

3. The relevant costs of quality improvement are the incremental costs incurred to implement the quality program. The relevant benefits are the savings in total costs and the estimated increase in contribution margin from the higher sales that will result from the quality improvements.

4. Nonfinancial measures of customer satisfaction include the number of customer complaints, the on-time delivery rate, and the customer-response time. Nonfinancial measures of internal performance include product defect levels, process yields, and manufacturing lead times.

5. Financial measures are helpful to evaluate trade-offs among prevention and failure costs. They focus attention on how costly poor quality can be. Nonfinancial measures help focus attention on the precise problem areas that need attention.

6. *Customer-response time* is the amount of time from when a customer places an order for a product or requests service to when the product or service is delivered to the customer. Lines and delays occur because of (a) uncertainty about when customers will order products or services, and (b) limited capacity and bottlenecks. Bottlenecks are operations at which the work to be performed approaches or exceeds the available capacity. The costs of lines and delays include lower revenues and increased inventory carrying costs.

7. The three main measurements in the theory of constraints are throughput contribution (equal to sales dollars minus direct materials costs); investments or inventory (equal to the sum of materials costs of direct materials inventory, work-in-process inventory and finished goods inventory; R&D costs; and costs of equipment and buildings); and operating costs (equal to all operating costs other than direct materials costs incurred to earn throughput contribution).

8. The four steps in managing bottlenecks are (a) recognize that the bottleneck operation determines throughput contribution, (b) search for and find the bottleneck, (c) keep the bottleneck busy and subordinate all nonbottleneck operations to the bottleneck operation, and (d) increase bottleneck efficiency and capacity.

▼ TERMS TO LEARN

This chapter and the Glossary at the end of this book contain definitions of the following important terms:

appraisal costs (p. 683)	manufacturing cycle time (694)
average waiting time (695)	manufacturing lead time (694)
bottleneck (694)	on-time performance (696)
cause-and-effect diagram (687)	Pareto diagram (687)
control chart (686)	prevention costs (683)
costs of quality (COQ) (683)	theory of constraints (TOC) (698)
customer-response time (693)	throughput contribution (698)
external failure costs (684)	time driver (694)
internal failure costs (684)	

▼ ASSIGNMENT MATERIAL

QUESTIONS

19-1 Describe some of the benefits of improving quality.

19-2 How does conformance quality differ from quality of design? Explain.

19-3 Name two items classified as prevention costs.

19-4 Distinguish between internal failure costs and external failure costs.

19-5 Describe three methods that companies use to identify quality problems.

19-6 "Companies should focus on financial measures of quality because these are the only measures of quality that can be linked to bottom-line performance." Do you agree? Explain.

19-7 Give two examples of nonfinancial measures of customer satisfaction.

19-8 Give two examples of nonfinancial measures of internal performance.

19-9 Distinguish between customer-response time and manufacturing lead time.

19-10 "There is no trade-off between customer-response time and on-time performance." Do you agree? Explain.

19-11 Give two reasons why waiting lines and delays occur.

19-12 "Companies should always make and sell all products whose selling prices exceed variable costs." Do you agree? Explain.

19-13 Describe the three main measures used in the theory of constraints.

19-14 Describe the four key steps in managing bottleneck resources.

19-15 Describe three ways to improve the performance of a bottleneck operation.

EXERCISES

19-16 Cost of quality program, nonfinancial quality measures. Baden Engineering manufactures automotive parts. A major customer has just given Baden an edict: "Improve quality or no more business." Hans Reichelstein, the controller of Baden Engineering, is given the task of developing a COQ program. He seeks your advice on classifying each of items a–g as (i) a prevention cost, (ii) an appraisal cost, (iii) an internal failure cost, or (iv) an external failure cost.

a. Cost of inspecting products on the production line by Baden quality inspectors.

b. Payment of travel costs for a Baden Engineering customer representative to meet with a customer who detected defective products.

c. Costs of reworking defective parts detected by Baden Engineering's quality-assurance group.

d. Labor cost of the product designer at Baden Engineering whose task is to design components that will not break under extreme temperature variations.

e. Cost of automotive parts returned by customers.

f. Seminar costs for "Vendor Day," a program aimed at communicating to vendors the new quality requirements for purchased components.

g. Costs of spoiled parts.

REQUIRED

1. Classify the seven individual cost items into one of the four categories of prevention, appraisal, internal failure, or external failure.

2. Give two examples of nonfinancial performance measures Baden Engineering could monitor as part of a total-quality-control effort.

19-17 Costs of quality analysis, nonfinancial quality measures. The Hartono Corporation manufactures and sells industrial grinders. The following table presents financial information pertaining to quality in 19_6 and 19_7 (in thousands):

	19_7	19_6
Sales	$12,500	$10,000
Line inspection	85	110
Scrap	200	250
Design engineering	240	100
Cost of returned goods	145	60
Product-testing equipment	50	50
Customer support	30	40
Rework costs	135	160
Preventive equipment maintenance	90	35
Product liability claims	100	200
Incoming materials inspection	40	20
Breakdown maintenance	40	90
Product-testing labor	75	220
Training	120	45
Warranty repair	200	300
Supplier evaluation	50	20

1. Classify the cost items in the table into prevention, appraisal, internal failure, or external failure categories.
2. Calculate the ratio of each COQ category to sales in 19_6 and 19_7. Comment on the trends in costs of quality between 19_6 and 19_7.
3. Give two examples of nonfinancial quality measures that Hartono Corporation could monitor as part of a total-quality-control effort.

19-18 Costs of quality analysis, nonfinancial quality measures. Ontario Industries manufactures two types of refrigerators, Olivia and Solta. Information on each refrigerator is as follows:

	Olivia	Solta
Units manufactured and sold	10,000 units	5,000 units
Selling price	$2,000	$1,500
Variable costs per unit	$1,200	$800
Hours spent on design	6,000	1,000
Testing and inspection hours per unit	1	0.5
Percentage of units reworked in plant	5%	10%
Rework costs per refrigerator	$500	$400
Percentage of units repaired at customer site	4%	8%
Repair costs per refrigerator	$600	$450
Estimated lost sales from poor quality	—	300 units

The labor rates per hour for various activities are as follows:

Design	$75 per hour
Testing and inspection	$40 per hour

REQUIRED

1. Calculate the costs of quality for Olivia and Solta classified into prevention, appraisal, internal failure, and external failure categories.
2. For each type of refrigerator, calculate the ratio of each COQ item as a percentage of sales. Compare and comment on the costs of quality for Olivia and Solta.
3. Give two examples of nonfinancial quality measures that Ontario Industries could monitor as part of a total-quality-control effort.

19-19 Quality improvement, relevant costs and revenues, service. The Sloan Corporation is a moving company that transports household goods from one city to another within the continental United States. It measures service quality in terms of (a) time required to transport goods, (b) on-time delivery (within two days of agreed-upon delivery date), and (c) lost or damaged shipments. Sloan is considering investing in a new scheduling and tracking system costing $160,000 per year that should help it improve performance with respect to items (b) and (c). The following information describes Sloan's current performance and the expected performance if the new system is implemented:

	Current Performance	Future Expected Performance
On-time delivery performance	85%	95%
Variable costs per carton lost or damaged	$60	$60
Number of cartons lost or damaged per year	3,000 cartons	1,000 cartons

Sloan expects that each percentage point increase in on-time performance will result in sales increases of $20,000 per year. Sloan's contribution margin percentage is 45%.

1. What are the annual additional costs to Sloan of choosing the new scheduling and tracking system?
2. What are the annual additional benefits of the new system?
3. Should Sloan acquire the new system?

19-20 Quality improvement, relevant costs, and relevant revenues. The Photon Corporation manufactures and sells 20,000 copiers each year. The variable and fixed costs of reworking and repairing copiers are as follows:

	Variable Costs	Fixed Costs	Total Costs
Rework costs per copier	$1,600	$2,400	$4,000
Repair costs per copier			
Customer-support costs	80	120	200
Transportation costs for repair parts	180	60	240
Warranty repair costs	1,800	2,600	4,400

Photon's engineers are currently working to solve the problem of copies being too light or too dark. They propose changing the lens of the copier. The new lens will cost $50 more then the old lens. Each copier uses one lens. Photon uses a 1-year time horizon for this decision, since it plans to introduce a new copier at the end of the year. Photon believes that even as it improves quality, it will not be able to save any of the fixed costs of rework or repair.

By changing the lens, Photon expects that it will (1) rework 300 fewer copiers, (2) repair 200 fewer copiers, and (3) sell 100 additional copiers. Photon's unit contribution margin on its existing copier is $6,000.

REQUIRED

1. What are the additional costs of choosing the new lens?
2. What are the additional benefits of choosing the new lens?
3. Should Photon use the new lens?

19-21 Waiting time, banks. Regal Bank has a small branch in Orillia, Canada. The counter is staffed by one teller. The counter is open for 5 hours (300 minutes) each day (the operational capacity). It takes 5 minutes to serve a customer (service time). The Orillia branch expects to receive 40 customers each day. (Note that the number of customers corresponds to the number of orders in the chapter discussion.)

REQUIRED

1. Using the formula on p. 695, calculate how long, on average, a customer will wait in line before being served.
2. How long, on average, will a customer wait in line if the branch expects 50 customers each day?
3. The bank is considering ways to reduce waiting time. How long will customers have to wait on average, if the time to serve a customer is reduced to 4 minutes and the bank expects to serve 50 customers each day?

19-22 Waiting time, relevant costs, and relevant revenues. The Orillia branch of Regal Bank is thinking of offering additional services to its customers. Its counter is open for 5 hours (300 minutes) each day (the operational capacity). If it introduces the new services, the bank expects to serve an average of 60 customers each day instead of the 40 customers it currently averages. It will take 4 minutes to serve each customer (service time) regardless of whether or not the new services are offered. (Note that the number of customers corresponds to the number of orders in the chapter discussion.)

REQUIRED

1. Using the formula on p. 695, calculate how long, on average, a customer will wait in line before being served.

2. Regal Bank's policy is that the average waiting time in the line should not exceed 5 minutes. The bank cannot reduce the time to serve a customer below 4 minutes without significantly affecting quality. To reduce average waiting time for the 60 customers it expects to serve each day, the bank decides to keep the counter open for 336 minutes each day. Verify that by keeping the counter open for a longer time, the bank will be able to achieve its goal of an average waiting time of 5 minutes or less.

3. The bank expects to generate, on average, $30 in additional operating income each day as a result of offering the new services. The teller is paid $10 per hour and is employed in increments of an hour (that is, the teller can be employed for 5, 6, 7 hours, and so on, but not for a fraction of an hour). If the bank wants average waiting time to be no more than 5 minutes, should the bank offer the new services?

19-23 Theory of constraints, throughput contribution, relevant costs. The Mayfield Corporation manufactures filing cabinets in two operations—machining and finishing. Additional information is as follows.

	Machining	Finishing
Annual capacity	100,000 units	80,000 units
Annual production	80,000 units	80,000 units
Fixed operating costs (excluding direct materials)	$640,000	$400,000
Fixed operating costs per unit produced ($640,000 ÷ 80,000; $400,000 ÷ 80,000)	$8 per unit	$5 per unit

Each cabinet sells for $72 and has direct materials costs of $32 incurred at the start of the machining operation. Mayfield has no other variable costs. Mayfield can sell whatever output it produces. The following requirements refer only to the preceding data; there is *no connection* between the situations.

REQUIRED

1. Mayfield is considering using some modern jigs and tools in the finishing operation that would increase annual finishing output by 1,000 units. The annual cost of these jigs and tools is $30,000. Should Mayfield acquire these tools?

2. The production manager of the Machining Department has submitted a proposal to do faster setups that would increase the annual capacity of the Machining Department by 10,000 units and cost $5,000 per year. Should Mayfield implement the change?

19-24 Theory of constraints, throughput contribution, relevant costs. Refer to the information in Exercise 19-23 in answering the following requirements; there is no connection between the situations.

REQUIRED

1. An outside contractor offers to do the finishing operation for 12,000 units at $10 per unit, double the $5 per unit that it costs Mayfield to do the finishing in-house. Should Mayfield accept the subcontractor's offer?

2. The Hunt Corporation offers to machine 4,000 units at $4 per unit, half the $8 per unit that it costs Mayfield to do the machining in-house. Should Mayfield accept the subcontractor's offer?

19-25 Theory of constraints, throughput contribution, quality. Refer to the information in Exercise 19-23 in answering the following requirements; there is no connection between the situations.

REQUIRED

1. Mayfield produces 2,000 defective units at the machining operation. What is the cost to Mayfield of the defective items produced? Explain your answer briefly.

2. Mayfield produces 2,000 defective units at the finishing operation. What is the cost to Mayfield of the defective items produced? Explain your answer briefly.

PROBLEMS

19-26 Quality improvement, relevant costs, and relevant revenues. The Thomas Corporation sells 300,000 V262 valves to the automobile and truck industry. Thomas has a capacity of 110,000 machine-hours and can produce 3 valves per machine-hour. V262's contribution margin per unit is $8. Thomas sells only 300,000 valves because 30,000 valves (10% of the good valves) need to be reworked. It takes 1 machine-hour to rework 3 valves so that 10,000 hours of capacity are lost in the rework process. Thomas's rework costs are $210,000. Rework costs consist of

Direct materials and direct rework labor (variable costs)	$3 per unit
Fixed costs of equipment, rent, and overhead allocation	$4 per unit

Thomas's process designers have come up with a modification that would maintain the speed of the process and would ensure 100% quality and no rework. The new process would cost $315,000 per year. The following additional information is available:

◆ The demand for Thomas's V262 valves is 370,000 per year.
◆ The Jackson Corporation has asked Thomas to supply 22,000 T971 valves if Thomas implements the new design. The contribution margin per T971 valve is $10. Thomas can make two T971 valves per machine-hour on the existing machine with 100% quality and no rework.

REQUIRED

1. Suppose Thomas's designers implemented the new design. Should Thomas accept Jackson's order for 22,000 T971 valves? Explain.
2. Should Thomas implement the new design?
3. What nonfinancial and qualitative factors should Thomas consider in deciding whether to implement the new design?

19-27 Quality improvement, relevant costs, and relevant revenues. The Tan Corporation makes multicolor plastic lamps in two operations, molding and welding. The molding operation has a capacity of 200,000 units per year; welding has a capacity of 300,000 units per year. Annual costs of quality information recorded by Tan is as follows:

◆ Design of product and process costs $240,000
◆ Inspection and testing costs   170,000
◆ Scrap costs (all in the molding department)   750,000

The demand for lamps is very strong. Tan will be able to sell whatever output quantities it can produce at $40 per lamp.

Tan can start only 200,000 units into production in the Molding Department because of capacity constraints on the molding machines. If a defective unit is produced at the molding operation, it must be scrapped, and the scrap yields no revenue. Of the 200,000 units started at the molding operation, 30,000 units (15%) are scrapped. Scrap costs, based on total (fixed and variable) manufacturing costs incurred up to the molding operation, equal $25 per unit as follows:

Direct materials (variable)	$16 per unit
Direct manufacturing labor, setup labor, and materials-handling labor (variable)	3 per unit
Equipment, rent, and other allocated overhead including inspection and testing costs on scrapped parts (fixed)	6 per unit
	$25 per unit

The good units from the Molding Department are sent to the Welding Department. Variable manufacturing costs at the Welding Department are $2.50 per unit. There is no scrap in the Welding Department. Therefore, Tan's total sales quantity equals the Molding Department's output. Tan incurs no other variable costs.

Tan's designers have determined that adding a different type of material to the existing direct materials would reduce scrap to zero, but it would increase the variable costs per unit in the Molding Department by $3. Recall that only 200,000 units can be started each year.

REQUIRED

1. What is the additional direct materials cost of implementing the new method?
2. What is the additional benefit to Tan from using the new material and improving quality?
3. Should Tan use the new material?
4. What other nonfinancial and qualitative factors should Tan consider in making a decision?

19-28 **Statistical quality control, airline operations.** Peoples Skyway operates daily round-trip flights on the London–New York route using a fleet of three 747s, the *Spirit of Birmingham*, the *Spirit of Glasgow*, and the *Spirit of Manchester*. The budgeted quantity of fuel for each round-trip flight is the mean (average) fuel usage. Over the last 12 months, the average fuel usage per round-trip is 100 gallon-units with a standard deviation of 10 gallon-units. A gallon-unit is 1,000 gallons.

Cilla Black, the operations manager of Peoples Skyway, uses a statistical quality control (SQC) approach in deciding whether to investigate fuel usage per round-trip flight. She investigates those flights with fuel usage greater than two standard deviations from the mean.

In October, Black receives the following report for round-trip fuel usage by the three planes operating on the London–New York route:

Flight	Spirit of Birmingham (Gallon-Units)	Spirit of Glasgow (Gallon-Units)	Spirit of Manchester (Gallon-Units)
1	104	103	97
2	94	94	104
3	97	96	111
4	101	107	104
5	105	92	122
6	107	113	118
7	111	99	126
8	112	106	114
9	115	101	117
10	119	93	123

REQUIRED

1. Using the $\pm 2\sigma$ rule, what variance investigation decisions would be made?
2. Present SQC charts for round-trip fuel usage for each of the three 747s in October. What inferences can you draw from them?
3. Some managers propose that Peoples Skyway present its SQC charts in monetary terms rather than in physical quantity terms (gallon-units). What are the advantages and disadvantages of using monetary fuel costs rather than gallon-units in the SQC charts?

19-29 **Compensation linked with profitability, on-time delivery, and external quality performance measures; balanced scorecard.** Pacific-Dunlop supplies tires to major automotive companies. It has two tire plants in North America, in Detroit and Los Angeles. The quarterly bonus plan for each plant manager has three components:

a. *Profitability performance.* Add 2% of operating income.
b. *On-time delivery performance.* Add $10,000 if on-time delivery performance to the ten most important customers is 98% or better. If on-time performance is below 98%, add nothing.

c. *Product quality performance.* Deduct 50% of cost of sales returns from the ten most important customers.

Quarterly data for 19_7 on the Detroit and Los Angeles plants are as follows:

	January–March	April–June	July–September	October–December
Detroit				
Operating income	$800,000	$850,000	$700,000	$900,000
On-time delivery	98.4%	98.6%	97.1%	97.9%
Cost of sales returns	$18,000	$26,000	$10,000	$25,000
Los Angeles				
Operating income	$1,600,000	$1,500,000	$1,800,000	$1,900,000
On-time delivery	95.6%	97.1%	97.9%	98.4%
Cost of sales returns	$35,000	$34,000	$28,000	$22,000

REQUIRED

1. Compute the bonuses paid each quarter of 19_7 to the plant managers of the Detroit and Los Angeles plants.
2. Discuss the three components of the bonus plan as measures of profitability, on-time delivery, and product quality.
3. Why would you want to evaluate plant managers on the basis of both operating income and on-time delivery?
4. Give one example of what might happen if on-time delivery were dropped as a performance-evaluation measure.

19-30 Waiting times, manufacturing lead times. The SRG Corporation uses an injection molding machine to make a plastic product, Z39. SRG makes products only after receiving firm orders from its customers. SRG estimates that it will receive 50 orders for Z39 (each order is for 1,000 units) during the coming year. Each order of Z39 will take 80 hours of machine time (4 hours to clean and prepare the machine, called setup, and 76 hours to process the order). The annual capacity of the machine is 5,000 hours.

REQUIRED

1. What percentage of the total available machine capacity does SRG expect to use during the coming year?
2. Calculate the average amount of time that an order for Z39 will wait in line before it is processed and the average manufacturing lead time per order for Z39.
3. SRG is considering introducing a new product, Y28. SRG estimates that, on average, it will receive 25 orders of Y28 (each order for 200 units) in the coming year. Each order of Y28 will take 20 hours of machine time (2 hours to clean and prepare the machine, and 18 hours to process the order). The average demand for Z39 will be unaffected by the introduction of Y28. Calculate the average waiting time for an order received and the average manufacturing lead time per order for each product, if SRG introduces Y28.
4. If SRG introduces Y28, on average what fraction of the total manufacturing lead time will each order of Y28 spend just waiting to be processed?
5. Briefly describe why delays occur in the processing of Z39 and Y28.

19-31 Waiting times, relevant revenues and relevant costs (continuation of 19-30). SRG is still deciding whether or not it should introduce and sell Y28. The following table provides information on selling prices, variable costs, and inventory carrying costs for Z39 and Y28. SRG will incur additional variable costs and inventory carrying costs for Y28 only if it introduces Y28. Fixed costs equal to 40% of variable costs are allocated to all products produced and sold during the year.

Product	Average Number of Orders	Average Selling Price per Order if Average Manufacturing Lead Time Is		Variable Costs per Order	Inventory Carrying Costs per Order per Hour
		Less than 320 Hours	More than 320 Hours		
Z39	50	$27,000	$26,500	$15,000	$0.75
Y28	25	8,400	8,000	5,000	0.25

REQUIRED

1. Should SRG manufacture and sell Y28? Show all your computations.
2. What is the cutoff price per order above which SRG should manufacture and sell Y28 and below which SRG should choose not to manufacture and sell Y28?

19-32 Waiting times, manufacturing lead times. The Casiopia Corporation makes wire harnesses for the aircraft industry. Casiopia is uncertain about when and how many customer orders will be received. Casiopia makes harnesses only after receiving firm orders from its customers. Casiopia has recently purchased a new machine to make two wire harnesses, G72 and R76. Casiopia's marketing manager, Peter Chalos, estimates that Casiopia will receive 125 orders for G72 during the coming year. Each order of G72 will take 40 hours of machine time. The marketing manager also estimates that Casiopia will receive 10 orders for R76 during the upcoming year. Each order of R76 will take 50 hours of machine time. The annual capacity of the new machine is 6,000 hours.

REQUIRED

1. Calculate the average manufacturing lead times per order of G72 and R76 if Casiopia manufactures both products.
2. Calculate the average manufacturing lead time per order if Casiopia only manufactures G72.

19-33 Waiting times, relevant revenues and relevant costs (continuation of 19-32). The following table provides information on the average number of orders, selling prices, variable costs, and inventory carrying costs for G72 and R76 for next year. Casiopia will incur additional variable costs and inventory carrying costs for R76 only if it produces R76. Fixed costs equal to 30% of variable costs are allocated to all products produced and sold.

Product	Average Number of Orders	Average Selling Price per Order if Average Manufacturing Lead Time Is		Variable Costs per Order	Inventory Carrying Costs per Order per Hour
		Less than 200 Hours	More than 200 Hours		
G72	125	$15,000	$14,400	$10,000	$0.50
R76	10	13,500	12,960	9,000	0.45

Peter Chalos and the CEO, Laura Minton, met to discuss which products the company should make and sell.

Laura Minton: The numbers indicate that both G72 and R76 are profitable products. I think we should manufacture and market both products.

Peter Chalos: I am not so sure. Since both products use a common machine, freeing up capacity—for example, by not producing and selling R76—could enable us to reduce the manufacturing lead time to make and sell G72 resulting in higher revenues per order of G72.

REQUIRED

1. Suppose Casiopia is choosing between the two following alternatives: (a) making and selling both G72 and R76, and (b) making and selling only G72. What should Casiopia do?

2. What is the cutoff price per order above which Casiopia should manufacture and sell R76 and below which Casiopia should not manufacture and sell R76?

3. What other factors should Casiopia Corporation consider in choosing among the alternatives described in requirement 1?

19-34 Theory of constraints, throughput contribution, relevant costs. Colorado Industries manufactures electronic testing equipment. Colorado also installs the equipment at the customer's site and ensures that it functions smoothly. Additional information on the Manufacturing and Installation Departments is as follows (capacities are expressed in terms of the number of units of equipment):

	Equipment Manufactured	Equipment Installed
Annual capacity	400 units per year	300 units per year
Equipment manufactured and installed	300 units per year	300 units per year

Colorado manufactures only 300 units per year because the Installation Department has only enough capacity to install 300 units. The equipment sells for $40,000 per unit (installed) and has direct materials costs of $15,000. All costs other than direct materials costs are fixed. The following requirements refer only to the preceding data; there is no connection between the situations.

REQUIRED

1. Colorado's engineers have found a way to reduce equipment manufacturing time. The new method would cost an additional $50 per unit and would allow Colorado to manufacture 20 additional units a year. Should Colorado implement the new method?

2. Colorado's designers have proposed a change in the direct materials that would increase direct materials costs by $2,000 per unit. This change would enable Colorado to install 320 units of equipment each year. If Colorado makes the change, it will implement the new design on all equipment sold. Should Colorado use the new design?

3. A new installation technique has been developed that will enable Colorado's engineers to install 10 additional units of equipment a year. The new method will increase installation costs by $50,000 each year. Should Colorado implement the new technique?

4. Colorado is considering how to motivate workers to improve their productivity (output per hour). One proposal is to evaluate and compensate workers in the Manufacturing and Installation Departments on the basis of their productivities. Do you think the new proposal is a good idea? Explain briefly.

19-35 Theory of constraints, throughput contribution, quality, relevant costs. Aardee Industries manufactures pharmaceutical products in two departments—Mixing and Tablet-Making. Additional information on the two departments follows. Each tablet contains 0.5 gram of direct materials.

	Mixing	Tablet Making
Capacity per hour	150 grams	200 tablets
Monthly capacity (2,000 hours available in each of mixing and tablet making)	300,000 grams	400,000 tablets
Monthly production	200,000 grams	390,000 tablets
Fixed operating costs (excluding direct materials)	$16,000	$39,000
Fixed operating costs per tablet ($16,000 ÷ 200,000; $39,000 ÷ 390,000)	$0.08 per gram	$0.10 per tablet

The Mixing Department makes 200,000 grams of direct materials mixture (enough to make 400,000 tablets) because the Tablet-Making Department has only enough capacity to process 400,000 tablets. All direct materials costs are incurred in the Mixing Department. Aardee incurs $156,000 in direct materials costs. The Tablet-Making Department manufactures only 390,000 tablets from the 200,000 grams of mixture processed; 2.5% of the direct materials mixture is lost in the tablet-making process. Each tablet sells for $1. All costs other than direct materials costs are fixed costs. The following requirements refer only to the preceding data; there is no connection between the situations.

REQUIRED

1. An outside contractor makes the following offer: If Aardee will supply the contractor with 10,000 grams of mixture, the contractor will manufacture 19,500 tablets for Aardee (allowing for the normal 2.5% loss during the tablet-making process) at $0.12 per tablet. Should Aardee accept the contractor's offer?

2. Another firm offers to prepare 20,000 grams of mixture a month from direct materials Aardee supplies. The company will charge $0.07 per gram of mixture. Should Aardee accept the company's offer?

3. Aardee's engineers have devised a method that would improve quality in the tablet-making operation. They estimate that the 10,000 tablets currently being lost would be saved. The modification would cost $7,000 a month. Should Aardee implement the new method?

4. Suppose that Aardee also loses 10,000 grams of mixture in its mixing operation. These losses can be reduced to zero if the company is willing to spend $9,000 per month in quality-improvement methods. Should Aardee adopt the quality-improvement method?

5. What are the benefits of improving quality at the mixing operation compared with the benefits of improving quality at the tablet-making operation?

19-36 **Quality improvement, Pareto charts, fishbone diagrams.** The Murray Corporation manufactures, sells, and installs photocopying machines. Murray has placed heavy emphasis on reducing defects and failures in its production operations. Murray wants to apply the same total-quality management (TQM) principles to managing its accounts receivables.

REQUIRED

1. On the basis of your knowledge and experience, what would you classify as failures in accounts receivables?

2. Give examples of prevention activities that could reduce failures in accounts receivables.

3. Draw a Pareto diagram of the types of failures in accounts receivables and a fishbone diagram of possible causes of one type of failure in accounts receivables.

19-37 **Ethics and quality.** Mary Hughes, the assistant controller of Grant Semiconductors, had recently prepared the following quality report comparing 19_8 and 19_7 quality performances.

	19_8	19_7
Sales	$90,000,000	$80,000,000
On-line inspection	$ 700,000	$ 600,000
Warranty liability	$ 2,250,000	$ 3,600,000
Product testing	$ 2,000,000	$ 1,000,000
Scrap	$ 2,700,000	$ 2,000,000
Design engineering	$ 1,800,000	$ 800,000
Percentage of customers complaining about quality	3%	4%

Just 2 days after preparing the report, John Emerson, the controller, had called Hughes into his office. "Our plant manager, Harry Davis, is quite upset with the recent costs of quality and nonfinancial measures of quality reports that you prepared. He feels his workers have made significant progress in improving quality at the plant but that our reports are just not showing this. He wants to apply for various quality awards that would bring a lot of prestige to Grant, but he obviously cannot do so on the basis of the numbers we are reporting. Can you look over these quality numbers, and see what you can do? I think Harry has a point. Nobody wants Grant to miss out on all the wonderful press we'd get if we won one of these quality awards." Hughes is quite certain that her numbers are correct. Yet she would very much like Grant to win these prestigious quality awards. She is confused about how to handle Emerson's request.

REQUIRED

1. Calculate the ratio of each costs of quality category (prevention, appraisal, internal failure and external failure) to sales in 19_7 and 19_8.
2. What do the reports indicate about the plant's quality performance?
3. Is John Emerson's suggestion to Hughes to recalculate her quality numbers unethical? Would it be unethical for Hughes to modify her analysis? What steps should Hughes take to resolve this situation?

COLLABORATIVE LEARNING PROBLEM

19-38 **Quality improvement, relevant costs, and relevant revenues.** The Wellesley Corporation makes printed cloth in two operations, weaving and printing. Direct materials costs are Wellesley's only variable costs. The demand for Wellesley's cloth is very strong. Wellesley can sell whatever output quantities it produces at $1,250 per roll to a distributor who then markets, distributes, and provides customer service for the product.

	Weaving	Printing
Monthly capacity	10,000 rolls	15,000 rolls
Monthly production	9,500 rolls	8,550 rolls
Direct material variable costs per roll of cloth processed at each operation	$500	$100
Fixed operating costs	$2,850,000	$427,500
Fixed operating costs per roll ($2,850,000 ÷ 9,500; $427,500 ÷ 8,550)	$300 per roll	$50 per roll

Monthly costs of quality information recorded by Wellesley are as follows:
◆ Product and process design costs $300,000
◆ Scrap costs in Weaving Department   392,500
◆ Scrap costs in Printing Department   883,500

Wellesley can start only 10,000 rolls of cloth in the Weaving Department because of capacity constraints at the weaving machines. If the weaving operation produces defective cloth, the cloth must be scrapped and yields zero net revenue. Of the 10,000 rolls of cloth started at the weaving operation, 500 rolls (5%) are scrapped. Scrap costs per roll, based on total (fixed and variable) manufacturing costs per roll incurred up to the end of the weaving operation, equal $785 per roll as follows:

Direct materials costs per roll (variable)	$500
Fixed operating costs per roll ($2,850,000 ÷ 10,000 rolls)	285
Total manufacturing costs per roll in Weaving Department	$785

The good rolls from the Weaving Department (called grey cloth) are sent to the Printing Department. Of the 9,500 good rolls started at the printing operation, 950 rolls (10%) are scrapped and yield zero net revenue. Scrap costs based on total (fixed and variable) manufacturing costs per unit incurred up to the end of the printing operation, equal $930 per roll calculated as follows:

Total manufacturing costs per roll in Weaving Department		$785
Printing Department manufacturing costs		
Direct materials costs per roll (variable)	$100	
Fixed operating costs per roll		
($427,500 ÷ 9,500 rolls)	45	
Total manufacturing costs per roll in Printing Department		145
Total manufacturing costs per roll		$930

The Wellesley Corporation's total monthly sales of printed cloth equals the Printing Department's output. The following requirements refer only to the preceding data; there is no connection between the situations.

INSTRUCTIONS

Form groups of three students to complete the following requirements.

REQUIRED

1. The Printing Department is considering buying 5,000 rolls of grey cloth from an outside supplier at $900 per roll. The Printing Department manager is concerned that the cost of purchasing the grey cloth is much higher than Wellesley's cost of manufacturing the grey cloth. The quality of the grey cloth acquired from outside is very similar to that manufactured in-house. The Printing Department expects that 10% of the rolls obtained from the outside supplier will be scrapped. Should the Printing Department buy the grey cloth from the outside supplier?

2. How much does Wellesley lose if a defective roll is produced in the Printing Department?

3. What is the expected loss to Wellesley if a defective roll is produced in the Weaving Department? Use the expected monetary value criterion described in the Appendix to Chapter 3 (p. 75–79).

4. Wellesley's engineers have developed a method that would lower the Printing Department's scrap rate to 6% at the printing operation. Implementing the new method would cost $350,000 per month. Should Wellesley implement the change?

5. The design engineering team has proposed a modification that would lower the Weaving Department's scrap rate to 3%. The modification would cost the company $175,000 per month. Should Wellesley implement the change?

6. From your answers to requirements 1–5, what general conclusions can you draw about implementing TQM programs?

20

OPERATION COSTING, JUST-IN-TIME SYSTEMS, AND BACKFLUSH COSTING

Changes in companies' production systems are leading to changes in their accounting systems. American Greetings recently invested in new information systems and technology to improve product flow and reduce work-in-process inventory, as in a just-in-time system. As companies implement such changes, they will also simplify their costing systems.

LEARNING OBJECTIVES

After studying this chapter, you should be able to

1. Explain how hybrid-costing systems develop in relation to production systems
2. Develop an understanding for an operation-costing system
3. Prepare journal entries for an operation-costing system
4. Describe a just-in-time production system
5. Identify the major features of a just-in-time production system
6. Explain how just-in-time systems simplify job costing
7. Describe journal entries for backflush-costing systems

Product-costing systems do not always fall into the neat categories of job costing or process costing. Product-costing systems must often be designed to fit the particular characteristics of different production systems. In this chapter, we examine two specific production systems—a hybrid production system with both job and process characteristics and a just-in-time production system—and the costing methods associated with them.

HYBRID AND SIMPLIFIED JOB-COSTING SYSTEMS

Hybrid-costing systems are blends of characteristics from both job-costing systems and process-costing systems. Recall that job-costing and process-costing systems are best viewed as opposite ends of a continuum:

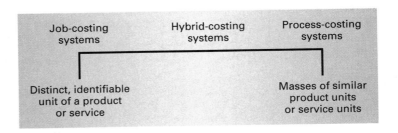

OBJECTIVE 1

Explain how hybrid-costing systems develop in relation to production systems

As we have seen, job costing usually accompanies the custom-order manufacturing of relatively heterogeneous (different) products or services (for example, printing posters, building custom-made machines, and constructing a homeowner's patio). In contrast, process costing usually accompanies the mass production and continuous-flow manufacturing of homogeneous (uniform) and standardized products (for example, printing rolls of wallpaper, stitching shirts, and bagging cement).

Obviously, a product-costing system should be tailored to the underlying production system. Hybrid-costing systems are developed to match hybrid production systems, which are blends of custom-order manufacturing and mass-production manufacturing. Manufacturers of a relatively wide variety of closely related standardized products tend to use a hybrid system. Consider the Ford Motor Company. Automobiles are manufactured in a continuous flow, but each can be customized with a special combination of motor, transmission, radio, and so on. Companies develop hybrid-costing systems to meet these individual needs.

An important and significant innovation in production systems in recent years is the Just-in-Time (JIT) system. JIT is designed to produce goods and services, as needed by customers, using minimal inventories. A feature of JIT systems and of holding minimal inventories is that the physical sequences of purchasing, production, and sales occur in quick succession. How do the unique features of JIT production affect the costing system? Streamlining the production process *simplifies job costing*—instead of costing products as they sequentially move from direct materials, to work in process and finished goods to sales, the recording of costs is often delayed until after the goods are completed or sold.

OPERATION COSTING

Overview of Operation Costing

OBJECTIVE 2

Develop an understanding for an operation-costing system

An **operation** is a standardized method or technique that is performed repetitively regardless of the distinguishing features of the finished good. Operations are usually conducted within departments. For instance, a suit maker may have a cutting operation and a hemming operation within a single department. The term *operation*, however, is often used loosely. It may be a synonym for a department or a process; for example, some companies may call their finishing department a finishing process or a finishing operation.

Operation costing is a hybrid costing system applied to batches of similar products. Each batch of products is often a variation of a single design and proceeds through a sequence of selected (though not necessarily the same) activities or operations. Within each operation, all product units are treated exactly alike, using identical amounts of the operation's resources. Batches are also termed *production runs*.

Consider a business that makes suits. Management may select a single basic design for every suit that the company manufactures. Depending on specifications, batches of suits vary from each other. One batch may use wool; another batch, cotton. One batch may require special hand stitching; another batch, machine stitching. Other products that are often manufactured in batches are semiconductors, textiles, and shoes.

An operation-costing system uses work orders that specify the needed direct materials and step-by-step operations. Product costs are compiled for each work order. Direct materials that are unique to different work orders are specifically identified with the appropriate work order as in job-costing systems. The conversion cost for each unit passing through a given operation is the same regardless of the work order. Why? Because each unit passing through an operation uses identical amounts of that operation's resources. A single average conversion cost per unit is calculated as in process costing. For each operation, this amount is computed by aggregating conversion costs and dividing by all units passing through that operation. Our examples assume only two cost categories, direct materials and conversion costs. Of course, operation costing can have more than two cost categories. The costs in each category are identified with work orders using job-costing or process-costing methods as appropriate.

Managers often find operation costing useful in cost management. Why? Because operation costing focuses on the physical processes, or operations, of a given production system. For example, in the manufacturing of clothing, managers are concerned with fabric waste, the number of fabric layers that can be cut at one time, and so on. Operation costing captures the financial impact of the control of physical processes. Feedback from an operation-costing system can therefore provide essential insight into the control of physical processes and the management of operational costs.

An Illustration of Operation Costing

Consider the Baltimore Company, a clothing manufacturer that produces two lines of blazers for department stores. Wool blazers use better-quality materials and undergo more operations than do polyester blazers. Let's look at the following operations in 19_7:

	Work Order 423	Work Order 424
Direct materials	Wool	Polyester
	Satin full lining	Rayon partial lining
	Bone buttons	Plastic buttons
Operations		
1. Cutting cloth	Use	Use
2. Checking edges	Use	Do not use
3. Sewing body	Use	Use
4. Checking seams	Use	Do not use
5. Machine sewing of collars and lapels	Do not use	Use
6. Hand sewing of collars and lapels	Use	Do not use

Suppose work order 423 is for 50 wool blazers and work order 424 is for 100 polyester blazers. The following costs are assumed for these two work orders, which were started and completed in March 19_7:

	Work Order 423	Work Order 424
Number of blazers	50	100
Direct materials costs	$ 6,000	$3,000
Conversion costs allocated:		
Operation 1	580	1,160
Operation 2	400	—
Operation 3	1,900	3,800
Operation 4	500	—
Operation 5	—	875
Operation 6	700	—
Total manufacturing costs	$10,080	$8,835

As in process costing, all product units in any work order are assumed to consume identical amounts of conversion costs of a particular operation. The Baltimore Company's operation-costing system uses a budgeted rate to calculate the conversion costs of each operation. For example, the costs of operation 1 might be budgeted as follows (amounts assumed):

$$\begin{array}{c}\text{Operation 1 budgeted}\\ \text{conversion cost}\\ \text{rate in 19\_7}\end{array} = \frac{\begin{array}{c}\text{Operation 1 budgeted}\\ \text{conversion costs in 19\_7}\end{array}}{\begin{array}{c}\text{Operation 1 budgeted}\\ \text{product units in 19\_7}\end{array}}$$

$$= \frac{\$232,000}{20,000 \text{ units}}$$

$$= \$11.60 \text{ per unit}$$

The budgeted conversion costs of operation 1 include labor, power, repairs, supplies, depreciation, and other overhead of this operation. If some units have not been completed so that all units in operation 1 have not received the same amounts of conversion costs, the conversion cost rate is computed by dividing budgeted conversion costs by the *equivalent units* of conversion costs, as in Chapters 17 and 18.

As goods are manufactured, conversion costs are allocated to the work orders processed in operation 1 by multiplying the $11.60 conversion costs per unit by the number of product units processed. The conversion costs of operation 1 for 50 wool blazers (work order 423) are $11.60 × 50 = $580, and for 100 polyester blazers (work order 424) are $11.60 × 100 = $1,160. If work order 424 contained 75 units, its total costs in operation 1 would be $870 ($11.60 × 75), 150% rather than 200% of the cost of work order 423. If equivalent units have been used to calculate the conversion cost rate, costs are allocated to work orders by multiplying the conversion cost per equivalent unit by the number of equivalent units in the work order. Direct materials costs of $6,000 for the 50 wool blazers (work order 423) and $3,000 for the 100 polyester blazers (work order 424) are specifically identified with each order as in a job-costing system. Note that operational unit costs are assumed to be the same regardless of the work order but direct materials costs vary across orders as the materials themselves vary.

OBJECTIVE 3

Prepare journal entries for an operation-costing system

Journal Entries

Actual conversion costs for operation 1 in March 19_7 (assumed to be $24,400) are entered into a Conversion Costs account:

1. Conversion Costs	24,400	
Various accounts (such as, Wages Payable and Accumulated Depreciation)		24,400

Summary journal entries for assigning costs to the polyester blazers (work order 424) follow. Entries for the wool blazers would be similar.

Of the $3,000 of direct materials for work order 424, $2,975 are used in operation 1. The journal entry for the use of direct materials, which are traced directly to particular batches, for the 100 polyester blazers is:

	2. Work in Process, Operation 1	2,975	
	Materials Inventory Control		2,975

The allocation of conversion costs to products in operation costing uses the budgeted rate $11.60 times the 100 units processed, or $1,160.

	3. Work in Process, Operation 1	1,160	
	Conversion Costs Allocated		1,160

The transfer of the polyester blazers from operation 1 to operation 3 (recall that the polyester blazers do not go through operation 2) would be journalized as follows:

	4. Work in Process, Operation 3	4,135	
	Work in Process, Operation 1		4,135

After posting, Work in Process, Operation 1 account, appears as follows:

Work in Process, Operation 1

2. Direct materials	2,975	4. Transferred to Operation 3	4,135
3. Conversion costs allocated	1,160		

The costs of the blazers are transferred through the pertinent operations and then to finished goods in the usual manner. Costs are added throughout the year in the Conversion Costs and Conversion Costs Allocated accounts. Any over- or underallocation of conversion costs is disposed of in the same way as over- or underallocated manufacturing overhead in a job-costing system. (See pp. 140–144 for discussion.)

Relation of Operation Costing to Other Costing Systems

Exhibit 20-1 presents an overview of the various costing systems described in this book. Since operation costing has features of both job and process costing, it is placed on the continuum of product costing between job costing and process costing. Below the continuum, we indicate that product costs under these three product-costing systems can be computed using actual costing, normal costing, extended-normal costing, and standard costing (which were compared in Exhibit 8-5, p. 269). The Baltimore Company operation-costing example used normal costing, but actual costing, extended-normal costing, or standard costing could have been used instead. Activity-based costing may be combined with any form or combination of product-costing systems. As Chapters 4 and 5 explain, using several different cost drivers, as in activity-based costing, leads to the most accurate information for evaluating the performance of activity areas and for building up product costs. For example, in an operation-costing system, managers may use an activity-based costing system with many cost pools and cost drivers to allocate manufacturing overhead costs to individual operations.

EXHIBIT 20-1
Variety of Cost Accounting Systems

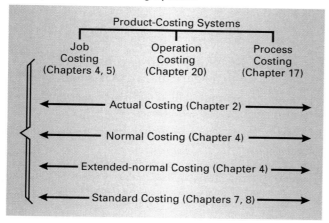

JUST-IN-TIME SYSTEMS

OBJECTIVE 4

Describe a just-in-time production system

Just-in-time refers to a system in which materials arrive exactly as they are needed. Demand drives the procurement or production of any needed materials, and immediate delivery eliminates waiting times and the need for inventory. Managers in such companies as AT&T, Honda Motors, Polaroid, Siemens, and Texas Instruments, which have implemented just-in-time systems, believe inventory is waste that can be minimized, and even eliminated, through careful planning. A key element of just-in-time is *just-in-time production*.

Just-in-time (JIT) production is a system in which each component on a production line is produced immediately as needed by the next step in the production line.[1] In a JIT production line, manufacturing activity at any particular workstation is prompted by the need for that station's output at the following station. Demand triggers each step of the production process, starting with customer demand for a finished product at one end of the process and working all the way back to the demand for direct materials at the other end of the process. In this way, demand pulls a product through the production line. The demand-pull feature of JIT production systems achieves close coordination among work centers. It smoothes the flow of goods, despite low quantities of inventory.

The demand-pull system sharply differs from the traditional push-through system of manufacturing. A push-through system, often described as a *materials requirement planning (MRP)* system, uses (a) demand forecasts for the final products; (b) a bill of materials outlining the materials, components, and subassemblies for each final product; and (c) the quantities of materials, components, subassemblies, and product inventories to predetermine the necessary outputs at each stage of production. Taking into account the lead time required to purchase materials and to manufacture components and subassemblies, a master production schedule specifies the quantity and timing of each item to be produced. Once scheduled production starts, the output of each department is pushed through the system whether it is needed or not. The result is often the accumulation of inventory by workstations that receive parts they are not yet ready to process.

There are many ways to implement the demand-pull feature of JIT production, but perhaps the most common is a Kanban system. *Kanban* is the Japanese term for a visual record or card. In the simplest Kanban system, workers at one operation use a Kanban card to signal those at another operation to produce a specified quantity of a particular part. For example, suppose the assembly department of a muffler manufacturer receives an order for ten mufflers. The assembly department triggers production of the ten metal pipes it needs to make the ten mufflers by sending a Kanban card to the machining department. Only after receiving the Kanban card does the machining department begin production of the pipes. When production is complete, the machining department attaches the Kanban card to the box containing the metal pipes and ships the package downstream to the assembly department. The assembly department starts the cycle over again when it receives the next customer order.

MAJOR FEATURES OF JIT PRODUCTION SYSTEMS

OBJECTIVE 5

Identify the major features of a just-in-time production system

There are five main features in a JIT production system:

◆ Production is organized in **manufacturing cells,** a grouping of all the different types of equipment used to manufacture a given product.

◆ Workers are trained to be multiskilled so that they are capable of performing a variety of operations and tasks.

◆ Total quality management is aggressively pursued to eliminate defects.

[1]A detailed discussion of JIT production management can be found in M. Schniederjans, *Topics in Just-in-Time Management* (Needham Heights, Mass.: Allyn and Bacon, 1992). For case studies, see R. M. Lindsay and S. Kalagnanam, *The Adoption of Just-in-Time Production Systems in Canada and Their Association with Management Control Practices* (Hamilton, Canada: Society of Management Accountants, 1993).

◆ Emphasis is placed on reducing *setup time*, which is the time required to get equipment, tools, and materials ready to start the production of a component or product, and *manufacturing lead time*, which is the time from when an order is ready to start on the production line to when it becomes a finished good.

◆ Suppliers are carefully selected to obtain delivery of quality-tested parts in a timely manner.

Organizing Manufacturing Cells

Conventional manufacturing plants generally have a *functional layout*, in which machines that perform the same function are located in the same area or department. JIT plants, however, organize machines in cells designed around products. Different types of machines that perform different functions needed to manufacture a product, or a family of products, are placed close to each other. Materials move from one machine to another where various operations are performed in sequence. Incoming and outgoing material stock points for individual cells are located near the cell rather than at a central location. Cells reduce materials handling costs. Forklifts and forklift operators are no longer needed to transport materials between central store rooms and between departments as in conventional manufacturing. Instead, workers or small conveyor belts carry materials from one cell station to the next.

Consider the manufacture of metal pipes for muffler assembly described earlier. Exhibit 20-2 contrasts the functional layout in conventional manufacturing with the cell layout in JIT plants in this case. Note the U-shaped layout of the cell. This layout ensures that all machines and workers are located near each other. Multi-skilled workers may then be able to operate more than one machine.

Multiskilled Workers

Workers in a cell are trained to perform all operations within the cell. Workers can then be assigned to different machines as needed to achieve smooth production flow.

EXHIBIT 20-2

Comparing Layouts of Conventional Manufacturing and JIT Plants for the Manufacture of Metal Pipes

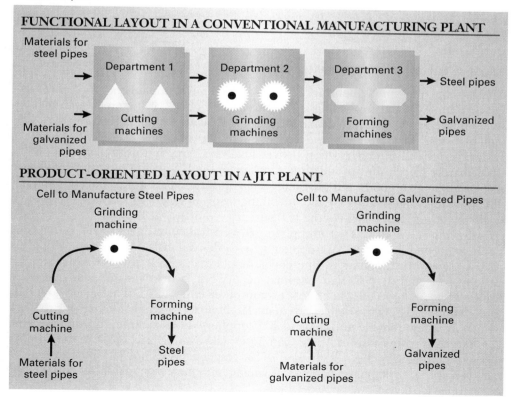

Workers are also trained and expected to perform minor repairs and do routine maintenance. Quality testing and inspection is also the responsibility of the workers in a cell rather than of a quality assurance department.

Total Quality Management

If a worker at any cell discovers a defect, he or she must set off an alarm to alert others of the problem and that operation is shut down. Because of the dynamics of the demand-pull system, when one operation shuts down, all production shuts down until the problem is solved. JIT creates an urgency for solving problems immediately and eliminating the root causes of defects as quickly as possible. Therefore, total quality management is an essential component of any JIT production system.

In contrast, in many traditional production systems, extra parts and subassemblies are held at workstations in anticipation of shortages or production breakdowns. These inventories can service a downstream operation even if a defect occurs. Consequently, there is less need for and emphasis on preventing rework and spoilage relative to JIT systems.

Reducing Manufacturing Lead Time and Setup Time

Reducing manufacturing lead time enables a company to respond better to changes in customer demand. For example, a short manufacturing lead time enables the Panasonic Corporation to rapidly restock those models of fax machines that, at any given time, are the most popular with consumers. An important aspect of reducing manufacturing lead time is reducing setup time. When setup time is long, plant managers tend to manufacture many units of a product because they want to spread the costs of the setup over as many units as possible. The higher production causes inventory to build up until such time that the units are eventually sold.

Reducing setup time makes production in smaller batches economical and worthwhile, which in turn reduces inventory levels. Companies use multiple approaches to reduce setup time. One way is to use manufacturing cells dedicated to the manufacture of a product or product family rather than multiple products. Another way is to improve setup processes and train workers to do setups more quickly. By far the most important way, however, is to automate the set up and production process by investing in *computer integrated manufacturing (CIM)*. In CIM plants, computers give instructions that automatically set up and run equipment.

Strong Supplier Relationships

Many companies implementing JIT production also implement *JIT purchasing*. **Just-in-time (JIT) purchasing** is the purchase of goods or materials such that delivery immediately precedes demand or use. JIT plants expect JIT suppliers to provide high-quality goods and make frequent deliveries of the exact quantities specified on a timely basis. Suppliers often deliver materials directly to the plant floor to be immediately placed into production. Consequently, JIT plants require suppliers to inspect their own goods and guarantee their quality. These procedures completely eliminate nonvalue-adding costs of incoming inspection, storage, inventory, and materials handling, and this saves the JIT purchaser money.

Strong relationships with suppliers are a critical component of JIT purchasing because production stops if a supplier fails to deliver materials on time. Building partnerships with suppliers is time-consuming and costly. It entails the negotiation of long-run contracts so that minimal paperwork is involved in each individual transaction. A single telephone call or computer entry (also called electronic data interchange) triggers the delivery of material. Hence JIT companies choose to work with only a few reliable and dependable suppliers. For example, in implementing JIT purchasing, divisions of Apple Computer, IBM, and Xerox reduced the number of their suppliers by 80%, 95%, and 97%, respectively. Since JIT purchasing demands a lot from supplier companies, many suppliers are unable to provide the needed service levels.

Financial Benefits of JIT

JIT tends to focus broadly on the control of *total manufacturing costs* instead of individual costs such as direct manufacturing labor. For example, idle time may rise because production lines are starved for materials more frequently than before. Nevertheless, many manufacturing costs will decline. JIT can provide many financial benefits, including

1. Lower investment in inventories
2. Reductions in carrying and handling costs of inventories
3. Reductions in risk of obsolescence of inventories
4. Lower investment in plant space for inventories and production
5. Reductions in setup costs and total manufacturing costs
6. Reduction in costs of waste and spoilage as a result of improved quality
7. Higher revenues as a result of responding faster to customers
8. Reductions in paperwork

Exhibit 20-3 summarizes the effects Hewlett-Packard reported from adopting JIT at several of its production plants.

Product-Costing Benefits of JIT

In reducing the need for materials handling, warehousing, inspection of supplies, and other activities, JIT systems reduce overhead costs. JIT systems also facilitate the direct tracing of some costs that were formerly classified as overhead. For example, the

OBJECTIVE 6

Explain how just-in-time systems simplify job costing

EXHIBIT 20-3

The Effects of JIT Production at Hewlett-Packard

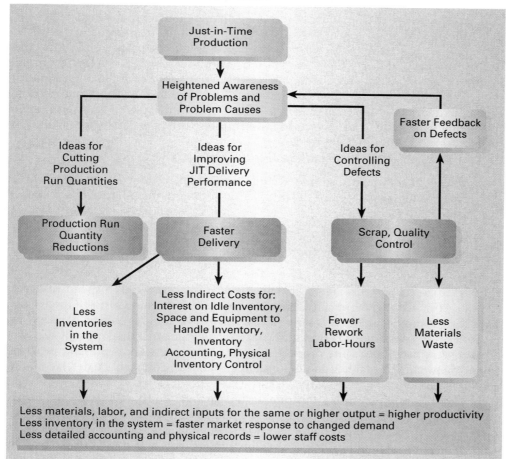

use of manufacturing cells makes it easy to trace materials handling and machine operating costs to specific products or product families made in specific cells. These costs then become direct costs of those products. Also, the use of multiskilled workers in these cells allows the costs of setup, minor maintenance, and quality inspection to become easily traced, direct costs.

BACKFLUSH COSTING

A unique production system such as JIT leads to its own unique costing system. Organizing manufacturing in cells, reducing defects and manufacturing lead time, and ensuring timely delivery of materials enables purchasing, production, and sales to occur in quick succession with minimal inventories. The absence of inventories makes choices about cost-flow assumptions (such as, weighted-average or first-in, first-out) or inventory costing methods (such as, absorption or variable costing) unimportant—all manufacturing costs of a period flow directly into cost of goods sold. The rapid conversion of direct materials to finished goods that are immediately sold simplifies job costing.

Simplified Budgeted or Standard Job Costing

Traditional and standard costing systems (discussed in Chapters 4, 7, and 8) use **sequential tracking** (also called **synchronous tracking**), which is any product-costing method in which the accounting system entries occur in the same order as actual purchases and production. These traditional systems track costs sequentially as products pass from direct materials, to work in process, to finished goods, and finally to sales. Sequential tracking is often expensive, especially if management tries to track direct materials requisitions and labor time tickets to individual operations and products.

An alternative to the sequential tracking approach in many costing systems is to delay the recording of journal entries until after the physical sequences have occurred. The term **backflush costing** (also called **delayed costing, endpoint costing**, or **post-deduct costing**) describes a costing system that delays recording changes in the status of a product being produced until good finished units appear; it then uses budgeted or standard costs to work backward to flush out manufacturing costs for the units produced. An extreme form of such delay is to wait until sale of finished units has occurred. Typically, no record of work in process appears in backflush costing.

In companies that adopt backflush costing, the following occurs:

1. Management wants a simple accounting system. Detailed tracking of direct costs through each step of the production system to the point of completion is deemed unnecessary.

2. Each product has a set of budgeted or standard costs.

3. Backflush costing reports approximately the same financial results as sequential tracking would generate.

If inventories are low, managers may not believe it worthwhile to spend resources tracking costs through Work in Process, Finished Goods, and Cost of Goods Sold. Backflush costing, therefore, is especially attractive in companies that have low inventories resulting from JIT. Backflush costing and sequential tracking will also produce approximately the same results, however, when inventory is present, provided inventories maintain stable values. Constant amounts of costs will be deferred in inventory each period.

The following examples illustrate backflush costing. To underscore basic concepts, we assume no direct materials variances in any of the examples. (We do, however, discuss variances in a separate section following Example 1.) These examples differ in the number and placement of points at which journal entries are made in the accounting system to accumulate production costs of units (also called trigger points):

	Number of Journal Entry Trigger Points	Location of Journal Entry Trigger Points
Example 1	2	1. Purchase of direct materials (also called raw materials)
		2. Completion of good finished units of product
Example 2	2	1. Purchase of raw materials
		2. Sale of good finished units of product
Example 3	1	1. Completion of good finished units of product

Implementing JIT Production and Backflushing at the Eaton Corporation

In the late 1980s, the Eaton Corporation's plant in Lincoln, Illinois, was in trouble. A few short years later, this plant, which manufactures breaker boxes, safety switches, and meter centers, is booming. The key reason? Implementing the demand-pull JIT production system in place of the push-through MRP system to streamline and simplify the production process. The Lincoln plant changed its physical layout to form cells, trained its workers in multiple skills, emphasized quality, and reduced manufacturing and setup time. Inventory was reduced by a third. But it did something else. It gave up-to-date information about customer orders, quantities in inventory, due dates, and financial results to teams of workers, empowered to operate the cells. Workers in turn decided what to work on, and who worked where, when, and for how long.

The plant controller, Al Houser, and his staff devised backflushing as an elementary way to track inventory in the new JIT environment. Rather than report on the flow of raw material and work in process through 15 or so manufacturing steps, the staff calculates product costs only when the product is completed and ready to be shipped. Gone is the tedious accounting of work in process. Eaton uses information from the bill of materials about the material content of every finished item and data from the list of operations performed to adjust inventory downward automatically.

The shipping dock prints bar-coded documents for each customer shipment. That single document backflushes inventory, creates the necessary accounting entries, generates customer invoices, and drives the computerized manifests for Eaton's freight carriers. Simultaneously, Eaton's divisional sales headquarters in Milwaukee receives the accounting information it needs in one transaction.

The results from JIT have been impressive. In a 3-year span, the plant's breakeven point has come down by 18%, its gross margins have become stronger, and its labor productivity has increased 26%. It can now fulfill a customer order in one day rather than five and has only once missed its goal of shipping 95% of its products on time.

Source: Adapted from P. Houston, "Old System, New Life: Eaton Corporation Utilizes Just-in-Time Manufacturing," *Corporate Computing*, November 1992.

Example 1: Trigger Points Are Materials Purchases and Finished Goods Completion

This example uses two trigger points to illustrate how backflushing can eliminate the need for a separate Work in Process account. A hypothetical company, Silicon Valley

Computer (SVC), produces keyboards for personal computers. For April, there were no beginning inventories of raw materials. Moreover, there is zero beginning and ending work in process.

SVC has only one direct manufacturing cost category (direct or raw materials) and one indirect manufacturing cost category (conversion costs). All labor costs at the manufacturing facility are included in conversion costs. From its bill of materials (description of the types and quantities of materials) and an operations list (description of operations to be undergone), SVC determines the April standard direct materials costs per keyboard unit of $19 and the standard conversion costs of $12. SVC has two inventory accounts:

Type	Account Title
Combined direct materials and any direct materials in work in process	Inventory: Raw and In-Process Control
Finished goods	Finished Goods Control

Trigger point 1 occurs when materials are purchased. These costs are charged to Inventory: Raw and In-Process Control.

Actual conversion costs are recorded as incurred under backflush costing, just as in other costing systems, and charged to Conversion Costs Control. Conversion costs are allocated to products at trigger point 2—the transfer of units to Finished Goods. This example assumes that under- or overallocated conversion costs are written off to cost of goods sold monthly.

SVC takes the following steps when assigning costs to units sold and to inventories.

Step 1: Record the Direct Materials Purchased During the Accounting Period Assume April purchases of $1,950,000:

Entry (a)	Inventory: Raw and In-Process Control	1,950,000	
	Accounts Payable Control		1,950,000

Step 2: Record the Incurrence of Conversion Costs During the Accounting Period Assume that conversion costs are $1,260,000:

Entry (b)	Conversion Costs Control	1,260,000	
	Various accounts (such as, Accounts Payable Control and Wages Payable)		1,260,000

Step 3: Determine the Number of Finished Units Manufactured During the Accounting Period Assume that 100,000 keyboard units were manufactured in April.

Step 4: Compute the Budgeted or Standard Costs of Each Finished Unit The standard cost is $31 ($19 direct materials + $12 conversion costs) per unit.

Step 5: Record the Cost of Finished Goods Completed During the Accounting Period In this case, 100,000 units × $31 = $3,100,000. This step gives backflush costing its name. Up to this point in the operations, the costs have not been recorded sequentially with the flow of product along its production route. Instead, the output trigger reaches back and pulls the standard costs of direct materials from Inventory: Raw and In-Process and the standard conversion costs for manufacturing the finished goods.

Entry (c)	Finished Goods Control	3,100,000	
	Inventory: Raw and In-Process Control		1,900,000
	Conversion Costs Allocated		1,200,000

Step 6: Record the Cost of Goods Sold During the Accounting Period Assume that 99,000 units were sold in April (99,000 units × $31 = $3,069,000).

Entry (d)	Cost of Goods Sold	3,069,000	
	Finished Goods Control		3,069,000

Step 7: Record Under- or Overallocated Conversion Costs Actual conversion costs may be under- or overallocated in any given accounting period. Chapter 5 (pp. 140–144) discussed various ways to account for under- or overallocated manufacturing overhead costs. Many companies write off underallocations or overallocations to cost of goods sold only at year-end; other companies, like SVC, do so monthly. Companies that use backflush costing typically have low inventories, so proration of under- or overallocated costs between finished goods and cost of goods sold is less often necessary. The journal entry for the $60,000 difference between actual conversion costs incurred and standard conversion costs allocated would be

Entry (e)	Conversion Costs Allocated	1,200,000	
	Cost of Goods Sold	60,000	
	Conversion Costs Control		1,260,000

The April ending inventory balances are

Inventory: Raw and In-Process	$50,000	
Finished Goods, 1,000 units × $31	31,000	
Total inventories	$81,000	

Exhibit 20-4, Panel A summarizes the journal entries for this example. Exhibit 20-5 provides an overview of this version of backflush costing. The elimination of the typical Work in Process account reduces the amount of detail in the accounting system. Units on the production line may still be tracked in physical terms, but there is "no attaching of costs" to specific work orders as they flow along the production cycle. In fact, there are no work orders or labor time tickets in the accounting system. Champion International uses a method similar to Example 1 in its specialty papers plant.

Accounting for Variances

The accounting for variances between actual costs incurred and standard costs allowed and the disposition of variances is basically the same under all standard costing systems. The procedures are described in Chapters 7 and 8. In Example 1, suppose the direct materials purchased had an unfavorable price variance of $42,000. Entry (a) would then be

Inventory: Raw and In-Process Control	1,950,000	
Raw Materials Price Variance	42,000	
Accounts Payable Control		1,992,000

Direct materials are often a large proportion of total manufacturing costs, sometimes over 60%. Consequently, many companies will at least measure the direct materials efficiency variance in total by physically comparing what remains in direct materials inventory against what should be remaining, given the output of finished goods for the accounting period. In our example, suppose that such a comparison showed an unfavorable materials efficiency variance of $90,000. The journal entry would be

Raw Materials Efficiency Variance	90,000	
Inventory: Raw and In-Process Control		90,000

The under- or overallocated manufacturing overhead costs may be split into various overhead variances (spending variance, efficiency variance, and production-volume

EXHIBIT 20-4
Journal Entries in Backflush Costing

PANEL A, EXAMPLE 1: TWO TRIGGER POINTS: PURCHASES OF RAW MATERIALS AND FINISHED UNITS PRODUCED

Transactions

a. Purchases of raw materials	Inventory: Raw and In-Process Control	1,950,000	
	Accounts Payable Control		1,950,000
b. Incur conversion costs	Conversion Costs Control	1,260,000	
	Various Accounts		1,260,000
c. Finished units produced	Finished Goods Control	3,100,000	
	Inventory: Raw and In-Process Control		1,900,000
	Conversion Costs Allocated		1,200,000
d. Finished units sold	Cost of Goods Sold	3,069,000	
	Finished Goods Control		3,069,000
e. Under- or overallocated conversion costs	Conversion Costs Allocated	1,200,000	
	Cost of Goods Sold	60,000	
	Conversion Costs Control		1,260,000

PANEL B, EXAMPLE 2: TWO TRIGGER POINTS: PURCHASES OF RAW MATERIALS AND FINISHED UNITS SOLD

Transactions

a. Purchases of raw materials	Inventory Control	1,950,000	
	Accounts Payable Control		1,950,000
b. Incur conversion costs	Conversion Costs Control	1,260,000	
	Various Accounts		1,260,000
c. Finished units produced	No entry		
d. Finished units sold	Cost of Goods Sold	3,069,000	
	Inventory Control		1,881,000
	Conversion Costs Allocated		1,188,000
e. Under- or overallocated conversion costs	Conversion Costs Allocated	1,188,000	
	Cost of Goods Sold	72,000	
	Conversion Costs Control		1,260,000

PANEL C, EXAMPLE 3: ONE TRIGGER POINT: FINISHED UNITS PRODUCED

Transactions

a. Purchases of raw materials	No entry		
b. Incur conversion costs	Conversion Costs Control	1,260,000	
	Various Accounts		1,260,000
c. Finished units produced	Finished Goods Control	3,100,000	
	Accounts Payable Control		1,900,000
	Conversion Costs Allocated		1,200,000
d. Finished units sold	Cost of Goods Sold	3,069,000	
	Finished Goods Control		3,069,000
e. Under- or overallocated conversion costs	Conversion Costs Allocated	1,200,000	
	Cost of Goods Sold	60,000	
	Conversion Costs Control		1,260,000

EXHIBIT 20-5
Overview of Backflush Costing, Example 1

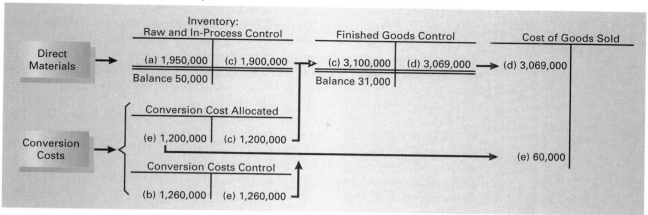

variance) as explained in Chapters 7 and 8. Using assumed numbers for the individual variances, entry (e) for the underallocated overhead of $60,000 would then be

Conversion Costs Allocated	1,200,000	
Conversion Costs Spending Variance	20,000	
Conversion Costs Production-Volume Variance	50,000	
Conversion Costs Efficiency Variance		10,000
Conversion Costs Control		1,260,000

If a company holds minimal Work in Process inventories, the backflush approach described in Example 1 closely approximates the costs computed using sequential tracking because the approach in Example 1 has no Work in Process inventory account.

Example 2: Trigger Points Are Materials Purchases and Finished Goods Sales

This example, also based on SVC and using the same data, presents a backflush costing system that, relative to Example 1, is a more dramatic departure from a sequential tracking inventory costing system. The first trigger point in this example is the same as the first trigger point in Example 1 (the purchase of direct materials), but the second trigger point is the sale—not the completed manufacture—of finished units. Toyota's cost accounting at its Kentucky plant is similar to this type of costing system. There are two justifications for this accounting system:

◆ To remove the incentive for managers to produce for inventory. If the value of finished goods inventory includes conversion costs, managers can bolster operating income by producing more units than are sold. Having trigger point 2 as the sale instead of the completion of production, however, reduces the attractiveness of producing for inventory by recording conversion costs as period costs instead of capitalizing them as inventoriable costs.

◆ To increase managers' focus on selling units.

This variation of backflush costing is sometimes called "supervariable costing" or "throughput costing" and is described in Chapter 9. The approach immediately expenses conversion costs. Allied Signal Limited, Skelmersdale, United Kingdom, uses this approach.

The inventory account in this example is confined solely to direct materials (whether they are in storerooms, in process, or in finished goods). There is only one inventory account:

Type	Account Title
Combined direct materials inventory and any direct materials in work in process and finished goods	Inventory Control

Exhibit 20-4, Panel B presents the journal entries in this case. Entry (a) is prompted by the same trigger point 1 as in Example 1, the purchase of direct materials. Entry (b) for the conversion costs incurred is recorded in an identical manner as in Example 1. Trigger point 2 is the sale of good finished units (not their production, as in Example 1), so there is no entry corresponding to entry (c) of Example 1. The cost of finished units is computed only when finished units are sold (which corresponds to entry (d) of Example 1): 99,000 units sold × $31 = $3,069,000, consisting of direct materials (99,000 × $19 = $1,881,000) and conversion costs allocated (99,000 × $12 = $1,188,000).

No conversion costs are inventoried. That is, compared to Example 1, Example 2 does not attach $12,000 ($12 per unit × 1,000 units) of conversion costs to finished goods inventory. Hence, Example 2 allocates $12,000 less in conversion costs relative to Example 1. Of the $1,260,000 in conversion costs, $1,188,000 is allocated at standard cost to the units sold. The remaining $72,000 ($1,260,000 − $1,188,000) of conversion costs is underallocated. Entry (e) in Exhibit 20-4, Panel B presents the journal entry if SVC, like many companies, writes off these underallocated costs monthly as additions to cost of goods sold.

The April ending balance of Inventory Control is $69,000 ($50,000 direct materials still on hand + $19,000 direct materials embodied in the 1,000 units manufactured but not sold during the period). Exhibit 20-6 provides an overview of this version of backflush costing. Entries are keyed to Exhibit 20-4, Panel B. The approach described in Example 2 closely approximates the costs computed using sequential tracking when a company holds minimal work in process and finished goods inventories because the approach in Example 2 does not maintain these inventory accounts.

Example 3: Trigger Point Is Finished Goods Completion

This example presents an extreme and simpler version of backflush costing. It has only one trigger point for making journal entries to inventory. The trigger point is SVC's completion of finished units. Exhibit 20-4, Panel C presents the journal entries in this case, using the same data as in Examples 1 and 2. Note that since the purchase of direct materials is not a trigger point, there is no entry corresponding to entry (a)—purchases of direct materials. Exhibit 20-7 provides an overview of this version of backflush costing. Entries are keyed to Exhibit 20-4, Panel C.

Compare entry (c) in Exhibit 20-4, Panel C with entries (a) and (c) in Exhibit 20-4, Panel A. The simpler version in Example 3 ignores the $1,950,000 purchases of direct materials [entry (a) of Example 1, p. 730]. At the end of April, $50,000 of direct materials purchased has not yet been placed into production ($1,950,000 − $1,900,000 = $50,000), nor has it been entered into the inventory costing system. The Example 3 version of backflush costing is suitable for a JIT production system

EXHIBIT 20-6
Overview of Backflush Costing, Example 2

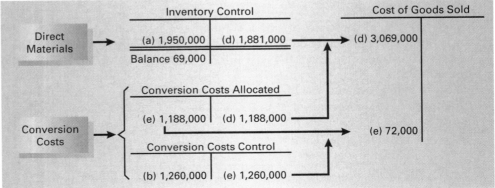

EXHIBIT 20-7
Overview of Backflush Costing, Example 3

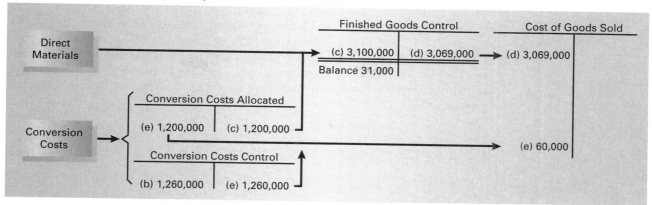

Adopt JIT and Simplify Your Life as a Management Accountant

Many companies adopting JIT production systems are reporting reductions in the complexity and detail of their management accounting systems. The results of a survey of 22 U.S. manufacturing companies implementing JIT support these claims. These manufacturers were made up of 11 machinery, 7 transportation, 2 computer, and 2 consumer products companies. On average, the companies had begun converting to JIT 4 years prior to the survey. At the time of the survey, they had converted an average 63% of their plant operations and inventory systems to JIT.

These are the key results from the survey:

1. Mean reductions in four key areas following JIT adoption were

   ◆ Number of vendors reduced by 67%
   ◆ Quantity of rework and scrap reduced by 44%
   ◆ Setup time for product changes on machines reduced by 47%
   ◆ Quantity in total inventory reduced by 46%

2. The types of cost accounting systems in use were

Type	Before JIT	After JIT
Job costing	70%	30%
Process costing	20	60
Hybrid costing	10	10

3. Cost accounting systems following implementation of JIT were

   ◆ Less complex 72.7%
   ◆ More complex 27.3%

4. Eight of the 22 companies adopted backflush costing after implementing JIT, eliminating accounting transactions for the movement of materials to work in process.

5. Performance measurement systems following implementation of JIT were

   ◆ Less complex 77.3%
   ◆ More complex 22.7%

Source: Adapted from Swenson and Cassidy, "The Effect of JIT." Full citation is in Appendix A.

with virtually no direct materials inventory and minimal work-in-process inventories because Example 3 does not maintain these inventory accounts. It is less feasible otherwise.

Extending Example 3, backflush costing systems could also use the sale of finished goods (instead of the production of finished goods) as the only trigger point. This version of backflush costing would be most suitable for a JIT production system with minimal direct materials, work in process, and finished goods inventories. Why? Because this backflush costing system would maintain no inventory accounts.

Special Considerations in Backflush Costing

The accounting illustrated in Examples 1, 2, and 3 does not strictly adhere to generally accepted accounting principles of external reporting. For example, work in process (an asset) exists but is not recognized in the accounting system. Advocates of backflush costing, however, cite the materiality concept in support of these versions of backflushing. They claim that if inventories are low or their total costs are not subject to significant change from one accounting period to the next, operating income and inventory costs developed in a backflush costing system will not differ materially from the results generated by a system that adheres to generally accepted accounting principles.

Suppose material differences in operating income and inventories do exist between the results of a backflush costing system and those of a conventional standard costing system. An adjustment can be recorded to make the backflush numbers satisfy external reporting requirements. For example, the backflush entries in Example 2 would result in expensing all conversion costs as a part of Cost of Goods Sold ($1,188,000 at standard costs + $72,000 write-off of under-allocated conversion costs = $1,260,000). But suppose conversion costs were regarded as sufficiently material in amount to be included in Inventory Control. Then entry (d), closing the Conversion Costs accounts, would change as shown below:

Original entry (d)	Conversion Costs Allocated	1,188,000	
	Cost of Goods Sold	72,000	
	Conversion Costs Control		1,260,000
Revised entry (d)	Conversion Costs Allocated	1,188,000	
	Inventory Control (1,000 units × $12)	12,000	
	Cost of Goods Sold	60,000	
	Conversion Costs Control		1,260,000

Criticisms of backflush costing focus mainly on the absence of audit trails—the ability of the accounting system to pinpoint the uses of resources at each step of the production process. The absence of large amounts of materials and work in process inventory means that managers can keep track of operations by personal observations, computer monitoring, and nonfinancial measures.

What are the implications of JIT and backflush costing systems for activity-based costing (ABC) systems? Simplifying the production process, as in a JIT system, makes more of the costs direct and so reduces the extent of overhead cost allocations. Simplified ABC systems are often adequate for companies implementing JIT. But even these simpler ABC systems can enhance backflush costing. Costs from ABC systems give relatively more accurate budgeted conversion costs per unit for different products, which are then used in the backflush costing system. The activity-based cost data are also useful for product costing, decision making, and cost management.

PROBLEM

A Dallas manufacturing company uses standard costs and an operation-costing system. It has a storeroom and several buffer stocks of parts and in-process inventories at various work centers along the production lines. No separate major cost category for direct manufacturing labor exists; all manufacturing labor is a part of conversion costs. For simplicity, assume that there are no beginning inventories and no standard cost variances of materials.

REQUIRED

1. Prepare summary journal entries (without disposing of under- or overallocated conversion costs) based on the following data (in thousands) for a given month.

Raw materials purchased	$35,000
Conversion costs incurred	22,000
Raw materials used	30,000
Conversion costs allocated	20,000
Costs transferred to finished goods	47,500
Cost of goods sold	40,000

For simplicity, you are not given the data to prepare journal entries for each underlying transfer from, say, Work in Process, Operation 1 to Work in Process, Operation 2 to Work in Process, Operation 3. Instead, assume that there is only a single account, Work in Process Control, that is supported by subsidiary Work in Process accounts for each operation.

2. Post the entries in requirement 1 to T-accounts for Inventories (Materials, Work in Process, and Finished Goods), Conversion Costs Control, Conversion Costs Allocated, and Cost of Goods Sold.

3. The plant adopts a JIT production system and a backflush costing system with two trigger points for journal entries: the purchase of materials and the completion of good finished units. Prepare summary journal entries based on the same data as in requirement 1. Note, however, that the raw materials used and the conversion costs assigned would be affected by the goods completed, not the work in process. Assume that 95% of the work placed in process is completed.

4. Post the entries in requirement 3 to T-accounts for Inventories (Raw and In-Process, and Finished Goods), Conversion Costs Control, Conversion Costs Allocated, and Cost of Goods Sold.

5. Compare the applicable inventory balances in requirements 2 and 4. Explain any differences.

SOLUTION

1. a. Materials Inventory Control 35,000

        Accounts Payable Control 35,000

  b. Conversion Costs Control 22,000

        Various Accounts 22,000

  c. Work in Process Control 30,000

        Materials Inventory Control 30,000

  d. Work in Process Control 20,000

        Conversion Costs Allocated 20,000

  e. Finished Goods Control 47,500

        Work in Process Control 47,500

  f. Cost of Goods Sold 40,000

        Finished Goods Control 40,000

2.

Materials Inventory Control	
(a) 35,000	(c) 30,000
Balance 5,000	

Work in Process Control	
(c) 30,000	(e) 47,500
(d) 20,000	
Balance 2,500	

Finished Goods Control	
(e) 47,500	(f) 40,000
Balance 7,500	

Cost of Goods Sold	
(f) 40,000	

Conversion Costs Control	
(b) 22,000	

Conversion Costs Allocated	
	(d) 20,000

3.

a.	Inventory: Raw and In-Process Control	35,000	
	Accounts Payable Control		35,000
b.	Conversion Costs Control	22,000	
	Various Accounts		22,000
c.	Finished Goods Control	47,500	
	Inventory: Raw and In-Process Control (0.95 × 30,000)		28,500
	Conversion Costs Allocated (0.95 × 20,000)		19,000
d.	Cost of Goods Sold	40,000	
	Finished Goods Control		40,000

4.

Inventory: Raw and In-Process Control	
(a) 35,000	(c) 28,500
Balance 6,500	

Finished Goods Control	
(c) 47,500	(d) 40,000
Balance 7,500	

Cost of Goods Sold	
(d) 40,000	

Conversion Costs Control	
(b) 22,000	

Conversion Costs Allocated	
	(c) 19,000

5.

	Sequential (Requirement 2)	Backflush (Requirement 4)
Materials inventory	$ 5,000	$ 0
Inventory: raw and in-process control	0	6,500
Work in process	2,500	0
Subtotal	7,500	6,500
Finished goods	7,500	7,500
Total inventories	$15,000	$14,000
Underallocated conversion costs	$ 2,000	$ 3,000
Cost of goods sold (at standard)	$40,000	$40,000

The $1,000 difference in inventories is explained by the accounting for conversion costs. Conversion costs assigned in operation costing were $1,000 greater than conversion costs allocated under backflush costing because the trigger point for assignment is work in process, not finished goods.

To ease comparisons between the journal entries for operation costing and backflush costing, the numbers used for the various inventory balances are identical except for the $1,000 difference just explained. Advocates of JIT using backflush costing, however, maintain that inventories would decline substantially under JIT, particularly inventories of raw materials and work in process.

The following points are linked to the chapter's learning objectives:

1. Each output unit can, in some extreme cases, be classified either (a) as a distinct, identifiable unit of a product or service, or (b) as identical to numerous other units from that production system. A job-costing system is well suited to a production system yielding the first type of products, while a process-costing system is well suited to the second type of products. Many production systems have elements of both (a) and (b), the mix of which changes over time. Hybrid costing systems, such as operation costing, are blends of characteristics from both job-costing systems and process-costing systems.

2. Just-in-time (JIT) systems streamline the production process and minimize inventories. JIT systems simplify job costing by delaying the recording of costs until after the goods are completed or sold.

3. Operation costing is a hybrid costing system applied to batches of similar products. Production costs are compiled for each work order that will be made up of two or more similar (in many cases, homogeneous) units of a product.

4. Journal entries in an operation-costing system focus on a work-in-process account for a batch of similar products. As the batch proceeds through various operations, direct costs (typically direct materials) are assigned to work in process, as in a job-costing system. Within each operation, all product units are treated exactly alike, and conversion costs per unit are calculated as in a process-costing system.

5. Just-in-time production is a system in which each component on a production line is produced immediately as needed by the next step in the production line.

6. The five major features of a JIT production system are (a) organizing production in manufacturing cells, (b) hiring and training multiskilled workers, (c) emphasizing total quality management, (d) reducing manufacturing lead time and setup time, and (e) building strong supplier relationships.

7. Journal entries in a backflush costing system are not made sequentially to match the flow of a product in a plant. No journal entries are made for work in process. The accounting system does not record details of the changes in a product being produced until at least finished units appear. Working backward, budgeted or standard costs are used to assign manufacturing costs to products.

TERMS TO LEARN

This chapter and the Glossary at the end of this book contain definitions of the following important terms:

backflush costing (p. 726)
delayed costing (726)
endpoint costing (726)
hybrid costing system (718)
just-in-time (JIT) production (722)
just-in-time (JIT) purchasing (724)

manufacturing cells (722)
operation (718)
operation costing (719)
post-deduct costing (726)
sequential tracking (726)
synchronous tracking (726)

ASSIGNMENT MATERIAL

QUESTIONS

20-1 "Hybrid production systems develop because there are hybrid costing systems." Do you agree? Explain.

20-2 "Operations and departments are synonyms." Do you agree?

20-3 "Operation costing means that *conversion costs* and *manufacturing overhead* are synonyms." Do you agree? Explain.

20-4 Give three examples of industries that are likely to use operation costing.

20-5 Identify (a) the major job-costing feature of operation costing, and (b) the major process-costing feature of operation costing.

20-6 Explain why JIT production systems simplify job costing.

20-7 Distinguish a demand-pull from a push-through system.

20-8 List five major features of JIT production systems.

20-9 Describe four financial benefits of implementing a JIT system.

20-10 Describe how JIT systems affect product costing.

20-11 Distinguish between the sequential tracking approach used in traditional budgeted or standard costing systems and the approach used in backflush costing.

20-12 Describe the essence of backflush costing.

20-13 Companies adopting backflush costing often meet three conditions. Describe these three conditions.

20-14 Outline how three different versions of backflush costing can differ.

20-15 "Backflush accounting should be prohibited. It is not in conformity with GAAP." Do you agree? Explain.

EXERCISES

20-16 Operation costing. The Gabriel Corporation produces a standard-sized window in four operations—framing, assembly, staining, and painting. The windows differ in the type of wood (pine, oak) and glass (regular, tempered) used. The framing and assembly operations are common to all windows, but thereafter they are either stained or painted but not both. The total conversion costs for the month of June are

	Framing	Assembly	Staining	Painting
Total conversion costs	$75,000	$105,000	$36,000	$54,000

There is no beginning or ending inventory of windows in the month of June. A total of 3,000 windows are produced in June, half of which are stained and half of which are painted. The conversion cost for each unit passing through a given operation is the same.

Details of two work orders processed in June are as follows:

	Work Order 626	Work Order 750
Number of windows	50	100
Direct materials costs	$5,500	$9,800
Finishing operation	Painting	Staining

REQUIRED

1. Tabulate the conversion costs of each operation, the total units produced, and the conversion cost per unit.
2. Calculate the total costs and the total cost per window of work order 626 and work order 750.

20-17 Operation costing, journal entries. The Omaha Desk Company specializes in making desks of varying shapes, materials, and sizes. It has a cutting operation, an assembly operation, and a staining operation. Some goods are sold unstained, so they do not go through the staining operation. Consider the following data for November:

Direct materials requisitioned by cutting		$200,000
Direct materials requisitioned by staining		20,000
Conversion costs of all operations (actual)		190,000
Conversion costs allocated:		
Cutting		50,000
Assembly		110,000
Staining		30,000

REQUIRED

Prepare the appropriate journal entries. Assume that there is no beginning or ending work in process and that all goods are transferred to Finished Goods. The total manufacturing costs of the products not undergoing staining were $60,000.

20-18 Operation costing. The Pafko Company, a small manufacturer, makes a variety of tool boxes. The company's manufacturing operations and their costs for November were

	Cutting	Assembly	Finishing	Total
Direct manufacturing labor	$2,600	$16,500	$4,800	$23,900
Manufacturing overhead	3,000	22,900	3,300	29,200
	$5,600	$39,400	$8,100	$53,100

Three styles of boxes were produced in November. The quantities and direct materials costs were

Style	Quantity	Direct Materials
Standard	1,200	$18,000
Home	600	6,660
Industrial	200	5,400
		$30,060

The company uses actual costing. It tracks direct materials to each style of box. It combines direct manufacturing labor and manufacturing overhead and allocates the conversion costs on the basis of all product units passing through an operation. All product units are assumed to receive an identical amount of time and effort in each operation. The Industrial style, however, does not go through the finishing operation.

REQUIRED

1. Tabulate the conversion costs of each operation, the total units produced, and the conversion costs per unit for November.
2. Calculate the total costs and the cost per unit of each style of box produced in November. Be sure to account for all the total costs.

20-19 Journal entries (continuation of 20-18).

REQUIRED

Prepare summary journal entries for each operation. For simplicity, assume that all direct materials are introduced at the beginning of the cutting operation. Also, assume that all units were transferred to finished goods when completed and that there was no beginning or ending work in process. Prepare one summary entry for all conversion costs incurred, but prepare a separate entry for allocating conversion costs in each operation.

20-20 Operation costing. The Penske Company manufactures a variety of plastic products. The company has an extrusion operation and subsequent operations to form, trim, and finish parts such as buckets, covers, and automotive interior components. Plastic sheets are produced by the extrusion operation. Many of these sheets are sold as finished goods directly to other manufacturers.

Additional direct materials (chemicals and coloring) are added in the finishing operation.

The company's manufacturing costs assigned to products for October were

	Extrude	Form	Trim	Finish	Totals
Direct materials	$650,000	$ 0	$ 0	$ 80,000	$ 730,000
Direct manufacturing labor	55,000	30,000	20,000	40,000	145,000
Manufacturing overhead	270,000	90,000	40,000	60,000	460,000
	$975,000	$120,000	$60,000	$180,000	$1,335,000

In addition to plastic sheets, two types of automotive products (firewalls and dashboards) were produced:

	Units	Plastic Sheet Direct Materials	Additional Direct Materials
Plastic sheets, sold after extrusion	10,000	$500,000	$ 0
Firewalls, sold after trimming	1,000	50,000	0
Dashboards, sold after finishing	2,000	100,000	80,000
	13,000	$650,000	$80,000

For simplicity, assume that all of the items and units produced received the same steps within each operation.

REQUIRED

1. Tabulate the conversion costs of each operation, the total units produced, and the conversion costs per unit for October.
2. Tabulate the total costs, the units produced, and the costs per unit. Be sure to account for all the total costs for October.

20-21 Backflush journal entries and JIT production. The Lee Company has a plant that manufactures transistor radios. The production time is only a few minutes per unit. The company uses a just-in-time production system and a backflush costing system with two trigger points for journal entries:
◆ Purchase of direct (raw) materials
◆ Completion of good finished units of product

There are no beginning inventories. The following data pertain to April manufacturing:

Direct (raw) materials purchased	$ 8,800,000
Direct (raw) materials used	8,500,000
Conversion costs incurred	4,220,000
Allocation of conversion costs	4,000,000
Costs transferred to finished goods	12,500,000
Cost of goods sold	11,900,000

REQUIRED

1. Prepare summary journal entries for April (without disposing of under- or overallocated conversion costs). Assume no direct materials variances.
2. Post the entries in requirement 1 to T-accounts for applicable Inventory Control, Conversion Costs Control, Conversion Costs Allocated, and Cost of Goods Sold.
3. Under an ideal JIT production system, how would the amounts in your journal entries differ from those in requirement 1?

20-22 Backflush costing and JIT production. The Acton Corporation manufactures electrical meters. For August, there were no beginning inventories of direct (raw) materials and no beginning and ending work in process. Acton uses a JIT production system and backflush costing with two trigger points for making entries in the accounting system:

- Purchase of direct materials debited to Inventory: Raw and In-Process Control
- Completion of good finished units of product debited to Finished Goods Control at standard costs

Acton's August standard costs per unit are direct materials, $25; conversion costs, $20. The following data apply to August manufacturing:

Direct (raw) materials purchased	$550,000
Conversion costs incurred	$440,000
Number of finished units manufactured	21,000
Number of finished units sold	20,000

REQUIRED

1. Prepare summary journal entries for August (without disposing of under- or overallocated conversion costs). Assume no direct materials variances.
2. Post the entries in requirement 1 to T-accounts for applicable Inventory Control, Conversion Costs Control, Conversion Costs Allocated, and Cost of Goods Sold.

20-23 Backflush, second trigger is sale. Assume the same facts as in 20-22. Assume that the second trigger point for the Acton Corporation is the sale—rather than the production—of finished units. Also, the Inventory Control account is confined solely to direct materials, whether these materials are in a storeroom, in work in process, or in finished goods. No conversion costs are inventoried. They are allocated at standard cost to the units sold. Any under- or overallocated conversion costs are written off monthly to Cost of Goods Sold.

REQUIRED

1. Prepare summary journal entries for August, including the disposition of under- or overallocated conversion costs. Assume no direct materials variances.
2. Post the entries in requirement 1 to T-accounts for applicable Inventory Control, Conversion Costs Control, Conversion Costs Allocated, and Cost of Goods Sold.

20-24 Backflush, one trigger point. Assume the same facts as in 20-22. Now assume that there is only one trigger point, the completion of good finished units of product, which are debited to Finished Goods Control at standard costs. Any under- or overallocated conversion costs are written off monthly to cost of goods sold.

REQUIRED

1. Prepare summary journal entries for August, including the disposition of under- or overallocated conversion costs. Assume no direct materials variances.
2. Post the entries in requirement 1 to T-accounts for applicable Inventory Control, Conversion Costs Control, Conversion Costs Allocated, and Cost of Goods Sold.

PROBLEMS

20-25 Operation costing, equivalent units. (CMA, adapted) Gregg Industries manufactures a variety of plastic products, including a series of molded chairs. The three models of molded chairs, which are all variations of the same design, are Standard (can be stacked), Deluxe (with arms), and Executive (with arms and padding). The company uses batch manufacturing and has an operation-costing system.

Gregg has an extrusion operation and subsequent operations to form, trim, and finish the chairs. Plastic sheets are produced by the extrusion operation, some of which are sold directly to other manufacturers. During the forming operation, the remaining plastic sheets are molded into chair seats and the legs are added. The Standard model is sold after this operation. During the trim operation, the arms are added to the Deluxe and Executive models and the chair edges are smoothed. Only the Executive model enters the finish operation, where the padding is added. All of the units produced receive the same steps within each operation.

The May production run had a total manufacturing cost of $898,000. The units of production and direct materials costs incurred are as follows:

	Units Produced	Extrusion Materials	Form Materials	Trim Materials	Finish Materials
Plastic sheets	5,000	$ 60,000	$ 0	$ 0	$ 0
Standard model	6,000	72,000	24,000	0	0
Deluxe model	3,000	36,000	12,000	9,000	0
Executive model	2,000	24,000	8,000	6,000	12,000
	16,000	$192,000	$44,000	$15,000	$12,000

Manufacturing costs of production assigned during the month of May were

	Extrusion Operation	Form Operation	Trim Operation	Finish Operation
Direct manufacturing labor	$152,000	$60,000	$30,000	$18,000
Manufacturing overhead	240,000	72,000	39,000	24,000

REQUIRED
1. For each product produced by Gregg Industries during the month of May, determine (a) the unit cost, and (b) the total cost. Be sure to account for all costs incurred during the month, and support your answer with appropriate calculations.
2. Without considering your answer in requirement 1, assume that 1,000 units of the Deluxe model produced during May remained in work-in-process at the end of the month. These units were 100% complete as to materials costs and 60% complete in the trim operation. Determine the cost of the 1,000 units of the Deluxe model in the work-in-process inventory at the end of May.

20-26 Operation costing with ending work in process and journal entries. The Galvez Company produces two models of video recorders. The deluxe units undergo two operations. The superdeluxe units undergo three operations. Consider the following:

	Production Order	
	For 1,000 Deluxe Units	For 500 Superdeluxe Units
Direct materials (actual costs)	$50,000	$54,000
Conversion costs allocated:		
Operation 1	20,000	10,000
Operation 2	?	?
Operation 3	—	5,000
Total manufacturing costs	?	?

REQUIRED
1. Operation 2 is highly automated. The budgeted conversion costs for 19_7 were $100,000 direct manufacturing labor and $440,000 manufac-

turing overhead. The budgeted production for 19_7 was 180,000 units. Each product unit receives the same conversion costs per unit in operation 2. Compute the total costs of processing the deluxe products and superdeluxe products in operation 2.

2. Compute the total manufacturing costs and the unit costs of the deluxe and superdeluxe products.

3. Prepare journal entries that track the costs of all 1,000 deluxe units through operations to Finished Goods.

4. Suppose that at the end of the year, 500 deluxe units were in process through operation 1 only and 300 superdeluxe units were in process through operation 2 only, but complete with respect to direct materials and conversion costs. Compute the cost of the ending work-in-process inventory. Assume that no direct materials are charged in operation 2 but that $4,000 of additional direct materials are to be charged to the 500 units processed in operation 3. (Ignore end-of-year variances.)

20-27 Operation costing, service sector, equivalent units. Union Bank uses an operation-costing system to determine the cost of opening two types of accounts (a checking account, and a checking account with an overdraft facility) and the cost of adding an overdraft facility to an existing checking account. Checking accounts are opened at the branch; overdraft facilities are approved by the Credit Department. Information for the month of March is as follows:

	Branch Costs	Credit Department Costs
Total service costs allocated to the account-opening and overdraft activity	$7,200	$14,850

In March, the bank signed up 600 checking account customers and 200 checking account customers with an overdraft facility. Furthermore, 100 customers added an overdraft facility to their existing checking accounts. All branch transactions related to opening accounts are assumed to receive an identical amount of time and effort. Similarly, the time and effort in the Credit Department to set up each overdraft facility are assumed to be the same.

REQUIRED

1. Calculate the total costs and the unit cost in March for opening a checking account, opening a checking account with an overdraft facility, or adding an overdraft facility to an existing checking account.

2. Suppose that at the end of March, the Credit Department had not completed setting up 40 of the 100 overdraft facilities for existing customers. Credit processing was 25% complete with respect to these 40 customers. There was no work pending in the Credit Department at the beginning of March, and the department had set up overdraft facilities for all other customers who wanted overdraft facilities during March. Calculate the total costs and the unit cost in March of opening a checking account, opening a checking account with an overdraft facility, and adding an overdraft facility to an existing checking account.

20-28 Backflush costing and JIT production. The Ronowski Company produces telephones. For June, there were no beginning inventories of raw materials and no beginning and ending work in process. Ronowski uses a JIT production system and backflush costing with two trigger points for making entries in its accounting system:

◆ Purchase of direct (raw) materials
◆ Completion of good finished units of product

Ronowski's June standard cost per unit of telephone product is direct materials, $26; conversion costs, $15. There are two inventory accounts:

◆ Inventory: Raw and In-Process Control
◆ Finished Goods Control

The following data apply to June manufacturing:

Raw materials purchased	$5,300,000
Conversion costs incurred	$3,080,000
Number of finished units manufactured	200,000
Number of finished units sold	192,000

REQUIRED

1. Prepare summary journal entries for June (without disposing of under- or overallocated conversion costs). Assume no direct materials variances.
2. Post the entries in requirement 1 to T-accounts for applicable Inventory Control, Conversion Costs Control, Conversion Costs Allocated, and Cost of Goods Sold.

20-29 Backflush, second trigger is sale. Assume the same facts as in 20-28. Assume that the second trigger point for the Ronowski Company is the sale—rather than the production—of finished units. Also, the inventory account is confined solely to direct materials, whether they would be in a storeroom, in work in process, or in finished goods.

No conversion costs are inventoried. They are allocated at standard cost to the units sold. Any under- or overallocated conversion costs are written off monthly to Cost of Goods Sold.

REQUIRED

1. Prepare summary journal entries for June, including the disposition of under- or overallocated conversion costs. Assume no direct materials variances.
2. Post the entries in requirement 1 to T-accounts for applicable Inventory Control, Conversion Costs Control, Conversion Costs Allocated, and Cost of Goods Sold. Explain the composition of the ending balance of Inventory Control.
3. Suppose conversion costs were sufficiently material in amount to be included in Inventory Control. Using a backflush system, show how your journal entries would be changed in requirement 1. Explain briefly.

20-30 Backflush, one trigger point. Assume the same facts as in 20-28. Now assume that there is only one trigger point, the completion of good finished units of product, which are debited to Finished Goods Control at standard costs. Any under- or overallocated conversion costs are written off monthly to Cost of Goods Sold.

REQUIRED

1. Prepare summary journal entries for June, including the disposition of under- or overallocated conversion costs. Assume no direct materials variances.
2. Post the entries in requirement 1 to T-accounts for applicable Inventory Control, Conversion Costs Control, Conversion Costs Allocated, and Cost of Goods Sold. Explain the composition of the ending balance of Inventory Control.
3. If you did Problem 20-28, compare and explain any differences between the results here and those in Problem 20-28.

20-31 Accounting for variances (continuation of 20-28). Suppose the same quantity of raw materials had additional costs as follows:

Price variance	$30,000 U
Efficiency variance	70,000 U

REQUIRED

1. Prepare summary journal entries (without explanations) to record the raw material variances.
2. Assume that under- or overallocated conversion costs are written off monthly to Cost of Goods Sold. Prepare the pertinent summary journal entry.

20-32 Just-in-time systems, ethics. Gail Daly, the plant manager at Daisy Electricals calls Linda Anwar, the plant controller, into her office. She had just finished reviewing Anwar's report on the financial benefits from implementing JIT. The report described the following annual benefits and costs.

	First Year After Implementation	Subsequent Years
Annual expected benefits from:		
Lower investment in inventories	$290,000	$350,000
Reductions in setup costs	110,000	150,000
Reduction in costs of waste, spoilage, and rework	200,000	250,000
Operating income from higher revenues as a result of responding faster to customers	180,000	300,000
Annual expected costs of implementing JIT	950,000	750,000

"We have been working on getting organized for JIT for almost a year now. Some of the financial benefits you have computed seem optimistic to me. I don't think we are quite there yet, but if you continue to use the financial numbers you have, we would be forced to implement JIT sooner than we should. Please look over the numbers and see what you can do. I think some of the numbers are rather soft anyway. I also understand that plant profitability might take a hit in the year JIT is first implemented. I retire next year and I don't want to go out with a losing record." Anwar is quite certain that her numbers are correct. She is also aware that Daly would lose most of her performance bonuses if plant earnings decrease next year. It does not seem fair to her that Daly should be penalized in the short term for what is in the long-run interest of the company.

REQUIRED

1. On the basis of Anwar's report, calculate the effect of JIT implementation on plant profitability in the first year after implementation and in subsequent years. On the basis of Anwar's report, should Daisy implement JIT?

2. Is Daly correct in characterizing some of the financial benefits as "soft." Which items do you think she is referring to? If the benefits you identify as "soft" are not realized, should Daisy implement JIT?

3. Is Daly being unfairly penalized if she implements JIT? What should Daly do? What should Anwar do?

COLLABORATIVE LEARNING PROBLEM

20-33 Backflushing. The following conversation occurred between Brian Richardson, plant manager at Glendale Engineering and Charles Cheng, plant controller. Glendale manufactures automotive component parts such as gears and crankshafts for automobile manufacturers. Richardson has been very enthusiastic about implementing JIT and about simplifying and streamlining the production and other business processes.

> Richardson: "Charles, I would like to substantially simplify our accounting in the new JIT environment. Can't we just record one accounting entry at the time we ship products to our customers? I don't want to have our staff spending time tracking inventory from one stage to the next, when we have as little inventory as we do."

> Cheng: "Brian, I think you are right about simplifying the accounting, but we still have a fair amount of raw material and finished goods inventory that varies from period to period depending on the demand for specific products. Doing away with all inventory accounting may be a problem."

Richardson: "Well, you know my desire to simplify, simplify, simplify. I know that there are some costs of oversimplifying, but I believe that, in the long run, simplification pays big dividends. Why don't you and your staff study the issues involved, and I will put it on the agenda for our next senior plant management meeting."

INSTRUCTIONS

Form groups of two or more students to complete the following requirements.

REQUIRED

1. What backflush costing method would you recommend that Cheng adopt? Remember Richardson's desire to simplify the accounting as much as possible. Develop support for your recommendation.

2. Think about the three examples of backflush costing described in this chapter. These examples differ with respect to the number and types of trigger points used. Suppose your goal of implementing backflush costing is to simplify the accounting, but only if it closely matches the sequential tracking approach. Which backflush costing method would you propose if
   a. Glendale had no raw materials or work-in-process inventories but did have finished goods inventory?
   b. Glendale had no work-in-process or finished goods inventories but did have raw material inventory?
   c. Glendale had no raw material, work-in-process, or finished goods inventories?

3. Backflush costing has its critics. In an article in the magazine *Management Accounting*, entitled "Beware the New Accounting Myths," R. Calvasina, E. Calvasina, and G. Calvasina state:

   The periodic (backflush) system has never been reflective of the reporting needs of a manufacturing system. In the highly standardized operating environments of the present JIT era, the appropriate system to be used is a perpetual accounting system based on an up-to-date, realistic set of standard costs. For management accountants to backflush on an actual cost basis is to return to the days of the outdoor privy.

   Comment on this statement.

CHAPTER 21

INVENTORY MANAGEMENT AND JUST-IN-TIME

Manufacturers are demanding more-frequent deliveries with shorter purchase-order lead times from their suppliers. To better service the companies who use their automotive products, Harman-Motive has invested in new information systems and technology. Better coordination and faster response times are helping Harman-Motive and its customers to reduce inventory levels.

LEARNING OBJECTIVES

After studying this chapter, you should be able to

1. Explain why cost management of materials is pivotal in many organizations

2. Identify five categories of costs associated with goods for sale

3. Explain the economic order quantity (EOQ) decision model and how it balances ordering costs and carrying costs

4. Explain the reorder point and safety stocks

5. Discuss why EOQ models are rarely sensitive to minor variations in cost predictions

6. Describe the potential conflicts that can arise between EOQ decision models and models used for performance evaluation

7. Compare EOQ and just-in-time (JIT) purchasing models

8. Determine the relevant benefits and relevant costs in JIT purchasing

9. Identify relevant benefits and relevant costs in JIT production

10. Describe measures for evaluating JIT production performance

Inventory management encompasses the planning, organizing, and control activities that focus on the flow of materials and inventory into, through, and from the organization. Many decisions fall under the inventory management umbrella. When is the best time to purchase materials or merchandise? How should purchasing arrangements be structured? Which is the best way to handle materials or merchandise inventories, once they are received?

Managing inventories and materials is important because, on average, the costs of materials account for more than 50% of total costs in manufacturing companies and over 70% of total costs in retail companies. Managers respond to the high costs of materials and inventory in several ways. In the last chapter, we saw managers adopting JIT systems to reduce inventory. Managers also focus on reducing the purchasing costs of materials. The 1990s have seen General Motors (GM) demand double-digit percentage price cuts from its suppliers. General Electric (GE) recently announced Target 10, an initiative that aims to cut GE's costs of purchases by 10%. To achieve these goals, GM and GE have offered to assist suppliers in reducing costs, and those suppliers who fail to cooperate will probably lose business.

Accounting information can play a key role in inventory management. This chapter illustrates the importance of accounting information in two areas:

1. The management of goods for sale in retail organizations
2. The management of materials, work in process, and finished goods in organizations with manufacturing operations

Inventory management is of little concern in service companies since these companies hold minimal materials and inventory.

MANAGING GOODS FOR SALE IN RETAIL ORGANIZATIONS

Cost of goods sold measures the costs of inventory sold, including the costs of purchasing and managing inventory. Cost of goods sold constitutes the largest single cost item for most retailers. For example, Kroger, a grocery retail store, reported the following breakdown of operations for 1994:

Sales		100.0%
Deduct costs:		
Cost of goods sold	75.8%	
Selling, general and administration costs	19.7	
Other costs, interest, and taxes	3.3	
Total costs		98.8
Net income		1.2%

The paper-thin net income percentage for Kroger, like other retail grocery stores, means that better decisions regarding the purchasing and managing of goods for sale can cause dramatic percentage increases in net income.

Costs Associated with Goods for Sale

The following cost categories are important when managing inventories and goods for sale.

1. *Purchasing costs:* **Purchasing costs** consist of the costs of goods acquired from suppliers including incoming freight or transportation costs. These costs usually make up the largest single cost category of goods for sale. Discounts for different purchase-order sizes and supplier credit terms affect purchasing costs.

2. *Ordering costs:* **Ordering costs** consist of the costs of preparing and issuing a purchase order. Related to the number of purchase orders processed are special processing, receiving, inspection, and payment costs.

3. *Carrying costs:* **Carrying costs** arise when a business holds inventories of goods for sale. These costs include the opportunity cost of the investment tied up in inven-

tory (see Chapter 11, pp. 395–396) and the costs associated with storage, such as storage-space rental and insurance, obsolescence and spoilage.

4. *Stockout costs:* A **stockout** occurs when a company runs out of a particular item for which there is customer demand. A company may respond to the shortfall or stockout by expediting an order from a supplier. Expediting costs of a stockout include the additional ordering costs plus any associated transportation costs. Alternatively, the company may lose a sale due to the stockout. In this case, stockout costs include the lost contribution margin on the sale plus any contribution margin lost on future sales hurt by customer ill-will caused by the stockout.

5. *Quality costs:* The *quality* of a product or service is its conformance with a preannounced or prespecified standard. As described in Chapter 19, four categories of costs of quality are often distinguished: (a) prevention costs, (b) appraisal costs, (c) internal failure costs, and (d) external failure costs.

The descriptions of the cost categories indicate that some of the relevant costs for making inventory decisions and managing goods for sale are not available in existing accounting systems. Opportunity costs, which are not typically recorded in accounting systems, are an important component in several of these cost categories.

The inclusion of costs from all five categories makes cost of goods sold substantial.[1] Advances in information-gathering technology, however, are attempting to increase the reliability and timeliness of inventory data and reduce costs in these five categories. For example, electronic data interchange (EDI) links a company to its suppliers via computers. An order is often initiated by a single keystroke, increasing timeliness and reducing costs of ordering. Similarly, barcoding technology allows a scanner to capture purchases and sales of individual units. This creates an instantaneous record of inventory movements and helps in the management of purchasing, carrying, and stockout costs.

Economic-Order-Quantity Decision Model

The first major decision in managing goods for sale is deciding how much of a given product to order. The **economic order quantity (EOQ)** decision model calculates the optimal quantity of inventory to order. The simplest version of this model incorporates only ordering costs and carrying costs into the calculation. It assumes the following:

OBJECTIVE 3

Explain the economic order quantity (EOQ) decision model and how it balances ordering costs and carrying costs

1. The same fixed quantity is ordered at each reorder point.

2. Demand, ordering costs, and carrying costs are certain. The **purchase-order lead time**—the time between the placement of an order and its delivery—is also certain.

3. Purchasing costs per unit are unaffected by the quantity ordered. This assumption makes purchasing costs irrelevant to determining EOQ, because purchasing costs of all units acquired will be the same, whatever the order size in which the units are ordered.

4. No stockouts occur. One justification for this assumption is that the costs of a stockout are prohibitively high. We assume that to avoid these potential costs, management always maintains adequate inventory so that no stockout can occur.

5. In deciding the size of the purchase order, management considers the costs of quality only to the extent that these costs affect ordering costs or carrying costs.

Given these assumptions, EOQ analysis ignores purchasing costs, stockout costs, and quality costs. To determine EOQ, we minimize the relevant ordering and carrying costs (those ordering and carrying costs that are affected by the quantity of inventory ordered):

Total relevant costs = Total relevant ordering costs + Total relevant carrying costs

[1]In some cases, inventory "shrinkage" from shoplifting and employee theft can also add to cost of goods sold.

EXAMPLE: Video Galore sells packages of blank video tapes to its customers; it also rents out tapes of movies and sporting events. It purchases packages of video tapes from Sontek at $14 a package. Sontek pays all incoming freight. No incoming inspection is necessary, as Sontek has a superb reputation for delivering quality merchandise. Annual demand is 13,000 packages, at a rate of 250 packages per week. Video Galore requires a 15% annual return on investment. The purchase-order lead time is 2 weeks. The following cost data are available:

Relevant ordering costs per purchase order		$200.00
Relevant carrying costs per package per year:		
Required annual return on investment, 15% × $14	$2.10	
Relevant insurance, materials handling, breakage, etc., per year	3.10	5.20

What is the economic order quantity of packages of video tapes?

The formula underlying the EOQ model is

$$EOQ = \sqrt{\frac{2DP}{C}}$$

where

EOQ = Economic order quantity

D = Demand in units for a specified time period (1 year in this example)

P = Relevant ordering costs per purchase order

C = Relevant carrying costs of 1 unit in stock for the time period used for D (1 year in this example)

The formula indicates that EOQ increases with demand and ordering costs and decreases with carrying costs.

We can use this formula to determine the EOQ for Video Galore as follows:

$$EOQ = \sqrt{\frac{2 \times 13{,}000 \times \$200}{\$5.20}} = \sqrt{1{,}000{,}000} = 1{,}000 \text{ packages}$$

Therefore, Video Galore should order 1,000 tape packages each time to minimize total ordering and carrying costs.

The total annual relevant costs (TRC) for any order quantity Q can be calculated using the following formula:

$$TRC = \begin{matrix} \text{Total annual relevant} \\ \text{ordering costs} \end{matrix} + \begin{matrix} \text{Total annual relevant} \\ \text{carrying costs} \end{matrix}$$

$$= \begin{matrix} \text{Number of} \\ \text{purchase orders} \\ \text{per year} \end{matrix} \times \begin{matrix} \text{Relevant} \\ \text{ordering costs per} \\ \text{purchase order} \end{matrix} + \begin{matrix} \text{Average inventory} \\ \text{in units} \end{matrix} \times \begin{matrix} \text{Annual relevant} \\ \text{carrying costs of 1} \\ \text{unit for a year} \end{matrix}$$

$$= \left(\frac{D}{Q}\right) \times P + \left(\frac{Q}{2}\right) \times C = \frac{DP}{Q} + \frac{QC}{2}$$

(Note that in this formula, Q can be any order quantity, not just the EOQ.)

When $Q = 1{,}000$ units,

$$TRC = \frac{13{,}000 \times \$200}{1{,}000} + \frac{1{,}000 \times \$5.20}{2}$$

$$= \$2{,}600 + \$2{,}600 = \$5{,}200$$

The number of deliveries each time period (in our example, 1 year) is

$$\frac{D}{EOQ} = \frac{13{,}000}{1{,}000} = 13 \text{ deliveries}$$

Exhibit 21-1 shows a graph analysis of the total annual relevant costs of ordering (DP/Q) and carrying inventory ($QC/2$) under various order sizes (Q), and illus-

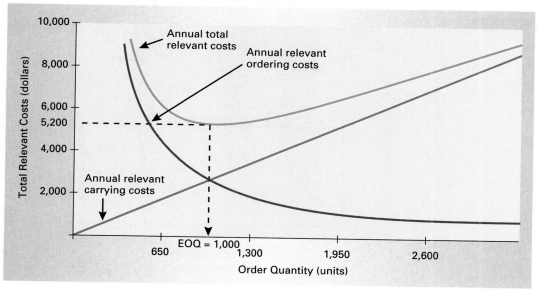

EXHIBIT 21-1
Ordering Costs and Carrying Costs for Video Galore

trates the trade-off between the two types of costs. The larger the order quantity, the higher the annual relevant carrying costs, but the lower the annual relevant ordering costs. *The total annual relevant costs are at a minimum where total relevant ordering costs and total relevant carrying costs are equal* (in the Video Galore example, each equals $2,600).

When to Order, Assuming Certainty

The second major decision in dealing with cost of goods for sale is when to order. The **reorder point** is the quantity level of the inventory on hand that triggers a new order. The reorder point is simplest to compute when both demand and lead time are certain:

$$\text{Reorder point} = \frac{\text{Number of units sold}}{\text{per unit of time}} \times \text{Purchase-order lead time}$$

OBJECTIVE 4

Explain the reorder point and safety stocks

Consider our Video Galore example. We choose a week as the unit of time:

Economic order quantity	1,000 packages
Number of units sold per week	250 packages
Purchase-order lead time	2 weeks

Thus,

$$\text{Reorder point} = \frac{\text{Number of units sold}}{\text{per unit of time}} \times \text{Purchase-order lead time}$$

$$= 250 \times 2 = 500 \text{ packages}$$

So, Video Galore will order 1,000 packages of tapes each time its inventory stock falls to 500 packages.

The graph in Exhibit 21-2 presents the behavior of the inventory level of tape packages, assuming demand occurs uniformly throughout each week.[2] If the purchase-order lead time is 2 weeks, a new order will be placed when the inventory level reaches 500 tape packages so that the 1,000 packages ordered are received at the time inventory reaches zero.

---

[2]This handy formula does not apply when the receipt of the order fails to increase inventory to the reorder-point quantity (for example, when the lead time is 3 weeks and the order is a 1-week supply). In these cases, orders will overlap.

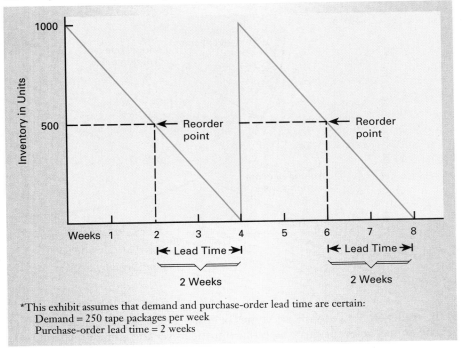

EXHIBIT 21-2
Inventory Level of Tape Packages for Video Galore*

*This exhibit assumes that demand and purchase-order lead time are certain:
Demand = 250 tape packages per week
Purchase-order lead time = 2 weeks

Safety Stock

So far, we have assumed that demand and purchase-order lead time are certain. When retailers are uncertain about the demand, the lead time, or the quantity that suppliers can provide, they often hold safety stock. **Safety stock** is inventory held at all times regardless of inventory ordered using EOQ. It is used as a buffer against unexpected increases in demand or lead time and unavailability of stock from suppliers. In our Video Galore example, expected demand is 250 packages per week, but the company's managers feel that a maximum demand of 400 packages per week may occur. If Video Galore's managers decide that the costs of stockout are prohibitive, they may decide to hold safety stock of 300 packages. This amount is the maximum excess demand of 150 packages per week for the 2 weeks of purchase-order lead time. The computation of safety stock hinges on demand forecasts. Managers will have some notion—usually based on experience—of the range of weekly demand.

A frequency distribution based on prior daily or weekly levels of demand provides data for computing the associated costs of maintaining safety stock. Assume that one of seven different levels of demand will occur over the 2-week purchase-order lead time at Video Galore.

Total Demand for 2 Weeks	Units						
	200	300	400	500	600	700	800
Probability (sums to 1.00)	0.06	0.09	0.20	0.30	0.20	0.09	0.06

We see that 500 is the most likely level of demand for two weeks because it is assigned the highest probability of occurrence. We also see that there is a 0.35 probability that demand will be between 600, 700, or 800 packages (0.20 + 0.09 + 0.06 = 0.35).

If a customer calls Video Galore to buy video tapes, and the store has none in stock, it can "rush" them to the customer at a cost to Video Galore of $4 per package. The relevant stockout costs in this case are $4 per package. The optimal safety stock level is the quantity of safety stock that minimizes the sum of the relevant annual stockout and carrying costs. Recall that the relevant carrying costs for Video Galore are $5.20 per unit per year.

Exhibit 21-3 presents the total annual relevant stockout and carrying costs when the reorder point is 500 units. We need only consider safety stock levels of 0, 100, 200 and 300 units, since demand will exceed the 500 units of stock available at reordering by 0 if demand is 500, by 100 if demand is 600, by 200 if demand is 700, and by 300 if demand is 800.[3] The total annual relevant stockout and carrying costs would be minimized at $1,352, when a safety stock of 200 packages is maintained. Think of the 200 units of safety stock as extra stock that Video Galore maintains. For example, Video Galore's total inventory of tapes at the time of reordering its EOQ of 1,000 units would be 700 units (the reorder point of 500 units plus the safety stock of 200 units).

Sontek does a similar analysis. Sontek too maintains safety stocks to meet unexpected demands from its customers. The net result is high levels of inventory in the supply chain consisting of the manufacturer and retailer. To reduce these inventories, companies are forming strategic partnerships. For example, Video Galore could contract with Sontek to manage Video Galore's inventory of tapes. Sontek could then better coordinate the flow of goods in the entire supply chain. For instance, Sontek could reduce its own inventory holdings when Video Galore is holding high quantities of inventory, and vice versa. Companies such as 3M, Procter & Gamble and Scott Paper have signed such agreements with WalMart, the largest retail company in the United States.

CHALLENGES IN ESTIMATING INVENTORY-RELATED COSTS AND THEIR EFFECTS

Considerations in Obtaining Estimates of Relevant Costs

Obtaining accurate estimates of the cost parameters used in the EOQ decision model is a challenging task. For example, the relevant annual carrying costs of inventory consist of *incremental* or *outlay costs* plus the *opportunity cost of capital*.

What are the relevant incremental costs of carrying inventory? Only those costs that vary with the quantity of inventory held—for example, insurance, property taxes, costs of obsolescence, and costs of breakage. Consider the salaries paid to clerks, storekeepers, and materials handlers. These costs are irrelevant if they are unaffected by changes in inventory levels. Suppose, however, that as inventories decrease, these salary costs also decrease as the clerks, storekeepers, and materials handlers are transferred to other activities or laid off. In this case, the salaries paid to these persons are relevant incremental costs of carrying inventory. Similarly, the costs of storage space owned that cannot be used for other profitable purposes as inventories decrease are irrelevant. But if the space has other profitable uses, or if rental cost is tied to the amount of space occupied, storage costs are relevant incremental costs of carrying inventory.

What is the relevant opportunity cost of capital? It is the return forgone by investing capital in inventory rather than elsewhere. It is calculated as the required rate of return multiplied by those costs per unit that vary with the number of units purchased and that are incurred at the time the units are received. (Examples of these costs per unit are purchase price, incoming freight, and incoming inspection.) Opportunity costs are not computed on investments, say, in buildings, if these

---

[3] If Video Galore is better (worse) off holding 100 units of safety stock rather than 0, it would prefer holding 100 (0) units rather than any number between 1 and 99 units. If Video Galore is better (worse) off holding 200 units of safety stock rather than 100, it would prefer holding 200 (100) units rather than any number between 101 and 199. If Video Galore is better (worse) off holding 300 units of safety stock rather than 200, it would prefer holding 300 (200) units rather than any number between 201 and 299. You can verify these statements by substituting different values of safety stock for 0, 100, 200, and 300 in Exhibit 21-3.

EXHIBIT 21-3
Computation of Safety Stock for Video Galore When Reorder Point is 500 Units

Safety Stock Level in Units (1)	Demand Realizations Resulting in Stockouts (2)	Stockout in Units* (3) = (2) − 500 − (1)	Probability of Stockout (4)	Relevant Stockout Costs† (5) = (3) × $4	Number of Orders per Year‡ (6)	Expected Stockout Costs§ (7) = (4) × (5) × (6)	Relevant Carrying Costs# (8) = (1) × $5.20	Total Relevant Costs (9) = (7) + (8)
0	600	100	0.20	$ 400	13	$1,040		
	700	200	0.09	800	13	936		
	800	300	0.06	1,200	13	936		
						$2,912	$ 0	$2,912
100	700	100	0.09	400	13	$ 468		
	800	200	0.06	800	13	624		
						$1,092	$ 520	$1,612
200	800	100	0.06	400	13	$ 312	$1,040	$1,352
300	—	—	—	—	—	$ 0‖	$1,560	$1,560

*Realized demand − inventory available during lead time (excluding safety stock), 500 units − safety stock.

†Stockout units × relevant stockout costs of $4.00 per unit.

‡Annual demand 13,000 ÷ 1,000 EOQ = 13 orders per year.

§Probability of stockout × relevant stockout costs × number of orders per year.

#Safety stock × annual relevant carrying costs of $5.20 per unit (assumes that safety stock is on hand at all times and that there is no overstocking caused by decreases in expected usage).

‖At a safety stock level of 300 units, no stockouts will occur and hence expected stockout costs = $0.

investment are unaffected by changes in inventory levels. In the case of stockouts, calculating the relevant opportunity costs requires an estimate of the lost contribution margin on that sale as well as on future sales hurt by customer ill-will resulting from the stockout.

Our discussion suggests that predicting relevant costs requires care and is difficult. Managers understand that their projections will seldom be flawless. This leads to the question, What is the cost of an incorrect prediction when actual relevant costs are different from the relevant predicted costs used for decision making?

Cost of a Prediction Error

Continuing our example, suppose Video Galore's relevant ordering costs per purchase order are $242 instead of the predicted $200. We can calculate the cost of this prediction error with a three-step approach.

OBJECTIVE 5

Discuss why EOQ models are rarely sensitive to minor variations in cost predictions

Step 1: Compute the Monetary Outcome from the Best Action that Could Have Been Taken, Given the Actual Amount of the Cost Input The appropriate inputs are $D = 13,000$ units, $P = \$242$, and $C = \$5.20$. The economic order quantity size is

$$EOQ = \sqrt{\frac{2DP}{C}}$$

$$= \sqrt{\frac{2 \times 13,000 \times \$242}{\$5.20}} = \sqrt{1,210,000}$$

$$= 1,100 \text{ packages}$$

The total annual relevant costs when EOQ = 1,100 is

$$TRC = \frac{DP}{Q} + \frac{QC}{2}$$

$$= \frac{13,000 \times \$242}{1,100} + \frac{1,100 \times \$5.20}{2}$$

$$= \$2,860 + \$2,860 = \$5,720$$

Step 2: Compute the Monetary Outcome from the Best Action Based on the Incorrect Amount of the Predicted Cost Input The planned action when the relevant ordering costs per purchase order are predicted to be $200 is to purchase 1,000 packages in each order. The total annual relevant costs using this order quantity when $D = 13,000$ units, $P = \$242$, and $C = \$5.20$ are

$$TRC = \frac{13,000 \times \$242}{1,000} + \frac{1,000 \times \$5.20}{2}$$

$$= \$3,146 + \$2,600 = \$5,746$$

Step 3: Compute the Difference Between the Monetary Outcomes from Steps 1 and 2

	Monetary Outcome
Step 1	$5,720
Step 2	5,746
Difference	$ (26)

The cost of the prediction error is only $26. Why? Because the total annual relevant costs curve in Exhibit 21-2 is relatively flat over the range of order quantities from 650 to 1,300. *An important feature of the EOQ model is that the total relevant costs are rarely sensitive to minor variations in cost predictions. The square root in the EOQ model reduces the sensitivity of the decision to errors in predicting its inputs.*

Goal-Congruence Issues

Goal-congruence issues can arise when there is an inconsistency between the decision model and the model used to evaluate the performance of the person implementing the decision. For example, the absence of recorded opportunity costs in conventional accounting systems raises the possibility of a conflict between the EOQ model's optimal order quantity and the order quantity that the purchasing manager, evaluated on conventional accounting numbers, regards as optimal.

If annual carrying costs are excluded when evaluating the performance of managers, the managers may favor purchasing a larger order quantity than the EOQ decision model indicates is optimal. Companies such as Coca Cola and WalMart resolve this conflict by designing the performance evaluation system so that the carrying costs, including a required return on investment, are charged to the appropriate manager.

JUST-IN-TIME PURCHASING

As we described in Chapter 20, organizations are giving increased attention to *just-in-time (JIT) purchasing*—the purchase of goods or materials such that a delivery immediately precedes demand or use. JIT purchasing requires organizations to restructure their relationship with suppliers and place smaller and more frequent purchase orders. We next explore the relationship between EOQ decision models and JIT purchasing.

Companies moving toward JIT purchasing argue that the full costs of carrying inventories (including inventory storage space, spoilage, and opportunity costs not recorded in the accounting system) have been dramatically underestimated in the past. At the same time, building close partnerships with suppliers and using computer-based systems (such as electronic data interchange or EDI) for order-related activities significantly reduce ordering costs.

EOQ Implications of JIT Purchasing

Exhibit 21-4 analyzes the sensitivity of Video Galore's EOQ to illustrate the economics of smaller and more frequent purchase orders. The analysis presented in Exhibit 21-4 supports JIT purchasing—that is, having a smaller EOQ and placing more frequent orders—as relevant carrying costs increase and relevant ordering costs per purchase order decrease.

Relevant Benefits and Relevant Costs of JIT Purchasing

The JIT purchasing model is not guided solely by the EOQ model. As discussed earlier (p. 749), the EOQ model is designed to emphasize only the trade-off between carrying and ordering costs. Inventory management extends beyond ordering and carrying costs to include purchasing costs, stockout costs, and quality costs (pp. 748–749). The quality of materials and goods and timely deliveries are important motivations for using JIT purchasing, and stockout costs are an important concern. We add these features as we move from the EOQ decision model to the JIT purchasing model.

Let us revisit the Video Galore example, and consider the following information. Video Galore has recently established an EDI hookup to Sontek. Video Galore triggers a purchase order for tapes by a single computer entry. Computer programs match receiving documents with purchase orders. Payments are made electronically for batches of deliveries rather than for each individual delivery. These changes make ordering costs negligible. Video Galore is negotiating to have Sontek deliver 100 packages of video tapes 130 times each year (5 times every 2 weeks) instead of delivering 1,000 packages 13 times each year as calculated in Exhibit 21-1. Sontek is willing to make these frequent deliveries, but it will tack on a small additional amount of $0.02 to the price per package. Video Galore's required return on investment remains 15%. Assume that relevant annual carrying costs of insurance, materials handling, breakage, and so on remain at $3.10 per package per year.

Porsche's Just-In-Time Revival

In 1993, Porsche was reeling. It had posted losses for three consecutive years and its sales in the United States had declined to 4,000 cars from 30,000 cars in 1986. But 2 short years later, Porsche is looking leaner and healthier as a result of slashing costs and revamping production and marketing. Wendelin Wiedeking, Porsche's CEO, credits the production turnaround to two former Toyota production engineers, Yoshiki Iwata and Chihiro Nakao, who introduced Porsche to JIT systems. When they first arrived at Porsche, Mr. Iwata remarked that Porsche looked like a shipping company, not a car factory, because workers spent less time assembling cars, and more time climbing up and down rows of inventory to find the parts they needed.

As a result of implementing JIT, Porsche freed up 100 million deutschmarks that had been tied up in inventory; slashed production time on its popular Carrera 911 model from 120 hours to 80; and reduced defects, scrap, and rework. By next year, production time is expected to be halved. Porsche also redesigned its cars to have 36% of parts common to its Boxster and 911 product lines. This reduced production, development, and inventory costs.

To get its JIT purchasing efforts on the road, Porsche has sharply reduced the number of suppliers. Porsche is working closely with its suppliers to have parts and components delivered just as they are needed, resulting in substantially lower direct materials inventories.

Source: Adapted from A. Choi, "Porsche, Once Near Collapse, Now Purrs; Automaker Cut Costs, Reduced Dependency on U.S.," *The Wall Street Journal*, Dec. 15, 1994, and Porsche's 1993/94 Annual Report.

Suppose that Video Galore incurs no stockout costs under its current purchasing policy because demand and purchase-order lead times over each 4-week period are certain. Video Galore's major concern is that lower inventory levels from implementing JIT purchasing will lead to more stockouts because demand variations, and delays in supplying tapes are more likely to occur in the short time intervals between supplies under JIT purchasing. Sontek assures Video Galore that its new manufacturing processes enable it to respond rapidly to changing demand patterns. Consequently, stockouts may not be a serious problem. Video Galore expects to incur stockout costs on 50 tape packages each year under a JIT purchasing policy. In the event of a stockout, Video Galore will have to rush-order tape packages at a cost of $4 per package. Should Video Galore implement JIT purchasing?

Exhibit 21-5 compares (1) the incremental costs Video Galore incurs when it purchases video tapes from Sontek under its current purchasing policy, with (2) the

EXHIBIT 21-4

Sensitivity of EOQ to Variations in Relevant Ordering and Carrying Costs for Video Galore*

Relevant Carrying Costs Per Package Per Year	Relevant Ordering Costs Per Purchase Order			
	$200	$150	$100	$30
$ 5.20	EOQ = 1,000	EOQ = 866	EOQ = 707	EOQ = 387
$ 7.00	862	746	609	334
$10.00	721	624	510	279
$15.00	589	510	416	228

*Assuming annual demand is always 13,000 packages.

EXHIBIT 21-5

Annual Relevant Costs of Current Purchasing Policy and JIT Purchasing Policy for Video Galore

Relevant Item	Incremental Costs Under Current Purchasing Relevant Item	Incremental Costs Under JIT Purchasing Policy
Purchasing costs		
$14 per unit × 13,000 units per year	$182,000.00	
$14.02 per unit × 13,000 units per year		$182,260.00
Required return on investment		
15% per year × $14 cost per unit × 500* units of average inventory per year	1,050.00	
15% per year × $14.02 cost per unit × 50† units of average inventory per year		105.15
Outlay carrying costs (insurance, materials handling, breakage, and so on)		
$3.10 per unit per year × 500* units of average inventory per year	1,550.00	
$3.10 per unit per year × 50† units of average inventory per year		155.00
Stockout costs		
No stockouts	0	
$4 per unit × 50 units per year		200.00
Total annual relevant costs	$184,600.00	$182,720.15
Annual difference in favor of JIT purchasing		$1,879.85

*Order quantity ÷ 2 = 1,000 ÷ 2 = 500
†Order quantity ÷ 2 = 100 ÷ 2 = 50

incremental costs Video Galore would incur if Sontek supplied video tapes under a JIT policy. The difference in the two incremental costs is the relevant savings of JIT purchasing. In other methods of comparing the two purchasing policies, the analysis would include only the relevant costs—those costs that differ between the two alternatives. Exhibit 21-5 shows a net cost savings of $1,879.85 per year from shifting to a JIT purchasing policy. Note that ordering costs are irrelevant and hence excluded from our analysis. Why? Because Video Galore will implement the new EDI hookup to make ordering costs negligible whether or not it shifts to JIT purchasing.

Supplier Evaluation and Relevant Costs of Quality and Timely Deliveries

As we saw in Chapter 20, costs of quality and timely deliveries are particularly crucial in JIT purchasing environments. Defective materials and late deliveries often bring the whole plant to a halt, resulting in forgone contribution margin on lost sales. Companies that implement JIT purchasing choose their suppliers carefully and pay special attention to developing long-run supplier partnerships. Some suppliers are very cooperative with a business's attempts to adopt JIT purchasing. For example, Frito-Lay, which has a large market share in potato chips and other snack foods, makes more frequent deliveries to retail outlets than many of its competitors. The company's corporate strategy emphasizes service to retailers and consistency, freshness, and quality of the delivered product.

When evaluating suppliers, companies have to pay special attention to quality costs of goods or materials (for example, incoming materials inspection costs, returns, scrap costs, and rework costs); costs of late deliveries (expediting costs, idle time on machines, and forgone contribution margin on lost sales); and costs of early deliveries (carrying costs). Consider Texas Instruments (TI). TI reports purchase costs of $0.55 per unit for its electrical connectors. If a connector is found to be defective, however, it costs TI $15 to replace this part during manufacturing, $57 to replace it during final testing, and $97 to replace it at the customer's site.[4] Not surprisingly, TI chooses its suppliers for electrical connectors carefully, paying a higher purchase price in exchange for higher quality. Purchase price is only one component in evaluating suppliers.

What are the relevant costs when choosing suppliers? Consider again our Video Galore example. The Denton Corporation also supplies video tapes. It offers to supply all of Video Galore's video tape needs at a price of $13.60 per package (less than Sontek's price of $14.02) under the same JIT delivery terms that Sontek offers. Denton proposes an electronic hookup identical to Sontek's that would make Video Galore's ordering costs negligible. Video Galore's relevant outlay carrying costs of insurance, materials handling, breakage, and so on per package per year is $3.10 if it purchases video tapes from Sontek and $3.00 if it purchases from Denton. Should Video Galore buy from Denton? Not before considering the relevant costs of quality and also the relevant costs of failing to deliver on time.

Video Galore has used Sontek in the past and knows that Sontek fully deserves its reputation for delivering quality merchandise on time. Video Galore does not, for example, find it necessary to inspect the tape packages that Sontek supplies. Denton, however, does not enjoy so sterling a reputation for quality. Video Galore anticipates the following negative aspects of using Denton:

◆ Video Galore would incur additional inspection costs of $0.05 per package.

◆ Average stockouts of 360 tape packages each year would occur, largely resulting from late deliveries. Denton cannot rush-order tape packages to Video Galore on short notice. Video Galore anticipates lost contribution margin per unit of $8 from stockouts.

◆ Customers would likely return 2% of all packages sold owing to poor quality of the tapes. Video Galore estimates its additional costs to handle each returned package is $25.

Exhibit 21-6 presents the relevant costs of purchasing from Sontek and from Denton. Even though Denton is offering a lower price per package, the total relevant costs of purchasing goods from Sontek are lower by $4,361.85 per year. Selling high-quality merchandise also has nonfinancial and qualitative benefits. For example, offering Sontek's high-quality tapes enhances Video Galore's reputation and increases customer goodwill, which may lead to higher future profitability.

INVENTORY COSTS AND ITS MANAGEMENT IN MANUFACTURING ORGANIZATIONS

Managers in companies with manufacturing facilities face the challenging task of producing high-quality products at competitive cost levels. Numerous systems have been developed to help managers plan and implement production and inventory activities. Chapter 20 described the two most basic types of systems:

◆ A *just-in-time (JIT) production system*, a "demand-pull" system under which products are only manufactured to satisfy a specific customer order.

◆ A *materials requirements planning (MRP) system*, a "push-through" system that manufactures finished goods for inventory on the basis of demand forecasts.

Before proceeding, you may wish to review MRP and JIT systems and the major features of JIT systems described in Chapter 20 (pp. 722–724).

---

[4]L. Carr and C. Ittner, "Measuring the Cost of Ownership," *Journal of Cost Management* (Fall 1992).

EXHIBIT 21-6
Annual Relevant Costs of Purchasing From Sontek and Denton

Relevant Item	Incremental Costs of Purchasing from Sontek	Incremental Costs of Purchasing from Denton
Purchasing costs		
$14.02 per unit × 13,000 units per year	$182,260.00	
$13.60 per unit × 13,000 units per year		$176,800.00
Inspection costs		
No inspection necessary	0	
$0.05 per unit × 13,000 units		650.00
Required return on investment		
15% per year × $14.02 × 50* units of average inventory per year	105.15	
15% per year × $13.60 × 50* units of average inventory per year		102.00
Outlay carrying costs (insurance, material handling, breakage, and so on)		
$3.10 per unit per year × 50* units of average inventory per year	155.00	
$3.00 per unit per year × 50* units of average inventory per year		150.00
Stockout costs		
$4 per unit × 50 units per year	200.00	
$8 per unit × 360 units per year		2,880.00
Customer returns costs		
No customer returns	0	
$25 per unit returned × 2% × 13,000 units returned		6,500.00
Total annual relevant costs	$182,720.15	$187,082.00

Annual difference in favor of Sontek $4,361.85

*Order quantity ÷ 2 = 100 ÷ 2 = 50

Companies implementing JIT production systems manage inventories by eliminating them. When inventories are present, as in MRP systems, the management accountant plays several important roles. First, the management accountant must maintain accurate and timely information pertaining to materials, work-in-process, and finished goods inventories. A major cause of unsuccessful attempts to implement MRP systems has been the problem of collecting and updating inventory records. Calculating the full cost of carrying finished goods inventory motivates other actions. For example, instead of storing product at six warehouses, National Semiconductor contracted with Federal Express to airfreight its microchips from a central location in Singapore to customer sites worldwide. The change enabled National to move products from factory to customer in 4 days rather than 45, and to reduce distribution costs from 2.6% to 1.9% of sales.

A second role of the management accountant consists of providing estimates of the costs of setting up each production run at a plant, the costs of downtime, and the costs of holding inventory. Costs of setting up the machine are analogous to ordering costs in the EOQ model. When the costs of setting up machines or sections of the production line are high (for example, as with a blast furnace in an integrated steel mill), processing larger batches of materials and incurring larger inventory carrying costs is the optimal approach because it reduces the number of times the machine must be set up. When setup costs are small, processing smaller batches is optimal because it reduces carrying costs. Similarly, when the costs of downtime are high, there can be sizable benefits from maintaining continuous production.

JIT Production, Quality, and Relevant Costs

OBJECTIVE 9

Identify relevant benefits and relevant costs in JIT production

Early advocates of JIT production emphasized the benefits of lower carrying costs of inventory. *An important benefit of lower inventories, however, is the heightened emphasis on eliminating the root causes of rework, scrap, and waste and on reducing the manufacturing lead time of their products.* In computing the relevant benefits and relevant costs of reducing inventories in JIT production systems, the cost analyst must consider all benefits.

Consider the Hudson Corporation, a manufacturer of brass fittings. Hudson is considering implementing a JIT production system. Suppose that to implement JIT production, Hudson must incur $100,000 in annual tooling costs to reduce setup times. Suppose further that JIT will reduce average inventory by $500,000. Also, relevant costs of insurance, space, materials handling, and setup will decline by $30,000 per year. The company's required rate of return on inventory investments is 10% per year. Should Hudson implement JIT? On the basis of the numbers provided, we would be tempted to say no. Why? Because annual relevant cost savings in carrying

SURVEYS OF COMPANY PRACTICE

JIT Performance Measures Around the Globe

What performance measures do companies around the globe use to evaluate their JIT systems? The following table ranks in order of importance (1 = most important) the performance measures that companies in four countries apply. The rankings also indicate the relative importance of the different reasons that motivated the companies to implement JIT in the first place.

	United States*	Canada[†]	Ireland[‡]	United Kingdom*
Inventory investment	1	1	3	1
Delivery performance	2	4	1	2
Quality measures	3	2	4	3
Manufacturing lead time	4	3	2	5
Labor productivity	5	—	—	4
Space utilization	6	5	—	6

Adapted from *Billesbach, Harrison, and, Croom-Morgan, "Just-in-Time." [†]Lindsay and Kalagnanam, "The Adoption." [‡]Clarke and O'Dea, "Management Accounting."

A pattern emerges. The most important reasons for JIT implementation are reducing inventory investment, getting deliveries on time, and improving quality. To a lesser extent, companies also view reducing manufacturing lead time as important.

A survey of Italian companies[§] also reveals extensive use of these performance measures. The survey, however, provides no information on the relative importance of individual measures.

One survey[#] also found distinct differences between management control systems in JIT and non-JIT companies. JIT companies are characterized by greater decentralization, more frequent and timely reporting, and increased worker responsibility and autonomy for starting and stopping production to ensure quality.

[§]Bartezzaghi, Turco, and Spina, "The Impact."
[#]Lindsay and Kalagnanam, "The Adoption." Full citations are in Appendix A.

costs amount to $80,000 [(10% of $500,000) + $30,000], which is less than the additional annual tooling costs of $100,000.

Our analysis, however, has not considered other benefits of lower inventories in JIT production. For example, Hudson estimates that implementing JIT will reduce rework on 500 units each year, resulting in savings of $50 per unit. Also, better quality and faster delivery will allow Hudson to charge $2 more per unit on the 20,000 units that it sells each year. The annual relevant quality and delivery benefits from JIT and lower inventory levels equal $65,000 (rework savings, $50 × 500 + additional contribution margin, $2 × 20,000). Total annual relevant benefits and cost savings equal $145,000 ($80,000 + $65,000), which exceeds annual JIT implementation costs of $100,000. Therefore, Hudson should implement a JIT production system.

Performance Measures and Control in JIT Production

OBJECTIVE 10

Describe measures for evaluating JIT production performance

To manage and reduce inventories, the management accountant must also design performance measures to evaluate and control JIT production. Examples of information the management accountant may use include:[5]

◆ Personal observation by production line workers and team leaders.
◆ Financial performance measures (such as inventory turnover ratios) and variances based on standard materials costs and conversion costs (for details, see Chapter 20, pp. 726–734, on backflush costing).
◆ Nonfinancial performance measures of time, inventory, and quality, such as
  Manufacturing lead time
  Units produced per hour
  Days inventory on hand

◆ $\dfrac{\text{Total setup time for machines}}{\text{Total manufacturing time}}$

◆ $\dfrac{\text{Number of units requiring rework or scrap}}{\text{Total number of units started and completed}}$

Personal observation and nonfinancial performance measures are the dominant methods of control. Why? Because they are the most timely, intuitive, and easy-to-comprehend measures of plant performance. Rapid, meaningful feedback is critical because the lack of buffer inventories in a demand-pull system creates added urgency to detect and solve problems quickly.

[5]See M. DeLuzio, "Management Accounting in a Just-in-Time Environment," *Journal of Cost Management* (Winter 1993).

PROBLEMS FOR SELF-STUDY

PROBLEM 1

The Complete Gardener (CG) is deciding on the economic order quantity for two brands of lawn fertilizer: Super Grow and Nature's Own. The following information is collected:

	Super Grow	Nature's Own
Annual demand	2,000 bags	1,280 bags
Relevant ordering costs per purchase order	$30	$35
Annual relevant carrying costs per bag	$12	$14

REQUIRED

1. Compute the EOQ for Super Grow and Nature's Own.
2. For the EOQ, what is the sum of the total annual relevant ordering costs and total annual relevant carrying costs for Super Grow and Nature's Own?
3. For the EOQ, compute the number of deliveries per year for Super Grow and Nature's Own.

SOLUTION 1

1.   SUPER GROW   NATURE'S OWN

$$EOQ = \sqrt{\frac{2(2,000)(\$30)}{\$12}} \qquad\qquad EOQ = \sqrt{\frac{2(1,280)(\$35)}{\$14}}$$

         = 100 Bags   = 80 Bags

2.   SUPER GROW   NATURE'S OWN

$$TRC = \frac{2,000(\$30)}{100} + \frac{100(\$12)}{2} \qquad TRC = \frac{1,280(\$35)}{80} + \frac{80(\$14)}{2}$$

         = \$1,200   = \$1,120

3.   SUPER GROW   NATURE'S OWN

$$\frac{2,000}{100} = 20 \text{ deliveries} \qquad\qquad \frac{1,280}{80} = 16 \text{ deliveries}$$

PROBLEM 2

CG signs a long-term contract with the Super Grow distributor, and they set up a new procedure for placing purchase orders. A single entry is made on an EDI hookup operated by the Super Grow distributor. CG will make no incoming inspection of bags; the distributor has guaranteed to maintain a 100% product quality level in return for CG's signing the long-term contract. CG's new relevant ordering costs per purchase order will be \$0.50. CG reexamined its materials-handling costs and revised its annual relevant carrying costs per bag upward to \$20.00.

REQUIRED

1. Consider the new relevant ordering costs per purchase order and the new relevant carrying costs per bag. Compute CG's economic order quantity and the number of deliveries per year for Super Grow.
2. How might your answers to requirement 1 provide insight into a JIT purchasing policy?

SOLUTION 2

1. For Super Grow, $D = 2,000$, $P = \$0.50$, and $C = \$20.00$:

$$EOQ = \sqrt{\frac{2(2,000)(\$0.50)}{\$20.00}}$$

         = 10 bags

$$\frac{D}{EOQ} = \frac{2,000}{10} = 200 \text{ deliveries}$$

2. A JIT purchasing policy involves the purchase of goods or materials such that delivery immediately precedes demand. The decrease in the EOQ for Super Grow from 100 bags to 10 bags increases the number of deliveries from 20 to 200. By restructuring relationships with its supplier, CG has dramatically reduced its ordering costs. This pattern is a familiar one for companies adopting JIT purchasing.

SUMMARY

The following points are linked to the chapter's learning objectives.

1. Managing costs of materials and other inventories is pivotal in many organizations because cost of goods sold constitutes the largest single cost item for most retail and manufacturing companies.

2. Five categories of costs associated with goods for sale are purchasing costs; ordering costs (costs of preparing a purchase order and receiving goods); carrying costs (costs of holding inventory of goods for sale); stockout costs (costs arising when a customer demands a unit of product and that unit is not readily available); and quality costs (prevention costs, appraisal costs, internal failure costs, and external failure costs).

3. The economic order quantity (EOQ) decision model calculates the optimal quantity of inventory to order. The larger the order quantity, the higher the annual carrying costs and the lower the annual ordering costs. The EOQ model includes those transactions routinely recorded in the accounting system and opportunity costs not routinely recorded.

4. The reorder point is the quantity level of inventory that triggers a new order. It equals the sales per unit of time multiplied by the purchase-order lead time. Safety stock is the buffer inventory held as a cushion against unexpected unavailability of stock from suppliers.

5. The EOQ model is not sensitive to minor variations in cost predictions. The square root in the EOQ model reduces the sensitivity of the decision to errors in predicting the inputs.

6. The EOQ model exemplifies the potential conflict between decision models and performance evaluation models. The opportunity cost of the forgone interest on the investment in inventory plays a key role in the EOQ decision model. Still, many organizations measure management performance on the basis of reported costs or conventional operating income, without providing for any opportunity cost of forgone interest.

7. Just-in-time (JIT) purchasing is the purchase of goods or materials such that delivery immediately precedes demand or use. EOQ models support smaller and more frequent purchase orders (as in JIT purchasing) as relevant carrying costs increase and relevant ordering costs per order decrease.

8. A relevant cost-benefit analysis of JIT purchasing includes relevant costs of purchasing, carrying inventory, ordering and stockout, quality-related costs of inspection and customer returns, and lost contribution margins due to late deliveries.

9. JIT production is a system in which each component on a production line is produced immediately as needed by the next step in the production line. Relevant benefits and relevant costs of JIT production include relevant costs of setup and carrying inventory, better quality, and faster delivery.

10. Performance measurements and control in JIT production systems emphasize personal observation and nonfinancial performance measures rather than financial performance measures.

This chapter and the Glossary at the end of this book contain definitions of the following important terms:

carrying costs (p. 748)
economic order quantity (EOQ) (749)
inventory management (748)
ordering costs (748)
purchase-order lead time (749)

purchasing costs (748)
reorder point (751)
safety stock (752)
stockout (749)

ASSIGNMENT MATERIAL

QUESTIONS

21-1 Give two examples of decisions that fall under the inventory management umbrella.

21-2 Why do better decisions regarding the purchasing and managing of goods for sale frequently cause dramatic percentage increases in net income?

21-3 Name five cost categories that are important in managing goods for sale in a retail organization.

21-4 Name two decisions that are central to the management of goods for sale in a retail organization.

21-5 What assumptions are made when using the simplest version of the economic order quantity (EOQ) decision model?

21-6 Give examples of costs included in annual carrying costs of inventory when using the EOQ decision model.

21-7 "Holding safety stocks needlessly ties up capital in inventory." Comment on this statement.

21-8 Give three examples of opportunity costs that typically are not recorded in accounting systems, although they are relevant to the EOQ model.

21-9 What are the steps in computing the cost of a prediction error when using the EOQ decision model?

21-10 "The practical approach to determining economic order quantity is concerned with locating a minimum cost range rather than a minimum cost point." Explain.

21-11 Why might goal-congruence issues arise when an EOQ model is used to guide decisions on how much to order?

21-12 Name two cost factors that can explain why an organization finds it cost-effective to make smaller and more frequent purchase orders.

21-13 "Accountants have placed inventories on the wrong side of the balance sheet. They are a liability, not an asset." Comment on this statement by a plant manager.

21-14 "Organizations should choose the supplier who can offer them the best price." Comment on this statement.

21-15 What roles can the accountant play in the operation of a materials requirements planning system?

21-16 EOQ for a retailer. The Cloth Center buys and sells fabrics to a wide range of industrial and consumer users. One of the products it carries is denim cloth, used in the manufacture of jeans and carrying bags. The supplier for the denim cloth pays all incoming freight. No incoming inspection of the denim is necessary because the supplier has a track record of delivering high-quality merchandise. The purchasing officer of the Cloth Center has collected the following information:

Annual demand for denim cloth	20,000 yards
Ordering costs per purchase order	$160
Carrying costs per year	20% of purchase cost
Safety stock requirements	None
Cost of denim cloth	$8 per yard

The purchasing lead time is 2 weeks. The Cloth Center is open 250 days a year (50 weeks for 5 days a week).

REQUIRED

1. Calculate the EOQ for denim cloth.
2. Calculate the number of orders that will be placed each year.
3. Calculate the reorder point for denim cloth.

21-17 EOQ for manufacturer. Beaumont Corporation makes air conditioners. It purchases 12,000 units of a particular type of compressor part, CU29, each year at a cost of $50 per unit. Beaumont requires a 12% annual return on investment. In addition, relevant carrying costs (for insurance, materials handling, breakage, and so on) are $2 per unit per year. Relevant costs per purchase order are $120.

REQUIRED

1. Calculate Beaumont's EOQ for CU29.
2. Calculate Beaumont's total ordering and carrying costs using EOQ.
3. Assume that demand is uniform throughout the year and is known with certainty. The purchasing lead time is half a month. Calculate Beaumont's reorder point for CU29.

21-18 EOQ, ordering and carrying costs. Dale Richmond, purchase manager at the Stellar Corporation, reports the following information for an electronic component, SSD1:

- Annual demand   8,000 units
- Ordering costs per order $100
- Carrying costs per unit per year $10

Richmond places orders for 200 units at a time.

REQUIRED

1. Calculate the economic order quantity for SSD1. Is Richmond's ordering policy optimal? What is the total annual ordering and carrying costs using the economic order quantity?
2. What is the total annual ordering and carrying costs of Richmond's policy?
3. What is the annual loss, if any, to Stellar of Richmond's ordering policy as opposed to the EOQ ordering policy?

21-19 Purchase-order size for retailer, EOQ, just-in-time purchasing. The 24-Hour Mart operates a chain of supermarkets. Its best-selling soft drink is Fruitslice. Demand in April for Fruitslice at its Memphis supermarket is estimated to be 6,000 cases (24 cans in each case). In March, the Memphis supermarket estimated the ordering costs per purchase order (*P*) for Fruitslice to be $30. The carrying costs (*C*) of each case of Fruitslice in inventory for a month were estimated to be $1. At the end of March, the Memphis 24-Hour Mart reestimated its carrying costs to be $1.50 per case per month to take into account an increase in warehouse-related costs.

During March, 24-Hour Mart restructured its relationship with suppliers. It reduced the number of suppliers from 600 to 180. Long-term contracts were signed only with those suppliers that agreed to make product-quality checks before shipping. Each purchase order would be made by linking into the suppliers' computer network. The Memphis 24-Hour Mart estimated that these changes would reduce the ordering costs per purchase order to $5. The 24-Hour Mart is open 30 days in April.

REQUIRED

1. Calculate the economic order quantity in April for Fruitslice. Use the EOQ model, and assume in turn that
   a. $D = 6,000; P = \$30; C = \$1$
   b. $D = 6,000; P = \$30; C = \$1.50$
   c. $D = 6,000; P = \$5; C = \$1.50$

2. How does your answer to requirement 1 give insight into the retailer's movement toward JIT purchasing policies?

21-20 Production batch size, EOQ. (CMA, adapted) Clyde Peterson, general manager for the Adam Furniture Company, is upset because the company exhausted its finished goods inventory of Style 103—Modern Desk twice during the previous month. These stockouts led to customer complaints and disrupted the normal flow of operations.

"We should plan better," declared Peterson. "Our annual sales demand is 18,000 units for this model or an average of 75 desks per day based upon our 240-day work year. Unfortunately, the sales pattern is not uniform. Our daily demand on that model varies considerably. When we run out of units, we cannot convert immediately because we would disrupt the production of our other products and cause cost increases. The setup process for this model costs $600. Once we get the line up, we can produce 200 units per day. I would prefer to have several planned runs of a uniform quantity rather than the short unplanned runs that are now required to meet unfilled customer orders."

The manager of the Cost Accounting Department has suggested that an EOQ model be adopted to determine optimal production runs and then a safety stock established to guard against stockouts. The cost data for the Modern Desk, which sells for $110.00, is readily available from the accounting records. The manufacturing costs are as follows:

Direct materials	$30.00
Direct manufacturing labor [1 direct manufacturing labor-hour (DMLH) × $14.00]	14.00
Variable manufacturing overhead (1 DMLH × $6.00)	6.00
Fixed manufacturing overhead (1 DMLH × $10.00)	10.00
Total manufacturing costs	$60.00

The Cost Accounting Department estimates that the company's carrying costs are 10.8% per year of the incremental manufacturing costs.

REQUIRED

1. Explain which costs the company would be attempting to balance if it adopted the EOQ model for its production runs.

2. Calculate Adam's optimal quantity for each production run of Style 103—Modern Desk.

3. Calculate the number of production runs of Modern Desks that the Adam Furniture Company would schedule during the year on the basis of the optimal quantity calculated in requirement 2.

21-21 Batch sizes for manufacturing, EOQ, just-in-time production. Donner Corporation machines steel bars into high-end components for the machine tool industry. The annual demand for one such component, MT15, is 5,000 units per year. Costs for setting up the machine to make MT15 are $400. Incremental unit manufacturing costs for MT15 are $250. Donner's carrying costs are 25.6% per year of the incremental manufacturing costs.

REQUIRED

1. Calculate the EOQ for MT15.

2. Donner's management is contemplating various changes in its production policies that would reduce setup costs of MT15. These changes will have no effect on MT15's incremental unit manufacturing costs. Donner's management also believes that it has underestimated annual carrying costs. Calculate the EOQ for MT15 under each of the following assumptions.

   a. Annual demand, 5,000 units; setup costs, $400; carrying costs equal to 30% per year of incremental manufacturing costs.

   b. Annual demand, 5,000 units; setup costs, $108; carrying costs equal to 30% per year of incremental manufacturing costs.

3. How do your answers to requirements 1 and 2 give insight about just-in-time production policies?

21-22 JIT purchasing, relevant benefits, relevant costs. (CMA, adapted) Agri-Corp sells farm equipment. AgriCorp's Service Division provides spare parts to various repair centers that repair AgriCorp's equipment. In an effort to reduce inventory costs, the Service Division implemented a JIT inventory program on January 1, 19_7. On January 1, 19_8, Janice Grady, the Service Division controller, decides to evaluate the effect the program has had on the Service Division's financial performance. Grady documents the following results:

◆ The Service Division's average inventory declined from $550,000 to $150,000.

◆ Projected annual insurance costs of $80,000 declined 60% owing to the lower average inventory.

◆ A leased 8,000-square-foot warehouse, previously used for materials storage, was not used at all during the year. The division paid $11,200 annual rent for the warehouse and was able to sublet the building to several tenants for $15,000.

◆ Two warehouse employees whose services were no longer needed were transferred on January 1, 19_7, to the Purchasing Department to assist in the coordination of the JIT program. The annual salary costs for these two employees totaled $35,000.

◆ The Service Division used overtime to manufacture 7,500 spare parts. The overtime premium incurred amounted to $5.60 per part manufactured. The use of overtime to fill spare parts orders was immaterial prior to January 1, 19_7.

◆ Lost sales due to stockouts totaled 3,800 spare parts. The contribution margin per spare part is $10.

AgriCorp's required rate of return for investment in inventory is 15% per year.

REQUIRED

1. Calculate the cash savings (loss) of AgriCorp's Service Division for 19_7 that resulted from the adoption of the JIT inventory program.

2. Identify and explain the nonfinancial and qualitative factors that should be considered by AgriCorp's Service Division before it implements a JIT program.

21-23 JIT purchasing, choosing suppliers. The Flavio Corporation and the Tyrus Corporation manufacture fairly similar remote-controlled toy cars. The Thurston Corporation, a retailer of children's toys, expects to buy and sell 4,000 of these cars each year. Both Flavio and Tyrus can supply all of Thurston's needs, and Thurston prefers to use only one supplier for these cars. An electronic hookup will make ordering costs negligible for either supplier. Thurston wants 80 cars delivered 50 times each year. Thurston obtains the following additional information.

	Flavio	Tyrus
Purchase price of the car	$50	$49
Relevant incremental carrying costs of insurance, materials handling, breakage, etc., per car per year	$11	$10
Expected number of stockouts per year resulting from late deliveries	20 cars	150 cars
Stockout costs per car	$25	$26
Expected number of cars sold that will be returned owing to quality and other problems	40 cars	140 cars
Additional costs to Thurston of handling each returned car	$21	$21
Inspection costs per delivery	$20	$28

Thurston requires a rate of return of 15% per year on investments in inventory.

REQUIRED

1. Which supplier should Thurston choose? Show all calculations.

2. What other factors should Thurston consider before choosing a supplier?

21-24 JIT production, relevant benefits, relevant costs. The Evans Corporation manufactures cordless telephones. Evans is planning to implement a JIT production system, which requires annual tooling costs of $150,000. Evans estimates that the following annual benefits would arise from JIT production.

a. Average inventory will decline by $700,000, from $900,000 to $200,000.

b. Insurance, space, materials handling, and setup costs, which currently total $200,000, would decline by 30%.

c. The emphasis on quality inherent in JIT systems would reduce rework costs by 20%. Evans currently incurs $350,000 on rework.

d. Better quality would enable Evans to raise the prices of its products by $3 per unit. Evans sells 30,000 units each year.

Evans's required rate of return on inventory investment is 12% per year.

REQUIRED

1. Calculate the net benefit or cost to the Evans Corporation from implementing a JIT production system.

2. What other nonfinancial and qualitative factors should Evans consider before deciding on whether it should implement a JIT system?

PROBLEMS

21-25 Effect of different order quantities on ordering costs and carrying costs, EOQ. Koala Blue retails a broad line of Australian merchandise at its Santa Monica store. It sells 26,000 Ken Done linen bedroom packages (two sheets and two pillow cases) each year. Koala Blue pays Ken Done Merchandise, Inc., $104 per package. Its ordering costs per purchase order are $72. The carrying costs per package are $10.40 per year.

Liv Carrol, manager of the Santa Monica store, seeks your advice on how ordering costs and carrying costs vary with different order quantities. Ken Done Merchandise, Inc., guarantees the $104 purchase cost per package for the 26,000 units budgeted to be purchased in the coming year.

REQUIRED

1. Compute the annual ordering costs, the annual carrying costs, and their sum for purchase-order quantities of 300, 500, 600, 700, and 900, using the formulas described in this chapter. What is the economic order quantity? Comment on your results.
2. Assume that Ken Done Merchandise, Inc., introduces a computerized ordering network for its customers. Liv Carrol estimates that Koala Blue's ordering costs will be reduced to $40 per purchase order. How will this reduction in ordering costs affect the EOQ for Koala Blue on their linen bedroom packages?

21-26 EOQ, quantity discounts. The Crofton Corporation buys and sells leather dog leashes. The annual demand is 10,000 units. Ordering costs are $120 per purchase order. The purchasing cost of each leash is $8. Carrying costs are 30% of purchasing cost per year.

REQUIRED

1. Calculate the EOQ for the leashes.
2. Calculate the total purchasing, ordering, and carrying costs for the year using the EOQ.
3. The supplier is willing to discount the price of the leash by $0.10 if Crofton will order 2,000 units or more per order. Calculate the total purchasing, ordering, and carrying costs if the order size is (a) 2,000 units, and (b) 2,500 units.
4. Considering your answers in requirements 2, 3a, and 3b, what order size should Crofton choose? Explain your answer briefly.

21-27 EOQ, uncertainty, safety stock, reorder point. (CMA, adapted) The Starr Company distributes a wide range of electrical products. One of its best-selling items is a standard electric motor. The management of the Starr Company uses the EOQ decision model to determine the optimal number of motors to order. Management now wants to determine how much safety stock to hold.

The Starr Company estimates annual demand (300 working days) to be 30,000 electric motors. Using the EOQ decision model, the company orders 3,000 motors at a time. The lead time for an order is 5 days. The annual carrying costs of one motor in safety stock are $10. Management has also estimated that the stockout costs are $20 for each motor they are short.

The Starr Company has analyzed the demand during 200 past reorder periods. The records indicate the following patterns:

Demand during Lead Time	Number of Times Quantity Was Demanded
440	6
460	12
480	16
500	130
520	20
540	10
560	6
	200

REQUIRED

1. Determine the level of safety stock for electric motors that the Starr Company should maintain in order to minimize expected stockout costs and carrying costs. When computing carrying costs, assume that the safety stock is on hand at all times and that there is no overstocking caused by decreases in expected demand. (Consider safety stock levels of 0, 20, 40, and 60 units.)

2. What would be the Starr Company's new reorder point?

3. What factors should the Starr Company have considered in estimating the stockout costs?

21-28 EOQ, cost of prediction error. Ralph Menard is the owner of a truck repair shop. He uses an EOQ model for each of his truck parts. He initially predicts the annual demand for heavy-duty tires to be 2,000. Each tire has a purchase price of $50. The incremental ordering costs per purchase order are $40. The incremental carrying costs per year are $4 per unit plus 10% of the supplier's purchase price.

REQUIRED

1. Calculate the EOQ for heavy-duty tires, along with the sum of annual relevant ordering costs and carrying costs.

2. Suppose Menard is correct in all his predictions except the purchase price. (He ignored a new law that abolished tariff duties on imported heavy-duty tires, which led to lower prices from foreign competitors.) If he had been a faultless predictor, he would have foreseen that the purchase price would drop to $30 at the beginning of the year and would be unchanged throughout the year. What is the cost of the prediction error?

21-29 JIT purchasing, relevant benefits, relevant costs. (CMA, adapted) The Margro Corporation is an automotive supplier that uses automatic turning machines to manufacture precision parts from steel bars. Margro's inventory of raw steel averages $600,000. John Oates, President of Margro, and Helen Gorman, Margro's controller, are concerned about the costs of carrying inventory. The steel supplier is willing to supply steel in smaller lots at no additional charge. Helen Gorman identified the following effects of adopting a JIT inventory program to virtually eliminate steel inventory.

◆ Without scheduling any overtime, lost sales due to stockouts would increase by 35,000 units per year. However, by incurring overtime premiums of $40,000 per year, the increase in lost sales could be reduced to 20,000 units. This would be the maximum amount of overtime that would be feasible for Margro.

◆ Two warehouses presently used for steel bar storage would no longer be needed. Margro rents one warehouse from another company under a cancelable leasing arrangement at an annual cost of $60,000. The other warehouse is owned by Margro and contains 12,000 square feet. Three-fourths of the space in the owned warehouse could be rented for $1.50 per square foot per year.

◆ Insurance and property tax costs totaling $14,000 per year would be eliminated.

Margro's projected operating results for the 19_8 calendar year follow. Long-term capital investments by Margro are expected to produce a rate of return of 20%.

Margro Corporation Budgeted Income Statement for the Year Ending December 31, 19_8 (in thousands)

Revenues (900,000 units)		$10,800
Cost of goods sold		
Variable costs	$4,050	
Fixed costs	1,450	
Total costs of goods sold		5,500
Gross margin		5,300
Marketing and distribution costs		
Variable costs	$ 900	
Fixed costs	1,500	
Total marketing and distribution costs		2,400
Operating income		$ 2,900

REQUIRED

1. Calculate the estimated dollar savings (loss) for the Margro Corporation that would result in 19_8 from the adoption of the JIT inventory control method.

2. Identify and explain other factors that Margro should consider before deciding whether to install a JIT system.

21-30 Choosing suppliers for JIT purchasing. Jeffrey Chang runs a print shop. Chang requires 100,000 boxes of printing paper each year. He wants his suppliers to deliver the boxes on a JIT basis in order quantities of 400 boxes. The Savoy Corporation currently supplies the paper to Chang. Savoy charges $100 per box and has a superb reputation for quality and timely delivery. Chang reports the following revenue and cost information for a typical print job:

Revenues	$100,000
Costs of printing paper ($100 per box × 400 boxes)	40,000
Other direct materials (ink, etc.)	2,000
Variable printing costs (other than materials)	3,000
Fixed printing costs	25,000
Variable marketing and distribution overhead	1,000
Fixed marketing and distribution overhead	12,000

The Bond Corporation has approached Chang with a proposal to supply all 100,000 boxes to Chang at a price of $95 a box. The savings in purchase costs are substantial, and Chang is tempted to accept Bond's offer, but before doing so, Chang decides to check on Bond's reputation for quality and timely delivery. The information Chang gathers is not all positive. Chang estimates that late deliveries from Bond would lead to his incurring overtime and subcontracting costs of $30,000 per job on ten jobs during the coming year. Chang also recognizes that Bond's paper quality is not uniformly high, and ink sometimes smudges after printing. Chang expects that smudging would occur on five jobs during the year. Chang would then have to buy paper in the open market at $110 per box and rerun the job. Chang does not expect both delivery problems and quality problems to occur on the same jobs. Chang requires a rate of return of 15% per year on investments in inventory.

REQUIRED

1. Calculate Chang's costs if he purchases paper from (a) Savoy, and (b) Bond. Which supplier should Chang choose only on the basis of the financial numbers given in the problem?

2. What other factors should Chang consider before choosing a supplier?

21-31 JIT production, operating efficiency. The Mannheim Group is a major manufacturer of metal-cutting machines. It has plants in Frankfurt and Stuttgart. The managers of these two plants have different manufacturing philosophies.

Richard Stehle, the recently appointed manager of the Frankfurt plant, is a convert to JIT production and has fully implemented JIT by January 19_8.

Frank Kohl, manager of the Stuttgart plant, has adopted a wait-and-see approach to JIT. He commented to Stehle: "In my time, I have forgotten more manufacturing acronyms than you have read about in your 5-year career. In 2 years' time, JIT will join the manufacturing buzzword scrapheap." Kohl continues with his "well-honed" traditional approach to manufacturing at the Stuttgart plant.

Summary operating data for the two plants in 19_8 are as follows:

	January–March	April–June	July–September	October–December
Manufacturing lead time (days)				
Frankfurt	9.2	8.7	7.4	6.2
Stuttgart	8.3	8.2	8.4	8.1
Total setup time for machines				
Total production time				
Frankfurt	52.1%	49.6%	43.8%	39.2%
Stuttgart	47.6	48.1	46.7	47.5
Number of units requiring rework				
Total number of units started and completed				
Frankfurt	64.7%	59.6%	52.1%	35.6%
Stuttgart	53.8	56.2	51.6	52.7

REQUIRED

1. What are the key features of JIT production?

2. Compare the operating performance of the Frankfurt and Stuttgart plants in 19_8. Comment on any differences you observe.

3. Stehle is concerned about the level of detail on the job-cost records for the cutting machines manufactured at the Frankfurt plant during 19_9. What reasons might lead Stehle to simplify the job-cost records?

21-32 Inventory management, ethics. (CMA, adapted) Belco Manufacturing builds and distributes industrial storage racks using a just-in-time system and maintaining minimal inventories. Belco's earnings increased sharply in 19_7, and earnings-based bonuses were paid to the management staff for the first time in several years. Ellen North, Belco's president, wants earnings to continue growing, even to the point that the 19_8 bonuses would be double those of 19_7.

Jim Kern, Belco's vice president of finance, met with Bill Keller of Pristeel, Inc., a primary vendor of Belco's manufacturing supplies and equipment. Kern asked Keller to invoice all of Belco's 19_8 purchases ($2 million in equipment and $3 million in supplies) as equipment. The reason Kern gave for his request was that Belco's president had imposed stringent budget constraints on operating costs but not on capital expenditures. Keller agreed to do as Kern asked. Belco expenses all supplies purchases immediately. It depreciates equipment on a straight-line basis over ten years, assuming a zero disposal price.

While analyzing the second-quarter financial statements, Gary Wood, Belco's controller, noticed that only equipment and no supplies had been purchased from Pristeel. Wood, who reported to Kern, immediately brought this matter to Kern's attention. Kern told Wood of President North's high expectations and of the arrangement made with Bill Keller of Pristeel. Wood requested that he be allowed to correct the accounts and urged that the arrangement with Pristeel be discontinued. Kern refused and told Wood not to become involved in the Pristeel arrangement.

After thinking about the matter for a while, Wood arranged to meet with Ellen North, and he disclosed the arrangement Kern had made with Pristeel.

REQUIRED

1. Calculate the effect on Belco's 19_8 operating income of showing supplies purchased in 19_8 as equipment purchases. Do you agree with Gary Wood, Belco's controller, that the supplies purchased from Pristeel, Inc., were accounted for improperly? Explain your answer.

2. Refer to the *Standards of Ethical Conduct for Management Accountants* described in Chapter 1 (pp. 10–11). Explain why the use of the alternative accounting method to manipulate reported earnings is unethical.

3. Without prejudice to your answers to requirements 1 and 2, assume that Jim Kern's arrangement with Pristeel, Inc., was in violation of the *Standards of Ethical Conduct for Management Accountants*. Discuss whether Wood's actions were appropriate.

COLLABORATIVE LEARNING PROBLEM

21-33 EOQ, JIT production, relevant costs, performance measurement. The Castle Rock Corporation makes many precision automotive components for cars in its Automotive Division. The question focuses on one representative component, CM95, which has an annual demand of 60,000 units. Making these high-precision components requires large setup times. Incremental setup costs are $900 per run (batch). Incremental cash manufacturing costs are $50 per unit and incremental carrying costs are $12 per unit per year [consisting of a required annual return on investment at 14% equal to $7 (14% × $50) and costs of insurance, materials handling, etc. of $5].

Susan Lau, Castle Rock's owner, is concerned about the high levels of inventory and would like John Delaney, the manager of the Automotive Division, to implement a JIT production system. Castle Rock operates in a decentralized manner so that John Delaney must make this decision. Delaney is evaluated and compensated on the basis of division operating income, which does not include any charge for a required return on investment made in the division.

Delaney estimates annual tooling costs to implement JIT will be $55,000. This expenditure will make setup time and setup costs negligible. To match customer demand patterns, Castle Rock will make the run size one-fifth its pre-JIT size and do five times as many runs. The JIT system's emphasis on quality will allow Castle Rock to raise the price of CM95 by $0.50 per unit.

Form groups of two or more students to complete the following requirements.

REQUIRED

1. For CM95, calculate the EOQ in the pre-JIT environment, the annual cost of the average inventory, and the total incremental setup and carrying costs per year.

2. Calculate the annual costs and benefits to Castle Rock of implementing the JIT system.

3. Will John Delaney be enthusiastic about implementing JIT? Explain your reasoning briefly.

4. What should Susan Lau do? Explain briefly.

Ritz-Carlton

You can usually tell when you've bought a quality product: It works the way it's supposed to and keeps on working for a long time. How, though, do you measure your stay at a hotel in terms of quality? That's the question managers at the Ritz-Carlton needed to answer. **1** The Ritz-Carlton is a symbol of luxury and elegance. Managers wanted it to be seen also as a symbol of quality. A stay at a hotel, though, comprises many different facets, and every facet must be excellent for a guest to feel he or she has had a quality experience. **2** The quality efforts of the hotel, therefore, must extend to every employee, from the valet parker that greets guests as they first arrive to the last person they see at the front desk when they check out. For example, housekeeping performance is critical to the quality of a guest's stay. **3** The Ritz-Carlton now uses teams of two housekeepers to service a guest room, completing the entire service in less than 11 minutes. Dining services are also crucial to a guest's perception of hotel quality.

1

2

3

4 Whether a guest has a formal meal in a dining room or **5** a casual meal on an outdoor terrace, the quality of the food and the quality of the service will leave a lasting impression. Other areas affecting a guest's experience range from the politeness of the concierge to the cleanliness of the pool. Managers determined nineteen such areas to study. The results of these studies were used to develop quality benchmarks, which managers now use to review performance on a daily and weekly basis. Also, managers empowered workers by organizing them into self-directed work teams. Because employees know best what happens each day in their respective work areas, managers felt that giving employees more control would result in better and more comfortable stays for all guests. As a result of its quality initiatives, the Ritz-Carlton became the first hotel company ever to win the prestigious Malcolm Baldrige National Quality Award. Earning this distinction, however, has not been the end of the company's quality efforts. Its goal is still 100% customer satisfaction. **6** Ritz-Carlton employees won't be happy until every guest to pass through the lobby at any one of the company's thirty-one hotels sees not only luxury, but quality as well.

RITZ-CARLTON HOTEL COMPANY
Quality

The Ritz-Carlton. The name alone evokes images of luxury and quality. At least, that's what the managers at their thirty-one hotels and resorts around the world hope. As the first hotel company ever to win the prestigious Malcolm Baldrige National Quality Award, the Ritz treats quality as more than a mere buzzword. Quality is the heartbeat of the company, and it means a daily commitment to meeting customer expectations and making sure each hotel is free of deficiency.

In the hotel industry, quality can be hard to quantify. Guests do not purchase a product when they stay at the Ritz; they buy an experience. So creating the right combination of elements to make the experience stand out is the challenge and goal of every employee, from maintenance to management.

Earning the Baldrige Award represented a major achievement for the company, but while the company was delighted to be selected, managers realized that work still remained to be done. Before applying for consideration, company management undertook a rigorous self-examination of its operations in an attempt to measure and quantify quality. Nineteen processes were studied, including room-service delivery, guest reservation and registration, message delivery, and breakfast service. This period of self-study included statistical measurement of process work flows and cycle times for areas ranging from room service delivery times and reservations, to valet parking and housekeeping efficiency. Each hotel focused on one of the nineteen areas for a year. The results were used to develop benchmarks of performance against which future activity could be measured.

With specific, quantifiable targets in place, managers at the Ritz-Carlton now focus on continuous improvement. The goal is 100% customer satisfaction. Each hotel and resort property is run as an independent business, so the general manager at each location takes ownership for monitoring quality and taking appropriate action to prevent problems from arising or affecting a guest. Performance is reviewed at both daily and weekly management meetings, and results are communicated back to employees. After all, if a guest's experience does not meet expectations, the Ritz-Carlton risks losing a valued guest to the competition.

One way the company has put more meaning behind its quality efforts is to organize its employees into "self-directed" work teams. The teams are formed within each functional area of the hotel, such as guest services, valet services, food and beverage, housekeeping, and maintenance. Managers no longer operate in command-and-control mode, where orders are dictated and expected to be carried out. Instead, the employee teams determine employee work scheduling, what work needs to be done, and what to do about quality problems in their areas. Managers are expected to become facilitators and resources for helping the teams achieve their quality goals. Employees are also given the opportunity to take additional training about how the hotel is run, so that they can see the relationship of their specific area's efforts to the overall goals of the hotel. Training topics range from budgets and purchasing to payroll and controllable costs. Employees are then tested and compensated for successful completion of training. Ritz-Carlton expects that a more educated and informed employee will be in a better position to make decisions that are in the best interest of the organization. ◆

QUESTIONS

1. In what ways could the Ritz-Carlton monitor its success at achieving quality?
2. Many companies say that their goal is to provide quality products or services. What actions might you expect from a company that intends quality to be more than a slogan or buzzword?
3. How does lack of quality, or missing a quality goal, affect the Ritz-Carlton's contribution margin?
4. Why might it cost the Ritz-Carlton less to "do things right" the first time?
5. How could control charts, pareto diagrams, and cause-and-effect diagrams be used to identify quality problems?
6. What are some nonfinancial measures of customer satisfaction that might be used by the Ritz-Carlton?

22
C H A P T E R

CAPITAL BUDGETING
AND COST ANALYSIS

When making capital budgeting decisions for highway overpasses, the
responsible government agencies
forecast construction costs, possible
revenues from tolls and operation
and maintenance costs. Discounted
cash flow and sensitivity analysis
helps these agencies to evaluate the
investment and financing options
available to them.

LEARNING OBJECTIVES

After studying this chapter, you should be able to

1. Differentiate between project-by-project orientation of capital budgeting and period-by-period orientation of accrual accounting

2. Explain the time value of money and opportunity costs

3. Identify the six stages of capital budgeting for a project and its predicted outcomes

4. Describe the two main discounted cash-flow (DCF) methods, the net present value (NPV) method, and the internal rate-of-return (IRR) method

5. Explain how the two main discounted cash-flow methods (NPV and IRR) differ

6. Identify relevant cash inflows and outflows for capital-budgeting decisions that use DCF methods

7. Describe the payback method

8. Explain the accrual accounting rate-of-return (AARR) method

9. Explain the breakeven time method

10. Recognize the impact of nonfinancial and qualitative factors in capital-budgeting decisions

11. Describe conflicts in using DCF for capital budgeting and accrual accounting for performance evaluation

Organizations are often required to make decisions whose consequences are felt over many future years. Such decisions frequently involve large investments of money and have uncertain actual outcomes that have long-lasting effects on the organization. For example, General Motors must decide whether it should spend billions of dollars developing a new minivan. USAir must decide whether it should invest millions of dollars in new Boeing 777 airplanes. The investments and the outcomes from those investments (which generally cover a number of years) are collectively referred to as **investment projects** or **investment programs.** Poor long-term investment decisions can affect the future stability of an organization because it is often difficult for organizations to recover money tied up in bad investments. Managers need a long-range planning tool or process to analyze and control investments with long-term consequences.

Capital budgeting is the process of making those long-term planning decisions for investments. Income determination and the planning and control of routine operations focus primarily on the current time period. Capital budgeting is a decision-making and control tool that focuses primarily on projects or programs whose effects span multiple time periods.

TWO FOCUSES OF COST ANALYSIS

OBJECTIVE 1

Differentiate between project-by-project orientation of capital budgeting and period-by-period orientation of accrual accounting

Recall a central theme of this book: different costs for different purposes. Capital-budgeting decisions focus on the project, which spans multiple time periods. There is a great danger in basing capital-budgeting decisions on the current accounting period's income statement, ignoring the future implications of investing in a project. Investment in a project might depress the current period's reported income, but it may still be a worthwhile investment because of the high future cash inflows that it is expected to generate.

Exhibit 22-1 illustrates two different dimensions of cost analysis: (1) the project dimension, and (2) the time dimension. Each project is represented in Exhibit 22-1 as a distinct horizontal rectangle. The life of each project is longer than one accounting period. Capital budgeting focuses on the entire life of the project in order to consider *all* cash inflows or cash savings from the investment. The white area in Exhibit 22-1 illustrates the accounting-period focus on income determination and routine planning and control. This cross section emphasizes the company's performance for the 1999 accounting period. Accounting income is of particular interest to the manager because bonuses are frequently based on reported income. Income reported in an accounting period is also important to a company because of its impact on the company's stock price. Excessive focus on short-run accounting income, however, can cause a company to forgo long-term profitability. Successful managers balance short-term accounting-period considerations and longer-term project considerations in their decision process.

EXHIBIT 22-1
The Project and Time Dimensions of Capital Budgeting

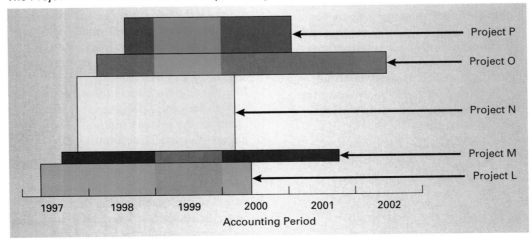

The accounting system that corresponds to the project dimension in Exhibit 22-1 is termed *life-cycle costing*. This system, described in Chapter 12, accumulates revenues and costs on a project-by-project basis. For example, a life-cycle costing statement for a new-car project at the Ford Motor Company could encompass a 4-year period and would accumulate costs for all business functions in the value chain, from R&D to customer service. This accumulation expands the accrual accounting system, which measures income on a period-by-period basis, to a system that computes income over the entire project covering many accounting periods.

Any system that focuses on the life span of a project must cover several years and thus must consider the time value of money. The *time value of money* takes into account the fact that a dollar (or any other monetary unit) received today is worth more than a dollar received tomorrow. The reason is that a $1 received today can be invested to start earning a return of 15% per year (say) so that it grows to $1.15 at the end of the year. The time value of money is the opportunity cost (the return of $0.15 forgone) from not having the money today.

Capital budgeting focuses on projects that can be accounted for using life-cycle costing and that must be evaluated taking into consideration the time value of money.

OBJECTIVE 2

Explain the time value of money and opportunity costs

STAGES OF CAPITAL BUDGETING

We describe six stages in capital budgeting.

Stage 1: Identification Stage *To distinguish which types of capital expenditure projects are necessary to accomplish organization objectives.* Capital expenditure initiatives are closely tied to the strategies of an organization or an organizational subunit. For example, an organization's strategy could be to increase revenues by targeting new products, customers, or markets, or to reduce costs by improving productivity and efficiency. Identifying which types of capital investment projects to invest in is largely the responsibility of line management.

Stage 2: Search Stage *To explore several alternative capital expenditure investments that will achieve organization strategies and goals.* Employee teams from all parts of the value chain evaluate alternative technologies, machines, and project specifications. Some alternatives are rejected early. Others are evaluated more thoroughly in the information-acquisition stage.

Stage 3: Information-Acquisition Stage *To consider the predicted costs and predicted consequences of alternative capital investments.* These consequences can be quantitative and qualitative. Capital budgeting emphasizes financial quantitative factors, but non-financial quantitative and qualitative factors are also very important.[1] Management accountants help identify these factors.

Stage 4: Selection Stage *To choose projects for implementation.* Organizations choose those projects whose predicted outcomes (benefits) exceed predicted costs by the greatest amount. The formal analysis includes only predicted outcomes quantified in financial terms. Managers reevaluate the conclusions reached on the basis of the formal analysis, using managerial judgment to take into account nonfinancial and qualitative considerations. Evaluating costs and benefits is often the responsibility of the management accountant.

OBJECTIVE 3

Identify the six stages of capital budgeting for a project and its predicted outcomes

[1] Surveys indicate that U.S. and Japanese managers regard both financial and nonfinancial factors as important in capital investment decisions. The five most important factors cited by U.S. managers were sales-quantity forecasts, unit variable manufacturing costs, and contribution margin (all financial factors) and improved quality and improved delivery time (both nonfinancial factors). See A. C. Sullivan and K. Smith, "Capital Investment Justification for U.S. Factory Automation Projects," *Journal of the Midwest Finance Association* (1994) and P. Scarbrough, A. Nanni, and M. Sakurai, "Japanese Management Accounting Practices and the Effects of Assembly and Process Automation," *Management Accounting Research 2* (1991).

Stage 5: Financing Stage *To obtain project funding.* Sources of financing include internally (within the organization) generated cash and the capital market (equity and debt securities). Financing is often the responsibility of the treasury function of an organization.

Stage 6: Implementation and Control Stage *To put the project in motion and monitor performance.* As the project is implemented, the company must evaluate whether capital investments are being made as scheduled and within the budget. As the project generates cash inflows, monitoring and control may include a postinvestment audit, in which the predictions made at the time the project was selected are compared with the actual results.

This chapter emphasizes the information-acquisition, selection, and implementation and control stages of capital budgeting because these are the stages in which the management accountant is most involved. Beyond the numbers, however, the ability of individual managers to "sell" their own projects to senior management is often pivotal in the acceptance or rejection of projects.

We use information from Lifetime Care Hospital to illustrate capital budgeting. Lifetime Care is a not-for-profit organization that is not subject to taxes. Chapter 23 introduces tax considerations in capital budgeting.

One of Lifetime Care's goals is to improve the productivity of its X-ray Department. To achieve this goal, the manager of Lifetime Care *identifies* a need to purchase a new state-of-the-art X-ray machine to replace an existing machine. The *search* stage yields several alternative models, but the hospital's technical staff focuses on one machine, XCAM8, as being particularly suitable. They next begin to *acquire information* for a more detailed evaluation. Quantitative financial information for the formal analysis follows:

> Regardless of whether the new X-ray machine is acquired or not, revenue will not change. Lifetime Care charges a fixed rate for a particular diagnosis, regardless of the number of X-rays taken. The only relevant financial benefit in evaluating Lifetime's decision to purchase the X-ray machine is the cash savings in operating costs. The existing X-ray machine can operate for another 5 years and will have a disposal price of zero at the end of 5 years. The required net initial investment for the new machine is $379,100. The initial investment consists of the cost of the new machine—$372,890—plus an additional cash investment in working capital (supplies and spare parts for the new machine) of $10,000 minus cash of $3,790 obtained from the disposal of the existing machine ($372,890 + $10,000 − $3,790 = $379,100).

> The manager expects the new machine to have a 5-year useful life and a disposal price of zero at the end of 5 years. The new machine is faster and easier to operate and has the ability to X-ray a larger area. This will decrease labor costs and will reduce the average number of X-rays taken per patient. The manager expects the investment to result in annual cash inflows of $100,000. These cash flows will generally occur throughout the year; however, to simplify computations, we assume that the cash flows occur at the end of each year. The cash inflows are expected to come from cash savings in operating costs of $100,000 for each of the first 4 years and $90,000 in year 5 plus recovery of working capital investment of $10,000 in year 5.

Managers at Lifetime Care also identify the following nonfinancial quantitative and qualitative benefits of investing in the new X-ray equipment:

1. *The quality of X-rays.* Higher-quality X-rays will lead to improved diagnoses and better patient treatment.
2. *The safety of technicians and patients.* The greater efficiency of the new machine would mean that X-ray technicians and patients are less exposed to the possibly harmful effects of X-rays.

These benefits are not considered in the formal financial analysis.

In the *selection* stage, managers must decide whether Lifetime Care should purchase the new X-ray machine. They start with financial information. This chapter discusses the following methods that they can use:

- ◆ Discounted cash-flow methods
    - Net present value (NPV) method
    - Internal rate-of-return (IRR) method
- ◆ Payback method
- ◆ Accrual accounting rate-of-return method
- ◆ Breakeven time method

DISCOUNTED CASH-FLOW METHODS

Discounted cash flow (DCF) measures the cash inflows and outflows of a project as if they occurred at a single point in time so that they can be compared in an appropriate way. The discounted cash-flow methods recognize that the use of money has an opportunity cost—return forgone. Because the DCF methods explicitly and routinely weight cash flows by the time value of money, they are usually the best (most comprehensive) methods to use for long-run decisions.

DCF focuses on *cash* inflows and outflows rather than on *operating income* as used in conventional accrual accounting. Cash is invested now with the expectation of receiving a greater amount of cash in the future. Try to avoid injecting accrual concepts of accounting into DCF analysis. For example, depreciation is deducted as an accrual expense when calculating operating income under accrual accounting. Depreciation is not deducted in DCF analysis because depreciation expense entails no cash outflow.

The compound interest tables and formulas used in DCF analysis are included in Appendix C (pp. 977–984). (Appendix C will be used frequently in Chapters 22 and 23.)

There are two main DCF methods:

1. Net present value (NPV)
2. Internal rate of return (IRR)

NPV is calculated using the **required rate of return (RRR)**, which is the minimum acceptable rate of return on an investment. It is the return that the organization could expect to receive elsewhere for an investment of comparable risk. This rate is also called the **discount rate, hurdle rate,** or **(opportunity) cost of capital.** When working with IRR, the RRR is used as a point of comparison. Chapter 23 discusses issues encountered in estimating this rate.

Assume that the required rate of return, or discount rate, for the Lifetime Care X-ray machine project is 8%. (This relatively low discount rate is not unusual for nonprofit institutions, which can borrow funds at low rates because lenders pay no income taxes on interest received from nonprofit institutions.)

Net Present-Value Method

The **net present-value (NPV) method** calculates the expected net monetary gain or loss from a project by discounting all expected future cash inflows and outflows to the present point in time, using the required rate of return. Only projects with a positive net present value are acceptable. Why? Because the return from these projects exceeds the cost of capital (the return available by investing the capital elsewhere). Managers prefer projects with higher NPVs to projects with lower NPVs, if all other things are equal. Using the NPV method entails the following steps:

Step 1: Sketch the Relevant Cash Inflows and Outflows   The right side of Exhibit 22-2 shows how these cash flows are portrayed. Outflows appear in parentheses. The sketch helps the decision maker organize the data in a systematic way. Note that Exhibit 22-2 includes the outflow for the new machine at year 0, the time of the

EXHIBIT 22-2
Net Present-Value Method: Lifetime Care Hospital

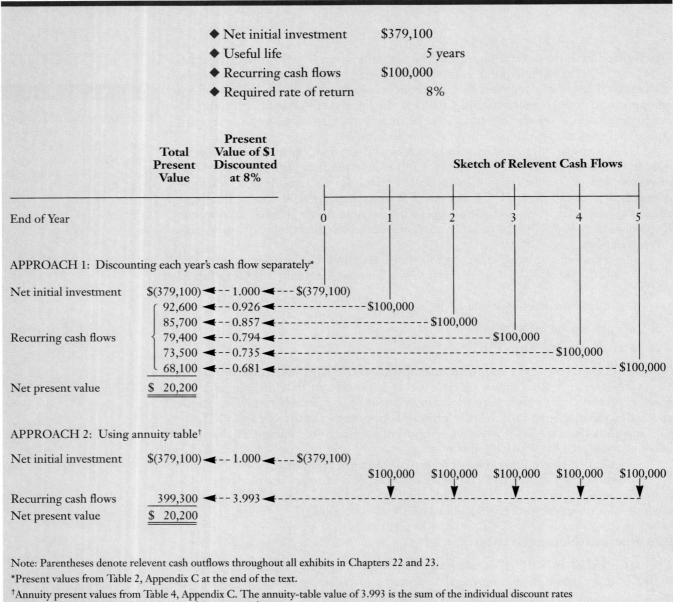

◆ Net initial investment $379,100
◆ Useful life   5 years
◆ Recurring cash flows $100,000
◆ Required rate of return   8%

	Total Present Value	Present Value of $1 Discounted at 8%	Sketch of Relevent Cash Flows

End of Year   0   1   2   3   4   5

APPROACH 1: Discounting each year's cash flow separately*

Net initial investment $(379,100) ◀--1.000◀---$(379,100)

Recurring cash flows   92,600 ◀--0.926◀--------------$100,000
                          85,700 ◀--0.857◀-----------------------$100,000
                          79,400 ◀--0.794◀-------------------------------$100,000
                          73,500 ◀--0.735◀--------------------------------------$100,000
                          68,100 ◀--0.681◀---$100,000

Net present value $ 20,200

APPROACH 2: Using annuity table†

Net initial investment $(379,100) ◀--1.000◀---$(379,100)

                                              $100,000 $100,000 $100,000 $100,000 $100,000

Recurring cash flows   399,300 ◀--3.993◀--
Net present value $ 20,200

Note: Parentheses denote relevent cash outflows throughout all exhibits in Chapters 22 and 23.

*Present values from Table 2, Appendix C at the end of the text.

†Annuity present values from Table 4, Appendix C. The annuity-table value of 3.993 is the sum of the individual discount rates 0.926 + 0.857 + 0.794 + 0.735 + 0.681, subject to rounding error.

acquisition. The NPV method focuses only on cash flows. NPV analysis is indifferent to where the cash flows come from (operations, purchase or sale of equipment, or investment or recovery of working capital) and to the accrual accounting treatments of individual cash-flow items (for example, depreciation costs on equipment purchases).

Step 2: Choose the Correct Compound Interest Table from Appendix C   In our example, we can discount each year's cash flow separately using Table 2 (Appendix C), or we can compute the present value of an annuity using Table 4 (Appendix C). If we use Table 2, we find the discount factors for periods 1–5 under the 8% column. Approach 1 in Exhibit 22-2 presents the five discount factors. Because the investment produces an annuity, a series of equal cash flows at equal intervals, we may use Table 4. We find the discount factor for five periods under the 8% column. Approach 2 in Exhibit 22-2 shows that this discount factor is 3.993 (3.993 is the sum of the five discount factors used in approach 1). To obtain the present-value figures, multiply the discount factors by the appropriate cash amounts in the sketch in Exhibit 22-2.

Step 3: Sum the Present-Value Figures to Determine the Net Present Value
If the sum is zero or positive, the NPV model indicates that the project should be accepted. That is, its expected rate of return equals or exceeds the required rate of return. If the total is negative, the project is undesirable. Its expected rate of return is below the required rate of return.

Exhibit 22-2 indicates an NPV of $20,200 at the required rate of return of 8%; the expected return from the project exceeds the 8% required rate of return. Therefore, the project is desirable. The cash flows from the project are adequate to (1) recover the net initial investment in the project, and (2) earn a return greater than 8% on the investment tied up in the project from period to period. Had the NPV been negative, the project would be undesirable on the basis of financial considerations.

Of course, the manager of the hospital must also weigh nonfinancial factors. Consider the reduction in the average number of individual X-rays taken per patient with the new machine. This reduction is a qualitative benefit of the new machine given the health risks to patients and technicians. Other qualitative benefits of the new machine are the better diagnoses and treatments that patients receive. Had the NPV been negative, the manager would need to judge whether the nonfinancial benefits outweigh the negative NPV.

It is important that you not proceed until you thoroughly understand Exhibit 22-2. Compare approach 1 with approach 2 in Exhibit 22-2 to see how Table 4 in Appendix C merely aggregates the present-value factors of Table 2. That is, the fundamental table is Table 2; Table 4 reduces calculations when there is an annuity—a series of equal cash flows at equal intervals.

Internal Rate-of-Return Method

The **internal rate of return (IRR)** is the discount rate at which the present value of expected cash inflows from a project equals the present value of expected cash outflows of the project. That is, the IRR is the discount rate that makes NPV = $0. IRR is sometimes called the **time-adjusted rate of return.** As in the NPV method, the sources of cash flows and the accrual accounting treatment of individual cash flows are irrelevant to the IRR calculations. We illustrate the computation of the IRR using the X-ray machine project of Lifetime Care. Exhibit 22-3 presents the cash flows and shows the calculation of the NPV using a 10% discount rate. At a 10% discount rate, the NPV of the project is zero. Therefore, the IRR for the project is 10%.

How do we determine the 10% discount rate that yields NPV = $0? In most cases, analysts solving capital-budgeting problems have a calculator or computer programmed to provide the internal rate of return. Without a calculator or computer program, a trial-and-error approach can provide the answer.

EXHIBIT 22-3
Internal Rate-of-Return Method: Lifetime Care Hospital

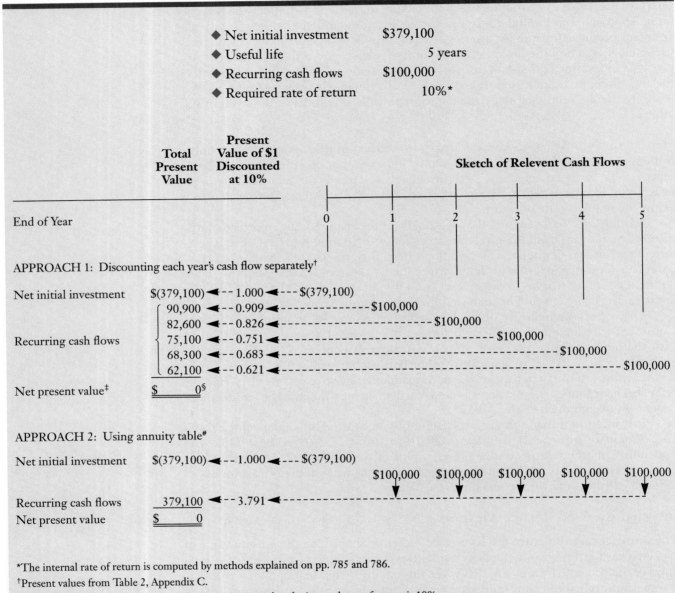

♦ Net initial investment $379,100
♦ Useful life   5 years
♦ Recurring cash flows $100,000
♦ Required rate of return   10%*

*The internal rate of return is computed by methods explained on pp. 785 and 786.
†Present values from Table 2, Appendix C.
‡The zero difference (subject to rounding error) proves that the internal rate of return is 10%.
§Sum is $(100) due to rounding errors. We round to $0.
#Annuity present values from Table 4, Appendix C. The annuity-table value of 3.791 is the sum of the individual discount rates of 0.909 + 0.826 + 0.751 + 0.683 + 0.621, subject to rounding error.

Step 1 Try a discount rate and calculate the NPV of the project using that discount rate.

Step 2 If the NPV is less than zero, try a lower discount rate. (A lower discount rate will increase the NPV; remember, we are trying to find a discount rate for which NPV = $0.) If the NPV is greater than zero, try a higher discount rate to lower the NPV. Keep adjusting the discount rate until NPV = $0. In the Lifetime Care example, a discount rate of 8% yields NPV of +$20,200 (see Exhibit 22-2). A discount rate of 12% yields NPV of −$18,600 (3.605, the present-value annuity factor from Table 4, × $100,000 − $379,100). Therefore, the discount rate that makes NPV = $0 must lie between 8% and 12%. We happen to try 10% and get NPV = $0. Hence, the IRR is 10%.

The step-by-step computations of an internal rate of return are easier when the cash inflows are equal, as in our example. Information from Exhibit 22-3 can be expressed in the following equation:

$379,100 = Present value of annuity of $100,000 at x% for 5 years

Or, using Table 4 (Appendix C) what factor F will satisfy the following equation?

$$379,100 = \$100,000F$$

$$F = 3.791$$

On the five-period line of Table 4, find the percentage column that is closest to 3.791. It is exactly 10%. If the factor F falls between the factors in two columns, straight-line interpolation is used to approximate the IRR. (For an illustration of interpolation, see requirement 1 of the Problem for Self-Study, pp. 800–802.)

A project is accepted only if the internal rate of return exceeds the required rate of return (the opportunity cost of capital). In the Lifetime Care example, the X-ray machine has an IRR of 10%, which is greater than the required rate of return of 8%. On the basis of financial factors, Lifetime Care should invest in the new machine. If the IRR exceeds the RRR, then the project has a positive NPV when project cash flows are discounted at the RRR. If the IRR equals the RRR, NPV = $0. If the IRR is less than the RRR, NPV is negative. Obviously, managers prefer projects with higher IRRs to projects with lower IRRs, if all other things are equal. The IRR of 10% means that the cash inflows from the project are adequate to (1) recover the net initial investment in the project, and (2) earn a return of exactly 10% on investment tied up in the project over its useful life.

Comparison of Net Present-Value and Internal Rate-of-Return Methods

This text emphasizes the NPV method, which has the important advantage that the end result of the computations is dollars, not a percentage. We can therefore add the NPVs of individual independent projects to estimate the effect of accepting a combination of projects. In contrast, the IRRs of individual projects cannot be added or averaged to derive the IRR of the combination of projects.

A second advantage of the NPV method is that we can use it in situations where the required rate of return varies over the life of the project. For example, suppose in the X-ray machine example, Lifetime Care has a required rate of return of 8% in years 1, 2, and 3 and 12% in years 4 and 5. The total present value of the cash inflows is as follows:

Year	Cash Inflows	Required Rate of Return	Present Value of $1 Discounted at Required Rate	Total Present Value of Cash Inflows
1	$100,000	8%	0.926	$ 92,600
2	100,000	8	0.857	85,700
3	100,000	8	0.794	79,400
4	100,000	12	0.636	63,600
5	100,000	12	0.567	56,700
				$378,000

Given the net initial investment of $379,100, NPV calculations indicate that the project is unattractive: It has a negative NPV of −$1,100 ($378,000 − $379,100). However, it is not possible to use the IRR method to infer that the project should be rejected. The existence of different required rates of return in different years (8% for years 1, 2, and 3 versus 12% for years 4 and 5) means there is not a single RRR that the IRR (a single figure) must exceed for the project to be acceptable.

SENSITIVITY ANALYSIS

To highlight the basic differences between the NPV and IRR methods, we have assumed that the expected values of cash flows will occur for certain. Obviously, managers know that their predictions are imperfect and thus uncertain. To examine how a result will change if the predicted financial outcomes are not achieved or if an underlying assumption changes, managers can use sensitivity analysis, a what-if technique first introduced in Chapter 3.

Sensitivity analysis can take various forms. For example, suppose Lifetime Care management believes forecasted savings are uncertain and difficult to predict. Management could then ask, What is the minimum annual cash savings that will cause us to invest in the new X-ray machine (that is, for NPV = $0)? For the data in Exhibit 22-2, let ACI = annual cash inflows and let NPV = $0. The net initial investment is $379,100, and the present-value factor at the 8% required rate of return for a 5-year annuity of $1 is 3.993. Then,

$$\text{NPV} = \$0$$

$$3.993 \times \text{ACI} - \$379,100 = \$0$$

$$3.993 \times \text{ACI} = \$379,100$$

$$\text{ACI} = \$94,941$$

Thus, at the discount rate of 8%, annual cash inflows can decrease to $94,941 (a decline of $100,000 − $94,941 = $5,059) before NPV falls below zero. If management believes it can attain annual cash savings of at least $94,941, it could justify investing in the new X-ray machine on financial grounds alone.

Computer spreadsheets enable managers to conduct systematic, efficient sensitivity analysis. Exhibit 22-4 shows how the net present value of the X-ray machine project is affected by variations in (1) the annual cash inflows, and (2) the required rate of return. NPVs can also vary with the useful life of a project. Sensitivity analysis helps a manager focus on those decisions that are most sensitive, and it eases the manager's mind about those decisions that are not so sensitive. For the X-ray machine project, Exhibit 22-4 shows that variations in either the annual cash inflows or the required rate of return have sizable effects on NPV.

EXHIBIT 22-4

Net Present-Value Calculations for Lifetime Care Hospital under Different Assumptions of Annual Cash Inflows and Required Rates of Return

		Annual Cash Inflows*				
		$80,000	$90,000	$100,000	$110,000	$120,000
Required	6%	$(42,140)	$ (22)	$42,100	$84,220	$126,340
Rate of	8%	(59,660)	(19,730)	22,200	60,130	100,060
Return	10%	(75,820)	(37,910)	0	37,910	75,820

*All entries in cells assume a useful project life of 5 years.

RELEVANT CASH FLOWS IN DISCOUNTED CASH-FLOW ANALYSIS

OBJECTIVE 6

Identify relevant cash inflows and outflows for capital-budgeting decisions that use DCF methods

The key point of discounted cash-flow methods is to focus exclusively on differences in expected future cash flows that result from implementing a project. All cash flows are treated the same, whether they arise from operations, purchase or sale of equipment, or investment in or recovery of working capital. The opportunity cost and the time value of money are tied to the cash flowing in or out of the organization, not to the source of the cash.

One of the biggest challenges in DCF analysis is determining those cash flows that are relevant to making the decision. Relevant cash flows are expected future cash flows that differ among the alternatives. At Lifetime Care, the alternatives are either to continue to use the old X-ray machine or to replace it with the new machine. The relevant cash flows are the *differences* in cash flows between continuing to use the old machine and purchasing the new one. *When reading this section, focus on identifying future expected cash flows of each alternative and differences in cash flows between alternatives.*

Capital investment projects (for example, purchasing a new machine) typically have five major categories of cash flows: (1) initial investment in machine and working capital, (2) cash flow from current disposal of the old machine, (3) recurring operating cash flows, (4) cash flow from terminal disposal of machine and recovery of working capital, and (5) income tax impacts on cash flows. We discuss the first four categories here, using Lifetime Care's purchase decision of the X-ray machine as an illustration. Income tax impacts are described in Chapter 23.

1. **Initial Investment**   Two components of investment cash flows are (a) the cash outflow to purchase the machine, and (b) the working-capital cash outflows.
   a. *Initial machine investment.* These outflows, made for purchasing plant, equipment, and machines, occur in the early periods of the project's life and include cash outflows for transporting and installing the item. In the Lifetime Care example, the $372,890 cost (including transportation and installation costs) of the X-ray machine is an outflow in year 0. These cash flows are relevant to the capital-budgeting decision because they will only be incurred if Lifetime decides to purchase the new machine.
   b. *Initial working-capital investment.* Investments in plant, equipment, and machines and in the sales promotions for product lines are invariably accompanied by incremental investments in working capital. These investments take the form of current assets, such as receivables and inventories (supplies and spare parts for the new machine in the Lifetime Care example), minus current liabilities, such as accounts payable. Working-capital investments are similar to machine investments. In each case, available cash is tied up.

      The Lifetime Care example assumes a $10,000 incremental investment in working capital (supplies and spare parts inventory) if the new machine is acquired. The incremental working-capital investment is the difference between the working capital required to operate the new machine (say, $15,000) and the working capital required to operate the old machine (say, $5,000). The $10,000 additional investment in working capital is a cash outflow in year 0.

2. **Current Disposal Price of Old Machine**   Any cash received from disposal of the old machine is a relevant cash inflow (in year 0) because it is an expected future cash flow that differs between the alternatives of investing and not investing in the new project. If Lifetime Care invests in the new X-ray machine, it will be able to dispose of its old machine for $3,790. These proceeds are included as cash inflow in year 0.

   Recall from Chapter 11 that the book value (original cost minus accumulated depreciation) of the old equipment is irrelevant. It is a past cost. Nothing can change what has already been spent or what has already happened.

   The net initial investment for the new X-ray machine, $379,100, is the initial machine investment plus the initial working-capital investment minus current disposal price of the old machine: $372,890 + $10,000 − $3,790 = $379,100.

3. **Recurring Operating Cash Flows**   This category includes all recurring operating cash flows that differ among the alternatives. Organizations make capital investments to generate cash inflows in the future. These inflows may result from producing and selling additional goods or services, or, as in the Lifetime Care example, from savings in operating cash costs. Recurring operating cash flows can be net outflows in some periods. For example, oil production may require large expenditures every 5 years (say) to improve oil extraction rates. Focus on operating cash flows, not on accrued revenues and costs.

To underscore this point, consider the following additional facts about the Lifetime Care X-ray machine example:

◆ Total X-Ray Department overhead costs will not change whether the new machine is purchased or the old machine is kept. The X-Ray Department overhead costs are allocated to individual X-ray machines—Lifetime has several—on the basis of the labor costs for operating each machine. Because the new X-ray machine will have lower labor costs, overhead allocated to it will be $30,000 less than the amount allocated to the machine it is replacing.

◆ Depreciation on the new X-ray machine using the straight-line method is $74,578 [(original cost, $372,890 – expected terminal disposal price, $0) ÷ useful life, 5 years].

The savings in operating cash flows (labor and materials) of $100,000 in each of the first 4 years and $90,000 in the fifth year are clearly relevant because they are expected future cash flows that will differ between the alternatives of investing and not investing in the new machine. But what about the decrease in allocated overhead costs of $30,000? What about depreciation of $74,578?

a. *Overhead costs.* The key question is, Do total overhead cash flows decrease as a result of acquiring the new machine? In our example, they do not. Total X-Ray Department overhead costs remain the same whether or not the new machine is acquired. Only the overhead allocated to individual machines changes. The overhead costs allocated to the new machine are $30,000 less. This $30,000 will be allocated to *other* machines in the department. No cash flow savings in total overhead occur. Therefore, the $30,000 should not be included as part of recurring operating cash inflows.

b. *Depreciation.* Absent income tax considerations, depreciation is irrelevant. It is a noncash allocation of costs whereas DCF is based on inflows and outflows of *cash*. In DCF methods, the initial cost of equipment is regarded as a *lump-sum* outflow of cash at year 0. Deducting depreciation from operating cash inflows would be counting the lump-sum amount twice.

4. **Terminal Disposal Price of Investment**   The disposal of the investment at the date of termination of a project generally increases cash inflow in the year of disposal. Errors in forecasting the terminal disposal price are seldom critical on long-duration projects because the present value of amounts to be received in the distant future is usually small. Two components of the terminal disposal price of an investment are (a) the terminal disposal price of the machine, and (b) the recovery of working capital.

a. *Terminal disposal price of machine.* At the end of the useful life of the project, the initial machine investment may not be recovered at all, or it may be only partially recovered in the amount of the terminal disposal price.

The relevant cash inflow is the difference in expected terminal disposal prices at the end of 5 years under the two alternatives—the terminal disposal price of the new machine (zero in the case of Lifetime Care) minus the terminal disposal price of the old machine (also zero in the Lifetime Care example).[2]

b. *Recovery of working capital.* The initial investment in working capital is usually fully recouped when the project is terminated. At that time, inventories

---

[2]The Lifetime Care example assumes that both the new and the old machine have a future useful life of 5 years. If instead the old machine only had a useful life of 4 years, management could choose to evaluate the investment decision over a 4-year horizon. In this case, Lifetime's management would need to predict the terminal disposal price of the new machine at the end of 4 years.

EXHIBIT 22-5

Relevant Cash Inflows and Outflows for Lifetime Care Hospital

End of Year		0	1	2	3	4	5
				Sketch of Relevant Cash Flows			
1. a. Initial machine investment		$ (372,890)					
b. Initial working-capital investment		(10,000)					
2. Current disposal price of old machine		3,790					
Net initial investment		(379,100)					
3. Recurring operating cash flows			$100,000	$100,000	$100,000	$100,000	$ 90,000
4. a. Terminal disposal price of machine							0
b. Recovery of working capital							10,000
Total relevant cash inflows and outflows as shown in Exhibits 22-2 and 22-3		$ (379,100)	$100,000	$100,000	$100,000	$100,000	$100,000

and receivables necessary to support the project are no longer needed. The relevant cash inflow is the difference in the expected working capital recovered under the two alternatives. If the new X-ray machine is purchased, Lifetime Care will recover $15,000 of working capital in year 5. If the new machine is not acquired, Lifetime will recover $5,000 of working capital in year 5, at the end of the useful life of the old machine. The relevant cash inflow in year 5 if Lifetime invests in the new machine is $10,000 ($15,000 – $5,000).

Some capital investments *reduce* working capital. Assume that a computer-integrated manufacturing project with a 7-year life will reduce inventories and hence working capital by $20 million from, say, $50 million to $30 million. This reduction will be represented as a $20 million cash inflow for the project at year 0. At the end of 7 years, the recovery of working capital will show a relevant cash *outflow* of $20 million. Why? Because the company recovers only $30 million of working capital under CIM rather than the $50 million of working capital it would have recovered had it not implemented CIM.

Exhibit 22-5 presents the relevant cash inflows and outflows for Lifetime Care's decision to purchase the new machine as described in items 1–4 in the preceding list. The total relevant cash flows for each year are the same as the relevant cash flows used in Exhibits 22-2 and 22-3 to illustrate the NPV and IRR methods.

PAYBACK METHOD

Uniform Cash Flows

We now consider a third method for analyzing the financial aspects of projects. The **payback method** measures the time it will take to recoup, in the form of net cash inflows, the net initial investment in a project. Like NPV and IRR, the payback method does not distinguish the sources of cash inflows (operations, disposal of equipment, or recovery of working capital). In the Lifetime Care example, the X-ray machine costs $379,100, has a 5-year expected useful life, and generates a $100,000 uniform cash inflow each year. The payback calculations[3] are as follows:

$$\text{Payback} = \frac{\text{Net initial investment}}{\text{Uniform increase in annual cash flows}}$$

$$= \frac{\$379,100}{100,000} = 3.791 \text{ years}$$

OBJECTIVE 7

Describe the payback method

[3]Cash savings from the new X-ray machine occur *throughout* the year, but for simplicity in calculating NPV and IRR, we assume they occur at the *end* of each year. A literal interpretation of this assumption would imply a payback of 4 years because Lifetime Care will only recover its investment when cash inflows occur at the end of the fourth year. The calculations shown in this chapter, however, better approximate Lifetime Care's payback on the basis of uniform cash flows throughout the year.

Under the payback method, organizations often choose a cutoff period for a project. The greater the risks of a project, the smaller the cutoff period. Why? Because faced with higher risks, managers would like to more quickly recover the investments they have made. For example, the Tesoro Petroleum Corporation uses a payback period of 3–4 years for investment decisions at its Kenai, Alaska, oil refinery. Projects with a payback period less than the cutoff period are acceptable. Those with a payback period greater than the cutoff period are rejected. If Lifetime's cutoff period under the payback method is 3 years, Lifetime will reject the new machine. If Lifetime uses a cutoff period of 4 years, Lifetime will consider the new machine to be acceptable.

The payback method highlights liquidity, which is often an important factor in capital-budgeting decisions. Managers prefer projects with shorter paybacks (more liquid) to projects with longer paybacks, if all other things are equal. Projects with shorter payback periods give the organization more flexibility because funds for other projects become available sooner. Also, managers are less confident about cash flow predictions that stretch far into the future. The shorter the payback, the more confident managers can feel that their forecasts are on target.

The major strength of the payback method is that it is easy to understand. Like the DCF methods described previously, the payback method is not affected by accrual accounting conventions such as depreciation. Advocates of the payback method argue that it is a handy measure when (1) estimates of profitability are not crucial and preliminary screening of many proposals is necessary, and (2) the predicted cash flows in later years of the project are highly uncertain.

Two major weaknesses of the payback method are (1) it neglects the time value of money, and (2) it neglects to consider project cash flows after the net initial investment is recovered. Consider an alternative to the $379,100 X-ray machine mentioned earlier. Assume that another X-ray machine, with a 3-year useful life and zero terminal disposal price, requires only a $300,000 net initial investment and will also result in cash inflows of $100,000 per year. First, compare the two payback periods:

$$\text{Payback period for Machine 1:} = \frac{\$379,100}{100,000} = 3.791 \text{ years}$$

$$\text{Payback period for Machine 2:} = \frac{\$300,000}{100,000} = 3.000 \text{ years}$$

The payback criterion would favor buying the $300,000 machine, because it has a shorter payback. In fact, if the cutoff period is 3 years, then Lifetime Care would not acquire machine 1 because it fails to meet the payback criterion. Consider next the NPV of the two investment options using Lifetime Care's 8% required rate of return for the X-ray machine investment. At a discount rate of 8%, the NPV of machine 2 is –$42,300 (2.577, the present-value annuity factor for 3 years at 8% from Table 4 × $100,000 = $257,700 – the net initial investment of $300,000). Machine 1, as we know, has a positive NPV of $20,200 (from Exhibit 22-2). The NPV criterion suggests that Lifetime Care should acquire machine 1. Machine 2, with a negative NPV, would fail to meet the NPV criterion. The payback method gives a different answer from the NPV method because the payback method (1) does not consider cash flows after the payback period, and (2) does not discount cash flows.

An added problem with the payback method is that choosing too short a cutoff period for project acceptance may promote the selection of only short-lived projects. The organization will tend to reject long-term, positive-NPV projects.

Nonuniform Cash Flows

The payback formula (presented on p. 791) is designed for uniform annual cash inflows. When annual cash inflows are not uniform, the payback computation takes a cumulative form. The years' net cash inflows are accumulated until the amount of the net initial investment has been recovered. Assume that Venture Law Group is considering purchase of a $1,500 fax machine for electronically transmitting documents to its clients. This machine is expected to produce a total cash savings of

$3,200 over the next 5 years (primarily due to a reduction in the use of express mail services). The cash savings occur evenly throughout each year but nonuniformly across 5 years, the life of the machine. Payback occurs during the third year:

Year	Cash Savings	Cumulative Cash Savings	Net Initial Investment Yet to be Recovered at End of Year
0	—	—	$1,500
1	$500	$ 500	1,000
2	600	1,100	400
3	800	1,900	—
4	700	2,600	—
5	600	3,200	—

Straight-line interpolation within the third year, which has cash savings of $800, reveals that the final $400 needed to recover the $1,500 investment (that is, $1,500 − $1,100 recovered by the end of year 2) will be achieved halfway through year 3 (in which $800 of cash savings occur):

$$\text{Payback} = 2 \text{ years} + \left(\frac{\$400}{\$800} \times 1 \text{ year} \right) = 2.5 \text{ years}$$

The fax machine example has a single cash outflow of $1,500 at year 0. Where a project has multiple cash outflows occurring at different points in time, these outflows are added to derive a total cash outflow figure for the project. No adjustment is made for the time value of money when adding these cash outflows in computing the payback period.

ACCRUAL ACCOUNTING RATE-OF-RETURN METHOD

We now consider a fourth method for analyzing the financial aspects of capital-budgeting projects. The **accrual accounting rate of return (AARR)** is an accounting measure of income divided by an accounting measure of investment. It is also called **accounting rate of return** or *return on investment (ROI)*. We illustrate AARR for the Lifetime Care example using the project's net initial investment as the denominator.

$$\text{AARR} = \frac{\text{Increase in expected average annual operating income}}{\text{Net initial investment}}$$

If Lifetime Care purchases the new X-ray machine, the increase in expected average annual savings in operating costs will be $98,000: This amount is the total operating savings of $490,000 ($100,000 for 4 years and $90,000 in year 5) ÷ 5. The new machine has a zero terminal disposal price. Straight-line depreciation on the new machine is $372,890 ÷ 5 = $74,578. The net initial investment is $379,100. The accrual accounting rate of return is equal to

$$\text{AARR} = \frac{\$98,000 - \$74,578}{\$379,100} = \frac{\$23,422}{\$379,100} = 6.18\%$$

The AARR method focuses on how investment decisions affect operating income numbers routinely reported by organizations. The AARR of 6.18% indicates the rate at which a dollar of investment generates operating income. Projects whose AARR exceeds an accrual accounting return required for the project are considered desirable. Managers using this method prefer projects with higher, rather than lower, AARR, if all other things are equal.

The AARR method is similar in spirit to the IRR method—both methods calculate a rate-of-return percentage. Whereas the AARR computation calculates return using operating income numbers after considering accruals, the IRR method calculates return on the basis of cash flows and the time value of money. For capital-budgeting decisions, the IRR method is conceptually superior to the AARR method described previously.[4]

The AARR computations are simple and easy to understand, and use routinely maintained accounting numbers. Unlike the payback method, the AARR method considers profitability. Unlike the NPV and IRR methods, however, the AARR focuses on operating income effects and hence considers accruals. It does not track

[4]Note that if depreciation is calculated as economic depreciation (the decline in the present value of future cash flows) under the AARR method, and if operating income and investment are adjusted each year for this depreciation, the AARR each year will equal the project's IRR. In practice, however, the book depreciation and investment value used in AARR computations are not calculated in this way.

International Comparison of Capital-Budgeting Methods

What methods do companies around the world use for analyzing capital investment decisions? The percentages in the following table indicate how frequently particular capital-budgeting methods are used in eight countries. The reported percentages exceed 100% because many companies surveyed use more than one capital-budgeting method.

	United States*	Australia†	Canada‡	Ireland§	Japan†	Scotland#	South Korea‖	United Kingdom†	Poland**
Payback	59%	61%	50%	84%	52%	78%	75%	76%	48%
IRR	52%	37%	62%	↑ 84% ↓	4%	58%	75%	39%	8%
NPV	28%	45%	41%		6%	48%	60%	38%	23%
AARR	13%	24%	17%	24%	36%	31%	68%	28%	11%
Other	44%	7%	8%	—	5%	—	—	7%	13%

*Adapted from Smith and Sullivan, "Survey of Cost." †Blayney and Yokoyama, "Comparative Analysis." ‡Jog and Srivastava, "Corporate Financial." §Clarke, "Management Accounting." #Sangster, "Capital Investment." ‖Kim and Song, "U.S., Korea, and Japan." **Zarzecki and "Wisniewski, "Investment Appraisal." Full citations are in Appendix A.

We make several observations:

1. Companies in the United States, Australia, Canada, Ireland, Scotland, South Korea, and the United Kingdom tend to use two methods to evaluate capital investments. (The sum of the capital-budgeting percentages in the columns for each of these countries is approximately 200%.)

2. Japanese and Polish companies tend to use only one method. (The sum of the capital-budgeting percentages for Japan and Poland is approximately 100%.)

3. The payback method is a very popular method among companies in all countries. Japanese companies and (to a lesser extent) Polish companies use the payback method as the primary method of analysis in their capital-budgeting decisions. Companies in the United States, Australia, Canada, Ireland, Scotland, South Korea, and the United Kingdom use the discounted cash-flow (DCF) methods, internal rate of return (IRR) and net present value (NPV), extensively.

4. The accrual accounting rate-of-return (AARR) method lags behind DCF methods in the United States, Australia, Canada, Ireland, Scotland, the United Kingdom, and Poland. It is on par with DCF methods in South Korea, and it is very much preferred to DCF methods in Japan.

cash flows and ignores the time value of money. Critics cite these arguments as major drawbacks of the AARR computations.

BREAKEVEN TIME AND CAPITAL BUDGETING FOR NEW PRODUCTS

Our final method for analyzing the financial aspects of capital-budgeting projects is breakeven time. **Breakeven time (BET)** is the time from when the initial concept for a new product is approved by management until the time when the cumulative present value of net cash inflows from the project equals the cumulative present value of net investment outflows. BET, on a time-adjusted basis, measures the length of time it takes to break even on a new product idea. It has features of the payback method with discounting. Hewlett-Packard's high-technology business uses BET as a capital-budgeting tool to evaluate new technologies and products.

OBJECTIVE 9

Explain the breakeven time method

Shorter BETs are important because shorter product life cycles have made products obsolete more quickly.[5] To be competitive, companies need to bring new products to market faster than competitors, reduce development costs, and sell products quickly and profitably. Many companies have reported spectacular reductions in new product development time—the amount of time from when the initial concept for a new product is approved by management to its market introduction—and hence costs. Deere and Co. reduced the time needed to develop new construction equipment from 7 to 4 years. Honeywell reduced development time on its thermostats from 4 years to less than a year. NCR reduced development time on its terminals from 4 years to 2 years. BET evaluates both how well a company has controlled product development time and costs, and how successfully the product has sold in the market place.

An Example of Bet Computations

The management of Thermax is considering the development of a new semiconductor manufacturing furnace (SP-108). Management is expected to approve the project on December 31, 1999. Because of other urgent commitments, the project is not expected to start until late in the year 2000. Information on the project is as follows:

1. The initial investment for the project consists of
   a. R&D costs for developing the furnace
   b. Product and process design costs, including the costs of designing, building, and testing product prototypes
   c. Manufacturing investments in special machines and additional working capital
   d. Marketing costs for market research and advertising
   Thermax's initial investment is expected to be $12 million. Assume for simplicity that $1 million of this investment will occur on December 31, 2000 and $11 million on December 31, 2001. The new furnace is expected to have a product life cycle of 4 years.

2. Thermax's expected annual cash inflows from sales of SP-108 will occur throughout the year, but to ease computations, we assume that they occur at the end of each year: 2002, $18 million; 2003, $33 million; 2004, $40 million; 2005, $14 million.

3. To generate sales, Thermax estimates incremental annual cash outflows of direct materials, direct manufacturing labor, manufacturing overhead, marketing, distribution and customer-service costs. Cash outflows are expected to occur throughout the year; but to ease computations, we again assume that they take place at the end of each year: 2002, $13 million; 2003, $24 million; 2004, $30 million; 2005, $11 million.

4. Thermax expects cash inflow from disposal of initial investment at the end of 2005 of $2 million.

5. Assume a 14% required rate of return for discounting cash flows on a before-tax basis. Ignore income taxes.

[5]The product life cycle is the time from initial R&D for a product to the time at which support to customers is withdrawn as the product dies.

EXHIBIT 22-6
Breakeven Time Computation for SP-108 at Thermax (in millions)

Year	PV Discount Factor at 14% (1)	Investment Cash Outflows (2)	PV of Investment Cash Outflows* (3) = (1) × (2)	Cumulative PV of Investment Cash Outflows* (4)	Cash Inflows from Product and Disposal of Investment (5)	PV of Product Cash Inflows* (6) = (1) × (5)	Cumulative PV of Product Cash Inflows* (7)
1999	1.000	—	—	—	—	—	—
2000	0.877	$ (1.000)	$(0.877)	$(0.877)			
2001	0.769	(11.000)	(8.459)	(9.336)			
2002	0.675				5.000	3.375	3.375
2003	0.592				9.000	5.328	8.703
2004	0.519				10.000	5.190	13.893
2005	0.456				3.000	1.368	15.261
	0.456				2.000†	0.912	16.173

*at December 31, 1999.
†Cash inflow from disposal of investment.

From items 2 and 3, product cash inflows in future years equal to sales cash inflows minus cash outflows incurred to generate sales are 2002, $5 million; 2003, $9 million; 2004, $10 million; 2005, $3 million. Exhibit 22-6 presents the computations necessary to calculate BET for SP-108. BET calculations cover the period of time beginning with the formation of the project investigation team on December 31, 1999, not the period of time beginning from when investment cash outflows start. Why? Because the goal of BET is to evaluate how quickly new ideas are converted into profitable products.

How long will it take Thermax to recover the $9.336 million cumulative present value of investment cash outflows? In present-value terms, Thermax will recover $8.703 million of its investment through product cash inflows by December 31, 2003, and $13.893 million by December 31, 2004. This means Thermax will recover the present value of its initial investment cash outflows of $9.336 million sometime in the year 2004. Thermax's present value of estimated product cash inflows during the year 2004 is $5.190 million, and it needs $0.633 million ($9.336 million − $8.703 million) to recover its investment. Thermax will thus take 4.12 years to recover the cumulative present value of investment cash outflows:

$$4 \text{ years (up to December 31, 2003)} + \frac{\$0.633 \text{ million}}{\$5.190 \text{ million}} = 4.12 \text{ years}$$

After 4.12 years, the cumulative present value of *all* project cash outflows will equal the cumulative present value of *all* project cash inflows.[6]

How does BET compare with payback? The investment cash outflows are expected to start on December 31, 2000 and to total $12 million. As product cash inflows occur, $5 million of this investment is expected to be recovered in the year 2002 and the remaining $7 ($12 − $5) million in 2003.

$$\text{Payback} = 2 \text{ years (up to December 31, 2002)} + \frac{\$7 \text{ million}}{\$9 \text{ million}} = 2.78 \text{ years}$$

Note that the payback period is shorter than BET (1) because the payback method starts counting time from when the initial investment was made (December 31, 2000), not from when management first approved the project (December 31, 1999); and (2) because the payback method does not discount future cash inflows.

[6]A literal interpretation of the assumption that cash flows will only occur at the end of each year will imply a BET of 5 years because Thermax will recover the present value of its investment only when cash inflows occur at the end of the fifth year. The calculations shown here, however, better approximate Thermax's actual BET computed on the basis of uniform cash flows.

Uses and Limitations of BET

BET is a capital-budgeting model for choosing among both design options and new development projects. For example, management may decide to consider only projects with a BET of less than 5 years. Further, management will prefer new product proposals with short BETs to new product proposals with longer BETs, if all other things are equal. Note, however, that shorter BETs could result from

- Undertaking short-run, unexciting projects rather than long-run, truly innovative projects based on new technology that generally have longer BETs.
- Choosing simpler projects rather than fundamentally improving the product development process.
- Investing in products and businesses that have inherently smaller investment needs and generate faster cash inflows.

Although BET is particularly well suited to budgeting for new product development, it is a form of discounted payback that can also be used to evaluate other capital-budgeting decisions such as investments in plant and equipment. The Self-Study Problem at the end of this chapter calculates the BET for Lifetime Care's decision to acquire a new X-ray machine.

By counting time from the point at which management approves a project, BET penalizes project delays to take into account lost opportunities from failing to develop products quickly. Two strengths of BET, like NPV and IRR, are that it focuses on cash flows and considers the time value of money. Payback does not consider the time value of money whereas AARR does not focus on cash flows. A weakness of BET is that, like payback, it ignores project cash flows after the net initial investment is recovered. NPV, IRR, and AARR all consider project profitability.

COMPLEXITIES IN CAPITAL-BUDGETING APPLICATIONS

In this section, we consider some challenging aspects of predicting outcomes in the information-acquisition stage and of choosing projects in the selection stage.

Consider a firm deciding whether to invest in computer-integrated manufacturing (CIM) technology. In CIM plants, computers give instructions that automatically set up and run equipment. Computers monitor the product and directly control the process to ensure defect-free, high-quality output. Applying CIM to its full extent can result in a highly automated plant, where the role of manufacturing labor is largely restricted to computer programming, engineering support, and maintenance of the robotic machinery. The amounts at stake in CIM decisions can be huge—in the billions of dollars for such companies as General Motors and Toyota. Two important factors when evaluating CIM investments are (1) predicting the full set of benefits and costs, and (2) recognizing the full time horizon of the project.

Predicting the Full Set of Benefits and Costs

The factors that companies consider in making CIM decisions are far broader than costs alone. For example, the reasons for introducing CIM technology—faster response time, higher product quality, and greater flexibility in meeting changes in customer preferences—are often to increase revenues and contribution margins. Ignoring the revenue effects underestimates the financial benefits of CIM investments. As we describe below, however, the revenue benefits of technology investments are often difficult to quantify in financial terms. Nevertheless, competitive and revenue advantages are important managerial considerations when introducing CIM.

Exhibit 22-7 presents examples of the broader set of factors that companies in the United States, Australia, Japan, and the United Kingdom weigh in evaluating CIM technology. The benefits[7] include:

OBJECTIVE 10

Recognize the impact of nonfinancial and qualitative factors in capital-budgeting decisions

[7]C. Sullivan and K. Smith, "Capital Investment Justification for U.S. Factory Automation Projects," *Journal of the Midwest Finance Association* (1994); M. Freeman and G. Hobbes, "Capital Budgeting: Theory versus Practice," *Australian Accountant* (September 1991); C. Drury, S. Braund, P. Osborne, and M. Tayles, *A Survey of Management Accounting Practices in U.K. Manufacturing Companies* (London: Certified Accountants Educational Trust, 1993); M. Sakurai, "The Change in Cost Management Systems in the Age of CIM," Working paper, Senshu University, 1992.

Examples of Financial Outcomes	Examples of Nonfinancial and Qualitative Outcomes
Lower direct labor costs	Reduction in manufacturing cycle time
Lower hourly support labor costs	Increase in manufacturing flexibility
Less scrap and rework	Increase in business risk due to higher fixed-cost structure
Lower inventory costs	Improved product delivery and service
Increase in software and related costs	Reduction in product-development time
Costs of retraining personnel	Faster response to market changes
	Increased learning by workers about automation
	Improved competitive position in the industry

1. *Faster response to market changes.* An automated plant can, for example, make major design modifications (such as switching from a two-door to a four-door car) relatively quickly. To quantify this benefit requires some notion of consumer-demand changes that may occur many years in the future and of the manufacturing technology choices made by competitors.

2. *Increased worker knowledge of automation.* If workers have a positive experience with CIM, the company can implement other automation projects more quickly and more successfully. Quantifying this benefit requires a prediction of the company's subsequent automation plans. Survey evidence emphasizes the importance of linking CIM decisions to a company's overall competitive strategies.

Predicting the full set of costs also presents problems. Three classes of costs are difficult to measure and are often underestimated:

1. Costs associated with a reduced competitive position in the industry. If other companies in the industry are investing in CIM, a company not investing in CIM will probably suffer a decline in market share because of its inferior quality and slower delivery performance. Several companies in the machine-tool industry that continued to use a conventional manufacturing approach experienced rapid drops in market share after their competitors introduced CIM.

2. Costs of retraining the operating and maintenance personnel to handle the automated facilities.

3. Costs of developing and maintaining the software and maintenance programs to operate the automated manufacturing activities.

Recognizing the Full Time Horizon of the Project

The time horizon of CIM projects can stretch well beyond 10 years. Many of the costs are incurred and are highly visible in the early years of adopting CIM. In contrast, important benefits may not be realized until many years after the adoption of CIM. A long time horizon should be considered when evaluating CIM investments.

Difficulties in predicting the full set of benefits and costs and long time horizons also arise in other investment decisions—for example, R&D projects and oil exploration.

Performance Evaluation and the Selection of Projects

OBJECTIVE 11

Describe conflicts in using DCF for capital budgeting and accrual accounting for performance evaluation

The use of the accrual accounting rate of return for evaluating performance can often deter a manager from using DCF methods for capital-budgeting decisions. Consider Peter Costner, the manager of the X-Ray Department at Lifetime Care Hospital. The NPV method for capital budgeting indicates that Peter should purchase the new X-ray machine since it has a positive NPV of $20,200.

Integrating Environmental Costs and Capital Budgeting at Niagara Mohawk and Ontario Hydro

Environmental laws seek to reduce the quantity and toxicity of pollution and impose penalties and fines for violating environmental standards. Capital investment decisions can significantly impact pollution and the environment. The key question is how the environmental effects of alternative pieces of equipment should be factored into capital budgeting choices.

Some environmental costs are easy to determine—for example, *prevention* or *compliance costs,* the costs incurred to install, operate, and maintain equipment and to train personnel to prevent pollution from occurring, and *appraisal costs,* the costs incurred to monitor and test for pollution and to report emission levels to government agencies. Other costs such as *failure costs* (the costs of environmental damage) are difficult to assess beyond the obvious penalties and fines for failing to comply with environmental laws. For example, what are the costs that a company should consider for human health problems, animal-herd losses, crop damage, and customer backlash from toxic air and water emissions?

Niagara Mohawk and Ontario Hydro have taken two different, equally innovative approaches to integrating environmental costs and capital budgeting. Niagara Mohawk considers environmental costs to equal the costs that need to be incurred to prevent any pollution from occurring. Niagara Mohawk thereby avoids the problem of determining the difficult-to-compute costs of environmental damage. The logic of this argument is that the costs of completely preventing pollution are a reasonable substitute for damage costs.

Ontario Hydro focuses on developing realistic estimates of the costs of environmental damage despite the associated uncertainties. Ontario Hydro uses innovative methods that consider (1) the decline in market prices of crops that have been damaged or lost due to toxic emissions, (2) estimates of differences in real-estate values or wage rates resulting from environmental pollution, and (3) survey responses about willingness-to-pay from "perpetrators" and willingness-to-accept from "victims" of environmental damage. Ontario Hydro requires capital-budgeting proposals to consider expected damage to ecosystems, communities, and human health, and not just the fact that it meets existing or proposed environmental regulations.

The Niagara Mohawk and Ontario Hydro examples highlight the importance and difficulties of acquiring information that would allow companies to integrate environmental impacts into capital-budgeting decisions more thoroughly. Without these approaches, companies cannot include environmental impacts as part of the formal analysis. They would then have to consider environmental pollution as a qualitative factor outside the financial analysis, making it more difficult to understand financial and environmental trade-offs.

Source: Adapted from M. Epstein, *Measures for Corporate Environmental Performance* (Chicago: Irwin, 1995).

Suppose top management of Lifetime Care uses the AARR for judging the X-Ray Department's performance. Peter Costner may consider not purchasing the new X-ray machine if the AARR of 6.18% on the investment reduces his overall AARR and so negatively affects his department's performance. The AARR on the new X-ray machine is low because the investment increases the denominator and, as a result of depreciation, also reduces the numerator (operating income) in the AARR computation.

Obviously, there is an inconsistency between citing DCF methods as being best for capital-budgeting decisions and then using a different method to evaluate subsequent performance. As long as such practice continues, managers will be tempted to make capital-budgeting choices on the basis of accrual accounting rates of return, even though such choices are not in the best interests of the organization. Such temptations become more pronounced if managers are frequently transferred (or promoted), or if annual operating income is important in their evaluations and their compensation plans. Why? Because the manager's performance is being evaluated over short time horizons. The manager has no motivation to use a DCF model to take into account cash flows that will occur in the distant future. Those cash flows will not influence the manager's performance evaluation.

MANAGING THE PROJECT

This section discusses stage 6 of capital budgeting, which deals with implementation and control. Two different aspects of management control are discussed—management control of the investment activity itself and management control of the project as a whole.

Management Control of the Investment Activity

Some initial investments such as purchasing an X-ray or fax machine are relatively easy to implement. Other initial investments such as building shopping malls or new manufacturing plants are more complex and take more time. In the latter case, monitoring and controlling the investment schedules and budgets is critical to the success of the overall project. The Appendix to this chapter describes methods used to control the investment activity itself.

Management Control of the Project—Postinvestment Audit

A postinvestment audit compares the predictions of investment costs and outcomes made at the time a project was selected to the actual results. It provides management with feedback about their performance. Suppose, for example, that actual outcomes (operating cash savings from the new X-ray machine in the Lifetime Care example) are much lower than predicted outcomes. Management must then investigate whether this occurred because the original estimates were overly optimistic or because there were problems in implementing the project. Both types of problems are a concern.

Optimistic estimates are a concern because they may result in the acceptance of a project that would otherwise have been rejected. To discourage optimistic estimates, companies such as DuPont maintain records comparing actual performance to the estimates made by individual managers when seeking approval for capital investments. DuPont believes that postinvestment audits discourage managers from making unrealistic forecasts. Problems in implementing a project are an obvious concern because the returns from the project will not meet expectations. Postinvestment audits can point to areas requiring corrective action.

Care should be exercised when performing a postinvestment audit. It should be done only after project outcomes have stabilized. Doing the audit early may give a misleading picture. Obtaining actual data to compare against estimates is often not easy. For example, actual labor cost savings from the new X-ray machine may not be comparable to the estimated savings because the actual number and types of X-rays taken may be different from the quantities assumed during the capital-budgeting process. Other benefits, such as the impact on patient treatment, may be difficult to quantify.

PROBLEM FOR SELF-STUDY

PROBLEM

Let us revisit the Lifetime Care X-ray machine project. Assume that the expected annual cash inflows are $130,000 instead of $100,000. All other facts are unchanged: a $379,100 net initial investment, a 5-year useful life, a zero terminal disposal price, and an 8% required rate of return. Year 5 cash inflows include $10,000 recovery of working capital. When calculating breakeven time, assume that the investment in the X-ray machine will occur immediately after management approves the project. Compute the following:

1. Discounted cash flow
   a. Net present value
   b. Internal rate of return
2. Payback period
3. Accrual accounting rate of return on net initial investment
4. Breakeven time

Assume (for calculation purposes) that cash outflows and cash inflows occur at the end of each period.

SOLUTION

1a. NPV = ($130,000 × 3.993) − $379,100
   = $519,090 − $379,100 = $139,990

b. There are several approaches to computing the IRR. One is to use a calculator with an IRR function; this gives an IRR of 21.18%. An alternative approach is to use Table 4 in Appendix C:

$$\$379,100 = \$130,000F$$

$$F = \frac{\$379,100}{130,000} = 2.916$$

On the five-period line of Table 4, the column closest to 2.916 is 22%. To obtain a more accurate number, straight-line interpolation can be used:

	Present Value	**Factors**
20%	2.991	2.991
IRR	—	2.916
22%	2.864	—
Difference	0.127	0.075

$$IRR = 20\% + \frac{0.075}{0.127}(2\%) = 21.18\%$$

2. Payback = $\dfrac{\text{Net initial investment}}{\text{Uniform increase in annual cash flows}}$

   = $379,100 ÷ $130,000 = 2.92 years

3.

$$AARR = \frac{\text{Increase in expected average annual operating income}}{\text{Net initial investment}}$$

$\begin{aligned}\text{Increase in expected average annual operating savings}\end{aligned}$ = [($130,000 × 4) + $120,000] ÷ 5

   = $128,000

Average annual depreciation = $372,890 ÷ 5 = $74,578

$\begin{aligned}\text{Increase in expected average annual operating income}\end{aligned}$ = $128,000 − $74,578 = $53,422

$$AARR = \frac{\$53,422}{\$379,100} = 14.09\%$$

4. Breakeven time computations are as follows:

Year	PV Discount Factor at 14% (1)	Investment Cash Outflows (2)	PV of Investment Cash Outflows* (3) = (1) × (2)	Cumulative PV of Investment Cash Outflows* (4)	Cash Inflows (5)	PV of Cash Inflows* (6) = (1) × (5)	Cumulative PV of Cash Inflows* (7)
0	1.000	$379,100	$379,100	$379,100			
1	0.926				$130,000	$120,380	$120,380
2	0.857				130,000	111,410	231,790
3	0.794				130,000	103,220	335,010
4	0.735				130,000	95,550	430,560
5	0.681				130,000	88,530	519,090

*At year 0.

$$\text{BET} = 3 \text{ years} + \frac{\$379,100 - \$335,010}{95,550}$$

$$= 3 \text{ years} + \frac{44,090}{95,550} = 3.46 \text{ years}$$

SUMMARY

The following points are linked to the chapter's learning objectives.

1. Capital budgeting is long-term planning for proposed capital projects. The life of a project is usually longer than 1 year, so capital-budgeting decisions consider revenues and costs over relatively long periods. In contrast, accrual accounting measures income on a year-by-year basis.

2. The time value of money takes into account this fact: A dollar received today can be invested to start earning a return (for example, interest), so it is worth more than a dollar received tomorrow. The time value of money is the opportunity cost (return forgone) from not having the money today.

3. Capital budgeting is a six-stage process: (a) the identification stage, (b) the search stage, (c) the information-acquisition stage, (d) the selection stage, (e) the financing stage, and (f) the implementation and control stage.

4. Discounted cash-flow (DCF) methods explicitly include all project cash flows and the time value of money in capital-budgeting decisions. Two DCF methods are the net present-value (NPV) method and the internal rate-of-return (IRR) method. The NPV method calculates the expected net monetary gain or loss from a project by discounting all expected future cash inflows and outflows to the present point in time, using the required rate of return. A project is acceptable if it has a positive NPV. The IRR method computes the rate of return (discount rate) at which the present value of expected cash inflows from a project equals the present value of expected cash outflows from a project. A project is acceptable if its IRR exceeds the required rate of return.

5. The NPV method has two advantages over the IRR method: (a) NPVs of individual projects can be added together to obtain a valid estimate of accepting a combination of projects, and (b) the NPV method accommodates different required rates of return across different years of the project.

6. Relevant cash inflows and outflows are expected future cash flows that differ among the alternatives. Only cash inflows and outflows matter. Accrual accounting concepts such as accrued revenues and accrued expenses are irrelevant for the discounted cash-flow methods.

7. The payback method measures the time it will take to recoup, in the form of cash inflows, the total amount invested in a project. The payback method neglects profitability and the time value of money.

8. The accrual accounting rate of return (AARR) is operating income divided by a measure of investment. The AARR considers profitability but ignores the time value of money.

9. The breakeven time (BET) method measures the time from when the initial concept for a new product is approved by management until the time when the cumulative present value of net cash inflows from the project equals the cumulative present value of net investment outflows.

10. Nonfinancial and qualitative factors, such as the effects of investment decisions on employee learning and on the company's ability to respond faster to market changes, are often not explicitly considered in capital-budgeting decisions. However, nonfinancial and qualitative factors can be extremely important. In making decisions, managers must at times give more weight to nonfinancial and qualitative factors than to financial factors.

11. The widespread use of accrual accounting for evaluating the performance of a manager or division impedes the adoption of DCF methods in capital budgeting. Frequently, the optimal decision made using a DCF method will not report good "operating income" results in the project's early years on the basis of accrual accounting methods, so managers are tempted to ignore DCF methods even though the decisions that stem from them would be optimal for the company over the long run.

APPENDIX: CONTROL OF JOB PROJECTS

A **job project** is a complex task that often takes months or years to complete and requires the work of many different departments, divisions, or subcontractors. Examples of job projects are building bridges, malls, and plants. Job projects are unique and nonrepetitive, have considerable uncertainties, use many skills and specialties, and require significant coordination over a long period. Examples of job projects in the service industry include preparing an advertising campaign or litigating complex class-action lawsuits.

This Appendix describes methods managers employ to control job projects. In a capital-budgeting context, "job project" refers to putting in place the initial investment. In the Thermax example described in this chapter, the job project was developing SP-108, the new semiconductor manufacturing furnace—a complex task expected to take more than a year to complete. The process of actually investing capital often takes months or years and needs regular monitoring and control.

To control job projects, managers generally focus on four critical success factors: (1) scope, (2) quality, (3) time schedule, and (4) costs. *Scope* is the technical description of the final product. Many job projects are subjected to engineering change orders as the work proceeds, so the features of the final product differ from those originally planned. Obviously, changes in scope usually also affect quality, time schedule, and costs. The long duration of job projects means that job project data on quality, time schedule, and costs need to be tracked over many time periods.

Project Variances

Midwest Bank is currently developing new software for its bank card and automatic teller machine (ATM) network. The job project, code-named Sabre, has a time horizon of 10 months (July 19_7 to April 19_8) and is expected to generate substantial cost savings in the future. The primary work on the job project consists of designing, writing, and testing new software. Midwest budgets $300,000 (4,000 engineering labor-hours at $75 per hour) to complete the job project. Exhibit 22-8 shows a cost performance report (CPR) for Sabre. Three variables are shown on Exhibit 22-8:

EXHIBIT 22-8
Cost and Schedule Performance Report for Project Sabre

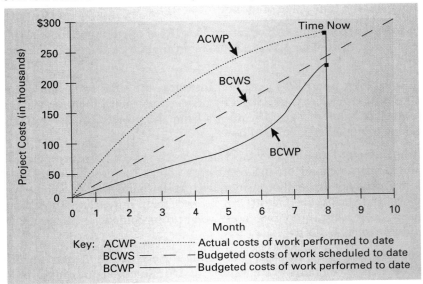

Key: ACWP ················· Actual costs of work performed to date
      BCWS — — — Budgeted costs of work scheduled to date
      BCWP ————— Budgeted costs of work performed to date

◆ BCWS—Budgeted costs of work *scheduled* to date. The Sabre project should be 80% complete by February 28, 19_8 (month 8 in project time), with budgeted costs of $240,000 ($240,000 ÷ $300,000 = 80%).

◆ BCWP—Budgeted costs of work *performed* to date. By February 28, 19_8, the Sabre project is only 75% complete. The budgeted costs of the 75% completed project are $225,000 ($225,000 ÷ $300,000 = 75%).

◆ ACWP—*Actual* cost of work performed to date, regardless of any budgets or schedules. By February 28, 19_8, costs assigned to the Sabre project total $280,000.

These three variables can be analyzed as follows:

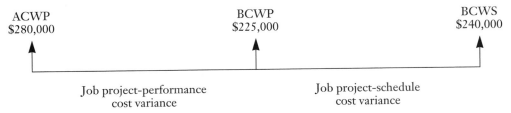

The **job project-performance cost variance** is the difference between the actual and the budgeted costs of work performed to date. It is a measure of the job project cost overrun (or underrun), controlling for the actual degree of completion to date on the project:

$$\text{ACWP} - \text{BCWP} = \$280,000 - \$225,000 = \$55,000 \text{ U}$$

where U refers to an unfavorable variance.

The Sabre project has a cost overrun of $55,000 (24.4% above the $225,000 budget). This is a serious (unfavorable) concern regarding cost management on the project.

The **job project-schedule cost variance** is the difference between the budgeted costs of work performed to date and the budgeted costs of work scheduled to date:

$$\text{BCWP} - \text{BCWS} = \$225,000 - \$240,000 = \$15,000 \text{ U}$$

The Sabre project is behind schedule (viewed as unfavorable). It is at only the 75% completion stage at February 28, 19_8, instead of the budgeted 80% stage. The job project-schedule cost variance of $15,000 measures the budgeted cost difference between the 75% and 80% project-completion stages.

These two major variances underscore that the cost performance report system should be more accurately labeled as a *cost and schedule performance report system*. Some managers may want to further investigate the reasons underlying the unfavorable job project-performance cost variance of $55,000 U. This variance can be subdivided into price and efficiency components (as in Chapter 7, p. 223–228). To illustrate this breakdown, we provide more details about BCWP and ACWP:

$$\text{BCWP} = \frac{\text{Budgeted hours allowed for}}{\text{actual work performed to date}} \times \frac{\text{Budgeted}}{\text{labor rate}}$$

$$\$225,000 = \qquad 3,000 \qquad \times \qquad \$75$$

$$\text{ACWP} = \frac{\text{Actual hours of work}}{\text{performed to date}} \times \frac{\text{Actual}}{\text{labor rate}}$$

$$\$280,000 = \qquad 3,500 \qquad \times \qquad \$80$$

We compute the price and efficiency variances using the columnar approach described in Chapter 7, (p. 228):

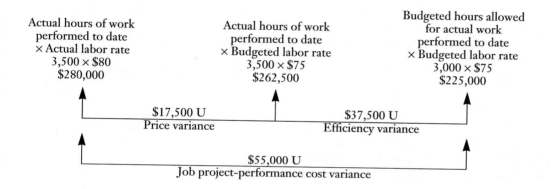

The job project manager can use the variance information to better manage and control job project performance. Even if little can be done to alter performance or profitability of the current project, the information gathered may be vital for the budgeting of costs of future projects.

Job projects, such as the development of new products and finding cures for diseases, are often undertaken despite high uncertainties and likely changes as work progresses. Should interim performance reports compare progress against the original budget or against a revised budget (much like a flexible budget)? Ideally, management should be provided with both comparisons. In this way, the performance of managers as planners can be assessed by comparing the original budget against the revised budget. Similarly, the performance of managers regarding control of operations can be assessed by comparing the actual results against the revised budget.

Many contractors and consultants who generate fee income from projects refer to Exhibit 22-8 as a *performance report*, an *earned value report*, or an *earned hours report*. The latter two labels are often used because control of the hours worked is the major determinant of success.

Focus on the Future

The graph in Exhibit 22-8 also illustrates another key aspect of job project control: a focus on what remains to be accomplished. Managers do not want surprises concerning future costs and the amount of time necessary for completing a job project. The "time now" label on the graph is the time of appraisal: Where has the project been, and where is it going? Appraisal may occur at scheduled intervals, such as weeks or months, or at designated stages of completion called *milestones*. An example of a milestone is the completion of the analysis and design of the software needed; a second milestone may be the completion of the coding; and so on.

In view of the unfavorable variances, the project manager might predict a late completion date and offer revised budgeted total final costs as follows:

Original budgeted total costs, 4,000 hours × $75	$300,000
Add: Unfavorable job project-performance cost variance to date	55,000 U
Subtotal	$355,000
Add: Projected unfavorable job project-performance cost variance (prediction is needed)	20,000 U (say)
Revised budget, total final costs	$375,000

TERMS TO LEARN

This chapter and the Glossary at the end of this book contain definitions of the following important terms:

accounting rate of return (p. 793)
accrual accounting rate of return (AARR) (793)
breakeven time (BET) (795)
capital budgeting (780)
discounted cash flow (DCF) (783)
discount rate (783)
hurdle rate (783)
internal rate of return (IRR) (785)
investment projects (780)
investment programs (780)

job project (803)
job project-performance cost variance (804)
job project-schedule cost variance (804)
net present-value (NPV) method (783)
opportunity cost of capital (783)
payback method (791)
required rate of return (RRR) (783)
time-adjusted rate of return (785)

ASSIGNMENT MATERIAL

QUESTIONS

22-1 "Capital budgeting has the same focus as accrual accounting." Do you agree? Explain.

22-2 List and briefly describe each of the six stages in capital budgeting.

22-3 What is the essence of the discounted cash-flow method?

22-4 "Only quantitative outcomes are relevant in capital-budgeting analyses." Do you agree? Explain.

22-5 List five methods of analyzing the quantitative and financial aspects of a capital-budgeting project.

22-6 What is the payback method? What are its main strengths and weaknesses?

22-7 Describe the accrual accounting rate-of-return method. What are its main strengths and weaknesses?

22-8 How is the breakeven time method of capital budgeting different from the payback method?

22-9 "When selecting new product development projects, companies should always choose the projects that have the shortest breakeven time." Do you agree? Explain.

22-10 "The trouble with discounted cash-flow techniques is that they ignore depreciation costs." Do you agree? Explain.

22-11 "Let's be more practical. DCF is not the gospel. Managers should not become so enchanted with DCF that strategic considerations are overlooked." Do you agree? Explain.

22-12 "The net present-value method is the preferred method for capital-budgeting decisions. Therefore, managers will always use it." Do you agree? Explain.

22-13 "All overhead costs are relevant in NPV analysis." Do you agree? Explain.

22-14 What is a postinvestment audit? Why is it important?

22-15 "Managers' control of job projects generally focuses on four critical success factors." Identify those factors.

EXERCISES

Throughout the assignment material, ignore the effects of income taxes.

22-16 **Exercises in compound interest.** To be sure that you understand how to use the tables in Appendix C at the end of this book, solve the following exercises. Ignore income tax considerations. (The correct answers, rounded to the nearest dollar, appear on pp. 818–819.)

REQUIRED

1. You have just won $5,000. How much money will you have at the end of 10 years if you invest it at 6% compounded annually? At 14%?
2. Ten years from now, the unpaid principal of the mortgage on your house will be $89,550. How much do you have to invest today at 6% interest compounded annually to accumulate the $89,550 in 10 years?
3. If the unpaid mortgage on your house in 10 years will be $89,550, how much money do you have to invest annually at 6% to have exactly this amount on hand at the end of the tenth year?
4. You plan to save $5,000 of your earnings at the end of each year for the next 10 years. How much money will you have at the end of the tenth year if you invest your savings compounded at 12% per year?
5. You have just turned 65, and an endowment insurance policy has paid you a lump sum of $200,000. If you invest the sum at 6%, how much money can you withdraw from your account in equal amounts each year so that at the end of 10 years (age 75) there will be nothing left?
6. You have estimated that for the first 10 years after you retire you will need an annual cash inflow of $50,000. How much money must you invest at 6% at your retirement age to obtain this annual cash inflow? At 20%?
7. The following table shows two schedules of prospective operating cash inflows, each of which requires the same net initial investment of $10,000 now:

	Annual Cash Inflows	
Year	Plan A	Plan B
1	$ 1,000	$ 5,000
2	2,000	4,000
3	3,000	3,000
4	4,000	2,000
5	5,000	1,000
Total	$15,000	$15,000

The required rate of return is 6% compounded annually. All cash inflows occur at the end of each year. In terms of net present value, which plan is more desirable? Show your computations.

22-17 **Comparison of approaches to capital budgeting.** The Building Distributors Group is thinking of buying, at a cost of $220,000, some new packaging equipment that is expected to save $50,000 in cash-operating costs per year. Its estimated useful life is 10 years, and it will have zero terminal disposal price. The required rate of return is 16%.

REQUIRED

1. Compute the payback period.
2. Compute the net present value.
3. Compute the internal rate of return.
4. Compute the accrual accounting rate of return based on net initial investment. Assume straight-line depreciation.

22-18 Comparison of approaches to capital budgeting. City Hospital, a non-taxable institution, estimates that it can save $28,000 a year in cash-operating costs for the next 10 years if it buys a special-purpose machine at a cost of $110,000. A zero terminal disposal price is expected. City Hospital's required rate of return is 14%.

REQUIRED
1. Compute the payback period.
2. Compute the net present value.
3. Compute the internal rate of return.
4. Compute the accrual accounting rate of return based on net initial investment. Assume straight-line depreciation.

22-19 Capital budgeting with uneven cash flows. Southern Cola is considering the purchase of a special-purpose bottling machine for $28,000. It is expected to have a useful life of 7 years with a zero terminal disposal price. The plant manager estimates the following savings in cash-operating costs:

Year	Amount
1	$10,000
2	8,000
3	6,000
4	5,000
5	4,000
6	3,000
7	3,000
Total	$39,000

Southern Cola uses a required rate of return of 16% in its capital-budgeting decisions.

REQUIRED
1. Compute the payback period.
2. Compute the net present value.
3. Compute the internal rate of return.
4. Compute the accrual accounting rate of return based on net initial investment. Assume straight-line depreciation. Use the average annual savings in cash-operating costs when computing the numerator of the accrual accounting rate of return.

22-20 Net present value, internal rate of return, sensitivity analysis. The Johnson Corporation is planning to buy equipment costing $120,000 to improve its materials handling system. The equipment is expected to save $40,000 in cash-operating costs per year. Its estimated useful life is 6 years, and it will have zero terminal disposal price. The required rate of return is 14%.

REQUIRED
1. Compute the net present value. Compute the internal rate of return.
2. What is the minimum annual cash savings that will make the equipment desirable on a net present value basis?
3. When might a manager calculate the minimum annual cash savings described in requirement 2 rather than use the $40,000 savings in cash-operating costs per year to calculate the net present value or internal rate of return?

22-21 Equipment replacement, net present value, relevant costs, payback. Monterey Corporation is a distributor of electronic measurement instruments. It is considering replacing one of its distribution trucks that it had purchased for $54,000 2 years ago. The truck has a current book value of $38,000 and a remaining useful life of 4 years. Its current disposal price is $26,000; in 4 years its terminal disposal price is expected to be $6,000. The annual cash-operating costs of the truck are expected to be $35,000 for each of the next 3 years and $40,000 in year 4.

Monterey is considering the purchase of a new truck for $56,000. Annual cash operating costs for the new truck are expected to be $25,000. The new truck has a useful life of 4 years and a terminal disposal price of $8,000.

Monterey Corporation depreciates all its trucks using straight-line depreciation calculated on the difference between the initial cost and the terminal disposal price divided by the estimated useful life. Monterey uses a rate of return of 14% in its capital budgeting decisions.

REQUIRED

1. Using a net present-value criterion, should Monterey Corporation purchase the new truck?
2. Compute the payback period for Monterey Corporation if it purchases the new truck.

22-22 **DCF, accrual accounting rate of return, working capital, evaluation of performance.** The Hammerlink Company has been offered a special-purpose metal-cutting machine for $110,000. The machine is expected to have a useful life of 8 years with a terminal disposal price of $30,000. Savings in cash-operating costs are expected to be $25,000 per year. However, additional working capital is needed to keep the machine running efficiently and without stoppages. Working capital includes such items as filters, lubricants, bearings, abrasives, flexible exhaust pipes, and belts. These items must continually be replaced so that an investment of $8,000 must be maintained in them at all times, but this investment is fully recoverable (will be "cashed in") at the end of the useful life. Hammerlink's required rate of return is 14%.

REQUIRED

1. **a.** Compute the net present value.
   b. Compute the internal rate of return.
2. Compute the accrual accounting rate of return based on the net initial investment. Assume straight-line depreciation.
3. You have the authority to make the purchase decision. Why might you be reluctant to base your decision on the DCF model?

22-23 **New product proposal, breakeven time, payback.** The Brooks Corporation is considering developing a new scientific instrument, MX-505. Management is expected to approve the project and form the project development team on December 31, 1998. Work on the new product is not expected to start until late in 1999 and will be completed in the year 2000. The initial investment is expected to be $15 million. Brooks estimates $2 million of this investment will be made on December 31, 1999, and the balance, $13 million, on December 31, 2000. The following data summarize the projected cash flows (in millions):

Year	Investment Cash Outflows	Product Cash Inflows*
1999	$ 2	
2000	13	
2001		$3
2002		6
2003		7
2004		8
2005		9

*Product cash inflows include cash inflows of $2 million from disposal of investment on December 31, 2005.

Brooks uses a 16% required rate of return for this investment. Ignore income taxes.

REQUIRED
1. Calculate the breakeven time for MX-505.
2. How could Brooks reduce BET?
3. Calculate the payback period for MX-505 and compare it to BET.

22-24 Sporting contract, net present value, payback, breakeven time. Milano Capri is an Italian soccer team with a long tradition of winning. However, the last 3 years have been traumatic. The team has not won a major championship, and attendance at games has dropped considerably. The Bennetelo Company is Milano Capri's major corporate sponsor. Rocky Agnelli, the president of Bennetelo, is also the president of Milano Capri. Agnelli proposes that the team purchase the services of Brazilian star, Bebeto. Bebeto would create great excitement for Milano's fans and sponsors. Bebeto's agent notifies Agnelli that terms for the superstar's signing with Milano Capri are a bonus of $3 million payable now (start of 1998) plus the following 4-year contract (assume all amounts are in millions and are paid at the end of each year):

	1998	1999	2000	2001
Salary	$4.500	$5.000	$6.000	$6.500
Living and other costs	1.000	1.200	1.300	1.400

Agnelli's initial reaction is one of horror. As president of Bennetelo, he has never earned more than $800,000 a year. However, he swallows his pride and decides to examine the expected additions to Milano Capri's cash inflows if Bebeto is signed for the 4-year contract (assume all cash inflows are in millions and are received at the end of each year):

	1998	1999	2000	2001
Net gate receipts	$2.000	$3.000	$3.000	$3.000
Corporate sponsorship	3.000	3.500	4.000	4.000
Television royalties	0.000	1.200	1.400	2.000
Merchandise income (net of costs)	0.600	0.600	0.700	0.700

Agnelli believes that a 12% required rate of return is appropriate for investments by Milano Capri.

REQUIRED
1. For Bebeto's proposed 4-year contract, compute (a) the net present value, (b) the payback period, and (c) the breakeven time.
2. What other factors should Agnelli consider when deciding whether to sign Bebeto to the 4-year contract?

22-25 Basic job project cost control. (Chapter Appendix) The Marketing, Manufacturing, and R&D Departments of the Perry Company have worked together in deciding which new products and components to develop. The R&D Department has launched a project to develop a new compressor for the Perry line of Frosty Refrigerators. Consider the following data:

Original budget to complete	30,000 hours
Budgeted average cost per hour	$120
Price variance to date	$0
Budgeted hours for work scheduled to date	22,100 hours
Budgeted hours for work performed to date (earned hours)	20,000 hours
Actual hours of work performed to date	21,200 hours
Price variance expected	$39,000 U

1. Compute the job project-performance cost variance and the job project-schedule cost variance.
2. Prepare a revised budget that is designed to predict actual final costs. Assume that the job project-performance cost variance will continue as unfavorable at the same rate as shown to date.

22-26 Basic job project cost control. (Chapter Appendix) The Northwest Corporation, a defense subcontractor, has a project to design and produce antiaircraft missiles. The original budget to complete the job was 25,000 hours. The budgeted hours for the work scheduled to date are 15,000 hours. The budgeted hours for the work performed to date (earned hours) are 13,750. The actual hours of work performed to date are 14,300. The budgeted cost is $70 per hour. There is no price variance.

REQUIRED

1. Compute the job project-performance cost variance and the job project-schedule cost variance.
2. Prepare a revised budget that is designed to predict actual final costs. Assume that the job project-performance cost variance will continue to be unfavorable at the same rate as shown to date.

PROBLEMS

22-27 Equipment replacement, relevant costs, sensitivity analysis. A toy manufacturer that specializes in making fad items has just developed a $50,000 molding machine for producing a special toy. The machine has been used to produce only one unit so far. The company will depreciate the $50,000 initial machine investment evenly over 4 years, after which production of the toy will be stopped. The company's expected annual costs will be direct materials, $10,000; direct manufacturing labor, $20,000; and variable manufacturing overhead, $15,000. Variable manufacturing overhead varies with direct manufacturing labor costs. Fixed manufacturing overhead, exclusive of depreciation, is $7,500 annually, and fixed marketing and administrative costs are $12,000 annually.

Suddenly a machine salesperson appears. He has a new machine that is ideally suited for producing this toy. His automatic machine is distinctly superior. It reduces the cost of direct materials by 10% and produces twice as many units per hour. It will cost $44,000 and will have a zero terminal disposal price at the end of 4 years.

Production and sales of 25,000 units per year (sales of $100,000) will be the same whether the company uses the old machine or the new machine. The current disposal price of the toy company's molding machine is $5,000. Its terminal disposal price in 4 years will be $2,600.

REQUIRED

1. Assume that the required rate of return is 18%. Using the net present-value method, show whether the new machine should be purchased. What is the role of the book value of the old machine in the analysis?
2. What is the payback period for the new machine?
3. As the manager who developed the $50,000 old molding machine, you are trying to justify not buying the new $44,000 machine. You question the accuracy of the expected cash operating savings. By how much must these cash savings fall before the point of indifference—the point where the net present value of investing in the new machine—reaches zero?

22-28 Payback, net present value, relevant costs, sensitivity analysis. The city of Los Angeles has been operating a cafeteria for its employees, but it is considering converting to a completely automated set of vending machines. If the change is made, the old equipment would be sold now for whatever cash it might bring.

The vending machines would be purchased immediately for cash. A catering firm would take complete responsibility for servicing and replenishing the vending machines and would pay the city a predetermined percentage of the gross vending receipts.

The present cafeteria equipment has 10 years of remaining useful life. The new vending machines have a 10-year useful life. The following data are available (in thousands):

Cafeteria cash revenues per year	$120
Cafeteria cash costs per year	$124
Present cafeteria equipment	
Net book value	$84
Annual depreciation cost	$6
Current disposal price	$4
Terminal disposal price (10 years from now)	$0
New vending machines	
Initial machine investment	$64
Terminal disposal price	$5
Expected annual gross receipts	$80
City's percentage share of receipts	10%
Expected annual cash costs (negligible)	
Present values at 14%	
$1 due in 10 years	$0.27
Annuity of $1 a year for 10 years	$5.20

The city of Los Angeles has a 14% required rate of return.

REQUIRED

Compute the following for the vending machine investment:

1. Expected increase in net annual operating cash inflows as a result of investing in the vending machines.
2. Payback period.
3. Net present value.
4. Point of indifference (zero NPV) in terms of annual gross vending machine receipts.

22-29 Relevant costs, replacement decisions performance evaluation. George Handley, the general manager of the Coronado Company, is contemplating replacing the existing assembly-line equipment in the Assembly Department with automated assembly equipment. Production output and revenues will be unaffected by the replacement decision. Transactions related to the capital investment are cash transactions that would occur today.

	Existing Assembly Equipment	New Automated Assembly Equipment
Original cost	$1,100,000	$1,200,000
Useful life	11 years	5 years
Current age	6 years	0 years
Useful life remaining	5 years	5 years
Accumulated depreciation	$600,000	$0
Book value	$530,000	Not acquired yet
Current disposal price (in cash)	$200,000	Not acquired yet
Terminal disposal price (in cash, in 5 years)	$0	$0
Average working capital needed	$120,000	$70,000

Current annual Assembly Department costs are as follows:

Direct materials	$ 600,000
Direct manufacturing labor	400,000
Depreciation	100,000
Maintenance and repairs	150,000
Other operating costs	50,000
Supervision (allocated as 10% of direct manufacturing labor costs)	40,000
Allocated rent (based on space used)	40,000
Allocated corporate overhead (based on direct manufacturing labor costs)	120,000
Total	$1,500,000

Additional information:

a. Coronado uses straight-line depreciation calculated on the difference between the initial equipment investment and the terminal disposal price of the equipment.

b. The new equipment will produce output more swiftly. Therefore, the average working-capital investment, if the new equipment is purchased, will decrease.

c. Of the total direct materials costs, $120,000 is waste and scrap. The new equipment is expected to reduce scrap costs to $20,000.

d. The new equipment is expected to reduce direct manufacturing labor costs by $150,000 each year.

e. Maintenance and repairs on the old equipment have been excessive. If the new equipment is acquired, maintenance and repair costs are expected to decrease to $100,000.

f. Coronado collects all supervision costs for all manufacturing departments in the plant into one cost pool. These costs are then allocated to departments on the basis of direct manufacturing labor costs. The Assembly Department has only one supervisor currently. The supervisor will continue in her current position if the new equipment is purchased.

g. The new equipment will reduce the space required for assembly operations by 20%, reducing allocated rent by $8,000. The Coronado Company has no alternative uses for this extra space.

h. Corporate overhead costs are allocated to each department at 30% of direct manufacturing labor costs of each department.

Handley estimates a required rate of return of 12% for this project.

REQUIRED

1. On the basis of the net present-value method, should Handley replace the existing assembly equipment?

2. Suppose that next year is the last year Coronado will offer the attractive bonus plan currently in place. Handley's bonus hinges on short-run accrual accounting income for that year. Will Handley be inclined to replace the Assembly Department equipment? Provide quantitative support for your answer.

3. What nonfinancial and qualitative factors should Handley consider in coming to a decision?

22-30 Special order, relevant costs, capital budgeting. (A. Spero, adapted). Toys, Inc., sells neon-coated "Nightglow" cars to several local toy stores. It has the capacity to make 250,000 of these units per year, but during the year ending December 31, 19_5, it made and sold 130,000 cars to its existing customers. It makes these cars by dipping its highly unsuccessful "Gander" model plastic toy cars into a vat of neon paint. It originally purchased 780,000 of the Ganders but has been unable to sell them as Ganders. These plastic cars originally cost $20 per unit, and 650,000 of them remain in inventory.

Toys' accountant has prepared the following cost sheet per Nightglow car:

Selling price per car		$59
Manufacturing costs per car		
Direct materials		
Plastic cars	$20	
Neon paint	6	
Boxes	3	29
Direct manufacturing labor		8
Vat depreciation		10
Allocated plant manager's salary		5
Manufacturing costs per car		52
Gross margin per car		7
Marketing costs per car ($2 of which is variable)		6
Operating margin per car		$ 1

On December 31, 19_5, the Tiny Tot chain asked Toys, Inc., to provide 100,000 Nightglow cars at a special price of $50 per car. Toys, Inc., will not need to incur any marketing cost for the Tiny Tot sale.

Toys, Inc., expected to sell the Nightglow cars to its existing customers for the next 4 years at the current level of demand of 130,000 units per year and none thereafter. At the end of 4 years, Toys, Inc., will dispose of the vat and whatever cars remain at zero net disposal price. If Toys accepts the Tiny Tot order, it is certain that its other customers will refuse to pay the current price of $59 and will demand a discount. Toys estimates a required rate of return of 16%.

REQUIRED
1. Should Toys accept the special order if it must also offer the same price of $50 to its existing customers for the next 4 years?
2. Suppose Toys is uncertain about the discount the existing customers would demand. Determine the price that Toys, Inc., would have to offer its existing customers for the next 4 years to be indifferent between accepting and rejecting Tiny Tot's special order.

22-31 Relevant costs, outsourcing, capital budgeting. The Strubel Company currently makes as many units of Part No. 789 as it needs. David Lin, general manager of the Strubel Company, has received a bid from the Gabriella Company for making Part No. 789. Current plans call for Gabriella to supply 1,000 units of Part No. 789 per year at $50 a unit. Gabriella can begin supplying on January 1, 19_5, and continue for 5 years, after which time Strubel will not need the part. Gabriella can accommodate any change in Strubel's demand for the part and will supply it for $50 a unit, regardless of quantity.

Jack Tyson, the controller of the Strubel Company, reports the following costs for manufacturing 1,000 units of Part No. 789:

Direct materials	$22,000
Direct manufacturing labor	11,000
Variable manufacturing overhead	7,000
Depreciation on machine	10,000
Product and process engineering	4,000
Rent	2,000
Allocation of general plant overhead costs	5,000
Total costs	$61,000

The following additional information is available:
a. Part No. 789 is made on a machine used exclusively for the manufacture of Part No. 789. The machine was acquired on January 1, 19_4, at a cost of $60,000. The machine has a useful life of 6 years and zero terminal disposal price. Depreciation is calculated on the straight-line method.
b. The machine could be sold today for $15,000.
c. Product and process engineering costs are incurred to ensure that the manufacturing process for Part No. 789 works smoothly. Although these

costs are fixed in the short run, with respect to units of Part No. 789 produced, they can be saved in the long run if this part is no longer produced. If Part No. 789 is outsourced, product and process engineering costs of $4,000 will be incurred for 19_5 but not thereafter.

d. Rent costs of $2,000 are allocated to products on the basis of the floor space used for manufacturing the product. If Part No. 789 is discontinued, the space currently used to manufacture it would become available. The company could then use the space for storage purposes and save $1,000 currently paid for outside storage.

e. General plant overhead costs are allocated to each department on the basis of direct manufacturing labor dollars. These costs will not change in total. But no general plant overhead will be allocated to Part No. 789 if the part is outsourced.

Assume that Strubel requires a 12% rate of return for this project.

REQUIRED

1. Should David Lin outsource Part No. 789? Prepare a quantitative analysis.
2. Describe any sensitivity analysis that seems advisable, but you need not perform any sensitivity calculations.
3. What other factors should Lin consider in making a decision?
4. Lin is particularly concerned about his bonus for 19_5. The bonus is based on Strubel's accounting income. What decision will Lin make if he wants to maximize his bonus in 19_5?

22-32 Capital budgeting, computer-integrated manufacturing, sensitivity. The Dynamo Corporation is planning to replace one of its production lines, which has a remaining useful life of 10 years, book value of $9 million, a current disposal price of $5 million, and a neglible terminal disposal price 10 years from now. The average investment in working capital is $6 million.

Dynamo plans to replace the production line with computer-integrated manufacturing (CIM) system at a cost of $45 million. Jeremy Burns, the production manager, estimates the following annual cash-flow effects of implementing CIM:

a. Cost of maintaining software programs and CIM equipment, $1.5 million.
b. Reduction in lease payments due to reduced floor-space requirements, $1 million.
c. Fewer product defects and reduced rework, $4.5 million.

In addition, Burns estimates the average investment in working capital will decrease to $2 million. The estimated disposal price of the CIM equipment is $14 million at the end of 10 years. Dynamo uses a required rate of return of 14%.

REQUIRED

1. Compute the net present value of the CIM proposal. On the basis of this criterion, should Dynamo adopt CIM?
2. Burns argues that the higher quality and faster production resulting from CIM will also increase Dynamo's revenues. He estimates additional cash revenues net of cash-operating costs from CIM of $3 million per year. Compute the net present value of the CIM proposal under this assumption.
3. Management is uncertain if the cash flows from additional revenues will occur. Compute the minimum annual cash flow from additional revenues that will cause Dynamo to invest in CIM on the basis of the net present-value criterion.
4. Discuss the effects of reducing the investment horizon for CIM to 5 years, Dynamo's usual time period for making investment decisions. Assume disposal prices at the end of 5 years of CIM line, $20 million; old production line, $4 million. Also assume additional cash revenues net of cash-operating costs from CIM of $3 million per year.

22-33 New product proposal, payback, breakeven time, relevant costs. Aircraft Engineering is planning to develop a new radar instrument RGS3. Management is expected to approve the project and form the project development team on December 31, 1998. Owing to lack of funding, the team is not expected to start working on the project until late in 1999. The following cash flows are projected over the life of the project (in millions). Note that the investment cash flows are spread out over 2 years. For simplicity, we assume all cash flows occur at the end of each year.

Year Ended	Initial Investment Outflow	Cash Revenues	Cash Outflows for Manufacturing, Marketing Distribution, and Customer Service
1999	$0.50		
2000	2.00		
2001		$0.50	$1.00
2002		2.20	1.20
2003		4.40	2.00
2004		3.50	1.80
2005		1.70	1.00

Additional Information

a. Each year, fixed-overhead costs are allocated to products at the rate of 1% of product revenues. For example, in 2001, 1% of $0.50 million ($0.005 million) is expected to be allocated to RGS3.

b. As a result of introducing RGS3, Aircraft Engineering estimates it will lose some sales of its existing radar device, R265, as follows: 2001, $0.40 million; 2002, $0.60 million; 2003, $0.70 million; 2004, $0.50 million; 2005, $0.30 million.

c. The cash contribution margin percentage on sales of R265 is expected to be 30%.

d. Aircraft Engineering uses a 12% required rate of return on this project. Ignore income taxes.

REQUIRED

1. Calculate the breakeven time for RGS3.
2. Why might Aircraft Engineering be interested in reducing the breakeven time on RGS3? What steps can Aircraft Engineering take to reduce breakeven time on the RGS3 project?
3. Calculate the payback period for RGS3.
4. Why does the payback period differ from the breakeven time?

22-34 **Project-cost control.** Consider a Grumman research project on a new wing design for a fighter aircraft. The original budget to complete the project was 30,000 hours at an average cost of $120 per hour. The budgeted hours for the work scheduled to date are 21,000 hours. The budgeted hours for the work performed to date (earned hours) were 22,000 hours. The actual hours of work performed to date were 21,500. Actual costs were $2,795,000.

REQUIRED

1. Compute in dollars the following: job project-performance cost variance, efficiency variance, price variance, and job project-schedule cost variance.
2. As the manager, how would you interpret these variances? If the job project-performance cost variance persists at the same rate as shown to date, what are the expected actual final costs?

22-35 **Ethics, capital budgeting.** (CMA, adapted) The Evans Company must expand its manufacturing capabilities to meet the growing demand for its products. The first alternative is to expand its current manufacturing facility, which is located next to a vacant lot in the heart of the city. The second alternative is to convert a warehouse, already owned by Evans, located 20 miles outside the city. Evans's controller, George Watson, assigns Helen Dodge, assistant controller, to use net present-value computations to evaluate both proposals.

Dodge obtains the following information. The investment in plant and equipment to expand the current manufacturing facility is $19 million, while a $22 million investment is required to convert the warehouse. At either site, Evans needs to invest $3 million in working capital. Cash revenues from products made in the new facility are expected to equal $13 million each year. If the warehouse is converted, cash-operating costs are expected to be $10 million per year. Expanding the current facility will result in some efficiencies: annual cash-operating costs, if the current facility is expanded, will be $1 million lower than the cash-operating costs if the warehouse is converted. Evans uses a 10-year period and a 14% required rate of return to evaluate manufacturing investments. The estimated terminal disposal price of the new facility (including recovery of working capital of $3 million) at the end of 10 years is estimated to be $8 million—regardless of where the plant is located. Evans depreciates the investment in plant and equipment using straight-line depreciation over 10 years on the difference between the initial investment and terminal disposal price.

Watson is upset at Dodge's conclusions. He returns the proposal to her with the comment, "You must have made an error. The warehouse proposal should look better and have a positive net present value. Work on the projections and estimates."

Dodge suspects that Watson is anxious to have the warehouse proposal selected because the choice of this location would eliminate his long commute into the city. Feeling some pressure, she checks her calculations but finds no errors. Dodge reviews her projections and estimates. These too are quite reasonable. Even so, she replaces some of her original estimates with new estimates that are more favorable to the warehouse proposal, although these new estimates are less likely to occur. The revised proposal still has a negative net present value. Dodge is confused about what she should do.

REQUIRED

1. Calculate the net present value of the proposals to expand the current manufacturing facility and to convert the warehouse. Which project should Evans choose based on the NPV calculations?
2. Was George Watson's conduct unethical when he gave Helen Dodge specific instructions on revising the proposal?
3. Was Helen Dodge's revised proposal for the warehouse conversion unethical?
4. Identify the steps Helen Dodge should take to resolve this situation.

COLLABORATIVE LEARNING PROBLEM

22-36 **Relevant costs, capital budgeting** (N. Melumad, S. Reichelstein, adapted). The Special Products Division (SPD) of Plastics Unlimited makes specially designed night goggles. Its main production machine broke down on January 1, 1998, and was no longer usable. SPD's manager requested $320,000 to acquire a new machine. Corporate management responded by requesting an analysis of the acquisition as well as an analysis of closing down SPD. SPD's 1997 income statement is as follows:

Special Products Division Income Statement for 1997

Sales (60,000 units)			$1,200,000
Deduct costs			
Variable production costs		$770,000	
Fixed production costs*			
Machine depreciation	$30,000		
Patent amortization	25,000		
Machine maintenance	20,000		
Building space	20,000		
Manager's salary	55,000		
Other fixed costs	15,000		
Total fixed production costs		165,000	
Variable marketing costs		130,000	
Total costs			1,065,000
Operating income			$ 135,000

*That do not vary with units produced and sold.

The externally reported book values of the division assets as of December 31, 1997 are

Cash	$190,000
Machine	60,000
Patent	125,000
Total	$375,000

All of SPD's transactions are cash transactions, and the division maintains no inventories. The contribution margin is expected to remain the same over the next 5 years if SPD continues to produce and sell goggles.

To make the goggles, the company had to acquire a patent 3 years ago for $200,000. The patent is being amortized (that is, written off on the income statement) evenly over its lifetime. If the company were to shut down SPD, the patent could be sold for $235,000 to an external buyer.

SPD purchased the existing machine 3 years ago for $150,000. It is depreciated on a straight-line basis over 5 years. The current disposal price of the broken machine is $4,000.

The new machine has a useful life of 5 years and an expected disposal price of $50,000. It would be depreciated under the straight-line method. Maintenance of the new machine would require $25,000 per year. Machine maintenance costs would not be incurred if SPD is closed down.

SPD uses 1,000 square feet of building space and is charged $20 per square foot by corporate management. If SPD is eliminated, the space can be rented externally for $30 per square foot.

Plastics Unlimited needs an assistant manager in another larger department. If SPD closes, its manager will take the assistant manager position at an annual salary of $60,000. If SPD continues operations, Plastics Unlimited will have to fill the assistant manager position with an outsider at an annual salary of $65,000.

Other fixed costs consist of miscellaneous items such as insurance and indirect labor that would remain at the same levels if SPD continues to produce the goggles and would not be incurred if SPD is closed down.

The firm uses a required rate of return of 16%. Ignore income taxes.

INSTRUCTIONS

Form groups of three students to complete the following requirements.

REQUIRED

1. On the basis of the net present-value criterion, should Plastics Unlimited purchase the new machine or close down SPD?
2. Suppose the manager making the decision is compensated on the basis of operating income earned by all divisions of Plastics Unlimited after gain or loss on disposal of assets. The manager will retire at the end of 1998. Which decision would the manager favor? Explain.

ANSWERS TO EXERCISES IN COMPOUND INTEREST (EXERCISE 22-16)

The general approach to these exercises centers on a key question: Which of the four tables in Appendix C should be used? No computations should be made until after this basic question has been answered with confidence.

1. *From Table 1.* The $5,000 is the present value P of your winnings. Their future value S in 10 years will be

$$S = P(1 + r)^n$$

The conversion factor, $(1 + r)^n$, is on line 10 of Table 1.

Substituting at 6%: $S = 5,000 \times 1.791 = \$8,955$

Substituting at 14%: $S = 5,000 \times 3.707 = \$18,535$

2. *From Table 2.* The $89,550 is an *amount of future worth*. You want the present value of that amount, which is $P = S \div (1 + r)^n$. The conversion factor, $1 \div (1 + r)^n$, is on line 10 of Table 2. Substituting,

$$P = \$89{,}550 \times 0.558 = \$49{,}969$$

3. *From Table 3.* The $89,550 is *future worth*. You are seeking the uniform amount (annuity) to set aside annually. Note that $1 invested each year for 10 years at 6% has a future worth F of $13.181 after 10 years, from line 10 of Table 3.

$$S_n = \text{Annual deposit} \times F$$

$$\$89{,}550 = \text{Annual deposit} \times 13.181$$

$$\text{Annual deposit} = \frac{\$89{,}550}{13.181} = \$6{,}794$$

4. *From Table 3.* You are seeking the *amount of future worth* of an annuity of $5,000 per year. Note that $1 invested each year for 10 years at 12% has a future worth F of $17.549 after 10 years.

$$S_n = \$5{,}000F \qquad \text{where } F \text{ is the conversion factor}$$

$$= \$5{,}000 \times 17.549 = \$87{,}745$$

5. *From Table 4.* When you reach age 65, you will get $200,000, a present value at that time. You must find the annuity that will exactly exhaust the invested principal in 10 years. To pay yourself $1 each year for 10 years when the interest rate is 6% requires you to have $7.360 today, from line 10 of Table 4.

$$P_n = \text{Annual withdrawal} \times F$$

$$\$200{,}000 = \text{Annual withdrawal} \times 7.360$$

$$\text{Annual withdrawal} = \frac{\$200{,}000}{7.360} = \$27{,}174$$

6. *From Table 4.* You need to find the present value of an annuity for 10 years. At 6%,

$$P_n = \text{Annual withdrawal} \times F$$

$$= \$50{,}000 \times 7.360$$

$$= \$368{,}000$$

At 20%,

$$P_n = \$50{,}000 \times 4.192$$

$$= \$209{,}600, \text{ a much lower figure}$$

7. Plan B is preferable. The net present value of plan B exceeds that of plan A by $980 ($3,126 − $2,146):

| | | Plan A | | Plan B | |
| | | | | | |
Year	PV Factor at 6%	Cash Inflows	PV of Cash Inflows	Cash Inflows	PV of Cash Inflows
0	1.000	$(10,000)	$(10,000)	$(10,000)	$(10,000)
1	0.943	1,000	943	5,000	4,715
2	0.890	2,000	1,780	4,000	3,560
3	0.840	3,000	2,520	3,000	2,520
4	0.792	4,000	3,168	2,000	1,584
5	0.747	5,000	3,735	1,000	747
			$ 2,146		$ 3,126

Even though plan B and plan A have the same total cash inflows over the 5 years, plan B is preferred to plan A because it has greater cash inflows occurring earlier.

23

CAPITAL BUDGETING: A CLOSER LOOK

Communication satellites are major long-term investments for companies such as AT&T, MCI, and Sprint. Companies consider taxes, the effects of inflation, and competitive factors when using discounted cash-flow analyses to evaluate these investments.

LEARNING OBJECTIVES

After studying this chapter, you should be able to

1. Identify three factors that influence the amount of depreciation claimed as a tax deduction
2. Explain why depreciation deductions are an important source of tax savings but do not themselves affect cash flows
3. Distinguish between the total project approach and the differential approach in capital-budgeting decisions
4. Give examples of five categories of cash flows considered in capital-budgeting analyses
5. Distinguish between the real rate of return and the nominal rate of return
6. Describe two internally consistent ways to account for inflation in capital budgeting
7. Describe alternative approaches used to recognize the degree of risk in capital-budgeting projects
8. Explain the excess present-value index and its usefulness in capital budgeting
9. Explain why the internal rate-of-return and the net present-value decision rules may rank projects differently

Benjamin Franklin said that two things in life are certain: death and taxes. We might add a third: changing prices. This chapter examines how managers analyze income taxes and changing prices in capital budgeting. (We also recognize death in this chapter, although only of projects, not of the individuals who select them!) We also cover risk and uncertainty in capital budgeting in this chapter, as well as capital budgeting in nonprofit organizations, and issues in implementing the net present-value and the internal rate-of-return decision methods.

INCOME TAX FACTORS

The Importance of Income Taxes

Income taxes often have a tremendous influence on decisions. For example, income taxes can sizably reduce the net cash inflows from individual projects and so change their relative desirability. Decisions to locate plants in certain countries such as Ireland or Puerto Rico are often motivated by the low tax rates in those countries. The benefits of lower taxes sometimes outweigh higher project operating costs.

Treatment of Depreciation for Tax Purposes

OBJECTIVE 1

Identify three factors that influence the amount of depreciation claimed as a tax deduction

Many tax rules regarding income measurement are the same as the generally accepted accounting principles (GAAP) used for preparing financial statements. Other rules, such as those pertaining to depreciation, differ. Income tax laws frequently allow taxpayers to use shorter useful lives for depreciation than GAAP permits.

We emphasize income tax provisions affecting depreciation. To provide focus, we confine our discussion to corporations, although the basic ideas apply to partnerships and individuals as well.[1] Tax laws for depreciation deductions both in the United States and in other countries typically cover three factors: the amount allowable for depreciation, the time period over which the asset is to be depreciated, and the pattern of allowable depreciation.

Amount Allowable for Depreciation In most cases, the amount allowable for depreciation is the original cost of (initial investment in) the asset; sometimes, however, the amount allowable for depreciation exceeds or is less than the original cost. In countries where corporations have the option of claiming an investment tax credit,[2] the amount allowable for depreciation may be reduced below the original cost of the asset acquired. Tax laws also permit corporations to write off more than the original cost (as measured by nominal monetary units) for depreciation purposes. For example, U.S. and Canadian tax laws have from time to time allowed companies to claim depreciation deductions that in total exceed the investments made in certain assets (for example, sulphur mines and oil and gas wells).

Time Period over Which the Asset Is To Be Depreciated Tax authorities in various countries permit three main methods of determining the depreciation time period:

1. The taxpayer estimates the useful life.

2. The tax authority estimates the useful life.

3. Tax law specifies a table of allowable lives. An example is the property-class life categories (recovery periods) used in the Modified Accelerated Cost Recovery Sys-

---

[1] A general framework for examining income tax factors in business decisions is presented in M. Scholes and M. Wolfson, *Tax and Corporate Financial Strategy: A Global Planning Approach*, (Englewood Cliffs, N.J.: Prentice-Hall, 1991).

[2] An **investment tax credit (ITC)** is a direct reduction of income taxes payable arising from the acquisition of depreciable assets. Governments use ITCs to stimulate investments in specific types of assets or in specific industries. To illustrate: If a company purchases an asset costing $100,000 and there is a 4% ITC, the company obtains an immediate tax credit of $4,000; this credit increases the net present value of the asset by $4,000. The depreciable amount of the asset would be $96,000 (the net cost, $100,000 – $4,000) or $100,000, depending on the specific tax law. In the United States, the ITC option has been made available (and then subsequently withdrawn) several times since 1962.

tem, described in the Appendix to this chapter, that is applicable in the United States at the time of this writing.

Other things being equal, the shorter the allowable (depreciable) life, the fewer the periods over which depreciation deductions can be claimed and the higher the depreciable amount per year. Higher depreciation deductions result in higher tax deductions and hence greater tax savings.

Pattern of Allowable Depreciation (for a Given Time Period) Tax authorities allow three main depreciation patterns:

1. **Straight-line depreciation (SL),** in which an equal amount of depreciation is taken each year.
2. Accelerated depreciation, such as the double-declining balance (DDB) method.[3] **Accelerated depreciation** is any pattern of depreciation that writes off more of the depreciable assets in the early years after investment than does straight-line depreciation.
3. Depreciation using a table of allowable percentage write-offs as specified by tax law.

Depreciation deductions are noncash costs that reduce taxable income and hence save taxes for profitable companies (which is the case we assume throughout this chapter). All other things being equal, companies prefer greater amounts of depreciation because they lead to greater tax savings. Companies also favor shorter allowable lives and more accelerated patterns of depreciation because they result in greater depreciation deductions and cash savings in the early years after the investment, when cash savings have higher present value.

> **EXAMPLE** Martina Enterprises, a newly formed corporation, is considering purchasing its first machine. The original cost of the machine is $90,000 payable in cash immediately. Martina predicts that the machine will have an expected useful life of 5 years and a zero terminal disposal price. No additional working capital will be required to run the machine. If the machine is purchased, Martina Enterprises estimates sales of $100,000 and operating costs (other than depreciation) of $62,000 each year. For simplicity, assume that all sales are cash sales and all operating costs (other than depreciation) are paid in cash. Although these cash flows generally occur throughout the year, to simplify calculations, assume that the cash flows occur at the end of each year. The following tax laws apply:
>
> ◆ *Amount allowable for depreciation.* Original cost of the machine minus any predicted terminal disposal price = $90,000 − $0 = $90,000.
> ◆ *Time period over which the asset is to be depreciated.* Computed on the basis of an estimate of useful life made by the taxpayer (Martina) = 5 years.
> ◆ *Pattern of allowable depreciation.* Only straight-line depreciation is permitted = ($90,000 − $0) ÷ 5 years = $18,000 per year.

The corporate income tax rate of 40% will apply each year. Martina uses the net present-value method to evaluate investments. Its after-tax required rate of return for this investment is 12%, which it uses to discount after-tax cash flows.

Panel A of Exhibit 23-1 shows the annual cash flow from operations, net of income taxes equal to $30,000, using two methods based on the income statement. The first method subtracts $62,000 *cash*-operating costs and $8,000 taxes paid from $100,000 cash sales. The second method starts with $12,000 net income and adds back $18,000 depreciation because depreciation is an operating cost that reduces net income but does not reduce cash outflow.

OBJECTIVE 2

Explain why depreciation deductions are an important source of tax savings but do not themselves affect cash flows

---

[3]**Double-declining balance (DDB) depreciation** is a form of accelerated depreciation in which first-year depreciation is twice the amount of straight-line depreciation when a zero terminal disposal price is assumed. The DDB method is illustrated on p. 830.

EXHIBIT 23-1
Basic Analysis of Cash Flow from Operations, Net of Income Taxes, for Martina Enterprises

PANEL A: TWO METHODS BASED ON THE INCOME STATEMENT

(S)	Sales (assumed to be all cash sales)			$100,000
(C)	Costs			
	All costs, excluding depreciation*		$62,000	
(D)	Depreciation (straight-line of $90,000 ÷ 5 years)		18,000	
	Total costs			80,000
(OI)	Operating income			20,000
(T)	Income taxes (Income tax rate, $t \times$ OI) = 40% × $20,000			8,000
(NI)	Net income			$ 12,000

Cash flow from operations, net of income taxes, is

Method 1. $S - C - T = \$100,000 - \$62,000 - \$8,000 = \$30,000$

or

Method 2. $\text{NI} + D = \$12,000 + \$18,000 = \$30,000$

PANEL B: ITEM-BY-ITEM METHOD

	Effect of cash-operating flows	
$(S - C)$	Sales – Cash costs: $100,000 – $62,000	$38,000
$t \times (S - C)$	Deduct income tax cash outflow at 40%	15,200
$(1 - t) \times (S - C)$	After-tax cash-operating flows	$22,800
	Effect of depreciation	
(D)	Straight-line depreciation: $90,000 ÷ 5 = $18,000	
$(t \times D)$	Income tax cash savings from depreciation deductions at 40% × $18,000	7,200
$(1 - t) \times (S - C) + (t \times D)$ or $S - (t \times S) - C + (t \times C) + (t \times D)$	Cash flow from operations, net of income taxes	$30,000

*All costs, other than depreciation, are assumed to be paid in cash (that is, depreciation is the only accrual accounting cost item).

Panel B of Exhibit 23-1 describes a third method that we will frequently use throughout this chapter to compute cash flow from operations, net of income taxes. The easiest way to interpret the third method is to think of the government as a 40% (equal to the tax rate) partner in Martina Enterprises. Every time Martina records sales of $S, its income is *higher* by S, and so it pays 40% of the sales (0.40S) in taxes. Similarly, every time Martina records a cost (C or D), its income is *lower* by C or D, and so it saves 40% of that cost (0.40C or 0.40D) in taxes. The tax cash savings appear as cash inflows. The examples in this chapter combine the cash-operating flows (those operating items that actually entail an inflow or outflow of cash) and the tax effects of those flows into a single term, *after-tax cash-operating flows*, equal to $(1-t)(S-C)$. Depreciation is considered separately. Depreciation cost itself does not affect cash flow because depreciation is a noncash cost. But depreciation reduces tax payments by (tD), and in this way it increases the company's cash flow by keeping cash that would otherwise be disbursed.

To emphasize the tax benefit from depreciation deductions, we compute the present values of the two streams of annual cash flows calculated in Panel B: (1) the after-tax cash-operating flows of $22,800, and (2) the income tax cash savings from depreciation deductions of $7,200.

Present value of after-tax cash operating flows, $22,800 × 3.605*	$82,194
Present value of income tax cash savings from depreciation deductions, $7,200 × 3.605*	25,956
Net initial investment in machine	(90,000)
Net present value of machine investment	$18,150

*Present value of an annuity of $1 for 5 years discounted at 12% is 3.605.

The positive net present value indicates that the machine investment is desirable. Had the tax benefits from depreciation deductions not been considered, the NPV would be negative and Martina would have concluded that the project is undesirable on the basis of financial considerations.

The tax benefit of depreciation offsets the net cash outflow of $90,000 over 5 years from purchasing and using the machine (original cost, $90,000 minus terminal disposal price, $0). This net cash outflow equals the depreciation cost of $90,000 over 5 years at $18,000 per year. The cash tax savings occur as depreciation cost is recognized, not when the cash of $90,000 is paid to purchase the machine. The tax savings from depreciation deductions are 40% of $90,000 spread over 5 years resulting in a present value of $25,956. The present value of the tax savings depends on the depreciation tax laws, the applicable tax rate, and the interest rate used for discounting future cash flows.

INCOME TAX CONSIDERATIONS IN CAPITAL BUDGETING

We turn now to a fuller discussion of how income taxes can affect cash inflows and outflows and also how they influence managers' decisions. We focus on the information-acquisition and selection stages of capital budgeting, highlight the effect of the tax deductibility of depreciation, and use the net present-value method for the formal financial analysis.

EXAMPLE Potato Supreme produces potato products for sale to supermarkets and other retail outlets. It is considering replacing an old packaging machine (purchased 3 years ago) with a new, more efficient packaging machine that has recently been introduced. The new machine is less labor-intensive and has lower operating costs than the old machine. For simplicity, we assume that

1. All cash outflows or inflows occur at the end of the year (even though cash-operating costs generally occur throughout the year).

2. The tax effects of cash inflows and outflows occur at the same time that the inflows and outflows occur.

3. The income tax rate is 30% each year.

4. Gains or losses on the sale of depreciable assets are taxed at the same rate as ordinary income.[4]

5. Both the old and the new machine have the same working capital requirements.

6. Potato Supreme is a profitable company. Tax savings from depreciation deductions occur in the year in which depreciation becomes available.

The following income tax laws apply to Potato Supreme for both the old and the new machines:

◆ *Amount allowable for depreciation.* Original cost is the basis for depreciation computations. Terminal disposal price is ignored when computing depreciation for either the old or the new machine. When a depreciable asset is sold, any difference between the disposal price and the book value (original cost minus accumulated depreciation at the time of the sale) is treated as ordinary income (or loss) for tax purposes.

---

[4]The example assumes that if the new machine is purchased, the old machine is sold outright for cash. When the old machine is traded in for a new machine of like kind, no gain or loss is recognized under U.S. tax laws in the year of the transaction. Rather, the new machine is capitalized at the book value of the old machine plus the cash paid in exchange. As a result, any gain or loss is spread over the life of the new machine through the new depreciation charges.

When the old machine is sold outright for cash, under U.S. tax laws, part of the gain may be taxed at ordinary income tax rates and part at capital-gains rates. The Appendix to this chapter describes the manner in which gains and losses on the sale of assets are taxed under U.S. tax laws. For simplicity, this chapter assumes that gains on disposal are taxed at ordinary income tax rates.

♦ *Time period over which the asset is to be depreciated.* Assets are depreciated over their useful lives. The old machine has a useful life of 7 years. It is 3 years old, so its remaining useful life is 4 years. The new machine has an expected useful life of 4 years because of the shorter product life cycles of new packaging machines.

♦ *Pattern of allowable depreciation.* Straight-line depreciation is used for the old machine. The new machine, however, would qualify for DDB depreciation.

Summary data for the two machines are as follows:

	Old Machine	New Machine
Original cost	$87,500	$200,000
Accumulated depreciation	$37,500	—
Current book value	$50,000	—
Current disposal price	$26,000	—
Terminal disposal price, 4 years from now	$6,000	$20,000
Annual cash-operating costs	$250,000	$150,000
Remaining useful life	4 years	4 years
After-tax required rate of return	10%	10%

OBJECTIVE 3

Distinguish between the total project approach and the differential approach in capital-budgeting decisions

Potato Supreme uses the net present-value method to evaluate whether it should replace the old packaging machine with the new packaging machine. As in the Lifetime Care example of Chapter 22, the key point in net present-value analysis is to identify the relevant cash flows. To emphasize the ideas of relevance, Chapter 22 used the **differential approach,** which analyzes only relevant cash flows—those future cash outflows and inflows that differ between or among alternatives. The differential approach is generally faster when there are only two alternatives.

When the number of alternatives is more than two, the differential approach becomes unwieldy. Why? Because it forces the analyst into difficult calculations of differences among multiple alternatives. Companies then use the *total project approach.* The **total project approach** calculates the present value of *all* future cash inflows and outflows under each alternative separately. It does not require the identification of cash flows that differ among alternatives. The total project approach has two steps:

Step 1 Calculate the present value of all cash inflows and outflows under the status quo alternative.

Step 2 Separately calculate the present value of all cash inflows and outflows under another alternative.

We use the Potato Supreme example to illustrate the two steps of the total project approach. We then use the differential approach to show that both approaches give the same net present value. Five categories of cash flows are considered in both approaches:

OBJECTIVE 4

Give examples of five categories of cash flows considered in capital-budgeting analyses

1. Initial machine investment
2. After-tax cash flow from current disposal of old machine
3. Recurring after-tax cash-operating flows (excluding depreciation effects)
4. Income tax cash savings from depreciation deductions
5. After-tax cash flow from terminal (at the end of the project) disposal of machine

Total Project Approach

Step 1. Calculate the Present Value of Total Cash Flows of Keeping the Old Packaging Machine Under this alternative, cash flow categories that specifically pertain to the new machine are not relevant.

a. *Initial machine investment.* No new investment is necessary if Potato Supreme keeps the old packaging machine. Exhibit 23-2, item 1, shows an initial machine investment of $0 in year 0.

EXHIBIT 23-2
Total Project Approach for Potato Supreme: After-Tax Analysis of Keeping Old Machine

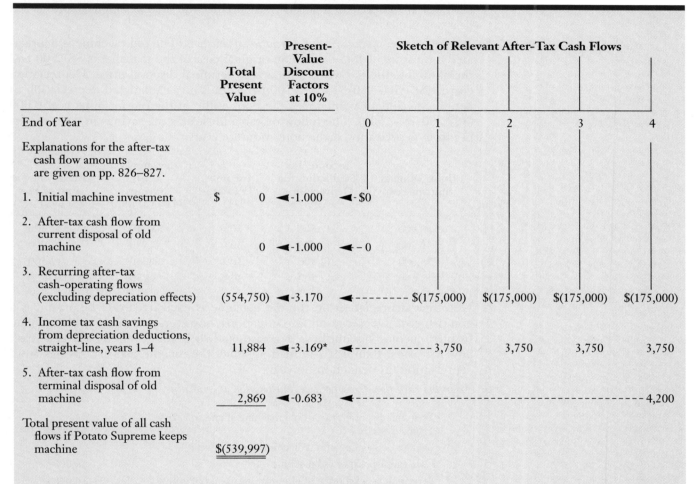

	Total Present Value	Present-Value Discount Factors at 10%	Sketch of Relevant After-Tax Cash Flows				
End of Year			0	1	2	3	4
Explanations for the after-tax cash flow amounts are given on pp. 826–827.							
1. Initial machine investment	$ 0	◄-1.000	◄-$0				
2. After-tax cash flow from current disposal of old machine	0	◄-1.000	◄-0				
3. Recurring after-tax cash-operating flows (excluding depreciation effects)	(554,750)	◄-3.170	◄-------- $(175,000)	$(175,000)	$(175,000)	$(175,000)	
4. Income tax cash savings from depreciation deductions, straight-line, years 1–4	11,884	◄-3.169*	◄------------ 3,750	3,750	3,750	3,750	
5. After-tax cash flow from terminal disposal of old machine	2,869	◄-0.683	◄-- 4,200				
Total present value of all cash flows if Potato Supreme keeps machine	$(539,997)						

Note: Parentheses denote relevant cash outflows throughout all exhibits in this chapter.
*Obtained by adding individual discount rates (0.909 + 0.826 + 0.751 + 0.683 = 3.169) to avoid discrepancies in item 4 between Exhibits 23-2 and 23-4.

b. *After-tax cash flow from current disposal of old machine.* Since the old machine is kept and not disposed of, Exhibit 23-2, item 2, shows after-tax cash flow from current disposal of old machine of $0 in year 0.

c. *Recurring after-tax cash-operating flows (excluding depreciation effects).*

Recurring cash-operating flows (costs) for the old machine	$(250,000)
Deduct income tax savings at 30% of $250,000	75,000
Recurring after-tax cash-operating flows	$(175,000)

After-tax cash-operating flows (excluding depreciation effects) of $(175,000) in years 1–4 appear as relevant cash outflows in Exhibit 23-2, item 3. Our example assumes that Potato Supreme's income tax rate is 30% each year. When future tax rates are uncertain, analysts must predict the tax rate applicable for each year of a project.

d. *Income tax cash savings from depreciation deductions.* The old machine is depreciated on a straight-line basis. The original cost of the machine is $87,500 and the allowable life is 7 years with a zero terminal disposal price. Depreciation cost is $(87,500 - $0) \div 7 = $12,500$ per year. The accumulated depreciation to date is $12,500 \times 3$ years $= $37,500$; book value of the old machine is $50,000 $($87,500 - $37,500)$. The following table illustrates the savings in taxes resulting from depreciation deductions in future years:

Year	Book Value at Start of Year (1)	Income Tax Deduction for Depreciation (2)	Income Tax Rate (3)	Income Tax Cash Savings (4) = (2) × (3)	Book Value at End of Year (5) = (1) - (2)
1	$50,000	$12,500	30%	$3,750	$37,500
2	37,500	12,500	30%	3,750	25,000
3	25,000	12,500	30%	3,750	12,500
4	12,500	12,500	30%	3,750	0

Note that depreciation on the old machine is itself irrelevant because it is a noncash cost. Depreciation tax deductions, however, decrease taxable income. In turn, income tax outflows decrease, and so Potato Supreme's overall cash flow increases. Exhibit 23-2, item 4, shows the income tax cash savings from depreciation tax deductions in years 1–4.

e. *After-tax cash flow from terminal disposal of old machine.*

Terminal disposal price of old machine at end of year 4 (given, see p. 826)	$6,000
Deduct book value of old machine at end of year 4	0
Gain on disposal of old machine	$6,000
Terminal disposal price of old machine at end of year 4	$6,000
Deduct taxes on gain (30% × $6,000)	(1,800)
After-tax cash inflow from terminal disposal of old machine	$4,200

The after-tax cash flow of $4,200 from the terminal disposal of the old machine appears as a cash inflow in year 4 of Exhibit 23-2, item 5.

Exhibit 23-2 presents all after-tax cash flows that would arise if Potato Supreme continued to use the old packaging machine. Each cash flow is multiplied by its corresponding present-value discount factor to give its present value. The total present value is $(539,997).

Step 2. Calculate the Present Value of Total Cash Flows of Replacing the Old Packaging Machine

a. *Initial machine investment.* The original cost of the new packaging machine is $200,000. This amount appears as a cash outflow in year 0 in Exhibit 23-3, item 1.

EXHIBIT 23-3
Total Project Approach for Potato Supreme: After-Tax Analysis of Purchasing New Machine

	Total Present Value	Present-Value Discount Factors at 10%	Sketch of Relevant After-Tax Cash Flows			
End of Year			0	1	2	3	4

Explanations for the after-tax cash flow amounts are given on pp. 828 and 830.

1. Initial machine investment — $(200,000) ◄-1.000◄-$(200,000)

2. After-tax cash flow from current disposal of old machine — 33,200 ◄-1.000◄- - 33,200
   Net initial investment — (166,800) — (166,800)

3. Recurring after-tax cash-operating flows (excluding depreciation effects) — (332,850) ◄-3.170◄- - - - - - - - - - - $(105,000) $(105,000) $(105,000) $(105,000)

4. Income tax cash savings from depreciation deductions (DDB)
   - Year 1 — 27,270 ◄-0.909◄- - - - - - - - - - - - 30,000
   - Year 2 — 12,390 ◄-0.826◄- 15,000
   - Year 3 — 5,633 ◄-0.751◄- 7,500
   - Year 4 — 5,122 ◄-0.683◄- 7,500

5. After-tax cash flow from terminal disposal of new machine — 9,562 ◄-0.683◄- -14,000

Total present value of all cash flows if Potato Supreme purchases new machine — $(439,673)

b. *After-tax cash flow from current disposal of old machine.*

Current disposal price of old machine (given, see p. 826)	$ 26,000
Deduct current book value of old machine (given, see p. 826)	50,000
Loss on disposal of machine	$(24,000)
Current disposal price of old machine	$ 26,000
Add tax savings on loss (30% × $24,000)	7,200
After-tax cash inflow from current disposal of old machine	$ 33,200

Review what is included in the present-value analysis. It is the *cash inflow* from asset disposal and the *cash savings* in taxes. The book value of the old machine and the loss on disposal do not themselves affect cash flow. The book value, however, enters into the calculation of the loss on disposal of the asset, which in turn affects the income tax cash flows.

The after-tax cash flow of $33,200 appears as a cash inflow in year 0 of Exhibit 23-3, item 2. The initial machine investment, $200,000, minus the after-tax cash inflow from current disposal of the old machine, $33,200, is the net initial investment of $166,800, shown as a cash outflow in year 0 in Exhibit 23-3.

c. *Recurring after-tax cash-operating flows (excluding depreciation effects).*

Recurring cash-operating flows (costs) for the new machine	$(150,000)
Deduct income tax savings (30% × $150,000)	45,000
Recurring after-tax cash-operating flows	$(105,000)

The after-tax cash-operating flows (excluding depreciation effects) of $(105,000) in years 1–4 appear as relevant cash outflows in Exhibit 23-3, item 3.

d. *Income tax cash savings from depreciation deductions.* Depreciation tax deductions result in tax savings that, in effect, partially offset the cost of acquiring the new packaging machine.

The following table illustrates (1) the calculation of depreciation on the new machine using the double-declining balance method,[5] and (2) the income tax savings arising each year from depreciation deductions.

Year	Book Value at Start of Year (1)	DDB Rate (2)	Income Tax Deduction for Depreciation (3) = (1) × (2)	Income Tax Rate (4)	Income Tax Cash Savings (5) = (3) × (4)	Book value at End of Year (6) = (1) - (3)
1	$200,000	50%	$100,000	30%	$30,000	$100,000
2	100,000	50%	50,000	30%	15,000	50,000
3	50,000	50%	25,000	30%	7,500	25,000
4	25,000	—	25,000	30%	7,500	0

Exhibit 23-3, item 4, shows the income tax cash savings from depreciation deductions in years 1–4.

Note that the initial investment in the asset of $200,000 is included in the capital-budgeting analysis as a *lump-sum* cash outflow in year 0 (see Exhibit 23-3,

---

[5]The DDB depreciation pattern is calculated as follows: (a) Compute the straight-line rate by dividing 100% by the years of useful life. Then double the rate. In the Potato Supreme example, 100% ÷ 4 years = 25%. The DDB rate would be 2 × 25% = 50%. (b) To compute the depreciation for any year, multiply the beginning book value at the start of the year (original cost minus any accumulated depreciaton) by the DDB rate (ignoring the terminal disposal price). In the Potato Supreme example, depreciation for the second year is 50% of $100,000 (book value of the packaging machine at the beginning of the second year) = $50,000. Unmodified, this method would never fully depreciate the existing book value. In the Potato Supreme example, for simplicity, we assume that the depreciation in the fourth (last) year is the book value at the start of that year. A more detailed DDB method would require a switch to straight-line depreciation applied to the undepreciated book value of the asset over the remaining useful life of the asset (ignoring the terminal disposal price) when straight-line depreciation first exceeds the amount in the DDB schedule.

item 1). Depreciation on the new machine is a noncash cost, as it was on the old machine. Depreciation tax deductions, however, decrease income tax outflows and so increase Potato Supreme's overall cash flow.

e. *After-tax cash flow from terminal disposal of new machine.*

Terminal disposal price of new machine at end of year 4 (given, see p. 826)	$20,000
Deduct book value of machine at end of year 4	0
Gain on disposal of new machine	$20,000
Terminal disposal price of new machine at end of year 4	$20,000
Deduct taxes on gain (30% × $20,000)	6,000
After-tax cash inflow from terminal disposal of new machine	$14,000

The after-tax cash flow of $14,000 from terminal disposal of the new machine appears as a cash inflow in year 4 of Exhibit 23-3, item 5.

Exhibit 23-3 summarizes the relevant after-tax cash flows that would occur if Potato Supreme replaced its old packaging machine. Present values are derived by multiplying cash flows by the corresponding present-value discount factors. The total present value of cash flows equals $(439,673). Recall from Exhibit 23-2 that the present value of after-tax cash flows of keeping the old packaging machine is $(539,997). The decision to replace the old machine with the new machine has a net present value of $100,324 ($539,997 − $439,673) and is therefore preferred.

Differential Approach

Unlike the two-step total project approach, the differential approach is a one-step method that includes only those cash inflows and outflows that *differ* between the two alternatives. The differential approach compares (1) the cash outflows arising from replacing the old machine with (2) the *savings* in future cash outflows resulting from using the new machine rather than the old machine. We will now examine the differences in cash flows between the keep and replace alternatives in the Potato Supreme example using the same five categories of cash flows that we described earlier.

1. *Initial machine investment* of $200,000 for the new machine (see Exhibit 23-3) appears as a cash outflow in year 0 in Exhibit 23-4, item 1.

2. *After-tax cash flow from current disposal of old machine* of $33,200 (see Exhibit 23-3) appears as a cash inflow in year 0 in Exhibit 23-4, item 2. The initial machine investment, $200,000, minus the after-tax cash flow from current disposal of the old machine, $33,200, is the net initial investment of $166,800, shown as a cash outflow in year 0 in Exhibit 23-4.

3. *Recurring after-tax cash-operating flows (excluding depreciation effects).* Replacing the old machine results in lower after-tax cash-operating costs, as follows:

Recurring after-tax cash-operating costs (excluding depreciation effects) if old machine kept (Exhibit 23-2, item 3)	$175,000
Deduct recurring after-tax cash-operating costs (excluding depreciation effects) if machine replaced (Exhibit 23-3, item 3)	105,000
Savings in recurring after-tax cash-operating costs (excluding depreciation effects) if machine replaced	$ 70,000

Exhibit 23-4, item 3, shows this $70,000 increase in recurring after-tax cash-operating flows (excluding depreciation effects) in years 1–4.

4. *Income tax cash savings from depreciation deductions.* Larger depreciation deductions are available on the new machine than on the old machine. The following table describes the additional tax savings resulting from the higher depreciation deductions allowed on the new machine:

EXHIBIT 23-4
Differential Approach for Potato Supreme: After-Tax Analysis of Replacing Old Machine

	Total Present Value	Present-Value Discount Factors at 10%	Sketch of Relevant After-Tax Cash Flows				
End of Year			0	1	2	3	4
Explanations for the after-tax inflow amounts are given on pp. 831 and 833.							
1. Initial machine investment	$(200,000) ◄ ─ ─	1.000 ◄ ─ ─	$(200,000)				
2. After-tax cash flow from current disposal of old machine	33,200 ◄ ─ ─ ─	1.000 ◄ ─ ─ ─ ─	33,200				
Net initial investment	(166,800)		(166,800)				
3. Recurring after-tax cash-operating flows (excluding depreciation effects)	221,900 ◄ ─ ─	3.170 ◄ ─ ─ ─ ─ ─ ─ ─ ─ ─ ─ ─ ─		$70,000	$70,000	$70,000	$70,000
4. Income tax cash savings from depreciation deductions							
Year 1	23,861 ◄ ─ ─ ─	0.909 ◄ ─ ─ ─ ─ ─ ─ ─ ─ ─ ─ ─ ─		26,250			
Year 2	9,293 ◄ ─ ─ ─	0.826 ◄ ─			11,250		
Year 3	2,816 ◄ ─ ─ ─	0.751 ◄ ─				3,750	
Year 4	2,561 ◄ ─ ─ ─	0.683 ◄ ─					3,750
5. After-tax cash flow from terminal disposal of machines	6,693 ◄ ─ ─ ─	0.683 ◄ ─					9,800
Net present value if new machine is purchased	$100,324						

Year	Income Tax Cash Savings from Depreciation Deductions on New Machine (Exhibit 23-3, Item 4) (1)	Income Tax Cash Savings from Depreciation Deductions If Old Machine Kept (Exhibit 23-2, Item 4) (2)	Increase in Income Tax Cash Savings from Depreciation Deductions If Machine Replaced (3) = (1) - (2)
1	$30,000	$3,750	$26,250
2	15,000	3,750	11,250
3	7,500	3,750	3,750
4	7,500	3,750	3,750

Exhibit 23-4, item 4, shows the increase in cash flow resulting from depreciation-related differential income tax savings in years 1–4.

5. *After-tax cash flow from terminal disposal of machines.*

After-tax cash inflow from terminal (at end of year 4) disposal of new machine (see Exhibit 23-3)	$14,000
Deduct after-tax cash inflow from terminal (at end of year 4) disposal of old machine (see Exhibit 23-2)	4,200
Increase in after-tax cash inflow from terminal disposal of machine if machine is replaced	$ 9,800

Exhibit 23-4, item 5, shows this relevant after-tax cash inflow from the disposal of the machines in year 4.

Both the total project approach (Exhibits 23-2 and 23-3) and the differential approach (Exhibit 23-4) result in a net present value of $100,324 in favor of replacing the old packaging machine with the new one. When comparing alternatives, these two approaches will always give the same net present value.

U.S. Income Tax Laws

Our general approach to analyzing income tax effects in capital budgeting applies to practices around the globe. The rules in effect in the United States at the time of this writing are called the **Modified Accelerated Cost Recovery System (MACRS)**. The two depreciation methods illustrated in the Potato Supreme example—straight-line and double-declining balance—and in the exercises and problems for this chapter are the main alternatives available under MACRS. The Appendix to this chapter summarizes some key provisions of U.S. tax laws for depreciable assets.

CAPITAL BUDGETING AND INFLATION

Inflation can be defined as the decline in the general purchasing power of the monetary unit (for example, the dollar in the United States or the yen in Japan). An inflation rate of 10% in 1 year means that what you could buy with $100 (say) at the start of the year will cost you $110 [$100 + (10% × $100)] at the end of the year. Prices increase as more money chases fewer goods. Some countries—for example, Brazil, Israel, Mexico, and Russia—have experienced annual inflation rates of 15% to over 100%. Even an annual inflation rate of 5% over, say, a 5-year period can result in sizable declines in the general purchasing power of the monetary unit over that time.

Why is it important to account for inflation in capital budgeting? Because declines in the general purchasing power of the monetary unit (dollars, say) will inflate future cash flows above what they would have been had there been no inflation. These inflated cash flows will cause the project to look better than it is, unless the analyst recognizes that the inflated cash flows are measured in dollars that have lesser value than the dollars that were initially invested. We now examine how inflation can be explicitly recognized in capital-budgeting analysis.

Real and Nominal Rates of Return

OBJECTIVE 5

Distinguish between the real rate of return and the nominal rate of return

When analyzing inflation, distinguish between the real rate of return and the nominal rate of return:

◆ **Real rate of return** is the rate of return required to cover only investment risk.

◆ **Nominal rate of return** is the rate of return required to cover investment risk and the anticipated decline, due to inflation, in the general purchasing power of the cash that the investment generates. The rates of return (or interest) earned on the financial markets are nominal rates, because they compensate investors for both risk and inflation.

We next describe the relationship between real and nominal rates of return. Assume that the real rate of return for investments in high-risk cellular data-transmission equipment at Network Communications is 20% and that the expected inflation rate is 10%. The nominal rate of return[6] is

$$\text{Nominal rate} = (1 + \text{Real rate})(1 + \text{Inflation rate}) - 1$$
$$= (1 + 0.20)(1 + 0.10) - 1$$
$$= [(1.20)(1.10)] - 1 = 1.32 - 1 = 0.32$$

The nominal rate of return is also related to the real rate of return and the inflation rate as follows:

Real rate of return	0.20
Inflation rate	0.10
Combination (0.20×0.10)	0.02
Nominal rate of return	0.32

Note that the nominal rate is slightly higher than the real rate (0.20) plus the inflation rate (0.10). Why? Because the nominal rate recognizes that inflation also decreases the purchasing power of the real rate of return earned during the year.

Net Present-Value Method and Inflation

OBJECTIVE 6

Describe two internally consistent ways to account for inflation in capital budgeting

The watchwords when incorporating inflation into the net present-value (NPV) method are *internal consistency*. There are two internally consistent approaches:

◆ *Nominal approach:* Predict cash inflows and outflows in nominal monetary units *and* use a nominal rate as the required rate of return.

◆ *Real approach:* Predict cash inflows and outflows in real monetary units *and* use a real rate as the required rate of return.

Consider an investment that is expected to generate sales of 100 units and a net cash inflow of $1,000 ($10 per unit) each year for 2 years *absent inflation*. If inflation of 10% is expected each year, net cash inflows from the sale of each unit would be $11 ($10 × 1.10) in year 1 and $12.10 [$11 × 1.10 or $10 × (1.10)^2] in year 2 resulting in net cash inflows of $1,100 in year 1 and $1,210 in year 2. The net cash inflows of $1,100 and $1,210 are nominal cash inflows because they include the impact of inflation. *These are the cash flows recorded by the accounting system.* The cash inflow of $1,000 each year are real cash flows because they exclude inflationary effects. Note that the real cash flows equal the nominal cash flows discounted for inflation, $1,000 = $1,100 ÷ 1.10 = $1,210 ÷ (1.10)^2. Many managers find the nominal approach easier to understand and use because they observe nominal cash flows in their accounting systems and the nominal rates of return on financial markets.

Let's revisit Network Communications, which is deciding whether to invest in equipment to make and sell a cellular data-transmission product. The equipment would cost $750,000 immediately. It is expected to have a 4-year useful life with a

---

[6]The real rate of return can be expressed in terms of the nominal rate of return as follows:

$$\text{Real rate} = \frac{(1 + \text{Nominal rate})}{(1 + \text{Inflation rate})} - 1 = \frac{(1 + 0.32)}{(1 + 0.10)} - 1 = 0.20$$

zero terminal disposal price. An annual inflation rate of 10% is expected over this 4-year period. Network Communications requires an after-tax real rate of return of 20% from this project or an after-tax nominal rate of return of 32% (see p. 834).

The following table presents the predicted amounts of real (assuming no inflation) and nominal (after considering cumulative inflation) net cash inflows from the equipment over the next 4 years (excluding the $750,000 investment in the equipment and before any income tax payments):

Year	Before-Tax Cash Inflows in Real Dollars (1)	Cumulative Inflation Rate Factor* (2)	Before-Tax Cash Inflows in Nominal Dollars (3) = (1) × (2)
1	$500,000	$(1.10)^1 = 1.1000$	$550,000
2	600,000	$(1.10)^2 = 1.2100$	726,000
3	600,000	$(1.10)^3 = 1.3310$	798,600
4	300,000	$(1.10)^4 = 1.4641$	439,230

*1.10 = 1.00 + 0.10 inflation rate.

The income tax rate is 40%. For tax purposes, the equipment will be depreciated using the double-declining balance method.[7]

Exhibit 23-5 presents the capital-budgeting approach for predicting cash flows in nominal dollars and using a nominal discount rate.[8] The calculations in Exhibit 23-5 exactly follow the calculations used in the Potato Supreme example for initial machine investment, recurring after-tax cash-operating flows (excluding depreciation effects), and income tax cash savings from depreciation deductions.

Exhibit 23-6 presents the approach of predicting cash flows in real terms and using a real discount rate. The calculations for item 2, recurring after-tax cash-operating flows (excluding depreciation effects), are basically the same as before except that the cash inflows are measured in real terms and discounted at real rates. Item 3 in Exhibit 23-6 describing income tax cash savings from depreciation deductions requires some clarification. U.S. tax laws restrict the amount allowed for depreciation to the asset's original cost in *nominal dollars*. That is, the depreciation cash saving in year 2, for example, will be $75,000 in nominal year 2 dollars, irrespective of the inflation that occurred in years 1 and 2. To express these depreciation tax savings in real dollars, we divide the nominal dollars by the cumulative rate of inflation.[9] The tax savings in real dollars are then discounted at the real rate.

[7]Given a 4-year useful life, the DDB factor is 0.5 (2 × 0.25). Depreciation each year will be as follows:

Year	Beginning Book Value	DDB Factor	Annual Depreciation
1	$750,000	0.5	$375,000
2	375,000	0.5	187,500
3	187,500	0.5	93,750
4	93,750	—	93,750

Assume for simplicity that the income tax deduction for depreciation in year 4 is the book value at the start of that year.

[8]The present-value discount factors in the example are calculated using six-decimal digits to eliminate doubt about the equivalence of the two approaches. In practice, the present-value discount factors (to three-decimal digits) can be obtained using Table 2 (present value of $1) of Appendix C at the end of the text. The Problem for Self-Study at the end of this chapter uses Table 2.

[9]The inflation factors used in Exhibit 23-6 to compute the tax savings in real dollars, given an inflation rate of 10%, are as follows:

Year	Inflation Factor Formula	Inflation Factor
1	$1 \div (1.10)^1$	0.909091
2	$1 \div (1.10)^2$	0.826446
3	$1 \div (1.10)^3$	0.751315
4	$1 \div (1.10)^4$	0.683013

EXHIBIT 23-5

Nominal Approach to Inflation for Network Communications: Predict Cash Inflows and Outflows in
Nominal Dollars and Use a Nominal Discount Rate*

		Total Present Value	Present Value Discount Factors at 32%†	Sketch of Relevant After-Tax Cash Flows				
End of Year				0	1	2	3	4

1. Initial equipment investment

Year	Investment Outflows
0	$(750,000)

$(750,000) ◄- 1.000000 ◄- $(750,000)

2. Recurring after-tax cash-operating flows
   (excluding depreciation effects)

Year (1)	Recurring Nominal Cash-Operating Inflows (2)	Income Tax Outflows (3) = 0.40 × (2)	Recurring Nominal After-Tax Cash-Operating Inflows (4) = (2) - (3)
1	$550,000	$220,000	$330,000
2	726,000	290,400	435,600
3	798,600	319,440	479,160
4	439,230	175,692	263,538

250,000 ◄- 0.757576 ◄--------- $330,000
250,000 ◄- 0.573921 ◄---------------- $435,600
208,333 ◄- 0.434789 ◄------------------------- $479,160
86,805 ◄- 0.329385 ◄-------------------------------- $263,538
795,138

3. Income tax cash savings from depreciation
   deductions

Year (1)	Depreciation (2)	Tax Cash Savings in Nominal Dollars (3) = 0.40 × (2)
1	$375,000	$150,000
2	187,500	75,000
3	93,750	37,500
4	93,750	37,500

113,636 ◄- 0.757576 ◄---------- 150,000
43,044 ◄- 0.573921 ◄-------------------- 75,000
16,305 ◄- 0.434789 ◄-------------------------- 37,500
12,352 ◄- 0.329385 ◄-------------------------------- 37,500
185,337

Net present value $ 230,475

*The nominal discount rate of 32% is made up of the real rate of interest of 20% and the inflation rate of 10%: [(1 + 0.20)(1 + 0.10)] − 1 = 0.32.
†Present-value discount factors are shown to six decimal digits to emphasize that the approaches to inflation in Exhibits 23–5 and 23–6 are equivalent. The formula on Table 2 of Appendix C is used to compute the present-value discount factor.

EXHIBIT 23-6

Real Approach to Inflation for Network Communications: Predict Cash Inflows and Outflows in Real Dollars and Use a Real Discount Rate

	Total Present Value	Present Value Discount Factors at 20%*	Sketch of Relevant After-Tax Cash Flows
			0 1 2 3 4

End of Year

1. Initial equipment investment

Year	Investment Outflows
0	$(750,000)

$(750,000) ◄- 1.000000 ◄- $(750,000)

2. Recurring after-tax cash-operating flows (excluding depreciation effects)

Year (1)	Recurring Real Cash-Operating Inflows (2)	Income Tax Outflows (3) = 0.40×(2)	Recurring Real After-Tax Cash-Operating Inflows (4) = (2)-(3)
1	$500,000	$200,000	$300,000
2	600,000	240,000	360,000
3	600,000	240,000	360,000
4	300,000	120,000	180,000

250,000 ◄- 0.833333 ◄-------- $300,000
250,000 ◄- 0.694444 ◄-------------- $360,000
208,333 ◄- 0.578704 ◄--------------------- $360,000
86,805 ◄- 0.482253 ◄---------------------------- $180,000
795,138

3. Income tax cash savings from depreciation deductions

Year (1)	Depreciation (2)	Tax Cash in Savings Nominal Dollars (3) = 0.40×(2)	Inflation Factor 10%† (4)	Tax Cash Savings in Real Dollars (5) = (3)×(4)
1	$375,000	$150,000	0.909091	$136,364
2	187,500	75,000	0.826446	61,983
3	93,750	37,500	0.751315	28,174
4	93,750	37,500	0.683013	25,613

113,636 ◄- 0.833333 ◄---------- 136,364
43,044 ◄- 0.694444 ◄----------------- 61,983
16,305 ◄- 0.578704 ◄----------------------- 28,174
12,352 ◄- 0.482253 ◄------------------------------ 25,613
185,337

Net present value $ 230,475

*Present-value factors are shown to six decimal digits and the present-value calculations rounded to emphasize that the approaches to inflation in Exhibits 23-5 and 23-6 are equivalent. The formula on Table 2 of Appendix C is used to compute the present-value discount factor.
†The computation of these inflation factors are explained in footnote 10, p. 838.

Both approaches show that the project has a net present value of $230,475 and should therefore be accepted. Why do the two approaches give the same answer? Because, for example, in going from the real approach to the nominal approach, the cash flows are multiplied by and the discount rates are divided by the same cumulative inflation factor.[10]

The most frequently encountered error when accounting for inflation in capital budgeting is stating cash inflows and outflows in real monetary units and using a nominal discount rate. This error understates the discounted present value of cash flows that occur in the future and therefore creates a bias against the acceptance of many worthwhile capital investment projects.

Inflation and Other Capital-Budgeting Methods

The concepts of the previous section apply equally forcefully to breakeven time and IRR methods. To calculate breakeven time, a company must either use nominal cash flows and a nominal discount rate or real cash flows and a real discount rate. Similarly, IRRs calculated on the basis of nominal cash flows must be compared to nominal required rates of return while IRRs calculated using real cash flows must be compared to real required rates of return. Payback and accrual accounting rate of return are generally computed using nominal dollars without any adjustment for inflation. Inflation effects on cash inflows will have the effect of reducing payback and increasing AARR. Managers using payback and AARR should recognize, however, that the dollars they are getting back have lower value (purchasing power) than the dollars they invested.

PROJECT RISK AND REQUIRED RATE OF RETURN

OBJECTIVE 7

Describe alternative approaches used to recognize the degree of risk in capital-budgeting projects

The *required rate of return* (RRR), which we discussed in Chapter 22, is a critical variable in discounted cash-flow analysis. It is the rate of return that the organization forgoes by investing in a particular project rather than in an alternative project of comparable risk. *Risk* here refers to the business risk of the project, *independent* of the specific manner in which the project is financed—whether with debt or with equity. Here is a safe generalization: The higher the risk, the higher the required rate of return and the faster management would want to recover the net initial investment. Why? Because higher risk means a greater chance that the project may lose money. Management would only be willing to take this added risk if it was compensated with a higher expected return.

The RRR used in discounted cash-flow analysis should be internally consistent with the approach applied to predict cash inflows and outflows. The options include various combinations of (1) the real rate and the nominal rate, and (2) the pretax and the after-tax rate. The differences among these rates can be sizable, given estimates of inflation that may exceed 10% and corporate tax rates of 30% or more.

Organizations typically use at least one of the following approaches in dealing with the risk factor of projects:

1. *Varying the required payback time.* Companies such as Nissan that use payback as a project-selection criterion vary the required payback to reflect differences in project risk. The higher the risk, the shorter the required payback time. When faced with higher risk, companies also evaluate their downside protection if the project is disbanded.[11]

2. *Adjusting the required rate of return.* Companies such as DuPont and Shell Oil use a higher required rate of return when the risk is higher. Estimating a precise risk fac-

---

[10]For example, recurring after-tax *real* cash-operating flow in year 2 of $360,000 in Exhibit 23-6 is multiplied by $(1.10)^2$ to give $435,600 in after-tax *nominal* cash-operating flows in year 2 in Exhibit 23-5. The *real* discount rate of 0.694444 in year 2 in Exhibit 23-6 is divided by $(1.10)^2$ to give the nominal discount rate of 0.573921 in year 2 in Exhibit 23-5.

[11]See J. Grinyer and N. Daing, "The Use of Abandonment Values in Capital Budgeting—A Research Note," *Management Accounting Research*, **4**(1993).

Risk Analysis in Capital Budgeting Decisions at Consumers Power

Consumers Power Co. (CP) owns pipelines to distribute natural gas to its customers. About 1,000 miles of the 20,000 miles of Consumers Power's main pipelines are made of cast iron. Most of CP's pipelines are made of cathodically protected coated and wrapped steel or of plastic. Gas leaks from cast-iron pipes are almost 10 times more than the other materials. An important capital budgeting decision for CP is how much of the cast-iron pipes it should replace and when. The benefits of replacing the pipes are lower repairs and maintenance costs and fewer claims following gas leaks, but the precise benefits are far from certain.

To incorporate uncertainty, Consumers Power estimates a range of values for key parameters—the number of times the pipeline might leak, the quantity of gas that may leak, the dollar claims that may have to be paid, and repairs and maintenance costs that may be incurred—under each replacement alternative. CP uses sensitivity analysis to identify the parameters and parameter values that most affect the decision and those that do not. It then develops probability distributions for the key parameters on the basis of structured interviews with experts in different subject areas. CP calculates net present values for the different alternatives by discounting the expected returns by a risk-adjusted required rate of return. CP computes net present values on an after-tax basis, using nominal cash flows and nominal discount rates to consistently consider the effects of inflation.

CP's analysis indicated that the optimal program was to replace the worst cast-iron pipes first and all cast-iron pipes over a 40-year period. In the absence of this detailed and thorough risk-based analysis, CP's managers would have favored replacing the cast-iron pipes sooner.

Source: Adapted from K. L. Elenbars and D. O'Neill, "Formal Decision Analysis Process Guides Maintenance Budgeting," *Pipeline Industry,* October 1994.

---

tor for each project is difficult. Some organizations simplify the task by having three or four general-risk categories (for example, very high, high, average, and low). Each project under consideration is assigned to a specific category. Management uses a predetermined discount rate, assigned to each category, as the required rate of return for projects in that category.

3. *Adjusting the estimated future cash inflows.* Some companies such as Dow Chemicals reduce the estimated future cash inflows of riskier projects. For example, they may systematically reduce the predicted cash inflows of very-high-risk projects by 30%, high-risk projects by 20%, and average-risk projects by 10%, and make no change to the projected cash inflows of low-risk projects. This approach is called the certainty equivalent approach. Since the cash flows for higher-risk projects have already been adjusted downward for their increased riskiness, the RRR used to evaluate those projects is the same as the RRR for low-risk projects. Note how this approach contrasts to adjusting the required rate of return. In that approach, the cash flows are not adjusted for risk, but the RRR is. In the certainty equivalent approach, the cash flows are adjusted for risk, but the RRR is not. Both adjusting the cash flows for risk and then using risk-adjusted RRRs would double-count the risk adjustment.

4. *Sensitivity (what-if?) analysis.* Companies such as the Consumers Power Company use this approach to examine the consequences of changing key assumptions underlying a capital-budgeting project.

5. *Estimating the probability distribution of future cash inflows and outflows for each project.* Companies such as Niagara Mohawk use the approach to uncertainty that was discussed in the Appendix to Chapter 3. The approach gives due weight to all possible cash flow outcomes to arrive at an expected cash flow and then discounts this amount at the risk-adjusted required rate of return for the investment. Estimating these probability distributions is difficult, but a practical guideline is to limit the number of outcomes under consideration to a small manageable set. Consider another benefit of estimating the probability distribution of future cash inflows and outflows. Suppose a project has a 60% likelihood of very high cash inflows and a 40% likelihood of minimal cash inflows in its early years. This 40% probability may prompt managers to establish lines of credit with a bank. If the low outcome occurs, these lines of credit would enable the company to avoid a short-run cash flow crisis.

APPLICABILITY TO NONPROFIT ORGANIZATIONS

Discounted cash flow analysis applies to both profit-seeking and nonprofit organizations. Almost all organizations must decide which investments in long-term assets will accomplish various tasks at the least cost. For example, U.S. federal agencies use a 7% required rate of return in capital budgeting for water projects (dams, irrigation, and so on) and 10% for all other projects.

Studies of the capital-budgeting practices of government agencies at various levels (federal, state, and local) and in several countries report that, as in the private sector, the following prevails:

1. Urgency is an important factor when allocating funds. For example, capital budgeting for roads is often motivated by physical deficiencies in an existing highway rather than a systematic analysis of alternative road construction projects.

2. Project estimates are sometimes systematically biased. For example, studies of irrigation projects by the U.S. Bureau of Reclamation report overestimates of the benefits, underestimates of the costs, and underestimates of the time it takes to construct dams and other irrigation infrastructures.

3. There is a tendency to cut capital-budget projects first when there is a strong push to balance a budget or reduce a deficit. Consider the effect of efforts to contain health-care costs in the United States. For example, Medicare, a government-run program that finances hospital care for the elderly, no longer fully reimburses hospitals for certain capital equipment expenditures.[12] As a result of these changes and the increased emphasis on controlling hospital charges through competition and regulation, hospitals are increasingly using analytical capital-budgeting methods (such as discounted cash-flow methods) and are also more carefully auditing the benefits of capital expenditures.

IMPLEMENTING THE NET PRESENT-VALUE DECISION RULE

OBJECTIVE 8

Explain the excess present-value index and its usefulness in capital budgeting

Executives in both profit-seeking and nonprofit organizations must frequently work within an overall capital-budget limit. This section discusses problems in using the net present-value method when there is a restriction on the total funds available for capital spending.

The **excess present-value index** (sometimes called the *profitability index*) is the total present value of future net cash inflows of a project divided by the total present value of the net initial investment. The following table illustrates this index for two software graphics packages—Superdraw and Masterdraw—that Business Systems is evaluating:

[12]S. Finkler, "Analytical Capital Budgeting," *Hospital Cost Management and Accounting* (March 1992).

Risk Adjustment Methods in Capital Budgeting

How do companies around the globe adjust for risk when evaluating capital investments? The percentages in the following table indicate how frequently particular risk adjustment methods are used in capital budgeting in four countries. The reported percentages exceed 100% because some companies use more than one risk adjustment method. Dashes indicate information was not disclosed in survey.

	United States*	Australia[†]	Canada[‡]	United Kingdom[§]	Taiwan[#]	Poland**
Sensitivity analysis	29%	57%	59%	63%	—	10%
Increase the required rate of return	18%	—	31%	42%	61%	13%
Shorten payback period	17%	—	24%	34%	72%	25%
Estimate probability distribution of future cash flows	12%	11%	18%	15%	—	13%
Compare optimistic and pessimistic forecasts	—	63%	—	—	—	—
Make subjective, nonquantitative assessment	54%	37%	29%	22%	69%	4%
Make no adjustments	37%	—	10%	—	—	—

The surveys indicate that the specific methods managers use vary among countries. A common feature, however, is that managers appear to favor simpler methods (for example, sensitivity analysis, shortening the payback period, increasing the required rate of return, and subjective, nonquantitative assessments) rather than more sophisticated techniques (for example, estimating the probability distribution of future cash flows).

*Adapted from Sullivan and Smith, "Capital Investment Justification."
[†]Freeman and Hobbes, "Capital Budgeting."
[‡]Jog and Srivastava, "Corporate Financial."
[§]Ho and Pike, "Risk Analysis."
[#]Ho and Yang, "Managerial Risk Taking."
**D. Zarzecki and T. Wisniewski, "Investment Appraisal." Full citations are in Appendix A.

Project	Present Value at 10% RRR (1)	Net Initial Investment (2)	Excess Present-Value Index (3) = (1) ÷ (2)	Net Present Value (4) = (1) - (2)
Superdraw	$1,400,000	$1,000,000	140%	$400,000
Masterdraw	3,900,000	3,000,000	130%	900,000

The excess present-value index or profitability index measures the cash-flow return per dollar invested. The index is particularly helpful in choosing among projects when investment funds are limited. Why? Because profitability indexes can identify the projects that will generate the most money from the limited capital available.

Suppose that the developers of each package require that Business Systems market only one software graphics package, so accepting one software package automatically means rejecting the other—that is, the packages are mutually exclusive. Which package should Business Systems choose?

Using the profitability index, Superdraw will be preferred over Masterdraw because it has a profitability index of 140%, which is higher than the 130% for

Masterdraw. But the profitability index analysis assumes that all other things, such as risk and alternative use of funds, are equal. For example, it assumes that choosing between Superdraw and Masterdraw has no effect on the other projects that Business Systems plans to implement. If "all other things" are not equal, which is often the case, the profitability index may not result in the optimal choice of investment projects.

Continuing the Business Systems example, assume that Business Systems has a total capital-budget limit of $5,000,000 for the coming year. It is considering investing in Superdraw or Masterdraw and in any one or more of eight other projects (coded B, C, . . . , H, I). Exhibit 23-7 presents two alternative combinations of these projects. Note that the project portfolio in alternative 2 is superior to alternative 1, despite the greater cash flow return per dollar invested in Superdraw compared with Masterdraw. Why? Because the $2,000,000 incremental investment in Masterdraw increases net present value (NPV) by $500,000. The $2,000,000 would otherwise be invested in projects E and B, which have a lower combined NPV of $256,000:

	Present Value	Net Initial Investment	Increase in Net Present Value
Masterdraw	$3,900,000	$3,000,000	
Superdraw	1,400,000	1,000,000	
Increment	$2,500,000	$2,000,000	$500,000
Project E	$ 912,000	$ 800,000	
Project B	1,344,000	1,200,000	
Total	$2,256,000	$2,000,000	$256,000

Note that other than Superdraw, alternative 2 includes projects with the highest excess present-value indexes and excludes those with the lowest excess present-value indexes. The excess present-value index is a useful guide for identifying and choosing projects that will offer the best return on limited capital and that will thereby maximize net present value. But managers cannot base decisions involving mutually exclusive investments of different sizes solely on the excess present-value index. The net present-value method is the best general guide.

EXHIBIT 23-7
Allocation of $5,000,000 Capital Budget: Comparison of Two Alternatives for Business Systems

Alternative 1				Alternative 2			
Project	Net Initial Investment	Excess Present-Value Index	Total Present Value at 10%	Project	Net Initial Investment	Excess Present-Value Index	Total Present Value at 10%
C	$ 600,000	167%	$1,002,000	C	$ 600,000	167%	$1,002,000
Superdraw	1,000,000	140%	1,400,000				
D	400,000	132%	528,000	D	400,000	132%	528,000
				Masterdraw	3,000,000	130%	3,900,000
F	1,000,000	115%	1,150,000	F	1,000,000	115%	1,150,000
					$5,000,000*		$6,580,000‡
E	800,000	114%	912,000	E	$ 800,000	114%	Reject
B	1,200,000	112%	1,344,000	B	1,200,000	112%	Reject
	$5,000,000*		$6,336,000†				
H	$ 550,000	105%	Reject	H	550,000	105%	Reject
G	450,000	101%	Reject	G	450,000	101%	Reject
I	1,000,000	90%	Reject	I	1,000,000	90%	Reject

*Total budget constraint.
†Net present value = $6,336,000 − $5,000,000 = $1,336,000.
‡Net present value = $6,580,000 − 5,000,000 = $1,580,000.

IMPLEMENTING THE INTERNAL RATE-OF-RETURN DECISION RULE

The NPV method always indicates the project (or set of projects) that maximizes the NPV of future cash flows. However, surveys of practice report widespread use of the internal rate-of-return (IRR) method. Why? Probably because managers find this method easier to understand and because, in most instances, their decisions would be unaffected by using one method or the other. In some cases, however, the two methods will not indicate the same decision.

Where mutually exclusive projects have unequal lives or unequal investments, the IRR method can rank projects differently from the NPV method. Consider Exhibit 23-8.[13] The ranking by the IRR method favors project X, while the ranking by the NPV method favors project Z. The projects ranked in Exhibit 23-8 differ in both life (5, 10, and 15 years) and net initial investment ($286,400, $419,200, and $509,200).

Managers using the IRR method implicitly assume that the reinvestment rate is equal to the indicated rate of return for the shortest-lived project. Managers using the NPV method implicitly assume that the funds obtainable from competing projects can be reinvested at the company's required rate of return. The NPV method is generally regarded as conceptually superior. Students should refer to corporate finance texts for more details on these issues, and on the problems of ranking projects with unequal lives or unequal investments.

[13]Exhibit 23-8 concentrates on differences in project lives. Similar conflicting results can occur when the terminal dates are the same but the sizes of the net initial investments differ.

EXHIBIT 23-8
Ranking of Projects Using Internal Rate of Return and Net Present Value

Project	Life	Net Initial Investment	Annual Cash Flow from Operations, Net of Income Taxes	IRR Method		PV of Annual Cash Flow from Operations, Net of Income Taxes	NPV Method	
				IRR	Ranking		NPV	Ranking
X	5	$286,400	$100,000	22%	1	$379,100	$ 92,700	3
Y	10	419,200	100,000	20	2	614,500	195,300	2
Z	15	509,200	100,000	18	3	760,600	251,400	1

PROBLEM FOR SELF-STUDY

This is a comprehensive review problem. It illustrates both income tax factors and capital budgeting with inflation.

PROBLEM

Stone Aggregates (SA) operates 92 plants producing a crushed stone that is used in many construction projects. Transportation is a major cost item. A scale clerk weighs the products and on a delivery ticket, records details of the product shipped: its weight, its freight charges, and whether or not it is taxed.

SA is considering a proposal to use computerized delivery ticket-writing equipment at each of its 92 plants. One plant has used the equipment as a pilot site for the past 12 months, generating cash-operating cost savings (before taxes) of $300,000 by improving productivity, and by reducing plant operating costs and excess shipments to customers. The cost analyst estimates that if the equipment had been in use at all of the company's plants for the past year, net cost savings would have been $25 million (expressed in today's dollars).

The cost of the equipment for all 92 plants is $45 million, which would be payable immediately. This equipment has an expected useful life of 4 years and a terminal disposal price of $10 million (expressed in today's dollars). Income tax laws applying to SA are as follows:

◆ *Amount allowable for depreciation.* The original cost of the equipment is the basis for depreciation computations. The predicted terminal disposal price is to be disregarded when computing depreciation. Any gain on disposal (in nominal dollars) will be taxed at the ordinary income tax rate in the year that disposal is made.

◆ *Time period over which the asset is to be depreciated.* Under a tax law designed to encourage investment, SA can use a 3-year write-off period for the equipment.

◆ *Pattern of allowable depreciation.* Straight-line depreciation is required. Given an original cost of $45 million and a 3-year write-off period, annual depreciation is $15 million.

Stone Aggregates expects a 30% income tax rate in each of the next 4 years.

REQUIRED

1. Does the proposal for the computerized delivery ticket-writing equipment meet SA's 16% after-tax required rate-of-return criterion? This rate of return includes an 8% inflation component. (The real rate of return is 7.4%; recall that nominal rate of return = $[(1 + 0.074)(1 + 0.08)] - 1 = 0.16$.) This 8% inflation prediction applies to both the cost savings and the terminal disposal price of the equipment. Compute the NPV using nominal dollars and a nominal required rate of return.

2. What other factors would you recommend that SA consider when evaluating the computerized delivery ticket-writing equipment?

SOLUTION

1. Exhibit 23-9 shows the NPV computations. To illustrate an alternative presentation found in practice, the format of Exhibit 23-9 differs from that of Exhibits 23-2, 23-3, and 23-4. The proposal for computerized delivery ticket-writing equipment has an NPV of $29.086 million, indicating that—on the basis of financial factors—it is an attractive investment. Note especially how the tax law enables SA to fully depreciate the equipment by the end of the third year. No depreciation occurs in year 4.

2. The analysis in Exhibit 23-9 assumes that net cash savings are $25 million each year. However, operating and implementation costs in the year of changeover to the computerized equipment are often 200% higher than in subsequent years. Consequently, net cash savings may be lower in the first year.

This problem is based on Vulcan Materials' adoption of computerized delivery ticket-writing equipment.[14] Vulcan reported the following benefits that SA should also consider:

◆ "Scale clerks have benefited through job enrichment and a much more predictable work load."

◆ "Communication between the scale-house microcomputers and the division office computers has reduced errors contained in the transaction data and reduced costs associated with making corrections. The system has also accelerated the issuance of Vulcan's invoices."

◆ "Faster flow of data has narrowed the time lag in detecting and correcting problems."

[14]J. Bush and R. Stewart, "Vulcan Materials Automates Delivery Ticket Writing," *Management Accounting* (August 1985).

EXHIBIT 23-9
Net Present-Value Analysis of Computerized Ticket-Writing System for Stone Aggregates (in millions; n.d. = nominal dollars)

	Total Present Value	End of Year 1	End of Year 2	End of Year 3	End of Year 4
Recurring After-Tax Cash-Operating Flows (Excluding Depreciation Effects)					
1. Recurring cash-operating savings (real dollars)	—	$25.000	$25.000	$25.000	$25.000
2. Cumulative inflation factor (from Table 1, Appendix C for 8%)	—	1.080	1.166	1.260	1.360
3. Cash-operating savings (n.d.): 1 × 2	—	$27.000	$29.150	$31.500	$34.000
4. Tax payments: 30% × 3	—	$8.100	$8.745	$9.450	$10.200
5. Recurring after-tax cash operating savings (n.d.): 3 − 4	—	$18.900	$20.405	$22.050	$23.800
6. Present-value discount factor (16% nominal)	—	0.862	0.743	0.641	0.552
7. PV of recurring after-tax cash-operating savings (n.d.): 5 × 6	$58.725	$16.292	$15.161	$14.134	$13.138
Income Tax Cash Savings from Depreciation Deductions					
8. Depreciation deductions	—	$15.000	$15.000	$15.000	—
9. Income tax cash savings from depreciation deductions: 30% × 8	—	$4.500	$4.500	$4.500	—
10. Present-value discount factor (16% nominal)	—	0.862	0.743	0.641	—
11. PV of income tax cash savings from depreciation deductions: 9 × 10	$10.106	$3.879	$3.343	$2.884	—
After-Tax Cash Flow from Terminal Disposal of Equipment					
12. Terminal disposal price of equipment at end of year 4 (n.d.)*	—	—	—	—	$13.600
13. Income tax on gain on disposal: 30% × 13.600[†]	—	—	—	—	$4.080
14. After-tax cash flow from terminal disposal of equipment	—	—	—	—	$9.520
15. Present-value discount factor (16%)	—	—	—	—	0.552
16. PV of after-tax cash flow from terminal disposal of equipment	$5.255	—	—	—	$5.255
PV of total cash inflows: 7 + 11 + 16	$74.086	$20.171	$18.504	$17.018	$18.393
Initial Equipment Investment					
PV of initial equipment investment	$(45.000)				
Net Present Value	$29.086				

*Terminal disposal price of $10 million in year 0 dollars will be $13.600 ($10 × 1.360) million in year 4 nominal dollars, from Table 1, Appendix C for 8%.

[†]Gain on disposal = Terminal disposal price of equipment at end of year 4 − Book value of equipment at end of year 4 = $13.600 − $0 = $13.600 million.

SUMMARY

The following points are linked to the chapter's learning objectives.

1. Three factors influence the amount of depreciation claimed as a tax deduction: (a) the amount allowable for depreciation, (b) the time period over which the asset is to be depreciated, and (c) the pattern of allowable depreciation.

2. Depreciation is a noncash cost. But depreciation is a deductible cost for calculating tax outflows. The taxes saved as a result of depreciation deductions increase cash flows in discounted cash-flow (DCF) computations.

3. The total project approach calculates the present value of all cash inflows and outflows under each alternative. The differential approach includes only those cash inflows and outflows that differ between or among the alternatives.

4. Five categories of cash flows considered in capital-budgeting analyses involving a machine are (a) initial machine investment, (b) after-tax cash flow from the current disposal of the old machine, (c) recurring after-tax cash-operating flows, (d) income tax cash savings from depreciation deductions, and (e) after-tax cash flow from the terminal disposal of the machine.

5. The real rate of return is the rate of return required to cover only investment risk. The nominal rate of return is the rate of return required to cover investment risk and the anticipated decline, due to inflation, in the general purchasing power of the cash that the investment generates.

6. Two internally consistent ways to account for inflation in capital budgeting are (a) to predict cash inflows and outflows in nominal terms and to use a nominal discount rate, and (b) to predict cash inflows and outflows in real terms and to use a real discount rate. The nominal and real approaches are equivalent: Both yield the same net present value, but many managers find the nominal approach easier to work with.

7. The higher the risk, the higher the required rate of return on an investment. Alternative approaches to recognizing project risk in capital-budgeting decisions are (a) reducing the required payback time, (b) increasing the required rate of return, (c) reducing estimated future cash inflows, (d) performing sensitivity analysis, and (e) estimating the probability distribution of future cash inflows and outflows.

8. The excess present-value index (profitability index) is the total present value of future net cash inflows of a project divided by the total present value of the net initial investment. It is a useful guide when allocating limited funds among projects, but it cannot be used as the sole criterion.

9. The net present-value and internal rate-of-return methods make different assumptions about the rate at which project cash inflows are reinvested. Consequently, the two methods may rank projects differently.

APPENDIX: MODIFIED ACCELERATED COST RECOVERY SYSTEM

The tax laws governing depreciation in the United States at the time of this writing are collectively called the Modified Accelerated Cost Recovery System (MACRS). MACRS is a modification of the tax laws first introduced in 1981, termed the Accelerated Cost Recovery System (ACRS). For most depreciable assets placed in service in the 1981–1986 period, the ACRS system applies. Assets acquired since 1987 are subject to MACRS. Both ACRS and MACRS have more accelerated depreciation schedules than existed with the prior tax laws. Some highlights of the current version of MACRS follow.

Amount Allowable for Depreciation

In general, the amount allowable for depreciation is the original cost of the asset. MACRS assumes that future disposal prices are zero. MACRS uses the phrase "cost recovery" to describe the amount allowable each year as a depreciation deduction.

For proceeds on disposal of an asset up to the original cost of the asset, the difference between the proceeds and the asset's book value is taxed at the same rate as ordinary income or loss (35% at the time of this writing). Proceeds greater than the original asset cost are taxed at special capital gains tax rates (28%).

Time Period over Which the Asset Is to Be Depreciated

The time period is specified in a "table of allowable lives" (termed *recovery periods*). Eight different recovery periods are possible: 3, 5, 7, 10, 15, 20, 27.5, and 31.5 years.

MACRS specifies the recovery periods for different assets. Exhibit 23-10 cites examples of assets in the 3-, 5-, 7-, and 10-year classes. These recovery periods do *not* necessarily reflect the estimated useful life of the assets included in each category.

Pattern of Allowable Depreciation (for a Given Time Period)

The depreciation method specified is a function of the recovery period. The eight different recovery periods and their depreciation methods are as follows:

Recovery Period	Depreciation Method
3, 5, 7, 10 years	Double-declining balance (also called 200% declining balance), or straight-line
15, 20 years	150% declining balance, or straight-line
27.5, 31.5 years	Straight-line

The MACRS depreciation rates for 3-, 5-, 7-, and 10-year recovery classes are described in Exhibit 23-10. The rates are based on the double-declining balance method with a conversion to straight-line depreciation, when straight-line depreciation results in a larger amount. The depreciation rates in Exhibit 23-10 are calculated assuming a *half-year convention* and a zero disposal price. The half-year convention computes depreciation for the first year *assuming* the asset was placed in service at the midpoint of the tax year, regardless of whether the asset was placed in service at the beginning, middle, or end of the year.

To see the calculations underlying Exhibit 23-10, consider a 3-year recovery-period asset with an original cost of $100. The following table describes depreciation under MACRS at a 200% double-declining balance rate of 66.66% (twice the straight-line depreciation rate of 33.33%) using the half-year convention.

EXHIBIT 23-10
Modified Accelerated Cost Recovery System Rates for Tangible Personal Property (Using Half-Year Convention)

	Recovery Classes			
Recovery Year	3-Year Tractors, Special Tools	5-Year Automobiles, Trucks, Computers	7-Year Most Machinery, Office Furniture, Fixtures, and Equipment	10-Year Ships, Petroleum and Food Processing Equipment
	200% Declining Balance	200% Declining Balance	200% Declining Balance	200% Declining Balance
1	33.33%	20.00%	14.29%	10.00%
2	44.45	32.00	24.49	18.00
3	14.81	19.20	17.49	14.40
4	7.41	11.52	12.49	11.52
5	—	11.52	8.93	9.22
6	—	5.76	8.92	7.37
7	—	—	8.93	6.55
8	—	—	4.46	6.55
9	—	—	—	6.56
10	—	—	—	6.55
11	—	—	—	3.28
	100.00%	100.00%	100.00%	100.00%

Year	Book Value at Beginning of Year (1)	Depreciation (2)	Book Value at End of Year (3) = (1) - (2)
1	$100.00	$\frac{1}{2}(66.66\% \times \$100) = \$33.33$	$66.67
2	66.67	$66.66\% \times \$66.67 = \$44.45$	22.22
3	22.22	$66.66\% \times \$22.22 = \$14.81$	7.41
4	7.41	$7.41	0

Under the half-year convention, only half of the first year depreciation of $66.66 (66.66% × $100) can be claimed as depreciation in year 1. Because of the half-year convention, depreciation on a 3-year recovery asset is actually spread over 4 years. The numbers in column (2) of the preceding table equal the depreciation rates described for 3-year assets in Exhibit 23-10.

MACRS offers companies the option of using straight-line depreciation instead of declining-balance depreciation for assets in the 3-, 5-, 7-, 10-, 15- or 20-year recovery-period class. This option is attractive for companies expecting to suffer tax losses in the early years of an asset's life.[15] The benefit of the straight-line option is that it defers more of the depreciation tax deductions to years in which the company expects to have taxable income.

[15] Loss carryforward provisions of the U.S. tax code restrict the number of years over which tax losses in a particular year can be used to offset taxable income in future years. The tax benefit of depreciation deductions can be lost if a company fails to earn sufficient income during the periods over which depreciation deductions can be carried forward.

▼ TERMS TO LEARN

This chapter and the Glossary at the end of this book contain definitions of the following important terms:

accelerated depreciation (p. 823)
differential approach (826)
double-declining balance (DDB) depreciation (823)
excess present-value index (840)
inflation (833)
investment tax credit (ITC) (822)

Modified Accelerated Cost Recovery System (MACRS) (833)
nominal rate of return (834)
real rate of return (834)
straight-line depreciation (SL) (823)
total project approach (826)

▼ ASSIGNMENT MATERIAL

QUESTIONS

23-1 Describe three factors that influence the amount claimed as a depreciation deduction for tax purposes.

23-2 "It doesn't matter what depreciation method is used. The total dollar tax bills are the same." Do you agree? Explain.

23-3 Give examples of four categories of cash flows considered in capital-budgeting analyses.

23-4 Distinguish between the total project approach and the differential approach to choosing between two capital-budgeting projects.

23-5 "Depreciation is an irrelevant factor in deciding whether to replace an existing delivery vehicle with a more energy-efficient vehicle." Do you agree? Explain.

23-6 "Income taxes only play a role in capital budgeting because of depreciation tax savings." Do you agree? Explain.

23-7 What are the main depreciation methods permitted under the Modified Accelerated Cost Recovery System (MACRS)?

23-8 Distinguish between the *nominal* rate of return and the *real* rate of return.

23-9 What are the two internally consistent approaches to incorporating inflation into DCF analysis?

23-10 What adjustments are needed for depreciation when using the real approach? Why are these adjustments necessary?

23-11 What approaches might be used to recognize risk in capital budgeting?

23-12 "In practice there is no single rate that a given company can use as a guide for sifting among all projects." Do you agree? Explain.

23-13 "Discounted cash-flow techniques are relevant only to profit-seeking organizations." Do you agree? Explain.

23-14 "The excess present-value index or profitability index is a useful guide when allocating limited funds among projects." Do you agree? Explain.

23-15 "The net present-value method and the internal rate-of-return method always rank different projects identically." Do you agree? Explain.

EXERCISES

23-16 Recapitulation of role of depreciation in Chapters 11, 22, and 23. Antonio Inoki, president of Yokohoma Steel, remarked, "I've read three chapters that have included discussions of depreciation in relation to decisions regarding the replacement of equipment. I'm confused. Chapter 11 said that depreciation on old equipment is irrelevant but that depreciation on new equipment is relevant. Chapter 22 said that depreciation was irrelevant in relation to discounted cash-flow models, but Chapter 23 indicated that depreciation was indeed relevant."

REQUIRED

Prepare a clear explanation for the president that would minimize his confusion.

23-17 New equipment purchase, taxation, straight-line, and DDB depreciation. Presentation Graphics prepares slides and other aids for individuals making presentations. It estimates it can save $35,000 a year in cash-operating costs for the next 5 years if it buys a special-purpose color-slide workstation at a cost of $75,000. The workstation will have a zero terminal disposal price at the end of year 5. Presentation Graphics has a 12% after-tax required rate of return. Its income tax rate is 40% each year for the next 5 years.

REQUIRED

1. Assume that Presentation Graphics uses straight-line depreciation on its tax return. Compute (a) net present value, (b) payback period, and (c) internal rate of return.
2. Assume that Presentation Graphics uses the double-declining balance method on its tax return with depreciation for the fifth year being the book value at the start of the fifth year. Compute (a) net present value, (b) payback period, and (c) internal rate of return.

23-18 Multiple choice, including straight-line depreciation. (CPA, adapted) The Apex Company is evaluating a capital-budgeting proposal for the current year. The relevant data are as follows:

Year	Present Value of an Annuity of $1 in Arrears at 15%
1	$0.870
2	1.626
3	2.284
4	2.856
5	3.353
6	3.785

The initial equipment investment would be $30,000. Apex would depreciate the equipment for tax purposes on a straight-line basis over 6 years with a zero terminal disposal price. The before-tax annual cash inflow arising from this investment is $10,000. The income tax rate is 40%, and income tax is paid the same year as incurred. The after-tax required rate of return is 15%. Choose the best answer for each question and show your computations.

1. What is the after-tax accrual accounting rate of return on Apex's initial equipment investment?
   (a) 10%, (b) 16⅔%, (c) 26⅔%, (d) 33⅓%.
2. What is the after-tax payback period (in years) for Apex's capital-budgeting proposal?
   (a) 5, (b) 3. 75, (c) 3, (d) 2.
3. What is the net present value of Apex's capital-budgeting proposal?
   (a) $(7,290), (b) $280, (c) $7,850, (d) $11,760.
4. How much would Apex have had to invest 5 years ago at 15% compounded annually to have $30,000 now?
   (a) $12,960, (b) $14,910, (c) $17,160, (d) cannot be determined from the information given.

23-19 Automated materials handling capital project, income taxes, DDB depreciation, sensitivity analysis. Ontime Distributors operates a large distribution network for health-related products. It is considering an automated materials handling (AMH) proposal for its major warehouse to reduce storage space, labor costs, and product damage. The before-tax net cash-operating savings from the automation are estimated to be $2.5 million a year. The AMH equipment will cost $6 million, payable immediately. The equipment has a useful life of 4 years and a zero terminal disposal price. The lease on the warehouse expires in 4 years and is not expected to be renewed. The company has an income tax rate of 40% and an after-tax required rate of return of 12%. Under existing tax laws, the $6 million equipment cost qualifies for use of the double-declining balance depreciation method with a 4-year useful life, with depreciation for the fourth year being the book value of the equipment at the start of the fourth year. The terminal disposal price of the equipment is included as a taxable income item in the year of its disposal.

REQUIRED

1. Compute (a) the net present value, and (b) the payback period on the automated materials handling project.
2. Calculate the minimum annual before-tax net cash-operating savings that will make the AMH equipment desirable from a net present-value standpoint.
3. What other factors should Ontime Distributors consider in its decision?

23-20 Total project versus differential approach, income taxes, straight-line depreciation. A manufacturer of automobile parts acquired a special-purpose shaping machine for automatically producing a particular part. The machine has been used for 1 year. It will have no useful economic life after 3 more years. The machine is being depreciated on a straight-line basis for income tax purposes. It cost $88,000, has a current disposal price of $29,000, and has a terminal disposal price of $6,000. However, a terminal disposal price of zero was assumed in computing straight-line depreciation for tax purposes.

A new machine has become available and is far more efficient than the present machine. It would cost $63,000, would cut annual cash-operating costs from $60,000 to $40,000, and would have zero terminal disposal price at the end of its useful life of 3 years. Straight-line depreciation would be used for tax purposes. The applicable income tax rate is 30%. The after-tax required rate of return is 14%.

REQUIRED

Using the net present-value method, show whether the new machine should be purchased (a) under a total project approach, and (b) under a differential approach.

23-21 Selling plant, income taxes, straight-line depreciation. (CMA, adapted) Waterford Specialties Corporation, a clothing manufacturer, has a plant that will become idle on December 31, 1995. John Landry, corporate controller, has been asked to look at three options regarding the disposition of the plant.

Option 1: The plant, which has been fully depreciated for financial reporting and tax purposes, can be sold immediately for $9 million.

Option 2: The plant can be leased to Auburn Mills, one of Waterford's suppliers for 4 years. Under the terms of the lease, Auburn would pay Waterford $200,000 per month in rent and would grant Waterford a special 10% discount off the normal price of $2 per yard on 2.37 million yards of fabric purchased by another Waterford plant. Auburn would cover all of the plant's ownership costs including property taxes. Waterford expects to sell this plant for $2 million at the end of the 4-year lease.

Option 3: The plant could be used for 4 years to make souvenir jackets for the 2000 Olympics. Fixed overhead, before any equipment upgrades, is estimated to be $200,000 annually for the 4-year period. The jackets are expected to sell for $42 each. Unit variable costs are expected to be as follows: direct materials, $20.80; direct manufacturing, marketing, and distribution labor, $6.40; variable manufacturing, marketing, and distribution overhead, $5.80.

   The following production and sales of jackets are expected: 1996, 200,000 units; 1997, 300,000 units; 1998, 400,000 units; 1999, 100,000 units. In order to manufacture the souvenir jackets, some of the plant equipment would have to be upgraded at an immediate cost of $1.5 million to be depreciated using straight-line depreciation over the 4 years it will be in use. Because of the modernization of the equipment, Waterford could sell the plant for $3 million at the end of 4 years.

   Waterford treats all cash flows as if they occur at the end of the year, and uses an after-tax cost of capital of 12%. Waterford is subject to a 40% tax rate.

REQUIRED
1. Would you use the total project approach or the differential approach to choose among the three options? Why?
2. Calculate the net present value of each of the options available to Waterford and determine which option Waterford should select using the net present-value criterion.
3. What nonfinancial and qualitative factors should Waterford consider before making its choice?

23-22 Project risk, required rate of return. Esso Petroleum is considering two investment projects. The first project, viewed as a high-risk investment, is drilling equipment for oil exploration activities. Esso expects the drilling equipment to cost $1 million and result in operating cash flows before taxes of $370,000 per year for 5 years. The equipment has a 5-year life, a terminal disposal price of zero, and is to be depreciated on a straight-line basis.

   The second project, viewed as a low-risk investment, is production equipment that will improve the yield in Esso's refinery. Esso expects the production equipment to cost $800,000 and result in operating cash flows before taxes of $300,000 per year for 4 years. The equipment has a 4-year life, a terminal disposal price of zero, and is to be depreciated on a straight-line basis. Esso's income tax rate is 30%.

REQUIRED
1. Which project has the higher net present value if Esso uses an after-tax required rate of return (RRR) of 12% for both projects?
2. A manager at Esso objects to the calculations in requirement 1 arguing that riskier investments should have a higher RRR. Suppose Esso

requires an 18% after-tax RRR for high-risk investments and a 12% after-tax RRR for low-risk investments. Which project has the higher net present value?

3. Which project do you favor? Why?

23-23 Income taxes, MACRS, inflation. James Delusio, plant manager of Peoria Metal Works, is considering an investment in special tools of $200,000 on December 31, 19_5. The tools have an estimated useful life of 4 years and a $20,000 terminal disposal price. The tools are in the 3-year property class under MACRS and will be depreciated as follows: 19_6, 33%; 19_7, 45%; 19_8, 15%, 19_9, 7%. The tools will enable Peoria to manufacture drill bits to very high tolerances without incurring any incremental costs, and to earn additional cash flows of $2 per unit in 19_6, $2.12 in 19_7, $2.25 in 19_8, and $2.38 in 19_9. Peoria expects to sell 35,000 units each year for the next 4 years. Peoria is subject to a 40% tax rate. The after-tax required rate of return is 18%.

REQUIRED

1. Compute the net present value of the project.
2. Delusio feels that inflation will persist for the next 4 years at the rate of 6% per year. However, the 18% minimum desired rate of return already includes a return required to cover the effects of anticipated inflation. Repeat requirement 1, to take inflationary effects into consideration.
3. Could you have taken inflation into account in a way different from what you did in requirement 2? Broadly describe how without actually performing any calculations.

23-24 Inflation and nonprofit institution, no tax aspects. Southern University is considering the purchase of a photocopying machine for $3,500 on December 31, 19_4. It has a useful life of 5 years, has a zero terminal disposal price, and is depreciated on a straight-line basis. The cash-operating savings are expected to be $1,000 annually, measured in December 31, 19_4 dollars. The required rate of return is 18.8%, which includes a return required to cover the effects of anticipated inflation of 10%. The university pays no taxes. The present values of $1 discounted at 18.8% received at the end of 1, 2, 3, 4 and 5 periods are 0.842, 0.709, 0.596, 0.502, and 0.423.

REQUIRED

1. A university official computed the net present value of the project using an 18.8% discount rate without adjusting the cash-operating savings for inflation. What net present-value figure did he compute? Is this approach correct? If not, how would you redo the analysis?
2. (a) What is the real rate of return required by Southern University for investing in the photocopying machine? (b) Calculate the net present value using the real rate of return approach to incorporating inflation.
3. Compare your analyses in requirements 1 and 2. Present generalizations that seem applicable about the analysis of inflation in capital budgeting.

23-25 Excess present-value index. The Bristol Company is a design engineering firm that specializes in designing different types of application-specific chips for the semiconductor industry. It is considering buying new design equipment and has identified two mutually exclusive options, Design Pro and Easychip. It is also considering other capital investments (coded C and D). The following table describes the financial characteristics of these projects.

Project	Present Value of Cash Inflows at 14% Required Rate of Return	Net Initial Investment
Design Pro	$ 750,000	$500,000
Easychip	1,050,000	750,000
Project C	585,000	450,000
Project D	320,000	200,000

1. For each project, calculate (a) the net present value, and (b) the excess present-value index. On the basis of the excess present-value index only, should Bristol choose Design Pro or Easychip?
2. Suppose Bristol must choose one of Design Pro or Easychip, and suppose Bristol has a capital investment budget of $950,000, which projects should Bristol choose?
3. Comment on your answers to requirements 1 and 2.

23-26 Comparison of projects with unequal lives. The manager of the Robin Hood Company is considering two investment projects that are mutually exclusive. The after-tax required rate of return of this company is 10%, and the anticipated cash flows are as follows:

		Cash Inflows			
Project No.	Investment Required Now	Year 1	Year 2	Year 3	Year 4
1	$10,000	$12,000	$0	$0	$ 0
2	10,000	0	0	0	17,500

REQUIRED

1. Compute the internal rate of return of both projects. Which project is preferable?
2. Compute the net present value of both projects. Which project is preferable?
3. Comment briefly on the results in requirements 1 and 2. Be specific in your comparisons.

PROBLEMS

23-27 Equipment replacement, income taxes. (CMA, adapted) VacuTech manufactures testing instruments for microcircuits. These instruments sell for $3,500 each. VacuTech incurs cash-operating costs of $2,450 to manufacture these instruments. On January 1, 19_2, VacuTech bought a vacuum pump for $400,000. VacuTech is considering the purchase of a new, more efficient pump on January 1, 19_6 (4 years later). The new pump costs $620,000. Under the income tax code, the original cost of the pump would be depreciated as follows: 19_6, 33%; 19_7, 45%; 19_8, 15%; 19_9, 7%. The new pump is expected to have a terminal disposal price of $80,000 at the end of 4 years. At current rates of production, the new pump's greater efficiency will result in annual cash savings of $125,000.

The old pump will be fully depreciated by December 31, 19_5, but it can still be used for another 4 years. It has a current disposal price of $50,000. If it is used for another 4 years, the pump's terminal disposal price will be zero.

VacuTech is able to sell all the testing instruments it produces. Because of the increased speed of the new pump, output is expected to increase by 30 units in 19_6, 50 units in 19_7 and 19_8, and 70 units in 19_9. Over and above the annual cash savings at current production levels, VacuTech's cash manufacturing costs will decrease by $150 per unit on all *additional* units produced.

VacuTech is subject to a 40% tax rate. VacuTech's after-tax required rate of return is 16%.

REQUIRED

1. Determine whether VacuTech should purchase the new pump by calculating the net present value at January 1, 19_6, of the estimated after-tax cash flows that would result from the acquisition.

2. Describe the nonfinancial and qualitative factors that VacuTech should consider before making the pump replacement decision.

23-28 Replacement of a machine, income taxes, straight-line depreciation, sensitivity. (CMA, adapted) The WRL Company operates a snack-food center at the Hartsfield Airport. On January 2, 19_3, WRL purchased a special cookie-cutting machine, which has been used for 3 years. WRL is considering purchasing a newer, more efficient machine. If purchased, the new machine would be acquired today on January 2, 19_6. WRL expects to sell 300,000 cookies in each of the next 4 years. The selling price of each cookie is expected to average $0.50.

WRL has two options: (1) continue to operate the old machine, or (2) sell the old machine and purchase the new machine. The seller of the new machine offered no trade-in. The following information has been assembled to help management decide which option is more desirable:

	Old Machine	New Machine
Initial machine investment	$80,000	$120,000
Terminal disposal price at the end of useful life assumed for depreciation purposes	$10,000	$ 20,000
Useful life from date of acquisition	7 years	4 years
Expected annual cash-operating costs		
Variable cost per cookie	$0.20	$0.14
Total fixed costs	$15,000	$ 14,000
Depreciation method used for tax purposes	Straight-line	Straight-line
Estimated disposal prices of machines:		
January 2, 19_6	$40,000	$120,000
December 31, 19_9	$ 7,000	$ 20,000

WRL has a 40% income tax rate. Assume that any gain or loss on the sale of machinery is treated as an ordinary tax item and will affect the taxes paid by WRL in the year in which it occurs. WRL has an after-tax required rate of return of 16%.

REQUIRED

1. Use the net present-value method to determine whether WRL should retain the old machine or acquire the new machine.
2. How much more or less would the recurring after-tax variable cash-operating savings have to be for WRL to exactly earn the 16% after-tax required rate of return? Assume all other data about the investment does not change.
3. Assume that the financial differences between the net present values of the two options are so slight that WRL is indifferent between the two proposals. Identify and discuss the nonfinancial and qualitative factors that WRL should consider.

23-29 Capital budgeting, make versus buy, income taxes, DDB depreciation, relevant costs. (CMA, adapted) The Jonfran Company manufactures three different models of paper shredders. Each has a waste container. Jonfran estimates the following number of waste containers needed over the next 5 years: 19_5, 50,000; 19_6, 50,000; 19_7, 52,000; 19_8, 55,000; 19_9, 55,000.

The equipment used to manufacture waste containers must be replaced because it has broken. The old equipment is fully depreciated and has a current disposal price of $1,500. The new equipment would cost $960,000. The equipment would go into service on January 1, 19_5, and would have a 5-year useful life. Under the prevailing tax laws, depreciation is calculated on the double-declining balance method over the 5 years, with depreciation in the fifth year being the book value of the equipment at the start of that year. The DDB method assumes a zero terminal disposal price at the end of 5 years, but the actual disposal price would be $12,000.

Jonfran's current manufacturing costs for waste containers are as follows:

Direct materials		$10.00
Direct manufacturing labor		8.00
Variable manufacturing overhead		4.00
Fixed manufacturing overhead		
Supervision	$2.00	
Depreciation on old equipment	3.00	
General administrative overhead	6.00	11.00
Total manufacturing cost per unit		$33.00

An outside supplier has offered to supply all the containers that Jonfran needs over the next 5 years at a fixed price of $29 per container. If the supplier's offer is accepted, Jonfran would not need to replace the equipment.

If the waste containers are purchased outside, the salary and benefits of one supervisor, included in the fixed overhead at $45,000, would be eliminated. There would, however, be no change in general administrative overhead. Jonfran has no alternative use for the extra space that would become available if the containers were purchased from outside. Working capital requirements are approximately the same whether the containers are made or purchased.

Jonfran has a 40% income tax rate. Its after-tax required rate of return on new equipment is 12%.

REQUIRED

1. Use a net present-value analysis to determine whether Jonfran should purchase the waste containers from the outside supplier or purchase the new equipment.
2. What nonfinancial and qualitative factors should Jonfran consider before coming to a decision?

23-30 **Capital budgeting, inventory changes.** (M. Wolfson, J. Harris, adapted) Total Fitness is a small company that makes products for physical fitness. The company is considering whether to add a new line of running shoes to be sold to retail stores. To produce these shoes, special machines costing a total of $109,200 must be acquired. The machines have a useful life of 4 years, with a combined terminal disposal price of $18,000. The new line of shoes would be dropped at the end of 4 years. The estimates for the new product line are as follows:

Year	Units Produced	Units Sold	Selling Price	Variable Manufacturing Costs per Unit
1	7,000	6,000	$25	$12
2	6,500	6,200	25	13
3	6,500	7,700	24	14
4	3,000	3,100	22	15
	23,000	23,000		

Variable marketing, distribution, and customer-service costs are estimated at $3 per unit and are not expected to change over the 4-year period. The selling price data and all cost estimates are expressed in nominal dollars. Accounts receivable and current liabilities are expected to be minimal.

For tax purposes, Total Fitness will use straight-line cost recovery (depreciation) on the machines, with a zero terminal disposal price. Manufacturing costs are deductible for tax purposes in the year when the related goods are sold. The company uses the first-in, first-out inventory method for its tax return. Marketing, distribution, and customer-service costs are deductible for tax purposes in the year when they are incurred. Assume a 40% tax rate. Also, assume that all operating cash flows and income tax payments occur at the end of the year. The after-tax nominal required rate of return is 16%.

Absorption costing must be used for tax purposes. Depreciation is allocated on the basis of the estimates of the units produced each year.

REQUIRED

1. Prepare a schedule of relevant cash flows, including income taxes, for each year.
2. Compute the net present value of adding the new line of running shoes.

23-31 Capital budgeting, inflation, taxation, straight-line depreciation. (J. Fellingham, adapted) Abbie Young is manager of the customer-service division of an electrical appliance store. Abbie is considering buying a repairing machine that costs $10,000 on December 31, 19_4. The machine will last 5 years. Abbie estimates that the incremental pretax cash savings from using the machine will be $3,000 annually. The $3,000 is measured at current prices and will be received at the end of each year. For tax purposes, she will depreciate the machine straight-line, assuming zero terminal disposal price. Abbie requires a 10% after-tax real rate of return (that is, the rate of return is 10% when all cash flows are denominated in December 31, 19_4 dollars). Use the 10% after-tax real rate of return when answering all four requirements.

REQUIRED

Treat each of the following cases independently.

1. Abbie lives in a world without income taxes and without inflation. What is the net present value of the machine in this world?
2. Abbie lives in a world without inflation, but there is an income tax rate of 40%. What is the net present value of the machine in this world?
3. There are no income taxes, but the annual inflation rate is 20%. What is the net present value of the machine? The cash savings each year will be increased by a factor equal to the cumulative inflation rate.
4. The annual inflation rate is 20%, and the income tax rate is 40%. What is the net present value of the machine?

23-32 Mining, income taxes, straight-line depreciation, inflation, sensitivity analysis. (CMA, adapted) VanDyk Enterprises has been operating a large gold mine for many years. The company wants to acquire equipment that will allow it to extract gold ore from a currently inaccessible area of this mine. Rich Salzman, VanDyk's controller, has gathered the following data to analyze the investment.

The initial cost of acquiring and installing the equipment is $3 million. The useful life of the specialized equipment is 5 years with no salvage value at the end of this period. VanDyk uses the straight-line depreciation method for this equipment.

Using the equipment, VanDyk estimates that an additional 300 pounds of gold (16 ounces per pound) will be extracted annually for the next 5 years. Salzman plans to use an estimated market price of $350 per ounce of gold in his analysis based on expert information. The price of gold is determined by many factors and represents a significant risk factor in this analysis.

The out-of-pocket variable costs to extract, sort, and pack the gold is $100 per ounce. Allocated fixed overhead costs are $40 per ounce.

Two skilled technicians will be hired to operate the new equipment. The total salary and fringe benefit costs for these two employees will be $110,000 annually over the next 5 years. Periodic maintenance on the equipment is expected to cost $50,000 per year in out-of-pocket costs.

When analyzing projects of this kind, VanDyk uses a 12% after-tax required rate of return and a 40% tax rate.

REQUIRED

1. Determine the payback period.
2. Calculate the after-tax net present value for VanDyk's proposed acquisition of the extraction equipment.
3. Determine the revenue per ounce of gold at which VanDyk's acquisition of the extraction equipment will break even from a net present-value perspective where VanDyk earns the 12% after-tax required rate of return.
4. Salzman feels that inflation will occur and persist for the next 5 years at the rate of 2% per year. Assume all the data given in the problem are already in nominal dollars and that the 12% minimum desired rate of return already includes an element attributable to anticipated inflation. Repeat requirement 2, to take inflationary effects into consideration.

23-33 **Robotics capital project, inflation, income taxes, DDB depreciation.** Rustbelt America, Inc., purchases secondhand pipeline equipment and "rehabilitates" it for resale. Rustbelt has experienced many industrial accidents involving workers at the spot-welding activity and is looking to invest in robots. The investment will cost $10 million payable immediately and will reduce labor costs, worker insurance costs, and materials usage costs by a total of $7 million (in January 1, 19_6 dollars) a year. The robots require an addition to annual cash-operating costs of $3 million (in January 1, 19_6 dollars) a year. Hence the net cash-operating savings from using the robots will be $4 million annually (in January 1, 19_6 dollars). Rustbelt believes that using the robots will eliminate industrial accidents involving workers at the spot-welding activity.

The robots have a 4-year useful life with a terminal disposal price of $1 million (in January 1, 19_6 dollars). The robots qualify for a 4-year recovery period using the double-declining balance depreciation method. Any terminal disposal price of the robots is treated as taxable income in the year of the disposal. Rustbelt anticipates inflation in its operating costs and in the terminal disposal price of the robots of 20% per year. It uses a 10% after-tax required rate of return for investments expressed in real dollars. Rustbelt's income tax rate is 40%.

REQUIRED

1. What is the nominal after-tax required rate of return of Rustbelt America for investments expressed in nominal dollars?
2. What is the net present value of the $10 million investment in robots? Use the approach of predicting cash inflows and outflows in nominal dollars and using a nominal discount rate.
3. What are the advantages of the approach to capital budgeting for inflation in requirement 2 relative to the approach of predicting real cash inflows and outflows and using a real discount rate?
4. What factors other than the net present-value figure in requirement 2 should Rustbelt America consider in deciding whether or not to invest in robots?

23-34 **Ranking projects.** (Adapted from NAA Research Report No. 35, pp. 83–85). Assume that six projects, A–F in the table that follows, have been submitted for inclusion in the coming year's budget for capital expenditures:

Project Cash Flows

	Year	A	B	C	D	E	F
Investment	0	$(100,000)	$(100,000)	$(200,000)	$(200,000)	$(200,000)	$(50,000)
	1	0	20,000	70,000	0	5,000	23,000
	2	10,000	20,000	70,000	0	15,000	20,000
	3	20,000	20,000	70,000	0	30,000	10,000
	4	20,000	20,000	70,000	0	50,000	10,000
	5	20,000	20,000	70,000	0	50,000	
Per year	6–9	20,000	20,000		200,000	50,000	
	10	20,000	20,000			50,000	
Per year	11–15	20,000					
Internal rate of return		14%	?	?	?	12.6%	12.0%

REQUIRED

1. Compute the internal rates of return (to the nearest half percent) for projects B, C, and D. Rank all projects in descending order in terms of the internal rate of return. Show your computations.
2. Based on your answer in requirement 1, state which projects you would select, assuming a 10% required rate of return (a) if $500,000 is the limit to be spent, (b) if $550,000 is the limit, and (c) if $650,000 is the limit.
3. Assuming a 16% required rate of return and using the net present-value method, compute the net present values and rank all the projects. Which project is more desirable, C or D? Compare your answer with your ranking in requirement 1.
4. What factors other than those considered in requirements 1–3 would influence your project rankings? Be specific.

23-35 **Ranking of capital-budgeting projects, alternative selection methods, capital rationing.** (CMA adapted) Brendan Rogers, division president of Wildwood Manufacturing, is preparing the 19_8 capital budget for submission to corporate headquarters at AmiBrands, Inc. AmiBrands has not yet told Rogers what the total amount of funds available for capital projects at Wildwood will be, but the after-tax required rate of return is 12%.

Each project is considered to have the same degree of risk. Projects A and D are mutually exclusive. If project A is chosen, project D cannot be chosen. If project D is chosen, project A cannot be chosen.

When analyzing projects, Wildwood assumes that any budgeted amount not spent on the identified projects will be invested at the after-tax required rate of return, and funds released at the end of a project can be reinvested at the hurdle rate. Further information about each of these projects is presented in the following schedule:

Wildwood Manufacturing Proposed Capital Projects

	Project A	Project B	Project C	Project D	Project E	Project F
Capital investment	$106,000	$200,000	$140,000	$160,000	$144,000	$130,000
Net present value at 12%	$ 69,683	$ 23,773	$ (10,228)	$ 74,374	$ 6,027	$ 69,513
Excess present-value index (profitability index)	1.66	1.12	0.93	1.46	1.04	1.53
Internal rate of return	35%	15%	9%	22%	14%	26%
Payback period	2.2 years	4.5 years	3.9 years	4.3 years	2.9 years	3.3 years
Economic life	6 years	8 years	5 years	8 years	6 years	8 years

1. Assume that Wildwood Manufacturing has no budget restrictions for capital expenditures and wants to maximize its value to AmiBrands. Identify the capital investment projects that Wildwood should include in the capital budget it submits to AmiBrands, Inc. Explain the basis for your selection.

2. Ignore your response to requirement 1. Assume that AmiBrands, Inc., has specified that Wildwood Manufacturing will have a restricted budget for capital expenditures, and that Wildwood should select the projects that maximize the company's value. Identify the capital investment projects Wildwood should include in its capital expenditures budget, and explain the basis for your selections, if the budget is (a) $450,000, and (b) $500,000.

23-36 Ethics, discounted cash-flow analysis, straight-line depreciation. Eric Griffey, manager of the Household Products Division of the Dudley Company is trying to decide whether to launch a new model of food blender, BF97. Griffey is particularly excited about this proposal because it calls for producing the product in the company's old plant at Beaverton, Griffey's home town. During the last recession, Dudley had to shut down this plant and lay off its workers, many of whom had grown up with Griffey and were his friends. Griffey had been very upset when the plant was closed down. If BF97 were produced in the new plant, most of the laid-off workers would be rehired.

Griffey asks Andrew Chen, the management accountant of the Household Products Division to analyze the BF97 proposal. Through the years the company has found that its products have a useful life of 6 years, after which the product is dropped and replaced by another new product. Chen gathers the following data.

a. BF97 will require new special-purpose equipment costing $900,000. The useful life of the equipment is 6 years, with a $140,000 estimated terminal disposal price at that time. However, the income tax authorities will not allow a write-off based on a life shorter than 9 years. Therefore, the new equipment would be written off over 9 years for tax purposes, using the straight-line depreciation method and assuming a zero terminal disposal price.

b. The old plant has a book value of $250,000 and is being depreciated on a straight-line basis at $25,000 annually. The plant is currently being leased to another company. This lease has 6 years remaining at an annual rental of $45,000. The lease contains a cancellation clause whereby the landlord can obtain immediate possession of the premises upon payment of $30,000 cash (fully deductible for income tax purposes).

c. Certain nonrecurring market-research studies and sales-promotion activities will amount to a cost of $300,000 at the end of year 1. The entire amount is deductible in full for income tax purposes in the year of expenditure.

d. Additions to working capital will require $200,000 at the outset and an additional $200,000 at the end of 2 years. This total is fully recoverable at the end of 6 years.

e. Net cash inflow from operations before depreciation and income taxes are expected to be $400,000 in years 1 and 2, $600,000 in years 3–5, and $100,000 in year 6.

The after-tax required rate of return is 12%. The income tax rate is 36%.

REQUIRED

1. Use a net present-value analysis to determine whether Chen should recommend launching BF97.

2. Chen learns that the working capital required will be twice the amounts estimated in d above. All other data remain unchanged. He revises his analysis and presents it to Griffey. Griffey is very unhappy with what he

sees. He tells Chen "Try different assumptions and redo your analysis. I have no doubt that this project should be worth pursuing on financial grounds." Chen is aware of Griffey's interest in supporting his home-town community. There is also the possibility that Griffey may be hired as a consultant by the new plant management after he retires next year. Why is Griffey unhappy with Chen's revised analysis? How should Chen respond to Griffey's suggestions? Identify the specific steps that Chen should take to resolve this situation.

COLLABORATIVE LEARNING PROBLEM

23-37 **Equipment replacement, income taxes, straight-line depreciation, un-equal project lives.** (CMA adapted) Instant Dinners, Inc. (IDI), makes microwaveable frozen foods. The company is considering purchasing an automated materials-movement system (AMMS) for its Western Plant. Bill Rolland, IDI's chief financial officer, has asked Lealand Forrest, assistant controller, to prepare a net present-value analysis for the proposal.

Rolland was instrumental in convincing the board of directors to open the Western Plant. Now, unless significant improvements in cost control and production efficiency are achieved, the Western Plant may be sold. Rolland is anxious to have the Western Plant continue to operate to maintain his credibility with the board and also to help Western's production manager, a long-time friend of Rolland.

The AMMS would replace a number of forklift trucks, eliminate the need for a number of materials handlers, and increase the output capacity of the Western plant.

Rolland has given Forrest the following information regarding the AMMS investment for the net present-value analysis:

Projected useful life	10 years
Purchase/installation	$4,400,000
Increased working capital needed	1,000,000
Increased annual operating costs (excluding depreciation) over current costs	200,000
Reduction in annual manufacturing costs over current costs	400,000
Reduction in annual maintenance costs over current costs	300,000
Increase in cash flow from higher sales revenue	700,000
Estimated disposal price at end of useful life	850,000
Estimated recovery of working capital at end of useful life	1,000,000

IDI uses straight-line depreciation for all its equipment assuming a zero terminal disposal price. The forklift trucks have a net book value of $480,000 with a remaining useful life of 8 years and a zero terminal disposal price. If IDI purchases AMMS now, it can sell the forklift trucks for $100,000. To make the 10-year project life of AMMS comparable to that of the forklift alternative, Forrest estimates that if IDI does not buy the AMMS, the company will lease new forklift trucks for the Western Plant for years 9 and 10 at a cost of $80,000 each year.

IDI has a 40% tax rate and requires a 12% after-tax rate of return on this project. Assume that tax effects and cash flows from equipment acquisition and disposal occur at the time of the transaction and that tax effects and cash flows from operations occur at the end of each year.

Roland was pleased with Forrest's initial analysis. After the initial analysis was completed, Forrest discovered that the estimated terminal disposal price of the AMMS should be $100,000, not $850,000, and that the useful life of the system was expected to be 8 years, not 10 years. Forrest prepared a revised, second analysis based on this new information. On seeing the second analysis, Rolland told Forrest to discard the revised analysis and not to discuss it with anyone at IDI or with the board of directors.

INSTRUCTIONS

Form groups of three students to complete the following requirements.

REQUIRED

1. What is the net present value of the decision to replace forklifts with the AMMS based on the *original estimates* Rolland gave to Forrest?

2. Using net present-value analysis, determine whether IDI should purchase and install the AMMS on the basis of the *revised estimates* that Forrest obtained.

3. Explain how Forrest, a management accountant, should evaluate Rolland's directives to conceal the revised analysis.

4. Identify the specific steps Forrest should take to resolve this situation.

Deer Valley Resort

It seems crazy to think that a company would be happy and proud to say that business has always been downhill. But for guests at the Deer Valley Ski Resort, going downhill is one of the main attractions. Deer Valley is a world-renowned ski resort located in Utah's Wasatch Mountains. **1** Guests are greeted and assisted by attendants immediately upon arrival. **2** They may then enjoy perfectly maintained ski slopes **3** and gourmet food. All in all, this would seem like a fabulous, even luxurious, experience. In 1995, though, Deer Valley undertook a $13 million capital budgeting project to make the experience even better. **4** The project renovated the base lodge, which was enlarged by almost 50,000 square feet.

1

2

3

4

5 A major component of this lodge renovation was the re-modeling and expansion of the resort's restaurants. Services at the resort were also renovated. **6** To attract family skiers, children's areas were expanded. **7** Ski storage and lockers were added at the resort's ski corral. **8** Even the resort's ski lift services were expanded and improved. Why would Deer Valley want to spend so much on improving an already popular resort? As with any capital budgeting project, management felt it was worth the cost. In this case, Deer Valley wanted to maintain and even improve its image as a world-class ski resort. It was management's hope that with every skier coming down their slopes, customer satisfaction, and profits, would keep going up.

DEER VALLEY RESORT
Capital Budgeting and Planning

From the moment you arrive until your departure, you can feel the difference at Deer Valley Resort. Nestled deep in the Wasatch Mountains near Park City, Utah, this world-class ski resort strives for excellence at every turn. Each winter since the resort's opening in 1980, a growing number of skiers have chosen to experience the "Deer Valley Difference"—meticulously groomed slopes, friendly staff, and gourmet cuisine. With owners and managers eager to pamper skiers beyond expectations, a $13 million renovation of the base lodge and facilities was approved for 1995.

The project began in April of 1995 and added close to 50,000 square feet of guest service space. The number of ticket windows doubled to sixteen, child-care space was expanded, and lockers and basket check service were added. The lodge's restaurants were remodeled and expanded, and new retail and ski rental spaces were built. The project was completed in December of 1995, just in time for a full opening to the 1995–96 ski season.

So how did the renovation project come into existence? Deer Valley management follows a structured approach to capital budgeting and planning. First, management maintains a rolling 10-year capital plan. This plan contains the master list of all projects planned for funding in the next 10 years. It is updated each spring, reflecting how well the resort performed during the preceding winter season.

In the identification stage, ideas for capital projects come from each major operating department: ski school,

food and beverage, mountain operations, accounting, and more. Each idea submitted must come with a description of the project, its anticipated benefits, and detailed cost estimates, including bids. During the search stage, proposed ideas are reviewed by the ski area's "Futures Committee," composed of senior management and area owners. Proposals are ranked and prioritized for funding. The final decision on how much to spend and which projects to pursue each year rests with the ski resort's general manager and owners.

The base lodge renovation was assigned a high priority in 1995 because the owners saw the direct and immediate benefit to enhancing Deer Valley's image and reputation through expanded restaurant and ski-lift services, as well as through reduced bottlenecks in guest service areas such as ticket sales and rentals.

For the information-acquisition stage in the capital budgeting process, managers considered which areas to renovate and where to add square footage to the lodge. Although preliminary plans and drawings were used to review the project for funding, management worked with architects to finalize the plans. Quantitative measures—such as return on skier days (increased demand), speed of lift-ticket and ski-school sales, increased child-care revenues, and greater food and beverage sales—were determined. Net present value and payback periods comprised part of the analysis. Qualitative measures—such as increased customer satisfaction and enhanced resort image—were considered as well. Deer Valley regularly ranks at or near the top of ski magazine consumer surveys in these areas. Since the base lodge is such an integral part of each guest's overall impression of their ski experience, the qualitative measures carried significant weight in the final decision to fund the project made in the selection stage of the capital budgeting process.

The financing stage came next. Deer Valley routinely starts and completes its capital projects between April and December of each year, so standing lines of credit at local banks were used for funding. Resort owners expect to pay off the balance owed on the project in 2 years, based on actual and planned increases in lift-ticket and restaurant revenues from additional skier days. With the renovation complete, a post-decision audit as part of the implementation and control stage is underway to evaluate project success and contribution to resort profitability and image. ◆

QUESTIONS

1. What other types of capital budgeting projects would you expect Deer Valley to have in its rolling 10-year plan? If you were making the decision to allocate funds for projects, what factors would you consider in your analysis?
2. What influence might competition and the coming 2002 Winter Olympics—to be held in Park City—have on Deer Valley's capital budgeting and planning?
3. What risks do you expect Deer Valley faced with the base lodge renovation project?
4. Deer Valley Resort is a partnership. How does this form of ownership make a difference in whether to consider the tax implications of a capital budgeting project?
5. Based upon the facts in the case, was the decision to pursue this project a good one? Why or why not?

24

MEASURING INPUT YIELD, MIX, AND PRODUCTIVITY

Ice creams contain multiple material ingredients. Ben & Jerry's Wavy Gravy ice cream, for example, has milk, cream, and different kinds of nuts. Managing the total quantity and mix of ingredients is essential to making high-quality ice cream at a competitive cost. Direct materials yield and mix variances help managers to achieve these goals.

LEARNING OBJECTIVES

After studying this chapter, you should be able to

1. Distinguish between variance analysis procedures where inputs cannot be substituted for one another and those where inputs can be so substituted

2. Understand how direct materials yield and mix variances highlight trade-offs among material inputs

3. Explain direct manufacturing labor yield and mix variances

4. Describe productivity and productivity measures

5. Discuss the benefits and drawbacks of partial productivity measures

6. Describe total factor productivity and its advantages and disadvantages

7. Describe how productivity changes can explain cost changes from one time period to the next

Comparing actual results with budgets can help managers evaluate operations and focus on areas that deserve more attention. Chapters 7 and 8 illustrated various uses of variance information relating to direct materials, direct manufacturing labor, direct marketing labor, manufacturing overhead, and marketing overhead. While Chapters 7 and 8 focused on a single input in each cost category (for example, only one direct material), this chapter considers multiple inputs in each cost category (for example, many types of direct materials). This chapter also develops another topic—productivity measurement. Because each of these topics can be studied independently, the chapter is divided into two parts.

Part One: Input Variances For illustrative purposes, we present yield and mix variances for each of two inputs—direct materials and direct manufacturing labor. These variances can readily be adapted to other inputs such as energy.

Part Two: Productivity Measurement We illustrate partial and total factor productivity measures using two inputs—direct materials and direct manufacturing labor. We also explore productivity's role in explaining the change in actual costs from one time-period to the next.

◆ PART ONE: INPUT VARIANCES

Here we focus on variance analysis for inputs in manufacturing organizations. Manufacturing processes often require that a number of different direct materials and different direct manufacturing labor skills be combined to obtain a unit of finished product. In the case of some materials and labor skills, this combination must be exact. For example, the manager of a Toshiba plant that assembles laptop computers prespecifies the type of chip to be used in each computer. Substituting a 486 chip for a Pentium chip will alter the final product. We refer to these materials as *nonsubstitutable* materials. In the case of other materials, a manufacturer has some leeway in combining the materials. For example, to manufacture fertilizers, Cargill Fertilizers can combine materials (for example, elemental phosphorus and acids) in varying proportions. Elemental phosphorus and acids are *substitutable* materials.

When inputs are substitutable, *mix* refers to the relative proportion or combination of the different inputs used within an input category such as direct materials or direct manufacturing labor to produce a quantity of finished output. *Yield* refers to the quantity of finished output units produced from a budgeted or standard mix of inputs within an input category. Yield and mix variances are useful when examining direct materials and direct-labor inputs. Recall from Chapter 7 that a *variance* is the difference between an actual result and a budgeted amount, when that budgeted amount is a financial variable reported by the accounting system. Budgeted figures discussed in this chapter can be obtained from

◆ Internally generated actual costs from the most recent accounting period, sometimes adjusted for expected improvement.
◆ Internally generated *standard* costs based on best performance standards or *currently attainable standards.*
◆ Externally generated *target cost* numbers based on an analysis of the cost structures of the leading competitors in an industry.

DIRECT MATERIALS YIELD AND MIX VARIANCES

When we initially examined materials and labor variances in Chapter 7, we saw that managers sometimes make trade-offs between price and efficiency variances. For example, an orange-juice bottler may use oranges whose juice content is lower than budgeted if their price is significantly lower than the price of oranges with the budgeted juice content. The yield and mix variances computed in this section provide additional insight into the effect that yield and mix factors have on operating income. Yield and mix variances divide the efficiency variance calculated in Chapter 7; hence, we start by reviewing efficiency and price variances.

Direct Materials Efficiency and Price Variances

Consider a specific example of multiple direct materials inputs and a single product output. The Delpino Corporation makes tomato ketchup. To produce ketchup of the desired consistency, color, and taste, Delpino mixes three types of tomatoes grown in three different regions—Latin American tomatoes (Latoms), California tomatoes (Caltoms), and Florida tomatoes (Flotoms). Delpino's production standards require 1.6 tons of tomatoes to produce 1 ton of ketchup, with 50% of the tomatoes being Latoms, 30% Caltoms, and 20% Flotoms. The direct materials input standards to produce 1 ton of ketchup are

0.80 (50% of 1.6) ton of Latoms at $70 per ton	$ 56.00
0.48 (30% of 1.6) ton of Caltoms at $80 per ton	38.40
0.32 (20% of 1.6) ton of Flotoms at $90 per ton	28.80
Total standard cost of 1.6 tons of tomatoes	$123.20

Budgeted cost per ton of tomatoes is $123.20 ÷ 1.6 tons = $77.

Because Delpino uses fresh tomatoes to make ketchup, no inventories of tomatoes are kept. Purchases are made as needed, so all price variances relate to tomatoes purchased and used. Actual results for June 19_7 show that a total of 6,500 tons of tomatoes were used to produce 4,000 tons of ketchup:

3,250 tons of Latoms at actual cost of $70 per ton	$227,500
2,275 tons of Caltoms at actual cost of $82 per ton	186,550
975 tons of Flotoms at actual cost of $96 per ton	93,600
6,500 tons of tomatoes	507,650
Standard cost of 4,000 tons of ketchup at $123.20 per ton	492,800
Total variance to be explained	$ 14,850 U

Given the standard ratio of 1.6 tons of tomatoes to 1 ton of ketchup, 6,400 tons of tomatoes should be used to produce 4,000 tons of ketchup. At the standard mix, the quantities of each type of tomato required are

Latoms	0.50 × 6,400 = 3,200 tons
Caltoms	0.30 × 6,400 = 1,920 tons
Flotoms	0.20 × 6,400 = 1,280 tons

Exhibit 24-1 presents the familiar approach to analyzing the flexible-budget direct materials variance discussed in Chapter 7. The direct materials price and efficiency variances are calculated separately for each input material and then added together. The variance analysis prompts Delpino to investigate the unfavorable price and efficiency variances—why did they pay more for the tomatoes and use greater quantities than they should have? Were the market prices of tomatoes higher, in general, or could the Purchasing Department have negotiated lower prices? Did the inefficiencies result from inferior tomatoes or from problems in processing?

The analysis in Exhibit 24-1 may suffice when the three direct materials used are not substitutes. Managers control each individual input, and no discretion is permitted regarding the substitution of materials inputs. For example, there is often a specified mix of parts needed for the assembly of cars, radios, and washing machines. A car needs both an engine and a transmission—one cannot be substituted for the other. In these cases, all deviations from the input-output relationships are due to efficient or inefficient usage of individual direct materials. Thus, the price and efficiency variances individually computed for each material typically provide the information necessary for decisions.

EXHIBIT 24-1
Direct Materials Price and Efficiency Variances for the Delpino Corporation for June 19_7

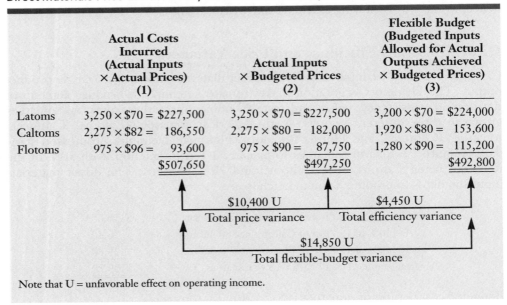

	Actual Costs Incurred (Actual Inputs × Actual Prices) (1)	Actual Inputs × Budgeted Prices (2)	Flexible Budget (Budgeted Inputs Allowed for Actual Outputs Achieved × Budgeted Prices) (3)
Latoms	3,250 × $70 = $227,500	3,250 × $70 = $227,500	3,200 × $70 = $224,000
Caltoms	2,275 × $82 = 186,550	2,275 × $80 = 182,000	1,920 × $80 = 153,600
Flotoms	975 × $96 = 93,600	975 × $90 = 87,750	1,280 × $90 = 115,200
	$507,650	$497,250	$492,800

$10,400 U
Total price variance

$4,450 U
Total efficiency variance

$14,850 U
Total flexible-budget variance

Note that U = unfavorable effect on operating income.

The Role of Direct Materials Yield and Direct Materials Mix Variances

OBJECTIVE 2

Understand how direct materials yield and mix variances highlight trade-offs among material inputs

Managers sometimes do have discretion to substitute one material for another. For example, the manager of Delpino's ketchup plant has some leeway in combining Latoms, Caltoms, and Flotoms without affecting quality. We will assume that to maintain quality, the mix percentages of each type of tomato can only vary up to 5% in the standard mix. For example, the percentage of Caltoms in the mix can vary between 25% and 35% (30% ± 5%). When inputs are substitutable, direct materials efficiency improvement relative to budgeted costs can come from two sources: (1) using less input to achieve a given output, and (2) using a cheaper mix to produce a given output. The direct materials yield and mix variances divide the efficiency variance into two variances: the yield variance focusing on total inputs used and the mix variance focusing on how the inputs are combined.

Given that the budgeted input mix is unchanged, the **total direct materials yield variance** is the difference between two amounts: (1) the budgeted cost of direct materials based on the actual total quantity of all direct materials inputs used, and (2) the flexible-budget cost of direct materials based on the budgeted total quantity of direct materials inputs for the actual output achieved. Given that the actual total quantity of all direct materials inputs used is unchanged, the **total direct materials mix variance** is the difference between two amounts: (1) the budgeted cost for the actual direct materials input mix, and (2) the budgeted cost if the budgeted direct materials input mix had been unchanged. The analysis of the direct materials yield and mix variances is conceptually very similar to the analysis of the sales-quantity and the sales-mix variances described in Chapter 16.

Exhibit 24-2 presents the total direct materials yield and mix variances for the Delpino Corporation. We start with column 3 and work our way to column 1.

Total Direct Materials Yield Variance Compare columns 3 and 2 of Exhibit 24-2. Column 3 calculates the flexible-budget cost based on the budgeted cost of the budgeted total quantity of all inputs used (6,400 tons of tomatoes) for the actual output achieved (4,000 tons of ketchup) times the budgeted input mix (Latoms, 50%; Caltoms, 30%; Flotoms, 20%). Column 2 also calculates costs using the budgeted

EXHIBIT 24-2

Total Direct Materials Yield and Mix Variances for the Delpino Corporation for June 19_7

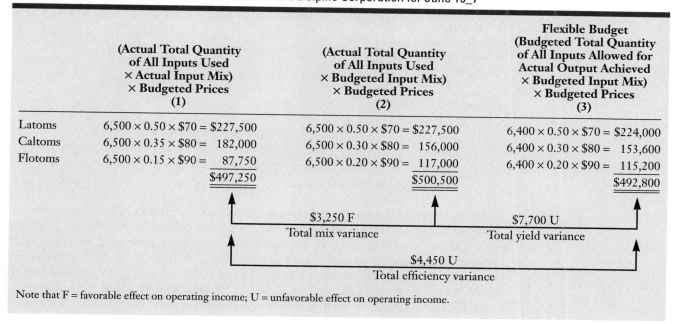

	(Actual Total Quantity of All Inputs Used × Actual Input Mix) × Budgeted Prices (1)	(Actual Total Quantity of All Inputs Used × Budgeted Input Mix) × Budgeted Prices (2)	Flexible Budget (Budgeted Total Quantity of All Inputs Allowed for Actual Output Achieved × Budgeted Input Mix) × Budgeted Prices (3)
Latoms	$6,500 \times 0.50 \times \$70 = \$227,500$	$6,500 \times 0.50 \times \$70 = \$227,500$	$6,400 \times 0.50 \times \$70 = \$224,000$
Caltoms	$6,500 \times 0.35 \times \$80 = 182,000$	$6,500 \times 0.30 \times \$80 = 156,000$	$6,400 \times 0.30 \times \$80 = 153,600$
Flotoms	$6,500 \times 0.15 \times \$90 = 87,750$	$6,500 \times 0.20 \times \$90 = 117,000$	$6,400 \times 0.20 \times \$90 = 115,200$
	$\$497,250$	$\$500,500$	$\$492,800$

$3,250 F
Total mix variance

$7,700 U
Total yield variance

$4,450 U
Total efficiency variance

Note that F = favorable effect on operating income; U = unfavorable effect on operating income.

input mix and the budgeted prices. The *only* difference in the two columns is that column 3 uses the *budgeted total quantity of all inputs used* (6,400 tons), while column 2 uses the *actual total quantity of all inputs used* (6,500 tons). Hence, the difference in costs between the two columns is the total direct materials yield variance, due solely to differences in actual and budgeted total input quantity used. The total direct materials yield variance is the sum of the direct materials yield variances for each input.

$$\begin{array}{l} \text{Direct} \\ \text{materials} \\ \text{yield variance} \\ \text{for each input} \end{array} = \left(\begin{array}{l} \text{Actual total} \\ \text{quantity of} \\ \text{all direct} \\ \text{materials} \\ \text{inputs used} \end{array} - \begin{array}{l} \text{Budgeted total} \\ \text{quantity of all} \\ \text{direct materials} \\ \text{inputs allowed} \\ \text{for actual} \\ \text{output achieved} \end{array} \right) \times \begin{array}{l} \text{Budgeted} \\ \text{direct materials} \\ \text{input mix} \\ \text{percentage} \end{array} \times \begin{array}{l} \text{Budgeted} \\ \text{price of} \\ \text{direct materials} \\ \text{input} \end{array}$$

The direct materials yield variances are

Latoms	$(6,500 - 6,400) \times 0.50 \times \$70 = 100 \times 0.50 \times \$70 = \$3,500$ U
Caltoms	$(6,500 - 6,400) \times 0.30 \times \$80 = 100 \times 0.30 \times \$80 = 2,400$ U
Flotoms	$(6,500 - 6,400) \times 0.20 \times \$90 = 100 \times 0.20 \times \$90 = 1,800$ U
Total direct materials yield variance	$\$7,700$ U

The total direct materials yield variance is unfavorable because Delpino uses 6,500 tons of tomatoes rather than the 6,400 tons that it should have used to produce 4,000 tons of ketchup. Holding constant the budgeted mix and budgeted prices of tomatoes, the budgeted cost per ton of tomatoes in the budgeted mix is $77 per ton (p. 867). The unfavorable yield variance represents the budgeted cost of using 100 more tons of tomatoes, $(6,500 - 6,400) \times \$77 = \$7,700$ U.

Total Direct Materials Mix Variance Compare columns 2 and 1 in Exhibit 24-2. Both columns calculate cost using the actual total quantity of all inputs used (6,500 tons) and budgeted input prices (Latoms, $70; Caltoms, $80; and Flotoms, $90). The *only* difference is that column 2 uses *budgeted input mix* (Latoms, 50%; Caltoms, 30%; and Flotoms, 20%), and column 1 uses *actual input mix* (Latoms, 50%; Caltoms, 35%; Flotoms, 15%). The difference in costs between the two columns is the total direct materials mix variance, attributable solely to differences in the mix of inputs used. The total direct materials mix variance is the sum of the direct materials mix variances for each input.

$$
\begin{pmatrix}
\text{Direct} \\
\text{materials} \\
\text{mix variance} \\
\text{for each} \\
\text{input}
\end{pmatrix}
=
\begin{pmatrix}
\text{Actual} & & \text{Budgeted} \\
\text{direct materials} & - & \text{direct materials} \\
\text{input mix} & & \text{input mix} \\
\text{percentage} & & \text{percentage}
\end{pmatrix}
\times
\begin{pmatrix}
\text{Actual total} \\
\text{quantity of all} \\
\text{direct materials} \\
\text{inputs used}
\end{pmatrix}
\times
\begin{pmatrix}
\text{Budgeted} \\
\text{price of} \\
\text{direct materials} \\
\text{input}
\end{pmatrix}
$$

The direct materials mix variances are

Latoms	$(0.50 - 0.50) \times 6,500 \times \$70 = 0 \times 6,500 \times \$70$	$= \$ \quad 0$
Caltoms	$(0.35 - 0.30) \times 6,500 \times \$80 = 0.05 \times 6,500 \times \$80$	$= \quad 26,000$ U
Flotoms	$(0.15 - 0.20) \times 6,500 \times \$90 = (-0.05) \times 6,500 \times \$90$	$= \quad \underline{29,250}$ F
Total direct materials mix variance		$\$ \ \underline{3,250}$ F

The favorable total direct materials mix variance (3,250 F) occurs because the average budgeted cost per ton of tomatoes in the actual mix [$497,250 (Exhibit 24-2, column 1) ÷ 6,500 = $76.50] is less than the average budgeted cost per ton of tomatoes in the budgeted mix [$500,500 (Exhibit 24-2, column 2) ÷ 6,500 = $77]. The favorable mix variance represents the difference in cost of the budgeted mix and the actual mix for the 6,500 tons of tomatoes used, ($76.50 − $77) × 6,500 = $3,250 F. The total direct materials mix variance helps managers understand how total budgeted costs change as the actual direct materials mix varies from the budgeted mix. The mix variance of an individual input is favorable (unfavorable) if Delpino uses a smaller (greater) percentage of that input in its actual mix relative to the budgeted mix. The individual variances help managers identify the reasons why the total mix variance is favorable— substituting some lower (budgeted) priced Caltoms ($80 per ton) in place of the more costly Flotoms ($90 per ton) while using the budgeted mix of Latoms reduces costs.

How should we interpret the analysis in Exhibit 24-2? The total direct materials yield variance is $7,700 U, and the total direct materials mix variance is $3,250 F. There was a trade-off among ingredients (perhaps because of the high cost or lack of availability of Flotoms) that reduced the (budgeted) cost of the mix of inputs used but hurt yield. That is, the benefit of the cheaper mix was more than offset by the lower yield. This analysis helps Delpino's managers to understand that using the cheaper mix of inputs in the future will only be worthwhile if they can improve yield. Managers would need to understand the reasons for the poor yield—for example, did the poor yield result from inadequate testing of the tomatoes received, from lax quality control during processing, or simply from using a cheaper mix? Identifying these reasons enables managers to find ways to overcome these problems and improve performance.

The direct materials variances computed in Exhibits 24-1 and 24-2 can be summarized as follows:

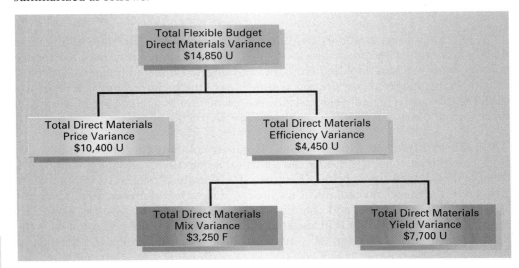

DIRECT MANUFACTURING LABOR YIELD AND MIX VARIANCES

Direct manufacturing labor variances are calculated in much the same way as direct materials variances. We again use the Delpino Corporation example to illustrate direct manufacturing labor price, efficiency, yield, and mix variances. Delpino has three grades of direct manufacturing labor: Grade 1, Grade 2, and Grade 3. Budgeted costs for June 19_7 follow:

OBJECTIVE 3

Explain direct manufacturing labor yield and mix variances

3,000 hours of Grade 3 labor at $24 per hour	$ 72,000
2,100 hours of Grade 2 labor at $16 per hour	33,600
900 hours of Grade 1 labor at $12 per hour	10,800
6,000 total hours	$116,400

Actual results for June 19_7 show that the work was completed in 5,900 hours:

3,245 hours of Grade 3 labor at $23 per hour	$ 74,635
1,770 hours of Grade 2 labor at $18 per hour	31,860
885 hours of Grade 1 labor at $13 per hour	11,505
5,900 total hours	118,000
Budgeted costs	116,400
Total direct manufacturing labor variance to be explained	$ 1,600 U

Exhibit 24-3 presents the direct manufacturing labor price and efficiency variances for each employee category and in total. The total price variance is unfavorable ($1,180 U) because of the higher wage rates paid to Grade 1 and Grade 2 labor. Managers would want to understand why the wage rates were higher—for example, did the higher rate result from a general shortage of Grade 2 labor or from factors specific to Delpino? The total efficiency variance is unfavorable ($420 U), primarily because of the greater number of hours worked by Grade 3 labor. The budgeted costs of these hours were only partially offset by the fewer hours worked by Grade 1 and Grade 2 labor and the fewer total hours worked. Delpino's managers would want to explore the reasons for the unfavorable efficiency variance—for example, was it caused by absenteeism, labor turnover, processing problems, or the change in the mix of workers? To further understand this last issue, the unfavorable total direct manufacturing labor efficiency variance of $420 may be divided into yield and mix

EXHIBIT 24-3
Direct Manufacturing Labor Price and Efficiency Variances for the Delpino Corporation for June 19_7

	Actual Costs Incurred (Actual Inputs × Actual Prices) (1)	Actual Input × Budgeted Prices (2)	Flexible Budget (Budgeted Inputs Allowed for Actual Outputs Achieved × Budgeted Prices) (3)
Grade 3 labor	3,245 × $23 = $ 74,635	3,245 × $24 = $ 77,880	3,000 × $24 = $ 72,000
Grade 2 labor	1,770 × $18 = 31,860	1,770 × $16 = 28,320	2,100 × $16 = 33,600
Grade 1 labor	885 × $13 = 11,505	885 × $12 = 10,620	900 × $12 = 10,800
	$118,000	$116,820	$116,400

$1,180 U
Total price variance

$420 U
Total efficiency variance

$1,600 U
Total flexible-budget variance

Note that U = unfavorable effect on operating income.

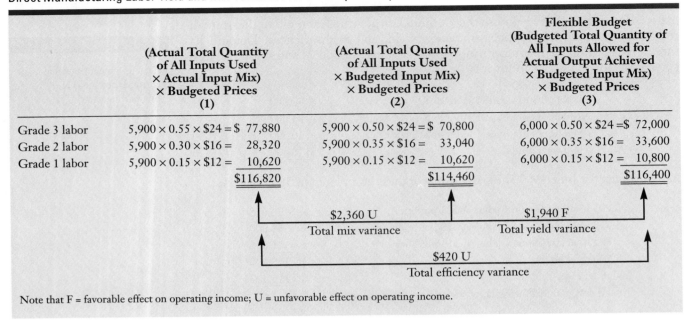

Note that F = favorable effect on operating income; U = unfavorable effect on operating income.

variances in the same way that we divided the direct materials efficiency variance in the preceding section.

Keeping the budgeted input mix unchanged, the **total direct manufacturing labor yield variance** is the difference between two amounts: (1) the budgeted cost of direct manufacturing labor based on the actual total quantity of all direct manufacturing labor used, and (2) the flexible-budget cost of direct manufacturing labor based on the budgeted total quantity of direct manufacturing labor for the actual output achieved. Taking the actual total quantity of all direct manufacturing labor used as given, the **total direct manufacturing labor mix variance** is the difference between two amounts: (1) the budgeted cost of inputs in the actual mix of direct manufacturing labor, and (2) the budgeted cost of inputs in the budgeted mix of direct manufacturing labor.

Exhibit 24-4 presents the computations for the *total direct manufacturing labor yield* and *mix variances* for the Delpino Corporation in columnar format. These variances can also be calculated as follows:

$$
\begin{pmatrix}
\text{Direct} \\
\text{manufacturing} \\
\text{labor yield} \\
\text{variance} \\
\text{for each} \\
\text{input}
\end{pmatrix}
=
\begin{pmatrix}
\text{Actual total} \\
\text{quantity of} \\
\text{all direct} \\
\text{manufacturing} \\
\text{labor inputs} \\
\text{used}
-
\text{Budgeted total} \\
\text{quantity of all direct} \\
\text{manufacturing labor} \\
\text{inputs allowed for} \\
\text{actual output} \\
\text{achieved}
\end{pmatrix}
\times
\begin{pmatrix}
\text{Budgeted} \\
\text{direct} \\
\text{manufacturing} \\
\text{labor input} \\
\text{mix} \\
\text{percentage}
\end{pmatrix}
\times
\begin{pmatrix}
\text{Budgeted} \\
\text{price of} \\
\text{direct} \\
\text{manufacturing} \\
\text{labor input}
\end{pmatrix}
$$

The direct manufacturing labor yield variances are

Grade 3 labor	$(5,900 - 6,000) \times 0.50 \times \$24 = (-100) \times 0.50 \times \$24 =$	$1,200 F
Grade 2 labor	$(5,900 - 6,000) \times 0.35 \times \$16 = (-100) \times 0.35 \times \$16 =$	560 F
Grade 1 labor	$(5,900 - 6,000) \times 0.15 \times \$12 = (-100) \times 0.15 \times \$12 =$	180 F
Total direct manufacturing labor yield variance		$1,940 F

$$
\begin{pmatrix}
\text{Direct} \\
\text{manufacturing} \\
\text{labor mix} \\
\text{variance} \\
\text{for each} \\
\text{input}
\end{pmatrix}
=
\begin{pmatrix}
\text{Actual direct} \\
\text{manufacturing} \\
\text{labor input} \\
\text{mix percentage}
-
\text{Budgeted direct} \\
\text{manufacturing} \\
\text{labor input} \\
\text{mix percentage}
\end{pmatrix}
\times
\begin{pmatrix}
\text{Actual total} \\
\text{quantity of} \\
\text{all direct} \\
\text{manufacturing} \\
\text{labor inputs} \\
\text{used}
\end{pmatrix}
\times
\begin{pmatrix}
\text{Budgeted} \\
\text{price of} \\
\text{direct} \\
\text{manufacturing} \\
\text{labor input}
\end{pmatrix}
$$

The direct manufacturing labor mix variances are

Grade 3 labor	$(0.55 - 0.50) \times 5,900 \times \$24 = 0.05 \times 5,900 \times \$24$	$= \$7,080$ U
Grade 2 labor	$(0.30 - 0.35) \times 5,900 \times \$16 = (-0.05) \times 5,900 \times \$16 =$	$4,720$ F
Grade 1 labor	$(0.15 - 0.15) \times 5,900 \times \$12 = 0 \times 5,900 \times \$12$	$= \underline{\hspace{0.6cm} 0}$
Total direct manufacturing labor mix variance		$\underline{\$2,360}$ U

The unfavorable mix variance occurs because a greater proportion of work was done by the more costly Grade 3 labor. Grade 3 labor accounted for 55% of the total actual direct manufacturing labor-hours but had been budgeted to handle only 50%. Grade 2 labor did a smaller proportion of the work. Delpino may have altered the mix of workers for reasons of availability or to achieve greater efficiency despite the higher costs. As a result of the change in mix, the average budgeted cost per direct manufacturing labor-hour in the actual mix [$116,820 (Exhibit 24-4, column 1) ÷ 5,900 = $19.80] was higher than the average budgeted cost per direct manufacturing labor-hour in the budgeted mix [$114,460 (Exhibit 24-4, column 2) ÷ 5,900 = $19.40]. The mix variance helps managers understand how budgeted costs change as the actual mix varies from the budgeted mix. The favorable yield variance indicates that the work was completed faster—in 5,900 actual total hours compared with 6,000 budgeted total hours. Perhaps this result is due to the extra time spent by Grade 3 labor. But did the mix-versus-yield trade-off reduce cost? No, because the overall direct manufacturing labor efficiency variance is unfavorable. The analysis helps managers understand that shifting to a higher skills mix will only be worthwhile if the total time taken can be further reduced. Managers would then have to consider ways to achieve this goal.

We could readily adapt the calculation of and insights gained from yield and mix variances to other inputs such as energy. For example, calculating these variances could further a company's understanding of how changing the mix of energy inputs—self-generated versus purchased—would affect operating income.

The examples we have presented involve no more than three direct materials inputs or three direct manufacturing labor inputs. Companies that have many direct materials or direct-labor inputs use computers to do the variance analysis.

◆ PART TWO: PRODUCTIVITY MEASUREMENT

Productivity measures the relationship between actual inputs used (both physical inputs and costs) and actual outputs achieved; the lower the inputs for a given set of outputs or the higher the outputs for a given set of inputs, the higher the level of productivity. Countries and companies pay great attention to productivity. Economists reason that productivity gains drive improvements in standards of living. The Bureau of Labor Statistics estimates that of the major industrialized nations, Japan has experienced the highest *growth* rate in labor productivity over the last 30 years, while U.S. labor productivity has grown at the slowest rate. However, U.S. workers still lead the world in labor productivity, although this lead has narrowed over the years. Chief executive officers consistently cite productivity improvement and cost containment as among the most important issues requiring their attention.

Productivity measures examine two aspects of the relationship between inputs and outputs. They evaluate (1) whether more inputs than necessary have been used to produce a given level of output, and (2) whether the best mix of inputs has been used to produce that output. Efficiency variances, discussed in Chapters 7 and 8, are one approach to getting at points 1 and 2, as are the yield variances discussed earlier in this chapter (point 1) and the mix variances (point 2). There are, however, two important features that distinguish productivity measurement from variance analysis. First, unlike the analysis of variances, productivity measures do not use information from budgets or standards. They compare the relation between actual inputs and actual outputs across similar organizations or over different time periods. Productivity comparisons over time periods provide an effective summary of an organization's effort at continuous improvement.

International Manufacturing Productivity Growth

Surveys across countries report wide differences in manufacturing productivity growth across countries and also over time. Annual average percentage change in manufacturing labor productivities (dollar value of output per hour) are as follows:

	1979–1985	1985–1990	1990–1993	1979–1993
United States	2.0%	2.7%	2.5%	2.4%
Canada	2.4	0.4	2.4	1.7
Japan	4.6	5.4	1.8	4.3
Germany	2.1	2.1	1.2	1.9
France	3.0	3.4	1.2	2.8
Italy	5.0	2.6	4.6	4.1
United Kingdom	4.1	3.8	4.5	4.1
Netherlands	4.2	1.9	0.9	2.6

The table indicates that while Japan has had the highest overall productivity growth from 1979 to 1993, its productivity growth has been slowing in recent years. In the 1990s, productivity growth has also slowed in Germany and France, but it has picked up noticeably in Canada, Italy, and the United Kingdom. Productivity growth in the United States has been steady in the 2–2.5% range over the different periods.

These differences in productivity growth are often explained by differences in capital investment, R&D, innovation, and employee training as well as changes in unit labor costs and currency exchange rates. For example, the higher U.S. productivity growth rates in the post-1985 period came during a period of the dollar's decline that made U.S. products more competitive internationally.

Countries differ considerably in whether higher output or fewer labor-hours contribute to the increase in productivity. For example, Japanese productivity growth is due entirely to rising output; in the United States, Canada, and the Netherlands rising output has contributed more than reductions in labor-hours; productivity gains in Italy arise equally from rising output and fewer labor-hours; and productivity increases in Germany, France, and the United Kingdom largely stem from a decrease in labor-hours. During the 1990s, however, almost all worldwide productivity growth has been accomplished by reducing the number of hours worked as companies have downsized and become more efficient.

Source: Greiner, Kask, and Sparks, "Comparative Manufacturing." Full citation is in Appendix A.

Second, yield and mix variance calculations only apply when substitutions occur *within* a given category of inputs—that is, within direct materials inputs (Latoms, Caltoms, and Flotoms), or within direct manufacturing labor inputs (as in the case of Grades 1, 2, and 3 labor). Often, however, substitutions can occur between direct materials and direct manufacturing labor. Garment manufacturers, for example, can substitute more costly snap fasteners for buttons thus saving the labor costs of making buttonholes. Substitutions may also occur between labor and capital. Manufacturing companies, for example, must decide on the extent of capital investment in automation that, in turn, reduces manufacturing labor costs. Productivity measures incorporate these more general substitutions among different types of inputs.

We illustrate productivity measures using data from Ramona, Inc., which makes wooden door handles. For simplicity, we focus on only two inputs, direct materials and direct manufacturing labor, which are partial substitutes for each other. Carving handles out of wooden boards creates trims and edges (the leftover portions of the board). These trims and edges could be reused, but they would require more care and attention and consequently more direct manufacturing labor time. Alternatively, trims and edges can be discarded, saving direct manufacturing labor time but increasing direct materials usage. Ramona provides the following information for the years 19_7 and 19_8:

	19_7	19_8
Wooden handles produced and sold	425,000	510,000
Direct manufacturing labor-hours used	34,000	37,400
Wages per hour	$14	$15
Direct materials used (in square feet)	170,000	219,500
Direct materials costs per square foot	$2.05	$2.00
Direct manufacturing labor costs (Direct manufacturing labor hours × Wages per hour)	$476,000	$561,000
Direct materials costs (Direct materials used × Direct materials costs per square foot)	$348,500	$439,000
Total input costs (Direct manufacturing labor costs + Direct materials costs)	$824,500	$1,000,000

Many factors can account for the change in Ramona's costs from 19_7 to 19_8—a change in the quantity of outputs produced, a change in the prices of inputs used, or a change in productivity (resulting from a change in the way inputs are converted into output). Our goal is to isolate the effect of any productivity change on costs. Management can use this information to evaluate actions aimed at improving productivity and reducing costs. These actions may include more training of workers and building better supplier relationships, among many others. To understand productivity changes, we consider both partial and total factor productivity measures.

PARTIAL PRODUCTIVITY MEASURES

Partial productivity compares the quantity of output produced with the quantity of a *single* input used. In its most common form, partial productivity is expressed as a ratio:

$$\text{Partial productivity} = \frac{\text{Quantity of output produced}}{\text{Quantity of input used}}$$

The higher the ratio, the greater the productivity. Partial productivity measures ignore all but one input, as well as the prices of all inputs.

Consider direct manufacturing labor productivity at Ramona in 19_7:

$$\begin{aligned}\text{Direct manufacturing} \atop \text{labor partial productivity} &= \frac{\text{Quantity of wooden handles produced during 19\_7}}{\text{Direct manufacturing labor-hours used to produce handles in 19\_7}} \\ &= \frac{425,000 \text{ handles}}{34,000 \text{ labor-hours}} \\ &= 12.5 \text{ handles per direct manufacturing labor-hour}\end{aligned}$$

Note that the direct manufacturing labor partial productivity measure is, indeed, a *partial* productivity measure. It ignores Ramona's second input, direct materials.

We can similarly define the direct materials partial productivity at Ramona for 19_7 as

$$\begin{aligned}\text{Direct materials} \atop \text{partial productivity} &= \frac{\text{Quantity of wooden handles produced during 19\_7}}{\text{Direct materials used to produce handles in 19\_7}} \\ &= \frac{425,000 \text{ handles}}{170,000 \text{ square feet}} \\ &= 2.5 \text{ handles per square foot of direct materials}\end{aligned}$$

By itself, a partial productivity measure has little meaning. It gains meaning only when comparisons are made that examine productivity changes over time, among several facilities, or relative to a benchmark.

The following table presents Ramona's direct manufacturing labor partial productivity and direct materials partial productivity for the years 19_7 and 19_8:

Partial Productivity	19_7	19_8
Direct manufacturing labor	$\dfrac{425,000}{34,000} = 12.50$	$\dfrac{510,000}{37,400} = 13.64$
Direct materials	$\dfrac{425,000}{170,000} = 2.50$	$\dfrac{510,000}{219,500} = 2.32$

Evaluating Changes in Partial Productivities and Their Relation to Efficiency Variances

The preceding table of partial productivities indicates that

◆ Direct manufacturing labor productivity increased by 9.12% [(13.64 − 12.5) ÷ 12.5].

◆ Direct materials productivity decreased by 7.20% [(2.32 − 2.5) ÷ 2.5].

Direct manufacturing labor partial productivity increased because workers made more handles per hour in 19_8 relative to 19_7. While the number of handles produced (the numerator) increased by 20% [(510,000 − 425,000) ÷ 425,000], the direct manufacturing labor-hours (the denominator) increased by only 10% [(37,400 − 34,000) ÷ 34,000].[1] Direct materials partial productivity decreased because workers used more wood per handle in 19_8 compared to 19_7. While the number of handles produced (the numerator) increased by 20%, the direct materials used (the denominator) increased by 29.12% [(219,500 − 170,000) ÷ 170,000].

A major advantage of partial productivity measures is that they focus on a single input; hence they are simple to calculate and easy to understand at the operations level. Managers and operators examine these numbers to understand the reasons underlying productivity changes from one period to the next. For example, Ramona's managers will evaluate whether the increase in direct manufacturing labor productivity from 19_7 to 19_8 was caused by better training of workers, lower absenteeism, lower labor turnover, better incentives, improved methods, or substitution of materials for labor. Isolating the relevant factors is important because it helps Ramona implement and sustain these practices in the future. Ramona can then set targets for gains in manufacturing labor productivity and monitor planned productivity improvements.

The efficiency variances calculated in Chapter 7 and in this chapter also focus on input-output relationships by comparing actual inputs with budgeted inputs for actual output produced. How do partial productivity measures differ from efficiency variances? Exhibit 24-5 indicates that Ramona has an *unfavorable* direct manufacturing labor efficiency variance (calculated using a standard costing system) in 19_8, while partial productivity *increased* from 19_7 to 19_8. The differences derive from the benchmark used—last year's actual performance in the case of productivity and an efficiency standard in the case of variance analysis. The higher partial productivity indicates that the workers' actual performance in 19_8 was better than it was in 19_7. The unfavorable efficiency variance arises because Ramona's workers did not perform at the standards set for 19_8. By looking at only the efficiency variance, Ramona's management could easily miss the fact that performance improved. Instead, management would simply see that standards for 19_8 were not met. The partial productivity measure thus complements the efficiency variance. It indicates that ac-

[1]The technical assumption underlying these calculations is that Ramona's production technology is a *constant returns to scale technology*. That is, absent any change in productivity, the direct manufacturing labor-hours (denominator) would have increased by the *same* 20% increase in the number of handles produced.

EXHIBIT 24-5

Comparison of Direct Manufacturing Labor Productivity and Direct Manufacturing Labor Efficiencies for Ramona, Inc., Based on a Standard Costing System

Year	Standard Direct Manufacturing Labor-hours per Output Unit (Numbers Assumed) (1)	Output Produced (2)	Actual Direct Manufacturing Labor-hours (3)	Standard Direct Manufacturing Labor-hours for Actual Output Achieved (4) = (1) × (2)	Standard Price Assumed to Equal Actual Price (5)	Direct Manufacturing Labor Efficiency Variance (6) = [(3) − (4)] × (5)	Direct Manufacturing Labor Partial Productivity (7) = (2) ÷ 3
19_7	0.084	425,000	34,000	35,700	$14	$(34,000 − 35,700) × 14 = $23,800 F	12.5
19_8	0.072	510,000	37,400	36,720	$15	$(37,400 − 36,720) × 15 = $10,200 U	13.64

tual performance did improve and prompts management to reevaluate whether the standards set were excessively demanding.

For all their advantages, partial productivity measures also have some serious drawbacks. Partial productivity focuses on only one input at a time rather than all inputs simultaneously and hence does not allow managers to evaluate the effect on overall productivity. For example, direct manufacturing labor partial productivity at Ramona *increased* from 19_7 to 19_8 while direct materials partial productivity *decreased*. The effect on overall productivity, however, is unclear. Partial productivity measures cannot evaluate whether the increase in direct manufacturing labor partial productivity offsets the decrease in direct materials partial productivity. *Total factor productivity (TFP)* or *total productivity* is a technique for measuring productivity that considers all inputs simultaneously.

TOTAL FACTOR PRODUCTIVITY

Total factor productivity (TFP) is the ratio of the quantity of output produced to the costs of *all* inputs used, where the inputs are combined on the basis of current period prices.

$$\text{Total factor productivity} = \frac{\text{Quantity of output produced}}{\text{Costs of all inputs used}}$$

TFP considers all inputs simultaneously and also considers the trade-offs across inputs based on current input prices. We often think of all productivity measures as physical measures lacking financial content—how many units of output are produced per unit of input. This is not the case. Total factor productivity is intricately tied to minimizing total cost—a financial objective. Our goal is to measure changes in TFP from one period to the next.

Calculating Total Factor Productivity and Change in Total Factor Productivity

We first calculate Ramona's TFP in 19_8, using 19_8 prices and 510,000 units of output produced.

$$
\begin{pmatrix} \text{Costs of} \\ \text{inputs used} \\ \text{in 19\_8 based} \\ \text{on 19\_8 prices} \end{pmatrix} = \begin{pmatrix} \text{Direct} \\ \text{manufacturing} \\ \text{labor-hours used} \\ \text{in 19\_8} \end{pmatrix} \times \begin{pmatrix} \text{Direct} \\ \text{manufacturing} \\ \text{labor rate} \\ \text{in 19\_8} \end{pmatrix} + \begin{pmatrix} \text{Direct} \\ \text{materials} \\ \text{used in} \\ \text{19\_8} \end{pmatrix} \times \begin{pmatrix} \text{Direct} \\ \text{materials} \\ \text{prices} \\ \text{in 19\_8} \end{pmatrix}
$$

$$= (37,400 \times \$15) + (219,500 \times \$2)$$
$$= \$561,000 + \$439,000$$
$$= \$1,000,000$$

$$
\begin{matrix} \text{Total factor} \\ \text{productivity} \\ \text{for 19\_8 using} \\ \text{19\_8 prices} \end{matrix} = \frac{\text{Quantity of output produced in 19\_8}}{\text{Costs of inputs used in 19\_8 based on 19\_8 prices}}
$$

$$= \frac{510,000}{\$1,000,000}$$

$$= 0.51 \text{ units of output per dollar of input}$$

By itself, the 19_8 TFP of 0.51 handles per dollar of input is not particularly helpful. We need something to compare the 19_8 TFP against. One alternative is to compare TFPs of other similar companies in 19_8. However, finding similar companies and obtaining accurate comparable data is often difficult. Companies therefore usually compare TFPs over time. In the Ramona example, the appropriate benchmark to compare 19_8 TFP against is the TFP from 19_7 calculated using 19_7's output but 19_8's prices. Why do we use 19_8 prices? Because using the current year's (19_8) prices in both calculations controls for input price differences, and focuses the analysis on the adjustments the manager made in the quantities and mix of inputs in response to changes in prices.

$$
\begin{pmatrix}
\text{Costs of} \\
\text{inputs used} \\
\text{in 19\_7 based} \\
\text{on 19\_8 prices}
\end{pmatrix}
=
\left(
\begin{array}{c}
\text{Direct} \\
\text{manufacturing} \\
\text{labor-hours used} \\
\text{in 19\_7}
\end{array}
\times
\begin{array}{c}
\text{Direct} \\
\text{manufacturing} \\
\text{labor rate} \\
\text{in 19\_8}
\end{array}
\right)
+
\left(
\begin{array}{c}
\text{Direct} \\
\text{materials} \\
\text{used in} \\
\text{19\_7}
\end{array}
\times
\begin{array}{c}
\text{Direct} \\
\text{materials} \\
\text{prices} \\
\text{in 19\_8}
\end{array}
\right)
$$

$$= (34{,}000 \times \$15) + (170{,}000 \times \$2)$$

$$= \$510{,}000 + \$340{,}000$$

$$= \$850{,}000$$

$$
\begin{array}{c}
\text{Total factor} \\
\text{productivity} \\
\text{for 19\_7 using} \\
\text{19\_8 prices}
\end{array}
=
\frac{\text{Quantity of output produced in 19\_7}}{\text{Costs of inputs used in 19\_7 based on 19\_8 prices}}
$$

$$= \frac{425{,}000}{\$850{,}000}$$

$$= 0.50 \text{ units of output per dollar of input}$$

Using 19_8 prices, total factor productivity increased 2% [(0.51 − 0.50) ÷ 0.50] from 19_7 to 19_8. The decrease in partial productivity of direct materials was more than offset by partial productivity gains in direct manufacturing labor.

Total factor productivity increased because Ramona produced more output per dollar of input in 19_8 relative to 19_7, measured in both years using 19_8 prices. While the number of handles produced (the numerator) increased by 20% [(510,000 − 425,000) ÷ 425,000], the cost of inputs based on 19_8 prices (the denominator) increased by only 17.65% [($1,000,000 − $850,000) ÷ $850,000].

Two sources account for gains in TFP from 19_7 to 19_8: (1) increases in partial productivities of individual inputs, and (2) changes to a cheaper mix of inputs in response to 19_8 input prices. TFP simultaneously measures the net effect of both sources of gains, but it does not separately measure the effect of each. Note that TFP increases are not due to differences in input prices; we used 19_8 prices to evaluate the input mix in both 19_7 and 19_8.[2]

Although our example has focused on direct materials and direct manufacturing labor, productivity measures also apply to overhead costs. To measure overhead productivity requires identifying cost drivers and cost driver rates for the overhead activity. Suppose, for example, that Ramona's operations were automated so that Ramona had no direct manufacturing labor. Instead, all labor was indirect support labor of a supervisory nature. The cost driver for indirect support labor costs is support labor-hours. Suppose indirect support labor-hours and wage rates are the same as those described earlier for direct manufacturing labor-hours. Then Ramona would calculate support labor partial productivities in terms of output per support labor-hour of 425,000 ÷ 34,000 = 12.50 in 19_7 and 510,000 ÷ 37,000 = 13.64 in 19_8. Total factor productivity of direct materials and support labor would also be calculated exactly as before: 0.50 units of output per dollar of input for 19_7 and 0.51 units of output per dollar of input for 19_8.

Using Partial and Total Factor Productivity Measures

A major advantage of TFP is that it measures the combined productivity of all inputs used to produce output and therefore explicitly considers gains from using fewer physical inputs as well as substitution among inputs. Managers analyze these numbers to understand the reasons for changes in TFP. For example, Ramona's managers will try to evaluate whether the increase in TFP from 19_7 to 19_8 was due to better

[2] We use 19_8 prices to evaluate the input mix in 19_7 and 19_8 rather than the 19_7 prices because we want to evaluate the manager's performance in the current year (19_8) by examining how the manager responded to changes in input prices that occurred between 19_7 and 19_8.

Productivity Improvement and Gain Sharing as Keys to Competitiveness at Whirlpool

Faced with intense competition and diminishing margins, the Whirlpool Corporation, a major manufacturer of home appliances, identified quality and productivity improvements as keys to better operating performance. In 1988, Whirlpool and the union at its Benton Harbor, Michigan, plant negotiated a contract that froze wages but tied bonus payments to a productivity-based gain-sharing program. The greater the labor productivity (output per hour of work), the larger the pool of money the company would share with its employees. The workers' share depended on the quality of output as measured by the number of rejected parts.

Has the gain-sharing program been effective? Very much so. For example, at the Benton Harbor plant, which manufactures agitator shafts and spin pinions for Whirlpool's washing machines, productivity has surged at a rate of 4% per year, the number of rejected parts has been reduced from 837 to a world-class level of 10 parts per million produced. During the first seven years of its existence, the gain-sharing program has increased hourly compensation from as low as 5.5% in one year to as high as 12% in two other years. The cost of an agitator shaft has decreased 13%, and the cost of a spin pinion has fallen 24%. Productivity gains have allowed Whirlpool to hold down its prices and bolster its operating results.

Whirlpool's productivity gains have not been achieved by simply spending millions of dollars on technological advances. Instead, Whirlpool's gains have come from overhauling manufacturing processes, training employees to improve quality, and empowering them to make decisions. Because of the success of gain sharing at Benton Harbor, the program has been extended to other Whirlpool manufacturing facilities around the world.

Source: R. Wartzman, "A Whirlpool Factory Raises Productivity—and Pay of Workers," *The Wall Street Journal*, May 4, 1992, and Whirlpool's 1995 Annual Report.

human resource management practices, quality of materials, improved manufacturing methods, or substitution of materials for labor. Ramona intends to implement the most successful practices and use TFP measures to set targets and monitor trends.

Many companies such as Monsanto, a manufacturer of fibers, Behlen Manufacturing, a steel fabricator, and Motorola, a chip manufacturer, use both partial and total factor productivity to evaluate performance. Partial productivity and TFP measures work best together. The methods complement each other because the strengths of one are the weaknesses of the other.

For example, although TFP measures are comprehensive, they are difficult to link across multiple periods. Consider the Ramona example. Our analysis used 19_8 prices to evaluate changes in total factor productivity between 19_7 and 19_8. To study the change in TFP between 19_8 and 19_9, we would use 19_9 prices. Because total factor productivity in each year is calculated using the prices in that year, we would compute the change from 19_7 to 19_9 using 19_9 prices only. Now the change in TFP between 19_7 and 19_9 will not be the same as the product of the changes in TFP (1) from 19_7 to 19_8, and (2) from 19_8 to 19_9. Why? Because the change in TFP for 19_8 is evaluated using 19_8 prices, while that for 19_9 is evaluated using 19_9 prices. Partial productivity measures, on the other hand, compare physical outputs to physical inputs and so can easily be compared across multiple periods.

Operations personnel find financial TFP measures more difficult to understand and less useful than physical partial productivity measures in performing their tasks. For example, physical measures of partial manufacturing labor productivity provide direct feedback to workers about output produced per labor-hour worked. Workers, therefore, often prefer to tie productivity-based bonuses to partial labor productivity. But this situation creates incentives for workers to substitute materials (and capital) for labor, which improves their own productivity measure, though possibly decreasing overall productivity of the company as measured by TFP. To overcome the possible incentive problems of partial productivity measures, some companies—for example, TRW, Eaton, and Whirlpool—explicitly adjust bonuses based on partial labor productivity for the effects of other factors such as investments in new equipment and higher levels of scrap; that is, they combine partial productivity with TFP-like measures.

ANALYSIS OF ANNUAL COST CHANGES

We now explore productivity's role in explaining Ramona's change in costs from 19_7 to 19_8. Exhibit 24-6 describes three components: the output adjustment component (difference between columns 3 and 4), the price change component (difference between columns 2 and 3), and the productivity change component (difference between columns 1 and 2) that together account for the cost changes. It is easiest to start with 19_7 actual costs and work our way toward 19_8 actual costs, so we start at the right side of the exhibit with column 4. A description of each component follows:

1. *Output adjustment component.* First, focus on columns 4 and 3. Compare the descriptions of the two columns. Only the *quantities of output produced* in 19_7 (425,000 handles) and in 19_8 (510,000 handles) *differ* between the two columns. Hence the corresponding amounts of inputs that would have been used to produce the 19_8 output quantity in 19_7 also differ. Both columns use 19_7 prices. We label the cost difference between the two columns as an output adjustment. Why? Because the cost increase of $164,900 (for all inputs) arises solely on account of differences in the output produced in 19_7 and the output produced in 19_8.

2. *Price change component.* Next, focus on columns 3 and 2. Each column computes costs using the inputs that would have been used in 19_7 to produce the 510,000 units of output that were produced in 19_8: 40,800 direct manufacturing labor-hours and 204,000 square feet of direct materials. The *only* difference between the columns is the use of *19_7 actual prices* in column 3 and *19_8 actual prices* in column 2. The increase in costs between columns 3 and 2 of $30,600 (for all inputs) is due solely to net increases in input prices in 19_8 over 19_7.

3. *Productivity change component.* Finally, focus on columns 2 and 1. Both columns use actual 19_8 input prices. Both columns calculate inputs used to produce the actual quantity of 510,000 handles in 19_8. The difference between the two columns arises solely because of differences in the quantities and mix of resources that would have been used in 19_7 (40,800 direct manufacturing labor-hours and 204,000 square feet of direct materials) and the quantities and mix of inputs used in 19_8 (37,400 direct manufacturing labor-hours and 219,500 square feet of direct materials). Ramona shows cost savings of $20,000 (for all inputs) as a result of productivity gains. Note that the 2% increase in TFP (p. 879) equals the $20,000 gain divided by the $1,000,000 of actual costs incurred in 19_8 (Exhibit 24-6, column 1).

The difference between Ramona's actual costs in 19_7 and in 19_8 can be explained as

Total change in costs	=	Change in costs due to output adjustment	+	Change in costs due to input price changes	+	Change in costs due to productivity change
$175,500 U	=	$164,900 U	+	$30,600 U	+	$20,000 F

EXHIBIT 24-6
Analysis of Change in Actual Costs from 19_7 to 19_8 for Ramona, Inc.

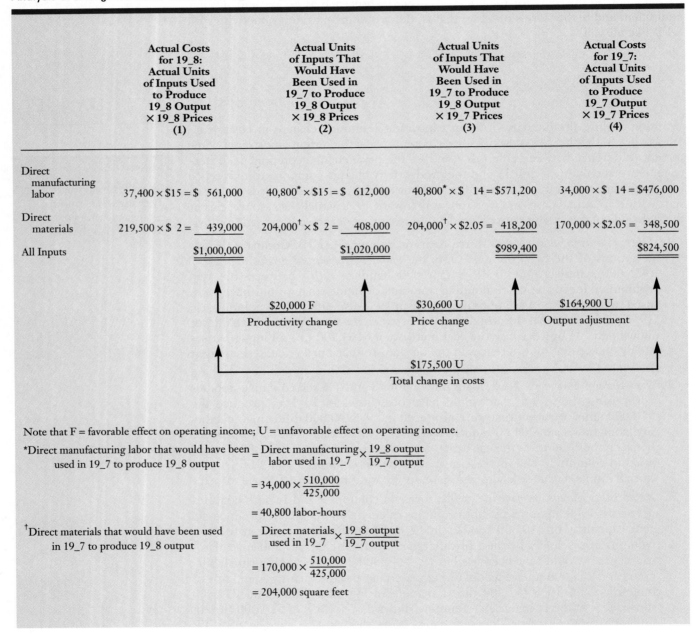

	Actual Costs for 19_8: Actual Units of Inputs Used to Produce 19_8 Output × 19_8 Prices (1)	**Actual Units of Inputs That Would Have Been Used in 19_7 to Produce 19_8 Output × 19_8 Prices (2)**	**Actual Units of Inputs That Would Have Been Used in 19_7 to Produce 19_8 Output × 19_7 Prices (3)**	**Actual Costs for 19_7: Actual Units of Inputs Used to Produce 19_7 Output × 19_7 Prices (4)**
Direct manufacturing labor	37,400 × $15 = $ 561,000	40,800* × $15 = $ 612,000	40,800* × $ 14 = $571,200	34,000 × $ 14 = $476,000
Direct materials	219,500 × $ 2 = 439,000	204,000† × $ 2 = 408,000	204,000† × $2.05 = 418,200	170,000 × $2.05 = 348,500
All Inputs	$1,000,000	$1,020,000	$989,400	$824,500

$20,000 F $30,600 U $164,900 U

Productivity change   Price change   Output adjustment

$175,500 U

Total change in costs

Note that F = favorable effect on operating income; U = unfavorable effect on operating income.

*Direct manufacturing labor that would have been used in 19_7 to produce 19_8 output $= \dfrac{\text{Direct manufacturing}}{\text{labor used in 19\_7}} \times \dfrac{\text{19\_8 output}}{\text{19\_7 output}}$

$= 34,000 \times \dfrac{510,000}{425,000}$

$= 40,800$ labor-hours

†Direct materials that would have been used in 19_7 to produce 19_8 output $= \dfrac{\text{Direct materials}}{\text{used in 19\_7}} \times \dfrac{\text{19\_8 output}}{\text{19\_7 output}}$

$= 170,000 \times \dfrac{510,000}{425,000}$

$= 204,000$ square feet

Note the following:

1. In calculating the cost difference due to the output adjustment, we hold input prices and the quantity and mix of inputs constant.
2. In calculating the cost difference due to input price changes, we hold output quantity and the quantities and mix of inputs constant.
3. In computing the cost difference resulting from productivity changes, we hold quantity of output and the input prices constant.

Of Ramona's $175,500 increase in costs from 19_7 to 19_8, $164,900 occurred because output expanded by 20%. Ramona's managers may not be particularly concerned about the cost increase resulting from growth because the higher output would presumably generate higher revenues, exceeding the increase in costs. The change in costs due to input price changes may be more of a concern. If markets are competitive, Ramona's managers may be unable to pass these price increases along to customers by way of higher output prices. This has been the experience of many companies operating in the semiconductor, computer, automobile, and copier industries. If higher input prices cannot be passed along, Ramona's managers must (1) seek to reduce direct materials and labor prices by renegotiating contracts and delivery terms for materials and job rates for workers, and (2) reduce the quantity and mix of inputs used to reduce costs via productivity gains. Ramona, for example, offset the $30,600 increase in costs from input price increases by productivity improvements that saved $20,000. As described earlier in the chapter, the next step is to put in place management practices and methods to sustain these improvements, and to set targets and monitor productivity improvements.

Exhibit 24-6 also shows how much of the cost change in each component is due to direct manufacturing labor and to direct materials. This additional information provides managers with more details about the underlying sources of the cost changes.

SERVICE-SECTOR PRODUCTIVITY

The service sector employs well over 60% of the work force in the United States and in most developed countries. In most of these countries, service-sector productivity growth (0.2% per year in the United States since 1970) has lagged behind growth in manufacturing productivity (2.6% per year in the United States since 1970), and has been a major reason for the slow rates of growth in overall productivity.[2] Overall productivity growth rates will continue to be low unless improvements occur in service or white-collar productivity.

The basic productivity measures used in the service sector are the same as the measures used in the manufacturing sector—the ratio of outputs produced to the costs of inputs used to produce the output. Some service industries have established output measures. For example, hospitals such as Massachusetts General use patient-days, and airlines such as Lufthansa use flight-miles as output measures. In service activities such as R&D output is more difficult to measure.

There are several ways to improve service-sector productivity.[3] A key step is to define all tasks carefully and to eliminate unnecessary ones. Bank lending productivity can be enhanced by reducing detailed analysis for small-value loans. Retail productivity can be enhanced by using bar codes to scan purchases electronically and by eliminating manual entry of customer's charges. Service-sector professionals, such as doctors, nurses, public accountants, and architects, can increase productivity by concentrating their efforts on professional responsibilities instead of administrative details.

[3]R. Schmidt, "Services: A Future of Low Productivity Growth?" *Federal Reserve Bank of San Francisco Weekly Letter*, Feb. 14, 1992, and "The Manufacturing Myth," *The Economist*, March 19, 1994.
[4]See P. Drucker, "The New Productivity Challenge," *Harvard Business Review* (Nov.–Dec. 1991), pp. 69–79; and H. D. Sherman, *Service Organization Productivity Management* (Hamilton, Ontario: The Society of Management Accountants of Canada, Nov. 1988).

PROBLEM

The Tilex Corporation specializes in installing floor tiles in houses, offices, and public places. It employs two types of labor—Grade 1 and Grade 2—to set the tiles, which are purchased by individual customers. Significant shifts in the wage structure occurred toward the end of 19_7. Grade 2 wages increased sharply while Grade 1 wages decreased a little.

Tilex uses a standard costing system. It adjusts its standards for 19_8 to represent the wage rates to be paid in 19_8. The 19_8 standards also recognize its strategy to reduce reliance, where possible, on the more costly Grade 2 labor without compromising quality. Tilex's standards for 19_8 are as follows:

Total standard hours of labor per square foot of tile laid	0.298
Budgeted percentage of Grade 2 labor	38%
Budgeted percentage of Grade 1 labor	62%
Budgeted Grade 2 labor wage rate	$22
Budgeted Grade 1 labor wage rate	$12

Actual results for 19_7 and 19_8 were

	19_7	19_8
Square feet of tile laid	50,000	62,500
Grade 2 labor-hours used	6,640	7,500
Grade 2 wages per hour	$19	$22
Grade 1 labor-hours used	8,660	11,250
Grade 1 wages per hour	$13	$12

REQUIRED

1. Calculate the total direct-labor efficiency variance for 19_8 and divide it into its mix and yield components.
2. Calculate the partial productivity measures for Grade 2 and Grade 1 labor in 19_7 and 19_8.
3. Calculate the total factor productivity for both types of labor in 19_8 and compare TFP performance in 19_8 to that in 19_7.
4. Divide the differences in actual costs between 19_7 and 19_8 into output adjustment, price change, and productivity change components.
5. Comment briefly on your analysis.

SOLUTION

1. Exhibit 24-7 presents the total direct-labor efficiency variance for 19_8 ($5,725 U) and its mix ($3,750 U) and yield ($1,975 U) components.

2.

Partial Productivities (square feet per labor-hour)	19_7	19_8
Grade 2	$\dfrac{50,000}{6,640} = 7.53$	$\dfrac{62,500}{7,500} = 8.33$
Grade 1	$\dfrac{50,000}{8,660} = 5.77$	$\dfrac{62,500}{11,250} = 5.56$

3. TFP calculations for 19_8 using 19_8 prices are as follows:

$$\begin{aligned}
\begin{matrix} \text{Costs of} \\ \text{inputs used} \\ \text{in 19\_8 based} \\ \text{on 19\_8 prices} \end{matrix} &= \left(\begin{matrix} \text{Grade 2} \\ \text{labor-hours} \\ \text{used in 19\_8} \end{matrix} \times \begin{matrix} \text{Grade 2} \\ \text{labor rate} \\ \text{in 19\_8} \end{matrix} \right) + \left(\begin{matrix} \text{Grade 1} \\ \text{labor-hours} \\ \text{used in 19\_8} \end{matrix} \times \begin{matrix} \text{Grade 1} \\ \text{labor rate} \\ \text{in 19\_8} \end{matrix} \right) \\[4pt]
&= (7,500 \times \$22) + (11,250 \times \$12) \\
&= \$165,000 + \$135,000 \\
&= \$300,000
\end{aligned}$$

$$\begin{aligned}
\begin{matrix} \text{Total factor} \\ \text{productivity} \\ \text{for 19\_8 using} \\ \text{19\_8 prices} \end{matrix} &= \frac{\text{Quantity of output produced}}{\text{Costs of inputs used in 19\_8 based on 19\_8 prices}} \\[8pt]
&= \frac{62,500}{\$300,000} \\[6pt]
&= 0.20833 \text{ square feet of tile laid per dollar of input}
\end{aligned}$$

TFP calculations for 19_7 using 19_8 prices are as follows:

$$\begin{aligned}
\begin{matrix} \text{Costs of} \\ \text{inputs used} \\ \text{in 19\_7 based} \\ \text{on 19\_8 prices} \end{matrix} &= \left(\begin{matrix} \text{Grade 2} \\ \text{labor-hours} \\ \text{used in 19\_7} \end{matrix} \times \begin{matrix} \text{Grade 2} \\ \text{labor rate} \\ \text{in 19\_8} \end{matrix} \right) + \left(\begin{matrix} \text{Grade 1} \\ \text{labor-hours} \\ \text{used in 19\_7} \end{matrix} \times \begin{matrix} \text{Grade 1} \\ \text{labor rate} \\ \text{in 19\_8} \end{matrix} \right) \\[4pt]
&= (6,640 \times \$22) + (8,660 \times \$12) \\
&= \$146,080 + \$103,920 \\
&= \$250,000
\end{aligned}$$

$$\begin{aligned}
\begin{matrix} \text{Total factor} \\ \text{productivity} \\ \text{for 19\_7 using} \\ \text{19\_8 prices} \end{matrix} &= \frac{\text{Quantity of output produced}}{\text{Costs of inputs used in 19\_7 based on 19\_8 prices}} \\[8pt]
&= \frac{50,000}{\$250,000} = 0.20 \text{ square feet of tile laid per dollar of input}
\end{aligned}$$

EXHIBIT 24-7
Direct-Labor Yield and Mix Variances for the Tilex Corporation for 19_8

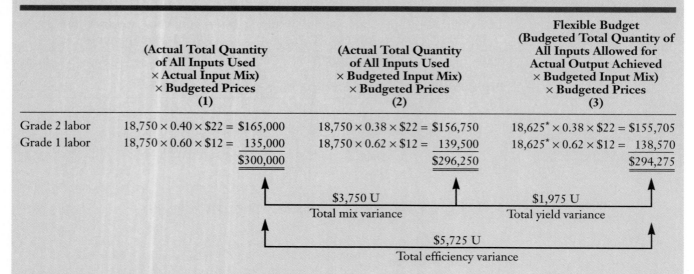

	(Actual Total Quantity of All Inputs Used × Actual Input Mix) × Budgeted Prices (1)	(Actual Total Quantity of All Inputs Used × Budgeted Input Mix) × Budgeted Prices (2)	Flexible Budget (Budgeted Total Quantity of All Inputs Allowed for Actual Output Achieved × Budgeted Input Mix) × Budgeted Prices (3)
Grade 2 labor	$18,750 \times 0.40 \times \$22 = \$165,000$	$18,750 \times 0.38 \times \$22 = \$156,750$	$18,625^* \times 0.38 \times \$22 = \$155,705$
Grade 1 labor	$18,750 \times 0.60 \times \$12 = \underline{135,000}$	$18,750 \times 0.62 \times \$12 = \underline{139,500}$	$18,625^* \times 0.62 \times \$12 = \underline{138,570}$
	$\$300,000$	$\$296,250$	$\$294,275$

$3,750 U \qquad $1,975 U
Total mix variance \qquad Total yield variance

$5,725 U
Total efficiency variance

*$18,625 = 0.298$ hours per square foot $\times 62,500$.
Note that F = favorable effect on operating income; U = unfavorable effect on operating income.

EXHIBIT 24-8
Analysis of Change in Actual Costs from 19_7 to 19_8 for the Tilex Corporation

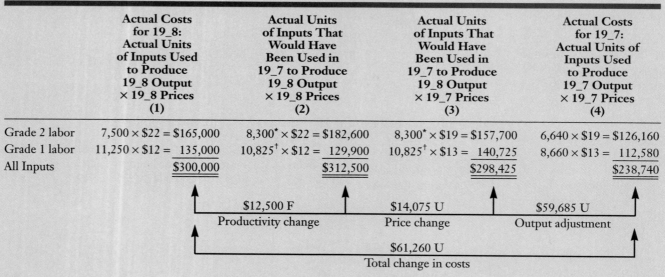

	Actual Costs for 19_8: Actual Units of Inputs Used to Produce 19_8 Output × 19_8 Prices (1)	Actual Units of Inputs That Would Have Been Used in 19_7 to Produce 19_8 Output × 19_8 Prices (2)	Actual Units of Inputs That Would Have Been Used in 19_7 to Produce 19_8 Output × 19_7 Prices (3)	Actual Costs for 19_7: Actual Units of Inputs Used to Produce 19_7 Output × 19_7 Prices (4)
Grade 2 labor	$7,500 \times \$22 = \$165,000$	$8,300^* \times \$22 = \$182,600$	$8,300^* \times \$19 = \$157,700$	$6,640 \times \$19 = \$126,160$
Grade 1 labor	$11,250 \times \$12 = \underline{135,000}$	$10,825^\dagger \times \$12 = \underline{129,900}$	$10,825^\dagger \times \$13 = \underline{140,725}$	$8,660 \times \$13 = \underline{112,580}$
All Inputs	$\$300,000$	$\$312,500$	$\$298,425$	$\$238,740$

$12,500 F \qquad $14,075 U \qquad $59,685 U
Productivity change \qquad Price change \qquad Output adjustment

$61,260 U
Total change in costs

Note that F = favorable effect on operating income; U = unfavorable effect on operating income.

*Grade 2 labor that would have been used in 19_7 to produce 19_8 output $= \dfrac{\text{Grade 2 labor}}{\text{used in 19\_7}} \times \dfrac{\text{19\_8 output}}{\text{19\_7 output}}$

$= 6,640 \times \dfrac{62,500}{50,000}$

$= 8,300$ labor-hours

$\dagger$Grade 1 labor that would have been used in 19_7 to produce 19_8 output $= \dfrac{\text{Grade 1}}{\text{labor used in 19\_7}} \times \dfrac{\text{19\_8 output}}{\text{19\_7 output}}$

$= 8,660 \times \dfrac{62,500}{50,000}$

$= 10,825$ labor-hours

4. Exhibit 24-8 analyzes the change in actual costs from 19_7 to 19_8 for Tilex.

5. The mix and yield variance calculations indicate that Tilex's performance was worse than budgeted. Tilex did not shift its mix away from Grade 2 labor as much as budgeted, and it used more labor than the budgeted amounts. Compared to the previous year, however, Tilex shows a significant improvement. Its TFP increased from 0.20 to 0.20833 square feet per dollar of inputs between 19_7 and 19_8. This increase of 4.17% was the joint effect of a change in the mix and in the use of fewer labor-hours per square foot of tile. The increase in the partial productivity of Grade 2 labor more than offset the decrease in partial productivity of Grade 1 labor. In summary, the variance and productivity analysis together indicate that Tilex's performance improved over 19_7, but not as much as anticipated. Tilex's management will review the standards, seek to understand the reasons for the improvement over last year's performance, and then chart a program for future improvement.

   Exhibit 24-8 shows that productivity improvements ($12,500 F) helped Tilex substantially offset the higher costs ($14,075 U) resulting from the price changes.

SUMMARY

The following points are linked to the chapter's learning objectives.

1. When inputs, such as three direct materials, are not substitutes, price and efficiency variances individually computed for each material typically provide the information necessary for decisions. In the case of substitutable inputs, however, various combinations of inputs can be used to produce the same output. Further splitting the efficiency variance into yield and mix variances provides additional information.

2. Many products use multiple direct materials that can be substituted for one another. In these cases, direct materials efficiency can come from two sources: (1) using fewer inputs of one or more of the materials and (2) using a cheaper mix of materials to produce output. The total direct materials yield and mix variances divide the total direct materials efficiency variance into two components, with the yield variance focusing on the total inputs used and the mix variance evaluating how the inputs are combined.

3. Multiple direct-labor inputs that are substitutes for one another are often used to manufacture a product or provide a service. The total direct manufacturing labor yield and mix variances indicate the sources of direct manufacturing labor efficiency. A favorable total direct manufacturing labor yield variance results when fewer total direct manufacturing labor-hours are used to produce a given quantity of product. A favorable total direct manufacturing labor mix variance results when a cheaper mix of direct manufacturing labor inputs is used to produce the actual quantity of product.

4. Productivity measures the relationship between actual inputs (both physical inputs and costs) and actual outputs achieved. Productivity measures frequently compare the quantities and mix of inputs (for example, direct materials and direct manufacturing labor) used to produce output over two or more periods.

5. Partial productivity measures compare the quantity of output produced with the quantity of a single input used. Partial productivity measures are simple to calculate and easily understood at the operations level. However, partial productivity measures do not focus on all inputs simultaneously and cannot evaluate trade-offs among inputs.

6. Total factor productivity measures the combined productivity of all inputs used to produce output by taking into account the relative prices of the inputs. A major advantage of total factor productivity is that it explicitly evaluates substitution possibilities among inputs. Two disadvantages are that total factor productivity measures are more difficult to understand at the operations level and that they are more difficult to link across multiple periods than are partial productivity measures.

7. Cost changes from one period to the next can be divided into changes in output adjustment, changes in input prices, and changes in productivity. The productivity change compares the cost to produce output in a particular period with what it would have cost to produce the same level of output in a previous period at current period input prices.

▼ TERMS TO LEARN

This chapter and the Glossary at the end of this book contain definitions of the following important terms:

partial productivity (p. 875)
productivity (873)
total direct manufacturing labor mix variance (872)
total direct manufacturing labor yield variance (872)

total direct materials mix variance (868)
total direct materials yield variance (868)
total factor productivity (TFP) (878)

▼ ASSIGNMENT MATERIAL

QUESTIONS

24-1 Distinguish between total direct materials yield and mix variances.

24-2 "Direct materials yield and mix variances are particularly useful when materials are substitutable." Do you agree? Explain.

24-3 Name three sources of the standards used in the total direct materials yield and mix variances.

24-4 "Changes in the mix of direct materials used from the budgeted mix always hurts yield." Do you agree? Explain.

24-5 Describe how an unfavorable total direct manufacturing labor mix variance can arise in a manufacturing plant using two categories of direct manufacturing labor.

24-6 How might managers use information about direct-labor yield and mix variances in improving the performance of a business?

24-7 Give an example of an input other than direct materials and direct labor where calculating yield and mix variances might be useful. Explain your reasoning briefly.

24-8 The manager of a highly automated plant that assembles desktop computers commented, "Yield and mix variance information is irrelevant to my cost management decisions." Give two possible reasons for the manager's statement.

24-9 Define productivity.

24-10 What is a partial productivity measure?

24-11 "Partial productivity measures and efficiency variances are identical because they both measure input-output relationships." Do you agree? Explain.

24-12 What is total factor productivity?

24-13 What information does total factor productivity provide that partial productivities do not?

24-14 Give one advantage and one limitation of total factor productivity.

24-15 "We are already measuring total factor productivity. Measuring partial productivities would be of no value." Do you agree? Comment briefly.

EXERCISES

24-16 Direct materials efficiency, yield and mix variances. (CMA adapted) The Energy Products Company produces a gasoline additive, Gas Gain, that increases engine efficiency and improves gasoline mileage. The actual and budgeted quantities (in gallons) of materials required to produce Gas Gain and the budgeted prices of materials in August 19_7 are as follows:

Chemical	Actual Quantity	Budgeted Quantity	Budgeted Price
Echol	24,080	25,200	$0.20
Protex	15,480	16,800	0.45
Benz	36,120	33,600	0.15
CT-40	10,320	8,400	0.30

REQUIRED

1. Calculate the total direct materials efficiency variance for August 19_7.

2. Calculate the total direct materials yield and mix variances for August 19_7.

3. What conclusions would you draw from the variance analysis?

24-17 Direct materials price, efficiency, yield, and mix variances. Greenwood, Inc., manufactures apple products such as apple jelly and applesauce. It makes applesauce by blending Tolman, Golden Delicious, and Ribston apples. Budgeted costs to produce 100,000 pounds of applesauce in November 19_7 are as follows:

45,000 pounds of Tolman apples at $0.30 per pound	$13,500
180,000 pounds of Golden Delicious apples at $0.26 per pound	46,800
75,000 pounds of Ribston apples at $0.22 per pound	16,500

Actual costs in November 19_7 are

62,000 pounds of Tolman apples at $0.28 per pound	$17,360
155,000 pounds of Golden Delicious apples at $0.26 per pound	40,300
93,000 pounds of Ribston apples at $0.20 per pound	18,600

REQUIRED

1. Calculate the total direct materials price and efficiency variances for November 19_7.

2. Calculate the total direct materials mix and yield variances for November 19_7.

3. Comment on your results in requirements 1 and 2.

24-18 Direct materials price and efficiency variances, direct materials yield and mix variances, perfume manufacturing. (SMA, adapted) The Scent Makers Company produces perfume. To make this perfume, Scent Makers uses three different types of fluids. Dycone, Cycone, and Bycone are used in standard proportions of 4/10, 3/10, and 3/10, and their standard costs are $6.00, $3.50, and $2.50 per pint, respectively. The chief engineer reported that in the past few months the standard yield has been at 80% on 100 pints of mix. The company maintains a policy of not carrying any direct materials, as inventory storage space is costly.

Last week, the company produced 75,000 pints of perfume at a total direct materials cost of $449,500. The actual number of pints used and costs per pint for the three fluids are as follows:

Direct Materials	Actual Pints	Costs per Pint
Dycone	45,000	$5.50
Cycone	35,000	4.20
Bycone	20,000	2.75

REQUIRED
1. Compute the total direct materials price and efficiency variances for perfume made in the last week.
2. Compute the total direct materials yield and mix variances for the last week.
3. Explain the significance of the price, yield, and mix variances from management's perspective.

24-19 **Direct nursing labor efficiency, yield and mix variances.** Riverside Hospital reports the following information for July 19_7 regarding its nursing staff consisting of registered nurses (RNs), licensed practical nurses (LPNs), and aides.

	Actual Hours	Budgeted Hours	Budgeted Rate per Hour
RNs	8,750	8,100	$25
LPNs	4,900	5,400	17
Aides	3,850	4,500	12

REQUIRED
1. Calculate the total direct nursing labor efficiency variance for July 19_7.
2. Calculate the total direct nursing labor yield and mix variances for July 19_7.
3. Briefly describe the conclusions you would draw from the variance analysis.

24-20 **Direct distribution labor price, efficiency variances, direct distribution labor yield and mix variances.** (CMA, adapted) The Memphis distribution center receives and distributes products for the Landeau Manufacturing Company. An analysis comparing the actual results with a flexible budget is prepared monthly.

The standard direct distribution labor rates in effect for the fiscal year ending June 30, 19_8, and the standard hours allowed for the April 19_8 output follow. The labor classes reflect different skill levels and different jobs: forklift operator, manual handler, and helper.

	Standard Direct Distribution Labor Rate per Hour	Standard Direct Distribution Labor-Hours Allowed for Actual Products Distributed
Distribution labor class III	$12.00	500
Distribution labor class II	10.00	500
Distribution labor class I	8.00	500

The actual direct distribution labor-hours worked and the actual direct distribution labor rates per hour for April 19_8 are as follows:

	Actual Direct Distribution Labor Rate per Hour	Actual Direct Distribution Labor-Hours
Distribution labor class III	$12.50	550
Distribution labor class II	10.50	650
Distribution labor class I	8.40	375
Total		1,575

REQUIRED

1. Calculate the total distribution labor price and efficiency variances for April 19_8.
2. Calculate the total distribution labor mix and yield variances for April 19_8.

24-21 Comparing efficiency and partial productivity measures. Vander Investments invests in stocks on behalf of its clients. Many of the transactions are done over the telephone. For the year 19_8, Vander expects its investment representatives to handle 10 calls per hour. In December 19_8, Vander buys a new client-information system that it expects will enable the representatives to handle 12 calls per hour. The standard and actual wages paid to investment representatives is $15 per hour. Vander obtains the following information about the performance of its representatives in June 19_8 and June 19_9.

◆ Representatives took 16,600 calls in 1,600 hours in June 19_8.
◆ Representatives took 18,360 calls in 1,600 hours in June 19_9.

REQUIRED

1. Calculate the direct-labor partial productivity in June 19_8 and June 19_9.
2. Calculate the direct-labor efficiency variances for June 19_8 and June 19_9.
3. Have both direct-labor partial productivity and efficiency measures improved in June 19_9 compared with June 19_8? Compare and comment on your answers to requirements 1 and 2.

24-22 Partial productivity measurement. The Hanover Corporation makes small parts from steel alloy sheets. Hanover's management has some ability to substitute direct materials for direct manufacturing labor. If workers cut the steel carefully, Hanover can manufacture more parts out of a metal sheet, but this will require more direct manufacturing labor-hours. Alternatively, Hanover can use fewer direct manufacturing labor-hours if it is willing to tolerate a larger quantity of direct materials waste. Hanover provides the following information for the years 19_8 and 19_9:

	19_8	19_9
Output units	400,000	520,000
Direct manufacturing labor-hours used	10,000	13,875
Wages per hour	$26	$25
Direct materials used (in tons)	160	190
Direct materials cost per ton	$3,187.50	$3,437.50

REQUIRED

1. Compute the partial productivity ratios for 19_8 and 19_9.
2. On the basis of the partial productivity ratios alone, can you conclude whether productivity improved overall in 19_9 relative to 19_8? Explain.

24-23 Total factor productivity and its comparison between two time periods (continuation of 24-22). Use the data given for the Hanover Corporation in Exercise 24-22.

REQUIRED

1. Calculate Hanover Corporation's total factor productivity in 19_9.
2. Compare Hanover's total factor productivity performance in 19_9 relative to 19_8.
3. What does the total factor productivity tell you that partial productivity measures do not?

24-24 **Analysis of cost changes.** Use the data given for the Hanover Corporation in Exercise 24-22.

REQUIRED

1. Calculate the actual costs incurred by the Hanover Corporation in 19_8 and 19_9.
2. Calculate how much of the difference in actual costs stems from the output adjustment component, the price change component, and the productivity change component.
3. Interpret your answers in requirement 2 to explain why Hanover's costs changed from 19_8 to 19_9.

PROBLEMS

24-25 **Direct materials price and efficiency variances, direct materials yield and mix variances, food processing.** Tropical Fruits, Inc., processes tropical fruit into fruit salad mix, which it sells to a food-service company. Tropical Fruits has in its budget the following standards for the direct materials inputs to produce 80 pounds of tropical fruit salad:

50 pounds of pineapple at $1.00 per pound	$50
30 pounds of watermelon at $0.50 per pound	15
20 pounds of strawberries at $0.75 per pound	15
100	$80

Note that 100 pounds of input quantities are required to produce 80 pounds of fruit salad. No inventories of direct materials are kept. Purchases are made as needed, so all price variances are related to direct materials used. The actual direct materials inputs used to produce 54,000 pounds of tropical fruit salad for the month of October were

36,400 pounds of pineapple at $0.90 per pound	$32,760
18,200 pounds of watermelon at $0.60 per pound	10,920
15,400 pounds of strawberries at $0.70 per pound	10,780
70,000	$54,460

REQUIRED

1. Compute the total direct materials price and efficiency variances in October.
2. Compute the total direct materials yield and mix variances for October.
3. Comment on your results in requirements 1 and 2.
4. How might the management of Tropical Fruits, Inc., use information about the direct materials yield and mix variances?

24-26 **Direct materials efficiency variance, mix and yield variances; working backward.** Agrichem Enterprises manufactures and sells fertilizers. Agrichem uses the following standard direct materials costs to produce 1 ton of fertilizer:

75% of the input materials is Base at $400 per ton	$360
25% of the input materials is Grade at $200 per ton	60
Total standard cost of 1.2 tons of inputs	$420

Note that 1.2 tons of input quantities are required to produce 1 ton of fertilizer. No inventories of direct materials are kept. Purchases are made as needed, so all price variances are related to direct materials used. Agrichem produced 2,000 tons of fertilizer in a particular period. The total direct materials yield variance for the period was $35,000 U. The actual input mix for the period was 50% of Base and 50% of Grade.

REQUIRED

1. Calculate the individual direct materials yield variances for the period.
2. Calculate the individual and total direct materials mix variances for the period.
3. Calculate the individual and total direct materials efficiency variances for the period.
4. Briefly describe the conclusions you would draw from the variance analyses.

24-27 **Direct service labor price, efficiency, yield and mix variances.** Wang and Associates, a firm of architects, has three levels of professional staff: principals (managers), who manage all aspects of the architectural job; senior architects, who are responsible for the main designs; and junior architects, who provide technical support. Budgeted costs for five architectural jobs done over a recent period are as follows:

600 principal-hours at $105 per hour	$ 63,000
1,800 senior-hours at $75 per hour	135,000
3,600 junior-hours at $25 per hour	90,000

Actual hours worked and the actual rates per hour to complete the five jobs are

295 principal-hours at $108 per hour	$ 31,860
2,360 senior-hours at $70 per hour	165,200
3,245 junior-hours at $30 per hour	97,350

REQUIRED

1. Calculate the total direct labor price and efficiency variances for the five jobs.
2. Calculate the total direct labor mix and yield variances for the five jobs.
3. Comment on your results in requirements 1 and 2.
4. How might managers use information about the direct labor yield and mix variances?

24-28 **Direct manufacturing labor price and efficiency variances, direct manufacturing labor yield and mix variances.** A supervisor in a sheet metal operation of Midwest Industries has the following direct manufacturing labor standard:

Direct manufacturing labor price per hour:	
2 artisans × $22	$44
3 helpers × $12	36
Total cost of standard combination of direct manufacturing labor	$80
Average price per direct manufacturing labor-hour ($80 ÷ 5)	$16
Standard direct manufacturing labor price per unit of output at 8 units per hour ($16 ÷ 8)	$ 2
Standard direct manufacturing labor cost of 20,000 units of output (20,000 × $2, or 2,500 × $16)	$40,000
Actual inputs, 2,900 hours consisting of	
900 hours of artisans × $23	$20,700
2,000 hours of helpers × $11	22,000
	$42,700

The supervisor had to pay a higher average wage rate to the artisans as the result of a bargained agreement.

1. Compute the total direct manufacturing labor price and efficiency variances.
2. Divide the total direct manufacturing labor efficiency variance into total direct manufacturing labor yield and mix variances.
3. What would the actual total cost have been if the standard direct manufacturing labor mix had been held constant given the actual direct manufacturing labor prices incurred? Comment on your answer.

24-29 Partial productivity measurement. Pittsburgh Industries makes chemical products using direct materials and direct manufacturing labor as substitutable inputs. It reports the following data for the last 2 years of operations:

	19_7	19_8
Output units	375,000	525,000
Direct manufacturing labor-hours used	7,500	9,500
Wages per hour	$20	$25
Direct materials used, in kilograms	450,000	610,000
Direct materials cost per kilogram	$1.20	$1.25

REQUIRED

1. Compute the partial productivity ratios for 19_7 and 19_8.
2. On the basis of the partial productivity ratios alone, can you conclude whether and by how much productivity improved overall in 19_8 relative to 19_7? Explain.
3. How might the management of Pittsburgh Industries use the partial productivity analysis?

24-30 Total factor productivity, its comparison between two time periods and analysis of cost changes (continuation of 24-29). Use the data given for Pittsburgh Industries in Problem 24-29.

REQUIRED

1. Compute Pittsburgh Industries' total factor productivity in 19_8.
2. Compare Pittsburgh's total factor productivity performance in 19_8 relative to 19_7.
3. Calculate the actual costs incurred by Pittsburgh Industries in 19_7 and 19_8 and indicate how much of the difference in actual costs is due to the output adjustment component, the price change component, and the productivity change component.
4. Interpret your answers in requirement 3 to explain why Pittsburgh's costs changed from 19_7 to 19_8.

24-31 Partial productivity measurement, budgeting. Quick Clean specializes in cleaning carpets in large office complexes. Its main inputs are cleaning labor, cleaning solution, and high-powered cleaning machinery that it leases on an as-needed basis. Partial productivities for 19_7 are as follows:

	19_7 Partial Productivity
Cleaning labor	1,000 square feet/labor-hour
Cleaning solution	1,200 square feet/gallon
Machine time	2,500 square feet/machine-hour

On the basis of these results, Quick Clean's manager, Mary Costas, is trying to formulate a sales plan and a budget for 19_8. Costas expects to have 15,000 labor-hours available in 19_8. She has been told by the equipment-leasing company that she can get up to 10,000 machine-hours. The partial productivity for the cleaning solution in 19_8 is expected to be 25% higher than its partial productivity in 19_7. No change in the partial productivities of other inputs is anticipated in 19_8. The cleaning solution is in plentiful supply in both 19_7 and 19_8. Assume that the demand for carpet-cleaning services is unlimited and profitable in both years.

REQUIRED

1. For how many square feet of carpet should Costas seek contracts in 19_8?
2. How much of each input should Costas plan to acquire?
3. Assume cleaning labor costs $22 per hour (wages and benefits), machine leasing is $45 per hour, and cleaning solution costs $12 per gallon in 19_8. If Quick Clean charges $0.08 per square foot of carpet cleaned, calculate its total contribution margin for 19_8.

24-32 Total factor productivity and analysis of cost changes (continuation of 24-31). Assume that in 19_8 Quick Clean obtained contracts to clean 15,000,000 square feet of carpet.

REQUIRED

1. Compute and comment on Quick Clean's total factor productivity in 19_8.
2. Suppose Quick Clean used 12,000 hours of cleaning labor in 19_7. Compare and comment on Quick Clean's total factor productivity performance in 19_8 relative to 19_7.
3. By how much did Quick Clean's total cost change because of productivity changes between 19_7 and 19_8?

24-33 Partial productivity and ethics. Donovan, Inc., manufactures valves for automobiles. In the latest round of negotiations, the union reluctantly agreed to give up regular increases in the hourly wage rate and to accept instead a productivity-based gain-sharing program. Under the gain-sharing program, wage rates were frozen at the 19_7 rates. A bonus of 1% of wages was to be paid to all manufacturing workers for each 1% improvement in the 19_7 direct manufacturing labor partial productivity. If direct manufacturing labor partial productivity declined, manufacturing workers were to be paid at their 19_7 base wage rates. The labor union leaders, however, continue to be skeptical about the gain-sharing program. They fear that management will try to avoid making bonus payments by incorrectly calculating the productivity numbers.

Donovan has just finished its first year under the gain-sharing program. Jerry Mason is the cost analyst in charge of maintaining productivity records and the data for calculating the bonus. Ken Hunter, the controller at Donovan, makes this comment to Mason: "I hope we show some productivity gains. The union already mistrusts our motives. If we don't pay at least some bonus, we are never going to get this productivity program off the ground. By the way, I think we classify too much of our labor as direct manufacturing labor. You may want to revisit this issue and reclassify some of the direct manufacturing labor as indirect manufacturing labor before calculating the direct manufacturing labor partial productivity." Mason believes the current manufacturing labor classification between direct and indirect is correct. He obtains the following information for 19_7 and 19_8:

	19_8	19_7
Valves produced	545,600 units	500,000 units
Direct manufacturing labor-hours	220,000 hours	200,000 hours
Direct manufacturing labor costs	?	$4,000,000

REQUIRED

1. Using Mason's numbers, (a) calculate the direct manufacturing labor partial productivity in 19_7 and 19_8, and (b) the direct manufacturing labor costs (including bonus payments, if any) for 19_8.

2. Evaluate whether Hunter's suggestion to Mason to consider reclassifying some of the direct manufacturing labor as indirect manufacturing labor is unethical. Would it be unethical for Mason to modify his analysis and calculations? What steps should Mason take to resolve this situation?

COLLABORATIVE LEARNING PROBLEM

24-34 Direct manufacturing labor price and efficiency variances, direct manufacturing labor yield and mix variances, productivity measures, externally based standard costs. Choshu Engineering assembles large-scale machining systems at plants in Tokuyama, Manchester, Memphis, and Singapore. Direct manufacturing labor, comprising the mix of Assembly Department direct manufacturing labor and Testing Department direct manufacturing labor, is a major cost category in each plant.

Data for the Memphis plant in 19_7 and 19_8 are as follows:

	19_7 Actual	19_8 Actual
Assembly Department		
Direct manufacturing labor-hours per machining system	52 hours	36 hours
Rate (price) per direct manufacturing labor-hour	$22	$25
Testing Department		
Direct manufacturing labor-hours per machining system	28 hours	24 hours
Rate (price) per direct manufacturing labor-hour	$15	$16

The standard direct manufacturing labor rates at the Memphis plant in 19_8 were $24 for the Assembly Department and $17 for the Testing Department. The Memphis plant assembled and tested 500 machining systems in both 19_7 and 19_8.

The 19_8 standard for direct manufacturing labor-hours of input per machining system assembled at the Memphis plant is based on the 19_7 actual results at the most efficient plant operated by Choshu Engineering, in Tokuyama. Results for the Tokuyama plant in 19_7 are as follows:

Assembly Department	
Direct manufacturing labor-hours per machining system	44 hours
Rate (price) per direct manufacturing labor-hour	$20
Testing Department	
Direct manufacturing labor-hours per machining system	20 hours
Rate (price) per direct manufacturing labor-hour	$18

Thus, the 19_8 standard cost for direct manufacturing labor for the Memphis Assembly Department is $1,056 ($24 × 44 hours) per machining system. The 19_8 standard cost for the Memphis Testing Department is $340 ($17 × 20 hours) per machining system.

INSTRUCTIONS

Form groups of two or more students to complete the following requirements.

REQUIRED

1. Why might Choshu Engineering use 19_7 actual results for direct manufacturing labor-hours of input per machining system at the Tokuyama plant when computing the 19_8 standard direct manufacturing labor cost per machining system at the Memphis plant?

2. Compute the total direct manufacturing labor price and efficiency variances at the Memphis plant for 19_8.

3. Compute the following for the Memphis plant for 19_8.
   a. Actual direct manufacturing labor mix and budgeted direct manufacturing labor mix percentages.
   b. Total direct manufacturing labor yield and total direct manufacturing labor mix variances.
4. Present a summary of the variances computed in requirements 2 and 3. Comment on your results.
5. Calculate the partial productivities for direct manufacturing labor in 19_7 and 19_8 in both the Assembly and Testing Departments of the Memphis plant.
6. Calculate the total factor productivity for Assembly and Testing direct manufacturing labor in 19_8 and compare it to the total factor productivity in 19_7 at the Memphis plant.
7. Comment on your answers to requirements 5 and 6. How does the productivity analysis differ from the variance analysis in terms of the insights that each provides?

25

CONTROL SYSTEMS, TRANSFER PRICING, AND MULTINATIONAL CONSIDERATIONS

Choosing transfer prices is an important aspect of transactions between internal divisions based in different countries. Companies consider tax as well as other factors—such as goal congruence, incentives, and autonomy—when determining transfer pricing policy. Transfer prices affect the profits reported in each division and are therefore of interest to division managers and tax officials in the different countries.

LEARNING OBJECTIVES

After studying this chapter, you should be able to

1. Describe a management control system
2. Describe three properties of effective management control systems
3. Describe the benefits and costs of decentralization
4. Identify three general methods for determining transfer prices
5. Understand how a transfer-pricing method can affect the operating income of individual subunits
6. Illustrate how market-based transfer prices generally promote goal congruence in perfectly competitive markets
7. Recognize why a transfer price based on full cost plus a mark up may lead to suboptimal decisions
8. Understand the range over which two divisions generally negotiate the transfer price when there is excess capacity
9. Present a general guideline for determining a minimum transfer price in transfer-pricing situations
10. Recognize income tax considerations in multinational transfer pricing

W hich company has the better management control system: the Ford Motor Company or the Toyota Motor Company? Michelin or Pirelli? Beyond the technical aspects, it is essential to consider how the system will influence the behavior of the people who use it. What role can accounting information play in management control systems? For example, how does cost and budget information help in planning and coordinating the actions of multiple divisions within these companies? This chapter develops the link between strategy, organization structure, management control systems, and accounting information. It examines the benefits and costs of centralized and decentralized organizational structures and looks at the pricing of products or services transferred between subunits of the same organization.

MANAGEMENT CONTROL SYSTEMS

OBJECTIVE 1

Describe a management control system

A **management control system** is a means of gathering and using information to aid and coordinate the process of making planning and control decisions throughout the organization and to guide employee behavior. The goal of the system is to improve the collective decisions within an organization.

Consider General Electric (GE). GE's management control system gathers and reports information for management control at various levels:

1. *Customer/market level*—for example, customer satisfaction, time taken to respond to customer requests for products, and cost of competitors' products.

2. *Total-organization level*—for example, stock price, net income, return on investment, cash flow from operations, total employment, pollution control, and contributions to the community.

3. *Individual-facility level*—for example, materials costs, labor costs, absenteeism, and accidents in various divisions or business functions (such as R&D, manufacturing, and distribution).

4. *Individual-activity level*—for example, the time taken and costs incurred for receiving, storing, assembling, and dispatching goods in a warehouse; scrap rates, defects, and units reworked on a manufacturing line; the number of sales transactions and sales dollars per salesperson; and the number of shipments per employee at distribution centers.

As the preceding examples indicate, management control systems collect both financial data (for example, net income, materials costs, and storage costs) and nonfinancial data (for example, the time taken to respond to customer requests for products, absenteeism and accidents). Some of the information is obtained from within the company (such as net income and number of shipments per employee); other information is obtained from outside the company (such as stock price and cost of competitors' products).

The levels indicate the different kinds of information that are needed by managers performing different tasks. For example, stock price information is important at the total-organization level but not at the individual-activity level in the warehouse, where information about the time taken for receiving and storing is more relevant. At the individual-activity level, management control reports focus on internal financial and nonfinancial data. At higher levels, management control reports also emphasize external financial and nonfinancial data.

Management control systems have both formal and informal components. The formal management control system of an organization includes those explicit rules, procedures, performance measures, and incentive plans that guide the behavior of its managers and employees. The formal control system itself consists of several systems. The management accounting system is a formal accounting system that provides information on costs, revenues, and income. Examples of other formal control systems are human resource systems (providing information on recruiting, training, absenteeism, and accidents), and quality systems (providing information on scrap, defects, rework, and late deliveries to customers).

The informal part of the management control system includes such aspects as shared values, loyalties, and mutual commitments among members of the organization and the unwritten norms about acceptable behavior for promotion that also influence employee behavior. Examples of slogans that reinforce values and loyalties are "At Ford, Quality Is Job 1," and "At Home Depot, low prices are just the beginning."

EVALUATING MANAGEMENT CONTROL SYSTEMS

To be effective, management control systems should be closely aligned to an organization's strategies and goals. Examples of strategies are doubling net income in 4 years, increasing market share by 50% in 2 years, or maximizing short-run income. Suppose management decides, wisely or unwisely, to emphasize maximizing short-run income as a strategy. Then the management control system must reinforce this strategy. It should provide managers with information that will help them make short-run decisions—for example, contribution margins on individual products. It should tie manager's incentives to short-run net income numbers.

A second important feature of management control systems is that they should be designed to fit the organization's structure and the decision-making responsibility of individual managers. For example, the management control information for the R&D manager at Glaxo Laboratories, a pharmaceutical company, should focus on the R&D activities required for different drug projects, the number of scientists needed, the scheduled dates for completing different projects, and the preparation of reports comparing actual and budgeted performance. On the other hand, consider a product-line manager responsible for the manufacture, sale, and distribution of ketchup at Heinz, a food products company. The management control system to support this manager should focus on information about customer satisfaction, market share, manufacturing costs and product-line profitability that helps the manager better plan and control the business. The manager of the Heinz ketchup product line requires very different information than the R&D manager at Glaxo Laboratories.

Finally, effective management control systems motivate managers and employees. **Motivation** is the desire to attain a selected goal (the goal-congruence aspect) combined with the resulting drive or pursuit toward that goal (the effort aspect).

Goal congruence exists when individuals and groups work toward the organization goals that top management desires—that is, managers working in their own best interest take actions that further the overall goals of top management. Goal-congruence issues have arisen in earlier chapters. For example, in capital-budgeting decisions, making decisions by discounting long-run cash flows at the required rate of return best achieves organization goals. But if the management control system evaluates managers on the basis of short-run accrual accounting income, managers will be tempted to make decisions to maximize accrual accounting income that may not be in the best interests of the organization.

Effort is defined as exertion toward a goal. Effort goes beyond physical exertion, such as a worker producing at a faster rate, to include all conscientious actions (physical and mental).

Management control systems motivate employees to exert effort toward attaining organization goals through a variety of incentives tied to the achievement of those goals. These incentives can be monetary (cash, stock, use of a company car, and membership of a club) or nonmonetary (power, self-esteem, and pride in working for a successful company).

To summarize, the primary criterion for evaluating a system is how it promotes the attainment of top management's goals in a cost-effective manner. Central to applying this criterion is how well the management control system fits the organization structure and the decision-making responsibility of individual managers, as well as how well it motivates individuals within the organization.

ORGANIZATIONAL STRUCTURE AND DECENTRALIZATION

As we have just seen, management control systems must fit an organization's structure. Many organizations have decentralized structures that give rise to an additional set of management control issues.

Top management makes decisions about decentralization that affect day-to-day operations at all levels of the organization. The essence of **decentralization** is the freedom for managers at lower levels of the organization to make decisions.

As we discuss the issues of decentralization, we use the term *subunit* to refer to any part of an organization. In practice, a subunit may be a large division (the Chevrolet Division of General Motors) or a small group (the two-person advertising department of a local clothing boutique).

Total decentralization *means minimum constraints and maximum freedom for managers to make decisions at the lowest levels of an organization.* Total centralization *means maximum constraints and minimum freedom for managers at the lowest levels.* Most companies' structures fall somewhere in between these two extremes.

Benefits of Decentralization

OBJECTIVE 3

Describe the benefits and costs of decentralization

How should top managers decide how much decentralization is optimal? Conceptually, they try to choose the degree of decentralization that maximizes the excess of benefits over costs. From a practical standpoint, top managers can seldom quantify either the benefits or the costs. Still, the cost-benefit approach helps them focus on the central issues.

Advocates of decentralizing decision making and granting responsibilities to managers of subunits claim the following benefits:

1. *Creates greater responsiveness to local needs.* Information is the key to intelligent decisions. Compared with top managers, subunit managers are better informed about their customers, competitors, suppliers, and employees, as well as about factors that affect the performance of their jobs such as ways to decrease costs and improve quality. Eastman Kodak reports that one advantage of decentralization is an "increase in the company's knowledge of the marketplace and improved service to customers."

2. *Leads to quicker decision making.* An organization that gives lower-level managers the responsibility for making decisions can make decisions quickly, creating a competitive advantage over organizations that are slower because they send the decision-making responsibility upward through layer after layer of management. Interlake, a manufacturer of materials-handling equipment, notes this important benefit of increased decentralization: "We have distributed decision-making powers more broadly to the cutting edge of product and market opportunity." Interlake's materials-handling equipment must often be customized to fit individual customers' needs. Delegating decision making to the salesforce allows Interlake to respond quickly to changing customer requirements.

3. *Increases motivation.* Subunit managers are usually more highly motivated when they can exercise greater individual initiative. Johnson & Johnson, a highly decentralized company, maintains that "Decentralization = Creativity = Productivity."

4. *Aids management development and learning.* Giving managers more responsibility promotes the development of an experienced pool of management talent—a pool that the organization can draw from to fill higher-level management positions. The organization also learns which people are not management material. Tektronix, an electronics instruments company, expressed this benefit as follows: "Decentralized units provide a training ground for general managers, and a visible field of combat where product champions may fight for their ideas."

5. *Sharpens the focus of managers.* In a decentralized setting, the manager of a small subunit has a concentrated focus. A small subunit is more flexible and nimble than a larger subunit and better able to adapt itself quickly to a fast-opening market opportunity. Also, top management, relieved of the burden of day-to-day operating decisions, can spend more time and energy on strategic planning for the entire organization.

Costs of Decentralization

Advocates of more centralized decision making point out the following costs of decentralizing decision making:

1. *Leads to **suboptimal** (also called **incongruent**) **decision making,*** *which arises when a decision's benefit to one subunit is more than offset by the costs or loss of benefits to the organization as a whole.* This cost arises because top management has given up some control over decision making.

   Suboptimal decision making may occur (1) when there is a lack of harmony or congruence among the overall organization goals, the subunit goals, and the individual goals of decision makers, or (2) when no guidance is given to subunit managers concerning the effects of their decisions on other parts of the organization. Suboptimal decision making is most likely to occur when the subunits in the organization are highly interdependent, such as when the end product of one subunit is the direct material of another subunit.

2. *Results in duplication of activities.* Several individual subunits of the organization may undertake the same activity separately. For example, there may be a duplication of staff functions (accounting, employee relations, and legal) if an organization is highly decentralized. Centralizing these functions helps to consolidate, streamline, and downsize these activities.

3. *Decreases loyalty toward the organization as a whole.* Individual subunit managers may regard the managers of other subunits in the same organization as external parties. Consequently, managers may be unwilling to share significant information or to assist when another subunit faces an emergency.

4. *Increases costs of gathering information.* Managers may spend too much time negotiating the prices for internal products or services transferred among subunits.

Comparison of Benefits and Costs

To choose an appropriate organization structure, top managers must compare the benefits and costs of decentralization, often on a function-by-function basis. For example, the controller's function may be highly decentralized for many attention-directing and problem-solving purposes (such as preparing operating budgets and performance reports) but highly centralized for other purposes (such as processing accounts receivables and developing income tax strategies). Decentralizing budgeting and cost reporting enables the marketing manager of a subunit, for example, to influence the design of product-line profitability reports for the subunit. Tailoring the report to the specific information that the manager may need helps the manager make better decisions and hence increases profits. Centralizing income tax strategies, on the other hand, allows the organization to trade off profits in some subunit with losses in others to evaluate the impact on the organization as a whole.

Surveys of U.S. and European companies report that the decisions made most frequently at the decentralized level and least frequently at the corporate level are related to sources of supplies, products to manufacture, and product advertising. Decisions related to the type and source of long-term financing are made least frequently at the decentralized level and most frequently at the corporate level.[1] Decentralized companies are generally large and unregulated, face great uncertainties in their environments, require detailed local knowledge for performing various jobs, and have few interdependencies among divisions.[2]

---

[1] *Evaluating the Performance of International Operations* (New York: Business International, 1989), p. 4; and *Managing the Global Finance Function* (London: Business International, 1992), p. 31.
[2] See A. Christie, M. Joye, and R. Watts, "Decentralization of the Firm: Theory and Evidence." Working Paper (University of Rochester, April 1991).

Decentralization in Multinational Companies

Multinational corporations are often decentralized. Language, customs, cultures, business practices, rules, laws, and regulations vary significantly across countries. Decentralization enables country managers to make decisions that exploit their knowledge of local business and political conditions and to deal with uncertainties in their individual environments. Phillips, a Dutch conglomerate, delegates marketing and pricing decisions for its television business in the Indian and Singaporean markets to its respective country managers. Multinational corporations often rotate managers between foreign locations and the home office. Job rotation combined with decentralization helps develop managers' abilities to operate in global environments.

Of course, there are several drawbacks to decentralizing multinational companies. One of the most important is the lack of control. Barings PLC, a British investment banking firm, went bankrupt and had to be sold when one of its traders in Singapore caused the firm to lose over £1 billion on unauthorized trades. Multinational corporations that implement decentralized decision making usually also design their management control systems to measure and monitor division performance. Information and communications technology eases the flow of data for reporting and control.

CHOICES ABOUT RESPONSIBILITY CENTERS

To measure the performance of subunits in centralized or decentralized organizations, the management control system uses one or a mix of the four types of responsibility centers presented in Chapter 6:

- *Cost center*—manager accountable for costs only.
- *Revenue center*—manager accountable for revenues only.
- *Profit center*—manager accountable for revenues and costs.
- *Investment center*—manager accountable for investments, revenues, and costs.

Centralization or decentralization is not mentioned in these descriptions. Why? Because each of these responsibility units can be found in either of the extremes of centralized and decentralized organizations.

A common misconception is that the term *profit center* (and, in some cases, *investment center*) is a synonym for a decentralized subunit and that *cost center* is a synonym for a centralized subunit. *Profit centers can be coupled with a highly centralized organization, and cost centers can be coupled with a highly decentralized organization.* For example, managers in a division organized as a profit center may have little leeway in making decisions. They may need to obtain approval from corporate headquarters for every expenditure over, say, $10,000 and may be forced to accept central-staff "advice." In another company, divisions may be organized as cost centers, but their managers may have great latitude on capital expenditures and on where to purchase materials and services. In short, the labels "profit center" and "cost center" are independent of the degree of decentralization in an organization.

TRANSFER PRICING

In decentralized organizations, individual subunits of an organization act as separate units. In these settings, the management control system often uses transfer prices to coordinate actions and to evaluate performance of the subunits.

An **intermediate product** is a product transferred from one subunit to another subunit of the same organization. This product may be processed further and sold to an external customer. A **transfer price** is the price one subunit (segment, department, division, and so on) of an organization charges for a product or service supplied to another subunit of the same organization. The transfer price creates revenue for the selling subunit and a purchase cost for the buying subunit, affecting operating income numbers for both subunits. The operating incomes can be used to evaluate the performance of each subunit and to motivate managers.

Alternative Transfer-Pricing Methods

There are three general methods for determining transfer prices:

OBJECTIVE 4

Identify three general methods for determining transfer prices

1. *Market-based transfer prices.* Upper management may choose to use the price of a similar product or service publicly listed in, say, a trade journal. Also, upper management may select, for the internal price, the external price that a subunit charges to outside customers.

2. *Cost-based transfer prices.* Upper management may choose a transfer price based on the costs of producing the product in question. Examples include variable manufacturing costs, manufacturing (absorption) costs, and full product costs. "Full product costs" include all production costs as well as costs from other business functions (R&D, design, marketing, distribution, and customer service). The costs used in cost-based transfer prices can be actual costs or budgeted costs.

3. *Negotiated transfer prices.* In some cases, the subunits of a company are free to negotiate the transfer price between themselves and then to decide whether to buy and sell internally or deal with outside parties. Subunits may use information about costs and market prices in these negotiations, but there is no requirement that the chosen transfer price bear any specific relationship to either cost or market-price data. Negotiated transfer prices are often employed when market prices are volatile and change occurs constantly. The negotiated transfer price is the outcome of a bargaining process between the selling and the buying divisions.

Ideally, the chosen transfer-pricing method should lead each subunit manager to make optimal decisions for the organization as a whole. As in all management control systems, transfer prices should help achieve an organization's strategies and goals, and fit its structure. In particular, it should promote *goal congruence* and a sustained high level of *management effort.* Sellers should be motivated to hold down costs of supplying a product or service, and buyers should be motivated to acquire and use inputs efficiently. If top management favors a high degree of decentralization, transfer prices should also promote a high level of subunit *autonomy* in decision making. **Autonomy** is the degree of freedom to make decisions.

AN ILLUSTRATION OF TRANSFER PRICING

Horizon Petroleum has three divisions. Each operates as a profit center. The Production Division manages the production of crude oil from a petroleum field near Matamoros, Mexico. The Transportation Division manages the operation of a pipeline that transports crude oil from the Matamoros area to Houston, Texas. The Refining Division manages a refinery at Houston that processes crude oil into gasoline. (For simplicity, assume that gasoline is the only salable product the refinery makes and that it takes two barrels of crude oil to yield one barrel of gasoline.)

OBJECTIVE 5

Understand how a transfer-pricing method can affect the operating income of individual subunits

Variable costs in each division are assumed to be variable with respect to a single cost driver in each division: barrels of crude oil produced by the Production Division, barrels of crude oil transported by the Transportation Division, and barrels of gasoline produced by the Refining Division. The fixed costs per unit are based on the budgeted annual output of crude oil to be produced and transported and the amount of gasoline to be produced. Horizon Petroleum reports all costs and revenues of its non-U.S. operations in U.S. dollars using the prevailing exchange rate.

- The Production Division can sell crude oil to outside parties in the Matamoros area at $13 per barrel.

- The Transportation Division "buys" crude oil from the Production Division, transports it to Houston, and then "sells" it to the Refining Division. The pipeline from Matamoros to Houston has the capacity to carry 40,000 barrels of crude oil per day.

- The Refining Division has been operating at capacity, 30,000 barrels of crude oil a day, using oil from Horizon's Production Division (an average of 10,000 barrels per day) and oil bought from other producers and delivered to the Houston Refinery (an average of 20,000 barrels per day, at $18 per barrel).

◆ The Refining Division sells the gasoline it produces at $52 per barrel.

Exhibit 25-1 summarizes Horizon Petroleum's variable and fixed costs per unit of the cost driver in each division, the external market prices of buying and selling crude oil, and the external market prices of selling gasoline. Consider the division operating income resulting from three transfer-pricing methods applied to a series of transactions involving 100 barrels of crude oil produced by Horizon's Production Division.

◆ Method A: Market-based transfer prices
◆ Method B: Cost-based transfer prices at 110% of full costs, where full costs are the cost of the transferred-in product plus the division's own variable and fixed costs
◆ Method C: Negotiated transfer prices

The transfer prices per barrel of crude oil under each method are as follows. The transferred-in cost component in method B is denoted by an asterisk (*).

◆ **Method A: Market-Based Transfer Prices**
  From Production Division to Transportation Division = $13
  From Transportation Division to Refining Division = $18

◆ **Method B: Cost-Based Transfer Prices at 110% of Full Costs** From Production Division to Transportation Division = 1.10($2 + $6) = $8.80
  From Transportation Division to Refining Division = 1.10($8.80* + $1 + $3) = $14.08

◆ **Method C: Transfer Prices Negotiated by Divisions to Be between Market-Based and Cost-Based Transfer Prices**
  From Production Division to Transportation Division = $10
  From Transportation Division to Refining Division = $16.75

Exhibit 25-2 presents division operating incomes per 100 barrels of crude oil reported under each transfer-pricing method. Transfer prices create income for the "selling" division and corresponding costs for the "buying" division that cancel out when divisional results are consolidated. The exhibit assumes that the different

EXHIBIT 25-1
Operating Data for Horizon Petroleum

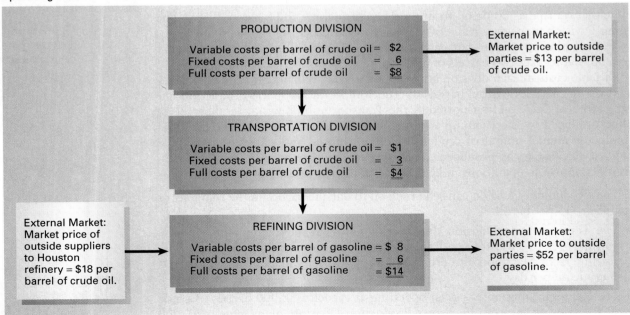

EXHIBIT 25-2
Division Operating Income of Horizon Petroleum for 100 Barrels of Crude Oil under
Alternative Transfer-Pricing Methods

	Method A	Method B	Method C
	Internal Transfers at Market Prices	**Internal Transfers at 110% of Full Costs**	**Internal Transfers at Negotiated Prices**
1. Production Division			
Revenues,			
$13, $8.80, $10, × 100 barrels crude oil	$1,300	$ 880	$1,000
Deduct:			
Division variable costs, $2 × 100 barrels crude oil	200	200	200
Division fixed costs, $6 × 100 barrels crude oil	600	600	600
Division operating income	$ 500	$ 80	$ 200
2. Transportation Division			
Revenues,			
$18, $14.08, $16.75, × 100 barrels crude oil	$1,800	$1,408	$1,675
Deduct:			
Transferred-in costs, $13, $8.80, $10, × 100 barrels crude oil	1,300	880	1,000
Division variable costs, $1 × 100 barrels crude oil	100	100	100
Division fixed costs, $3 × 100 barrels crude oil	300	300	300
Division operating income	$ 100	$ 128	$ 275
3. Refining Division			
Revenues,			
$52 × 50 barrels gasoline	$2,600	$2,600	$2,600
Deduct:			
Transferred-in costs, $18, $14.08, $16.75, × 100 barrels crude oil	1,800	1,408	1,675
Division variable costs, $8 × 50 barrels gasoline	400	400	400
Division fixed costs, $6 × 50 barrels gasoline	300	300	300
Division operating income	$ 100	$ 492	$ 225

transfer-pricing methods have no effect on the decisions and actions taken by the Production, Transportation, and Refining Division managers. Horizon Petroleum's total operating income from producing, transporting, and refining the 100 barrels of crude oil is therefore the same, $700 (revenues of $2,600 minus costs of $800 in production, $400 in transportation, and $700 in refining), regardless of internal transfer prices used. Keeping total operating income the same focuses attention on the effects of different transfer-pricing methods on division operating incomes. These incomes differ under the three methods. The operating income amounts span a $420 range ($80–$500) in the Production Division; a $175 range ($100–$275) in the Transportation Division; and a $392 range ($100–$492) in the Refining Division. Note that each division would choose a different transfer-pricing method if its sole criterion were to maximize its own division operating income: the Production Division would choose market prices, the Transportation Division would favor negotiated prices, and the Refining Division would choose 110% of full costs. Little wonder that division managers take considerable interest in the setting of transfer prices, especially those managers whose compensation or promotion directly depends on division operating income.

Exhibit 25-2 maintains companywide operating income at $700 and illustrates how the choice of a transfer-pricing method divides the companywide operating income pie among individual divisions. Subsequent sections of this chapter illustrate that the choice of a transfer-pricing method can also affect the decisions that individual division managers make and hence the size of the operating income pie itself. We consider this effect as we expand our discussion of market-based, cost-based, and negotiated transfer prices.

MARKET-BASED TRANSFER PRICES

Perfectly Competitive Market Case

Transferring products or services at market prices generally leads to optimal decisions when three conditions are satisfied: (1) the intermediate market is perfectly competitive, (2) interdependencies of subunits are minimal, and (3) there are no additional costs or benefits to the corporation as a whole in using the market instead of transacting internally. A **perfectly competitive market** exists when there is a homogeneous product with equivalent buying and selling prices and no individual buyers or sellers can affect those prices by their own actions. By using market-based transfer prices in perfectly competitive markets, a company can meet the criteria of goal congruence, management effort, and (if desired) subunit autonomy.

Reconsider the Horizon Petroleum example, assuming that there is a perfectly competitive market for crude oil in the Matamoros area. As a result, the Production Division can sell and the Transportation Division can buy as much crude oil as each wants at $13 per barrel. Horizon would like its managers to buy or sell crude oil internally. Think about the decisions that Horizon's division managers would make if each had the option to sell or buy crude oil externally. If the transfer price between Horizon's Production Division and Transportation Division is set below $13, the manager of the Production Division will be motivated to sell all production to outside buyers at $13 per barrel. If the transfer price is set above $13, the manager of the Transportation Division will be motivated to purchase all its crude oil requirements from outside suppliers. A transfer price of $13 will motivate the Production Division and the Transportation Division to buy and sell internally.

Suppose each division manager is motivated to maximize his or her own division operating income. The Production Division will sell (either internally or externally) as much crude oil as it can profitably sell, and the Transportation Division will buy (either internally or externally) as much crude oil as it can profitably transport. At a transfer price of $13, the actions that maximize division operating income are also the actions that maximize operating income of Horizon Petroleum as a whole. Market prices also serve to evaluate the economic performance and profitability of each division individually.

Distress Prices

When supply outstrips demand, market prices may drop well below their historical average. If the drop in prices is expected to be temporary, these low market prices are sometimes called "distress prices." Deciding whether a current market price is a distress price is often difficult. The market prices of several agricultural commodities, such as wheat and oats, have stayed for many years at what observers initially believed were temporary distress levels.

Which transfer-pricing method should be used for judging performance if distress prices prevail? Some companies use the distress prices themselves, but others use long-run average prices, or "normal" market prices. In the short run, the manager of the supplier division should meet the distress price as long as it exceeds the incremental costs of supplying the product or service; if not, the supplying division should stop producing and the buying division should buy the product or service from an outside supplier. These actions would increase overall companywide operating income. If the long-run average market price is used, forcing the manager to buy internally at a price above the current market price will hurt the buying division's short-run performance and understate its profitability. If, however, prices remain low in the long run, the manager of the supplying division must decide whether to dispose of some manufacturing facilities or shut down and have the buying division purchase the product from outside.

COST-BASED TRANSFER PRICES

Cost-based transfer prices are helpful when market prices are unavailable, inappropriate, or too costly to obtain. For example, the product may be specialized or unique, price lists may not be widely available, or the internal product may be different from the products available externally in terms of quality and service.

Full-Cost Bases

In practice, many companies use transfer prices based on full costs. These prices, however, can lead to suboptimal decisions. Assume that Horizon Petroleum makes internal transfers at 110% of full cost. The Houston Refining Division purchases, on average, 20,000 barrels of crude oil per day from a local Houston supplier, who delivers the crude oil to the refinery. Purchase and delivery cost $18 per barrel. To reduce crude oil costs, the Refining Division has located an independent producer in Matamoros who is willing to sell 20,000 barrels of crude oil per day at $13 per barrel, delivered to Horizon's pipeline in Matamoros. Given Horizon's organization structure, the Transportation Division would purchase the 20,000 barrels of crude oil in Matamoros, transport it to Houston, and then sell it to the Refining Division. The pipeline has excess capacity and can ship the 20,000 barrels at its variable costs of $1 per barrel without affecting the shipment of crude oil from Horizon's own Production Division. Will Horizon Petroleum incur lower costs by purchasing crude oil from the independent producer in Matamoros or by purchasing crude oil from the Houston supplier? Will the Refining Division show lower crude oil purchasing costs by using oil from the Matamoros producer or by using its current Houston supplier?

The following analysis shows that operating income of Horizon Petroleum as a whole would be maximized by purchasing oil from the independent Matamoros producer. The analysis compares the incremental costs in all divisions under the two alternatives.

- ◆ *Alternative 1:* Buy 20,000 barrels from Houston supplier at $18 per barrel.
  Total costs to Horizon Petroleum = 20,000 × $18 = $360,000

- ◆ *Alternative 2:* Buy 20,000 barrels in Matamoros at $13 per barrel and transport it to Houston at $1 per barrel variable costs.
  Total costs to Horizon Petroleum = 20,000 × ($13 + $1) = $280,000

There is a reduction in total costs to Horizon Petroleum of $80,000 by using the independent producer in Matamoros.

In turn, suppose the Transportation Division's transfer price to the Refining Division is 110% of full cost. The Refining Division will see its reported division costs increase if the crude oil is purchased from the independent producer in Matamoros:

$$\text{Transfer price} = 1.10 \times \left(\begin{array}{c} \text{Purchase price} \\ \text{from Matamoros} \\ \text{producer} \end{array} + \begin{array}{c} \text{Unit variable cost} \\ \text{of Transportation} \\ \text{Division} \end{array} + \begin{array}{c} \text{Unit fixed cost} \\ \text{of Transportation} \\ \text{Division} \end{array} \right)$$

$$= 1.10 \times (\$13 + \$1 + \$3) = 1.10 \times \$17 = \$18.70$$

- ◆ *Alternative 1:* Buy 20,000 barrels from Houston supplier at $18 per barrel.
  Total costs to Refining Division = 20,000 × $18 = $360,000

- *Alternative 2:* Buy 20,000 barrels from the Transportation Division of Horizon Petroleum that are purchased from the independent producer in Matamoros. Total costs to Refining Division = 20,000 × $18.70 = $374,000

As a profit center, the Refining Division can maximize its short-run division operating income by purchasing from the Houston supplier ($360,000 versus $374,000).

The transfer-pricing method has led the Refining Division to regard the fixed cost (and the 10% markup) of the Transportation Division as a variable cost. Why? Because the Refining Division looks at each barrel that it obtains from the Transportation Division as a variable cost of $18.70—if 10 barrels are transferred, it costs the Refining Division $187; if 100 barrels are transferred, it costs $1,870. From the point of view of Horizon Petroleum as a whole, its variable costs per barrel are $14 ($13 to purchase the oil from the independent producer and $1 to transport it to Houston). The remaining $4.70 ($18.70 − $14) per barrel are fixed costs and markups of the Transportation Division. Buying crude oil in Houston costs Horizon Petroleum an additional $18 per barrel. For the company, it is cheaper to buy from Matamoros. But the Refining Division sees the problem differently. From its standpoint, it prefers buying from the Houston supplier at a cost of $360,000 (20,000 barrels × $18 per barrel) because buying from Matamoros costs the division $374,000 (20,000 barrels × $18.70). Goal incongruence is induced by the transfer price based on full cost plus a markup.

What transfer price will promote goal congruence for both the Transportation Division and the Refining Division? The minimum transfer price is $14 per barrel; a transfer price below $14 does not provide the Transportation Division with an incentive to purchase crude oil from the independent producer in Matamoros while a transfer price above $14 generates contribution margin to cover fixed costs. The maximum transfer price is $18 per barrel; a transfer price above $18 will cause the Refining Division to purchase crude oil from the external market rather than from the Transportation Division. A transfer price between the minimum and maximum transfer prices of $14 and $18, respectively, will promote goal congruence—both divisions will increase their own reported division operating income by purchasing crude oil from the independent producer in Matamoros. In particular, a transfer price based on the full costs of $17 without a markup will achieve goal congruence. The Transportation Division will show no operating income and will be evaluated as a cost center. Surveys indicate that managers prefer to use full-cost transfer pricing because it yields relevant costs for long-run decisions and because it facilitates pricing on the basis of full product costs.

Using full-cost transfer prices that include an allocation of fixed overhead costs raises other issues. How are indirect costs allocated to products? Have the correct activities, cost pools, and cost drivers been identified? Are the chosen overhead rates actual or budgeted rates? The issues here are similar to the issues that arise in allocating fixed costs (Chapters 13 and 14). Full-cost-based transfer prices calculated using activity-based cost drivers can provide more refined allocation bases for allocating costs to products. Using budgeted costs and budgeted rates lets both divisions know the transfer price in advance. Also variations in the quantity of units produced by the selling division do not affect the transfer price.

Prorating the Difference between Minimum and Maximum Transfer Prices

An alternative cost-based approach is for Horizon Petroleum to choose a transfer price that splits the $4 difference between the maximum transfer price the Refining Division is willing to pay and the minimum transfer price the Transportation Division wants on some equitable basis. Suppose Horizon Petroleum allocates the $4 difference on the basis of the budgeted variable costs incurred by the Transportation Division and the Refining Division for a given quantity of crude oil. Using the data in Exhibit 25-2 (p. 907), the variable costs are as follows

Transportation Division to transport 100 barrels of crude oil	$100
Refining Division to refine 100 barrels of crude oil	400
	$500

The Transportation Division gets to keep $\frac{\$100}{\$500} \times \$4.00 = \$0.80$, and the Refining Division gets to keep $\frac{\$400}{\$500} \times \$4.00 = \$3.20$ of the $4 difference. That is, the transfer price between the Transportation Division and the Refining Division would be $14.80 per barrel of crude oil ($13 purchase cost + $1 variable costs + $0.80 that the Transportation Division gets to keep). Essentially, this approach is a budgeted variable cost plus transfer price; the "plus" indicates the setting of a transfer price above variable costs.

To decide on the $0.80 and $3.20 allocation of the $4.00 contribution to total corporate operating income per barrel, the divisions must share information about their variable costs. In effect, each division does not operate (at least for this transaction) in a totally decentralized manner. Because most organizations are hybrids of centralization and decentralization anyway, this approach deserves serious consideration when transfers are significant. Note, however, that each division has an incentive to overstate its variable costs in order to receive a more favorable transfer price.

Dual Pricing

There is seldom a *single* transfer price that simultaneously meets the criteria of goal congruence, management effort, and subunit autonomy. Some companies turn to **dual pricing,** using two separate transfer-pricing methods to price each interdivision transaction. An example of dual pricing arises when the selling division receives a full cost plus markup-based price and the buying division pays the market price for the internally transferred products. Assume that Horizon Petroleum purchases crude oil from the independent producer in Matamoros at $13 per barrel. One way of recording the journal entry for the transfer between the Transportation Division and the Refining Division is

1. Credit the Transportation Division (the selling division) with the 110%-of-full-cost transfer price of $18.70 per barrel of crude oil.
2. Debit the Refining Division (the buying division) with the market-based transfer price of $18 per barrel of crude oil.
3. Debit a corporate cost account for the $0.70 ($18.70 − $18.00) difference between the two transfer prices for the cost of crude oil borne by corporate rather than the Refining Division.

The dual-price method promotes goal congruence because it makes the Refining Division no worse off if it purchases the crude oil from the Transportation Division rather than from the outside supplier. In either case, the Refining Division's cost is $18 per barrel of crude oil. This dual-price system essentially gives the Transportation Division a corporate subsidy. The results of dual pricing? The operating income for Horizon Petroleum as a whole is less than the sum of the operating incomes of the divisions.

Dual pricing is not widely used in practice even though it reduces the goal-congruence problems associated with a pure cost-plus-based transfer-pricing method. One concern of top management is that the manager of the supplying division does not have sufficient incentive to control costs with a dual-price system. A second concern is that the dual-price system confuses division managers about the level of decentralization top management seeks. Above all, dual pricing tends to insulate managers from the frictions of the marketplace. Managers should know as much as possible about their subunits' buying and selling markets, and dual pricing reduces the incentive to gain this knowledge.

NEGOTIATED TRANSFER PRICES

Negotiated transfer prices arise as the outcome of a bargaining process between selling and buying divisions. Consider again the choice of a transfer price between the Transportation and Refining Divisions of Horizon Petroleum. The Transportation Division has excess capacity that it can use to transport oil from Matamoros to Houston. The Transportation Division will only be willing to "sell" oil to the Refin-

Domestic and Multinational Transfer-Pricing Practices

What transfer-pricing practices are used around the world? The following tables indicate how frequently particular transfer-pricing methods are used in different countries.

TRANSFER-PRICING METHODS

A. Domestic

Methods	United States*	Australia[†]	Canada[‡]	Japan*	India[§]	United Kingdom[#]	New Zealand[‖]
1. Market-price-based	37%	13%	34%	34%	47%	26%	18%
2. Cost-based							
Variable costs	4	—	6	2	6	10	10
Absorption or full costs	41	—	37	44	47	38	61
Other	1	—	3	—	—	1	—
Total	46	65	46	46	53	49	71
3. Negotiated	16	11	18	19	—	24	11
4. Other	1	11	2	1	—	1	—
	100%	100%	100%	100%	100%	100%	100%

B. Multinational

Methods	United States*	Australia[†]	Canada[‡]	Japan*	India[§]	United Kingdom**	New Zealand[‖]
1. Market-price-based	46%	—	37%	37%	—	31%	—
2. Cost-based							
Variable costs	3	—	5	3	—	5	—
Absorption or full costs	37	—	26	38	—	28	—
Other	1	—	2	—	—	5	—
Total	41	—	33	41	—	38	—
3. Negotiated	13	—	26	22	—	20	—
4. Other	0	—	4	—	—	11	—
	100%	—	100%	100%	—	100%	—

The surveys indicate that managers in all countries use cost-based transfer prices more frequently than market-price-based transfer prices for domestic transfer pricing. For multinational transfer pricing, managers use market-price-based and cost-based methods equally frequently.

What factors do executives consider important in decisions on domestic transfer pricing? Survey evidence indicates the following (in order of importance): (1) performance evaluation, (2) management motivation, (3) pricing and product emphasis, and (4) external market recognition.[††]

Factors cited as important in decisions on multinational transfer-pricing policy are (in order of importance) (1) overall income of the company, (2) income tax rate and other tax differences among countries, (3) income or dividend repatriation restrictions, and (4) competitive position of subsidiaries in their respective markets.[‡]

Note: Dashes indicate information was not disclosed in survey.
*Adapted from Tang, Walter, and Raymond, "Transfer Pricing."
[†]Joye and Blayney, "Cost and Management Accounting."
[‡]Tang, "Canadian Transfer."
[§]Govindarajan and Ramamurthy, "Transfer Pricing."
[#]Drury, Braund, Osborne, and Tayles, *A Survey of Management Accounting.*
[‖]Hoque and Alam, "Organization Size."
**Mostafa, Sharp, and Howard, "Transfer Pricing." Full citations are in Appendix A.
[††]Price Waterhouse, *Transfer Pricing Practices.*

ing Division if the transfer price equals or exceeds $14 per barrel of crude oil (its variable costs). The Refining Division will only be willing to "buy" crude oil from the Transportation Division if the cost equals or is below $18 per barrel (the price at which the Refining Division can buy crude oil in Houston).

From the viewpoint of Horizon Petroleum as a whole, operating income would be maximized if the Refining Division purchased from the Transportation Division rather than from the Houston market (incremental costs of $14 per barrel versus incremental costs of $18 per barrel). Both divisions would be interested in transacting with each other if the transfer price is set between $14 and $18. For example, a transfer price of $16.75 per barrel will increase the Transportation Division's operating income by $16.75 − $14 = $2.75 per barrel. It will increase the Refining Division's operating income by $18 − $16.75 = $1.25 per barrel because Refining can now "buy" the oil for $16.75 inside rather than for $18 outside.

The key question is where between the $14 and $18 will the transfer price be. The answer depends on the bargaining strengths of the two divisions. Negotiations become particularly sensitive if Horizon evaluates each division's performance on the basis of divisional operating income. The price negotiated by the two divisions will, in general, have no specific relationship to either costs or market price. But cost and price information are often useful starting points in the negotiation process.

OBJECTIVE 8

Understand the range over which two divisions generally negotiate the transfer price when there is excess capacity

A GENERAL GUIDELINE FOR TRANSFER-PRICING SITUATIONS

Is there an all-pervasive rule for transfer pricing that leads toward optimal decisions for the organization as a whole? No. Why? Because the three criteria of goal congruence, management effort, and subunit autonomy must all be considered simultaneously. The following general guideline, however, has proven to be a helpful first step in setting a minimum transfer price in many specific situations:

OBJECTIVE 9

Present a general guideline for determining a minimum transfer price in transfer-pricing situations

$$
\begin{array}{c}
\text{Minimum} \\
\text{transfer price}
\end{array} =
\begin{array}{c}
\text{Additional \textit{incremental} or \textit{outlay costs} per} \\
\text{unit incurred up to the point of transfer}
\end{array} +
\begin{array}{c}
\textit{Opportunity costs} \text{ per unit} \\
\text{to the supplying division}
\end{array}
$$

The term *incremental* or *outlay costs* in this context represents the additional costs that are directly associated with the production and transfer of the products or services. *Opportunity costs* are defined here as the maximum contribution forgone by the supplying division if the products or services are transferred internally. For example, if the supplying division is operating at capacity, the opportunity cost of transferring a unit internally rather than selling it externally is equal to the market price minus variable costs. We distinguish incremental costs from opportunity costs because the accounting system typically records incremental costs but not opportunity costs. We illustrate the general guideline in some specific situations using data from the Production and Transportation Divisions of Horizon Petroleum.

1. *A perfectly competitive market for the intermediate product exists, and the supplying division has no idle capacity.* If the market for crude oil is perfectly competitive, the Production Division can sell all the crude oil it produces to the external market at $13 per barrel, and it will have no idle capacity. The Production Division's incremental costs (see Exhibit 25-1, p. 906) are $2 per barrel of crude oil. The Production Division's opportunity cost per barrel of transferring the oil internally is the contribution margin per barrel of $11 (market price, $13 − variable cost, $2) forgone by not selling the crude oil in the external market. In this case,

$$
\begin{array}{c}
\text{Minimum transfer} \\
\text{price per barrel}
\end{array} =
\begin{array}{c}
\text{Incremental costs} \\
\text{per barrel}
\end{array} +
\begin{array}{c}
\text{Opportunity costs} \\
\text{per barrel}
\end{array}
$$

$$
= \$2 + \$11 = \$13 = \text{Market price per barrel}
$$

Market-based transfer prices are ideal in perfectly competitive markets when there is no idle capacity.

2. *An intermediate market exists that is not perfectly competitive, and the supplying division has idle capacity.* In markets that are not perfectly competitive, capacity utilization can only be increased by decreasing prices. Idle capacity exists because decreasing prices is often not worthwhile—it decreases operating income.

If the Production Division has idle capacity, its opportunity cost of transferring the oil internally is zero because the division does not forgo any external sales and hence does not forgo any contribution margin from internal transfers. In this case,

$$\frac{\text{Minimum transfer}}{\text{price per barrel}} = \frac{\text{Incremental costs}}{\text{per barrel}} = \$2 \text{ per barrel}$$

Note that any transfer price between $2 and $13 (the price at which the Transportation Division can buy crude oil in Matamoros) motivates the Production Division to produce and sell crude oil to the Transportation Division and the Transportation Division to buy crude oil from the Production Division. In this situation, the company could either use a cost-based transfer price or allow the two divisions to negotiate a transfer price between themselves.

In general though, in markets that are not perfectly competitive, the potential to influence demand and operating income through prices makes measuring opportunity costs more complicated. The transfer price depends on constantly changing levels of supply and demand. There is not just one transfer price; rather, a transfer-pricing schedule yields the transfer price for various quantities supplied and demanded, depending on the incremental costs and opportunity costs of the units transferred.

3. *No market exists for the intermediate product.* This would occur, for example, in the Horizon Petroleum case if oil from the production well flows directly into the pipeline and cannot be sold to outside parties. Here, the opportunity cost of supplying crude oil internally is zero because the inability to sell crude oil externally means no contribution margin is forgone. At the Production Division of Horizon Petroleum, the minimum transfer price under the general guideline would be the incremental costs per barrel of $2. As in the previous case, any transfer price between $2 and $13 will achieve goal congruence. If the transfer price is set at $2, of course, the Production Division would never record positive operating income and would show poor performance. One approach to overcoming this problem is to have the Transportation Division make a lump-sum payment to cover fixed costs and generate some operating income for the Production Division while the Production Division continues to make transfers at incremental costs of $2 per barrel.

MULTINATIONAL TRANSFER PRICING AND TAX CONSIDERATIONS

Transfer prices often have tax implications. Tax factors include not only income taxes, but also payroll taxes, customs duties, tariffs, sales taxes, value-added taxes, environment-related taxes, and other government levies on organizations. Full consideration of tax aspects of transfer-pricing decisions is beyond the scope of this book. Our aim here is to highlight tax factors and, in particular, income taxes as an important consideration in transfer-pricing decisions.

Consider the Horizon Petroleum data in Exhibit 25-2. Assume that the Production Division based in Mexico pays Mexican income taxes at 30% of operating income and that both the Transportation and Refining Divisions based in the United States pay income taxes at 20% of operating income. Horizon Petroleum would minimize its total income tax payments with the 110%-of-full-costs transfer-pricing method, as shown in the following table:

Transfer-Pricing Method	Operating Income for 100 Barrels of Crude Oil			Income Tax on 100 Barrels of Crude Oil		
	Production Division (1)	Transportation and Refining Divisions (2)	Total (3) = (1) + (2)	Production Division (4) = 0.30 × (1)	Transportation and Refining Divisions (5) = 0.20 × (2)	Total (6) = (4) + (5)
A. Market Price	$500	$200	$700	$150	$ 40	$190
B. 110% of full costs	80	620	700	24	124	148
C. Negotiated price	200	500	700	60	100	160

Tax considerations raise additional issues that may conflict with other objectives of transfer pricing. Suppose that the market for crude oil in Matamoros is perfectly competitive. In this case, the market-based transfer price achieves goal congruence and provides effort incentives. It also helps Horizon to evaluate the economic profitability of the Production Division. But it is costly from an income tax standpoint.

Horizon Petroleum would favor using 110% of full costs for tax reporting. Tax laws in the United States and Mexico constrain this option. In particular, the Mexican tax authorities are fully aware of Horizon Petroleum's incentives to minimize income taxes by reducing the income reported in Mexico. They would challenge any attempts to shift income to the Transportation and Refining Divisions through a low transfer price.

Section 482 of the U.S. Internal Revenue Code governs taxation of multinational transfer pricing. Section 482 requires that transfer prices for both tangible and intangible property between a company and its foreign division or subsidiary be set to equal the price that would be charged by an unrelated third party in a comparable transaction. Section 482 recognizes that transfer prices can be market-price-based or cost-plus-based (where the plus represents margins on comparable transactions).[3]

The perfectly competitive market for crude oil in Matamoros would probably force Horizon Petroleum to use the market price for transfers from the Production Division to the Transportation Division. Horizon Petroleum might successfully argue that the transfer price should be set below the market price because the Production Division incurs no marketing and distribution costs when "selling" crude oil to the Transportation Division. Under the U.S. Internal Revenue Code, Horizon Petroleum could obtain advanced approval of the transfer pricing arrangements from the tax authorities.

Consider another example of a U.S. company that manufactures and sells products from Ireland. Tax and other incentives offered by Ireland results in the Irish division paying lower taxes on its income in Ireland. Therefore, the company has an incentive to set the transfer price for transfers into the United States as high as possible. Why? To maximize income reported in Ireland where tax rates are lower and reduce income reported in the United States that is taxed at rates as high as 40%. Section 482 restricts the company's transfer-pricing choices to the price that would be charged by an unrelated third party.

To meet multiple transfer-pricing objectives, a company may choose to keep one set of accounting records for tax reporting and a second set for internal management reporting. The difficulty here is that tax authorities may interpret two sets of books as suggestive of the company manipulating its reported taxable income to avoid tax payments.

Additional factors that arise in multinational transfer pricing include tariffs and customs duties levied on imports of products into a country. The issues here are similar to the income tax considerations discussed earlier—companies will have incentives to lower transfer prices for products imported into a country to reduce the tariffs and customs duties that those products will attract.

In addition to the various motivations for choosing transfer prices described so far, multinational transfer prices are sometimes influenced by restrictions that some countries place on the payment of income or dividends to parties outside their national borders. By increasing the prices of goods or services transferred into divisions in these countries, companies can increase the funds paid out of these countries without appearing to violate income or dividend restrictions.

---

[3]Business International Corporation, *International Transfer Pricing* (New York, 1991); A. King, "The IRS's New Neutron Bomb," *Management Accounting* (Dec. 1992); Coopers and Lybrand, *Tax Topics Advisory* (Jan. 21, 1993); P. Rooney and N. Suit, "IRS Relaxes Transfer Pricing Rules," *International Tax Review* (Oct. 1994); and D. K. Dolan, and D. Bower, "Final Transfer Pricing Regulations," *Tax Management International Journal* (July 1994).

U.S. Internal Revenue Service, Japanese National Tax Agency, and Transfer Pricing Games

Tax authorities and government officials all over the world pay close attention to taxes paid by foreign corporations operating within their boundaries. In the United States, the huge Federal budget deficit has heightened interest in whether foreign corporations pay their fair share of U.S. taxes. At the heart of the issue: the transfer prices that companies use to transfer products from one country to another.

In 1993, the U.S. Internal Revenue Service (IRS) investigated and concluded that Nissan Motor Company had minimized U.S. taxes by setting transfer prices on passenger cars and trucks imported from Japan at "unrealistically" high levels. Nissan argued that it had maintained low margins in the United States to increase long-run market share in a very competitive market. Eventually, Nissan agreed to pay the IRS $170 million. But Nissan suffered no loss. The Japanese National Tax Agency (NTA), Japan's tax authority, refunded Nissan the full amount of the IRS payment.

In May 1994, Japan's NTA alleged that Coca-Cola Corporation had deliberately under-recorded profits earned in Japan both by charging "excessive" transfer prices to its local subsidiary for materials and concentrate imported from the parent company and by levying "excessive" royalty payments on its Japanese subsidiary. The NTA imposed taxes and penalties of $150 million. The NTA also took similar action against three European pharmaceutical companies, Ciba-Geigy, Roche, and Hoechst.

The dispute over what is a "fair" transfer price arises in each of these cases because of the absence of an easily observable market price for the transferred product. Multinational transfer pricing disputes are likely to remain a significant issue given the substantial and increasing amounts of multinational investments.

Source: Adapted from C. Pass, "Transfer Pricing in Multinational Companies," *Management Accounting,* September, 1994.

PROBLEM

The Pillercat Corporation is a highly decentralized company. Each division manager has full authority for sourcing decisions and selling decisions. The Machining Division of Pillercat has been the major supplier of the 2,000 crankshafts that the Tractor Division needs each year.

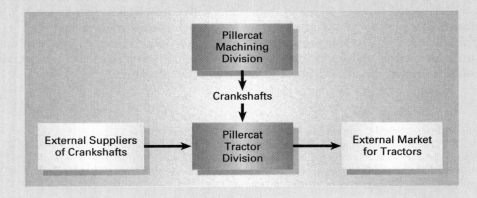

The Tractor Division, however, has just announced that it plans to purchase all its crankshafts in the forthcoming year from two external suppliers at $200 per crankshaft. The Machining Division of Pillercat recently increased its price for the forthcoming year to $220 per unit (from $200 per unit in the current year).

Juan Gomez, manager of the Machining Division, feels that the 10% price increase is fully justified. It results from a higher depreciation charge on some new specialized equipment used to manufacture crankshafts and an increase in labor costs. Gomez wants the president of Pillercat Corporation to direct the Tractor Division to buy all its crankshafts from the Machining Division at the price of $220. The additional incremental costs per unit that Pillercat incurs to produce each crankshaft is the Machining Division's variable costs of $190. Fixed costs per crankshaft in the Machining Division equals $20.

REQUIRED

1. Compute the advantage or disadvantage (in terms of monthly operating income) to the Pillercat Corporation as a whole if the Tractor Division buys crankshafts internally from the Machining Division under each of the following cases.
   a. The Machining Division has no alternative use for the facilities used to manufacture crankshafts.
   b. The Machining Division can use the facilities for other production operations, which will result in monthly cash operating savings of $29,000.
   c. The Machining Division has no alternative use for the facilities, and the external supplier drops its price to $185 per crankshaft.
2. As the president of Pillercat, how would you respond to Juan Gomez's request to order the Tractor Division to purchase all of its crankshafts from the Machining Division? Would your response differ according to the scenarios described in parts a, b, and c of requirement 1? Why?

SOLUTION

1. Computations for the Tractor Division buying crankshafts internally.

	Case		
	(a)	(b)	(c)
Total purchase costs if buying from an external supplier (2,000 × $200, $200, $185)	$400,000	$400,000	$370,000
Total incremental costs if buying from the Machining Division (2,000 × $190)	380,000	380,000	380,000
Total opportunity costs of the Machining Division	—	29,000	—
Total relevant costs	380,000	409,000	380,000
Monthly operating income advantage (disadvantage) to the Pillercat Corporation of buying from the Machining Division	$ 20,000	$ (9,000)	$ (10,000)

The general guideline that was introduced in the chapter as a first step in setting a transfer price can be used to highlight the alternatives:

Case	Additional Incremental Costs per Unit Incurred to Point of Transfer	+	Opportunity Costs per Unit to the Supplying Division	=	Transfer Price	External Market Price
(a)	$190	+	$0	=	$190	$200
(b)	$190	+	$14.50 ($29,000 ÷ 2,000)	=	$204.50	$200
(c)	$190	+	$0	=	$190	$185

The Tractor Division will maximize monthly operating income of Pillercat Corporation as a whole by purchasing from the Machining Division in Case (a) and by purchasing from the external supplier in Cases (b) and (c).

2. Pillercat Corporation is a highly decentralized company. If no forced transfer were made, the Tractor Division would use an external supplier, resulting in an optimal decision for the company as a whole in Cases (b) and (c) of requirement 1 but not in Case (a).

Suppose that in Case 1(a), the Machining Division refuses to meet the price of $200. This decision means that the company will be $20,000 worse off in the short-run. Should top management interfere and force a transfer at $200? This interference would undercut the philosophy of decentralization. Many top managements would not interfere because they would view the $20,000 as an inevitable cost of a suboptimal decision that occasionally occurs under decentralization. But how high must this cost be before the temptation to interfere would be irresistible? $30,000? $40,000?

Any top management interference with lower-level decision making weakens decentralization. Of course, such interference may occasionally be necessary to prevent costly blunders. But recurring interference and constraints simply transform a decentralized organization into a centralized organization.

SUMMARY

The following points are linked to the chapter's learning objectives.

1. A management control system is a means of gathering and using information to aid and coordinate the process of making planning and control decisions throughout the organization, and to guide employee behavior.

2. Effective management control systems are closely aligned to the organization's strategy, fit the organization's structure, and motivate managers and employees to give effort to achieve the organization's goals.

3. The benefits of decentralization include (a) greater responsiveness to local needs, (b) gains from quicker decision making, (c) increased motivation of subunit managers, (d) greater management development and learning, and (e) sharper management focus. The costs of decentralization include (a) dysfunctional decision making (control loss), (b) duplication of activities, (c) decreased loyalty toward the organization, and (d) increased costs of information gathering.

4. Transfer prices can be (a) market-based, (b) cost-based, or (c) negotiated.

5. Different transfer-pricing methods produce different revenues and costs for individual subunits, and hence different operating incomes for them.

6. In perfectly competitive markets, there is no idle capacity, and division managers can buy and sell as much as they want at the market price. Setting the transfer price at the market price motivates division managers to deal internally and to take exactly the same actions as they would if they were dealing in the external market.

7. A transfer price based on full cost plus a markup may lead to suboptimal decisions because it leads the "buying" division to regard the fixed costs and the markup of the selling division as variable costs.

8. When there is excess capacity, the transfer price range for negotiations generally lies between the minimum price at which the selling division is willing to sell (its variable costs) and the maximum price the buying division is willing to pay (the price at which the product is available from outside suppliers).

9. The general guideline for transfer pricing states that the minimum transfer price equals the incremental costs per unit incurred up to the point of transfer *plus* the opportunity costs per unit to the supplying division resulting from transferring products or services internally.

10. Transfer prices can reduce income tax payments by recognizing more income in low tax rate countries and lower income in high tax rate countries.

This chapter and the Glossary at the end of this book contain definitions of the following important terms:

autonomy (p. 905)

decentralization (902)

dual pricing (911)

effort (901)

goal congruence (901)

incongruent decision making (903)

intermediate product (904)

management control system (900)

motivation (901)

perfectly competitive market (908)

suboptimal decision making (903)

transfer price (904)

▼ **ASSIGNMENT MATERIAL**

QUESTIONS

25-1 What is a management control system?

25-2 Describe three criteria you would use to evaluate whether a management control system is effective.

25-3 What is the relationship among motivation, goal congruence, and effort?

25-4 Name three benefits and two costs of decentralization.

25-5 "Organizations typically adopt a consistent decentralization or centralization philosophy across all their business functions." Do you agree? Explain.

25-6 "Transfer pricing is confined to profit centers." Do you agree? Why?

25-7 What are the three general methods for determining transfer prices?

25-8 What properties should transfer-pricing systems have?

25-9 "All transfer-pricing methods give the same division operating income." Do you agree? Explain.

25-10 Under what conditions is a market-based transfer price optimal?

25-11 What is one potential limitation of full-cost-based transfer prices?

25-12 Give two reasons why a dual-price approach to transfer pricing is not widely used.

25-13 "Cost and price information play no role in negotiated transfer prices." Do you agree? Explain.

25-14 "Under the general transfer-pricing guideline, the minimum transfer price will vary depending on whether the supplying division has idle capacity or not." Do you agree? Explain.

25-15 Why should managers consider income tax issues when choosing a transfer-pricing method?

EXERCISES

25-16 Goals of public accounting firms. All personnel, including partners, of public accounting firms must usually turn in biweekly time reports, showing how many hours were devoted to their various duties. These firms have traditionally looked unfavorably on idle or unassigned staff time. They have looked favorably on heavy percentages of chargeable (billable) time because this maximizes revenue.

REQUIRED

What effect is such a policy likely to have on the behavior of the firm's personnel? Can you relate this practice to the problem of goal congruence that was discussed in this chapter? How?

25-17 Decentralization, goal congruence, responsibility centers. Hexton Chemicals consists of seven operating divisions that each operate independently. The operating divisions are supported by a number of support divisions such as R&D, labor relations, and environmental management. The environmental management group consists of 20 environmental engineers. These engineers must seek out business from the operating divisions—that is, the projects they work on must be mutually agreed to and paid for by one of the operating divisions. Under Hexton's rules, the environmental group is required to charge the operating divisions for environmental services at cost.

REQUIRED
1. Is the environmental management organization centralized or decentralized?
2. What type of responsibility center is the environmental management group?
3. What benefits and problems do you see in structuring the environmental management group the way Hexton has? Does it lead to goal congruence and motivation?

25-18 Multinational transfer pricing, effect of alternative transfer-pricing methods, global income tax minimization. User Friendly Computer, Inc., with headquarters in San Francisco, manufactures and sells desk-top computers. User Friendly has three divisions, each of which is located in a different country:
a. China Division—manufactures memory devices and keyboards.
b. South Korea Division—assembles desk-top computers, using internally manufactured parts and memory devices and keyboards from the China Division.
c. U.S. Division—packages and distributes desk-top computers.

   Each division is run as a profit center. The costs for the work done in each division that is associated with a single desk-top computer unit are as follows:

China Division:	Variable costs = 1,000 yuan
	Fixed costs = 1,800 yuan
South Korea Division:	Variable costs = 240,000 won
	Fixed costs = 320,000 won
U.S. Division:	Variable costs = $100
	Fixed costs = $200

Chinese income tax rate on China Division's operating income	40%
South Korean income tax rate in South Korea Division's operating income	20%
U.S. income tax rate on U.S. Division's operating income	30%

Each desk-top computer is sold to retail outlets in the United States for $3,200. Assume that the current foreign exchange rates are

8 yuan = $1 U.S.

800 won = $1 U.S.

   Both the China and the South Korea divisions sell part of their production under a private label. The China division sells the comparable memory/keyboard package used in each User Friendly desk-top computer to a Chinese manufacturer for 3,600 yuan. The South Korea division sells the comparable desk-top computer to a South Korean distributor for 1,040,000 won.

REQUIRED
1. Calculate the after-tax operating income per unit earned by each division under each of the following transfer-pricing methods: (a) market price, (b) 200% of full costs, and (c) 300% of variable costs. (Income taxes are *not* included in the computation of the cost-based transfer prices.)

2. Which transfer-pricing method(s) will maximize the net income per unit of User Friendly Computer, Inc?

25-19 Transfer-pricing methods, goal congruence. British Columbia Lumber has a Raw Lumber Division and Finished Lumber Division. The variable costs are

◆ Raw Lumber Division: $100 per 100 board-feet of raw lumber
◆ Finished Lumber Division: $125 per 100 board-feet of finished lumber

Assume that there is no board-feet loss in processing raw lumber into finished lumber. Raw lumber can be sold at $200 per 100 board-feet. Finished lumber can be sold at $275 per 100 board-feet.

REQUIRED

1. Should British Columbia Lumber process raw lumber into its finished form?
2. Assume that internal transfers are made at 110% of variable costs. Will each division maximize its division operating income contribution by adopting the action that is in the best interests of British Columbia Lumber?
3. Assume that internal transfers are made at market prices. Will each division maximize its division operating income contribution by adopting the action that is in the best interests of British Columbia Lumber?

25-20 Effect of alternative transfer-pricing methods on division operating income. (CMA, adapted) Ajax Corporation has two divisions. The Mining Division makes toldine, which is then transferred to the Metals Division. The toldine is further processed by the Metals Division and is sold to customers at a price of $150 per unit. The Mining Division is currently required by Ajax to transfer its total yearly output of 400,000 units of toldine to the Metals Division at 110% of full manufacturing cost. Unlimited quantities of toldine can be purchased and sold on the outside market at $90 per unit. To sell the toldine it produces at $90 per unit on the outside market, the Mining Division would have to incur variable marketing and distribution costs of $5 per unit. Similarly, if the Metals Division purchased toldine from the outside market, it would have to incur variable purchasing costs of $3 per unit.

The following table gives the manufacturing costs per unit in the Mining and Metals Divisions for the year 19_7:

	Mining Division	Metals Division
Direct materials	$12	$ 6
Direct manufacturing labor costs	16	20
Manufacturing overhead costs	32*	25†
Manufacturing costs per unit	$60	$51

*Manufacturing overhead costs in the Mining Division are 25% fixed and 75% variable.
†Manufacturing overhead costs in the Metals Division are 60% fixed and 40% variable.

REQUIRED

1. Calculate the operating incomes for the Mining and Metals Divisions for the 400,000 units of toldine transferred under each of the following transfer-pricing methods: (a) market price, and (b) 110% of full manufacturing costs.
2. Suppose Ajax rewards each division manager with a bonus, calculated as 1% of division operating income (if positive). What is the amount of bonus that will be paid to each division manager under each of the transfer-pricing methods in requirement 1? Which transfer-pricing method will each division manager prefer to use?
3. What arguments would Brian Jones, manager of the Mining Division, make to support the transfer-pricing method that he prefers?

25-21 Goal congruence, negotiated transfer prices. Refer to the information in Exercise 25-20. Suppose that the Mining Division is not required to transfer its yearly output of 400,000 units of toldine to the Metals Division.

REQUIRED

1. From the standpoint of Ajax Corporation as a whole, what quantity of toldine should the Mining Division transfer to the Metals Division?
2. Now suppose each division manager acts autonomously to maximize the division's operating income. What range of transfer prices will result in managers of the Metals and Mining Divisions achieving the actions determined to be optimal in requirement 1? Explain your answer.
3. Would you recommend that Ajax allow the divisions to buy and sell toldine in the open market, and to negotiate the transfer price between themselves? Explain your answer.

25-22 Multinational transfer pricing, global tax minimization. The Mornay Company manufactures telecommunications equipment at its Wisconsin factory in the United States. The company has marketing divisions throughout the world. A Mornay marketing division in Vienna, Austria, imports 1,000 units of a particular equipment called Product 4A36 from the United States. The following information is available:

U.S. income tax rate on the U.S. division's operating income	40%
Austrian income tax rate on the Austrian division's operating income	44%
Austrian import duty	10%
Variable manufacturing cost per unit of Product 4A36	$350
Full manufacturing cost per unit of Product 4A36	$500
Selling price (net of marketing and distribution costs) in Austria	$750

Suppose the U.S. and Austrian tax authorities only allow transfer prices that are between the full manufacturing cost per unit and a market price of $650 based on comparable imports into Austria. The Austrian import duty is charged on the price at which the product is transferred into Austria. Any import duty paid to the Austrian authorities is a deductible expense for calculating Austrian income taxes due.

REQUIRED

1. Calculate the after-tax operating income earned by the U.S. and Austrian divisions from transferring 1,000 units of Product 4A36 at (a) full manufacturing cost per unit, and (b) market price of comparable imports. (Income taxes are *not* included in the computation of the cost-based transfer prices.)
2. Which transfer price should the Mornay Company select to minimize the total of company import duties and income taxes? Recall that the transfer price must be between the full manufacturing cost per unit of $500 and the market price of $650 of comparable imports into Austria. Explain your reasoning.

25-23 Multinational transfer pricing, goal congruence (continuation of 25-22). Suppose that the U.S. division could sell as many units of Product 4A36 as it makes at $600 per unit in the U.S. market , net of all marketing and distribution costs.

REQUIRED

1. From the viewpoint of the Mornay Company as a whole, would after-tax operating income be maximized if it sold the 1,000 units of Product 4A36 in the United States or in Austria?
2. Suppose each division manager acts autonomously to maximize their division's after-tax operating income. Will the transfer price calculated in requirement 2 of Exercise 25-22 result in the U.S. division manager taking the actions determined to be optimal in requirement 1 of this exercise? Explain.
3. What is the minimum transfer price that the U.S. division manager would agree to? Does this transfer price result in the Mornay Company as a whole paying more import duty and taxes than the answer to requirement 2 of Exercise 25-22? If so, by how much?

25-24 Transfer-pricing dispute. The Allison-Chambers Corporation, manufacturer of tractors and other heavy farm equipment, is organized along decentralized lines, with each manufacturing division operating as a separate profit center. Each division manager has been delegated full authority on all decisions involving the sale of that division's output both to outsiders and to other divisions of Allison-Chambers. Division C has in the past always purchased its requirement of a particular tractor-engine component from Division A. However, when informed that Division A is increasing its selling price to $150, Division C's manager decides to purchase the engine component from outside suppliers.

Division C can purchase the component for $135 on the open market. Division A insists that, because of the recent installation of some highly specialized equipment and the resulting high depreciation charges, it will not be able to earn an adequate return on its investment unless it raises its price. Division A's manager appeals to top management of Allison-Chambers for support in the dispute with Division C and supplies the following operating data:

C's annual purchases of tractor-engine component	1,000 units
A's variable costs per unit of tractor-engine component	$120
A's fixed costs per unit of tractor-engine component	$20

REQUIRED

1. Assume that there are no alternative uses for internal facilities. Determine whether the company as a whole will benefit if Division C purchases the component from outside suppliers for $135 per unit.
2. Assume that internal facilities of Division A would not otherwise be idle. By not producing the 1,000 units for Division C, Division A's equipment and other facilities would be used for other production operations that would result in annual cash-operating savings of $18,000. Should Division C purchase from outside suppliers?
3. Assume that there are no alternative uses for Division A's internal facilities and that the price from outsiders drops $20. Should Division C purchase from outside suppliers?

25-25 Transfer-pricing problem (continuation of 25-24). Refer to Exercise 25-24. Assume that Division A can sell the 1,000 units to other customers at $155 per unit with variable marketing costs of $5 per unit.

REQUIRED

Determine whether Allison-Chambers will benefit if Division C purchases the 1,000 components from outside suppliers at $135 per unit.

25-26 Transfer pricing, goal congruence. (CMA, adapted) Nogo Motors, Inc., has several regional divisions that often purchase component parts from each other. The company is fully decentralized, each division buying and selling to other divisions or in outside markets. Each division makes its decision on where to buy and sell in conformity with division goals. Igo Division purchases most of its airbags from Letgo Division. The managers of these two divisions are currently negotiating a transfer price for the airbags for next year, when the airbag will be standard equipment on all Igo vehicles. Letgo Division prepares the following financial information for negotiating purposes:

Costs per airbag	
Direct materials costs	$ 40
Direct manufacturing labor costs	55
Variable manufacturing overhead costs	10
Fixed manufacturing overhead costs	25
Variable marketing costs	5
Fixed marketing costs	15
Fixed administrative costs	10
Total costs per airbag	$160

Letgo Division is currently working at 80% of its capacity. Letgo's policy is to achieve an operating income of 20% of sales.

There has been a drop in the price of airbags. The current market price is $130 per unit.

REQUIRED

Consider each of the requirements independently.

1. If Letgo Division desires to achieve its operating income goal of 20% of sales, what should the transfer price be?
2. Assume that Letgo Division wants to maximize its operating income. What transfer price would you recommend that the Letgo Division negotiate?
3. What is the transfer price that you believe Letgo Division should charge if overall company operating income is to be maximized?

PROBLEMS

25-27 Pertinent transfer price. Europa, Inc., has two divisions, A and B, which manufacture expensive bicycles. Division A produces the bicycle frame, and Division B assembles the rest of the bicycle onto the frame. There is a market for both the subassembly and the final product. Each division has been designated as a profit center. The transfer price for the subassembly has been set at the long-run average market price. The following data are available to each division:

Estimated selling price for final product	$300
Long-run average selling price for intermediate product	200
Incremental costs for completion in Division B	150
Incremental costs in Division A	120

The manager of Division B has made the following calculation:

Selling price for final product		$300
Transferred-in costs (market)	$200	
Incremental costs for completion	150	350
Contribution (loss) on product		$ (50)

REQUIRED

1. Should transfers be made to Division B if there is no excess capacity in Division A? Is the market price the correct transfer price?
2. Assume that Division A's maximum capacity for this product is 1,000 units per month and sales to the intermediate market are now 800 units. Should 200 units be transferred to Division B? At what transfer price? Assume that for a variety of reasons, A will maintain the $200 selling price indefinitely; that is, A is not considering lowering the price to outsiders even if idle capacity exists.
3. Suppose Division A quoted a transfer price of $150 for up to 200 units. What would be the contribution to the company as a whole if the transfer were made? As manager of Division B, would you be inclined to buy at $150?

25-28 Pricing in imperfect markets (continuation of 25-27). Refer to Problem 25-27.

REQUIRED

1. Suppose the manager of Division A has the option of (a) cutting the external price to $195 with the certainty that sales will rise to 1,000 units, or (b) maintaining the outside price of $200 for the 800 units and transferring the 200 units to Division B at some price that would produce the same operating income for Division A. What transfer price would produce the same operating income for Division A? Does that price coincide

with that produced by the general guideline in the chapter so that the desirable decision for the company as a whole would result?

2. Suppose that if the selling price for the intermediate product is dropped to $195, outside sales can be increased to 900 units. Division B wants to acquire as many as 200 units if the transfer price is acceptable. For simplicity, assume that there is no outside market for the final 100 units of Division A's capacity.

   a. Using the general guideline, what is (are) the minimum transfer price(s) that should lead to the correct economic decision? Ignore performance-evaluation considerations.

   b. Compare the total contributions under the alternatives to show why the transfer price(s) recommended lead(s) to the optimal economic decision.

25-29 Effect of alternative transfer-pricing methods on division operating income. Oceanic Products is a tuna fishing company based in San Diego. It has three divisions:

a. Tuna Harvesting—operates a fleet of 20 trawling vessels.

b. Tuna Processing—processes the raw tuna into tuna fillets.

c. Tuna Marketing—packages tuna fillets in 2-pound packets that are sold to wholesale distributors at $12 each.

The Tuna Processing Division has a yield of 500 pounds of processed tuna fillets from 1,000 pounds of raw tuna provided by the Tuna Harvesting Division. The Tuna Marketing Division has a yield of 300 2-pound packets from every 500 pounds of processed tuna fillets provided by the Tuna Processing Division. (The weight of the packaging material is included in the 2-pound weight.) Cost data for each division are as follows:

Tuna Harvesting Division	
Variable costs per pound of raw tuna	$0.20
Fixed costs per pound of raw tuna	$0.40
Tuna Processing Division	
Variable costs per pound of processed tuna	$0.80
Fixed costs per pound of processed tuna	$0.60
Tuna Marketing Division	
Variable costs per 2-pound packet	$0.30
Fixed costs per 2-pound packet	$0.70

Fixed costs per unit are based on the estimated quantity of raw tuna, processed tuna, and 2-pound packets to be produced during the current fishing season.

Oceanic Products has chosen to process internally all raw tuna brought in by the Tuna Harvesting Division. Other tuna processors in San Diego purchase raw tuna from boat operators at $1 per pound. Oceanic Products has also chosen to process internally all tuna fillets into the 2-pound packets sold by the Tuna Marketing Division. Several fish-marketing companies in San Diego purchase tuna fillets at $5 per pound.

REQUIRED

1. Compute the overall operating income to Oceanic Products of harvesting 1,000 pounds of raw tuna, processing it into tuna fillets, and then selling it in 2-pound packets.

2. Compute the transfer prices that will be used for internal transfers (i) from the Tuna Harvesting Division to the Tuna Processing Division, and (ii) from the Tuna Processing Division to the Tuna Marketing Division under each of the following transfer-pricing methods:

   a. *200% of variable costs.* Variable costs are the costs of the transferred-in product (if any) plus the division's own variable costs.

   b. *150% of full costs.* Full costs are the costs of the transferred-in product (if any) plus the division's own variable and fixed costs.

   c. *Market price.*

3. Oceanic rewards each division manager with a bonus, calculated as 10% of division operating income (if positive). What is the amount of the bonus that will be paid to each division manager under each of the three transfer-pricing methods in requirement 2? Which transfer-pricing method will each division manager prefer to use?

25-30 Goal-congruence problems with cost-plus transfer-pricing methods, dual-price method (continuation of 25-29). Assume that Oceanic Products uses a transfer price of 150% of full cost. Pat Forgione, the company president, attends a seminar on the virtues of decentralization. Forgione decides to implement decentralization at Oceanic Products. A memorandum is sent to all division managers: "Starting immediately, each division of Oceanic Products is free to make its own decisions regarding the purchase of its direct materials and the sale of its finished product."

REQUIRED

1. Give two examples of goal-congruence problems that may arise if Oceanic continues to use the 150%-of-full-costs transfer-pricing method and a policy of decentralization is adopted.

2. Forgione is investigating whether a dual transfer-pricing policy will reduce goal-congruence problems at Oceanic Products. Transfers out of each selling division will be made at 150% of full cost; transfers into each buying division will be made at market price. Using this dual transfer-pricing policy, compute the operating income of each division for a harvest of 1,000 pounds of raw tuna that is further processed and marketed by Oceanic Products.

3. Compute the sum of the division operating incomes in requirement 2. Why might this sum not equal the overall corporate operating income from the harvesting of 1,000 pounds of raw tuna and its further processing and marketing?

4. What problems may arise if Oceanic Products uses the dual transfer-pricing system described in requirement 2?

25-31 Multinational transfer pricing, global tax minimization. Industrial Diamonds, Inc., based in Los Angeles, has two divisions:

a. *Philippine Mining Division*—operates a mine in the Philippines containing a rich body of raw diamonds.

b. *U.S. Processing Division*—processes the raw diamonds into polished diamonds used in industrial applications

The costs of the Philippine Mining Division are
◆ Variable costs, 2,500 pesos per pound of raw industrial diamonds.
◆ Fixed costs, 5,000 pesos per pound of raw industrial diamonds.

Industrial Diamonds has a corporate policy of further processing diamonds in Los Angeles. Several diamond-polishing companies in the Philippines buy raw diamonds from other local mining companies at 10,000 pesos per pound. Assume that the current foreign exchange rate is 25 pesos = $1 U.S.

The costs of the U.S. Processing Division are
◆ Variable costs, $200 per pound of polished industrial diamonds.
◆ Fixed costs, $600 per pound of polished industrial diamonds.

Assume that it takes 2 pounds of raw industrial diamonds to yield 1 pound of polished industrial diamonds. Polished diamonds sell for $4,000 per pound.

REQUIRED

1. Compute the transfer price (in $U.S.) for 1 pound of raw industrial diamonds transferred from the Philippine Mining Division to the U.S. Processing Division under two methods: (a) 300% of full costs, and (b) market price.

2. Assume a world of no income taxes. One thousand pounds of raw industrial diamonds are mined by the Philippine Division and then processed and sold by the U.S. Processing Division. Compute the operating income (in $U.S.) for each division of Industrial Diamonds, Inc., under each transfer-pricing method in requirement 1.

3. Assume that the corporate income tax rate is 20% in the Philippines and 35% in the United States. Compute the after-tax operating income (in $U.S.) for each division under each transfer-pricing method in requirement 1. (Income taxes are not included in the computation of the cost-based transfer price. Industrial Diamonds does not pay U.S. taxes on income already taxed in the Philippines.)

4. Which transfer-pricing method in requirement 1 will maximize the total after-tax operating income of Industrial Diamonds?

5. What factors, in addition to global tax minimization, might Industrial Diamonds consider in choosing a transfer-pricing method for transfers between its two divisions?

25-32 Multinational transfer pricing and taxation. (Richard Lambert, adapted) Anita Corporation, headquartered in the United States, manufactures state-of-the-art milling machines. It has two marketing subsidiaries, one in Brazil and one in Switzerland, that sell its products. Anita is building one new machine, at a cost of $500,000. There is no market for the equipment in the United States. The equipment can be sold in Brazil for $1,000,000, but the Brazilian subsidiary would incur transportation and modification costs of $200,000. Alternatively, the equipment can be sold in Switzerland for $950,000, but the Swiss subsidiary would incur transportation and modification costs of $250,000. The U.S. company can sell the equipment to either its Brazilian subsidiary or its Swiss subsidiary but not to both. The Anita Corporation and its subsidiaries operate in a very decentralized manner. Managers in each company have considerable autonomy, with each manager interested in maximizing company income.

REQUIRED

1. From the viewpoint of Anita and its subsidiaries taken together, should the Anita Corporation manufacture the equipment? If it does, where should it sell the equipment to maximize corporate operating income? What would the operating income for Anita and its subsidiaries be from the sale? Ignore any income tax effects.

2. What range of transfer prices will result in achieving the actions determined to be optimal in requirement 1? Explain your answer.

3. The effective income tax rates for this transaction are as follows: 40% in the United States, 60% in Brazil, and 15% in Switzerland. The tax authorities in the three countries are uncertain about the cost of the intermediate product and will allow any transfer price between $500,000 and $700,000. If Anita and its subsidiaries want to maximize after-tax operating income, (a) should the equipment be manufactured, and (b) where and at what price should it be transferred?

4. Now suppose managers act autonomously to maximize their own company's after-tax operating income. The tax authorities will allow transfer prices only between $500,000 and $700,000. Which subsidiary will get the product and at what price? Is your answer the same as your answer in requirement 3? Explain why or why not.

25-33 Transfer price, goal congruence. (Nahum Melumad, adapted) The Cheap Shot Company has three divisions (A, B, and C) organized as decentralized profit centers. Division A produces the basic chemical Aldon (in multiples of 1,000 pounds) and transfers it to Divisions B and C. Division B processes Aldon into the final chemical product Baxon, and Division C processes Aldon into the final chemical product Calmite. No material is lost during processing.

Division A's costs are as follows:

Fixed costs per pound	$0
Variable costs per pound of Aldon	$0.18

Division A has a capacity limit of 10,000 pounds; Divisions B and C have capacity limits of 4,000 and 6,000 pounds, respectively. Given the high cost of storing Aldon, Baxon, and Calmite, Cheap Shot's divisions produce no more than the quantities they plan to sell. Divisions B and C sell their final product in separate markets.

The total revenues minus processing costs (net revenues) for each division are summarized in the following tables. Observe that the net revenues change for each incremental 1,000 pounds of Aldon converted to Baxon or to Calmite.

Pounds of Aldon Processed in B	Division B Revenues—Processing Costs from Selling Baxon
1,000	$ 500
2,000	850
3,000	1,100
4,000	1,200

Pounds of Aldon Processed in C	Division C Revenues—Processing Costs from Selling Calmite
1,000	$ 600
2,000	1,200
3,000	1,800
4,000	2,100
5,000	2,250
6,000	2,350

REQUIRED

1. Suppose there is no external market for Aldon. What quantity of Aldon should Cheap Shot produce to maximize Cheap Shot's operating income? How should this quantity be allocated between the two processing divisions?
2. What range of transfer prices will motivate Divisions B and C to demand the quantities that maximize Cheap Shot's operating income as determined in requirement 1, as well as motivate Division A to produce the sum of those quantities?

25-34 **Transfer prices, goal congruence, external markets, capacity constraints.** Refer to the information in Problem 25-33.

REQUIRED

1. Suppose that Division A has the option of selling as much Aldon as it wants for $0.33 per pound. Divisions B and C must buy the Aldon produced in Division A. They cannot buy Aldon from the open market. To maximize Cheap Shot's operating income, how many pounds of Aldon should Division A transfer to Division B and to Division C, and how many pounds should it sell in the external market?
2. What range of transfer prices will result in Divisions A, B, and C taking the actions determined as optimal in requirement 1? Explain your answer.
3. Assume the same scenario as in requirement 1, except that Division A's capacity constraint limits production to only 4,000 pounds of Aldon. To maximize Cheap Shot's operating income, how many pounds of Aldon should Division A transfer to Division B and to Division C, and how many pounds should it sell in the external market?
4. What range of transfer prices will result in Divisions A, B, and C taking the actions determined as optimal in requirement 3? Explain your answer.

25-35 **Ethics, transfer pricing.** The Winchester Division of Boston Industries makes two component parts, X23 and Y99. It supplies X23 to the Dearborn Division to be used in the manufacture of car engines and supplies Y99 to the Flint Division to be used in the manufacture of car transmissions. The Winchester Division is the only supplier of these specialized components. When transfers are made in-house, Boston Industries transfers products at full cost (calculated using an activity-based cost system) plus 10%. The unit cost information for X23 and Y99 are as follows:

	X23	Y99
Variable costs per unit	$11	$8
Allocated fixed costs per unit	$14	$7

The Dearborn Division feels that the price for X23 is too high and has told Winchester that it is trying to locate an outside vendor to supply the part at a lower price. Cliff Malone, Winchester Division's management accountant, calls Sam Fraser, his assistant, into his office. "We can't afford to lose the Dearborn Division business. Our fixed costs won't go away even if we stop supplying Dearborn, and this means that the costs of supplying Y99 to Flint will increase. Then they'll start wanting to buy from outside. We're seriously looking at possibly shutting down the entire division if we lose the Dearborn business. See if you can find a different method of allocating fixed costs that will decrease X23's transfer price to $23.65. I think Flint will be willing to pay a somewhat higher price for Y99."

Fraser is uncomfortable making any changes because he knows that any other allocation method would violate corporate guidelines on overhead cost allocation. Still, he believes that changing the fixed-cost allocations is in the best interest of Boston Industries. Fraser is confused about what he should do.

REQUIRED
1. Calculate the transfer prices for X23 and Y99.
2. Calculate the fixed cost per unit that Fraser would have to allocate to X23 to enable Winchester to transfer X23 at $23.65 per unit.
3. Evaluate whether Cliff Malone's suggestion to Fraser to change the fixed-cost allocations is ethical. Would it be ethical for Fraser to revise the fixed-cost allocations at his boss's urging? What steps should Fraser take to resolve this situation?

COLLABORATIVE LEARNING PROBLEM

25-36 **Goal congruence, taxes, different market conditions.** The San Ramon Corporation makes water pumps. The Engine Division makes the engines and supplies them to the Assembly Division where the pumps are assembled. San Ramon is a successful and profitable corporation that attributes much of its success to its decentralized operating style. Each division manager is compensated on the basis of division operating income.

The Assembly Division currently acquires all its engines from the Engine Division. The Assembly Division manager could purchase similar engines in the market for $400.

The Engine Division is currently operating at 80% of its capacity of 4,000 units and has the following particulars:

Direct materials ($125 per unit × 3,200 units)	$400,000
Direct manufacturing labor ($50 per unit × 3,200 units)	160,000
Variable manufacturing overhead costs ($25 per unit × 3,200 units)	80,000
Fixed manufacturing overhead costs	520,000

All the Engine Division's 3,200 units are currently transferred to the Assembly Division. No engines are sold in the outside market.

The Engine Division has just received an order for 2,000 units at $375 per engine that would utilize half the capacity of the plant. The order has either to be taken in full or rejected totally. The order is for a slightly different engine than what the Engine Division currently makes but takes the same amount of manufacturing time. To produce the new engine would require direct materials per unit of $100, direct manufacturing labor per unit of $40, and variable manufacturing overhead costs per unit of $25.

INSTRUCTIONS

Form groups of two or three students to complete the following requirements.

REQUIRED

1. From the viewpoint of the San Ramon Corporation as a whole, should the Engine Division accept the order for the 2,000 units?

2. What range of transfer prices will result in achieving the actions determined to be optimal in requirement 1, if division managers act in a decentralized manner?

3. The manager of the Assembly Division has proposed a transfer price for the engines equal to the full cost of the engines including an allocation of overhead costs. The Engine Division allocates overhead costs to engines on the basis of the total capacity of the plant used to manufacture the engines.

   a. Calculate the transfer price for the engines transferred to the Assembly Division under this arrangement.

   b. Do you think that the transfer price calculated in requirement 3a will result in achieving the actions determined to be optimal in requirement 1, if division managers act in a decentralized manner?

   c. Comment in general on one advantage and one disadvantage of using full costs of the producing division as the basis for setting transfer prices.

4. Now consider the effect of taxes.

   a. Suppose the Assembly Division is located in a state that imposes a 10% tax on income earned within its boundaries, while the Engine Division is located in a state that imposes no tax on income earned within its boundaries. What transfer price would be chosen by the San Ramon Corporation to minimize tax payments for the corporation as a whole? Assume that only transfer prices that are greater than or equal to full manufacturing costs and less than or equal to the market price of "substantially similar" engines are acceptable to the taxing authorities.

   b. Suppose that the San Ramon Corporation announces the transfer price computed in requirement 4a to price all transfers between the Engine and Assembly Divisions. Each division manager then acts autonomously to maximize division operating income. Will division managers acting in a decentralized manner achieve the actions determined to be optimal in requirement 1?

5. Consider your responses to requirements 1–4 and assume the Engine Division will continue to have opportunities for outside business as described in requirement 1. What transfer pricing policy would you recommend San Ramon use and why? Would you continue to evaluate division performance on the basis of division operating incomes?

CHAPTER 26

SYSTEMS CHOICE: PERFORMANCE MEASUREMENT, COMPENSATION, AND MULTINATIONAL CONSIDERATIONS

Hotels, such as the Sheraton in Tasmania, aim to maximize return on investment by increasing the income earned on each dollar of revenue and by increasing revenue per dollar of investment. Hotel managers' performance measures generally include both financial performance measures such as return on investment and nonfinancial performance measures such as occupancy levels.

LEARNING OBJECTIVES

After studying this chapter, you should be able to

1. Provide examples of financial and nonfinancial measures of performance
2. Describe the steps in designing an accounting-based performance measure
3. Understand the DuPont method of profitability analysis
4. Describe the motivation for using the residual-income measure
5. Describe the economic value added method
6. Distinguish between present-value, current-cost, and historical-cost asset measurement methods
7. Indicate the difficulties that arise when comparing the performance of divisions operating in different countries
8. Recognize the role of salaries and incentives in compensation arrangements
9. Describe the management accountant's role in helping organizations provide better incentives
10. Describe the incentive problems that can arise when employees perform multiple tasks as part of their jobs

We have discussed performance measurement in many of the earlier chapters, each time within a specific accounting context. Chapter 11, for example, described situations where the correct decision based on a relevant-cost analysis (buying new equipment, say) may not be implemented because the performance measurement system induced the manager to act differently. This chapter discusses the design, implementation, and uses of performance measures more generally.

Performance measures are a central component of a management control system. Making good planning and control decisions requires information about how different subunits of the organization have performed. To be effective, management control systems must also motivate managers and employees to strive to achieve organization goals. Performance evaluation and rewards are key elements for motivating employees.

Performance measurement of an organization's subunits should be a prerequisite for allocating resources within that organization. When a subunit undertakes new activities, it forecasts revenues, costs, and investments. Periodic comparisons of the actual revenues, costs, and investments with the budgeted amounts can help guide top management's decisions about future allocations.

Performance measurement of managers is used in decisions about their salaries, bonuses, future assignments, and career advancement. Moreover, the very act of measuring their performance can motivate managers to strive for the goals used in their evaluation.

This chapter examines issues in designing performance measures for different levels of an organization and for managers at these different levels. We discuss both financial and nonfinancial performance measures.

FINANCIAL AND NONFINANCIAL PERFORMANCE MEASURES

Chapter 25 noted how the information used in a management control system can be financial or nonfinancial. Many common performance measures such as operating income rely on internal financial and accounting information. Increasingly, companies are supplementing internal financial measures with measures based on external financial information (for example, stock prices), internal nonfinancial information (such as manufacturing lead time), and external nonfinancial information (such as customer satisfaction). In addition, companies are benchmarking their financial and nonfinancial measures against other companies that are regarded as the "best performers." To compete effectively in the global market, companies need to perform at or near the "best of the breed."

Some companies present financial and nonfinancial performance measures for various organization subunits in a single report called the *balanced scorecard* (see Chapter 19, p. 693). Different companies stress various elements in their scorecards, but most scorecards include (1) profitability measures; (2) customer-satisfaction measures; (3) internal measures of efficiency, quality, and time; and (4) innovation measures.[1]

Conner Peripherals, a manufacturer of hard disk drives, identifies the following measures within each category:

- *Profitability measures*—operating income and revenue growth.
- *Customer-satisfaction measures*—market share, customer-response time, on-time performance, and product reliability.
- *Efficiency, quality, and time measures*—direct materials efficiency variance, overhead spending variance, defects, yield, manufacturing lead time, head count, and inventory.

[1]See R. Kaplan and D. Norton, "The Balanced Scorecard—Measures That Drive Performance," *Harvard Business Review* (Jan.–Feb. 1992), S. Hronec, *Vital Signs* (New York: American Management Association, 1993), and R. Kaplan and D. Norton, "Using the Balanced Scorecard as a Strategic Management System," *Harvard Business Review* (Jan.–Feb. 1996).

Nonfinancial Measures of Performance

Companies around the world supplement financial performance measures with nonfinancial information. The following table ranks nonfinancial measures used in five countries in order of importance (1 = most important):

	United States*	Australia[†]	Ireland[‡]	Japan[†]	United Kingdom[†]
Product quality and defects	1	1	3	1	1
Delivery performance	2	2	4	2	2
Schedule attainment	3	—	—	—	—
Output per hour	4	—	1	—	—
Absenteeism	—	3	—	4	3
New-product time	—	4	—	3	4
Plant utilization	—	—	2	—	—

Adapted from *Smith and Sullivan, "Survey of Cost." [†]Blayney and Yokoyama, "Comparative Analysis." [‡]Clarke, "Management Accounting Practices." Full citations are in Appendix A.

The surveys indicate that these nonfinancial performance measures are used extensively. Product quality is the most important nonfinancial/internal performance measure overall. Delivery performance is the most important nonfinancial/external measure of performance.

◆ *Innovation measures*—number of new patents, number of new product launches, and new product development time.

The balanced scorecard highlights trade-offs that the manager may have made. For example, it indicates whether improvements in financial performance resulted from sacrificing investments in new products or from on-time delivery. The specific nonfinancial measures chosen signal to employees the areas that top management views as critical to the company's success.

Some performance measures, such as the number of new patents developed, have a long-run time horizon. Other measures, such as direct materials efficiency variances, overhead spending variances, and yield, have a short-run time horizon. We focus on the most widely used performance measures covering an intermediate to long-run time horizon. These are internal financial measures based on accounting numbers routinely maintained by organizations.

DESIGNING AN ACCOUNTING-BASED PERFORMANCE MEASURE

Designing an accounting-based performance measure requires the following steps:

Step 1: Choosing the Variable(s) that Represents Top Management's Financial Goal(s) Does operating income, net income, return on assets, or revenues, for example, best measure a division's financial performance?

Step 2: Choosing Definitions of the Items Included in the Variables in Step 1 For example, should assets be defined as total assets or net assets (total assets minus total liabilities)?

Step 3: Choosing Measures for the Items Included in the Variables in Step 1 For example, should assets be measured at historical cost, current cost, or present value?

OBJECTIVE 2

Describe the steps in designing an accounting-based performance measure

Step 4: Choosing a Target Against which to Gauge Performance For example, should all divisions have as a target the same required rate of return on assets?

Step 5: Choosing the Timing of Feedback For example, should manufacturing performance reports be sent to top management daily, weekly, or monthly?

These five steps need not be done sequentially. The issues considered in each step are interdependent, and a decision maker will often proceed through these steps several times before deciding on an accounting-based performance measure. The answers to the questions raised at each step depend on top management's beliefs about how cost effectively and how well each alternative fulfills the behavioral criteria of goal congruence, employee effort, and subunit autonomy discussed in Chapter 25.

DIFFERENT PERFORMANCE MEASURES

This section presents step 1 by describing four measures commonly used to evaluate the economic performance of organization subunits. Good performance measures promote goal congruence with the organization's objectives and facilitate comparisons across different subunits. We illustrate these measures using the example of Hospitality Inns.

Hospitality Inns owns and operates three motels, located in San Francisco, Chicago, and New Orleans. Exhibit 26-1 summarizes data for each of the three motels for the most recent year (19_8). At present, Hospitality Inns does not allocate to the three separate motels the total long-term debt of the company. Exhibit 26-1 indicates that the New Orleans motel generates the highest operating income, $510,000. The Chicago motel generates $300,000; the San Francisco motel, $240,000. But is this comparison appropriate? Is the New Orleans motel the most

EXHIBIT 26-1
Annual Financial Data for Hospitality Inns for 19_8

	San Francisco Motel (1)	Chicago Motel (2)	New Orleans Motel (3)	Total (4) = (1) + (2) + (3)
Motel revenues (sales)	$1,200,000	$1,400,000	$3,185,000	$5,785,000
Motel variable costs	310,000	375,000	995,000	1,680,000
Motel fixed costs	650,000	725,000	1,680,000	3,055,000
Motel operating income	$ 240,000	$ 300,000	$ 510,000	1,050,000
Interest costs on long-term debt at 10%	—	—	—	450,000
Income before income taxes	—	—	—	600,000
Income taxes at 30%	—	—	—	180,000
Net income	—	—	—	$ 420,000
Average book values for 19_8				
Current assets	$ 400,000	$ 500,000	$ 600,000	$1,500,000
Long-term assets	600,000	1,500,000	2,400,000	4,500,000
Total assets	$1,000,000	$2,000,000	$3,000,000	$6,000,000
Current liabilities	$ 50,000	$ 150,000	$ 300,000	$ 500,000
Long-term debt	—	—	—	4,500,000
Stockholders' equity	—	—	—	1,000,000
Total liabilities and stockholders' equity				$6,000,000

"successful"? Actually, the comparison of operating income ignores potential differences in the *size* of the investments in the different motels. **Investment** refers to the resources or assets used to generate income. The question then is not how large operating income is per se, but how large it is given the resources that were used to earn it.

Three approaches include investment in performance measures: return on investment (ROI), residual income (RI), and economic value added (EVA®). A fourth approach measures return on sales (ROS).

Return on Investment

Return on investment (ROI) is an accounting measure of income divided by an accounting measure of investment.

OBJECTIVE 3

Understand the DuPont method of profitability analysis

$$\text{Return on investment (ROI)} = \frac{\text{Income}}{\text{Investment}}$$

ROI is the most popular approach to incorporating the investment base into a performance measure. ROI appeals conceptually because it blends all the major ingredients of profitability (revenues, costs, and investment) into a single number. ROI can be compared with the rate of return on opportunities elsewhere, inside or outside the company. Like any single performance measure, however, ROI should be used cautiously and in conjunction with other performance measures.

ROI is also called the accounting rate of return or the accrual accounting rate of return (see Chapter 22). Managers usually use the term ROI in the context of evaluating the performance of a division or subunit, and accrual accounting rate of return when evaluating a project. Companies vary in the way they define both the numerator and the denominator of the ROI. For example, some firms use operating income for the numerator. Other firms use net income. Some firms use total assets in the denominator. Others use total assets minus current liabilities.

Hospitality Inns can increase ROI by increasing revenues or decreasing costs (both these actions increase the numerator), or by decreasing investments (decreases the denominator). ROI can often provide more insight into performance when it is divided into the following components:

$$\frac{\text{Revenues}}{\text{Investment}} \times \frac{\text{Income}}{\text{Revenues}} = \frac{\text{Income}}{\text{Investment}}$$

This approach is widely known as the *DuPont method of profitability analysis*. The DuPont approach recognizes that there are two basic ingredients in profit making: using assets to generate more revenue and increasing income per dollar of revenue. An improvement in either ingredient without changing the other increases return on investment.

Consider the ROI of each of the three Hospitality motels in Exhibit 26-1. For our calculations, we are using the operating income of each motel for the numerator and total assets of each motel for the denominator.

Motel	Operating Income	÷	Total Assets	=	ROI
San Francisco	$240,000	÷	$1,000,000	=	24%
Chicago	$300,000	÷	$2,000,000	=	15%
New Orleans	$510,000	÷	$3,000,000	=	17%

Using these ROI figures, the San Francisco motel appears to make the best use of its total assets.

Assume that the top management at Hospitality Inns adopts a 30% target ROI for the San Francisco motel. How can this return be attained? The DuPont method illustrates the present situation and three alternatives:

	$\dfrac{\text{Revenues}}{\text{Total Assets}}$	$\times$	$\dfrac{\text{Operating Income}}{\text{Revenues}}$			=	$\dfrac{\text{Operating Income}}{\text{Total Assets}}$
Present Situation	$\dfrac{\$1,200,000}{\$1,000,000}$	$\times$	$\dfrac{\$240,000}{\$1,200,000}$	=	1.20×0.20	=	0.24 or 24%
Alternatives							
A. Decrease assets (for example, receivables) keeping revenues and operating income per dollar of revenue constant.	$\dfrac{\$1,200,000}{\$800,000}$	$\times$	$\dfrac{\$240,000}{\$1,200,000}$	=	1.50×0.20	=	0.30 or 30%
B. Increase revenues (by selling more rooms) keeping assets and operating income per dollar of revenue constant.	$\dfrac{\$1,500,000}{\$1,000,000}$	$\times$	$\dfrac{\$300,000}{\$1,500,000}$	=	1.50×0.20	=	0.30 or 30%
C. Decrease costs (for example, via efficient maintenance) to increase operating income per dollar of revenue, keeping revenues and assets constant.	$\dfrac{\$1,200,000}{\$1,000,000}$	$\times$	$\dfrac{\$300,000}{\$1,200,000}$	=	1.20×0.25	=	0.30 or 30%

Other alternatives such as increasing the selling price per room could increase both the revenue per dollar of total assets and the operating income per dollar of revenue.

ROI highlights the benefits that managers can obtain by reducing their investments in current or fixed assets. Some managers are conscious of the need to boost revenues or to control costs but pay less attention to reducing their investment base. Reducing investments means decreasing idle cash, managing credit judiciously, determining proper inventory levels, and spending carefully on fixed assets.

Residual Income

OBJECTIVE 4

Describe the motivation for using the residual-income measure

Residual income is income minus a required dollar return on the investment.

$$\text{Residual income} = \text{Income} - (\text{Required rate of return} \times \text{Investment})$$

The required rate of return multiplied by investment is also called the *imputed cost* of the investment. **Imputed costs** are costs recognized in particular situations that are not regularly recognized by accrual accounting procedures. An imputed cost is not recognized in accounting records because it is not an incremental cost but instead represents the return forgone by Hospitality Inns as a result of tying up cash in various investments of similar risk. Assume that each motel faces similar risks. Hospitality Inns defines residual income for each motel as motel operating income minus a required rate of return of 12% of the total assets of the motel:

Motel	Operating Income	$-$	Required Rate of Return $\times$ Investment		=	Income
San Francisco	$240,000	$-$	$120,000 (12% $\times$ $1,000,000)		=	$120,000
Chicago	$300,000	$-$	$240,000 (12% $\times$ $2,000,000)		=	$ 60,000
New Orleans	$510,000	$-$	$360,000 (12% $\times$ $3,000,000)		=	$150,000

Given the 12% required rate of return, the New Orleans motel is performing best in terms of residual income.

Some firms favor the residual-income approach because managers will concentrate on maximizing an absolute amount (dollars of residual income) rather than a percentage (return on investment). The objective of maximizing residual income assumes that as long as a division earns a rate in excess of the required return for investments, that division should expand.

The objective of maximizing ROI may induce managers of highly profitable divisions to reject projects that, from the viewpoint of the organization as a whole, should be accepted. To illustrate, assume that Hospitality's required rate of return on investment is 12%. Assume also that an expansion of the San Francisco motel will increase its operating income by $160,000 and increase its total assets by $800,000. The ROI for the expansion is 20% ($160,000 ÷ $800,000), which makes it attractive to Hospitality Inns as a whole. By making this expansion, however, the San Francisco manager will see the motel's ROI decrease:

$$\text{Preexpansion ROI} = \frac{\$240,000}{1,000,000} = 24\%$$

$$\text{Postexpansion ROI} = \frac{(\$240,000 + \$160,000)}{(\$1,000,000 + \$800,000)} = \frac{\$400,000}{1,800,000} = 22.2\%$$

The annual bonus paid to the San Francisco manager may decrease if ROI is a key component in the bonus calculation and the expansion option is selected. In contrast, if the annual bonus is a function of residual income, the San Francisco manager will view the expansion favorably:

$$\text{Preexpansion residual income} = \$240,000 - (12\% \times \$1,000,000) = \$120,000$$

$$\text{Postexpansion residual income} = \$400,000 - (12\% \times \$1,800,000) = \$184,000$$

Goal congruence is more likely to be promoted by using residual income rather than ROI as a measure of the division manager's performance.

Both ROI and residual income represent the results for a single time period (such as a year). Managers could take actions that cause short-run increases in ROI or residual income but are in conflict with the long-run interests of the organization. For example, managers may curtail R&D and plant maintenance in the last 3 months of a fiscal year to achieve a target level of annual operating income. For this reason, some companies evaluate subunits on the basis of ROI and residual income over multiple years.

Economic Value Added (EVA®)[2]

OBJECTIVE 5

Describe the economic value added method

Economic value added (EVA®) is a specific type of residual income calculation that has recently attracted considerable attention. **Economic value added (EVA®)** equals after-tax operating income *minus* the (after-tax) weighted-average cost of capital *multiplied* by total assets minus current liabilities.

$$\begin{matrix} \text{Economic value} \\ \text{added (EVA®)} \end{matrix} = \begin{matrix} \text{After-tax} \\ \text{operating income} \end{matrix} - \left[\begin{matrix} \text{Weighted-average} \\ \text{cost of capital} \end{matrix} \times \left(\begin{matrix} \text{Total} \\ \text{assets} \end{matrix} - \begin{matrix} \text{Current} \\ \text{liabilities} \end{matrix} \right) \right]$$

EVA® substitutes the following numbers in the residual-income calculations: (1) income equal to after-tax operating income (2) a required rate of return equal to the weighted-average cost of capital, and (3) investment equal to total assets minus current liabilities. We use the Hospitality Inns data in Exhibit 26-1 to illustrate EVA®.

The key calculation is the weighted-average cost of capital (WACC), which equals *after-tax* average cost of all the long-term funds used by Hospitality Inns. The company has two sources of long-term funds—long-term debt with a market and book value of $4.5 million issued at an interest rate of 10%, and equity capital that has a market value of $3 million (and a book value of $1 million).[3] Since interest costs are tax-deductible, the after-tax cost of debt financing equals $0.10 \times (1 - \text{Tax rate}) = 0.10 \times (1 - 0.30) = 0.10 \times 0.70 = 0.07$, or 7%. The cost of equity capital is the opportunity cost to investors of not investing their capital in another investment that

---

[2]G. B. Stewart III, "EVA®: Fact and Fantasy," *Journal of Applied Corporate Finance* (Summer, 1994); B. Birchard, "Mastering the New Metrics," *CFO* (Oct. 1994); S. Tully, "The Real Key to Creating Wealth," *Fortune* (Sept. 27, 1993).

[3]The market value of Hospitality Inns equity exceeds book value because book values, based on historical costs, do not reflect the current values of the company's assets and because various intangible assets, such as the company's brand name, are not shown at current value on the balance sheet.

is similar in risk to Hospitality Inns. Suppose that Hospitality's cost of equity capital is 15%. The WACC computation, which uses market values of debt and equity, is as follows:

$$\text{WACC} = \frac{(0.07 \times \$4,500,00) + (0.15 \times \$3,000,000)}{\$4,500,000 + \$3,000,000}$$

$$= \frac{\$315,000 + \$450,000}{\$7,500,000} = \frac{\$765,000}{\$7,500,000}$$

$$= 0.102 \text{ or } 10.2\%$$

The company applies the same WACC to all its motels since each motel faces similar risks.

Long-term assets minus current liabilities (see Exhibit 26-1) can also be computed as:

$$\text{Total assets} - \text{Current liabilities} = \text{Long-term assets} + \text{Current Assets} - \text{Current liabilities}$$

$$= \text{Long-term assets} + \text{Working capital}$$

where working capital = current assets − current liabilities. After-tax motel operating income is

$$\frac{\text{Motel operating}}{\text{income}} \times (1 - \text{Tax rate}) = \frac{\text{Motel operating}}{\text{income}} \times (1 - 0.30) = \frac{\text{Motel operating}}{\text{income}} \times 0.70$$

EVA® calculations for Hospitality Inns are as follows:

Motel	After-Tax Operating Income	−	[Weighted-Average Cost of Capital × (Total Assets − Current Liabilities)]		=	Economic Value Added (EVA®)
San Francisco	$240,000 × 0.7	−	[10.2% × ($1,000,000 − $50,000)]	= $168,000 − $96,900	=	$71,100
Chicago	$300,000 × 0.7	−	[10.2% × ($2,000,000 − $150,000)]	= $210,000 − $188,700	=	$21,300
New Orleans	$510,000 × 0.7	−	[10.2% × ($3,000,000 − $300,000)]	= $357,000 − $275,400	=	$81,600

The New Orleans motel has the highest EVA®. EVA®, like residual income, charges managers for the cost of their investments in long-term assets and working capital. Value is created only if after-tax operating income exceeds the cost of investing the capital. To improve EVA®, managers must earn more operating income with the same capital, use less capital, or invest capital in high-return projects. After implementing EVA®, CSX, a railroad company, began running trains with three locomotives instead of four by scheduling arrivals just-in-time for unloading, rather than having trains arrive at their destination several hours in advance. The result? Higher profits because of lower fuel costs, and less capital invested in locomotives. Chief executive officers of companies, such as AT&T, Briggs & Stratton, Coca-Cola, CSX, Equifax, FMC, and Quaker Oats, credit the EVA® concept with motivating decisions that have increased shareholder value.

Return on Sales

The income-to-revenue (sales) ratio—often called return on sales (ROS)—is a frequently used financial performance measure. ROS is one component of ROI in the DuPont method of profitability analysis. To calculate the ROS of each of Hospitality's motels, we use operating income divided by revenues. The ROS for each motel is

Motel	Operating Income	÷	Revenues (Sales)	=	ROS
San Francisco	$240,000	÷	$1,200,000	=	20.0%
Chicago	$300,000	÷	$1,400,000	=	21.4%
New Orleans	$510,000	÷	$3,185,000	=	16.0%

The following table summarizes the performance and ranking of each motel under each of the four performance measures:

Motel	ROI (Rank)	Residual Income (Rank)	EVA® (Rank)	ROS (Rank)
San Francisco	24% (1)	$120,000 (2)	$71,100 (2)	20.0% (2)
Chicago	15% (3)	$60,000 (3)	$21,300 (3)	21.4% (1)
New Orleans	17% (2)	$150,000 (1)	$81,600 (1)	16.0% (3)

The residual-income and EVA® rankings differ from the ROI and ROS rankings. Consider the ROI and residual-income rankings for the San Francisco and New Orleans motels. The New Orleans motel has a smaller ROI. Although its operating income is only slightly more than twice that of the San Francisco motel ($510,000 versus $240,000), its total assets are three times as large ($3 million versus $1 million). The return on assets invested in the New Orleans motel is not as high as the return on assets invested in the San Francisco motel. The New Orleans motel has a higher residual income because it earns a higher operating income after covering the 12% required return on investment. The Chicago motel has the highest ROS but the lowest ROI. Why? Because although it earns very high income per dollar of revenue, it generates very low revenues per dollar of assets invested. Is any one method superior to the others? No, because each evaluates a slightly different aspect of performance. For example, in markets where revenue growth is limited, return on sales is the most meaningful indicator of a subunit's performance. To evaluate overall aggregate performance, ROI or residual-income-based measures are more appropriate since they consider both income earned and investments made. Residual-income and EVA® measures overcome some of the goal-congruence problems that ROI measures might introduce. Some managers favor EVA® because it explicitly considers tax effects while pre-tax residual-income measures do not. Other managers favor pre-tax residual-income because it is easier to compute, and because it often leads to the same conclusions as EVA®.

Surveys of U.S. and Japanese companies indicate extensive use of net income as a performance measure. After net income measures, U.S. companies favor ROI over ROS, while Japanese companies use ROS more than ROI. More recently, many large U.S. companies have begun using EVA®, which also focuses on income and investment. These differences are also consistent with differences in pricing practices in the two countries. Japanese companies emphasize sales margins, while U.S. companies emphasize return on investment.[4] Some researchers speculate that Japanese managers favor ROS because it is easier to calculate and because achieving a sufficient sales margin will be likely to benefit ROI sooner or later. Deemphasizing ROI has other advantages. Managers are not induced to delay investment in facilities or equipment because of the negative effects it might have on ROI in the short run. Exhibit 26-2 presents the key financial performance measures used by eleven companies. Note the diversity in the use of income-based measures, ROS, ROI and EVA®.

ALTERNATIVE DEFINITIONS OF INVESTMENT

We use the different definitions of investment that companies use to illustrate step 2 when designing accounting-based performance measures. Definitions include the following:

1. *Total assets available*—includes all business assets, regardless of their particular purpose.

2. *Total assets employed*—defined as total assets available minus idle assets and minus assets purchased for future expansion. For example, if the New Orleans motel in Exhibit 26-1 has unused land set aside for potential expansion, the total assets employed by the motel would exclude the cost of that land.

[4]See K. Smith and C. Sullivan, "Survey of Cost Management Systems in Manufacturing," Working paper, Purdue University, 1990; and P. Scarbrough, A. Nanni, and M. Sakurai, "Japanese Management Accounting Practices and the Effects of Assembly and Process Automation," *Management Accounting Research* 2(1991).

EXHIBIT 26-2
Company Examples of Key Financial Performance Measures

Company Name	Country Headquarters	Product/ Business	Key Financial Performance Measures
Dow Chemical	U.S.	Chemicals	Income
Xerox	U.S.	Photocopiers	ROS and ROI
Ford Motor	U.S.	Automotive	ROS and ROI
Quaker Oats	U.S.	Food products	EVA®
AT&T	U.S.	Telecommunications/ computers	EVA®
Guinness	U.K.	Consumer products	Income and ROS
Krones	Germany	Machinery/equipment	Sales and income
Mayne Nickless	Australia	Security/transportation	ROI and ROS
Mitsui	Japan	Trading	Sales and income
Pirelli	Italy	Tires/manufacturing	Income and cash flow
Swedish Match	Sweden	Consumer products	ROI

Source: Business International Corporation, *Evaluating the Performance of International Operations* (New York, 1989); Business International Corporation, *101 More Checklists for Global Financial Management* (New York, 1992); and G.B. Stewart, "EVA®: Fact and Fantasy," *Journal of Applied Corporate Finance* (Summer, 1994).

3. *Working capital (current assets minus current liabilities) plus long-term assets*—this definition excludes that portion of current assets financed by short-term creditors.

4. *Stockholders' equity*—use of this definition for each individual motel in Exhibit 26-1 requires allocation of the long-term liabilities of Hospitality Inns to the three motels, which would then be deducted from the total assets of each motel.

Most companies that employ ROI, residual income, or EVA® for performance measurement use either total assets available or working capital plus long-term assets as the definition of investment. However, when top management directs a division manager to carry extra assets, total assets employed can be more informative than total assets available. The most common rationale for using working capital plus long-term assets is that the division manager often influences decisions on the short-term debt of the division.

MEASUREMENT ALTERNATIVES FOR ASSETS

To illustrate step 3 in the design of accounting-based performance measures consider different ways to measure assets included in the investment calculations. Should they be measured at historical cost, present value, current cost, or current disposal price? Should gross book value or net book value be used for depreciable assets? We now examine these issues.

Present Value

Chapters 22 and 23 discuss the relevance of discounted cash-flow (DCF) analysis for both asset acquisition and disposal decisions. **Present value** is the measure of assets based on DCF estimates. Consider an existing motel with an expected useful life of 10 years, expected net cash inflows of $1,200,000 each year, and an expected terminal disposal price of $2,000,000. The required rate of return is 12%. The present value of the motel would be $7,424,000 (the present-value factors are from Tables 2 and 4, Appendix C):

Present value of annuity of $1,200,000 for 10 years discounted at 12%: $1,200,000 × 5.650			$6,780,000
Present value of $2,000,000 disposal price 10 years from now discounted at 12%: $2,000,000 × 0.322			644,000
Present value of motel			$7,424,000

The present-value analysis is useful because it measures the economic value of the investment based on future cash flows rather than its accounting value. The difficulty in implementing present-value analysis is estimating the expected net cash flows. For this reason, few organizations systematically incorporate total present-value (and disposal price) information into their routine accounting reports. Nevertheless, managers make periodic attempts to approximate present values and current disposal prices in judging the desirability of investments in assets. Otherwise, managers may overlook opportunities to invest or dispose of investments that will improve the value of the company. The decision rule to dispose of investments compares the total present value with the current disposal price. If the current disposal price exceeds the total present value, the asset(s) should be sold now.

Current Cost

Current cost is the cost of purchasing an asset today identical to the one currently held. It is the cost of purchasing the services provided by that asset if an identical asset cannot currently be purchased. Of course, measuring assets at current costs will result in different ROIs compared to the ROIs calculated based on historical costs.

We illustrate the current-cost ROI calculations using the Hospitality Inns example (see Exhibit 26-1) and then compare current- and historical-cost-based ROIs. Assume the following information about the long-term assets of each motel:

	San Francisco	Chicago	New Orleans
Age of facility (at end of 19_8)	8 years	4 years	2 years
Gross book value	$1,400,000	$2,100,000	$2,800,000
Accumulated depreciation	$800,000	$600,000	$400,000
Net book value (at end of 19_8)	$600,000	$1,500,000	$2,400,000
Depreciation for 19_8	$100,000	$150,000	$200,000

Hospitality Inns assumes a 14-year estimated useful life, assumes no terminal disposal price for the physical facilities, and calculates depreciation on a straight-line basis.

An index of construction costs for the 8-year period that Hospitality Inns has been operating (19_0 year-end = 100) is as follows:

Year	19_1	19_2	19_3	19_4	19_5	19_6	19_7	19_8
Construction cost index	110	122	136	144	152	160	174	180

Earlier in this chapter, we computed an ROI of 24% for San Francisco, 15% for Chicago, and 17% for New Orleans (see p. 935). One possible explanation of the high ROI for San Francisco is that this motel's long-term assets are expressed in terms of 19_0 construction price levels (8 years ago) and that the long-term assets for the Chicago and New Orleans motels are expressed in terms of the higher, more recent construction price levels, which depress ROIs for these motels.

Exhibit 26-3 illustrates a step-by-step approach for incorporating current-cost estimates for long-term assets and depreciation into the ROI calculation. The aim is to approximate what it would cost today to obtain assets that would produce the same expected operating income that the subunits currently earn. (Similar adjustments to represent current costs of capital employed and depreciation can also be made in the residual income and EVA® calculations.) The current-cost adjustment dramatically reduces the ROI of the San Francisco motel.

Step 1: Restate long-term assets from gross book value at historical cost to gross book value at current cost as of the end of 19_8.

$$\text{Gross book value of long-term assets at current cost at the end of 19\_8} = \text{Gross book value of long-term assets at historical cost} \times \frac{\text{Construction cost index in 19\_8}}{\text{Construction cost index in year of construction}}$$

San Francisco	$1,400,000 × (180 ÷ 100) = $2,520,000
Chicago	$2,100,000 × (180 ÷ 144) = $2,625,000
New Orleans	$2,800,000 × (180 ÷ 160) = $3,150,000

Step 2: Derive the net book value of long-term assets at current cost as of the end of 19_8. (The estimated useful life of each motel is 14 years.)

$$\text{Net book value of long-term assets at current cost at the end of 19\_8} = \text{Gross book value of long-term assets at current cost at the end of 19\_8} \times \frac{\text{Estimated useful life remaining}}{\text{Estimated total useful life}}$$

San Francisco	$2,520,000 × (6 ÷ 14) = $1,080,000
Chicago	$2,625,000 × (10 ÷ 14) = $1,875,000
New Orleans	$3,150,000 × (12 ÷ 14) = $2,700,000

Step 3: Compute the current cost of total assets at the end of 19_8. (Assume that the current assets of each motel are expressed in 19_8 dollars.)

$$\text{Current cost of total assets at the end of 19\_8} = \text{Current assets at the end of 19\_8 (from Exhibit 26-1)} + \text{Net book value of long-term assets at current cost at the end of 19\_8 (from step 2)}$$

San Francisco	$400,000 + $1,080,000 = $1,480,000
Chicago	$500,000 + $1,875,000 = $2,375,000
New Orleans	$600,000 + $2,700,000 = $3,300,000

Step 4: Compute the current-cost depreciation expense in 19_8 dollars.

$$\text{Current-cost depreciation expense in 19\_8 dollars} = \text{Gross book value of long-term assets at current cost at the end of 19\_8 (from step 1)} \times \frac{1}{\text{Estimated total useful life}}$$

San Francisco	$2,520,000 × (1 ÷ 14) = $180,000
Chicago	$2,625,000 × (1 ÷ 14) = $187,500
New Orleans	$3,150,000 × (1 ÷ 14) = $225,000

Step 5: Compute 19_8 operating income using 19_8 current-cost depreciation.

$$\text{Operating income for 19\_8 using 19\_8 current-cost depreciation} = \text{Historical-cost operating income} - \left(\text{Current-cost depreciation expense in 19\_8 dollars (from step 4)} - \text{Historical-cost depreciation} \right)$$

San Francisco	$240,000 − ($180,000 - $100,000) = $160,000
Chicago	$300,000 − ($187,500 - $150,000) = $262,500
New Orleans	$510,000 − ($225,000 - $200,000) = $485,000

Step 6: Compute the ROI using current-cost estimates for long-term assets and depreciation.

$$\text{ROI using current-cost estimates} = \frac{\text{Operating income for 19\_8 using 19\_8 current cost depreciation (from step 5)}}{\text{Current cost of total assets at the end of 19\_8 (from step 3)}}$$

San Francisco	$160,000 ÷ $1,480,000 = 10.81%
Chicago	$262,500 ÷ $2,375,000 = 11.05%
New Orleans	$485,000 ÷ $3,300,000 = 14.70%

	Historical-Cost ROI	Current-Cost ROI
San Francisco	24%	10.81%
Chicago	15%	11.05%
New Orleans	17%	14.70%

Adjusting for current costs negates differences in the investment base caused solely by differences in construction price levels. Consequently, compared to historical-cost ROI, current-cost ROI is a better measure of the current economic returns from the investment. For example, current-cost ROI indicates that taking into account current construction price levels, investing in a new motel in San Francisco will result in an ROI closer to 10.81% rather than 24%. If Hospitality Inns were to invest in a new motel today, investing in one like the New Orleans motel offers the best ROI.

A drawback of the current-cost method is that obtaining current-cost estimates for some assets can be difficult.[5] Why? Because the estimate requires a company to consider technological advances when determining the current cost of assets needed to earn today's operating income.

Long-Term Assets: Gross or Net Book Value?

Because historical-cost investment measures are used often in practice, there has been much discussion about the relative merits of using gross book value (original cost) or net book value (original cost minus accumulated depreciation). Using the data in Exhibit 26-1 and page 934, the ROI calculations using net book values and gross book values of plant and equipment are as follows:

	San Francisco	Chicago	New Orleans
ROI for 19_8 using net book value of total assets given in Exhibit 26-1 and calculated earlier.	$\frac{\$240,000}{\$1,000,000} = 24\%$	$\frac{\$300,000}{\$2,000,000} = 15\%$	$\frac{\$510,000}{\$3,000,000} = 17\%$
ROI for 19_8 using gross book value of total assets obtained by adding accumulated depreciation from p. 941 to net book value of total assets in Exhibit 26-1.	$\frac{\$240,000}{\$1,800,000} = 13.33\%$	$\frac{\$300,000}{\$2,600,000} = 11.54\%$	$\frac{\$510,000}{\$3,400,000} = 15\%$

Using the gross book value, the ROI of the older San Francisco motel (13.33%) is lower than that of the newer New Orleans motel (15%). Those who favor using gross book value claim that it enables more accurate comparisons across subunits. For example, using gross book value calculations, the return on the original plant and equipment investment is higher for the newer New Orleans motel than for the older San Francisco motel. This probably reflects the decline in earning power of the San Francisco motel. In contrast, using the net book value masks this decline in earning power because the constantly decreasing base results in a higher ROI (24%); this higher rate may mislead decision makers into thinking that the earning power of the San Francisco motel has not decreased.

The proponents of using net book value as a base maintain that it is less confusing because (1) it is consistent with the total assets shown on the conventional balance sheet, and (2) it is consistent with net income computations that include deductions for depreciation. Surveys of company practice report net book value to be the dominant asset measure used by companies in their internal performance evaluations.

---

[5]When a specific cost index, such as the construction cost index, is not available, companies use a general index, such as the consumer price index, to approximate current costs.

Choosing Targets to Compare Performance

We next consider step 4 and the setting of targets to compare actual performance against. Recall that historical-cost-based accounting measures are often inadequate for evaluating economic returns on new investments and sometimes create disincentives for new expansion. Despite these problems, historical-cost ROIs *can* be used to evaluate current performance by adjusting target ROIs. Consider our Hospitality Inns example. The key is to recognize that the motels were built at different times, which in turn means they were built at different levels of the construction-cost index. Top management could adjust the target historical cost ROIs accordingly, perhaps setting San Francisco's ROI at 26%, Chicago's at 18%, and New Orleans' at 19%.

Nevertheless, the alternative of comparing actual to target performance is frequently overlooked in the literature. Critics of historical cost have indicated how high rates of return on old assets may erroneously induce a manager not to replace assets. Regardless, the manager's mandate is often "Go forth and attain the budgeted results." The budget, then, should be carefully negotiated with full knowledge of historical-cost accounting pitfalls. *The desirability of tailoring a budget to a particular subunit and a particular accounting system cannot be overemphasized.* For example, many problems of asset valuation and income measurement (whether based on historical cost or current cost) can be satisfactorily solved if top management gets everybody to focus on what is attainable in the forthcoming budget period—regardless of whether the financial measures are based on historical costs or some other measure, such as current costs.

Top management often sets continuous improvement targets. Consider companies implementing EVA®. These companies have generally found it cost-effective to use historical-cost net assets rather than estimates of market or replacement values. Why? Because top management evaluates operations on year-to-year changes in EVA®, not on absolute measures of EVA®. Evaluating performance on the basis of *improvements* in EVA® makes the initial method of calculating EVA® less important.

Timing of Feedback

The fifth and final step in designing accounting-based performance measures is the timing of feedback. Timing of feedback depends largely on how critical the information is for the success of the organization, the specific level of management that is receiving the feedback, and on the sophistication of the organization's information technology. For example, motel managers responsible for room sales, will want information on the number of rooms sold each day on a daily or, at most, weekly basis. Why? Because a large percentage of motel costs are fixed costs, so that achieving high room sales and taking quick action to reverse any declining sales trends are critical to the financial success of each motel. Supplying managers with daily information about room sales would be much easier if Hospitality Inns had a computerized room reservation and check-in system. Senior management, on the other hand, in their oversight role may look at information about daily room sales only on a monthly basis. In some instances, for example, because of concern about the low sales to total assets ratio of the Chicago motel, they may want the information weekly.

PERFORMANCE MEASUREMENT IN MULTINATIONAL COMPANIES

Comparing the performance of divisions of a multinational company operating in different countries creates additional difficulties.[6]

◆ The economic, legal, political, social, and cultural environments differ significantly across countries.

[6]M. Z. Iqbal, T. Melcher, and A. Elmallah, *International Accounting—A Global Perspective* (Cincinatti: Southwestern ITP, 1996).

- Governments in some countries may impose controls and limit selling prices of a company's products. For example, developing countries in Asia, Latin America, and Eastern Europe impose tariffs and duties to restrict the import of certain goods.
- Availability of materials and skilled labor, as well as costs of materials, labor, and infrastructure (power, transportation, and communication) may also differ significantly across countries.
- Divisions operating in different countries keep score of their performance in different currencies. Issues of inflation and fluctuations in foreign currency exchange rates then become important.

We focus on the last of these issues next.

Calculating the Foreign Division's ROI in the Foreign Currency

Suppose Hospitality Inns invests in a motel in Mexico City. The investment consists mainly of the costs of buildings and furnishings. The following information is available:

- The exchange rate at the time of Hospitality's investment on December 31, 19_7 is 3 pesos = $1.
- During 19_8, the Mexican peso suffers a steady and steep decline in its value.
  The exchange rate on December 31, 19_8 is 6 pesos = $1.
  The average exchange rate during 19_8 is $[(3 + 6) \div 2] = 4.5$ pesos = $1.
  The investment (total assets) in the Mexico City motel = 9,000,000 pesos.
  The operating income of the Mexico City motel in 19_8 = 1,800,000 pesos.

What is the historical-cost-based ROI for the Mexico City motel in 19_8?

Some specific questions arise. Should we calculate the ROI in pesos or in dollars? If we calculate the ROI in dollars, what exchange rate should we use? How does the ROI of Hospitality Inns Mexico City (HIMC) compare with the ROI of Hospitality Inns New Orleans (HINO), which is also a relatively new motel of roughly the same size? Hospitality Inns may be interested in this information for making future investment decisions.

$$\text{HIMC's ROI (calculated using pesos)} = \frac{\text{Operating income}}{\text{Total assets}} = \frac{1{,}800{,}000 \text{ pesos}}{9{,}000{,}000 \text{ pesos}} = 20\%$$

HIMC's ROI of 20% is higher than HINO's ROI of 17% (computed on p. 935). Does this mean that HIMC outperformed HINO on the ROI criterion? Not necessarily. Why? Because HIMC operates in a very different economic environment than does HINO.

The peso has declined steeply in value relative to the dollar in 19_8. Research studies show that the peso's decline is correlated with correspondingly higher inflation in Mexico relative to the United States.[7] A consequence of the higher inflation in Mexico is that HIMC will charge higher prices for its motel rooms, which will increase HIMC's operating income and lead to a higher ROI. Inflation clouds the real economic returns on an asset and makes ROI calculated on historical cost of assets unrealistically high. Why? Because had there been no inflation, HIMC's room rates and hence operating income would have been much lower. Differences in inflation rates between the two countries make a direct comparison of HIMC's peso-denominated ROI with HINO's dollar-denominated ROI misleading.

Calculating the Foreign Division's ROI in U.S. Dollars

One way to achieve greater comparability of historical-cost-based ROIs is to restate HIMC's performance in dollars. But what exchange rate(s) should we use to make the comparison meaningful? Assume operating income was earned evenly through-

[7] W. Beaver and M. Wolfson, "Foreign Currency Translation Gains and Losses: What Effect Do They Have and What Do They Mean?" *Financial Analysts Journal* (March–April 1984); F. D. S. Choi, "Resolving the Inflation/Currency Translation Dilemma," *Management International Review* (Vol. 34, Special Issue, 1994).

out 19_8. We use the average exchange rate of 4.5 pesos = $1 to convert the operating income from pesos to dollars: 1,800,000 pesos ÷ 4.5 = $400,000. The effect of dividing the operating income in pesos by the higher pesos to dollar exchange rate is that any increase in operating income in pesos as a result of inflation is undone when converting back to dollars.

At what rate should we convert HIMC's total assets of 9,000,000 pesos? At the exchange rate prevailing when the assets were acquired on December 31, 19_7, namely, 3 pesos = $1. Why? Because HIMC's book value of assets is recorded at the December 31, 19_7 cost, and is not revalued as a result of inflation in Mexico in 19_8. Since the book value of assets is unaffected by subsequent inflation, so should the exchange rate used to convert it into dollars. Using exchange rates after December 31, 19_7 would be incorrect because these rates incorporate the higher inflation in Mexico in 19_8. Total assets would be converted to 9,000,000 pesos ÷ 3 = $3,000,000. Then,

$$\text{HIMC's ROI (calculated using dollars)} = \frac{\text{Operating income}}{\text{Total assets}} = \frac{\$400,000}{\$3,000,000} = 13.33\%$$

These adjustments make the historical-cost-based ROIs of the two motels comparable because they negate the effects of any differences in inflation rates between the two countries. HIMC's ROI of 13.33% is less than HINO's ROI of 17%.

Residual income calculated in pesos suffers from the same problems as ROI calculated using pesos. Instead, calculating HIMC's residual income in dollars adjusts for changes in exchange rates and facilitates comparisons with Hospitality's other motels:

$$\text{HIMC's residual income} = \$400,000 - (12\% \times \$3,000,000)$$

$$= \$400,000 - \$360,000 = \$40,000$$

which is also less than HINO's residual income of $150,000. In interpreting HIMC's and HINO's ROI and residual income, note that they are historical-cost-based calculations. They do, however, pertain to relatively new motels.

DISTINCTION BETWEEN MANAGERS AND ORGANIZATIONAL UNITS[8]

As noted before in this and several earlier chapters, the performance evaluation of a manager should be distinguished from the performance evaluation of an organization subunit, such as a division of a company. For example, historical-cost-based ROIs for a particular division can be used to evaluate a manager's performance relative to a budget or over time, even though historical-cost ROIs may be unsatisfactory for evaluating economic returns earned by the subunit. But using historical-cost ROIs to compare the performance of managers of different subunits can be misleading. In the Hospitality Inns example, Hospitality Inns New Orleans's (HINO's) ROI of 17% exceeds Hospitality Inns Mexico City's (HIMC's) ROI of 13.33% after adjusting for the higher inflation in Mexico. The ROIs may give some indication of the economic returns from each motel but do not mean that the manager of HINO performed better than the manager of HIMC. Why? Because among other factors, HIMC's ROI may have been adversely affected relative to HINO's ROI because of legal, political, and government regulations as well as economic conditions in Mexico over which the HIMC manager has no control.

Consider another example. Companies often put the most skillful division manager in charge of the weakest division in an attempt to change its fortunes. Such an effort may take years to bear fruit. Furthermore, the manager's efforts may result merely in bringing the division up to a minimum acceptable ROI. The division may continue to be a poor profit performer in comparison with other divisions, but it would be a mistake to conclude from the poor performance of the division that the manager is necessarily performing poorly.

[8]The presentations here draw (in part) from teaching notes prepared by S. Huddart, N. Melumad, and S. Reichelstein.

This section focuses on developing basic principles for evaluating the performance of a division manager of an individual subunit. The concepts we discuss apply, however, to all organization levels. Later sections consider specific examples at the individual-activity level and the total-organization level. For specificity, we use the residual-income (RI) performance measure throughout.

The Basic Trade-off: Creating Incentives versus Imposing Risk

OBJECTIVE 8

Recognize the role of salaries and incentives in compensation arrangements

The performance evaluation of managers and employees often affects their compensation. Compensation arrangements run the range from a flat salary with no direct performance-based bonus (as in the case of some government officials) to rewards based only on performance (as in the case of employees of real estate agencies). Most often, however, a manager's total compensation includes some combination of salary and a performance-based bonus. An important consideration in designing compensation arrangements is the trade-off between creating incentives and imposing risk. We illustrate this trade-off in the context of our Hospitality Inns example.

Sally Fonda owns the Hospitality Inns chain of motels. Roger Brett manages the Hospitality Inns San Francisco (HISF) motel. Assume that Fonda uses RI to measure performance. To achieve good results as measured by RI, Fonda would like Brett to control costs, provide prompt and courteous service, and reduce receivables. But even if Brett did all those things, good results are by no means guaranteed. HISF's RI is affected by many factors outside Fonda's and Brett's control, such as a recession in the San Francisco economy, or recent earthquakes that might negatively affect HISF. Alternatively, noncontrollable factors might have a positive influence on HISF's RI. Noncontrollable factors make HISF's profitability uncertain and risky.

Fonda is an entrepreneur and does not mind bearing risk, but Brett does not like being subject to risk. One way of insuring Brett against risk is to pay Brett a flat salary, regardless of the actual amount of residual income attained. All the risk would then be borne by Fonda. There is a problem here, however, because the effort that Brett puts in is difficult to monitor, and the absence of performance-based compensation will provide Brett with no incentive to work harder or undertake extra physical and mental effort beyond what is necessary to retain his job or to uphold his own personal values.

Moral hazard[9] describes contexts in which an employee prefers to exert less effort (or report distorted information) than the effort (or information) desired by the owner because the employee's effort (or information) cannot be accurately monitored and enforced. In some repetitive jobs—for example, in electronic assembly—a supervisor can monitor the workers' actions, and the moral hazard problem may not arise. However, the manager's job is often to gather information and exercise judgment on the basis of the information obtained, and monitoring a manager's effort is thus considerably more difficult.

Paying no salary and rewarding Brett *only* on the basis of some performance measure—RI, in our example—raises different concerns. Brett would now be motivated to strive to increase RI because his rewards would increase with increases in RI. But compensating Brett on RI also subjects Brett to risk. Why? Because HISF's RI depends not only on Brett's effort, but also on random factors such as the local economy over which Brett has no control.

To compensate Brett (who does not like being subject to risk) for taking on uncontrollable risk, Fonda must pay Brett some extra compensation within the structure of the RI-based arrangement. Thus, using performance-based incentives will cost Fonda more money, *on average*, than paying Brett a flat salary. Why "on average"? Because Fonda's compensation payment to Brett will vary with RI outcomes. When averaged over these outcomes, the RI-based compensation will cost Fonda more than would paying Brett a flat salary. The motivation for having some salary

---

[9]The term *moral hazard* originated in insurance contracts to represent situations where insurance coverage caused insured parties to take less care of their properties than they might otherwise. One response to moral hazard in insurance contracts is the system of deductibles (that is, the insured pays for damages below a specified amount).

and some performance-based bonus in compensation arrangements is to balance the benefits of incentives against the extra costs of imposing uncontrollable risk on the manager.

OBJECTIVE 9

Describe the management accountant's role in helping organizations provide better incentives

Intensity of Incentives and Financial and Nonfinancial Measurements

What dictates the intensity of the incentives? That is, how large should the incentive component be relative to salary? A key question is, How well does the performance measure capture the manager's ability to influence the desired results?

Measures of performance that are superior change significantly with the manager's performance and not very much with changes in factors that are beyond the manager's control. Consequently, superior performance measures motivate the manager but limit the manager's exposure to uncontrollable risk and hence reduce the cost of providing incentives to get the manager to accept the incentive program. On the other hand, measures of performance are inferior if they fail to capture the manager's performance and fail to induce managers to improve. When owners have superior performance measures available to them, they place greater reliance on incentive compensation.

Suppose Brett has no authority to determine investments. Further suppose revenue is determined largely by external factors such as the local economy. Brett's actions influence only costs. Using RI as a performance measure in these circumstances subjects Brett's bonus to excessive risk because two components of the performance measure (investments and revenues) are unrelated to his actions. The management accountant might suggest that, to create stronger incentives, Fonda consider using a different performance measure for Brett—perhaps HISF's costs—that more closely captures Brett's effort. Note that in this case, RI may be a perfectly good measure of the economic viability of HISF, but it is not a good measure of Brett's performance.

The benefits of tying performance measures more closely to a manager's efforts encourage the use of nonfinancial measures. Consider two possible measures for evaluating the manager of the Housekeeping Department at one of Hospitality's motels—the costs of the Housekeeping Department and the average time taken by the housekeeping staff to clean a room. Suppose housekeeping costs are affected by factors such as wage rates, which the housekeeping manager does not determine. In this case, the average time taken to clean a room may more precisely capture the manager's performance.

The salary component of compensation dominates in the absence of good measures of performance (as in the case of some corporate staff and government officials). This is not to say, however, that incentives are completely absent; promotions and salary increases do depend on some overall measure of performance, but the incentives are less direct. Employers give stronger incentives when superior measures of performance are available to them and when monitoring the employee's effort is very difficult (real estate agencies for example, reward employees mainly on commissions on houses sold).

Benchmarks and Relative Performance Evaluation

Owners can use benchmarks to evaluate performance. Benchmarks representing best practice may be available inside or outside the overall organization. In our Hospitality Inns example, benchmarks could be other similar motels, either within or outside the Hospitality Inns chain. Suppose Brett has authority over revenues, costs, and investments. In evaluating Brett's performance, Fonda would want to use as a benchmark, a motel of a similar size that is influenced by the same uncontrollable factors—for example, location, demographic trends, and economic conditions—that affect HISF. *Differences* in performances of the two motels occur only because of differences in the two managers' performances, not because of random factors. Thus, benchmarking, also called *relative performance evaluation*, "filters out" the effects of the common noncontrollable factors.

Kidder Peabody's Paper Profits and High Compensations

Incentives based on superior performance measures motivate managers and employees to work hard because these measures change significantly with actions that the senior management wants managers and employees to take. At no time should employees be able to manipulate performance measures to make their performance look better than what it is. Besides being unethical, such measures fail to achieve the objectives of the company.

In April 1994, Kidder Peabody, a Wall Street investment banking firm and a subsidiary of General Electric, made a dramatic announcement. It dismissed its chief government bond trader alleging fraudulent trading apparently intended to inflate profits and the trader's performance bonus in 1993. Kidder Peabody said $350 million in profits it recorded in 1993 never existed. The trader alleged that his superiors had suggested and were aware of the scheme, and that they also benefited from big bonuses resulting from it.

The problems arose with respect to trades in government bonds (debt issued by the U.S. Government) and zero-coupon bonds (bonds that accumulate and pay interest only when the bond is finally paid off). Kidder alleged that the trades took advantage of the difference in the accounting for government bonds and zero-coupon bonds in Kidder's system. For zero-coupon bonds, Kidder's accounting recognized future interest yet to be earned as paper profits today, boosting income. "Creating" profits increased employee bonuses based on those profits when the firm itself earned no cash or real economic profit. The trades had another effect. They shrank Kidder's assets by $73 billion making the firm's return on assets look better to its parent company, General Electric.

Kidder stated that as the profits of the government trading division grew, it started its own internal examination and uncovered the phony trades. It responded by strengthening its accounting controls for trading in government and zero-coupon bonds. Kidder also began reexamining its incentive compensation and goal setting programs to ensure that performance measures could not be manipulated in the future.

Source: Adapted from S. Hansell, "Kidder Reports Fraud and Ousts a Top Trader," *New York Times*, April 18, 1994, L. Spiro, L. Himelstein, and M. Schroeder, "They Said, He Said at Kidder Peabody," *Business Week*, August 8, 1994.

Can the performance of two managers responsible for running similar operations within a company be benchmarked against one another? Yes, but one problem is that the use of these benchmarks may reduce incentives for these managers to help one another. That is, a manager's performance evaluation measure improves either by doing a better job or by making the other manager look bad. Not working together as a team is not in the best interests of the organization as a whole. In this case, using benchmarks for performance evaluation can lead to goal incongruence.

PERFORMANCE MEASURES AT THE INDIVIDUAL ACTIVITY LEVEL

This section focuses on incentive issues that arise in the context of individual activities. The principles described here, however, can be applied at all levels of the organization.

Performing Multiple Tasks

Most employees perform more than one task as part of their jobs. Marketing representatives sell products, provide customer support, and gather market information. Other jobs have multiple aspects to them. Manufacturing workers, for example, are

OBJECTIVE 10

Describe the incentive problems that can arise when employees perform multiple tasks as part of their jobs

responsible for both the quantity and quality of their products. Employers want employees to allocate their time and effort intelligently among various tasks or aspects of their jobs.

Consider, for example, mechanics at an auto repair shop. Their jobs have at least two distinct and important aspects. The first aspect is the repair work. Performing more repair work would generate more revenues for the shop. The second aspect is customer satisfaction. The higher the quality of the job, the more likely the customer will be pleased. If the employer wants an employee to focus on both these aspects, then the employer must measure and compensate performance on both.

Suppose the employer can easily measure the quantity of auto repairs but not their quality. If the employer rewards workers on a piece-rate system—which pays workers only on the basis of the number of repairs actually performed—mechanics will likely increase the number of repairs they make at the expense of quality. Sears, Roebuck and Co. experienced this problem when they introduced by-the-job rates for its mechanics. Sears' management responded by taking the following steps to motivate workers to balance both quantity and quality: (1) Management dropped the piece-rate system and paid mechanics an hourly salary, a step that deemphasized the quantity of repair. Mechanics' promotions and pay increases were determined on the basis of management's assessment of each mechanic's overall performance regarding quantity and quality of repairs. (2) Management began evaluating employees, in part, using data such as customer-satisfaction surveys, the number of dissatisfied customers, or the number of customer complaints. (3) Management also employed independent staff to randomly monitor whether the repairs performed were of high quality.

Note that nonfinancial measures (such as customer-satisfaction measures) play a central role in motivating mechanics to emphasize both quantity and quality. The goal is to measure both aspects of the mechanics' jobs and to balance incentives so that both aspects are properly emphasized.

Team-Based Compensation Arrangements

Many manufacturing, marketing, and design problems require employees with multiple skills, experiences, and judgments to pool their talents. In these situations, a team of employees achieves better results than individuals acting on their own.[10] Companies give incentives and bonuses to individuals on the basis of team performance. Team incentives encourage cooperation, with individuals helping one another as they strive toward a common goal. The blend of knowledge and skills needed to change methods and improve efficiency puts a team in a better position than a lone individual to respond to incentives. Eaton, TRW, Whirlpool, Monsanto, Dana, and Analog Devices in the United States and Nissan Motors and Nippon Steel in Japan are examples of companies that use some form of team-based incentives.

Whether team-based compensation is desirable depends, to a great extent, on the culture and management style of a particular organization. One criticism of teams, especially in the United States, is that individual incentives to excel are dampened, harming overall performance.

EXECUTIVE PERFORMANCE MEASURES AND COMPENSATION

The principles of performance evaluation described in the previous sections also apply to executive compensation plans at the total-organization level. Executive compensation plans are based on both financial and nonfinancial performance measures and consist of a mix of (1) base salary; (2) annual incentives (for example, cash bonus based on yearly net income); (3) long-term incentives [for example, stock options (described later in this section) based on achieving a specified return by the end of a 5-year period]; and (4) fringe benefits (for example, life insurance, an office with a view, or a personal secretary). Designers of executive compensation plans

---

[10]J. Katzenbach and D. Smith, *The Wisdom of Teams* (Boston: The Harvard Business School Press, 1993).

emphasize three factors: achievement of organization goals, administrative ease, and the likelihood that affected managers will perceive the plan as fair.

Well-designed plans use a compensation mix that carefully balances risk, and short-term and long-term incentives. For example, evaluating performance on the basis of annual ROI would sharpen an executive's short-term focus. Using ROI and stock option plans over, say, 5 years would motivate the executive to take a long-term view as well.

Stock options give executives the right to buy company stock at a specified price (called the exercise price) within a specified period. Suppose on June 1, 1995, Marriott International gave its chief executive officer (CEO) the option to buy 200,000 shares of Marriott stock at any time before June 30, 1999, at the June 1, 1995, market price of $35 per share. If Marriott's stock price rises to, say, $50 per share on March 24, 1997, and the CEO chooses to exercise his option on all 200,000 shares, he will earn $3 million. (The CEO would exercise his right to buy Marriott stock from the company on March 24, 1997, for $35 per share and sell it in the market at $50 per share, earning $15 per share on 200,000 shares.) If Marriott's stock price stays below $35 the entire period, the CEO will simply forgo his right to buy the shares. Hence, by linking CEO compensation to increases in the stock price, the stock option plan serves to motivate the CEO to improve the company's long-term performance.

In late 1995, the Financial Accounting Standards Board (FASB) issued Statement Number 123 for the accounting of stock options. For most stock options granted, the exercise price of the option equals or exceeds the market price of the stock on the day the options are granted. In these cases, Statement 123 encourages, but does not require, a company to record a compensation cost in its income statement. The company can choose not to recognize cost even though the company has sacrificed something of value—the potentially large income the executive will receive if the price of the stock increases. If the company records no cost, it must disclose in a footnote to the financial statements the effect on net income and earnings per share had the company recognized cost equal to the estimated fair market value of the options on the date they were granted.[11]

Responding to some concerns about executive compensation packages that were unrelated to performance, the Securities and Exchange Commission (SEC), in October 1992, issued new rules requiring more detailed disclosures of the compensation arrangements of top-level executives. In complying with these rules in 1996, Marriott International, for example, disclosed a summary compensation table showing the salary, bonus, stock options, other stock awards, and other compensation earned by its top five officers during the 1993, 1994, and 1995 fiscal years.

The SEC rules also require companies to disclose the principles underlying their executive compensation plans and the performance criteria—such as profitability, sales growth, and market share—used in determining compensation. In its annual report, Marriott International described these principles as "building a strong correlation between stockholder return and executive compensation, offering incentives that encourage attainment of short-term and long-term business goals, and providing a total level of pay that is commensurate with performance." Marriott uses cash flow, earnings per share, and guest satisfaction as performance criteria to determine annual cash incentives for its executives. In complying with other mandated SEC disclosures, Marriott also disclosed how well its stock performed relative to the overall market and stocks of other motels and hotels over a 5-year period.

ENVIRONMENTAL AND ETHICAL RESPONSIBILITIES

Managers in all organizations shoulder environmental and ethical responsibilities. Environmental violations (such as water and air pollution) and unethical and illegal

---

[11]If the exercise price is less than the market price of the stock on the date the options are granted, the company must recognize compensation cost equal to the difference. This amount is less than the fair market value of the options. The company can choose to either recognize the full fair market value as a cost or disclose its impact in a footnote.

practices (such as bribery and corruption) carry heavy fines and are prison offenses under the laws of the United States and other countries. But environmental responsibilities and ethical conduct extend beyond legal requirements.

Socially responsible companies set aggressive environmental targets and measure and report their performance against them. German, Swiss, Dutch, and Scandinavian companies report on environmental performance as part of a larger set of social responsibility disclosures (which include employee welfare and community development information). Some companies, such as DuPont and Lockheed, make environmental performance a line item on every employee's salary appraisal sheet. The Duke Power Company appraises employees on reducing solid waste, cutting emissions and discharges, and implementing environmental plans. The result: Duke Power has met all its environmental goals.

Ethical behavior on the part of managers is paramount. In particular, the numbers that subunit managers report should not be tainted by "cooking the books"—they should be uncontaminated by, for example, padded assets, understated liabilities, fictitious sales, and understated costs.

Codes of business conduct are circulated in some organizations to signal appropriate and inappropriate individual behavior. The following is a quote from Caterpillar Tractor's "Code of Worldwide Business Conduct and Operating Principles":

> The law is a floor. Ethical business conduct should normally exist at a level well above the minimum required by law. . . . Caterpillar employees shall not accept costly entertainment or gifts (excepting mementos and novelties of nominal value) from dealers, suppliers and others with whom we do business. And we won't tolerate circumstances that produce, or reasonably appear to produce, conflict between personal interests of an employee and interests of the company.

Division managers often cite enormous top-management pressures "to make the budget" as excuses or rationalizations for not adhering to ethical accounting policies and procedures. A healthy amount of motivational pressure is not bad—as long as the "tone from the top" simultaneously communicates the absolute need for all managers to behave ethically at all times. Management should promptly and severely reprimand unethical conduct irrespective of the benefits that accrue to the company from such actions. Some companies such as Lockheed emphasize ethical behavior by routinely evaluating employees against a business code of ethics.

PROBLEM FOR SELF-STUDY

PROBLEM

Budgeted data of the baseball manufacturing division of Home Run Sports for February 19_7 are as follows:

◆ Current assets	$ 400,000
◆ Long-term assets	600,000
◆ Total assets	$1,000,000
◆ Production output	200,000 baseballs per month
◆ Target ROI (operating income ÷ total assets):	30%
◆ Fixed costs:	$400,000 per month
◆ Variable costs:	$4 per baseball

REQUIRED
1. Compute the minimum unit selling price necessary to achieve the 30% target ROI.
2. Using the selling price from requirement 1, separate the target ROI into its two components using the DuPont method.
3. Pamela Stephenson, division manager, receives 5% of the monthly residual income of the baseball manufacturing division as a bonus. Compute her bonus

for February 19_7, using the selling price from requirement 1. Home Run Sports uses a 12% required rate of return on total division assets when computing division residual income.

SOLUTION

1.

$$\text{Target operating income} = 30\% \text{ of } \$1,000,000$$
$$= \$300,000$$

Let P = Selling price

$$\text{Sales} - \text{Variable costs} - \text{Fixed costs} = \text{Operating income}$$
$$200,000P - (200,000 \times \$4) - \$400,000 = \$300,000$$
$$200,000P = \$300,000 + \$800,000 + \$400,000 = \$1,500,000$$
$$P = \$7.50$$

Proof:		
Sales, 200,000 × $7.50		$1,500,000
Variable costs, 200,000 × $4		800,000
Contribution margin		700,000
Fixed costs		400,000
Operating income		$ 300,000

2.

$$\frac{\text{Revenues}}{\text{Investment}} \times \frac{\text{Income}}{\text{Revenues}} = \frac{\text{Income}}{\text{Investment}}$$

$$\frac{\$1,500,000}{\$1,000,000} \times \frac{\$300,000}{\$1,500,000} = \frac{\$300,000}{\$1,000,000}$$

$$1.5 \quad \times \quad 0.2 \quad = 0.30 \text{ or } 30\%$$

3. Residual income = Operating income − Required return on investment

$$= \quad \$300,000 \quad - (0.12 \times \$1,000,000)$$
$$= \quad \$300,000 \quad - \$120,000$$
$$= \quad \$180,000$$

Stephenson's bonus is $9,000 (5% of $180,000).

SUMMARY

The following points are linked to the chapter's learning objectives.

1. Financial measures such as return on investment and residual income can capture important aspects of both manager performance and organization-subunit performance. In many cases, however, financial measures are supplemented with nonfinancial measures of performance, such as those relating to customer service time, number of defects, and productivity.

2. The steps in designing an accounting-based performance measure are (a) choosing variables to include in the performance measure, (b) defining the terms, (c) measuring the items included in the variables, (d) choosing a target for performance, and (e) choosing the timing of feedback.

3. The DuPont method describes return on investment (ROI) as the product of two components: revenues divided by investment and income divided by revenues. ROI can be increased in three ways—increase revenues, decrease costs, and decrease investment.

4. Residual income is income minus a required dollar return on the investment. Residual income was designed to overcome some of the limitations of ROI. For example, residual income is more likely than ROI to promote goal congruence. That is, actions that are in the best interests of the organization maximize residual income. The objective of maximizing ROI, conversely, may induce managers of highly profitable divisions to reject projects that, from the viewpoint of the organization as a whole, should be accepted.

5. Economic value added (EVA®) is a specific type of residual income calculation. It equals the after-tax operating income minus the after-tax weighted-average cost of capital multiplied by total assets minus current liabilities.

6. Present value is a measure of assets based on discounted cash-flow (DCF) estimates. The current cost of an asset is the cost now of purchasing an identical asset to the one currently held. Historical-cost asset measurement methods consider the original cost of the asset net of accumulated depreciation.

7. Comparing the performance of divisions operating in different countries is difficult because of legal, political, social, economic, and currency differences. ROI calculations for subunits operating in different countries need to be adjusted for differences in inflation between the two countries and changes in exchange rates.

8. Organizations create incentives by rewarding managers on the basis of performance. But managers may face risks because random factors beyond the managers' control may also affect performance. Owners choose a mix of salary and incentive compensation to trade off the incentive benefit against the cost of imposing risk.

9. Obtaining measures of employee performance that are superior is critical for implementing strong incentives. Many management accounting practices, such as the design of responsibility centers and the establishment of financial and nonfinancial measures, have as their goal better performance evaluation.

10. Most employees perform multiple tasks as part of their jobs. In some situations, one aspect of a job is easily measured (for example, the quantity of work done), while another aspect is not (for example, the quality of work done). Creating incentives to promote the aspect of the job that is easily measured (quantity) may cause workers to ignore an aspect of their job that is more difficult to measure (quality).

▼ TERMS TO LEARN

This chapter and the Glossary at the end of this book contain definitions of the following important terms:

current cost (p. 941)	moral hazard (947)
economic value added (EVA®) (937)	present value (940)
imputed cost (936)	residual income (936)
investment (935)	return on investment (ROI) (935)

▼ ASSIGNMENT MATERIAL

QUESTIONS

26-1 Give two examples of financial performance measures and two examples of nonfinancial performance measures.

26-2 What are the five steps in designing an accounting-based performance measure?

26-3 What factors affecting ROI does the DuPont method highlight?

26-4 "Residual income is not identical to ROI although both measures incorporate income and investment into their computations." Do you agree? Explain.

26-5 Describe economic value added.

26-6 Give three definitions of investment used in practice when computing ROI.

26-7 Distinguish between measuring assets based on present value, current cost, and historical cost.

26-8 What special problems arise when evaluating performance in multinational companies?

26-9 Why is it important to distinguish between the performance of a manager and the performance of the organization subunit for which the manager is responsible? Give examples.

26-10 Describe moral hazard.

26-11 "Managers should be rewarded only on the basis of their performance measures. They should be paid no salary." Do you agree? Explain.

26-12 Explain the management accountant's role in helping organizations design stronger incentive systems for their employees.

26-13 Explain the role of benchmarking in evaluating managers.

26-14 Explain the incentive problems that can arise when employees have to perform multiple tasks as part of their jobs.

26-15 Describe two disclosures required by the SEC with respect to executive compensation.

EXERCISES

26-16 Return on investment; comparisons of three companies. (CMA, adapted) Return on investment is often expressed as follows:

$$\frac{\text{Income}}{\text{Investment}} = \frac{\text{Revenues}}{\text{Investment}} \times \frac{\text{Income}}{\text{Revenues}}$$

REQUIRED

1. What advantages are there in the breakdown of the computation into two separate components?
2. Fill in the following blanks:

	Companies in Same Industry		
	A	**B**	**C**
Revenue	$1,000,000	$500,000	?
Income	$ 100,000	$ 50,000	?
Investment	$ 500,000	?	$5,000,000
Income as a percentage of revenue	?	?	0.5%
Investment turnover	?	?	2
Return on investment	?	1%	?

After filling in the blanks, comment on the relative performance of these companies as thoroughly as the data permit.

26-17 Analysis of return on invested assets, comparison of three divisions. Quality Products, Inc., is a soft-drink and food-products company. It has three divisions: soft drinks, snack foods, and family restaurants. Results for the past 3 years are as follows (in millions):

	Soft-Drink Division	Snack-Foods Division	Restaurant Division	Quality Products, Inc.
Operating Revenues				
19_7	$2,800	$2,000	$1,050	$5,850
19_8	3,000	2,400	1,250	6,650
19_9	3,600	2,600	1,530	7,730
Operating Income				
19_7	120	360	105	585
19_8	160	400	114	674
19_9	240	420	100	760
Total Assets				
19_7	1,200	1,240	800	3,240
19_8	1,250	1,400	1,000	3,650
19_9	1,400	1,430	1,300	4,130

Use the DuPont method to explain changes in the operating income to total assets ratio over the 19_7 to 19_9 period for each division. Comment on the results.

26-18 ROI and residual income. (D. Kleespie) The Gaul Company produces and distributes a wide variety of recreational products. One of its divisions, the Goscinny Division, manufactures and sells "menhirs," which are very popular with cross-country skiers. The demand for these menhirs is relatively insensitive to price changes. The Goscinny Division is considered to be an investment center and in recent years has averaged a return on investment of 20%. The following data are available for the Goscinny Division and its product:

Total annual fixed costs	$1,000,000
Variable costs per menhir	$300
Average number of menhirs sold each year	10,000
Average operating assets invested in the division	$1,600,000

REQUIRED
1. What is the minimum selling price per unit that the Goscinny Division could charge in order for Mary Obelix, the division manager, to get a favorable performance rating? Management considers an ROI below 20% to be unfavorable.
2. Assume that the Gaul Company judges the performance of its investment center managers on the basis of residual income rather than ROI, as was assumed in requirement 1. The company's required rate of return is considered to be 15%. What is the minimum selling price per unit that the Goscinny Division should charge for Obelix to receive a favorable performance rating?

26-19 Pricing and return on investment. Hardy, Inc., assembles motorcycles and uses long-run (defined as 3–5 years) average demand to set the budgeted production level and costs for pricing. Prices are then adjusted only for large changes in assembly wage rates or direct materials prices. You are given the following data:

Direct materials, assembly wages, and other variable costs	$1,320 per unit
Fixed costs	$300,000,000 per year
Target return on investment	20%
Normal utilization of capacity (average output)	1,000,000 units
Investment (total assets)	$900,000,000

REQUIRED
1. What operating income percentage on revenues is needed to attain the target return on investment of 20%? What is the selling price per unit?
2. Using the selling price per unit calculated in requirement 1, what rate of return on investment will be earned if Hardy assembles and sells 1,500,000 units? 500,000 units?
3. The company has a management bonus plan based on yearly division performance. Assume that Hardy assembled and sold 1,000,000, 1,500,000, and 500,000 units in three successive years. Each of three people served as division manager for 1 year before being killed in an automobile accident. As the principal heir of the third manager, comment on the bonus plan.

26-20 Financial and nonfinancial performance measures, goal congruence. (CMA adapted) Summit Equipment specializes in the manufacture of medical equipment, a field that has become increasingly competitive. Approximately 2 years ago, Ben Harrington, president of Summit, decided to revise the bonus plan (based, at the time, entirely on operating income) to encourage division managers to focus on areas that were important to customers and that added value without increasing cost. In addition to a profitability incentive, the revised plan also includes incentives for reduced rework costs, reduced sales returns, and on-time deliveries. Bonuses are calculated and awarded semi-annually on the following basis. A base bonus is calculated at 2% of operating income. The bonus amount is then adjusted by the following amounts:

a. (i) Reduced by excess of rework costs over 2% of operating income.
   (ii) No adjustment if rework costs are less than or equal to 2% of operating income.
b. Increased by $5,000 if over 98% of deliveries are on time, by $2,000 if 96–98% of deliveries are on time, and by $0 if on-time deliveries are below 96%.
c. (i) Increased by $3,000 if sales returns are less than or equal to 1.5% of sales.
   (ii) Decreased by 50% of excess of sales returns over 1.5% of sales.

Note: If the calculation of the bonus results in a negative amount for a particular period, the manager simply receives no bonus, and the negative amount is *not* carried forward to the next period.

Results for Summit's Charter and Mesa Divisions for the year 19_7, the first year under the new bonus plan, follow. In the previous year, 19_6, under the old bonus plan, the Charter Division manager earned a bonus of $27,060 and the Mesa Division manager, a bonus of $22,440.

	Charter Division		**Mesa Division**	
	January 1, 19_7 to June 30, 19_7	**July 1, 19_7 to December 31, 19_7**	**January 1, 19_7 to June 30, 19_7**	**July 1, 19_7 to December 31, 19_7**
Sales	$4,200,000	$4,400,000	$2,850,000	$2,900,000
Operating income	$462,000	$440,000	$342,000	$406,000
On-time delivery	95.4%	97.3%	98.2%	94.6%
Rework costs	$11,500	$11,000	$6,000	$8,000
Sales returns	$84,000	$70,000	$44,750	$42,500

REQUIRED

1. Why did Harrington need to introduce these new performance measures? That is, why does Harrington need to use these performance measures over and above the operating income numbers for the period?
2. Calculate the bonus earned by each manager for each 6-month period and for the year 19_7.
3. What effect did the change in the bonus plan have on each manager's behavior? Did the new bonus plan achieve what Harrington desired? What changes, if any, would you make to the new bonus plan?

26-21 ROI residual income, economic value added. (D. Solomons, adapted) Consider the following data for the two geographical divisions of the Potomac Electric Company that operate as profit centers:

	Atlantic Division	**Pacific Division**
Total assets	$1,000,000	$5,000,000
Current liabilities	250,000	1,500,000
Operating income	200,000	750,000

REQUIRED

1. Calculate the return on investment (ROI) using operating income as the measure of income and using total assets as the measure of investment.
2. Potomac Electric has used residual income as a measure of management success, the variable it wants a manager to maximize. Using this criterion,

what is the residual income for each division using operating income and total assets if the required rate of return on investment is 12%?

3. Potomac Electric has two sources of funds: long-term debt with a market value of $3,500,000 and an interest rate of 10%, and equity capital with a market value of $3,500,000 at a cost of equity of 14%. Potomac's income tax rate is 40%. Potomac applies the same weighted-average cost of capital to both divisions, since each division faces similar risks. Calculate the economic value added. Which of the measures calculated in requirements 1, 2, and 3 would you recommend Potomac Electric use? Why? Explain briefly.

26-22 Residual income, economic value added. The Burlingame Transport Company operates two divisions, a Truck Rental Division that rents to individuals, and a Transportation Division that transports goods from one city to another. Results reported for the last year are as follows:

	Truck Rental Division	Transportation Division
Total assets	$650,000	$950,000
Current liabilities	120,000	200,000
Operating income before tax	75,000	160,000

REQUIRED

1. Calculate the residual income for each division using operating income before tax and investment equal to total assets minus current liabilities. The required rate of return on investments is 12%.

2. The company has two sources of funds: long-term debt with a market value of $900,000 at an interest rate of 10% and equity capital with a market value of $600,000 at a cost of equity of 15%. Burlingame's income tax rate is 40%. Burlingame applies the same weighted-average cost of capital to both divisions, since each division faces similar risks. Calculate the economic value added (EVA®) for each division.

3. Using your answers to requirements 1 and 2, what would you conclude about the performance of each division? Explain briefly.

26-23 Various measures of profitability. When the Coronet Company formed three divisions a year ago, the president told the division managers that an annual bonus would be paid to the most profitable division. However, absolute division operating income as conventionally computed would not be used. Instead, the ranking would be affected by the relative investments in the three divisions. Options available include ROI and residual income. Investment can be measured using gross book value or net book value. Each manager has now written a memorandum claiming entitlement to the bonus. The following data are available:

Division	Gross Book Value of Division Assets	Division Operating Income
Mastex	$400,000	$47,500
Banjo	380,000	46,000
Randal	250,000	30,800

All the assets are fixed assets that were purchased 10 years ago and have 10 years of useful life remaining. A zero terminal disposal price is predicted. Coronet's required rate of return on investment used for computing residual income is 10% of investment.

REQUIRED

Which method for computing profitability did each manager choose? Make your description specific and brief. Show supporting computations. Where applicable, assume straight-line depreciation.

26-24 Multinational performance measurement, ROI. The Sandvik Corporation manufactures electric motors in the United States and Sweden. The U.S. and Swedish operations are organized as decentralized divisions. The following information is available for 19_7:

	U.S. Division	Swedish Division
Operating income	$1,200,000	6,552,000 kronas
Total assets	$8,000,000	42,000,000 kronas

The exchange rate at the time of Sandvik's investment in Sweden on December 31, 19_6 was 6 kronas = $1. During 19_7, the Swedish krona declined steadily in value so that the exchange rate on December 31, 19_7 is 7 kronas = $1. The average exchange rate during 19_7 is $[(6 + 7) \div 2] = 6.5$ kronas = $1.

REQUIRED

1. Calculate the U.S. Division's return on investment for 19_7.
2. Calculate the Swedish Division's return on investment for 19_7 in kronas.
3. Senior management at Sandvik wants to know which division earned a better return on investment in 19_7. What would you tell them? Explain your answer.

26-25 Multinational performance measurement, ROI, residual income. Loren Press operates two printing presses that operate as separate divisions, one located in Durham, North Carolina, and the other in Lyon, France. The following information is available for 19_8. The required rate of return on investments is 15%.

	Durham Division	Lyon Division
Operating income	$765,000	3,600,000 francs
Total assets	$4,500,000	20,000,000 francs

Both investments were made on December 31, 19_7. The exchange rate at the time of Loren's investment in France on December 31, 19_7 was 4 francs = $1. During 19_8, the French franc declined steadily in value reaching an exchange rate on December 31, 19_8 of 5 francs = $1. The average exchange rate during 19_8 is $[(4 + 5) \div 2] = 4.5$ francs = $1.

REQUIRED

1. (a) Calculate Durham Division's return on investment for 19_8. (b) Calculate Lyon Division's return on investment for 19_8 in French francs. (c) Which division earned a better return on investment in 19_8? Explain.
2. Senior management wants to compare the performance of the two divisions using residual income. Which division do you think had the better residual-income performance? Explain your answer.
3. On the basis of your answers to requirements 1 and 2, which division is performing better? If you had to promote one of the division managers to the vice president's position, which manager would you choose? Explain.

26-26 Risk sharing, incentives, benchmarking, multiple tasks. The Dexter Division of AMCO sells car batteries. AMCO's corporate management gives Dexter management considerable operating and investment autonomy in running the division. AMCO is considering how it should compensate Jim Marks, the general manager of the Dexter Division. Proposal 1 calls for paying Marks a fixed salary. Proposal 2 calls for paying Marks no salary and compensating him only on the basis of the division's ROI (calculated based on operating income before any bonus payments). Proposal 3 calls for paying Marks some salary and some bonus based on ROI. Assume that Marks does not like bearing risk.

1. (a) Evaluate each of the three proposals, specifying the advantages and disadvantages of each.

   (b) Suppose that AMCO competes against Tiara Industries in the car battery business. Tiara is roughly the same size and operates in a business environment that is very similar to Dexter's. The senior management of AMCO is considering evaluating Marks on the basis of Dexter's ROI minus Tiara's ROI. Marks complains that this approach is unfair because the performance of another firm, over which he has no control, is included in his performance evaluation measure. Is Marks's complaint valid? Why or why not?

2. Now suppose that Marks has no authority for making capital investment decisions. Corporate management makes these decisions. Is return on investment a good performance measure to use to evaluate Marks? Is return on investment a good measure to evaluate the economic viability of the Dexter Division? Explain.

3. Dexter's salespersons are responsible for selling and providing customer service and support. Sales are easy to measure. Although customer service is very important to Dexter in the long run, it has not yet implemented customer-service measures. Marks wants to compensate his salesforce only on the basis of sales commissions paid for each unit of product sold. He cites two advantages to this plan: (a) It creates very strong incentives for the salesforce to work hard, and (b) the company pays salespersons only when the company itself is earning revenues and has cash. Do you like his plan? Why or why not?

PROBLEMS

26-27 Relevant costs, performance evaluation, goal congruence. Pike Enterprises has three operating divisions. The managers of these divisions are evaluated on their divisional operating income, a figure that includes an allocation of corporate overhead *proportional to the revenues of each division*. The operating income statement (in thousands) for the first quarter of 19_8 is as follows:

	Andorian Division	Orion Division	Tribble Division	Total
Revenues	$2,000	$1,200	$1,600	$4,800
Cost of goods sold	1,050	540	640	2,230
Gross margin	950	660	960	2,570
Division overhead	250	125	160	535
Corporate overhead	400	240	320	960
Division operating income	$ 300	$ 295	$ 480	$1,075

The manager of the Andorian Division is unhappy that his profitability is about the same as the Orion Division's and is much less than the Tribble Division's, even though his revenues are much higher than either of these other two divisions. The manager knows that he is carrying one line of products with very low profitability. He was going to replace this line of business as soon as more profitable product opportunities became available, but he has kept it because the line is marginally profitable and uses facilities that would otherwise be idle. That manager now realizes, however, that the sales from this product line are attracting a fair amount of corporate overhead because of the allocation procedure, and maybe the line is already unprofitable for him. This low-margin line of products had the following characteristics for the most recent quarter (in thousands):

Revenues	$800
Cost of goods sold	600
Avoidable division overhead	100

1. Prepare the operating income statement for Pike Enterprises for the second quarter of 19_8. Assume that revenues and operating results are identical to the first quarter except that the manager of the Andorian Division has dropped the low-margin product line from his product group.
2. Is Pike Enterprises better off from this action?
3. Is the Andorian Division manager better off from this action?
4. Suggest changes for Pike's system of division reporting and evaluation that will motivate division managers to make decisions that are in the best interest of Pike Enterprises as a whole. Discuss any potential disadvantages of your proposal.

26-28 Alternative measures for the investment base of gasoline stations. ARCO is having trouble in deciding whether to continue to use its old gasoline stations and in evaluating the performance of these stations and their managers in terms of return on investment. Top management has explored various ways of measuring investment for the stations:

a. *Historical cost*—original cost of land and buildings minus accumulated depreciation (sometimes called net book value).
b. *Current cost*—cost to currently replace the operating cash inflows provided by the existing gasoline station.
c. *Current disposal price*—the net proceeds from selling the gasoline station to another company.

Information on three gasoline stations was collected to help clarify the issues:

	Fresno Station	Las Vegas Station	Modesto Station
Operating income	$100,000	$120,000	$60,000
Historical cost of investment	$400,000	$200,000	$260,000
Current cost of investment	$640,000	$480,000	$290,000
Current disposal price of investment	$600,000	$2,500,000	$300,000
Age	6 years	15 years	2 years

The Las Vegas station is located next to the largest casino on the Las Vegas Strip and was purchased before the current boom in casinos. The current-cost estimate of the Las Vegas station is for a site 1 mile away from the existing site. The new site would generate the same amount of operating income as the old site. The current-cost estimates for the Fresno and Modesto stations are for the same site as the existing station in each city.

REQUIRED

1. Which of the three measures of investment is relevant for deciding whether to dispose of any one (or more) of the gasoline stations? Why?
2. Compute the ratio of operating income to investment for the Fresno, Las Vegas, and Modesto stations under each of the three measures of investment.
3. Which of the three measures is applicable for judging the performance of a gasoline station as an investment activity?
4. Which of the three measures is applicable for judging the performance of the manager of a gasoline station? Is your answer the same as, or different from, your answers in requirements 1 and 3?
5. What measures of performance, in addition to ROI, might be used to evaluate the performance of a manager of a gasoline station?

26-29 ROI performance measures based on historical cost and current cost. Mineral Waters Ltd. operates three divisions that process and bottle sparkling mineral water. The historical-cost accounting system reports the following data for 1998:

	Calistoga Division	Alpine Springs Division	Rocky Mountains Division
Revenues	$500,000	$ 700,000	$1,100,000
Operating costs (excluding depreciation)	300,000	380,000	600,000
Plant depreciation	70,000	100,000	120,000
Operating income	$130,000	$ 220,000	$ 380,000
Current assets	$200,000	$ 250,000	$ 300,000
Fixed assets—plant	140,000	900,000	1,320,000
Total assets	$340,000	$1,150,000	$1,620,000

Mineral Waters estimates the useful life of each plant to be 12 years with a zero terminal disposal price. The straight-line depreciation method is used. At the end of 1998, the Calistoga plant is 10 years old, Alpine Springs plant is 3 years old, and Rocky Mountains plant is 1 year old.

An index of construction costs of plants for mineral water production for the 10-year period that Mineral Waters has been operating (1988 year-end = 100) is

1988	1995	1997	1998
100	136	160	170

Given the high turnover of current assets, management believes that the historical-cost and current-cost measures of current assets are approximately the same.

REQUIRED

1. Compute the ROI (operating income to total assets) ratio of each division using historical-cost measures. Comment on the results.
2. Use the approach in Exhibit 26-3 (p. 942) to compute the ROI of each division, incorporating current-cost estimates as of 1998 for depreciation and fixed assets. Comment on the results.
3. What advantages might arise from using current-cost asset measures as compared with historical-cost measures for evaluating the performance of the managers of the three divisions?

26-30 **Evaluating managers, ROI, value-chain analysis of cost structure.** User Friendly Computer is one of the largest personal computer companies in the world. The board of directors was recently (March 19_8) informed that User Friendly's president, Brian Clay, was resigning to "pursue other interests." An executive search firm recommends that the board consider appointing Peter Diamond (current president of Computer Power) or Norma Provan (current president of Peach Computer). You collect the following financial information on Computer Power and Peach Computer for 19_6 and 19_7 (in millions):

	Computer Power		Peach Computer	
	19_6	19_7	19_6	19_7
Total assets	$360.0	$340.0	$160.0	$240.0
Revenues	$400.0	$320.0	$200.0	$350.0
Costs				
R&D	36.0	16.8	18.0	43.5
Design	15.0	8.4	3.6	11.6
Production	102.0	112.0	82.8	98.6
Marketing	75.0	92.4	36.0	66.7
Distribution	27.0	22.4	18.0	23.2
Customer service	45.0	28.0	21.6	46.4
Total costs	300.0	280.0	180.0	290.0
Operating income	$100.0	$ 40.0	$ 20.0	$ 60.0

In early 19_8, a computer magazine gave Peach Computer's main product five stars (its highest rating on a five-point scale). Computer Power's main product was given three stars, down from five stars a year ago because of customer-service problems. The computer magazine also ran an article on new-product introductions in the personal computer industry. Peach Computer received high marks for new products in 19_7. Computer Power's performance was called "mediocre." One "unnamed insider" of Computer Power commented: "Our new-product cupboard is empty."

REQUIRED

1. Use the DuPont method to analyze the ROI of Computer Power and Peach Computer in 19_6 and 19_7. Comment on the results.
2. Compute the percentage of costs in each of the six business-function cost categories for Computer Power and Peach Computer in 19_6 and 19_7. Comment on the results.
3. Rank Diamond and Provan as potential candidates for president of User Friendly Computer.

26-31 ROI, residual income, investment decisions. The Media Group has three major divisions:

a. Newspapers—owns leading newspapers on four continents
b. Television—owns major television networks on three continents
c. Film studios—owns one of the five largest film studios in the world

Summary financial data for 19_6 and 19_7 are as follows (in millions):

	Operating Income		Revenues		Total Assets	
	19_6	19_7	19_6	19_7	19_6	19_7
Newspapers	$900	$1,100	$4,500	$4,600	$4,400	$4,900
Television	130	160	6,000	6,400	2,700	3,000
Film studios	220	200	1,600	1,650	2,500	2,600

The manager of each division has an annual bonus plan based on division return on investment (ROI). ROI is defined as operating income divided by total assets. Senior executives from divisions reporting increases in ROI from the prior year are automatically eligible for a bonus. Senior executives of divisions reporting a decline in the division ROI have to provide persuasive explanations for the decline to be eligible for a limited bonus.

Ken Kearney, manager of the Newspapers Division, is considering a proposal to invest $200 million in fast-speed printing presses with color-print options. The estimated increment to 19_8 operating income would be $30 million. The Media Group has a 12% required rate of return for investments in all three divisions.

REQUIRED

1. Use the DuPont method to explain differences among the three divisions in their 19_7 division ROI. Use 19_7 total assets as the denominator.
2. Why might Kearney be less than enthusiastic about the fast-speed printing press investment proposal?
3. Rupert Prince, chairman of the Media Group, receives a proposal to base senior executive compensation at each division on division residual income. Compute the residual income of each division in 19_7.
4. Would adoption of a residual income measure reduce Kearney's reluctance to adopt the fast-speed printing press investment proposal?

26-32 Division managers' compensation (continuation of 26-31). Rupert Prince seeks your advice on revising the existing bonus plan for division managers of the Media Group. Assume division managers do not like bearing risk. He is considering three ideas:

◆ Make all of each division manager's compensation depend on division ROI.

♦ Make all of each division manager's compensation depend on company-wide ROI.

♦ Use benchmarking, and compensate each division manager on the basis of his or her own division's ROI minus the average ROI of the other two divisions.

REQUIRED

Evaluate each of the three ideas Prince has put forth using performance evaluation concepts described in this chapter. Indicate the positive and negative features of each proposal.

26-33 ROI, residual income, management incentives. (CMA, adapted) The Jump-Start Company (JSC), a subsidiary of Mason Industries, manufactures go-carts and other recreational vehicles. Family recreational centers, featuring go-cart tracks and miniature golf, batting cages, and arcade games have increased in popularity. As a result, JSC has been receiving some pressure from the Mason management to diversify into some of these other recreational areas. Recreational Leasing, Inc. (RLI), one of the largest companies that leases arcade games to these family recreational centers, is looking for a friendly buyer. Mason's top management believes that RLI's assets could be acquired for an investment of $3 million and has strongly urged Bill Grieco, division manager of JSC, to consider acquiring RLI.

Grieco has reviewed RLI's financial statements with his controller, Marie Donnelly, and they believe that the acquisition may not be in JSC's best interest. "If we decide not to do this, the Mason people are not going to be happy," said Grieco. "If we could convince them to base our bonuses on something other than return on investment, maybe this acquisition would look more attractive. How would we do if the bonuses were based on residual income using the company's 15% required rate of return on investment?"

Mason has traditionally evaluated all of its divisions on the basis of return on investment, which is defined as the ratio of operating income to total assets. The management team of any division reporting an annual increase in the return on investment is automatically eligible for a bonus. The management team of any division reporting a decline in the return on investment must provide convincing explanations for the decline to be eligible for a limited bonus.

Presented here are condensed financial statements for both JSC and RLI for the fiscal year ended May 31, 19_8:

	JSC	RLI
Revenues	$10,500,000	—
Leasing revenue	—	$2,800,000
Variable costs	7,000,000	1,000,000
Fixed costs	1,500,000	1,200,000
Operating income	$ 2,000,000	$ 600,000
Current assets	$ 2,300,000	$1,900,000
Long-term assets	5,700,000	1,100,000
Total assets	$ 8,000,000	$3,000,000
Current liabilities	$ 1,400,000	$ 850,000
Long-term liabilities	3,800,000	1,200,000
Stockholders' equity	2,800,000	950,000
Total liabilities and stockholders' equity	$ 8,000,000	$3,000,000

REQUIRED

1. If Mason Industries continues to use return on investment as the sole measure of division performance, explain why the Jump-Start Company (JSC) would be reluctant to acquire Recreational Leasing, Inc., (RLI). Be sure to support your answer with appropriate calculations.

2. If Mason Industries could be persuaded to use residual income to measure the performance of JSC, explain why JSC would be more willing to acquire RLI. Be sure to support your answer with appropriate calculations.

3. Discuss how the behavior of division managers is likely to be affected by the use of

   a. Return on investment (ROI) as a performance measure

   b. Residual income (RI) as a performance measure

26-34 Division manager's compensation, risk sharing, incentives (continuation of 26-33). The management of Mason Industries is considering the following alternative compensation arrangements for Bill Grieco, the division manager of JSC.

◆ Make Grieco's compensation a fixed salary without any bonus. Mason's management believes that one advantage of this arrangement is that Grieco will be less inclined to reject future attractive acquisitions like RLI just because of their impact on ROI or RI.

◆ Make all of Grieco's compensation depend on the division's residual income. The benefit of this arrangement is that it creates incentives for Grieco to aggressively seek and accept all proposals that increase JSC's residual income.

◆ Evaluate Grieco's performance using benchmarking by comparing JSC's RI against the RI achieved by managers of other companies that also manufacture and sell go-carts and recreational vehicles and have comparable levels of investment. Mason's management believes that the advantage of benchmarking is that it focuses attention on Grieco's performance relative to peers rather than on the division's absolute performance.

REQUIRED

1. Assume Grieco is risk averse and does not like bearing risk. Using concepts about performance evaluation described in this chapter evaluate each of the three proposals that Mason's management is considering. Indicate the positive and negative features of each proposal.

2. What compensation arrangement would you recommend? Explain briefly.

26-35 Ethics, manager's performance evaluation. (A. Spero, adapted) The Caffi Mug Company is a maker of ceramic coffee mugs. It imprints company logos and other sayings on the mugs for both commercial and whole-sale markets. The firm has the capacity to produce 3,000,000 mugs per year, but the recession has cut production and sales last year to 1,500,000 mugs. The summary operating statement for 19_7 was as follows:

Sales (1,500,000 × $2)	$3,000,000
Cost of goods sold	2,700,000
Gross Margin	300,000
Marketing, distribution and administration costs (fixed)	400,000
Operating income	$ (100,000)

Cost of goods sold consists of variable costs of $750,000 (or $0.50 per mug) and fixed costs of $1,950,000 (or $1.30 per mug). There was no beginning and no ending inventory of finished goods in 19_7.

Concerned about the loss, the board of directors hired a new CEO, Derek Johnson, and offered him an incentive-based compensation contract rather than the fixed-wage contract of the previous CEO. Johnson's contract paid $50,000 per year in salary plus a 15% bonus on the firm's operating profits (if any) before deducting the bonus. Operating profits are calculated using full absorption costing—that is, fixed manufacturing costs per unit manufactured are inventoried and expensed only when the goods are sold.

Johnson took the following actions for 19_8:

a. Increased production to 2,500,000 mugs.

b. Increased sales to 1,800,000 mugs.

c. Increased marketing, distribution and administration costs to $650,000. (Johnson's salary of $50,000 is included in these costs.)

The selling price per mug in 19_8 of $2, the variable manufacturing costs per mug of $0.50, and total fixed manufacturing costs of $1,950,000 were all unchanged from 19_7.

At the end of 19_8, Johnson met with the board of directors and announced that he had accepted another job. He noted that he had gotten Caffi successfully on track and thanked the board for the opportunity. His new job was to turn around another struggling company.

REQUIRED

1. Calculate Johnson's bonus for 19_8.
2. Evaluate Johnson's performance. Did he do as good a job as the numbers in requirement 1 suggest? Explain.
3. Did Johnson behave ethically? Explain your answer.

COLLABORATIVE LEARNING PROBLEM

26-36 ROI, residual income, investment decisions, division manager's compensation. (CMA adapted) Raddington Industries is a manufacturer of tool and die machinery. Raddington is a vertically integrated company that is organized into two divisions. The Reigis Steel Division manufactures alloy steel plates. The Tool and Die Machinery Division uses the alloy steel plates to make machines. Raddington operates each of its divisions as an investment center.

Raddington monitors its divisions on the basis of return on investment (ROI) with investment defined as average operating assets employed. Raddington uses ROI to determine management bonuses. All investments in operating assets are expected to earn a minimum return of 11% before income taxes. For many years, Reigis's ROI has ranged from 11.8% to 14.7%. During the fiscal year ended December 31, 19_8, Reigis contemplated a capital acquisition with an estimated ROI of 11.5%; division management, however, decided against the investment because it believed that the investment would decrease Reigis's overall ROI.

Reigis's 19_8 operating income statement follows. The division's operating assets employed were $15,750,000 at December 31, 19_8, a 5% increase over the 19_7 year-end balance.

Reigis Steel Division Operating Income Statement for the Year Ended December 31, 19_8

Revenue		$25,000,000
Cost of goods sold		16,500,000
Gross margin		8,500,000
Operating costs		
Administrative	$3,955,000	
Marketing	2,700,000	
Operating costs		6,655,000
Operating income		$ 1,845,000

INSTRUCTIONS

Form groups of two or three students to complete the following requirements.

REQUIRED

1. Calculate the return on investment in average operating assets employed (ROI) for 19_8 for the Reigis Steel Division.
2. Compute Reigis Steel Division's residual income on the basis of average operating assets employed.
3. Would the management of Reigis Steel Division have been more likely to accept the investment opportunity it had in 19_8 if residual income were used as a performance measure instead of ROI? Explain.

4. James Chen, the chairman of Raddington Industries, is considering one of four alternative ways to compensate division managers.
- ◆ Pay each division manager only a flat salary and no bonus.
- ◆ Make all of each division manager's compensation depend on division residual income.
- ◆ Make all of each division manager's compensation depend on companywide (Raddington Industries) residual income rather than division residual income.
- ◆ Use benchmarking and compensate each division manager on the basis of his or her own division's residual income minus the residual income of the other division. Assume the two divisions have comparable levels of investment and required rates of return.

Assume that division managers are risk averse and do not like bearing risk. Evaluate each of the four alternatives Chen is considering, in the context of the structure and businesses of Raddington Industries. Indicate the positive and negative features of each proposal.

5. What compensation arrangement would you recommend? Explain your answer briefly.

Dell Computer

There are numerous programs to measure your computer's performance, but how do you measure the performance of a computer company? Dell Computer Corporation uses both financial and nonfinancial performance measures. **1** Assembly workers would no doubt concentrate more on nonfinancial measures such as the number of computers assembled per hour, but all employees must pay close attention to both sets of measures. Financial measures at Dell include operating income, net income, and return on invested capital. Nonfinancial measures can range from the number of computers assembled per hour to more general concerns, such as quality. To best track its overall performance, Dell uses both internal and external nonfinancial performance measures. **2** An example of an internal measure is Dell's "out-of-box" audit. Inspectors pull at least 5% of finished, boxed units off the assembly line to ensure that computers have been assembled to customer order. Dell's most important external measure is its customer satisfaction survey. Information gleaned from these surveys can affect every aspect of Dell's operations, from research and development to customer service. **3** For example, managers could use feedback from customer surveys to help decide whether or not to run an ad touting the ability of Dell's laptop computers to withstand coffee spills. Dell issues monthly, weekly and even daily reports tracking both financial and nonfinancial performance.

1

2

3

4

5

6

4 These reports track overall company performance, as well as performance in key areas such as assembly. Managers can use the information in the reports to keep employees focused on their performance targets. Of course, the best way to keep employees focused on their targets is to offer incentives. Dell offers incentives for all levels of employees. **5** For management, bonuses can be significant, especially for high-level managers such as CEO Michael Dell. For nonmanagement employees, Dell offers a profit sharing plan. **6** Manufacturing's product assembly work cell employees participate in the program and are rewarded for their cost reduction efforts.

DELL COMPUTER CORPORATION
Management Control Systems

Measuring performance is one of many important activities undertaken by organizations. But the phrase "performance measurement" takes on different meanings depending on a specific organization's structure and management views. For instance, companies may choose to use financial measures, such as operating income, net income, or return on investment. They may also choose to use nonfinancial measures, such as market share, customer satisfaction, and product manufacturing lead times. Dell Computer Corporation uses a combination of financial and nonfinancial measures to gauge corporate performance.

At Dell, financial performance is measured, in part, by examining the ratio of "return on invested capital." Return is defined as operating income, and invested capital consists of working capital plus fixed assets minus an adjustment for cash. This calculation is a refinement of return on the investment and return on asset measures. Nonfinancial performance is evaluated by examining both internal and external measures. An example of an internal measure is Dell's "out-of-box audit," which is performed on a sample of at least 5 percent of finished goods. Product auditors pull finished, boxed units that are ready to ship off the line to check for customer-order accuracy. A significant external measure is "field incident rate." As an indicator of product quality, this measure tracks warranty items and flaws after products have been delivered to the customer. Dell's target in this area is to achieve significant improvement each year, in keeping with their total quality

management efforts. Another important external measure of performance for Dell is customer satisfaction surveys. Dell has repeatedly scored at or near the top of annual J.D. Power consumer surveys, and the company also regularly makes the "best buy" lists in computer trade magazines.

Dell has used several different time intervals for reporting performance results back to managers. In the initial stages of company growth, planning was done two quarters in advance, with measurement of performance against plan done monthly. Dell believed that forecasting beyond two quarters out held little value because the business environment was so volatile. More than a decade later, the company still faces a volatile business environment, but it has come a long way in both planning and measuring its performance against those plans. For example, managers used to examine performance using monthly reports. When they found that monthly financial reports were not timely enough for decision making, Dell added daily and weekly reports, containing nonfinancial measures in addition to financial information. More weight in reporting and decision making has now been given to the weekly report, which shows performance in key metric areas. These key metrics are tied to major corporate initiatives, such as product leadership, quality, cost and productivity, and globalization. The principal part of this report shows sales information, such as what products are selling best, and lead times of inventory and product delivery. The daily reports focus on such items as sales revenues, order rates, order cancellation rates, and inventory levels.

Incentives for achieving target levels of performance are offered to employees at every level. For managers, Dell has a Management Incentive Bonus Plan, tied to achieving corporate initiatives. The bonuses paid to managers are based on predetermined targets, such as profitability. Depending on managerial level in the organization, bonuses can be a significant percentage of the target. For employees who do not participate in the Management Incentive Bonus Plan, there is a profit sharing program. Every employee is eligible, and, like management, Dell employees also are given targets. Stock option plans are also used as an incentive to meet goals. These have been quite successful not only in helping Dell achieve its performance goals, but also in retaining motivated employees. ◆

QUESTIONS

1. Identify various performance measures that Dell finds useful.

2. How might Dell's internal information systems affect managers' ability to measure performance?

3. What risks does Dell face in offering performance incentives?

4. How might Dell measure the contribution toward goal achievement by individual employees who perform multiple tasks or work in teams?

5. Dell prepares a rolling five-quarter plan for performance, against which variance analysis is performed. What types of variances would you expect Dell to analyze, and why?

SURVEYS OF COMPANY PRACTICE

This appendix provides the full citations to the individual publications cited in the many Surveys of Company Practice boxes included in the text.

American Electronics Association, *Operating Ratios Survey 1993-94*, (Santa Clara, CA: American Electronics Association, 1993)—cited in Chapters 8 and 18.

Armitage, H., and R. Nicholson, "Activity-Based Costing: A Survey of Canadian Practice," Supplement to *CMA Magazine* (1993)—cited in Chapter 4.

APQC/CAM-I, *Activity Based Management Consortium Study* (American Productivity and Quality Center/CAM-I, 1995)—cited in Chapter 4.

Asada, T., J. Bailes, and M. Amano, "An Empirical Study of Japanese and American Budget Planning and Control Systems," (Working Paper, Tsukuba University and Oregon State University, 1989)—cited in Chapter 6.

Ask, U., and C. Ax, "Trends in the Development of Product Costing Practices and Techniques—A Survey of the Swedish Manufacturing Industry," (Working Paper, Gothenburg School of Economics, Gothenburg, Sweden, 1992)—cited in Chapters 7 and 9.

Atkinson, A., *Intrafirm Cost and Resource Allocations: Theory and Practice*, (Hamilton, Canada: Society of Management Accountants of Canada and Canadian Academic Accounting Association Research Monograph, 1987)—cited in Chapter 13.

Bartezzaghi, E., F. Turco, and G. Spina, "The Impact of the Just-in-Time Approach on Production System Performance: A Survey of Italian Industry," *International Journal of Operations & Production Management* (Vol. 12, No. 1, 1992)—cited in Chapter 21.

Berenheim, R.E., *Corporate Ethics Practices* (New York: The Conference Board, 1992)—cited in Chapter 2.

Billesbach, T., A. Harrison, and S. Croom-Morgan, "Just-in-Time: A United States United Kingdom Comparison," *International Journal of Operations & Production Management* (Vol. 11, No. 10, 1991)—cited in Chapter 21.

Blayney, P., and I. Yokoyama, "Comparative Analysis of Japanese and Australian Cost Accounting and Management Practices," (Working Paper, The University of Sydney, Sydney, Australia, 1991)—cited in Chapters 2, 5, 6, 9, 12, 13, 15, 22, and 26.

Boons, A., and F. Roozen, "Symptoms of Dysfunctional Cost Information Systems: Some Preliminary Evidence from the Netherlands," (Working Paper, Erasmus Universiteit, Rotterdam, Netherlands, 1992)—cited in Chapter 14.

Clarke, P., "Management Accounting Practices and Techniques in Irish Manufacturing Firms," (Working Paper, Trinity College, Dublin, Ireland, 1995)—cited in Chapters 4, 7, 22, and 26.

Clarke, P., and T. ODea, "Management Accounting Systems: Some Field Evidence from Sixteen Multinational Companies in Ireland," (Working Paper, Trinity College, Dublin, Ireland, 1993)—cited in Chapter 21.

Cohen, J., and L. Paquette, "Management Accounting Practices: Perceptions of Controllers," *Journal of Cost Management* (Fall 1991)—cited in Chapter 5.

Cooper, R., "Does Your Company Need a New Cost System?" *Journal of Cost Management* (Spring 1987)—cited in Chapter 14.

Cornick, M., W. Cooper, and S. Wilson, "How Do Companies Analyze Overhead," *Management Accounting* (June 1988)—cited in Chapters 7 and 12.

Cotton, W., "Activity Based Costing in New Zealand," (Working paper, SUNY Genesco, 1993)—cited in Chapter 4.

Dean, G., M. Joye, and P. Blayney, *Strategic Management Accounting Survey*, (Sydney, Australia: The University of Sydney, 1991)—cited in Chapter 13.

de With, E., and E. Ijskes, "Current Budgeting Practices in Dutch Companies," (Working Paper, Vrije Universiteit, 1992, Amsterdam, Netherlands)—cited in Chapter 6.

Drury, C., S. Braund, P. Osborne, and M. Tayles, *A Survey of Management Accounting Practices in UK Manufacturing Companies*, (London, U.K.: Chartered Association of Certified Accountants, 1993)—cited in Chapters 7, 12, and 25.

Freeman, M., and G. Hobbes, "Capital Budgeting: Theory versus Practice," *Australian Accountant* (September 1991)—cited in Chapter 23.

Fremgen, J., and S. Liao, *The Allocation of Corporate Indirect Costs* (New York: National Association of Accountants, 1981)—cited in Chapter 13.

Gaumnitz, B., and F. Kollaritsch, "Manufacturing Variances: Current Practice and Trends," *Journal of Cost Management* (Spring 1991)—cited in Chapter 7.

Govindarajan, V., and B. Ramamurthy, "Transfer Pricing Policies in Indian Companies: A Survey," *Chartered Accountant* (November 1983)—cited in Chapter 25.

Grant, Thornton, *Survey of American Manufacturers*, (New York: Grant Thornton, 1992)—cited in Chapter 12.

Greiner, M., C. Kask, and C. Sparks, "Comparative Manufacturing Productivity and Unit Labor Cost," *Monthly Labor Review* (February 1995)—cited in Chapter 24.

Hanson, K., "Unavoidable Ethical Dilemmas in a Business Career," (Stanford University, 1995)—cited in Chapter 2.

Ho, S., and R. Pike, "Risk Analysis in Capital Budgeting Contexts: Simple or Sophisticated?" *Accounting and Business Research* (Vol. 21, No. 83, 1991)—cited in Chapter 23.

Ho, S., and L. Yang, "Managerial Risk Taking and Handling in Corporate Investment: An Exploratory Study in Taiwan," *Proceedings of the Second International Conference on Asian-Pacific Financial Markets*, (September 1991)—cited in Chapter 23.

Hoque, Z., and M. Alam, "Organization Size, Business Objectives, Managerial Antonomy, Industry Conditions, and Management's Choice of Transfer Pricing Methods: A Contextual Analysis of New Zealand Companies," (Working Paper, Victoria University of Wellington, Wellington, New Zealand)—cited in Chapter 25.

Innes, J., and F. Mitchell, "A Survey of Activity-Based Costing in the U.K.'s Largest Companies," *Management Accounting Research* (June 1995)—cited in Chapters 4 and 16.

Inoue, S., "A Comparative Study of Recent Development of Cost Management Problems in U.S.A., U.K., Canada, and Japan," *Kagawa University Economic Review* (June 1988)—cited in Chapters 7 and 9.

Jog, V., and A. Srivastava, "Corporate Financial Decision Making in Canada, *Canadian Journal of Administrataive Sciences* (June 1994)—cited in Chapters 20 and 21.

Joye, M., and P. Blayney, "Cost and Management Accounting Practices in Australian Manufacturing Companies: Survey Results," (Accounting Research Centre, The University of Sydney, 1991)—cited in Chapters 10, 17 and 25.

Kim, I., and J. Song, "U.S., Korea, and Japan: Accounting Practices in Three Countries," *Management Accounting* (August 1990)—cited in Chapters 22 and 23.

Lindsay, R., and S. Kalagnanam, *The Adoption of Just-in-Time Production Systems in Canada and Their Association with Management Control Practices*, (Hamilton, Canada: Society of Management Accountants of Canada, 1993)—cited in Chapter 21.

Management Accounting Research Group, "Investigation into the Actual State of Target Costing, Corporate Accounting," (Working Paper, Kobe University, Japan, May 1992)—cited in Chapter 12.

Mills, R., and C. Sweeting, "Pricing Decisions in Practice: How Are They Made in U.K. Manufacturing and Service Companies?" (London, U.K.: Chartered Institute of Management Accountants, Occasional Paper, 1988)—cited in Chapter 12.

Mostafa, A., J. Sharp, and K. Howard, "Transfer Pricing—A Survey Using Discriminant Analysis," *Omega*, (Vol. 12, No. 5, 1984)—cited in Chapter 25.

Mowen, M., *Accounting for Costs as Fixed and Variable* (National Association of Accountants: Montvale, NJ, 1986)—cited in Chapter 2.

NAA Tokyo Affiliate, "Management Accounting in the Advanced Manufacturing Surrounding: Comparative Study on Survey in Japan and U.S.A.," (Tokyo, Japan, 1988)—cited in Chapter 10.

Price Waterhouse, *Transfer Pricing Practices of American Industry* (New York: Price Waterhouse, 1984)—cited in Chapter 25.

Ramadan, S., "The Rationale for Cost Allocation: A Study of U.K. Divisionalised Companies," *Accounting and Business Research* (Winter 1989)—cited in Chapter 13.

Sangster, A., "Capital Investment Appraisal Techniques: A Survey of Current Usage," *Journal of Business Finance & Accounting* (April 1993)—cited in Chapter 22.

Scarbrough, P., A. Nanni, and M. Sakurai, "Japanese Management Accounting Practices and the Effects of Assembly and Process Automation," *Management Accounting Research* (March 1991)—cited in Chapter 7.

Slater, K., and C. Wooton, *A Study of Joint and By-Product Costing in the UK* (London, U.K.: Institute of Cost and Management Accountants, 1984)—cited in Chapter 15.

Smith, K., and C. Sullivan, "Survey of Cost Management Systems in Manufacturing," (Working Paper, Purdue University, West Lafayette, Indiana, 1990)—cited in Chapters 22 and 26.

Sullivan, C., and K. Smith, "Capital Investment Justification for U.S. Factory Automation Projects," *Journal of the Midwest Finance Association* (1994)—cited in Chapter 23.

Swenson, D., and J. Cassidy, "The Effect of JIT on Management Accounting," *Journal of Cost Management* (Spring 1993)—cited in Chapter 20.

Tang, R., "Canadian Transfer Pricing in the 1990s," *Management Accounting* (February 1992)—cited in Chapter 25.

Tang, R., C. Walter, and R. Raymond, "Transfer Pricing—Japanese vs. American Style," *Management Accounting* (January 1979)—cited in Chapter 25.

Zarzecki, D., and T. Wisniewski, "Investment Appraisal Practice in Poland," (Working Paper, Szcecin University, Szczecin, Poland, 1995)—cited in Chapters 22 and 23.

RECOMMENDED READINGS

The literature on cost accounting and related areas is vast and varied. The following books illustrate recent publications that capture current developments:

Brimson, J., *Activity Accounting: An Activity-Based Costing Approach*. New York: Wiley, 1991.

Connell, R., *Measuring Customer and Service Profitability in the Finance Sector*. London, U.K.: Chapman & Hall, 1995.

Cooper, R., and R. Kaplan, *The Design of Cost Management Systems*. Englewood Cliffs, NJ: Prentice-Hall, 1991.

Ditz, D., J. Ranganathan, and R. Banks, *Green Ledgers: Case Studies in Corporate Environmental Accounting*. World Resources Institute, 1995.

Hronec, S., *Vital Signs*. New York: American Management Association, 1993.

Johnson, T., *Relevance Regained*. New York: Free Press, 1992.

Miller, J., *Implementing Activity-Based Management in Daily Operation*. New York: Wiley, 1996.

Player, S., and D. Keys, *Activity-Based Management*. New York: MasterMedia Limited, 1995.

Schweitzer, M., E. Trossmann, and G. Lawson, *Break-even Analyses: Basic Model, Variants, Extensions*. Chichester, U.K.: Wiley, 1992.

Shank, J., and V. Govindarajan, *Strategic Management Accounting*. New York: The Free Press, 1993.

Books of readings related to cost or management accounting include:

Aly, I., ed., *Readings in Management Accounting*. Dubuque, Iowa: Kendall/Hunt, 1995.

Brinker, B., ed., *Emerging Practices in Cost Management*. Boston, MA: Warren, Gorham, and Lamont, 1995.

Ratnatunga, J., J. Miller, N. Mudalige, and A. Sohalled, eds., *Issues in Strategic Management Accounting*. Sydney, Australia: Harcourt Brace Jovanovich, 1993.

Young, M., ed., *Readings in Management Accounting*. Englewood Cliffs, N.J.: Prentice-Hall, 1995.

The Harvard Business School series in accounting and control offers important contributions to the cost accounting literature, including:

Anthony, R., *The Management Control Function*. Boston: Harvard Business School Press, 1988.

Berliner, C., and J. Brimson, eds., *Cost Management for Todays Advanced Manufacturing: The CAM-I Conceptual Design*. Boston: Harvard Business School Press, 1988.

Bruns, W., ed., *Performance Measurement, Evaluation, and Incentives*. Boston: Harvard Business School Press, 1992.

Bruns, W., and R. Kaplan, eds., *Accounting and Management: Field Study Perspectives*. Boston: Harvard Business School Press, 1987.

Cooper, R., *When Lean Enterprises Collide*. Boston: Harvard Business School Press, 1995.

Johnson, H., and R. Kaplan, *Relevance Lost: The Rise and Fall of Management Accounting*. Boston: Harvard Business School Press, 1987.

Kaplan, R., ed., *Measures for Manufacturing Excellence*. Boston: Harvard Business School Press, 1990.

Merchant, K.A., *Rewarding Results: Motivating Profit Center Managers*. Boston: Harvard Business School Press, 1989.

Productivity Press publishes many books with a global focus on cost and management accounting, including:

Monden, Y., *Cost Management in the New Manufacturing Age: Innovations in the Japanese Automotive Industry*. Cambridge, MA: Productivity Press, 1992.

Sakurai, M., *Integrated Cost Management*. Portland, OR: Productivity Press, 1996.

The Institute of Management Accountants publishes monographs and books covering cost accounting topics, such as:

Atkinson, A., J. Hamburg, and C. Ittner, *Linking Quality to Profits*, Montvale, NJ: Institute of Management Accountants and Milwaukee, WI: ASQC Quality Press, 1994.

Cooper, R., R. Kaplan, L. Maisel, E. Morrissey, and R. Oehm, *Activity-Based Cost Management: Moving from Analysis to Action*. Montvale, NJ: Institute of Management Accountants, 1992.

Dhavale, D., *Management Accounting Issues in Cellular Manufacturing and Focused-Factory Systems*. Montvale, NJ: Institute of Management Accountings, 1996.

Epstein, M., *Measuring Corporate Environmental Performance*. Montvale, NJ: IMA Foundation of Applied Research, 1995.

Klammer, T., *Managing Strategic and Capital Investment Decisions*. Burr Ridge, IL: Irwin & IMA, 1994.

Martinson, O., *Cost Accounting in the Service Industry*. Montvale, NJ: Institute of Management Accountants, 1994.

Noreen, E., D. Smith, and J.T. Mackey, *The Theory of Constraints and Its Implications for Management Accounting*. Great Barrington, MA: North River Press, 1995.

The Financial Executives Research Foundation publishes monographs and books concerning topics of interest to financial executives, such as:

Howell, R., J. Shank, S. Soucy, and J. Fisher, *Cost Management for Tomorrow: Seeking the Competitive Edge*. Morristown, NJ: Financial Executives Research Foundation, 1992.

Keating, P., and S. Jablonsky, *Changing Roles of Financial Management*. Morristown, NJ: Financial Executives Research Foundation, 1990.

The Chartered Institute of Management Accountants publishes monographs and books, including:

Drury, C., ed., *Management Accounting Handbook*. London, U.K.: Butterworth Heinemann and Chartered Institute of Management Accountants, 1992.

Ezzamel, M., C. Green, S. Lilley, and H. Willmott, *Changing Managers and Managing Change*. London, UK: Chartered Institute of Management Accountants, 1995.

Friedman, A., and S. Lylne, *Activity-Based Techniques: The Real Life Consequences*. London, UK: Chartered Institute of Management Accountants, 1995.

Murphy, C., J. Currie, M. Fahy, and W. Golden, *Deciding the Future: Management Accountants as Decision Support Personnel*. London, UK: Chartered Institute of Management Accountants, 1995.

Ward, K., *Strategic Management Accounting*. Oxford, U.K.: Butterworth and Chartered Institute of Management Accountants, 1992.

Jai Press publishes *Advances in Management Accounting* on an annual basis. It is edited by M. Epstein and K. Poston and includes a broad cross-section of research articles and case studies.

Case books on cost and management accounting include:

Rotch, W., B. Allen, and E. Brownlee, *Cases in Management Accounting and Control Systems*. Englewood Cliffs, NJ: Prentice-Hall, 1995.

Shank, J., *Cases in Cost Management: A Strategic Emphasis*. Cincinnati, Ohio: South-Western, 1996.

The following are detailed annotated bibliographies of the cost and management accounting research literatures:

Clancy, D., *Annotated Management Accounting Readings*. Management Accounting Section of the American Accounting Association, 1986.

Deakin, E., M. Maher, and J. Cappel, *Contemporary Literature in Cost Accounting*. Homewood, IL: Richard D. Irwin, 1988.

Klemstine, C., and M. Maher, *Management Accounting Research: 1926-1983*. New York: Garland Publishing, 1984.

The *Journal of Cost Management for the Manufacturing Industry* contains numerous articles on modern management accounting. It is published by Warren, Gorham, and Lamont, 210 South Street, Boston, MA 02111.

Two journals bearing on management accounting are published by sections of the American Accounting Association, 5717 Bessie Drive, Sarasota, FL 34233: *Journal of Management Accounting Research* and *Behavioral Research in Accounting*.

Professional associations that specialize in serving members with cost and management accounting interests include:

- *Institute of Management Accountants*, 10 Paragon Drive, P.O. Box 433, Montvale, NJ 07645. Publishes the *Management Accountant* journal.

- *Financial Executives Institute*, 10 Madison Avenue, P.O. Box 1938, Morristown, NJ 07960. Publishes *Financial Executive*.

- *Society of Cost Estimating and Analysis*, 101 South Whiting Street, Suite 313, Alexandria, VA 22304. Publishes the *Journal of Cost Analysis* and monographs related to cost estimation and price analysis in government and industry.

- *The Institute of Internal Auditors*, 249 Maitland Avenue, Altamonte Springs, FL 32701. Publishes *The Internal Auditor* journal. Also publishes monographs on topics related to internal control.

- *Society of Management Accountants of Canada*, 154 Main Street East, MPO Box 176, Hamilton, Ontario, L8N 3C3. Publishes the *CMA Magazine*.

- *The Chartered Institute of Management Accountants*, 63 Portland Place, London, WIN 4AB. Publishes the *Management Accounting* journal. Also publishes monographs covering cost and managerial accounting topics.

In many countries, individuals with cost and management accounting interests belong to professional bodies that serve members with financial reporting and taxation, as well as cost and management accounting, interests.

NOTES ON COMPOUND INTEREST AND INTEREST TABLES

Interest is the cost of using money. It is the rental charge for funds, just as renting a building and equipment entails a rental charge. When the funds are used for a period of time, it is necessary to recognize interest as a cost of using the borrowed ("rented") funds. This requirement applies even if the funds represent ownership capital and if interest does not entail an outlay of cash. Why must interest be considered? Because the selection of one alternative automatically commits a given amount of funds that could otherwise be invested in some other alternative.

Interest is generally important, even when short-term projects are under consideration. Interest looms correspondingly larger when long-run plans are studied. The rate of interest has significant enough impact to influence decisions regarding borrowing and investing funds. For example, $100,000 invested now and compounded annually for 10 years at 8% will accumulate to $215,900; at 20%, the $100,000 will accumulate to $619,200.

INTEREST TABLES

Many computer programs and pocket calculators are available that handle computations involving the time value of money. You may also turn to the following four basic tables to compute interest.

Table 1—Future Amount of $1

Table 1 shows how much $1 invested now will accumulate in a given number of periods at a given compounded interest rate per period. Consider investing $1,000 now for three years at 8% compound interest. A tabular presentation of how this $1,000 would accumulate to $1,259.70 follows:

Year	Interest per Year	Cumulative Interest Called Compound Interest	Total at End of Year
0	$ —	$ —	$1,000.00
1	80.00	80.00	1,080.00
2	86.40	166.40	1,166.40
3	93.30	259.70	1,259.70

This tabular presentation is a series of computations that could appear as follows:

$$S_1 = \$1,000(1.08)^1$$

$$S_2 = \$1,000(1.08)^2$$

$$S_3 = \$1,000(1.08)^3$$

The formula for the "amount of 1," often called the "future value of $1" of "future amount of $1," can be written

$$S = P(1 + r)^n$$

$$S = \$1,000(1 + .08)^3 = \$1,259.70$$

S is the future value amount; P is the present value, $1,000 in this case; r is the rate of interest; and n is the number of time periods.

Fortunately, tables make key computations readily available. A facility in selecting the *proper* table will minimize computations. Check the accuracy of the preceding answer using Table 1, p. 981.

Table 2—Present Value of $1

In the previous example, if $1,000 compounded at 8% per year will accumulate to $1,259.70 in 3 years, then $1,000 must be the present value of $1,259.70 due at the end of 3 years. The formula for the present value can be derived by reversing the process of *accumulation* (finding the future amount) that we just finished.

$$S = P(1 + r)^n$$

If

$$P = \frac{S}{(1 + r)^n}$$

then

$$P = \frac{\$1,259.70}{(1.08)^3} = \$1,000$$

Use Table 2, p. 982, to check this calculation.

When accumulating, we advance or roll forward in time. The difference between our original amount and our accumulated amount is called *compound interest*. When discounting, we retreat or roll back in time. The difference between the future amount and the present value is called *compound discount*. Note the following formulas (where $P = \$1,000$):

$$\text{Compound interest} = P[(1 + r)^n - 1] = \$259.70$$

$$\text{Compound discount} = S\left[1 - \frac{1}{(1 + r)^n}\right] = \$259.70$$

Table 3—Amount of Annuity of $1

An (ordinary) *annuity* is a series of equal payments (receipts) to be paid (or received) at the *end* of successive periods of equal length. Assume that $1,000 is invested at the end of each of 3 years at 8%:

End of Year	Amount
1st payment	$1,000.00 ➤ $1,080.00 ➤ $1,166.40, which is $1,000(1.08)^2
2nd payment	$1,000.00 ➤ 1,080.00, which is $1,000(1.08)^1
3rd payment	1,000.00
Accumulation (future amount)	$3,246.40

The preceding arithmetic may be expressed algebraically as the amount of an ordinary annuity of $1,000 for 3 years = $1,000(1 + r)^2 + $1,000(1 + r)^1 + $1,000.

We can develop the general formula for S_n, the amount of an ordinary annuity of $1, by using the example above as a basis:

1. $$S_n = 1 + (1 + r)^1 + (1 + r)^2$$

2. Substitute: $$S_n = 1 + (1.08)^1 + (1.08)^2$$

3. Multiply (2) by $(1 + r)$: $$(1.08)S_n = (1.08)^1 + (1.08)^2 + (1.08)^3$$

4. Subtract (2) from (3): $$1.08S_n - S_n = (1.08)^3 - 1$$
Note that all terms on the right-hand side are removed except $(1.08)^3$ in equation (3) and 1 in equation (2).

5. Factor (4): $$S_n(1.08 - 1) = (1.08)^3 - 1$$

6. Divide (5) by $(1.08 - 1)$: $$S_n = \frac{(1.08)^3 - 1}{1.08 - 1} = \frac{(1.08)^3 - 1}{.08}$$

7. The general formula for the amount of an ordinary annuity of $1 becomes: $$S_n = \frac{(1 + r)^n - 1}{r} \text{ or } \frac{\text{Compound interest}}{\text{Rate}}$$

This formula is the basis for Table 3, p. 983. Look at Table 3 or use the formula itself to check the calculations.

Table 4—Present Value of an Ordinary Annuity of $1

Using the same example as for Table 3, we can show how the formula of P_n, the *present value of an ordinary annuity*, is developed.

End of Year		0	1	2	3
1st payment	$\frac{1,000}{(1.08)^1} = \$\ 926.14$		$1,000		
2nd payment	$\frac{1,000}{(1.08)^2} = \$\ 857.52$			$1,000	
3rd payment	$\frac{1,000}{(1.08)^3} = \$\ 794.00$				$1,000
Total present value	$\$2,577.66$				

For the general case, the present value of an ordinary annuity of $1 may be expressed as:

1. $$P_n = \frac{1}{1+r} + \frac{1}{(1+r)^2} + \frac{1}{(1+r)^3}$$

2. Substitute $$P_n = \frac{1}{1.08} + \frac{1}{(1.08)^2} + \frac{1}{(1.08)^3}$$

3. Multiply by $\frac{1}{1.08}$: $$P_n\frac{1}{1.08} = \frac{1}{(1.08)^2} + \frac{1}{(1.08)^3} + \frac{1}{(1.08)^4}$$

4. Subtract (3) from (2): $$P_n - P_n\frac{1}{1.08} = \frac{1}{1.08} - \frac{1}{(1.08)^4}$$

5. Factor: $$P_n\left(1 - \frac{1}{(1.08)}\right) = \frac{1}{1.08}\left[1 - \frac{1}{(1.08)^3}\right]$$

6. or $$P_n\left(\frac{.08}{1.08}\right) = \frac{1}{1.08}\left[1 - \frac{1}{(1.08)^3}\right]$$

7. Multiply by $\dfrac{1.08}{.08}$:
$$P_n = \frac{1}{.08}\left[1 - \frac{1}{(1.08)^3}\right]$$

The general formula for the present value of an annuity of $1.00 is:

$$P_n = \frac{1}{r}\left[1 - \frac{1}{(1+r)^n}\right] = \frac{\text{Compound discount}}{\text{Rate}}$$

Solving,

$$P_n = \frac{.2062}{.08} = 2.577$$

The formula is the basis for Table 4, p. 984. Check the answer in the table. The present value tables, Tables 2 and 4, are used most frequently in capital budgeting.

The tables for annuities are not essential. With Tables 1 and 2, compound interest and compound discount can readily be computed. It is simply a matter of dividing either of these by the rate to get values equivalent to those shown in Tables 3 and 4.

TABLE 1
Compound Amount of $1.00 (The Future Value of $1.00)
$S = P(1 + i)^n$. In this table $P = \$1.00$

Periods	2%	4%	6%	8%	10%	12%	14%	16%	18%	20%	22%	24%	26%	28%	30%	32%	40%	Periods
1	1.020	1.040	1.060	1.080	1.100	1.120	1.140	1.160	1.180	1.200	1.220	1.240	1.260	1.280	1.300	1.320	1.400	1
2	1.040	1.082	1.124	1.166	1.210	1.254	1.300	1.346	1.392	1.440	1.488	1.538	1.588	1.638	1.690	1.742	1.960	2
3	1.061	1.125	1.191	1.260	1.331	1.405	1.482	1.561	1.643	1.728	1.816	1.907	2.000	2.097	2.197	2.300	2.744	3
4	1.082	1.170	1.262	1.360	1.464	1.574	1.689	1.811	1.939	2.074	2.215	2.364	2.520	2.684	2.856	3.036	3.842	4
5	1.104	1.217	1.338	1.469	1.611	1.762	1.925	2.100	2.288	2.488	2.703	2.932	3.176	3.436	3.713	4.007	5.378	5
6	1.126	1.265	1.419	1.587	1.772	1.974	2.195	2.436	2.700	2.986	3.297	3.635	4.002	4.398	4.827	5.290	7.530	6
7	1.149	1.316	1.504	1.714	1.949	2.211	2.502	2.826	3.185	3.583	4.023	4.508	5.042	5.629	6.275	6.983	10.541	7
8	1.172	1.369	1.594	1.851	2.144	2.476	2.853	3.278	3.759	4.300	4.908	5.590	6.353	7.206	8.157	9.217	14.758	8
9	1.195	1.423	1.689	1.999	2.358	2.773	3.252	3.803	4.435	5.160	5.987	6.931	8.005	9.223	10.604	12.166	20.661	9
10	1.219	1.480	1.791	2.159	2.594	3.106	3.707	4.411	5.234	6.192	7.305	8.594	10.086	11.806	13.786	16.060	28.925	10
11	1.243	1.539	1.898	2.332	2.853	3.479	4.226	5.117	6.176	7.430	8.912	10.657	12.708	15.112	17.922	21.199	40.496	11
12	1.268	1.601	2.012	2.518	3.138	3.896	4.818	5.936	7.288	8.916	10.872	13.215	16.012	19.343	23.298	27.983	56.694	12
13	1.294	1.665	2.133	2.720	3.452	4.363	5.492	6.886	8.599	10.699	13.264	16.386	20.175	24.759	30.288	36.937	79.371	13
14	1.319	1.732	2.261	2.937	3.797	4.887	6.261	7.988	10.147	12.839	16.182	20.319	25.421	31.691	39.374	48.757	111.120	14
15	1.346	1.801	2.397	3.172	4.177	5.474	7.138	9.266	11.974	15.407	19.742	25.196	32.030	40.565	51.186	64.359	155.568	15
16	1.373	1.873	2.540	3.426	4.595	6.130	8.137	10.748	14.129	18.488	24.086	31.243	40.358	51.923	66.542	84.954	217.795	16
17	1.400	1.948	2.693	3.700	5.054	6.866	9.276	12.468	16.672	22.186	29.384	38.741	50.851	66.461	86.504	112.139	304.913	17
18	1.428	2.026	2.854	3.996	5.560	7.690	10.575	14.463	19.673	26.623	35.849	48.039	64.072	85.071	112.455	148.024	426.879	18
19	1.457	2.107	3.026	4.316	6.116	8.613	12.056	16.777	23.214	31.948	43.736	59.568	80.731	108.890	146.192	195.391	597.630	19
20	1.486	2.191	3.207	4.661	6.727	9.646	13.743	19.461	27.393	38.338	53.358	73.864	101.721	139.380	190.050	257.916	836.683	20
21	1.516	2.279	3.400	5.034	7.400	10.804	15.668	22.574	32.324	46.005	65.096	91.592	128.169	178.406	247.065	340.449	1171.356	21
22	1.546	2.370	3.604	5.437	8.140	12.100	17.861	26.186	38.142	55.206	79.418	113.574	161.492	228.360	321.184	449.393	1639.898	22
23	1.577	2.465	3.820	5.871	8.954	13.552	20.362	30.376	45.008	66.247	96.889	140.831	203.480	292.300	417.539	593.199	2295.857	23
24	1.608	2.563	4.049	6.341	9.850	15.179	23.212	35.236	53.109	79.497	118.205	174.631	256.385	374.144	542.801	783.023	3214.200	24
25	1.641	2.666	4.292	6.848	10.835	17.000	26.462	40.874	62.669	95.396	144.210	216.542	323.045	478.905	705.641	1033.590	4499.880	25
26	1.673	2.772	4.549	7.396	11.918	19.040	30.167	47.414	73.949	114.475	175.936	268.512	407.037	612.998	917.333	1364.339	6299.831	26
27	1.707	2.883	4.822	7.988	13.110	21.325	34.390	55.000	87.260	137.371	214.642	332.955	512.867	784.638	1192.533	1800.927	8819.764	27
28	1.741	2.999	5.112	8.627	14.421	23.884	39.204	63.800	102.967	164.845	261.864	412.864	646.212	1004.336	1550.293	2377.224	12347.670	28
29	1.776	3.119	5.418	9.317	15.863	26.750	44.693	74.009	121.501	197.814	319.474	511.952	814.228	1285.550	2015.381	3137.935	17286.737	29
30	1.811	3.243	5.743	10.063	17.449	29.960	50.950	85.850	143.371	237.376	389.758	634.820	1025.927	1645.505	2619.996	4142.075	24201.432	30
35	2.000	3.946	7.686	14.785	28.102	52.800	98.100	180.314	327.997	590.668	1053.402	1861.054	3258.135	5653.911	9727.860	16599.217	130161.112	35
40	2.208	4.801	10.286	21.725	45.259	93.051	188.884	378.721	750.378	1469.772	2847.038	5455.913	10347.175	19426.689	36118.865	66520.767	700037.697	40

TABLE 2 (*Place a clip on this page for easy reference.*)
Present Value of $1.00.

$$P = \frac{S}{(1+r)^n}. \text{ In this table } S = \$1.00.$$

Periods	2%	4%	6%	8%	10%	12%	14%	16%	18%	20%	22%	24%	26%	28%	30%	32%	40%	Periods
1	0.980	0.962	0.943	0.926	0.909	0.893	0.877	0.862	0.847	0.833	0.820	0.806	0.794	0.781	0.769	0.758	0.714	1
2	0.961	0.925	0.890	0.857	0.826	0.797	0.769	0.743	0.718	0.694	0.672	0.650	0.630	0.610	0.592	0.574	0.510	2
3	0.942	0.889	0.840	0.794	0.751	0.712	0.675	0.641	0.609	0.579	0.551	0.524	0.500	0.477	0.455	0.435	0.364	3
4	0.924	0.855	0.792	0.735	0.683	0.636	0.592	0.552	0.516	0.482	0.451	0.423	0.397	0.373	0.350	0.329	0.260	4
5	0.906	0.822	0.747	0.681	0.621	0.567	0.519	0.476	0.437	0.402	0.370	0.341	0.315	0.291	0.269	0.250	0.186	5
6	0.888	0.790	0.705	0.630	0.564	0.507	0.456	0.410	0.370	0.335	0.303	0.275	0.250	0.227	0.207	0.189	0.133	6
7	0.871	0.760	0.665	0.583	0.513	0.452	0.400	0.354	0.314	0.279	0.249	0.222	0.198	0.178	0.159	0.143	0.095	7
8	0.853	0.731	0.627	0.540	0.467	0.404	0.351	0.305	0.266	0.233	0.204	0.179	0.157	0.139	0.123	0.108	0.068	8
9	0.837	0.703	0.592	0.500	0.424	0.361	0.308	0.263	0.225	0.194	0.167	0.144	0.125	0.108	0.094	0.082	0.048	9
10	0.820	0.676	0.558	0.463	0.386	0.322	0.270	0.227	0.191	0.162	0.137	0.116	0.099	0.085	0.073	0.062	0.035	10
11	0.804	0.650	0.527	0.429	0.350	0.287	0.237	0.195	0.162	0.135	0.112	0.094	0.079	0.066	0.056	0.047	0.025	11
12	0.788	0.625	0.497	0.397	0.319	0.257	0.208	0.168	0.137	0.112	0.092	0.076	0.062	0.052	0.043	0.036	0.018	12
13	0.773	0.601	0.469	0.368	0.290	0.229	0.182	0.145	0.116	0.093	0.075	0.061	0.050	0.040	0.033	0.027	0.013	13
14	0.758	0.577	0.442	0.340	0.263	0.205	0.160	0.125	0.099	0.078	0.062	0.049	0.039	0.032	0.025	0.021	0.009	14
15	0.743	0.555	0.417	0.315	0.239	0.183	0.140	0.108	0.084	0.065	0.051	0.040	0.031	0.025	0.020	0.016	0.006	15
16	0.728	0.534	0.394	0.292	0.218	0.163	0.123	0.093	0.071	0.054	0.042	0.032	0.025	0.019	0.015	0.012	0.005	16
17	0.714	0.513	0.371	0.270	0.198	0.146	0.108	0.080	0.060	0.045	0.034	0.026	0.020	0.015	0.012	0.009	0.003	17
18	0.700	0.494	0.350	0.250	0.180	0.130	0.095	0.069	0.051	0.038	0.028	0.021	0.016	0.012	0.009	0.007	0.002	18
19	0.686	0.475	0.331	0.232	0.164	0.116	0.083	0.060	0.043	0.031	0.023	0.017	0.012	0.009	0.007	0.005	0.002	19
20	0.673	0.456	0.312	0.215	0.149	0.104	0.073	0.051	0.037	0.026	0.019	0.014	0.010	0.007	0.005	0.004	0.001	20
21	0.660	0.439	0.294	0.199	0.135	0.093	0.064	0.044	0.031	0.022	0.015	0.011	0.008	0.006	0.004	0.003	0.001	21
22	0.647	0.422	0.278	0.184	0.123	0.083	0.056	0.038	0.026	0.018	0.013	0.009	0.006	0.004	0.003	0.002	0.001	22
23	0.634	0.406	0.262	0.170	0.112	0.074	0.049	0.033	0.022	0.015	0.010	0.007	0.005	0.003	0.002	0.002	0.000	23
24	0.622	0.390	0.247	0.158	0.102	0.066	0.043	0.028	0.019	0.013	0.008	0.006	0.004	0.003	0.002	0.001	0.000	24
25	0.610	0.375	0.233	0.146	0.092	0.059	0.038	0.024	0.016	0.010	0.007	0.005	0.003	0.002	0.001	0.001	0.000	25
26	0.598	0.361	0.220	0.135	0.084	0.053	0.033	0.021	0.014	0.009	0.006	0.004	0.002	0.002	0.001	0.001	0.000	26
27	0.586	0.347	0.207	0.125	0.076	0.047	0.029	0.018	0.011	0.007	0.005	0.003	0.002	0.001	0.001	0.001	0.000	27
28	0.574	0.333	0.196	0.116	0.069	0.042	0.026	0.016	0.010	0.006	0.004	0.002	0.002	0.001	0.001	0.000	0.000	28
29	0.563	0.321	0.185	0.107	0.063	0.037	0.022	0.014	0.008	0.005	0.003	0.002	0.001	0.001	0.000	0.000	0.000	29
30	0.552	0.308	0.174	0.099	0.057	0.033	0.020	0.012	0.007	0.004	0.003	0.002	0.001	0.001	0.000	0.000	0.000	30
35	0.500	0.253	0.130	0.068	0.036	0.019	0.010	0.006	0.003	0.002	0.001	0.001	0.000	0.000	0.000	0.000	0.000	35
40	0.453	0.208	0.097	0.046	0.022	0.011	0.005	0.003	0.001	0.001	0.000	0.000	0.000	0.000	0.000	0.000	0.000	40

TABLE 3
Compound Amount of Annuity of $1.00 in Arrears* (Future Value of Annuity)

$$S_n = \frac{(1+r)^n - 1}{r}$$

Periods	2%	4%	6%	8%	10%	12%	14%	16%	18%	20%	22%	24%	26%	28%	30%	32%	40%	Periods
1	1.000	1.000	1.000	1.000	1.000	1.000	1.000	1.000	1.000	1.000	1.000	1.000	1.000	1.000	1.000	1.000	1.000	1
2	2.020	2.040	2.060	2.080	2.100	2.120	2.140	2.160	2.180	2.200	2.220	2.240	2.260	2.280	2.300	2.320	2.400	2
3	3.060	3.122	3.184	3.246	3.310	3.374	3.440	3.506	3.572	3.640	3.708	3.778	3.848	3.918	3.990	4.062	4.360	3
4	4.122	4.246	4.375	4.506	4.641	4.779	4.921	5.066	5.215	5.368	5.524	5.684	5.848	6.016	6.187	6.362	7.104	4
5	5.204	5.416	5.637	5.867	6.105	6.353	6.610	6.877	7.154	7.442	7.740	8.048	8.368	8.700	9.043	9.398	10.946	5
6	6.308	6.633	6.975	7.336	7.716	8.115	8.536	8.977	9.442	9.930	10.442	10.980	11.544	12.136	12.756	13.406	16.324	6
7	7.434	7.898	8.394	8.923	9.487	10.089	10.730	11.414	12.142	12.916	13.740	14.615	15.546	16.534	17.583	18.696	23.853	7
8	8.583	9.214	9.897	10.637	11.436	12.300	13.233	14.240	15.327	16.499	17.762	19.123	20.588	22.163	23.858	25.678	34.395	8
9	9.755	10.583	11.491	12.488	13.579	14.776	16.085	17.519	19.086	20.799	22.670	24.712	26.940	29.369	32.015	34.895	49.153	9
10	10.950	12.006	13.181	14.487	15.937	17.549	19.337	21.321	23.521	25.959	28.657	31.643	34.945	38.593	42.619	47.062	69.814	10
11	12.169	13.486	14.972	16.645	18.531	20.655	23.045	25.733	28.755	32.150	35.962	40.238	45.031	50.398	56.405	63.122	98.739	11
12	13.412	15.026	16.870	18.977	21.384	24.133	27.271	30.850	34.931	39.581	44.874	50.895	57.739	65.510	74.327	84.320	139.235	12
13	14.680	16.627	18.882	21.495	24.523	28.029	32.089	36.786	42.219	48.497	55.746	64.110	73.751	84.853	97.625	112.303	195.929	13
14	15.974	18.292	21.015	24.215	27.975	32.393	37.581	43.672	50.818	59.196	69.010	80.496	93.926	109.612	127.913	149.240	275.300	14
15	17.293	20.024	23.276	27.152	31.772	37.280	43.842	51.660	60.965	72.035	85.192	100.815	119.347	141.303	167.286	197.997	386.420	15
16	18.639	21.825	25.673	30.324	35.950	42.753	50.980	60.925	72.939	87.442	104.935	126.011	151.377	181.868	218.472	262.356	541.988	16
17	20.012	23.698	28.213	33.750	40.545	48.884	59.118	71.673	87.068	105.931	129.020	157.253	191.735	233.791	285.014	347.309	759.784	17
18	21.412	25.645	30.906	37.450	45.599	55.750	68.394	84.141	103.740	128.117	158.405	195.994	242.585	300.252	371.518	459.449	1064.697	18
19	22.841	27.671	33.760	41.446	51.159	63.440	78.969	98.603	123.414	154.740	194.254	244.033	306.658	385.323	483.973	607.472	1491.576	19
20	24.297	29.778	36.786	45.762	57.275	72.052	91.025	115.380	146.628	186.688	237.989	303.601	387.389	494.213	630.165	802.863	2089.206	20
21	25.783	31.969	39.993	50.423	64.002	81.699	104.768	134.841	174.021	225.026	291.347	377.465	489.110	633.593	820.215	1060.779	2925.889	21
22	27.299	34.248	43.392	55.457	71.403	92.503	120.436	157.415	206.345	271.031	356.443	469.056	617.278	811.999	1067.280	1401.229	4097.245	22
23	28.845	36.618	46.996	60.893	79.543	104.603	138.297	183.601	244.487	326.237	435.861	582.630	778.771	1040.358	1388.464	1850.622	5737.142	23
24	30.422	39.083	50.816	66.765	88.497	118.155	158.659	213.978	289.494	392.484	532.750	723.461	982.251	1332.659	1806.003	2443.821	8032.999	24
25	32.030	41.646	54.865	73.106	98.347	133.334	181.871	249.214	342.603	471.981	650.955	898.092	1238.636	1706.803	2348.803	3226.844	11247.199	25
26	33.671	44.312	59.156	79.954	109.182	150.334	208.333	290.088	405.272	567.377	795.165	1114.634	1561.682	2185.708	3054.444	4260.434	15747.079	26
27	35.344	47.084	63.706	87.351	121.100	169.374	238.499	337.502	479.221	681.853	971.102	1383.146	1968.719	2798.706	3971.778	5624.772	22046.910	27
28	37.051	49.968	68.528	95.339	134.210	190.699	272.889	392.503	566.481	819.223	1185.744	1716.101	2481.586	3583.344	5164.311	7425.699	30866.674	28
29	38.792	52.966	73.640	103.966	148.631	214.583	312.094	456.303	669.447	984.068	1447.608	2128.965	3127.798	4587.680	6714.604	9802.923	43214.343	29
30	40.568	56.085	79.058	113.263	164.494	241.333	356.787	530.312	790.948	1181.882	1767.081	2640.916	3942.026	5873.231	8729.985	12940.859	60501.081	30
35	49.994	73.652	111.435	172.317	271.024	431.663	693.573	1120.713	1816.652	2948.341	4783.645	7750.225	12527.442	20188.966	32422.868	51869.427	325400.279	35
40	60.402	95.026	154.762	259.057	442.593	767.091	1342.025	2360.757	4163.213	7343.858	12936.535	22728.803	39792.982	69377.460	120392.883	207874.272	1750091.741	40

*Payments (or receipts) at the end of each period.

TABLE 4 (*Place a clip on this page for easy reference.*)
Present Value of Annuity $1.00 in Arrears*.

$$P_n = \frac{1}{r}\left[1 - \frac{1}{(1+r)^n}\right]$$

Periods	2%	4%	6%	8%	10%	12%	14%	16%	18%	20%	22%	24%	26%	28%	30%	32%	40%	Periods
1	0.980	0.962	0.943	0.926	0.909	0.893	0.877	0.862	0.847	0.833	0.820	0.806	0.794	0.781	0.769	0.758	0.714	1
2	1.942	1.886	1.833	1.783	1.736	1.690	1.647	1.605	1.566	1.528	1.492	1.457	1.424	1.392	1.361	1.331	1.224	2
3	2.884	2.775	2.673	2.577	2.487	2.402	2.322	2.246	2.174	2.106	2.042	1.981	1.923	1.868	1.816	1.766	1.589	3
4	3.808	3.630	3.465	3.312	3.170	3.037	2.914	2.798	2.690	2.589	2.494	2.404	2.320	2.241	2.166	2.096	1.849	4
5	4.713	4.452	4.212	3.993	3.791	3.605	3.433	3.274	3.127	2.991	2.864	2.745	2.635	2.532	2.436	2.345	2.035	5
6	5.601	5.242	4.917	4.623	4.355	4.111	3.889	3.685	3.498	3.326	3.167	3.020	2.885	2.759	2.643	2.534	2.168	6
7	6.472	6.002	5.582	5.206	4.868	4.564	4.288	4.039	3.812	3.605	3.416	3.242	3.083	2.937	2.802	2.677	2.263	7
8	7.325	6.733	6.210	5.747	5.335	4.968	4.639	4.344	4.078	3.837	3.619	3.421	3.241	3.076	2.925	2.786	2.331	8
9	8.162	7.435	6.802	6.247	5.759	5.328	4.946	4.607	4.303	4.031	3.786	3.566	3.366	3.184	3.019	2.868	2.379	9
10	8.983	8.111	7.360	6.710	6.145	5.650	5.216	4.833	4.494	4.192	3.923	3.682	3.465	3.269	3.092	2.930	2.414	10
11	9.787	8.760	7.887	7.139	6.495	5.938	5.453	5.029	4.656	4.327	4.035	3.776	3.543	3.335	3.147	2.978	2.438	11
12	10.575	9.385	8.384	7.536	6.814	6.194	5.660	5.197	4.793	4.439	4.127	3.851	3.606	3.387	3.190	3.013	2.456	12
13	11.348	9.986	8.853	7.904	7.103	6.424	5.842	5.342	4.910	4.533	4.203	3.912	3.656	3.427	3.223	3.040	2.469	13
14	12.106	10.563	9.295	8.244	7.367	6.628	6.002	5.468	5.008	4.611	4.265	3.962	3.695	3.459	3.249	3.061	2.478	14
15	12.849	11.118	9.712	8.559	7.606	6.811	6.142	5.575	5.092	4.675	4.315	4.001	3.726	3.483	3.268	3.076	2.484	15
16	13.578	11.652	10.106	8.851	7.824	6.974	6.265	5.668	5.162	4.730	4.357	4.033	3.751	3.503	3.283	3.088	2.489	16
17	14.292	12.166	10.477	9.122	8.022	7.120	6.373	5.749	5.222	4.775	4.391	4.059	3.771	3.518	3.295	3.097	2.492	17
18	14.992	12.659	10.828	9.372	8.201	7.250	6.467	5.818	5.273	4.812	4.419	4.080	3.786	3.529	3.304	3.104	2.494	18
19	15.678	13.134	11.158	9.604	8.365	7.366	6.550	5.877	5.316	4.843	4.442	4.097	3.799	3.539	3.311	3.109	2.496	19
20	16.351	13.590	11.470	9.818	8.514	7.469	6.623	5.929	5.353	4.870	4.460	4.110	3.808	3.546	3.316	3.113	2.497	20
21	17.011	14.029	11.764	10.017	8.649	7.562	6.687	5.973	5.384	4.891	4.476	4.121	3.816	3.551	3.320	3.116	2.498	21
22	17.658	14.451	12.042	10.201	8.772	7.645	6.743	6.011	5.410	4.909	4.488	4.130	3.822	3.556	3.323	3.118	2.498	22
23	18.292	14.857	12.303	10.371	8.883	7.718	6.792	6.044	5.432	4.925	4.499	4.137	3.827	3.559	3.325	3.120	2.499	23
24	18.914	15.247	12.550	10.529	8.985	7.784	6.835	6.073	5.451	4.937	4.507	4.143	3.831	3.562	3.327	3.121	2.499	24
25	19.523	15.622	12.783	10.675	9.077	7.843	6.873	6.097	5.467	4.948	4.514	4.147	3.834	3.564	3.329	3.122	2.499	25
26	20.121	15.983	13.003	10.810	9.161	7.896	6.906	6.118	5.480	4.956	4.520	4.151	3.837	3.566	3.330	3.123	2.500	26
27	20.707	16.330	13.211	10.935	9.237	7.943	6.935	6.136	5.492	4.964	4.524	4.154	3.839	3.567	3.331	3.123	2.500	27
28	21.281	16.663	13.406	11.051	9.307	7.984	6.961	6.152	5.502	4.970	4.528	4.157	3.840	3.568	3.331	3.124	2.500	28
29	21.844	16.984	13.591	11.158	9.370	8.022	6.983	6.166	5.510	4.975	4.531	4.159	3.841	3.569	3.332	3.124	2.500	29
30	22.396	17.292	13.765	11.258	9.427	8.055	7.003	6.177	5.517	4.979	4.534	4.160	3.842	3.569	3.332	3.124	2.500	30
35	24.999	18.665	14.498	11.655	9.644	8.176	7.070	6.215	5.539	4.992	4.541	4.164	3.845	3.571	3.333	3.125	2.500	35
40	27.355	19.793	15.046	11.925	9.779	8.244	7.105	6.233	5.548	4.997	4.544	4.166	3.846	3.571	3.333	3.125	2.500	40

*Payments (or receipts) at the end of each period.

COST ACCOUNTING IN PROFESSIONAL EXAMINATIONS

This appendix describes the role of cost accounting in professional examinations. We use professional examinations in the United States, Canada, Australia, Japan, and the United Kingdom to illustrate the role.[1] A conscientious reader who has solved a representative sample of the problems at the end of the chapters will be well prepared for the professional examination questions dealing with cost accounting. This appendix aims to provide perspective, install confidence, and encourage readers to take the examinations.

AMERICAN PROFESSIONAL EXAMINATIONS

CPA and CMA Designations

Many American readers may eventually take the Certified Public Accountant (CPA) examination or the Certified Management Accountant (CMA) examination. Certification is important to professional accountants for many reasons, such as:

1. Recognition of achievement and technical competence by fellow accountants and by users of accounting services

2. Increased self-confidence in one's professional abilities

3. Membership in professional organizations offering programs of career-long education

4. Enhancement of career opportunities

5. Personal satisfaction

The CPA certificate is issued by individual states; it is necessary for obtaining a state's license to practice as a Certified Public Accountant. A prominent feature of public accounting is the use of independent (external) auditors to give assurance about the reliability of the financial statements supplied by managers. These auditors are called Certified Public Accountants in the United States and Chartered Accountants in many other English-speaking nations. The major U.S. professional association in the private sector that regulates the quality of external auditing is the American Institute of Certified Public Accountants (AICPA).

---

[1] We appreciate help from Tom Craven (United States), Bill Langdon (Canada), John Goodwin (Australia), Michi Sakurai (Japan), and Louise Drysdale and Andrea Jeffries (U.K.).

The CMA designation is offered by the Institute of Management Accountants (IMA). The IMA is the largest association of management accountants in the world.[2] The major objective of the CMA certification is to enhance the development of the management accounting profession. In particular, focus is placed on the modern role of the management accountant as an active contributor to and a participant in management. The CMA designation is gaining increased stature in the business community as a credential parallel to the CPA designation.

The CMA examination consists of 4 parts taken during 2 days (16 hours):

◆ Part 1: Economics, finance, and management
◆ Part 2: Financial accounting and reporting
◆ Part 3: Management reporting, analysis, and behavioral issues
◆ Part 4: Decision analysis and information systems

Questions regarding ethical issues will appear on any part of the examination. A person who has successfully completed the U.S. CPA examination is exempt from Part 2.

Cost/management accounting questions are prominent in the CMA examination. The CPA examination also includes such questions, although they are less extensive than questions regarding financial accounting, auditing, and business law. On the average, cost/managerial accounting represents 35% to 40% of the CMA examination and 5% of the CPA examination. This book includes many questions and problems used in past CMA and CPA examinations. In addition, a supplement to this book, *Student Guide and Review Manual* [John K. Harris and Dudley W. Curry (Englewood Cliffs, NJ: Prentice Hall, 1997)], contains over one hundred CMA and CPA questions and explanatory answers. Careful study of appropriate topics in this book will give candidates sufficient background for succeeding in the cost accounting portions of the professional examinations.

The IMA publishes *Management Accounting* monthly. Each issue includes advertisements for courses that help students prepare for the CMA examination.[3]

CANADIAN PROFESSIONAL EXAMINATIONS

Three professional accounting designations are available in Canada:

Designation	Sponsoring Organization
Certified Management Accountant (CMA)	Society of Management Accountants (SMA)
Certified General Accountant (CGA)	Certified General Accountants' Association (CGA)
Chartered Accountant (CA)	Canadian Institute of Chartered Accountants

The SMA represents over 27,000 certified management accountants employed throughout Canadian business, industry, and government.

The CMA Entrance Examination is a two-day examination, divided into three broad categories:

1. Management accounting area   50%–60%
2. Financial accounting area   20%–30%
3. Management studies   15%–25%

Objective questions comprise 40% to 50% and cases 50% to 60% of the exam. Topics covered on recent examinations in the management accounting area include rele-

---

[2]The IMA has a wide range of activities driven by many committees. For example, the Management Accounting Practices Committee issues statements on both financial accounting and management accounting. The IMA also has an extensive continuing-education program.

[3]Other U.S. professional associations also require detailed knowledge of cost accounting. For example, the Certified Cost Estimator/Analyst (CCEA) program is administered by the Society of Cost Estimating and Analysis, 101 South Whiting Street, Suite 313, Alexandria, VA 22304. The society's primary purpose is to improve the effectiveness of cost estimation and price analysis. Special attention is given to contract cost estimation.

vant costing, transfer pricing, capital budgeting, performance measures, activity-based costing, cost allocation, and productivity.

The Society of Management Accountants publishes CMA: *The Management Accounting Magazine* monthly. This magazine includes details of courses that assist students in preparing for the CMA examination.

AUSTRALIAN PROFESSIONAL EXAMINATIONS

The Australian Society of Certified Practising Accountants is the largest body representing accountants in Australia. Their professional designation is termed a CPA (Certified Practising Accountant). The basic entry requirements for Associate membership of the Society are having an approved Bachelors degree. Associates of the Society can advance to CPA status by passing the CPA program and having the required amount of relevant work experience. There are two compulsory core segments in the program. Core I covers the practical application of the more common accounting standards and ethics, while more technical standards (such as foreign currency translation) are covered in the Core II segment. Candidates are then required to take three segments from seven elective subjects. These subjects are: (1) external reporting, (2) insolvency and reconstruction, (3) management accounting, (4) management of information systems, (5) auditing, (6) treasury, and (7) taxation. Personal Financial Planning and Superannuation is a new elective subject which will soon be added to the electives.

The management accounting segment topics include:

1. Management accounting in the contemporary business environment
2. Accounting for strategic management
3. Long-term project planning and management
4. Costing for decision making
5. Performance measurement and reward systems.

The Australian Accountant, published each month (except January), includes advertisements for courses that help students prepare for the CPA examination.

The Institute of Chartered Accountants in Australia (ICAA) has membership requirements that include passing four core modules (Taxation, Accounting I, Accounting II, and Ethics) and one elective module (one of which is Advanced Management Accounting). Management related topics are in both the Accounting 2 and Advanced Management Accounting modules. These include:

◆ purpose and perspective (including strategic and operational management; organizations, goals, ethics; operational environments; cost concepts);

◆ strategic management accounting (including strategic applications, project evaluation and capital budgeting);

◆ operational management accounting (including decision analysis, financial planning and management, product and service costing, control and performance evaluation).

JAPANESE PROFESSIONAL EXAMINATIONS

There are two major management accounting organizations—Japanese Industrial Management and Accounting Association and Enterprise Management Association. The JIMAA is the oldest, largest, and most authoritative accounting organization of its kind in Japan. It directs a School of Cost Control and a School of Corporate Tax Accounting. There are two courses in the School of Cost Control—Preparatory Course and Cost Control Course. These courses are taught by university professors and executives from member corporations. The Enterprise Management Association is the Japanese chapter of the U.S.-based Institute of Management Accountants.

UNITED KINGDOM PROFESSIONAL EXAMINATIONS

The Chartered Institute of Management Accountants (CIMA) is the largest professional management accounting body in the United Kingdom. CIMA provides a wide range of services to members in commerce, education, government, and the accounting profession.

The syllabus for the CIMA examination consists of four stages:

1. Preparation for business and accounting (including "foundation costing")
2. The tools of management accounting (including "operational cost accounting")
3. The rules of a profession (including "management accounting applications")
4. The application of knowledge to business management and finance (including "strategic management accounting" and "management accounting control systems")

Management Accounting, published monthly by CIMA, includes details of courses assisting students in preparing for their examinations.

Management accounting topics are also covered by several other professional bodies. The syllabus for the examinations of the Chartered Association of Certified Accountants (ACCA) has three stages: I (Foundation), II (Certificate), and III (Professional). Skills examined in III include information for control and decision making, management and strategy, and financial strategy. Other accounting bodies include the Institute of Chartered Accountants in England and Wales (ICAEW) and the Institute for Chartered Accountants of Scotland (ICAS). Both institutes have requirements that cover proficiency in "general management" topics as well as professional accounting topics.

GLOSSARY

Abnormal spoilage. Spoilage that is not expected to arise under efficient operating conditions; it is not an inherent part of the chosen production process. (653)

Absorption costing. Inventory costing method in which all variable manufacturing costs and all fixed manufacturing costs are included as inventoriable costs. (298)

Accelerated depreciation. Depreciation method in which the pattern of depreciation writes off more of the depreciable assets in the early years after investment than straight-line depreciation. (823)

Account analysis method. Approach to cost estimation that classifies cost accounts in the ledger as variable, fixed, or mixed with respect to the cost driver. Typically, qualitative rather than quantitative analysis is used in making these classification decisions. (341)

Accounting rate of return. See *accrual accounting rate of return (AARR).* (793)

Accrual accounting rate of return (AARR). Accounting measure of income divided by an accounting measure of investment. Also called *accounting rate of return* or *return on investment (ROI).* (793)

Activity. An event, task, or unit of work with a specified purpose. (107)

Activity-based budgeting. Approach to budgeting that focuses on the costs of activities necessary to produce and sell products and services. (189)

Activity-based costing (ABC). Approach to costing that focuses on activities as the fundamental cost objects. It uses the cost of these activities as the basis for assigning costs to other cost objects such as products, services, or customers. (107)

Actual costing. A costing method that traces direct costs to a cost object by using the actual direct cost rate(s) times the actual quantity of the direct cost input(s) and allocates indirect costs based on the actual indirect cost rate(s) times the actual quantity of the cost allocation base. (96)

Actual costs. Costs incurred (historical costs), as distinguished from budgeted or forecasted costs. (26)

Allowable cost. Cost that the parties to a contract agree to include in the costs to be reimbursed. (517)

Appraisal costs. Costs incurred in detecting which of the individual units of products do not conform to specifications. (683)

Artificial costs. See *complete reciprocated cost.* (487)

Attention directing. Management accountant's function that involves making visible both opportunities and problems on which managers need to focus. (9)

Autonomy. The degree of freedom to make decisions. (905)

Average cost. See *unit cost.* (32)

Average waiting time. The average amount of time that an order will wait in line before it is set up and processed. (695)

Backflush costing. Costing system that delays recording changes in the status of a product being produced until good finished units appear; it then uses budgeted or standard costs to work backward to flush out manufacturing costs for the units produced. Also called *delayed costing, endpoint costing,* or *post-deduct costing.* (726)

Batch-level costs. The costs of resources sacrificed on activities that are related to a group of units of products or services rather than to each individual unit of product or service. (151)

Benchmark. Point of reference from which comparisons may be made. (218)

Benchmarking. The continuous process of measuring products, services, or activities against the best levels of performance. (235)

Black hole demand spiral. See *downward demand spiral.* (520)

Book value. The original cost minus accumulated depreciation of an asset. (400)

Bottleneck. An operation where the work required approaches or exceeds the available capacity. (694)

Breakeven point. Quantity of output where total revenues and total costs are equal; that is where the operating income is zero. (62)

Breakeven time (BET). The amount of time from when the initial concept for a new product is approved by management until the time when the cumulative present value of net cash inflows from the project equals the cumulative present value of net investment outflows. (795)

Budget. The quantitative expression of a plan of action and an aid to the coordination and implementation of the plan. (4)

Budgetary slack. See *padding.* (183)

Budgeted costing. See *extended normal costing.* (101)

Bundled product. A package of two or more products or services, sold for a single price, where the individual components of the bundle may be sold as separate items, each with their stand-alone prices. (578)

Business function costs. The sum of all the costs in a particular business function. (389)

Byproduct. Product from a joint process that has a low sales value compared with the sales value of the main or joint product(s). (544)

Capital budgeting. The process of making long-term planning decisions for investments. (780)

Capitalized costs. Costs that are first recorded as an asset (capitalized) when they are incurred. (35)

Capitalized inventoriable costs. Specific type of capitalized costs. Those capitalized costs associated with the purchase of goods for resale (in the costs of merchandise inventory) or costs associated with the acquisition and conversion of materials and all other manufacturing inputs into goods for sale (in the case of manufacturing inventories). Also called inventoriable costs. (36)

Capitalized noninventoriable costs. Specific type of capitalized costs. Those capitalized costs associated with any aspect of business other than inventory. (36)

Carrying costs. Costs that arise when a business holds inventories of goods for sale. (748)

Cash budget. Schedule of expected cash receipts and disbursements. (197)

Cash cycle. See self-liquidating cycle. (198)

Cause-and-effect diagram. Diagram that identifies the potential causes of failures or defects. Four major categories of potential causes of failure are identified human factors, methods and design factors, machine-related factors, and materials and components factors. Also called a fishbone diagram. (687)

Certified Management Accountant (CMA). The professional designation for management accountants in the United States. (9)

Chief financial officer (CFO). The senior officer empowered with overseeing of the financial operations of an organization. Also called finance director. (7)

Choice criterion. Objective that can be quantified in a decision model. (75)

Coefficient of determination (r^2). Measures the percentage of variation in a dependent variable explained by one or more independent variables. (359)

Collusive pricing. Companies in an industry conspire in their pricing and output decisions to achieve a price above the competitive price. (450)

Combined variance analysis. Approach to overhead variance analysis that combines variable-cost and fixed-cost variances. (264)

Common cost. The cost of operating a facility, operation, activity area, or like cost object that is shared by two or more users. (489)

Complete reciprocated cost. The actual cost incurred by the service department plus a part of the costs of the other support departments that provide services to it; it is always larger than the actual cost. Also called artificial cost of the service department. (487)

Composite product unit. A hypothetical unit of product with weights related to the individual products of the company. (584)

Conference method. Approach to cost estimation that develops cost estimates on the basis of analysis and opin-

ions gathered from various departments of an organization (purchasing, process engineering, manufacturing, employee relations, and so on). (341)

Constant. The component of total costs that, within the relevant range, does not vary with changes in the level of the cost driver. Also called intercept. (337)

Constant gross-margin percentage NRV method. Joint cost allocation method that allocates joint costs in such a way that the overall gross-margin percentage is identical for all the individual products. (551)

Constraint. A mathematical inequality or equality that must be satisfied by the variables in a mathematical model. (407)

Continuous improvement budgeted cost. Budgeted cost that is successively reduced over succeeding time periods. (229)

Contribution income statement. Income statement that groups line items by cost behavior pattern to highlight the contribution margin. (63)

Contribution margin. Revenues minus all costs of the output (a product or service) that vary with respect to the number of output units. (71)

Contribution margin percentage. Total contribution margin divided by revenues. (72)

Control. Covers both the action that implements the planning decision and the performance evaluation of the personnel and operations. (4)

Control chart. Graph of a series of successive observations of a particular step, procedure, or operation taken at regular intervals of time. Each observation is plotted relative to specified ranges that represent the expected distribution. (686)

Controllability. The degree of influence that a specific manager has over costs, revenues, or other items in question. (192)

Controllable cost. Any cost that is primarily subject to the influence of a given manager of a given responsibility center for a given time span. (192)

Controller. The financial executive primarily responsible for both management accounting and financial accounting. (7)

Conversion costs. All manufacturing costs other than direct materials costs. (41)

Cost. Resource sacrificed or forgone to achieve a specific objective. (26)

Cost accounting. Measures and reports financial and other information related to the organization's acquisition or consumption of resources. It provides information for both management accounting and financial accounting. (2)

Cost Accounting Standards Board (CASB). Has the exclusive authority to make, promulgate, amend, and rescind cost accounting standards used to guide contracts with U.S. government. (517)

Cost accumulation. The collection of cost data in some organized way through an accounting system. (26)

Cost allocation. The assigning of indirect costs to the chosen cost object. (27)

Cost-allocation base. A factor that is the common denominator for systematically linking an indirect cost or group of indirect costs to a cost object. (94)

Cost assignment. General term that encompasses both (1) tracing accumulated costs to a cost object and (2) allocating accumulated costs to a cost object. (26)

Cost-benefit approach. Primary criterion for choosing among alternative accounting systems, which is how each system achieves organizational goals in relation to the cost of those systems. (6)

Cost center. A responsibility center in which a manager is accountable for costs only. (191)

Cost driver. Any factor that affects total costs. That is, a change in the cost driver will cause a change in the level of the total cost of a related cost object. (28)

Cost estimation. The measurement of past cost relationships. (338)

Cost hierarchy. Categorization of costs into different cost pools on the basis of different classes of cost drivers, or different degrees of difficulty in determining cause-and-effect (or benefits received) relationships. (150)

Cost incurrence. Occurs when a resource is sacrificed or used up. (438)

Cost management. Actions by managers undertaken to satisfy customers while continuously reducing and controlling costs. (3)

Cost object. Anything for which a separate measurement of costs is desired. (26)

Cost-plus contract. Contract in which reimbursement is based on actual allowable cost plus a fixed fee. (517)

Cost pool. A grouping of individual cost items. (94)

Cost predictions. Forecast of future costs. (338)

Costs of quality (COQ). Costs incurred to prevent or rectify the production of a low-quality product. (683)

Cost tracing. The assigning of direct costs to the chosen cost object. (27)

Cost-volume-profit (CVP). Examines the behavior of total revenues, total costs, and operating income as changes occur in the output level, selling price, variable costs, or fixed costs; a single revenue driver and a single cost driver are used in this analysis. (60)

Cumulative average-time learning model. Learning curve model in which the cumulative average time per unit declines by a constant percentage each time the cumulative quantity of units produced is doubled. (351)

Current cost. Asset measure based on the cost of purchasing an asset today identical to the one currently held. It is the cost of purchasing the services provided by that asset if an identical asset cannot currently be purchased. (941)

Customer-cost hierarchy. Categorization of costs related to customers into different cost pools on the basis of different classes of cost drivers or different degrees of difficulty in determining cause-and-effect (or benefits received) relationships. (595)

Customer life-cycle costs. Focuses on the total costs to a customer of acquiring and using a product or service until it is replaced. (449)

Customer-profitability analysis. Examines how individual customers, or groupings of customers, differ in their profitability. (590)

Customer-response time. Amount of time from when a customer places an order for a product or requests a ser-

vice to when the product or service is delivered to the customer. (693)

Customer revenues. Inflows of assets from customers received in exchange for products or services being provided to those customers. (590)

Customer service. The support activities provided to customers. (3)

Decentralization. The freedom for managers at lower levels (subunits) of the organization to make decisions. (902)

Decision model. Formal model for making a choice under uncertainty, frequently involving quantitative analysis. (75)

Decision table. Summary of the contemplated actions, events, outcomes, and probabilities of events in a decision. (78)

Delayed costing. See *backflush costing*. (726)

Denominator level. Quantity of the allocation base used to allocate fixed overhead costs to a cost object. Also called a *production denominator level* or a *production denominator volume*. (261)

Denominator-level variance. See *production-volume variance*. (263)

Dependent variable. The cost variable to be predicted in a cost estimation or prediction model. (342)

Design of products, services, or processes. The detailed planning and engineering of products, services, or processes. (3)

Designed-in costs. See *locked-in costs*. (438)

Differential approach. Approach to decision making and capital budgeting that analyzes only those future cash outflows and inflows that differ among alternatives. (826)

Differential cost. Difference in total cost between two alternatives. Also called *net relevant cost*. (386)

Direct allocation method. Method of support cost allocation that ignores any service rendered by one support department to another; it allocates each support department's total costs directly to the operating departments. Also called *direct method*. (484)

Direct costing. See *variable costing*. (300)

Direct costs of a cost object. Costs that are related to the particular cost object and that can be traced to it in an economically feasible way. (27)

Direct manufacturing labor costs. Compensation of all manufacturing labor that is considered to be specifically identified with the cost object (say, units finished or in process) and that can be traced to the cost object in an economically feasible way. (40)

Direct materials costs. The acquisition costs of all materials that eventually become part of the cost object (say, units finished or in process) and that can be traced to that cost object in an economically feasible way. (40)

Direct materials inventory. Direct materials in stock and awaiting use in the manufacturing process. (38)

Direct method. See *direct allocation method*. (484)

Discounted cash flow (DCF). Capital budgeting method that measures the cash inflows and outflows of a project as if they occurred at a single point in time so that they can be compared in an appropriate way. (783)

Discount rate. See *required rate of return*. (783)

Discretionary costs. Arise from periodic (usually yearly) decisions regarding the maximum outlay to be incurred. They are not tied to a clear cause-and-effect relationship between inputs and outputs. (279)

Distribution. The mechanism by which products or services are delivered to the customer. (3)

Double-counting. Occurs when a cost item is included in a contract reimbursement report both as a direct cost item and as part of an indirect cost pool allocated to the contract using a budgeted rate. (517)

Double-declining balance (DDB) depreciation. Accelerated depreciation method in which the first-year depreciation is twice the amount of straight-line depreciation when a zero terminal disposal price is assumed. (823)

Downward demand spiral. Continuing reduction in demand that occurs when prices are raised and then raised again in an attempt to recover fixed costs from an ever-decreasing customer base. Also called *black hole demand spiral*. (520)

Dual pricing. Approach to transfer pricing using two separate transfer-pricing methods to price each interdivision transaction. (911)

Dual-rate cost-allocation method. Allocation method that first classifies costs in one cost pool into two sub-pools (typically into a variable-cost sub-pool and a fixed-cost sub-pool). Each sub-pool has a different allocation rate or a different allocation base. (480)

Dumping. Under U.S. laws, occurs when a non-U.S. company sells a product in the United States at a price below the market value in the country of its creation, and this action materially injures or threatens to materially injure an industry in the United States. (450)

Economic order quantity (EOQ). Decision model that calculates the optimal quantity of inventory to order. Simplest model incorporates only ordering costs and carrying costs. (749)

Economic value added (EVA®). After-tax operating income minus the (after-tax) weighted average cost of capital multiplied by total assets minus current liabilities. (937)

Effectiveness. The degree to which a predetermined objective or target is met. (228)

Efficiency. The relative amount of inputs used to achieve a given level of output. (228)

Efficiency variance. The difference between the actual quantity of input used (such as yards of materials) and the budgeted quantity of input that should have been used, multiplied by the budgeted price. Also called *input-efficiency variance* or *usage variance*. (223)

Effort. Exertion toward a goal. (901)

Endpoint costing. See *backflush costing*. (726)

Engineered costs. Costs that result specifically from a clear cause-and-effect relationship between costs and outputs. (278)

Equivalent units. Measure of the output in terms of the physical quantities of each of the inputs (factors of production) that have been consumed when producing the units. It is the physical quantities of inputs necessary to produce output of one fully complete unit. (615)

Estimated net realizable value (NRV) method. Joint cost allocation method that allocates joint costs on the basis of the relative estimated net realizable value (expected final sales value in the ordinary course of business minus the expected separable costs of production and marketing of the total production of the period). (550)

Events. A possible occurrence in a decision model. (75)

Excess capacity. See *unused capacity*. (518)

Excess present value index. Capital budgeting measure in which the total present value of future net cash inflows of a project is divided by the total present value of the net initial investment. (840)

Expected monetary value. See *expected value*. (76)

Expected value. Weighted average of the outcomes of a decision with the probability of each outcome serving as the weight. Also called *expected monetary value*. (76)

Experience curve. Function that shows how full product costs per unit (including manufacturing, distribution, marketing, and so on) decline as units of output increase. (351)

Extended normal costing. A costing method that traces direct costs to a cost object by using the budgeted direct-cost rate(s) times the actual quantity of the direct-cost input and allocates indirect costs based on the budgeted indirect-cost rate(s) times the actual quantity of the cost allocation base. Also called *budgeted costing*. (101)

External failure costs. Costs incurred when a nonconforming product is detected after it is shipped to customers. (684)

Facility-sustaining costs. The costs of resources sacrificed on activities that cannot be traced to specific products or services but support the organization as a whole. (152)

Factory overhead costs. See *indirect manufacturing costs*. (40)

Favorable variance. Variance that increases operating income relative to the budgeted amount. Denoted F. (218)

Finance director. See *chief financial officer (CFO)*. (7)

Financial accounting. Focuses on external reporting that is guided by generally accepted accounting principles. (2)

Financial budget. That part of the master budget that comprises the capital budget, cash budget, budgeted balance sheet, and budgeted statement of cash flows. (180)

Financial planning models. Mathematical representations of the relationships among all operating activities, financial activities, and financial statements. (187)

Finished goods inventory. Goods fully completed but not yet sold. (39)

First-in, first-out (FIFO) process-costing method. Method of process costing that assigns the cost of the earliest equivalent units available (starting with the equivalent units in beginning work-in-process inventory) to units completed and transferred out, and the cost of the most recent equivalent units worked on during the period to ending work-in-process inventory. (623)

Fixed cost. Cost that does not change in total despite changes in a cost driver. (29)

Flexible budget. A budget that is developed using budgeted revenues or cost amounts; when variances are computed, the budgeted amounts are adjusted (flexed) to recognize the actual level of output and the actual quantities of the revenue and cost drivers. (218)

Flexible-budget variance. Difference between the actual result and the flexible budget amount for the actual output achieved. (222)

Full product costs. The sum of all the costs in all the business functions R&D, design, production, marketing, distribution, and customer service. (390)

Goal congruence. Exists when individuals and groups work toward the organization goals that top management desires. (901)

Gross margin. Revenues minus cost of goods sold. (71)

Gross margin percentage. Gross margin divided by revenues. (72)

High-low method. Method used to estimate a cost function that entails using only the highest and lowest observed values of the cost driver within the relevant range. (344)

Homogeneous cost pool. Cost pool in which all the activities whose costs are included in the pool have the same or a similar cause-and-effect relationship or benefits-received relationship between the cost allocator and the costs of the activity. (479)

Hurdle rate. See *required rate of return*. (783)

Hybrid costing system. Blends of characteristics from both job costing systems and process costing systems. (718)

Imputed costs. Costs recognized in particular situations that are not regularly recognized by accrual accounting procedures. (936)

Incongruent decision making. See *suboptimal decision making*. (903)

Incremental cost-allocation method. Cost allocation method requiring that one user be viewed as the primary party and the second user be viewed as the incremental party. (490)

Incremental costs. Additional costs to obtain an additional quantity over and above existing or planned quantities of a cost object. Also called *outlay* or *out of pocket costs*. (388)

Incremental revenue-allocation method. Revenue allocation method that ranks the individual products in a bundle and then uses this ranking to allocate the bundled revenues to these individual products. (580)

Incremental unit-time learning model. Learning curve model in which the incremental unit time (the time needed to produce the last unit) declines by a constant percentage each time the cumulative quantity of units produced is doubled. (351)

Indirect costs of a cost object. Costs that are related to the particular cost object but cannot be traced to it in an economically feasible way. (27)

Indirect manufacturing costs. All manufacturing costs considered to be part of the cost object (say, units finished or in process) but that cannot be individually traced to that cost object in an economically feasible way. Also called *manufacturing overhead costs* and *factory overhead costs*. (40)

Industrial engineering method. Approach to cost estimation that first analyzes the relationship between inputs and outputs in physical terms. Also called *work measurement method*. (340)

Inflation. The decline in the general purchasing power of the monetary unit. (833)

Infrastructure costs. Costs that arise from having property, plant, equipment, and a functioning organization. (279)

Input-efficiency variance. See *efficiency variance*. (223)

Input-price variance. See *price variance*. (223)

Insourcing. Process of producing goods or providing services within the firm rather than purchasing those same goods or services from outside vendors. (390)

Institute of Management Accountants (IMA). The largest association of management accountants in the United States. (9)

Intercept. See *constant*. (337)

Intermediate product. Product transferred from one subunit to another subunit of the organization. This product may be processed further and sold to an external customer. (904)

Internal failure costs. Costs incurred when a nonconforming product is detected before it is shipped to customers. (684)

Internal rate of return (IRR). Discount rate at which the present value of expected cash inflows from a project equals the present value of expected cash outflows of the project. The IRR is the discount rate that makes NPV = \$0. Also called the *time-adjusted rate of return*. (785)

Inventoriable costs. See *capitalized inventoriable costs*. (36)

Inventory management. The planning, organizing, and control activities focused on the flow of materials into, through, and from the organization. (748)

Investment. Resources or assets used to generate income. (935)

Investment center. A responsibility center in which a manager is accountable for investments, revenues, and costs. (191)

Investment programs. See *investment projects*. (780)

Investment projects. Investments and outcomes from those investments (which generally cover a number of years). Also called *investment programs*. (780)

Investment tax credit (ITC). A direct reduction of income taxes payable arising from the acquisition of depreciable assets. (822)

Job-costing system. Costing system in which the cost of a product or service is obtained by assigning costs to a distinct unit, batch, or lot of a product or service. (95)

Job cost record. Source document that records and accumulates all the costs assigned to a specific job. Also called *job cost sheet*. (134)

Job cost sheet. See *job cost record.* (134)

Job project. Complex task that often takes months or years to complete and requires the work of many different departments, divisions, or subcontractors. (803)

Job project-performance cost variance. Difference between the actual costs of work performed to date and the budgeted costs of work performed to date. (804)

Job project-schedule cost variance. Difference between the budgeted costs of work performed to date and the budgeted costs of work scheduled to date. (804)

Joint cost. Cost of a single process that yields multiple products simultaneously. (544)

Joint products. Products from a joint process that have relatively high sales value and are not separately identifiable as individual products until the splitoff point. (544)

Just-in-time (JIT) production. Production system in which each component on a production line is produced immediately as needed by the next step in the production line. (722)

Just-in-time (JIT) purchasing. The purchase of goods or materials such that delivery immediately precedes demand or use. (724)

Kaizen budgeting. Budgetary approach that explicitly incorporates continuous improvement during the budget period into the resultant budget numbers. (188)

Key success factors. Factors that directly affect customer satisfaction such as cost, quality, time, and innovative products and services. (14)

Labor-paced operations. Worker dexterity and productivity determine the speed of production. (514)

Labor time record. Record used to charge departments and job cost records for labor time used on a specific job. (135)

Learning curve. Function that shows how labor-hours per unit decline as units of production increase. (351)

Life-cycle budgeting. Budget that incorporates the revenues and costs attributable to each product from its initial R&D to its final customer servicing and support in the market place. (446)

Life-cycle costing. System that tracks and accumulates the actual costs attributable to each product from start to finish. (446)

Line management. Managers directly responsible for attaining the objectives of the organization. (7)

Linear cost function. Cost function in which the graph of total costs versus a single cost driver forms a straight line within the relevant range. (336)

Locked-in costs. Costs that have not yet been incurred but that will be incurred in the future on the basis of decisions that have already been made. Also called *designed-in costs.* (438)

Machine-paced operations. Machines conduct most (or all) phases of production, such as movement of materials to the production line, assembly and other activities on the production line, and shipment of finished goods to the delivery dock areas. (514)

Main product. When a single process yielding two or more products yields only one product with a relatively high sales value, that product is termed a main product. (544)

Make-or-buy decisions. Decisions about whether a producer of goods or services will produce goods or services within the firm or purchase them from outside vendors. (390)

Management accounting. Measures and reports financial information as well as other types of information that assist managers in fulfilling the goals of the organization. (2)

Management by exception. The practice of concentrating on areas that are not operating as expected and placing less attention on areas operating as expected. (5)

Management control system. Means of gathering and using information to aid and coordinate the process of making planning and control decisions throughout the organization and to guide employee behavior. (900)

Manufacturing cells. Grouping of all the different types of equipment used to manufacture a given product. (722)

Manufacturing lead time. Time from when an order is ready to start on the production line (ready to be set up) to when it becomes a finished good. (514)

Manufacturing overhead allocated. All manufacturing costs that are assigned to a product (or service) using a cost allocation base because they cannot be traced to a product (or service) in an economically feasible way. (139)

Manufacturing overhead costs. See *indirect manufacturing costs.* (40)

Manufacturing-sector company. Provide to their customers tangible products that have been converted to a different form from that of the products purchased from suppliers. (36)

Margin of safety. Excess of budgeted revenues over the breakeven revenues. (66)

Marketing. The manner by which individuals or groups (a) learn about and value the attributes of products or services and (b) purchase those products or services. (3)

Market-share variance. The difference between (a) the budgeted amount at budgeted mix based on the actual market size in units and the actual market share, and (2) the budgeted amount at budgeted mix based on actual market size in units and the budgeted market share. (586)

Market-size variance. The difference between (1) the budgeted amount based on the actual market size in units and the budgeted market share and (2) the static-budget amount based on the budgeted market size in units and the budgeted market share. (586)

Master budget. Budget that summarizes the financial projections of all the organizations individual budgets. It describes the financial plans for all value-chain functions. (176)

Master-budget utilization. The denominator-level concept based on the anticipated level of capacity utilization for the coming budget period. (314)

Materials requisition record. Record used to charge departments and job cost records for the cost of the materials used on a specific job. (134)

Merchandising-sector company. Provide to their customers tangible products they have previously purchased in the same basic form from suppliers. (36)

Mixed cost. A cost that has both fixed and variable elements. Also called a *semivariable cost.* (337)

Modified Accelerated Cost Recovery System (MACRS). United States regulation describes depreciation methods for determining federal income taxes. (833)

Moral hazard. Describes contexts in which an employee prefers to exert less effort (or report distorted information) than the effort (or information) desired by the owner because the employee's effort (or information) cannot be accurately monitored and enforced. (947)

Motivation. The desire to attain a selected goal (the goal-congruence aspect) combined with the resulting drive or pursuit toward that goal (the effort aspect). (901)

Multicollinearity. Exists when two or more independent variables in a regression model are highly correlated with each other. (366)

Multiple regression. Regression model that uses more than one independent variable to estimate the dependent variable. (345)

Negotiated static budget. Budget in which a fixed amount of costs is established through negotiations before the start of the budget period. (280)

Net income. Operating income plus nonoperating revenues (such as interest revenues) minus nonoperating costs (such as interest costs) minus income taxes. (61)

Net present value (NPV) method. Discounted cash-flow method that calculates the expected net monetary gain or loss from a project by discounting all expected future cash inflows and outflows to the present point in time, using the required rate of return. (783)

Net relevant cost. See *differential cost.* (386)

Nominal rate of return. Rate of return required to cover investment risk and the anticipated decline due to inflation, in the general purchasing power of the cash that the investment generates. (834)

Noncapitalized costs. Costs that are recorded as expenses of the accounting period when they are incurred. (35)

Nonlinear cost function. Cost function in which the graph of total costs versus a single cost driver does not form a straight line within the relevant range. (348)

Nonvalue-added cost. A cost that, if eliminated, would not reduce the value customers obtain from using the product or service. (254)

Normal costing. A costing method that traces direct costs to a cost object by using the actual direct cost rate(s) times the actual quantity of the direct cost input and allocates indirect costs based on the budgeted indirect cost rate(s) times the actual quantity of the cost allocation base. (98)

Normal spoilage. Spoilage that arises under efficient operating conditions; it is an inherent result of the particular production process. (653)

Normal utilization. The denominator-level concept based on the level of capacity utilization that satisfies average customer demand over a period (say, two or three years) that includes seasonal, cyclical, or other trend factors. (314)

Objective function. Expresses the objective to be maximized (for example, operating income) or minimized (for example, operating costs) in a decision model, for example, a linear programming model. (407)

On-time performance. Situations in which the product or service is actually delivered at the time it is scheduled to be delivered. (696)

Operating budget. The budgeted income statement and its supporting schedules. (180)

Operating costs. All costs associated with generating revenues, other than cost of goods sold. (36)

Operating cycle. See *self-liquidating cycle.* (198)

Operating department. A department that adds value to a product or service that is observable by a customer. Also called a *production department* in manufacturing organizations. (483)

Operating income. Operating income is total revenues from operations minus total costs from operations (excluding income taxes). (61)

Operation. A standardized method or technique that is performed repetitively regardless of the distinguishing features of the finished good. (718)

Operation costing. Hybrid costing system applied to batches of similar products. Each batch of products is often a variation of a single design and proceeds through a sequence of selected (though not necessarily the same) activities or operations. Within each operation all product units use identical amounts of the operations resources. (719)

Opportunity cost. The contribution to income that is forgone (rejected) by not using a limited resource in its best alternative use. (394)

Opportunity cost of capital. See *required rate of return.* (783)

Ordering costs. Costs of preparing and issuing a purchase order. (748)

Ordinary incremental budgets. Budget based on the budget of the previous period and actual results as well as expectations for the new period. (280)

Organizational structure. The arrangement of lines of responsibility within the entity. (191)

Outcomes. Predicted consequences of the various possible combinations of actions and events in a decision model. (78)

Outlay costs. See *incremental costs.* (388)

Out-of-pocket costs. See *incremental costs.* (388)

Output-level overhead variance. See *production-volume variance.* (263)

Output unit-level costs. The costs of resources sacrificed on activities performed on each individual unit of product or service. (150)

Outsourcing. Process of purchasing goods and services from outside vendors rather than producing the same goods or providing the same services within the firm. (390)

Overabsorbed indirect costs. See *overallocated indirect costs.* (140)

Overallocated indirect costs. Allocated amount of indirect costs in an accounting period is greater than the actual (incurred) amount in that period. Also called *overapplied indirect costs* and *overabsorbed indirect costs*. (140)

Overapplied indirect costs. See *overallocated indirect costs*. (140)

Padding. The practice of underestimating budgeted revenues (or overestimating budgeted costs) in order to make budgeted targets more easily achievable. Also called *budgetary slack*. (183)

Pareto diagram. Diagram that indicates how frequently each type of failure (defect) occurs. (687)

Partial productivity. Measures the quantity of output produced with the quantity of a single input used. (875)

Payback method. Capital budgeting method that measures the time it will take to recoup, in the form of net cash inflows, the net initial investment in a project. (791)

Peak-load pricing. Practice of charging a higher price for the same product or service when demand approaches physical capacity limits. (446)

Peanut-butter costing. A costing approach that uses broad averages to uniformly assign (spread or smooth out) the cost of resources to cost objects (such as products, services, or customers) when the individual products, services, or customers in fact use those resources in a nonuniform way. (102)

Perfectly competitive market. Exists when there is a homogeneous product with equivalent buying and selling prices and no individual buyers or sellers can affect those prices by their own actions. (908)

Physical measure method. Joint cost allocation method that allocates joint costs on the basis of their relative proportions at the splitoff point, using a common physical measure such as weight or volume of the total production of each product. (548)

Planning. Choosing goals, predicting results under various ways of achieving those goals, and then deciding how to attain the desired goals. (4)

Post-deduct costing. See *backflush costing*. (726)

Practical capacity. The denominator-level concept that reduces theoretical capacity for unavoidable operating interruptions such as scheduled maintenance time, shutdowns for holidays and other days, and so on. (313)

Predatory pricing. Company deliberately prices below its costs in an effort to drive out competitors and restrict supply and then raises prices rather than enlarge demand or meet competition. (449)

Present value. An asset measure based on DCF estimates. (940)

Prevention costs. Costs incurred in precluding the production of products that do not conform to specifications. (683)

Previous department costs. See *transferred-in costs*. (630)

Price discounting. The reduction of selling prices below listed levels in order to encourage an increase in purchases by customers. (591)

Price discrimination. Practice of charging some customers a higher price than is charged to other customers. (445)

Price variance. The difference between actual price and budgeted price multiplied by the actual quantity of input in question. Also called *input-price variance*, *rate variance* (especially when those variances are for direct labor categories). (223)

Prime costs. All direct manufacturing costs. (41)

Priority incremental budgets. Similar to an ordinary incremental budget, with the inclusion of a description of incremental changes if the budget were increased or decreased by, say, 10%. (281)

Probability. Likelihood or chance of occurrence of an event. (75)

Probability distribution. Describes the likelihood (or probability) of each of the mutually exclusive and collectively exhaustive sets of events. (76)

Problem solving. Management accountant's function that involves comparative analysis to identify the best alternatives in relation to the organization's goals. (9)

Process-costing system. Costing system in which the cost of a product or service is obtained by using broad averages to assign costs to masses of similar units. (95)

Product. Any output sold to a customer that has a positive sales value (or an output used internally that enables an organization to avoid incurring costs). (544)

Product cost. Sum of the costs assigned to a product for a specific purpose. (43)

Product-cost cross-subsidization. Costing outcome where at least one miscosted product is resulting in the miscosting of other products in the organization. (103)

Production. The coordination and assembly of resources to produce a product or deliver a service. (3)

Production denominator level. See *denominator level*. (261)

Production denominator volume. See *denominator level*. (261)

Production department. See *operating department*. (483)

Production-volume variance. Difference between budgeted fixed overhead and the fixed overhead allocated. Fixed overhead is allocated based on the budgeted fixed overhead rate times the budgeted quantity of the fixed-overhead allocation base for the actual output units achieved. Also called *denominator-level variance* and *output-level overhead variance*. (263)

Productivity. Measures the relationship between actual inputs used (both physical inputs and costs) and actual outputs achieved; the lower the inputs for a given set of outputs or the higher the outputs for a given set of inputs, the higher the level of productivity. (873)

Product life cycle. Spans the time from initial R&D to the time at which support to customers is withdrawn. (446)

Product line. A grouping of similar products. (107)

Product overcosting. A product consumes a relatively low level of resources but is reported to have a relatively high total cost. (102)

Product-sustaining costs. The costs of resources sacrificed on activities undertaken to support specific products or services. (151)

Product undercosting. A product consumes a relatively high level of resources but is reported to have a relatively low total cost. (102)

Profit center. A responsibility center in which a manager is accountable for revenues and costs. (191)

Pro forma statements. Budgeted financial statements of an organization. (179)

Proration. The spreading of underallocated or overallocated overhead among ending inventories and cost of goods sold. (142)

Purchase-order lead time. Amount of time between the placement of an order and its delivery. (749)

Purchasing costs. Cost of goods acquired from suppliers, including freight and transportation costs. (748)

PV graph. Shows the impact on operating income of changes in the output level. (65)

Qualitative factors. Outcomes that cannot be measured in numerical terms. (386)

Quantitative factors. Outcomes that are measured in numerical terms. (386)

Rate variance. See *price variance*. (223)

Real rate of return. The rate of return required to cover only investment risk. (834)

Reciprocal allocation method. Method of support-cost allocation that explicitly includes the mutual services rendered among all support departments. (486)

Refined costing system. Costing system that results in a better measure of the nonuniformity in the use of resources by jobs, products, and customers. (105)

Regression analysis. Statistical model that measures the average amount of change in the dependent variable that is associated with a unit change in one or more independent variables. (345)

Relevant costs. Expected future costs that differ among alternative courses of action. (385)

Relevant range. Range of the cost driver in which a specific relationship between cost and driver is valid. (30)

Relevant revenues. Expected future revenues that differ among alternative courses of action. (385)

Reorder point. The quantity level of the inventory on hand that triggers a new order. (751)

Required rate of return (RRR). The minimum acceptable rate of return on an investment; the return that the organization could expect to receive elsewhere for an investment of comparable risk. Also called *discount rate*, *hurdle rate*, and *opportunity cost of capital*. (783)

Research and development (R&D). The generation of, and experimentation with, ideas related to new products, services, or processes. (3)

Residual income. Income minus a required dollar return on the investment. (936)

Residual term. The difference between the actual and predicted amount of a dependent variable (such as a cost) in a regression model. Also called the *disturbance term* or *error term*. (346)

Responsibility accounting. System that measures the plans (by budgets) and actions (by actual results) of each responsibility center. (191)

Responsibility center. A part, segment, or subunit of an organization whose manager is accountable for a specified set of activities. (191)

Return on investment (ROI). See *accrual accounting rate of return*. (793)

Revenue allocation. The assigning of revenues that are related, but not traceable to, individual products (services, customers, etc.) in an economically feasible (cost-effective) way. A revenue allocation base is used to make this assignment. (576)

Revenue center. A responsibility center in which a manager is accountable for revenues only. (191)

Revenue driver. Any factor that affects revenues. (60)

Revenue mix. The relative contribution of quantities of products or services that constitutes total revenues. See *sales mix*. (69)

Revenues. Inflows of assets received in exchange for products or services provided to customers. (60)

Revenue tracing. The tracings of revenues that can be identified with an individual product (service, customer, etc.) in an economically feasible (cost-effective) way. (576)

Reworked units. Unacceptable units of production that are subsequently reworked and sold as acceptable finished goods. (652)

Rolling budget. Budget or plan that is always available for a specified future period by adding a month, quarter, or year in the future as the month, quarter, or year just ended is dropped. (179)

Safety stock. Inventory held at all times regardless of inventory ordered using EOQ. It is a buffer against unexpected increases in demand or lead time and unexpected unavailability of stock from suppliers. (752)

Sales mix. See *revenue mix*. (69)

Sales-mix variance. The difference between (1) the budgeted amount for the actual sales mix, and (2) the budgeted amount if the budgeted sales mix had been unchanged. (583)

Sales-quantity variance. The difference between (1) the budgeted amount based on actual quantities sold of all products and the budgeted-mix, and (2) the amount in the static budget (which is based on the budgeted quantities to be sold of all products and the budgeted-mix). (583)

Sales value at splitoff method. Joint cost allocation method that allocates joint costs on the basis of the relative sales value at the splitoff point of the total production in the accounting period of each product. (547)

Sales-volume variance. Difference between the flexible-budget amount and the static-budget amount; unit selling prices, unit variable costs, and fixed costs are held constant. (222)

Scorekeeping. Management accountant's function that involves accumulating data and reporting reliable results to all levels of management. (8)

Scrap. Product that has a minimal (frequently zero) sales value. (544)

Segment. Identifiable part or subunit of an organization. (522)

Self-liquidating cycle. The movement of cash to inventories to receivables and back to cash. (198)

Selling-price variance. Flexible-budget variance that pertains to revenues; arises solely from differences between the actual selling price and the budgeted selling price. (222)

Semivariable cost. See *mixed cost.* (337)

Sensitivity analysis. A what-if technique that examines how a result will change if the original predicted data are not achieved or if an underlying assumption changes. (65)

Separable costs. Costs incurred beyond the splitoff point that are assignable to one or more individual products. (544)

Sequential allocation method. See *step-down allocation method.* (484)

Sequential tracking. Product-costing method in which the accounting system entries occur in the same order as actual purchases and production. Also called *synchronous tracking.* (726)

Service department. See *support department.* (483)

Service-sector company. Provide services or intangible products to their customers—for example, legal advice, or an audit. (35)

Service-sustaining costs. The costs of resources sacrificed on activities undertaken to support specific services. (151)

Simple regression. Regression model that uses only one independent variable to estimate the dependent variable. (345)

Single-rate cost-allocation method. Allocation method that pools all costs in one cost pool and allocates them to cost objects using the same rate per unit of the single allocation base. (480)

Slope coefficient. Coefficient term in a cost estimation model indicates how much total costs change for each unit change in the cost driver within the relevant range. (336)

Source documents. The original records that support journal entries in an accounting system. (97)

Specification analysis. Testing of the assumptions of regression analysis. (361)

Splitoff point. Juncture in the process when one or more products in a joint-cost setting become separately identifiable. (544)

Spoilage. Unacceptable units of production that are discarded or sold for net disposal proceeds. (652)

Staff management. Managers who provide advice and assistance to line management. (7)

Stand-alone cost-allocation method. Cost allocation method that allocates the common cost on the basis of each users percentage of the total of the individual stand-alone costs. (490)

Stand-alone revenue-allocation method. Revenue allocation method that uses product-specific information pertaining to products in the bundle to determine the weights used to allocate the bundled revenues to those individual products. (579)

Standard. Carefully predetermined amount; it is usually expressed on a per-unit basis. (218)

Standard cost. Carefully predetermined cost. Standard costs can relate to units of inputs or units of outputs. (224)

Standard costing. Costing method that traces direct costs to a cost object by multiplying the standard price(s) or rate(s) times the standard inputs allowed for actual outputs achieved and allocates indirect costs on the basis of the standard indirect rate(s) times the standard inputs allowed for the actual outputs achieved. (269)

Standard error of the estimated coefficient. Regression statistic that indicates how much the estimated value is likely to be affected by random factors. (360)

Standard input. Carefully predetermined quantity of inputs (such as pounds of materials or hours of labor time) required for one unit of output. (224)

Static budget. Budget that is based on one level of output; when variances are computed at the end of the period, no adjustment is made to the budgeted amounts. (218)

Step allocation method. See *step-down allocation method.* (484)

Step cost function. A cost function in which the cost is constant over various ranges of the cost driver, but the cost increases by discrete amounts (that is, in steps) as the cost driver moves from one range to the next. (350)

Step-down allocation method. Method of support cost allocation that allows for partial recognition of services rendered by support departments to other support departments. Also called *step* or *sequential allocation method.* (484)

Stockout. A stockout arises when a supplier runs out of a particular item for which there is customer demand. (749)

Straight-line depreciation (SL). Depreciation method in which an equal amount of depreciation is taken each year. (823)

Strategic analysis. Considers how an organization best combines its own capabilities with the opportunities in the market place to accomplish its overall objectives. (177)

Suboptimal decision making. Decisions in which the benefit to one subunit is more than offset by the costs or loss of benefits to the organization as a whole. Also called *incongruent decision making.* (903)

Sunk costs. Past costs that are unavoidable because they cannot be changed no matter what action is taken. (402)

Super-variable costing. See *throughput costing.* (308)

Support department. A department that provides the services that maintain other internal departments (operating departments and other support departments) in the organization. Also called a *service department.* (483)

Synchronous tracking. See *sequential tracking.* (726)

Target cost per unit. Estimated long-run cost per unit of a product (or service) that when sold at the target price enables the company to achieve the targeted income per unit. Target cost per unit is derived by subtracting the target operating income per unit from the target price. (436)

Target operating income per unit. Operating income that a company wants to earn on each unit of a product (or service) sold. (436)

Target price. Estimated price for a product (or service) that potential customers will be willing to pay. (436)

Target rate of return on investment. The target operating income that an organization must earn divided by invested capital. (442)

Theoretical capacity. The denominator-level concept that is based on the production of output at maximum efficiency for all of the time. (313)

Theory of constraints (TOC). Describes methods to maximize operating income when faced with some bottleneck and some nonbottleneck operations. (698)

Throughput contribution. Revenues minus all variable direct materials costs. (698)

Throughput costing. Inventory costing method that treats all costs except those related to variable direct materials as costs of the accounting period in which they are incurred; only variable direct materials costs are inventoriable. Also called *super-variable costing*. (308)

Time-adjusted rate of return. See *internal rate of return (IRR)*. (785)

Time driver. Any factor where change in the factor causes a change in the speed with which an activity is undertaken. (694)

Total direct manufacturing labor mix variance. The difference between the budgeted cost for the actual direct manufacturing labor input mix and the budgeted cost if the budgeted direct labor input mix had been unchanged for the actual total quantity of all direct manufacturing labor used. (872)

Total direct manufacturing labor yield variance. The difference between the budgeted cost of direct manufacturing labor based on actual total quantity of all direct manufacturing labor used and the flexible budget cost of direct manufacturing labor based on the budgeted total quantity of direct manufacturing labor inputs for the actual output achieved, given that the budgeted labor input mix is unchanged. (872)

Total direct materials mix variance. The difference between the budgeted cost for the actual direct materials input mix and the budgeted cost if the budgeted direct materials input mix had been unchanged, for the actual total quantity of all direct material inputs used. (868)

Total direct materials yield variance. The difference between the budgeted cost of direct materials based on actual total quantity of all direct materials inputs used and the flexible-budget cost of direct materials based on the budgeted total quantity of direct materials inputs for the actual output achieved, given that the budgeted materials input mix is unchanged. (868)

Total factor productivity (TFP). The ratio of the quantity of output produced to the costs of all inputs used, where the inputs are combined on the basis of current period prices. (878)

Total project approach. Approach to decision making that incorporates all relevant revenues and relevant costs under each alternative. In capital budgeting decisions, calculates the present value of all future cash inflows and outflows under each alternative separately. (826)

Transfer price. Price one subunit (segment, department, division, etc.) of an organization charges for a product or service supplied to another subunit of the same organization. (904)

Transferred-in costs. Costs incurred in a previous department that are carried forward as part of the product's cost as it moves to a subsequent department for processing. Also called *previous department costs*. (630)

Uncertainty. The possibility that an actual amount will deviate from an expected amount. (66)

Underabsorbed indirect costs. See *underallocated indirect costs*. (140)

Underallocated indirect costs. Allocated amount of indirect costs in an accounting period is less than the actual (incurred) amount in that period. Also called *underapplied indirect (overhead) costs* or *underabsorbed indirect costs*. (140)

Underapplied indirect costs. See *underallocated indirect costs*. (140)

Unfavorable variance. Variance that decreases operating income relative to the budgeted amount. Denoted U. (218)

Unit cost. Computed by dividing some total cost (the numerator) by some number of units (the denominator). Also called *average cost*. (32)

Unused capacity. The difference between the productive capacity available and the productive capacity required to meet consumer demand in the current period. Also called *excess capacity*. (518)

Usage variance. See *efficiency variance*. (223)

Value-added activities. Activities that customers perceive as adding value to the products or services they purchase. (28)

Value-added cost. A cost that, if eliminated, would reduce the value customers obtain from using the product or service. (254)

Value chain. The sequence of business functions in which utility (usefulness) is added to the products or services of an organization. (3)

Value engineering. Systematic evaluation of all aspects of the value-chain business functions, with the objective of reducing costs while satisfying customer needs. (436)

Variable cost. Cost that changes in total in proportion to changes in a cost driver. (29)

Variable costing. Inventory costing method in which all variable manufacturing costs are included as inventoriable costs. All fixed manufacturing costs are excluded from inventoriable costs; they are costs of the period in which they are incurred. Also called *direct costing*. (298)

Variable-cost percentage. Total variable costs (with respect to units of output) divided by revenues. (72)

Variable-overhead efficiency variance. The difference between the actual and budgeted quantity of the variable-overhead cost allocation base allowed for the actual output units achieved times the budgeted variable overhead cost allocation rate. (258)

Variable-overhead spending variance. The difference between the actual amount of variable overhead incurred and the budgeted amount allowed for the actual quantity of the variable-overhead allocation base used for the actual output units achieved. (259)

Variance. Difference between an actual result and a budgeted amount when that budgeted amount is a financial variable reported by the accounting system. (5)

Weighted-average process-costing method. Method of process costing that assigns the average equivalent unit cost of all work done to date (regardless of when it was done) to equivalent units completed and transferred out, and to equivalent units in ending inventory. (620)

Working-capital cycle. The movement from cash to inventories to receivables and back to cash. (198)

Work-in-process inventory. Goods partially worked on but not yet fully completed. Also called *work in progress inventory*. (39)

Work-in-progress inventory. See *work-in-process inventory*. (39)

Work measurement. Careful analysis of a task, its size, the method used in its performance, and the efficiency with which it is performed. (280)

Work-measurement method. See *industrial-engineering method*. (340)

Zero-based budgeting (ZBB). Budgeting from the ground up, as though the budget were being prepared for the first time. Every proposed expenditure comes under review. (281)

AUTHOR INDEX

COMPANY INDEX

SUBJECT INDEX

optimal solution in, 407
simplex method in, 407*n*
trial-and-error approach to, 408–9
Line management, 7
Locked-in costs, 438
Long-term assets, measuring, 943

Machine-paced operations, 514
Main product, 544
Make-or-buy decisions, 390–92
Management
  budget support by, 178–79
  by exception, 5
  line, 7
  staff, 7
Management accountant(s)
  attention-directing function of, 9
  organization structure and, 7–9
  problem-solving function of, 9
  professional ethics for, 9–13
  scorekeeping function of, 8–9
Management accounting, 2–3
  Just-in-Time system and, 733
Management control system(s), 4–6, 900–901
  decentralization and, 901–4
  organization structure and, 901–4
  planning and control in, 4–6
  responsibility center choices and, 904
  transfer pricing and, 904–16. (*see also* Transfer pricing)
Management themes evolving around globe, 12, 14–15
Managers
  environmental responsibilities of, 951–52
  ethical responsibilities of, 951–52
  performance evaluation of
    organization unit evaluation distinguished from, 946–49
Manufacturing
  activity-based costing in, 144–50
    cost refinement with, 146–48
    in designing costing system, traditional approach versus, 152–55
    end-period adjustments and, 149–50
    insights available with, 148
  cost hierarchy in, 150–52
  job costing in, 132–40
    illustration of, 135–40
Manufacturing cells in JIT system, 722
Manufacturing costs, 40–42
  classifications of, 40–41
Manufacturing labor, direct, yield and mix variances for, 871–73
Manufacturing lead time, 514, 694
Manufacturing organization, inventory cost/management in, 759–62
Manufacturing overhead allocated, 139
Manufacturing overhead budget in operating budget preparation, 185
Manufacturing overhead (MOH) costs
  cost allocation bases and rates for, in electronics industry, 255
  fixed, 267
  variable, 266
    static-budget and flexible-budget analyses of, 257–58
Manufacturing overhead variances, proration of, 274–76
Manufacturing productivity growth, international, *874*
Manufacturing sector
  companies in, 36
    financial statements of, 38–40
    difference between contribution margin and gross margin in, 72

Manufacturing variances, proration of, using standard costs, 273–78
Market, perfectly competitive, transfer prices based on, 908
Market-based approach to long-run pricing, 435
Market-based transfer prices, 905, 908–9
Marketing in value chain, 3, *4*
Market-share variance, 584, 586–87
Market-size variance, 584, 586–87
Master-budget utilization, 314
Materials, direct
  efficiency and price variances for, 867, *868*
  mix variances for, 866–70
    role of, 869–70
  price variances for, 867–68
  yield variances for, 866–70
    role of, 868–69
Materials requisition record, 134
Measurement
  productivity, 873–88
  work, engineered costs and, 280
Measures
  of performance. *See* Performance, measures of
  productivity, 873–88
Merchandising, activity-based costing in, 107–12
Merchandising sector
  companies in, 36
    financial statements of, 36–37
    difference between contribution margin and gross margin in, 72
Mixed cost, 337
Mix variances
  direct manufacturing labor, 871–73
  direct materials, 866–70
    role of, 869–70
Modified Accelerated Cost Recovery System (MACRS), 833
Moral hazard
  compensation and, 947
  insurance and, 947*n*
Motivation in management control system evaluation, 901
Multicollinearity, 366
Multinational companies
  decentralization of, 904
  performance measurement in, 944–46
  transfer pricing in, tax considerations on, 914–15
Multiple countries, variance analysis for, 587–90
Multiple products, variance analysis and, 581–87
Multiple regression, cost hierarchies and, 363–66
Multiple regression analysis, 344–45

Negotiated static budgets, 279
  discretionary costs and, 280–81
Negotiated transfer prices, 905, 911, 913
Net book value in measuring assets, 943
Net present-value decision rule in capital budgeting, 840–42
Net present-value (NPV) method
  of capital budgeting, inflation and, 834–38
  of discounted cash-flow calculation, 783–85
    internal rate-of-return method compared with, 786, 788
Nominal rate of return, 834
Noncapitalized costs, 35
Nonfinancial performance measures, 268–69, 932–33
Nonlinear cost functions, 348–50

learning curves and, 351–54
Nonmanufacturing settings, overhead cost variances in, 264–65
Nonproduction costs budget in operating budget preparation, 186
Nonprofit institutions/organizations
  capital budgeting in, 840
  cost-volume-profit (CVP) analysis and, 71
Nonvalue-added cost, 254
Normal costing, 98–100, 269
  extended, 101–2
Normal utilization, 314

Objective function of linear program, 407
Objectivity, ethical standards for, 11
One-time-only special order(s), 387–89
  pricing and, 431–33
1–variance analysis, 264
On-time performance, 696
Operating budget, 180
  preparation of
    budgeted income statement in, 187
    cost of goods sold budget in, 186
    direct manufacturing labor budget in, 184–85
    direct materials purchases budget in, 184
    direct materials usage budget in, 184
    ending inventory budget in, 185–86
    manufacturing overhead budget in, 185
    other (nonproduction) budget in, 186
    production budget in, 183
    revenue budget in, 182–83
    steps in, 182–87
Operating costs, 36
Operating cycle, 198
Operating department, 483
Operating income
  under absorption vs. variable costing, 304–5
  denominator level concepts and, 315
  production and, 305–6
  sales and, 305–6
  target, per unit, 436
Operation costing, 718–21
  illustration of, 719–20
  journal entries for, 720–21
  relation of, to other costing systems, 721
Opportunity cost(s)
  of capital, 783
  contracting and, 397
  outsourcing and, 392–96
Optimal solution in linear programming, 407
Ordering costs, 748
Ordinary incremental budgets, 280
Organization(s)
  decentralization of, 901–4
  evaluation of, manager evaluation distinguished from, 946–49
  service, job costing in, using actual costing, 96–97, *98*
  structure of, 901–4
    management accountant and, 7–9
Organization-structure cost hierarchy, 521–22
Outcomes
  in decision model, 75
  good, distinguishing between good decisions and, 78–79
Outlay costs, 388
Out-of-pocket costs, 388
Output(s)
  equivalent units of, 615–16
    computing output in terms of, in process costing, 619
  costs of, computing, in process costing, 619